Icon: The Life, Times, and Films of **Marilyn Monroe**

Volume 2

1956 to 1962 & Beyond

by Gary Vitacco-Robles

Icon: The Life, Times, and Films of
Marilyn Monroe
Volume 2
1956 to 1962 & Beyond

Published in the USA by:

BearManor Media
P.O. Box 71426
Albany, Georgia 31708
www.BearManorMedia.com

ISBN-10: 1-59393-778-4 (alk. paper)
ISBN-13: 978-1-59393-778-2 (alk. paper)

Cover photo by Glenn Embree/MPTVimages.com

Design and Layout: Valerie Thompson

Table of Contents

Acknowledgements . . . 1

Introduction: Goddess, Legend, Icon . . . 9

Part I: Mrs. Arthur Miller . . . 15

Chapter One: *The Prince and the Showgirl* . . . **17**

Chapter Two: Manhattan, Autumn 1956/Winter & Spring 1957 . . . **65**

Chapter Three: Amagansett, Summer 1957 . . . **85**

Chapter Four: Connecticut & Manhattan, Autumn & Winter 1957 . . . **103**

Chapter Five: January to July 1958 . . . **117**

Part II: Living Legend . . . 127

Chapter Six: *Some Like It Hot* Part I . . . **129**

Chapter Seven: *Some Like It Hot* Part II . . . **147**

Chapter Eight: November–December 1958 . . . **167**

Chapter Nine: 1959 . . . **171**

Chapter Ten: *Let's Make Love* . . . **197**

Chapter Eleven: Spring & Summer 1960 . . . **233**

Chapter Twelve: *The Misfits* Part I . . . **243**

Chapter Thirteen: *The Misfits* Part II . . . **283**

Chapter Fourteen: October–December 1960 . . . **301**

Chapter Fifteen: January–June 1961 . . . **311**

Chapter Sixteen: June–December . . . **343**

Part III: The Last Months . . . 371

Chapter Seventeen: *Something's Got to Give* . . . **373**

Chapter Eighteen: January 1962 . . . **389**

Chapter Nineteen: *Cursum Perficio*: February 1962 . . . **397**

Chapter Twenty: Robert F. Kennedy . . . **405**

Chapter Twenty-One: February–March 1962 . . . **413**

Chapter Twenty-Two: March–April 1962 . . . **431**

Chapter Twenty-Three: President John F. Kennedy . . . **439**

Chapter Twenty-Four: April to May 1962 . . . **447**

Chapter Twenty-Five: The JFK Birthday Gala . . . **461**

Chapter Twenty-Six: May to June 1962 . . . **479**

Chapter Twenty-Seven: Life on Fifth Helena Drive . . . **497**

Chapter Twenty-Eight: The Last Days/July–August 3, 1962 . . . **515**

Chapter Twenty-Nine: August 4, 1962 . . . **533**

Part IV: Icon . . . 551

Chapter Thirty: The Death of Marilyn Monroe . . . **553**

Chapter Thirty-One: The World Mourns . . . **563**

Chapter Thirty-Two: The Funeral . . . **573**

Chapter Thirty-Three: The Investigation & Results of the Autopsy . . . **585**

Chapter Thirty-Four: Studio without Its Queen . . . **591**

Chapter Thirty-Five: Aftermath . . . **595**

Chapter Thirty-Six: The Estate . . . **609**

Chapter Thirty-Seven: The Legend & the Myth . . . **621**

Chapter Thirty-Eight: Those She Left Behind . . . **651**

Part V: Legacy . . . 663

Chapter Thirty-Nine: The Marilyn Monroe Half-centennial Memorial . . . **665**

Appendix: Selected Marilyn Monroe Film Synopses . . . 679

NOTES . . . 711

BIBLIOGRAPHY . . . 785

INDEX . . . 845

ABOUT THE AUTHOR . . . 885

Acknowledgments

The Life, Times, and Films of Marilyn Monroe is the result of a decade of research culminating in two volumes reviewing five decades of literature on this extraordinary woman. My previous book, *Cursum Perficio: Marilyn Monroe's Brentwood Hacienda,* resonated with her many fans across the globe who contacted me with appeals to write an unabridged biography. I extend appreciation to the many people who have supported this project.

Christelle Montagner graciously served as my overseas volunteer research assistant. She created a timeline of Marilyn's life and organized her archive of electronically scanned documents and photographic images into a visual biography. Christelle was especially helpful in identifying the context of Marilyn's life through photographs and electronic scans of letters written by Marilyn.

Prolific author Michelle Morgan served as my advisor, cheerleader, and coach. As a researcher and biographer of film stars of the Golden Age of filmmaking, she related to my frenzied excitement over finding an obscure article published nearly seventy years ago containing a tidbit of information—and she always validated such discoveries as well-worth a day of investigation. From across the Atlantic Ocean, Michelle took my hand and wisely guided me to Ben Ohmart of BearManor Media who believed in and accepted my manuscript. My thanks also go out to Beth Jacques at Mptvimages.com who facilitated the licensing of the cover 1962 photograph by Glenn Embree.

I am grateful to those who participated in interviews:

My friend, Greg Schreiner of *Marilyn Remembered,* provided a private tour of his exceptional collection of Marilyn's personal property and archive and served as a consultant.

Scott Fortner of *The Marilyn Monroe Collection* also permitted my access to his colossal archive of Marilyn's documents and personal property, which had recently been displayed with Greg Schreiner's at the Hollywood History Museum in Los Angeles. Both collections serve as artifacts documenting a "personal archeology."

The late Evelyn Moriarty spoke to me at length about Marilyn's generosity and the productions of *Let's Make Love, The Misfits,* and *Something's Got to Give.*

Marilyn's internist, Dr. Hyman Engelberg, corresponded with me and requested that I write questions on index cards and mail them to him. Like a devoted pen pal, the retired physician jotted down his responses on the cards and returned them.

Joshua Greene of *The Archives of Milton Greene* and his mother, Amy Greene, spoke at Marilyn Monroe's fiftieth anniversary memorial service about their personal memories of Marilyn as a member of their household.

Patricia Newcomb, Marilyn's close friend and publicist, spoke with me about Marilyn's personal relationships, vulnerability, and strength. She took an interest in my work as a psychotherapist and its influence on my perspective of Marilyn. We discussed the duty of confidentiality in our respective professions and strayed to the topic of our mutual love of opera. After our conversation, I felt appreciative of Marilyn having Ms. Newcomb as a loyal friend and confidante.

James Haspiel provided consultation through a surprise long distance telephone call on New Year's Eve 1999 and discussed his memories of Marilyn in Manhattan.

Stylist Mickey Song invited me into his home in Los Angeles and recounted his encounter with Marilyn at President Kennedy's birthday gala in 1962.

Jason Dow discussed his adolescent encounter with Marilyn and Joe DiMaggio on North Redington Beach, Florida, in March 1961.

Family friend Sal Arena discussed Marilyn as a customer in his pet shop in Manhattan where she regularly purchased canine vitamins for Hugo, her Basset Hound.

The following participated in interviews during the Fiftieth Anniversary Memorial Service for Marilyn Monroe held in Los Angeles on August 5, 2012: Deborah Bakker, Ramon Bertolini,

Morgan Blackbyrne, Gianandrea Colombo, Jackie Craig, Shar Daws, Jessica Dunn, Shaney and Aimee Evans, Ernesto Galindo, Marijane Gray, Roy Harvey, Leslie Kasperowicz, Suzie Kennedy, Paul Maggs, David Marshall, Joel Morgan, Hanna Nixon, Niva Pemberton, Mary Sims, James Spada, Greg and Sunny Thompson, Manel Torquet-Oliva, Marco van der Munnik, and Janet Wheeler.

James Dougherty exchanged email messages with me and shared fond personal memories of his young bride, Norma Jeane. Our communication branched into many other topics until his passing.

Phyllis Goddard, who managed an archival website dedicated to William Spratling, discussed the American expatriate's friendship with Marilyn and her trip to Mexico.

Margot Stipe of *The Archives of Frank Lloyd Wright* at Taliesin West in Scottsdale, Arizona, shared with me floor plans of Wright's design for the Monroe-Miller house, and we often digressed to stories about our mutual love for dogs.

Eric Monroe Woodard assisted with information about Marilyn's Brentwood hacienda and ill-fated production of *Rain* for the NBC television network. Eric also provided a fateful introduction to Greg Schreiner of *Marilyn Remembered.*

Michael Greenwald discussed the history of Brentwood, Los Angeles.

Ceasar Vasallo shared his expansive archive including a photograph of Marilyn's childhood pet dog, Tippy.

George Bailey, Niagara's local historian, discussed the production of *Niagara* (1953). He also honored me by serving as best man at my wedding in Niagara-on-the-Lake.

Ernie Garcia nurtured my interest in Marilyn during the twentieth anniversary of her death and provided articles dating back to 1962; it was during the editing process of this project thirty years later that we reunited via social media.

Marilyn Monroe has an international following of devoted fans who generously offered to share their astounding knowledge of the details of her life. Through the Internet, I was able to reach across the globe to consult with many experts to clarify a date, a name, or an event. Their enthusiastic willingness to answer a question or identify a source at any hour of the day or night is greatly appreciated. The lovely Mary Sims, President of *Immortal Marilyn Fan Club,* assisted in researching rare and vintage periodicals.

Special thanks to the following who aided in research: Jackie Craig, Dorothy Bartlett, Sebastien Cauchon, Ashlee Davis, Shar Daws, Marijane Gray, Jane Guy, Tara Hanks, Brandon Heidrick, Roman Hryniszak, Michelle Justice, Leslie Kasperowicz, Melody Lockard, David Marshall, Hanna Nixon, Angie Paul, Tony Plant, Judy Stetson, Rebecca Swift, Roy Turner, Miguel Angel Gomora Vazquez, Marco van der Munnik, Peggy Wilkins, and Peter L. Winkler. Please forgive any oversight in acknowledgment of every "Monrologist" who answered a question or pointed me in the right direction.

I am indebted to the biographer Sarah Churchwell who provided encouragement via email across the Atlantic; she generously permitted me to include quotations from the definitive *The Many Lives of Marilyn Monroe.* Sarah's observations about Marilyn are priceless gems, which were essential as textural source material.

I am grateful to Joshua Greene for permission to include Marilyn's own words from her 1954 autobiography, *My Story.* The photographic archive of Milton H. Greene, his father, can be accessed at www.archivesmhg.com.

I am also appreciative to Mona Rae Miracle, Marilyn's niece, for her authorization to include quotations from *My Sister Marilyn.* Please see www.MonaRaeMiracle.com.

Additional thanks to Jonas Mekas for permission to quote extensively from his poetic review of *The Misfits*; Luke Yankee for permission to quote extensively from his memoir, *Just Outside the Spotlight: Growing Up with Eileen Heckart*; and TIME/LIFE for permission to quote from Richard Meryman's interview with Marilyn from the August 3, 1962 issue of *Life.* Thank you, Amy Wong of TIME/LIFE, for assistance.

Carl Rollyson granted permission for excerpts from his scholarly biography *Marilyn Monroe: A Life of the Actress* as he completed his latest work on our shared subject, *Marilyn Day By Day.* He reviewed my manuscript and offered valuable advice on the publishing process.

Social and political activist Gloria Steinem permitted my inclusion of quotations from *Marilyn Monroe: Norma Jean*, and actress/journalist Sheila O'Malley allowed a passage from her review of *Don't Bother to Knock* (1952) from her classic film blog *The Sheila Variations.*

Joann Schwendemann, representing Dover Publications, arranged for permission to include the excerpt from the Molly Brown soliloquy in James Joyce's *Ulysses* and Kevin Neelan, CEO/Founder of Digireads.com Publishing granted permission for the excerpt from Eugene O'Neill's *Anna Christie.*

Having been born three years after Marilyn Monroe's death, I first discovered her through the *4:30 Movie* on WABC-TV's Channel 7 and in a *Funk and Wagnalls Encyclopedia* in my childhood home in New York, circa 1973. In an article about the American motion industry, her portrait appeared with three other iconic actresses: Katharine Hepburn, Joan Crawford, and Bette Davis. Marilyn's image seemed more approachable than the others. Then I saw her image of her in photographer Milton Greene's famous "ballerina session." Looking into her eyes, I did not see a sex symbol. Instead, I felt as though I peered in the soul of a fascinating and complex young woman. Marilyn seemed to follow me everywhere, and I've chased her ever since. She looms in my consciousness like a deceased relative whom I never met—but wish I had—and about whom I had heard so much.

This biography critically cites from genuine research and credible sources, and purposefully excludes speculative and unreliable material.

The first book I read on this remarkable woman was Fred Lawrence Guiles' *Norma Jean: The Life of Marilyn Monroe.* In 1967, Guiles had adapted his 1963 screenplay, *Goodbye, Norma Jean*, into a series for *Ladies' Home Journal*—the magazine in which Marilyn had longed to be featured—titled "The Final Summer of Marilyn Monroe." Guiles expanded the piece into this definitive biography in 1969.

Shortly thereafter, I discovered Norman Mailer's *Marilyn: A Biography*, illustrated with mesmerizing photographs of his subject by Eve Arnold, Lawrence Schiller, Bert Stern, Milton Greene, and others. Another Norman, poet Norman Rosten, published his affectionate memoir, *Marilyn: An Untold Story*, as a rebuttal and shared a personal insight into his family's relationship with Marilyn during the last seven years of her life. Rosten later collaborated with photographer Sam Shaw, another friend of Marilyn's—whose family had also embraced her—to produce *Marilyn Among Friends.*

In the late 1960s and early 1970s, the culture had rediscovered Marilyn as a serious talent and cultural icon while acknowledging her irreplaceable role in film. Equality activist Gloria Steinem published an article, "The Woman Who Died Too Soon," in a 1972 issue of *Ms.* magazine and offered the first exploration of Marilyn's journey from a feminist perspective. Steinem followed up with *Marilyn: Norma Jean* fourteen years later.

Later, Marilyn was often the target of literary exploitation aimed to profit at the expense of her dignity. Too often would she be reduced to sensational speculation about her alleged relationships and theories about the circumstances of her death. This tabloid focus overshadowed her extraordinary life and accomplishments.

The scales tipped in Marilyn's favor when scholar Carl Rollyson honored and validated her talent and performances in *Marilyn Monroe: A Life of An Actress.* Donald Spoto's landmark, *Marilyn Monroe: The Biography*, replaced Guiles' work as a definitive biography as its title asserts. Later, Donald H. Wolfe's *The Last Days of Marilyn Monroe* and Barbara Leaming's *Marilyn Monroe* offered additional insights. In the new millennium, Sarah Churchwell's similarly academic *The Many Lives of Marilyn Monroe* summarized four decades of biographies.

Marilyn evolved as less of an archetype and more of a living, breathing woman in housekeeper Eunice Murray's *Marilyn: The Last Months*, Susan Strasberg's *Marilyn and Me: Sisters, Rivals, Friends*, and Berniece Miracle and Mona Rae Miracle's *My Sister Marilyn: A Memoir of Marilyn Monroe.* These treatments dispelled myths created by those who seem to have made scurrilous claims about their alleged associations with Marilyn. Most of those in whom Marilyn actually confided remained silent over the decades and spoke only to defend her. Time would reveal she chose her confidantes wisely. Ralph Roberts and Inez Melson never published their manuscripts yet were arguably closer to Marilyn than many other published authors.

Interestingly, Maurice Zolotow's first scholarly biography, *Marilyn Monroe*, remains accurate and salient fifty-four years after its original release and rivals many of its 600-odd subsequent challengers. With similar relevance, *My Story*, Marilyn's 1954 autobiography, written in collaboration with Ben Hecht, was finally published in 1974 and gave us Marilyn's own voice. Marilyn's voice resonated again in Lois Banner and Mark Anderson's *MM-Personal: From the Private Archive of Marilyn Monroe* and *Fragments: Poems, Intimate Notes, Letters*, edited by Stanley Buchthal and Bernard Comment.

Anthony Summers' exhaustive research culminated into *Goddess: The Secret Lives of Marilyn Monroe*. Though I question the credibility of many of the subjects he interviewed and sometimes disagree with his conclusions and implications, Summers provided an unprecedented depth of detail. Sandra Shevey, Richard Buskin, and Michelle Morgan interviewed many of Marilyn's co-stars and directors in their late years and documented their insights respectively in *The Marilyn Scandal, Blonde Heat: The Sizzling Screen Career of Marilyn Monroe*, and *Marilyn Monroe: Private and Undisclosed*.

I direct those interested in further reading to the plethora of above-mentioned works in addition to actual interviews with Marilyn by Richard Meryman, Georges Belmont, George Barris, and Alan Levy. My researched relied upon all of these legitimate sources.

I thank Michelle Levy for her exceptional editing and patience. Our videoconferences on Skype often digressed to enjoyable personal conversations about dogs, family, and life in general. Thanks also to Valerie Thompson for her beautiful cover designs and layouts for both volumes. *Molte grazie* to Mary Monson for being my second set of eyes; it is no coincidence that her initials are MM.

Personal thanks to my wonderful parents, Gloria and Frank Vitacco; my supportive brother, Mark Vitacco; my beloved aunt, Priscilla Muralo; my longtime friend and mentor, Courtenay O'Connell-Sims; Penny Himmler Vitacco; Oscar Vitacco-Robles—my spouse and eternal soulmate—who selflessly and lovingly supported this project while enduring the massive amount of time and attention it required; and Oscar's family, who has become my family in the last twenty-four years: Gloria and Bob Ward; Mitzi Robles; and David, Tori, and Wyatt Robles.

Finally, I dedicate this book to Norma Jeane, the resilient little girl who became Marilyn Monroe, and the many girls and young women who have also survived trauma and are reaching for their dreams.

GARY VITACCO-ROBLES
TRINITY, FL
JUNE 1, 2014

Introduction: Goddess, Legend, Icon

Marilyn Monroe survived a childhood marked by neglect, chaos, and sexual abuse to become a psychological, cultural, and spiritual phenomenon of the Twentieth Century.

Born Norma Jeane Baker, Marilyn Monroe (1926-1962) battled depression, anxiety, sexism, and addiction to prescribed medication while establishing herself as a shining star, accomplished motion picture actress, and historical figure. Marilyn continues to illuminate the world and fascinate young people with her remarkable story. Marilyn's idiosyncratic style of requesting supportive energy from her friends was to say, "Please hold a good thought for me." On the half-centennial of her untimely death, a new generation continues to hold a good thought for this beloved cinematic and cultural icon and admire her legacy of vulnerability, strength, talent, and beauty.

Marilyn's screen image was often in contrast to her soulful, shy, and introspective personality. Close friends witnessed a conscious and spontaneous transformation from her real self to persona when she asked them, "Do you want me to be her?" Denied a sense of grounding by the unfortunate circumstances of her childhood, Marilyn searched for identity through a personal journey toward growth, culture, knowledge, and love.

As she was in the 1950s, Marilyn remains frozen in time as stunningly beautiful, desirable, charismatic, forever smiling, and carefree. She was the last modern love goddess, a cultural archetype of idealized feminine sexuality. Paradoxically, she is also our icon for a tragic and premature death. She is simultaneously the embodiment of desire and death.

Part of Marilyn's enduring appeal may be the empathy that her pain and life experiences evoke in each of us. She inspires us to project our own subjective interpretations onto her extraordinary life. Volumes of biographies are published each year analyzing the events in Marilyn's life and their impact on her personal and professional functioning. We hear repeatedly of her illegitimate birth, mentally ill mother, three marriages, divorces, and multiple miscarriages. Authors provide varying perceptions of Marilyn's professional triumphs, personal suffering, and tragic death. She commonly emerges as a virtually parentless waif who grows up to become the America's sweetheart—a Cinderella who transforms and goes to the ball. "I knew I belonged to the public and to the world," Marilyn wrote, aware of the emotional chord she struck in her audience, "not because I was talented or even beautiful, but because I had never belonged to anything or anyone else."

Marilyn was decades ahead of her time and greatly misunderstood during her lifetime. She was the first public figure to disclose childhood sexual abuse, and one of the few female stars to establish her own production company. She also suffered from symptoms consistent with the diagnoses of Bipolar Disorder long before it had an effective treatment.

An insecure and often introverted woman, Marilyn generally avoided dressing in furs and jewels and attending the lavish parties and public spectacles of Hollywood's social circuit. She preferred wearing Capri slacks, no make-up, and discussing literature and acting theory in the kitchens of her New York intellectual friends. She engaged in intense relationships with a small number of motion picture technicians whose contributions took place behind the camera. The actress walked with poets, authors, politicians, liberals and artists, but her funeral was attended by non-celebrities upon whom she had depended for loyalty and friendship.

In the last weeks of Marilyn's life, a housekeeper greeted her at the door of a host's home and stared with surprise. "No one will believe me when I say I met and shook hands with Marilyn Monroe," the housekeeper gasped. "I can hardly believe it myself." "Well, I can't believe it, too," Marilyn replied, joining in the maid's astonishment. "I guess I am. Everybody says I am." Marilyn's response suggests that she identified with her audience and felt detached from her own celebrity.

Through twenty-nine films released during a sixteen-year career, Marilyn left behind a legacy of brilliance that has established her as the motion picture industry's reigning actress icon. She possessed enormous charisma and a powerful screen presence that made the audience focus on every nuance of her performance.

Marilyn's screen roles demonstrated a wide range within typecasting. Her early portrayals of the 'dumb blonde' elevated the two-dimensional archetype into a textured, satirical parody, and even in her most minor roles, she emerged as an adroit comedienne and dramatic artist whose personal depth radiated through often limited scripts. Later, screenwriters altered Marilyn's roles to reflect the sensitive artist beneath the sexual facade maintained by her screen image. Her characterizations were wise, gentle and nurturing; they engendered goodness and compassion, taught lessons, and united opposing forces.

Despite the motion picture industry's goal to limit Marilyn's range and exploit her physical attraction, she was obsessively driven to evolve into a serious, dramatic actress. She courageously risked ridicule and her career by rebelling against her studio and rejecting its imposed direction. She embarked on study of the controversial Method Acting technique at Lee Strasberg's Actor's Studio in New York City, while collaborating with photographer Milton Greene to produce her own films.

Although the Academy of Motion Picture Arts and Sciences snubbed Marilyn's critically acclaimed performances in *Bus Stop* (1956) and *The Misfits* (1961), she received significant laurels from other corners. In March 1960, Marilyn was presented the Golden Globe Award for Best Actress in a Musical or Comedy for her performance as Sugar Kane in *Some Like It Hot* (1959). At one point, the public speculated Marilyn's career was declining, but when she received the Golden Globe Award as World Film Favorite of 1961 in March 1962, she proved them wrong. Three years earlier, Marilyn was awarded both the French and Italian film industries' respective Crystal Star and David di Donatello Award for her performance as Elsie Marina in *The Prince and the Showgirl* (1957). (These European honors for Best Foreign Actress were equivalent to the Oscar). In 1999, the American Film Institute ranked Marilyn Monroe sixth among the list of legendary screen actresses behind

Katharine Hepburn, Audrey Hepburn, Bette Davis, Ingrid Bergman, and Greta Garbo.

Ultimately, Marilyn's impact on the world overshadows the contribution of many statesmen. Her extraordinary life elicits strong emotional reactions and is celebrated and respected in our popular culture today. "She was (and still is) adored by men and women alike," wrote Nancy Valentino, "and the depths to which she can stir the emotions of both sexes indicate a profound sense of humanity."

In the five decades following her death, Marilyn Monroe has resonated as a legend, a myth, and the subject of apocrypha. "A religious metaphor like apocrypha seems particularly apt in the case of Marilyn, our ultimate goddess, divinity, icon, idol," wrote Sarah Churchwell, the first to document to scale of the myth of Marilyn Monroe and its reflection on our cultural values and our attitudes about women, celebrity, sex, and death.

With her rags to riches story, Marilyn embodies the American dream. She proved that no matter how meager one's background, with hard work and determination, one could achieve one's dreams. Feminist Gloria Steinem acknowledges Marilyn as an inspiration to women because she exemplified almost celestial energy and—in spite of evident vulnerability—exerted her will, strength, and intelligence.

Marilyn's story has been reproduced in an estimated six hundred books written since her death in 1962. They include traditional biographies, biographical novels, and fictionalized autobiographies; collections of photographs, trivia, and quotations; encyclopedias, film reviews, essays, and elegies; dramatic interpretations of her life in the form of plays, musicals, operas, and films. She is also frequently the subject of documentary films. Many books and documentaries address only speculation about the circumstances of her death. "Marilyn has gone from sex symbol to a symbol of mourning, from a promise of the liberation of sex to a cautionary tale about the dangers of loneliness and spinsterhood," wrote Churchwell. "And chiefly it is the writing and rewriting of her life story that has achieved this transformation."

Marilyn Monroe was a character created and honed by Norma Jeane Baker. She performed as this character in films and in public life, reserving her authentic personality for private life. It is due to our lack of knowledge about Marilyn the woman, not Marilyn the star that has made her character flourish posthumously through the legend and myth surrounding her life.

Despite all the tomes and dramatic interpretations of Marilyn Monroe's life based upon both truth and fiction, she remains an enigma in part because she left behind no definitive autobiography or televised or filmed interview of any merit. Her partially ghost-written memoir, *My Story*, depicts only snapshots of her childhood and life until 1954. In a brief *Person to Person* interview with Edward R. Murrow in 1955, Marilyn appears vacuous and mirrors her screen persona as she speaks in the affected baby doll voice in responses to mindless and trite questions such as, "What was your smallest part in a film?"

Marilyn's more substantial interviews with Georges Belmont in 1960 and Richard Meryman in 1962 more effectively capture the real woman and her intellect, but these were preserved only in audiotapes and remain obscure. In the first interview, conducted on the set of *Let's Make Love*, Marilyn speaks maturely and seriously in her natural voice about her past, her work, aspirations, routine, relationships, philosophy, and personal struggles. Her responses sound spontaneous and thoughtful with a hint of an underlying depressed mood.

In the latter interview conducted for *Life* shortly before her death, Marilyn seems rehearsed in her responses. She punctuates witty remarks with a giggle that culminates into a nervous laugh and sounds manic. Journalists recorded Marilyn's most cerebral discussions in text form, and no audiotapes of these interviews have been released to the public. The true depth of Marilyn Monroe's psyche is not revealed in these interviews or in the plethora of biographies, but rather, through the archive of her journals, diaries, poems, and letters published or auctioned as historic documents decades after her death. Reproduced in auction catalogues, the prose echoes Marilyn's inner voice in a stream of consciousness and private confessions. Through them, her now silenced voice is strong and clear. Herein lay the truth.

Part I:

Mrs. Arthur Miller

CHAPTER ONE: *THE PRINCE AND THE SHOWGIRL*

Director Joshua Logan considered the collaboration of Marilyn Monroe and Sir Laurence Olivier "the best combination since black and white." By producing her first independent film playing opposite a distinguished British thespian, Marilyn hoped to gain legitimacy as a serious artist. In turn, she offered Olivier an opportunity to rejuvenate his dimming film career with her youth, vibrancy, and commercial appeal.

"[Olivier's] position at one time in England was that he was like a kind of God," said cinematographer Jack Cardiff. "He ruled the theatre world. And when it was proposed that he would work with Marilyn Monroe, it tickled the press. What a combination—Laurence Olivier, the great Shakespearean actor working with this American cream puff." After a long negotiation conducted through countless transatlantic cables, Olivier accepted the role on the condition that he co-produce and direct the film.

Twenty years older than Marilyn, Laurence Olivier (1907-1989) was the quintessential, classical actor of the British stage. He had earned Oscars for film versions of Shakespearian dramas such as *Henry V* (1945) and *Hamlet* (1948). As an adolescent, Marilyn had admired his Oscar-nominated performances as the romantic Healthcliff in *Wuthering Heights* (1939) and as a tormented widower trying to start a new life in *Rebecca* (1940). In 1947, King George VI bestowed Olivier with the title of Knighthood. "She had idealized Olivier," Arthur Miller wrote, "who as the great and serious artist must be above mortal considerations of the kind so common among the Hollywood fleshmongers she thought she had escaped."

According to Miller, Marilyn originated the idea of co-starring with Olivier long before her corporation acquired a suitable property for her first completely independent production. Charles Feldman had sought the film rights for Terrance Rattigan's play, *The Sleeping Prince*, with Marilyn in mind. Once the rights became available, Marilyn envisioned herself as the sweet and diplomatic showgirl—an innate sage—who reconciles members of a royal family and prevents a world war. She was amused by the casting of Olivier as the pompous, arrogant Balkan Regent of Carpathia whose cold heart the showgirl thaws. Across the Atlantic, Vivien Leigh, Olivier's wife, shared Marilyn's vision of this preposterous pairing in the very same property.

Marilyn pursued the purchase of the property from Rattigan (1911-1977) while he traveled from London to New York by sending a message to him at an airport lounge, inviting him to join her for cocktails at the Barberry Room, a Manhattan bar. She swept in with Milton Greene, the vice president of her production corporation; Jay Kanter, her agent; and Irving Stein, her corporation's attorney. According to Rattigan's biographer, Michael Darlow, "[Marilyn] was prepared to write out a contract on the bar table there and then." The experiences of Rattigan's father as the official host to a Moroccan dignitary during the coronation of George V at the time of the author's birth inspired the plot. With the exception of *The Sleeping Prince*, much of Rattigan's work contained coded references to his sexual orientation during an era when gay and lesbian people were forced to keep their true identities secret. His previous work included *The Winslow Boy* (1946), *The Browning Version* (1948), *The Deep Blue Sea* (1952), and *Separate Tables* (1954).

Warner Brothers Studios would distribute the film, and for publicity, Jack Warner welcomed Marilyn and Milton Greene to the lot to present her with a bouquet of roses and a symbolic key to the studio. Director Billy Wilder and actor James Stewart, on a break from filming *The Charles Lindberg Story*, joined many others present in congratulating her. Arthur P. Jacobs assigned a young female publicist on his staff, Patricia Newcomb, to cover the event but Marilyn took an immediate dislike to her and requested a replacement. Jacobs would appoint Newcomb to Marilyn in late 1960, and the two women would eventually form a close bond.

With serious ambition, Marilyn—aided by Milton Greene—took Rattigan's three-act drawing-room comedy out of the drawing room but essentially kept the plot intact. The story takes place in the city of London in 1911, where American actress Elsie Marina is performing in a play starring Maisie Springfield. Following a performance, the cast is introduced to the Regent of Carpathia from the Balkan kingdom. Elsie makes an impression on the Regent upon their meeting when the strap of her dress snaps as she curtsies. Later, she receives a formal invitation to a reception at the Carpathian embassy. Upon arrival, she realizes it is a private affair and suspects the Regent is trying to seduce her. She outlines the steps the Regent will use in his seduction attempt to Mr. Northbrook, the British liaison coordinating the affair. While fleeing the embassy, the Regent arrives and convinces her to stay.

The stiff and irritable sovereign alternates between delight and consternation with his beautiful guest who rebuffs his sexual advances and displays no tolerance for the vodka he serves. Driven by her open emotions and American ideals, Elsie challenges his beliefs about love and politics. His plans of a sex-filled evening cast aside, the Regent becomes exasperated by her confrontation of his repressive politics and difficulties with intimacy. His attempts to send Elsie home are delayed by King Nicolas, the Regent's teen son (Jeremy Spenser) with reformist principals, and the Queen dowager (Sybil Thorndike), the hearing-impaired mother of the Regent's deceased wife.

Both are entirely enchanted with Elsie's warm and child-like charm. The dowager speaks French to Elsie who fakes understanding and inadvertently leads the elderly lady into believing Elsie is the friend of the great actress Sarah Bernhardt. Elsie accepts the dowager's invitation to accompany the royal family to the coronation of King George V, and later accepts the young king's invitation to the coronation ball. Gradually softened by Elsie's blunt honesty and democratic values, the Regent falls in love with her.

Originally from Milwaukee, Elsie is fluent in German and overhears the young King's plans to overthrow his father's government. This grants her the inadvertent role of preventing a World War, reconciling a royal family, and softening of the Regent's hardened heart.

Elements of the plot paralleled Marilyn's relationship with her audience. The public, like the Regent, initially saw her as merely a sex symbol; and Marilyn, like Elsie, is humanized when she reveals intelligence and soulfulness beneath an attractive surface.

"Some people have been unkind," Marilyn sighed to Dorothy Manning, a reporter for *Photoplay*, about her aspirations to be taken seriously. "If I say I want to grow as an actress, they look at my figure. If I say I want to develop, to learn my craft, they laugh. Somehow they don't expect me to be serious about my work. I'm more serious about that than anything. But people persist in thinking I've pretensions of turning into a Bernhardt or a Duse—that I want to play Lady Macbeth. And what they'll say when I work with Sir Laurence, I don't know."

Elsie offered Marilyn a transition from her dumb-blonde showgirl characters to more serious, three-dimensional roles. "Marilyn's Elsie is a marvelous portrait," wrote Donald Spoto, "alternately feisty and independent, not to be had for the price of caviar and champagne, wise in the ways of monocled playboys and entirely capable of mediating an international crisis."

Rattigan's story was a simple spin on fairy tales such as *Sleeping Beauty* and *Snow White*, that both involved a sleeping princess awaiting a kiss by a noble prince. However, the playwright reversed the characters' genders, replacing the noble prince with an instinctively wise and benevolent showgirl. In the words of the playwright, "The play is about a man who has been asleep—at least his emotional side; but little by little a relationship builds up between him and this American chorus girl. He begins to stir in his sleep."

Scarcely starry-eyed, Rattigan's Grand Ducal Highness is a cantankerous cynic interested in short-term sexual encounters and dalliances with actresses of the stage. The character is an arrogant and chauvinistic cad who regards the showgirl with downright contempt. Rattigan worried that Marilyn's adaptation would romanticize the Regent: "Where I had feared that my Prince Uncharming would inevitably become Prince Utterly Irresistible those fears were forever laid to rest when…I went into [Olivier's] dressing room…to be confronted by a rather dull-looking little man, with an anemic complexion…a thin, prissy, humorless mouth, hair parted in the middle and plastered repulsively downwards over his ears, and a sad-looking monocle glued over his right eye."

Two decades earlier, Olivier and British actress Vivien Leigh (1913-1967) both were married to other partners but engaged in a public love affair after appearing together in *Fire Over England* (1937). Leigh accompanied Olivier to the United States in 1938 where director David O. Selznick cast her as the feisty American southern belle, Scarlett O'Hara, in his epic masterpiece *Gone with the Wind*. Leigh would earn her first of two Best Actress Oscars as Scarlett O'Hara, the second for Blanche DuBois in *A Streetcar Named Desire* (1951).

Olivier and Leigh lived openly together in Hollywood and married in 1940. The relationship became strained after a miscarriage four years later followed by Leigh's excessive alcohol consumption. She was eventually diagnosed with Bipolar Disorder and had likely been self-medicating her severe symptoms. In 1953, Vivien Leigh was cast in *Elephant Walk* with actor Peter Finch.

While working with Finch, Vivien suffered a severe manic episode marked by hallucinations, compulsions to clean, angry outbursts, and disrobing in public. She became increasingly more psychotic, reciting lines from *A Streetcar Named Desire*, directing her assistants to procure sexual partners, and identifying Finch as Olivier. During a horrific flight to London, Vivien became hysterical, disrobed, and tried to jump out of the plane. The studio promptly replaced her with Elizabeth Taylor, and Vivien entered Netherne, a psychiatric hospital in Surrey, for intensive treatment. Mood stabilizing drugs such as Lithium were not yet available, and the course of treatment was electroshock therapy to the brain.

Olivier believed that working with his wife might salvage their troubled marriage. Enter Terence Rattigan, who tailored *The Sleeping Prince* for the troubled couple. Opening in London at the Phoenix Theatre in November 1953—during Vivien's fortieth birthday—the play was designed as a courtier's offering to Queen Elizabeth II in her coronation year.

Olivier's success in the film adaptation of *The Sleeping Prince* would depend upon his ability to inject passion and animation into the role of the prince, and who could better inspire him than Marilyn Monroe?

Warner Brothers Studios submitted Rattigan's screenplay to the

Breen Office for censorship approval, and it failed on the basis of the Code forbidding seduction as a subject for a comedy, inferred that "low forms of sex relationship are accepted or common thing." Rattigan protested that his plot contained a moral turn in its "awakening of a sleeping prince from a low view of love to a higher one." In a brave move, Olivier wrote to Greene suggesting they forfeit the Breen Office seal, as did United Artists in release of *The Moon Is Blue* (1952)—the first American film to contain the word "virgin."

Jack Warner sent Motion Picture Code Administrator, Geoffrey Shurlock, to London to meet with Rattigan and Olivier. The playwright agreed to insert a scene in which Elsie informs Northbrook that she spent the night wandering outside the Carpathian Embassy to avoid any implication of her spending the night in bed with the Regent. To sidestep adultery, Rattigan replaced the married regent with a widowed one and replaced the wife with a mother-in-law.

Marilyn and Olivier selected cinematographer Jack Cardiff (1914-2009) who had won Oscars for *Black Narcissus* (1946) and *The African Queen* (1951) and had earned artistic success with his cinematic compositions for *The Red Shoes* (1948) and *The Barefoot Contessa* (1954). He had worked with Olivier in *As You Like It* (1936) and would become especially close to Marilyn during the production. "[Marilyn] was practically perfect to photograph," Cardiff said. "If you could measure Marilyn's eyes and facial features, they were almost perfect. The end of her nose was tipped a bit, but it was charming, and she was absolutely lovely. She photographed perfectly from any direction."

Tony Bushell served as associate director who took the helm when Olivier performed in front of the cameras. Bushell had directed British films of the 1930s in addition to Olivier's *Hamlet*. Third assistant director Colin Clark (1932-2002), a young graduate from the prestigious Eton College in Berkshire, maintained a diary during the production. Published in 1996, his notes display insight and compassion for Marilyn's struggles with Olivier's rigidity and snobbery.

Marilyn's co-stars were primarily classically trained actors of the British stage with scant motion picture experience. With twenty-six films behind her, Marilyn found herself the most polished film veteran among her troupe. Dame Sybil Thorndike (1886-1976) portrayed the sagacious, hearing-impaired Queen Dowager. Born in Lincolnshire and trained in the United States at Ben Greet's Academy, she first performed on the British stage in 1904. Dame Sybil appeared in several of George Bernard Shaw's plays, including *Candida* (1920) and in the leading role of Joan of Arc in *Saint Joan* in 1933, the latter written specifically for her. She would reprise this role with great success well into her sixties.

Dame Sybil and her husband, Welsh actor and director Lewis Casson, were both politically liberal and together toured Welsh mining villages in Shakespearean productions produced by the Council for the Encouragement of the Arts. King George V appointed her Dame Commander of the British Empire in 1931. Having episodically suffered from nervous anxiety, Dame Sybil was completely sympathetic to Marilyn. While she was a young woman, the elder actress' musical career as a concert pianist ended as the result of a wrist injury.

Early in her career, after performing in one hundred twelve roles during a three-year Shakespearean repertory, Dame Sybil experienced symptoms of anxiety leading to acute laryngitis, and this experience would make her especially empathic toward Marilyn's neuroses. Dame Sybil immediately attached herself to Marilyn. "[Marilyn] has an innocence which is so extraordinary," she said, "whatever she plays, however brazen a hussy, it always comes over as an innocent girl. I remember Sir Laurence saying one day during the filming: 'Look at her face—she could be five years old!'"

British character actor, Richard Wattis (1912-1975), who played the British liaison Mr. Northbrook, was well known in roles as annoying government officials in films such as *The Happiest Days of Your Life* and *The Great St. Trinian's Train Robbery.* He shared nearly as much screen time with Marilyn as Olivier. Jeremy Spenser (born 1937) portrayed the King of Carpathia, the Regent's sixteen-year-old son. He had appeared in the film *Portrait of Clare* (1950). Paul Hardwick had a small but effective part as Majordomo, the head butler of the prince's household.

Daphne Anderson (1922-2013) was cast as Fanny, Elsie's friend and the dresser in her play, *The Coconut Girl.* She appeared in *Hobson's Choice* (1953) with Charles Laughton, *The Beggar's Opera* (1953) with Olivier, and *A Kid for Two Farthings* (1955). "She was withdrawn and I couldn't get anywhere near her as a person," Anderson remembered of Marilyn. "I don't think she was trying to be a star, she was just remote, probably because she lacked confidence, especially among stage people like Sir Laurence Olivier and Dame Sybil Thorndike." Anderson imagined Marilyn feeling like she was in another world among the British world of filmmaking and interpreted her appearing an hour late every day as the result of terror.

Jean Kent (1921-2013) was cast as Maisie Springfield, the star of Elsie's play and the Regent's long-term sex interest. She had performed in British films such as *Sleeping Car to Trieste* (1945), *The Woman in Question* (1950), and Rattigan's *The Browning Version* (1951). Maxine Audley (1923-1992) had a small part as Lady Sunningdale, the Regent's elegant lady friend and suggested lover. Mostly known as a stage actress, one of her few films included *The Sleeping Tiger* (1954).

Beatrice "Bumble" Dawson received screen credit for ladies costume design, although some reports indicate Edith Head actually designed Marilyn's Edwardian white gown and crepe wrap. Colin Clark remembered Dawson as a "jolly, ginny neurotic old bird" who "smokes continuously and grinds her teeth." Amy Greene had suggested Dawson after seeing the designer's period costumes in *The Importance of Being Ernest* (1952).

Aside from her stage costume in her first scene and her undergarments in the next, Elsie wears the white gown during the majority of the film covering a period of two days. In fact, the Queen Mother remarks to her, "You are imitating the divine Sarah Bernhardt, no doubt...but even she, I am told, changes her dress occasionally." Milton Greene believed Marilyn's hourglass figure befitted the period film. Her figure would expand each weekend as she gained weight drinking champagne and eating with her husband. By midweek, Marilyn returned to her normal size through the use of diuretics. Dawson designed several versions of the white gown in various sizes to accommodate Marilyn's fluctuations in weight. "I have two ulcers from this film," Dawson would complain to Amy Greene, "and they're both monogrammed MM."

Allan Snyder designed Marilyn's makeup and traveled to England to teach the process of application to the British beauticians who would attend to her during the long production. Sydney Guilaroff was credited for designing Marilyn's period hairstyles and instructing the British stylists recreating them during the production. "MGM agreed to loan me out to do Marilyn's hair on the condition that she agree to attend the upcoming premiere of *Gigi*," Guilaroff would write. "After letting her out of their grasp a few years before, Metro now knew the drawing power Marilyn possessed wherever she went."

Carmen Dillon, the art director, and Roger Furse, set designer, created the neo-classical Carpathian Embassy and its purple drawing room with mauve furnishings, described by Colin Clark as a setting for a 19th century operetta, to contrast with Marilyn's white costume.

Rattigan suggested an incidental musical soundtrack, but Olivier disagreed; Marilyn wanted a continuous romantic melodic background to the plot. Richard Addinsell (1904-1977) composed the film's score and, at the direction of Greene, wrote two songs for Marilyn to sing. Only one, "I Found a Dream," survived to the final cut. Strangely, Miller exerted influence against his wife's singing in the production. The dance sequences included a ballroom scene featuring the main musical theme set to a waltz and Elsie's short but charming dance to a distant organ grinder's tune. Billy Chappell choreographed the dances for the stars and many extras in period costumes.

Marilyn insisted upon Paula Strasberg's services as acting coach during the production. In Marilyn's eyes, Lee's wife was his representative but was no substitute for her mentor. Lee required Paula to receive $25,000 for ten weeks' work plus expenses and overtime, eventually amounting to $38,000. To compensate for Paula's high rate, Marilyn agreed to reduce her own salary.

Marilyn Monroe Productions had secured the most illustrious and serious British actor as its president's co-star and director, a celebrated cinematographer, highly seasoned designers, and a superb cast from the British stage. With these provisions in place, how could Marilyn lose?

* * *

Magnum photographer Eve Arnold rarely documented motion picture press conferences, finding them uninspired, predictable, and insignificant. However, when Marilyn invited her to the public announcement of her latest production at the Plaza Hotel in New York on February 9, 1956, Arnold marked her calendar without hesitation. (Marilyn appealed to the photographer's sense of humor.) Arnold was less expecting to take interesting shots and more curious to observe Marilyn's mastery of the press.

Arnold would be both enchanted and impressed by Marilyn's command of the situation and creative manipulation of the press. She briefly met with Marilyn as she prepared for the event and complimented her striking appearance, not realizing her subject's rigging of a costume malfunction unmatched until Janet Jackson's exposure of a breast during the half-time entertainment at the 2004 Super Bowl.

At eleven o'clock in the morning, Marilyn arrived at the Plaza wearing a black velvet dress with thin spaghetti straps, a matching cape designed by John Moore, a diaphanous scarf draped around her neck, a coat over her shoulders, and black gloves. She graciously thanked Arnold for attending and added rather mischievously, "Just watch me."

With Olivier at her side in a dark suit, dark tie, and white shirt, Marilyn made a grand entrance from a balcony like the fairy tale characters she and Olivier would portray. The couple descended the sweeping stairs as the press below engulfed them. "It has long been my hope and dream to act with Sir Laurence," Marilyn said, seated at a small table next to her future co-star. "He has always been my idol." Olivier controlled the microphone, often clutching it with both hands, and rephrased the reporters' questions. This delay allowed Marilyn time to formulate her witty responses.

"She is a brilliant comedienne," remarked Olivier, "and therefore an extremely good actress. She has the cunning gift of being able to suggest one minute that she is the naughtiest little thing, and the next minute that she is beautifully dumb and innocent. The audience leaves the theatre gently titillated into a state of excitement by not knowing which she is and thoroughly enjoying it."

"Is it true you want to play *The Brothers Karamazov*?" one incredulous reporter asked. Arthur Miller would later describe the implication behind the query as a suggestion that Marilyn planned to grow a beard and portray one of the leading male roles.

"I don't want to play the brothers," Marilyn explained. "I want to play Grushenka. She's a girl."

"How do you spell Grushenka?" a reporter asked.

"I think it begins with a G," Marilyn demurely responded. "Look it up."

The press could not permit Marilyn the "the simple dignity of a performer announcing a new project," lamented Miller with rancor nearly thirty years later.

Marilyn did not back down, though. Instead, she asserted, "*My* corporation owns *The Sleeping Prince*." When asked what inspired her to study acting, Marilyn quickly replied, "Seeing my own pictures." The reporters burst into applause. And then Marilyn unleashed her unparalleled magic.

As she leaned forward, the fragile spaghetti strap of Marilyn's dress broke. Her hand swiftly rose to her breast, avoiding public exposure. "Shall I take my coat off, boys?" Olivier wryly asked the journalists. "Suddenly, the ambience changed," remembered Eve Arnold, "by Marilyn creating hilarity." Everyone laughed, film critic Judith Crist of the *New York Herald Tribune* offered a safety pin, and Marilyn strategically gained control. Arnold was amazed by Marilyn's cleverness and rejoiced that she had agreed to come along. When one reporter asked how it felt when the strap broke, Marilyn retorted, "How would you feel if something of yours broke in front of a whole room of a lot of strangers?" Olivier marveled at Marilyn's command of the press conference. Out of the gate, they were off to a good start.

It had been love at first sight when Olivier met Marilyn in February 1956 at her Sutton Place apartment. Rattigan and Olivier's agent Cecil Tennant witnessed the sparks. "By the end of the day one thing was clear to me," Olivier wrote, "I was going to fall most shatteringly in love with Marilyn, and what was going to happen? There was no question about it, it was inescapable, or so I thought; she was so adorable, so witty, such incredible fun and more physically attractive than anyone I could have imagined. I went home like a lamb reprieved from the slaughter just for now, but next time...Wow! For the first time now it threatened to be 'poor Vivien'!" Amy Greene suspected that if Marilyn weren't married, she would have had an affair with Olivier. Marilyn was initially thrilled with the actor, and since his marriage was collapsing, he was vulnerable to a romantic diversion.

Olivier did his homework before directing Marilyn. He began with a transatlantic phone conversation with her most recent director,

Joshua Logan. She would be worth any trouble, the director of *Bus Stop* (1956) advised, just load the camera with film, position Marilyn in front of it, and keep Paula Strasberg off the set. Logan enjoyed a personal relationship with the Strasbergs and recognized Marilyn's belief that Paula provided something she needed even though he disagreed.

Logan gave Olivier specific instructions based upon his experience and success in facilitating what many critics praised as Marilyn's finest performance. "Please, don't tell her what to do," he begged. "She probably knows more about acting in films than anyone in the world. Don't order her about...Please do not expect her to behave like the average actress you have worked with. For instance, don't tell her exactly how to read a line. Let her work it out some way herself no matter how long it takes."

"I will not get upset if I don't get everything my way," Olivier assured Logan. "I will iron myself out every morning like a shirt, hoping to get through the day without a wrinkle." Within a few months, however, Olivier would abandon the metaphoric iron, and his fabric would turn into a wrinkled mess.

* * *

As executive producer, Milton Greene attended to the details of production and the agreement between Marilyn Monroe Productions and Laurence Olivier's production company. He arranged for the large crew of Americans to fly to Great Britain for lodgings.

Third assistant director Colin Clark (1932-2002) was tasked with finding housing for the Millers in close proximity to both Pinewood Studios and central London for the eighteen weeks of production. The couple had specified a secluded residence off the main roads, surrounded by gardens, with a minimum of three bedrooms and three bathrooms and ample servants' quarters. The twenty-three-year-old son of historian Lord Kenneth Clark found himself in exciting but unfamiliar territory as a go-fer on a film crew and feverishly jotted his daily experiences in a personal diary.

Initially, Clark previewed Tibbs Farm, across from Ascot Racecourse, for use by the production team. Owned by Mr. Cotes-Preedy and his wife, the estate would rent at one hundred pounds a week. Clark took precautions and leaked the story to the *Evening Standard* as a decoy to safeguard the Millers' privacy. The residence became a temporary home for Milton and Amy Greene.

For the Millers, Clark reserved Parkside House, a Georgian mansion at Englefield Green, Surrey, the country estate of Lord Garrett Moore, publisher of the *Financial Times*, and his wife Joan Carr, a concert pianist. Clark wrote, "*Moore fancies himself as God's gift to women...*" and "*secretly thinks that he will get to meet [Marilyn] and that she will be unable to resist his languid charms.*" The residence was built on ten acres of royal ground adjoining Windsor Park. The park included maze pathways and rose gardens. The home contained eleven bedrooms and servants' quarters, but at one hundred twenty pounds per week, lacked amenities. In fact, Marilyn found it cold and damp; these conditions led to her catching viral infections that would delay production. Milton Greene arranged to have the master bedroom painted in white, Marilyn's preference, and installed special blinds to facilitate her sleep.

Clark also coordinated security with the airport and law enforcement in preparation for Marilyn's arrival. The London police were still reeling from pandemonium caused by screaming adolescent fans when singer Johnny Ray arrived three years earlier. "*They all want to be the one who stands next to MM and protect her from the mob,*" Clark wrote of the police officers he met. William Hickey of *Daily Express* interviewed officials of the Ministry of Civil Aviation who quickly differentiated London Airport from Idlewild in New York and predicted no screaming fans. The British don't participate in the "ballyhoo" of American publicity, a spokesperson asserted, and Marilyn would be treated as "just another arrival."

During a rain drizzle, Marilyn and Miller arrived at London's Heathrow Airport on July 14, 1956, with their twenty-seven pieces of luggage, three of which belonged to Miller. For their five hundred ninety-seven pounds of assorted suitcases, the couple incurred $1,500 in excess baggage charges. Accompanied by three hundred journalists, reporters and press photographers, as well as seventy-five police officers, Olivier and Vivien Leigh greeted the couple as they deplaned.

Marilyn wore a light-colored raincoat over her shoulders and a light-colored, long-sleeved, high-necked, clinging sheath with matching pumps and short white gloves. Despite her hair appearing somewhat flat from sleeping on the long flight from New York, Marilyn's radiance defied the gloomy day. Miller wore a light sports coat, dark trousers, shirt and tie. Vivien wore a matronly, two-piece suit with a pleated skirt, long gloves, and a hat. At the age of forty-two, she was pregnant, as reported by the press a few days earlier. Amy Greene would claim the pregnancy was fictitious based upon a confidential conversation with Leigh, but biographers document the pregnancy as fact.

Miller recalled the madness of the arrival at the airport with an enduring "solid wall of white light" formed by a multitude of camera flashes that made even the photographers burst into laughter. The event dominated newspapers and overshadowed British Prime Minister Anthony Eden's speech about an ensuing economic crisis. "She is here. She walks. She talks," *The London Evening News* announced. "She really is as luscious as strawberries and cream." Contrastingly, Miller was described as "cold as a refrigerated fish in his personal appearance. Not like a hot lover—more like a morgue keeper lift with a royal cadaver."

"*The Customs officers had lost their heads and had been swept away,*" Colin Clark wrote in his diary of the melee created by airport employees rather than the mob of fans. "*I suppose the very thought of searching MM's person had been too much for them.*" After clearance through Customs, the Millers and Oliviers spoke with the press in an airport lounge. When the reporters instructed Marilyn to kiss her new husband for the cameras, she demurely refused. Eventually, Miller patted her hand, conveying permission for a kiss. One of the photographers was hospitalized after he fell at Marilyn's feet and his stampeding colleagues trampled him.

"Are all your press conferences like this?" asked Vivien.

"Actually, this is a little quieter than some of them," Marilyn responded with a smile.

A reporter asked if Marilyn would be the Oliviers' houseguest. "Marilyn *will not* be staying with us," Vivien asserted, a bit too indignantly. "She will weekend with us sometimes at our country home in Buckinghamshire…Miss Monroe desires vacant possession of her little bit of England…"

One reporter asked if Marilyn would be godmother to the Olivier child. "That's an interesting idea," Sir Laurence replied.

After the Millers' arrival, additional members of Marilyn's entourage landed at Heathrow: the Strasbergs, Amy Greene with her son Joshua, Hedda Rosten—in tow as Marilyn's secretary—and Allan Snyder. Colin Clark observed: "*MM is carrying quite a lot of other burdens as well—a husband who is unsupportive and away; a manager who could be seen as exploiting her; and 'best friends' who are sycophantic and weak.*"

A limousine transported the Millers, Greene, and Arthur P. Jacobs to Surrey with four policemen on motorcycles in close formation. The Oliviers followed in a Bentley, separated by a third vehicle carrying Colin Clark and Inspector Plod by several press cars. When Clark arrived at Parkside House, he discovered several policemen guarding the gate from the press. Marilyn had shed her coat, and Miller changed his shirt, tie and trousers. Twelve years younger than Leigh, Marilyn radiated in a modern outfit, her breasts prominently lifted and outlined in the dress that clung to her contours.

Marilyn intended to thank the police on motorcycles, and inadvertently allowed Donald Zec of the *Daily Mirror* on the property. They were photographed smiling and laughing when one of Zec's photographers jumped out from the landscaping. Miller eventually permitted some of the press to come up the gravel drive outside the front door where the two couples posed for a last round of photos.

"We are going to bed," Miller announced. Colin Clark considered the comment vulgar and observed Marilyn's expression of displeasure before pretending not to have heard it. Once inside Park House, Lord Moore gave the couple an awkwardly long tour of the home while staring at Marilyn the entire time.

The Millers were given a cook and butler, Hungarian refugees, who tried to organize their temporary household. Miller would later describe them as "a pair of bewildered pigeons." The regiment proved too rigid for the couple, and the servants were dismissed and replaced. Roger Hunt from Scotland Yard served as Marilyn's bodyguard during her travels and at all times she was at Parkside House. Colin Clark, who remembered Inspector Plod as the bodyguard, wrote that the gentleman received a huge salary to leave his family and live in-house to protect America's biggest star. When Clark asked Plod about his wife's feelings about his new charge, the inspector replied,

"I hope she's jealous."

Marilyn and Arthur sometimes slept in separate bedrooms since she had to awaken at five o'clock in the morning for work. In the evening, Miller collected her at Pinewood Studios in a chauffeured limousine. The newlyweds would often stroll in the garden before dinner with the bodyguard trailing at a respectful but watchful distance.

A second press conference was scheduled on July 15, the day following Marilyn's arrival, in the Lancaster Room at the Savoy Hotel in London. Olivier, his agent Cecil Tennant, and Rupert Allan took their seats in the ballroom and awaited Marilyn's arrival. Two hundred reporters, four thousand fans, two inspectors, a sergeant, six constables, and four teams of police also eagerly anticipated Marilyn's presence. The mass outnumbered the turnout for former President Harry S. Truman.

Marilyn's tardiness was not her fault. Three hundred villagers mobbed her car as it drove through the gates of Parkside House. As a human chain of policemen joined hands to hold back the crowd, Marilyn stepped out of the limousine forty minutes after the press conference was scheduled to begin. She looked ravishing in a sleeveless black sheath with a diaphanous, chiffon midriff, white gloves, and black pumps. Her gravitational pull commanded all attention, allowing American actress Ava Gardner to pass unnoticed through the hotel lobby.

Olivier took a seat between Marilyn and Miller on the ballroom dais, and the press bombarded them with questions documented by Maurice Zolotow, Donald Spoto, and various British newspapers.

"Do you still sleep only in *Chanel No. 5*?"

"Considering I'm in England now," Marilyn replied, "let's just say I am now sleeping in Yardley's English Lavender."

"What parts do you want to play?"

"Lady Macbeth," she said. "But, please quote me correctly. I don't mean I'd like to play her right now, but sometime...at present that is just a dream for me. I know how much work I must do before I could undertake such a role."

"What inspired you to study acting?" a reporter asked.

"Seeing my own pictures," Marilyn said with a smile, a line she had used before that elicited a loud round of applause.

"What is your taste in music?"

"I like Louis Armstrong and Beethoven."

"Which Beethoven numbers in particular, Miss Monroe?"

"I have a terrible time with numbers. But I know it when I hear it."

Marilyn discussed her interest in starring in a screen version of *My Fair Lady*, which was currently running in New York with Julie Andrews and Rex Harrison. Before the event ended, representatives of the *Daily Sketch* presented her with a bicycle to ride through the Royal Park.

A third and final press conference took place with Marilyn and Olivier fielding the questions. This time Marilyn wore the monochromatic black suit, blouse, silk tie, gloves, and shoes that she donned upon arrival to Los Angeles when filming *Bus Stop*. "*Compared to California, England seems tiny and quaint with its little toy trains chugging through the miniature countryside...*" Marilyn wrote to a friend back home. "*I am dying to walk bareheaded in the rain. I want to eat real roast beef and Yorkshire pudding as I believe only the English can cook it. I want to buy a tweed suit that fits me—I have never worn a tailored suit in my life. I want to ride a bicycle, and I'd like someone to explain the jokes in Punch—they don't seem funny to me.*"

At eight o'clock that evening, a group of about eighty students from nearby Shoreditch Teacher Training College, an all-male institution specialized in preparing physical education instructors, hiked two miles to Parkside House. While chanting, "We want Marilyn," the mob lifted the front gates off their hinges to trespass on the grounds where they took position under Marilyn's bedroom window and serenaded her with the Twenty-third Psalm accompanied by musical instruments. Miller brought a sleepy Marilyn to the window and pointed to the mass of choirboys in blazers. She queried of him what to do. Miller suggested she put on a robe and wave to them.

"All for me?" Marilyn gasped.

"My darling," Miller replied. "You can't think they're singing to me."

Marilyn sighed in exhaustion.

Before production commenced, the Millers made a point to socialize with their British hosts. Vivien Leigh was appearing in *South Sea Bubble*, and Marilyn and Arthur expressed interest in seeing the production at the Lyric Theatre. With little explanation to the Millers, Olivier had made arrangements for them to accompany him to a performance. During the show, Miller suddenly realized the leading lady was Vivien. He immediately leaned toward Olivier, seated next to him, and asked who directed. Olivier identified himself. The two broke into laughter. After the performance, the Millers accompanied the Oliviers to their London home at Lowndes Place, Westminster, where they visited until after midnight.

Milton Greene, Olivier, and Jack Cardiff filmed Marilyn's makeup and wardrobe tests on July 18, 19, and 20. Cardiff recalled her appearance as a lovely vision in white, wearing the snowy makeup from *Bus Stop*. The cinematographer disagreed with this choice, warning of its effect of making her teeth look dark. Marilyn protested, but the tests proved his point. "After that we changed it," Cardiff said, "but she was a piece of cake to photograph, absolutely marvelous." Dismissing the cinematographer's tact, Olivier rather bluntly instructed Marilyn to brush her teeth with baking soda.

Olivier encouraged Terrance Rattigan to host a party for the film's principals to mingle with British notables. On July 24, the playwright hosted a formal event that took place at his Georgian country house, Little Court, in Sunningdale, Berkshire, overlooking Wentworth golf course. He served a buffet dinner of lobster curry and encouraged dancing in a large drawing room. Although ranking as the highlight of the social season, Rattigan's after-theatre supper dance struck Colin Clark "*as formal and artificial as his plays.*" Guests included the United States Ambassador and Mrs. Winthrop Aldrich, Dame Margot Fonteyn, the Duke and Duchess of Baccleuch, Lady Diana Cooper, Sir Terence and Lady Nugent, Dame Sybil Thorndike and Lewis Casson, Sir John Gielgud, Mary and John Mills, Anthony Qualye, Alan Webb, and Douglas Fairbanks, Jr.

Marilyn arrived at a quarter to eleven wearing a costume designed by Beatrice Dawson, a ball gown of white chiffon with a pale blue ribbon. Olivier took one look at her and grimaced. Reading his disapproval of her wearing a costume originally intended for the film, Marilyn explained the gown had been rejected.

A receiving line formed in the garden, with the guests greeting Marilyn and Miller beneath a rose-entwined arbor. Oddly, American columnist Louella Parsons stood beside Marilyn like a proud mother.

Sir John Gielgud (1904-2000)—winner of an Oscar, Emmy, Grammy, and Tony Award—may be best remembered for his roles in *Beckett* (1966), *Murder on the Orient Express* (1974), and as the fatherly valet in *Arthur* (1981) with Dudley Moore. He described the moment to Michelle Morgan:

> [Marilyn] held court in a tent in the garden, where everyone queued up to shake her hand. As I was speaking to her, a rather formidable-looking lady in black suddenly appeared at Marilyn's side and introduced herself as Louella Parsons. Arthur Miller kept at a discreet distance. I had no opportunity of talking further with Marilyn, but remember how graceful she looked, dancing with Terry Rattigan as I took my departure.

Although the event was an overall success, there were moments of tension. When Marilyn made a compassionate remark about animals, actor Anthony Quayle snapped at her, "And what about the poor little animals whose skins you're wearing on your back?" Also, the guests thought it odd that Olivier declined to ask Marilyn to dance, which foreshadowed the disdain for her that he would later harbor.

An orchestra played American music in the formal salon where Marilyn danced the waltz and fox trot with Miller. "How marvelous that you two have come together," Louella Parsons told the Millers. "We all love Marilyn, it's so wonderful to know that she's happy at last. And she does look really and truly happy." Sidney Guilaroff and Rattigan joined Marilyn in dancing the 1920s Charleston. The party ended at four o'clock in the morning. Marilyn thanked Rattigan with a poetic letter on Parkside stationery, commenting on their memorable display on the dance floor.

Rehearsals began on July 30, and filming commenced on August 7 at Pinewood Studios, located about twenty miles west of London and nestled among pine trees on the former estate of Heatherden Hall in Buckinghamshire. Within weeks, the studio would serve as a battleground.

The January 30, 1956 issue of *Time* quoted Olivier on Monroe: "I regard her as an actress and a comedienne of the first order..." Decades after production ended—and long after Marilyn was gone and unable to defend herself—he would refer to her as "a thoroughly ill-mannered and rude girl..." and bash her to Barbara Walters in a televised interview.

* * *

The production's clash of egos, cultures, and acting styles would inspire a book based upon Colin Clark's diary, *The Prince, the Showgirl, and Me* (1996) and his follow-up account, *My Week with Marilyn* (2000). The latter would be adapted into both a BBC documentary in 2004 and a feature film in 2011.

Olivier, an intelligent but arrogant man quite similar to the role he was playing, made every effort to exert his power and control while demeaning his co-star and co-producer. He engendered no sense of collaboration and built no bridges. From the start, Olivier treated Marilyn like a subordinate. His style was manipulative and sneaky. He appeared overtly charming and welcoming, but conveyed covert messages that Marilyn deserved no respect, her opinion was worthless, and that she was regarded as an amateur act. According to Clark, Marilyn initially seemed "*enchantingly unspoilt.*"

Olivier's disdain for his co-star was evident from the first day of production on August 7, when he gathered the cast and crew for a welcome at the studio and condescendingly took Marilyn by the hand to introduce her to his colleagues. He urged them to be patient with their guest. In a patronizing tone, he explained that his co-producer would require time to get accustomed to their way of doing things and to learn their method of acting.

Hedda Rosten told her husband that Olivier and Marilyn were off to a bad start with their first important interaction on the set. Although overtly polite and gracious, Olivier came across as talking down to her. According to Hedda, his tone changed from that of "clubby professionalism" when speaking to the rest of the cast to an "almost elementary explanation" when speaking to Marilyn. Frankly, it appeared patronizing and grossly inappropriate.

This humiliation ruptured what could have been a brilliant and amiable association. Later that evening, Clark penned in his diary, "*None of his demeaning subtleties escaped MM's finely tuned vibe barometer.*" Clark hoped Olivier would treat Marilyn as an equal business partner.

Olivier perceived Marilyn as an unruly child under his total power and supervision and pushed her emotional buttons. He provoked her feelings of disgrace and betrayal. Marilyn now mistrusted him and relied solely upon Paula. Olivier criticized her reaction: "Her manner to me got steadily ruder and more insolent; whenever I patiently labored to make her understand an indication for some reading, business or timing she would listen with ill-disguised impatience, and when I had finished would turn to Paula...A very short way into filming, my humiliation had reached depths I would not have believed possible."

Olivier lacked insight into the consequences of his behavior. He passive-aggressively insulted and belittled Marilyn in the presence of the cast and crew, then acted dismayed and confused by her disengagement with him. Olivier unrealistically expected her to feel trust and ease toward him while he bullied and metaphorically slugged her in the presence of his loyal friends, and he derided her for reacting to his mean-spiritedness.

From the way he treated Marilyn, one gets a sense of how Olivier may have treated his own wife, another woman in his life who suffered from Bipolar Disorder. Perhaps he projected negative feelings about Vivien toward Marilyn. Based upon his later writings, Olivier may simply have been disappointed in Marilyn's failure to live up to his fantasy and deliver the extramarital diversion he was seeking. On her honeymoon, Marilyn was interested in her husband, not her co-star. This may have come as a blow to Olivier's ego.

"He talks to me as if he's slumming," Marilyn complained about her interactions with Olivier, her expectations clearly unfulfilled. Although she had hired Olivier as co-star and director, Marilyn began to feel as though the film was his and not hers. She was out of her comfort zone and on Olivier's territory, surrounded by mostly a British crew and British actors loyal to him. On her personal copy of the working script auctioned by Julien's in 2005, Marilyn scribbled, "*What am I doing here with this strange man?*"

Marilyn's second major humiliation also occurred early in filming. "All you have to do is be sexy, dear Marilyn," Olivier offered as directorial motivation to his Method actress. Her idol—the man she trusted to direct her transition to more serious roles—now revealed himself as a chauvinist. Marilyn was devastated and bolted to the nearest telephone to call Lee Strasberg. In an emotional meltdown, she frantically asked questions about how to be sexy, and the coach suggested Olivier might have facetiously intended the remark. Susan Strasberg's version of this incident depicts Marilyn assertively responding to Olivier: "Larry, I don't have to act sexy. I am sexy."

Paula Strasberg was appalled by the great actor sinking to such depth of spite. She, too, found herself on the receiving end of Olivier's ridicule. He lambasted her for motivating Marilyn during the flirtatious scene between the Regent and Elsie with a suggestion to think of Coca-Cola and Frank Sinatra. One can imagine Olivier's mortification regarding Marilyn Monroe's need to fantasize about another man while filming a love scene with him, and her substituting a rowdy, street-wise man from New Jersey who was alleged to have ties to organized crime.

Miller seemed to side with Olivier and find fault in Paula's coaching. He believed in Marilyn as an adroit comedienne who often appeared perplexed by "half-digested, spit-balled imagery and pseudo-Stanislavskian parallelisms" that only disabled her from relying upon her own natural exuberance. At the end of the working day, Miller and Olivier would share a drink at the studio and commiserate about returning home to their respective marital challenges. Colin Clark overheard Miller confiding to Olivier that his wife was devouring him.

Olivier's directorial style involved explaining to Marilyn how to deliver a line of dialogue and then acting it out for her to mimic in her breathy voice. This method proved to be another huge mistake because Marilyn made no effort to disguise her impatience with his actions, and instead deferred to Paula for guidance. This infuriated Olivier even further.

During a visit by Joshua Logan, Olivier asked him how he coped with Marilyn's reaction to his demonstrations. Logan tactfully replied that he couldn't respond as he never attempted to read a line for her. He reminded Olivier that he had urged him to allow Marilyn to play scenes in her own way as she was "terribly" talented and on "intimate" terms with the camera. Logan acknowledged Olivier's mastery of technical acting and directorial skills and advised him to honor Marilyn's "brilliant instincts" which seemed as inexplicable as "a frightened unicorn."

At Pinewood Studios, the greatest combination since black and white was now embroiled in a bitter battle between classical and Method acting—the established school versus the new school, the pre-war acting generation versus the post-war generation. Olivier believed in a technical approach: delivering a line and executing a movement. As a devout Method actress, Marilyn engaged in a peculiar hand-shaking exercise for about fifteen minutes, and explored her own sense-memories to discover her character's motivation, and flesh out character development. She searched for realism in her performance while Olivier was trained in memorizing lines verbatim and pretending.

"For God's sake, Marilyn, there is no motivation!" Olivier repeatedly said. "Just say the word and let's get on with this scene." Having worked with Huston, Hawks, Wilder, Lytess, and Strasberg, Marilyn had never received such pragmatic direction. Olivier typically instructed her to sit, count to three, and then speak her line. When Marilyn shut down, he would bark, "Can't you count either?" Obviously, Olivier was also unable to sit still, take a deep breath, and count to ten.

"[Marilyn's] system was spontaneity," Jack Cardiff told Sandra Shevey. "So there was a complete clash. She didn't trust anything but herself and her Method acting. It is like asking a Catholic to forget about the Virgin Mary." Since Marilyn had converted to a devout Method actress, she searched deep into her own emotional reservoir for the motivation behind her character's every move and line. Sandra Shevey attributes the co-stars' individual differences in their conceptualization of the film, not their irreconcilable schools of acting, as the major catalyst in their escalating feud. Marilyn questioned Olivier's resistance to allowing her to develop the character with her own nuances and mannerisms instead of re-creating Vivien's interpretation on the stage. Susan Strasberg concurred with this impression: "[Vivien Leigh] was a wonderful actress but miscasted as the sexy, naïve American showgirl, a part for which Marilyn was perfect." Marilyn could play the role while sleepwalking, but Olivier demanded that she perform it exactly as Leigh had and was therefore infuriated with Paula's influence and presence on the set.

Feeling insecure and threatened, Marilyn confronted Olivier's staging of more close-ups of himself rather than an equal amount of close-ups for her. She believed that he was trying to compete with her like another woman to draw the audience's focus away from her. To make matters worse, each actor's best side was the right side of the face, and Olivier positioned the camera so it would film his best side when he and Marilyn played scenes facing each other.

Apparently, Marilyn's insecurities were not all based on paranoia. "I sensed Sir Laurence was irritated because his co-star was coming across far better on the screen than he," Sydney Guilaroff wrote, "and he was no doubt jealous of all the attention she was receiving in his homeland." Despite Guilaroff's deep respect of Olivier, he acknowledged the director as "unduly critical of every aspect of Marilyn's appearance." Olivier vetoed one dress in particular because he considered it too revealing, but Guilaroff sensed the reason behind the rejection was that the dress was eye-catching, and Olivier didn't want the audience focused on Marilyn wearing it.

Olivier would receive honest feedback and chiding from Dame Sybil Thorndike. "Don't you realize what a strain this poor girl is under?" the aged and wise actress asked. "She hasn't had your years of experience. She is far from home in a strange country, trying to act a strange part. Are you helping or bullying?"

When Marilyn arrived late for a scene with Dame Sybil on August 10, Olivier led her by the hand to her co-star and demanded that she apologize. Marilyn's efforts to make amends was interrupted. "My dear, you mustn't concern yourself," Dame Sybil insisted, embarrassed by Olivier's punitive act. "A great actress like you has other things than time on her mind, doesn't she?" Marilyn beamed in appreciation, but Olivier must have boiled with ire. Colin Clark wrote in his diary: "*[Dame Sybil] has become MM's dear old granny and this spills over into the part.*"

Dame Sybil had always supported the underdog. She came to the rescue of her friend and colleague Sir John Gielgud when he was arrested for picking up another man in a public restroom. The two had been appearing together in a play in which Gielgud was acting and directing and at the end performance following the arrest, Gielgud stood frozen in the wings during the curtain call, expecting the audience to heckle him for the arrest when he took a bow. "Come on, John darling," Dame Sybil said, taking him by the arm and leading him to the stage, "they won't boo me." Gielgud received a standing ovation.

During a televised interview for the BBC in 1957, the commentator asked Dame Sybil if Marilyn was difficult. "No, not at all," she vehemently protested. "She's a dear, and she's a most charming person. She's got a wonderful instinct. I don't think she takes direction really well, but then I don't see why she should. [Larry] wanted her to do certain things. Why don't you leave her alone? She is married to the camera. She knows exactly. She's a darling girl. I never found any difficulties with her. I don't know if anybody has. I think they must be difficult themselves perhaps."

To her experienced theatrical company, Marilyn's work seemed subtle and nearly imperceptible on the set. It was not until they viewed the daily rushes that they came to appreciate her tremendous cinematic acting skill. During a screening, Dame Sybil turned to Olivier and said, "Larry, you did well in that scene but with Marilyn up there, nobody will be watching you. Her manner and timing are just too delicious. And don't be hard about her tardiness, dear boy. We need her desperately. She's really the only one of us who knows how to act in front of the camera."

Daphne Anderson watched Marilyn on set and believed it appeared as if she were doing nothing. "But when I saw the film, it just knocked me over," she later admitted. "[Marilyn] had this amazing quality in front of the camera." Other accomplished actors of the stage with minimal film experience shared similar impressions. "When working, on the set, I thought, surely she won't come over," Dame Sybil said, "she's so small scale, but when I saw her on the screen, my goodness how it came over. She was a revelation. We theatre people tend to be so outgoing. She was the reverse. The perfect film actress, I thought. I have seen a lot of her films since then, and it's always there—that perfect quality."

Cinematographer Jack Cardiff observed the unit respecting Olivier as a great actor and director but respecting Marilyn less because of her chronic tardiness. However, like Dame Sybil, he supported Marilyn and sympathized with her vulnerability and psychological issues. Cardiff often filmed a dozen takes of a scene when Marilyn faltered on her lines. Suspecting the takes were bad but hoping they could be salvaged with proper editing, Olivier ordered them to be printed. However, when he and Cardiff viewed the rushes, Marilyn's extraordinary screen presence overshadowed any minor flaws they had observed on set.

Leigh arranged to privately view the daily rushes with Olivier's agent, Cecil Tennant, and Amy Greene. "I didn't think she would be that beautiful," she said. "It's magic. She has it and I don't." The tears behind this confession broke Amy's heart.

* * *

With Marilyn's idealism of Olivier shattered, she felt deeply disappointed and lost respect for him. The collapse of the relationship led to her nightly insomnia and increased intake of barbiturates. She started openly addressing Olivier as "Mister Sir."

Marilyn now realized the mistake of her relinquishing editing rights to Olivier. He insisted on the lengthy coronation sequence, but Marilyn believed it slowed the story and would bore the audience. She tried to advise him of American audiences being unmoved by belabored shots of stained glass windows at Westminster Abbey, but was unsuccessful.

Marilyn's painful menstrual cramps resulting from endometriosis caused excessive tardiness and delayed production during the fifty-four days she worked. Fully aware of the condition, Paula secretly nursed her in the middle of the night. During the day, though, Olivier thought Marilyn was misbehaving out of opposition and defiance. When she felt well, Milton Greene observed Miller keeping Marilyn away from the production by spending lengths of time in her dressing room reading aloud reviews of his play while the cast and crew waited on the set.

Paula's role in Marilyn's entourage evolved from acting coach to a combination of nurturing Jewish mother, protector, and defender. At times, she served as interpreter for communication between Marilyn and Olivier, who seemed to be speaking two distinct languages. When Olivier grew impatient with Marilyn's creative process, Paula warned him not to rush her, citing the eight month period that Charles Chaplin required in completing a movie. The prospect of working with Marilyn for eight months was not an option for Olivier, however. In his estimation, Paula lacked credibility, and her perpetual presence on the set alarmed him. "She was no actress, no director, no teacher, no advisor—except in Marilyn's eyes," he said. "For she had one talent—she could butter Marilyn up." And buttering up, Marilyn now needed.

Colin Clark overheard Paula praising Marilyn's talents. "All my life, Marilyn, I have prayed for a great actress who I could help and guide..." she gushed. "[God] has given me you, and you are the great actress..." Olivier told Fred Lawrence Guiles of overhearing similar accolades from Paula while driving in a car with the coach and Marilyn. Guiles published Olivier's quotation of Paula, though possibly exaggerated:

> My dear, you really must recognize your own potential; you haven't even yet any idea of the importance of your position in the world. You are the greatest sex symbol in human memory. Everybody knows and recognizes that, and you should too. It's a duty which you owe to yourself and to the world; it's ungrateful not to accept it. You are the greatest woman of your time, the greatest human being of your time, you name it. You can't think of anybody, I mean—no one, not even Jesus—except you're more popular.

On the early morning of August 17, Marilyn and Olivier filmed a charming scene during which Elsie serves herself from the buffet while the prince takes an urgent telephone call. Bored with the evening, she begins talking to herself and drinking champagne, slowly becoming intoxicated. Marilyn was required to eat caviar and chicken salad in the multiple takes, so Olivier suggested she mime eating. Marilyn insisted on the reality of consuming the food but requested apple juice as a substitute for champagne. Elaine Schreyeck, responsible for script continuity, assisted Marilyn in directing the scene while Olivier acted in the background. Donald Spoto called the sequence "a masterpiece of improvisation" and compared Marilyn's comic talent to Billie Burke's in *Dinner at Eight* and Miriam Hopkins' in *Trouble in Paradise.* Once again, Marilyn stole the scene from Olivier.

Though mostly fraught with tension, the production experienced a fair number of light and comic episodes. During one, Colin Clark stood prepared to open the set doors for Marilyn's entrance, but he forgot that the doors opened inward and not into the corridor where the couple waited for Marilyn's cue. At the proper moment, he pulled the doors' handles, but nothing happened. Clark and Marilyn burst into giggles. "*The more they cursed from the other side of those nice strong doors, the more we laughed,*" he wrote. "*She really can be adorable when she is human like that.*"

British comedian Norman Wisdom, also making a film at Pinewood Studios, relished Marilyn's delightful and frequent visits when she was not required on set by Olivier. Wisdom shared his memories with biographer Michelle Morgan:

> She quite unintentionally ruined a couple of takes. Obviously, of course, once the director has said, "Action" everyone must remain silent, no matter how funny the situation might be, but Marilyn just could not help laughing, and on two occasions she was politely escorted off the set. The nicest thing that happened was that we passed each other in the long hallway one lunchtime; it was crowded, but she still caught hold of me, kissed me and hugged me and walked away laughing.

On the day the coronation scene was being filmed, Colin Clark barged into Marilyn's dressing room to locate her script and came face to face with her in the nude, wearing only a white towel around her head.

"*All I could see were beautiful white and pink curves,*" he jotted in his diary. "*I must have gone as red as a beetroot.*" Marilyn innocently smiled. "Oh Colin," she said. "And you an old Etonian!" Clark wondered how Marilyn knew he had attended the all-boys boarding school. Amused and amazed by her wit, Clark wrote later that night about what fun it might be to make a film with Marilyn if she felt supported by those around her.

Following both good and bad days at Pinewood, Marilyn's chauffeured car passed Margaret Gillon's home near Parkside House. The neighbor stood waving and smiling at her door like clockwork. Marilyn came to rely upon this warm gesture of kindness.

* * *

Early into the production, an incident irrevocably damaged the Millers' fledgling marriage. While searching for her script, Marilyn discovered Miller's diary, open to a page containing a passage. Intrigued, she began reading her husband's most intimate thoughts. Curiosity turned to shock when she read Miller's confession of regret for marrying her and his newfound perception of her; in his opinion, she was becoming unpredictable and neurotic. In Marilyn's description of the entry to others, Miller expressed feeling both disillusioned by her and pitying her. What he had discovered was a child and not a woman, which made him fear for his own creative life and how it would be sacrificed by her boundless emotional neediness. Bart Mills quoted Marilyn's version of the inscription in *Marilyn on Location*:

> *It was something about how disappointed he was in me, how he thought I was some kind of angel but now he guessed he was wrong—that his first wife had let him down, but I had done something worse. Olivier was beginning to think I was a troublesome bitch, and Arthur said he no longer had a decent answer....*

Marilyn long struggled with her insecurities and belief of being worthless and unlovable and Miller's love had challenged this belief, but she lived in the fear of his discovering she was not worthy of his affection. To Marilyn, the diary only verified what she held as the truth about herself; her worst fear was now realized. Miller never really loved her; there was nothing to love. He was now ashamed of being married to her and rejected her as others had done since her birth. Marilyn cried to the Strasbergs, "It's so terrible, so terrible."

Paula tried to convince Marilyn that people explore both positive and negative thoughts in their diaries; what they write does not necessarily reflect what they really mean or feel. In her memoir *Marilyn and Me: Sisters, Rivals, Friends*, Susan Strasberg offered the following paraphrased dialogue between Marilyn and Paula:

"Marilyn, don't you sometimes have secret thoughts that you don't want anyone to know?" Paula asked.

"Of course, but I don't say it out loud to the person I'm thinking about," Marilyn rebutted. "Perhaps it's a Freudian slip. Arthur wanted me to read what he was thinking about me."

"You must admit that Freud himself said, 'Sometimes a cigar is just a cigar,'" replied Paula in a motherly tone.

"Maybe that's true, Paula," Marilyn insisted. "But this cigar was on purpose; I don't believe it was merely an accident."

Marilyn would later confide in Ralph Roberts that Miller's inscription triggered a flashback to a childhood trauma in foster care and served as the catalyst for abuse of sedative drugs. Suddenly, she was back in a religious fundamentalist household and was being punished for singing before breakfast. Marilyn would also recount to Roberts that during this crisis she called a friend for a sleeping pill that did not work, and had used pills ever since.

According to Robert Josephy, Miller's friend in Connecticut, Marilyn was most hurt by her husband's realization of his having married two women with similar flaws. This devastated Marilyn as Miller had once told her he hated his first wife. In Marilyn's black and white 'all or nothing' style of thinking, if he hated his former wife, this meant he hated her, too.

Miller would include a parallel incident in his play *After the Fall*, which suggested Marilyn attributed his journal entry to her subsequent episodes of suicidal impulses. Maggie, the character based upon Marilyn, confronts her husband, Quentin, and unmasks his underlying hatred. She pinpoints reading a message in his diary two months after their wedding as the trigger for her wish to die. In the play, Maggie recounts searching for a pen to sign autographs on Quentin's desk where he usually sits. She glances at her husband's open journal, and reads—in his handwriting—a confession about loving only his daughter. Maggie accuses Quentin of being ashamed of her and playing God. Quentin, Miller's obvious counterpart, admits that his "letter from hell" reveals his incapacity to love.

Perhaps seeking retail therapy on August 25, Marilyn shopped in Regent Square, an arcade in London's West End where she acquired suits, camel hair coats, cashmere sweaters in autumnal shades, Oxford dictionaries for Miller, and clothing and gifts for her stepchildren. When fans mobbed Marilyn, she fainted. The cause of her emotional anguish remained unknown, and an underlying medical issue had not yet been diagnosed.

When Miller's daughter, Janie, became ill, he departed for New York. Photographers captured close-ups of the couple in a car as they said goodbye on August 30. Wearing dark glasses and a scarf over her hair, Marilyn cried as her husband departed. No amount of reassurance could have convinced her that Miller would not permanently leave her, and his leaving soon after she discovered his diary must have only fuelled her panic. Without his protection and presence, Marilyn emotionally crashed, so much so that she failed to appear at the Venice Film Festival where she was scheduled to attend the European premiere of *Bus Stop.*

On the day of Miller's departure, Marilyn penned her thoughts on Parkside House stationery. She identified feeling restless, nervous, and unfocused. The most disturbing insight recorded is the realization of having felt depressed her entire life, as long as she could remember. Marilyn's inspiration for portraying Elsie came from a few happy memories experienced at age fourteen while living with "Aunt" Ana Lower.

Marilyn discovered she was pregnant in late August 1956. Attorney Irving Stein's daily memorandum of phone calls contains documentation of contact with two London doctors confirming the pregnancy on August 31. Similarly, Colin Clark noted a rumor of the pregnancy on September 2; six days later, he recorded the bodyguard revealing she had been pregnant for a month and miscarried. Sadly, Marilyn lost the fetus in September while Miller visited his children in the United States. This incident adding to her depression, she continued to emotionally unravel. Oddly, Olivier was never informed of her emotional state. Instead, he thought Marilyn was just being difficult.

Thankfully, a ray of bright light emerged from the gathering storm clouds to offer Marilyn some solace when *Bus Stop* opened on August 31 to rave reviews. "Miss Monroe is a talented comedienne, and her sense of timing never forsakes her," proclaimed the *London Times.* "She gives a complete portrait, sensitively and sometimes even brilliantly conceived. There is a waif-like quality about her, an underlying note of pathos which can be strangely moving." This professional success should have bolstered Marilyn's self-esteem but her worries had begun to consume her; she feared the ending of her marriage and grieved the overwhelming loss of her unborn child while separated from her husband.

Acting as both friend and executive producer, Milton Greene contacted Dr. Margaret Hohenberg in New York and requested an intervention to stabilize his leading lady and avoid a lengthy disruption of the production. The psychoanalyst referred Marilyn to Anna Freud (1895-1982) for several sessions in London. As the sixth and last child of Sigmund and Martha Freud, Anna specialized in the field of psychoanalytic child psychology. She researched and practiced at Maresfield Gardens in Hampstead, now the Anna Freud Center, and the home where her family escaped the Nazi annexation of Austria in 1938. Here, Anna had cared for her father as he suffered from jaw cancer until his death the following year.

Anna Freud's credentials and studies on the effect of the deprivation of parental care on children fully prepared her to respond to Marilyn's crisis. Freud's center accepted children separated by their parents by the war or orphaned by the Holocaust and created opportunities for them to develop healthy attachments through substitute relationships. With a collaborator, Anna published her observations on the impact of parental absence on children and their resiliency through connecting with peers.

In 1987, Paula Fichtl (1902-1989) published *Day to Day Life with the Freud Family: The Reminiscences of Paula Fichtl*, a memoir of her experience as Anna Freud's chambermaid. She referenced Marilyn's intensive treatment at the center during a leave of absence from production. When Marilyn arrived at Maresfield Gardens, Freud invited her to the nursery where she readily played and joked with the children. The analyst began the session by engaging Marilyn in a game of marbles, a modality used with her child patients. Allegedly, a note card documenting Freud's brief assessment of Marilyn remains in her archive: "*Adult patient. Emotional instability, exaggerated impulsiveness, constant need for external approval, inability to be alone, tendency to depression in case of rejection.*" Marilyn improved with Freud's interventions and returned to work within a week.

Notes found on Parkside House stationery during this period possibly reflect Marilyn's processing of the deep, emotional wound caused by reading Miller's diary. She wrote of feeling terrified to be a wife and based these feelings on her life experience having taught her that a person is incapable of loving another "*ever, really.*" She recorded feeling hurt, "*merciless pain*", and a profound lack of joy in her life. Marilyn also referenced "*shapes of monsters*" emerging in her darkest thoughts. The "letter from hell" would remain a wedge between Marilyn and Miller for the duration of their five-year marriage. To Marilyn, it foreshadowed an eventual abandonment. "She had dropped the experience into some dark space in her unconscious," Susan Strasberg observed, "where it could sprout like a seed and fertilize future battlegrounds."

While Anna Freud brought some relief to her, Marilyn still felt betrayed by her husband and disillusioned by her co-star; she needed a shining white knight on a horse to rescue her more than ever. A short, balding, Jewish man in a suit onboard a plane en route to London would soon play this role; Lee Strasberg and his daughter, Susan, arrived and drove straight to Pinewood Studios to comfort Marilyn. Milton stopped them at the gate and warned of Olivier banning the Method Acting guru from the soundstage. Olivier had sparred with Strasberg during the London production of *A Streetcar Named Desire* and had no intention of reliving that experience or permitting Marilyn another ally.

In an apparent gesture of reconciliation, Olivier and Vivien invited the Strasberg family to their home for a luncheon. According to Susan, her parents suspected their hosts staged this social call as a calculated means for Olivier to engage them in instructing Marilyn to submit to his control. Susan recalled their impeccably appointed rooms, silver tea set, and emotional coolness. Olivier talked at them rather than to them, she would recall. While outwardly charming, he lacked genuine interpersonal warmth. Lee remained reserved and Paula overcompensated by laughing too loudly and overeating. The following day, Vivien's miscarriage—fact or fabricated—was reported by the British press.

Lee believed *The Sleeping Prince* could have been an outstanding and classic film had Olivier infused more romance and compromised with Marilyn's vision. "Larry has no right to say he had a terrible time with her," Strasberg said. "I was there. We had a terrible time with him; he just wouldn't listen."

According to Lee Strasberg, Olivier never allowed Marilyn to find her performance; instead he gave orders and expected her to obey. Moreover, Olivier appeared too cold in the early scenes, which made the later romantic theme unconvincing. Olivier's notion of a good performance was an artificial performance, Strasberg opined. The motion picture media allowed a more intimate approach to what the actor had achieved on stage. Herein lay the crux of the battle; Marilyn envisioned a film adaptation of a play while Olivier designed to film the play.

Several biographers accused Milton Greene of trying to control Marilyn just as Miller and Strasberg had tried. Other allegations say that he made arrangements with Amy's New York physician,

Mortimer Weinstein, to ship both sedative and stimulant drugs to Marilyn. If this is true, no evidence appeared in her performance preserved on celluloid.

On September 19, Miller returned to London a week earlier than planned and picked up the pieces of his damaged marriage. Escorted by her husband, Marilyn made her first public appearance since the miscarriage by attending the Berliner Ensemble's German language performance of Bertolt Brecht's play, *Caucasian Chalk Circle*, at the Palace Theatre.

Ten days later, Marilyn shined at Pinewood Studio in the scene of Elsie entering the Carpathian Embassy. The sequence contained a stretch of dialogue while the prince and the showgirl ascend the winding grand staircase. Olivier set up one continuous shot with a camera mounted on a crane. Lasting about forty-five seconds, the sequence required multiple takes when it could have been broken down into smaller, more manageable setups. At the end of the day, Marilyn made a distressed phone call to Lee Strasberg.

In early October, Paula flew back to New York with her husband and daughter, and Olivier hired another American crewmember in her absence. Unbeknownst to Marilyn and Paula, Britain's Eady Plan restricted the number of American crewmembers on the production's payroll. Olivier's filling of the quota would prevent Paula to return at the scheduled time at the end of the month. In Paula's absence, Marilyn and Olivier got along splendidly; suggesting the climate on set had the two worked directly with each another from the start. This harmony shattered upon Marilyn learning of Paula's roadblock in returning, which she regarded as yet another dagger thrown by Olivier. Eventually, Olivier gave in and arranged for Paula's return to the payroll in hope of restoring some sense of peace. Marilyn's insecurities now extended beyond her relationships with Olivier and Miller. She suspected Milton Greene of purchasing expensive antiques and charging them to her production company. With Hedda Rosten and Lee Strasberg back in New York, her support system dwindled. Marilyn now felt she could trust no one.

* * *

The British press broadcasted its disappointment with the Millers' self-imposed isolation during their stay by publishing statements rife with resentment and contempt. Marilyn declined many public appearances, which could have been advantageous media events. She refused the BBC's invitation to perform in Aristophane's comedy, *Lysistrata*, and Miller turned down a request to appear on *The Brains Trust.*

Marilyn received a letter from ABC television network offering her a part in the television production of *The Brothers Karamazov*—what she had been dreaming about for so long—and NBC invited the Millers to speak on television about how the television should be used for the education of children. Oddly, they declined both invitations. In Marilyn's defense, she faced pressures unknown to those outside the walls of Parkside House and Pinewood Studios. She carried the film with a significant portion of screen time, appearing in nearly every scene and working long hours. She had long speeches to memorize and was ill or pregnant during the production.

Additionally, the Millers were on a honeymoon, and the new marriage was shaken when Marilyn felt betrayed by her husband and miscarried. On good days, the Millers bicycled in Windsor Great Park, watched a Polo match, and strolled the seaside streets of Brighton. While lounging with Miller on the vast lawn of Parkside House, Marilyn seemed more hopeful as she discussed a desire to return to New York to study history and literature and be a wife and mother.

The British media were poised for the debut of Miller's new play, *A View from the Bridge*, at the Comedy Theatre in London's West End, and its prospect of inciting a scandal across Europe. Originally banned due to its references to homosexuality, the play contained a provocative scene in which a male character kissed another male on the lips. The play was being produced by the New Watergate Theatre Club, a membership-based organization dedicated to protesting all forms of censorship in the arts by presenting banned plays. The Millers became members of the club in order to attend the performance and staged a media event during which Marilyn visited the club to purchase her membership.

At the opening on October 11, Marilyn—not Miller's play—made scandalous headlines by wearing a skin-tight, blood-red, silk strapless gown designed by De Rachelle with matching wrap and opera gloves. Did Marilyn purposely wear a daring outfit to distract from the controversial themes in her husband's latest work? Miller remembered the evening beginning with a pleasant gathering at Olivier's apartment where he, Marilyn, and their hosts consumed generous portions of chilled oysters. Despite several months of conflict at Pinewood Studios, on this night Marilyn acted warmly and friendly toward Olivier, and Olivier appeared excited by the activation of her movie star aura. In *Timebends*, Miller seemed to confuse this event with an introduction to the Queen of England. Following the performance, the Millers took a bow onstage and met backstage with the cast.

The following day, the Millers and Greenes read Marilyn's scathing review by The Associated Press along with those of the play. Associated Press criticized Marilyn's appearance: "Marilyn Monroe's close-fitting dress turned the London opening of her husband's latest play into a near riot..." Marilyn responded by telling the press she had chosen the dress because it was her husband's favorite color. Appreciative of the publicity, Miller came to his wife's defense: "Why should someone like Marilyn pretend to be dressing like somebody's old aunt?"

Marilyn declined an invitation from British ballerina Dame Margot Fonteyn (1919-1991) to attend the Bolshoi Theatre Ballet along with the Oliviers and reunite with Dame Edith Sitwell, whom she had met in Los Angeles in 1954. The eccentric poet and critic regularly held court in the hushed atmosphere of the liberal Sesame, Imperial, and Pioneer Club on Grosvenor Street, where she also maintained a residence. Hearing Marilyn was in London, Sitwell invited the Millers and others to a luncheon. Lady Natasha Spender, British pianist and author, recalled the meeting: "[Sitwell] clearly regarded Marilyn Monroe as an intelligent waif who was 'young and good' and she rejoiced to see her safeguarded and blossoming in marriage."

Marilyn discussed with Sitwell her reaction to British poet Gerard Manley Hopkins (1844-1889) and Welsh poet Dylan Thomas (1914-1953) as she had been reading the work of both men during her sleepless nights at Parkside House. For her hostess, Marilyn recited Hopkins' *Terrible Sonnets*: "*I wake and feel the fell of dark, not day/What hours, O what black we have spent/This night.*" Sitwell later commented on Marilyn having related to the poet's despair.

"She was very quiet and had great natural dignity... and was extremely intelligent," Sitwell said, as quoted by Victoria Glendinning in *Edith Sitwell: A Unicorn Among Lions.* "She was also exceedingly sensitive.... In repose, her face was at moments strangely, prophetically tragic, like the face of a beautiful ghost—a little spring-ghost, an innocent fertility-daemon, the vegetation spirit that was Ophelia." Equally impressed with her hostess, Marilyn said, "She was what my mother would have called a Lady."

Another intellectual encounter took place during Marilyn's interview with British critic Tom Hutchinson. She spoke about Franz Kafka's *The Trial,* a novel published in 1925 about a man arrested for a crime against the state that is never explained to him. "It's like we all feel this sense of guilt," Marilyn explained. "I know they say it's the Jewish thing with Kafka—that's what Arthur says anyway—but it goes beyond that. It's about all men and women. This sense that we have fallen or something."

Marilyn also participated in a local charity event by donating a whimsical self-portrait in yellow watercolor titled, "Myself Exercising," signed Marilyn Monroe Miller and dated September 1956. Purchased at auction by Terrence Rattigan, the work depicted Marilyn in profile, bending over to touch her toes. The outline of her body is clear and strong, perhaps nude, with her breast visible. Her long hair hangs over her face. A circular shape encapsulates the waist and legs, possibly suggesting either a full skirt or movement of the body.

* * *

If *The Sleeping Prince* was indeed a fairy tale about a prince falling in love with a commoner, life imitated art when Marilyn dressed like a princess, went to the royal ball and—like Cinderella—met the queen. Coupled with working with Sir Laurence Olivier in her own production, an introduction to royalty would undeniably elevate Marilyn's position in the film industry. Alan Arnold, a British publicist, received a confidential memorandum requesting his investigation of an appropriate occasion for Marilyn to meet the members of the royal family.

The Royal Film Performance of *The Battle of the River Plate* at the Empire Theatre, Leicester Square, on October 29 would serve as the proper event to bring Marilyn face to face with a monarch. Queen Elizabeth II, also born in 1926, was fascinated by Marilyn and had probed Rattigan to learn more about her. He described Marilyn as "a shy exhibitionist, a Garbo who likes to be photographed."

Flanked by actors Victor Mature and Anthony Quayle in a receiving line at the Empire Theatre, a poised Marilyn looked regal in a gold lame gown with topaz straps accessorized by a gold cape, opera gloves, and two-inch platform shoes. Gordon Bond had styled her hair in a simple, elegant bun. Other luminaries lined to meet the queen included Brigitte Bardot, Joan Crawford, and Anita Ekberg.

In a transatlantic phone conversation, Anne Karger told Marilyn to look the monarch in the eye and think, "I am just as pretty as you are!" Marilyn clearly took the advice. In newsreels, she stands with confidence in total command, her head held high. The Queen of England and the Queen of Hollywood look each other directly in the eye and smile warmly at each other. Elizabeth's eyes run up and down Marilyn's dress, which fell to the ground in Grecian folds. Upon the Queen's offering her hand, Marilyn gently takes it with her gloved fingers and bows. Maurice Zolotow and the British press recorded their conversation. "That's a very proper curtsy," beamed the Queen.

"Curtsying isn't difficult for me anymore," replied Marilyn. "I learned how to do it for the film." The Queen asked her about the accommodations at Windsor and acknowledged that they were neighbors. Marilyn replied that she thought Her Majesty lived at Buckingham Palace.

"You see, we often live at Windsor Castle," the monarch explained before describing how a park bridged the castle with Parkside House. "That makes us neighbors, doesn't it?" Marilyn replied to the Queen that she and Miller had a permit to walk and bicycle in Her Majesty's park.

"Do you really bicycle, Mrs. Miller?" asked Princess Margaret, who had joined the conversation.

"I love riding a bicycle. Unfortunately, I haven't had much time lately to enjoy it."

"How long will you be staying in our country, Mrs. Miller?" asked the Queen, lingering with Marilyn longer than with the other actors.

"Only two more weeks. We must leave as soon as I finish the picture."

Princess Margaret expressed interest in attending a performance of *A View to a Bridge*, a controversial move for a member of royalty. Afterward, Marilyn spoke of the Queen as warm-hearted and sweet and re-enacted her curtsy for press photographers, saying, "She radiates a wonderful womanly essence and softness."

The event was Milton Greene's best effort in public relations, and Marilyn rebounded after having disappointed the British press in previous months. "Marilyn Monroe, the sleek, the pink and the beautiful, captured Britain," *The Daily Mirror* announced. She had lived up to her reputation by embodying "diplomacy, mischief and bubbling sense of fun." Similarly, *The Spectator* found Marilyn "as intelligent as she was pleasant as she was pretty."

Joan Crawford disagreed with both publications. "The Queen is a lady and expects to meet other ladies," the formidable fifty-one year-old actress said to a reporter from the *Daily Herald* in a tirade as she criticized the younger contemporary actresses for uncouth behavior and criticizing Marilyn's curtsy.

In contrast, one of the ingénues disapproved by Crawford stood in awe of Marilyn. "That evening was one of the most important ones in my life, above all," twenty-two year-old French actress Brigitte Bardot said, "because I was finally able to see Marilyn in the flesh and blood. She wasn't as I had imagined her; you could see that she was fragile besides being very beautiful. I've never seen an ethereal beauty like hers again. She actually looked luminous, her sheer presence made you hold your breath."

Decades later, Bardot regretted not having introduced herself and telling Marilyn of how much she admired her. She surmised that Marilyn might have needed to hear such praise. Earlier in 1956, Bardot mesmerized male audiences on both sides of the Atlantic in *And God Created Woman*. Her iconic table-dancing scene rivaled Marilyn's dress-blowing subway scene and established Bardot as a Gallic version of free-spirited female sensuality.

* * *

On November 6, President Eisenhower won a second term in a rematch against democratic opponent Adlai Stevenson whom he defeated in 1952. It was the last election in which the contenders had been born in the previous century.

Almost two weeks later, *The Sleeping Prince* was completed in less time than scheduled, came in $35,000 under budget, required only two days of reshoots and wrapped on November 17. Olivier met with the Millers and offered to reshoot two scenes, including the first meeting of their characters, in two days if Marilyn promised not to demand multiple takes. He struggled to infuse wit and sparkle into the scene of their meeting and eventually conceded that Paula's Method approach of inspiring Marilyn by instructing her to think of Coca Cola and Frank Sinatra was indeed the best one. "God! Don't tell me they would have been right and I was wrong throughout this whole thing?" Olivier wrote. "Needless to say it worked; enough to make a man cut his throat, enough for this man, anyway."

On the last day of production, Marilyn stood before the cast and crew and delivered a heartfelt, public apology for her delays and tardiness. "I hope you will all forgive me," she said. "It wasn't my fault. I've been sick all through the picture. Please, please don't hold it against me." She also presented gifts to all associated with the production.

Jack Cardiff imparted insight into Marilyn's demeanor on the set, debunking the myth of her being rude, drugged, and erratic: "[Marilyn] was impeccable and fastidious in every possible way. She was always to me 'clean'—if you know what I mean. The average film star (and I have worked with many) were hooker types in their language (they'd swear and stuff). You knew from the way they talked that they were Hollywood types, and that they had slept all over the place. From Marilyn I can never once remember hearing a four-letter word. On the set she was professional. She never burst into tears or rows."

The Millers arrived one hour early to Heathrow Airport en route to New York on November 20. The British media reported, "[Marilyn's] triumphal visit to Britain ended today on a note like the thud of a soggy crumpet." Wearing a high-neck black dress and fur coat, she seemed eager to return home. "It's the British who are supposed to be so stiff but Marilyn Monroe outclasses us," lamented the press, voicing disappointment in the fact that Marilyn's screen image differed from her demure and sedate demeanor during her visit to the United Kingdom. "She was about as approachable as a crown jewel."

The feeling was mutual. Marilyn described the British press as sex-starved schoolboys to her closest friends and vowed never again to return. "It seemed to be raining the whole time," she said. "Or maybe it was me." In contrast, her closing comments to the press were respectful and courteous: "I want to thank everyone for our treatment when we were in Britain."

Photographers captured a beaming Marilyn sandwiched between the Oliviers as each of them kissed her warmly on the cheek before she and Miller boarded the plane. The couple had given Marilyn an expensive engraved watch as a farewell gift. "Miss Monroe's a wonderful person," Olivier said. "She's been feeling really poorly since she's been here, but I'd make a film with her again." True to character, Miller remained silent.

After the Millers' plane touched the runway at Idlewild Airport in New York, Margaret Gillon received an autographed photograph of Marilyn as a token of appreciation for the woman's friendly wave each evening as Marilyn was driven from Pinewood Studio to Parkside House.

* * *

In late 1956, Olivier brought a rough cut of the film to Hollywood so that Jack Warner, the president of Warner Brothers Studios and the film's distributer, could view it. Apprehensive about its slow pace, Warner changed the title to *The Prince and the Showgirl*, hoping a reference to Marilyn's character would draw a larger audience. "I wished I had got better stuff out of Marilyn," Olivier said after the screening. "Other directors had, and it lay uneasy on my conscience that I had not. I began to admit to myself that I had not achieved greater perfection because I had shirked the probability of more rows."

Back in New York, Greene organized a sitting for publicity photographs of Monroe and Olivier. The battling co-stars returned to their pre-production amicability thanks to Greene's staging a sexy atmosphere with mood music, caviar sandwiches, and cocktails at his vast studio on Lexington Avenue. Images of Olivier in a silk lounging robe embracing Marilyn in modern gown with a plunging halter-top depicted a fictitious scene never filmed at Pinewood Studios. Greene seemed inspired by the current spicy advertising campaign for Elia Kazan's *Baby Doll* that included billboards of Carroll Baker wearing baby doll lingerie in a crib and sucking her thumb.

* * *

On April 1, 1957, Marilyn viewed an edited print of the film and wished someone were merely playing an April Fool's Day joke on her. In response, she angrily dictated a letter to Jack Warner later published by Donald Spoto. It was no longer the same film she had watched during an early screening with him in New York, Marilyn insisted, and she predicted it would not be as successful as the first edited version, which they had both approved. She objected to the slow pacing of the first third of the film and believed the comedic scenes had been "*flattened out*" by a substitution of "*inferior*" takes with "*flatter performances lacking the energy and brightness that you saw in New York.*"

Marilyn also took exception with the editing: "*Jump cutting kills the points, as in the fainting scene.*" She added, "*The story gets lost in the coronation scene,*" as it seemed longer than in the previous version, and that "*American audiences are not as moved by stained glass windows as the British are, and we threaten them with boredom.*" In addition, the sparse soundtrack shocked her, as the intention was to make a romantic film. She concluded the memo by begging Warner to "*make every effort to save our picture.*"

Warner Brothers Studios made no major editing changes. Without salvation, *The Prince and the Showgirl* proceeded for a summer release. Greene was to be credited as executive producer, but Olivier believed he didn't earn the title. Upon release, Greene was credited as such, but in subsequent prints, his name was removed. Marilyn and Olivier appeared on the cover of the international edition of the July 8, 1957 issue of *Life* magazine, and crawling news tickers in New York's Time Square promoted the film's release.

For the world premiere, Warner Brothers and Marilyn Monroe Productions chose the masterpiece of American Modernist and Art Deco design, Radio City Music Hall, located on Sixth Avenue between Fiftieth and Fifty-First Streets. Designed by Donald Deskey and built by John D. Rockefeller, Jr. in 1932, the venue boasts the largest indoor theatre in the world with nearly six thousand spectator seats. A sweeping proscenium arch, measuring sixty feet high and one hundred feet long, frames the Great Stage and cinema screen. The stunning movie palace is said to need no performers, but this night, it provided a lavish backdrop for one of the decade's most dazzling entertainers.

On June 13, 1957, the hall's marquee, a full city block long, advertised Monroe and Olivier opening in Warner Brother's re-titled film. To Olivier, *The Prince and the Showgirl* sounded like a third-rate Edwardian musical, but the film's trailer called it a "spicy adventure" with Marilyn "in her happiest role." Taglines on the lobby posters read, "Some countries have a medal for *Everything*." The premiere, a charity event for The Milk Fund for Babies, earned $32,250. Two rows of Honor Guards dressed in period British uniforms from the Seventy-first Regiment lined both sides of the red carpet where Ed Sullivan interviewed those in attendance.

The doors of a tail-finned Cadillac limousine opened, and Marilyn stepped onto the red carpet in a champagne-colored, form-fitting satin mermaid gown flared into a full skirt at the knee with matching wrap, clutch purse, drop earrings, and long opera gloves. The gown's structure suggested a modern version of the Edwardian period costume she wore throughout most of the film. Miller wore a tuxedo and bow tie and frequently wiped his brow with a white handkerchief. Marilyn approached Amy Greene standing next to Milton, and threw her arms around her friend, now pregnant with a second son, Anthony. Marilyn asked to feel the baby before placing her hands on Amy's bulging stomach.

Suddenly, a friendly crowd broke through the cordon of honor guards and fifteen policemen and someone snatched off Marilyn's earring while another scratched at her gown. Ed Sullivan assisted in recovering the jewel and returning it to her while Marilyn straightened the towering hat and chinstrap of an honor guard who had intervened.

"That crowd nearly finished me off," she exclaimed to Sullivan. "Wasn't it wonderful?"

"Marilyn can always make me forget my troubles," Miller told the reporters, "but I don't have to go to movie premieres for her to distract me."

The celebrities rose from their seats when Marilyn entered the auditorium. Before the film was shown, the Music Hall's Rockettes, an all-female precision line dance company, performed a lavish stage production featuring high kicks in perfect unison. When the film ended, actor Red Buttons told a reporter in the lobby that Marilyn was the greatest comedienne of the day. "Only she has more than that," Buttons said. "There's a charm which you can't describe."

Afterward, the Millers attended a formal dinner dance at the Waldorf Astoria Hotel. New York City mayor, Robert F. Wagner (1910-1991) and his wife sat at the Millers' table along with Jack Warner. African-American vocalist Eartha Kitt (1927-2008), who had recently been performing in the musical *Shinbone Alley* at the Broadway Theatre, chatted with Marilyn at length after the dinner.

The following morning, the *New York Times* lamented the film's lack of the scene that showed Olivier in a silk lounging robe and kissing Marilyn's shoulder. Actually it was not a scene but a provocative publicity photograph taken by Milton Greene, with Marilyn wearing a contemporary sequin gown. The advertisement's text read, "There's only one Marilyn Monroe but there isn't one Marilyn Monroe picture that teases and tickles like Marilyn Monroe starring with Laurence Olivier..."

The public reaction to the film was largely positive, and most of Marilyn's reviews were favorable. The film ranked tenth in the year's top moneymakers and garnered many awards in Europe and Great Britain. Marilyn was nominated for Best Foreign Actress by the British Academy Awards and the film received nominations for the British Academy Award in the categories of Best British Actor, Best British Film, Best British screenplay, and Best Film from any source. Marilyn received both the Italian David Di Donatello Prize and the French Crystal Star Award for Best Foreign Actress. "When you look at the film," observed Miller's sister, Joan Copeland, "it is apparent who won the battle, and it wasn't Olivier."

"Marilyn Monroe...has never seemed more in command of herself as a person and comedienne," lauded the *New York Post*. "She manages to make her laughs without sacrificing the real Marilyn to play-acting. This, of course, is something one can expect from great, talented and practiced performers. It comes as a most pleasant surprise from Marilyn Monroe, who has been half-actress, half-sensation." On the heels of Marilyn's critical triumph in *Bus Stop*, her latest achievement only solidified her stature as an actress."This, I am sure, is Miss Monroe's best cinema effort," proclaimed the *Los Angeles Times*. "Under Olivier's direction, she reveals a real sense of comedy. Miss Monroe also proves that she can command attention now by other means than her famous hip-swinging walk." Critics finally saw beyond her body and celebrated the skills she had mastered at the Actor's Studio.

"Marilyn Monroe's acting promise soars to a triumphant peak in *The Prince and the Showgirl...*" announced the *New York World-Telegram and Sun*. "The movie is also a comic delight, matching the surprise bestowed upon us by Marilyn. As her co-star and director, Laurence Olivier brings out qualities none of her films ever summoned. She is captivatingly kittenish in her infectious mirth. Her love scenes are played as a girlish game. She romps through slapstick and turns solemn moments into part of her fun." None of the on-set tension between the stars transcended to film, and Olivier received credit for extracting from Marilyn the spontaneity that he had only inhibited and which had been summoned through whispered conferences with Paula Strasberg.

Unfortunately, not everyone was as complimentary. "*The Prince and the Showgirl* lifts Marilyn Monroe to the probable ceiling of her serious career as a comedienne," *Time* concluded, "It also leaves her ankle-high to such giants of the theatre as her fellow performers, Producer-Director Laurence Olivier (her co-star) and cloud-capped Dame Sybil Thorndike...Marilyn is alternately spirited and lethargic."

For some, the plot was lackluster. "Miss Monroe never gets out of that dress and Mr. Rattigan never swings out of the circle in which he has permitted this thin plot to get stuck..." reported Bosley Crowther of *The New York Times*, "He has not let his story do much more than go around and around, and then come to a sad end."

"*The Prince and the Showgirl* is great fun if you don't take it seriously," advised *New York Herald Tribune*. "Certainly its author doesn't. Terence Rattigan is just playing a game, amusing us for two hours, and the actors enjoy the charade immensely. They try to look earnest but a twinkle in the eye betrays them. In the case of Olivier, the twinkle must fight its way through a thick monocle to reach the outside world and it does. This is a performance of rich, subtle humor...Marilyn's role has no such fine shadings. This is a dumb, affable showgirl and nothing more, and Miss Monroe goes through the motions with mirth, childish innocence, squeals of pleasure, pouts of annoyance, eyes big as golf balls, and many a delighted toss of her rounded surfaces." At least one reviewer was distracted by

Marilyn's curves, but future film critics would regard her performance as one of her best.

Film historian Foster Hirsch observed that Monroe and Olivier "play beautifully together, and the obvious difference in their style of performance enhances the thin material," but the film, "with its confined drawing-room setting and its artificial storyline, looks unmistakably like a theatre piece transported uncomfortably to an alien and resistant medium." This is exactly the effect Marilyn hoped to avoid.

Having attacked Marilyn in the press in the decades after her death, Olivier finally made some inner peace with his deceased co-star after he viewed the film with some young colleagues in the 1980s. In his autobiography, he admitted without rancor: "I just don't think I tried terribly hard to get on with her." Towards the end of his life, Olivier offered an honest and accurate summary of their experience: "No one had such a look of unconscious wisdom, and her personality was strong on the screen. She gave a star performance. Maybe I was tetchy with Marilyn and with myself, because I felt my career was in a rut...I was fifty. What a happy memory it would have been if Marilyn had made me feel twenty years younger..." In the end, Olivier concisely and accurately assessed their performances: "I was good as could be; and Marilyn! Marilyn was quite wonderful, the best of all. So. What do you know?"

"It's making money, but that's the crazy thing," Marilyn would tell George Barris about the film a few weeks before her death. "I've been asked to sell it to TV but I've refused. I feel it's one of my financial assets and I want to hold onto it...it did very well in Europe; I got the French and Italian award."

* * *

Five years after publishing his memoir, *The Prince, the Showgirl and Me*, Colin Clark penned a follow-up, *My Week With Marilyn*, in which he alluded to having engaged in an affair with Marilyn during her working honeymoon with Miller. No mention of the affair in the first book led many to disbelieve his claims. None of the surviving cast and crew of the film had witnessed intimate interactions between the two and they doubted the veracity of his allegations. Jean Kent (Maisie Springfield), interviewed by

Amy Kaufman of *Los Angeles Times*, asserted Marilyn and Miller "were glued together on set all the time."

When the author mentioned Colin Clark's name to Amy Greene in 2012, she covered her ears with her hands and cried, "No!" Greene shuddered at the sound of Clark's name and dismissed his allegations. She had been present during the entire production and described the third assistant director as a mere "gopher" who had limited access to Marilyn and had never spent a week alone with her.

"The Marilyn legend had already been exaggerated and twisted and turned," actor Kenneth Branagh, who portrayed Olivier in the film adaptation of Clark's memoir, told Kaufman. "He took a view on his own youth, and perhaps wrote what he thought made for a good story—not necessarily the absolute truth."

In *The Prince and the Showgirl*, Marilyn holds the viewer's interest with her expressions and physical comedy and has more screen time than in any of her previous films. The film proves the adage that whenever she appears on screen, other actors cease to exist.

* * *

[For a synopsis of *The Prince and the Showgirl*, please see **Appendix: Selected Marilyn Monroe Film Synopses**]

Chapter Two: Manhattan, Autumn 1956/Winter & Spring 1957

After the Thanksgiving holiday of 1956, Marilyn recovered emotionally and physically from the four months of the tense production in England and the fissure in her new marriage. With no professional commitments on the horizon, she returned to her role as an advocate for the Actors Studio and its alumni during the remainder of the year. In December, Marilyn made a public appearance at the Actors Studio to promote the upcoming benefit premiere of *Baby Doll.* Orchestra seats sold for $50 to see Marilyn as a celebrity usherette and Carroll Baker on the screen in the role Marilyn coveted.

On December 18, Marilyn and Miller attended Kazan's premiere of the film at the Victoria Theatre and the $350-per-seat benefit dance for the Actors Studio at the Waldorf-Astoria. Under her ermine coat, Marilyn wore an ill-fitting plum sequin gown with halter-top and plunging neckline purchased off the rack at a dress shop on Eighth Avenue. The dress ordered had not arrived on time and despite its poor fit, the $87 replacement photographed well in several shoots and formal events. During the dance, Marilyn gave a rare radio interview.

On New Year's Day 1957, Marilyn received the Award of Achievement from the *Motion Picture Herald*, a motion picture industry trade publication, for her rank as one of the "Top Ten Money Making Stars" of 1956. The Quigley Poll, as it was known, was regarded as one of the most reliable indicators of a star's real box-office draw because the theatre owners whose livelihood depended on exhibiting the films that attracted audiences determined its honorees. This was the last year that Marilyn appeared on the Top Ten List.

The future of MMP seemed uncertain with Miller, Milton Greene, and Lee Strasberg competing for control over Marilyn's career. Amid the escalating tension, Kermit Bloomgarden, Miller's producer, suggested Marilyn make her Broadway debut in *Maiden Voyage*, a Paul Osborn comedy about Greek gods. The role he had in mind for Marilyn was Hera, wife of Zeus and goddess of marriage who protects wives and punishes adulterers. Scheduled to open in the winter of 1957, the play never reached the stage. Even though he believed his wife would be a great stage actress, Miller told Bloomgarden that she was exhausted and preferred to enjoy a quiet life now that she completed two films back to back. "Just be her husband!" Greene shouted to Miller. "Marilyn and I can run the corporation."

As the weeks passed, Miller continued to drive a wedge between his wife and her business partner. After six months in the blinding spotlight of her fame, he wanted her to take a break and focus on becoming a wife and mother. Greene's dreams for Marilyn's career threatened Miller's plan for his personal life, and he found himself being edged out. Greene told Fred Lawrence Guiles of Miller angrily shouting at him on the telephone. Greene said that he had told Miller he would refuse to listen if Miller continued to yell. When Miller escalated his tone further, Greene abruptly ended the call.

At thirty, Marilyn heard the biological clock tick away at the remaining time for starting a family and was faced with a difficult decision. Avid to please her husband and become a mother, Marilyn put her aspiration of becoming a great actress on hold. "She was ultrasensitive, and very dedicated to her work, whether people realize this or not," Greene would say of Marilyn. "She came through magnificently in *The Prince and the Showgirl* and she was great in *Bus Stop*. All I did was believe in her. She was a marvelous, living, wonderful person who I don't think many people understood."

Perhaps as a corrective experience for their strained working honeymoon in England, on January 3, Marilyn and Miller arrived in Moot Point, Jamaica, where they vacationed for sixteen days at the seaside villa of British aristocrat Lady Pamela Bird. "Marriage makes me feel more womanly, more proud of myself," Marilyn said early in the year. "It also makes me feel less frantic. All my life I've been alone. Now for the first time I have a feeling of being sheltered. It's as if I have come in and out of the cold...There's a feeling of being together—a warmth and tenderness. I don't mean a display of affection or anything like that. I mean just being together."

"Marilyn is a perfectionist and she makes impossible demands of herself," Miller said of his wife both as a homemaker and actress. "I do, too. You can never reach what you're after. I try to help Marilyn accept this truth, and she helps me...I've learned a lot about living from her." With a deepened appreciation of his wife, Miller hoped her life as his wife would provide more emotional contentment.

With a completed film behind her, Marilyn rested in the Caribbean and reflected upon the fruits of her driving ambition to reach two major priorities: to establish herself as a serious actress and to become a mother. With *Bus Stop*, she achieved critical acclaim, but the experience of producing her own film with a director who demeaned her had only chipped away at her self-worth. An early screening of *The Prince and the Showgirl* had left her disappointed and unsure of the film's potential for success.

Marilyn now detached from her career and focused on her role of housewife and becoming a mother. She longed to love and nurture a child, hoping to lavish it with all she had been denied by her own parents. The first step was to find a property where she and Miller could start a family. With $29,500 in proceeds from the sale of Miller's Roxbury farmhouse, the couple scoured Manhattan for a suitable luxury apartment.

During a respite from touring pre-war apartment buildings on the Upper East Side with realtors, Marilyn attended what would become her final photo shoot with Milton Greene. Against a black backdrop, Marilyn posed seductively in a red halter dress from Jax with full skirts of layered chiffon, a scarlet version of the white dress from *The Seven Year Itch*, and matching red Ferragamo pumps. Now that Marilyn was married to a man who exercised control over her and her career, the dynamic between she and Milton during this shoot was changed. Lounging sensuously and playing with the sheer chiffon layers of her skirt, she appeared serene and content as a newly married lady surrendering her control to her husband.

The indelible billboard image of The Girl from *The Seven Year Itch* standing over the subway grating with her skirt flying toward the sky paved the way for a new breed of entertainers whose sexual expression defied the period's prevailing notion of conservatism and restrictiveness. Early in January, during Elvis Presley's third appearance on *The Ed Sullivan Show*, censors insisted that the singer be filmed from the waist up in a claustrophobic, tight frame to prevent the public from exposure to the provocative thrusts of his pelvis as he sang a medley of his rock and roll songs.

Even though the censors tried to prevent the world from Elvis' moves that would eventually become legendary, they had no problem with the crude emphasis on Jayne Mansfield's breasts in Fox's *The Girl Can't Help It*, currently in release. Director Frank Tashlin filmed Jayne Mansfield walking down the street carrying two milk bottles in front of her chest. As she passes the milkman, who is also holding a bottle of milk, the cap pops off and milk overflows with ejaculatory gusto. Professionally, Marilyn was a sexual trailblazer, but personally, she assumed the role of traditional Jewish housewife and sophisticated New York social hostess.

Our collective consciousness of life in the 1950s evokes images of post-war economic prosperity; a rising white, middle-class population; intact families with mother, father, and children; a migration to the suburbs, comprised of nearly identical single-family homes; and a domesticated lifestyle exemplified by backyard barbeques and cocktail parties.

The iconic 1950s American woman was a housewife in a full-skirt, high-heeled shoes, and white apron. She wore dramatic cosmetics, and was never seen without her hair styled and lacquered. She would spend her days at home, raising the children and completing household chores while her husband worked outside the home. Although retrospectively perceived as revolutionary and ahead of her time, Marilyn held many of the values and beliefs of the period and was equally susceptible to the formidable conformist pressures. "Movies are my business," she said, "but Arthur is my life. Wherever he is, I want to be. When we're in New York, Arthur is the boss."

During this era, the social and cultural expectation of a woman's role was that of a perfect wife and mother who obeyed her husband. The media reinforced this role by steering women away from the work force and back in the home. Black and white television shows of the times further reinforced the ideal of domestic bliss: *Father Knows Best, The Donna Reed Show,* and *Leave It To Beaver.* Popular magazine articles primed women in looking attractive for the purpose of catching or keeping a husband, child rearing, and keeping marriages happy and fresh.

In December 1956 and January 1957, the precise time Marilyn and Miller set up household together, popular *Life* magazine published two issues devoted to the "American Woman: Her Achievements and Troubles." Its main feature, "Changing Roles in Modern Marriage," explored a growing sexual ambiguity's ruination of marriage. The author cited a trend of men taking on more traditionally feminine qualities, and woman taking on more traditionally masculine qualities. In the following fifty years, society and culture evolved in this androgynous direction, but during mid-twentieth century America, a blending of gender roles was radical, even menacing. The author interviewed Dr. Ralph Greenson, a psychiatrist in practice in Beverly Hills, who speculated that they lost their identities due to having "had mothers that were fatherly and fathers who were motherly." Three years after the publication, Marilyn would present challenges to Dr. Greenson when she became his patient.

In a 1954 issue of *Esquire*, Merle Miller attacked "that increasing and strident minority of women who are doing their damndest to wreck marriage and home life in America...Those who insist on having both a husband and a career. They are a menace and they have to be stopped." Two year later, in *Life*, readers were warned of the "disease of working women" eroding American men's self-respect. The article concluded that no man wanted to be "out-distanced by his wife." Marilyn was the primary breadwinner in the Miller marriage. Arthur had experienced a dry spell in his writing, and the couple was living off the income from Marilyn's contract with Fox, the recent sale of her rights to the screenplay *Horns for the Devil*, and a percentage of profit from *The Prince and the Showgirl*. A 1950s American most certainly could accuse Marilyn of emasculating her playwright husband.

* * *

In January, Marilyn and Arthur purchased a three-bedroom, two and one-half bath apartment on the thirteenth floor of a handsome, 15-story, red brick apartment building at 444 East Fifty-Seventh Street. Erected in 1927, the structure had a four-story rusticated limestone base with a canopied entrance, two-story-high columns, sidewalk landscaping, a doorman, a vaulted lobby with marble floor, some decorative balconies, and forty-five condominium apartments. Over the years, it would serve as home to numerous celebrities including Bill Blass, the designer, and Bobby Short, cabaret pianist. The building stood beside a corner apartment house at the intersection of Sutton Place where Marilyn had been living, so the move was literally next-door and around the corner. In the New York phone book, the Millers' telephone number (Eldorado 5 2325) was listed under "Marilyn, Monroe" opposed to "Monroe, Marilyn."

Beamed ceilings, ornate moldings, windows in all of the rooms, and views of the Queensborough Bridge only added to the charm of what Miller called a "surprisingly inexpensive but spacious apartment right off the East River." The apartment would remain Marilyn's primary residence until her death. A single entry door opened to a gallery with a black and white checkerboard marble floor. To the immediate left was a butler's pantry leading to a kitchen, breakfast room, maid's room, and bath. A service entrance next to the bath accessed a rear corridor and service elevator. To the left of the entrance gallery, beyond the entry to the pantry, was the living room with fireplace and window facing the street. It opened to the formal dining room to the left, also with a window facing the street.

The dining room connected with the breakfast room and kitchen. To the right of the entrance gallery, a hall led to three bedrooms and two baths. Down the hall on the left was the master bedroom with a fireplace and en suite bath with soaking tub. Further down the hall, also on the left, was the second bedroom. This bedroom, the master bedroom, and master bath had views of Fifty-Seventh Street. The third bedroom, across the second bedroom, was next to the guest bath with tub and shower. Across the hall from the master bedroom was a walk-in closet.

Designer John Moore helped Marilyn decorate in shades of white, beige, and chocolate. Eventually, Marilyn had a wall removed between the living and dining rooms and mounted floor-to-ceiling mirrors on several walls. George Gruner installed white wall-to-wall carpeting over the hardwood floors, making the apartment resemble a 1930s movie set. When the job was done, Marilyn gave Gruner two signed photographs for him and his son, Peter. "One day they may be worth a little cash for you and your family," she said. Gruner's children, Laurie and Peter Gruner, auctioned the photographs in 2010.

Elegantly furnished in French provincial, Marilyn's Manhattan apartment contained the possession she valued the most. The white-lacquered baby grand piano given to Marilyn in childhood by her mother dominated the living room. It had to be hoisted from the street and brought directly into the living room window. When Marilyn's mother was institutionalized, the piano had been sold. As a starlet, Marilyn diligently searched for the instrument and recovered it from an auction house. She carried the piano to each new address, providing continuity to her roving lifestyle. She entertained guests by playing "To a Wild Rose," "Spinning Wheel," and "Fur Elise." Marilyn prominently displayed the triptych with her portrait by Cecil Beaton on the white piano.

Beside the piano, she placed a 1930s white plaster Serge Roche floor lamp in the shape of palm tree. Under the living room window, Marilyn placed a traditional sofa of white on white damask, round French side tables, and a Louis XV provincial fruitwood coffee table with marbled surface. Matching damask draperies covered the windows in the living and dining rooms. Marilyn flanked the sofa with a pair of Regency beech wood chairs. Rich chocolate colored satin covered the chairs and accompanying ottomans. A Louis XV cut glass sunburst wall clock with a gilt metal dial hung over the fireplace mantel. Bookshelves flanked the fireplace. A marble statue depicting a headless and limbless female torso rested on the windowsill behind the sofa.

In the apartment, Marilyn also displayed a lithograph of her childhood idol Abraham Lincoln and a framed portrait of scientist Albert Einstein. The physicist's picture carried a personal inscription: "*To Marilyn, with respect and love and thanks. Albert Einstein.*" Many biographers speculated an encounter between the two, but Eli Wallach took credit for executing this practical joke.

The second bedroom offered two twin beds for Miller's children, Jane and Robert, when they visited from their mother's home in Brooklyn. A pair of Louis XV provincial style grey and cream painted bedside tables completed the room's furnishings.

Marilyn converted the third bedroom into a writing study for Miller and whispered to visitors to keep their voices low as not to disturb her husband's concentration. "I never intrude except to bring him a second cup of coffee," she said. "I need to be here to get my husband's breakfast and to make him a cheerful mid-morning cup of coffee occasionally. Writing's such a lonely kind of work..." Jack Cardiff's sensual portrait of Marilyn with her hair casually astray and covering one heavy-lidded eye hung on the wall near a chess set suspended in mid-play. "That's Marilyn," Miller said of the image. "I like the tenderness in it, her dreaming quality, and I like it because she is relaxed. Not many people ever see her that way."

The study also housed her library of over four hundred books varying in subjects, reflecting an insatiable thirst for widespread knowledge. Her laden bookshelves held works of literature, art, drama, poetry, politics, philosophy, psychology, theology, history, and biography. From Camus to Tolstoy, many classic volumes represented Marilyn's interest in serious literature and spilled out of the study and onto the bookshelves flanking the living room fireplace.

The master bedroom featured a quilted and buttoned upholstered headboard in ivory silk and a king-size bed. Moderne mirrored bedside cabinets and matching dresser reflected Marilyn's image as she lounged in bed listening to Ella Fitzgerald and Frank Sinatra record albums. That year, the crooner released *Come Fly with Me*, featuring escapist songs with accompaniment by the Billy May orchestra. "I know it's considered chic for a husband and wife to have separate bedrooms," Marilyn told journalist Radie Harris, "but I'm an old-fashioned girl who believes a husband and wife should share the same bedroom and bed."

The Millers frequently attended the theatre, dinner parties, and cocktail parties. The couple hosted many soirees themselves. Marilyn's guests delighted in her quick wit, charisma, and talent for lively conversation. Maurice Zolotow described her as a "charming and hospitable hostess." Marilyn welcomed columnist Radie Harris into the apartment for an interview and served tea like a proper hostess, influenced by her recent trip to England. Harris found her "deliriously happy in her new role as housewife." Miller proudly announced to friends that Marilyn waxed the floors herself.

Marilyn called her husband Art, Arturo, Papa, and Poppy Pa. Arthur called her Penny Dreadful, Sugar Finney, and Gramercy 5. The latter referenced his affinity for clarinetist Artie Shaw's 1940s jazz combo whose recordings of "Summit Ridge Drive," "Smoke Gets in Your Eyes," and "My Blue Heaven" were among Miller's favorites.

Miller's children, Bobby, age nine, and Jane, age twelve, frequently visited. Marilyn adored them and in return, they maintained affection for her and appreciated her imaginative spirit. "I take a lot of pride in them," Marilyn would say of her three stepchildren, including Joe DiMaggio, Jr. "Because they're from broken homes too, and I think I can understand them. I've always said to them that I didn't want to be their mother or stepmother...I just wanted to be their friend...I think I love them more than anyone."

Marilyn got Bobby and Jane off to school in the morning and planned fun things for them to do on the weekends, holidays, and during the summers. Rupert Allan remembered Marilyn hosting Bobby's first birthday party when he turned eleven and invited his friends to the apartment. They parked their bicycles in the lobby of the apartment building and took the elevator to the thirteenth floor to enjoy cake, ice cream and party games. In a letter to Nobel and Pulitzer Prize-winning author Saul Bellow (1915-2005), Miller stated his children were in love with his new wife and reluctant to return home to their mother when the weekends ended.

To manage her life and household finances, Marilyn hired May Reis as a private secretary. At age 53, Reis had been a caretaker for her mother and infirmed grandmother since the death of her father when she was only nine. Reis came well recommended, having worked for Miller and Elia Kazan. "May was alone in this world and had no family—and so Marilyn became her existence, her profession, her commitment," sister-in-law Virginia Reis told Donald Spoto. The petite and mild-mannered secretary answered Marilyn's mail, kept the schedule, took calls, and communicated with agents and publicists. "*May is steadfastly loyal to Marilyn,*" Berniece Miracle wrote after observing the secretary's abhorrence for gossip earn Marilyn's unyielding trust. Marilyn also employed Hattie Stevenson, an African-American cook who spoke in a British accent and had recently left the household of a diplomat in London.

On weekends, the Millers drove across the bridge to Brooklyn to visit Arthur's parents. Isidore adored Marilyn and carried around a faded newspaper picture of himself with her. "*He had the vulnerability of age, which moved her to a flowing tenderness with him,*" Miller wrote. All of Marilyn's chronic worries disappeared when she cuddled beside Isidore on the sofa.

Marilyn's relationship with Milton Greene deteriorated in the months following their return to the United States as she aligned with her husband and detached from her business partner. Amy later admitted her husband always put Miller down to Marilyn, intentionally and inadvertently, creating a further wedge between the two men. Miller would later describe Marilyn as a woman who immersed herself in a relationship with the particular person she needed; yet, when he talked with her about such an apparent powerful connection, she downplayed it as quite the opposite. Inferring Marilyn was an opportunist, he may not have realized she may merely have been affirming her loyalty to him by downplaying these relationships. According to Amy Greene, Miller resented Milton's involvement in his wife's business and financial affairs and wanted more control in these areas of her life. He finally gave his wife an ultimatum to end the partnership.

To further distance herself from Milton, Marilyn terminated sessions with Dr. Hohenberg because she was also Greene's doctor. Marilyn contacted Anna Freud in London for a referral and received a recommendation to work with Dr. Marianne Kris. Beginning in April, Marilyn saw the analyst five times a week. Kris practiced out of her apartment in the Langham Building, which also housed the Strasberg's residence. Following therapy sessions, Marilyn took the elevator to the Strasberg's floor for private acting sessions with Lee.

Born in Vienna on May 27, 1900, Dr. Marianne Kris graduated in medicine from the University of Vienna in 1925. Her father, Dr. Oskar Rie (1863-1931), had been a close friend and associate of Sigmund Freud and had served as pediatrician to Freud's children. After two years of psychiatric and psychoanalytic training in Berlin, Marianne returned to Vienna and married Ernst Kris (1900-1957), a fellow psychoanalyst and lecturer at the Vienna Psychoanalytic Institute. She was active in Anna Freud's research on analytic treatment of children. When the Nazis took over in Austria in 1938, Kris relocated with her husband and children to London.

With help from Joseph P. Kennedy, the United States Ambassador to London, the Krises eventually settled in New York in 1940 where Marianne joined the New York Psychoanalytic Institute and practiced as one of the few analysts specializing in the treatment of children. Ernst and Marianne's research led to the creation of the

Child Study Center at Yale University. When Ernst died early in 1957, Marianne took over the journal he founded, *The Psychoanalytic Study of the Child.*

Kris' approach to Marilyn's treatment focused on exploration of her childhood, deliberately returning Marilyn to her painful history five days per week. Marilyn remained stuck in her past trauma like a mastodon trapped in a tar pit. The treatment would prove self-defeating. Since Marilyn took acting lessons with Strasberg after nearly every therapy session, she left Kris' office only to face Strasberg's exercises in sense memory, instructing her to go back into her past for inspiration on tackling a role or to elicit raw emotions. It was a recipe for psychic disaster. Marilyn increasingly viewed herself as a victim, and her depression worsened.

During some of her visits to the Strasberg apartment after her acting sessions with Lee, Marilyn enjoyed engaging in word plays with Paula and Susan. An example was published in Susan's memoir, *Marilyn and Me: Sisters, Rivals, Friends*:

> "Mother, your sauce is delicious," Susan said.
>
> "People have always told me that I'm a good *sauceress*," Paula replied.
>
> Marilyn joined in: "*Witch* kind?"

Although Marilyn painfully struggled in her treatment reliving childhood trauma, at times she was able to relax with those she trusted and enjoy genuine, spontaneous fun.

On February 18, the Academy of Motion Picture Arts and Sciences announced the Oscar award nominations for 1956. Marilyn's co-star in *Bus Stop*, Don Murray, earned a nomination for Best Actor in his film debut. Nominations for Best Actress went to Ingrid Bergman in *Anastasia*, Carroll Baker in Baby Doll, Katharine Hepburn in *The Rainmaker*, Nancy Kelly in *The Bad Seed*, and Deborah Kerr in *The King and I.* Columnist Sheilah Graham believed the snub was "cruelly effective punishment" for Marilyn's past professional behavior and abandonment of Hollywood for the Actors Studio. Marilyn was intensely disappointed. "The two things she most wanted during that era—an Oscar and a baby—were just to escape her grasp," Graham wrote. "To her, it meant that they felt she wasn't good enough."

Things weren't looking good for Miller either. On the same day, a federal grand jury indicted Miller on two counts of contempt of Congress due to Miller's refusal to name names. On March 1, he pled not guilty in his arraignment before Judge Charles F. McLaughlin in Washington and was released after posting a thousand dollar bond. As Miller battled legal woes, Milton Greene approached Marilyn with a two million dollar deal to perform weekly in a television series. At the time, television was a medium for aging, has-been film stars like Lucille Ball, Loretta Young, and Donna Reed, who forged second careers and great success on the small screen. Miller waged war against Greene, and Marilyn obediently turned over her business dealing to her new husband and his minions.

The Fourteenth annual Golden Globe Award ceremony was held in Los Angeles on February 28. Marilyn was nominated for *Bus Stop* in the category of Best Actress in a Musical or Comedy along with Judy Holliday in *The Solid Gold Cadillac*, Debbie Reynolds in *Bundle of Joy*, Machiko Kyo in *The Teahouse of the August Moon*, and Deborah Kerr in *The King and I.* Marilyn remained in New York, passing on attending the award ceremony in Los Angeles and missing Deborah Kerr receive the honor.

"It seems Marilyn doesn't want to go ahead with the program we planned," Greene told the *Los Angeles Times.* "I'm getting lawyers to represent me. I don't want to do anything now to hurt her career, but I did devote about a year and a half exclusively to her, I practically gave up photography. You can't just make a contract with someone and then forget it."

On April 11, Robert H. Montgomery released a statement alleging Greene had grossly mismanaged Marilyn Monroe Productions. Within days, Marilyn held a meeting and announced that Greene, Irving Stein, and accountant Joseph Carr were dismissed and replaced by Montgomery, Arthur's childhood friend; George Kupchik, Miller's brother-in-law; and George Levine, a friend of Miller's. Montgomery remembers Marilyn drinking vermouth during the meeting, rambling about Greene failing her, and relating this betrayal to her childhood sexual abuse by an adult male. The latter disclosure shocked the attorney.

Next, Marilyn dissolved the partnership. Greene and Irving Stein went to the offices of Millers' attorneys where they met to negotiate the contract. The Millers greeted them. Greene asked for only his initial $100,000 investment, and Marilyn urged him to "take more." He calmly insisted that he wanted to be the only person in her life never to take more. Within an hour of the meeting's end, Marilyn and Greene returned to their respective homes and were crying to each other over the telephone.

"Arthur took away the only person I ever trusted," Marilyn cried to Amy Greene. Milton had appointed his friends as corporate officers and now Arthur was doing the same. It would take another year before the partnership was officially dissolved with Marilyn buying out Milton's share of the corporation for a mere one hundred thousand dollars.

According to Amy, Arthur harbored an unwarranted jealousy of Milton and wanted him out of Marilyn's life. Amy, on the other hand, respected Marilyn and Milton's bond and believed no one should come between it. If Miller had believed the same, Amy would say, he and Marilyn could have had a happier and longer life together. As for Miller, he would never speak publicly of Milton. Miller would tell Fred Lawrence Guiles that he considered Amy a "highly ambitious person" who couldn't "feel anything profound." Attorney Irving Stein sued MMP for $22,100 for services for which he claimed nonpayment before Marilyn ousted him from her board of directors. The case was resolved the following year by the Appellate Division of the Supreme Court of the State of New York.

Marilyn was all smiles on April 12 at the April in Paris Ball, a charity ball held at the Waldorf Astoria Hotel, co-hosted by Elsa Maxwell (1883-1963), gossip columnist and renowned orchestrator of high society events, and Claude Philippe, manager of the ball's venue. The thirteen hundred in attendance raised $170,000 for French and American charities and included French film actors Gerard Philippe and Jean Marais, French actress Françoise Arnoul, the Duke and Duchess of Windsor, and Senator John Kennedy and his wife Jacqueline.

Maxwell strategically seated Marilyn beside Winthrop Aldrich, former U.S. Ambassador to Britain. Philippe decorated the Waldorf

Astoria's grand ballroom with thirty-foot chestnut tresses in artificial bloom kept fragrant by atomizers and staged a reenactment of New York's reception in honor of the Marquis of Lafayette during his visit to the city in 1824, a symbol of Franco-American friendship, complete with a horse-drawn carriage.

"Mrs. [Millicent] Hearst [wife of media tycoon William Randolph Hearst] wanted Marilyn Monroe to come to the party," Maxwell explained to Mike Wallace in a televised interview several months later, "because she was giving an affair with her afterwards, and Marilyn Monroe said to her it's wonderful to be here and no one ever notices us, no one pays any attention to us any more, Arthur and I can walk in the streets and no one bothers us, so I said well then come to my ball tomorrow...She came in and pandemonium... and it was a bombshell." Maxwell credited Marilyn as the facilitator of a truce to the feud between herself and the Duchess of Windsor, who had sold tickets to the soiree. Marilyn and Arthur danced closely together, publicly kissed, and held hands throughout the evening.

After the ball, Marilyn's schedule was filled with more publicity-related events. Notes by secretary May Reis dated April 22 document nine interviews or photo layouts for *Look, Week, Redbook, Esquire,* and *The Mirror.* Topics ranged from life at home with Miller, a birthday party for Earl Wilson, publicity for *The Prince and the Showgirl,* and a Manhattan cocktail party for *Publisher's Weekly.* In full demand, Marilyn's professional priority was promotion for her unreleased film.

In her most significant photographic session since 1955, Marilyn arrived at fashion photographer Richard Avedon's Madison Avenue studio on May 6 for a session of publicity photos for *The Prince and the Showgirl.* She wore the dark plum sequined gown previously donned for the premiere of *Baby Doll* and the April in Paris Ball. She posed with a grey fur, on a leather sofa, and on the floor with a tiger rug—complete with animal head—and with a stuffed white tiger. She even did a burlesque dance with white plume fans. Her smile was radiant, and her eyes sparkled.

"Marilyn Monroe was an invention of hers," Avedon said. "A genius invention that she created like an author creates a character. So when Marilyn Monroe put on a sequin dress and danced in the studio—

I mean, for hours she danced, and sang, and flirted, and did this thing. There is no describing what she did. She did Marilyn Monroe. And then there was the inevitable drop because she was someone who went very high up and went way, way down."

Avedon's portrait bearing the most posthumous interest is one he snapped of a serious Marilyn, out of character, with an anguished expression. "The famous portrait that resulted from this session is a study of the complex nature of celebrity," wrote Maria Morris Hambourg and Mia Fineman in *Avedon's Endgame.* "Entombed in her body, Avedon's Marilyn is a secular Madonna mourning some indefinable loss. The picture is imbued with a sense of inferiority that seems worlds away from the rigid mask in Andy Warhol's posthumous silk screens of Marilyn as a gaudily glamorous pop icon…Avedon's portrait foreshadowed the tragic figure Marilyn would soon become in the popular imagination…Yet neither Avedon's humanist portrayal of a sad seductress nor Warhol's lurid canonization of her vivacious, wet-lipped counterpart reveals the real Marilyn Monroe. The truth of Avedon's portrait lies in a new character, a melancholy heroine collaboratively created by the photographer and his subject."

Marilyn was back in character on May 12, when over twenty-two thousand spectators filled the stands at Ebbets Field in Brooklyn, home of the Dodgers baseball team, for a soccer game between Hapoel Tel Aviv of Israel and the American Soccer Leagues All Star Team. The match served as a fund-raiser for Israel, and many in the massive crowd came to watch a newly converted Jewish Marilyn perform the honorary kick-off. "The Israelis were asked what they wanted to see during their visit," said Dennis D'Agostino, a public relations employee for the New York Mets. "Their response: 'As athletes, we'd like to meet the Brooklyn Dodgers; as men we'd like to meet Marilyn Monroe.'"

In a tight, royal blue dress with a plunging neckline and a carnation tucked into her cleavage, Marilyn waved to the crowds in an open car slowly circling the field and escorted by a troupe of Boy Scouts. At the start of the game, flanked by a group of athletes including former Belgium player Eddie Wauters now playing for the American league, Marilyn walked onto the field. She gingerly lifted her skirt and sprinted a few feet in high-heeled pumps before kicking the soccer ball for photographers. Stubbing her toes, Marilyn hopped on one foot as the pain subsided. At the end of the match, she awarded a trophy to Israel's winning team. It was a uniting moment between Israel and the United States. "Sign her up!" announced Soccer Star magazine. "We'd hear no more of falling attendance figures..."

On the morning of May 13, the Millers left New York to attend the trial in Washington. The press surrounded the couple as they exited the apartment and got into their convertible Thunderbird. With a facial expression as serious as her severe upswept hairstyle and dark glasses, Marilyn managed a demure wave to photographers as Miller drove away with the top down. In Washington, they stayed with Joe and Olie Rauh on Appleton Street. Marilyn stayed away from the courthouse to avoid publicity and spent time with Olie in the townhouse. She studied transcripts of the proceedings delivered to the house each evening. Afraid to show any sign of weakness or emotion to his wife, Miller simply shut down. Marilyn tried to support him during the six-day trial, but met with what she perceived as rejection.

Under oath in Judge Charles F. McLaughlin's court, Miller admitted to attending five or six meetings of Communist writers in 1947 but refused to identify others attending the meetings. "I could not use the name of another person and bring trouble on him," Miller asserted. Rauh argued that the identity of those attending the Communist writers' meeting was irrelevant to the issue of passport abuse.

On May 23, Marilyn faced the press in a brown and white horizontal striped dress emphasizing the weight she had gained during the past six months. Needing a manicure and presuming one of the female reporters would notice and comment in the paper, Marilyn donned short white gloves. "A wife's place is with her husband," she softly told the press, appearing more aloof than customary. When asked how she was spending her time, Marilyn replied: "Mostly reading all of the time. Just odds and ends from Mr. Rauh's library. And I've been pouring over the court records, learning a little about law." With resolve in her voice, she announced, "I would like to say that I am fully confident that in the end my husband will win this case." When asked if the trial affected her career, she responded, "No, I haven't been working recently." Asked about her future plans, Marilyn stated, "We hope to go back to our normal life."

When the Miller's returned to their "normal life" in Manhattan, the court found Arthur guilty on two counts contempt of Congress for failing to answer two questions during the hearing. Miller's attorneys swiftly appealed. In a subsequent Supreme Court decision in *Watkins v. the United States*, Chief Justice Earl Warren supported Watkins' views, asserting that the power of the United States Congress is not unlimited in conducting investigations, and that there was no authority given to expose individuals' private affairs. In response to this decision, Judge MacLaughlin modified his verdict by reducing Miller's charges to one count, fining him $500, and suspending a one-month jail sentence.

Miller's legal battle waged as Marilyn faced her own monsters. In May, *Confidential* magazine released an article titled "The Ordinary Joe Sure Made Time on that Couch with Marilyn Monroe!" quoting Robert Slatzer on his claim of a torrid affair during Marilyn's courtship with DiMaggio. The magazine pioneered a combination of Hollywood tabloid and right-wing politics. *Time* magazine described its journalistic approach in 1955: "By sprinkling grains of fact into a cheesecake of innuendo, detraction and plain smut, *Confidential* creates the illusion of reporting the 'lowdown' on celebrities. Its standard method: dig up one sensational 'fact' and embroider it for 1,500 to 2,000 words. If the subject thinks of suing, he may quickly realize that the fact is true, even if the embroidery is not."

Celebrities such as pianist Liberace, heiress Doris Duke, and actress Dorothy Dandridge successfully sued *Confidential* for libel in the 1950s, amounting to twelve million dollars in damages at one point. In her 2004 autobiography, actress Maureen O'Hara recounted her litigation against the magazine for falsely accusing her of having sex in the balcony of Hollywood's Grauman's Chinese Theatre in a March 1957 issue. During the trial, her passport proved that she was in Spain on the date alleged by *Confidential.* Liberace and O'Hara's large settlements instigated the magazine's eventual demise. Slatzer laid low until after Marilyn's death, and when he could no longer be sued for slander, published a scurrilous tale of a marriage to her. He banked on the public forgetting the allegations sold to *Confidential.* Marilyn's reaction to the original article is undocumented, but she assumingly could not have been pleased.

The readers of *Confidential* had no idea what realities actually filled Marilyn's time in Manhattan and might have been surprised by the observations of a middleclass housewife who had befriended her around the time the article had been published. Dalia Leeds, a young Israeli woman living in New York, frequently took her newborn son to the riverside Sutton Place Park at end of East Fifty-Seventh Street, a short walk from the Millers' apartment.

During one visit in the spring, Leeds sat on a bench beside a woman wearing sunglasses, hair curlers under a handkerchief, and a fur coat. The woman introduced herself as Mrs. Miller asked if she could hold the baby. Leeds remembered her as timid and gentle. Mrs. Miller's voice revealed her true identity to Leeds and the other mothers, but they respected her privacy by never acknowledging her as Marilyn Monroe. Over time, the two women frequently met at the park and engaged in many pleasant conversations about children, living in the city, and mutual feelings of loneliness. Leeds told Gloria Steinem:

> *She talked mostly about children. She was very curious about being pregnant, about what you fed a child, how you diapered it—everything...She never confided in me about what difficulties she was having, but she very much wanted to have a child...She would play with the kids, hold them in her lap, and they adored having her. I think the park became a cozy place for her.*

In late June, Marilyn told Leeds, "I want you to know that you won't be seeing me." She explained plans to go away for the summer with her husband and hope to return the following year. Leeds decided never again to trust gossip magazines since Marilyn was really an "ordinary woman who was shy, curious, and lonely."

A child of her own, Miller wrote, "was a crown with a thousand diamonds" in Marilyn's eyes. Finally, that coveted jewel seemed to be within Marilyn's reach. In response to the fertility treatments at Doctor's Hospital, she had conceived sometime in the late spring or early summer. The physician warned of a high-risk pregnancy, but Marilyn was hopeful and "deaf to his cautionary tone." Miller observed in his wife "a new kind of confidence, a quietness of spirit I had never seen in her." Susan Strasberg remembered Marilyn as "thrilled, euphoric" about the pregnancy. "I really hope my baby is as happy and excited about having me as a mother as I am about having him as my child," she said while patting her expanding belly. When Marilyn later viewed photographs taken during the pregnancy she would refer to this time as the happiest of her life.

On June 12, Sam Shaw followed the Millers through New York for a photo essay published in the October 1 issue of *Look* magazine. Marilyn wore a white cotton sleeveless dress with eyelet trim around the neckline and shoulder straps and short white gloves; Miller wore a light sports coat over darks slacks, a shirt and tie.

Shaw photographed the couple strolling hand in hand along East River Drive against the background of the Queensborough Bridge, eating hot dogs purchased from a street vendor at Battery Park, driving through the financial district in Marilyn's Ford Thunderbird, rowing a canoe in the lake in Central Park, shopping at Tiffany's, selecting neck ties at a men's store, and drawing a crowd by the Pulitzer Fountain in Grand Army Plaza. At the fountain, across from the Plaza Hotel, Marilyn slipped off her backless mules and bathed her feet in the water.

As Shaw walked with the Millers through Central Park, Marilyn discussed the Method Acting technique of sense memory and its use in theatrical improvisation. Shaw challenged Marilyn to demonstrate an improvisation on the spot. Immediately, she picked up a copy of the *New York Times* and walked toward a bench where a young couple sat engaged in conversation, the man's arm around the woman's shoulder. Sitting beside them, Marilyn acted "oblivious" to their intimate moment. She unfolded the paper and improvised the "small personal world" of a reader in the park who read the columns from top to bottom and turned the pages with gusto. In reality, the man seated beside Marilyn was asking his girlfriend to marry him. Unknowingly, Marilyn upstaged the proposal. Shaw captured the performance on film with his camera.

The following day, early in the afternoon, Marilyn posed for more photographs with various young beneficiaries of the Milk Fund for Babies who took turns sitting on her lap. She and the children sipped milk through long straws from a large glass goblet. When questioned about rumors of being pregnant, Marilyn would only respond, "No comment." The premiere for *The Prince and the*

Showgirl, scheduled that evening at Radio City Music Hall, was a benefit for the organization founded in part by Millicent Hearst, who had acquired all the first mezzanine seats.

Chapter Three: Amagansett, Summer 1957

Marilyn rested from the toll of her personal and professional life while waiting for a good script to come along. For once, Susan Strasberg would say, Marilyn's life—and not her career—became her priority. Marilyn now approached her personal life with the same intensity as she did her work. She relished in the anonymity of life in New York but at times collided with the press and sought refuge with her husband and non-celebrity friends in rural Long Island.

Paparazzi camped outside the Fifty-Seventh Street Apartment, snooped through the Millers' garbage, and ambushed a disheveled Marilyn while she was wearing Miller's ankle-high shoes during a late-night walk with Hugo, the Basset Hound. Covering her face with her hand, Marilyn ran down the sidewalk to evade them, the dog trotting behind her on a leash.

On weekends during the spring, the Millers packed up the black Thunderbird, put down its convertible top, and drove to Amagansett, a sleepy hamlet of rustic cedar shake and clapboard houses on the south fork of Long Island in the Hamptons. Upon arrival, a wind-tousled Marilyn told the local press she and her husband needed a place to escape. Along with Hugo, the newlyweds rented a weather-worn, shingled cottage on Stony Hill Farm, a 100-acre beachfront estate on Hamlin Lane nestled between riding stables and potato fields, owned by theatre stage manager Jeffrey Potter, and his wife, Penny.

The Potters and their six year old son, Job, lived in the main house, later owned by another famous Hollywood couple, Alec Baldwin and Kim Basinger. The Millers stayed in the Hill House, once the caretaker's cottage and one of the smaller structures on the property, facing green fields but just a short walk to the ocean. "I was gaga," Job Potter would tell the *New York Times* of his memories of Marilyn. He remembered a helicopter landing on the property's front field for Marilyn, likely for her appearance for the groundbreaking ceremony of the Time Life Building in New York City, and described her as "lovely, feminine and sweet." Finding any excuse to visit Marilyn, Job once knocked on the cottage door and sold her boxes of his sister's left over Girl Scout cookies in an attempt to spend time with her.

By summer, the Millers extended their respite beyond weekends. Amagansett provided the couple with a retreat from the limelight where they enjoyed marital intimacy and socialized with friends who also owned or rented nearby summer properties. The Rostens' cottage was located minutes north in Springs, close to the home of married artists Jackson Pollock (1912-1956) and Lee Krasner (1908-1984). The recently deceased Pollock, arguably the leader of the Abstract Expressionistic movement, created his masterpieces out back in the barn during his "drip technique period." The eccentric artist poured, dripped, and flung liquid paint onto long canvases on the floor as he physically moved about in dancelike movements.

One of the Millers' neighbors was another artist, Willem de Kooning (1904-1997), who lived in Red House in Bridgehampton where he painted his "Woman" series of abstract impressionistic portraits of females. De Kooning's painting of Marilyn, reduced to blonde tresses, red lips, a beauty mark and big breasts, which is displayed at New York's Museum of Modern Art, offended Miller. Other neighbors included Sardinian sculptor Constantino Nivola and his family, whose home became a gathering place for de Kooning and Pollock; twice-widowed Mary Bass, editor of *Ladies' Home Journal*, and her young son, with whom the Millers spent many afternoons on Bass' patio; and Broadway producer Kermit Bloomgarden and his wife.

Bloomgarden's press agent, Merle Debuskey, and Christine, his fiancée, lived in nearby Montauk. Debuskey handled the publicity for more than three hundred Broadway productions, more than any other press agent in Broadway history, and later became Lincoln Center Theater's first press representative. He found Marilyn completely devoted to her "Arturo," whom she sometimes called "Papa."

Debuskey and his fiancée confided to the Millers their concerns about finding a rabbi to marry them as Merle was Jewish and Christine was gentile. "I can arrange for Chris to be converted and it isn't going to make her feel terrible," Marilyn told the couple, eager to bring them closer to matrimony. "In fact it was one of the most rewarding experiences of my life, I'm so happy I did. I know a marvelous rabbi who has a congregation in Connecticut—a brilliant man. He marched in Selma, he's very anti HUAC. He's open minded and scholarly about Jewish history. He understands what makes sense in religion and what doesn't."

Perhaps Marilyn's desire to bring a couple closer to matrimony stemmed from enjoying her own marriage and pregnancy. She seemed to have forgiven Miller for his journal entry in London. Photographer Sam Shaw captured images of Marilyn and Miller, seemingly smitten and in love, in spontaneous and unguarded moments; talking on the phone and playing at the beach. In a blue polka-dot sundress, Marilyn picked daisies and wild flowers and played with Hugo. She danced among the tall oak trees in her full-skirted, white lace dress and rested on the ground with Miller under the shade of branches.

Even Miller seemed to loosen up. "I don't think I ever saw two people so dizzy with love for each other," Jim Proctor told Maurice Zolotow. Having known the playwright for many years, Proctor considered Marilyn a miracle-worker for making his introspective friend so outgoing.

Marilyn embraced the role of housewife and relished cooking for her husband and friends. Her specialty was Yiddish dishes such as borscht, chicken soup, matzo balls, and gefilte fish, which she learned from mother-in-law Augusta. She and Miller frequently feasted on thick steaks, homemade angel food cake, pound cake, and ice cream. After Marilyn's death, hand-written recipes for beef bourguignon (Mary Bass') and rum cake would be found between the pages of her well-worn copy of the 1953 edition of *The Joy of Cooking*. The notations she penned in the margins of her 1951 edition of *The New Fannie Farmer Boston Cooking-School Cook Book*, auctioned at her estate sale, serve as further clues to her skills in the kitchen.

"[Marilyn] made all the meals, and she's a hell of a cook," Miller's friend Jim Proctor told Maurice Zolotow. She baked bread and made her own noodles for noodle soup. One evening, Proctor watched her roll the dough, cut it into strips, and dry the noodles with a portable hair dryer. That night, she served a delicious meal of bluefish soufflé with fresh caught fish, noodle soup, and a chocolate meringue pie. After, Marilyn invited her dinner guests to dance. With a few drinks, Miller would attempt a loping fox trot, "perilously off-balance," according to Norman Rosten.

After her death, Marilyn's recipe for a stuffing for chicken or turkey scrawled on stationery from City Title Insurance Company was the subject of a *New York Times* article verifying that not only did she cook, but cooked "confidently and with flair." The recipe, likely dating back to the DiMaggio marriage, outlined a laborious, two-hour process of soaking and shredding a loaf of sourdough bread, peeling hard-boiled eggs, simmering liver, and browning meat. Marilyn specified eleven ingredients including five herbs and spices, three kinds of nuts, and three animal proteins.

The *Times* cited both Marilyn's culinary flexibility and absence of measurement as the hallmark of an experienced and fluent cook (she provides only the instruction of "1 handful" of grated Parmesan). The chefs in the food section of the *Times* attempted the challenge of restoring Marilyn's half-century-old stuffing recipe for Thanksgiving 2010 and noted it yielded twenty cups, implying Marilyn served it for a large dinner party or a holiday meal. "We were amazed to discover one of the most handsome stuffings we've encountered," wrote Matt and Ted Lee. The odd combination of ingredients, such as raisins and chopped egg, created pleasant color contrasts and delicious flavor.

Food historian Anne Mendelson speculated that the stuffing originated in San Francisco based upon the Sutter Street address on the letterhead and the use of sourdough bread, a staple in the Bay area. The Boudin Bakery, the city's oldest continuously running company, specialized in sourdough bread. Mendelson identified the profusion of raisins, pine nuts, and grated Parmesan as Italian in derivation and most likely influenced by the women in the DiMaggio family.

When not toiling in the kitchen, Marilyn spent her time horseback riding, painting watercolors, and going to the beach. Sometimes she served as Miller's personal barber by trimming his hair with scissors while he sat outside in the sunshine. Although insomnia kept her awake throughout the night and into the morning, she usually pulled herself together by the afternoon and took daily bike rides north up Abraham's Path to Springs to visit Norman and Hedda Rosten and their daughter, Patricia.

In a babushka, striped pedal pushers and a white blouse, Marilyn enjoyed playing badminton with Patricia and taking long walks with Hedda. Sometimes Sam and Anne Shaw joined them with their three children, Meta, Edie, and Larry. The Rosten and Shaw families' photo albums soon filled with candid snap shots of their mutual movie star friend. In one photo, Marilyn and Hedda created a human chain by holding hands with Patricia and the Shaw's children as they all walked along the shore. "Marilyn had enough of the child within her to be acutely conscious of the needs of children," Norman Rosten wrote. She instinctively sensed when they were joyful or sad and was especially generous toward Patricia.

In their new Jeep, Marilyn and Arthur drove to the beaches at Louise Point and Barnes Landing. In grey swimming trunks and a beige cap, Miller fly casted in the surf while Marilyn, in a one-piece white bathing suit, hugged him around the waist from behind. Tall, lean and lanky, Miller was physically different from the athletic and muscular DiMaggio. Marilyn frolicked and splashed in the foamy white water and walked hand in hand with Miller along the beach.

In 2008, Author Julia Nasser interviewed the few surviving locals who crossed paths with Marilyn during the summers of 1957 and 1958. A former lifeguard recalled digging her jeep out of the beach, and the owner of White's Pharmacy remembered her frequent trips to the make-up counter where she sat in a chair and applied products like a little girl playing dress-up. Another woman told Nasser of her knocking on the Millers' front door at the age of twelve to encounter a friendly Marilyn in dark sunglasses and a bathrobe. She came outside and chatted gregariously with the preteen until Miller sternly ordered her inside. "Okay, Papa," Marilyn replied like a scolded child.

Bobby and Jane visited on some weekends and during school vacations. Marilyn enjoyed documenting their youth with her camera.

She took photographs of Bobby playing with Hugo, the children on the beach with their father, and the children horseback riding. The Millers permitted Norman Rosten to use their apartment when he had business in the city, and Marilyn left him humorous notes and poems on the refrigerator to welcome him along with loving messages to his wife and daughter.

Author Norman Mailer expressed an interest in meeting Marilyn and asked Rosten to arrange an introduction on Long Island. At first she made excuses. "Come on," Rosten urged. "He's the nicest ogre you'll ever meet." Marilyn eventually extended an invitation, but by the time she consented, Mailer had dropped contact with Rosten.

In 1972, Mailer would write a biography of Marilyn that would be criticized for blending facts with fiction. In his autobiography, Miller remembered her rejecting the idea of inviting Mailer, saying she 'knew those types' and wanted to start a new life among "civilians" who were not "obsessed" with the images of themselves or others. Miller would someday read Mailer's volume about Marilyn and note its "grinning vengefulness toward both of us—skillfully hidden under a magisterial aplomb." Miller believed Mailer would not have written with such negativity had Marilyn hosted Mailer for dinner and permitted him to "confront her humanity, not merely her publicity."

Before Marilyn's pregnancy, Miller had been driving her back into the city to Doctor's Hospital for fertility treatments, but some of these inpatient admissions were possibly for the treatment of depression. Marilyn told the Strasbergs that her moods fluctuated from the extremes of euphoria and anguish, indicating alternations of possible recurrent major depressive episodes and episodes of mania. Miller witnessed in his wife the disturbing symptoms of Bipolar Disorder, the mental illness that affected her maternal grandmother.

It would be another fifty years before a filial link was proven, but Marilyn had feared the correlation since she was a young woman. In a 2009 study tracking Bipolar Disorder and Schizophrenia within families, the Karolinska Institute in Sweden offered the first evidence of the disorders sharing a common genetic cause. Parents, their children and siblings with either diagnosis would be found at increased odds for both disorders. Marilyn's mother's diagnosis of Schizophrenia only further illustrated this intergenerational genetic connection in the Monroe family.

Other friends also observed signs of a serious mood disorder. During a dinner party with music and dancing hosted by the Rostens at their rental property, Norman Rosten found Marilyn on the front porch in tears and asked what was wrong. "I can't tell you," Marilyn sobbed. "I feel terrible, maybe it's the weather." Norman encouraged her to return to the group, uneasy leaving her alone crying. "Make believe I was just out here powdering my nose or something, okay?" she asked him. "Arthur will only get upset."

Further supporting Marilyn's fluctuating moods, Susan Strasberg would recall her frequently paraphrasing a quotation by Goethe from *The Diary of Anne Frank* with which she had identified: "*I'm either in the heights of elation or the depths of despair.*" Hyman Engelberg, Marilyn's internist in Los Angeles, would confirm after her death that she likely suffered from an undiagnosed Bipolar Disorder.

In a lighter moment, the Millers celebrated their first anniversary in July with Miller sending Marilyn three dozen Lady Beautiful red roses from Goldfarb Flowers and Gifts. A pregnant Marilyn retired early that evening in preparation for a public event the following day, July 2, 1957. Nonetheless, she arrived two hours late, wearing a full-skirted, white lace sundress with fitted bodice at the groundbreaking ceremony at the Rockefeller Center Sidewalk Superintendents Club. Fifteen hundred mirthful spectators, forty photographers, twenty law enforcement officers, and Laurence S. Rockefeller (1910-2004) waited patiently for her arrival. Rockefeller was photographed looking at his wristwatch when Marilyn finally appeared, apologetic and complaining of stomach discomfort resulting from the celebration of her one year wedding anniversary the previous night. "We celebrated with champagne," she told reporters, "but instead of it going to my head, it went to my stomach." This white lie concealed the symptom of morning sickness.

At the groundbreaking ceremony, Marilyn ignited a firecracker detonating dynamite in an excavation pit at the site of the planned forty-eight-story Time-Life Building on Sixth Avenue (completed in 1959 as the tallest slab-formed skyscraper in the city and the first building in the Rockefeller Center Extension). Startled by a spray of sparks from the firecracker, she raised her hand to protect her face. After the official groundbreaking, Marilyn was given a tour of the *New York Times* headquarters on West Forty-Third Street. Typesetting machine operator, Carl Schlesinger, later a published author on the history of printing, demonstrated Linotype technology for Marilyn and gave her a bar of type cast with her name on the surface. "Marilyn seemed interested," Schlesinger said. "At the end of my demonstration she thanked me and leaned over me...and kissed the top of my balding head." A group of co-workers broke into applause. Marilyn followed up with a letter thanking Schlesinger for his kindness.

At the end of the day, a helicopter returned Marilyn to the cottage in Amagansett. From the window of his studio where Miller was working at his typewriter, he watched Marilyn exit the helicopter, her hair and sundress tousled by the draft of the blades, and walk across the lawn, still carrying a bouquet of flowers. Miller recalled this moment with a combination of awe and resentment in *Timebends*: "What a frightening power she had! The event seemed like the intrusion of a gross iron hand into the vulnerable flesh of our existence and yet at the same time signified her triumph, proof of the immense public importance she had won." To Miller, there was no other woman in the world the media giant would have flown to New York and back for only a few publicity photos.

During the summer, Marilyn became a founding member of SANE, created by Norman Cousins of *The Saturday Review*, Coretta Scott King (wife of civil rights leader Dr. Martin Luther King, Jr.), Dr. Albert Schweitzer, Dr. Benjamin Spock, and others in an effort to educate the public on the danger of the nuclear arms race and the Eisenhower administration's testing of nuclear weapons in the western states. Eric Fromm's book *The Sane Society* inspired the organization's name. SANE's full-page ad, published in the November 15 issue of *The New York Times*, incited a nationwide response. When its member grew to over 25,000, SANE formally incorporated in July 1958.

On the morning of August 1, Marilyn was gardening in Amagansett when she collapsed to the ground in excruciating agony and screamed for Miller's assistance. She lost consciousness, and Miller called for an ambulance. With her husband at her side, Marilyn endured incessant pain and emotional distress when she woke up during the one hundred mile drive to the city. At Doctor's Hospital, Miller explained Marilyn had recently been digging for clams and swimming, but had not suffered a fall or any other trauma that could have triggered a miscarriage. Dr. Bernard Berglass and Dr. Hilliard Dubrow evaluated Marilyn and diagnosed an ectopic pregnancy. The fetus had developed in the fallopian tube rather than the uterus, and an emergency termination of the pregnancy was necessary to save Marilyn's life. Dr. Dubrow performed the surgery in the late evening, and his patient required a blood transfusion. The fetus was male.

The next day, Miller faced the press. "Marilyn wants as many [children] as she can get," he said, "I feel the same way." Depressed and grieving, Marilyn lay in the hospital bed for ten days. When Kermit Bloomgarden and his wife, actress Virginia Kaye, visited, Kaye sensed Marilyn felt ashamed of losing the child. James Haspiel visited Marilyn in the hospital, and remembered entering a darkened room overlooking the East River and illuminated only by a small light from a radio playing classical music at low volume. A sheet was pulled to her chest, and Miller was seated in a chair beside the bed, holding her hand. A few days later, the young fan received a note mailed to him in a secretary's handwriting and not Marilyn's. It read: "*Thank you for the lovely card. It is so nice to know that there are so many people, whom I have never met, who think of me. Warm regards, Marilyn Monroe Miller.*"

Sam Shaw also visited Marilyn and Miller at the hospital. Afterward, Shaw and Miller strolled outside the hospital and sat in a nearby park. The photographer shared plans to adapt *Paris Blues* into a screenplay. The conversation turned to Miller's short story, "The Misfits" (subtitled: "Chicken Feed: The Last Frontier of the Quixotic Cowboy"), and Shaw encouraged him to adapt the material into a screenplay with a part for Marilyn. It could be a great film, Shaw advised, and Marilyn could do justice to the role of Roslyn.

While recuperating at the hospital on August 9, Marilyn typed an eleven-paragraph letter to Bobby Miller at summer camp. The letter was reproduced in entirely in Lois Banner's *MM—Personal from the Private Archive of Marilyn Monroe*:

I am glad you are enjoying camp so much...Hugo has been up to all kinds of mischief. He loves people so much that he goes visiting...One day he brought home a woman's shoe and the other day he came in with a child's toy—a little stuffed dog. We are thinking of calling him Klepto...

Marilyn playfully asks Bobby to conspire with her to plan a surprise birthday party for his sister and solicits his suggestions for gifts. She also acknowledges the usefulness of his gift of a barometer. In conclusion, Marilyn tells the boy that she and his father miss him and promises to send anything he might need while at summer camp.

On August 10, Marilyn was released from the hospital. She emerged from the facility in the white, full-skirted, sleeveless lace dress previously worn to the Time-Life Building's groundbreaking event. She held on fiercely to her husband's hand. Marilyn's hair was casually styled, and she wore make-up. "I'm feeling wonderful," Marilyn told the press in a performance worthy of an Oscar nomination. "I definitely still plan to have a large family. I'm going to rest, rest and more rest."

Photographers clamored at the ambulance windows as hospital attendants strapped her onto a stretcher for a three-hour drive back to Amagansett. "A baby makes a marriage, it makes a marriage perfect," Marilyn said. "But doctors have assured me that I can have children. Oh, I'm looking forward to having a family of my own." Once the ambulance entered onto the highway, Marilyn's demeanor changed. "There were no words anymore that could change anything for her," Miller later wrote of the seemingly endless drive home to Connecticut in silence. "She lay there sad beyond sadness, watching the traffic pass the cautiously driven ambulance."

The loss of the baby plunged Marilyn into a serious depressive episode. She felt like a failure as a woman, a disappointment as a wife, and an ineffective muse for her husband. Landlord and friend Jeffrey Potter observed the revival of Miller's urgency to protect her when he took the couple to Devon Yacht Club in late August. "There was a great sadness...and Arthur hung on her every word. He would have physically merged with her and taken her sadness on if he could."

Back in Amagansett, Marilyn grieved the loss of her child and seemed hypersensitive to the natural process of the life cycle. She wept at the sight of wounded seagulls on the shore, stopped her car to rescue stray dogs on the side of the road, and denounced killing as a sport when the beginning of deer-hunting season entered conversation. "Whatever the reasons, her inability to have a child was to loom as a crucial disappointment in her life," Norman Rosten wrote. "The love goddess, the woman supreme, unable to create a baby; it was a dagger at her ego. There was something wrong with her, inside her, a defect, an evil. Nor would pills erase this sense of failure."

The miscarriage only intensified Marilyn's feelings of sanctity for all living things. While strolling with Miller along the beaches of Long Island, Marilyn observed fishermen tossing runt fish out of their nets onto the sand and was horrified by the site of fish flopping out of the water. Miller found inspiration for a short story as he watched her tireless efforts to save the fish stranded onshore by gathering them up with her hands and throwing them back into the sea.

Titled "Please Don't Kill Anything" and first published in 1960, the piece explores a man's feelings about the sensitive woman he loves as he watches her rescue fish. It is one of the few pieces completed during their marriage and acknowledges, in Miller's words, "her fierce tenderness" toward living things. Here Miller reverently writes a testament of how deeply he loved Marilyn despite her eccentricities and seems to sense her desperation or a pending emotional collapse.

As Miller celebrated beauty in Marilyn's acute empathy for living things, he witnessed the lack of empathy she had for herself. One day, Miller discovered her collapsed in a chair and breathing irregularly. Marilyn had overdosed on barbiturates prescribed for sleep, and the drugs labored her respiration. He summoned medical help, and Marilyn's stomach was pumped. Susan Strasberg observed the cycle of Marilyn's pain evolving into depression and then hopelessness. Losing the baby made her want to escape by numbing herself. Afterward, Marilyn expressed affection toward her husband in gratitude for saving her life, showing her appreciation by reaching for his hand and kissing it repeatedly.

Miller cites Marilyn's overdose in *Timebends* but does not indicate if her intention was suicide. In *Marilyn: The Untold Story*, Norman Rosten documents a suicide attempt without a specific date, but the period seems sometime between 1957 and 1958. Also unclear is whether it was the one referenced by Miller or yet another. In Mailer's version, Miller summoned a private doctor who pumped Marilyn's stomach, and the maid called the Rostens in the early morning hours to alert them. When Norman and Hedda rushed over and entered Marilyn's bedroom, she was quietly sobbing. He gently asked how she was feeling.

"Alive," she said. "Bad luck. Cruel, all of them, all those bastards." Rosten wondered to whom his groggy friend was referring.

Shortly thereafter, Marilyn's alcohol consumption increased while her tolerance stopped at one or two drinks. She usually drank champagne and avoided liquor because it upset her stomach. On one occasion, Marilyn rode a horse across the property of a local farmer while intoxicated and fell off the horse. The farmer and his field hands carried her back to the cottage uninjured.

Marilyn also relied upon prescribed tranquilizers for her chronic insomnia and mood disturbances. Initially, this did not alarm Miller or others in her life. At this time in history, doctors wrote over forty million prescriptions for tranquilizers. Meprobamate, marketed under the brand name Miltown, promised to decrease housewives' anxiety but instead led to the first documented drug abuse phenomena in the American middle class. Its advertising promised a "happier pregnancy," and on the streets it was coined a "dehydrated Martini." The drug was later discovered to cause serious birth defects.

Marilyn's use of alcohol and drugs may not have yet roused the concern of Miller and others in her circle due to the era's norm of social drinking and use of prescribed tranquilizers, but she had begun a downward spiral of regular drug use. This early stage in the development of dependence or addiction is deceptive as the user is able to stop independently and feels in control of the drug. How closely Marilyn's prescribing physicians monitored her during this period is unknown.

Unable to respond to his wife's anguish and perceiving her as consuming him, Miller disappeared into his writing to support his wife in the only way he knew how, to adapt his short story, "The Misfits", into a script for her. Marilyn, needing her husband's emotional presence during those dark days, felt as though he was withdrawing from her, spending hours in isolation, hammering out the script on his typewriter as the intensity of her paranoia and grief escalated.

Since their marriage, Miller began at least two plays, neither materializing into anything worthy of further development and so they were tossed into the fireplace. This creative drought ended with his motivation to create something for Marilyn, so he produced a rough script with an idealized portrait of her; a homemade valentine. Marilyn's initial reaction was cautious. Despite laughing "delightedly" at some of the cowboys' lines, she felt shock over his quotations of her actual thoughts.

For some time, Marilyn did not fully commit to the part. To her, love meant Miller had to accept both her light and dark sides. His idealized portrait of her in the character of Roslyn struck her as rejection of a part of her; he could not fully love her if he loved only a part of her. Marilyn also possessed an uncanny knowledge of film scripts and an ability to assess a script's ability to translate into film. She pegged the screenplay as static, too "talky," and flawed in its plot and thin characterizations. Above all, Marilyn disliked Roslyn's passivity.

Marilyn put aside Miller's attempts at a script and turned to her own writing. On August 22, while recuperating, Marilyn typed loving letters in the voice of Hugo to Miller's children away at summer camp. It is easy to see what made Bobby Miller fall in love with Marilyn through the care she takes in appealing to the child's imagination, referencing his experiences, and capturing the longing tone of his loyal canine companion [the letter is published in its entirely in *MM—Personal from the Private Archive of Marilyn Monroe*]:

> *Bob, I was wondering if you could make me some kind of toy while you are up in Camp. I realize it might be impossible but in case you could make something for me to play with, so I wouldn't chew on your baseballs, etc., at least I might not feel so lonely while you are away, especially with something from you. But if you can't, I'll understand…*

"Hugo" closes the letter with love and "slurpy kisses" from Bobby's friend and "ankle-chewer" and adds a postscript sending love from Miller and Marilyn.

Marilyn's ability to apply Method Acting to thrusting herself in the role of a canine is evident in her lengthy and affectionate letter to Jane Miller:

> *Janie, I really am trying to be a good dog—one that you would be proud of—but I make mistakes sometimes, but other times I don't... What makes me the saddest is that I can't see you and Bobby and what would make me the gladdest is if I could see you both... P.P.S. Daddy and Marilyn send their love...*

Around Labor Day, the Millers hosted a thirteenth birthday party for Jane in Amagansett, remembered by Elizabeth Kaye in an article for *Premiere* magazine in August 1988. (Elizabeth's divorced mother was marrying a man who wrote songs for Broadway shows and was a friend to Kermit and Virginia Bloomgarden.) Elizabeth, age twelve at the time, came along with her two younger sisters. She asked her mother if she could bring an autograph book, but her mother told her to leave it at home as asking Marilyn for an autograph would be rude. When the children arrived, Elizabeth felt disappointed that Marilyn was not yet present and observed Jane as "outshone even by her stepmother's absence." Marilyn suddenly appeared in no makeup with a thin coating of Vaseline on her face. "I had never seen anyone as beautiful," Elizabeth wrote. "I still haven't."

Marilyn sat on the floor and asked Elizabeth the typical questions of grown-ups. Most noteworthy, she called each of the children by name. When the adults arrived, Marilyn sat on Miller's lap. Later, she went over to Elizabeth and invited her to see the animals on her farm.

Taking Elizabeth by the hand, Marilyn led her to see Hugo, some cats, and a pen of sheep. Together, they picked dandelions and Marilyn taught the girl how to weave a dandelion chain. Finally, Marilyn took three Polaroid photographs of the girl beside the sheep pen. When they went back to the house, Elizabeth watched Marilyn place the photos in a scrapbook.

As she was leaving the party, Elizabeth saw on a table in the entrance hall a glamorous photo of Marilyn, which in no way resembled the woman with whom she had just spent time. "Magic is best served by ignorance," Elizabeth wrote as a forty-two year old woman, "since what we believe things to be is often more wonderful than what they actually are. That is something she too must have known."

Among Marilyn's possessions discovered after her death was an envelope filled with photographs of the party Elizabeth Kaye described. Janie sits on the lawn surrounded by her brother and friends, including Kaye and Patricia Rosten, and opens birthday presents. Marilyn, operating the camera, appears only in two shots with Janie. Smiling broadly, she gazes adoringly at her step-daughter.

As summer ended, Bobby and Jane returned to their mother's home in Brooklyn to prepare for the start of school. Ever passionate about civil rights, Marilyn's attention joined with the nation's on a racial incident brewing in the South's school system. Arkansas governor Orval Faubus called the National Guard to prevent nine African-American students from entering the recently desegregated Central High School on September 4. President Eisenhower federalized the Guard and directed the 101st airborne division to protect the students, known as the Little Rock Nine, from a hostile mob of white racist students.

Television cameras looked into the ugly faces of intergenerational prejudice and hate as the mob spat on the students, tore at their clothing, and called for a lynching. Marilyn's library included a first edition of Ralph Ellison's 1952 novel *Invisible Man* about the experiences of an African American man. The book's theme, the invisibility of the underdog, resonated with Marilyn, who related to the main character because of the racial stereotype that made him seem not like a real person.

As the leaves in the trees in Amagansett turned orange and red, the Millers returned to East Fifty-Seventh Street. That autumn, Marilyn purchased a hardcover copy of Jack Kerouac's latest work, *On the Road*, a cross-country odyssey written during a three-week creative or drug-induced burst on twelve-foot long rolls of paper. Critics hailed the work as a literary version of a jazz improvisation. Marilyn's library was expanding with other counter-culture work such as Woody Guthrie's *Bound for Glory*, Harold Flender's *Paris Blues*, and Harrison Salisbury's *The Shook-Up Generation.*

Miller noted Marilyn's frustration with the country's lack of social consciousness during the late 1950s and listened to her complaints that films, books, and plays failed to educate the public on matters she considered important. "Marilyn possessed a revolutionary idealism, regardless—or probably because—of her difficulties," he would write. They met during a conservative era in American history, when social consciousness had waned and before it resurged. Marilyn was disillusioned with herself and her country.

The Millers soon found a property in Connecticut to replace the cottage rental in Amagansett. Today, the cottage remains perched high on Stony Hill surrounded by the dignified oaks under which Marilyn, Arthur, and Hugo sought shade and posed for Sam Shaw's camera more than a half century ago. Currently owned by Joe and Lucy Kazickas, the house is three times its original size of 1500 square feet.

Journalist T.J. Clemente toured the former Miller cottage in 2007 and noted its changes over the decades. The Miller bedroom is now a guest room and the original bathtub remains in the adjoining bath. Marilyn's kitchen is now a mudroom and retains its orignal back door. The old icehouse is transformed into a luxurious sauna with showers, seating, and a television. The wood-burning stove is gone, but the wide-planked knotty pine floors look very much the same as when Marilyn and Arthur danced together on them during summer dinner parties. The Kazickas display framed prints of Shaw's portraits of Marilyn seated in a corner of the same room. In one, Marilyn's foot rests beside a large pine knot still visible on the flooring. The old school desk at which Shaw photographed Marilyn talking on the telephone remains in homage to the former lady of the house. In Shaw's timeless portraits, she plays with her hair and, in a graceful motion of her hand, covers her face from his lens.

In his later years, Miller would drive to the cottage he had shared with Marilyn whenever he experienced despair and then would come home saying, "I'm a new man." Shortly before his death in 2005, Miller requested to be chauffeured throughout the small town of Amagansett, where his sister and her son still had a home, and to the Stony Hill farmhouse. Seated in a vehicle outside the farmhouse, the aged author experienced a flood of memories as vivid as Sam Shaw's classic photographs. Quietly, Miller reminisced about the days when he and Marilyn were in love, hopeful about starting a family, and grieving the loss of a child.

Singer Sammy Davis, Jr., who most certainly had a more casual connection to Marilyn, declared, "[she] still hangs like a bat in the heads of the men who met her, and none of us will ever forget her." As the themes of his later writing revealed, Marilyn would eternally serve as Miller's muse.

Chapter Four: Connecticut & Manhattan, Autumn & Winter 1957

"What do you think of Miss Monroe as architecture?" Mike Wallace satirically asked architect Frank Lloyd Wright in a televised interview in 1957. "I think Miss Monroe's architecture is extremely good architecture," Wright responded, "and she's a very natural actress and a very good one." Wallace pressed Wright to confirm rumors about Marilyn's retaining him to design a home. "For Mrs. Miller and Mr. Miller I'll be very happy to design a house," Wright remarked, "but they haven't asked me in so many words yet."

They were perhaps the most prominent, celebrated twentieth century icons of their respective fields; Wright was as a revolutionary and abundantly creative genius of architecture, and Marilyn reigned as the postwar era's fresh, cinematic embodiment of feminine sensuality and childlike innocence. Wright preached the beauty of natural materials and insisted that structures integrate naturally with their surroundings, a concept he called "organic architecture." He liberated Americans from the compartmentalized spaces of nineteenth century Victorian boxes and helped create the open plan with rooms that flowed and opened out to each other.

By changing the spaces in which Americans lived, Wright revolutionized the modern American lifestyle for the twentieth century. "Whether people are fully conscious of this or not," he said, "they actually derive countenance and sustenance from the 'atmosphere' of the things they live in or with. They are rooted in them just as a plant is in the soil in which it is planted." For a brief time in 1957, Marilyn's legendary path crossed with Wright's in New York City. Living with Miller in Midtown Manhattan, Marilyn was recovering from a serious depression triggered by the miscarriage but she mustered enough courage to continue her quest to start a family with Miller. "Since I lost my last baby," Marilyn told Susan Strasberg, "I couldn't bring myself to hope any more, but I do now, all the time."

Throughout the summer, the couple searched for a property in rural Connecticut to replace the home Miller sold. In October, they used mostly Marilyn's funds to purchase an eighteenth-century three-story house once a dairy farm on three hundred-fifty acres in Roxbury, Connecticut, a sparsely populated, rural area with cows, white wooden farms from the 18th Century, stone low walls, red barns, and grain silos. Roxbury, in Litchfield County, had been a farming town with silver and iron mines in the 1800s, and now it offered a landscape of hilltops and pastures.

At 323 Tophet Road, the sagging farmhouse described by Marilyn as "a kind of old saltbox with a kitchen extension" was walking distance from Miller's former home where he lived with his first wife. Built in 1783 and belonging to the Tanner family for over one hundred seventy-five years, the home had high ceilings and thick beams made from ship timbers. Marilyn and Miller modernized the interior and restored the fireplace with stone from a local quarry.

In the attic, Marilyn and Arthur found photographs of the previous families who had once lived in the home along with nineteenth century portraits in gilded frames. In an interview with Radie Harris, Marilyn expressed feelings of comfort in learning about the former residents: "We do long so much for a child, but that will come I'm sure. I look at our house, and I know that it has been home for other families, back through all those years. And it's as if some of their happiness has stayed there even after they went away, and I can feel it around me."

The Miller's new neighbors included Alexander Calder, an artist specializing in mobiles, and his wife; Actors Studio alumnus Eli Wallach and his wife, Anne Jackson; and Marilyn's former co-star, Richard Widmark. The immediate neighbors, the Diebolds, took an immediate liking to Marilyn at a cocktail party and treated her as one of their adult children. The local community would nominate her as an alternate delegate to the 1960 National Democratic Convention.

By mid-autumn, Marilyn visualized the construction of a new

home on the property reflecting her current priorities: children and husband. There would be grand-scale nurseries and a well-appointed study. While Frank Lloyd Wright was staying at the Plaza Hotel during the construction of the radically designed Guggenheim Museum; his concept resembled a white ribbon curled into a cylindrical stack, slightly wider at the top than the bottom. There, Marilyn approached him about designing a home for her anticipated family on three hundred-fifty acres.

Marilyn met with Wright several more times at his office in the Plaza Hotel, sharing with him her vision of open spaces for children at play and a study for Miller's writing. She discovered a kindred spirit in the architect, a fellow Gemini. Together, their creative energies elevated to a near eccentric level and extended well beyond the Monroe-Miller budget. Legal fees escalated for Miller's defense against accusations of Communist Party affiliation, and the playwright doubted the ability to finance the building project.

"Her impulse was royal, in part a kind of gift to me of a unique home," wrote Miller. He refrained from questioning their ability to afford Wright's design in fear of seeming ungrateful. Both Marilyn and the architect ignored costs, so Miller decided to wait for Wright's final proposal and allow Marilyn to judge its practicality.

On a cool autumn morning, Marilyn and Miller collected Wright in the city and drove him out to Connecticut to view the property and surrounding landscape. Nearly age ninety, Wright slept soundly during the two-hour drive. Awaking in Roxbury, he perused the crest of woodland where the home would rise and recommended against patching an old home on the land.

Weeks later, Wright presented the Millers with seven architectural drawings of a proposed residence based upon his 1949 design of a home for Robert Windfohr of Fort Worth, Texas, that was never built. The design's center was a circular living room, sixty-feet in diameter, surrounded by ovoid columns of fieldstone five feet thick and topped by a dramatic domed ceiling. Glass doors opened to a curved veranda surrounding the room and overlooking a seventy-foot swimming pool. Wright's curvaceous design, with circular rooms and few straight lines or right angles, seemed inspired by Marilyn's physical form. In fact, it has been described as resembling Marilyn supine. To some, the ultra-modern center dome suggested a space ship.

A graveled forecourt led to an entrance to the living room. The domed living room featured a circular projection booth, with a motion picture screen recessed into the ceiling when not in use, and a seating booth beside the screen. The living room's design consisted of three concentric, tiered sections, each one slightly lower than the other and declining toward the center. Wright envisioned a large crystal chandelier in the center of the dome's skylight ceiling, and a gold aluminum-covered roof.

Two wings of equal length extended from the central dome structure. The longer wing contained a kitchen, an oval dining room with vaulted ceiling extending to the second story, a breakfast room, separate china and silver storage rooms, and a card room. The dining room, with seating for twenty-four, featured a built-in buffet. A conservatory across from the dining room faced the forecourt. Four pairs of glass doors in the card room opened to a half-circle pavilion, with a large, triangular pool sandwiched between the pavilion and living room. The pool was designed to jet forth from the downhill slope of the hill.

The other wing, at a near 130-degree angle to the first, was also designed to connect to the living room dome. This wing contained male and female restrooms, a library for Miller, a storage room with separate luggage storage, chauffeur quarters, a multi-vehicle carport, a guest room with en suite bath and a private terrace. Off a glass walled gallery, and opposite the library and guest room, a ramp led to the second story. The absence of stairs suggests that the Millers requested safety features for their expected children.

The second level's design contained a circular children's room, a children's dressing room and bath, a loggia, and a curved sitting room with fireplace. Behind the fireplace would be the master bedroom wardrobe connecting to the master bedroom, master bath, and dressing room. Wright labeled the master bedroom as "Mrs. Miller's bedroom." His exclusion of reference to Mr. Miller in the plans illustrated Marilyn's power in the planning process. Off the master bedroom was a sewing room and elaborate nursery with bath and curved fireplace, with a circular costume vault behind. Twenty-one pairs of glass doors, set at close intervals opened to a balcony extending along most of the second level and providing a spectacular view of the woodlands.

Miller recalled Wright's inclusion of a conference room with a long boardroom table flanked by twelve high-backed chairs, the highest being at the head where Miller thought the architect envisioned Marilyn sitting "like a reigning queen of a small country." Although existing drawings in the Frank Lloyd Wright Foundation's archive do not show the conference room, perhaps Miller was referring to the dining room doubling as a meeting room for Marilyn Monroe Productions.

Miller enjoyed Wright's impressionistic watercolor rendering of the home's exterior elevation, depicting a 1920s limousine in the driveway. Wright estimated the cost at $250,000, but Miller judged that would cover merely the cost of the swimming pool, since its supporting walls would be over twenty feet high. Miller stated it was far too elaborate for his and Marilyn's needs. Wright's revival of an earlier design for Windfohr, modified for the Millers, returned to the shelf and remained unrealized for over three decades.

With the Wright design eliminated, the Millers decided to repair the eighteenth century farmhouse, ignoring advice to demolish it. Marilyn told journalist Radie Harris: "All our friends agreed the land was beautiful, but they said the house was just uninhabitable. I looked at it and thought how it had been standing there, weathering everything for more than one hundred and eighty years. And I just hated the idea of its being torn down or even left unoccupied. So Arthur and I ignored everybody's advice and got to work…It's the place where we hope to live until we die."

With $100,000 earned from *Showgirl*, Marilyn and Arthur renovated the house. They installed dormer windows on the top floor and raised the roofline over one wing to create a room above the kitchen, keeping the original ceiling beams intact. They also installed sliding glass doors in the living room opening to the long verandah to enjoy the view to the hill and man-made pond beyond. With renewed hope, Marilyn christened the added wing as the nursery. She decorated the living and dining rooms with modern furnishings and filled the sunroom with photos of Arthur and posters of his plays. Arthur mounted a faulty dispenser of insect repellent on the eaves of the roof. Instead of spraying into the air, it doused the Millers while they lounged on the deck. Miller had better luck with building a cabin a few yards from the house to be used as a retreat for his writing.

During the renovation, workers raised plaster dust that covered nearly everything in the house. Known by her Roxbury friends as a fastidious housekeeper, Marilyn dusted the furniture and vacuumed the rugs and floors every day. She was pleased with the progress on the house but unhappy with the curved asphalt driveway, as she preferred the elegant sound of loose stones under car tires like the homes in southern California. Miller insisted the heavy snows each winter made a gravel driveway impractical.

Marilyn was most dissatisfied with the construction of a low stone wall in front of the property. She felt guilty about masons cutting through the oak trees and damaging them. "It's all my fault for wanting the wall," Marilyn lamented to Norman Rosten while surveying the injury. When the trees didn't bloom the next spring, she told him they were "punishing" her for not appreciating them.

She pressured Miller in purchasing an adjoining property of three hundred fifteen acres which he completed the following year. This purchase increased the property to three hundred forty acres of prime Connecticut real estate deeded in Marilyn's name along with the house. Miller planted pine trees on the land that grew into a forest at the time of his death in 2005. For the next four years, the New York apartment would be known as Marilyn's apartment, and the home in Connecticut would be known as Arthur's farm. "All the time I was married to Arthur Miller," Marilyn said, "four years, our life was set in a definite pattern. Summers in Connecticut, no deviation. Winters in our New York apartment. Then back to Connecticut..."

Plagued by night terrors and insomnia, Marilyn remained awake during most of the night, and often climbed out of bed in the early morning hours to start her day. After sunrise, she tooled around Roxbury's single lane roads in a motor scooter. On typical days, she rode to Mr. Birchall's farm in the mornings to watch him milk cows, returned home to finally sleep until early afternoon, and then went to the center of Roxbury to shop at Hodge's general store on Route 67.

In nearby Belle Haven, Old Greenwich, Miller's friend Frank Taylor and his wife, Nan, maintained a summer house. Taylor met Miller when Mary Grace Slattery, Miller's first wife, was his secretary in the New York publishing house, Reynal and Hitchcock. In 1945, Taylor published Arthur's first novel, *Focus*, and remained a close friend of his for many years. In 1948, Taylor temporarily left publishing to produce movies at MGM with Dore Schary. He returned to the edition in 1952 and purchased a town house in Greenwich Village.

The Taylors and their four sons often visited Marilyn and Arthur in Roxbury. Two of the sons, Curtice (called Tucky) and Mike, sometimes stayed at the Millers' home when Arthur's children visited. Marilyn enjoyed a solid relationship with the family who sold her a horse named Ebony. Taylor's son, Mark, gave Marilyn instructions on riding.

Curtice Taylor remembers Marilyn vacuuming upstairs during a family visit when Miller read Frank Taylor his screenplay. "She eventually came down and she was very sweet," Curtice told Michelle Morgan. "She liked children, and she was very drawn to my brother Mark, who had the most problems out of all the children. She immediately recognized that and made an extra effort to reach out to him—she recognized people in trouble and would reach out to them in some way." After Marilyn served lunch, she invited Curtice to sit beside her and swing on the hammock. He lay down on the hammock with her, and his brothers were jealous. Eventually, they all got a turn on the hammock with Marilyn.

Roxbury's rural setting suited Marilyn's love for animals. When a pregnant Siamese cat stumbled into the garden, Marilyn adopted her and bestowed the name Sugar Finney after a character in a folk story. She soon assisted in the delivery of kittens on the kitchen floor. Marilyn also rescued a starving dog and nursed it back to health under the guidance of a local veterinarian. She named the dog Cindy and presented it to Patricia Rosten. On the vast farmland, Miller erected feeding stations for birds in a maple tree. Inside their country house, Marilyn had two caged talking parakeets, Bobo and Butch. She would often travel with them on planes. To the surprise of other passengers, the birds would squawk out in mid-flight, "I'm Marilyn's bird, Marilyn's bird."

While spending a week with the Millers, Mark Taylor stumbled upon their tenant farmer loading a calf into a truck. A cow had just given birth to a male. Knowing Marilyn would be thrilled to see the calf, he ran back to the house and brought her back. "Where are you taking the black calf?" Marilyn asked the tenant farmer. "He might return on your dinner table next week as veal cutlets," the farmer responded, so young Mark had to explain to Marilyn that the male calf was going to the slaughterhouse. "The calf lives here!" Marilyn protested in horror. "You can't take him away from his mother!"

With the boy in tow, Marilyn rushed back to the house and routed through her purse only to find twenty dollars in cash to buy the calf from the farmer. The man refused her money and explained he had to do his job. Mark successfully convinced Marilyn that even if it were enough money, it wouldn't solve the problem. The farmer would raise at least one male calf every six months; would she buy every one? And if she did, what would she do with them? Miller would reference this event in *The Misfits* when the character of Roslyn attempts to buy the freedom of the wild Mustangs from Gay, an aging cowboy.

Mark wasn't the only Taylor boy to witness their sensitive friend's attempt at rescue. Curtice watched Marilyn observing a hawk circling above some swallow chicks nesting on her front porch. She spent hours throwing rocks at the hawk to chase it away from the fledglings. Marilyn explained that she could not relocate the nest in fear of the mother bird abandoning her young if it were disrupted.

James Haspiel, Marilyn's teen fan and friend in Manhattan, also corroborated her determination to protect vulnerable birds. On a walk in the city with young Haspiel, Marilyn observed a group of boys on Fifty-Eighth Street trapping pigeons. She begged them to release the birds from the cages. The boys told her they earned fifty cents per pigeon. She paid the boys to release the captive birds and returned every week to pay the ransom for their freedom.

Curtice continued to experience Marilyn's empathy for all living things, animal and human, when he visited her back in the city. "Marilyn decided she had to go out to get some shopping done, so she took me with her," he later recounted. "She wore a crazy disguise—dark wig and dark glasses, and people were looking because of it. She walked like Marilyn but didn't look like her. There was a homeless man, and Marilyn walked right up to him, not at all afraid. 'Things are not going well at the moment, are they?' she said. 'No, they're not,' he said. She opened her purse and gave him five dollars before walking on."

* * *

After the divorce, Miller retained the farmhouse where he would later live with his third wife, Inge Morath, until her death in 2002. Miller's archival consultant, Andreas Brown, begged him to secure his papers, stored in files cabinets in an old barn on the property, fearing the barn could catch fire. While cataloguing the manuscripts, Brown discovered a small package of brown paper sealed with wax. Miller explained that it contained about one hundred letters from Marilyn. Miller eventually deposited the letters in a bank strong box. Brown's prediction came true when fire gutted the house in Connecticut in 1983 while Miller directed the revival of his play, *Death of a Salesman*, in China. Miller lost most of his books to the fire, but his manuscripts survived in the barn. Upon her death, Inge was buried in a modest grave on the property, and her memorial service took place in the barn, which had been her photography studio.

* * *

Marilyn hadn't worked for a year but *The Prince and the Showgirl* maintained her relevance during 1957. It ranked tenth among the top-grossing films of the year behind *Bridge On the River Kwai, Peyton Place, A Farewell to Arms, Raintree County,* and Elvis Presley's *Jailhouse Rock.*

During her absence from Hollywood, every studio found its own Monroe imitator. Universal Studios had Mamie Van Doren, and Columbia Studios had Kim Novak, born Marilyn Novak, who was forced to change her name since Monroe trumped. The British film industry had Diana Dors and Fox even offered Sheree North and Jayne Mansfield. Other major roles for actresses that year included Joanne Woodward's in *The Three Faces of Eve* and Lana Turner's in the melodramatic soap opera *Peyton Place.*

Fox hadn't assigned Marilyn a film since the new contract was signed in 1955. She was now thirty-one years old, married again, and actively working toward becoming a mother. The studio saw the need to collect on their investment before the public began to perceive her as a wife and mother and no longer a sex symbol. There was also the fear of her aging and no longer being bankable as a leading lady. In Hollywood, roles for women over forty dwindled, and so the studio likely projected less than a decade remaining for Marilyn's reign as a box office draw.

Fox studio executive Lew Schreiber approached Marilyn about a remake of *Blue Angel*, the first major German sound film directed by Josef von Sternberg in 1930. The original brought Marlene Dietrich international fame and introduced her signature song, Friedrich Hollaender's "Falling in Love Again." Schreiber tried to sell Marilyn on Curt Jurgens or Fredric March as co-star and Charles Vidor as director, but Vidor's name did not appear on Marilyn's list of approved directors. Her interest peaked when Spencer Tracy (1900-1967) expressed enthusiasm in playing the male lead. Over the course of thirty years, the gruff Tracy made nine films with Katharine Hepburn, his long-time mistress, and had recently completed *Desk Set*, a film about a computer replacing an entire crew of library information researchers during the Christmas holidays.

The plot of *Blue Angel*, vaguely similar to *Of Human Bondage*, traces Immanuel Rath's transformation from respected professor at a college preparatory high school to an impoverished vagrant. Rath's downfall begins when he reprimands a group of his students for distributing photographs of a beautiful singer, Lola Lola, performing at a local cabaret, The Blue Angel. In an attempt to entrap the students, Professor Rath goes to the club later that evening, but forgets about his original plan when he falls under Lola's seductive spell. Frenzied with desire, Rath returns to the cabaret the following evening and spends a night of passion with her. The next morning, he arrives late to school to find his classroom in chaos and the principal incensed by his irresponsible behavior. Rath resigns from the school and marries Lola, but their happiness diminishes as his savings exhaust.

Rath is forced to work as a clown in Lola's traveling cabaret act and becomes jealous of the audience's lust for his beautiful and desirable wife. When the act returns to Rath's hometown, the patrons of the Blue Angel mock him. As Rath performs for the people he once judged as lustful, he sees Lola kiss one of her former lovers and erupts into a violent rage. He attempts to strangle Lola, but is subdued and confined to a strait jacket. Later freed, Rath returns to his former classroom where he dies in remorse for having abandoned his noble career for the unrequited love of a wanton woman.

Surprisingly, Marilyn was eager to perform in *Blue Angel*, despite the role's similarity to characters from which she had worked diligently to distance herself such as Rose Loomis in *Niagara*. (Perhaps she was drawn to the serious plot and the prospect of reinterpreting Marlene Dietrich's powerful dramatic performance.)

When Marilyn arrived at Fox's New York offices on West Fifty-Sixth Street in October, she told the executives she preferred to wait for Spencer Tracy to become available as her co-star when he finished filming an adaptation of Hemingway's *The Old Man and The Sea.* In the meantime, Marilyn met with Spyros Skouras, despite his refusal to intervene with Representative Donald Jackson to support Miller's legal challenges. Her motivation to make nice with Skouras was clearly intended to peddle him the rights to the newly completed *The Misfits. Blue Angel* was placed on hold.

Also in October, the Millers hired a maid, an immigrant from Italy with poor proficiency in the English language. This deficit made Lena Pepitone (1925-2011) a perfect fit for the position, as Marilyn and Arthur guarded their privacy. Ironically, Pepitone would exploit her employers in 1979 when she allowed William Stadiem to ghost-write an apparently scurrilous "memoir" of the days she spent cleaning the apartment on Fifty-Seventh Street.

Comprised of lengthy dialogue and obviously written for easy adaptation into a screenplay, Pepitone's book, *Marilyn Monroe Confidential: An Intimate Personal Account*, contained many glaring inaccuracies. Over the years, other sources have quoted Marilyn from this memoir, but Pepitone and her ghostwriter revealed unconvincing credibility. Pepitone's appearance on *The Mike Douglas Show* in 1980 suggested she was incapable of writing the book or quoting Marilyn with any precision, and that Stadiem was likely largely responsible for both. The former maid spoke to Douglas in elementary and broken English.

Clutching her handbag in her lap—her legs shaking with nervousness—Pepitone described Marilyn as a "wonderful" and "good person" who suffered from depression during the Miller years in New York and later reconciled with her true love, DiMaggio, following the divorce from Miller. Pepitone also acknowledged Marilyn's generosity to her and her family. According to Pepitone, Marilyn had a "good heart" and would "give you anything you want." Marilyn lavished the maid's two young sons with gifts of toys and the maid and her husband with cash. Mike Douglas guided Pepitone throughout the interview, helping her navigate intelligible responses in English.

* * *

During Marilyn's residency in New York in the late 1950s, Broadway was in the midst of a golden age. A thriving economy and ample creative talent delivered new stage musicals, and the 1957 season premiered some of the essential musical theatre repertory enjoyed in revivals into the next century. The Millers frequently attended the New York theatre during this exciting period in its history. Mary Martin opened in *The Sound of Music*, a Rodgers and Hammerstein musical about the Austrian von Trapp Family Singers during the ascent of the Third Reich. Six years later, Fox adapted the musical into an adored blockbuster that would save the studio from bankruptcy.

Other musical successes included *The Music Man* with Robert Preston that won the Tony Award for Best Musical and Leonard Bernstein and Stephen Sondheim's *West Side Story*. The last reinterpreted Shakespeare's *Romeo and Juliet* by retelling the story with an interracial couple amid a backdrop of clashing Caucasian and Latino gangs and relocating the action from Verona to New York City. On November 18, the Millers were members of the audience during a performance of Noel Coward's musical *Conversation Piece* at the Barbizon-Plaza Theatre, starring Arthur's sister, Joan Copeland, in the role of Melanie.

Marilyn continued attending cocktail parties with celebrities and intellectuals visiting from California and Europe and sustained her role as a consummate New York society hostess. With assistance from secretary May Reis and cook Hattie Stevenson, Marilyn meticulously planned elegant dinner parties down to the minute details as evidenced by her surviving handwritten notes, guest lists, and menus. Miller was amazed at how she could spontaneously invite six to eight friends to the apartment and serve them an impressive meal. Her leg of lamb was the best he had ever tasted, and he especially liked her chicken with wine sauce. Marilyn often hired Milton Greene's employees, Kitty and Clyde Owens, to help her serve during these soirees.

Her personal property auctioned in 1999 included chic glassware, a vast array of entertaining pieces, and cooking utensils. Marilyn's personal diary included her notes on preparing for hosting an elaborate dinner in honor of the birthday of the wife of Isidor Schneider, a Ukraine-born novelist and critic who was a reader for Grove Press. Schneider and his wife, Helene, were also friends of the Rostens.

Other guests included poet and playwright Ettore Rella; his wife, Jesse; publisher George Braziller; and his wife, Marsha.

When Marilyn's brother-in-law, Paris Miracle, traveled with coworkers Robert Peacock and Dan Polar on a business trip to New York City, her half-sister, Berniece, insisted on tagging along so that she could visit Marilyn. Paris told her none of the other wives were traveling with their husbands, so her presence would appear inappropriate. Paris called ahead, and Marilyn warmly invited him and his colleagues to her apartment. Miller entertained the men until she arrived with an armful of flowers. Serving cocktails in highball glasses, Marilyn continuously forgot the other men's names, and the group found her predicament charmingly funny. Joining in their laughter, she called one gentleman "Mr. Polar Bear" and the other "Mr. Bird." The delightful evening ended with Marilyn giving all of them autographed portraits. She inscribed the one to Berniece's husband: "*For Paris, Love & Kisses from your sister-in-law, Marilyn.*"

On December 4, Marilyn typed a letter to Mary Bass (1905-1996), executive editor of the *Ladies' Home Journal*, and mentioned her extended renovation of the apartment ("*we are in the middle of knocking down walls*"), culinary successes ("*Everyone thinks I am a marvelous cook, thanks to you*"), and Bass' eleven-year-old son, Richardson. Marilyn expressed sincere appreciation for Bass being "*so wonderful*" to her and Arthur during the summer and fondly recalled their spending quality time together while relaxing on the Bass family's patio.

On Hanukkah 1957, Marilyn lit a candle on a gold menorah—its base played the Israeli National Anthem—each day of the festival of lights. She gave Arthur the *Encyclopedia Britannica*, presented record albums and books to Lee Strasberg, and re-gifted a pearl necklace (allegedly from the Emperor of Japan) to Paula. As her eyes filled with joyous tears, Paula ran around the living room brandishing the offering and squealing about Marilyn knowing how much she had admired the necklace. Marilyn's gifts to the Strasberg children peaked extravagance. Susan received an original Chagall sketch, and Marilyn offered John ownership of her Ford Thunderbird. Arthur had purchased a white Jaguar while in England the previous year.

Initially, John resisted Marilyn's kindness, citing his inability to afford the excessive cost of insurance, but she assured him that her corporation would continue payment. "There were so few, so very few people who were generous like that," John would say. "Especially to me, who couldn't do anything for her." John Strasberg would later tell Patricia Bosworth that only Marilyn recognized how he had been overlooked and even ignored. He believed that kind of care, especially from someone as warm as Marilyn, saved his life.

CHAPTER FIVE: JANUARY TO JULY 1958

In the New Year, the Court of Appeals ruled that oral arguments for Miller's appeal would not begin until the Supreme Court ruled on a related case. This pending legal problem made him a pariah in the eyes of Fox executives and ruled out the possibility of their purchasing his screenplay. Since the studio was only interested in Marilyn without Miller, the couple announced to the press that *The Misfits* would be produced as an independent film.

Conferences between Fox and Marilyn's representation at MCA led to a draft of a contract for *Blue Angel* to begin production in June with George Cukor as director and Spencer Tracy's name appearing before hers in the credits. Meanwhile, Marilyn's attorneys declared that Fox's failure to cast her in a film in 1957 entitled her to $100,000. Studio vice president Joseph Moskowitz argued that Marilyn was responsible for postponing *Blue Angel* and owed the studio three more films to fulfill her contract. Eventually, Fox conceded by releasing Marilyn from *Blue Angel* and paying her for an unmade film. The studio now faced another deadline of January 14, 1959 to cast her in another film.

Meanwhile, Marilyn posed for photographer Carl Perultz, modeling a variety of hats for an Easter bonnet feature in the April issue of *The American Weekly*. The magazine published artist Jon Whitcomb's painting of Marilyn based upon one of Perultz's portraits, which remained unseen by the public until their discovery in a derelict building on East Eighteenth Street in Manhattan. *Playboy* published the original portraits in its January 1980 issue.

On January 28, Marilyn appeared as one of the models at the Annual March of Dimes Fashion Show at the Waldorf-Astoria Hotel, a charity event held to support the organization's mission to improve the health of babies by preventing birth defects, premature birth, and infant mortality. Marilyn was photographed being kissed by Lindy and Sandy Sue Solomon, six-year-old twins appearing on posters promoting charitable contributions. Both girls were diagnosed with polio, and one walked with crutches. Marilyn appeared on stage holding their hands. She modeled a champagne colored two-piece long silk dress, designed by John Moore (1928-1996) with fitted jacket, wide lapels and white gloves.

The show also featured fashions by members of the couture group of the New York Dress Institute and other designers from New York, California, and Italy. As a protégé of one of Marilyn's favorite designers, Norman Norell, Moore started out at Elizabeth Arden's Salon in the late 1940s, was at Jane Derby for a short while, and designed for Mattie Talmack throughout the 1950s before opening his own design house in 1963.

The topic of motherhood was revisited when Stella Yuska of Huntington Beach, California, contacted Miller with an offer to facilitate their adoption of a two-month old female born to an unwed mother and living in a foster home. She described the infant as healthy and beautiful and relayed that the mother "feels that you people would really make a good happy home for her." It is unknown if the Millers explored this offer further or considered adoption as an option, but Yuska's letter was found in Marilyn's filing cabinet after her death.

In February, MGM brought Russian author Fyodor Dostoyevsky's *The Brothers Karamazov* to the screen with Australian actress Maria Schell in Marilyn's coveted role of Grushenka opposite Yul Brynner as Dimitri. Originally, the studio wanted to cast Marilyn and Marlon Brando, but Marilyn's pregnancy, miscarriage, and subsequent depression prevented her from working during the summer of 1957.

"I can't imagine that Marilyn Monroe wanted to do this role," Maria Schell had told syndicated reporter Bob Thomas. "If she did, why wouldn't the studio have moved heaven and earth to sign her? I must write her to tell her how sorry I am." While Marilyn lay in the hospital grieving the loss of her child in 1957, Schell spoke with reporter Aline Mosby about her belief that Marilyn had been done an injustice by the critics. "She is an honest actress in her expressions,"

Schell said. "She can really look at something with an honest innocence. I saw *The Prince and the Showgirl* and was delighted...I don't understand why some people say she is not an actress. She is, in her field. She is sweet and funny. If she wants to be a dramatic actress and break the circle, she would have to watch a few things. But right now, what she sells on the market is first quality."

After seeing Schell's performance, Marilyn graciously returned her kindness and told the press that Maria was wonderful in the part. However, critical reception of the film was lukewarm as the adaptation's excessively edited version failed to capture the passion of Dostoyevsky's last novel. Published in 1880, *The Brothers Karamazov*, is a story of three brothers implicated in the murder of their corrupt father, named Fyodor. Dmitri, his eldest son, is a soldier, stalled in a life of debauchery. Middle son Ivan is a student disturbed by the irrationality of the world. Alexei, the youngest, is an idealistic novice monk. Both Dmitri and his father, Fyodor, fight for the affections of Grushenka, a peasant girl who has risen to the status of courtesan.

Russian actress Anna Sten (1908-1993), who portrayed Grushenka in the 1931 German film adaptation, believed Marilyn would have been "fascinating" in the role. Having studied alongside Marilyn at the Actors Studio, Sten described her as a "searching soul who probed for characterization...very deep and very lovely, giving and taking at the same time—and that's a very rare quality."

By the spring of 1958, Marilyn was heavily drinking champagne at Roxbury. On one occasion, she slipped and fell down a flight of stairs, bruised her ankle, and cut the palm of her hand on a drinking glass. In a telephone conversation a few days later, she told half-sister Berniece that she accidently lacerated herself while slicing a ham. Berniece's husband, Paris, suspiciously queried about the Millers' apparent deviation from a Kosher diet, implying he began to suspect Marilyn's drinking.

Marilyn's indulgence in comfort food resulted in a gain of fifteen to twenty pounds. Her increased weight during pregnancies and during the Miller marriage eventually led to the next generation's urban myth that she was a US size 16 and criticism of her being obese by contemporary standards. The debate began decades following Marilyn's death during an era when the prevailing perception of attractive body size was emaciated, boyish, and anorexic. It also originated in a British newspaper article that referenced dress sizes converted to the UK system.

"Contrary to received wisdom, she was not a voluptuous size 16 (a size 12 in the US)," wrote Sara Buys of *The Sunday Times*, a British newspaper, "quite the opposite. While she was undeniably voluptuous—in possession of an ample bosom and a bottom that would look at home gyrating in a Jennifer Lopez music video—for most of the early part of her career, she was a size 8 (US 4) and even in her plumper stages, was no more than a 10 (US 6). I can tell you this from experience because a few weeks ago, I tried on her clothes."

Buys slipped on Marilyn's costumes and dresses owned by David Gainsborough Roberts, a retired investment banker whose collection was on display at the Jersey Heritage Museum in 2009. The curator charged with caring for the pieces described Marilyn as having an unusually narrow back and rib cage with ample breasts that would approximate a bra size 30E (US 30DD). Marilyn stood five-feet, five and one-half inches tall and usually ranged in weight from 112 in the early 1950s to 135 pounds at her heaviest (1959-1960). Based upon the clothing in the collection, Buys estimated Marilyn as just over 115 pounds (eight stone) with a Body Mass Index of 21.

"[Marilyn] didn't have a long body," Buys wrote, "and although her legs were a lovely shape (beautiful bony ankles and knees) they weren't particularly long. She had a very short rise (the distance from waist to crotch), but what made her body so extraordinary was the 13-inch difference between her breast and hip measurements and her waist. In her younger years her vital statistics would have come in at 36-23-35, and although her weight fluctuated throughout her career, she always maintained that out-of-this-world body ratio." The waist size of surviving belts and clothing from early in Marilyn's career ranged from 22 to 26 inches.

The museum's curator ordered a custom mold for the mannequins used to display the collection because none of the standard measurements matched Marilyn's extreme hourglass shape. Curators of Christie's Auction House met with a similar challenge during the 1999 exhibition of Marilyn's wardrobe. "One of the smallest mannequins we found in the U.S. was still not the correct size to fit [Marilyn's] Happy Birthday dress," Nancy Valentino told *People* magazine in 1999. "Marilyn was much more petite than people realized." Valentine had to reach across the Atlantic to custom-order a slim mannequin from London to display the gown worn for President Kennedy's birthday gala in New York in 1962.

In June 2011, when actress Debbie Reynolds auctioned her collection of Marilyn's costumes from 1954 at the Profiles in History Auction House in Los Angeles, the mannequin displaying the white halter dress from *The Seven Year Itch* had to be carved down from a standard size 2 to accommodate the tiny waist. According to Lisa Urban, who displayed the four Monroe costumes in the collection (from 1952-1954) and took their measurements, the average waist measurement was a mere twenty-two inches. The bust measurements averaged thirty-four inches.

Weight issues aside, the increase in Marilyn's consumption of champagne only worsened her symptoms of depression. She even resorted to the bottle to lift Hugo's spirits. Bassett Hounds are known for their droopy eyes and ears, visually suggesting an expression of sadness, but Marilyn sensed a real depression in her canine and perhaps projected her own symptoms on her beloved pet. She consulted with the Hugo's veterinarian who advised her to dose the dog with a shot of whiskey. In the presence of Norman Rosten, Marilyn administered the booze with a teaspoon.

The dog, sneezed, wobbled, and—according to Marilyn's perception—smiled. Her concern about the pet only intensified. Given Hugo's body stature, short-legged and a belly low to the ground, Marilyn worried about injuries to his genitals as he raced along the rough terrain of her Connecticut farm. "Be careful, Hugo!" she warned like an anxious mother. In Manhattan, she browsed through Sal Arena's pet store looking for other remedies and purchased some of the first available canine vitamins.

Marilyn's mood brightened in April, when she was photographed wearing a taupe sack dress with large white collar designed by John Moore. "A sack allows you to move," she explained." And it moves with you. And movement is—well, movement is good." The global response was overwhelmingly negative. "She shouldn't wear it," advised the Associated Press, "she looks awful." The German press reported Marilyn looked like she was wearing a barrel. "But I've never even been to West Berlin!" she replied. When auctioned at Sotheby's in

2011 by half-sister Berneice, the dress revealed alterations that had ensured a more snug fit. (Perhaps Marilyn heeded the advice of the international media who had a fondness for garments that clung to her physical attributes.) Marilyn was also photographed in her apartment wearing a more slenderizing black silk cocktail dress, also designed by Moore, with a large ivory organza bow in the front center of the bodice, stockings, black pumps, and white opera gloves. She posed in the living room leaning on her white piano against the backdrop of white damask draperies and also sitting on an ottoman.

While Marilyn spent time returning to her love of modeling, Miller sought material for a new play; unfortunate circumstances brought him inspiration. Barbara Leaming wrote of a mentally ill student from Latin America accosting Miller at Columbia University in the spring. Believing in the occult, the young man had read *The Crucible* and had taken the topic of witchcraft literally instead of as a metaphor for the Communist "witch hunts." He found a way to meet the playwright and was subsequently hospitalized for psychosis. Miller felt a strong empathy for the young man, which inspired his next piece, *After the Fall*, a biographic "memory play" with a protagonist named Quentin, clearly a representation of its author.

After the Fall originally included characters such as a cold and unforgiving wife, inspired by Mary Miller, and a fragile, unstable man, inspired by the student. After Miller decided to leave Marilyn, he morphed the fragile character into Maggie, later perceived by audiences and critics as Marilyn. According to Leaming, Miller had abandoned writing the play and resumed only because of his emotional need to "reassure himself, and the audience, of his own goodness."

The first film loosely based upon Marilyn's childhood and rise to fame, *The Goddess*, opened at the Fifty-fifth Street Playhouse in June. Paddy Chayefsky's script seemed to settle a score for Marilyn passing on an offer to star in the film adaptation of his play *Middle of the Night*. In *The Goddess*, unloved and neglected Emily Ann (remindful of Norma Jeane), played by eight-year-old Patty Duke, copes with her pain and low self-esteem by dreaming about a career as a glamorous movie star. As a woman (portrayed by Actors Studio alum Kim Stanley), she is briefly married to a moody soldier (shades of Jim Dougherty). Emily Ann changes her name to Rita Shaw and goes to Hollywood where she is transformed into a sexy, blonde starlet. Rita's charisma lands her a few small acting parts, and a film executive seductively invites her to his house to discuss the terms of her contract (Johnny Hyde, perhaps).

She marries a boxing champion, Dutch Seymore (an athlete like DiMaggio) who retires from the ring. Rita becomes a superstar, suffers a nervous breakdown, and reconnects with her religious zealot mother (a reference to Gladys Baker). She ultimately winds up alone in a big, empty house and laments about the burden of wealth and fame. After her mother's death, Rita's life is controlled by a secretary/nurse who monitors her self-destructive behavior. Was Chayefsky predicting Marilyn's psychiatric hospitalizations in 1961 and the future roles of Eunice Murray and Patricia Newcomb in her life?

It didn't take a rocket scientist to see the parallel between Rita Shaw and Marilyn Monroe. "It might vaguely appear that Mr. Chayefsky had a particular sexy star in mind," wrote Bosley Crowther in the *New York Times.* Marilyn's reaction is not documented, but some biographers assert she was offered the role and Miller persuaded her not to play it. Ironically, Miller's sister, Joan Copeland, portrayed the role of Rita's drama coach patterned after Natasha Lytess. As for the fate of Chayefsky's *Middle of the Night* after Marilyn's rejection, Columbia Studios cast Kim Novak as the younger love interest of an elderly clothes manufacturer, played by Frederic March, in the mildly controversial 1959 film.

Eager to produce the next Monroe film, Fox executives sent Marilyn scripts for a loose adaptation of William Faulkner's novel, *The Sound and the Fury*; a French-themed musical, *Can Can*, with songs by Cole Porter; and a drama, *Some Came Running.* Marilyn passed on all, opening the door for Shirley MacLaine's casting in two of the films. MacLaine co-starred with Frank Sinatra and Dean Martin in *Some Came Running* and earned an Oscar nomination for her performance as Ginny, the simple-minded trollop who sacrifices her life by taking a bullet for Sinatra. Directed by Vincente Minnelli, the film was released in 1958. MacLaine was also cast in *Can Can* (1960) with Frank Sinatra, Maurice Chevalier, and Louis Jordan, but the musical flopped. In *The Sound and the Fury*, Joanne Woodward portrayed Quentin opposite Yul Brynner (performing with hair) as members of a once-proud Southern family just barely surviving both financially and emotionally.

There had also been talk of Marilyn and Montgomery Clift starring in *Cat on a Hot Tin Roof* in the roles eventually played by Elizabeth Taylor and Paul Newman. The screenplay adaptation of Tennessee Williams' play only sunk to the bottom of a stack of scripts accumulating on Marilyn's desk. Amid this clutter was an envelope containing a two-page summary of an old German farce with a return address from Billy Wilder. It was titled *Not Tonight, Josephine!* Its leading female character, Sugar Kane, would become Marilyn's next role, and the film would become her most commercially successful.

Foremost on Marilyn's mind that spring was a baby, not another picture. Sadly, only one of her goals would come to fruition. Marilyn continued experiencing hysterical pregnancies during which she would gain weight. During one episode, she wrote to Norman Rosten: "*I think I've been pregnant for about three weeks or maybe two. My breasts have been sore to even touch—I've never had that in my life before, also they ache—also I've been having cramps and slight [blood] staining since Monday—now the staining is increasing and the pain is increasing by the minute.*" Facing the reality of not carrying a child after all only thrust Marilyn into deeper sadness and self-loathing.

Young parents wheeling their newborn baby daughter in a carriage along the East River promenade watched an attractive woman and a tall man walk toward them from the opposite direction. The attractive woman's eyes focused directly on the carriage. She stopped and asked the young couple, "May I see the baby?" The young mother immediately recognized Marilyn Monroe but pretended not to notice and pulled the baby's blanket down. Marilyn smiled at the baby for a long time. "You don't know how lucky you are to have such a wonderful baby," she said with tears in her eyes. "Take good care of her." The young woman never forgot Marilyn's words and told the story to a magazine long after her infant daughter was a mother herself.

On May 22, 1958, *Life* photographers documented Broadway producer Kermit Bloomgarden's visit to the Miller apartment. Flanked by Marilyn and Bloomgarden, Miller played the piano. In the photographs, Marilyn appears childlike as she sits and hugs her husband around the waist as he stands above her. Later, the men sat in the living room with their feet resting on an ottoman as Marilyn sat on the floor in a black dress and pumps at her husband's feet. Conversation centered on Bloomgarden's interest in producing *After the Fall* with actor Jason Robards, Jr. in the role of Quentin. The projected opening date was December 18, 1958. Miller also recounted having sent a copy of *The Misfits* to French director Rene Clement who had passed on the opportunity.

Marilyn's criticism of *The Misfits* was on target. It was talky, static, and thin on both character and action. She recommended a rewrite. Having sent a copy of the script to Norman Rosten in hope of validation, Marilyn followed up with a phone call to his Brooklyn home with Miller listening on the extension. "I want this speech rewritten," Rosten remembered her barking. "Norman agrees with me. I object to the whole stupid speech!" Marilyn complained that Roslyn was coming across too passive, and she grew increasingly disinterested in playing the character. She expected her husband to write a role different to the two-dimensional ones Fox offered her and one more worthy of her dramatic potential.

On May 27, Miller was inducted as a member of the National Institute of Arts and Letters and received its Gold Metal of Drama. Marilyn devotedly accompanied him to the award ceremony in a black silk sleeveless cocktail sheath with gathered neckline, three strings of pearls, and long white gloves. Outside the American Academy of Arts and Letters, she gaily signed autographs for fans. During the ceremony, as Marilyn sat beside seventy-eight-year-old Irish writer Padraic Colum, she adoringly watched her husband receive an accolade when only a few days earlier she had criticized his latest work. Miller sounded pious in his acceptance speech, calling the gold metal "an honor which the artist perhaps would not part with, but never truly takes as his own, because labor freely given and the joyful misery of creating cannot be translated into a prize."

After the ceremony, the members of the academy, usually reserved intellectuals, swarmed around his wife like giddy schoolgirls. The honor may have encouraged Miller to continue laboring on *The Misfits*, but before Marilyn could dive into the dramatic role crafted especially for her, her husband's mounting legal bills needed to be paid and another professional commitment loomed.

Part II:

Living Legend

CHAPTER SIX: *SOME LIKE IT HOT* PART I

In 2000, the American Film Institute honored *Some Like It Hot* as the "Best Comedy of All Time." In the five decades after its release, the film achieved acclaim worldwide as one of the greatest movie comedies ever made, ranking number fourteen on the America Film Institute's list of the 100 Best American Films of All Time. It has also been deemed "culturally significant" by the United States Library of Congress and selected for preservation in the national Film Registry. However, the road to such greatness was paved with pain and frustration.

In 1958, this masterpiece's working title was based on a line of dialogue: *Not Tonight Josephine!* According to Tim Dirk, the title was borrowed from Napoleon Bonaparte's alleged response when refusing sex with Empress Josephine. Inspired by a 1951 German film *Fanfaren der Liebe* (*Fanfares of Love*), the remake of the 1935 film *Fanfare d'Amour*, the screenplay recycled the basic plot element of two musicians who travel about disguised as gypsies, African-Americans and women to suit the venues of their diverse gigs.

Collaborators Billy Wilder and I.A.L. Diamond scripted the unemployed jazz musicians in drag out of necessity rather than choice. Chased by mobsters after witnessing a gangster massacre in Prohibition-era Chicago, the characters join an all-female band, *Sweet Sue and Her Society Syncopaters*, and escape to Florida. "We had to find the hammerlock," Diamond told Sandra Shevey. "We had to find the ironclad thing so these guys trapped in women's clothes cannot just take the wigs off...And that's where the idea for the St. Valentine's Day murder came. If they got out of the women's clothes, they would be killed..."

Wilder and Diamond's fast-paced, satirical story romanticized the Matt Sennett and Marx Brothers screwball comedies of the 1920s and 1930s. Rich in *double-entendres* and risqué dialogue, the script bravely and precariously wobbled from a cliff with the censors. Because the male leading characters masquerade as women, their sexualized dialogue passed Production Code censorship. The brilliant script's complex, multiple layers included witty sexual innuendo and themes of homosexuality, bisexuality, transvestism, androgyny, and impotence. Amid all the outrageous humor, the underlying plot addressed serious issues of alcoholism, gangland murder, and sexual harassment of women.

Some Like It Hot satirizes the stereotyping of female and male roles by reversing them throughout the plot, a radical statement during the conservative 1950s, an era of rigid gender roles. Joe, a saxophone-playing womanizer, becomes attracted to the band's lead singer, Sugar Kane (Marilyn's role), and devises a way to court her while out of his female disguise and in the disguise of a male millionaire. He creates a male identity, Junior, based on Sugar's ideal, by employing a vocal imitation of actor Cary Grant, a 1950s male sex symbol.

Junior, an intellectual millionaire who wears corrective lenses, complies with Sugar's theory that "men who wear glasses are so much more gentle and sweet and helpless." As Junior, Joe fakes impotence to lower Sugar's defenses and further his romance with her. He takes a passive role—literally on his back—in the seduction scene, and Sugar becomes the dominant aggressor in an attempt to "cure" his bogus sexual dysfunction.

Both Joe and his sidekick, Jerry, who plays the bass fiddle, transform during the gender-reversal. Moved by Sugar after he becomes her friend and confidante as Josephine, Joe eventually commits to her, shedding his pattern of notorious womanizing. Jerry actually enjoys being feminine to the point of accepting the proposal of a rich, old millionaire. Having originally re-named himself Geraldine, Jerry changes the name of his drag identity to Daphne as he begins to identify with his new feminine persona. For Jerry, his feminine side deserves humanity because as he experiences it, he sees it as more than a mere disguise. As Jerry befriends Sugar, he acquires many of her qualities and grows interested in her as more than a sexual object. This blending of male and female roles and perspectives would not occur in the culture until the last decades of the twentieth century.

I.A.L. Diamond (1915-1988) was born Itek Dommnici in Romania and known as Iz in Hollywood; he often joked that his initials stood for "Interscholastic Algebra League." In 1957, Diamond began a collaborative relationship with Wilder on the film *Love in the Afternoon. Some Like It Hot* was their most successful endeavor. The pair had an additional six hits including *The Apartment* (1960), *One Two Three* (1961), *Irma La Douce* (1963), *The Fortune Cookie* (1966), and *The Private Life of Sherlock Holmes* (1970). Diamond had co-written screenplays for Marilyn's early comedies *Love Nest, Let's Make It Legal,* and *Monkey Business.* "Sometimes I would run into [Marilyn] and get a big greeting;" Diamond recalled, "other times, she would look at me blankly, as if she'd never seen me before in her life. It was like trying to communicate with someone through a plate-glass window."

Jack Lemmon (1925-2001) was always Wilder's first choice for the role of Jerry, but the Mirisch Company desired a bigger name such as Frank Sinatra or Danny Kaye. Lemmon became Wilder's favorite actor, later starring in *The Apartment, Irma La Douce*, and *Avanti* (1972). Lemmon gained attention in *It Should Happen to You* (1954) with Judy Holliday, and he was the first actor to have been honored with Oscars for both Best Supporting Actor for *Mister Roberts* (1955) and Best Actor for *Save the Tiger* (1973). In 1988, the American Film Institute presented him its Lifetime Achievement Award. Lemmon was stunned by Marilyn's knowledge of his career and would attest he soon came to love her.

Frank Sinatra lost his opportunity to participate in the project when he failed to meet Wilder for a scheduled lunch date. Wilder turned to Tony Curtis (1925-2010), who thirsted to work with one of the industry's best and most talented directors, and signed him to play Joe. Born Bernard Schwartz, Tony Curtis was the son of Jewish Hungarian immigrants. Shedding a beefcake image in his early career, Curtis established himself as a competent actor in *Sweet Smell of Success* (1957) with Burt Lancaster and *The Defiant Ones* (1958) with Sidney Poitier.

Mitzi Gaynor was originally considered as the leading lady, a supporting role as "straight man" to Lemmon and Curtis' wild comic antics but Gaynor was busy completing the musical film *South Pacific* released in 1958. The script describes the female lead, Sugar Kane, as "the dream girl of every red-blooded American male who ever read College Humor." It was the weakest part, according to Wilder, so the trick was to give it the strongest casting. For Wilder, no one but Marilyn Monroe projected the mixture of innocence and provocation absolutely crucial for the film's success. Marilyn's agreement would also assure the fiscally focused producers of star power, this ushering Wilder to cast lesser box office draw Lemmon.

As the film director, Wilder persistently courted Marilyn to accept the role and reunite after their collaborative success with *The Seven Year Itch*, bringing Curtis and Lemmon to her apartment to coax her into the project. Lemmon told biographer Carl Rollyson that at the first meeting, Marilyn immediately embraced and kissed him warmly. She impressed him with knowledge of his screen performances and positive critiques of each, making him feel "wonderful." Rollyson describes Curtis as especially charming and solicitous toward Marilyn during the early stages of planning. Following the meeting, Wilder spoke to the press about Marilyn's appreciation of the script: "She gets the point right away. She is exceptionally keen."

Joe E. Brown (1892-1973) came out of retirement to work with Marilyn and to dance on the screen in the role of the aging millionaire, Osgood Fielding III. Known for his infectious grin and cavernous mouth, Brown began acting on stage in the 1920s after touring the country on both the circus and vaudeville circuits as one of a troupe of tumblers known as the Five Marvelous Astons. He transitioned into a comedian, catching the attention of Warner Brothers Studios. With his "rubber face" repertoire of expressions, Brown preceded Jim Carey as the lovable and zany film comedian of his era, and became one of the top ten box office earners in 1933 and 1936. He starred in the stage production of *Harvey* and appeared in the film version of *Show Boat* (1951). Brown's performance in *Some Like It Hot* renewed public interest in the faded star, and he penned an autobiography, *Laughter is a Wonderful Thing*, the year the film was released. Brown immortalized himself in his brilliant delivery of the film's final, hilarious line, "Nobody's perfect."

Wilder paid tribute to the great gangster movies of the 1930s with subtle gags in the movie's script and the casting of the Mobsters. The name of the crime lord, Little Bonaparte, is borrowed from *Little Caesar* (1931). George Raft (1895-1980), cast as Spats Columbo, threatens to smash a grapefruit in the face of one of his henchmen, a reference to James Cagney's famous scene in *The Public Enemy* (1931). He later grabs a coin from the air when another gangster repeatedly flips it, a gesture from the actor's role in *Scarface* (1932). Raft was born in Hell's Kitchen, New York, and based his gangster portrayals on actual underworld figures such as his childhood friend, Owney Madden, who became a powerful mobster during the Prohibition Era.

The cast also included Edward G. Robinson Jr. (whose father portrayed gangsters in the 1930s and 40s), Pat O'Brien (1899-1983) as the Irish Police Sergeant, and George E. Stone as Toothpick Charlie. Originally a dancer from Poland, Stone performed in dozens of Warner Brothers Studios' urban films and musicals from 1929 to 1936. By the time he worked with Wilder and Marilyn, the actor was nearly blind. The loss of sight seriously affected his ability to work as an actor, and he was later cast as the Court Clerk in the television series *Perry Mason*, requiring him to sit silently at a desk and occasionally hold up a Bible before a witness. Lastly, Joan Shawlee (1926-1987) was cast as Sweet Sue, described in the script as a "flashily-dressed broad, who has seen thirty summers and a few hard winters." Shawlee worked again with Wilder in *The Apartment* and *Irma La Deuce*.

Interiors would be filmed at the Samuel Goldwyn Studios (now the Warner-Hollywood Studios) on Santa Monica Boulevard and Formosa Avenue in Hollywood, formerly the Pickford-Fairbanks Studio. Silent screen stars and spouses Mary Pickford and Douglas Fairbanks partnered with fellow actor Charles Chaplin and director D.W. Griffith in 1919 to create United Artists Corporation, liberating themselves from studio contracts. These mavericks, like Marilyn herself, aimed to control distribution and their own independently produced films. In 1924, Goldwyn joined the partnership, and the studio bore his name in 1935. Many of the classic musicals enjoyed by Norma Jeane were filmed at the studio.

Both Miller and Spyros Skouras urged Marilyn to accept the

film. Marilyn's management, MCA, and Fox agreed she needed to be working and Wilder's comedy was predicated to be a huge hit. Although produced by the Mirisch Brothers and distributed by United Artists, an independent film company, Fox would benefit by the film's enhancement of Marilyn's reputation, especially since *The Prince and the Showgirl* had failed at the box office.

Ralph Roberts, John Springer, and Rupert Allan recalled Marilyn loving the role. She possessed an instinctive critical sense of what would play well onscreen and what would not. Marilyn assessed the script and production ensemble as nothing shy of brilliant. In his evaluation of another author's work, Miller described Sugar Kane as "a tasteless and characterless ingénue" and a "worthless" role. According to Miller, Marilyn begrudgingly accepted the part, something she considered an "affront," and diligently made "something out of nothing" to offset the couple's mounting legal expenses incurred from his contempt charges and his lack of significant income since their marriage.

By most accounts, Marilyn's initial reluctance stemmed from her confusion about her character's motivation. "I've got a real problem, Lee," Marilyn confided to her mentor in the living room of his Central Park West apartment. "I just can't believe in the central situation. I'm supposed to be real cozy with these two newcomers, who are really men in drag. How can I possibly feel a thing like that without just being too stupid? After all, I know the two men."

Strasberg offered Marilyn an insight into her own life to apply to the role. He reminded her of her challenges in having relationships with other women because of their jealousy over the attention men gave her. "You've never really had a girlfriend," Strasberg said. "Now here suddenly are two women and they want to be your friend. They like you. For the first time in your life, you have two girlfriends." Marilyn's eyes widened as she discovered the motivation for her character.

As Wilder pursed his leading lady, Marilyn, she was in the midst of a contract dispute with Fox. In reviewing her 1955 contract, MCA claimed that Fox's failure to cast her in a film in 1957 resulted in the studio sacrificing of one of the three remaining films of which she was legally obligated. The catalyst for going over Marilyn's contract with a fine toothcomb may have been Miller, who was desperate for cash due to his skyrocketing legal expenses and lack of income. When Miller offered to sell Fox the rights to produce *The Misfits* in late 1957, Spyros Skouras refused to acquire them unless the court reversed Miller's contempt conviction. Finally, Marilyn's agents and Fox reached agreement on April 15. She would make three more films for Fox and be released of the obligation to appear in *Blue Angel*.

With the Mirisch Company courting his highest revenue-producing star, Skouras agreed to pay Marilyn $100,000 for the film she never made at Fox. Fox had until January 14, 1959 to cast her in a film, and Wilder's production schedule established a completion date before the end of the year. Capitalizing on a win-win situation for all parties involved, Skouras gave Marilyn his blessing to appear in *Some Like It Hot*. Now, the door opened for Marilyn to appear in Wilder's outrageous farce.

On April 25, 1958, Marilyn signed the contract with the Mirisch Company. The press photographed her meeting with Walter Mirisch and signing of the contract. In the photographs, Marilyn was in a sack-styled taupe dress with a high, broad collar, snuggling up to Mirisch on a sofa in the office. [Marilyn's half-sister and niece, Berniece and Mona Miracle, auctioned the dress, designed by John Moore for Talmack New York, at Sotheby's in 2001]. Marilyn would receive $100,000 plus ten percent of the profits from this independent project. The bulk of Marilyn's financial assets in 1962 ($593,675.88) originated from her share of *Some Like It Hot*.

In the study of the New York apartment, Arthur sublimated his strong emotions about the marriage through work on the draft of his play, *After the Fall*, while Marilyn taught herself to play the ukulele in the darkness of their bedroom and spoke on the telephone with Judy Garland about ways to approach her musical numbers.

As Marilyn prepared to travel to the west coast, she suspected she had conceived a baby. Ambivalent about continuing with the film, she turned to her confidante, poet Norman Rosten, and said: "*Should I do my next picture or stay home and try to have a baby again? That's what I want most of all, the baby, I guess, but maybe God is trying to tell me something...Arthur says he wants it, but he's losing his enthusiasm. He thinks I should do the picture...*" Rosten responded through a poem; its final line read: "*We watched and bought her anguish with our coins."*

However, there were no signs of anguish on July 8, when Marilyn arrived at the Los Angeles Airport accompanied by May Reis and Paula Strasberg. "An apparition in white materialized in the doorway," reported the *Los Angeles Times*, "white hair aswirl in the propwash of another plane; white silk shirt open at the powdered white throat; white, tight, silk skirt; white shoes; white gloves. Marilyn Monroe blinked big, sleepy eyes at the world...began descending—slowly and wickedly—down the steps. 'I'm so sorry,' she cooed. 'I was asleep.'" She carried three books: *The Importance of Living* by Lin Yutand, Shirley Jackson's *Life Among the Savages*, and *To the Actor* by Michael Chekhov.

Physicians confirmed Marilyn's pregnancy, but she kept the condition secret from the press given her history of miscarriages. When reporters teased her about her weight, Marilyn replied, "It's still in the right places, isn't it?" She added, "My weight goes up and down like everyone else's, but I'll be in good shape in two weeks because I intend to do lots of walking and exercising."

"Why do reporters ask if I'm happy or unhappy?" sighed Marilyn after another question from the press. "Making movies is just one part of my life. My ambition is to grow old gracefully like Marie Dressler, who was my idol." [Marie Dressler (1868-1934), a robust woman with coarse and plain features, became one of Metro-Goldwyn-Mayer Studios' biggest box office character actresses past the age of sixty. Her films included *Anna Christie* with Greta Garbo, *Tugboat Annie*, and *Dinner at Eight* with Jean Harlow. Dressler earned an Oscar for Best Supporting Actress of 1931 for *Min and Bill.* Her autobiography was titled *The Life Story of an Ugly Duckling.*]

When quizzed about bringing along acting coach Paula Strasberg, Marilyn explained:

> *You see, I'm not a quick study, but I'm very serious about my work and am not experienced enough as an actress to chat with friends and workers on the set and then go into a dramatic scene. I like to go directly from a scene into my dressing room and concentrate on the next one and keep my mind in one channel. I envy these people who can meet all comers and go from a bright quip and gay laugh into a scene before the camera. All I'm thinking of is my*

performance, and I try to make it as good as I know how. And Paula gives me confidence.

Producer Harold Mirisch hosted a lavish press conference and dinner party in Marilyn's honor at the Beverly Hills Hotel, inviting Hollywood's A-list for cocktails at seven and dinner directly following. Marilyn arrived late wearing a three-quarter-length dress of black silk crepe with a plunging neckline, cap sleeves, and a "pouff" hemline accessorized with long, white gloves. "She is more touching than ever, and in many ways more beautiful than ever," observed Earl Leaf, who photographed the event, "but there's a delicacy about her that is new—as though she has less physical strength and less inner force. Her smile breaks your heart. She seems no longer of this world." Marilyn demurely socialized with her director and co-stars, enjoyed hors d'oeuvre with Tony Curtis, and gingerly sipped a cocktail.

Marilyn had been absent from Los Angeles for two years and the Hollywood community welcomed her back with an avalanche of invitations. She accepted two before filming began. On July 9, Marilyn accompanied Louella Parsons to a reception held in honor of composer Jimmy McHugh. Marilyn was photographed walking hand in hand with the formidable gossip columnist. The following day, an unescorted Marilyn attended the premiere of the musical *Gigi* (later recipient of the Oscar for Best Motion Picture) at the Paramount Theatre, now El Capitan, on Hollywood Boulevard. She wore a red lace gown with a black tulle wrap and black satin opera gloves.

Back at his office at the Goldwyn Studios, Wilder envisioned his tribute to 1920s gangster films in monochromatic black and white. For two days, Marilyn persistently reminded him of her 1955 contract stipulating she would perform only in color films. He persuaded her to concede by demonstrating how color film read the male leads' heavy drag make-up.

Marilyn would shimmer in cinematographer Charles Lang Jr.'s textured black and white photography. Lang may have used a double Obie lighting technique to halo Marilyn, who virtually glowed on film with her sparkling eyes, platinum hair, iridescent make-up, and glittering costumes by Jack Orry-Kelly. Orry-Kelly (1897-1964), formerly an illustrator of title cards for silent films who had ascended to design stage and film wardrobes, recreated the vintage styles of the Jazz Age. With two Oscar awards for costume design, Orry-Kelly would win his third honor for *Some Like It Hot.*

Marilyn's most luminous costume was a cocktail dress of tulle adorned with sequins and silver fringing with a heart shape embroidered on the derrière. It clung to her breasts, appearing diaphanous if not for strategically placed sequins. A similar frock in black tulle was spotlighted at the end of the film. Some of Marilyn's other Orry-Kelly creations included a long-sleeve, V-neck black silk dress with fringe at the hemline (now displayed at the Museum of Moving Image in London, it shows evidence of having been altered to accommodate the bulge of Marilyn's pregnancy); a short, black lace negligee with sheer bed jacket; and a white day dress with beading. Given the period of the film, Marilyn's most modest outfit was a 1920s bathing suit.

The film also highlighted Marilyn singing three 1920s songs: "Runnin' Wild," "I Wanna Be Loved By You," and "I'm Through With Love." She also recorded an original piece, "Some Like It Hot," intended for the main titles, but the number was deleted and replaced with a snappy instrumental medley of "Runnin' Wild" and "Sugar Blues," Sugar's theme song. Marilyn's deleted performance appeared on the film's soundtrack record album. Miller apparently enjoyed Marilyn's recordings, especially the soulful torch song "I'm Through With Love."

Written by Herbert Stothart and Harry Ruby with lyrics by Bert Kalmar, "I Wanna Be Loved By You" was featured in the 1928 musical, *Good Boy.* It was first performed by Helen Kane (1904-1966), dubbed the "Boop-Boop-a-Doop Girl" because of the song's tag line sung in her squeaky, baby voice with Bronx dialect. She inspired the 1930s Betty Boop cartoon character, also modeled after Brooklyn-born Clara Bow, Hollywood's "It Girl" ("it" being a term for the quality of absolute attraction).

"Runnin' Wild," written by A. H. Gibbs, Joe Grey, and Leo Wood was recorded in 1922 by Miss Patricola, a vaudeville singer. Fud Livingston's 1931 composition "I'm Through With Love," written with Matty Malneck and Gus Kahn, actually missed the film's period setting by two years. Malneck (1903-1981) wrote "Some Like It Hot" in 1920s style especially for the film.

Sugar's theme, "Sugar Blues," was written in 1920 by Clarence Williams and Lucy Fletcher and recorded by Leona Williams and her Dixie Band two years later. Clyde McCoy's 1930 instrumental version—with a growling "wah-wah" jazz mute trumpet—inspired the version on the film's soundtrack.

Adolph Deutsch (1896-1980) composed the energetic, jazz-oriented soundtrack, and Matty Malneck and his Orchestra performed with Marilyn. Having last performed a full musical number four years before in *There's No Business Like Show Business*, Marilyn turned to her friend Judy Garland for coaching on phrasing. Despite this expert guidance, she struggled in the recording studio.

Usually an adequate vocalist who could sell a song, Marilyn's voice could be strong, but her insecurities and self-doubt triggered paralyzing anxiety. Self-conscious, Marilyn asked sound editor Eve Newman not to look directly at her while recording, so Newman hid behind a potted tree to avoid Marilyn's line of eye contact. Marilyn satisfied Malneck by the third take on "Runnin' Wild" but begged for another. Malneck selected the final attempt.

On July 16, Marilyn sat at a desk at the Beverly Hills Hotel and typed a letter to Bobby Miller (it entirely is published in *MM—Personal from the Private Archive of Marilyn Monroe*). She references taking ukulele lessons and suggests he accompany her on the guitar, proposing they charge admission. Marilyn also recounts having accepted the gift of a ten-month old, housebroken golden-haired Cocker Spaniel puppy named Walter. Unfortunately, Marilyn learned the dog had only recently bitten a woman on the throat, so she returned it to the owner. Marilyn also shares several private jokes and seems thoroughly engaged in Bobby's life, referring to his friends by name and specific interests. Her tone is warm and personal and she gently prompts the boy to write to his father and even encloses stamps.

On August 4, the year anniversary of Marilyn's miscarriage, she arrived on the set with her entourage: acting coach, hairdresser, make-up artist, and press agent. Camouflaging bereavement with an infectious enthusiasm for the film, Marilyn expressed delight at discovering a sign Wilder had jokingly posted on her dressing room door: "*Marilyn Monroe on loan from Dostoevsky.*" Another sign announced, "*Come on the Billy Wilder set and smoke your little hearts out, some like it hot*!" This referenced prohibition of smoking on the Goldwyn lot since the neighboring *Porgy and Bess* set had burned down due to a carelessly thrown cigarette.

The first scene was Marilyn's entrance in the train station—nothing especially notable. Sugar Kane was introduced as just another member of the girls' band boarding the Pullman for Florida. After shooting, Wilder cried, "Cut!" He turned to Strasberg, standing off camera and wearing her typical black dress and black hat. "How was that for you, Paula?" he queried, strategically setting the tone for Strasberg's involvement in the film. For a director known to be ruthless, bombastic and insulting, Wilder initially treated Marilyn with dignity and respect, honoring her trust in a personal coach.

Lemmon and Curtis also had a coach of their own; retired female impersonator Barbette, chosen by Wilder to facilitate the men's feminized walk and gestures. Barbette had been born in Texas as Vander Clyde and longed to join the circus. An opportunity presented when he was offered to star in an aerial act contingent upon his willingness to cross-dress. Wilder had watched the act while in Europe in the 1930s.

While viewing the rushes of Sugar's first scene, Marilyn felt dissatisfied and immediately generated ideas for its improvement. "She had a tremendous sense of a joke, as good a delivery as Judy Holliday, and that's saying a lot," said Wilder. "She had a kind of inner sense of what will play, what will work. She called me after the first daily rushes because she did not like her introductory scene." After hanging up, the director called Diamond who agreed it wasn't a good enough entrance to for Marilyn, so they created a new introduction.

In the revision, at Marilyn's suggestion, Sugar clips down the train platform, carrying a valise and a ukulele case and accompanied by the soundtrack's raucous jazz tune played by a muted trumpet. As she wiggles on her high-heeled pumps past the two men in drag, the train emits a puff of steam toward Sugar's swinging buttocks. She quickens her pace. Lemmon's character turns to Curtis' and observes that she moves like "Jell-O on springs." With its allusion to the subway breeze lifting her skirt in *The Seven Year Itch*, this reworked scene is one of Marilyn's most memorable entrances. She was absolutely correct, Wilder conceded.

On August 7, workers renovating the Roxbury farmhouse surprised Miller with a case of beer and bottle of whiskey to celebrate the good news: his conviction was overturned. Marilyn called her husband from the Bel Air Hotel. "Neither I nor my husband ever had any doubt about the outcome of the case," she told the press. "I have been studying Thomas Jefferson for years, and according to Thomas Jefferson, this case had to turn out this way." She victoriously strummed "Happy Days are Here Again" on her ukulele, sounding slightly flat to one reporter.

Marilyn entertained Curtis' parents, Emanuel and Helen Schwartz, when they visited the set, and was photographed snuggling with the family outside her dressing room. In drag, Curtis vaguely resembled his mother, both sharing a strong jaw and prominent nose. The actor took pride in his performance as Josephine, basing it upon his dignified and aloof mother melded with Grace Kelly. He later told film critic Leonard Maltin that he hoped his characterization would complement Lemmon's "twenty cent tart" depiction of Jerry as Daphne.

Porgy and Bess was in production in the adjacent soundstage under the direction of Otto Preminger, and actors Sidney Poitier, Sammy Davis Jr., and Dorothy Dandridge—a friend of Marilyn's from earlier in her career—often visited the *Some Like It Hot* set. Poitier had recently worked with Curtis in *The Defiant Ones.* Maurice Chevalier, star of *Gigi*, made a special visit to see Marilyn, who had recently attended the musical's premiere in New York.

Henry Fonda's daughter, twenty-year-old Jane Fonda (born 1937), also visited the set with her friend, Susan Strasberg. In *My Life So Far*, the two-time Oscar-winning actress, political activist, and physical fitness guru would reflect back upon meeting Marilyn long before Fonda performed in front of a camera:

> Into the darkness stepped Marilyn Monroe, bringing the light with her, shimmering, in her hair and on her skin...I saw a scared, wide-eyed child...There was a vulnerability that radiated from her and allowed me to love her right there and feel glad that she had someone wide and soft, like Paula, to mama her. She was very sweet to Susan and me...

Fonda would consider the coincidence of Paula's coaching Marilyn as the catalyst of her big break into show business. Coincidently, during the production of *Some Like It Hot*, the Strasberg family rented a house in Malibu a few blocks from the beach home rented by Henry Fonda and his fourth wife, Baronessa Afdera Franchetti. In the summer of 1958, Jane was on vacation from New York and visiting her father and his wife. Lee, visiting his wife, would meet Jane and accept her into his private classes in New York.

Filming continued with increasing challenges when Marilyn faced the camera and her director. Usually tardy and unpredictable, she fluctuated from requiring multiple takes to nailing a scene in one take. Of course, this fits the profile of a woman battling Bipolar Disorder while pregnant. Chemically, hormonally, and emotionally, Marilyn must have been completely unregulated, but in 1958, she was perceived as neurotic, unprofessional, temperamental, and—sometimes—mean.

Wilder's next frustration with his star stemmed from opposing interpretations of her character's role. The scene involves Sugar's flask accidentally dropping from her garter belt onto the floor in front of the bandleader who prohibits alcohol consumption. Wilder gently told Marilyn she did not express a proper degree of surprise, and they repeated the scene. "*Cut!*" he said. "You still haven't got it, dear. Don't strain for it. It's a very simple reaction."

Marilyn darted offset to Paula, whispered, and conferred with her coach for twenty minutes. Wilder made an effort to appear busy, but Marilyn and Paula's discussion lengthened to what seemed an eternity. Even Miller perceived that Marilyn's keeping the director waiting for thirty minutes was a "great humiliation." However, Wilder's professional ego was not yet bruised. This would change in the upcoming months.

Journalist Donald H. Wolfe, present on the set, believes Marilyn was determined to combat Wilder's interpretation of Sugar Kane as a "Betty Boop" cartoon character. If she were reduced to playing a dumb blonde role, there would be none of Wilder's broad gags. Instead, she would create the portrayal of a three-dimensional character with a heart and soul; a textured performance that would provide the glue to make this farce a cohesive film. "The constant flubbing, and drying up, and forgetting lines were the exhaustive process Marilyn went through until Wilder gave up," wrote Wolfe. "By take twenty-nine, Marilyn's way began looking good to the frustrated director."

Marilyn's co-star experienced considerable difficulty in his performance, but his challenges remained secret from the press for decades after the film's success. Tony Curtis could not reach a high registered voice as Josephine. Paul Frees, known as the "Man of a Thousand Voices," dubbed all of Curtis' feminine lines as Josephine, a majority of his performance. Frees would later provide the voice of Boris Badenov in the animated *Rocky and Bullwinkle* shorts.

Marilyn's delays plagued the production and achieved a legendary reputation for the remainder of her career. She worked more slowly in her performance, but the results were more powerful. She demanded repeated takes even when Wilder was satisfied. Take after take, Marilyn would say she was "relaxing a little more…" and promised to "go a bit further on the next try." Wilder, Lemmon, and Curtis found this unique process tedious and incensing. Marilyn's perfectionism reflected both her insecurities and professional goals. In reality, she could film three pages of dialogue without a flaw but then get stuck with one line in another scene.

"I have to make contact with Sugar Kane," Marilyn pleaded to her director in an interaction that must have sounded equally humorous as the script they were filming—if not for the pain we now know she experienced. "Go ahead and make contact with Sugar Kane,' Wilder replied in his thick accent, "but for God's sake, could you contact her a little faster?"

"She was a sweet lady who was clearly going through some kind of hell on earth," Lemmon told biographer Graham McCann. "I didn't know all the reasons, but I saw she was suffering—suffering and still producing that magic on film. It was a courageous performance, really courageous. Most actors only occasionally use all their talent, but Marilyn was using hers *constantly*, giving everything she had till it hurt, struggling to be better. Sure, it was infuriating for us at times, but I was really fascinated to watch her work."

"It used to be you'd call her at 9:00 a.m. and she'd show up at noon," Wilder said of Marilyn's chronic tardiness. "Now, you call in May and she shows up in October." For Marilyn, a 9:00 a.m. call required her awaking by 5:00, arriving at the studio at 6:30 for hairdressing, face and body make-up application, and reporting to wardrobe by 9:00. Since her chronic insomnia could not be treated with sedatives because of the pregnancy, Marilyn would usually fall asleep between two and three in the morning, resulting in a total of two hours of sleep. Once on the set, she would be irritable, unfocused, and forgetful.

On some mornings, Marilyn arrived at eleven o'clock in the morning for a nine o'clock call. On bad days, she arrived after the cast and crew had eaten lunch. On occasion, she arrived at three in the afternoon. The following year, Wilder observed Marilyn arrive several hours early at Fox's banquet for visiting Soviet Premier Nikita Khrushchev. "I vowed then that if I did another picture with her," Wilder joked, "I'd hire Khrushchev to hang around the set so she'd show up on time."

Tony Curtis would remember Wilder's gentle treatment of Marilyn when she finally arrived on the set, to the consternation of some of her co-stars. Once when Wilder suggested how to read a line, she snapped: "Don't talk to me now. I'm thinking about how I'm going to play the scene." On the set, Wilder could be capable of passive-aggressive behavior toward Marilyn. On several occasions, Wilder spitefully called a lunch break following Marilyn's delayed arrival. Eve Newman remembered Marilyn arriving in her car at 11:00 for a 9:00 call while 150 extras stood waiting; Wilder told the entire company to break for lunch.

Concerned about the health of his wife and their unborn baby, Miller pleaded later with Wilder to allow her to leave the set each evening at four-thirty. It was already four o'clock, and the director still couldn't print a take. Marilyn arrived half past eleven, Wilder explained, and wasn't ready to perform until one. "Arthur, you get her here at nine, ready to work," Wilder bargained. "I'll let her go at noon."

Despite Wilder's moments of impatience, he recognized the worth of enduring Marilyn's idiosyncrasies and peculiarities. In his more tolerant moments, he kept a rational perspective: "I have an aunt in Vienna, also an actress. Her name, I think, is Mildred Lachenfarber. She always comes to the set on time. She knows her lines perfectly. She never gives anyone the slightest trouble. At the box office she is worth fourteen cents. Do you get my point?"

"Maybe it's a psychological hurdle," Wilder hypothesized of Marilyn's frequent inability to remember lines. "I've noticed that if she gets past the first two or three lines she sometimes can go on and on, even if it's a long speech. She doesn't seem to get tired. She'll do take after take. She poops out the other actors. But Marilyn blooms as the day goes on, and she's at her best in the late afternoon, when the other actors are dropping like flies."

For a film about men gaining insight into the psychology of women as they impersonate them, the subject matter failed to register with the men present on the soundstage, where male supremacy reigned. Some of the principal males working on the film behaved insensitively to the principal female who was struggling with a high-risk pregnancy, emotional and psychological problems. Biographer Sandra Shevey confronts the sexist bias in a subsequent evaluation of the politics on the set of *Some Like It Hot*: "Diamond…was a fastidious screenwriter; so much so that if an actor messed up *one* word, even a syllable, he would request that Wilder ask them to do it again."

While Marilyn was letter-perfect while filming long, mentally demanding scenes (such as the one with Lemmon in the train's upper berth and one on the beach with Curtis), she had trouble remembering three words in shorter scenes requiring an alleged forty-seven takes. Biographer Donald H. Wolfe suggests this was Marilyn's way of proving to her director that she was, indeed, capable of memorizing and delivering lines in one take.

Marilyn and Lemmon completed the hilarious upper birth bed scene on the Pullman train on the first take on the morning of August 28. Having learned to pace himself with his co-star, Lemmon was prepared to shoot the entire day. At 9:05 in the morning, the day's work was done. However, the day before, Marilyn required thirty-seven takes for her two lines. There were tortuous days when the director could have strangled her, Wilder would tell Donald Spoto, but there were also marvelous days when he knew she was brilliant.

Chapter Seven: *Some Like It Hot* Part II

Monroe biographies unanimously emphasize the tumultuous aspects of the production of *Some Like It Hot*, but journalists on the set reported a lighter atmosphere in magazines of the day. In an article for *Cosmopolitan*, columnist Jon Whitcomb documented no overt signs of tension in the Goldwyn soundstages. "I have never watched a film put together in the midst of so much hilarity," he reported. Whitcomb also observed the crew worshipping the ground Marilyn walked on. Those most inconvenienced by her delays staunchly defended her. He quotes them describing her as "prompt, cordial, and cooperative" as well as "fragile and maligned by the press."

Wardrobe mistress Ann Landers told him: "MM is really all woman, warm and generous. Unlike every other actress I've ever known, she is completely without jealousy." When Whitcomb referred to Marilyn's comeback performance, Wilder challenged this perception with tenacity: "Marilyn, contrary to what you may have heard, is absolutely tireless. She always thinks she can do a scene better than before. Her face will light up and she'll say, 'Can we do it again?' It's silly to speak of this film as a 'comeback' for her."

In September, the production moved two hours south on location in San Diego at the Hotel del Coronado. In the fall of 1958, the resort was frozen in time. Opened in 1888 on a sagebrush peninsula across the bay from San Diego and known as "the Del," it boasted turrets, verandahs, gingerbread detailing, red roofs and white-framed structures. The resort also had a rich history. It hosted twelve U.S. presidents, several major films, and was the rumored location of Edward VIII's introduction to Mrs. Wallace Simpson. Marilyn and Miller stayed in one of the resort's exclusive Vista Mar cottages on

Gloriana Bay. As a sign of the times, the production manager warned the Del's manager that Marilyn brought along her African-American maid, Ida Mae Zanders. In a memo, he wrote, "*This situation you will handle with your usual diplomacy.*"

For the next seven days, Marilyn was at her most brilliant, amazing the young actresses who portrayed members of the all-girls orchestra. To these women, their leading lady's eccentricities were neither angering nor frustrating. "Marilyn Monroe was dynamite!" exclaimed Sandra Warner, who played Emily. Virginia Butterfield interviewed these co-stars decades later when they returned to the famed resort for *San Diego Online*. "She had a childlike naiveté," said Warner. "A sad childhood...foster homes...and that innocence about her. You had to love her. I have never seen anybody with such magic." The group was unanimous in their adoration. "She was beautiful and an inspiration to all of us," said Grace Lee Whitney, who did not have a speaking part. "She was a tremendous actress. I didn't realize her problems until later, when I heard the stories."

Members of *Sweet Sue's Society Syncopaters* reunited in 2001 for MGM Home Entertainment for an interview for the DVD release of the film. Marion Collier who played Olga, the clarinet player; Laurie Mitchell who portrayed Mary Lou, the trumpet player; and Joan Nicholas, Betty on the saxophone, shared fond and glowing reminiscences of Marilyn. "Marilyn Monroe was magic, she really lit up the screen..." remembered Sandra Warner. "She was absolutely adorable..."

"This will be great for the baby!" exclaimed a refreshed Marilyn on the white sandy beachfront of the Del. Indeed, she was pregnant and now openly discussing her condition with coworkers. Between takes, Marilyn stood on the verandah and took long breaths of sea air. She dreamed of the day in June 1959 when she would give birth to her first child. Ever precautious of the safety of her developing fetus, Marilyn retired early and studied her scenes in bed.

Gynecologist Leon Krohn accompanied her on location and remained on call to monitor the pregnancy. Home movies capture Marilyn covering her mouth and possibly gagging or vomiting as she was escorted off set with Miller to a trailer. The source for this moment of distress is unclear. Could she be experiencing nausea, morning sickness, or debilitating anxiety? Marjorie Pletcher told

Anthony Summers that Marilyn was so obsessed about looking and acting correctly that she became physically incapable of leaving her trailer: "It was the ultimate stage fright. She had great talent, but she never felt sure of herself, never could believe in herself."

The location itself replaced Marilyn as the source of delays and disruption during the production of a scene with lengthy dialogue between Sugar and Joe posing as Junior. Every ten minutes, a jet from nearby Naval Air Station North Island flew over the beach. "I thought it would take about four days to shoot that scene," Wilder said. "I tried to film between take-offs, but then on the second take everything was there; every sentence of two pages. Not one letter, not one comma was left out. We were finished in less than twenty minutes." Two and one-half minutes of color home movies of this scene were filmed by a sailor and auctioned in Australia for an estimated $60,000 in 2008.

Marilyn's abilities had evolved and refined in the four years since she had worked with Wilder, but he believed her study of Method Acting both crippled an innate talent and alienated the actress from other actors and crewmembers with whom she worked. Wilder's assessment as told to Maurice Zolotow:

> She has become a better actress, even a deeper actress, since Strasberg. But I still believe she was developing herself naturally and would have become greater as she matured, even without him....Before, she was like a tightrope walker who doesn't know there's a big pit down there she could fall into. Now she knows about the pit and she's more careful on the tightrope. She's more self-conscious; I'm still not convinced she needed training. God gave her everything.

Tony Curtis was joined on location by his wife, Janet Leigh, pregnant with their daughter, Jamie Lee Curtis, who would eventually become an actress herself. "Marilyn was tortured by insecurity," Leigh empathically wrote in her autobiography. "This exquisite creature, so talented, so vulnerable, so irretrievable, labored just to come on the set. She was there at the studio, but was hard put to muster the courage to appear. It was not malicious game playing or status tactics but just plain terror that forced her to retreat."

In the editing room, Wilder's artistic and creative loyalty was to his fragile leading lady. In the early takes, Curtis' performance is strong and Marilyn's is weak. In later takes, she is superb, and Curtis is weak. As a director, Wilder admitted to using Marilyn's best takes at the risk of garnering Curtis' resentment. Wilder had no choice but to favor Marilyn because when she appeared on the screen, audiences could not take their eyes off her.

Wilder may have been accused of objectifying Marilyn's sexuality in their two films together, but he consistently praised her ability over her more obvious physical attributes. "The greatest thing about Monroe is not her chest," he declared with sincerity. "It is her ear. She is a master of delivery. She can read comedy better than anyone else in the world."

Some stories about the film's production rose to a mythic level and have become folklore in Hollywood history and apocrypha in the Monroe legend. One anecdote surrounds the scene in which a jilted Sugar enters Daphne and Geraldine's hotel room and searches the dresser drawers for the liquor she had sworn off in happier times. "Where's the bourbon?" is her famous line. Its delivery, depending upon the source, took Marilyn anywhere from thirty, forty-seven, fifty-nine, or even eighty-three takes, implying that her drug use was out of control. Wilder pasted the line in each of the dresser drawers to compensate for Marilyn's apparent memory and concentration deficits.

Biographer Sarah Churchwell observes that the scene was filmed with Marilyn's back to the camera, enabling her to easily dub the line in postproduction. Wilder's demand for repeated takes suggests an overt power struggle between director and star. Donald H. Wolfe theorizes that Marilyn staged the repeated takes in order to control the interpretation of her character and as a way to defy Wilder's direction. She would deliver an incorrect line in the manner Wilder instructed for a series of takes ("Where's the whiskey?" "Where's the bottle?") and purposefully wear down her director. In later takes, she would deliver the line verbatim to the script in the manner in which she believed fit her characterization. Donald H. Wolfe observed: "She knew she was right and believed that a star of her stature had the prerogative of playing a scene the way she felt it." It was a battle of the wills but in the end, Marilyn won.

Another apocryphal story depicts Tony Curtis nibbling on a

pheasant leg on the yacht set while Marilyn recites her lines of their dialogue. According to many accounts, her inability to deliver the lines required him to consume several dozen legs to the point of his abhorring poultry for years (this anecdote may be more legendary than fact, as it seems unlikely the property master predicted the problem and supplied dozens of servings of pheasant legs). "I knew we were in mid-flight," Wilder lamented, "and there was a nut on the plane."

Over the years, stories emerged about an exasperated Wilder having Marilyn's lines written in inconspicuous spots on the set so she could read them. According to folklore printed on the cover of the 2001 DVD release, it is possible to see Monroe's eyes move back and forth during the scene where she talks to Curtis' character on the phone in her hotel room. Allegedly, she was reading from a chalkboard positioned behind the camera. Such allegations have become part of Marilyn's legend.

"There was a method to her madness," wrote Wolfe of Marilyn's purposeful flubbing of lines in order to play scenes according to her own interpretation, "but unfortunately, cinema mythology preferred to repeat the myriad stories of Marilyn Monroe's inability to remember a simple line..." Wilder, an intelligent man, must have recognized Marilyn's transparent manipulation. The closest he came to publicly acknowledging it was to comment on the quality of Marilyn's final product: "Anyone can remember lines, but it takes a real artist to come on the set and not know her lines and yet give the performance she did!"

On September 11, Marilyn typed a letter to Norman Rosten on Coronado del Mar stationery. Its letterhead featured an illustration of the resort, coastline and sea. She drew a figure, visible from the waist up in the water, with breasts, a bow in the hair, and arms extended upward. Marilyn also inscribed a caption over the figure's head: "Help." The time spent at the beach inspired a metaphor for the state of her marriage, the production of the film, or both:

Don't give up the ship while we're sinking. I have a feeling this boat is never going to dock. We are going through the Straits of Dire. It's rough and choppy...

Marilyn references a poem by Yeats: "*...only God, my dear/Could love you for yourself alone/And not your yellow hair.*" At the bottom of the page, she handwrites a note about typing instead of writing because her hand was trembling.

Off-set, Marilyn reviewed Miller's tribute to her written to accompany a *Life* magazine spread. The year-end holiday issue (December 22, 1958), dedicated to entertainment, featured Marilyn as photographed by Richard Avedon in poses imitating her illustrious predecessors of the stage and screen: Lillian Russell, Theda Bara, Clara Bow, Jean Harlow, and Marlene Dietrich. According to Donald Spoto, Marilyn reacted negatively to Miller's tribute, focusing on her qualities of naiveté and sexual truth. On the evening of September 12, she telephoned her husband in New York as he spent the weekend with Jane and Bobby.

Donald Spoto examined a letter Miller wrote to Marilyn also dated September 12, possibly penned directly following the telephone conversation in an effort to express feelings he had been unable to verbalize. Miller addressed his wife as "Darling Girl," and referred to her as his ideal partner. He apologized for things he had not done in their relationship and for those he had. He also reported some progress in psychotherapy with Dr. Loewenstein and insight into his emotional blockage. Miller wrote that tears flowed from his eyes in love for her and concluded with a plea for her to love him and understand his mental confusion.

After the telephone conversation, Marilyn ingested too many sleeping pills and vomited violently. Although the overdose was not life threatening, Paula admitted her to a hospital for the weekend and Marilyn returned to work Monday morning. Several days later, she was admitted to Cedars of Lebanon Hospital for "nervous exhaustion." Wilder and Diamond had not yet written the film's ending but had to shoot around her.

In the final scene, Wilder's camera focuses on a close-up of Lemmon and Brown in the front seat of the motorboat. Marilyn and Curtis are not visible behind them, although they were shown kissing in the boat's rear seat in the previous sequence. This lack of continuity is due to Marilyn's absence during the filming of Lemmon and Brown's exchange. Wilder instructed Curtis to bend Marilyn out of the shot during the kiss to explain their invisibility in the film's last scene.

On October 27, Marilyn again wrote to Rosten on Bel Air Hotel stationary:

Thank you for your Halloween wishes. It's too bad we can't be together. I might scare you...it's so spooky here! Arthur looks well though weaker—from holding me up. Whatever happened to the "Mister Johnson Club"? Is Ben still giving free gas?

Marilyn signed the letter "e.e. cummings" whose poetry she enjoyed. The Johnson club was a private joke referencing Marilyn and other friends who invested in Rosten's failed play. Ben, Rosten's friend who owned a gas station, had once given Marilyn a tank of gas for no charge and had inducted him as an honorary member of the club.

On October 1, the production moved to soundstage 3 at the Goldwyn Studios. In the studio's screening theatre, Tony Curtis, Paula Strasberg, and others watched rushes of the hilarious yacht scene between Curtis' Joe as Junior and Sugar. Someone turned to Curtis and commented that he seemed to enjoy kissing Marilyn. "Kissing Marilyn is like kissing Hitler!" Curtis allegedly shot back. When the screening room lights came on, Paula was crying. "Why would you say such a terrible thing about her?" she sobbed. "Paula, you act with her," Curtis purportedly responded. "Then we'll see how you feel."

In the context of the era, a Jewish man using Hitler's name—the tyrant who imprisoned and murdered thousands of innocent Jews just over a decade before—as a reference for Marilyn to her mentor, a Jewish woman, was a flaming insult. Marilyn—who had converted to Judaism, married a Jew, and whose social support consisted of many Jewish people—was deeply hurt and offended. At the time, Marilyn's official response seemed in good humor: "He only said that because I wore prettier dresses than he did."

Marilyn didn't understand the basis for Curtis' betrayal given his kindness to her face. She told Rupert Allan that Curtis visited her dressing room every morning, complimented her appearance, and expressed excitement about their work. Allan believed the only thing Marilyn did to provoke Curtis' wrath was to tell Jack Lemmon at the end of production that it was wonderful working with him and her character should have ended up with him instead of Curtis.

Curtis' remarks about smooching Marilyn appeared in the *Cumberland Times* in May 1960, a year after the film's release, inciting many actors in Hollywood to announce their willingness to film love scenes with her. In a June 1960 interview for the *Deseret News*, Charlton Heston imparted his interest in trading Biblical roles for comedy scenes with Monroe: "I'd really like to do a picture with Marilyn," he said, "even if Tony Curtis says kissing her is like kissing Hitler." Perhaps critic Roger Ebert said it best when commenting about Curtis' remark, "When you watch that scene, all you can think is that Hitler must have been a terrific kisser."

Although Curtis would later deny insulting Marilyn, he continued to bash her to the press in the 1970s and 1980s. He was quoted in *Time Out* magazine: "She would come and tell *me* that I was funnier than Jack Lemon, then she'd tell Jack she wished she were ending up with *him* at the end of the movie...She was a 600-pound gorilla, y'know. About 680 pounds, actually..." Perhaps Curtis had forgotten his co-star was pregnant.

Time and age seemed to have softened Curtis' perception of Marilyn, though. As his career declined and public interest in Marilyn grew in the years following her death, Curtis began to praise Marilyn as a means to remain relevant through connection to her legend. By the time *Some Like It Hot* was touted as the Best Comedy of All Time and released on DVD, Curtis told critic Leonard Maltin that working with Marilyn was "fabulous...wonderful..."

Curtis published his second autobiography, *American Prince: A Memoir* in 2008 and *The Making of Some Like It Hot* in 2009. In the latest book, Curtis preposterously alleges that he was the father of the child Marilyn was carrying during the production. In a review for the *San Francisco Chronicle*, Mick LaSalle wrote of Curtis "underscore[ing] one of the unsung advantages of longevity: If you live long enough, you can claim to have had sex with any of your contemporaries, so long as they're not around to deny it." A personal note written by Marilyn and discovered posthumously in one of her filing cabinets may support this: "*There is only one way he could comment on my sexuality and I'm afraid he has never had the opportunity!*"

In her last interview for *Life*, Marilyn expressed lingering pain over Tony Curtis' alleged insult. "You've read there was some actor that once said about me that kissing me was like kissing Hitler," Marilyn said with a sad laugh. "If I have to do intimate love scenes with somebody who really has these kinds of feelings toward me, then my fantasy can come into play. In other words, out with him, in with my fantasy." In the audiotapes of the interview, Marilyn's voice begins to shake with intensity: "He was never there."

Another frequently cited incident illustrated Marilyn's uncharacteristic behavior during this period. In her dressing room, Marilyn was reading Thomas Paine's *Rights of Man* (1791), advocating a liberal worldview and challenging political oppression. Assistant Director Hal Polaire knocked on the dressing room door. "We're ready for you, Miss Monroe," he said. The degree of offensiveness in Marilyn's abrupt reply varies according to the source: "Drop dead," Edwin P. Hoyt reported in *Marilyn: The Tragic Venus*. "Go screw!" Miller told Fred Lawrence Guiles, as recounted by Marilyn. "Fuck you!" according to Billy Wilder. "Go fuck yourself!" quotes Norman Mailer.

"Maybe she doesn't consider that directors and assistant directors have rights," commented Wilder, referring to the topic of the book she was reading during the incident. "Or maybe she doesn't consider us men." Biographer Norman Mailer viewed this episode as Marilyn's anticipation of "how a future generation of women would evaluate the rights of men." In Guiles' 1969 biography, Wilder attributed Marilyn's profanity as "adamant refusal to be caught up in the studio pressure surrounding any film production." In Guiles' 1984 edition, he wonders if Marilyn's obscenity stems from a split personality as she is performing as a sexy, cheerful girl, but—in reality—she feels rage.

Biographer Sarah Churchwell identifies sexist bias in attributing the discrepancy between Marilyn's screen performance and her on-set behavior to dissociation. "The effect of this is to deny the reality of her arrogance, to refuse her the dignity of her own rage," argues Churchwell. "Would a biographer ask the same question about a male actor who told a director to go fuck himself? Frank Sinatra evidently said it all the time, and no one calls him schizoid, just arrogant. End of story."

The true testament of Marilyn's fine acting is the image she projected on the screen, at times incongruent with her emotional state during the actual performances. For instance, Marilyn appears delightful and effervescent in *The Seven Year Itch* while her marriage to DiMaggio was ending and she is enchanting in *The Prince and the Showgirl*, despite having been degraded by her director and betrayed by her husband. Co-star Jack Lemmon seemed to empathize most with Marilyn's inner torment while honoring her ability to create a characterization separate from the turmoil the actress was experiencing in her personal and professional life. "It *was* moving," he would say. "Acting with her on that picture, I felt she was, inside, deeply unhappy. She was no 'giddy blonde'. She had a certain intelligence in and about her work, and she was smart enough to use herself to make Sugar come alive."

Photographer Earl Leaf also admired Marilyn's best work rendered at a time of intense psychological and emotional distress. "It makes one think of the last paintings of Van Gogh or the mid-Fifties recordings of Bud Powell," he later wrote. "The marvel is that one living such a hell could work at all, much less work greatly. It speaks again of the strength of Marilyn Monroe's gifts. Something within this woman was uncannily resilient and determined." The production's final scenes required strenuous physical effort in high temperatures, and Marilyn risked her own health and the health of her unborn baby. To avoid a complication in the pregnancy, she returned to the hospital and took to her bed at the hotel.

Shooting wrapped on November 6. Wilder exacted his revenge by excluding Marilyn from the dinner party he held for the rest of the cast, but she had more serious concerns. Her miscarriage started twelve hours after filming ended, when she collapsed and was taken by ambulance to Cedars of Lebanon where a doctor determined the baby was in grave danger. Released, Marilyn returned to the Bel Air Hotel where she was ordered to a week's bed rest to save her unborn child. When Anne Karger arrived at the suite for a visit before the Millers left for the east coast, Marilyn stood to embrace her. "It's the least I can do when someone I love comes to see me," Marilyn explained.

Marilyn and Miller traveled to the airport by ambulance and then back home to New York. The New York maid, Lena Pepitone, arranged a framed photograph of Marilyn's mother on her night table next to a miniature cradle and a toy for the baby. Upon returning home and discovering this loving gesture, Marilyn burst into tears.

While Miller worked in his study, he heard Marilyn scream in agony. An ambulance transported the couple to Polyclinic Hospital where Marilyn's worst fear was realized and she lost their baby. On December 17, the Millers announced it to the press. Marilyn perceived the miscarriage as a personal failure and sign that she was unlovable, unworthy and even, cursed.

* * *

The closing scene of *Some Like It Hot* is one of the most memorable finales in motion picture history; the final line competes with Clark Gable's "Frankly, my dear, I don't give a damn" and Vivien Leigh's, "After all, tomorrow is another day" in *Gone With the Wind.* In Wilder's farce, Daphne/Jerry attempts to convince Osgood that she is an unsuitable spouse, but Osgood is undaunted. Daphne confesses that she smokes; Osgood doesn't care. Daphne confesses to having lived with a saxophone player; Osgood forgives her. Daphne announces she can never have children; Osgood offers to adopt. Finally, Jerry rips off his wig, and in his male voice, reveals that he is a man. Oblivious, Osgood replies, "Well—nobody's perfect." I.A.L. Diamond wrote this final punch line the night before the scene was filmed. In the original script, Wilder and Diamond added, "But that's another story—and we're not quite sure the public is ready for it."

Publicity posters for *Some Like It Hot* announced "Marilyn Monroe and her bosom companions Tony Curtis and Jack Lemmon" starring in a Billy Wilder Production that was "too HOT for words." Sandra Warner actually posed for publicity photos wearing Marilyn's costumes alongside the male leads in drag because Marilyn's advanced pregnancy prevented her appearance. Long before digital technology, meticulous touch-up artists inserted images of Marilyn's head onto Warner's body.

In December 1958, *Some Like It Hot* had a sneak preview at Bay Theatre in Pacific Palisades. It followed the featured film *Suddenly Last Summer*, a drama by Tennessee Williams with references to lobotomies and cannibalism and starring Katharine Hepburn, Montgomery Clift, and Elizabeth Taylor. At the film's climax, Taylor's character discloses that her brother lured the young men of the town into sexual situations during a trip to Spain the previous summer and was subsequently killed and mutilated:

> *He was lying naked on the broken stone...It looked as if...as if they had devoured him! As if they'd torn or cut parts of him away with their hands, or with knives, or those jagged tin cans they made music with. As if they'd torn bits of him away in strips!*

Following this riveting trifecta of insanity, trauma, and homicidal homophobia, the comedy about two cross-dressing men played. According to Jack Lemmon, it was the worst preview he had attended. In response, Wilder cut just one sequence from his film, wherein Sugar accepts Josephine's offer to trade berths, as she cannot sleep above the ever-snoring Bienstock. Curtis' character delivers a pricelessly racy line, "I can fall asleep anywhere, anytime, over anybody." Jerry sneaks into what he believes to be Sugar's berth only to confess his feminine disguise to a furious Joe. Despite the debacle at the Bay Theatre, however, news was far worse in New York, where Marilyn suffered a miscarriage at Polyclinic Hospital.

Tides turned when the film was shown in Westwood Village on December 17th. "You could not hear anything going on from one minute into that film," recalled Lemmon. "All the kids, their parents, whoever, were screaming with laughter. It was an absolute smash, and it was the same film." On the same day, Marilyn's miscarriage was announced to the press. Wilder acknowledged Marilyn as a trouper: "She insisted on going on until we were ready to finish." The actress saved the film at the expense of her losing her baby; her anguish was inconsolable, and no one could blame her.

From a window in the Goldwyn Studios, photographer Phil Stern had secretly taken photos of an obviously pregnant Marilyn arriving on the set and walking with Paula Strasberg. She appears about five or six months pregnant. Before the photographs could be published, Marilyn was grieving the loss of her baby. She had been convinced its gender was female.

Having contained much of his escalating frustration and anger toward Marilyn during the production, Wilder sought revenge through an interview with Joe Hyams of the *New York Herald Tribune*. Initially, he made an allusion to his feelings about Monroe: "I am eating better. My back doesn't ache anymore. I am able to sleep for the first time in months. I can look at my wife without wanting to hit her because she's a woman." Then the floodgates opened; Wilder announced he was the only director to have made two films with Marilyn Monroe and earned a Purple Heart from the Screen Actor's Guild.

When Hyams asked if Wilder would be interested in making a third film with Marilyn, he replied, "Well, I have discussed this project with my doctor and my psychiatrist, and they tell me I'm too old and too rich to go through this again."

Several days after reading Wilder's published remarks, Marilyn overdosed. Lena Pepitone summoned Norman and Hedda Rosten to the apartment. By the time the couple arrived from Brooklyn, the doctor had discreetly pumped Marilyn's stomach, and Miller put her to bed. Miller took offense by what he perceived as Wilder's lack of empathy and denigration of Marilyn, whose performance greatly contributed to the success of both the film and its director.

In a subsequent telegram to Wilder, Miller defended his wife's honor, sparking an escalating argument through a series of irate correspondence published in Maurice Zolotow's *Billy Wilder in Hollywood* and Sandra Shevey's *The Marilyn Scandal*.

Wilder was officially informed by Marilyn's physician that she was pregnant and unable to work a full day, Miller wrote with anger. He went on to accuse the director of ignoring this justification and intentionally failing to mention it in his public "attack" on her. Miller cited Wilder's criticism as "contemptible" since the film's success was due largely to Marilyn's performance and guaranteed the director a sizeable profit. Miller confronted Wilder as an "unjust" and "cruel" man. The telegram ended with a tribute to his wife: "Despite you, her beauty and humanity shine through as they always have."

Wilder expressed his condolences about the miscarriage but rejected the implication that "overwork or inconsiderate treatment" was responsible for the miscarriage. He further claimed the entire company had essentially "coddled" Marilyn, and if Miller polled the cast crew, he would face his wife's "overwhelming lack of popularity."

Wilder refused to back down and wrote that if Miller had been subjected to such indignities, he would have "thrown her out on her can, thermos bottle and all." The reference to a line from the film relating to the band manager threatens to throw Sugar off the train for sneaking liquor from the flask hidden in her garter implies Marilyn spiked her coffee with alcohol.

"She did her job and did it superbly," Miller responded, "while your published remarks create the contrary impression without any mitigation." In one telegram, Miller referred to Marilyn as "the salt of the earth." Wilder responded that the salt of the earth told an assistant director "to go fuck himself."

Finally, Wilder conceded with some remorse and good humor, borrowing from the film's final line: "I hereby acknowledge that good wife Marilyn is a unique personality and I am the beast of Belsen [a reference to the Nazi concentration camp, mirroring Curtis' insulting claim that kissing Marilyn was like kissing Hitler] but in the immortal words of Joe E. Brown quote nobody is perfect end quote."

The flurry of angry telegrams between the Pulitzer Prize winning playwright and celebrated screenwriter/director ended with a truce, but journalist Art Buchwald confronted Wilder on his harsh commentary. Wilder responded with his usual sardonic humor, claiming to have spoken "under duress" and the "influence of barbiturates," and that he was "suffering from high blood pressure," and had been "brainwashed."

Marilyn seemed most hurt by Wilder's rant about not wanting to work with her again as she hoped they would collaborate in the future. While having lunch with Marilyn at Romanoff's, Rupert Allan called Wilder and confronted him about what Marilyn had been reading in newspapers and magazines. Wilder told Allan not to believe "that shit they put in the papers" and confirmed he would "love" to work with her again. Allan handed the receiver to Marilyn, and she had a joyous conversation with the director. According to Allan, she "roared" with laughter.

In the 1980s, Marilyn's publicist John Springer recounted that Marilyn had been deeply hurt by Wilder's negative remarks, but that the director had sung her praises after the film's release. "She is a very great actress," he would assert in 1960. "Better Marilyn late than most of the others on time." Marilyn may have eventually forgiven Wilder, but his remarks wounded her nonetheless. Three years later, she clearly referred to the incident in her final interview with Richard Meryman for *Life*. "You're always running into people's unconscious," Marilyn said. "Let's take some actors—or directors. Usually they don't say it to me, they say it to the newspapers because that's a bigger play. You know, if they're only insulting me to my face that doesn't make a big enough play because all I have to do is say, 'See you around, like never.' But if it's the newspapers, it's coast to coast and on around the world...I don't understand why people aren't a little more generous with each other," She offered an explanation for Curtis' and Wilder's biting remarks saying. "I don't like to say this, but I'm afraid there is a lot of envy in this business."

Sarah Churchwell identified a misogynistic basis for each man's resentment of Marilyn's power. Wilder wanted to "beat her into submission," and Curtis stated that power "made her a monster." Both responses, noted Churchwell, disturbingly associated Marilyn's power with violence.

As time distanced Wilder from the experience on set, his feelings for Marilyn softened, and he hoped to work with her again. "I miss her," he said after her death. "It was like going to the dentist, making a picture with her. It was hell at the time, but after it was over, it was wonderful." When Wilder accepted the American Film Institute's Lifetime Achievement Award in 1986, he included Marilyn in the list of colleagues he singled out with appreciation. "We just happen to miss her like hell..." a tearful Wilder would tell a biographer. "Never a week passes when I don't wish she was still around... Because that whole category of films is lost. Her kind of genius is a lost art...Unless you have nerves of iron and total dedication, like climbing the Himalayas, let's turn back. But you go on with Marilyn, and it's worth it. The luminosity of that face!" The celebrated director's definitive analysis of Marilyn is a loving tribute expressed long after her death:

She was an absolute genius as a comic actress, with an extraordinary sense for comic dialogue. It was a God-given gift. Believe me, in the last fifteen years there were ten projects that came to me, and I'd start working on them and I'd think, "It's not going to work, it needs Marilyn Monroe. Nobody else is in that orbit; everyone else is earthbound by comparison.

Some Like It Hot premiered on March 29, 1959, as the inaugural attraction of the newly renovated Loew's Capitol Theatre on Broadway and 45th Street in the heart of New York's Times Square. Advertisements boasted the "new easy-chair orchestra lounger seats properly spaced, new multi-channel hi-fi stereo sound, new robot-controlled all-weather air-conditioning..."

Marilyn emerged from a black Cadillac limousine as a luminous vision in silver and white on the arm of Miller as the police held back a mob of onlookers. She looked absolutely magnificent and was the epitome of a glamorous Hollywood movie icon. Her platinum hair was teased in a bouffant style. She wore pendant rhinestone earrings, a silver dress, and stole of white chiffon was trimmed with white fox fur. Her dazzling full-length evening sheath of ivory crepe was embroidered with silvered clear bugle beads, its skirt adorned with shimmering pendant bugle beads. Its halter neckline had shoe-string straps and a plunging rear décolletage. The dangling bugle beads swayed with the undulation of Marilyn's graceful walk as she glided along the red carpet.

Contrastingly, Miller looked stoic in a bow tie, tuxedo, topcoat and hat. He managed to smile for the press photographers and newsreel cameramen. Marilyn appeared visibly nervous while interviewed in the lobby and she regressed to her childhood stammer. The brief conversation focused on the mob scene outside, but Marilyn used this public opportunity to praise Jack Lemon as "the funniest man in the world."

Lena Pepitone's ostensibly ghostwritten memoir erroneously claims that Marilyn, horrified by her noticeable weight gain on the screen, had a hysterical screaming fit after the New York premiere. Pepitone seems unaware that her employer had been pregnant during the production. In reality, Marilyn was joyous. James Haspiel published a stunning photograph of a triumphantly smiling Marilyn, wearing her spangled evening dress, en route to the premiere celebration at the Strasbergs' Central Park West apartment. Pepitone's ghostwriter William Stadiem arguably had not adequately researched his subject before writing the dramatic scene, overlooking Marilyn and Miller's attendance at an advance screening of the film on February 5 at Loew's State Theatre. The couple was photographed arriving at the event and during their viewing of the completed film.

Published photographs captured the Millers joining in the audience's laughter. Professionally, the subsequent official premiere was one of Marilyn's most shining hours. "To get down to cases, Marilyn does herself proud," announced the *New York Post*, "giving a performance of such intrinsic quality that you begin to believe she's only being herself and it is herself who fits into that distant period and this picture so well."

"As the band's somewhat simple singer-ukulele player, Miss Monroe, whose figure simply cannot be overlooked, contributes more assets than the obvious ones to this mad-cap romp," opined A. H. Weiler of *The New York Times*. "As a pushover for gin and the tonic effect of saxophone players, she sings a couple of whispery old numbers...and also proves to be the epitome of a dumb blonde and a talented comedienne." Weiler's rave was overshadowed when the newspaper's persnickety critic Bosely Crowther later called Marilyn a "superb" comedienne.

"*Some Like It Hot*, directed in masterly style by Billy Wilder is probably the funniest picture of recent memory," *Variety* reported. "It's a wacky, clever, farcical comedy that starts off like a firecracker and keeps on throwing off lively sparks till the very end...To coin a phrase, Marilyn has never looked better. Her performance as 'Sugar', the fuzzy blonde who likes saxophone players and men with glasses, has a deliciously naïve quality. She's a comedienne with that combination of sex appeal and timing that can't be beat."

Some Like It Hot ran $500,000 over budget and was produced for a total cost of $2.8 million. It grossed $20 million upon the initial release and came in third behind *Auntie Mame*, starring Rosalind Russell, and *The Shaggy Dog* as biggest films of 1959—a time when the average admission cost fifty-one cents. In 2014, the average admission price was $8.35; in today's prices, the film grossed over $327 million. It also out-grossed all other films for first six months of 1959 and for many years held the record for comedy success at the box office. Residuals on *Some Like It Hot* earned Marilyn's estate an average of $55,077 per year through 1980, before VHS sales commenced. By 1999, two years before its release on DVD, the film grossed over $47 million, earning $4,500,000 for Marilyn Monroe's heirs.

Marilyn appeared on the cover of *Life* on April 20, 1959, with the kicker, "A Comic Marilyn Sets Movie Aglow." In the photograph by Richard Avedon, she playfully bites on a dangling earring. The magazine also published a photograph of Wilder demonstrating for Marilyn how to swish through the puff of steam from the train. "Directing Marilyn Monroe in a movie is not the unalloyed delight a man might think," *Life* told the world. "She often reports late for work. Sometimes she doesn't report at all. When she does report she is likely to go off in a corner to commune with her soul. She wants to hear music. She does not want to hear cursing. Marilyn has filled his movie with fun and set it afire—and last week, its run just starting, it was top moneymaker in the key cities of the nation."

Cosmopolitan magazine spotlighted a portrait of Marilyn by writer Jon Whitcomb on its March 1959 cover in wardrobe as Sugar with her mole prominently visible on her chin rather than her cheek. The article, also penned by Whitcomb, "The New Marilyn," announced the film as her comeback. Other articles advertised on the cover addressed topics such as "our moral revolt" over the past forty years, citing spouse swapping, sex education, and the rising divorce rate.

The Kansas Board of Review censored one hundred five feet of film from the seduction scene aboard the yacht, and the Roman Catholic Legion of Decency rated the film "Class C" in part due to Marilyn's costumes. Formed in 1934 by Catholic bishops, this archconservative watchdog group instructed parishioners to avoid films rated as objectionable. The Legion published rating lists in which films were designated as Class A, unobjectionable; Class B, objectionable in part; and the dreaded Class C, condemned. Condemnation was reserved for films containing suggestive dialogue or lack of moral compensation. The following year, Alfred Hitchcock's classic thriller *Psycho* would earn the same rating. As the film did not receive Production Code approval, it was released without the Motion Picture Association of America's logo in the title sequence and credits.

During the consecutive months of April, May, and June 1959, *Some Like It Hot* was the most popular movie in the United States and around the world. Marilyn's universal appeal made the film popular in Latin America, Asia, the Middle East, and Europe. Critics and audiences unanimously agreed. From the moment Sugar Kane appeared onscreen until the final fade out, one could easily fall in love with Marilyn Monroe for the first time or all over again. The role captured many of the actress' most endearing traits: innocence, mischievousness, sweetness, determination, hopefulness, and vulnerability. "Monroe steals [the film]," wrote contemporary film critic Roger Ebert, "as she walked away with every movie she was in. It is an act of will to watch anyone else."

Some Like It Hot garnered six nominations by the Academy of Motion Picture Arts and Sciences in the categories of Best Director (Billy Wilder), Best Actor (Jack Lemmon), Best Adapted Screenplay (Wilder and I.A.L. Diamond), Best Black and White Cinematography (Charles Lang, Jr.), Best Black and White Art Direction/Set Decoration (Ted Haworth), and Best Black and White Costume Design (Orry-Kelly).

It would win only one for its costumes. The Hollywood Foreign Press Association honored the film with three Golden Globe Awards in all the categories in which it was nominated: Best Comedy Film, Best Actor (Jack Lemmon), and Best Actress (Marilyn Monroe). The soundtrack would even be nominated for a Grammy Award. Just as *Some Like It Hot* was a derivative of earlier work, it spawned similar incarnations, most notably *Tootsie* (1982) and *Mrs. Doubtfire* (1993), respectively with Dustin Hoffman and Robin Williams in drag.

"*Some Like It Hot* was like the perfect soufflé ever made," Sandra Warner concluded in 2001. "It had the perfect ingredients. It has the greatest script, a great cast, a great director—Billy Wilder was the best chef."

* * *

[For a synopsis of *Some Like It Hot*, see **Appendix: Selected Marilyn Monroe Film Synopses**]

CHAPTER EIGHT: NOVEMBER–DECEMBER 1958

In November, when the production of *Some Like It Hot* ended in sunny southern California, a pregnant Marilyn returned to the autumn chill of New York. Marilyn was greeted home with a telegram from L'Academie du Cinema in Paris announcing her as the recipient of the Crystal Star Award for Best Foreign Actress of 1957. On November 26, 1958, she sent the following edited version of a rambling response that led to both a postponement and relocation of the presentation ceremony:

> *Because of some recent complications in regards to the pregnancy, my doctor has forbidden travel of any kind...I hope you will understand that only a circumstance so important to me as this could have possibly kept me from coming...my warmest thanks again for this great honor.*

For its December 1958 year-end holiday special issue, *Life* magazine's movie editor Mary Leatherbee needed a splashy centerpiece while fashion editor Sally Kirkland wanted a photographic essay on the cosmetic trend of the year, thick black eyeliner. Brainstorming sessions generated the idea that Marilyn's soon-to-be-released period film would meet the needs of both editors. In the resultant article, "A Recreation of Fabled Enchantresses," Marilyn impersonated a few of the iconic females in the entertainment industry: Lillian Russell (1860-1922), Theda Bara (1885-1955), Clara Bow (1905-1965), Marlene Dietrich (1901-1992), and Jean Harlow (1911-1937).

Life engaged fashion photographer Richard Avedon to capture the images during an evening shoot at Marilyn's request. Robert Mackintosh designed the costumes, elaborate set designs, props, and makeup, and Petty Nelson Blake was the stylist. Marilyn approached the assignment as a Method actress. "Between exposures she didn't hide her sense of humor," Avedon told *Life*, "but then in a split second she would become the actress she was portraying."

In every generation, the entertainment industry produces an enchantress who embodies the fancies of men, *Life* announced in a photographic spread of Marilyn's stunning impersonations of her predecessors. Representing the modern female ideal, Marilyn also posed as herself in a contemporary sequin gown worn previously in promotional photographs for *The Prince and the Showgirl*. The accompanying essay celebrated each of the enchantresses as unique and original. "In our time," wrote *Life*, "Marilyn is their heiress."

The piece was a huge success and generated the sale of over six million issues, the highest circulation figure at the time in the magazine's history. Marilyn would still be talking about it to Simone Signoret with extreme pride during the filming of *Let's Make Love* in the spring of 1960. The *Life* article also included a portrait of Marilyn embracing a seated Miller from behind, her cheek pressed against his. Smiling under his wife, Miller appears somewhat childlike. Miller penned a tribute to Marilyn especially for the piece, noting the "beauty of the spirit in her everyday actions, playing with their dog, styling the housekeeper's hair, or bursting into a room to report exciting news." Miller also honored his wife's "*spontaneous joy*" in observing children and her respect for the elderly.

Miller was most amazed by his wife's impersonation of Clara Bow. Dressed in period costume and a red wig, Marilyn walked onto the set filled with the sound of recorded music of the 1920s. Avedon started shooting, and Marilyn performed as if she were making a film. "Her miraculous sense of sheer play had been unloosed," Miller wrote.

Excitement about the photographic essay ended abruptly with Marilyn's miscarriage shortly before the Christmas holidays. Poet and author Louis Untermeyer of Newton, Connecticut sent Marilyn a heartfelt note of sympathy on December 20:

It's grimly ironic that while the rest of the country was enjoying the comedy of your impersonations in LIFE, you were going through your personal tragedy. We hope you are not taking the irony too bitterly, and we hope, moreover, that you will have sufficiently recovered to get some pleasure from the holidays...Everyone loves you—especially now.

J. Randy Taraborrelli interviewed an unidentified friend who recounted her memory of helping Marilyn search through her closet to find something to wear for dinner shortly after the miscarriage. When Marilyn discovered a maternity blouse, she begged her friend to dispose of it for her. Moments later, Marilyn found more maternity garments and gasped. She started removing all the maternity clothes from the closet and wept. All she had wanted was to wear a pretty outfit. Marilyn shipped the maternity clothes to half-sister Berniece with a request that Mona, Berniece's daughter, receive them, and successfully become a mother someday.

During this period, Marilyn and Miller went backstage at The Mocambo to meet singer Diahann Carroll, who was pregnant with her daughter, Suzanne. Marilyn asked permission to touch her tummy. Delighted, Carroll took Marilyn's hand and placed it against her swelling belly. "You pat right here, sweetheart, and say a prayer and a wish," the singer said, "and I'll hope with all my heart that your dreams come true." Marilyn looked at Carroll with tears in her eyes.

Marilyn's depression and irritability only worsened after the miscarriage. As Miller emotionally withdrew, she became increasingly angry and resentful toward him, creating a toxic cycle. Susan Strasberg remembered Marilyn frequently contradicting her husband and insulting him. "Get my mink coat!" Marilyn shrieked at Miller. One of Susan's actor friends confronted the behavior. "Then why didn't he slap me?" Marilyn asked, now feeling guilty. "He should have slapped me." Perhaps due to physical abuse in her childhood and domestic violence during her marriage to DiMaggio, Marilyn sadly believed that she deserved violent retaliation for her behavior.

When tensions arose in the Miller apartment, Marilyn had no family members to seek out for solace. On occasion, she would take a cab to the Strasberg apartment where she sought comfort and nurturing from parental figures who attempted to soothe and support her through the crisis. With her head slumped, Marilyn sat at the kitchen table while Paula mothered her with advice and food and Lee reassured her like a patient, loving father. Marilyn was "preprogrammed" for rejection and betrayal, Paula told Susan. If anyone looked at her with a harsh expression, made a sudden move, or had a certain tone in his voice, Marilyn would be reminded of a traumatic childhood event.

When Marilyn was inconsolable, the Strasbergs invited her to spend the night in John's bed, displacing him to the sofa. Once, in the middle of the night while John was not sleeping at home, Susan couldn't sleep and went out into the hall on her way to the kitchen for a glass of milk. She saw a half-naked Marilyn in a drugged state crawl on her hands and knees to Lee and Paula's bedroom and scratch on the door like an animal. Lee came out in an old blue bathrobe, carried her back to John's room and left the door partly open. Susan felt resentful at the sight of her father cradling Marilyn in his arms and singing a lullaby he had sung when his own daughter was a little girl.

Marilyn feared the rage inside her and felt more comfortable stuffing it or turning it against herself rather than unleashing it on others. "If I expressed everything inside me," she confessed to Susan. "I'd explode like Hiroshima, and I'd probably kill someone...maybe myself."

It was during this period that Marilyn shared with Norman Rosten a disturbing poem she had written in her journal:

Help help
Help I feel life coming closer
When all I want to do is die

Marilyn expressed her ambivalent feelings about life and death through prose that insightfully acknowledges her innate resiliency. In *Life—I Am of Both Your Directions*, she identifies as a sheer cobweb hanging downward in cold frost and celebrates her strength in having survived both strong winds and leaping flames.

CHAPTER NINE: 1959

Author Fred Kaplan touts 1959 as a pivotal year in the cultural shift from pre-World War II traditions to the world we know today. He cites its major events as catalysts for changes in sexual behavior, citizens' views of the government, and information exchange. During the year, the Federal Drug Administration approved the birth control pill, American soldiers were killed in Vietnam, and Texas Instruments' introduction of the microchip heralded the approaching Information Age of personal computers, cell phones, and digital technology. Kaplan points to the year's noteworthy architectural, musical, and literary works as examples of deviation from convention: the completion of Frank Lloyd Wright's innovatively designed Guggenheim Museum in New York City, the release of Miles Davis' revolutionary jazz album *Kind of Blue*, and the publishing of William Burroughs' radical novel, *Naked Lunch*.

The courts also expanded the scope of what Americans would be allowed to see and read. Grove Press fought legal battles to publish D.H. Lawrence's 1928 novel *Lady Chatterley's Lover*, previously banned in the United States due to graphic sexual content. Simultaneously, the United States Supreme Court reversed the New York censors' refusal to license a French film based on the same work.

Jack Kerouac and Allen Ginsberg, writers of the beat generation, revolted against the conformity and conservatism of American white, middle-class, heterosexual, Christian life of the staid 1950s. *The Sick Humor of Lenny Bruce*, a comic record album—devoid of conventional jokes but filled with observations about sex, religion and politics—crossed the boundaries of what was considered appropriate material for entertainment and public discussion. *Breathless*, the first film to employ New Wave cinematography, utilized hand-held cameras and jump shots, commonplace techniques in twenty-first century film and television.

Pan American World Airways' Boeing 707 passenger airplane provided the first nonstop jet flight across the Atlantic Ocean. NASA selected its first *Mercury 7* astronauts and led the space race to land the first man on the moon. Madison Avenue's advertising industry used phrases like "jet age," "space age," and "the countdown to tomorrow" to sell products ranging from automobiles to floor wax.

For Marilyn, the first days of this watershed year were shrouded by a deepening depression. Looking out her apartment window on East Fifty-Seventh Street, she observed gray skies, bare trees, and sidewalks covered in snow. Emotionally, she felt barren and numb. Norman Rosten wrote of finding Marilyn sitting on a windowsill in Willard Maas' penthouse overlooking the Brooklyn Bridge. Allegedly, Maas—an experimental filmmaker and poet—and his wife, Marie Menken, inspired Edward Albee's battling couple in *Who's Afraid of Virginia Woolf?* On that evening, Rosten felt more concern over Marilyn's mental state than his hosts' turbulent marriage.

Marilyn told Rosten it was a quick fall down to the pavement from the window. This was the first time she had disclosed suicidal thoughts to him. "Who'd know the difference if I died?" she asked. "I would and all the people in this room who care," Rosten said, lovingly gripping her shoulder. "They'd hear the crash." Marilyn laughed. The pair jokingly made a pact: if one of them considered suicide, he or she would phone the other. There by the window, Marilyn and Rosten promised to talk each other out of suicide.

A letter from Rosten, postmarked January 6, 1959, implies that Marilyn's closest friends considered the role of Sugar in the soon-to-be released *Some Like Hot* as trivial and appears to have referenced Marilyn's recent suicidal thoughts. Rosten's cavalier reference in the letter indicates that he did not perceive his friend's disclosure as serious: "*About the movie—don't jump!...it is a completely enjoyable film, full of fun and YOU...I feel it is a shame you didn't get more to do, and better lines for what you did do...nothing could really destroy your wonderful quality that gives the film the one touch of "seriousness" (humanity) it needs for any sort of balance.*"

When not suffering from episodes of serious symptoms of depression, Marilyn's typical routine throughout the year consisted of awaking at 8:30 in the morning to take Hugo for a walk while the cook made breakfast. When the cook wasn't working, Marilyn got up early to cook. She believed a married man should never have to prepare his own meals. "I'm very old-fashioned that way," she told French journalist Georges Belmont. "I also don't think a man should carry a woman's belongings, like her high-heeled shoes or her purse or whatever."

Marilyn usually enjoyed a long bath after breakfast to differentiate her nonworking days from the days she rose early and had a cold shower to get to the studio on time. While soaking in the tub, she read the *New York Times* and listened to music. On Tuesdays and Fridays, Marilyn attended the Actors Studio at eleven o'clock in the morning; on Mondays, Wednesdays and Thursdays, she attended private classes with Lee Strasberg. Marilyn normally returned home for lunch and ate dinner there with Miller and played classical or jazz music during their meal.

"I like to cook..." Marilyn said of her household routine. "I can make bread and noodles—you know, roll them up and dry them, and prepare a sauce. Those are my specialties. Sometimes I invent recipes. I love lots of seasonings. I love garlic, but sometimes it's too much for other people."

On occasion, fellow students from the Actors Studio visited, and Marilyn served them breakfast or tea while they studied. Her daytime schedule was generally full, but she reserved her evenings for quality time with Miller. After dinner, the couple often attended theatre or the cinema. They occasionally entertained friends or visited others. When the weather in New York was mild, they strolled in Central Park.

"I like people," Marilyn said, "but sometimes I wonder how sociable I am. I can easily be alone and it doesn't bother me. I don't mind it—it's like a rest, it kind of refreshes myself...I have a gay side to me and also a sad side. That's a real problem. I've very sensitive to that. That's why I love my work. When I'm happy with it, I feel more sociable. If not, I like to be alone."

Marilyn remained selective of her friends and preferred the company of Norman and Hedda Rostens, Sam and Anne Shaw, Frank and Nan Taylor, and the Strasbergs. She described herself as impetuous and exclusive to journalist Georges Belmont, intentionally avoiding public appearances as they attracted media intrusion. "I like people, but when it comes to friends, I only like a few. And when I love, I'm so exclusive that I really have only one idea in my mind."

Novelist Carson McCullers (1917-1967) invited the Millers to her home in in Nyack-on-Hudson, New York, on February 5 for a luncheon and discussion on poetry. McCullers wrote fiction exploring the isolation of misfits of the south in work such as *The Heart Is A Lonely Hunter* and *Reflections in a Golden Eye* and had been a friend since Marilyn arrived in New York in 1955. The two women had been neighbors at the Gladstone Hotel on East Fifty-Second Street. McCullers related to Marilyn's vulnerability and bouts of depression, and shared Marilyn's resilience and creativity.

McCuller suffered from several illnesses, including rheumatic fever and cerebral hemorrhages, leaving her left side paralyzed by the age of thirty-one. She married a soldier and author, Reeves McCullers, and they each engaged in same-gender love relationships before divorcing and remarrying. Carson attempted suicide in 1948. Five years later, Reeves tried to draw her into a suicide pact, but she left him once again, and he overdosed on sleeping pills in a Paris hotel. Director John Huston described Carson as "a fragile thing with great shining eyes, and a tremor in her hand as she placed it in mine. It wasn't palsy, rather a quiver of animal timidity. But there was nothing timid or frail about the manner in which Carson McCullers faced life. And as her afflictions multiplied, she only grew stronger."

The Millers collected Isak Dineson (1885-1962), known as Baroness Karen Blixen, and her secretary, Clara Svendsen, at a hotel in New York City and drove them to McCullers' home to attend the engagement. Dineson, the author of *Out of Africa* and *Babette's Feast*—both adapted into Academy Award winning films in the 1980s—was on a lecture tour of America. She had lived in Kenya where she operated a coffee plantation. "I think Marilyn is bound to make an almost overwhelming impression on the people who meet her the first time," Dineson wrote to writer Fleur Cowles Meyer in 1961. "It is not that she is pretty, but she radiates, at the same time, unbounded vitality and a kind of unbelievable innocence. I have met the same in a lion-cub, which my native servants in Africa brought me."

Eager to accept an invitation to join his cousin, McCullers, at the gathering for Dineson and to meet Marilyn Monroe, author Jordan

Massee asked his boss for the day off. "Well, you can take the week off if you want to," the boss advised, "just remember everything [Marilyn] says." Massee introduced himself to Marilyn as the person who lent his photos of Eleanora Duse to Sam Shaw to copy for her. "She was most charming and very animated and appreciative," Masse recalled. "She was absolutely delightful. Of course, everyone had to take second fiddle to Isak Denisen who talked non-stop." Dinesen enthralled the group with her story of the first lion she had killed in Kenya and having sent its skin to the King of Denmark.

According to McCullers' biographer, Virginia Carr, Marilyn charmed the group assembled in honor of Dineson with her marvelous sense of humor and an entertaining anecdote from her own kitchen. With a clever delivery, she poked fun at herself making homemade noodles for Arthur and their guests the way Arthur's mother made them. The attempt was such a failure that she feared losing not only a meal, but also a husband. Since the noodles hadn't dried by the time for the dinner party, she used a hair dryer to speed the process. When the enjoyable dinner party at McCullers' home had concluded, Marilyn and Miller returned to the city and attended the preview of *Some Like It Hot* at Loew's Lexington Theatre, where Marilyn wore the same black dress and jacket with fur collar from the luncheon.

In early 1959, Marilyn also spent time with poet Carl Sandburg (1878-1967), whom she met during the production of *Some Like It Hot.* He was a frequent guest at the Miller apartment and remained a friend until her death. Sandburg was a successful journalist, poet, historian, biographer, and autobiographer. During the course of his career, he won the Pulitzer Prize for his biography of Abraham Lincoln and for *The Complete Poems of Carl Sandburg.* "We agreed on a number of things," Sandburg said. "She sometimes threw her arms around me like people do who like each other very much. Too bad I was forty-eight years older—I couldn't play her leading man."

"Carl Sandburg, who's in his eighties—you should see his vitality," Marilyn would tell *Life*, "what he has contributed. Why, he could play the guitar until three in the morning. You can meet Carl Sandburg and he is so pleased to meet you. He wants to know about you and you want to know about him. Not in any way has he ever let me down."

On February 26, the French Film Industry presented Marilyn with its Crystal Star Award for Best Foreign Actress in *The Prince and the Showgirl* albeit late due to delays caused by her pregnancy and subsequent miscarriage. Wearing a black suit with pronounced fur collar, Marilyn accepted the award at the French Ambassador's Consulate on Fifth Avenue in New York and was enchanted by Georges Auric (1899-1983), the French composer, and the Ambassador's two Dachshunds. Following the presentation ceremony, the Ambassador hosted a champagne reception during which Marilyn cuddled and fussed over the dogs and was photographed holding one in each arm.

Marilyn had invited James Haspiel to her apartment after the event to celebrate his twenty-first birthday and to plant a kiss on his cheek. Dressed in a suit and tie, he arrived at the lobby of the Miller apartment accompanied by members of the Monroe Six. Miller seemed impatient when the group gathered to take photographs with his wife. It was the youth's birthday, Marilyn explained, and so she wanted to kiss him. After the peck, Marilyn stepped back to examine James' cheek and voiced disappointment at not leaving a lipstick print. She kissed him once more and whispered into his ear that she could remember when he was seventeen. The affectionate experience would remain unforgettable in Haspiel's memory.

On a Saturday afternoon in March, journalist Evan Michaels spotted Marilyn, wearing a loose camel's hair polo coat, strolling on Fifty-Seventh Street. He followed her for several hours as she shopped, and later interviewed clerks and proprietors who had waited on her. Michaels documented his observations in an article for *Photoplay* magazine and offered a glimpse into Marilyn's days in New York.

Joe Yulstra, a tall Dutch day doorman in Marilyn's apartment building, told Michaels, "The first time I saw her she was coming from the grocer's with a big bag. And some little boy said, 'Marilyn, Marilyn give me your autograph.' And do you know, she put her big package down and smiled and signed the little boy's notebook. Now isn't that something nice for her to do?"

The night-man, Jimmy McQuade, said in his charming Irish brogue, "She's the most sociable of anybody. She just loves kids. She wants a baby more than anything. Everybody says so. She'll always say hello to a little kid on the street or in the elevator. And you should see the way she treats Mr. Miller's two children. Just like she was their mother. She's always buttoning up Robert's coat if it's a cold day, and she goes out shopping with Jane for pretty dresses and things." To further the standpoint that Marilyn was unlike any typical movie star, when the maid was sick, Marilyn scrubbed her own floors and told a neighbor that hard work never hurt anyone.

Michaels tailed Marilyn to the 400 Cake Shop on First Avenue, where he later spoke with a server named Alma. Marilyn had a passion for poppy seed rolls and rye bread but avoided chocolate. She often purchased cheesecakes, macaroons, strawberry tarts, and layer cakes. Marilyn also shopped at Gristede Brothers Superior Market and was excited by new products like instant soup or unusual cheeses. She ordered meat personally to assure a prime cut.

Marilyn also frequented Sutton Place Stationers on First Avenue where she borrowed books from the rental library. Proprietor Jack Newman said, "She doesn't come in here too often by herself. Usually, she's with Mr. Miller, and she's holding his arm. I don't know why, but to me she's never seemed like Marilyn Monroe, the sexy girl in the movies. She's just like an everyday housewife who's crazy about her husband." Newman carried *The Collected Plays of Arthur Miller* and noted that Marilyn liked to point to it when they visited the shop together, and both of them would smile. The collection, published in 1957, was dedicated to Marilyn.

At Schrafft's Restaurant on Fifty-Seventh Street, Michaels observed Marilyn ordering an ice cream soda and then browsing in the nearby antique shops. A salesman at the French Antiques Store on Third Avenue told him that she loved antiques and enjoyed touching the surfaces of old chests to feel their smooth finishes.

With Michaels on her heels, Marilyn entered Bloomingdale's and headed to the housewares department. She handled bright yellow and green enameled pots and pans from Europe (possibly the Le Crueset set that was auctioned at her estate sale in 1999). Marilyn also watched a chef demonstrate how to bake French pastries. She picked up a recipe sheet and folded it into her coat pocket. Overhearing two middle-aged housewives discussing a shop that sold delicious polish sausages on Third Street, Marilyn slipped outside and hailed a taxi. Michaels followed close behind in another taxi to their destination, a parking lot. Marilyn stepped out of the taxi and seemed confused; Michaels stood discreetly nearby.

"Hey, mister," Marilyn called to Michaels. "Is this 685 Third Avenue?" He nodded. "But somebody said this is where they sold Polish sausage," Marilyn said with disappointment, "and I wanted to get some. My husband's crazy about it." Michaels remarked that the building might have been demolished. "Oh they're tearing down this whole city, and it makes me mad," she replied. "Isn't it a shame to see everything go?" Michaels marveled at how this typical housewife searching for her husband's favorite kielbasa morphed into a glamorous movie star the following week when he saw her at the premiere of *Some Like It Hot.*

In early April, Marilyn boarded an American Airlines plane at Idlewild Airport en route to Chicago for a promotional roadshow to publicize *Some Like It Hot.* She arrived at the Ambassador East Hotel in a turtleneck sheath, fur coat, and pumps. The film had premiered in New York City on March 29, and she garnered attention in the press for the remainder of the year.

Marilyn connected with her husband's friend, Jewish-American writer Saul Bellow (1915-2005), recipient of the Pulitzer Prize and Nobel Prize for Literature and professor at the Committee on Social Thought at the University of Chicago. He escorted her to the Ambassador's Pump Room restaurant where she signed the guest book with the inscription, "*Proud to be the guest of the Chicago writer Saul Bellow.*"

"*I have yet to see anything in Marilyn that isn't genuine,*" Bellow wrote in a letter to his Editor, Pascal Covici. "*Surrounded by thousands, she conducts herself like a philosopher.*" The writer found Marilyn particularly witty in the way she told him about her bodyguard leaving the bathroom door ajar—as the man was ordered not to let her out of his sight—and about her ten-inch sculptured bust of Carl Sandburg by Joseph Konzal (now a part of the Taper Collection owned by the Abraham Lincoln Presidential Library and Museum). "I always felt she had picked up some high-tension cable and couldn't release it," Bellow would say. "She couldn't rest, she found no repose in anything."

Marilyn delighted the midwestern newsmen with her views on underwear ("*I have no prejudice against it.*"), intellectualism ("*I don't consider myself an intellectual...this is not one of my aims...but I admire intellectual people.*"), and her public role as a sex symbol to men ("*How do I know about man's need for a sex symbol? I'm a girl.*").

Mervin Block, a reporter with the *Chicago American*, who attended a press luncheon with Marilyn at the Ambassador East, shared memories with biographer Donald Spoto: "Even when a nervous photographer spilled a drink all over the front of her dress, she remained calm, showed no anger, didn't act like the great star she was." Marilyn continued gaining weight on the roadshow as evidenced in photographs of her at the film's premiere in New York City in March. Regardless of whispers about changes in her figure, Marilyn enjoyed the enormous success of the film.

In 1956, crusty *New York Times* film critic Bosley Crowther announced that Marilyn Monroe had proven herself an actress, but with the success of *Some Like It Hot*, she achieved respect as an established performer at the peak of her career. She appeared in *Who's Who Current Biography 1959* and was lauded as having "successfully managed the difficult transition from star to actress." The article also quoted Wilder on Marilyn: "Her appeal stems from many things, including voice, grace of movement, and personality. She's an actress improving all the time."

While Fox continued searching for a property for Marilyn, executives scanned her list of approved directors. Former lover Elia Kazan, included in her list, voiced an interest in casting her in *Time and Tide*. The plot, about the 1930s Tennessee Valley Authority, was based on the novels *Mud on the Stars* by William Bradford Huie and *Dunbar's Cove* by Borden Deal. At the time, Kazan was in New York directing Tennessee Williams' *Sweet Bird of Youth*. Fox had officially assigned Marilyn to the film with a report date of April 14. Kazan requested that Fox hire Paul Osborn, who had written the screenplay for Kazan's masterpiece, *East of Eden*, to rewrite *Time and Tide*. Meanwhile, Marilyn was instructed to remain in New York while her salary commenced as scheduled.

As the weeks passed, Kazan announced that he preferred to cast Lee Remick, rejecting Marilyn as he had done for the role in *Baby Doll*. Movie magazines had already announced the project as her next film. Marilyn Monroe Productions sent a telegram reminding Fox that its star's obligation to perform in *Time and Tide* had expired. In her contract, Paragraph 8 stipulated that principal photography would begin no later than ten weeks after the film's start date. Marilyn demanded $100,000 for this film and *Blue Angel,* as well as release from the remaining three films required by the contact. She seemed to be severing her ties to the studio. On August 26, Fox made payment to Marilyn for the two films she never made but required her services for the three remaining films.

On May 13, Marilyn belatedly received the David di Donatello award for Best Actress for her performance in *The Prince and the Showgirl.* Over four hundred people attended the presentation at the Italian Consulate on Park Avenue. Filipo Donini, director of the Italian Cultural Institute, presented the award. Italian actress Anna Magnani, winner of the 1955 Academy Award for Best Actress in *The Rose Tattoo*, also participated in the event and warmly embraced Marilyn. Escorted by Miller, Marilyn wore a form-fitted sleeveless dress with a bodice of flesh colored chiffon embroidered with black scrolling foliage and beading, accompanied by a bolero jacket. Her Italian maid, Lena Pepitone, allegedly attended the event. Following the award presentation, the press interviewed Marilyn in a very warm location within the Consulate.

"Do you have a couple of words in your language for the Italian viewers?" a reporter asked. Marilyn covered the microphone with her hand and whispered in conference with Anna Magnani for a few seconds before responding: "*Sono commossa…grazie.* [I am touched…thank you.]"

"How do you feel about all this madness every time you come out and make a public appearance?" asked another reporter. "It looks as if we're all going to die of suffocation in here. Does it bother you that you cause such turmoil?"

"I'm honored," she replied.

"What's responsible for the improvement in your keeping time better than you did before?"

"I believe in improvement."

"You have been improving. There's no doubt about it. What or who inspired it?"

"I guess maturity inspires it."

"You mean about getting here on time?"

"Yes, I was punctual."

"Does this mean you turned over a new leaf?"

"I hope so."

"You're going to be prompt from now on?"

"Yes...Who gave...? Someone handed me a glass of water."

"They thought you looked pretty warm," a reporter explained, "and thought this would cool you a little bit."

"Oh, that's sweet," Marilyn whispered.

"Marilyn, you got an award from the Italians. Do you feel they know the most about movie making in the world?"

"Well, they've made some of the greatest pictures that have ever been made. I can't tell you how deeply moved I am that they've awarded me this... award...that they take very seriously, and I receive it the same way."

"Would you say that you take acting very seriously?"

"I'm afraid I do," Marilyn replied with a smile before graciously bidding farewell and leaving. Afterward, Miller escorted her to an acting class at the Capital Theatre Building.

* * *

Lauded for her last three performances, Marilyn's career was thriving but she had not yet reached the coveted dramatic pinnacle. The choice of her next screen role was crucial. On the wave of a recent success with a comedy, should she return to the genre or select a more serious role?

Hoping to work again with Marilyn, Fox producer Jerry Wald presented her with *The Story on Page One,* a courtroom drama by Clifford Odets (who also wrote *Clash By Night*, which Wald also produced). The role appeared to outline Marilyn's own life. Jo Morris is a lonely, attractive woman who is raised in foster care, unprotected and abused. She is a survivor who recognizes her inner resources aside from her beauty, marries an older man, and tries to have children. Jo's dreams are shattered when her husband becomes jealous and abusive. In May and June, Marilyn was actively involved in casting plans, but Rita Hayworth eventually played the role.

On June 1, James Haspiel observed Marilyn buying her own birthday cake. When asked by a journalist about whether or not her husband ever bought her flowers, Marilyn responded, "I can buy flowers on my own." Their father may have slacked on organizing a birthday celebration for his wife, but Bobby and Jane presented her with a subscription to *Horticulture* magazine which they would renew each year. An issue was found on her nightstand after her death.

"I'm sorry to report that I'm not pregnant again," Marilyn told the press, "I feel fine now, but it takes time to get over the feeling of loss." The Millers packed up Arthur's Jaguar and drove to Roxbury for the summer. Miller's children were visiting Europe with their mother, and Bobby took home movies of his adventures and sent them to Marilyn. She told a journalist of having only traveled abroad to England, Korea, and Japan, and wanting to see Paris and other European countries through Bobby's eyes. She was very attached to her stepchildren and looked forward to their visits. Bobby seemed especially close to his famous stepmother and mailed her affectionate notes of appreciation for her hospitality and including specific instructions on how to contact him through his bedroom phone if she ever needed him.

When Bobby and Jane returned to New York from Europe, Marilyn drove from Connecticut to the apartment to retrieve a television set with MCA agent Joe Wohlhandler and friend Hollis Alpert. The three couldn't fit the set in the car, so Marilyn called upon Frank Taylor to lend a hand. Taylor, who lived and worked in the city and spent weekends and summers in Connecticut, used the mission as an opportunity to discuss *The Misfits* with Miller.

Following the Independence Day holiday, Taylor brought his wife and sons to the Millers' farmhouse where Arthur greeted them alone and read aloud the screenplay of *The Misfits*, acting out all the parts by changing his voice. Possibly communicating her indifference to the project from upstairs, Marilyn vacuumed plaster dust from the home's renovation, creating a cacophonous soundtrack for her husband's thespian efforts. Some biographers have interpreted Marilyn's noisemaking as a sardonic comment on Miller's script. One of the Taylor boys would remember Marilyn eventually coming downstairs to entertain them and serve lunch. Frank Taylor was moved by Miller's oral presentation and recommended John Huston as director and Clark Gable as male lead.

If Miller failed to enlist Huston (Marilyn Monroe Productions had neglected to offer him *The Prince and the Showgirl*), Marilyn might not participate and the film might not be made without her, so Taylor sent Huston a telegram lauding the script as "magnificent." However, there was no need to worry about Huston feeling slighted and refusing to work with Marilyn as he had recently hired Jean-Paul Sartre to write a script about the life of Sigmund Freud and envisioned Marilyn as the female lead.

Huston read *The Misfits* in a hotel in Paris while he was directing *The Roots of Heaven* and immediately contacted Elliott Hyman of United Artists, who was coincidently staying in a room on the same floor. Huston was interested in directing and approached Hyman about producing the property through his company, Seven Arts Productions, a subsidiary of United Artists. Huston arrived in New York on December 14 and suggested to Miller a substantial revision of the screenplay and a start date of April 6, 1960. The validation of Miller's work by a director she respected and trusted renewed Marilyn's interest in portraying Roslyn.

Marilyn's two major life goals might now be realized: a serious dramatic role and motherhood. On June 22, Marilyn entered Lenox Hill Hospital for gynecological surgery scheduled the following day. Dr. Mortimer Rodgers operated to correct chronic endometriosis, abnormally painful menstrual periods, and severe bleeding. He confirmed to the press Marilyn had not been pregnant. J. Randy Taraborelli interviewed the daughter of Dr. Oscar Steinberg, the physician who delivered to Marilyn the terrible news that she could not have children. Before he could open his mouth, Marilyn expressed intuitively knowing her status and took it very badly. Before leaving Marilyn's hospital room, Steinberg told her that he would name his firstborn daughter after her, a promise he kept. She was extremely sad, Steinberg's daughter, Melissa, told Taraborrelli, and her father was seriously worried about her. Allegedly, the gynecologist observed Miller as rude, dismissive, and treating his wife like an inferior.

Relying on her acting skills to cover her pain, Marilyn emerged smiling from the hospital three days later on the arm of Miller and wearing a casual blouse, skirt and a coat over her shoulders. The smile masked an emotional devastation over the failure of the procedure. Later that summer, Marilyn was riding in a car with Susan Strasberg and admitted that if she didn't have work, she'd jump out of the car. Marilyn threw herself back into performing scenes at the Actors Studio and concealed her deep sadness to her classmates during gatherings at local diners and parties at members' homes.

Marilyn's journal entries reveal the extent of the rupture in her relationship with Miller and a depression that had lingered since the winter. She wrote of feeling lonely and hopeless and described her eyes as looking "*dead.*" She now depended only upon herself and promised to take better care of herself. Disillusioned with life in Roxbury, she painfully lamented, "*There is no love here anymore.*"

This was clearly evident to the Strasbergs who, along with Susan, made the two and one-half hour drive from the city to visit. Miller opened the door with an uncomfortably cold greeting, and Marilyn wandered downstairs an hour later to give them a lackluster tour of the renovated home. Susan immediately felt the couple's distance and noticed they no longer gazed adoringly into each other's eyes. In fact, Marilyn seemed downright guarded in her husband's presence. Most indicative of personal problems, she hadn't prepared a meal for her guests and went to the freezer to take out a frozen piece of meat that would take hours to thaw and cook. The Strasbergs cut short their visit, and Marilyn invited them back soon. Hungry, the family headed to a local restaurant to have dinner and process their reaction to the upsettingly deteriorated marriage.

As she waited for her next film, Marilyn filled her time strolling along the dirt roads of Roxbury lined with low stone walls, poking in the antique shops of Woodbury, giving her husband haircuts, and chasing after Hugo, who habitually wandered off her property. One afternoon, she visited neighbor, Percy Beardsley, who gave her a tour of his sizeable coal cellar. His father, Nate, had filled it decades before with cows and steer and permitted its use as the set for a silent film starring Norma Talmadge, the wife of Fox Studio's mogul Joseph Schenck. Norma had left her white gloves on a cider barrel where they remained coated in dust. Nate, and later Percy, preserved the gloves and delighted in showing them to guests while sharing the story of the visiting Hollywood royalty. Percy also preserved the marks on the coal cellar's dirt floor left by Marilyn's spike heels as remnants of yet another film goddess' presence.

Marilyn's mood began to brighten by fall. "I've been scared all my life, really until now," she said. "Scared about so many things, even picking up the phone to make a call. That is the sort of thing I'm getting over at last. My philosophy now is 'Enjoy the day.' I don't fear the future anymore."

At a boisterous Actors Studio party in a Greenwich Village apartment, the host and guests watched a barefoot Marilyn, in a clinging black dress, undulating with Paul Newman, lean and muscled in tight chinos and a T-shirt. A few years earlier, while practicing a dance sequence for *Picnic*, director Joshua Logan had instructed Newman to move more suggestively by wiggling his behind with his dance partner, Joanne Woodward, the understudy for the leading lady. Newman must have hit the mark, as he divorced his wife and married Woodward.

Cheryl Crawford moved around the room introducing everyone to Patricia Bosworth, who recently auditioned for the Actors Studio and had been accepted as a member, but no one shifted their eyes away from the sexy dancing couple. "They seemed to be dancing with such rapture; they both kept changing rhythms and sometimes they walk-stepped to the beat," Bosworth later wrote. "They didn't dance for very long—maybe three minutes—but what a hot, pulsing three minutes it was!" When they finished dancing, Marilyn curtsied, and Newman bowed before stepping into the kitchen for a bottle of beer.

Back in the city fulltime, Marilyn rehearsed a scene from Tennessee Williams' *A Streetcar Named Desire* for a performance at the Actors Studio. The role of Blanche DuBois, a genteel school teacher who arrives in New Orleans' French Quarter to visit the home of her sister and her new husband, had been mastered on the stage by Jessica Tandy and on the screen by Vivien Leigh. The plot contained Williams' trademark blend of sexuality and tragedy. Blanche and Stella are the last descendants from an aristocratic southern family that has lost its property and fortune. Stella has married Stanley, a working class man whom Blanche considers an animal. She judges Stella's purely sexual attraction to him but behind Blanche's façade of snobbery and propriety lies an insecure, aging Southern belle who agonizes about her fading beauty. She is transparent to Stanley, who investigates her past and reveals her hypocrisy. Indeed, Blanche is lustful underneath her morally upright veneer.

Scene five, chosen by Marilyn, prepares the audience for the approaching truth about the circumstances of Blanche's departure from Mississippi. She had become sexually involved with one of her young male students, and the locals banished her from the town. In the scene, Blanche acts seductively toward the young man who comes to her door collecting for a newspaper subscription. Marilyn's scene partner was eighteen year old John Strasberg.

Marilyn portrayed Blanche's loneliness and sensuality as the character creates a romanticized fantasy life since she cannot face the grim reality of her own. She powerfully delivered her line: "*Young man! Has anyone ever told you that you look like a young Prince out of the Arabian nights?*" Marilyn had done her homework. She decorated the stage with props and applied bizarre makeup to her face. When John looked at Marilyn onstage, he saw desperation in her expression which made him anxious enough to want to leave the stage. This created perfect motivation for his role since that is what the young boy felt. Lee Strasberg loved Marilyn's performance, and John later described it as "fantastic."

* * *

Earlier in the year, the American National Exhibition had opened in Moscow. Designer Charles Eames asked Billy Wilder for an excerpt of Marilyn for an exhibit about American motion pictures. Wilder told Fred Lawrence Guiles: "I gave him a close-up of Monroe from *Some Like It Hot*, where she smiles [and winks], and it appeared on sixteen screens, this great close-up of Monroe. Forty thousand people a day would come to see her in that sequence...The Russians had not seen a Monroe film before. For the first time they were confronted with Marilyn, and they broke into applause." Wilder would soon witness his star's momentous introduction to the Russians' leader.

On September 19, Soviet Premier Nikita Khrushchev and his wife, Nina, commenced a historic tour of America. The film industry sponsored a banquet at Fox's lavish commissary, Café de Paris, well appointed in finery for the occasion. The menu featured squab, wild rice, Parisian potatoes, and peas with pearl onions. Fox excluded agents and stars' spouses. The only couples invited were actors Tony

Curtis and Janet Leigh, Dick Powell and June Allyson, Elizabeth Taylor and Eddie Fisher. Spyros Skouras demanded assurance of Marilyn's attendance. "She *has* to be there!" he insisted. The studio mogul was prideful of his most successful contract player and appointed her to represent the corporation.

Marilyn asked Miller to escort her, but he feared the public's reaction if he traveled across the country to meet the communist leader after having been recently acquitted on charges of being a communist. Instead, Frank Taylor served as Marilyn's escort for the event.

"I think it's a very wonderful thing and I'm happy to be here," Marilyn told the press as she deplaned the Trans World Airlines jet in a tight black suit. Taylor remembered Marilyn jutting out her chest with pride as she spoke with the press, and a photograph of her arrival reflects this interesting posture.

"Do you think [Khrushchev] wants to see you?" a reporter asked. "I hope he does," replied Marilyn, taken aback by the comment. Marilyn settled into the Beverly Hills Hotel, where her entourage began her two-hour transformation into a movie star. Agnes Flanagan applied body makeup, Ralph Roberts provided a relaxing massage, Allan Snyder applied face makeup, and Sydney Guilaroff styled her hair. Marilyn wore one of her favorite cocktail suits, previously worn when she accepted the David di Donatello Award. She would wear it again in *Let's Make Love* and in screen tests for *Something's Got to Give.* The suit would be auctioned in 1999 for $79,500.

Marilyn and Taylor arrived at 12:05 pm in a sleek, black, tail-finned limousine, one of a few vehicles in the Fox parking lot. "We must have come too late!" Marilyn cried, "It ended, and everyone left." On this historic occasion, Marilyn surprised herself by arriving early. Reporters descended upon her and complimented her punctuality for the second time in the year.

Fox placed Marilyn in an honorary seat at a table with directors George Cukor, Billy Wilder, William Wyler, and Joshua Logan. Judy Garland, Producer David Brown, and actor Henry Fonda also sat nearby. Fonda listened to a baseball game through an earpiece attached to a transistor radio. Newlyweds Elizabeth Taylor and Eddie Fisher sat at table 15. Fox event coordinators purposefully placed Fisher's ex-wife, Debbie Reynolds, at a distance at table 21.

Judy Garland raised her glass and announced, "I think we'll all get blind drunk and hiss and boo and carry on."

After a series of speeches, Skouras presented Khrushchev to Marilyn as Fox's goodwill emissary on the arm of director George Cukor. "You are a very lovely young lady," said Khrushchev shaking her hand so hard and long that it ached for days. "There should be more of this kind of thing," replied Marilyn. "It would help both our countries understand each other."

"My husband Arthur Miller, the playwright, sends you his greetings," Marilyn continued. "Ah, yes, Arthur Miller, your husband," said the short, bald, course-looking dictator. "I am honored. Your husband is a great man, your husband. We think highly of him in my country."

Ever prepared for social events, Marilyn had consulted with Natalie Wood, of Russian heritage, to communicate a few rehearsed phrases in Russian. The aged Communist leader and the youthful blonde actress even discussed Dostoevsky's *The Brothers Karamazov.* He was so delighted by the encounter that he invited Marilyn to visit Russia. For a moment in history, the Cold War warmed a few degrees.

"I very much would like to go to Disneyland," Khrushchev later told the crowd from the podium. Elizabeth Taylor climbed on the table to get a better look. "But then, we cannot guarantee your security, they say. Then what must I do? Commit suicide? What is it? Is there an epidemic of cholera there or something? Or have gangsters taken hold of the place that can destroy me?" Sinatra turned to those seated around him and facetiously suggested taking the dictator and his wife to the theme park.

After the meal and speeches, Khrushchev and his wife were invited onto the set of *Can Can* to watch an extravagant French musical number performed by Shirley MacLaine, Frank Sinatra, and other dancers. Marilyn had passed on both MacLaine's and Juliette Prowse's roles in the film [designer Donfeld's concept sketches of her costumes were auctioned in 2002]. During the performance, a group of female dancers in the chorus performed the French can-can, which involved lifting their full skirts to expose their undergarments. "It was the worst choice imaginable," Wiley T. Buchanan, State Department Chief of Protocol, said of Fox's exhibition. "When the male dancer dived under [MacLaine's] skirt and emerged holding what seemed to be her red panties, the Americans in the audience gave an audible gasp of dismay, while the Russians sat in stolid, disapproving silence." Fox's spectacle bombed, but Marilyn projected demure poise.

Reporters overheard Marilyn's conversation with Khrushchev and excerpts were published in the press, reflecting Marilyn's grace and dignity. At the airport a few days later, Marilyn told reporters, "I feel this is a historic occasion for the nation and for the film industry. I think Mr. Khrushchev's visit is a wonderful thing. Maybe now we can learn to be friends." As she walked up the steps to the plane, members of the press applauded. Upon departure, Marilyn received the respect denied by the impertinent reporter during her arrival.

Before leaving Los Angeles, Marilyn launched a campaign to land what might become her next role, effervescent Holly Golightly, in the film adaptation of Truman Capote's 1958 novella *Breakfast at Tiffany's.* Indeed, Capote envisioned Marilyn in the role when he sold the film rights to Paramount Studios. According to Barry Paris, Capote said, "Marilyn was always my first choice to play the girl." George Axelrod was hired to tailor the screenplay for Monroe as he had for *The Seven Year Itch*, and John Frankenheimer was originally considered to direct her even though his name did not appear on her list of approved directors.

Back in New York, Marilyn prepared two scenes from the screenplay with actor Michael Pollard in Strasberg's private class and performed them for Capote who found her "terrifically good." Marilyn was a natural for the quirky, free-spirited Holly, who earned her living as a courtesan or escort, referenced by accepting fifty dollars from her gentlemen companions when she excused herself to visit the ladies room (during mid-twentieth century, it was customary to tip an attendant in the ladies room for providing linen; the implication being Holly was really an escort since she kept a large amount of money left over after tipping the attendants). Similarly, the leading male role in this modern love story was equally tarnished by being kept by an older, married woman. The Strasbergs discouraged Marilyn from taking the role of an escort at this point in her career.

When the studio turned to one of their contracted stars instead of Marilyn, Capote snapped: "Paramount double-crossed me in every way and cast Audrey [Hepburn]." Even Hepburn considered herself inappropriately cast and, throughout the production, could feel Capote's disappointment for her not being Marilyn. Released in the fall of 1961, *Breakfast at Tiffany's* earned an Oscar for Best Song, "Moon River," and Audrey Hepburn earned a best actress nomination. In her Givenchy wardrobe, Holly Golightly became Hepburn's iconic role; and with all due respect to Hepburn, the role could have become Marilyn's definitive performance as well.

While Paramount hammered out the details of *Breakfast at Tiffany's*, across town on Pico Boulevard, Fox cast Marilyn in the musical comedy, *The Billionaire*. It was important for Fox to capitalize on its star's recent success for a rival film studio. However, she was more interested in negotiating a film adaptation of *Paris Blues* with Marlon Brando, which never came to fruition.

Meanwhile, on September 27, Marilyn and Miller accepted an invitation from The American Friends of Hebrew University for a fundraiser at the Bellevue Stratford Hotel in Philadelphia. Executive director Rabbi Robert Goldburg counted on Marilyn's presence for the success of the event, and she didn't disappoint him as she had two years earlier when he invited her to attend the United Jewish Appeals conference in Miami. At the time, he had ghostwritten her speech about her conversion to Judaism and her endorsement of Jewish institutions. Marilyn declined her invitation when Miller's was withdrawn directly following his charge for contempt of Congress. Oddly, the Jewish playwright lost credibility and his formerly Christian Scientist wife gained it.

Two days later, Lester Markel, the Sunday editor of the *New York Times*, escorted Marilyn on a tour of the newspaper's headquarters at One Times Square. The building featured a famous electric news ticker display near the base of the building, and dropped an illuminated ball from its rooftop flagpole at midnight on New Year's Eve. Marilyn watched the typesetters and printers at work, and Markel brought her to the Lively Morgue, the newspaper's vast archive of clippings and photographs. "Earthquakes, storms, wars, and murders cause only ripples in the Sunday and news department," noted the paper's *Times Talk* newsletter, "but the passing of Miss Monroe rocked the eighth and third floors." Countless notable guests had toured the facility, but none had left such a wake. It took hours for the copyrighters and printers to settle down after her departure. "The *Times* is such a friendly place," Marilyn told Markel.

The November 9, 1959 cover of *Life* featured a photograph of Marilyn defying gravity: whimsically jumping in a spangled gown (a black version of the one worn to the premiere of *Some Like It Hot*) against a blue background. The cover story focused on photographer Philippe Halsman's *Jump Book*, a collection of photographs of prominent personalities from the arts, politics and immortalized in stop-motion jumping poses and a tongue-in-cheek study of "jumpology."

Halsman's playfulness and mischievousness inspired the jump shots during a photo session of the Ford automobile family taken to celebrate the company's fiftieth anniversary in 1952. After the session, Halsman relaxed with a drink offered by Mrs. Edsel Ford and asked the matronly lady if she would indulge him by jumping for his camera. "With my high heels?" she asked. Amused, Mrs. Ford slipped off her pumps and leaped into the air, followed by her daughter-in-law, Mrs. Henry Ford II.

Over the next several years, Halsman ended his portrait sessions by asking his subjects to spring into the air. A huge accomplishment, considering few of his subjects were known for public displays of self-humor, aside from a few celebrities. Halsman successfully persuaded senator Richard Nixon; the Duke and Duchess of Windsor; eighty-something-year-old Unites States Judge Learned Hand; and scientist Robert Oppenheimer, creator of the atomic bomb. Former President Hubert Hoover and pianist Van Cliburn flatly refused.

"In a burst of energy the subject overcomes gravity," Halsman told *Life*. "He cannot also control all his muscles. The mask falls. The real self becomes visible, and one needs only to snap it with a camera." Halsman predicted a day when psychiatrists would no longer diagnose hidden characteristics with the painstakingly slow Rorschach test.

How did Halsman analyze Marilyn by her style of jumping with her fists closed and knees bent? "When an adult woman jumps with bent knees like a little girl," he observed, "it shows that, during the jump at least, she has become a girl again." In a rare moment,

Halsman captured himself on celluloid in mid-air holding Marilyn's hand and joining her airborne.

With her feet on the ground that autumn, Marilyn resumed a friendship with down-to-earth Ralph Roberts (1916-1999), a stage actor and masseur to entertainment industry luminaries. Standing six foot, three inches and weighing two hundred fifteen pounds, Roberts was a gentle giant with broad shoulders and Native American features. Following military service in World War II and the Korean War, he studied at the Actors Studio and played the role of executioner in *The Lark* and in its television adaptation. Onstage, he played the masseur in the opening scenes of *Will Success Spoil Rock Hunter?* with Jayne Mansfield and in *Bells Are Ringing* (and its 1960 film adaptation) with close friend Judy Holliday.

In Roberts, Marilyn found a kindred spirit and arguably her closest confidante and friend for the remainder of her life. She referred to him as "Rafe" and "The Brother." Roberts may also have been a gay man, as Marilyn told Truman Capote, suggesting she found safety in their nonthreatening relationship.

Marilyn and Roberts met in the Strasbergs' kitchen apartment a few years earlier. He had just finished giving Susan a massage and they were enjoying a cup of hot tea. Roberts heard Lee talking to a woman in the hall and was taken aback when Marilyn entered the kitchen. She was the most "radiantly beautiful creature" Roberts had ever seen. Aside from her physical beauty, she had an inner glow that illuminated the Strasbergs' high-ceilinged kitchen.

Lee prepared the stunning woman a glass of tea and stood at the sink sharing funny stories about his experiences in the theatre. Roberts, Susan, and the woman exchanged glances as they giggled in amusement. When Roberts left for another appointment, Susan walked him to the door, and he asked the identity of the woman. She told him the woman was Marilyn Monroe and apologized for neglecting to introduce them.

Roberts saw Marilyn again at the Strasbergs' New Year's Eve party. A few weeks later, he was walking east on Fifty-fourth Street with blonde comedic actress Judy Holliday on their way to attend a party for Jule Styne, the songwriter, and as they crossed Park Avenue, a woman standing on the median called out: "Miss Holliday, you're wonderful! I saw you on *The Perry Como Show* the other night doing an imitation of me. I loved it." In Holliday's act, she lampooned Marilyn mispronouncing *The Brothers Karamazov*.

The gushing fan was Marilyn who stood beside an unidentified male. Judy blushed and replied how wonderful she thought Marilyn was. The streetlights changed, and Marilyn and her escort said good-bye. Roberts and Holliday crossed the street and met two other friends, Milton Goldman and Arnold Weissberger, who had been unabashedly following Marilyn. Holliday's male friends explained they had just seen Marilyn as they left a nearby restaurant. Like zombies, the two men slowly turned and followed her for a few blocks. Holliday would later invite Marilyn to her apartment at the Dakota for tea, where Marilyn coached her on makeup application and gestures for future impersonations.

The first time Ralph Roberts massaged Marilyn was in November. He arrived early for the nine o'clock appointment when she and Miller had just finished dinner. The three visited until Miller retired to the bedroom. Marilyn suggested setting the table in front of a glowing fire and turning off the lights. She climbed on the table, lay face up under two towels, and closed her eyes.

Fifteen minutes into the massage, Roberts' mind drifted to a book he had been reading, *The Professor's House* by Willa Cather. Marilyn opened her eyes for the first time. "Do you know an author named Willa Cather?" she asked. Startled, he responded that she was his favorite author. Marilyn explained Cather's *Lost Lady* was one of her favorite books and she longed to adapt it to film.

As Roberts massaged Marilyn's body, he thought of a friend in New York, singer Janice Mars, who owned a nightclub on Sixth Avenue called Baq Room. Mars had been actress Maureen Stapleton's roommate in a brownstone on Fifty-Second Street where Marlon Brando had also lived. Having been silent for over twenty minutes, Marilyn asked Ralph if he knew an actress, Janice Mars, from the Actors Studio. "She's one of my closest friends!" he exclaimed.

For the first of many more times to follow, Roberts wondered if Marilyn could read his mind. While filming on location in Reno, she confessed a suspicion that he could do the same to her. Marilyn admitted to having frequently thought of a random subject after which Roberts had made a related remark, which showed the closeness of their connection.

Wearing a tailored gray suit and a spotted fur stole, Marilyn arrived in Los Angeles on Miller's arm on November 2. Roberts reunited with her when he arrived to begin work in a role in MGM's film adaptation of *Bells Are Ringing* with Judy Holliday. Director Vincente Minnelli's production was fraught with delays caused by Holliday's depression and illness, considered psychosomatic by some. The talented actress, who—like Marilyn—had perfected the dumb blonde screen image, would soon be diagnosed with cancer and died in 1965.

On December 4, 1959, Richard D. Zanuck (1934-2012), the son of Marilyn's nemesis, wrote her a letter offering her the role of Temple Drake in a film adaptation of William Faulker's novel, *Requiem for a Nun*, later adapted into a play, *The Sanctuary*. "*I have always felt you would be perfect for the part and, needless to say, I'd be more than delighted if you were to share my feelings*," Zanuck wrote from the story department of his father's motion picture studio. Lee Remick and Yves Montand would be cast in *Sanctuary* (1961) shortly after Montand completed *Let's Make Love* (retitled from *The Billionaire*) with Marilyn. Eventually fired by his father, Zanuck set up his own film company with David Brown and produced *Jaws* (1975), *Cocoon* (1985), and *Driving Miss Daisy* (1989).

In October, poet Sylvia Plath (1932-1963), best known for her semi-autobiographical novel *The Bell Jar*, awoke after a dream in the Yaddo artist colony in Saratoga Springs, New York, and recorded it in a journal. Marilyn had appeared as "*fairy godmother*" and gave the writer an expert manicure. Sylvia told Marilyn how much she and Miller meant to her and her husband before she asked her to recommend a hairdresser. Marilyn extended an invitation to visit her during the Christmas holidays and promised her "*a new flowering life*." Unfortunately, she never found the chance because in 1963, Plath took her own life by carbon monoxide poisoning when she placed her head deep into an oven in the kitchen of her London flat.

As Marilyn embarked upon a "new flowering life" during the holiday season, the popular Christmas gift for girls was the new Barbie Doll. Eleven inches tall with a waterfall of blond hair and dressed in a black and white striped bathing suit, Barbie was the first mass-produced toy doll in the United States modeled with adult features.

While most little girls of the era played with baby dolls like urinating Betsy Wetsy and talking Chatty Cathy, Barbie was patterned after a sexy German doll, Lilli—based on a comic strip character with large breasts and sexy clothing—and marketed as a gag gift for adult men. The Barbie doll veered from the culture's ideal of a voluptuous female form and later incited criticism for its unrealistic body dimensions. In 1997, Mattel released a collection of Marilyn Monroe Barbie dolls dressed in costumes from her Fox films and featuring her signature beauty mark.

CHAPTER TEN: *LET'S MAKE LOVE*

"Marilyn Monroe is the greatest farceuse in the business," Fox film producer Jerry Wald asserted, "a female Chaplin." In the summer of 1959, Wald approached Marilyn with *The Billionaire*, a musical comedy by Norman Krasna who had scripted the sophisticated *Indiscreet* (1958) for Ingrid Bergman and Cary Grant. Professionally, Marilyn was hot, and Fox wanted to capitalize on the success of its own star whose last two films were made for rival studios. In fact, Marilyn hadn't worked on the Fox lot in over three years.

The studio wanted Billy Wilder to direct, clearly hoping to recreate the magic of *Some Like It Hot*, but he was filming *The Apartment* at his home studio, Paramount. George Cukor (1899-1983), another director on Marilyn's approved list, was the next choice. Cukor, a talented gay man known as a "women's director," had a string of successes including *The Women* (1939), *The Philadelphia Story* (1940), *Born Yesterday* (1950), and *A Star is Born* (1954) and had worked with Joan Crawford, Norma Shearer, Katharine Hepburn, Judy Holliday, and Judy Garland. "[Marilyn] had this absolutely unerring touch with comedy," Cukor would later say. "In real life she didn't seem funny, but she had this touch. She acted as if she didn't quite understand why it was funny, which is what made it so funny."

The film is a backstage story about a billionaire who learns his Casanova reputation is being satirized in an off-Broadway musical. Dismissing his attorney's urge to shut down the production, the billionaire instead heeds the advice of his public relations agent and visits the theater during rehearsals to show good humor. At the theater, he is mistaken for an inexperienced actor auditioning for his part. Dazzled by the production's leading female performer, Amanda Dell, the billionaire accepts the part of the playboy in an effort to court her.

Amanda, who attends night school, is serious about self-improvement and voices a strong prejudice against wealthy playboys. She is more interested in the art of acting, men who are awkward with women, and the show's male singer. Amanda begins to coach this would-be impersonator whose disguise prevents him from relying upon money and power to impress her. The billionaire hires famous virtuosos in comedy, singing and dancing to assist him in stirring Amanda, but discovers he is utterly untalented. Realizing he has found a woman who actually cares for him and not just his money, the billionaire reveals his identity to the disbelieving showgirl.

The plot is a recycled treatment of *On the Avenue*, a 1937 film starring Dick Powell and Alice Faye; however, the original featured a wealthy female and a male performer. Borrowing from the formula of *Around the World in 80 Days*, Fox production manager Buddy Adler envisioned a lush production filmed on location in New York, Europe, and the West Indies and an all-star cast with uncredited cameo performances. To add sex appeal, Fox eventually changed the title to *Let's Make Love*.

The story's premise also borrows from the previous year's hit *Pillow Talk* with Doris Day and Rock Hudson, in which a man pursues a woman disinterested in his playboy reputation by disguising himself as more sensitive and approachable. Day and Hudson repeated the formula in the subsequent film *Lover Come Back* (1961). Even *Some Like It Hot* was a more skewed variation on the formula. *Let's Make Love* would even co-star Tony Randall, a staple in the Day-Hudson romantic comedies of the late 1950s and early 1960s. The film could have been a vehicle for Doris Day, whose career in mostly musical and comedies Marilyn's was beginning to mirror hers. One can imagine Marilyn in Day's *Midnight Lace* (1960), *That Touch of Mink* (1962), and *The Thrill of It All* (1963). Marilyn's next comedy, *Something's Got to Give*, would eventually be re-worked into Day's *Move Over Darling* (1963), with Day in Marilyn's role.

On Sunday, September 20, following the Khrushchev luncheon, Marilyn spent four hours in a meeting with Wald, Krasna, and Cukor to discuss the film. Although cautious about the thinness of the script, she expressed enthusiasm about working with the male lead, Gregory Peck, who had already been cast while Fox courted her for *Time and Tide*. Perhaps Marilyn's underlying motivation was to complete another obligatory film to fulfill her contract. She requested Jack Cole as choreographer and Harry Stradling as cinematographer (the latter had impressed her with his work in *A Streetcar Named Desire*). The production was slated to commence on January 18, 1960. With Marilyn sealed as leading lady, the script was modified to bolster her role.

Deemed by Miller as "not worth the paper it was typed on," the screenplay of *Let's Make Love* seriously concerned Marilyn, who had an innate sense of what would work on screen and what would not. (Miller's re-writes likely delayed both the production and the anticipated start date for *The Misfits*.) With equal motivation to start and end the film on time and within budget, Fox hired Miller for $15,000 to develop Marilyn's role and resuscitate the plot. Miller earned an additional $5,000 for a second revision and finally another $7,500 for a third.

In *Timebends*, Miller rather arrogantly implied that Marilyn failed to demonstrate the gratitude he expected for his sacrificing "blocks of time" in an attempt to save her from "complete catastrophe." He later concluded it was a "bad miscalculation" that failed to bring them closer to each other. Miller's inflation of Marilyn's role diminished Gregory Peck's, and so the actor returned an advance of $100,000 to Fox and walked away from the project. With Peck off the film, Miller's scriptwriting inadvertently thrust his wife into the arms of a European lover.

Fox considered pairing Marilyn with five other contenders who were each hot property in 1959. Yul Brynner, the studio's Oscar-winning "King of Siam," had three films in release, *The Journey, The Sound and the Fury* with Joanne Woodward, and *Solomon and Sheba*. Cary Grant was currently appearing on cinema screens running for his life through a cornfield to escape killers as a low-flying crop-dusting plane sprayed him with pesticide in Alfred Hitchcock's suspense masterpiece *North By Northwest*. James Stewart had recently co-starred with Kim Novak in *Vertigo* and *Bell, Book and Candle* and with Lee Remick in *Anatomy of a Murder*. Since *Ben-Hur*, Charlton

Heston was equally in demand.

The logical casting for chemistry and box office return was clearly Rock Hudson; to quote Marilyn's character when Clement is selected from a group of lookalikes to portray himself, "No doubt about it." Hudson was now Marilyn's male counterpart as an international sex symbol after the recent success of *Pillow Talk.* An eager Universal Studios offered Hudson to Fox in exchange for Marilyn's appearance in Universal's heavy drama *Freud*, based on the life and work of the eminent Viennese psychoanalyst.

Ironically, as Marilyn returned to New York Miller was arranging her introduction to the French actor and vocalist who would become her co-star and lover. Although Yves Montand (1921-1991) was born near Florence, Italy, the film's trailer promoted him as "the greatest gift France has sent to us since the Statue of Liberty." With his prominent nose, Montand bore a slight resemblance to Joe DiMaggio.

France's singing sensation Edith Piaf (1915-1963) discovered Montand and hired him in her nightclub act at Moulin Rouge. She quickly became his lover and mentor, and launched his film career by casting him in her film *Star Without Light* (1946). Piaf was an iconic national treasure whose vocal style mirrored Judy Garland's but whose mass appeal paralleled that of America's King of Rock and Roll, Elvis Presley. In 1953, Montand and his wife, Simone Signoret (1921-1985), the husky-voiced star of French cinema, performed as John and Mary Proctor in the French stage production of Miller's *The Crucible.* They shared Miller's political views and got along well with him when the three met in France.

Now touring the United States in concert, the French troubadour was scheduled to perform *An Evening with Yves Montand* at the Henry Miller Theatre on Broadway. Miller, unable to attend because he was completing the screenplay of *The Misfits*, asked Montgomery Clift to escort Marilyn to the opening night on September 22. Clift would soon be leaving for Tennessee to begin production of *Time and Tide*, re-titled *Wild River.* On the arm of her dear friend, Marilyn arrived at the theater wearing the silver spangled gown and white fur wrap she had worn to the premiere of *Some Like It Hot*.

The next evening, Marilyn returned to the Henry Miller Theatre with her husband and Norman and Hedda Rosten. Afterward, the two couples joined Montand and Signoret in his dressing room and laughed uproariously at Montand's fly buttons gleaming in spotlight whenever he put his hands in his trouser pockets during the show. An immediate connection formed between the three couples. Later that evening, the Millers hosted a dinner in their apartment for the Montands and Rostens. "He comes from good Italian peasant stock," Miller said of Montand to *Look* magazine, "and looks like the richest man who ever lived." With assistance from her husband, Marilyn had found her next leading man.

Montand's forty-two performances on Broadway commanded rave reviews, elevated his position to that of a French version of Frank Sinatra, and secured his first role in an American film opposite its biggest female star. Having seen him on *The Dinah Shore Show*, Jerry Wald concurred with the Millers' endorsement and offered Montand the role of the billionaire, rewritten as a Frenchman named Jean-Marc Clement.

Simone Signoret was known as brighter and wittier than her husband. Starring in the complex French thriller *Les Diaboliques* (1955), she played the mistress of a sadistic director of a boarding school who teaches alongside his passive, ailing wife. Signoret's character constantly wears sunglasses to conceal the bruise on her eye from her lover's abuse. The two women conspire to drown him in the school's swimming pool. (To provider further detail would be an unnecessary spoiler but the film earned a cult following and is considered a classic.)

The Hollywood buzz predicted Signoret was a contender for a Best Actress Oscar for her performance in *Room at the Top*, the first British New Wave film. Gritty and realistic, the film earned an "X" certificate due to its strong sexual content, and its advertising promised "a savage story of lust and ambition." Laurence Harvey co-starred as Joe, a ruthlessly ambitious young working class man who falls in love with Susan, the daughter of an industrialist. When Susan's father sends her abroad, Joe turns to Alice (Signoret), an older, unhappily married woman. Susan returns to Joe, but he chooses Alice. Soon, Joe discovers that Susan is pregnant, and her father forces Joe to marry her. Alice is devastated and goes on a drinking binge that ends with an automobile accident and her tragic death. The character's abandonment and suffering at the hand of an exploitative young opportunist guaranteed Signoret an Oscar nomination.

The role of Amanda in *Let's Make Love* offered Marilyn no opportunity for an award, but she co-starred with a seasoned cast. Tony Randall (1920-2004), cast as Jean-Marc Clement's publicist Alex Coffman, found success in the aptly titled *Will Success Spoil Rock Hunter?* (1957) and *The Mating Game* (1959). Frankie Vaughn (1928-1999), "the singing idol of England," played Tony Danton, a cabaret singer. Vaughan released more than eighty recordings over the course of his career, mostly covers of American songs, before retiring in 1985. "[Marilyn] was always on time for rehearsals," Vaughan told Tom Hutchinson. "There were none of those notorious late starts. When she arrived, everybody smartened up, as if her presence was the light that fell on everyone. Certainly she seemed to me very professional."

As Clement's protective attorney Mr. Wales, Wilfrid Hyde-White (1903-1991) was a British actor eventually best remembered for his role in *My Fair Lady* (1964). He amused Marilyn with a story he heard of a man visiting the wilds of Africa who told a savage tribesman that he was from America, and the head-hunter responded, "America—Marilyn Monroe." Screen legends Milton Berle (1908-2002), Bing Crosby (1903-1977), and Gene Kelly (1912-1996) portrayed themselves in cameos as the comedian, singer and dancer who coach Clement.

Dubbed "Mr. Television" and America's "Uncle Miltie," Berle was the first major star and comedian of small screen after his long-term radio career transitioned to NBC's *Texaco Star Theatre* from 1948-1955. "The wide-eyed naïve Marilyn I had first known was gone," Berle observed. "This Marilyn was more beautiful than ever." Paving the way for Sinatra, Dean Martin and Perry Como, crooner Bing Crosby had a musical style with a conversational ease in phrasing. Selling over one hundred million copies, Crosby's recording of *White Christmas* remains a holiday staple.

He enjoyed a long career as a popular recording artist and actor in films such as *Going My Way* (1944), *The Bells of St. Mary's* (1945), and *The Country Girl* (1954). Crosby partnered with comic Bob Hope in a series of musical comedies in various locations referred to as the "Road To" films since their titles included these words before the name of the destination. Well into the spring, Marilyn aggressively pursued Frank Sinatra for a cameo in place of Crosby, but he declined, missing another opportunity to make a film with her; Sinatra was completing *Can-Can* and scheduled to begin *Ocean's 11* with his Rat Pack cronies.

Gene Kelly was an innovative dancer, singer, actor, choreographer, and director who transformed the Hollywood musical film. Energetic, athletic and handsome, Kelly starred in Metro-Goldwyn-Mayer Studios' *Anchors Aweigh* (1945), *On the Town* (1949), and *An American in Paris* (1951). The later won six Oscars and featured his show-stopping eighteen-minute ballet with Leslie Caron. Kelly is best remembered for his iconic dance sequence twirling an umbrella, splashing in the puddles, and swirling on a lamppost in *Singin' in the Rain* (1952). He and Marilyn enjoyed a warm rapport and would search for more projects in which to work together.

Madge Kennedy (1891-1987), a stage and movie actress of the silent era, had a small part as Clement's staid secretary. She had recently appeared in *North By Northwest* (1959). Comedian Joe Besser (1907-1988), best remembered as one of the Three Stooges comedy act, portrayed joke writer Charlie Lamont. In 1956, Besser joined the trio in short subject films for Columbia Studios when Shemp Howard died suddenly.

In late October, Cukor, accompanied by songwriters Sammy Cahn and Jimmy Van Heusen and musical director, Lionel Newman, traveled to the Millers' Manhattan apartment to audition the musical score for Marilyn. She proudly introduced her husband's son, Bobby, present for the preview. Using Marilyn's white baby grand piano in the corner of the living room, the team sang four original songs created for the film: "Specialization," "Incurably Romantic," "Hey You with the Crazy Eyes," and "Let's Make Love." The four men had a rare glimpse of Marilyn as a stepmother when, in middle of a song, she jumped up and answered the door to personally welcome the boy's friend. As the two boys left together, Marilyn ascertained that Bobby had his keys and confirmed the time he was expected to return home.

On December 17th, Marilyn reported to the studio in Los Angeles to film hairstyle and costume tests. While on set, Buddy Adler viewed them and became greatly disturbed by how different his leading lady looked compared to her previous Fox films. Her hair was upswept, her make–up was pale, and Dorothy Jeakins' costumes seemed odd and unflattering. Adler arranged for those responsible to review Marilyn's more familiar styles.

Either Marilyn heard Adler's negative feedback or concluded for herself that the hairstyling and costumes were not effective. Regardless, she called in sick to the studio the following week and through Christmas Eve. For the first time in her career, Marilyn faced harsh criticism of her physical appearance. To improve matters, she authorized Fox to deduct $2,500 from her salary to make additional payments to hairstylist Sydney Guilaroff for his work during the production.

Dorothy Jeakins designed a variety of dance costumes including a Beatnick ensemble consisting of a sheer black leotard body suit under a blue knitted sweater and black pumps (the sweater, as we shall see, would provoke ire), and a black, laced corset over a leotard. Some of her other designs included a blue chiffon strapless gown with gathered fabric at the bodice, to emphasize Marilyn's bosom and matched with rhinestone pumps, a taupe cocktail dress, a white gown with a fitted bodice, and a halter dress with a full skirt of orange and red chiffon. Jeakins' designs deviated from the William Travilla's fashions for Marilyn in Fox films from 1952-1956. Jeakins' wardrobe for Marilyn also included two garments she wore previously: the silver gown from the premiere of *Some Like It* and the Jean Louis black suit most recently worn to the Khrushchev luncheon.

While wardrobe and make-up artists returned to the drawing board, Lionel Newman made progress supervising the vocal recording sessions for the soundtrack. With her hair disheveled and wearing no make-up, Marilyn worked diligently for several days with the orchestra, conducted by Dominic Frontiere. "She was nothing but a pro with us, the musicians," Newman would tell Lawrence Crown. Typical of Marilyn, she was cooperative with technicians and crew, if not with directors. She especially endeared herself to a gentleman who operated the boom and microphone. He was a fan who was so excited about working with Marilyn that he asked Newman if he might photograph her with his personal camera. Newman relayed his request to Marilyn, who joyfully consented. Wearing no make-up and her hair unstyled, Marilyn smiled and played to his amateur camera.

Bobby and Jane visited during the Christmas holidays, and Marilyn arranged activities for them while she juggled family time and pre-production work. She asked Ralph Roberts to assist her in obtaining passes to MGM studios where he was filming *Bells Are Ringing*. Roberts' co-star, Judy Holliday, arranged for the Miller family to tour the MGM soundstages. After the New Year, the Millers set up residence at the Beverly Hills Hotel in an upper level bungalow complex, number twenty while Yves Montand and Simone Signoret settled next door in number twenty-one. Reclusive Howard Hughes and his wife, Jean Peters, Marilyn's co-star in *Niagara*, inhabited the lower level bungalow.

In a hospitable, neighborly act, the Millers invited the Montands to a homemade pasta dinner, where Marilyn used the DiMaggio family recipe for her sauce. Signoret was charmed by this gracious gesture; she fondly remembered it as her introduction to America. They sat on the floor in casual clothes, drank red wine, and ate spaghetti. The Miller's dinner invitation was the Montand's first intimate gathering the couple had attended since their arrival in Hollywood. Signoret admired Marilyn and appreciated her warm welcome.

"Marilyn was a smiling, bubbling, beautiful hostess," Sidney Skolsky wrote of his friend's cocktail party press event held at Fox Studio's elegant commissary, Café de Paris, on Friday, January 15. "She still has the old glamour, the magic." That evening, Marilyn looked ravishing in a Jax dress of pearl silk jersey with halter neck and full skirt of layered chiffon. Contrastingly, Signoret wore a sedate sheath and chic fur hat and chain-smoked cigarettes. Photographs of the event show Marilyn standing between Miller and Montand, her arms linked with each of theirs. Miller played along for the cameras by gently kissing her cheek; Montand repeated the action, kissing her other cheek. These photographs foreshadowed the impending triangle exploited by the studio to publicize the film. Journalist Jae Lyle reported that the co-stars spent an "eternity" of forty-seven minutes staring at each other in mutual adoration.

"Next to my husband and along with Marlon Brando," Marilyn told the press that evening, seated at a banquet under the Art Deco mural that spanned the commissary walls, "I think Yves Montand is the most attractive man I've ever met." Montand spoke similarly of his co-star, "There is nobody like her in Europe. We have Brigitte Bardot, yes, but she is more famous for the body." Miller commented on the charisma of each co-star: "They possess internal engines which emit indescribable rays of energy."

On Monday, January 25, the crew assembled on Fox studio's Soundstage 11 for Marilyn's opening number, a Beatnick version of Cole Porter's standard "My Heart Belongs to Daddy". The six-minute sequence was on the scale of "Diamonds Are a Girl's Best Friend" and "Heat Wave". Immortalized by Mary Martin in her stage debut in *Leave it to Me* (1938), the song was updated to include jazzy "ba-da-da" back-up male vocals. The melody of the chorus is in a minor key while the bridge is in major. Marilyn delivered staccato phrasing with precise pitch.

As the number begins, the camera focuses on a series of firehouse poles as Marilyn's legs appear from above, opening and closing as she shimmies down a pole and into frame before whispering, "Boys!" Ten male dancers in casual beige outfits join her. Wearing the bulky blue Aran sweater over a black leotard body suit and black pumps, Marilyn announces, "*My name is...Lolita, and I'm not supposed to play...with boys.*" This phrase calls to mind Vladimir Nabokov's controversial book about a twelve-year-old girl seduced by her step-father. Furthering the image, Marilyn plays jacks and crawls across the floor between the spread legs of a row of male dancers.

Once again, she portrays a sexualized child, recapitulating her childhood sexual abuse. As in *Diamonds*, the male dancers chase, lift, and carry her around the stage. She climbs up and spins around the poles. It is a vigorously acrobatic number, probably the most difficult of her career. Cukor shot the sequence slowly in fifteen second takes while Marilyn mimicked the dance moves modeled off-set by Jack Cole and his assistant, Maggie Banks. When Cole accidently caught his foot in a camera dolly, Marilyn grimaced and clutched her chest in exact imitation of her choreographer. The number took eleven days to shoot.

The blue sweater, ordered by Dorothy Jeakins from Ireland for $75, created more controversy on the set than Marilyn. "What you paid your money to see Marilyn in on the screen you would never see in that sweater with those tights underneath it," said Rupert

Allan. "She rehearsed in it and every time she wore it, it got another inch longer." The wardrobe department made the mistake of ordering only one sweater, and Cukor had to shoot other scenes while a replacement was knitted in western Ireland. Fox eventually air-expressed four extra sweaters to the wardrobe department.

Buddy Adler screened the rushes of the dance number and found further fault with Marilyn's appearance. At start of filming, Marilyn was slender, having lost the weight gained during her pregnancy in late 1958. However, Adler now complained that Marilyn looked pregnant in the infamous blue sweater. Jerry Wald insisted the audience would never notice her belly in the fast-paced sequence. In actuality, Marilyn's sweater gave the illusion of middle fullness as it was sewn into her black leotard to prevent it from riding up during the highly physical dance moves.

Despite the drama of the sweater, Marilyn was a trouper who endeared herself to the dancers. "She was very nice and comfortable but very childlike," Bob Banas told Michele Morgan. "She was not like some other big stars, with closed doors...She was very happy to talk, and when I brought people on the set to get autographs, Marilyn was very nice about it and spent time with them." She presented all the dancers with personally inscribed and autographed pictures at the end of the production.

Banas remembered having so much grease on his hair, that when Marilyn ran her fingers through it and swirled around the pole, the lubricant made her fly quickly to the point of alarm. She jokingly called out to Cukor, "I don't want to say but someone has too much grease on his hair!" Cukor sent Banas back to wardrobe to have his hair shampooed. Later, when filming the part of the number in which Marilyn kissed Banas, her lip gloss caused her to slide off his face. Banas jokingly announced Marilyn was wearing too much grease on her lips. She burst into laughter.

"She's one of the few stars who doesn't act as if she's made it," Jerry Wald said of Marilyn during the production of grueling musical numbers. "She does not coast. She worked harder in *Let's Make Love* than she did in *Clash by Night.* She's still the same person." Marilyn, now approaching her mid-30s, was working with accomplished singers and dancers and rose to the challenge despite her usual insecurities. Journalist Richard Gehman visited the set and published in *The American Weekly* an excerpt he read from Marilyn's personal diary: "*What am I afraid of? Do I think I can't act? I know I can act but I am afraid. I am afraid and I should not be and I must not be.*"

"Marilyn is not a great dancer and she knows it," Jack Cole told *Life* magazine. "The motivation is a terrible fear of failure. She is a great star without the background or experience. She is afraid and insecure. That's why she is late. That's why she stalls. She is always looking for more time—a hem out of line, a mussed hair, a scene to discuss, anything to stall facing the specter, the terrible thing of doing something for which she feels inadequate."

Marilyn appreciated Jack Cole's patience. She sent him a greeting card and enclosed a check for $1500 and a note that read, "*I really was awful, it must have been a difficult experience, please go someplace nice for a couple of weeks and act like it all never happened.*" A few days later, Cole received another card with a check for $500 and an inscription that said, "*Stay three more days.*" This was Marilyn's way of expressing love and apologizing. Cole responded with a telegram: "*The universe sparkles with miracles but none among them shines like you. Remember that when you go to sleep tonight. Tomorrow will be fun, there is no other way. All my love.*"

According to Barbara Leaming, Marilyn greeted Montand on their first day of work together, January 29, with the declaration that he was about to experience working "with the worst actress in the world."

"You are just scared," Montand reflected. "But I am lost." He was correct. Not fluent in English, Montand received a copy of the script in French and learned his lines phonetically, not always aware of the gist of their meaning.

Before playing a scene, Marilyn would shake her hands in a manner Cukor compared to a pianist preparing for a concert. Unlike Billy Wilder, he found her stronger in earlier takes, even though Marilyn disagreed. After word-perfect delivery, she insisted on retakes, and frequently begged, "Can we please do it again?" Cukor maintained a positive relationship with Paula Strasberg who earned $50,000 for coaching Marilyn. Miller resentfully remarked that Paula cleared more income than Marilyn on the film.

"Everything she does is original," remarked Montand in broken English to journalist Stanley Gordon, "even just standing and talking to you. I never see anybody who concentrates so hard. She is very conscientious. She do scene again and again and again, but is not satisfied. An actor needs patience with her. In her mind is only professional conscience, not caprice. I try to help all I can because if she is good, it is good for me too. Nobody makes picture by himself."

Like Dame Sybil Thorndike, Montand regarded Marilyn as a seasoned, professional film actor. Marilyn rarely experienced such reverence from co-stars. Montand would later describe Marilyn's on-set torment to Shirley MacLaine. Marilyn actually arrived hours before the rest of the cast, but after an arduous ritual of make-up and hairstyling, felt unworthy of being a star, untalented, and ashamed. What people called Marilyn's tardiness and temperament was actually her humiliation, MacLaine would later conclude. During the production, Miller interpreted his wife's artistry and humility for the press: "In a whole picture, there may be only two scenes in which she is really proud...She has her own very definite concept of the best way to play a role and she follows it."

Unlike her behavior at Pinewood Studios in London, Marilyn was particularly friendly and interactive with cast and crew, endearing herself to all. Her kindness was reciprocated by their gift of a pearl necklace presented on her birthday. Marilyn established immediate rapport with her stand-in, Evelyn Moriarty (1926-2008), whose role was to take Marilyn's position on the set under the bright lights for tedious lighting set-up and camera blocking. Moriarty was unsure of how to approach Marilyn, but it was Marilyn who sensed her stand-in's apprehension and broke the ice one morning. While cradling her cat, Serafina, Marilyn sweetly introduced Moriarty to the pet.

"She was a wonderful person," Moriarty would say of Marilyn. "I believe when she woke up in the morning, she wondered who she could help. She was very generous and fantastic." The women would share a close and genuine friendship until Marilyn's death, even after. Moriarty remained vehemently protective of her friend's reputation and shared touching anecdotes with biographers. "She treated me more like a friend than a studio associate," Moriarty said. "Before I would go into a scene to stand in for her, she would come over and fix my hair and my clothes and she'd give me the motivation for a scene, so I would know what I was doing. She was my Paula Strasberg."

Marilyn often exercised her power to help with little things, especially when Fox closed down a vendor who had long been serving refreshments to cast and crew on the studio's soundstages. When Marilyn learned of this, she went to the studio brass and advocated for the vendor's return. Her efforts were successful, and she posed for photos at the vendor's counter sipping coffee with Montand and Gene Kelly. Marilyn was especially attentive to the children of cast and crew who visited the set that winter and spring. She charmed Frankie Vaughan's young son David and spent time with two little girls whose sister had recently been killed in an accident.

Marilyn would later delete from her last *Life* interview transcript a comment about anonymously donating money to needy individuals. Knowledge of her generosity was only shared with the public after her death. Moriarty recalled Marilyn's anonymous donation of one thousand dollars toward the funeral expenses of a crewmember's deceased wife during the filming of *Let's Make Love*. In addition, Jack Cole's assistant remembered seeing Marilyn hand a crewmember a roll of bills to help pay for his loved one's surgery. The crewmember cried, which made Marilyn hug him before she silently walked away.

"If she walked on the set and someone admired a sweater she was wearing," summed Moriarty, "the next day, that person received the sweater off her back." Rather spontaneously, Marilyn treated Moriarty to a shopping spree in New York in the middle of production, warranting a telegram of apology to Cukor signed with love from Amanda/Marilyn:

> *My next weekend off I will do any painting cleaning brushing you need around the house. I can also dust. Also I am sending you something...I beg you to understand. Dear Evelyn sends her best... we're both city types.*

Each evening at the Beverly Hills Hotel, Marilyn and Signoret took turns cooking for the foursome. "When Arthur was in town and had dinner with them, I was never invited," Sidney Skolsky wrote. "When he was out of town, I was invited to dinner every night. I really found it amusing watching these sexy, glamorous ladies running across the little porch asking how you went about cooking this dish or that dish. They took risks making the dinner."

To publicize the growing intimacy between the Millers and Montands, Fox commissioned Bruce Davidson to photograph the two couples sharing a home-cooked meal in bungalow 21. "I am always drawn to something that's unexpected, that might open a door to some kind of truth," Davidson explained in a February 2001 article in *Gourmet Magazine* reprinting his work, which his photographs depict. In Davidson's photographs, Montand and Miller visited in the living room as their wives moved into the kitchenette. Signoret, in Scotch-plaid Capri slacks, cooked spaghetti and sauce in two pans on the small stove; Marilyn, in an off-the-shoulder black cocktail dress, set the table, served the meal, and cleared the table.

Marilyn sipped a glass of wine while dreamily reading the liner notes on a Montand record jacket. In one picture, Marilyn sits at the table with the others, a quart of milk at her elbow, symbolizing her femininity, juxtaposed with a bottle of Chateau Lafite-Rothschild but she looked depressed. "Marilyn had an openness and a vulnerability," recalled Davidson, "where the others were worldly sophisticates."

While their spouses "made love" on the set, Miller worked on the screenplay for *The Misfits* in bungalow 20, and Simone busied herself as a housewife in number 21. In the late afternoon, when he finished writing, Miller would stroll across the hall and visit Signoret. She described herself and Marilyn as two women "who lived together as neighbors, as one does in any apartment house anywhere." Marilyn usually wore a blue polka-dotted rayon dressing gown, no makeup or false eyelashes, with her feet bare. Signoret thought she looked like "the most beautiful peasant girl imaginable from Ile-de-France." Marilyn had no fond memories to share about her film work, but instead delighted in hearing Signoret's. Marilyn's happiest professional experience, her new friend learned, was Richard Avedon's photograph session for *Life* in 1958.

On weekends, Marilyn hosted Signoret in the kitchenette of her bungalow for their bonding ritual, when their hair would be dyed blonde by Marilyn's personal colorist, Pearl Porterfield. Thirty years earlier, Porterfield, affectionately called Porter, worked for Metro-Goldwyn-Mayer where she had been a hairdresser to Jean Harlow and perfected her platinum blonde tone. Now the elderly woman lived in retirement in San Diego. Marilyn, at her own expense, had

Porterfield flown to Los Angeles to dye her hair a similar "pillow white," ensuring that the elderly hairdresser continued to feel relevant in the current film industry. On Friday evenings, Marilyn told Simone, "Meet me in the kitchen tomorrow morning at eleven."

On Saturday morning, a limousine collected Porterfield at the airport and drove her to the Beverly Hills Hotel where Marilyn prepared a buffet meal in the kitchenette. Before getting down to business, Porterfield ate with gusto. While coloring, she shared stories of old Hollywood, usually ending with Harlow's funeral. While Porterfild talked, Marilyn and Signoret basked in nostalgia and winked at each other when the elderly woman paused with emotion. Signoret came to realize Marilyn hung on every word of her colorist, interested in the life of her childhood idol. Signoret believed Marilyn had reached out to a worker in the film industry who had long been forgotten.

During one of these beauty treatments, Signoret urged Marilyn to purchase the rights of *They Shoot Horses, Don't They?* and to star in its film adaptation. Unbeknownst to Signoret, silent screen star Charles Chaplin owned the screen rights for this story about a group of contestants in a Depression-era dance marathon, and had expressed the desire to work with Marilyn. In fact, years before, he considered casting her with his son in the film because he felt Marilyn would be believable as the suicidal Gloria, the role Jane Fonda would play nearly a decade later.

When the Hollywood Foreign Press announced its nomination for Best Actress in a Musical or Comedy on February 2, Marilyn was elated to see her nomination for *Some Like It Hot* along with Shirley MacLaine in *Ask Any Girl*, Doris Day in *Pillow Talk*, Dorothy Dandridge in *Porgy and Bess*, and Lilli Palmer in *But Not For Me*. By now, Marilyn clearly knew *Let's Make Love* was evolving into an inferior follow-up to her latest comedy smash.

Meanwhile, on February 8, the Hollywood Chamber of Commerce unveiled the Hollywood Walk of Fame in an official mass dedication ceremony honoring 1,558 personalities from the worlds of radio, recording, television, and film. In one sweeping installation, the sidewalks on each side of Hollywood Boulevard were embedded with pink terrazzo five-point stars rimmed with bronze. Each star contained the inlaid name of an honoree in bronze. Beginning as part of a neighborhood improvement program, the Walk of Fame would continue, immortalizing each generation of luminaries. Even though Marilyn did not attend the event, her star was placed at 6774 Hollywood Boulevard, between Highland and McCadden Avenues. Today the stars of actor Arsenio Hall and actor/former Governor of California Arnold Schwarzenegger flank Marilyn's.

On February 10, Miller traveled to Ireland to meet with John Huston regarding his direction of *The Misfits.* Marilyn worked the next day but left early and worked intermittently in the days to follow. On the evening of the 17th, Signoret entertained Marilyn long into the night with anecdotes about her film work in France and got the impression Marilyn was acting like a "a kid who's delaying the moment for lights out."

The next day, Marilyn failed to report to work and failed to contact the studio. Everyone at the studio feared for her safety when there was no answer at her bungalow. The hotel switchboard operator reported she made an outgoing call, and everyone's concern changed to irritation. An agitated Montand sent Signoret to knock on the door. There was no response. The couple composed a letter and slid it halfway under her door. They watched it slowly disappear into the bungalow.

> "*You can do whatever you like to Spyros Skouras and the Fox studio if that's what you want,*" *the couple had written.* "*But next time you decide to hang around too late listening to my wife tell you stories instead of going to bed, because you've decided not to get up the next morning and go to the studio, please tell me! Don't leave me to work for hours on end on a scene you've already decided not to do the next day. I'm not the enemy. I'm your pal and capricious little girls have never amused me, Best, Yves.*"

Later that evening, Miller called the Montands' bungalow explaining that Marilyn felt ashamed and remorseful. He asked Signoret to rescue his wife by knocking on her door. Signoret agreed, and suddenly, Marilyn appeared and collapsed in her friend's arms. "Please forgive me," she wept. "I won't do it again." The Montands immediately forgave her and found humor in Marilyn having phoned Miller in Dublin so he could he could make a long-distance call to her next-door neighbors. The incident illustrates Marilyn's emotional paralysis and inability to reach out when in crisis.

On the Fox lot, a publicist introduced Marilyn to a young photographer, Lawrence "Larry" Schiller from *Look*. "Hi, Larry from *Look*," she said warmly to the twenty-three-year-old man with two Leica cameras hanging from his neck, "I'm Marilyn." The photographer playfully identified himself as "the Big Bad Wolf." With a smile, Marilyn told Schiller he looked too young to be so bad and invited him into her dressing room. He started shooting as Allan "Whitey" Snyder applied her makeup. Marilyn looked at the photographer through the large mirror and suggested he move to another location where the light was better and the angle was more flattering. It was then that Schiller realized she probably understood photography better than he did and had mastered being its subject.

Marilyn was the first of Schiller's many subjects to observe that he did not close his left eye when he looked into the lens of the camera with his right, making it hard to take a good photograph. Schiller recounted that as a boy, an umbrella fell through a dumbwaiter, injuring his eye and costing its sight. With her eyes tearing, Marilyn acknowledged the loss having changed him.

On March 7, the Screen Actors Guild and the Writers Guild went on strike against the studios in protest of non-payment for the television broadcast of films. All productions in Hollywood shut down. The following day, the Hollywood Foreign Press presented the Golden Globe Awards at the famed Ambassador Hotel. The ceremony was broadcast locally on KTTV Los Angeles.

Sam Shaw came into town to photograph John Wayne and visited the Miller bungalow on the evening of the award ceremony. He found Miller sitting across from the Montands in the living room, all three silent and stoic. Unshaven and disheveled, Miller stared at a steak delivered by room service, and slowly began to cut it. He had returned from Ireland at the end of February. The bizarre silence ended when Marilyn cheerfully called to Shaw from the bathtub where she was soaking nude in ice.

The ice bath was intended to lift and tighten her body to squeeze into a snug gown. Marilyn emerged nude from the tub, and Shaw complimented her figure. The pair chatted in the bedroom as Marilyn dressed and Allan Snyder applied her make-up. Shaw observed

Miller as a doting husband as he helped carry the long train of his wife's gown down the path to an awaiting limousine. Strangely, Miller did not escort her to this momentous event in her career; instead, Rupert Allan accompanied Marilyn to the dinner and ceremony.

At the Ambassador Hotel, where Marilyn had once posed in a bikini at the swimming pool for the Blue Book Modeling Agency, she returned in a tail-finned Cadillac limousine as an accomplished actress with one Golden Globe already on display in her Manhattan Apartment and two nominations. She looked every inch a movie star when she entered the Coconut Grove banquet hall wearing an elegant strapless white gown, white fur, and long gloves. Glenn Ford read the names of the nominees: Dorothy Dandridge, Doris Day, Shirley MacLaine, Lilli Palmer, and Marilyn Monroe.

When he read Marilyn's name as the winner, she demurely navigated on high-heeled shoes up the steps to the stage, while balancing a fur around her shoulders and carrying the long train of her tight gown. Her rhythmic undulation made this feat look effortless. "Thank you with all my heart," Marilyn said at the end of her acceptance speech as Ford and Tony Randall stood behind her on the stage. Later, Marilyn posed for photographs snuggling the award and even kissing it. *Some Like It Hot* swept the Golden Globes with Best Musical or Comedy film, Best Actor and Best Actress in a Musical or Comedy. It was Marilyn's night, and her husband was sitting at home with the Montands. Murmurs in Hollywood started to circulate about the relationship beginning to unravel.

Shelley Winters was nominated for Best Supporting Actress in *The Diary of Anne Frank* but lost earlier in the evening to Susan Kohner for *Imitation of Life* (Winters would later win an Oscar for her performance). Photographed together, Marilyn gently touched Winters' cheek as the two friends smiled and congratulated each other.

On the heels of Marilyn's success, the Academy of Motion Picture Arts and Sciences announced the nominations for Best Actress of 1959: Doris Day in *Pillow Talk*, Audrey Hepburn in *The Nun's Story*, Katharine Hepburn in *Suddenly, Last Summer*, Elizabeth Taylor in *Suddenly, Last Summer*, and Simone Signoret in *Room at the Top*. Glaringly absent was Marilyn's seriocomic performance in *Some Like It Hot*. All the nominated performances, with the exception of Day's, were in dramatic films.

As the Millers left the Beverly Hills Hotel en route to New York and Roxbury to wait out the writers' strike, Marilyn embraced Signoret warmly and said, "I know you're going to win!" Never competitive in her career, Marilyn genuinely rooted for her friend and expressed no bitterness about her lack of a nomination. In fact, she was always the first to bring Signoret newspaper clippings predicting her Oscar win. Deep down, however, Marilyn felt deeply disappointed for being professionally invalidated once again.

During the remainder of the writers' strike, the Millers returned to their farmhouse in Connecticut, where Arthur continued to work on his screenplay. Rupert Allan provided insight to the state of their marriage: "For him to snub his nose at the strike confused [Marilyn] and then made her lose respect for him. She had thought of him as a principled person, an Abraham Lincoln." According to Allan, because Miller flaunted his intelligence to the cast and crew and turned against Marilyn, people began to dislike and avoid him. Suddenly, Marilyn grew ashamed of her husband.

In Connecticut, Marilyn involved herself in local politics and was appointed the Democratic Party's Alternate Delegate to the Fifth Congressional District. The 1960 presidential campaign primaries were in full swing. During the early spring, she became more active in her role as a sponsor of SANE, the National Committee for a Sane Nuclear Policy, along with Marlon Brando, Shirley MacLaine, and Gene Kelly. In an interview for *Redbook* in 1962, Alan Levy asked Marilyn to identify her worst nightmare. "The H-bomb," she responded. "What's yours?"

On hiatus, Marilyn continued her correspondence with Lester Markel, the sixty-year-old Sunday editor of *The New York Times*. After his death, Markel's daughter discovered a letter from Marilyn, dated March 29, stuffed in the back of a desk drawer, and it would be published in its entirety in Lois Banner's *MM-Personal: From the Private Archive of Marilyn Monroe*. Marilyn opens with an expression of fondness for the editor and compliments his March 27th article on Sean O'Casey, the Irish playwright who had recently turned eighty. She also revisits a recent political conversation with Markel and concedes her original opinion of the lack of a strong presidential candidate for the *New York Times'* endorsement.

Marilyn suggests Rockefeller as a viable candidate based upon his sharing Republican partisanship with the newspaper and his being "more liberal than many of the Democrats." She also names Hubert Humphrey as viable, despite her inability to unearth information about him, and parenthetically clarifies this is not an accusation against Markel's newspaper. Marilyn also rules out Adlai Stevenson as too intellectual for the masses. She personally endorses Supreme Court Justice William O. Douglas—a civil libertarian who would serve the longest term on the high court—but disqualifies him on the basis of being divorced. In an apparent burst of inspiration, Marilyn suggests the ticket of Douglas for President and Kennedy for Vice President so that the Catholics who would reject Douglas' divorce would still vote for the ticket based upon the Irish-Catholic Kennedy.

Therefore, she concludes, Stevenson could serve more appropriately as Secretary of State. Marilyn segways to the topic of Fidel Castro, Cuban Communist revolutionary and politician who served as Prime Minister of Cuba from 1959 to 1976. She asserts her belief in democracy and chides the United States for turning its back on Cuba after the revolution excised the regime of Dictator Fulgencio Battista in 1959, and the newspaper for biased reporting. Marilyn excuses television personality John Daly's recent ridiculing of Castro appearance at a fundraiser out of his typical army fatigues and in a tuxedo as unequally biased given his national role as an entertainer.

The letter's conclusion becomes more personal. Marilyn asks about Merkel and his wife's wellbeing and assumes the latter is happy since "she sits at the foot of your table." Marilyn also inquires if the couple's amaryllis bloomed this season, as hers had not. "It's a little like me," she writes. "But there's still hope." Marilyn confirmed rumors that she had been visiting Merkel's building to see her "wonderful" doctor and playfully explains she had avoided him for a specific reason. "I didn't want you to get a glimpse of me, though, until I was wearing my Somali leopard," she writes the elderly man with harmless flirtation. "I want you to think of me as a predatory animal." In the postscript, Marilyn adds her presidential race slogans for 1960: "Nix on Nixon," "Over the hump with Humphrey;" "Stymied with Symington," "Back to Boston by Xmas—Kennedy". She clearly had little faith in Kennedy's bid for the party's nomination.

The thirty-second Academy Award Ceremony was held at the RKO Pantages Theatre on Hollywood Boulevard on Monday, April 4. *Some Like It Hot* only received one award, for costume design. *Ben-Hur* eclipsed all other films that year, winning a total eleven awards—of twelve nominations—including Best Picture, Best Director, Best Actor, and Best Supporting Actor. Costing over $15 million, *Ben-Hur* broke the previous year's all-time record winner, *Gigi*, and remained the most Oscar-honored film until *Titanic* (1997) and *Lord of the Rings: Return of the King* (2003) joined it in a tie for eleven awards. *Ben-Hur* may have received almost a dozen awards, but *Some Like It Hot* proved to age better because in 1998, the American Film Institute announced the top 100 films of all time, and placed *Some Like It Hot* fourteenth and *Ben-Hur* seventy-second.

Later, when director Vincente Minnelli approached Montand, Montand says, "The next Oscar is for best actress, and Marilyn say my wife is going to get it." Marilyn's prediction rang true, and Rock Hudson placed the golden statue in Simone Signoret's hands. Never jealous of the success of her female peers, Marilyn was thrilled by Signoret's recognition, even though she was slighted by not being nominated for *Some Like It Hot.*

Meanwhile, Miller, accompanied by producer Frank Taylor and scenic designer Steven Grimes, left New York for Reno to scout locations for *The Misfits*. Riding the wave of her success, Signoret departed for Rome to begin a film. As fate would allow, Marilyn and Montand would be left without chaperones to shoot loves scenes at Fox during the day and to return each night to side-by-side bungalows.

On April 11, Marilyn returned to Los Angeles weighing considerably more than when she left. She reported to the studio the following day, and it soon became clear that the wardrobe department needed to alter her costumes. However, more than Marilyn's weight changed during the break, and the buzz in the studio's commissary focused on the deterioration of her emotional state. Tony Randall told Barbara Leaming that when Cukor yelled "Action!" Marilyn's face lit up and her eyes brightened. When he yelled "Cut!" her shoulders drooped in "desperate depression." Marilyn reminded him of a deflated tire, with her head down when the camera was not rolling. Randall observed her getting into a limousine and slumping down into the back seat; he sensed her self-loathing and pitied her plight.

On the heels of her Golden Globe win, Rupert Allan arranged for Marilyn to be interviewed by the French magazine *Marie Claire*. Editor Georges Belmont brought along a tape recorder as he promised to strictly transcribe her words for publication in the October 1960 issue. "I just let her go ahead and speak," he explained. "The only pressure I exerted was silence. When she was silent, I didn't say anything either, and when she couldn't stand it any longer and continued talking, she usually said something very important, something very moving." It was a lengthy and intimate interview. On audiotape, Marilyn sounded serious and thoughtful in her natural voice, different from her screen persona. She was also quite articulate. At times she broke into a laugh. Occasionally, there was conversation and laughter in the background. When it grew louder, Marilyn cautioned, "Shh, excuse us—it's being taped."

Marilyn spoke at length about her childhood, her work, her marriages, her goals, her daily routine, and her personal philosophy. When she spoke about work, she stated, "My one desire is to do my best, the best that I can from the moment the camera starts until it stops. That moment I want to be perfect, as perfect as I can make it." She was also quoted saying about marriage, "When I dreamt of love, that was also something that had to be as perfect as possible."

When Belmont asked if she were happy, Marilyn commented in a sincere tone on the relativity of happiness and reflected the question back to him. Belmont told her that he thought she was happy. "If I'm generally anything," Marilyn replied, "I'm miserable." She punctuated the statement with a laugh. Finally, she indicated a degree of happiness: "I'm only thirty-four and have a few years to go, yet I hope to have time to become better and happier, professionally and in my personal life. That's my one ambition. Maybe I'll need a long time, because I'm slow. I don't want to say that it's the best method, but it's the only one I know and it gives me the feeling that in spite of everything life is not without hope."

Belmont inquired about her social life and support system. Marilyn explained:

> I like people, but sometimes I wonder how sociable I am. I can easily be alone and it doesn't bother me...I think there are two things about human beings—at least, I think there are about

> me: they want to be alone and they also want to be together. I have a gay side to me and also a sad side. That's a real problem.

A lasting theme in this stage of Marilyn's life is emotional maturity and honesty. She was no longer the giddy starlet wearing a mask of happiness and convincing the interviewer that everything is fine. "Above all," Marilyn asserted, "I want to be treated like a human being." Marilyn also synthesized her life down to two issues that mattered most to her that she must resolve: "Love and work are the only things that really happen to us. Everything else doesn't really matter. I think that one without the other isn't so good—you need both."

While Marilyn shared her philosophies with Georges Belmont, Miller continued to travel, scouting locations for *The Misfits*. "*I have never known her so happy at work*," Miller wrote to Cukor in a letter filled with loving thoughts of his wife. "*You must know now some of the reasons why she is so precious to me...*" He concluded with dread of being away from Marilyn in a work-imposed "bachelorhood."

When Miller returned, Marilyn invited Montand to dinner. Miller elected instead to go east to visit his children during their spring vacation; he asked Montand to attend to Marilyn. By now Miller represented betrayal to his wife, and he believed she was beyond his help. He would later say that anyone capable of making Marilyn laugh during this period was a blessing to him.

Montand couldn't understand Miller leaving him in charge of Marilyn and sought the advice of her friend, Doris Vidor. Didn't Miller see that Marilyn was beginning to throw herself at her co-star? Vidor speculated that Miller, indeed, sent his wife directly toward Montand's open arms. Marilyn and Montand's notorious affair lasted from April to June. They joined the ranks of many co-stars whose onscreen romance spilled into reality. Eddie Fisher had recently cheated on wife Debbie Reynolds with the widow of his best friend, Elizabeth Taylor, garnering a mountain of unfavorable publicity for the illicit lovers. Montand was the only co-star with whom Marilyn had an affair while she was married.

The affair sparked when Marilyn was ill, feverish, and resting in her bungalow. "Say good-night to Marilyn," Paula Strasberg instructed Montand. "It'll make her feel better." "It was the dullest exchange you can imagine..." Montand later wrote of his subsequent visit to bungalow number twenty, "I still had a half-page to work on for the next day. I bent down to put a good-night kiss on her cheek. And her head turned, and my lips went wild. It was a wonderful, tender kiss. A kiss of fire. I was half stunned, stammering. I straightened up, already flooded with guilt, wondering what was happening to me. I didn't wonder for long." Montand later admitted feeling "this powerful radiation, the impact of the amazing charisma!" The details remain undocumented. Rumors swept through the Beverly Hills Hotel, ranging from Marilyn visiting Montand's bungalow the next day wearing nothing under her mink to Marilyn permitting the room service delivery waiter to see her in Montand's bedroom.

In *My Lucky Stars*, Shirley MacLaine, Montand's soon future co-star and lover, provided insight to the aroused climate of film studios and on-location productions. "Locations in those days, before AIDS," she writes, "were a byword for sexual freedom...Sometimes [the] antics were hilarious. Most of [the stars] had secure and long-term marriages, but monogamy was not the accepted role of the day...It was kind of experimental swapping of working partners for the duration of the film."

The Monroe-Montand affair coincided with what many social historians argue was the catalyst for both the Sexual Revolution and the Modern Women's Movement: the introduction of the first oral contraceptive for women. On May 9, the Food and Drug Administration announced approval of Enovid, commonly referred to as "the pill." Revolution seems an overstatement as contraception for even married couples remained illegal in several states until 1965, and unmarried women were unable to access the pill in all fifty states until a decade after Marilyn's death.

However, the morals of Hollywood in 1960 certainly did not reflect those of the general population. The contraceptive pill for women created unprecedented controversy in Western culture, forcing Americans to revisit attitudes and beliefs regarding sexual morality and women's roles. American women now had a similar sexual freedom as men in the elimination of their worry about unwanted pregnancy. This freedom also created opportunities for economic independence and power. Ready or not, the culture took a huge step toward gender equality.

Marilyn struggled with her own recent sexual choice and attended a long psychiatric session with psychiatrist Romeo "Ralph" Greenson during the first week of the affair. She also turned to her friend Elia Kazan (in town working on *Splendor in the Grass* with Natalie Wood) and confided her resentment of Miller's pattern of regarding himself as morally superior to others. Kazan, himself once romantically involved with Marilyn during the time Miller was interested in her, contacted Miller in an act of compassion.

The difference between this affair and the one in her previous marriage was Marilyn's lack of secrecy. With Hal Schaeffer, Marilyn was discreet; DiMaggio was prone to violence. With Montand, Marilyn was blatant; she had lost respect for her husband and had no reason to fear for her physical safety, as Miller had never battered her. Instead, he was rejecting and arguably emotionally abusive. Marilyn was already detached from her marriage, and may have been planning her escape through another relationship. She might also have felt justified in infidelity or sought to express her detachment through it. Miller had already betrayed her through his exposed diary entry four years earlier. The affair with Montand may have served both as Marilyn's retaliation and disengagement.

Among Marilyn's possessions preserved after her death was a note she wrote to Paula Strasberg during this time, possibly while they sat together in silence: "*When he sees me on the screen, he can't wait to get me home…but I'm there, Paula, I'm right there.*" The exact date and context are unknown, but one can imagine Marilyn passing notes to Paula on the film set. The passage implies a partner's arousal to her screen persona and personal feelings of rejection by the same partner. Is she referring to Miller? Does she imply that Miller was now primarily sexually responsive only to her screen image?

Columnists blasted Montand for exploiting Marilyn's vulnerability for, in Signoret's understanding words, "what may have happened during my weeks in Rome and Miller's weeks in New York between a man, my husband, and a woman, my pal, who were working together, living under the same roof, and consequently sharing their solitudes, their fears, their moods, and their recollections of childhood poverty."

David O. Selznick, producer of *Gone with the Wind*, and his actress wife, Jennifer Jones, invited about forty guests to a dinner buffet in May, including Cheryl Crawford. Crawford wanted to see Montand in a Broadway musical and used this opportunity to orchestrate an introduction to Selznick, who was now producing theatrical shows. In acknowledgement of Montand and Marilyn as a couple, Crawford took them along to the dinner. Montand, in turn, asked Doris Vidor to tag along, and she observed the lovers inciting gawks from the other guests.

According to Fred Lawrence Guiles, Marilyn gravitated to a drawing room where film industry attorney Gregson Bautzer discussed Joseph Schenck's failing health following a stroke three years earlier. As Schenck was dying, he asked for Marilyn. Allegedly, Marilyn vowed she would never forgive herself if she didn't go visit him.

Bautzer, intoxicated, was particularly hateful toward Marilyn. "You're too damned late!" he allegedly shouted at her. Later, Montand found Marilyn trembling in a corner and left, ordering Rudy, the chauffeur, to return for his two female companions. When Marilyn realized Montand left, she ran down the steep slope to the street, shouting that she'll catch up with the car. The chauffeur returned and collected Marilyn, who some time later remembered Doris Vidor and asked him to turn back.

Rupert Allan recounted another version of the evening to Sandra Shevey. The Selznicks' party was the first time he saw Marilyn stand up for herself when harshly confronted rather than bursting into tears. "I have been to see Mr. Schenck last week," she told Bautzer. "I had a long visit with him." Allan remembered accompanying Marilyn to visit the dying man because she did not want to go alone. She felt an obligation to him, although there was never a romance between the two, because he had been kind to her while she lived at the Hollywood Studio Club.

A nurse escorted Marilyn to Schenck's deathbed while Allan waited outside with Schenck's brother. The men heard laughter through the wall for the duration of the visit. "I don't understand it," the brother told Marilyn when she emerged from the room. "I have been here ten days. Some days he won't even see me. It is the first time I have heard my brother laugh in years. It is the best thing in the world. It is the best treatment anyone can give. Please come back." Harry Brand followed up with a letter to Marilyn dated June 2nd expressing appreciation for visiting Schenck and cheering him.

June 1 marked Marilyn's thirty-fourth birthday during the filming of the "Specialization" number. At the end of the workday, the cast and crew gathered to celebrate around a banquet table set with a cake, a greeting card, and a display created by studio artists. The display featured dolls depicting each member of the cast in the "Specialization" number including the impersonators for Elvis Presley, Maria Callas, and Van Cliburn surrounding a miniature piano. The Marilyn doll, perched on the greeting card, wore black tights, a mole, and a miniature replica of her pearl necklace. The Elvis figurine was complete with a guitar. The cast and crew contributed two dollars each to present Marilyn with a seed pearl necklace. Joseph Krutak drew the birthday card depicting Marilyn wearing a black leotard and graduation mortarboard as she holds open a book by Alexander Dumas.

Signatures on the card include studio maid Hazel Washington, Cukor, Montand, Agnes Flanagan, Jack Cole, Marjorie Pletcher, John Gatto "Little Elvis", Bunny Gardel, and limousine driver, Rudy Kautzky. After serving the cake, Marilyn sat in a folding chair in her spangled gown and visited with some children of the cast and crew. Playwright Tennessee Williams and his mother, Edwina, visited the set that day and wished Marilyn well. Edwina had been the inspiration for her son's masterpiece *The Glass Menagerie.* She complimented Marilyn as "a real southern girl."

Afterward, Rupert Allan hosted a birthday party for Marilyn in his Benedict Canyon villa on Seabright Place. A few weeks earlier, she previewed the invitation list (including playwright Clifford Odets, Tennessee Williams, Williams' mother, Jack Lemmon, James Stewart, and Gary Cooper) and thought the party would be a disaster because none of the guests knew each other. "They all know you," Allan replied. "Besides, they'll be interested in meeting one another." When Allan telephoned the Russian author Nabokov to invite him, Mrs. Nabokov abruptly declined, citing her husband was working hard and didn't need such a distraction. More open to a diversion, Xenia Chekhov, the widow of Marilyn's former acting coach, Michael Chekhov, accepted the invitation along with Marilyn's former mime coach, Lotte Goslar.

The party was a smashing success. Marilyn spent most of the evening engrossed in discussion about American dramatic theater with Odets and Williams, Odets staying until four o'clock in the morning reading palms. Songwriter Sammy Cahn, one of the guests, followed up with a letter to Marilyn thanking her for a "marvelous time" and soliciting a future invitation.

Gary Cooper, recovering from surgery related to prostate and colon cancer, expressed his regret at declining her invitation in a typed letter. "*It was your good thoughts, good deed, and good wishes that helped me get out of the hospital in record time*," he wrote. "*The roses were beautiful and I can't tell you how much I appreciate the trouble you went to. I just want to thank you with all my heart.*" Rupert Allan followed up by hosting an intimate dinner party for Marilyn, Tennessee Williams, Williams' mother and brother. Marilyn shared a great sense of humor with the gay playwright, and they laughed so uproariously that they nearly fell off the sofa.

* * *

By most accounts, Marilyn and Elvis Presley never met. However, according to Alanna Nash, the King of Rock and Roll was on the Fox lot for costume fittings for a period western, *Flaming Star*, and fleetingly crossed paths with the studio's reigning queen. Interested in meeting Marilyn—and perhaps curious to see the three actors impersonating him in her film—Presley and two "barely civilized" members of his entourage rode bicycles to the soundstage where *Let's Make Love* was in production. "How are you, Miss Monroe?" Presley politely asked upon encountering Marilyn in a bathrobe. She smiled, but her expression changed to fear and disgust upon noticing his disorderly companions. Marilyn quickly excused herself with a complaint of a headache caused by allergies.

Cukor filmed the last musical number on June 10th. Frankie Vaughn and Marilyn's characters rehearse "Let's Make Love," their cabaret show's title song, with Tony and Amanda pursuing each other on a minimalistic stage set with modern swiveling sofas. At times they are nearly positioned horizontally. The censors deemed their amorous actions, in combination with the lyrics, completely unacceptable by reason of "offensive sex suggestiveness." Marilyn argued with her natural good humor that they could be having sex standing up.

Marilyn completed her scenes on June 16. After an exhausting six months of production, the film wrapped twenty-eight days over schedule. Wilfred Hyde-White kissed Marilyn's cheek and thanked her "for the longest and most remunerative contract I've ever had." On June 24 she and Montand previewed a roughly edited version of the film. Marilyn and Montand now regularly appeared together in public as a couple. Affairs between co-stars have always been common, and so the Hollywood community didn't flinch. Wrapped in a mink coat and on the arm of her lover, Marilyn attended the premiere of Billy Wilder's *The Apartment* at Grauman's Chinese Theatre on June 21st. Afterward, United Artists hosted a huge party at Romanoff's where Marilyn entered, warmly embraced Wilder, and gushed about the film and her desire to work with him again. Wilder and the Mirisch Company pursued her for the leading role in *Irma La Douce* with Charles Laughton as co-star.

"I'm possibly mad, but that's who I want," Wilder would tell Roderick Mann a few weeks later. "All right, I know that after *Some Like It Hot* I swore I'd never use her again. She's like my smoking. I keep swearing off cigarettes but I still get through sixty a day." *Some Like It Hot* was a challenging act to follow, but Wilder struck gold again with *The Apartment.* The plot is pure Wilder and Diamond, further pushing the envelope with a satire about sexual infidelity, abusive male power over females, and climbing the corporate ladder. Jack Lemmon is C. C. Baxter, a lonely drone working for an insurance company in Manhattan who advances in the company by loaning his apartment to four executives requiring a place to conduct their extramarital affairs.

Marilyn would have been effective in the role of Fran Kubelik, (played by Shirley MacLaine) who was the elevator operator and object of Lemmon's affection who is having an affair with the company's married personnel director, Mr. Sheldrake (Fred MacMurray). However, Wilder was unlikely to cast her again in his next project after her challenges during *Some Like It Hot.* Apparently, Marilyn was amused with Wilder's nod to her when he cast a Monroe imitator, Joyce Jameson, in a brief scene in which one executive, Ray Walston (later known in the television series *My Favorite Martian*) urgently calls Baxter from a bar for the use of his apartment because the woman he has just met and wants to hook up with "looks like Marilyn Monroe!"

Baxter begins to resent his role in the shenanigans when he learns Miss Kubelik is the woman being used by his superior. Miss Kubelik attempts suicide by overdosing on sleeping pills in the apartment on Christmas Eve after Sheldrake gives her cash in place of a gift and rushes home to his family to celebrate the holiday. Baxter nurses her back to health and provides well-intentioned counseling while the pair plays gin rummy. In the end, Miss Kubelik decides Baxter is the man for her and leaves Sheldrake for him on New Year's Eve. In the final scene, when Baxter declares his love for Miss Kubelick over a hand of gin rummy, MacLaine delivers the famous final line, *a la* Joe E. Brown in *Some Like It Hot*: "Shut up and deal." *The Apartment* would win the Academy Award for Best Picture and its plot involving a woman's ill-fated relationship with a married man would foreshadow Marilyn's destiny with Montand. Miss Kubelik's lover had no intention of leaving his wife, and neither did Montand.

None of Marilyn's biographers offer an explanation of the affair's demise, but we are told she believed Montand would soon leave his wife. In her fantasy, Marilyn didn't want to hurt Signoret and hoped to retain their friendship after she and Montand married. At the end of August, Hedda Hopper interviewed Montand and published his statements in early September. "She is simple without any guile," Montand allegedly said, as quoted by Hopper. "Perhaps I was too tender and thought she was as sophisticated as some of the other ladies I have known. Had Marilyn been sophisticated, none of this would have happened…she is known throughout the world, but she is still a child. Perhaps she had a schoolgirl crush. If she did, I'm sorry. But nothing will break up my marriage."

Signoret doubted her husband ever uttered these words to Hopper. His lack of proficiency in English prevented him from such grammar and pronunciation, she argued. Perhaps Hopper had taken "her revenge." Signoret denounced the gossip maven for terrorizing those she disliked in Hollywood and breaking marriages through her column. Signoret also told the press: "The real problem is that when a woman feels the physical attraction of a man who is not her husband, she must also feel she is in love to justify it. It is no longer casual even in passing. A man, on the other hand, doesn't feel he has to confuse an affair with eternal love and make it a crisis in marriage." The Montands aligned in their marital bond and implied Marilyn was foolish to expect the affair to be anything more than a meaningless fling. Marilyn felt ashamed, hurt, and humiliated. *Paris Match* ignored Montand's complicity and concluded, "The Montands had survived Hurricane Marilyn." "Marilyn was wracked with guilt and embarrassment," Rupert Allan recalled. "I remember her saying, 'I shouldn't have done it because he's married.' I think she felt shame about it." Marilyn's infidelity to Miller seemed a secondary concern, but her strong reaction to the public disclosure of an affair must have been mortifying, given her reclusion to the bungalow in response to Montand's reprimand for not reporting to work.

As condescending as their statements sound, Montand and Signoret actually spoke the truth. Marilyn was unlike other famous actresses who engaged in meaningless affairs with their co-stars. She fell in love with Montand and assumed he felt similarly; she expected to live with him happily ever after. It may have been devastating to sacrifice her marriage with the hope of another relationship only to learn her lover was interested in nothing more than a transient sexual connection and nothing more. The Montands' European attitudes about an "open" marriage contrasted with Marilyn's notion of an American romance, something both she and Hollywood were selling in movies in the 1950s. Montand would later express tender feelings for Marilyn, but long after she was gone.

As Montand gained perspective in the years after Marilyn's death, he wrote: "Not for a moment did I think of breaking with my wife, but if she had slammed the door on me, I would probably have made my life with Marilyn, or tried to. That was the direction we were moving in. Maybe it would have lasted only two or three years. I didn't have too many illusions. Still, what years they would have been!"

How did the storm leave the Miller marriage? Miller would omit the affair from his autobiography. Some sources assert the couple civilly and mutually concluded the marriage was over, but agreed to remain together temporarily to complete *The Misfits.* Marilyn would pine after Montand until she left Los Angeles to begin her next film.

The Fox publicity machine launched a campaign to lure audiences away from the television news reports covering the impending presidential election. The July 5 issue of *Look* featured a story titled "Marilyn Meets Montand" with a casual portrait of the co-stars smiling brightly on the cover. Marilyn wears a striped turtleneck sweater and Montand, in a cardigan, resembles DiMaggio. An extreme close-up of the couple in the throes of passion from the film's final scene appeared on the August 15 cover of *Life*, Marilyn with eyes closed and Montand embracing her from behind, his lips caressing her neck.

Fox promised "The Best Entertainment Offer You've Had in Years!" and organized a premiere in Reno, where Marilyn was scheduled to film *The Misfits*. Rather ominously, the city experienced an electrical blackout on the evening of the event. The premiere was canceled and never rescheduled. Fox released the film nationally on September 8, and for the most part, the critics panned it. Indeed, it had shortcomings because the supporting characters were dull, the script was trite, Cukor's direction was rather unfocused, the pacing was slow, and the editing was rough at times.

With all its deficits, the film is average; but the public expected a Marilyn Monroe film to produce above average results. Regardless, Marilyn is delightful and approachable in the role. She speaks in her natural voice, her manner is natural and unaffected, she portrays Amanda as the real Monroe. However, not all the critics seemed to like the real Monroe.

"The old Monroe dynamism is lacking in the things she is given to do by the cliché-clogged script," announced crusty Bosley Crowther in *The New York Times*. "It doesn't seem very important that she is finally brought together with Mr. Montand." He goes on to comment on Marilyn's lack of purpose, "fumbling" on the sidelines and "sighing" songs.

For the first time, reviews lambasted Marilyn for having gained weight. "In the acting department, Miss Monroe is not impressive as in comedy-type roles," observed *Hollywood Citizen News*. It gets harsh: "She plays a straight part here and does little. Visually? Marilyn offers her famous curves, not a little on the fleshy side. Diet, anyone?"

Conversely, *New York World-Telegram and Sun* noticed the public's positive response to her musical performance: "Marilyn Monroe is geared for some of the loudest laughter of her life...It is a gay, preposterously and completely delightful romp...Marilyn actually dares comparison with Mary Martin by singing 'My Heart Belongs to Daddy' in the first scene. The night I saw it, the audience broke into the picture with applause."

Bosley Crowther found Montand's charisma lacking and his French accent a "poor excuse for charm." In the end, Crowther concluded that Uncle Miltie effortlessly walked away with an "ambling and shambling" film in its first hour before his entrance, "Who (aside from his mother) would ever have expected to see Milton Berle steal a show, without much effort, from Marilyn Monroe and Yves Montand?" *Let's Make Love* received an Oscar nomination for best scoring of a musical but lost to *Song without End*, the story of composer Franz Liszt, directed by Charles Vidor. However, it received a Golden Globe nomination for Best Musical Motion Picture and a nomination for Best Written American Musical by the Writers Guild of America.

In her autobiography, *Nostalgia Isn't What It Used to Be* (1978), Signoret wrote a loving portrait of Marilyn: "She never knew to what degree I never detested her." Signoret continued to cherish a gift Marilyn had given her and wrote about forgiving Marilyn's betrayal in metaphor: "She's gone without ever knowing that I never stopped wearing the champagne colored silk scarf she'd lent me one day... It's a bit frayed now, but if I fold it carefully, the fray doesn't show."

Signoret also wrote of fireside chats with Miller at the Beverly Hills Hotel in 1960 in which he recounted how Marilyn extricated him from the Communist witch hunts. Miller had explained how Marilyn announced to the press that she loved him because he was a good and respectable man. "One of two things could [have] happened," Signoret wrote, "her total destruction, or the rehabilitation in the eyes of the public of a man." When Spyros Skouras told Marilyn that Fox might destroy her if she stayed with Miller, she told the film mogul to go ahead; they would flee to Europe. Signoret declared it was "well worth an act, or a scene, or a few lines" in Miller's *After the Fall*, an unflattering, semi-autobiographical play about the marriage that was performed after Marilyn's death.

"I think [Marilyn and Montand] both felt attraction," Shirley MacLaine recalled, "and didn't mean to hurt anyone with it." Montand went on to co-star with Shirley MacLaine in *My Geisha* (1962), Norman Krasna's next screenplay, and engaged in an affair with her as well. Later on, she probed him about the relationship with Marilyn. "It was a sweet adventure," Montand would reply before going on to describe Marilyn's insecurity about her beauty, her acting, and herself. Moved, MacLaine would realize her questions had been "intrusive and insensitive."

MacLaine ended the affair when she learned Montand had bet her husband that he would seduce her. When she confronted Montand, he said nothing to defend himself, and seemingly acknowledged the trouble he had caused with his affair with Marilyn. MacLaine would write: "He knew he had been insensitive in his public reaction to her ongoing adoration of him." MacLaine acknowledged Montand's placement of Signoret in an undefended position by hurting her pride, but Signoret still loved him. Montand would continue dalliances with other women, and Hollywood questioned Signoret's sexual orientation in light of her tolerance for his conduct.

Montand remained unfaithfully married to Signoret until her death in 1985 from pancreatic cancer. He remarried two years later and had a child at age sixty-seven. Subsequently, another woman accused Montand of fathering her daughter, but he refused to cooperate with a court order for a DNA sample. In 1991, Montand died of a heart attack immediately after shooting his last scene in *The Island of Pachyderms*, a film about a man who dies of a heart attack. The paternity suit persisted after his death and resulted in the exhumation of his body. Post mortem DNA testing ultimately proved Montand was not the girl's father, but the dramatic and publicized sex life of France's aging sex symbol did not end there. Montand's stepdaughter, Signoret's daughter, published an autobiography titled *World Upside Down*, alleging that he sexually abused her beginning at age five.

On the twentieth anniversary of Marilyn's death, the *Good Morning America* television program would interview Montand, who struggled to eulogize Marilyn with limited English proficiency but apparent authenticity:

> She was somebody very exceptional. She helped me a lot... She came and I came from low classes in the society...[and this commonality contributed to] a very tender relationship. I try to be the most sincere. I came today because—for twenty years I refused to talk about Marilyn officially—because I'm hearing and I read some unbelievable, awful, incredible things that make me mad...She was very intelligent more than intelligent for me. She [had] good sense. Inside, she had [the

feelings] of a child—something rare for a human being—with this fantastic, wonderful body...I made her laugh often, and when Marilyn laughed it meant something...She was very deep[ly] sad. She was like this [pointing his finger up and down to illustrate high and low emotions]. When she was sad, she was very, very sad...For me she was more than an actress, not just for me but for millions of people.

* * *

[For a synopsis of *Let's Make Love*, see **Appendix: Selected Marilyn Monroe Film Synopses**]

Chapter Eleven: Spring & Summer 1960

When Marilyn's affair with Montand plunged her into confusion and crisis on the set of *Let's Make Love*, Dr. Marianne Kris called from Manhattan and recommended a colleague in Los Angeles, Dr. Ralph Greenson. His credentials seemed impressive: Clinical Professor of Psychiatry at the University of California Medical School at Los Angeles, Dean of the Training School at the Los Angeles Institute for Psychoanalysis, a member of the Medical Advisory Board of the Reiss-Davis Clinic, and psychoanalyst to Frank Sinatra. Perhaps Greenson's connection to the singer convinced Marilyn of his credibility.

At forty-nine, Greenson was an attractive man and fatherly figure with salt and pepper hair receding at the temples, a long nose, and rather sensuous lips beneath a neatly trimmed mustache. In photographs, his penetrating and deeply inset dark eyes convey compassion and empathy. He veered from the Freudian approach by facing his patients in session rather than sitting behind the couch. Outspoken and confrontational, Greenson spoke in a New York accent and may have reminded Marilyn of Lee Strasberg with a medical degree.

The son of Russian Jewish immigrants Joel and Katharine Greenschpoon from Minsk, Russia, Marilyn's new psychiatrist was born Romeo Greenschpoon on September 20, 1911, the fraternal twin to Juliet, in the Brownsville neighborhood of Brooklyn, New York. Known as the Red District, Brownsville drew Marxist socialists who protested the local economic and social conditions of largely first generation European immigrants who worked in factories. Brownsville produced luminaries such as George Gershwin, composer; Phil Silvers and Jerry Lewis, comedians; and Shelley Winters, actress.

Joel worked as a pharmacist, and Katharine served as his assistant. The couple later settled in a tenement in the Lower East Side of Manhattan where they became prominent members of the Labor Lyceum, a social and political forum where early advocates for unionizing gathered and later organized the International Ladies Garment Workers' Union. Katharine booked speakers and concert artists to the Lyceum including Frederick Vanderbilt Field, a leader in the labor movement. Field and his wife would befriend Marilyn in Mexico in the last months of her life.

When his twin children were age three, Joel graduated from Columbia University with a medical degree. Subsequently, siblings Elizabeth and Washington were born. Katharine, an accomplished pianist, passed on to most of her children a gift of music. Elizabeth became a piano virtuoso, and Romeo played violin. A boy named Romeo who played violin was an easy target of teasing on a Brooklyn school playground, so in fifth grade, Romeo (called Romi by his friends) solved the problem by unofficially changing his name to Ralph.

Greenson graduated medical school in 1932 and studied psychoanalysis in Vienna with Wilhelm Stekel (1868-1940), a founding member of the Vienna Psychoanalytic Society with Freudian-Marxist beliefs. A student of Freud, Stekel contributed to the theory of fetishism and coined the word "paraphilia" to replace "perversion." Sadly, he committed suicide in London by taking an overdose of aspirin.

Ralph served an internship at Cedars of Lebanon Hospital in Hollywood along with intern Hyman Engelberg, whom he befriended. After legally changing his name to Ralph R. Greenson in 1937, he opened a practice on Wilshire Boulevard. That same year, Hilde gave birth to a son, Daniel, followed by a daughter, Joan, in 1941. Greenson joined the Southern California Psychoanalytic Study Group formed by Ernst Simmel and Otto Fenichel.

According to Donald H. Wolfe, Colonel John M. Murray, Commanding Officer of Fort Logan's Psychiatric Unit, approached Greenson to establish a teaching hospital in psychiatry. The author speculates this may be the same John Murray who married Eunice J. Murray, Marilyn's housekeeper in the last year of her life. Wolfe's research revealed the Colonel's military records indicating he was born in 1897 (the same year as Eunice's husband) and studied in Vienna in 1932.

Discharged in 1946, Greenson re-established his practice and founded the Los Angeles Psychoanalytic Society with ties to Anna Freud in London. The following year, he and Hildi purchased a home at 902 Franklin Street, Santa Monica, from John and Eunice Murray. He also served as Clinical Professor of Psychiatry at UCLA Medical School and as Supervising Analyst at the Los Angeles Psychoanalytic Society and Institute.

By 1960, Greenson practiced in a penthouse office at 405 North Bedford Drive in Beverly Hills, shared with Dr. Milton Wexler. After suffering a heart attack in 1955, Greenson often worked from his home in the afternoons, offering privacy to many of his famous clients. Aside from Frank Sinatra, he treated Tony Curtis, Peter Lorre, Vincente Minnelli, and Vivien Leigh. Greenson published his insight into working with this unique population in the article "Special Problems in Psychotherapy with the Rich and Famous."

When Greenson arrived at Marilyn's bungalow at the Beverly Hills Hotel during the production of *Let's Make Love*, he noted that she was conditioned to go straight to the couch for a session of Freudian therapy. However, Greenson did not sit behind his patients' heads and take notes. He met with his patients face-to-face, which took Marilyn out of her safety zone. Greenson's correspondence with colleagues examined by Anthony Summers revealed that Marilyn initially appeared too fragile for psychoanalysis, so the psychiatrist assessed her daily life and provided supportive therapy.

Marilyn expressed feeling abandoned by both her husband and by Paula Strasberg, whom she perceived as preoccupied with her own daughter. She described Miller as "cold and unresponsive," attracted to other women, dominated by his mother, and neglectful of his elderly father and children. Additionally, Marilyn complained of chronic insomnia for which she perceived the need for powerful drugs. She demonstrated an extensive knowledge of pharmaceuticals but described having dangerously mixed drugs obtained from several doctors. Greenson learned Marilyn was able to occasionally discontinue drugs without withdrawal symptoms but was well on the road to developing an addiction.

Like many entertainers, Marilyn struggled with chemical dependency during an era when little was known about addiction and options for recovery were scarce. Marilyn did not engage in recreational drug use with illegal substances such as marijuana, cocaine, or heroin but she regularly used barbiturate sedatives and stimulant amphetamine drugs prescribed by studio physicians and personal physicians, which were, and still are, just as dangerous. Physicians employed by motion picture studios gave stars injections of amphetamines to increase energy to perform for long hours and then prescribed oral barbiturates to induce sleep. The resulting morning hangover was combated with another injection of amphetamines, and the cycle would continue. Amphetamines were also used in weight reduction. Like many who abuse prescription drugs, Marilyn self-medicated her symptoms of depression and chronic pain caused by endometriosis.

Greenson educated Marilyn on the body's ability to build a tolerance to the effect of barbiturates, requiring an increased dosage to continue providing the same effect. Over time, physical dependence to the drug results in withdrawal symptoms if the drug is not taken. Symptoms include insomnia, irritability, memory problems, panic attacks, headaches, nausea, constipation, and even hallucinations. The long-term use of amphetamines can result in symptoms of depression, creating a circular problem.

After the initial assessment, Greenson interviewed Miller and assessed him as "rapidly coming to the end of his rope." He believed Miller wanted to support his wife but simultaneously appeared angry and rejecting of her while Marilyn appeared to be searching for the protection of an idealized father and required the unconditional love and devotion Miller was no longer able or willing to provide.

Greenson's treatment plan was to limit Marilyn's intake of prescribed drugs and restrict her to obtaining medications only through one prescribing physician. "I promised she would sleep with less medication," he wrote, "if she would recognize she is fighting sleep as well as searching for some oblivion which is not sleep." Greenson responded as a healing but firm father figure and set clear parameters with Marilyn. He told her that he would not assist her in killing herself, targeting her husband with malevolence, or self-medicating with drugs. "Let us be modest about what we want to achieve here," he concluded. "We don't have time to make deep change since you'll soon return to New York and your analyst there."

Marilyn followed up with Greenson by a visit to his office. She requested to lie on the couch as she did with Dr. Kris, but the analyst redirected her to a face-to-face session. Marilyn seemed guarded and distant. Having previously been treated by Margaret Hohenberg and Kris, she had never worked with a male analyst, so new issues arose from Greenson's gender.

"I'm hurt because you didn't think I was modest," Marilyn announced in her second session with Greenson, having literally interpreted his comment from the first session. Greenson clarified that he had not meant she was behaving in an overtly sexual manner but had instead referred to the formation of realistic expectations for their brief work together. Reassured, Marilyn began to self-disclose, describing herself as emotionally "taking a beating, like a soldier in a war." The metaphor likely resonated with Greenson whose former patients included traumatized veterans. "I remember things from my childhood that burn in my mind," she said.

Greenson quickly observed Marilyn repeating a dynamic in her relationships, noting them in a letter to a colleague: "As she becomes more anxious, she begins to act like an orphan, a waif, and she masochistically provokes [others] to mistreat her and to take advantage of her. As fragments of her past history came out, she began to talk more and more about the traumatic experiences of an orphan child."

"You're both narcissists, and I think you'll get along fine together," Greenson told Marilyn when he recommended she appoint Hyman Engelberg (1913-2005) as her personal doctor of internal medicine. While a medical student at Cornell University in the early 1930s, Engelberg joined the Communist Party. He taught at the People's Education Center and participated in the Hollywood Arts, Sciences, and Professions Committee, both known as Communist fronts. Engelberg was married to Esther Goldstein, and Donald H. Wolfe discovered both their names on documentation of party meetings stored in the Archives of the Los Angeles Communist Party.

Marilyn continued seeing Dr. Greenson and Dr. Engelberg in Los Angeles during the summer of 1960 as she prepared for her next film. That summer, Chubby Checker's song, "The Twist," introduced the decade's first of many dance crazes, while Percy Smith's instrumental theme, "A Summer Place," became the number one instrumental hit. Alfred Hitchcock's *Psycho* opened with Anthony Perkins and Janet Leigh. The leading lady's pivotal murder by stabbing in the shower of a roadside motel room amid composer Bernard Hermann's shrieking violins occurred only forty-seven minutes into the film and created an iconic cinematic image of horror.

At the time, Marilyn was reading Harper Lee's southern gothic novel *To Kill A Mockingbird.* Depicting racial prejudice through the eyes of the six-year-old daughter of an attorney who represents a black man unjustly accused of rape in 1930s Alabama, the book would win the Pulitzer Prize and be adapted into a film starring Gregory Peck in 1962.

Marilyn still had an obligation to complete post-production dubbing of about fifty lines of dialogue for *Let's Make Love* before she could begin *The Misfits.* Yves Montand also owed Fox dubbing services. Herein lay the groundwork for Marilyn's plan to salvage the relationship. On June 30, Montand's plane left Los Angeles and arrived in New York where he would connect with another flight for Paris. Marilyn wasted no time in designing a rendezvous. According to some sources, she reserved a hotel near Idlewild Airport; according to others, she arrived in a limousine prepared for his layover with champagne, caviar, and flowers.

A bomb threat heightened the drama by extending Montand's layover, giving Marilyn more time with him as investigators searched the plane for explosives. Allegedly, the couple chatted in the back seat of the limousine. According to Sandra Shevey, Montand's publicist, Marilyn Reiss escorted him to the airport's VIP lounge where Marilyn Monroe popped out from behind a pillar dressed in beige, wearing dark glasses and a scarf around her hair. To complicate matters, Monroe had May Reis in tow. Montand was surrounded by three women, two having the first name Marilyn, and two having last names that sounded identical. When the women referred to each other, he couldn't tell whom each meant. Now less concerned about the bomb but anticipating a media detonation, Marilyn Reiss suggested the group discreetly move to a nearby hotel and assisted in transporting the champagne and caviar with May Reis's help.

Marilyn Reiss asked Monroe to remain in the limousine to prevent the media and the public from seeing the couple enter the hotel together, but the latter was not in a discreet mood. Monroe stepped out of the elevator toward Montand's suite. Reiss blurted, "I told you to wait in the car." Monroe merely laughed. Montand also found humor in the situation, confused by the three females with similar names.

During the visit, Marilyn frequently went into the suite's bedroom to call Miller and update him on the bomb-scare investigation. A reporter from *Variety* magazine soon arrived to interview Montand and believed the mysterious woman in the other room was Kim Novak. Marilyn Reiss had no impetus to rectify the misunderstanding.

Sometime during the melee, Montand told Marilyn he planned to return to Simone. He then nonchalantly invited her and Arthur to visit him and his wife in France. The message was clear: the fling was over. Marilyn had said that love and work were life's only two motivations. Now she had no choice but to throw herself into work.

On July 1, Fox assigned Marilyn to *Goodbye, Charlie* with a start date scheduled after completion of *The Misfits.* George Axelrod adapted his 1959 stage comedy starring Lauren Bacall for Monroe as he had done successfully with *The Seven Year Itch* and *Bus Stop.* Charlie, a cavorting Hollywood writer, is killed by the husband of the woman with whom he was having an affair. His spirit is instantly reincarnated into the body of a sexy adult woman. Charlie convinces his best male friend of his true identity. The comedy is based on Charlie's spirit initially resisting his new gender and later using it to his advantage to marry into money with help from the friend. In the end, Charlie is killed again, only to be reincarnated into a dog. (It was smart casting to give the nation's leading female sex symbol the role of a lecherous man aroused by discovering the ample breasts of his new feminine body.)

Marilyn's contract stipulated that she must start production by April 14, 1961, with George Cukor as director and James Garner as co-star. Donfeld (born Donald Lee Feld) began designing her costumes, including a low-cut, form-fitting white gown with embroidered black lace and beading, accessorized by a white fur wrap, and black opera gloves. Marilyn liked the costume designs but balked at the role. Lee Strasberg discouraged her from accepting this light comedy on the heels of *The Misfits* and urged her to select a drama.

Marilyn would express her misgivings about the project in an interview with Sheilah Graham published in October, citing dislike of the concept of playing a man in a woman's body, but admitted having carefully observed hyper-masculine Clark Gable during their work together as a reference. When Marilyn told him about the possibility of her playing a male character, Gable laughed and said, "You don't have that kind of equipment."

When another obligation for MGM forced Cukor to withdraw from directing *Goodbye, Charlie*, Fox entered into negotiations with Strasberg, offering him $22,500. Suddenly, Strasberg held at a counteroffer of $50,000 and supported Marilyn's casting in a comedy. Ultimately, Strasberg's obstinacy cost him the film.

Milton Rudin pointed Marilyn toward Vera Caspary's *Illicity*, and Richard Zanuck, mailed letters with his interest in her committing to *Sanctuary*, Montand's next project. Meanwhile, Tennessee Williams pressed her to accept *Celebration*, Jerry Wald's project, an adaptation of William Inge's unsuccessful 1959 stage play, *A Loss for Roses.*

Inge had Marilyn's success in the film adaptation of his earlier work *Bus Stop*, when he wrote the part of Lila in *Celebration*. Lila, a dancer and actress, returns to her hometown in the Midwest during the Great Depression when her traveling show closes and her troupe looks for work in Kansas City. Out of work, Lila stays with a friend in her forties, Helen, a church-going widow, and the woman's twenty-one-year-old son, Kenny, who is drinking and running around with girls.

In a crucial scene, Lila confides to Helen her sordid past: multiple men, a failed marriage, sexual abuse, social stigma, an attempted suicide, and psychiatric institutionalization. Due the economic downshift of the Depression, she was forced to survive through moral degradation. Despite all her misfortune, Lila is loving and hopeful. Kenny makes advances toward Lila who rebuffs with sisterly compassion but their relationship evolves into an affair. When Helen learns of this, Lila attempts to slash her wrists. In the adaptation, Lila relinquishes both Kenny and her career to establish a more stable life.

In *Celebration*, for the first time, Marilyn would be playing a mature woman in love with a younger man. Jerry Wald wanted singer and actor Pat Boone (born 1934). According to Louella Parson's column, Fox put the film on hold so that Marilyn could complete *Goodbye, Charlie* and Boone could complete *State Fair*, a musical with Ann-Margret.

On July 8, Marilyn invited James Haspiel and the Monroe Six to the Fox-Movietone Studio on West Fifty-Fourth Street in New York to watch her film costume, hair, and makeup tests for *The Misfits* with Miller and Huston. Haspiel shot color home movies of her as she stepped down the stoop of the building and crossed the street with Miller to an awaiting car. The group of young people followed and begged her to return for photographs with them. Marilyn turned to her husband and explained needing to get out of the car and allowing Haspiel to take her picture. She demonstrated her devotion to fans by returning to the stoop and submissively taking direction from Haspiel on how he wanted her to pose for his camera.

On July 13, Marilyn searched out Ralph Roberts at Maureen Stapleton's apartment, where he was playing poker. Marilyn pleaded with him to give her a massage before her departure in the morning to Los Angeles. When Roberts arrived at Marilyn's apartment, she was alone in the living room watching the Democratic primary election on television with the volume turned low while Miller slept in the bedroom on the other side of the wall. Roberts was wearing a Stevenson campaign button, and Marilyn asked him to keep it on during the massage. She didn't discuss the candidates and focused instead on preparation for her next film. After finishing the massage, Roberts left the apartment with a strong feeling that her marriage was on the rocks. "The night of the most important Democratic Convention for many years, one of the most proclaimed liberals, went to bed," Roberts wrote. "He might have had a prescient [sic] most didn't."

With fifty lines of dialogue to dub before beginning *Sanctuary*, Montand returned to Los Angeles on July 15. Marilyn arrived the following day in a city abuzz with the Democratic National Convention taking place at the Los Angeles Coliseum. Forty-three-year-old John F. Kennedy accepted the nomination and delivered his "New Frontier" speech. The enigmatic senator's progressive designs for transitioning the country into a new decade invigorated the younger generation and stirred the establishment:

> It is time, in short, for a new generation of leadership. All over the world, particularly in the newer nations, young men are coming to power, men who are not bound by the traditions of the past, men who are not blinded by the old fears and hates and rivalries—young men who can cast off the old slogans and the old delusions...We stand today on the edge of a New Frontier... the frontier of unfilled hopes and unfilled threats... The New Frontier is here whether we seek it or not. Beyond that frontier are uncharted areas of science and space, unsolved problems of peace and war, unconquered problems of ignorance and prejudice, unanswered questions of poverty and surplus.

Five days later, Marilyn boarded a plane to Reno to begin *The Misfits.* She would have less than a week's rest for what would become a grueling on-location production fraught with emotional turmoil and extreme physical challenges.

CHAPTER TWELVE: *THE MISFITS* PART I

Producer Frank Taylor announced that *The Misfits* would be the "ultimate motion picture," and one of Hollywood's original independent productions, the joint vision of a leading American playwright and his internationally prominent wife. It originated as a short story, titled "The Misfits or Chicken Feed: The Last Frontier of the Quixotic Cowboy," published in *Esquire* magazine in May 1957. Miller later adapted it into a screenplay—a "Valentine" for Marilyn and a vehicle intended to advance her dramatic acting career. The character of Roslyn was Miller's idealized representation of Marilyn.

He documented elements of her personality into monologues she had actually spoken and incorporated into the script personal and painful situations excised from her life; art would imitate life. Numerous obstacles delayed the couple's film project, so by the time the production began the Valentine had faded and the marriage was disintegrating. What began as a love-inspired collaboration ended with the spouses struggling against each other in a production laden with tension and spite.

The Millers expected to begin production in the autumn of 1959, but Marilyn was obligated to film *Let's Make Love* for Fox. The start date was pushed forward to March 1960, but the writers' strike delayed it yet another four months. Finally, in July 1960, the production was ready in time for the sweltering summer heat of Nevada, the film's location, with temperatures in excess of one hundred ten degrees in the shade. Conversely, the emotional temperature in the Miller's Reno hotel suite would be freezing cold.

Long before divorce was common as the sun rising each morning, there was Reno. Along the Truckee River, the once largest city in

Nevada offered a solution to those seeking to untie the marriage knot. Unhappy couples across the country migrated to Reno to "take the cure"—early twentieth century speak for divorce. Columnist Walter Winchell waggishly referred to a Reno divorce as "Reno-vation." While other states' divorce laws required long waiting periods and proof of adultery, a 1931 Nevada law gained the city's notoriety as the divorce capital of the United States. The law permitted a plaintiff to divorce contingent upon that plaintiff's declaration to make the state his or her permanent home and the testimony from a witness, typically a landlord, confirming that the plaintiff had been a continuous resident in the state for six weeks.

Miller obtained his 1956 divorce from Mary Slattery by establishing residency in a cabin outside of Reno on Pyramid Lake. There he met three aging cowboys who inspired his short story who explained to him how they made a living capturing wild Mustangs and selling them to dealers who in turn sold them as riding horses, but now the dealers had begun to sell the Mustangs to companies that used them as meat in the production of dog food. Once running through the desert by the hundreds, the wild Mustangs dwindled to a few scattered family units. The misfit cowboys, like the misfit horses, were vanishing along with their way of life.

The adapted screenplay, in apparent western genre, is confusing by its lack of a hero, usually a staple in true westerns. "It's supposed to be a Western, but it's not, is it?" leading man Clark Gable asked Miller after originally reading the screenplay. "It's sort of an Eastern Western," the author explained. "It's about our lives' meaninglessness and maybe how we got to where we are." Despite rodeo scenes, roping wild horses, and the characters camping in the desert, *The Misfits* was not a contemporary western in the way John Wayne's films were historic period westerns. Miller's cowboys are metaphors for those wishing to roam free and resist societal changes. Modern urbanization had eroded their masculine roles much in the same way suburbanization had changed the role of the American male. "I've always felt a misfit," Miller said of his personal link to the cowboys. "I've always identified with those fellows, even down in the middle of New York."

The plot involves a triangle between Gay, Roslyn, and Guido, counterparts for Miller, Marilyn and Elia Kazan ten years earlier.

Roslyn is an interpretive jazz dancer from Chicago divorcing her estranged husband. She meets Guido, a widower and pilot who dropped bombs in the war. Through Guido, Roslyn meets Gay, an aging, strong-willed cowboy coming to terms with the vanishing old frontier, and who avoids working for the man. He, too, is divorced and estranged from his adult children. Gay is immediately attracted to Roslyn, but she is reticent to start a relationship so soon after her divorce. Eventually, they partner as a couple and live together in the unfinished home Guido had been building for his wife before her death.

The three attend a Rodeo in Dayton along with Roslyn's older friend and landlady, Isabelle, a divorcee who long ago arrived in Reno to get rid of her husband and remained to establish a new life. At the rodeo, the group connects with Perce, a sensitive cowboy estranged from his mother. The three men mount a plan to capture wild Mustangs, known as misfit horses, and sell them for dog food meat. The shallow plot only serves as a canvas for the four leading characters' exploration of their inner conflicts and attempt to connect and relate to each other. Each exposes scars from negative life events and searches for meaning in his or her life.

Roslyn, a character never actually appearing in the short story but merely referenced by the cowboys, is the center of film. As an outsider to their world, she impacts each of the men by questioning their long-held and unchallenged beliefs. Roslyn struck Marilyn as a character too passive and idealized, whose performance would give the role a darker side and a complex backstory absent from the script. In the character, Miller referenced biographical parallels to Marilyn's life: Roslyn's abandonment by her parents, her continuous search for security; her perceived image by others as the essence of femininity, sensitivity, love for life (but is simultaneously sad and anxious), and that each man who falls for her honors her good qualities. Ultimately, she becomes a feminine metaphor for life and hope.

Gay, on the other hand, represents the idealized masculine role. He is afforded freedom and independence by his trade as an itinerant cowboy but now faces revolution. "He's the same man," Huston explained, "but the world has changed. Then he was noble. Now he is ignoble." Widowed Guido, the most intelligent and educated of the cowboys, is also bitter and cynical. He feels alienated from others and guilty about his violent acts as a soldier in war. With a blending of masculine and feminine traits, Perce yearns for mothering and nurturing after having had experienced rejection by his mother. She remarried after the death of his father and gave her new husband the family farm. Isabelle, Roslyn's older divorced landlady, represents survival and female resiliency. She is adaptive and thick-skinned. She loves to drink and laugh and accepts life as it is without trying to change it.

Throughout the film, Roslyn is a source of light and a point of reference. Whatever happens to someone in Roslyn's life, Guido says, happens to her. She ministers to each misfit man and is herself a misfit. Gay tells Roslyn that she is the saddest girl he ever met, a line Miller uttered when he first met Marilyn in Hollywood. "You have the gift of life, Roslyn," Guido says. Perce wonders aloud how she retains the trust of a newly born child.

In Roslyn's voice, we hear a new morality signaling an emerging counterculture later exemplified by the Feminist Movement and the protest against the Vietnam War. She confronts the killing of the Mustangs as barbaric, something the cowboys never pondered, and identifies with the horses as victims of the men's brutality. Ultimately, Gay—a man of an older generation—finds a way to embrace the new morality and transforms without losing himself.

Miller's highly cerebral themes are clearly literary and akin to a book rather than to a motion picture. According to Donald Spoto, the characters "mumble arid aphorisms" such as "Maybe you're not supposed to remember anybody's promises;" "I can't make a landing, and I can't get up to God;" and "A man afraid to die is afraid to live." Marilyn recognized this upon early review of the screenplay and expressed serious doubts about its cinematic merit.

Marilyn's opinion mattered. After all, Marilyn Monroe Productions, although uncredited onscreen, partnered with Seven Arts Productions, a subsidiary of United Artists, to produce *The Misfits* and distribute it globally. MCA agent George Chasin represented both the Millers and Clark Gable, so the leading man's contract negations ran smoothly. Marilyn earned $300,000 and ten percent of the film's revenue while Gable commanded a salary of $750,000 and ten percent of revenue. He was the only cast member afforded both script approval and overtime salary.

Miller wanted Frank Taylor, his personal friend and former publisher, as producer. "I want you to do it," Marilyn pleaded to Taylor. "You're an old friend of Arthur's, so we trust you. All films need the independent eye of a producer." John Huston, with whom Marilyn had great affinity, was selected as director. In the decade since he worked with her on *The Asphalt Jungle*, Huston directed *Moulin Rouge* (1953), *Heaven Knows, Mr. Allison* (1957), and the Oscar-winning *The African Queen* (1951), starring Humphrey Bogart and Katharine Hepburn. Marilyn had reconnected with Huston in the mid-1950s, and she expressed appreciation for him giving her a first break. "There was a depth in her, and she could not do anything as an actress simply," Huston told Fred Lawrence Guiles. "By that I mean she had to feel it and it had to come from her insides. She couldn't just with technique give it that surface shine. That wasn't enough."

"Working with John ten years later is very good," Marilyn said. "He's helpful in a personal way as well as professionally...He's an artist with a camera—he sees it like a painter. He watches for the reality of a situation and he leaves it alone, and he waits until he needs less or more before he comes in." In discussing the cast with the media, Taylor said, "Each of them...is the person they play." Cast as Isabelle, supporting actress Thelma Ritter agreed, "If anyone were average, it wouldn't work. You've read the script. What would it be like if it were cast out of an agent's office?" The leading actors were archetypes themselves, perfectly suited for Miller's archetypal characters.

Robert Mitchum turned down the role as Marilyn's leading man based upon his assessment of the script as incomprehensible. Again, art imitated life when the Millers cast Clark Gable (1901-1960) as Gaylord Langland. He had been Norma Jeane's childhood idol and fantasy father and at fifty-nine, Gable was the undisputed King of Hollywood. Portraying virile, likeable charmers, he was the leading box office actor of the 1930s. A signature thin mustache and prominent ears made him look like a taxicab driving down the street with both doors open. When Judy Garland sang "You Made Me Love You" to a framed photograph of Gable in *Broadway Melody of 1938*, twelve-year-old Norma Jeane Baker imagined herself doing the same. At a party following the completion of *The Seven Year Itch*, a twenty-eight year-old Marilyn had danced with Gable and told him about her childhood fantasy of his being her father. Marilyn worshipped him, and Gable loved her for it and took a paternal interest in her.

As Gable's punishment for protesting roles as villains and gangsters, Metro-Goldwyn-Mayer Studios' president Louis B. Mayer loaned him out to Columbia Studios for a romantic comedy with Claudette Colbert. The plan backfired. *It Happened One Night* (1934) became the first film to sweep five major Oscar awards, and Gable received the Best Actor Oscar. His most iconic role was Rhett Butler in the biggest film of all time, *Gone With the Wind* (1939). This Civil War epic, based on the best-selling novel by Margaret Mitchell, clocked in at two hundred twenty-two minutes and forever sealed Gable as a legend. He made five films with Jean Harlow, including her last, *Saratoga* (1937). No stranger to tragedy, Gable lost his third wife, actress Carole Lombard, in a plane crash during a 1942 war bond selling tour in Nevada.

As the Millers' marriage crumbled, Gable's fifth marriage remained stable. His wife, Kay, had become pregnant in June with a son who the general public would know as his only child. Posthumously, the media revealed that Gable had fathered a child with co-star Loretta Young during the filming of *Call of the Wild* in 1934.

Marilyn urged Miller to cast her friend Montgomery Clift (1920-1966) as man-child Perce Howland. By the summer of 1960, Clift had bought a townhouse on East Sixty-First Street, near the Millers' apartment, and had already earned three of his total four Oscar nominations for portraying moody, sensitive young men. Known by his friends as Monty, Clift starred in *A Place in the Sun* (1951), *From Here to Eternity* (1953), *Raintree County* (1957), and *Suddenly, Last Summer* (1959). He had recently completed *Wild River*, a film that was originally intended for Marilyn as his co-star.

As a closeted gay man, Clift struggled with internalized homophobia. "He's the only person I know who's in worse shape than I am," Marilyn said of Clift. "I look at him and see the brother I never had and feel brave and get protective." Clift said of her: "I have the same problem as Marilyn. We attract people the way honey does bees, but they're generally the wrong kind of people."

While filming *Raintree County* in 1956, Monty frequently socialized with co-star Elizabeth Taylor and her husband, Michael Wilding. On the evening of May 12, Clift dismissed his driver for the night. Taylor called and invited him to her home for dinner. Clift declined, but Taylor called back and insisted he reconsider. Finally, Clift surrendered and drove to the couple's home in a Chevrolet he hadn't driven in several months. The Wildings' other guests included Rock Hudson and his wife, Phyllis Gates, and Kevin McCarthy. As the dinner party ended, Clift expressed apprehension about driving his car down the steep hill to Sunset Boulevard. McCarthy offered to guide him by driving his own car ahead of Clift's Chevrolet.

Clift lost control of his vehicle and crashed head-on into a telephone pole, sustaining a broken nose, fractured jaw, crushed sinus cavity, facial lacerations, severe cerebral concussion, and spine injuries. McCarthy drove back to the house and instructed Taylor to call an ambulance. Instead of calling for help, she ran down the hill to rescue her gravely injured friend. Taylor entered the mangled car through the rear door, crawled over the front seat, and found Clift wedged under the dashboard. She cradled his bloody face in her lap. Choking, Clift motioned to his neck. Several of his teeth had been knocked loose and lodged in the back of his throat. Taylor reached into his mouth and extracted the teeth. Finally, Clift received emergency medical care at nearby Cedars of Lebanon Hospital, but his painful recovery lasted nine months.

Clift's long recovery led to an addiction to painkilling medication that became a gateway to other addictive drugs and alcohol abuse. Although surgeons repaired his face, Clift was no longer the arrestingly handsome young man with a flawless complexion who garnered claustrophobic close-ups in *A Place in the Sun*. The tragic, disfiguring accident resulted in what many have called the "the longest suicide in Hollywood." By May 1960, Clift developed alcoholic hepatitis and had been admitted to Mount Sinai Hospital in New York. He had also been diagnosed with hypothyroidism resulting in poor balance, memory loss, premature cataracts, and mood swings. Insurance companies would no longer underwrite him in a film, but made an exception based upon Miller's and Huston's vouching.

Marilyn also cast her friend from the Actors Studio, Eli Wallach (1915-2014) as Guido, a former armed forces pilot turned auto mechanic. Wallach, the film's longest-surviving cast member, made his Broadway debut in 1945 and earned a Tony Award for his performance on stage in Tennessee Williams' *The Rose Tattoo* in 1951. Originally cast in *From Here to Eternity*, he was replaced by Frank Sinatra. Wallach won a Golden Globe nomination for his film debut in *Baby Doll* (1956).

Thelma Ritter (1902-1969) was the same age as Gladys Baker, and her maternal role in Roslyn's life mirrored the older women to whom Marilyn turned for maternal comfort and support: Ann Karger, Natasha Lytess, Paula Strasberg, and May Reis. Ritter was a supporting and character actress who gained attention in her first brief, uncredited role in *Miracle on 34th Street* (1947). She played a frustrated mother unable to find a toy at Macy's department store during the Christmas shopping season and was especially resentful of the department store's Santa Claus having promised the toy to her son. Ritter appeared with Marilyn in *All About Eve* (1950) and *As Young As You Feel* (1951).

British stage and screen actress Estelle Winwood (1883-1984) turned age seventy-seven when cameras rolled on *The Misfits* and would outlive Marilyn by twenty-two years. She was casted as an elderly woman soliciting church charity donations from rowdy patrons at a cowboy bar. Winwood had recently performed in *Darby O'Gill and the Little People* (1959). A close friend of Tallulah Bankhead, Winwood relocated to the United States late in her career. In later years, she appeared on television talk shows and became noted for her longevity. By 1979, ninety-six-year-old Winwood was the documented oldest working actor. She died at age one hundred one years, as the oldest member in the history of the Screen Actors Guild. On her hundredth birthday when asked how it felt to have lived so long, Winwood quipped, "How rude of you to remind me!" She was interred near Marilyn's crypt in Westwood Village Memorial Park.

Square-jawed actor Kevin McCarthy (1914-2010) played Raymond Tabor, Roslyn's husband. McCarthy had starred as Biff, the older son of Willy Lowman, in the London production of Miller's *Death of a Salesman* and earned an Oscar nomination in the same role in the 1951 film adaptation. He was best known for his role in the science fiction film *Invasion of the Body Snatchers* (1956) about an alien takeover of a community, wherein citizens were replaced with unemotional, inhuman replicas grown from seedpods. This allegory addressed the 1950s paranoia of the spread of Communism and mass hysteria culminating from Senator Joseph McCarthy's Communist "witch hunts." Coincidently, Kevin McCarthy not only considered himself a friend of Clift, but he grew up with Frank Taylor's wife, Nan, in Deerwood, Minnesota.

In minor roles, Philip Mitchell, the sound recorder for *The Misfits*, portrayed Isabelle's husband, and Marilyn's personal masseur, Ralph Roberts, had a walk-on part as an ambulance driver. Rex Bell (1903-1962), then the Lieutenant Governor of Nevada who had once been an actor and married to actress Clara Bow, was cast in a bit part that would be his final film appearance. Many residents of Reno and Dayton served as extras in the crowd scenes, some with speaking parts.

John Huston cast his mistress, socialite Marietta Peabody Tree (1917-1991), in the walk-on part of Susan, Gay's most recent love interest who boards a train to return to her hometown following a Reno divorce. At the time of production, Huston was married to Enrica Soma and had two children, Anjelica and Walter Antony. Anjelica would become an Oscar-winning actress in the 1980s, and Walter Antony's son, Jack Huston, would continue the family's tradition by becoming an actor known for his vampire role in the *Twilight* film series.

Cinematographer Russell Metty (1906-1978) took a black and white documentarian approach in his treatment of *The Misfits*. After scouting Nevada locations of sparse, almost lunar landscape, he told Miller, "They're not going to pay to get into this movie to see scenery." Metty would rapidly set up scenes using only three lights, and in the days before cell phones, he would spend the remainder of his time near a phone booth awaiting news about an oil well in which he had invested. Metty's work included *Touch of Evil* (1958), *Imitation of Life* (1959), *Spartacus* (1960), and *Flower Drum Song* (1961).

Miller called on Alex North (1910-1991) to compose the film's score. The two had met through Elia Kazan when North scored the film version of *A Streetcar Named Desire*. The same year, North scored the film version of Miller's *Death of a Salesman*. By the summer of 1960, the composer had spent most of the year on Stanley Kubrick's *Spartacus*. North collaborated with Henry Brant, who orchestrated the film's score.

North composed a main theme establishing high drama and pathos, consisting of four descending phrases and accentuated by a percussive piano toward the end. The film called for several pieces of source music including "Rendezvous," a light jazz arrangement for the lounge scene where Gay meets Roslyn. "Paddleball," a raucous rock and roll tune with saxophone and horns, livens the bar scene in which Roslyn displays her prowess with a child's toy. A jazz version of the main theme, titled "Roslyn," serves as music playing from a car radio when Roslyn dances with Gay and Guido in the cabin. For the climatic rounding up of horses with lassos and ropes, North composed a classic dance, inspired from years of writing music for interpretive dancers such as Martha Graham. "Round-Up Suite" is comprised of four movements unified by a high-energy tempo. North would score more of Huston's films including *Prizzi's Honor* (1985) and the director's last, *The Dead* (1987).

Dorothy Jeakins, who dressed Marilyn in *Niagara* (1953) and *Let's Make Love* (1960), was originally hired as the costume designer. She suggested the use of several wigs on location due to the wind, dirt, and dryness of the desert and to reduce the time required each morning for hairdressing. The film's hair stylist Sydney Guilaroff concurred, but Jeakins and Marilyn had a falling out. Jean-Louis would replace the designer. They continued with Jeakin's idea, though, agreeing that instead of stopping a scene to straighten or curl Marilyn's hair, the hairdresser would merely remove Marilyn's wig and apply another one already styled."

Marilyn's appearance diverged from her signature look with an emphasis on heavy mascara—a new style—and wigs of long, straight, one-length hair, parted on the side, and flipped on the ends. Marilyn's hair was typically curled, styled into a pageboy, or teased. During an era when women's hair was teased higher and higher into elaborate bouffant styles, this flatter, more casual look seemed youthful and predictive of styles that would arise in the latter part of the decade.

Jean-Louis' designs for Marilyn's wardrobe included a champagne silk full slip adorned with black lace and an ecru bikini. For the early scenes, Louis designed a black sleeveless cocktail sheath of black silk jersey with irregular neckline threaded with a jersey band and a matching bolero jacket. The ensemble was accessorized with a black veiled headpiece. His most memorable creation for the film remains a sleeveless silk jersey dress of ivory with a pattern of scattered cherries. Its V-neckline and skirt draped onto the hip showcased Marilyn's hourglass figure and adeptly camouflaged her increased weight. The dress was accessorized with a short white jacket with white fur collar. For the last third of the film, Marilyn wore plain white shirts, snug denim jeans, a denim jacket, and cowboy boots, the latter acquired at auction by designer Tommy Hilfiger in 1999.

Frank Taylor took a leave from his position as editor in chief at Dell Books to produce the film. In the late 1940s, he and his wife, Nan, moved to Hollywood with hopes of adapting F. Scott Fitzgerald's *Tender is the Night* to the big screen. When the project failed to materialize, they returned east with their four sons. *The Misfits* offered a corrective experience for him. Tall and stylish, Taylor frequently donned loud color sports coats, checkered trousers, and Tyrolean hats on location in Reno.

Taylor told *Time* that Miller's script was the best he had read. To further publicize the film, Taylor ordered an open set and permitted author John Goode full access to his cast and set for a simultaneous book documenting the production. Goode's journal was published three years later as *The Story of The Misfits*. W.J. Weatherby of Britain's *Manchester Guardian* also had authorized access to the entire company and later wrote of his experience as "standing in a minefield among all those manic-depressive people."

Granted exclusive rights to shoot a photo essay of the production and its mercurial stars, legendary French photographer Henri Cartier-Bresson (1908-2004), co-founder of Magnum Photos, arrived on location with photographer Eve Arnold. With a perception strikingly different from Weatherby's, Cartier-Bression said of Marilyn:

> There's something extremely alert and vivid in her, an intelligence...I had the pleasure of having dinner next to her and I saw that these things came fluidly all the time...all these amusing remarks, precise, pungent, direct. It was flowing all the time... In her you feel the woman, and also the great discipline as an actress.

Austrian photographer Inge Morath (1923-2002), Cartier-Bresson's protégé, considered Marilyn "a photographic phenomenon." Morath insisted that Marilyn could not photograph badly even if the photographer tried and said, "She would surpass the expectations of the lens. She had a shimmering quality like an emanation of water, and she moved lyrically." Marilyn took an immediate liking to the Austrian photographer and the flattering portraits she had taken, sensing a genuine affection in them.

Huston's style differed from many of Marilyn's former directors. If a location or set is to appear at the beginning and ending of a film, the director films all scenes using that location and set before moving to another location and set, requiring actors to perform out of plot sequence. This saves time and expense. Huston's atypical style of production for *The Misfits* involved no rehearsals and filming the script in chronological sequence—an expensive undertaking—so that the actors developed their characters as the plot unfolded, something Marilyn appreciated.

* * *

A United Airlines DC-7 jet carrying Marilyn Monroe and her entourage landed at two forty-five on the afternoon of July 20 at Reno Airport where hundreds of fans had assembled along with members of the media and a welcoming committee that included Miller, Frank Taylor, Rupert Allan, and local dignitaries. The airport had been expanded to accommodate the 1960 Winter Olympics in nearby Squaw Valley and had recently seen a steady procession of luminaries in the entertainment and sports fields.

Thirty minutes after the jet touched down on the runway, Marilyn emerged from the cabin freshly coiffed by Sydney Guilaroff. She wore a white, long-sleeve silk blouse, a white pencil skirt, and white pumps as she carried white gloves, with her hair piled high and ringlets on each side of her face. Marilyn gave Miller a warm greeting, but seemed happier to see Gail Sawyer, the young daughter of Nevada Governor Grant Sawyer. Accompanied by her mother, the youth presented Marilyn with a bouquet of two dozen red roses. Mayor Bud Baker presented her with a ceremonial key to the city.

Following the welcome ceremony, Marilyn climbed into the rear seat of Taylor's rented red convertible Thunderbird for a motorcade through downtown Reno. With Taylor behind the wheel, Miller beside him, and Allan beside Marilyn, the car drove under Reno's arched sign announcing, "The Biggest Little City in the World." Marilyn waved to her fans crowding both sides of Virginia Street until the car arrived at the Mapes Hotel, the first skyscraper built in the west since World War II, styled in Art Deco design. Built in 1947, the Mapes was the first resort-casino hotel that would multiply and dominate the Nevada landscape in nearby Las Vegas. It featured the Sky Room, a glass promenade and show bar on the top floor where both Liberace and Sammy Davis, Jr. debuted. Here the company lodged for three months of location shooting.

Soon after settling into corner suite 614, Marilyn experienced gastrointestinal pain on her right side, a symptom that had begun earlier in the summer. She took a dose of pain killing medication prescribed by Dr. Engelberg and rested. By the following year, the condition would be accurately diagnosed as gallstones and corrected by surgery. Physically and emotionally exhausted, Marilyn complained to anyone who listened about her necessity to jump from one long film production to another without an ample pause. When photographer Eve Arnold greeted her, Marilyn exclaimed, "I'm thirty-four-years-old, I've been dancing for six months, I've had no rest, I'm exhausted. Where do I go from here?" Despite her fatigue, Marilyn was ready to work; however, Miller's script remained unfinished.

Within days, Marilyn was joined by her entourage: Paula Strasberg, acting coach; Ralph Roberts, masseur; May Reis, personal secretary; Allan "Whitey" Snyder, cosmetician; Agnes Flanagan, hairdresser; Rudy Kautzsky, chauffer from Carey Limousine Company in Los Angeles; Evelyn Moriarty, stand-in; Bunny Gardel, body cosmetician; Shirlee Strahm, wardrobe mistress; Augusta "Gussie" Wyler, seamstress; and Hazel Washington, personal maid. Eve Arnold observed that Marilyn's inner circle of employees were fiercely dedicated to her.

Angela Allen, the British crewmember responsible for script continuity, had worked with Huston on *The African Queen*, and immediately disliked Marilyn and her entourage. "They're devouring her," she told Fred Lawrence Guiles. Allen interpreted Marilyn's tardiness as deliberate retaliation for a deprived childhood. Allen's impression of Marilyn softened once she experienced the actress' impact. "What was so amazing about her was the thing she projected on the screen," Allen said after first viewing the daily rushes at the Crest Theatre in Reno. "She seemed so ordinary when doing a scene, and then you'd go to the rushes and see her up there, so different, like no one else." Although the two women never connected, Allen appreciated Marilyn's talent.

When Ralph Roberts arrived at the Mapes, the fuss described by Allen was in full force. The hotel buzzed with the excitement of a film crew's arrival and temporary residency. Roberts found his accommodations on the sixth floor, down the hall from the Millers and around the corner from Paula Strasberg. Negotiating the crowded corridor, he nearly bumped into a cautious Paula. "Trouble has already begun," she warned. "I'm so relieved you're here. Marilyn needs your help." Roberts also met May Reis for the first time and found her to be a bright, articulate, and charming woman extremely protective of Marilyn's privacy. "What I do for Marilyn is out of pure love," May told Fred Lawrence Guiles.

Montgomery Clift arrived accompanied by his makeup artist and companion, Frank LaRue, and press agent, Harry Mines. Clift had been researching his role by working in a rodeo in Pocatello, Idaho, where he had bruised the bridge of his nose. Coincidently, the injury was exactly the type his character was supposed to have in the film.

Gable passed on a jet plane to drive his silver Mercedes coupe from California to Reno. Along the journey, he and his wife celebrated their wedding anniversary in Minden, where they had been married five years earlier. Gable would also pass on a company limousine to transport him to the daily work location. Instead, he tried to beat his driving time up the mountain road from Reno every morning. Marilyn eagerly anticipated performing with Gable. "I'm working with Rhett Butler!" she prattled.

The Millers joined Huston and the main cast for a press reception in the Sky Room at the Mapes. Marilyn wore a sleeveless ivory silk jersey dress with V-neckline and pleated onto the center waistband, its pattern of peacock feather eyes. *Esquire* photographer Alice McIntyre found her "astonishingly beautiful. Like nothing human you have ever seen or dreamed!" However, in newsreels, Marilyn appears wan and exhausted as she interacts with her co-stars. She had been working nonstop since rehearsals for *Let's Make Love* in the fall, and the long hours of production, combined with a failed love affair and no respite between films, took their toll.

Afterward, the company celebrated Huston and Kay Gable's birthdays at a formal dinner. Marilyn and Miller sat at a table with Huston and Clark and Kay Gable; Paula and Roberts were seated at another table. Paula voiced annoyance at being excluded from Marilyn's table. When Marilyn spotted her two friends nearby, she kissed her hand and blew them a kiss.

The shooting schedule required Marilyn to work six days a week in desert temperatures soaring over one hundred ten degrees. Given her reputation for lateness since *Some Like It Hot,* Huston scheduled Marilyn's daily call for ten o'clock in the morning, but she often arrived later. Physical pain from an undiagnosed gastrointestinal condition and Miller's nightly re-writes of scenes to be filmed the next morning contributed to this tardiness. When Miller handed Marilyn a stack of pages with new lines to memorize before going to bed, she panicked and found it harder to fall asleep.

Marilyn would take a sleeping pill at seven or eight o'clock, Allan "Whitey" Snyder recounted decades later, and went to bed early. If she couldn't fall asleep, she would take another at nine or ten. If Marilyn awoke, she took yet another pill around midnight or later. By dawn, the cumulative effect of the pill would leave her drugged, so much so that Snyder allowed her to lie in bed while he applied her makeup.

According to legend, Marilyn's pattern of exceeding the dosage of her sedative drugs, estimated at sometimes three times the prescribed dosage, impaired her functioning and delayed production. To some degree, this appears accurate, but she was not the only member of the cast and crew who struggled with substances. Gable allegedly consumed two quarts of whiskey per day and got the shakes when he wasn't drinking. Clift, allegedly dependent on painkilling medication prescribed since his car accident, drank Whiskey Sours concealed in a thermos on the set.

After a day's work, members of the production routinely caroused at the numerous casinos open for their enjoyment twenty-four hours. Snyder remembered both cast and crew frequently waking up in the morning after a night of excessive drinking "with screaming headaches" and prayed Marilyn would be late again. Even Paula Strasberg was taking large dosages of narcotic drugs for bodily pain and migraine headaches. Unbeknownst to all, she was in the early stages of the bone marrow cancer that would kill her six years later.

Undisciplined, Huston had little control over his cast and crew. He, too, arrived late to the set after spending all night gambling at the casinos. In *Timebends*, Miller recalled leaving a casino late one night and observing Huston in his bush jacket, scarf around his neck, a glass of scotch in his hand, losing immense sums of money—in excess of twenty-five thousand dollars. Miller returned to the casino for breakfast only to find Huston wearing the same bush jacket and holding another glass of scotch. The director had won back the money and was trying to win more. Miller would also observe him falling asleep in his director's chair behind the camera and losing track of which scene he was shooting. Chaos had befallen.

Marilyn, Wallach, and Ritter arrived at the Reno USO building at ten o'clock in the morning of July 21 to film the first scene. The old frame structure was dressed as a boarding home with a white 1959 Cadillac Biarritz convertible parked in the driveway. The car displayed body damage, the result of crewmembers attacking it with crowbars and sledgehammers. The scene introduces Roslyn as she prepares for a divorce hearing. The car was a gift from her husband in an attempt to save the marriage. Roslyn's landlady, Isabelle, tells the mechanic that local male drivers crash into her attractive tenant's new car "just to start a conversation." Metty had difficulty lighting the small room where Marilyn and Ritter filmed their dialogue in the USO building, and the interior temperature soared over one hundred degrees.

The next day, Marilyn filmed at scene at the courthouse with Ritter, McCarthy, and Wallach in which Roslyn's husband attempts to dissuade her from divorce and later where Roslyn tosses her wedding band into the river after the court proceedings. "You're not there, Raymond," Roslyn tells her husband. "If I'm going to be alone, I want to be by myself." Life was now imitating art, as Marilyn's own marriage was crumbling even as she portrayed a divorcing young woman. "Marilyn had the difficult scene, the blast-off for the picture," Wallach said. "She had considerable anxiety but like a wise child she uses it."

Miller sensed Marilyn's disappointment in both her character's and her own marriage and conferred with her after the second take. When he complimented her performance, Marilyn gazed up at him as if he lied. Deep down, Miller believed they still had a future together, and he thought their working together on the film would only strengthen their relationship. "It was far from accidental that by the end of the film Roslyn does find it possible to believe in a man and in her own survival," he would write.

Sydney Guilaroff also remembered Marilyn's despair that day as she recited lines mirroring her own life. Watching her tremble, the hairdresser went to her side. "I'm so lonely," she lamented. "So lonely, so alone." Days later, when he was attending to her wig, Marilyn said, "You know, Sydney, I wish I was married to you. You're so kind and so sweet to me, and you understand me better than anybody else." "Marilyn, I could be your father," he said softly.

Marilyn hid her nervousness and personal pain as she happily chatted with the spectating teenagers on summer vacation from high school, who lined the sidewalks in front of the courthouse. One striking girl, slightly older than the students, caught Marilyn's attention, and the two chatted privately. When Marilyn learned the girl was performing locally as the only female in a vocal group called the Suttletones and dreamed of a film career, she offered the novice encouragement.

The girl's name was Ann-Margret (born 1941), and would soon gain the attention of comedian George Burns while she was playing the maracas in a lounge at the Dunes Hotel in nearby Las Vegas. Burns hired her that Christmas to perform in his nightclub act, and she subsequently landed a recording contract with RCA and debuted as Bette Davis' daughter in *Pocketful of Miracles* (1961). Following Marilyn's death, Fox would promote the sexy, hip-swiveling actress-singer as the "next Monroe" and launched her early career as a "sex kitten" in *State Fair* (1962). Ann-Margret followed up with starring roles in youth-oriented films such as the musical, *Bye Bye Birdie* (1963), and Elvis Presley's *Viva Las Vegas* (1964). Expected to ascend the throne vacated by Marilyn in death, Ann-Margret sang at President Kennedy's forty-sixth birthday gala just as Marilyn had the year before.

At the Reno train station, Gable filmed a brief scene with Marietta Peabody Tree, who portrayed Susan, a divorcee departing for St. Louis. Tree never intended to act in a film. She had merely come to town to hook up with her lover who happened to be directing and offered her a role. The day before filming, Tree and Gable read the scene together three times. Later, she went to dinner with Huston and rehearsed it another twenty times, with Huston playing the part of Susan. "The next morning I was called for makeup at six-fifteen," Tree told James Goode. "I was shown how to make up my own mouth, which came to me as a revelation." After three rehearsals, Tree completed the scene in only one take.

Shortly thereafter, Marilyn's trailer arrived in front of Harrah's Reno Club's casino, a city block of gambling stations between Virginia and Center Streets, open twenty-four hours daily. Huston was filming an interior scene where Roslyn and Isabelle coincidently reunite with Guido and meet his friend, Gay. Driven to the location by Rudy Kautzsky, Marilyn was accompanied by Rupert Allan, Paula, and May.

For this scene, Marilyn didn't have to worry about her chronic insomnia and difficulty with waking for an early morning shoot. Huston filmed the long exchange of dialogue at three o'clock in the morning, at the time when Marilyn's intake of Nembutal would finally take effect. Filming unexpectedly extended to an additional day due to delays created by the three-year-old trained hunting dog cast as Gay's pet, Tom Dooley. Nevertheless, Marilyn read her lines perfectly. She was professional and effective, Miller would later write, and he celebrated her accepting his gift of a script that she could bring to life.

"[Paula] kept saying that she wanted to be invisible," Eve Arnold remembered, "but her get-up was a very strong silhouette against the stark desert sandscape." Believing black clothing would shield her from the blazing sun, Paula Strasberg appeared on location every day wearing black dresses, black sandals, and a black conical hat resembling a dunce cap or witch's hat. The crew nicknamed her "Black Bart." Some of them teased her by first pressing their hands in the abundant desert sand and then laying their hands on her back, leaving a print of sand.

Miller remembered Huston tolerating Paula by listening to her with "seriousness so profound as to be ludicrous." Huston rarely told an actor how to read a line and never explained the motivation behind the line; instead, he cast the actor appropriate to the role. According to Miller, Huston believed Marilyn possessed an adequate capacity for a dramatic performance and allowed her to activate her own internal resources. Paula provided inspiration through metaphoric suggestions such as, "You're a branch on a tree...You're a bird in the sky." When Huston couldn't get Marilyn to turn away from Wallach with an expression of disdain, Paula successfully elicited the desired response by merely saying to her, "Imagine he's eaten garlic."

A man of considerable patience, Huston resolved to avoid power struggles with Paula and Marilyn. When Marilyn begged for more takes to improve upon her performance, he simply indulged her. In the end, he had the ultimate power to select the take for final print during the editing process. "When she was herself, she could be marvelously effective," Huston recalled. "She wasn't acting—I mean, she was not pretending to an emotion. It was the real thing. She would go deep down within herself and find it and bring it up into consciousness. But maybe that's what truly good acting consists of. It was profoundly sad to see what was happening to her. She had no technique. It was all the truth, it was only Marilyn. But it was Marilyn, plus. She found things, found things about womankind in herself."

As the Democratic and Republican parties waged a presidential campaign across the country, *The Misfits* company played their own political games and chose sides. "If you were pro-Marilyn, you were said to be anti-Arthur," British journalist W.J. Weatherby wrote. "If you were pro-Huston, you were anti-Paula Strasberg." Two hostile camps organized: Marilyn's and Miller's. Marilyn's camp included May Reis, Montgomery Clift, Frank LaRue, Paula Strasberg, Ralph Roberts, Agnes Flanagan, Rudy Kautzsky, and Evelyn Moriarty. Miller criticized Marilyn for consorting with people whom he considered of small importance. To Marilyn, these were her loyal friends and sources of support. Eventually, Gable gravitated toward her side. According to Rupert Allan, Marilyn was "desperately unhappy" at having to read lines written by Miller that so obviously documented her personal pain. Regardless of the constant encouragement by her faction, Marilyn felt lonely, isolated, abandoned, and worthless.

Miller's camp consisted of Angela Allen, Eli Wallach, Frank and Nan Taylor, and Edward Parone, Taylor's assistant. Eventually, even Huston would join them, although quite innocently. Writer Arnold Schulman observed Miller "sulking around like a two-year-old, glowering at everybody, particularly at Paula." Taylor believed the coach's tactic was to divide and conquer, so he, Miller, and Huston avoided her.

Aside from the splitting created by the deterioration of the Monroe-Miller marriage, other frictions developed. Gable's character was supposed to be the best friend of Eli Wallach's, but Gable never warmed to his co-star. According to film historian Frank Miller, the two men seemed uncomfortable with each other initially had difficulty remembering lines in their scenes together. Wallach attempted humor by asking, "Hey, King, can you lower my taxes?" Gable once joked about Wallach's Jewish heritage by stating boiled ham would be served for lunch in Wallach's honor.

Although the men kept a distance from each other, they portrayed chemistry onscreen. Similarly, while the other males competed to win Huston's approval, Gable viewed him as a rival. Although he once shared Huston's propensity for drinking, hunting, and womanizing, Gable had settled down in his fifth marriage and was expecting a child. He couldn't relate to the director's reckless gambling and marital infidelities.

On July 27, the production moved to Quail Canon Ranch, surrounded by hills of sage and off Pyramid Highway, to film scenes at Guido's ranch. Miller had spent time with the original cowboys in a house on the ranch owned by a Mrs. Styx. Art imitated life when the production used Mrs. Styx house as Guido's. Necessitating more space for the cameras, the crew sawed through the corners of the house to make them removable by turning a few bolts. Miller later wrote about feeling disturbed by the fact that the walls of the same house where he had visited with the real cowboy and his girlfriend could now be unbolted and repositioned to bring in the light of the open sky. The set designers had also swiftly planted a vegetable garden required by the script.

After Guido and Gay bring Roslyn and Isabelle to the house Guido had built for his now deceased wife, they all enjoy cocktails and listen to music as the men compete for Roslyn's attention. Gay asks her to dance, and then an intoxicated Guido cuts in. According to Ralph Roberts, Marilyn believed Wallach was upstaging her and became annoyed.

Watching from off camera, Paula suddenly grabbed Roberts' arm and whispered, "What is Eli doing?" Roberts didn't understand

Paula's reaction and thought Wallach was doing a good job acting drunk. Huston wanted another take.

Afterward, Marilyn approached Paula and Roberts and asked if they noticed Wallach's behavior. Paula advised Marilyn to address it with Huston. "He's leading me in a way so that his face is always toward the camera," Marilyn hissed. "Nobody is going to look at his face if I'm jiggling my rear." Suddenly, Marilyn's attitude toward Wallach turned emotionally cold.

Roslyn becomes intoxicated and performs a dreamlike ballet in the moonlight under the trees. As Huston filmed, Inge took photographs of Marilyn's barefoot interpretive dance that culminated into an embrace of a large oak tree: "She was the master of the still camera," the photographer said with awe as she watched the actress' graceful movements. "She was the animal trainer and the photographer was the beast. She always struggled with the film camera, but with the still camera she was free."

In the Styx house, Roslyn and Gay's relationship evolves into a romantic one. Guido offers Roslyn' the unfinished house for the remainder of her stay in Nevada, and soon Gay moves in with her. Censorship prohibited Huston from showing the couple together in bed to signify their new intimacy, so he staged a scene in which Gay, fully dressed, leans over the bed to awaken Roslyn with a kiss. Marilyn shot the scene nude under the sheets. During one take, the sheet dropped, and part of the side of Marilyn's breast was revealed to the camera. Huston elected to use a different take.

"Let's get the people away from the television sets," Marilyn protested. "I love to do things the censors won't pass." She believed that censorship would gradually lessen, but not in her lifetime. United Artists' executive Max Youngstein shared Marilyn enthusiasm and exclaimed that the provocative scene was UA's ammunition against the takeover of television.

In the next sequence, Gay and Roslyn enjoy a breakfast he has cooked for her. Again, Marilyn was letter-perfect, and Huston embraced her. The moment was captured in a photograph. Later, when Marilyn viewed the picture, her relationship with the director soured. Marilyn sarcastically instructed someone to save the photograph so that she could show it when Huston said mean things about her.

Each evening, Ralph Roberts went to Marilyn's suite to massage her in preparation for sleep. They would engage in intimate discussions of her most private thoughts and feelings. By the time Roberts prepared for his own rest, she would sometimes summon him for another massage of her neck and feet until she fell asleep. On especially difficult nights, Marilyn would call on his services yet again instead of taking sedatives. Roberts would return the next morning to massage Marilyn's neck and shoulders as she sipped herbal tea. The scene would be repeated each work day with Allan Snyder applying Marilyn's makeup, Agnes Flanagan fitting her wig, and Paula reading lines with her. When Marilyn was fully prepared, she and Paula rode together in a limousine driven by Rudy Kautzsky to the set location. They would continue reading lines and discussing Marilyn's performance.

Marilyn requested Roberts' presence on the set, and he would drive to the location with May Reis and Clift's publicist, Harry Mines. Frequently, Roberts served as chauffeur to an assortment of personal secretaries, publicists, and photographers who would come along as passengers. During the long lapses in work, common with on-location productions, Marilyn would silently meditate as Roberts provided a foot or shoulder massage. Massages seemed to sweep the company as evidenced by the images captured by Magnum photographers. One depicts a massage chain: Clift massaging Roberts massaging Marilyn.

For weeks, Marilyn avoided an interview with W. J. Weatherby of the *Manchester Guardian*. The journalist spent time with Miller, Huston, Gable, and Clift before she consented. Believing Marilyn's reputation as a vapid movie star, Weatherby expected to dislike her. Instead, he found her charming, witty, and articulate. Soon Weatherby found himself a member of the Monroe camp. Each day after work, Marilyn handed out silver dollars to each member of her entourage for gambling at the Mapes casino's roulette wheel. When Weatherby first lost his silver dollar, she invited him to her suite and made him a salami sandwich as consolation.

Taylor made many attempts to assemble his mercurial cast of principal actors, Huston and Miller for a group portrait series. Photographers Elliott Erwitt and Ernst Haas rigged a backdrop under a tarp in the desert and waited for the right moment to lure them, along with Taylor, in front of the lens. After three days, Erwitt asked the group to convene. "Marilyn and Monty were intrigued and played around and joked," Taylor remembered. "It was fun and spontaneous and suddenly it was done."

At center of the cast portrait, Marilyn sits demurely on a stool, her legs crossed and wrapped around each other, her hands poised gracefully on her knees. She is surrounded by her male costars and Huston. Clift sits on an electrician's box, his chin resting on his fist; Marilyn looms maternally beside him. Gable stands paternally beside her, leaning close, his one foot resting on a crate. Huston stands powerfully over Marilyn, his arms folded. Wallach sits on a ladder next to Huston. Taylor stands under a ladder in the rear. Wearing a cowboy hat, Miller stands on a ladder, towering above all as creator.

As the summer progressed, the number one song on the popular music charts was "Itsy Bitsy Teeney Weeney Yellow Polka Dot Bikini." Simultaneously, Jean-Louis' ecru bikini costume was making its debut as Marilyn filmed a scene with Gable at Pyramid Lake. Miller noticed that the area had changed dramatically in the four years since he visited while awaiting his divorce. The lake was now filled with motorboats, and the shore lined with refreshment huts. The phone booth where he had spoken nightly to Marilyn, disguising herself as Mrs. Leslie, was no longer standing.

Marilyn sat in the bikini, draped in a white terrycloth towel as Agnes Flanagan braided her wig in two short ponytails. Marilyn was experiencing her menstrual period and contractually could not refuse to film the beach scene along with another in which she rides horseback. She confided dread to Ralph Roberts that the bikini would show her bloatedness but was determined to fulfill her obligation.

Tensions escalated again when the cast and crew relocated forty miles south of Reno to Dayton for the rodeo scenes, where many of the town's two hundred fifty residents watched the production or worked as extras. The Odeon Hall Building on Pike Street, now Mia's Restaurant, served as the location for interior saloon scenes. Montgomery Clift's character is introduced in Dayton. Many on the film were concerned about Clift's ability to perform, particularly since the first scene he was scheduled to shoot was a long telephone scene in which he calls his mother on a pay phone as the other characters watch in the background.

According to Frank Miller, Clift described the shot as an "audition in front of the gods and goddesses of the performing arts," but he mastered it in one take. "I look at him and see the brother I never had," Marilyn told Miller. According to Fred Lawrence Guiles, Clift and Marilyn were "psychic twins" who "recognized disaster in each other's faces and giggled about it."

In Dayton, Gable clashed with Clift while filming a scene driving to the rodeo in a station wagon. Portraying Perce's excitement, Clift slapped Gable's back from the back seat. From the driver's seat, Gable asked him to stop as he had spine problems. In repeated takes, Clift persisted with the slaps. Finally, Gable yelled, "If you do that again, you little bastard, I'll land one on you!" Clift burst into tears.

At Odeon Bar, the cast filmed a scene of Roslyn displaying her talent at the paddle ball as her cronies accept bets from the other customers on her ability to continue hitting the ball and win money from those gawking at her. Huston's lens focuses on her swaying buttocks and jiggling breasts. Miller's scene appears exploitative, but he may have been making a statement about his wife having been misused by studio executives who profited from displaying her body. The Millers appeared to be on civil terms when they strolled together through Dayton. "We're only going for a walk," Marilyn told a reporter, "just like everyday people." For another sequence filmed in the bar, Miller danced with his wife to demonstrate how he wished for Clift to lead her in a Texas two-step. The observing cast and crew cheered with delight.

Huston insisted on using real wild horses for the rodeo scene. The horse selected for Clift was too wild, but Huston insisted that he sit on it in the bullpen chute for a close shot. The horse lost control and threw Clift against the side of the chute, ripping his shirt. Later, Clift impressed Gable with his performance after the character is injected with painkilling medication after an injury. Gable said, "He had a wild look in his eye that could only have come from morphine...and booze...and the steer..."

Marilyn and Gable climbed into a white Chrysler station wagon to film a scene in which Roslyn is crying over Perce's injuries. The temperature inside soared over one hundred twenty degrees. Evelyn

Moriarty believed Huston was sadistic for requiring Marilyn to shoot for two hours in the roasting vehicle. Huston was notorious for his unrealistic demands from his actors. Thelma Ritter, for instance, had recently completed her work and required hospitalization for exhaustion.

Shirlee Strahm stepped out of Marilyn's trailer when it rocked, not from passion, but from heated arguments. In spite of the congenial Texas two-step a few days prior, the Millers' interactions degenerated into an angry dance with Marilyn externalizing her feelings and Miller resorting to a more passive aggression. Nan Taylor overheard Marilyn telling Miller she loved Montand and that he planned to leave Signoret for her. Marilyn only grew more infuriated when Miller gently insisted this was simply not true. Rumors persisted of an affair between Miller and Inge Morath and of Marilyn moving out of the corner suite and into Paula's room. W. J. Weatherby contradicted the first allegation. The Millers separated once they returned to Los Angeles and were registered at the Beverly Hills Hotel. By the middle of the summer, rumors of a Miller affair had him in bed with Angela Allen.

"We hear you're Arthur's girlfriend now," someone joked to the script supervisor. "Are you having fun?"

Allen asked the jester to relay a message to Marilyn: "If she knows that much, then she must know how much I am enjoying it."

Marilyn and Gable's relationship remained intact and unspoiled throughout the production. According to Miller, Gable behaved as though Marilyn were experiencing physical pain. He was a gentleman, opening doors for Marilyn and bringing her a chair while other men sat as she stood. "The place was full of so-called men," Marilyn said, "but Clark was the one who brought a chair for me between takes."

As the two leading stars passed time together waiting for a cloud to cover the sun so they might film a scene, they chatted about personal matters. Marilyn expressed pride in Gable's wanting her to be the first in the company to know that his wife was expecting his baby. She was thrilled about his becoming a father for the first time late in life and almost as excited as if she were expecting a child. Marilyn was in awe of her idol, treating him with reverence and charmed by his chivalry. "With Gable [Marilyn] was at her best," Eve Arnold remembered, "considerate, gracious and amusing." Marilyn would soon learn of Gable's vulnerability. "We were rehearsing a very long scene, and he started to tremble, just the slightest bit," she told a reporter. "I can't tell you how endearing that was to me. To find somebody—my idol—to be, well, *human.*"

During a break in filming the scene when Roslyn and Gay tend to their vegetable garden, Marilyn and Paula rested in the shade while Roberts massaged Marilyn's neck. Gable brought his chair beside Marilyn's and commented on their work together. "I had reservations about working with you because of what I hear about your temperament," he said. "But from what I see, you're the least temperamental person on the set."

"Thank you, Clark," Marilyn replied. "I'm so grateful to have had you as a father figure all these years. My feelings for you are just like the lyrics to the song Judy Garland sang to you." In *Broadway Melody of 1938*, a teenaged Garland sang "You Made Me Love You" to a framed portrait of Gable. Marilyn revealed to Ralph Roberts how much she loved working with Gable and how he fulfilled her ideal by making her feel safe and protected. When Marilyn suffered from abdominal pain and violently vomited, Gable personally took her back to the hotel and insisted she rest despite her protests and promise to Huston to get the shot.

Magnum photographers documented Marilyn's warm and close relationships with cast and crew. In dozens of pictures, she is touching and hugging the men or sitting on their laps. In one instance, Eli Wallach parks himself on her lap as she embraces him from behind. Marilyn affectionately grabs onto Gable's arm as he faces over her shoulder; she sits on the doorstep of her trailer with Gable beside her. Marilyn and Paula gaze adoringly at an infant lying on a blanket on a store counter; Marilyn eats tacos with the locals, rests on the grass with Miller, and lounges in amusingly exaggerated movie star poses on the hood of a white Cadillac along with Shirlee Strahm and Bunny Gardel. Marilyn embraces and speaks with young children of the crew, present with their mothers during summer vacation from school. In none of these celluloid images does Marilyn appear drugged, temperamental, or unstable.

She also appears steady and cheerful in color home movies filmed by Stanley Kilarr, a blackjack dealer in Reno who worked in a nonspeaking part as a drunk in a bar scene (the reel was auctioned by his surviving great-niece at Julien's Auction House in 2008). Kilarr was granted close access to the stars and had his cowboy hat signed by all of the principal actors. Marilyn complied with his camera and blew kisses to him.

The first weekend off from production, Ralph Roberts and May Reis drove to Virginia City, the most important settlement between Denver and San Francisco during the nineteenth century's mining boom and the site of the Comstock Lode, the world's largest silver strike. With saloons and buildings dating back to the 1860s, the town draws tourists to its preserved authenticity of the old west. When May Reis suggested a picnic and Roberts stopped for directions to a catering establishment, they were directed to The Country Inn and Restaurant owned by Edith Palmer, a renowned innkeeper, avid gardener, and accomplished cook. Palmer prepared a picnic lunch with pitchers of Martinis and iced tea and invited them to enjoy the feast in her tranquil garden. Roberts and Reis returned to the Mapes and raved to Marilyn about their experience.

Marilyn begged Roberts to take her back to Virginia City with him, remembering her visit with Fred Karger when it was only a tourist ghost town. Roberts brought her to the Chollar Mansion, commissioned in 1860 by the discoverer of the Chollar silver lode, and to the Country Inn. Mrs. Palmer was tending to her lush garden when Marilyn approached the fence and admired the plantings. "You have such a lovely garden," Marilyn remarked. "May I come in and admire it?" Palmer gave her a grand tour, and Marilyn fell in love with its warm hospitality.

For the next three months of production, the Country Inn served as Marilyn's haven. She routinely met her entourage there twice each week after work for dinner in the dining room, once a cider factory and surrounded by thick stone walls. Palmer prepared lunches and delivered them to Marilyn at the filming location. "Marilyn loved the food I prepared so much," Palmer told Fred Lawrence Guiles. "She was a gourmet, you know...She came to dinner often... 'My oasis in the desert,' she called our place...I often sit here and think about her. What a sad thing. Such a beautiful, lovely person. So sensitive." Because of Marilyn's love for The Country Inn, it now features a Marilyn Monroe inspired guestroom.

Twenty miles south, another charming host awaited Marilyn. Frank Sinatra invited the entire company of *The Misfits* to his Cal-Neva Lodge Resort on the north shore of Crystal Bay, Lake Tahoe, to see his show on the evening of Saturday, August 13 and to spend the night. Along with partners Sam Giancana and Mickey Rudin, Sinatra had recently purchased the property from reputed gangsters Elmer "Bones" Renner and Bert "Wingy" Grober. The resort—comprised of chalets, cabins, restaurants, lounges and a casino—straddled the border of California and Nevada.

In fact, the state line crossed through the massive stone fireplace in the Indian Room as well as the kidney-shaped swimming pool. Sinatra renovated the rustic complex, nicknamed the "Lady of the Lake," by adding a Native-American themed celebrity showroom and a helicopter pad on its roof. Allegedly, mobsters and celebrities moved through tunnels beneath the resort to avoid contact with the general public. The tunnels were built during Prohibition to smuggle liquor onto the property.

Escorted by her husband, Marilyn arrived at the showroom in a costume from the film: Jean-Louis' black dress, adorned by a five-strand necklace of black beads and a white ribbon tied to her shoulder strap. With her hair up-styled, she resembled a blonde version of Audrey Hepburn in *Breakfast at Tiffany's.* Gable and his wife sat beside Miller, and Clift sat next to Marilyn. After the performance, Sinatra displaced Clift by sitting beside Marilyn. Photographers, including Magnum's Elliot Erwitt, snapped photos of Miller, Marilyn, and Sinatra. Reno Photographer Don Donero's picture of Marilyn seated beside Sinatra, with Bert Gober (hired back as club manager) standing between them, is frequently used as "evidence" of a Monroe-Sinatra affair and of her alleged visits to Lake Tahoe in 1962. Miller is evidently cropped from the photograph.

In preparation for the premiere of *Let's Make Love* on Sunday, August 21 at the Crest Theatre in Reno, Marilyn planned a trip to Los Angeles with Roberts and Reis. To face critics, reporters, photographers, and celebrities from all over the world, Marilyn wanted to have her hair colored by Pearl Porterfield, retrieve a dress for the occasion, and obtain a supply of medication. She could travel on Thursday and return in time for the premiere. Marilyn told her friends they were certain to feel disappointed as she believed *Let's*

Make Love wouldn't be a good film.

"I want to get away from this morass of miasma," Marilyn told Roberts, the word miasma reminding her of having played a word game in New York with Montgomery Clift. She told her friend about having combined her two favorite words—miasma and mimosa—during the game. One meant a toxic air, and the other was the name of a lovely flower. Marilyn had played her turn with the phrase "mimosas give me asthma."

On the evening the Monroe-Montand musical was scheduled for screening, forest fires raged seventeen miles from Reno in the Sierras Mountains, burning power lines and causing an electrical blackout of the surrounding area. There would be no premiere, and the event would not be rescheduled. Jaded by recent negative press, Marilyn sarcastically wondered aloud if she would be blamed for the fire and fretted about the destruction of animals and trees.

Due to the blackout, the lights and the elevators at the Mapes didn't work, and the hotel was bathed in pitch darkness. Miller had the maintenance crew carry a power line from a generator in the basement to his suite so he could use the electric typewriter to produce script revisions for the next day's work.

Roberts joined Agnes Flanagan in the wardrobe room, opposite a stairway, freshening wigs by candlelight. They transformed a work-table into a bar and lined it with glowing candles. Marilyn found them and said she wanted to visit with the "happy people," insinuating misery with Miller in her suite. She sat on a wardrobe trunk and asked permission to join the small party. When Marilyn noticed they had no ice for their drinks, she asked Roberts to go to her suite to fetch some. "He's such a sweet man," Marilyn told Agnes. "I'd be lost without him."

Roberts returned with the ice, and Marilyn asked if he saw "Grouchy Grumps." Roberts replied that Miller had been lying on the sofa. She explained that Arthur typically moved from the desk to the sofa and then back again, until he fell asleep. Marilyn also quipped that Roberts was fortunate to have gotten some ice out of that room, implying the lack of positive outcomes during exchanges with her husband.

A couple walking down the darkened corridor passed the open door of the wardrobe room, and the woman peeked inside. She asked Flanagan if the young blonde woman was Marilyn Monroe. Marilyn grabbed Estelle Winwood's wig, placed it over her hair, and made an embellished dance movement. "No!" she cried. "I'm Mitzi Gaynor!" Marilyn started singing Gaynor's song from *South Pacific*, "I'm Gonna Wash That Man Right Out of my Hair." Roberts believed the choice of song implied her delight in ridding Miller.

While drinking with her friends in the candlelight, Marilyn reminisced about Johnny Hyde and confessed how not a day passed that she didn't think of him. She thanked him in prayer whenever feeling pleased with her own performance. "The big Reno blackout," Marilyn remarked with mirth as the evening ended. With the premiere of *Let's Make Love* sabotaged by the fires, she had enjoyed relaxing with her friends in the darkness. "This has turned out to be so much fun."

Beginning on Monday, August 22, Marilyn enjoyed two consecutive nights of sound sleep. The next day, Inge Morath photographed the Millers at the window in the suite at the Mapes. Marilyn stands, partially draped in the sheer curtain fabric, in the corner window at far left with her back toward the camera. Miller stands at far right in profile with a cigarette dangling from his lips, his hand in his pocket. A lamp with a large shade at center acts as a barrier between them. Marilyn's head is downcast as she looks to the street below, her body conveying despondency although her facial expression is unseen. This haunting, poignant photograph captures the widening rift in their marriage.

As the rancor in the Monroe-Miller marriage peaked, so did hostilities between Miller's camp and Paula Strasberg; even Paula's friend Eli Wallach resented Marilyn's dependence upon the dramatic coach. While filming a scene, he chastised Marilyn, asking what pearls of wisdom Paula could provide that Marilyn didn't already have. Arguably, Paula enabled Marilyn's troublesome habits and was held accountable by those who were negatively impacted by them. When Marilyn arrived tardy to the set, Paula joked, "You can afford to be late, but when you become a big star like Sandra Dee, you'll have to come on time." [At the time, Sandra Dee was a seventeen-year-old ingénue who had appeared in *Imitation of Life* and *A Summer Place* in 1959]. Even groggy from a barbiturate hangover, Marilyn giggled at this remark.

Lee Strasberg boarded a plane headed for Reno along with his daughter, Susan, for a western showdown with Miller in Paula's honor. The diminutive guru even dressed the part in a braided shirt, jeans, pointed-toe boots, and a cowboy hat. Susan paraphrased her father's confrontation of Miller: "I can't tolerate this behavior toward Paula. She's an artist. She's worked with many stars and never been treated like this. If something doesn't change, I'm afraid I'll have to pull her off the picture. She has to be shown some respect."

Miller remembered a content Paula sitting on the sofa and smirking. He held disgust for the Strasbergs, Lee for his petty focus on Paula and apathy over Marilyn's plight, and Paula for her self-absorption in light of Marilyn's plight. There is no evidence that Miller's camp treated Paula any differently after the confrontation, but Paula remained at Marilyn's side. Lee may never have intended to enforce the ultimatum as Marilyn's production company was paying Paula three thousand dollars a week for coaching services. The incident appears to reinforce Miller's perception of the Strasbergs as parasites.

Miller's most damning picture of Paula as an enabler of addiction is recounted in his autobiography, *Timebends*. Paula led him to Marilyn's bedroom where she lay in bed while a local doctor injected her hand with Amytal, a barbiturate used in the treatment of severe sleeping disorders. The drug was generally only prescribed to patients who are already taking barbiturates due to the high risk for dependence and addiction. Marilyn started yelling at her husband to leave, but he briefly conferred with the doctor who expressed shock that she was still alert and talking. "She was a flower of iron to survive this onslaught," Miller wrote. He feared Marilyn couldn't complete *The Misfits*, and this failure would confirm her worst fear of losing control of her life. He also thought Paula looked somewhat guilty for colluding with Marilyn to obtain the drug.

Ralph Roberts' unpublished manuscript details his observation of Marilyn's tormented struggle to achieve sleep when Miller called him to their suite. When Roberts approached the Millers' door, he could hear Marilyn moaning in "agonizing pain." He entered the suite as Miller was leaving the bedroom and shaking his head. Roberts went to the bedroom and found Marilyn barely aware of his presence. "Raffe, oh, Raffe," she cried. "I can't bear it." After a thirty-minute massage from her friend, she finally fell asleep.

"I was not an observer—I was part of the whole," May Reis told Eve Arnold of her chilling experience with Marilyn's troubles. "It's too painful to remember those moments. I am filled with things seen and unseen, done and undone, spoken and untold. I cannot talk. I'm filled with sadness. No matter what people saw on the surface, there was always anxiety and uncertainty."

Two people's addictions were losing control and threatening to derail the film: Marilyn's prescription medication and Huston's gambling. While Marilyn managed to function, Huston hit rock bottom. "We had the Errol Flynn of directors," remembered Evelyn Moriarty. "He had dames imported from Europe, and when they weren't available there'd be the hookers from Reno. Big John was a playboy, and he was also into the gambling tables."

On August 16, Huston had lost $16,000 at the roulette table, bringing his total debt to over $50,000 owed to Harrah's and the Mapes Hotel and Casino. With the casinos demanding payment, a panicked Huston requested an advance of twenty-five thousand dollars from Universal Studio for his next directorial assignment, *Freud*. This was not enough money to remunerate the amassed debt. Next, Huston expended production money, depleting all of the entire funds in the production's bank account. Now there was no money to complete the film.

Oblivious to the financial crisis, the company continued filming. Gable filmed a scene in which a drunken Gay climbs on the hood of a car in front of the saloon as he calls for his adult children and falls to the ground. Crewmembers pulled away the mattress breaking Gable's fall as Huston's camera panned down in one shot to reveal Gable lying on the dirt street. Screaming at high pitch, Marilyn runs and kneels before him, cradling his head. A burst of applause from the crew and spectators marked the success of the scene in one hundred fifteen degree temperature. Marilyn told Gable how wonderfully he performed before climbing into a Cadillac. Rudy Kautzsky drove her back to the Mapes Hotel.

On August 25, Max Youngstein, responsible for financing and distribution, discovered the production had exceeded its budget and contacted executives at United Artists to request the release of additional funds. There was no option but to suspend production. Humiliated, Huston requested his mismanagement be hushed from the cast. However, as investors, Marilyn and Miller were informed.

As the production went on hiatus, Marilyn's circumstances remained unclear. According to Ralph Roberts, Marilyn's Cadillac took her from the location with Gable to the Mapes and then to the airport. He remembered her being prepared for the suspension and making traveling plans to Los Angeles where she checked into the Beverly Hills Hotel, attended dinner with Doris Vidor, and visited the dying Joe Schenck. In contrast, rumors have since persisted alleging that Paula had found Marilyn unconscious in the hotel suite and called for paramedics to pump her stomach. Many biographers point to cinematographer Russell Metty telling Huston he couldn't shoot close-ups of Marilyn because her eyes wouldn't focus due the influence of sedative drugs, resulting in a medical decision to hospitalize her.

In recent years, information emerged about United Artists having covered Huston's gambling tracks by persuading Dr. Greenson to admit Marilyn to Westside Hospital on La Cienega Boulevard in Los Angeles. In the now accepted version, on Sunday, August 28, Marilyn met with Dr. Greenson and Dr. Engelberg who advised a week's rest at the expense of United Artists' insurance. Interest in Marilyn's well-being, however, did not motivate the decision for her to undergo detoxification. With the insurance carrier paying a claim based on the leading lady's health crisis, United Artists dodged the need to withdraw its cash.

Serving as a scapegoat for Huston bankrupting the production, Marilyn checked into Westside Hospital under care of Dr. Greenson and Dr. Engelberg. The ruse saved the film at the cost of Marilyn's reputation. Regardless, she received appropriate intervention for an addiction that was no fabrication. A few days after admission, Engelberg told the *New York Times* Marilyn needed about a week's rest. The official word was acute exhaustion.

Evelyn Moriarty remembered Frank Taylor gathering the company for a meeting and announcing Marilyn having suffered a breakdown. Miller rose from his chair and stormed out of the room. Moriarty told Donald Spoto that everyone knew Taylor's report was a ruse and Marilyn's troubles were unfairly exaggerated to cover for Huston's gambling of production funds. According to the stand-in, Marilyn was an easy scapegoat. Representatives of the Mapes gathered around the airplane taking the crew back to Los Angeles during the hiatus. Several carried signs with messages such as "We love you, Marilyn," "Come back soon, Marilyn," and "The Misfits need you."

Miller contacted Roberts and asked him to drive to Los Angeles because a reporter had trespassed Marilyn's private hospital room despite the heavy security. Roberts drove with Lee and Susan Strasberg as his passengers as Miller, Paula, May, and Rupert Allan took a plane. "She was a ghost of herself," Susan Strasberg thought upon first seeing Marilyn in the hospital. With a pale white complexion, Marilyn lay "helpless" on white sheets looking like an "overgrown child" and as if a "vampire had drained her life force."

Marilyn appreciated her friends rallying around her and accepted gifts of magazines to pass the time. Rupert Allan and May Reis screened every magazine to protect her from the sensational media reaction to Hedda Hopper's published interview with Yves Montand on September 1. Having successfully evaded Marilyn during her recent sojourns to Los Angeles, Montand met with the gossip columnist and disclosed: "Had Marilyn been more sophisticated, none of this would have happened. I did everything I could for her when I realized that mine was a very small part. The only things that could stand out in my performance were my love scenes. So, naturally, I did everything I could to make them good." Montand revealed himself as the last in a long line of users.

Wounded and publicly humiliated, Marilyn accepted supportive visits from Joe DiMaggio and regular phone calls from Frank Sinatra and Marlon Brando. Clark and Kay Gable sent a large bouquet of flowers and an encouraging note. Miller rushed to her side with hope of saving the marriage. He believed they still had a future together, and working on the film would only enhance their marriage. It was no coincidence, Miller later wrote, that in the end of his plot, Roslyn finds it possible to trust a man and believe in her own survival.

According to Barbara Leaming, Greenson discontinued Marilyn's barbiturates and substituted mild dosages of chloral hydrate, Librium, and Placidyl. Unlike the typical addict, she experienced no withdrawal symptoms. Now sober and revitalized, Marilyn was ready to return to work. Following discharge, she visited DiMaggio in San

Francisco before catching a flight back to Nevada. The couple would remain in constant contact for the remainder of her life.

On the evening of September 5, Marilyn arrived at the Reno Airport wearing white slacks, a caftan, white pumps, and a straw Peruvian hat purchased en route for a dollar. Protective Reno law enforcement officers playfully brandished their firearms as they escorted her through the airport, where she was met by Frank and Nan Taylor and by Miller, who did not embrace her. Crewmembers with welcome signs swarmed the plane in an attempt to quell the rumors of a drug overdose. "I'm looking forward to getting back to work," Marilyn told the press. "I'm feeling better. I guess I was just worn out."

Marilyn quickly resumed work "looking wonderfully self-possessed if not bright-eyed," according to her husband. Miller later wrote: "Her incredible resilience was almost heroic to me now." Marilyn allegedly felt ashamed of her behavior and demonstrated awareness of her addiction. She asked Huston and Gable for their forgiveness.

Huston continued filming the rodeo scenes in Dayton where Marilyn walked dogs with Bob Plummer Jr., age thirteen, and Gene Walmsley, age 8, who brought back their friends to introduce them to her. Toni Westbrook-Van Cleave, age six at the time, still remembers Marilyn strapping on a toy gun belt and playing cowboys and Indians with her young brother during a break in filming. When a female fan admired Marilyn's diamond ring, Marilyn bought her one.

What exactly was Marilyn's mental state at the time? While driving to Virginia City, Ralph Roberts' passenger—television comedienne Imogene Coco (1908-2001)—asked him what Miss Monroe was really like. Very much like Coco, Maureen Stapleton, and Judy Holliday, he replied. In fact, Marilyn was like most women he knew in the theater. The only difference was the extremes in her mood and the depth of her depression. Roberts observed Marilyn's withdrawal into a darkened bedroom for days but at the same time, he never experienced anyone laughing more or being more joyous about life.

Anthony Summers published Rupert Allan's memory of strolling with Marilyn along the Truckee River and explaining to her the life cycle of salmon, swimming upstream to spawn only to eventually get eaten by raccoons. "That's terrible," Marilyn gasped. "I can relate to the salmon because I've felt like them." As she did with Norman Rosten in New York, Marilyn made a pact with Allan never to kill herself. If despondent, they agreed to call one another and utter the code, "Truckee River."

* * *

One of the most difficult scenes in *The Misfits* involved lengthy dialogue between Marilyn and Clift. Huston wanted to shoot the scene in one take; the longest single take in his entire directorial career. It takes place behind the saloon, where Roslyn sits on a decayed seat from an old automobile and Perce lays on the ground, his head resting in her lap. Surrounded symbolically by a mound of empty liquor bottles, beer cans, broken cartons, and assorted trash, the characters reflect upon betrayal in their lives.

"When the 10,000-watt lights were switched on, the flies buzzing about, and the stench vile, it was like some nether hell," Eve Arnold wrote. The crew sprayed fly repellent as Marilyn shielded Clift's eyes with her hand and he cracked bad jokes. Expecting the actors to concentrate under such circumstances seemed "diabolical" to the photographer. None of the crew believed the two actors, notorious for their problems in remembering lines, could get through the scene. To increase her concentration, Marilyn requested that no one stand in her line of vision. "Working with her was fantastic...like an escalator," Clift said. "You would meet her on one level and then she would rise higher and you would rise to that point, and then you would both go higher."

To everyone's amazement, they completed the scene in a mere six takes, producing two perfect takes. Two takes were disrupted when Marilyn thought she shifted Clift's head bandage out of place and Clift incorrectly read a line. She complimented Clift when they finished without missing any lines in the long dialogue. According to Carl Rollyson, "Compared to the multiple takes of much shorter scenes, this long, beautifully modulated exchange...was performed with extreme economy and grace."

The company traveled thirty miles north of Reno and twenty miles east of Dayton to film the climatic horse roping sequences amid the lunar landscape on a dry lake near Stagecoach, an area is now known as Misfits Flat. The town derived its name from the Overland Stagecoach station at Desert Well. In 1857, the station served for a dual stop for the Overland Mail Company and the Pony Express.

Jim Palen, trained roper and stand-in for Gable, sustained injuries from a horse kicking him in the face and began spitting blood. Huston insisted for another take, and Gable grew furious. "You can all go to hell," he shouted while walking off the set in disgust. "They don't care if we live or die." Gable insisted on performing all the stunts except the most dangerous ones, even allowing himself to be dragged repeatedly (albeit heavily padded) behind a truck doubling as a runaway horse for four hundred feet over the desert floor."

"People like to manufacture myths," Eli Wallach confided to Richard Buskin in response to rumors that Gable's subsequent fatal heart attack was caused by the stunts, as well as by Marilyn's tardiness. According to Wallach, Gable's being pulled by the truck was neither dangerous nor exhausting. What's more, he understood Marilyn and Clift's neuroses and never lost his temper. Gable left the set at five o'clock in the afternoon, regardless of a scene's incompletion; this stipulation was in his contract. Moreover, Wallach asserts, Gable was ecstatic about becoming a father for the first time and rushed home to his expectant wife.

The horse-roping scenes were equally challenging for Clift. According to Frank Miller, when the crew overlooked providing him with leather gloves, the actor had to hold the ropes with his bare hands, making them raw and bloody. Even the horses weren't spared injury. Marilyn insisted a horse be freed from further work when she discovered it bleeding from a minor wound.

Marilyn, too, was required to participate in physically taxing activity when Roslyn attempts to pull the rope away from Gay as he wrangles the stallion. He pushes her off, and she hits the ground with force and rolls onto her back. Earlier in the shoot, Marilyn rode a horse that became entangled by electrical wire and lurched. Marilyn lost her grip on the reins and the horse broke into a wild gallop. Whitey Snyder grabbed the dragging reins and gained control of the animal.

W. J. Weatherby nearly bumped into Marilyn one afternoon while leaving the dry lake and marveled at her composure. Considering all that she had supposedly experienced in recent weeks, the journalist thought she looked "wonderful." Later that day, he interviewed an intoxicated, incoherent Clift in the Mapes' lounge. Marilyn spied from a distance, in the words of Weatherby, like a "concerned mother hen."

The time had arrived for Marilyn's triumphant climatic scene on October 11, an overcast day. The cowboys wrestle the mare to the ground and tie its legs together. Roslyn watches, her heart breaking as the mare's colt stands helplessly beside its mother. She erupts in a raw emotional outburst. "Butchers! Killers! Murderers!" she shrieks. "You liars. All of you, liars! You're only happy when you can see something die! Why don't you kill yourselves and be happy? You and your God's country. Freedom! I pity you. You're three dear, sweet dead men. Butchers! Murderers! I pity you! You're three dead men!"

Expecting Miller to allow Roslyn to intelligently articulate her cause, Marilyn resented the speech. Nevertheless, the histrionic explosion presents a more suitable dramatic climax. Having captured close-ups of Marilyn emoting pain while watching the roping, Huston chose to film her speech from a considerable distance. The volume of her voice and her body motions would carry the performance, as the camera would not read facial expressions. Miller disagreed with the camera set-up, but Huston argued her voice would be a cry from the wilderness. They compromised by filming the scene from both a medium shot and from fifty yards away and later choosing the most effective one.

Early in the morning, Evelyn Moriarty stood out on the flat while Russell Metty focused the camera and the crew arranged the lighting for Marilyn's big scene. Watching from behind the camera, Marilyn sipped from a thermos of hot tea, lemon, and honey to soothe her. Once Evelyn completed her function as stand-in, Marilyn hit her mark on the flat. When Huston yelled, "Action," Marilyn began screaming in a voice never before heard by her fans in a powerful performance unlike any of her previous comedy roles and early dramas. Carl Rollyson describes Marilyn's delivery: "These words come up from the pit of suppressed resentment she barely manages to articulate...In projecting her profound sense of alienation to Gay, to his male companions, to men in general, and to the whole of existence, Roslyn is both triumphant and defeated. She is the ultimate cinematic embodiment of Monroe's double bind."

In a still photograph by Inge Morath, Marilyn stands with her legs spread apart, her torso leaning forward in rage, her fists clenched at her side. Her head is thrust forward with her mouth open. Her forehead is furrowed, her hair hangs limp with perspiration. No longer is she the sex symbol pin-up; instead she is a serious, dramatic actress. This photograph evokes the impact Huston could have achieved through a close-up. The extreme distance of Huston's camera minimizes Marilyn's effect by recording a fraction of her intensity; had Huston filmed this powerful performance in a close-up or used the alternate medium shot, Marilyn arguably may have been nominated for an Academy Award.

Weatherby observed Marilyn filming the scene several times as she was "jumping in and out of a state of high emotion without any preparatory passages." He wrote that the "wear and tear" on her psyche "must have been savage." Between takes, Weatherby described Marilyn as a boxer in the corner of the ring, waiting to come out fighting when the bell sounded. Amazingly, later that afternoon, the journalist met her shopping in Reno with Ed Parone, Taylor's assistant, and was shocked that she looked relaxed and composed in a dress befitting her public image. Marilyn spontaneously consented to an interview shortly thereafter and made a date to meet Weatherby in the Mapes' lounge.

In the interview published in both *Manchester Guardian* and *Conversations with Marilyn*, Marilyn expressed her identification and respect for Betty Grable and praised Michael Chekhov's performance in *Spellbound*, reverently recalling his playing King Lear opposite her Cordelia. Weatherby shared his own admiration of the deceased actor in the Hitchcock classic, and Marilyn begged him to tell Chekhov's widow directly since the elderly woman seldom heard people mention him. "The public in America is fickle," Marilyn bemoaned. She gave Weatherby Xenia Chekov's address and phone number in Los Angeles.

Marilyn also shared her desire to someday portray Lady Macbeth and impressed Weatherby with her intelligence and down to earth persona. When Weatherby referred to her day's work as a big scene, Marilyn disagreed. All scenes are equally important, she believed, contingent upon working with a good director. "And if you aren't working with a good director," she warned, "nothing will matter anyway."

Chapter Thirteen: *The Misfits* Part II

Biographers paint a largely black picture of the production, but Marilyn and other members of the company enjoyed light moments on and off the set. On a blistering afternoon, Taylor brought a man to Marilyn's dressing-room trailer whose role was to design the concept for the film's trailer, a brief advertising preview of the film. "Marilyn, here is the gentleman who is going to handle the trailer," Taylor said. "I am so happy to see you!" Marilyn exclaimed without missing a beat. "My air conditioning doesn't work."

Aside from frequent visits to Virginia City, members of the company spent weekends in nearby cities. Marilyn, Roberts, Clift, Frank LaRue, Snyder, and Flanagan traveled to Lake Tahoe in a caravan of Cadillac sedans. Marilyn also stopped at a resort on the lake where she had stayed with DiMaggio and lingered by the largest of its cabins until a boy spotted her and called for his family. She quickly ran to her waiting car. Marilyn sometimes joined May Reis, Eve Arnold, and Roberts for cocktails on the weekends. She often coaxed May to do an imitation of Marlene Dietrich with her legs crossed as if she were sitting on a piano and singing. "Look at those legs!" Marilyn squealed. "I wish I had legs like that."

Roberts' most recent film, *Bells Are Ringing*, with Judy Holliday was playing at a drive-in theatre in Reno. He and Paula, both residents of New York City, had never been to such a venue and decided it would be exciting to go together. Marilyn heard about their plans and asked to accompany them. In a rented car and with barrels of popcorn and gallons of Coca Cola, the trio watched Roberts' brief performance. Marilyn was mesmerized. Afterward, they dined at a

Mexican restaurant, and Marilyn praised Roberts' performance, suggesting that he play the character of Lennie in *Of Mice and Men*. She begged him to perform a scene from the play with her at the Actors Studio when they returned to New York.

On Wednesday before Huston filmed the final roping scenes on the salt flats, Miller told Marilyn that the second unit would be working during the weekend and she would be free from Friday until Monday. She decided to travel to San Francisco and asked Roberts, Snyder, Paula, May and Agnes to join her for the adventure, making reservations for all to fly with her and stay at the Huntington Hotel on Nob Hill. Clift privately made a reservation for himself on the same flight and at the Fairmont Hotel.

On the plane, Marilyn and Paula sat beside each other while May and Roberts sat behind them. Clift entered the plane hiding his face and talked to the pilot. He slipped on a flight attendant's jacket and cap and winked at Roberts. Clift began walking down the aisle and reviewing the passenger's boarding passes. When he paused at Marilyn's row, she looked at him, turned to May, who had the tickets, did a double take, and burst into laughter.

Marilyn had arranged for tickets to see Ella Fitzgerald perform at the Fairmont and asked Roberts if he liked her. He facetiously replied, "Yes, but she's no Janice Mars and no Gertrude Niesen." Thereafter, this became their comparison reference: How does something or someone rate on the scale of one to Janice Mars or Gertrude Niesen? After Fitzgerald's performance, Marilyn and Clift visited the vocalist's suite for about a half-hour while Agnes and her husband explored the city and May, Paula, and Roberts rested in the lobby. Paula became tired and returned to the Huntington.

Marilyn joined her entourage without Clift, and the three began walking back to the hotel. It was an exceptionally lovely night, and Marilyn impulsively suggested a stroll through the city. When an empty cable car stopped in front of them, May suggested they go for a ride. Although a frequent visitor to San Francisco, Marilyn had never ridden a cable car. The three climbed aboard and sat silently watching the city in lights. At the end of the line, a group of people boarded, and the trio helped turn the car around. They rode back without Marilyn being recognized by any of the other passengers.

During the trip, Marilyn walked to Fisherman's Wharf and visited Joe DiMaggio's restaurant, where she reunited with his brother, sister, and friend, Lefty O'Doul. DiMaggio was in New York at the time. A young sailor who had been following her for several blocks quickly fled upon O'Doul's bellowing a greeting.

On another evening, Marilyn joined Clift, Roberts, May, Paula, Frank LaRue, Allan Snyder, Agnes Flanagan and Agnes' husband for dinner at the Blue Fox. Founded in 1933, this landmark in the city's financial district was renowned for its alley entrance, attentive service, and trend-setting cuisine. It was owned by the Fassio family since 1948 and closed in 1993 when its luxury and formal, slow-paced dining experience became obsolete. The hostess threw her arms around Marilyn, practically crying with joy. She was a relative of DiMaggio's and had been close to Marilyn during the marriage.

The next evening, Clift reserved a table at Finocchio's, a famous nightclub featuring the finest female impersonators, several of whom parodied celebrities. One of the drag queens routinely imitated Marilyn. The group arrived incognito wearing dark glasses, and planned to rush out, leaving Frank LaRue to pay the check if either Marilyn or Clift were recognized. As Marilyn sat at her party's table in the second row, Snyder warned her to remember that the lampoon would be in good humor. Marilyn had enjoyed Edie Adams' impersonations of her on the *Ernie Kovacs Show.*

Aleshia Brevard (born 1937), then known professionally as Lee Shaw, performed at Finocchio's from 1950 to 1962, leaving to undergo gender reassignment surgery. In her signature number, "My Heart Belongs to Daddy," patterned after Marilyn's performance in *Let's Make Love*, Brevard peeled off a red knit sweater to reveal a red lace corset. Audiences loved it. Photos of Brevard as Lee Shaw show her as a beautiful blonde with sparkling eyes and a sweet face. Wearing a gown and a wig teased high, she had a notable resemblance to Marilyn.

Brevard unknowingly played to her inspiration in the audience, and a few of the patrons noticed the original Marilyn sans disguise. Marilyn turned to Roberts and whispered that she felt as though she were looking at herself in one of her films. At the curtain call, all the drag queens lined up on stage, and Brevard suddenly recognized Marilyn. She whispered to the performer beside her, and word spread along the line. Marilyn's group rose for their swift departure, and Marilyn blew Brevard a kiss as she exited the building before the audience could spot her.

Roberts and Marilyn also attended a performance by June Ericson featuring the songs of Harold Arlen ("Over the Rainbow"). Afterward, possibly at the *hungry i* nightclub in North Beach, they remained for the second-act comedian, then unknown Lenny Bruce (1925-1966). Marilyn sat back in her seat and laughed more than Roberts had observed in a long time. At the end of the act, someone handed Bruce a note, and his expression changed. With intense emotion, he stuttered a farewell: "I'm sorry. The greatest lady in the whole world is in the audience today—I can't bear it." Overcome with emotion for Marilyn, Bruce abruptly left the stage.

At five o'clock in the morning, on Sunday, October 1st, director Blake Edwards filmed the opening scene of *Breakfast at Tiffany's* on the corner of Fifty-Seventh Street and Fifth Avenue, seven blocks west of the Millers' apartment. A taxicab glided down the desolate street and delivered Audrey Hepburn, in the role Marilyn coveted, to Tiffany's. With her hair piled high, adored with a tiara and wearing a Hubert Givenchy black sleeveless gown and sunglasses, the actress exited the vehicle. She gazed up at the jewelry store's iconic sign, approached a window, and admired the diamonds on display as she sipped black coffee and nibbled a croissant. The film premiered the following autumn without Marilyn in the role for which Truman Capote had assiduously campaigned for her.

On Monday, October 10, Marilyn hosted a dinner party for eighteen at Edith Palmer's Country Inn in honor of Frank LaRue. Miller was not invited. Gable drove Marilyn to the inn in his silver Mercedes. Never one to take sides, he had one drink, kissed Marilyn, and left. One of the other patrons that night was Fred Lawrence Guiles (1920-2000), a writer from San Francisco, who was writing a book on Marilyn and had come up to Reno in hopes of interviewing her. He and a friend had driven to Virginia City to have dinner and were staying nearby at the Silver Dollar Hotel. They made no attempt to intrude but observed from a nearby table. In his biography, *Norma Jean: The Life and Death of Marilyn Monroe*, Guiles acknowledged "Mrs. Florence Edwards in whose hospitable inn in Virginia City this all began."

The company hosted a surprise birthday party for Miller, turning forty-five, and Monty Clift, five years younger, on the following Monday evening at the Christmas Tree Inn & Casino. The event also served as a wrap party. Clift told Roberts that the evening was a highlight of his life, and sadly, this was a true statement. Within two years, Clift experienced a major depressive episode and lived virtually as a hermit, drinking heavily and sustaining on canned baby food.

Marilyn, in a pearl dress from the party she hosted for Yves Montand before the start of *Let's Make Love*, sat beside Clift and expertly twirled fettuccini alfredo on a spoon as only the former wife of an Italian-American could. Russell Metty made the toast: "Arthur writes scripts and John shoots ducks. First Arthur screwed up the script and now his wife is screwing it up. Why don't you wish him a Happy Birthday, Marilyn?...This is truly the biggest bunch of misfits I ever saw." Marilyn smiled but shook her head in negation. After dinner, the party gambled in the casino. At the roulette table, Marilyn teamed with Eve Arnold. Huston handed Marilyn a pair of green dice.

"What should I ask the dice for, John?" she asked.

"Don't think, honey, just throw," Huston replied. "That's the story of your life. Don't think, do it."

The following day, October 18, location filming ended. The morning after a farewell venison dinner in the Mapes Sky Room, the company returned to Los Angeles. Marilyn and Miller registered together in a suite at the Beverly Hills Hotel. The few remaining process scenes, mostly of the characters' dialogue in trucks and cars with a projection screen in the background, took place on Stage 2 at Paramount Studios.

Miller still had no ending for his film. In one draft, Roslyn pairs with Perce, the cowboy most sensitive to her values. Marilyn, however, had her own ideas about a suitable conclusion. Since Gay and Roslyn served as the Millers' fictional counterparts, Marilyn may have been suggesting the dissolution of her own marriage when she told her husband the leading characters should break up in the end. Though several biographers pinpoint the Millers' separation in Reno, evidence places it at the Beverly Hills Hotel with Frank Taylor, May Reis, and Ralph Roberts helping to relocate Arthur's possessions to another hotel. The irony was too harsh, Miller wrote, regarding Marilyn's desire to end the relationship of the characters that represented them. The film he created to reassure Marilyn that she could find peace apparently backfired.

On Soundstage 2, Marilyn filmed a critical scene with Wallach. Believing Roslyn's relationship with Gay has ended, Guido asks her to give him a reason to double-cross his friend and release the roped horses. Marilyn's speech is poignant as she confronts Wallach's selfishness with disgust and acrimony:

> You, a sensitive fellow…so sad for his wife. Crying to me about the bombs you dropped and the people you killed. You have to *get* something to be human? You never felt anything for anybody in your life. All you know is the sad words. You could blow up the world and all you'd feel is sorry for *yourself*.

Marilyn skillfully used her Method Acting approach in summoning her recent feelings toward Wallach as motivation for the scene, but she was beginning to let go of some of the bitterness. "I've loved him like a brother, and I shouldn't let something like this come between us," she told Roberts. "I feel betrayed. It's the same feeling I used to have as a child." Marilyn eventually resolved her differences with Wallach and gave him a book of Einstein's letters inscribed: "*To my dear brother*."

* * *

"Whitey, do you remember our first photo session?" Marilyn asked her cosmetician as she faced a large makeup mirror in the portrait studio at Paramount. "We had hope then." It was October 29, and Marilyn was posing for Eve Arnold for the film's promotional studio portraits. May Reis attended for moral support, and Patricia Newcomb, filling in for Rupert Allan, supervised. Standing behind Marilyn, the group lifted their flutes of champagne and toasted the session through a reflection in her mirror.

Arnold staged some campy shots of Marilyn in the Jean-Louis bikini and lace full-slip and others of her nude and draped in a white sheet. The inspiration was Botticelli's painting, *The Birth of Venus*, not cheesecake photography. While preparing for the session in Arnold's studio, Marilyn walked around with her Jax Capri slacks unzipped in the rear as Arnold took candid shots of her. Protective of how Marilyn would appear in the shots, Newcomb followed Marilyn about, pulling up the zipper before Arnold could get another shot.

On Halloween, director Henry Hathaway found the star of his film, *Niagara*, crying outside a Paramount soundstage. "All my life I've played Marilyn Monroe, Marilyn Monroe, Marilyn Monroe," she bemoaned. "I've tried to do a little better and find myself doing an imitation of myself. I so want to do something different. That was one of the things that attracted me to Arthur when he said he was attracted to me. When I married him, one of the fantasies in my mind was that I could get away from Marilyn Monroe through him, and here I find myself back doing the same thing, and I just couldn't take it, I had to get out of there. I just couldn't face having to do another scene with Marilyn Monroe." Miller's character of Roslyn plainly failed to meet Marilyn's expectation of a departure of her previous roles. If her Pulitzer Prize winning husband's independent film couldn't deliver Marilyn from the sexy dumb blonde image, how could she establish a dramatic career in the Hollywood system?

Ralph Roberts offers an unsettling memory of the production's final day. As Rudy Kautzsky drove Marilyn and Paula to Paramount Studios on November 4, the two women sat peacefully in silence in the back seat. Huston was reshooting the final scene between Roslyn and Gay. With no need to memorize lines already committed to memory for the film's final scene, Marilyn was reading five newly added pages of Miller's script sent to her that morning, involving the reshooting of an earlier scene in the film. Suddenly, she let out a scream that nearly caused Kautzky to send the Cadillac off the road. Paula tried comforting her, but Marilyn only cried. "I have no protection," she cried, recalling her husband's former betrayal in London. "It's like another open page of his diary."

In adding material to an earlier scene in *The Misfits*, Miller betrayed her once again. The newly added pages of script exposed his eleventh-hour plan to reshoot the opening scene in Isabel's home to establish Guido as Roslyn's former lover. Unknown to Marilyn, Miller's camp had already scouted for a similar structure in Los Angeles. Marilyn felt her husband transformed her character into a tramp, thus branding her the same, and changed the entire tone of the film. She would protest the change, but meanwhile, she had to produce the film's final scene with Gable at Paramount Studios.

None of the cast and crew recognized it at the time, but the scene filmed on Soundstage 2 would end an era in motion picture history and contained the last completed on-screen performances of the industry's biggest legends. In the cab of a truck positioned in front of a large projection screen, Gable looked lovingly at Marilyn. When Huston yelled, "Cut," Miller offered Gable feedback that his expression seemed understated. "You can't overdo," Gable explained, "because it's being magnified hundreds of times on the theater screen."

In the next shot, Roslyn leans against Gay as he places his arm around her and drives into the night. She asks how he finds his way home in the dark.

"Just head for that big star straight on," Gable gently replies. "The highway's under it—it'll take us right home."

These prophetic final lines created the perfect capstone for two stars in their last completed film performances. The last scene was done in one take. The final shot would be the night sky with a star prominently illuminated.

The previous day, Frank Taylor had viewed a rough cut of the film minus a musical soundtrack. Seated alongside him in the screening room at Paramount were Huston; Huston's mother, Nan; and Max Youngstein. When the lights came on, the group discussed their reactions. Nan loved Marilyn's performance. "It's a spiritual autobiography," Taylor said. "This is who she is. This is why life is so painful for her and always will be."

Youngstein felt differently and voiced disappointment in the film. In turn, Huston blamed Miller, who started rewriting the earlier scene. Allegedly, Wallach had already conferred with Miller and Huston to change his part and the ending, suggesting Guido as the hero, Gay an alcoholic, and Roslyn a promiscuous woman.

Gable was the only member of the cast who was granted the power of script approval, so Miller needed to convince him of the merit of these alterations. Ralph Roberts stood outside Gable's trailer talking with Frank Prehoda when both men were startled by Gable's profanity. Gable had read Miller's rewritten scenes and, fearing the mutilation of a good film, adamantly refused to perform in them. Immediately, Gable made a telephone call demanding a screening of all the assembled footage.

Next, Gable marched to Marilyn's trailer and found her equally distraught. He comforted her with assurance of exercising his contractual power to refuse any modification of the screenplay. Marilyn begged Gable not to sway under Huston or Miller's influence. Her contract provided no power to prevent the changes. Gable met with Miller and Huston and told them that he was finished with the film. Miller tried to persuade him that the rewrites improved the film and asked if he had taken the time to read them. Gable confirmed he had, but the picture was sound as it had been filmed, and he felt proud to have been involved. Gable thanked Frank Taylor and proclaimed: "I now have two things to be proud of in my career: *Gone With the Wind* and this." Before leaving Paramount, Gable bade farewell to Marilyn and embraced her as photographers took photographs.

Before leaving the studio, Marilyn announced to Huston that she respectfully passed on his offer to cast her in the film biography of Sigmund Freud. Screenwriter Jean-Paul Sartre wanted her to portray Cecily, the sexually repressed and hysterical patient who manifests many neuroses and recovers through hypnosis. Although she wanted to appear in the film, Marilyn explained, Anna Freud disapproved of the project. Aligned with the Freud family, Dr. Greenson also disapproved and allegedly influenced his patient's decision to decline the role. Montgomery Clift went on to star as the founder of psychoanalysis, and Susanna York portrayed his neurotic patient.

"I do believe it was essential for me to be with her on this picture…" Paula Strasberg announced, laying closure on the entire experience before taking a flight back to New York, "because so much of it was close to her, also because she is a creative actress, not a personality… I feel that I have contributed to every frame of *The Misfits.* If it doesn't work out, that's something I must share with her. My work is not a mystery. This is my twenty-fourth picture. My work is evident on the screen."

In the end, Huston shared none of Billy Wilder's criticisms of Marilyn. Instead, he praised her to the *Sunday Press*: "The real trouble with Monroe is that she is over-dedicated…She read and re-read her lines in order to appear word perfect on the set. If she felt she didn't know her lines, that was just your hard luck. You just had to wait, but you knew you were waiting for the best." *The Misfits* wrapped forty days behind schedule and clocked in over budget at $3,955,000, earning the distinction of the most expensive black and white film of Hollywood history at the time.

In time, a curse having fallen on *The Misfits* would become Hollywood folklore as all but one of the film's major actors would be deceased before the end of the decade. Gable would die twelve days after production ended; Marilyn would die twenty-seven months later; Clift and Paula six years later; and Ritter by 1969. On a day he wasn't working in Reno, Eli Wallach appeared on set costumed as Sigmund Freud in tribute to Huston's next film. Marilyn clutched his arm and lovingly said, "Eli you're going to be working all your life." Her prediction would ring true as Wallach would be the last surviving principal cast member, continuing to work past age ninety in *Wall Street: Money Never Sleeps* (2010) and *The Ghost Writer* (2010).

Frank Taylor rushed the film into post-production for eligibility for the 1960 Academy Awards. Surely, Gable would be posthumously nominated. However, Alex North could not score the film in time.

Playing on a literal interpretation of the title, print advertisements featured a graphic motif of puzzle pieces with the tagline: "It shouts and sings with life...explodes with love!" The trailer juxtaposed Magnum's portraits of each of the principal cast with brief scenes featuring each performance without the typical voiceover. Emphasis was placed on the paddleball scene and nude bedroom scene with a jazz soundtrack providing a sexy but tawdry undercurrent, divulging little of the plot. In the end, Gable's death was the most effective lure. The January 31, 1961 issue of *Look* magazine contained a cover with Gable and Monroe and an article titled "Gable's Last Movie: Prelude to Tragedy."

Taylor's next hurdle was to appease the censors. The Legion of Decency gave the film a "B" rating and ordered the slapping of Marilyn's buttocks in the paddleball scene be reduced from six slaps to two. Censors conceded that Gay's asking Roslyn to marry him compensated for their "illicit relationship," but identified two additional violations including the bikini costume and "an over-emphasis of nudity on the part of Marilyn Monroe in her bedroom scene." Overall the censors found no redeeming qualities. The Legion of Decency asserted: "The low moral tone, highly suggestive costuming and degrading situations which permeate this film tend to obscure and nullify any alleged serious dramatic purpose of the picture makers."

Despite the film's alleged depravity, a gala premiere was held on January 31, 1961, at the Capitol Theatre on Broadway and Fifty-First Street in New York, in honor of Gable. Simultaneously, the film opened at the Granada Theatre in Reno. Freshly divorced, Miller attended the New York premiere with his children; Montgomery Clift escorted Marilyn. The initial grosses were good, indicating the film would be United Artist's all-time largest earner, but admission sales slumped after the film failed to garner Oscar nominations. In 1962, the Hollywood Foreign Press presented Marilyn with a Golden Globe award for World Film Favorite, indirectly acknowledging her most recent screen performance in *The Misfits*.

Ahead of the times, this disturbing and melancholy film failed to resonate with mainstream critics and audiences alike. Damian Cannon of *Movie Reviews UK* summarized its troubled reception: "Seemingly misunderstood by contemporary critics, *The Misfits* is an adequate swan song. What seems to have floored viewers of the time is the lack of a clear-cut hero, the absence of a solid central figure…Most of Miller's intellect is spent rooting through the personal misfortune of his characters…The audience has nothing concrete to hold onto, to identify with in a halfway pleasurable manner…"

Flaws in the plot notwithstanding, the critics could not dismiss the potency of the stars' individual performances. "Gable has never done anything better on screen, nor has Miss Monroe," heralded the *New York Daily News*. "Gable's acting is vibrant and lusty, hers true to the character as written by Miller…The screen vibrates with emotion during the latter part of the film, as Marilyn and Gable engage in one of those battle of the sexes that seem eternal in their constant eruption. It is a poignant conflict between a man and a woman in love, with each trying to maintain individual characteristics and preserve a fundamental way of life."

Hollis Alport of *Saturday Review* lauded *The Misfits* as a "powerful experience..." with "characters at once more lifelike and larger-than-life than we are ordinarily accustomed to in American movies... [Monroe] gets pathos into the role, and a very winning sweet charm into a great many of her scenes. She shows range, too, and it can be plainly announced that acting has by no means spoiled Marilyn Monroe. On the other hand, we lack the information about her that Miller has given the other characters. Her past, in a word, is amorphous. Not so with the others. It is almost as though Miller has thought of Roslyn more in terms of American myth than of reality. Real she becomes, though, as the story progresses...There is also the effect of ensemble playing usually missing from any but European movies...It's a most unusual movie to have come out of the Hollywood system..."

"A picture that I can only call superb..." proclaimed Paul V. Beckley of *New York Herald Tribune.* "After the long drought of vital American pictures one can now cheer, for *The Misfits* is so distinctively American nobody but an American could have made it...It augurs well for the future of American films...There is evidence in the picture that much of it has a personal relationship to Miss Monroe, but even so her performance ought to make those dubious of her acting ability reverse their opinions. Here is a dramatic, serious, accurate performance; and Gable's is little less than great."

"In this era when sex and violence are so exploited that our sensibilities are in danger of being dulled," Beckly continued, "here is a film in which both elements are as forceful as in life but never exploited for themselves. Here Miss Monroe is magic but not a living pin-up dangled in skin-tight satin before our eyes...And can anyone deny that in this film these performers are at their best? You forget they are performing and feel that they 'are.'"

Bosley Crowther of *New York Times* disagreed. Although he praised the wrangling scenes "vivid" and "thrilling," he found Marilyn "completely blank" and "unfathomable," even when she "kicks up such a ruckus." Crowther applauds Roslyn ending the audience's "breathless horror" of animal cruelty by persuading Gay to free the horses, but reckons the film's structure is weakened by "everything turn[ing] upon her." He concludes the plot is pointless; therefore, the film "just doesn't come off."

"At face value, *The Misfits* is a robust, high-voltage adventure drama, vibrating with explosively emotional histrionics," declared *Variety*, "conceived and executed with a refreshing disdain for superficial technical and photographic slickness in favor or an uncommonly honest and direct cinematic approach." Though *Variety* highlighted the Millers' innovative and rogue approach to filmmaking, it also pin-pointed where the audience got lost in the plot: "...Nuances of which may seriously confound general audiences and prove dramatically fallible for patrons unable to cope with author Arthur Miller's underlying philosophical meanings..."

Time was particularly brutal: "Terrible...a routine bland opera... [a] clumsy western... [a] pseudosociological study of the American cowboy in the last, disgusting stages of obsolescence...a woolly lament for the loss of innocence in American life." As if this weren't enough of a bashing, the magazine called it a "glum...fatuously embarrassing psychoanalysis" of Monroe, Miller, and their failed marriage. The critic used Marilyn's line from the film's "dullest point" to summarize his reaction: "'Help.'"

For the first time in her career, Marilyn earned downright scathing reviews about her physical appearance as if she had failed her audience by not being slim and glamorous in a role that required neither attribute.

"Miss Monroe has seldom looked worse," announced *Hollywood Reporter*, "the camera is unfailingly unflattering. But there is a delicacy about her playing, and a tenderness that is affecting." *Limelight* observed: "Marilyn Monroe (in a bikini yet) looks like an aunt of Mae West who has been eating intemperately at Luchow's [a New York restaurant]. She mopes around with a moronic preoccupation and is, for reasons known only to the author, considered a life symbol."

"Miss Monroe plays the stripper without any of her erstwhile sexual magic," declared Henry Hart in *Films in Review*. "Her body is still provocative, but the last vestiges of youth have gone from her face. An inexplicable lassitude has invaded her, and, ineptly coiffured and mascara-ed, and burdened with inappropriate Strasbergian mannerisms, she dead-panned the Miller magniloquence in an uninteresting and increasingly tiresome way."

Leaving no survivors, *Films in Review* also blasted Huston, Miller and Metty: "Mediocre...Rather venally conceived, amateurishly written, and perfunctorily directed, photographed and edited.

[Huston] sinks so low, trying to compensate for his perfunctory direction, that he makes Miss Monroe bare her breasts and shake her buttocks as though she were a stripper not only in this film but in real life as well."

Lithuanian-born filmmaker Jonas Mekas (born 1922) raved about Marilyn's performance. In 1958, he began writing the "Movie Journal" column for *The Village Voice* after serving as editor of *Film Culture*. In the early 1960s, Mekas would co-found Film-Makers' Cooperative and the Filmmaker's Cinematheque, the latter eventually growing into Anthology Film Archives, one of the world's largest repositories of avant-garde films. Mekas' reaction to *The Misfits*—written in the rhythm of a Beat poem—remains one of Marilyn's best critiques and insinuates the film's appeal to the counterculture:

> Marilyn Monroe, the Saint of Nevada Desert...she haunts you, you'll not forget her. It is MM that is the film. A woman that has known love, has known life, has known men, has been betrayed by all three, but has retained her dream of man, and love, and life...She finds love everywhere, and she cries for everyone, when everybody is so tough, when toughness is everything. It's MM that is the only beautiful thing in the whole ugly desert, in the whole world, in this whole dump of toughness, atom bomb, death...All the tough men of the world have become cynics, except MM. And she fights for her dream, for the beautiful, innocent, and free...It is MM that tells the truth in this movie, who accuses, judges, reveals. And it is MM who runs into the middle of the desert and in her helplessness shouts: "You are all dead, you are all dead!"—in the most powerful image of the film—and one doesn't know if she is saying those words to Gable and Wallach or to the whole loveless world...There is such a truth in her little details, in her reactions to cruelty, to false manliness, nature, life, death—everything—that is overpowering, that makes her one of the most tragic and contemporary characters of modern cinema, and another contribution to The Woman as a Modern Hero in Search of Love...No drama, no ideas, but a human face in all its nakedness—something that no other art can do. Let's watch this face, its movements, its shades; it is

this face, the face of MM that is the content and story and idea of the film...

Arguably, the film's failure stemmed from the fact that Miller and Huston did not deliver the product audiences expected. *The Misfits* appeared as a Western at face value but did not follow the formula of the genre. At the time, television Westerns permeated the medium, and the public had a specific standard when they saw cowboys and horses on the big and small screens. Additionally, as one of the first independent films or "indies," *The Misfits* did not follow the formula cranked out by American film studios.

The average filmgoer may not have comprehended the metaphoric cowboys; in fact, without a supplementary explanation from the author, neither did Robert Mitchum or Clark Gable. The dialogue and theme more closely resembled the French New Wave of film-making exemplified by Jean-Luc Godard's *Breathless* (1959), Alain Resnais' *Hiroshima, Mon Amour* (1959), and the Italian style perfected by Federico Felini in films such as *La Dolce Vita* (1960). However, Huston's direction and Metty's cinematography paralleled the traditional style of American film, perhaps causing the audience to miss the distinction.

Moreover, Frank Taylor's hype of making the greatest American film backfired. Promotion of the film as somewhat innovative or introducing a new style of American film might have more accurately reflected what audiences were going to see. Ultimately, as iconic figures, the leading stars and their repertoire of films following the Hollywood studio formula drew an audience with a high expectation for entertainment congruent with those iconic images and their previous work. After all, Gable had already appeared in great American dramas such as *It Happened One Night* (1934) and *Gone With the Wind* (1939), and Marilyn had recently won the Golden Globe Award for Wilder's "great American comedy."

The Misfits earned increased acclaim over time as the film industry evolved. Today it seems an outlier in 1960s cinema and representative of later films made during the 1970s and 1980s. In evaluations by modern critics, the film embodies the advent of the "indie" film, now commonplace. Marilyn's performance has also received retroactive praise.

"As Roslyn, Marilyn carries the film," wrote Joan Mellen a decade after Marilyn's death. "The other characters are male stereotypes but she is a person without guile, role-playing, or hypocrisy. Her feelings are close to the surface, and her vulnerability inspires decency."

"The more tormented Monroe's private and professional existence became, the more remarkable was her work and appearance on the screen," wrote Carl E. Rollyson fifteen years later. "As Roslyn, she had undeniably become an actor of depth and subtlety and power which transcended a role which was not entirely realized in the writing."

The production was torturous for Marilyn, Miller would later say. He marveled at how well she performed under the circumstances, and Marilyn would have likely appreciated his empathetic hindsight. "I had to use my wits, or else I'd have been sunk—and nothing is going to sink me," Marilyn said of the experience.

Montgomery Clift displayed a strong, negative reaction to the film in the final hours of his life. (Perhaps its association with the early deaths of his costars was too painful for him.) On July 22, 1966, Clift spent most of the day in his bedroom in his townhouse on East Sixty-First Street in Manhattan where he lived with his personal secretary Lorenzo James. The pair had not spoken much during that day. At one in the morning, Lorenzo went to Clift's bedroom to ask him if he wanted to watch *The Misfits* on television. "Absolutely not!" Clift replied, his last spoken words. At 6 a.m. the next morning, Lorenzo went to wake him but found the bedroom door locked. Unable to break it down, he ran down to the garden and climbed a ladder to the bedroom window. When he got inside, he found Clift dead. He was undressed, lying on his back in bed, wearing eyeglasses, with fists clenched.

"Clark [Gable] was one of the kindest men I ever worked with," Marilyn would tell Louella Parsons, summarizing her experience of making *The Misfits*. "I was so miserable during most of the picture, unhappy and sick—but he always understood and was never impatient even when we had to stop shooting. By the time we finished, after all the heat and the delays and my personal problems, I was completely run down and even more unhappy than I remember being at any time in my life."

* * *

[For a synopsis of *The Misfits*, see **Appendix: Selected Marilyn Monroe Film Synopses**]

CHAPTER FOURTEEN: OCTOBER–DECEMBER 1960

On Sunday, October 30, the *New York Times Book Review* contained the article "How Cinderella Became a National Institution." William K. Zinsser reviewed Maurice Zolotow's 340-page biography of Marilyn Monroe, the first of its kind, published by Harcourt, Brace & Company. Featuring a dust jacket with a photograph of a Marilyn taken during the announcement of her divorce from DiMaggio, the book went on sale across the nation at $5.75 per copy. Zinsser wrote: "Proof of her eminence is the fact that she is now the subject of a long and serious biography, an honor that doesn't ordinarily fall to 34-year-olds."

Marilyn's reputation benefitted from the biography, but little is known of her reaction aside from an inscription she wrote in James Haspiel's copy. Zolotow had written: "*To Jim Hapsiel—Who would have written a better book about MM.*" Under the message, Marilyn penned: "*That's right!*"

In their quest to further promote Marilyn's positive image, the Arthur P. Jacobs Company reassigned Rupert Allan to Princess Grace of Monaco and assigned Patricia Newcomb as Marilyn's personal press representative. Marilyn had objected to Newcomb during the production of *Bus Stop*, but consented to the transfer. Margot Patricia Newcomb (born 1930 in Washington, D.C.) was the daughter of Carmen Adams Newcomb and Lillian Lee. Her mother was a social worker, and her father was a lobbyist who represented large corporations of the coal industry, including the Great Lakes Coal and Coke Corporation owned by George Skakel, Jr., father of Attorney General Robert Kennedy's wife, Ethel Skakel Kennedy.

Newcomb spent her childhood in Chevy Chase, Maryland and relocated with her parents to Los Angeles in 1946 where she graduated from Immaculate Heart High School two years later. She subsequently attended Mills College in Oakland, where she was enrolled in courses by Pierre Salinger (1925-2004), a journalist for the *San Francisco Chronicle*, contributing editor for *Collier's* magazine, and later White House Press Secretary for Presidents Kennedy and Johnson. Newcomb graduated with a Major in Psychology in 1952 and Salinger quickly hired her as a researcher of corruption in the Teamsters Union for a series of articles. Salinger introduced her to Robert Kennedy and she would serve as Kennedy's campaign manager during the 1968 presidential election.

In April 1954, the Arthur P. Jacobs Company hired Newcomb as a publicist and writer at $50 per week. Beginning in 1957, she worked in public relations as an employee of Rogers and Cowan Company until May 1960, when she returned to Arthur P. Jacobs Company as an account executive. Newcomb was living at 120 South Canon Drive in Beverly Hills and was described as intelligent, witty, and appreciated by her clients for her discretion. She was especially passionate about civil rights.

While appointing Newcomb, Arthur Jacobs maintained John Springer's assignment as Marilyn's press manager. A graduate of Marquette University with a journalism degree, Springer (1916-2001) was hired by RKO Studios as a publicist in the late 1940s. He later worked for Fox as a magazine publicity director and met Marilyn in 1952. In 1960, Springer began working for Arthur P. Jacobs. Following Marilyn's death, Springer established his own firm, John Springer and Associates, and tapped his encyclopedic memory to become a film historian. Although he wrote five books about the industry, Springer refused to publish his memoir about his famous clients. "I don't care how long Marilyn Monroe or Judy Garland are dead," he would say. "They've trusted me. Trust is what it is all about. I grew up with the nuns and Jesuits, and I feel my obligation is something like the seal of a confessional."

* * *

On November 4, Clark Gable and Marilyn filmed the happy ending scene together, and *The Misfits* wrapped forty days behind schedule. Gable kissed Marilyn goodbye and drove home to his ranch in Encino. Marilyn returned to the Beverly Hills Hotel to start packing for her flight back east that weekend.

Roberts planned to drive his car across the country to New York. He packed several Native American rugs Marilyn had purchased in Reno and Miller's typewriter in the trunk of his car to deliver to the couple's apartment. He went to the Beverly Hills Hotel to say goodbye to them. Miller shook his hand and thanked him for his contribution to Marilyn's ability to finish the film. Marilyn begged him to drive carefully and offered him cash for the trip.

The following day, while changing the tire of his jeep, Gable began perspiring profusely and suffered extreme chest pains. He entered the house, and Kay Gable thought he looked exhausted. She suggested he eat dinner and retire early to bed. In the middle of the night, Gable awoke with a splitting headache and symptoms mistaken as indigestion. Kay gave him seltzer and aspirin. While dressing the next morning, Gable collapsed and was rushed by ambulance to Hollywood Presbyterian Hospital where he was diagnosed with a coronary thrombosis.

In 1960, doctors prescribed oxygen and hospital rest for heart attack victims. Medicine had not yet advanced to bypass surgery, or insertion of stints or pacemakers. Kay stayed with Gable in an adjoining room; he seemed to recover and reportedly sat up in bed, chatted with nurses, and even smoked cigarettes.

On November 11, the Millers flew back to New York City on separate flights. Pat Newcomb and May Reis accompanied Marilyn. Miller felt relieved to have slipped back into anonymity without his wife. An elderly man walking down the aisle of the plane stopped and pointed to him. Miller claimed to *look* like the famous playwright, but alleged to be someone else. The man then asked if he were Morris Green. "Who's Morris Green?" Miller asked. "Who's Morris Green!" the man repeated as if this was a household name. "*Morris Green*, Poughkeepsie. Green's Hardware."

Eight months earlier, Miller and Marilyn passed on their boring food in the kitchenette of the Beverly Hills Hotel bungalow and went to a restaurant without a reservation. To avoid being recognized, Miller took off his eyeglasses; Marilyn hid behind dark sunglasses and a headscarf. They were refused service. Miller considered putting on his glasses and asking Marilyn to take off hers. Leaving the restaurant, the couple laughed about seeking anonymity only to contemplate using the power of celebrity to go to the head of the line.

Marilyn returned to the apartment at east Fifty-Seventh Street. Miller registered at the Adams Hotel, where she phoned him. "Are you coming home?" she asked. "Only to collect my things," Miller replied. As soon as Monroe and Miller's representatives released news of the separation and ensuing divorce to columnist Earl Wilson, reporters and paparazzi staked out in the lobby of Marilyn's building waiting for her next departure. When the elevator doors opened, Marilyn and Newcomb stood inside.

The thunder of camera shutters exploded. A young couple stepped aside to permit the women to pass, but their young son entered the elevator as Marilyn rushed out and before Patricia could exit. The boy looked confused about the commotion in the lobby of his apartment building. The two women ran the gauntlet of reporters to the front doors and toward an awaiting limousine. Reporters asked questions about Marilyn's future plans, and one insolent man asked if she felt guilty about causing Gable's heart attack. Looking visibly distressed, Marilyn replied, "I will not discuss my personal life." A reporter thrust a microphone into her face and accidently tapped her tooth, nearly chipping it.

On November 12, the *New York Daily News* published a photograph of a solemn Marilyn seated in the back seat of the limousine, clutching the high collar of her mink coat close to her neck, her hair covered by a scarf. The headline announced the news in all capitals: "MILLER WALKS OUT ON MARILYN." A few days later, Marilyn mustered enough courage to unlock Miller's study. Opening the door, she noticed his cleared desk and the empty spaces on the bookshelves. Marilyn's eyes raised to her framed portrait taken by Jack Cardiff displayed on the wall. Taken in London, it was Miller's favorite picture of his wife with her hair casually tossed, her eyes heavily lidded, and her mouth sensuously open. Seeing her own image staring at her made Marilyn feel mocked and abandoned. Miller leaving the portrait behind, she told friends, was a final act of vengeance.

Across town, Miller ran into Inge Morath on the street and struck up a conversation. Unable to recall her name, he called Nan Taylor to refresh his memory. Morath would become his third and final wife. "The breakup of [their] marriage is a great pity," Simone Signoret told the media. "It's strange, you know, people go to the theatre to the movies and they laugh and cry at lovers on the screen. But when those same stars are living real-life heartbreak, the same public becomes cruel."

Newcomb told the press Marilyn had not yet retained an attorney for the divorce, but the time had come, and so she hired Aaron Frosch (1924-1989). Without bitterness and rancor, the Millers agreed to an amicable and collaborative divorce. Marilyn would retain the New York apartment as her primary residence, and Miller would retain the farmhouse in Connecticut. Miller would also gain custody of Hugo, the Basset Hound, who enjoyed a more rural lifestyle.

Eve Arnold dodged the press outside Marilyn's apartment to deliver the contact sheets, a jeweler's loupe to magnify the images, and grease pencils to mark the rejects. The two women spent a week reviewing the contact sheets, working from noon to five o'clock, with Marilyn frequently disappearing into the kitchen to blend and serve guacamole dip. When the task ended, Arnold gave Marilyn a box of Botticelli prints from the Uffizi museum in Florence inscribed: "*To the other Venus.*"

On November 16, columnist Earl Wilson wrote to Marilyn asking her for an interview in response to Zolotow's biography rapidly selling off the shelves of bookstores across the country and hearing positive early reviews of her latest film:

> *I hear from a couple of very good sources that "The Misfits" is an excellent picture—that you in particular are excellent—and I have so written in today's column...I would like to see you for a story on your future plans when you are ready...I think the sooner the better. I am at your service.*

At 10:30 p.m. that evening, Kay Gable kissed Clark goodnight to retire to an adjoining hospital room as he read a magazine in bed. Twenty minutes later, a private duty nurse observed Gable lay his head back on the pillow and peacefully die of a second coronary. His years of smoking three packs of cigarettes a day, hard drinking, and yo-yo dieting before the start of a new film had finally taken their toll.

A reporter from the Associated Press called Marilyn at two o'clock in the morning and found her still awake. He informed her of Gable's death and requested a statement. Marilyn grew hysterical and incoherent. She hung up the phone and immediately contacted DiMaggio, who rushed to her side. The following morning, newspaper headlines announced: "The King Is Dead." Marilyn called Rupert Allan, who advised her to return the reporter's call and issue a statement. She replied publicly to George Carpozi: "Clark Gable was one of the finest men I ever met. He was one of the most decent human beings anyone could have encountered anywhere. He was an excellent guy to work with. Knowing him and working with him was a great personal joy. I send all my love and deepest sympathy to his wife, Kay."

Initially, the press blamed Gable's refusal for a stunt double to film his strenuous scenes in *The Misfits*. Later, newspaper and magazine articles erroneously and ruthlessly held Marilyn responsible due to her chronic tardiness, botched lines, and need for multiple takes of scenes. However, Gable had received a letter from Severn Arts Productions on February 25, 1960 that read: "*You have recently submitted to a physical examination...because of the fact that such examination disclosed a hypertension condition, the insurance company declined to issue cast insurance...*" The note continues with a directive for Gable to submit to another exam and declaration that the production company would not be liable for any of his health issues during filming of *The Misfits.*

Gable's funeral was at Forest Lawn Memorial Park, where he was interred in the crypt beside his third wife, actress Carole Lombard (1908-1942). Arthur Miller and Frank Taylor attended with two hundred other mourners. Marilyn wouldn't attend for fear of collapsing and becoming a spectacle; and she didn't want to be unfair to Gable's pregnant widow.

"I kept him waiting—kept him waiting for hours and hours on that picture," she cried to Sidney Skolsky. "Was I punishing my father? Getting even for all of the years he kept me waiting?" Marilyn ruminated over the possibility she had subconsciously substituted Gable as her father, displaced her hurt onto him, and punished her father through him. Too many years of Freudian therapy taught Marilyn to search for subconscious motivation behind her behavior. Others were quick to point a finger at her. Marilyn told her half-sister someone shouted to her from a passing car, "How does it feel to be a murderer?"

John Springer's assistant at Arthur P. Jacobs Company, Diane Stevens, allegedly called Marilyn one evening to check on her. Marilyn confessed she was feeling responsible for Gable's death. Stevens insisted it was not Marilyn's fault and advised that self-blaming would only make her feel worse. Marilyn lamented her inability to find a way to go on living. Alarmed, Stevens called John Springer, who, in turn, called May Reis. Springer called Stevens back and reported that Reis had said Marilyn was safe and sleeping.

The release of *Cosmopolitan* magazine's December issue on November 23 could not have been more inappropriately timed. Jon Whitcomb's article highlighted the positive working relationship between Marilyn and Miller while on location in Reno and in the article Marilyn had also discussed her self-assessment of not yet reaching the goal of being a good wife. Through the rest of December, Marilyn attended sessions with Dr. Kris every weekday and participated in the classes at the Actors Studio. She seemed to be doing better emotionally and financially. Marilyn received a fifty thousand dollar payment residual for *Some Like It Hot*, $100,000 of $300,000 owed to her for the performance in *The Misfits*, and her fee as uncredited co-producer.

During this period, a column by Art Buchwald titled "Let's Be Firm on Monroe Doctrine," satirically escalated Marilyn's availability to national interest. "Who will be the next ambassador to Monroe?" Buchwald wrote. "This is one of the many problems President-elect Kennedy will have to work on in January. Obviously you can't leave Monroe adrift. There are too many greedy people eyeing her, and now that Ambassador Miller has left she could flounder around without any direction." Kennedy had recently won the presidential election without Marilyn's vote; she hadn't returned to Roxbury, Connecticut, where she was registered to vote, and made no provision to cast a ballot as an absentee voter.

As Christmas approached, Gladys sent her famous daughter a holiday greeting card with the formal inscription: "*Loving good wishes, Gladys Pearl Eley.*" Diane Stevens would recall Marilyn discussing a positive phone call with her mother during the holiday. Apparently, Marilyn's own miscarriages provided insight into the depth of her mother's pain. She detailed the circumstances of Gladys' ex-husband kidnapping her children and surmised the event as a catalyst for her mother's subsequent psychosis.

Marilyn spent Christmas Eve with the Strasbergs. She lavished Jane and Bobby Miller with gifts and gave Patricia Newcomb a mink coat. Marilyn returned to her apartment on Christmas night, where Newcomb waited for her to celebrate, to find a "forest-full" of poinsettias delivered by a local florist. Marilyn recounted the evening's dialogue to Dr. Greenson in a letter a few months later. "Who sent the flowers?" Marilyn asked Patricia. "The card just says 'Best, Joe,'" she replied. Marilyn smiled wearily and said, "Pat, there is only one Joe in my life."

V.H. Monette, Incorporated, a global supplier of merchandise for Military Post Exchange stores now employed Joe DiMaggio as corporate vice president. The retired athlete earned $100,000 annually as a goodwill ambassador, traveling to army bases and presiding at exhibition baseball games, and was given a suite at the Lexington Hotel in New York. Marilyn called DiMaggio that night and asked why he had sent me the flowers. "First of all," he said, "because I thought you would call me to thank me. Besides, who in the hell also do you have in the world? I know I was married to you and was never bothered of any in-law."

Aware of Marilyn's separation from Miller and his love for her still strong, DiMaggio reached out and invited Marilyn to join him somewhere for a drink. She told him that she thought he no longer drank, and DiMaggio admitted to occasionally taking a drink. She remarked they would need to meet in a very dark place to avoid being recognized together. "What are you doing Christmas?" DiMaggio inquired. "Nothing," Marilyn replied. "I'm just visiting with a friend." DiMaggio offered to pick her up and take her back to his hotel. "*I must say I was bleary and depressed,*" Marilyn wrote to Dr. Greenson, "*but somehow still glad he was coming over.*"

DiMaggio told Marilyn she had saved his life by encouraging him to engage in psychotherapy with an analyst recommended by Dr. Kris. With new insight, DiMaggio admitted he, too, would have wanted a divorce if he had been in her position. This heartfelt revelation served as a catharsis for the couple. Marilyn remained in DiMaggio's company through the holidays, edging out her new press agent. Patricia Newcomb, aware of her role as the third wheel, boarded a plane back to Los Angeles on New Year's Eve and penned a letter to Marilyn during the four-hour flight. She expressed sympathy for Marilyn's recent stressors and a hope to share a lifelong friendship with her. Indeed, their friendship would last for the remaining twenty months of Marilyn's life. DiMaggio would remain equally loyal, transcending her death.

The depth of Marilyn's relationship with DiMaggio is reflected in the numerous original telephone messages recorded by telephone operators at the Hotel Lexington in New York between December 27, 1960 and her death in August 1962. Sold by Hunt Auctions in May 2006, the messages are notated as coming from "Mrs. Miller" and "Mrs. Norman." They also document Marilyn having frequently called DiMaggio two to three times per day and often as late as three o'clock in the morning. DiMaggio deeply loved Marilyn, and her attraction to him remained strong. "Marilyn knew where she stood with him," Lois Weber Smith said. "He was always there, she could call on him, lean on him, depend on him, be certain of him. It was a marvelous feeling of comfort for her."

CHAPTER FIFTEEN: JANUARY–JUNE 1961

Living alone in New York, Marilyn surrounded herself with loyal staff for support and companionship. Hattie Stevenson continued to prepare Marilyn's meals, and Hedda Rosten managed the enormous volume of fan mail. Marjorie Stengel, formerly Montgomery Clift's secretary, left her post due to his escalating drug and alcohol problems and started working for Marilyn when May Reis left. When not at home, Marilyn visited the Strasbergs' apartment on Central Park East, where she passed time playing with their Yorkshire terrier and male cat. According to Susan Strasberg, the feline usually had its mouth open and actually resembled Marilyn. When Stengel's hairdresser begged for tidbits of information about the new employer, the secretary said, "In twenty-four hours your life is busier and more glamorous then Marilyn Monroe's is in two weeks."

Hollywood attorney Milton Rudin encouraged Marilyn to hire Cherie Redmond to manage her finances, deposited in accounts spread across the city at Colonial Trust Company, Irving Trust Company, Excelsior Savings Bank, Chemical Bank Trust Company, and First National City Bank of New York. Her income tax report for 1961 claimed a total income of $72,919.54. In addition to a payment of $300,000 for her performance in *The Misfits*, Marilyn received ten percent of its earnings, and the film was making significantly more money in Europe than in the United States.

Marilyn needed professional vigilance in guarding her financial interests, and Cherie Redmond served as a fierce protector. The secretary initially suspected accountant Julius Winokur of embezzling money from the accounts; in turn, he accused Jack Ostrow, employed by Marilyn's new attorney, Aaron R. Frosch (1924-1989). "*The fewer people who know about the state of MM's finances...the better,"* Redmond typed in a memo to Rudin's secretary, authorizing the woman to open envelopes addressed to the attorney marked "personal." Eventually, Redmond came to suspect Frosch of pocketing some of Marilyn's money.

On January 14, Marilyn signed her last will and testament in preparation for her divorce in the presence of Aaron Frosch and Louise H. White. Marilyn bequeathed $10,000 each to Bernice Miracle and May Reis and $5,000 to Norman and Hedda Rosten to be used for the education of their daughter, Patricia. She willed all of her personal possessions and clothing to Lee Strasberg with instructions to distribute them "*in his sole discretion, among my friends, colleagues, and those to whom I am devoted.*"

Additionally, she bequeathed to her trustee, Frosch, $100,000 to manage and invest to provide annual incomes for Gladys and Xenia Chekhov (the widow of acting coach Michael Chekhov), respectively at $5,000 and $2,500 annually. Following their deaths, she stipulated the principal remaining trust go to Dr. Marianne Kris "*to be used by her for the furtherance of the work of such psychiatric institutions or groups as she shall elect.*" The real and personal remainder of the estate would be divided in twenty-five percent each to Reis and Kris and fifty percent to Strasberg. She appointed Frosch as executor.

Marilyn's recent correspondence with Marlon Brando focused on their exploration of material for a project together. *Paris Blues* (1961), produced by Sam Shaw, had sparked their interest. The racially sensitive screenplay centered on the friendship between two pairs, one African-American and the other white. The men, American jazz musicians, live and perform in Paris. Their carefree lifestyle of playing through the night and sleeping all day is interrupted by the arrival of two women on vacation who attend their performances.

Marilyn and Brando never secured the property, and it was now in production in Paris with Paul Newman, Joanne Woodward, Sydney Poitier, and Diahann Carrol. Shaw kept Marilyn informed of his progress. "*I don't think those squares will like the picture,*" Shaw wrote on February 10, "*but thank God you've got round curves (on your head). You'll love it...*" He ended with an invitation to disregard their current time difference and contact him: "*You can call in the middle of the night...I don't mind.*"

With limited control over her assignments at Fox, Marilyn turned to the developing medium of television, which offered her increased creative control through a cooperative network and sponsor. NBC's project on the table was a ninety-minute color television drama based on an adaptation of the short story *Rain* by gay author Somerset Maugham (1874-1965), best known for *Of Human Bondage* and female characters depicted as sexual beings. Adapted for the stage by John Colton in 1923, *Rain* had starred Jeanne Eagels, who died at thirty-six of an overdose of alcohol, chloral hydrate, and heroin. Rod Serling, creator of *The Twilight Zone* series, had adapted the play into a television screenplay.

The network would air *Rain* on Sunday, October 29, paired with a sixty-minute episode of the documentary series *Project XX*, titled *The World of Bob Hope*. The project's executive producer was Anne Marlowe, whose soprano voice was familiar to radio audiences because of the jingle in commercials for Rinso laundry detergent long before she produced *Somerset Maugham TV Theatre* anthology for CBS, beginning in 1950. Marlowe produced fifteen Maugham scripts, culminating in the highly rated 1959 teleplay *The Moon and Sixpence* starring Laurence Olivier and Jessica Tandy. This would mark Marilyn's first experience working with a female producer.

The most enticing of NBC's amenities was not the $150,000 salary for the first run of the show—and an additional $75,000 if it were repeated—but the network's consideration of Lee Strasberg as director. Columnist Mike Connolly reported Marilyn and the Strasbergs had incorporated as partners to produce television films.

The plot of *Rain* involved passengers of a ship stranded on the South Pacific island of Pago Pago and required some censorship for early 1960s television, which depicted married couples sleeping in separate beds. Self-righteous missionary, Alfred Davidson, and his wife encounter a prostitute, Sadie Thompson, on the run from police in San Francisco. Davison observes Sadie cavorting with American Marines on the island and vows to redeem her. Sadie also catches the attention of Marine Sergeant O'Hara, who falls in love with her. Following a confrontation with Davidson, Sadie experiences a religious conversion and agrees to return to San Francisco to face criminal charges. O'Hara proposes to her and plans their escape to Australia. Under the influence of Davidson, Sadie refuses. Davidson seduces her and soon after he commits suicide. Disillusioned, Sadie chooses to go to Australia with O'Hara.

Rain had already been adapted in three film versions: *Sadie Thompson* (1928), a silent film with Gloria Swanson and Lionel Barrymore; *Rain* (1932), a sound version with Joan Crawford and Walter Huston; and *Miss Sadie Thompson* (1953), a 3-D musical version with Rita Hayworth and José Ferrer.

Interestingly, now that Strasberg was involved in negotiations to direct the project, he and Paula supported Marilyn in the role of a prostitute; a huge departure from their balking at the allusion of Holly Golightly accepting cash from the men who dated her in *Breakfast at Tiffany's.* Quite possibly, their change of heart was financially prompted, due to Marilyn's arranging for them to receive $25,000 and $12,500 respectively for directing and coaching her.

Lee remembered Jeanne Eagels' performance and believed Marilyn would more brilliantly interpret Sadie's disappointment upon realizing the preacher was an imperfect man who wanted what every other man wanted from her. "I felt Marilyn could do that wonderfully and in certain ways, even more so [than Eagels]...I thought she could do that quite superbly. And that's what I saw in the part—a kind of colorfulness, a strange romantic quality, mainly this gauzelike quality, this tremulousness, together with the other things which she had that didn't need to be worked for."

NBC television network secured Fredric March (1897-1975), the original owner of the white baby grand piano in Marilyn's living room—purchased by Gladys in 1933—as the missionary Reverend Davidson. March had starred in the original version of *A Star is Born* (1937) and the film version of Miller's *Death of a Salesman* (1951), and won an Oscar for *Dr. Jekyll and Mr. Hyde* (1932). March's wife, Florence Eldridge (1901-1988), accepted the role of the missionary's wife. Robert Loggia, a student at the Actors Studio appearing on Broadway in *Toys in the Attic*, screen-tested as Sadie's love interest, Sergeant O'Hara.

Rod Serling, hired by NBC to write the teleplay, won his second of six Emmy Awards for an episode of CBS' *Playhouse 90* titled "Requiem for a Heavyweight." As the writer, host, and narrator of *The Twilight Zone* science fiction anthology season for five seasons, Serling successfully addressed controversial subjects on national television by shrouding them in fantasy. "I went back to the Maugham story, never looked at the play," he reported. "But, my Sadie Thompson is not exactly Maugham's—she's a beautiful lost woman; she's Monroe."

NBC granted Marilyn final control over the producer, executive producer, script, set designer, wardrobe designer, and costume designer. Exercising newfound power denied in the film industry, Marilyn selected Sydney Guilaroff to create her hairstyles, Whitey Snyder for makeup, Agnes Flanagan for execution of Guilaroff's designs, and Evelyn Moriarty as stand-in. Each would receive $350 per week plus expenses.

With a script deadline of February 18, NBC tentatively scheduled the filming production between March 27 and April 2. Anticipating a superb performance from Marilyn, Ward Morehouse composed a love letter to her in his column: "My hope is Marilyn Monroe will have the triumph of her life as the put-upon but indestructible Sadie. And that soon after she conquers television, she will go on to conquer Broadway." When Morehouse and his wife, journalist Rebecca Franklin, visited the set of *The Misfits*, Marilyn accidently spilled buttermilk on him and wiped it off his shoe.

While negotiations waged for *Rain*, Marilyn privately sustained her relationship with DiMaggio. He regularly and quietly accessed the service elevator of her building, entering her apartment through the kitchen door, and left the same way at dawn. On January 7, DiMaggio escorted Marilyn to the Eugene O'Neill Theatre for the final performance of Brendan Behan's *The Hostage*—chaperoned by Susan Strasberg and George Solotaire—and dined at Le Pavillon, Henri Soule's French restaurant on East Fifty-Seventh Street. Despite DiMaggio's discretion, the media caught wind of his visits. Three days later, John Springer issued a statement to the press confirming the friendship while downplaying a romance.

On a few occasions, Patricia Newcomb accompanied a gloomy Marilyn on the Staten Island ferry to view the Manhattan skyline. They ate hot dogs and gazed into the water. Newcomb stepped closer when Marilyn appeared a bit too focused on the murky depths of the river. In an attempt to lift Marilyn's spirits, director and actor José Ferrer called her a few times. He sounded despondent about the slump in his acting career, and the two commiserated about

Hollywood. Despite the original reason behind Ferrer's call, Marilyn ended up cheering him.

The Millers mutually agreed to an expedient dissolution of their marriage. New York courts recognized quick Mexican divorces, and Mexican courts had no residency requirement so like many affluent New Yorkers, Marilyn and Arthur planned to secure freedom from each other south of the border. Marilyn retained Aaron R. Frosch to represent her.

Patricia Newcomb chose January 20 as the day to depart from New York for the divorce proceedings in Mexico. It was no coincidence that she selected the day when the thirty-fifth president's inauguration would be taking place in Washington DC. This significant political and historic event would eclipse the Monroe-Miller divorce and attract the undivided attention of the media, allowing Marilyn to end her marriage in privacy.

With Newcomb and Frosch beside her as traveling companions, Marilyn arrived at Idlewild Airport in a black suit and a flowerpot hat. The plane was temporarily grounded due to a raging blizzard, so the trio watched the President deliver the inaugural address on a black and white television in the airport. "Let the word go forth from this time and place," Kennedy proclaimed in his Bostonian accent as weary travelers crowded in front of the screens scattered in airport lounges, "to friend and foe alike, that the torch has been passed to a new generation of Americans, born in this century, tempered by war, disciplined by a hard and bitter peace, proud of our ancient heritage, and unwilling to witness or permit the slow undoing of those human rights to which this nation has always been committed, and to which we are committed today at home and around the world."

Listening to the news broadcast on his car radio while driving to an emergency massage appointment, Ralph Roberts heard a report of the crash of a plane en route to Mexico City, and no further details. Horrified, he pulled over to the curb and considered canceling the appointment. After giving what he considered the worse massage of his career, Roberts called May Reis. "I've been expecting you to call," she said, "but Marilyn missed the plane and had taken another." Tardiness had saved her life.

The blizzard subsided, and the plane was cleared for take-off in

New York as the inaugural parade proceeded in the bitter cold of Washington, DC. It landed in El Paso, Texas, at seven in the evening, where a car carried Marilyn, Patricia, and Frosch across the border into Juarez, Mexico. In an arranged night court session, Judge Miguel Gomez listened to attorney Arturo Soa Aguilar cite "incompatibility of character" as the basis for divorce.

Arthur Miller signed a waiver, choosing not to appear at the court proceeding. Instead, he accepted an invitation from the forty-two-year-old President to attend the inauguration, accompanied by his attorney, Joseph Rauh, and his wife, Olie. During the inauguration, Olie told Miller how sorry she felt about the divorce. Miller replied that he, too, felt sorry, as did Marilyn. However, if Miller hadn't have left, he feared his own demise. Olie joked about Miller making an advance toward the new, thirty-year-old First Lady; the only woman the pair supposed could top Marilyn.

After spending the night in Mexico, Marilyn returned to New York the following day, where Lee Strasberg welcomed her back. "I am upset and I don't feel like being bothered by publicity right now," she told reporters at the airport, "but I would love to have a plate of tacos and enchiladas—we didn't have time for food in Mexico!" Marilyn called Roberts to announce her return and to invite him to her apartment where DiMaggio, Patricia, and Aaron Frosch were celebrating the divorce, although the decree would be granted three days later. She also contacted Norman and Hedda Rosten with concern about their friendship surviving the divorce and received reassurance.

According to Roberts, Marilyn had been besieged with invitations, flowers, and telegrams from "every kind of celebrity, non-celebrity, would-be celebrity" from around the globe since the announcement of the divorce. Roberts claimed only two pursuers particularly fascinated her: Frank Sinatra and President Kennedy. Marilyn appreciated the calls and messages from Sinatra, known to come to the aid of his friends experiencing a crisis. She continued to play his records in her dressing room to create the mood for her acting. Marilyn also confided to Roberts that Sinatra had been interested in an affair with her years ago, but she had declined. Now, Marilyn was willing to consider him as a lover.

Senator Kennedy's overtures offended Marilyn, but she found

herself somewhat attracted to him. According to Roberts, Marilyn commented on the President having "everything"—a wife and children—but he didn't appeal to her romantically. However, Marilyn was "intrigued" with television footage of the President riding in an open limousine in Palm Beach, playing with his young son, and waving to a crowd after leaving a church.

On January 31, Ham the Astrochimp became the first chimpanzee launched into outer space in a Project Mercury capsule from Cape Canaveral in Florida. Scientists trained him to perform simple, timed tasks in response to electric lights and sounds, proving that humans could accomplish similar tasks in space. Ham safely returned to earth following a sixteen-minute mission, and his flight contributed to Alan Shepard's becoming the first American to travel into space on May 5.

Also on January 31, author W. Somerset Maugham typed Marilyn a letter thanking her for a "*charming telegram of good wishes on my birthday.*" He expressed joy in hearing she would play Sadie Thompson on television and ended with an endorsement: "*I am sure you will be splendid.*"

That evening, Marilyn attended the world premiere of *The Misfits* escorted by Montgomery Clift at the Capitol Theatre on Broadway. Marilyn looked elegant and demure in a black fitted cocktail dress with fur-trimmed wrap and hem and black gloves. Hairdresser Kenneth Batelle had styled her hair, longer than usual, in a bouffant. Soon after the premiere, Marilyn called Miller to arrange for her collection of some things from the farm in Roxbury. She felt disappointed to find her former husband gone from the home when she arrived; he had moved into Chelsea Hotel in New York. "It was sad," Marilyn told Norman Rosten. "Even a little smile would do." She had expected Miller to invite her in for coffee since they had spent several happy years in the house. Marilyn learned the reason for Miller's avoidance when she discovered another woman's perfume on her fur coat stored in one of the closets. She quickly disposed of the coat. Norman Rosten had never seen Marilyn so depressed.

Hairdresser George Masters traveled from Los Angeles to New York to style Marilyn's hair for another event. When he arrived at the apartment, she greeted him at the door in a worn terry cloth bathrobe and apologized as she handed him a consolatory check for two thousand dollars. Marilyn kept her depression a secret, muttered something about feeling too tired to attend the event, and sent him home.

Marilyn met with Dr. Kris forty-seven times in two months. During a session shortly after she had read a gossip column's scurrilous quote attributed to Kay Gable and holding her responsible for Clark Gable's death, Marilyn confessed a recent suicide gesture. She also repeated it to Ralph Roberts as quoted by Fred Lawrence Guiles, the only documented account of the episode in Marilyn's own words:

> *I opened the living room window as wide as I could and I leaned out. I knew that I had to make up my mind inside the room. If I climbed out onto the ledge, someone below would be certain to recognize me and there'd be a big spectacle. I squeezed my eyes shut at the open window, clenched my fists. I remembered reading somewhere that people who fall from heights lose consciousness before they hit the ground. Then when I looked down, I saw a woman walking along the sidewalk near the building. She was wearing a brown dress and I knew her.*

Coincidently, Gene Tierney, another Fox beauty who once faced a similar brush with death, lived directly across the street from Marilyn's apartment. Tierney had starred in *Laura* (1944) and, like Marilyn, battled mental illness. Three years earlier, Tierney contemplated suicide on the ledge of her apartment window and was spotted by a neighbor. Consequently, she received treatment at a facility in Kansas. Before this suicide gesture, Tierney underwent nearly thirty electric shock treatments in hospitals in New York and Connecticut, causing significant memory loss. In her 1979 autobiography, Tierney claimed a brief affair with John Kennedy before his marriage to Jacqueline Bouvier. Marilyn, too, would soon face psychiatric treatment.

Greatly alarmed for her patient's safety, Kris convinced Marilyn to voluntarily admit herself to Cornell University-New York Hospital's psychiatric unit, Payne Whitney Clinic. The next day, February 5, Kris drove Marilyn to the facility on East Sixty-Eighth Street where she signed the admission forms as Mrs. Faye Miller. The hospital later confirmed to the media that she was admitted "for the study and treatment of an illness of undisclosed origin."

Outside, John Springer faced the reporters with a statement: "Marilyn was admitted for a period of rest and recuperation following a very arduous year in which she completed two films and had to face marital problems...it is expected her stay will not be prolonged." Incited by spreading rumors of a mental breakdown or a suicide attempt, reporters pressed at what happened in Marilyn's apartment to necessitate a hospitalization.

Inside, staff escorted Marilyn into a locked unit for moderately disturbed patients. Wearing a fur coat, casual blouse, and brightly colored plaid slacks, she passed through several locked doors and surrendered her personal possessions and clothing. The admissions staff searched her for materials or objects that could be used to inflict self-injury. Dr. Kris had not prepared Marilyn for this level of security. "What are you doing to me?" Marilyn gasped. "*What kind of a place is this?*"

Marilyn would later describe the secured environment, where light switches, dresser drawers, and bathroom and closet doors were locked. Steel bars covered the windows. The doors to the private rooms contained unobstructed windows so that the staff could visibly monitor patients at all times. She observed on the walls evidence of past violence and scrawled messages from former patients. Marilyn also heard the disturbing sound of screaming female patients echoing through the halls. They "screamed out when life was unbearable," she surmised.

Placed in seclusion in a cement block room on the sixth floor deemed for "very disturbed depressed patients," Marilyn clung to the locked door. According to an admissions nurse, for over an hour, Marilyn calmly but endlessly pleaded: "Please open that door. Just open that door. I won't make any trouble, just let me out. Please. Open that door."

A psychiatrist gave Marilyn a physical examination including a manual examination of her breasts for lumps. She objected to this and stated that a physician, Dr. Lipkin, from another department in the same facility, had completed an examination within the last thirty days. After the psychiatrist left her room, a nurse entered and explained to Marilyn that she had been admitted to the hospital's psychiatric unit. When members of the staff asked Marilyn why she seemed unhappy with the arrangements, she responded, "I'd have to be nuts if I like it here."

"There was no empathy at Payne-Whitney," Marilyn would later write, "it had a very bad effect...I was in some kind of prison for a crime I hadn't committed. The inhumanity there I found archaic... They pride themselves in having a home-like atmosphere." Apparently, a doctor boasted that the psychiatric unit had wall-to-wall carpeting and modern furnishings. Marilyn shot back:

> *Well, that any good interior decorator could provide...but since they are dealing with human beings why couldn't they perceive even an interior of a human being...Men are climbing to the moon but they don't seem interested in the beating human heart.*

When the staff later recommended to Marilyn that she mingle with other patients in occupational therapy, she asked what they expected her to do. "Well, Miss Monroe," a nurse replied, "You may sew or play checkers. You can even play cards or knit." Marilyn reacted with indignance:

> *I tried to explain the day I did that they would have a nut on their hands. These things were furthest from my mind.*

Marilyn interacted with a fellow female patient—"a pathetic and vague creature"—who disclosed having slashed her throat and wrists multiple times. The woman sensed Marilyn's sadness and suggested she telephone a friend. Marilyn explained that the staff had told her telephones were prohibited on the floor, but the patient escorted her to one, and Marilyn stood in line for her turn. When she reached for the receiver, though, a guard "strong-armed" the telephone and explained that she was prohibited from making calls.

Angry about the staff's dishonesty, Marilyn returned to her room and considered her next step. She approached the situation by imagining it as a scenario in an acting improvisation. "I figured, it's a squeaky wheel that gets the grease," Marilyn would recount. "I admit it was a loud squeak but I got the idea from a movie I made once called *Don't Bother to Knock*."

Marilyn picked up a chair and slammed it against the window on the door of her room. At first the glass did not shatter, so she continuously slammed the chair until the glass broke. Marilyn concealed a small shard of glass in her hand and quietly sat on the bed waiting for attendants to respond to her outburst. "If you are going to treat me like a nut," she announced, "I'll act like a nut."

Marilyn would later confide to Greenson that her strategy seemed "corny" and was inspired by her role as psychotic Nell Forbes. She had demanded to be discharged and threatened to harm herself if denied. Self-mutilation was "the furthest thing from my mind," Marilyn asserted. "Dr. Greenson, I'm an actress and would never intentionally mark or mar myself, I'm just that vain." To support this claim, she described a previous suicide attempt in which she had swallowed ten capsules of Seconal and ten Tuonal.

When Marilyn refused to go quietly, two male and two female attendants lifted her by her arms and legs and carried her face down to the elevator and up to the seventh floor, where she was placed in a cell. One of the female attendants—described by Marilyn as an "ox of a woman"—instructed her to take a bath. Marilyn reported having just taken one on the sixth floor. The attendant explained that a change of floors required another bath.

The hospital administrator, whom Marilyn thought resembled a "high-school principal type," interviewed her and concluded she was "a very, very sick girl" and had been one "for many years." Marilyn felt demeaned when he asked how she could possibly work in such a debilitated condition. "Don't you think that perhaps Greta Garbo and Charlie Chaplin perhaps and perhaps Ingrid Bergman had been depressed when they worked sometimes?" she replied. "It's like saying a ball player like DiMaggio if he could hit the ball when he was depressed."

In 1966, Richard Meryman interviewed an unidentified admissions nurse who attended to Marilyn. Breaking confidentiality, the nurse described her colleagues' reactions to their famous patient: "We felt so protective toward her. She made us all feel like we wanted to hold her in our laps. We wanted to soothe her, wanted to say, 'It's all right now.' It was the feeling lonely, small children give you. You know—sort of dry their tears and pat them on the head and hold their hands."

"It was like a nightmare..." Marilyn would tell Gloria Romanoff. She was bound by restraints and sedated, but aware of what was happening. During the night, there was a steady procession of hospital personnel, doctors, and nurses gawking at her. With her arms bound, Marilyn was powerless. "I was a curiosity piece," she said. "No one had my interests at heart."

According to the *New York World Telegram*, on Monday morning, a psychiatrist assessed Marilyn as "extremely disturbed" and "potentially self-destructive." She had been transferred to a unit for the most disturbed, psychotic patients, where she spent forty-eight hours in a padded cell. Panicked, Marilyn cried, screamed, and banged her fists on the door. The staff assumed she was completely psychotic.

On February 8, the Strasbergs received a frantic letter from Marilyn written in pencil on a piece of paper obtained from a nurse:

> *Dr. Kris has put me in the hospital under the care of two idiot doctors. They both should not be my doctors. I'm locked up with these poor nutty people. I'm sure to end up a nut too if I stay in this nightmare. Please help me. This is the last place I should be. I love you both. Marilyn*
>
> *P.S. I'm on the dangerous floor. It's like a cell. They had my bathroom door locked and I couldn't get their key to get into it, so I broke the glass. But outside of that I haven't done anything that is uncooperative.*

Marilyn was finally permitted to make a telephone call to DiMaggio on February 9th. Fiercely loyal and protective, he swiftly arrived the next day. The doctors recommended against Marilyn's leaving, but DiMaggio threatened to take the hospital apart "brick by brick" if they did not release her to him. Shortly after this ordeal, Marilyn filed a legal document requiring the notification of DiMaggio, Frosh, and Reis before she could ever be involuntarily confined to a hospital.

On February 10th, Frank Taylor's wife, Nan, wrote an encouraging letter of support to Marilyn:

It seems to me again, as it did last summer, very sad that we who have been given so much by you but we cannot give you even what little we might in return. You have my admiration for your courage, my gratitude for the many delights of charm and beauty and humor your presence has meant, and my deep sorrow for your troubles. I believe in your strength, Marilyn, as I believe in the sun. If at any time I can help in any way, please let me.

Walter Winchell sent Marilyn an uplifting telegram addressing her by the nickname given by Andre de Dienes: "*Turkey foot. Stop feeling sorry for yourself. Get out of the hospital. Let's go driving and hiking through the Redwoods, incognito, and take beautiful pictures like nobody could ever take. It will cure you of all your ills. Call me up. Love, WW.*"

On February 10th, Ralph Roberts collected Marilyn at the hospital with Dr. Kris in his car, and drove Marilyn home. The ride across town seemed to last an eternity as Marilyn confronted her analyst. Roberts described Marilyn as a "hurricane unleashed," and Kris had never seen her patient so enraged. Later, Roberts drove the unsettled psychoanalyst home. As they inched in traffic along the West Side Highway, Kris trembled and repeated, "I did a terrible thing, a terrible thing. Oh, God. I didn't mean to. I'd didn't mean to, but I did."

Marilyn maintained her sanity during the hospitalization by imagining what Marlon Brando would have done in her position. She confided to Ralph Roberts that she knew her friend would have done more and worse in protest. While Marilyn channeled Brando, Brando reached out to her:

The best reappraisals are born in the worst crisis. It has happened to all of us in relative degrees. Be glad for it and don't be afraid of being afraid. It can only help. Relax and enjoy it. I send you my thoughts and my warmest affections.

Marilyn later confided to the Strasbergs that she had always feared she would go crazy like her mother, but once surrounded by truly mentally disturbed people, her perspective changed. Marilyn realized she had serious problems, indeed; however, she wasn't as disturbed as the psychotic patients on the ward.

According to the admission nurse, Marilyn had been deemed high risk for suicide and had been on an appropriate suicide precaution watch. Upon news of her death eighteen months later, some of the staff members at Payne Whitney believed if Marilyn had remained for nine months of intensive treatment, her death could likely have been prevented.

It became clear to all involved that although the admission was a disaster, Marilyn needed inpatient treatment. With guidance from Dr. Kris, DiMaggio arranged for an admission to facility Marilyn would find more humane. She agreed to enter the Neurological Institute of Columbia-Presbyterian Medical Center contingent upon DiMaggio's promise to visit her daily.

In the late afternoon of February 11th, Marilyn was admitted to the institute on West One Hundred Sixty-Eighth Street and placed in room 719, where she received treatment until March 5. "She had a hell of a year," John Springer told reporters. "She had been exhausted, really beat down." The hospital issued a statement denying rumors of a diagnosis of Schizophrenia and said she was admitted for "just rest and a checkup."

From her private room—during a twenty-four hour period between March 1st and 2nd—Marilyn reached out to Dr. Greenson in Los Angeles. She recorded a detailed account of her harrowing experience at Payne Whitney Clinic in a letter now archived in the Ralph R. Greenson Papers collection at UCLA's Department of Special Collections and closed from access until 2039. First published by Donald Spoto and later in *Fragments*, the letter conveyed Marilyn's insight and intelligence during one of the lowest points of her life:

> *Just now, when I looked out the hospital window where the snow had covered everything, suddenly everything is kind of a muted green. The grass, shabby evergreen bushes—though the trees give me a little hope—the desolate bare branches promising maybe there will be spring and maybe they promise hope...as I started to write this letter about four quiet tears had fallen...last night I*

was awake all night again. Sometimes I wonder what the night time is for. It almost doesn't exist for me—it all seems like one long, long horrible day.

Marilyn discussed having recently read the published letters of Sigmund Freud, and relating to a portrait of the pioneering psychoanalyst in the book, she wrote she saw, "*I see a sad disappointment in his gentle face.*"

In a postscript, Marilyn updated Greenson on her most recent romantic relationships. The first unnamed lover is likely Frank Sinatra or DiMaggio. Marilyn writes about the doctor disapprovingly frowning with his mustache and looking up at the ceiling whenever she mentioned the lover's name in session. She begs for the doctor to trust her instincts, as he has been "secretly" a "tender" friend:

It was sort of a fling on the wing. I had never done that before but now I have—but he is very unselfish in bed...From Yves, I have heard nothing—but I don't mind since I have such a strong, tender, wonderful memory...I am almost weeping...

The letter suggests that Marilyn spent a considerable time processing and recovering from her experience in the first hospital, a trauma that might have overshadowed the reason for her admission in the first place. If Marilyn had been depressed and suicidal, the manner in which the professionals had treated her elicited an anger that propelled her out of depression and gave her a reason to fight for her life.

Nonetheless, Norman and Hedda Rosten visited Marilyn and sensed their friend's deep sadness. Marilyn wearily raised her arm to greet them, but Norman observed the illness spreading "from her body to her mind to her soul." She told the Rostens about a recent assessment by a psychiatrist. "Why are you so unhappy?" the doctor had inquired. Outraged by what she perceived as minimalizing her issues, Marilyn retorted, "I've been paying the best doctors a fortune to find out why, and you're asking *me*?"

Twenty-three days after her second admission, Marilyn was finally discharged. Accompanied by six guards, Patricia Newcomb, May Reis, and John Springer, she emerged from the hospital smiling warmly and walked past four hundred members of the press, fans, and gawkers. Newsreel footage documented sheer pandemonium resembling a riot as Marilyn exited the hospital doors with Newcomb beside her. A reporter offered her a newspaper with a headline announcing Elizabeth Taylor's near death experience. Even in Marilyn's fragile state, Lloyd's of London, a leading conglomerate of insurance companies, was willing to insure her as the prime replacement for the higher-risk Taylor in *Cleopatra*.

Amid all the chaos, Marilyn appeared joyful and at ease. (Perhaps she was acting.) She had clearly lost weight and wore a longer, casual hairstyle, white silk blouse, tight white skirt, and matching pumps. "I feel wonderful," she said, "I had a nice rest."

The entourage of Newcomb and Springer created a human shield around Marilyn as they held on to her, pushed through the crowd, brushed against the exterior wall of the hospital, and led her to an awaiting vehicle. The hungry crowd—eager to photograph Marilyn or capture a comment with a microphone—pushed, shoved, and shouted. In the calamity, some reporters were pinned against Marilyn's vehicle. One reporter fell backward onto the cab of the car, and a photographer rested his news camera against the reporter's chest to get a shot. The audio shares Marilyn calmly responding to the questions of one reporter following beside her. In white, she resembles an icon of a saint being carried by a mob during a boisterous religious festival. Holding her white gloves in hand, Marilyn gave a radiant celebrity smile and waved to the fans lined up across the street before escaping into the Lincoln Continental.

Believing the media only trivialized her tribulations, Marilyn told Susan Strasberg that she couldn't even have a nervous breakdown in private. In imparting to her young friend that war might someday become theater, Marilyn closely predicted entertainment's evolution into the twenty-first century's reality television. The press even staked out Marilyn's apartment, where she greeted them again before retiring to her home.

Across town, Isidore Miller was admitted to another hospital in preparation for a second attempt at prostate surgery when his wife, Augusta, suddenly died of a heart attack at age sixty-eight on March 7th. Having survived breast cancer and diabetes, Augusta's health had begun to decline earlier in the year, but she rebounded to care for Isidore after his heart momentarily stopped beating during a previous operation. "Well I put [him] in the hospital today," she told a neighbor. "He's going to be all right, the doctor says, and now I can die." She died peacefully in her sleep later that night.

Isidore's surgery was postponed for the second time, and in the Jewish tradition, his wife was buried the following day. Barely out of the hospital herself, Marilyn attended the funeral service at Riverside Memorial Chapel in Brooklyn accompanied by May Reis. Marilyn's former father-in-law was surprised to see her. She sat beside him and held his hand throughout the service. Arthur's nephew, Ross, thought Marilyn demonstrated tremendous courage in attending the funeral. When Isidore eventually underwent surgery, Marilyn called him relentlessly during the hospitalization, spoke with his physicians, and sent flowers.

Marilyn's relationship with Dr. Kris suffered following the hospitalization. She felt betrayed by the psychoanalyst's decision to recommend a voluntary admission, but whether or not Marilyn came to understand the necessity and resume treatment is unclear. For Kris to have taken action in increasing Marilyn's level of care, she must have determined her patient as in imminent risk for self-harm or suicide.

Robert Stewart, senior editor at Charles Scribner's Sons publishers, knew Kris and spoke with author Lucy Freeman about the obvious quality of Marilyn's therapeutic relationship with her analyst: "Marilyn must have found a genuine mother in Marianne Kris, who was perhaps the first person in her troubled life to be somewhat of a mother to her...My guess is that Marianne felt genuine love for Marilyn but kept the boundaries as an analyst should... Leaving part of her estate to Marianne was a sign of indebtedness. Somehow Dr. Kris had the capacity to move Marilyn and show affection for her in a realistic, believable way." Marilyn's provision for Kris in her will— although executed before this perceived betrayal—was never reversed, suggesting her continued value of the therapeutic relationship as well as confidence in Kris' judgment to direct the funds "for the furtherance of the work of such psychiatric institutions or groups as [Dr. Kris] shall elect."

In mid-March Margaret Parton of *Ladies' Home Journal* arrived at Marilyn's apartment for an interview, armed with a bag filled with yarn and knitting needles in the event Marilyn remained true to her reputation for tardiness. Patricia Newcomb briefed the journalist for an hour, emphasizing exclusion of any questions pertaining to the past. Following the hospitalization, Marilyn's protective entourage focused her on the future, not the past.

When Marilyn finally spoke to Parton, she announced, "I'm beginning to look at things...I want to find out what it's all about. Life. Love. The world. People. Everything." Marilyn wore a beige skirt and sleeveless beige blouse with high neckline, adorned by a necklace of amber and topaz stones. While serving sherry and caviar canapés, she spoke of shopping plans in preparation of hosting intimate candlelight dinner parties. She envisioned a crystal chandelier with real candles suspended over her mirrored dining table and two large comfortable club chairs "for a man to sit in!" A woman cannot be alone, she told the journalist, because a man and a woman "support and strengthen" each other. A woman "just can't do it by herself," Marilyn said, and added that she was seeking love, strength, and reassurance in her next relationship. With a giggle, Marilyn quoted author John Steinbeck once telling her that the most wonderful thing about a wife is the fact that "she's *there*!"

Marilyn referenced her anticipation of portraying Sadie Thompson and drew a parallel to a quality shared with the character: "She was a girl who knew how to be gay, even when she was sad. And that's important—you know?" Parton immediately empathized with Marilyn's vulnerability.

Later, Parton described leaving the apartment "with a sense of having met a sick little canary instead of a peacock. Only when you pick it up in your hand to comfort it...beneath the sickness, the weakness and the innocence, you find a strong bone structure, and a heart beating. You *recognize* sickness, and you *find* strength."

The magazine's editors, Bruce and Beatrice Gould, considered Parson's piece too sympathetic. "If you were a man," Bruce Gould told her, "I'd wonder what went on that afternoon in Marilyn's apartment."

While the Goulds misperceived Marilyn as pining for a new man in her life, nothing could be farther from the truth. During a major snowstorm in March, she spent a weekend with DiMaggio in his suite at the Lexington Hotel. Marilyn called Ralph Roberts to collect a "care package" prepared by her cook, Hattie, and bring it to them. "I know that station wagon of yours is like that sign on the front of the post office," Marilyn said, "'neither rain nor snow...'"

Instead of driving the station wagon, Roberts walked from his apartment on Fifty-First Street to Marilyn's on Fifty-Seventh Street and then to the hotel. On the way, he stopped at a grocery store for additional food and bumped into actress and vocalist Lena Horne and her husband, composer Lennie Hayton, both covered with snowflakes. Lena asked Roberts about Marilyn's well-being. Upon hearing he was en route to bring a box of provisions to Marilyn, Horne picked up a package of Hersey's chocolate Candy Kisses and asked him to deliver them to Marilyn as a token of her affection. When Roberts arrived at the Lexington Hotel, he found Marilyn standing at the lobby entrance. She told him DiMaggio was watching a game upstairs and had chastised her for imposing upon Roberts in such inclement weather.

On March 13, John Springer escorted Marilyn to an Actors Studio benefit at the Roseland Ballroom on West Fifty-Second Street. She wore a black spangled sheath gown—donned for the November 1959 cover of *Life*—accessorized with black gloves and a fur wrap. Photographs provide evidence that Marilyn announced into a microphone the winning tickets for door prizes, selected by director Joshua Logan from a rotating raffle drum. She also danced with debonair actor Franchot Tone (1905-1968), who left the Group Theatre in New York for Hollywood, where he forged a screen career at MGM and was briefly married to Joan Crawford.

In late March, Marilyn and DiMaggio escaped the cold of New York and traveled to North Redington Beach, Florida, to rest and watch the Yankees' spring training at Al Lang Field in nearby Saint Petersburg. They registered in separate guest rooms across from each other in the main building of the exclusive Tides Resort and Bath Club on the Gulf of Mexico.

During the day, the couple lounged under one of the many blue canvas cabanas lining the property's shore, attracting curious residents from the neighboring beach communities. Word spread, and large crowds flocked the public beach for a glimpse of the actress and retired baseball player. Eventually, the resort's management relocated the famous couple to the rooftop for more private sunbathing. "MM—pale of figure and serene in the face of a crowd of gaping onlookers," announced the *St. Petersburg Times*, "played a singles radiance match with the Florida sun yesterday afternoon. There is no doubt who outshone whom."

Marilyn and DiMaggio appeared reconciled to most onlookers. Photographers captured them snuggling beside each other in the press box at a baseball-training field, collecting seashells on the beach, and strolling along the shore while holding hands. In the evenings, the couple dined intimately at the White House Restaurant, now the Wine Cellar, on Gulf Boulevard. Jason Dow, age thirteen, was the only male to lure Marilyn away from DiMaggio during the vacation. She helped the boy build a sand castle while asking him questions about his family until DiMaggio urged her to prepare for a dinner engagement with the city's mayor.

In the local press, the staff of the Tides disclosed mundane details of Marilyn's vacation. B.C. Clark, a longtime server at the resort, described her alcohol consumption: "The only time I remember her taking anything to drink was one night she sent down for two champagne cocktails to be sent to her room." Server Harold Esque divulged her typical breakfast of buttermilk and a soft-boiled egg.

When the romantic holiday ended on April 2, Marilyn and DiMaggio took a red-eye flight back to New York, where DiMaggio frequently spent the night at her apartment, keeping a pair of his pajamas in her bedroom dresser drawer. The couple attended the opening game of baseball season, between the Yankees and the Minnesota Twins at the New York Yankee Stadium on April 11. As the guests of co-owner Dan Topping and his wife, Marilyn and DiMaggio sat in the press box and attracted media attention.

Also on April 11, Kay Gable poured her heart out to Marilyn in a letter:

> *Do let me know when you plan to return to California. I'll let you be the second nanny in charge. Later you may take him fishing. Guess I will be the one to teach him to shoot ducks. My work is really cut out for me. I feel certain his dearest father is watching his every move from heaven.*

The warm and friendly tone of Kay's letter dispels the gossip about her holding Marilyn accountable for Gable's heart attack and subsequent death. Moreover, Kay invited Marilyn and DiMaggio to visit her at the ranch. "*It would be so pleasant...*" she concluded. "*Give my best to May [Reis]. I hope this letter finds your heart full of happiness. Love, Kay.*" The letter also affirms common knowledge of Marilyn's rekindled relationship with DiMaggio that was being splashed across magazine covers. The day after Kay wrote her letter, James Bacon mentioned in his column having seen the pair dining together at Four Seasons near the elegant restaurant's white marble pool with bubbling fountain.

At the thirty-third Academy Awards Ceremony, held at the Santa Monica Civic Auditorium on April 17, Master of Ceremonies Bob Hope dedicated the song of the year nominee "The Second Time Around" (from *High Time*) to Marilyn and DiMaggio. Elizabeth Taylor, recovering from a near-fatal bout of pneumonia that had brought on a coma, had won back public favor and earned the award for Best Actress for *Butterfield 8*. Taylor considered the honor a consolation prize for a role she disliked. Shirley MacLaine, nominated for *The Apartment*, allegedly said, "I lost to a tracheotomy." The Academy nominated both Taylor and MacLaine for their portrayals of unmarried, sexually active and kept women, invalidating the Strasbergs' ongoing apprehension of Marilyn's accepting such roles. "I was the slut of all times!" Taylor screams to her mother in one harrowing scene from *Butterfield 8*.

On April 23 at 8:30 in the evening, Judy Garland performed a milestone concert at Carnegie Hall on Seventh Avenue. Marilyn's posthumously auctioned appointment book reveals her attendance among a rapt audience of nearly three thousand. Critic Rex Reed claimed he had never seen an audience of celebrated people in such a state of mass adulation. As Garland sang several encores, including "Over the Rainbow" (a song Marilyn chose for her funeral when drawing up her will earlier in the year), the crowd called out song titles. "I know, I know," Garland cried. "I'll sing 'em all, and we'll stay all night!" A recording of the performance, *Judy at Carnegie Hall*, appeared on the music charts for a total of ninety-five weeks, including thirteen weeks at number one. It won four Grammy Awards including Album of the Year and Best Female Vocal of the Year.

Garland's resiliency may have been an inspiration to Marilyn. Garland suffered her own addictions to stimulant and sedative drugs, brought upon by medication MGM Studio doctors had prescribed. The intention was to keep her energetic by day to perform in a string of musicals, to help her sleep soundly at night, and to ensure that she was able to repeat the high level of animation the next day. Garland was only a teenager when the doctors started issuing prescriptions, and in 1947 she was admitted to a private sanitarium. A few months later, she made a suicide gesture by superficially lacerating her wrists with a broken glass, and was subsequently hospitalized for two weeks in at the Austen Riggs Center, a psychiatric hospital in Massachusetts.

Mental illness, an addiction to prescribed barbiturates, and illicit use of morphine prevented Garland from completing several films. MGM subsequently suspended her and replaced her with other actresses. Garland made another suicide gesture by superficially lacerating her throat. "All I could see ahead was more confusion," Garland later said of this desperate act. "I wanted to black out the future as well as the past. I wanted to hurt myself and everyone who had hurt me." Garland reinvented herself and gave exceptional performances in the musical remake of *A Star is Born* (1954) and in *Judgment at Nuremberg* (1961), and was nominated for an Oscar for both. Her final film, *I Could Go On Singing* (1963), about a self-destructive international vocalist, paralleled her own life in the way *The Misfits* mirrored Marilyn's.

Three days after Garland's concert, negotiations ended for Fox's next Monroe film, *Goodbye, Charlie*. George Cukor remained unavailable, and Marilyn's contract stipulated she would work with only one of her sixteen approved directors. Fox rebuffed Strasberg's salary demands, and the death of production chief Buddy Adler in the summer of 1960 led to additional delays. "The studio people want me to do *Goodbye, Charlie...*" Marilyn told the press. "But I'm not going to do it. I don't like the idea of playing a man in a woman's body—you know? It just doesn't seem feminine." In the end, Fox had failed to successfully secure Marilyn by the deadline. Spyros Skouras released her and postponed the start day for her remaining obligation to begin a film to November 15, allowing her ample time to complete *Rain* for NBC.

In preparation for a return to film work, Marilyn left New York for Los Angeles in May and registered at the Beverly Hills Hotel.

She later accepted an invitation as a guest in Frank Sinatra's apartment. Meanwhile, back in New York, Paula Strasberg began experiencing psychological distress in the form of recurring nightmares about the death of an unidentified person in her life. She was now taking on Marilyn's qualities and illnesses in a possible transference relationship or *folie a deux*, likely in response to anxieties related to Lee's alleged sexual affairs.

Marilyn resumed treatment with Dr. Greenson, who worried about her association with his former patient, Frank Sinatra. Marilyn noticed the psychoanalyst's facial expression whenever she spoke of Sinatra in session; he would twist his mouth into a disapproving frown and lift his eyes to the ceiling. His insights into Sinatra's dark side and unhealthy relationship patterns with women, combined with a commitment to protect Marilyn's best interests, caused him to redirect her from this relationship.

In a letter to Dr. Kris dated May 1961, Greenson expressed his disapproval of Sinatra:

> *Above all, I try to help her not to be lonely, and people, who will engaged in some sort of sado-masochistic relationship with her...This is the kind of planning you do with an adolescent girl who needs guidance, friendliness, and firmness, and she seems to take it very well...She said, for the first time, she looked forward to coming to Los Angeles, because she could speak to me. Of course, this does not prevent her from canceling several hours to go to Palm Springs with Mr. F.S. She is unfaithful to me as one is to a parent...*

In her hometown, Marilyn also reconnected with old friends such as Clifton Webb, Lotte Goslar, Xenia Chekov, Dean Martin and his wife Jeanne, and a new friend, twenty-two-year-old singer Connie Francis. Marilyn enjoyed Francis' recent recordings: "Everybody's Somebody's Fool" and "Where the Boys Are." Webb, a gay man who had lived with his mother until her death at age ninety-one in 1960, was in the process of grieving, prompting playwright Noël Coward to flippantly comment, "It must be terrible to be orphaned at 71."

Carl Sandburg, who had an office at Fox to write some dialogue for *The Greatest Story Ever Told*, continued to call and correspond with Marilyn. She attended parties hosted by Sandburg and his lady friend Mildred Norton, a classical music critic for *Los Angeles Daily News*, at Norton's Los Angeles home. Here, the poet serenaded Marilyn with folk music strummed on a guitar purchased at a local pawnshop. G.W. Campbell called on Sunday nights and typically chatted with her for an hour about philosophy. He would later tell Eunice Murray, Marilyn's future housekeeper, that these conversations forced him to frequently consult an encyclopedia.

Marilyn went to the Crescendo Club, a two-hundred-seat intimate jazz venue on Sunset, to see Ella Fitzgerald and Ray Charles perform American standard songs sometime between May 11 and May 21. One of the performances was released as *Ella in Hollywood*, under direction of Norman Granz, including the songs of Harold Arlen, Irving Berlin, Rodgers and Hart, Cole Porter, Duke Ellington, Johnny Mercer, and Ira Gershwin.

Walter Winchell's column of May 8 referenced the long delay of *Rain*: "We hear Marilyn Monroe's version of 'Rain' on TV will be different. Reverend Davidson gets tired of waiting for Marilyn to show up at rehearsal and goes back to his wife." Fox eliminated another barrier by communicating to Marilyn Monroe Productions willingness to begin *Goodbye, Charlie* after October 30 so that she might complete the teleplay. Hedda Hopper's column concurred with Marilyn's earlier dislike of Fox's project, citing Marilyn as the least suitable actress to play a man reincarnated as a woman. Ultimately, Vincente Minnelli would direct Debbie Reynolds and Tony Curtis in the 1964 film.

On May 24, Dr. Leon Krohn admitted Marilyn to Cedars of Lebanon Hospital for a fifth gynecological operation to remove tissue in her pelvic and abdominal organs damaged by endometriosis. Other reports claim on May 26 Marilyn underwent surgery for the removal of part of the pancreas. Across the hall in the VIP section of the hospital, Marion Davies lay dying of stomach cancer. The aging actress, once Hollywood reigning blonde comedienne, told columnist Hedda Hopper, "We blondes seem to be falling apart."

Davies would sadly succumb to cancer by the fall, but Marilyn celebrated her thirty-fifth birthday on June 1 by dining with some friends. She also sent a telegram to Dr. Greenson: "*Dear Dr. Greenson:*

In this world of people I'm glad there's you. I have a feeling of hope though today I am three five. Marilyn."

"I'm very happy to have reached this age," she told Jonah Rudd of *The London Daily Mail.* "I feel I'm growing up. It was wonderful being a girl, but it's more wonderful being a woman."

Remembering Marilyn's birthday and having read that she was ensconced at the Beverly Hills Hotel, photographer Andre de Dienes called and hummed the "Happy Birthday" song. Marilyn joyfully invited him to her hotel suite to celebrate. Fox had hosted a cocktail party in her honor, but she departed early. Reunited in Marilyn's hotel suite, de Dienes found her preoccupied with betrayals. "When I just can't take it anymore, they think I'm being temperamental," she said, "they can't understand what's it's like to be so tired that it's impossible to get out of bed in the morning." Marilyn sadly added that she had been exploited, tossed away, and now had "nothing."

Noticing the covers had been thrown back on Marilyn's bed, de Dienes impulsively thrust himself upon her. Bursting into tears, Marilyn protested: "Oh, please, don't! You of all people." De Dienes later regretted his brutish behavior so shortly after Marilyn had undergone a major operation. "I was ashamed of myself," he would write. He bade her farewell and wished her well. What makes de Dienes' claim believable is his admission that their last contact didn't turn into a sexual encounter. He appears honest in taking responsibility for a thwarted sexual advance.

Walking to his car, de Dienes watched the light go out from Marilyn's window immediately after he left. The next day, he sent her a basket of fruit. Marilyn responded by sending him a bouquet of flowers with several of her latest portraits. Obviously, Marilyn wasn't receptive to sexual intimacy as a way to cope with sadness, betrayal, and loneliness but forgave her friend; perhaps she was making progress with Dr. Greenson.

Former suitor Frank Sinatra escorted Marilyn on dates to Don the Beachcomber's Tiki Lounge and the Dunes Club in Palm Springs even though she continued seeing his former friend, DiMaggio, when home in New York. Sinatra was leader of The Rat Pack, a male ensemble epitomizing the hip, cool image of the early 1960s male and executing it with both swagger and panache. The men told racy jokes, boozed, smoked, and womanized—even when all were married. The group also included Dean Martin, singer and actor; Sammy Davis, Jr., singer and dancer; Peter Lawford, actor and President Kennedy's brother-in-law; and Joey Bishop, comedian. Shirley MacLaine became an honorary mascot after she appeared in *Some Came Running* with Sinatra and Martin. At times, actress Angie Dickenson and dancer Juliet Prowse served as female mascots.

Actor Humphrey Bogart originally formed the group, and Lauren Bacall, his wife, bestowed its moniker. "You look like a goddamned rat pack!" she allegedly told her husband when he and his pals came home to her Holmby Hills estate in a state of disarray and intoxication after a night of carousing on the town. After Bogart's death in 1957, Sinatra ascended to ringleader.

For two months in 1960, the hard drinking, hard-living Rat Pack filmed *Oceans 11,* filmed mostly on location at the iconic Sands on the Las Vegas Strip, a hotel-casino in which Sinatra and Martin had invested. The property was comprised of a series of low-rise buildings, suites and bungalows, beneath a futuristic 1950s neon sign that bore the slogan, "A Place in the Sun" (now the site of the Venetian Hotel Casino). Sinatra dually produced the film and starred as Danny Ocean, the mastermind of a casino heist executed by his World War II cronies.

By day, the Rat Pack filmed, and by night, they held court on stage in the Sands' Copa Room, packing in audiences with a powerful collective chemistry. Their lounge act was a combination of impromptu singing, suggestive humor, irreverent impressions, and ad-libbed banter. Sinatra would christen the Sands performances as "Rat Pack Summits" after the President Kennedy's summit meeting with Nikita Khrushchev in Vienna in June.

Senator John F. Kennedy was a member of the audience during his presidential campaign and invited Sinatra, Davis, Lawford, and MacLaine to sing *The National Anthem* at the Democratic National Convention in Los Angeles. Sinatra even recorded a version of "High Hopes" as Kennedy's campaign song. The bond between politics, entertainment, and celebrity was born; a trend that has continued in subsequent elections.

While Sinatra filmed *Sergeants 3* in Utah, he invited Marilyn to join him in nearby Las Vegas, where he was scheduled to perform at the Sands on June 7 in honor of Dean Martin's forty-fifth birthday;

a private celebration would follow the show. "I've never had such a good time ever—in Hollywood," Marilyn would later gush.

J. Randy Taraborrelli obtained memos from the Sands' advertising and promotional director and publicity director prohibiting Sinatra and Monroe from being photographed backstage together. Marilyn arrived at the celebration in the black Jean-Louis sheath with nude illusion from *Let's Make Love*, the Khrushchev welcome reception, and the David di Donatello Award Ceremony, a dress that got much mileage. Sinatra had her seated at a table placed at the edge of the elevated stage in the Copa Room with Milton Berle seated beside her and Dean and Jeanne Martin placed across from them. Elizabeth Taylor and Eddie Fisher sat beside the Martins. Others at the table included Jean Kennedy Smith (President Kennedy's sister) and her husband, Patricia Kennedy Lawford (President Kennedy's sister) and Peter Lawford, and Sammy Davis, Jr.

While smoking four cigarettes and sipping a cup of coffee, Sinatra sang thirteen songs including the tender ballad "Someone to Watch Over Me." As Sinatra sang, Marilyn leaned against the short railing running the perimeter of the stage and stared into his legendary blue eyes. When the music swelled up-tempo, she clapped along. When Sinatra cracked a few jokes, she slapped her hand on the stage floor above her in delight. But as the evening progressed, Marilyn had difficulty keeping up with this hard-drinking crowd and became intoxicated. Jack Entratter, former manager of the Stork Club in Manhattan and now overseeing the Sands Casino, had no prohibition against himself being photographed with Marilyn. He stood behind her chair and posed for a series of photographs in which Marilyn appears visibly inebriated.

"All eyes were on Marilyn as she swayed back and forth to the music and pounded her hands on the stage, her breasts falling out of her low-cut dress," Eddie Fisher recalled. "She was so beautiful—and so drunk. She came to the [after-] party later that evening, but Sinatra made no secret of his displeasure at her behavior, and she vanished almost immediately." Elizabeth Taylor allegedly turned to a reporter and remarked that Marilyn should refrain from drinking if she were incapable of holding her liquor.

According to J. Randy Taraborrelli, as Taylor threw back a martini, she slurred a prideful claim of holding her liquor and made clear her comments about Marilyn were "off the record." Lawford, Fisher, and comic Joey Bishop joined Sinatra on stage to serenade Martin with a personalized birthday song by Sammy Cahn before wheeling out a five-foot birthday cake shaped like a J & B scotch bottle. Martin showed his appreciation by throwing the first slice of cake at Cahn.

A few days after Martin's birthday celebration, Marilyn made a hundred-eighty degree turnabout from reveling in Las Vegas with playboy Sinatra to participating in a formal Catholic sacrament in the San Fernando Valley with a much younger male. Kay Gable had invited Marilyn to the Christening of her six-month-old son, John Clark Gable, at St. Cyril of Jerusalem Church in Encino on Sunday, June 11. *The Los Angeles Times* reported, "Even Marilyn Monroe was there, slipping quietly through the throng in a subdued black dress." Home movies of the event show Marilyn demurely arriving alone with her head covered by a simple black tulle veil, required of women entering a Catholic Church during the era. Other guests included Fred Astaire, Jack Benny, Robert Stack, Cesar Romero, Louella Parsons, and Hedda Hopper. According to Anthony Summers, Marilyn made the other guests feel uncomfortable when she held the baby for an inappropriately long period of time after the baptism.

In the October issue of *Modern Screen*, Louella Parsons would report on "Marilyn Monroe's Life as a Divorcee," largely taken from a conversation at the reception at Kay Gable's home after the Christening of John Clark Gable. Parsons grilled Marilyn for comments about the former and current men in her life. Marilyn glowed at the mention of Frank Sinatra's name, but was quick to say, "Oh, we're just old friends. He has always been nice to me." She also underplayed her relationship with DiMaggio: "I've always been able to count on him after that first bad bitterness of our parting faded," Marilyn confessed. "I just like being with Joe. We have a real understanding—something we didn't share when we were married. When I was ill in New York, there wasn't a day he didn't come to the hospital to visit me. It is a fine thing to be able to call someone your—friend. That's what Joe and I are. Friends."

When the conversation turned to Miller, Marilyn responded with her typical positive spin: "Arthur is a brilliant man. A wonderful writer. Maybe it wasn't his fault that he was a much better writer than he was a husband. I am sure that his writing is the most important thing in his life." She was quick to clarify that their separation was too recent to permit settling into a friendship.

Parsons noted how Marilyn seemed at ease and enjoying herself, even though she had now merited a reputation for dressing like a widow by wearing a consistent uniform of black sheaths to even informal public events. "For the first time in many years I am completely free to do exactly as I please." Marilyn relayed, "To come and go as I see fit—make my own decisions. And this new freedom has made me happier."

Marilyn told Parsons about having met Mrs. Gary Cooper, Elizabeth Taylor, and Eddie Fisher in Las Vegas, liking them all, and appreciating their invitations to parties. "It's always seemed strange to me," Parsons wrote, "the marked gratitude Marilyn always shows to anyone who is thoughtful of her. More than any other trait in her character, it shows the innate loneliness of this girl who has the world at her feet."

"That's my real love," Marilyn said as she blew a kiss to John Clark Gable. "Wonderful...kind of sad, too. My real love; he's the big man in my life, even if he is a little young for me...Clark would have given everything in the world just to see that baby one time."

Shortly after attending the christening, Marilyn flew to Rancho Mirage, Palm Springs, to Frank Sinatra's ultra-modern house in the exclusive residential community surrounding the Tamarisk Country Club. The visit was most likely romantic, and the couple spent time with members of the Rat Pack when not sexually occupied with each other.

Sinatra could be cruel and rude to the women in his life when intoxicated, a state he regularly sought while socializing with friends. During this particular visit, Sinatra showed Marilyn the darker side of a dual nature described by his wife Barbara Marx as "Jekyll and Hyde." When Marilyn grumbled about her miserable childhood to Sammy Davis, Jr. and Dean Martin, an intoxicated Sinatra grumbled, "Oh, not that again." Now when he disagreed with her, Sinatra allegedly snapped, "Shut up, Norma Jeane. You're so stupid you don't know what you're taking about." To Marilyn, her current lover turned on her much in the same way Fred Karger had, confirming her devalued sense of self and unhealthy patterns by experiencing the pairing of love with emotional and verbal abuse.

As Marilyn vacillated between romances with DiMaggio and Sinatra, an article appeared in the *Hutchinson News* about Fox's production of *Celebration.* On the table since the previous summer, it was scheduled to film scenes in the Kansas town, forty miles northwest of Wichita. Jennifer Jones, Kim Novak, or Marilyn would star under José Ferrer's direction. However, Ferrer's name did not appear on Marilyn's list of approved directors, so producer Jerry Wald was courting Joshua Logan. Devoutly Christian Pat Boone refused the role on grounds that it compromised his conservative morals. "Believe me, I would have loved to play opposite Marilyn Monroe," Boone told reporters. "I went to the studio boss Buddy Adler and said I've got a lot of teenage fans, and they would be upset if I played a person who has an affair with an older woman. I can't do that." Utimately, Fox retitled the film *The Stripper* (1963) and cast Joanne Woodward and Richard Beymer.

Given the long delay in negotiations for *Rain*, Fredric March and Florence Eldridge withdrew from the production in fear it would now interfere with a planned vacation with their grandchildren, who were visiting from Italy. Additionally, March was scheduled to begin rehearsals for *Gideon* on Broadway. In an attempt to retain them, Marilyn told Vernon Scott in his May 1 column, "I've always wanted to play Sadie Thompson in 'Rain'...I told NBC I would tape the show on two conditions. One, that Lee Strasberg would have artistic control of the production and two, that Fredric March would be my leading man."

When Marilyn arrived in New York on June 15, NBC had rescheduled the taping at its studio in Brooklyn from four weeks in March—pre-empted from her psychiatric hospitalization—to the entire month of July. With only two weeks to a possible starting date, she quickly received writer Rod Serling (1924-1975) in her apartment for a script conference. As they spoke into the early hours of the morning, Serling chain-smoked Chesterfield cigarettes as Marilyn explained her preference for John Colton's adaptation, from which she had prepared her performance. The former boxer and paratrooper was an intense and angry man who spoke in a deep voice with distinctive diction. "I've seen so much of the old *Rain*, I'm waterlogged," he told columnist Marie Torre. "I accepted the assignment on the understanding that they wanted an updated story."

Louella Parson's column on June 23 announced Richard Burton would be signing a contract to portray Reverend Davidson opposite Marilyn. "That is a coup if I ever heard one," the gossip maven declared. Burton purportedly declined; worried that Marilyn's tardiness would interfere with his ability to arrive on time at the Majestic Theatre for his evening performance in *Camelot* opposite Julie Andrews.

On June 27, NBC's deal with Marilyn terminated when the network rejected Lee Strasberg and assigned George Roy Hill, who would later direct Robert Redford in both *Butch Cassidy and the Sundance Kid* (1969) and *The Sting* (1973). "It's not that I have any concern about the director or any criticism of the director," Marilyn told the press, "but I don't know what his ideas are or will be. I only know what Lee's ideas are, and those are the ideas I want to put into the thing. I don't again want to go into something and then find myself in something totally different from what I expected or what I hoped for." Loyal to Lee Strasberg, Marilyn abandoned the project and would never again have an opportunity to show the world how well she could portray Sadie Thompson or to transition to television drama.

Chapter Sixteen: June–December 1961

On the morning of June 28, Marilyn awoke in her bedroom in New York with excruciating gastric pain, and she called May Reis and Joe DiMaggio. Reis called Marilyn's physician who ordered immediate hospitalization.

Frequent indigestion and a chronic pain on Marilyn's right side had plagued her throughout the production of *The Misfits*, causing her to self-medicate with large doses of barbiturates, but the source of the symptoms was never properly diagnosed. Within minutes, an ambulance arrived in front of 444 East Fifty-Seventh Street, and its medical crew delivered Marilyn to Manhattan Polyclinic on West Fiftieth Street.

The media were already in front of the hospital, photographing her arrival on a stretcher with her face covered by a pillow and DiMaggio and Reis at her side. *Life* published a photograph of Joe grimacing sorrowfully in its July 7 issue. Marilyn was admitted under the name Norma Jean Baker and was soon diagnosed with an inflamed gallbladder and impacted gallstones.

The following day, she underwent a two-hour cholecystectomy by Dr. Richard Cottrell with DiMaggio beside her the entire time. Marilyn was also suffering from an ulcerated colon speculated to be caused by chronic anxiety. The doctor allegedly found her "highly nervous, frightened, and confused." Marilyn awoke to two dozen roses from DiMaggio. *The New York Daily Mirror* announced this was her fourth hospitalization in five months.

"During the days immediately preceding her operation, I saw Marilyn two or three times daily," Dr. Cottrell told *Ladies' Home Companion.* "Often she would be sitting moodily as I entered, but as always she suddenly seemed cheered whenever anyone came to see her. Sometimes she would be sitting and gazing out at the skyline visible from her room's window. When she did, her mood seemed to be that of a caged wilting fawn yearning to return to a freer life outside."

Preferring to look after herself rather than accept care, Marilyn began visiting patients in the ward. She gravitated to the room of an elderly Jewish woman who had no visitors. The patient beamed as she told nurses of Marilyn's visits and showed off gifts such as candy or magazines. In her private room, Marilyn told Cottrell, "Look at the stars. They are all up there shining brightly, but each one must be so very much alone...It's a make-believe world, isn't it?"

Marilyn called upon hairdresser Kenneth Batelle (1927-2013) of Lilly Daniche's salon to style her hair the morning of her discharge from Polyclinic Hospital. Kenneth teased Marilyn's platinum hair into an asymmetrical bouffant with an exaggerated flip on the right side. With John Springer at her side, Marilyn was released on the morning of July 11 amid chaos on the street outside the hospital doors. She wore a tangerine Pucci dress with a white coat draped over her shoulders, short white gloves, and white pumps. Before leaving the ward, Marilyn thanked each aide and nurse while touching his or her hands, until she was instructed to take a seat in a wheelchair. An attendant wheeled her out of the hospital entrance doors to an awaiting ambulance.

Upon exiting the hospital, Marilyn experienced a crush of reporters and spectators. Cameras and microphones were thrust in her face before the attendants could assist her out of the wheelchair and to her feet. As she approached the vehicle, Marilyn's glowing smiled turned into a fearful expression. "It was scary," Marilyn said. "I felt for a few minutes as if they were just going to take pieces out of me. Actually it made me feel a little sick. I mean I appreciated the concerns and their affection and all that, but—I don't know—it was a little like a nightmare. I wasn't sure I was going to get into that car safely and get away!" When the ambulance arrived at her apartment on Fifty-Seventh Street, a group of attendants from the hospital and law enforcement officers escorted Marilyn into the lobby of her building.

Eve Arnold and Marilyn had planned a photographic session with hairdresser Kenneth Batelle at the apartment upon her arrival home. "She looked fresh and rested, and she and Kenneth played up for the camera," Arnold later wrote, "she teasing him about his showing the more photogenic side of his face. Not wanting to tire Marilyn, Arnold shot only one roll of film. Marilyn pressed Arnold about doing more photographic essays on her. Arnold explained this would be a challenge as she was now living in London, traveling between continents, and under contract to the *Sunday Times* in England, but Arnold and her editors would devise a project. They promised to keep in touch with each other. "That was the last time I saw her and the last roll of film I exposed of her," the photographer would write.

As Arnold exited Marilyn's building, media photographers lurched toward her. "What was it like to photograph her?" one reporter asked. Arnold didn't respond until she published her own account. "It was like watching a print come up in the developer," Arnold later wrote in the photographic memoir *Marilyn and Eve.* "The latent image was there—it needed just her time and temperature controls to bring it into being. It was a stroboscopic display, and all the photographer had to do was to stop time at any given instant and Marilyn would bring forth a new image."

The media held vigil outside Marilyn's building. In a move designed to appease rumors as well as reporters' thirst, Marilyn sent a coal scuttle filled with bottles of beer to the mostly male reporters on the sidewalk on July 25. She included a note inscribed, "*Dear fellas, I know it's been a long, hot vigil so have a beer on me. I swear I'm not leaving, I'm staying—single.*" As she convalesced, Marilyn sent a telegram to Dr. Greenson, dated July 14 with well wishes on his twenty-sixth wedding anniversary. "*I hope all your roses are in bloom today including the blackest red ones,*" she wrote. "*Happy, happy anniversary to you and Mrs. Greenson.*"

Marilyn had anticipated the need for surgery shortly before her emergency admission to Polyclinic Hospital. "I need you to be with me," she told Berniece in a long-distance phone call to Tennessee. After the surgery, Marilyn needed someone to tend to her, especially during the night. The opportunity would allow the sisters to talk intimately in person instead of on the telephone.

Berniece booked a flight under a pseudonym and arrived at Marilyn's apartment. She was greeted by May Reis and walked into a living room filled with vases of tropical anthuriums, or flamingo flowers. Marilyn welcomed Berniece with a warm embrace and settled her in the third bedroom, formerly Arthur's study. During her visit, Berniece accompanied Marilyn to Arthur's farmhouse in Connecticut to deliver the twin beds in the guest room where Jane and Bobby used to spend weekends, and which was now under renovation. Marilyn had recently placed a bronze bust of her friend, Carl Sandburg, in the study. "Thank goodness he's not too heavy," she told her half-sister. "I keep carrying him from room to room. I want him everywhere!" Marilyn hoped to introduce Berneice to the poet and invited her to read his published work stored on a shelf in the study.

Berniece documented her visit to New York in her memoir, *My Sister Marilyn*, in 1994. Marilyn was the first to arise each morning and stepped barefoot into the hallway for the newspaper. Lena Pepitone, the maid, arrived at eight in the morning through the kitchen entry and hand washed Marilyn's bras and hung them to dry. She served the sisters broiled steak for breakfast and prepared Marilyn's new diet consisting of four raw beaten eggs each day and the prohibition of alcohol. Pepitone spent the rest of her shift in the kitchen.

Marilyn's doctor visited each night for about twenty minutes, and she personally served him a cocktail. After the doctor's departure, DiMaggio regularly arrived for dinner served by the maid, and George Solotaire joined them each night of Berniece's visit. Berniece, accustomed to a typical suburban life, noted the absence of television and radio in the evening. Marilyn entertained her guests with conversation and served DiMaggio's favorite after dinner beverage, hot tea, intended to soothe his ulcers.

Berniece vehemently discredited the utterly tasteless memoir penned by Lena Pepitone's ghostwriter in 1979. Her experience contradicted Pepitone's allegations written long after Marilyn was dead and unable to defend herself. "Marilyn told me she never talked to anyone about her personal life," Berniece wrote. "And I never observed her discussing intimate matters with her employees. The truest thing that has been written about her since her death is that she had a wall around her."

According to Berniece, DiMaggio continued to carefully scrutinize Marilyn's bills and monitor her finances. At one point, she was furious to discover a receipt with a charge nearly doubled. "Whatever anybody did for her," Berniece wrote, "they charged her three times what they should have." Charities incessantly pressured Marilyn for donations. If Marilyn refused, she incurred bad publicity, Berniece remembered. The only solution was to make a donation to everyone who approached her. During this period, Marilyn generously cashed her AT&T stocks and gifted the proceeds to the Strasbergs for their visit to Japan.

Marilyn made a concerted effort to pamper Berniece, including arranging for Kenneth to style her hair in a bouffant pixie. She also gave her several dresses from her closets. In intimate conversations, Marilyn discussed her love for Joe DiMaggio Jr., Miller's children, and Patricia Rosten. She expressed feeling closest to DiMaggio's son, now twenty, who called her frequently to talk or for advice. At face value, Berniece's visit may have seemed cozy but there were moments of tension between the two women. Loud noises from workers remodeling the building next door disrupted their conversations at all hours of the day and night.

When Berniece questioned Marilyn's large intake of prescribed medication, Marilyn sharply insisted she needed the pills to get rest. Marilyn appeared preoccupied at times and frequently muttered about having "many problems—so many problems." Although Berniece was concerned about Marilyn, DiMaggio confronted Marilyn with his suspicion of her sister's wanting money from Marilyn, an impression shared by May Reis. "I've known my sister longer than I've known you," she insisted. "Besides, if she did want my money, she can have it. What am I going to do with it when I'm gone?"

Before the visit ended, Marilyn and Berniece piled into Ralph Roberts' station wagon and drove them to Arthur Miller's farmhouse in Connecticut to collect an RCA television from the second floor and other odds and ends. Marilyn had signed over the house to him, and without her income, the playwright had resorted to selling original versions of his manuscripts to pay the high taxes.

In the sunroom, Arthur hospitably served them tea while puffing a pipe. He acknowledged Marilyn's foresight in encouraging him to invest in more land, despite his reluctance to do so. After small talk,

Marilyn escorted Berniece on a tour of the remodeling she had done to the property with a combination of pride and sadness. Ironically, she explained to her half-sister that the work had finally been completed at the time of the couple's separation.

While Roberts and Berniece loaded boxes of jelly jars into the car (Marilyn thought they would make charming drinking glasses), the divorced couple stood alone in the driveway, Marilyn wearing moccasins that Miller thought made her look about fourteen. "I faced Marilyn, and we grinned at each other and at the absurdity," he recorded of this bittersweet visit in *Timebends* with a mixture of resolve and melancholy. She lifted her blouse to reveal bandages on the side of her abdomen. "That's why I was always in pain," Marilyn explained in defense of her ailments during the production of *The Misfits*. Miller remembered Marilyn smiling and waving goodbye as the station wagon drove off. There is no documentation of the couple ever meeting in person again.

A new male entered Marilyn's life at this time and provided her with much joy and loyalty. He was different from the current males in her life. He didn't have DiMaggio's jealous temper or Sinatra's penchant for alcohol. Born on a Scottish farm, the puppy had been raised by the housekeepers of artists Vanessa Bell and Duncan Grant at Charleston in Sussex. Actress Natalie Wood's mother, Maria Gurdin, purchased the pet and had him shipped to California. According to some sources, Gurdin gave the dog to Frank Sinatra, who in turn, presented it to Marilyn. Other sources point to Patricia Newcomb giving him to Marilyn as companionship following the divorce and during her convalescence from surgeries. Apparently, the publicist intended the fluffy white puppy to prevent Marilyn from feeling lonely ever again.

Marilyn named the dog Maf-Honey in honor of Frank Sinatra and his alleged connection to the organized crime of the Italian mafia. A New York pet registration dated July 18, 1961, noted the dog as a five-month old Poodle, although license issued in Los Angeles dated July 9, 1962 categorized him as a Maltese, implying that he might have been a mixture of both breeds. In 2010, Andrew O'Hagan published a fanciful and fictional account of Marilyn's last years through the eyes of Maf-Honey: *The Life and Opinions of Maf the Dog, and of His Friend Marilyn Monroe*.

The book mirrored Marilyn penning the thoughts of Hugo the Basset Hound for Miller's children during the summer of 1957. Maf would serve as Marilyn's loyal companion for the last two years of her life, outliving his famous mistress by over a decade, and was eventually adopted by Gloria Lovell, Sinatra's secretary. According to Andrew O'Hagan, Maf died on the morning of President Richard Nixon's resignation in 1974 as the result of running into the path of a dairy van delivering fresh milk in Washington, D.C.

On a tip from Sinatra, Marilyn contacted Jane Zeigler, daughter of her former landlady Viola Mertz, regarding the availability of a rental at 882 Doheney Drive. The building stood at the corner of Cynthia Drive, bordering West Hollywood and Beverly Hills. On August 8, Marilyn moved into the garden apartment across from Gloria Lovell's. Behind a black enamel entry door, Marilyn's space essentially consisted of one room with a kitchenette and bath. For anonymity, Marilyn posted her secretary's name, "Marjorie Stengel," next to the doorbell, effectively confusing curious fans and visitors. In actuality, Stengel had declined Marilyn's request to relocate to Los Angeles with her.

Marilyn placed the bed in the apartment's living room, in what her friends considered a shrine to sleeping. A decorator installed heavy electric blue draperies, a matching bedspread with tassels at each of its four corners, a hand-carved Italian settee, and two matching chairs. Outside was a narrow garden with potted plants and a fountain. When Marilyn noticed a visitor staring at the décor, she apologized and confessed, "I made the decorator stop when I saw what he was doing."

Loyal Ralph Roberts relocated from New York to Los Angeles to be near his friend, driving his car cross-country. He continued to provide Marilyn with massage therapy and chauffeured her to sessions with Dr. Greenson. Roberts typically spent time with Marilyn from early in the morning until late into the evening. He cooked steaks on the grill, and they dined together most nights. Greenson appeared heavily influential—even controlling—of Marilyn's life; and she seriously considered his recommendation to sever many relationships and place herself entirely in his hands. Roberts noted that Marilyn seemed unhappier than she had been in New York under Dr. Kris' care.

Patricia Newcomb also gave up her apartment in New York and followed Marilyn to the West Coast, settling in a nearby apartment in a similarly austere two-story, modern brick building at 120 South Canon Drive in Beverly Hills. One evening, Pat received a frantic telephone call from Marilyn, rushed to Doheney Drive in minutes, finding Marilyn holding an embossed silk greeting card from the man she believed was her father, extending best wishes for an early recovery. Marilyn read the inscription to her, "*From the man you tried to see nearly ten years ago. God forgive me.*" It had been forwarded from Polyclinic Hospital in New York. With tears in her eyes, Marilyn asked Pat what it meant but then concluded the communication came too late. Pat stayed the night, but Marilyn made no mention of the card the next day.

* * *

Later in August, Marilyn joined Sinatra, Dean and Jeanne Martin, and Mike and Gloria Romanoff on a four-day cruise to Catalina Island aboard the Romanoff's yacht. Mike owned the Beverly Hills restaurant that bore his name, where Marilyn often dined with Johnny Hyde. Age sixty-one, Mike had been married to his thirty-seven-year-old business manager, Gloria, for thirteen years. Everyone but Marilyn seemed to be enjoying himself or herself, but a cloud of sadness always seemed to hang above her.

A few of the attendees noticed this change in Marilyn, and she seemed disoriented and over-medicated during the cruise. "It was such a sad sight," Gloria remembered of Marilyn as she assisted her in dressing. "I didn't take my eyes off her for a second because I was afraid she would slip and fall. You can't know how difficult this was unless you knew Marilyn and what a lovely woman she was, how nice she was to everyone. You wanted her to be all right, but on this day during this party, it struck me that she was not all right."

Friends continued to worry about Marilyn's mental state. While dining with her at a restaurant, Maureen Stapleton perceived Marilyn as paranoid. "[She] thought the waiter was reading her mind. At first, she said he was a secret agent or something, she said, 'He's one of the bad guys,' and then she said, 'He knows what I'm thinking now, we have to leave.' Now, you have to keep in mind we were *all* [New York actors] a little loopy back then—but that was particularly strange."

To add to the extremity of Marilyn's declining mental state, earlier in the summer Berniece had seen Marilyn throw away complimentary food sent to her by a local restaurant, thinking it was poisoned. Diane Stevens from John Springer's office told J. Randy Taraborrelli of having witnessed a similar suspicion of tainted food during a late night meeting attended by her employer, Marilyn, and Joe. When the food arrived, Marilyn refused to eat it, and Joe became impatient.

If the food were poisoned, Joe said, he would be dead because of having eaten it. Marilyn looked at him very suspiciously and explained she was the one they wanted to poison, not him. Stevens and Springer sat silently, unsure of how to respond, much in the same way Maureen Stapleton had reacted during Marilyn's earlier episode of paranoia. Finally, Springer gently reasoned it was all the same food. Marilyn told them to enjoy it but—sounding like her mother—announced she wasn't taking any chances. A combination of dieting and possible suspicion of contaminated food led to Marilyn's loss of a considerable amount of weight. As a result, she no longer fit into the wardrobe of mostly straight-lined, brightly colored Emilio Pucci sheaths she had purchased in the beginning of the year.

Marilyn resumed consistent treatment with Dr. Greenson and presented a clinical challenge to the prominent psychoanalyst. Fellow psychoanalyst Milton Wexler, who shared Greenson's penthouse office, co-facilitated several of Marilyn's sessions and suggested Greenson invite her into his home and family to provide an example of the healthy family life she lacked in childhood. Wexler recommended Greenson and his wife virtually re-parent his patient. "I felt it would alleviate her separation anxiety if she knew she had a place to return to," Wexler explained.

In today's age, Greenson's treatment modalities with Marilyn seem controversial. He violated professional ethics and boundaries by inviting his famous patient into his personal life and encouraging his family to treat her as a member of the family, but firmly rationalized these surrogate family relationships were therapeutic. Unfortunately, in his dual role as psychotherapist and foster father, Greenson may have also crossed an ethical boundary by assuming an overinvolved, controlling, and paternal role in her life.

In 2007, Stanley J. Coen explored the rarely studied danger of an analyst's narcissistic neediness; steering treatment away from the patient's needs and toward the analyst's own needs, seemingly describing Dr. Greenson and Marilyn's dynamic. An analyst may find a patient "impressive" by her celebrity, power, wealth, attractiveness, sexiness, and youth. He may inflate one or more of these features into making the impressive patient and himself somehow special and wanted to share the patient's world. The analyst may also attempt to manage his own feelings of both envy of and separateness from his impressive patient by overly identifying with her. Coen pinpointed the intensity of the analyst's excitement and arousal as the warning of a problem in the therapeutic relationship, and through the analyst's lack of self-awareness, the patient may be led to compromised treatment.

Marilyn's special relationship with Greenson's children, Joan and Daniel, exemplified her ability to relate to young people and simultaneously illustrated their father's blurred professional boundaries. In 1961, Joan was a twenty-year-old student at Otis Art Institute. Her brother, Daniel, was a twenty-four-year-old medical student at University of California at Berkley. The siblings shared fond memories of Marilyn's role in their family. "She treated me as a younger sister," Joan remembered in the documentary *The Last Days of Marilyn Monroe* (1985). "She never let me see pictures of her nude, would never allude she slept with anybody. She presented herself to me as a very virginal creature."

Joan met Marilyn for the first time in early 1960 when Greenson asked Joan to collect a prescription and deliver it to the Miller bungalow at the Beverly Hills Hotel. Next, the young woman's role advanced to greeting Marilyn at the door of the Greenson home on Franklin Street and taking her on strolls through the garden until the doctor was ready to receive his patient. Greenson had been successful in engaging a young male patient diagnosed with Schizophrenia after he involved Joan in driving the patient home from sessions. Apparently, the contact with another young person facilitated the young man's connection to others and social skills.

On the evenings Greenson taught at UCLA, he would often arrive home late for the appointment, and so Joan accompanied Marilyn on walks around the nearby lake overlooking Santa Monica and beyond to the Pacific Ocean. Joan remembered their first awkward conversation in which she gushed about Marilyn's performance in *The Misfits*. She discovered Marilyn as fragile, artistic, intuitive, and fun loving. "She would give me older sisterly advice about men and about life," Joan told Christopher Turner of the *UK Telegraph* in an article in 2010 when she and her brother auctioned their father's Freudian couch. "And at other times, it seemed like I was the older one and more experienced, and I would give her sisterly advice."

Greenson scheduled Marilyn as the last appointment of the day and frequently invited her afterward to join the family for dinner. She kept a bottle of Dom Perignon champagne at the Greenson home for personal use when having cocktails with the psychiatrist and his wife. Afterward, she'd always help wash the dishes, and sometimes she assisted Hilde in preparing the meal. "Good Lord," Daniel once exclaimed, "who would believe I just left home for the evening where Marilyn was peeling potatoes as I gave her a peck on the cheek?"

The Greensons prominently displayed a grand piano in their living room just as Marilyn displayed hers in the Manhattan apartment. Greenson's twin sister, Juliet, a concert pianist, often visited and played the instrument, accompanied by her brother on the violin. On Sunday afternoons with the assistance of several other musically inclined friends, the siblings entertained guests such as Celeste Holm (1917-2012), actress; Henry Weinstein (1924-2000), producer; Lillian Hellman (1905-1984), playwright (*The Children's Hour, The Little Foxes, Toys in the Attic*); Katharine Greenschpoon, Greenson's mother; and Hanna Fenichel, psychoanalyst and educator known for her work in the field of early child development and for her association with The School for Nursery Years in Los Angeles. Marilyn regularly attended these gatherings, and Hilde shared with Lucy Freeman her memories of a mesmerized Marilyn curled in a blue velvet chair, graciously moving her hand to the classical music in an almost dance.

Greenson's other sister, Elizabeth, was married to attorney Milton Rudin. A blatant conflict-of-interest developed when Greenson referred Marilyn to his brother-in-law's law firm. Not only did he create her surrogate family, but he linked her to another professional personally connected to his family, to ensure Marilyn's protection by those he believed would advocate for her best interests. Future biographers would question whose needs were being met through the patient-doctor relationship, even though Greenson seemed unaware of his own countertransference issues as he behaved like an overly protective parent.

Wearing a black wig, Marilyn assisted Daniel in hunting for an apartment when he left home for the first time. During this crusade, they discovered common liberal social values. Daniel came to realize his father's treatment plan was far from a knee-jerk reaction to Marilyn's vulnerability and neediness. "Until she came along [my father] was assiduous in not saying anything about who his patients were,' he would say. "She was the only person I ever met who was in treatment with him at the same time. It was very much a thought-through process—to have her hang out with us—and we'd do things together and go places."

Marilyn avoided driving in Los Angeles so Joan would take her around the city in a decrepit compact Hillman Minx convertible. Once as they sat at a red light, a truck driver pulled alongside them and attempted to flirt with Marilyn. When she remained nonresponsive, the driver snapped, "Who the hell do you think you are—Marilyn Monroe?" Marilyn would repeat the story with a laugh in her last interview for *Life*. "When you're famous you kind of run into human nature in a raw kind of way...It stirs up envy, fame does. People you run into feel that, well, who does she think she is, Marilyn Monroe?"

According to Joan, Marilyn took her under her wing and reciprocated the love and attachment the family bestowed upon her. "She gave me self-confidence, she taught me how to dance and stuff like that," Joan told the *UK Telegraph*. "So it was a two-way street. It was sort of like having a very bizarre sister that I never had. It was always complex—partly because she was complex, her moods up and down, but also because of her fame: everything became complicated."

On one occasion, Joan was invited to a friend's party and the friend's father made her feel bad because she did not have a date for the event. Marilyn responded by arranging for Marlon Brando to escort Joan, but he unfortunately had another commitment. Marilyn would not permit her friend to arrive alone and humiliated. Instead, she arrived at the Greenson home in full Hollywood movie star attire and accompanied Joan to the party. To further boost

Joan's reputation among her friends, Marilyn announced at the party that afterward, she would be bringing Joan to a Hollywood soiree.

Ralph and Hilde Greenson found Marilyn fiercely protective of their children and empathic to the feelings of others, in sharp contrast with the Hollywood myth that she was narcissistic. Greenson related evidence of this to Norman Rosten by describing an observation occurring when Marilyn hosted a surprise birthday party for Joan on July 19. While dancing the Twist with the young guests who flocked around her, Marilyn noticed a rather shy African-American girl. Before Marilyn arrived and stole the spotlight, all the boys had been dancing with this girl. Marilyn asked the girl to teach her a new dance step and cleverly shifted the attention away from herself and back toward the girl.

"It may have been foolhardy," Joan would later concede of her father's unorthodox interventions, "but he was willing to take a risk." Daniel eventually became an analyst and acknowledged his father's lapse in judgment: "My father's heart was in the right place, but his mind wasn't...I think he was backed into a corner and he couldn't give up on the idea that he could help her, but then the whole thing came down. The fact is, it didn't work. I mean, she killed herself."

Even at the young age of twenty, Joan recognized the traits of Borderline Personality in Marilyn: "She never saw things except in black and white which made a relationship tenuous, though never with me. Sometimes she argued strongly with others and they were dead in the water if they disagreed, as far as she was concerned."

"I was her therapist, the good father who would not disappoint her and who would bring her insights, and if not insights, just kindness," Dr. Greenson would write of Marilyn in a letter to Marianne Kris two weeks after her death. "I had become the most important person in her life...I also felt guilty that I put a burden on my family. But there was something very lovable about this girl and we all cared about her and she could be delightful."

As the direction of Marilyn's treatment challenged those invested in her personal wellbeing, her career path was laden with obstacles. Fox continued to search for a film for Marilyn. The studio had taken an option to acquire the rights of *Of Human Bondage*, an adaptation of Somerset Maugham's story about a medical student with a club-foot who falls in love with a vulgar waitress previously portrayed on film by Bette Davis. Fox executive Joseph Moskowitz envisioned Marlon Brando as the medical student because he remained interested in performing with Marilyn and suggested Paul Schofield in the event Brando was not available.

Originally, Moskowitz approached José Ferrer as director but decided upon Henry Hathaway. When the studio vetoed Marilyn, Hathaway withdrew from the project, and the film was remade in 1964 with Kim Novak playing the part intended for Marilyn. "I firmly believe she'd be alive today if she had played *Of Human Bondage*," Hathaway told Hedda Hopper shortly after Marilyn's death. "It would have given her the role she longed for and which I know she could have done."

* * *

Top 40 disc jockey Tom Clay entertained radio audiences with nostalgic stories about his past and childhood on his show *Million Dollar Request Radio* on station KDAY in Santa Monica. In early September, he began receiving late-night phone calls from a woman with a soft voice. Clay asked the woman, as he did all his callers, to disclose her name, a requirement for him to broadcast the call on his show, but she refused. When the woman eventually revealed her identity as Marilyn Monroe, Clay disbelieved her and abruptly hung up. The woman called back, and the two chatted several times over the phone before she invited him to her apartment for an early morning cup of coffee. Intrigued, Clay accepted the invitation and arrived at the address provided on Doheney Drive. There he met a sad Marilyn Monroe in her bathrobe, clearly not interested in romance. Over the course of three weeks, Clay visited her almost every other day, staying for about an hour each time.

Clay would tell Anthony Summers of Marilyn's avid interest in his family life with his wife and children. She especially wanted to hear "every word she could" about Clay's children. Marilyn confided in the disc jockey her intense feelings of isolation. "Have you ever been in a house with forty rooms?" she asked him rhetorically. "Well, multiply my loneliness by forty." Dr. Greenson wrote of feeling "appalled at the emptiness of her life in terms of object relations" during this period and expressed concern to a colleague about her "terrible loneliness."

Agnes Flanagan also described to Edwin P. Hoyt the depth of Marilyn's lonesomeness and despair, observed during a social call. The studio hairdresser had been married for twenty years to an electrician at Warner Brothers and had two children. During Marilyn's visit to their home, Marilyn watched the family and said aloud that she wished for a family of her own, to which Agnes told Marilyn she would always be a member of their household.

According to Dr. Greenson, Marilyn may have experienced another major depressive episode in September. "She went through a severe depressive and paranoid reaction," Greenson wrote. "She talked about retiring from the movie industry, killing herself, etc. I had to place nurses in her apartment day and night and keep strict control over the medication since I felt she was potentially suicidal." An entry in a ledger for nursing care dated September 26, 1961 found among Marilyn's financial records in 2008 corroborates this claim.

When Marilyn traveled to New York on September 22, the plane she was flying encountered problems upon take off and returned to Los Angeles. Having faced death at the hand of machinery and not her own, a shaken Marilyn immediately sent a Western Union telegram to DiMaggio at the Lexington Hotel, where he awaited her arrival in the city:

> *Dear Dad Darling: Airplane developed engine trouble plus all oil ran out of same plane so we had to turn back and land back in LA. Leaving again on another plane at 5PM arrive New York 1PM. When plane was in trouble I thought about two things you and changing my will. Love you, I think more than ever. Mrs. Norman*

Marilyn took another flight to New York to visit DiMaggio. When she finally arrived, she occasionally met with W.J. Weatherby in a bar on Eighth Avenue in New York. They had become friendly during *The Misfits*, and Marilyn trusted him. In one meeting, she arrived plainly in a depressed state evidenced by a disheveled appearance and a faint body odor. When the conversation turned to the recent suicide of author Ernest Hemingway, Marilyn aggressively maintained a person's "privilege" to take his or her own life. "I don't believe it's a sin or a crime..." she said, "although it doesn't get you anywhere."

In late September, Rabbi Robert Goldburg met with Marilyn and learned of her psychoanalytic treatment with Dr. Greenson as they discussed the teachings of Freudian revisionist Dr. Bernard Robbins. The spiritual advisor followed up with a lengthy letter to Marilyn subtly steering her from a fundamentalist interpretation of Freud's work. He advised her against reading about psychiatry while undergoing treatment but recommended *The Morality of Sigmund Freud* by Phillip Rief. Rabbi Goldburg also invited her to his home or to specific restaurants on any Thursday evening for a non-alcoholic beverage and more serious discussion.

After returning to Los Angeles, Marilyn reconnected with Sinatra, who reintroduced her to his strikingly handsome friend, Peter Lawford (1923-1984), whom he referred to as "Brother-in-Lawford," the husband of Patricia Kennedy Lawford (1924-2006). "Pat" Lawford was the sixth child of Joseph and Rose Kennedy and the second younger sister of President Kennedy. She liked Marilyn upon their first documented meeting at the Sands in Las Vegas in June. Marilyn had originally met Peter at Metro Goldwyn Mayer Studios in 1950 while she was filming *Hometown Story* and they went on one unsuccessful date. An attractive and desirable playboy in his youth, Lawford had been romantically linked to Rita Hayworth, Lana Turner, and Ava Gardner. Marilyn never truly liked or trusted him but shared a friendly association with his wife.

Born Peter Sydney Vaughn Aylen (1923-1984) to British aristocratic parents, Lawford spent his childhood in France before arriving in Hollywood in 1940. His combination of good looks, debonair appearance, and distinct accent secured a contract with MGM and a string of roles as young British soldiers in a series of war-themed films. After the war, Lawford co-starred with Sinatra in *It Happened in Brooklyn* (1947), Judy Garland in *Easter Parade* (1948), and Elizabeth Taylor in *Little Women* (1949). MGM chose not to renew his contract in 1952, relegating him to television roles, until Sinatra invited him into the Rat Pack.

Lawford married Patricia Kennedy in 1954, much to the chagrin of her father, Joseph Kennedy. The couple's oldest child, Christopher, told CBS that his father was his maternal grandfather's worst nightmare because he was British, Protestant, and an actor. Joseph Kennedy gave Patricia one million dollars upon her turning age twenty-five, and so when Lawford married her five years after she received the fortune, he seemed an opportunistic gold-digger to many.

When Marilyn entered their lives in the autumn of 1961, Peter and Patricia, respectively ages thirty-eight and thirty-seven, had four young children ranging in age from infancy to six. The family occupied an estate at 625 Beach Road on Santa Monica Beach, steps away from the Pacific Ocean. The sprawling stucco mansion in Neo-Spanish motif with a red tile roof had been built by movie mogul Louis B, Mayer, once president of MGM Studios, and Lawford's former boss. It boasted a motion picture screen that rose from the living room floor at the touch of a button, and onyx and marble bathrooms.

When President Kennedy visited Los Angeles, he officially stayed at the Beverly Hilton Hotel, but relaxed at Peter and Patricia's beachfront estate, now dubbed the Western Branch of the White House. The couple entertained lavishly around their fresh water swimming pool, which overlooked the ocean. Patricia tolerated her husband's heavy drinking and extramarital affairs much in the same way her mother role-modeled acceptance of her father's affair with actress Gloria Swanson.

Patricia was smitten with Marilyn's celebrity, and like most of her friends, wanted to protect and take care of her. For Marilyn, Patricia had all she desired: a close-knit family of origin, an education, a husband, children, and an independent personality. Patricia was vibrant, lighthearted, and acerbic. She especially enjoyed making Marilyn laugh. According to J. Randy Taraborrelli, Patricia's personality and laughter reminded Marilyn of Grace Goddard. Eunice Murray, Marilyn's housekeeper in the last nine months of her life, overheard Marilyn's telephone conversations with Patricia and perceived the president's sister as Marilyn's best friend.

"[Marilyn] had a quiet voice and she would smile at me and head out to walk on the sand with my mom," Christopher Lawford, Peter and Patricia's oldest son, wrote. "My mother told me Marilyn was like her 'little sister.' It surprised her that Marilyn was so open with her. My mom didn't come from an environment where emotions and feelings were openly shared. Marilyn Monroe trusted my mother's love for her."

Marilyn's connection to the Lawfords afforded an introduction to President Kennedy. On November 18, Kennedy delivered a speech at a Democratic Party dinner held in his honor at the Hollywood Palladium in Los Angeles. According to some sources, afterward, he allegedly visited the Lawfords' beach house and met Marilyn for the first time. However, that same evening, Douglas Kirkland was photographing Marilyn at the Bel-Air Hotel. In another version, biographer Donald Spoto placed their first meeting earlier, and published an account of Allan "Whitey" Snyder delivering Marilyn to the beach house in his Volkswagen Beetle for a dinner party honoring the President in October. Spoto cited Snyder as his source.

* * *

Dr. Greenson advised Marilyn to hire a housekeeper and companion; not any housekeeper and companion, but one selected specifically by him. Marilyn obeyed and scheduled an interview with the woman in early November. This housekeeper and companion would allegedly be the last person to see Marilyn alive and would be present in her home the night of her death. Eunice Murray (1902-1994), described as a quiet, matronly widow by most of Marilyn's biographers, lived in apartment number eleven in a narrow Spanish apartment complex at 933 Ocean Avenue, facing the vast Pacific Ocean in Santa Monica, a more modest area south of the Lawford estate.

She was born Eunice Joerndt in Chicago, on March 3, 1902, the year of Gladys' birth, to Wilhelm and Mary, devout members of the Jehovah's Witness faith. The family relocated to Ohio, where Eunice and her sister, Carolyn (four years older), attended Urbana School and Academy, a private institution founded on the Swedenborgian religion, based upon mysticism and the teachings of Swedish theologian Emanuel Swedenborg. Carolyn unfortunately contracted Spanish influenza. When the Joerndts learned their daughter had received medical care against their beliefs, the couple legally disowned her, and the academy's staff assumed the adolescent's guardianship.

According to Donald Spoto, Eunice's education ended just prior to her sixteenth birthday due to emotional problems related to a severe fear of abandonment engendered by their rejection of her sister. In the early 1920s, Carolyn married Franklin Blackmer, a Swedenborgian minister who was president of Urbana College, and Eunice married John Murray, a World War I veteran who was the son of a Swedenborgian minister. Murray had left divinity school to become a carpenter and eventually was elected vice president of the United Brotherhood of Carpenters and Joiners. Eunice and John had three daughters, Jacqueline, Patricia, and Marilyn. All were close in age to Marilyn Monroe.

Despite lacking adequate education, Eunice referred to herself as a nurse in telephone directories as John traveled to Mexico for his involvement in trade unions. They built a five-bedroom Monterey-style home on Franklin Street in Santa Monica in 1946. Murray turned out to be an absentee husband and father. He left Eunice unable to afford the monthly mortgage payments, and she was forced to sell the home after only four months of residency. She divorced Murray in 1950 and he died eight years later. His brother, Churchill Murray, an expatriate living in Mexico, maintained contact with Eunice. After Carolyn's death in 1972, Eunice married her widowed brother-in-law and moved to Bath, Maine. Her second husband died shortly thereafter.

Eunice Murray apparently befriended the new owners of her former home, Ralph and Hilde Greenson, in the hope of remaining connected to it. Greenson, in turn, often placed Eunice in the homes of his patients as a monitor and companion in exchange for her reporting back to him the details of the patients' private lives. He would assign her to this covert role in Marilyn's life, whereby she doted on the actress and treated her with a degree of condescension.

Mrs. Murray's overt duties included arranging Marilyn's household schedule around daily sessions with Greenson, light housekeeping, sewing, and chauffeur services. Murray addressed Marilyn by her first name, but Marilyn felt comfortable addressing her housekeeper only as Mrs. Murray. Patricia Newcomb and other friends considered Murray strange in demeanor and an inappropriate companion for Marilyn.

When Eunice knocked on the black enamel door of apartment number three on Doheny Drive for her interview, Marilyn appeared in a red kimono. She apologized for making the woman wait and graciously invited her inside the apartment. To Murray, Marilyn seemed entirely capable in the small kitchenette as she demonstrated the preparation of her meals based upon a newly prescribed diet. The housekeeper noted her new employer's "sensuous catlike grace of motion" as she carried out her routine in the dark apartment. Marilyn soon put Murray to work altering her wardrobe to accommodate the actress's drastic reduction in weight.

Mrs. Murray soon became aware of the incongruity between Marilyn and DiMaggio, with whom Marilyn continued spending considerable time. "Marilyn, despite her lack of education, was an extremely bright girl with an intuitive intelligence that was most unusual," the housekeeper later wrote in her memoir, *Marilyn: The Last Months.* "She had a real feeling for people and what was going on. Joe was just not interested in those things. He enjoyed sports. And that just wasn't Marilyn at all." Murray also noted Marilyn's dimming interest in her other suitor. When Marilyn reviewed a package of photographs from the cruise to Catalina Island with Frank Sinatra aboard the Romanoffs' yacht, she told Murray that she was not sending him prints because she had "already given him enough."

Marilyn shared with Murray her challenges as a single, attractive woman known to the world as a sex symbol, recounting a recent event that had particularly alarmed her. Motivated by maternal instinct, Marilyn had invited a cold and hungry taxi driver into her apartment for hot soup after he had driven her home in the rain. She panicked when he made a pass at her. Murray also observed Marilyn's personal value of substance over superficiality. The housekeeper would write that Marilyn received more pleasure from confidences than from "fawning or flattery."

With Murray firmly secured as Marilyn's new carefully selected companion, Greenson subsequently maneuvered to distance Ralph Roberts from his patient. One November afternoon as Roberts sat in his car parked at the curb outside the house on Franklin Street waiting to drive Marilyn home from a session, she climbed into his car sobbing. "Dr. Greenson thinks you should go back to New York," she wept. "He has chosen someone else to be a companion for me. He said that two Ralphs in my life are one too many..." Trusting Greenson's judgment, neither Marilyn nor Roberts protested.

Neighbor Gloria Lovell told Roberts, who returned to Marilyn's apartment the following morning, that she heard Marilyn crying throughout the night through their common wall. Both women experienced sleeplessness that night due to a wild party at a nearby residence. A group of revelers from the bash had stood under Marilyn's window and called her name, coaxing her to join them.

Roberts grew alarmed when Marilyn did not respond to his persistent ringing of her doorbell, so he used the garden hose to spray water against her bedroom window. Marilyn emerged and reassured him she was not in danger. Due to the disturbance, she had, indeed, taken a larger overdose of medication, but not enough to harm her.

According to Donald Spoto, one of the revelers who had disturbed Marilyn's sleep was a thirty-one year old blonde model, trick golfer, and television actress named Jeanne Carmen (1930-2007). In the 1980s, Carmen made preposterous claims in the media of having been Marilyn's friend and confidante. Most of her claims focused on witnessing Marilyn's alleged affairs with both President Kennedy and Attorney General Robert Kennedy. Shortly before her death, Brandon James, Carmen's son, published a book seemingly written by his mother in first person expanding her claims to include that she, too, had affairs with both Kennedy brothers and Sinatra. The author's disclaimer, however, notes the book is "an artistic interpretation of the extraordinary true life story of the amazingly beautiful American Icon Jeanne Carmen—my mother."

Most important in assessing the veracity of Carmen's claims, her name is absent from Marilyn's surviving telephone and address books from the time period, and no photographs of the women together nor written correspondence between them have ever surfaced. The only known published reference to Carmen's connection to Marilyn appeared in the article "Housekeeper Discloses: Mystery Phone Call Received by Marilyn," in the *Los Angeles Times* on August 7, 1962. Carmen was mentioned as "a neighbor" of Monroe's who had seen her two weeks earlier. She was quoted as saying Marilyn had "looked like death."

* * *

Look magazine commissioned a portrait session of Marilyn by Canadian photographer, Douglas Kirkland, for its twenty-five year anniversary issue, scheduled to be published on January 16, 1962.

At age twenty-four, Kirkland (born 1934) was hired as a staff photographer for *Look* and became famous for this iconic Monroe session. He later joined the staff of *Life* magazine.

For the anniversary issue, *Look* predicted American life twenty-five years into the future. A feature article identified four women in film who could still be relevant and in the limelight in 1987: Elizabeth Taylor, Shirley MacLaine, Marilyn Monroe, and Judy Garland. *Look* prophesized that Monroe would be a future sex symbol of age, similar to Mae West. Only two of the magazine's predictions came to fruition. MacLaine remained relevant as a character actress, winning an Oscar for *Terms of Endearment* (1983) at age fifty and having a string of good roles into the 1990s and early 2000s; Elizabeth Taylor transitioned from film to television in the 1970s and bravely dedicated her time in the 1980s to increase both awareness of AIDS and funding for its treatment when the Reagan administration ignored the epidemic as a "gay plague." *Look* failed to forecast Monroe's death within the year and Garland's fatal overdose of barbiturates in her London flat in 1969.

In the memoir, *An Evening with Marilyn*, Kirkland described his first meeting with Marilyn on Doheny Drive. He found her "amazingly pleasant and playful." Marilyn seemed like the sister he would have liked to have or "the girl next door," not at all intimidating as he had imagined her. Marilyn warmly greeted Kirkland and his *Look* colleagues, Jack Hamilton and Stanley Gordon. She directed the other men to sit on the only two chairs in the room, and playfully looked at Kirkland and patted the bed. "Sit here," Marilyn said with a giggle. "I think of it as a sofa." Unaware of Marilyn's primary residence being in Manhattan the photographer was struck by the simplicity of her life and appraised her apartment as slightly larger than a "deluxe" hotel room with a kitchenette. "[Marilyn's] smile and easy manner also relaxed me almost immediately," Kirkland would write. "It felt as though I were with a real person, not a superstar."

Marilyn sensed Kirkland's anxiety and put him at ease by sitting beside him and making small talk. "I was young and did not know how to ask her to pose for the sexy images I hoped to get," he wrote, "but she simplified it all by suggesting, 'I should get into bed with nothing on but white silk," and requested Frank Sinatra music and chilled Dom Perignon champagne to set a romantic mood for the shoot.

On November 17, Kirkland patiently waited with Jack Hamilton, Stanley Gordon, and John Springer in a two-story loft at the Bel Aire Hotel. Kirkland's concept was to shoot from the second level, looking down upon Marilyn in a bed covered in white silk sheets and white pillows. A white backdrop covered the floor beneath the bed. Marilyn, with her pale skin and platinum hair, would be surrounded by a white aura. At 9:30 in the evening, Marilyn had not yet arrived for the seven o'clock session. An assistant took a photograph of Kirkland and the other assistant sitting slouched and cross-legged in chairs awaiting Marilyn's arrival. "She's sometimes a little late," Springer explained after hours of small talk, "but she always shows up."

Upon her late arrival, Marilyn did not disappoint. She struck Kirkland as almost ghostlike. He described her as "more spiritual than mortal" and moving in a "floating slow motion." Once Marilyn changed into a white robe, slid under the sheets, and removed the robe, Kirkland began shooting. "I think I should be alone with this boy," she announced after this warm-up. "I find it usually works better that way!" The result suggests a playful and sensuous fantasy with the point of view of a lover above during a night of lovemaking. Perched over the railing of the loft, Kirkland strained for the quintessential portrait for *Look.* "Why don't you come down here with me?" Marilyn asked at the end. Kirkland declined. When he finally came down to the first level, he sat on the floor and shot up at Marilyn in the bed.

Afterward, Kirkland lay down on floor, hands behind his head, as Marilyn remained nude in bed. The pair sipped champagne as the assistant continued to shoot a scene resembling two lovers' pillow talk after lovemaking. "We talked about simple things," Kirkland later wrote. "All sorts of things that we'd experienced in our different worlds, and also what we believed in. We talked for about twenty minutes, and then I said that we should let everybody come back in. When they returned, my assistant took a few more pictures and then we got up."

"When I worked in a factory I'd go to the movies on a Saturday night and sit alone in the back row watching," Marilyn said of her own role as a consumer with desire for fantasy from the film industry. "If the film was good, I mean really great, that movie would carry me through the entire next week on my dreary job in the plant. That's what I think movies should be all about, giving people that kind of fantasy!"

Kirkland could not hide his excitement when he arrived at the Doheny Drive apartment a few days later with a light box filled with the results of the session to review with his subject. Wearing dark glasses and a scarf, Marilyn appeared the antithesis of the goddess he had photographed only days earlier. She sent him to a drug store on Sunset Boulevard for a magnifying glass, a grease pencil, and a pair of scissors. When he returned, Kirkland watched Marilyn's precise process of selection. She described the pictures as mediocre before examining them more closely with a jeweler's loupe and grew more enthusiastic upon discovering several good shots, including the iconic image of her hugging a pillow that was ultimately selected for the article. "I like this girl because she's the kind of woman that every man would like to be in there with," Marilyn announced in third person. "The kind of girl a truck driver would like to be in bed with." She ended the meeting by giving Kirkland a peck on the cheek and expressing a desire to work together again.

Marilyn also posed for a portrait sitting for photographer Eric Skipsey with Maf-Honey at the Beverly Hills Hotel. This time, it wasn't she who held up the session. Patricia Newcomb was forty-five minutes late. They passed the time chatting, joking, and sipping champagne. When Patricia finally arrived, she turned to Skipsey and said, "You have ten minutes." Marilyn retorted Skipsey had as much time as he wished, as the pictures were hers, not Patricia's. They worked together for another hour, and Marilyn offered additional time. Skipsey would later recall this attitude was typical of her, as she was considerate and did not behave like a diva.

Further proof of Marilyn's thoughtfulness was exemplified by her having arranged the session with Skipsy to fulfill a request by fourteen year-old Barbara Heinz, an avid collector of toy dogs who lay dying of bone cancer at Wisconsin's Appleton Memorial Hospital. Given just a few months to live, the child had written with a wish for a photograph of her favorite star with the dog recently publicized in the press. Marilyn's personalized portrait with Maf-Honey arrived at the child's hospital room inscribed: "*From Marilyn Monroe to Barbara Heinz. With love.*"

As a nurse handed Barbara Heinz an envelope containing the photograph from Marilyn, a currier from Fox delivered a comedy script titled *Something's Got to Give* to the Doheney Drive apartment. Marilyn read it during the long Thanksgiving weekend, but was preoccupied with steering her career in a new direction.

Marilyn spent her last Thanksgiving on Thursday, November 23 at the apartment of her friend and neighbor Gloria Lovell. The event was documented by Marilyn's autograph and inscription on a napkin adorned with a printed turkey design and a letter typed on corporate letterhead (from the firm Riss & Company, Inc., in Kansas City, Missouri) by a woman named Jo. Both pieces were auctioned in 2009.

"*I know that writing on the little napkin is hard to read, I'll try and get a better one...*" Jo's letter reads. "*If you can't make it out it's Marilyn Monroe, she was at Gloria's Thanksgiving dinner. There were six of us including Gloria.*" The letter references others in attendance: Janet Roth, comedian Danny Thomas' secretary; Jimmy Morrissey, Gloria's hairdresser; and Inez Melson. Jo described her impressions of Marilyn in detail:

> *Marilyn is no more like she is on screen than anything...I did not know who she was, hardly...Her voice is different, although she has that little high pitched note, it's most exaggerated in her [films]. She is as tall as I, but oh so slender, thin face, little bucket, small breasts, wears size 12...she looks...times that [large] on screen...is very sweet, nice as can be, very down to earth, not a bit stuck up or anything...just folks. She had on a [black] short skirt, [black] pumps, a silk jersey pull on sweater, hair tied up in white silk scarf, said [her hair] did not look good in back so did not take it off. You'd like her. She wore the most elegant, sheared white beaver coat I have ever seen...*

In early December, photographer Len Steckler chatted with Carl Sandburg in Sandburg's apartment in New York when the poet announced he was expecting a visitor. When the doorbell rang, Steckler offered to receive the guest so that his eighty-one-year-old host could remain seated. Standing at the door was Marilyn. "I'm sorry I'm late," she said, "I was at the hairdressers', matching my hair to Carl's." Marilyn ran to greet her friend, and they embraced and sat for hours engrossed in conversation. Steckler photographed the visit and captured Marilyn's youthful hand holding the aged poet's.

On December 19, Marilyn typed a lucid, articulate, and well-organized letter to Lee Strasberg published in *Fragments: Poems, Intimate Notes, Letters by Marilyn Monroe.* It reveals no evidence of the depressive episode from earlier in the year. On the contrary, it is filled with hopes and dreams. "*For years I have been struggling to find some emotional security with little success, for many different reasons,*" she wrote. "*It is true that treatment with Dr. Greenson has had its ups and downs, as you know. However, my overall progress is such that I have hope of finally establishing a piece of ground for myself to stand on, instead of the quicksand I have always been in. But Dr. Greenson agrees with you, that for me to live decently and productively, I must work!*"

Marilyn surmised that her future plans as an artist depended upon Strasberg's role in her plan to establish another independent film production company along with Marlon Brando. In the third paragraph, she outlined a position for Strasberg as a consultant, which would permit him the freedom of pursuing his teaching and other interests. Marilyn wished to avoid appearing "*presumptuous*" in asking Strasberg to relocate to Los Angeles for her alone unless she could offer him significant personal and professional incentive. Marilyn realistically acknowledged the lofty aspects of her aspirations and clarified that the production company would make films with other performers, offering opportunities for Strasberg's daughter, Susan, and son, John. In closing, she referenced plans for further meetings with Brando and her attorneys.

In a more desperate undated note to Brando written on stationery from the Los Angeles Institute for Psychoanalysis, Marilyn urged him to help her persuade Strasberg to move from New York to Los Angeles to set up the company. "*Dear Marlon, I need your opinion about a plan for getting Lee out here on more than a temporary basis,*" she wrote. "*Please phone me as soon as possible. Time is of the essence, Marilyn.*" Brando responded to Marilyn's urgency with a telegram dated January 13, 1962: "*Tried to reach you by fone (sic). Must leave city this weekend. Sorry. Marlon.*"

During the Christmas holiday in Los Angeles, Marilyn's celebrity image retreated into the background as DiMaggio, the baseball hero, became center of attention at a Christmas Eve dinner at the Greenson home. "Who would believe that there were four or five men sitting next to Marilyn Monroe, and they didn't give a darn?" Joan Greenson rhetorically asked Fred Lawrence Guiles when they discussed the evening. Joe and Marilyn spent Christmas Day together in the apartment on Doheny Drive. DiMaggio had bought Marilyn a Christmas tree, and they shopped for traditional Mexican ornaments at Olvera Street, a historic Mexican marketplace.

"All the kids in the house got presents but me," Marilyn told Mrs. Murray while reminiscing about a childhood Christmas in foster care. "One of the other kids gave me an orange." Marilyn wouldn't let the holiday slip by without sending gifts for Miller's children. Bobby's mother vetoed the telephone Marilyn shipped to him in New York, believing it an inappropriate gift for a twelve-year-old boy.

Joan and Daniel Greenson visited Marilyn and DiMaggio after midnight on New Year's Eve at the apartment on Doheney Drive. As they drank champagne and roasted chestnuts, Joan likened the experience to visiting "an old married couple."

A few weeks earlier in New York, Paula Strasberg's astrologer had completed a chart for Marilyn's upcoming year. The forecast was tumultuous. "I can't give it to her," Paula told her daughter, Susan, "she'll get too depressed." Susan pressed her for details. "It's not fatal," Paula said, shaking her head, "it doesn't have to be fatal."

Part III:

The Last Months

Chapter Seventeen: *Something's Got to Give*

Marilyn effectively dodged *Blue Angel* and *Goodbye, Charlie*, but she still owed Fox two films to fulfill her contract. After satisfying this obligation, she would have the freedom to pursue her own productions, select dramatic roles in quality films, and demand script approval. Beginning in the early 1960s, studios discontinued hiring and grooming performers through confining "slave" contracts and dismissed on-site casting directors and talent departments. Instead, they contracted freelance casting directors to pursue now freelance actors. Dr. Greenson encouraged Marilyn to resume working and fulfill her contractual duties in return for increased power and range of choice.

By early 1962, Marilyn would be one of Fox's remaining twelve contract players; the studio had boasted fifty-five the previous year. However, her title as the queen of the studio offered no solace; both actress and studio harbored mutual animosity. Marilyn wanted out, and the studio seemed to want the same, but only after she delivered on her contract for two final films. When Spyros Skouras assigned George Cukor as director of Marilyn's next film, Cukor protested by sending harsh telegrams to Darryl Zanuck in Europe. Zanuck responded: "If I could, I would launch a torpedo from here—aimed directly at her dressing room."

Even before Dr. Greenson's urging, Marilyn recognized her need to get back to work. At thirty-five in 1961-1962, her days as a sex symbol were waning, and the natural aging process would soon limit her opportunities for romantic leading female roles. Today, romantic leading actresses' careers reach over age 50, but in the previous century, the approach of age 40 generally signaled the end of a career. Clara

Bow, Joan Crawford, and Greta Garbo—sexy and glamorous stars of the 1920s and 1930s—experienced a significant decline in their careers at thirty-six.

Potentially, Marilyn's maturity might afford an opportunity for a wider range of characters or dramatic roles, but even those roles were now scarce for actresses who had thrived playing them. At 53, two-time Oscar-winning Bette Davis experienced a professional drought and placed a tongue in cheek ad in the "Situations Wanted" section of *Variety* in early 1962. "I want to grow old without face-lifts," Marilyn bravely told W.J. Weatherby decades before cosmetic surgery, Botox injections, and liposuction became the norm for celebrities and average citizens alike. "They take the life out of a face, the character. I want to have the courage to be loyal to the face I've made."

Some blondes had achieved relevance in their fourth decade. Lana Turner at 41, six years older than Marilyn, maintained success in a string of melodramas. Doris Day, at 40, had been cast in a series of hit formula romantic comedies. Day's career more closely mirrored Marilyn's and suggested a possible path for professional longevity. According to Quigley's Annual Top Ten Money-Makers Poll, Day rated first in 1960 and for three consecutive years beginning in 1962. Marilyn had dropped off the Quigley Top Ten List in 1956, so this was a pivotal point in her career.

Fox faced an equally crucial crossroads as its star. In 1961, the studio had lost nearly $22 million due to the production turmoil of *Cleopatra*, in production in London since 1960 and costing $150,000 a day. By the first quarter of 1962, studio stocks fell from $39 to $20 per share. Fox had paid Elizabeth Taylor $1,000,000 to portray the seductive Queen of the Nile, the highest salary for an actress at the time, which ballooned to $7 million (equivalent to about $47 million today) due to production delays.

In return, she incited a scandal by engaging in an adulterous affair with Richard Burton, her married co-star who portrayed Marc Antony. Taylor was married to Eddie Fisher, and three years prior, the press had blamed her for stealing him from Debbie Reynolds. Moral outrage from the Vatican and other conservative organizations created bad publicity for the film but offered the potential for morbid curiosity to generate ticket sales.

Marilyn had allegedly campaigned for the role of Cleopatra by sending the studio Richard Avedon's photographs of her impersonating Theda Bara in the original 1917 silent film version. Marilyn was virtually unrecognizable in a black wig, heavily lined eyes, Egyptian headdress with a simulated cobra, flimsy harem pants, and revealing gold snake-coil breast-cups. With her midriff bare, Marilyn's abdomen was surprisingly flat. By most accounts, she was never a serious contender for the role of the shrewd and charismatic monarch.

Six months into production of *Cleopatra*, under the direction of Rouben Mamoulian, Elizabeth Taylor became life-threateningly ill and was rushed to a London hospital where doctors performed a tracheotomy to save her. As a result, the film was shut down. When the English weather proved detrimental to Taylor's recuperation and responsible for the deterioration of expensive sets, Fox relocated the production to Rome under the direction of Joseph L. Mankiewicz. He inherited a film with no usable footage despite being already $5 million over budget. Originally budgeted at $2 million, *Cleopatra* would ultimately cost $44 million, the equivalent of about $320 million today, mostly due to the exceptionally long duration of filming and the construction of two complete sets in two different European countries.

When Marilyn arrived at Fox in 1946, the studio earned $185 million per year, owned three hundred acres, sixteen soundstages, and lay claim to four thousand employees. Fifteen years later and due to the unbridled production costs of one film, the studio terminated two-thirds of its workforce, closed its commissary and talent school, and stopped watering its lawns and gardens. Now, only nine hundred employees remained on fifty acres.

Reeling from the shenanigans of Taylor, and nearly bankrupted by a film gone awry, Fox turned to its tried and true contract player, Marilyn Monroe, adept at appealing to the public and making money. Her last film for the studio, *Let's Make Love*, tied with *Swiss Family Robinson* as the top moneymaker of 1960. Fully aware of her box office draw, Fox strategically assigned her *Something's Got to Give* on October 16, 1961, in return for a salary of $100,000, a meager one-tenth of Taylor's and arguably a metaphoric slap in the face. The studio depended upon an anticipated autumn release of a Monroe blockbuster to begin recuperating from the fiscal losses of

Cleopatra. Marilyn Monroe Productions would not be a co-producer; Fox would pay her salary to the corporation as a tax shelter.

Ten days later, Milton Rudin negotiated with studio executives for a contract for his other client, Frank Sinatra, and used this opportunity to advocate for Marilyn. He minimized Marilyn's desire for salary and approvals, voiced her concern about shabby treatment, desire to be taken seriously and have more control over her roles and scripts. Marilyn's former agent, Charles Feldman, lacked Rudin's insight into her mindset afforded by the latter's relationship with her psychoanalyst. Fox still refused to allow her script approval and instead, the studio offered a bonus if Marilyn finished the film on time and emphasized that Arnold Schulman had specifically tailored for her the original script by Frank Tashlin. Having not yet received a copy of the script, Marilyn was apprehensive.

Something's Got to Give was a remake of RKO Studio's *My Favorite Wife* (1940), a screwball comedy starring Gary Grant, Irene Dunne, Randolph Scott, and Gail Patrick. The project had already been recycled from *Too Many Husbands* (adapted from W. Somerset Maugham's 1919 play *Home and Beauty* and released two months before the Grant-Dunne film), starring Jean Arthur, Fred MacMurray, and Melvyn Douglas.

The property offered Marilyn a chance to portray a sexy mother and wife, Ellen Arden, who returns to her family after being declared lost at sea for five years. The film opens in a courtroom where Ellen's husband, Nick, has petitioned for a judge to declare her legally dead. Ellen, a professional photographer, had taken pictures of a sail boat race off the Hawaiian Islands and fell overboard during a gathering storm. Immediately following the declaration of death, the judge begrudgingly officiates Nick's civil wedding to Bianca, a neurotic woman dependent upon her psychoanalyst, Dr. Herman Schlick.

On the day she is declared legally dead, Ellen is rescued by a United States submarine crew and returned to Honolulu after spending the last five years stranded on a deserted island in the South Pacific. She calls home from a payphone and speaks to her children, Timmy and Lita, who tell her their father has married and gone to Hawaii with their new stepmother. Ellen checks into the Honolulu resort where she and Nick spent their honeymoon and spots Nick entering an elevator with his new bride. Nick appears to recognize his "dead" wife but dismisses the vision as guilt for his remarriage.

Ellen checks into the resort and buys a new wardrobe, charging everything to Nick's account. Nick tells Bianca he is going to the hotel barber shop for a shave and finds Ellen. The couple reunites. Ellen tells Nick of her experience on the island and recent rescue, and they recommit their love for each other. When Nick wants to have sex, Ellen resists, insisting that he tell Bianca about her return. When Nick and Ellen reunite at the resort, he asserts his fidelity to Ellen, but avoids telling his new overly reactive wife the truth. The screwball comedy employs Nick bouncing from Ellen's suite to his unsuspecting new wife's suite. Finally, he feigns a back injury to evade consummation of the marriage. Bianca spends much of her honeymoon alone, consulting over the telephone with her analyst regarding her suspicion of Nick having a sexual dysfunction.

Incensed, Ellen returns home to San Francisco to reclaim her role in the family and reunite with her children. She immediately establishes rapport with Timmy and Lita but discovers they have no memory of her. Ellen is crushed to learn she is only recognized by the family Cocker Spaniel, Tippy, and that Bianca is replacing her as a wife and mother. Cautious not to shock the children, she tells them she is a family friend. The children tell her that their mother drowned in the ocean and that they bring flowers to her memorial.

Ellen poses as the household's Swedish nanny, Miss Ingrid Tic, complete with accent. She adjusts to civilization while bonding with the children and teaching them about survival in the South Pacific as well as the culture of island natives. Nick and Bianca return home shortly thereafter to find the children building a hut in the back yard in preparation for the South Pacific rainy season and a new and sexy member of the household.

Tension ensues as Ellen schemes to disrupt Nick's new marriage and grows agitated by his shirking responsibility to clarify the situation for his new wife. Bianca becomes angry at her husband's disinterest in her and new interest in the blonde nanny. Bianca continues her attempts to seduce her husband while Ellen skinny-dips in the family pool at night under the moon, her routine on the island for the last five years. Nick is mortified, and demands that she get out of the pool and put on a robe.

That evening, an insurance agent visits Nick at home to resolve the issue of his company having paid Ellen's life insurance claim and a report of a woman fitting Ellen's description being recently rescued. The agent shares details of an investigation into Ellen's experience as a castaway: she had not spent the last five alone, but her companion on the island was a muscular and athletic playboy, Stephen Burkett, who had participated in the boat race. According to Burkett's statement in the report, the couple addressed each other as "Adam and Eve," implying sexual involvement in the tropical Eden. The insurance agent leaves and catches Ellen emerging from the pool. This leads to a confrontation between Nick and Ellen, each insistent upon their respective fidelity during the separation.

Suspecting Ellen of infidelity, Nick consults with his secretary, Miss Worth, over a hypothetical case of a wife having an affair. What should the husband do, he asks her. She replies that he should forgive his wife. When Nick asks her attitude toward a husband who strays, she insists that is a completely different situation because the husband has a wife waiting for him at home.

To allay her husband's doubts about her fidelity, Ellen recruits a mousy shoe salesman to pose as Burkett. Meanwhile, Nick has already sought out and confronted the playboy at the local yacht club. Ellen presents the show salesman to Nick as "Adam." Nick plays along as Ellen and the imposter stumble along in describing the island and their struggle for survival. Soon after, Burkett arrives at the home at Nick's invitation. Ellen is mortified that Nick was aware of her deception with the shoe salesman, and the couple quarrel. Burkett learns about Nick's remarriage and proposes to Ellen who reveals that he relentlessly chased her on the island as she resisted his advances.

Since Nick delays confronting Bianca with the truth, Ellen threatens to marry the playboy in retaliation. Ending the drama, detectives from the District Attorney's Office arrest Nick for bigamy, leading to a climactic courtroom scene—akin to screwball comedy—before the judge who declared Ellen dead and officiated Nick's new marriage. Ellen requests to be declared alive and seeks a divorced based upon Nick's failure to unconditionally love her. Accompanied by her psychoanalyst, Bianca requests an annulment based upon an unconsummated marriage. The judge declares Ellen as alive and annuls Nick's marriage to Bianca. Bianca partners with her analyst, and Burkett proposes to Ellen. Ellen convinces Burkett to help her resolve problems with Nick.

The film ends with Ellen returning home to find her husband in the pool with the children, and the children acknowledging her as their mother, evidence of Nick telling them the truth. Ellen jumps into the pool and embraces her family.

* * *

In November Marilyn was invited to lunch at the Beverly Hills Hotel by the new studio production chief, Peter Levathes, who replaced Robert Goldstein, to discuss *Something's Got to Give*. Fox's head of production, Darryl F. Zanuck, had resigned in 1956 and relocated to Paris where he continued his success as an independent producer. According to the tabloids, Mrs. Zanuck had finally discovered her husband's affair with Bella Darvi and threatened to divorce him in California, a state recognizing the community property of married couples. Avoiding a financial meltdown, Zanuck stayed out of the country while Fox's president, Spyros Skouras, hired a series of production executives.

Peter Levathes (1911-2002) joined Fox in 1937 as a legal assistant to Spyros Skouras and worked at Fox's motion picture chain headquarters in New York. Levathes had told Marilyn she was ordered to the Fox lot for work on November 15, 1961. The production schedule included ten days of shooting at a hotel in Honolulu. She appeared at the studio two days before the start date but refused to proceed without a script. (At the time, she was still considering Tennessee Williams' *Celebration*.) As evidenced by a note she received from Paula Strasberg dated November 4, 1961, the Strasbergs were advising her about a suitable role to increase the momentum of her career. Paula wrote:

> *This is just a reminder that we miss you and love you. From the tone of your voice, we sense that whatever you are doing is important and right. When I mentioned the script of Celebration, it is only because we want you to do what possibly would be the right parts and scripts. That's all. Please call whenever you want to, and we'll see you soon I'm sure.*

Something's Got to Give would also mark David Brown's debut as producer. He served as director of Fox's story department and was the husband of *Cosmopolitan* magazine's future editor, Helen Gurley Brown. Brown admired Marilyn and later told Donald Spoto that she was "a thorough professional, whatever her personal problems." He hired Arnold Schulman to adapt the original screenplay by Sam and Bella Spewack. "He was a great writer," Brown said in the documentary *Marilyn Monroe: The Final Days*, "but I was somewhat alarmed when I passed his office and saw that he had removed his desk, and was writing in a yoga position."

The film's prospective director, Frank Tashlin, had a string of successes with *Will Success Spoil Rock Hunter?* and several Jerry Lewis comedies for Paramount. However, Tashlin's name did not appear on Marilyn's list of approved directors, so Brown considered Italian director, Vittorio De Sica (1901-1974), whose masterpiece *The Bicycle Thief* (1948) earned an Academy Award as Best Foreign Film. Ultimately, George Cukor took the helm. Marilyn's contract contained Cukor's name on her list of directors, so she could not disapprove, but she vetoed his color film consultant. She also campaigned for Charles Lang Jr. as cinematographer but lost to Franz Planer (1894-1963) whose work included *Roman Holiday* (1953), *A Nun's Story* (1959), and *Breakfast at Tiffany's* (1961). *Something's Got to Give* would be Planer's last of one hundred-thirty films.

Brown pursued James Garner (born 1928) whose rugged good looks made him suitable for the role of Marilyn's husband, but she campaigned for Dean Martin. Before his success in *The Rockford Files* television series of the 1970s and *Victor/Victoria* (1982), Garner portrayed professional gambler Bret Maverick in the Western series *Maverick* from 1957 to 1960. On screen, he had co-stared with Brando in *Sayonara* (1957) and with Kim Novak in *Boys' Night Out*, not yet released. Garner's most recent film was the adaptation of Lillian Hellman's *The Children's Hour* (1961) with Audrey Hepburn and Shirley MacLaine about a spiteful student accusing two female teachers at a private girls' school of being involved in a lesbian relationship. Garner demanded $200,000, but Fox declined and cast Dean Martin for $300,000. Martin's production company, Claude Productions, would co-produce.

Since his friendship with Marilyn in the early 1950s, Dean Martin had ended his partnership with comic sidekick Jerry Lewis and took on dramatic roles in *The Young Lions* (1958) and *Some Came Running* (1958). Most recently, he costarred in a musical comedy, *Bells Are Ringing* (1960), an ensemble piece with his Rat Pack cronies, *Ocean's 11* (1960). Martin smooth voice and laid-back image made him a popular crooner, and his recording career on the Capitol Records label soared during the 1950s and early 1960s. His popular hits included "That's Amore," "Memories Are Made of This," "Volare," "Mambo Italiano," "Ain't That a Kick in the Head?" "Return to Me," and "Sway." Nick Arden's simultaneous marriage to two women made the role a good fit for Martin, whose image as a heavy drinker and womanizer afforded few roles as a devoted husband.

Four days before Christmas 1961, a copy of the script dated November 22 arrived in a brown envelope at Marilyn's apartment. Auctioned in 1999, the script by Arnold Schulman bore Marilyn's disapproving annotations in pencil: "*Not a story for MM*;" "*It's for a man and just any two girls*;" and "*Not funny.*" She made notes about modifying the plot so that her character does not chase after her newly remarried husband but instead manipulates him into chasing her. "*At one point in the story two women like each other but hate the man*," Marilyn scribbled, "*all the fags are going to love it.*"

On a revised script by Nunnally Johnson dated February 12, 1962, Marilyn writes: "*We've got a dog here—so we've got to look for impacts in a different way, or as Mr. [Nunnally] Johnson says, the situation.*" In annotations on another revised script, Marilyn relates Ellen's rage toward her husband for not telling his new wife that his first wife has returned to a song from My Fair Lady: "*I can do without you, or just you wait, Henry Higgins, just you wait.*" Instead of Johnson's scenario of Ellen banging on the wall of her husband's honeymoon suite to interrupt the consummation of his marriage to the new wife, Marilyn pencils her suggestion: "*She plays a record player very loud—and she does a twist and at certain beats in time with the music she bumps him against the wall/Ellen is getting tired her bumps are getting less enthusiastic and sad to put it mildly.*" Next to the lame line, "*You know the old saying—cast your broad upon the waters*," Marilyn writes, "*Not funny.*"

As writers modified the script, Marilyn remained cautious. On a script dated April 16, 1962, Marilyn inscribes comments alongside the scene between Ellen and her children: "*Too flat/it's painting black on black so to speak/We don't have to worry about Heart/I have one/Believe it or not/Either they have to trust me to play the scenes with heart or we are lost.*" Above the scene between Ellen and her crying son, she writes, "*sentimental schmaltz.*"

Much of the script's action takes place on production designer Gene Allen's set, a reproduction of George Cukor's six-acre estate and opulent pool at 9166 Cordell Drive in Beverly Hills, costing $100,000 (Marilyn's salary for the film). In 1935, Cukor had remodeled the home as an Italian villa with assistance from silent film star turned interior designer William "Billy" Haines. Openly gay, but nonetheless discreet, Cukor served as an unofficial leader of Hollywood's elite gay subculture and entertained closeted members of the film industry at legendary Sunday afternoon parties in his luxurious home. His guests brought along attractive young men they met at local bars and gyms. The parties often gravitated around the Roman-Greco pool, providing opportunities for many attractive and well-built gay men to gather in bathing suits.

Since the late 1950s, Cukor had been partnered with a considerably younger man, George Towers, and the two men lived together in the original version of the house that would be duplicated for Nick and Ellen Arden on Stage 14. Cukor posed for a photograph sitting in front of the replica of his home and pool, planning to use it as his Christmas greeting card but would scratch the idea as tasteless in the wake of Marilyn's death.

As crewmembers completed finishing work on the elaborate set, the studio made last-minute changes in the film's personnel to control its unpredictable star. At the urging of Dr. Greenson, executives removed David Brown and replaced him with Greenson's friend, Henry Weinstein. Both Greenson and Weinstein guaranteed Marilyn's punctuality contingent upon the change. The psychoanalyst haughtily told the executives there was no need to worry; he could get Marilyn to do whatever he wanted.

Marilyn may have not been aware of her psychoanalyst's influence as evidenced by her annotation on her of the script dated November 22: "*New producer...How come?*" Brown lost his first opportunity to produce but rebounded with great success in the ensuing decades. In 1972, he partnered with Richard Zanuck to create an independent production company and became the father of summer blockbuster films by producing *The Sting* (1973), *Jaws* (1975), *Cocoon* (1985), and *Driving Miss Daisy* (1989).

Henry Weinstein (1924-2000) was raised in Brooklyn, graduated from City College, and received a master's degree in drama from Carnegie Institute of Technology. He was a Broadway theater producer who had only one film under his belt, *Tender is the Night* (1962). When Marilyn arrived exhausted at Weinstein's office for a story conference estimated to last the entire afternoon, he offered her to lie down on his sofa. "You know, Henry," Marilyn replied, "you're the first producer to tell me to lie down for a rest and really mean it." Marilyn grew to trust Weinstein and frequently called his Beverly Hills home late at night. "Before you, Henry," she said, "it was just me against them."

Marilyn would find a similar ally in Nunnally Johnson, who was hired to rewrite Schulman's script. He had written *The Three Faces of Eve* and previously worked with Marilyn on *We're Not Married.* Johnson's wife, Dorris, was a public relations attaché for the Valmore Monette Corporation where DiMaggio was now employed. Remembering her refusal to accept Johnson's script, *How to Be Very, Very Popular*, and aware of his disparaging comments about her in the press, Marilyn felt the need to extend an olive branch to him. Johnson was touched by this act of humility from a big star and agreed to a meeting at the famed Polo Lounge of the Beverly Hills Hotel. She asked Johnson if he, too, had been "trapped" into the film.

Johnson disputed Marilyn's perception of the film as a trap and argued the merits of the script, eventually convincing her it was suitable material. Intrigued with his enthusiasm, Marilyn started suggesting changes in the script, and Johnson readily accepted them. She confided her need for a good role in a good film since her popularity had slipped since *Some Like It Hot.*

After three hours of lively brainstorming over three bottles of champagne, Johnson regretted having ever thought badly of Marilyn. He marveled at her humor and uncanny ability to identify weaknesses in the storyline. Marilyn suggested ideas for her character's adjustment to civilization such as eating with her hands and discarding of shoes since she went barefoot on the island. Most of all, Johnson recognized Marilyn's concern about Cukor's attitude toward her and her inability to veto his assignment because his name appeared on her list of directors.

At the end of the meeting, Johnson told Marilyn he was leaving for England in the morning. Marilyn requested to meet with him one last time before his early morning flight. Johnson consented but doubted she would show at the appointed time of 7:45 am. To his surprise, Marilyn arrived at promptly in lobby of the Beverly Hills Hotel. When the front desk staff declined her request to go to his room, she called him from the lobby. Johnson instructed Marilyn to announce that she was a call girl for whom he had summoned, and she begrudgingly complied. Marilyn was immediately permitted upstairs.

When Johnson opened his door, Marilyn stood before him without makeup, holding two bottles of Dom Perignon, and offered to take him to the airport in her chauffeured rented car in gratitude for being helpful to her. They chatted about the film during the entire ride to the airport, never opening a bottle of champagne. After arriving in London, Johnson wrote to his wife: "She was quick. She was gay. She probed certain aspects of the story with the sharpest of perceptions."

When Cukor learned of the meeting between Marilyn and Johnson, he resented this collaboration and demanded reversion to the original 1940 script. Cukor's contract stipulated script approval; Marilyn's did not. Although covertly hired to protect Marilyn's best interest, Weinstein conceded, and the studio hired Walter Bernstein, at Cukor's insistence, to change the dialogue. Weinstein had minimal experience as a producer, and Johnson warned that if he permitted the director to have power over a writer on the set, Weinstein would lose control of the film. Johnson's predictions would ring true.

Threatened, Marilyn invited Bernstein to her home to align with him. She served him tea and offered him the only chair in the room, sitting cross-legged on the floor in front of him. Bernstein would recall Marilyn as "perfectly pleasant" and "darling" when she erupted in "oohs" and "ahhs" when he introduced her to his infant son.

"There's no contest!" Marilyn insisted, because the story was a struggle between two women for the love of one man, and she was playing one of the women. Her self-confidence overflowed, but she wanted to protect her career from what she sensed as sabotage by Cukor. "Remember, you've got Marilyn Monroe," she advised Bernstein. "You've got to use her."

Bernstein dismissed many of Marilyn's suggestions but heeded the advice to take advantage of her sexual appeal. He added a scene with Ellen greeting her husband dressed in a negligee at the resort in Honolulu, another featuring her swimming nude in the family pool, and yet another in which she falls fully dressed in a pool and removes her wet clothes from under a sheet as Nick and Burkett watch.

By now, Fox spent nearly $400,000 on a recycled and heavily reworked script that still had no ending. This monumental waste of money seems ludicrous in light of the studio's dismal financial condition and demonstrates Fox's poor management. With Dean Martin secured as the leading man and his fellow Rat-Packer Frank Sinatra slated to sing the title song over the main titles, Fox searched for a second female lead who would not upstage their sexy star. Cast as Bianca Russell, Ellen's elegant but neurotic rival, Cyd Charisse (1922-2008) received $50,000 for her performance, half of Marilyn's salary.

Charisse had recovered from childhood polio to study ballet and dance across the screen with Fred Astaire and Gene Kelly in musicals such as *Singin' in the Rain* (1952), *The Band Wagon* (1953), *Brigadoon* (1954), and *Silk Stockings* (1957). Metro-Goldwyn-Mayer Studios reputedly insured her legs for one million dollars each, placing her in the Guinness Book of World Records for "Most Valuable Legs," but Charisse later said this claim was merely the invention of the studio's publicity department. In the 1980s, Charisse came out of retirement to perform in a music video with Janet Jackson. At the time the cameras rolled on Stage 14 at Fox, Charisse was age 40, four years older than Marilyn.

Before Fox cast Tom Tryon (1926-1991) in the role of Steven Burkett, Ellen's male companion on the island, he played the title role in the Disney television series *Texas John Slaughter* (1958-1961). Alfred Hitchcock had considered him for the role of Janet Leigh's lover, Sam Loomis, in *Psycho*, but passed in favor of John Gavin. Tryon and Dean Martin had recently worked together at Fox among an impressive ensemble cast in the World War II epic, *The Longest*

Day (1962), about the invasion of Normandy, scheduled for theatrical release in the fall. By the end of the decade, Tryon would retire and write mystery and suspense novels, successfully transitioning from handsome movie star to published author.

His best-known work is *The Other* (1971), about a boy whose evil twin brother is suspected of killing several residents in a small rural community. The novel was adapted as a film the following year. Tryon's other book, Harvest Home, was eventually adapted into *The Dark Secret of Harvest Home* (1978), a television mini-series starring Bette Davis. During the 1970s, Tryon was in a longtime romantic relationship with Clive Clerk, the interior designer who had decorated Tryon's Manhattan apartment and one of the original cast members of *A Chorus Line.* Later, Tryon was involved in a relationship with Calvin Culver, also known as Casey Donovan, a star of gay pornography.

Marilyn passionately campaigned for comedic actor Wally Cox (1924-1973) over Don Knotts in the role of the meek shoe salesman who Ellen attempts to pass as her companion on the island. Knotts had recently achieved both notoriety and an Emmy Award as the bug-eyed, anxiety-ridden deputy, Barney Fife, in CBS's hit comedy series, *The Andy Griffith Show.* Cox and Marilyn shared a mutual friend in Marlon Brando. In fact, Cox had been Brando's roommate, and Brando encouraged him to study acting with Stella Adler. Cox performed in early television comedy-variety programs between 1949 and 1951, culminating to national stardom in a starring role as a well-meaning but bumbling policeman on *Philco Television Playhouse* in 1951. In death, Cox's ashes would be mingled with those of Brando before being scattered in Death Valley, California.

As the insurance adjuster who informs Nick Arden that his wife was stranded on the island with a muscular male companion, Phil Silvers (1911-1985) was a two-time Tony Award-winning comedian of the stage and screen. Best known for starring in *The Phil Silvers Show*, a 1950s situation comedy set on an Army post in which he played Sergeant Bilko. Silvers contributed to the show's three consecutive Emmy Awards as Outstanding Comedy Series.

Steve Allen (1921-2000), cast as Bianca's psychiatrist, Dr. Herman Schlick, was a television personality, musician, and comedian who first hosted *The Tonight Show* from 1954 to 1957 on NBC, and pioneered the concept of the television "talk show." He hosted numerous game and variety shows, including *The Steven Allen Show, I've Got a Secret, The New Steve Allen Show,* and was a regular panel member on *What's My Line?*

For owl-faced character actor John Irwin McGiver (1913-1975), the brief role as the judge in *Something's Got to Give* would be one of his five film performances in 1962 along with *Period of Adjustment, The Manchurian Candidate, Who's Got the Action?* and *Mr. Hobbs Takes a Vacation.* He would make more than a hundred appearances in television and motion pictures over a two-decade span beginning in 1955. Most notable was the part of the gracious salesman who accommodates Audrey Hepburn's meager $10 budget by suggesting to her a gold plated telephone dialer in *Breakfast at Tiffany's* (1961).

Fox borrowed the film's title from a popular song written and composed by Johnny Mercer for Fred Astaire and featured in the Fox musical *Daddy Long Legs* (1955). The lyrics use a principle in physics: an irresistible force meets an immovable object, as a metaphor for a relationship between an effervescent young woman and an older, reserved man. The song mirrors the plot of the film in which Astaire portrays a reserve, older man attracted to a younger woman, Leslie Caron. Strangely, the scenario does not reflect the plot of the Monroe-Martin screenplay.

When the Monroe film was incomplete and shelved, its title would be used in a 2003 film starring Jack Nicholson and Diane Keaton. In this version, an aged music industry executive with a penchant for younger women suffers a heart attack in the home of his younger trophy girlfriend's mother. Under the care of a woman closer to his age, the executive falls in love with her and creates an awkward love triangle. All ends well when the trophy girlfriend falls in love with a man closer to her age. If she had lived to become an older actress, Marilyn would have been suitable in Keaton's role.

Chapter Eighteen: January 1962

The optimism of the Kennedy era exploded in 1962 with the Space Race, Civil Rights Movement, and emerging youth culture. It was a romantic period of colossal creative expression, hope, and style in America. Post-war economic prosperity prevailed, the Vietnam War had not yet polarized the younger and middle-age generations, and the tremendous cultural changes that would mark the end of the decade had not yet shaken the country. This would also be the last calendar year of Marilyn's life.

A beautiful new female face from the East Coast now competed with Marilyn and Elizabeth Taylor for magazine covers. At age 32, First Lady Jacqueline Bouvier Kennedy (1928-1994) was the youngest wife of a president to occupy the White House. She had attended Vassar College, the University of Grenoble, the Sorbonne in Paris, George Washington University, and Georgetown University. Poised and eloquent, with finishing school refinement, she spoke in a whispery, Monroe-like voice filtered through a New England accent. By winning *Vogue* magazine's Prix de Paris contest, Kennedy served as junior editor in Paris. Subsequently, she was employed as the Inquiring Camera Girl for the *Washington Times-Herald*, photographing and interviewing local citizens on topics that became increasingly more political.

As the mother of a four-year-old daughter, Caroline, and toddler, John Jr., Jacqueline Kennedy brought youth and vitality into the White House. Born in Southampton to an affluent Wall Street stock-broker and his French-Anglo-descendant wife, Kennedy revolutionized taste, promoted culture and arts, and embarked upon well-received goodwill tours abroad. Upon her and the President's return from

Europe, JFK proudly announced, "I am the man who accompanied Jacqueline Kennedy to Paris." Jacqueline also redefined fashion for modern young women with her suits designed by Oleg Cassini in bright solid colors like pink, red, yellow, and pistachio. She also wore pillbox hats, A-line dresses, and Capri slacks. Her style was mass-produced for the average woman. At the 1962 Manhattan Easter's Parade, the press reported on mobs of women dressed like her on the street, but young women across the nation and around the world looked to Kennedy for more than just her sleek wardrobe and hairstyles; the President's wife served as a role model for the modern woman.

In 1962, women's issues only simmered beneath the veneer of the traditional, domesticated female role paved by the Eisenhower era. Betty Freidan (1921-2006) had been conducting a survey of her former Smith College classmates fifteen years after their graduation and discovered a widespread pattern of unhappiness with their lives as housewives which she coined "the problem that has no name." She interviewed other suburban homemakers and mothers as she researched the impact of psychology, the media, and advertising on women's roles; publishing her findings in the groundbreaking book, *The Feminine Mystique*, early the following year.

Before the Civil Rights Movement, the Modern Women's Movement, and the Equal Opportunity Act, it was a "man's world." The centrality of both the nuclear family and post-war economic prosperity of the early 1960s placed married men as sole-breadwinners with supreme social and political authority. These were the last days of the traditionally dominant narrative of American life being based on white, heterosexual males and exclusion of women, nonwhites, and gays. *Playboy* magazine romanticized a swinging bachelor lifestyle characterized by cool cocktails, sports cars, Space Age bachelor pads, and plenty of no-strings-attached sex. No group of men better exemplified the playboy archetype than Frank Sinatra and his Rat Pack cronies.

Fashion for men also evolved during the Kennedy Era by borrowing from the smolderingly seductive European role models who replaced John Wayne's cowboy archetype. American men began emulating Italian actor Marcello Mastroianni, as men's suits became more tight fitting. Influenced by Italian designers, the new look was a single-breasted, two-button suit with short tailored jacket and narrow lapels worn with a narrow-collared shirt and thin tie; the shorter jackets were originally designed not to touch the seat of Vespa or Lambretta motor scooters, the main mode of transportation for stylish and affluent men living in Rome and Milan. Fashionable young American men also wore narrow pants with pointed-toe "winklepicker" shoes. Crew cuts and longer hair slicked back with oil and gel were now standard.

Sherri Finkbine, a thirty-year-old mother, decided to terminate her fifth pregnancy after discovering that tranquilizers she had taken in the first few weeks after conception contained the drug Thalidomide known for causing severe fetal deformities such as missing limbs, deafness and blindness. As the hostess of a Phoenix children's television program, *Romper Room*, Finkbine became the focus of an intense anti-abortion campaign and received worldwide public condemnation.

In the Space Race, Lieutenant Colonial John H. Glenn (born 1921) became the first American to orbit the Earth on February 20. He did so three times in four hours, fifty-five minutes. AT&T's Telstar, the world's first commercial communications satellite, was launched into orbit and activated transmission of global television, telephone, facsimile, and photography at high speed for the approaching Information Age.

In Hollywood, Peter O'Toole starred as T. E. Lawrence in the Columbia Pictures film that would win the 1962 Best Picture Oscar, *Lawrence of Arabia*. Anne Bancroft was portraying Annie Sullivan opposite Patty Duke as Helen Keller in United Artists' adaptation of *The Miracle Worker*. At Warner Brothers Studios, Mervyn LeRoy was directing Natalie Wood as Gypsy Rose Lee and Rosalind Russell as Momma Rose in *Gypsy*. At Universal Studios, Gregory Peck was filming the adaptation of *To Kill A Mockingbird* while Doris Day and Cary Grant were making *That Touch of Mink*. The buzz on the Fox lot concentrated on the new Monroe-Martin comedy being produced by a studio newcomer, Henry Weinstein.

* * *

On Saturday, January 20, Weinstein and his wife invited Marilyn to their home at North Rexford Drive along with Carl Sandburg and another couple. In Arnold Newman's photographs taken that evening, Marilyn appears somewhat disheveled in a magenta Pucci sheath with matching sheer kerchief covering her unstyled hair. She sat beside Sandburg on the sofa, both sipping champagne and engrossed in conversation. In Newman's photos, Sandburg's elderly, weathered face is juxtaposed with Marilyn's youthful, smooth skin, but their connection is evident despite the disparity in ages. "There is something naïve and lovely about her," Sandburg said, "and yet, there is a sagacity there."

Marilyn and Sandburg resumed where they had left off in New York in December. "Marilyn was a good talker," he said. "There were realms of science, politics and economics in which she wasn't at home, but she spoke well on the national scene, the Hollywood scene, and on people who are good to know and people who ain't...She never talked about her husbands." At one point, she rested her head on his shoulder like a young granddaughter expressing love to her grandfather. They engaged in some mock playacting and even danced together.

As the evening progressed, Sandburg prescribed and demonstrated to Marilyn and Henry's wife a series of exercises to alleviate insomnia. Marilyn kicked off her pumps and mirrored the poet's movements, stretching toward the ceiling and crouching close to the floor. Marilyn then led Weinstein's wife and the other couple in a group line dance, possibly from a Broadway musical. Henry watched and later joined in Marilyn's merriment. "The bigger the people are or the simpler the people are, the more they are not awed by you," Marilyn would tell *Life*. "They don't feel they have to be offensive, they don't have to insult you. You can meet Carl Sandburg, and he is so pleased to meet you. He wants to know about you, and you want to know about him. Not in any way has he let me down." "There were no pretenses about Marilyn Monroe...." Sandburg would tell *Look* magazine shortly after her death. "She had a genuine quality. She was good to know offstage."

While Sandburg's platonic companionship delighted Marilyn, her romantic bond with an ex-husband deepened after Frank Sinatra had become engaged to Juliet Prowse, whom he had originally met on the set of *Can Can*. A two-page note from Joe DiMaggio on Hotel Lexington stationery dated January 27 and addressed to "Miss Marge Stengel," Marilyn's pseudonym on Doheny Drive, cites the couple's continued intimacy following their cozy holiday celebration. Auctioned by Christie's in 2007, it references the first American to orbit the Earth aboard *Friendship 7*:

A beautiful Saturday morning for New York, and no place to go, but to sit back on my desk and scribble you a note. Shouldn't that be proof enough where my thoughts are? There's so much going 'on' this quiet morning, like the hot water for the tea, radio etc. The report on the radio now says that the astronaut [John Glenn] will not attempt the orbital flight until Thursday or Friday. Fog and broken clouds were the reasons for this morning's cancellation. It must be tough on the astronaut's nerves, being all set to go and the last minute to be cancelled out—and knowing it still has to be attempted...I just remembered I have an appointment with my accountant this afternoon. And me in my robe, not shaved or bathed. Guess my opening line about this being a note was not exaggerated. However, I'll drop you another note tonight. Forgiven for the "shorty"? You sound great on the phone. Keep yourself well!

Marilyn also received a letter from syndicated personal advice columnist Ann Landers, real name Esther Pauline Friedman Lederer (1918-2002), indicating a friendship between the two. Under the pen name Abigail Van Buren, Landers' twin sister, Pauline Esther Friedman wrote a similar advice column titled "Dear Abby." Dated January 24, the letter would be auctioned by Bonhams in 2005:

Just read where you are back in Hollywood. Since I haven't seen or heard from you in so long a time—naturally wondering how you are. Am sorry I wasn't able to be with you on your last picture but my husband had a stroke at that time and was afraid to leave him. Would like very much to talk to you in person but don't know how to reach you by phone—If you care to call me my number is still TH5-4823. If you make another film in Hollywood I hope I can be with you again. Wishing you a happy and prosperous 1962. With kindest regards and warm wishes.

On February 10, Willy Rizzo photographed a casual Marilyn lounging poolside at Frank Sinatra's luxurious leased house in the

Chatsworth district of the San Fernando Valley. Commissioned by Chase Manhattan Bank heiress Dora Hutchinson and designed by the architectural firm of Pereira & Luckman (responsible for the Los Angeles International Airport), the steel and glass house provided an ultramodern backdrop for Rizzo's shoot. With her hair teased high and wearing white Capri slacks, a lavender Pucci blouse—later given to Joan Greenson—and a similar one in tangerine, Marilyn posed on patio furniture and sprawled on cushions on the pool deck. She applied her make-up herself and appeared somewhat weary in this third attempt to complete the session. "Marilyn was immensely sad," Rizzo would recall. "And that sadness was very visible on the pictures."

The grandson of a Neapolitan magistrate, Rizzo (1928-2013) had been an artistic director for *Paris Match* and now served as the French magazine's photographic correspondent. He wanted to capture Marilyn in the morning light, but Patricia Newcomb nixed this suggestion and scheduled the session in the afternoon. On the day of their appointment, Newcomb called to apologize for Marilyn's inability to attend, as she was not feeling well. They rescheduled for the following afternoon, but Marilyn arrived late at six o'clock in the evening. "I'm really sorry, I'm so tired," she said in a face-to-face apology and gave him a peck on the cheek. "I'll be here tomorrow, I promise." Rizzo replied, "For you, I would wait a week." His informal portraits appeared five months later in the French magazine's June 23, 1962 issue.

There was another man willing to wait for Marilyn—one far more powerful. Presidential aides invited her to join John Fitzgerald Kennedy in Manhattan for a black-tie, thousand-dollar per plate political fundraiser at the Park Avenue penthouse apartment of Fifi Fell, the widow of a prominent investment banker, John Randolph Fell. Some sources claim the fundraiser took place in early December 1961, coinciding with Marilyn's visit with Carl Sandburg, when Kennedy attended the National Football Foundation and Hall of Fame at Waldorf-Astoria Hotel and received the organization's gold medal for his promotion of the role of athletics. Other sources place the event in February or April of 1962. This may have been Kennedy and Marilyn's first or second meeting. Many sources place their introduction at the Lawford beach house in the autumn of 1961.

Milton Ebbins, joined with David Powers, the presidential aide, were charged with the uneasy feat of getting Marilyn to arrive on time. Ebbins recounted to J. Randy Taraborrelli helping Marilyn slip into a skin-tight black gown in the bedroom of the Fifty-Seventh Street Apartment and sneaking her disguised into Mrs. Fell's building. Ebbins and Powers failed in their national mission to deliver Kennedy's date on time. "When she walked in, Christ Almighty, it was like the parting of the Red Sea," Ebbins said. "There were about twenty-five people in there, and the crowd divided into halves as she walked through the room." According to actress Arlene Dahl, a guest at the event, Kennedy greeted Marilyn with a big smile. "Finally! You're here!" he said. "There are some people here who are dying to meet you." Dahl would recall: "Then she was descended upon. People just wanted to stand near her, smell her fragrance, breathe the same air as she."

During this fundraiser, the President allegedly invited Marilyn to join him in Palm Springs in March. Sidney Skolsky, who remained Marilyn's confidante in Los Angeles, knew about their close relationship, and she told him the president was going to invite her to a dinner at the White House in March. Marilyn planned to bring Skolsky as her escort. "She was overjoyed with this bit of news," Skolsky would write in his 1975 memoir. "I couldn't help wondering whether she nurtured a fantasy of visiting a room in the White House other than a dining room with the President."

At the age of forty-three, the thirty-fifth president was the youngest elected to the office, and the second-youngest president (after Theodore Roosevelt who became president following William McKinley's assassination), and the first president to have been born in the 20th century. Kennedy was also the first Catholic president, and is the only president to have won a Pulitzer Prize (for *Profiles in Courage* in 1957).

Kennedy entered Harvard in 1936. While playing football on the junior varsity team, Kennedy ruptured a disk in his spine and continued to have back pain the remainder of his life. This would not be his only serious injury. After graduating, Kennedy joined the Navy and was assigned to the Solomon Islands in the South Pacific as commander of a patrol torpedo boat *PT-109*. On August 2, 1943, a Japanese warship rammed *PT-109*, splitting it in two and killing two men. Seriously injured, Kennedy managed to jump into the water and swam off to find survivors while the boat sank in flames. Clinging to a piece of the boat, he led the surviving crew to an island several miles away and later received a Purple Heart for his injuries and the Navy and Marine Corps Medal for heroic conduct.

After military service, Kennedy represented Massachusetts's 11th congressional district in the United States House of Representatives as a Democrat from 1947 to 1953. Subsequently, he was elected to the United States Senate and served from 1953 until 1960. In September 1953, Senator Kennedy married Jacqueline Bouvier, a writer for the *Washington Times-Herald*, in Newport, Rhode Island. The couple's daughter, Caroline, was born in 1957. A son, John, Jr., followed after Kennedy won the 1960 presidential election.

Kennedy was also an attractive and athletic man with a long list of paramours. Nancy Dickerson, who dated Kennedy when he was a bachelor and before she became NBC's first female news anchor, wrote in her memoir, *Among Those Present*: "Sex to Jack Kennedy was like another cup of coffee, or maybe dessert." His father, Joseph Kennedy, modeled extramarital interest in actresses. In *Swanson on Swanson*, silent screen star Gloria Swanson claimed having an affair with the patriarch during his business trips to Hollywood while his wife, Rose, at home in Massachusetts. Marilyn idealized the President as an epic hero, another Lincoln—not a womanizer—who would change history.

CHAPTER NINETEEN: *CURSUM PERFICIO*: FEBRUARY 1962

In a haunting inscription in a guest book at a reception, beside her name, in the column marked for addresses, Marilyn wrote, "*Nowhere.*" The inscription reveals Marilyn's lack of emotional grounding since childhood. "To put it bluntly, I seem to have a whole superstructure with no foundation" she would insightfully tell journalist Alan Levy. "But I'm working on the foundation..."

Perhaps one of the definitive testaments of Marilyn Monroe's modest nature, simple tastes, and spirituality was her selection of a home in which to settle at age thirty-five. Having lived a nomadic lifestyle since birth, Marilyn sought permanence and stability through the purchase of a property at 12305 Fifth Helena Drive in Brentwood, Los Angeles. It was the first home she owned independent of a husband. While many motion picture celebrities of Marilyn's stature indulged in ostentatious mansions in Beverly Hills, Marilyn chose to nest in a snug Spanish Colonial residence in upscale Brentwood, befitting an upper middle class professional.

"She was not the usual movie idol," said poet Carl Sandburg. "There was something democratic about her. Why, she was the type who would join in and wash the supper dishes even if you didn't ask her." Daniel Greenson agreed: "In no way was she put on or artificial, she had real warmth."

A stable home environment had evaded Marilyn throughout her childhood. Settling down in this house in adulthood empowered her to correct the past by recreating it. She described the house as a "fortress where I can feel safe from the world." Following Marilyn's death, the house on Fifth Helena Drive has grown to symbolize her unfulfilled dreams and unfinished life, just as the sparsely-furnished home itself was still in need of some restoration at the time of Marilyn's sudden, unexpected death.

The genesis of Marilyn's plans to ground and center herself through the purchase of a home is hypothesized by her legion of biographers. According to Fred Lawrence Guiles, Marilyn's purchase may have been motivated by the dissolution of her five-year marriage to Arthur Miller and a personal choice to channel her energies into becoming a more independent single woman.

Marilyn retained the apartment in New York where she preferred to reside, but her motion picture career summoned her to the West Coast. The efficiency apartment on Doheny Drive afforded only a transient lifestyle and little opportunity to establish roots. Her purchase of the Brentwood home has been interpreted as a woman taking control of her life. However, Donald Spoto suggests that Dr. Greenson attempted to control his famous patient by instructing her to buy a house and hire as a housekeeper the woman who had once owned Greenson's home. Spoto also hypothesizes that the 59-year-old housekeeper, Eunice Murray, vicariously lived her own domestic fantasies through Marilyn. Greenson recommended that Marilyn settle in a neighborhood in proximity to his own, and Murray previewed properties situated just a few blocks from the Greensons' residence, where Marilyn attended daily treatment sessions in the doctor's study.

"The doctor thought the house would take the place of a baby or a husband, and that it would protect her," Murray later said. In 1966, Greenson recalled, "I encouraged her to buy the house. She said she had no interest in remaining in California or making it her residence. She said that after her next picture she would go back to New York, which she considered her permanent home." Stand-in Evelyn Moriarty recalled Marilyn explaining that Murray and Greenson talked her into buying the house.

Murray's memoir, *Marilyn: The Last Months*, chronicled the journey from Marilyn's first interest in a home to her death in meticulous detail. Mrs. Murray's version begins with her driving Marilyn in a green 1957 Dodge Coronet along a tree-lined residential street. Marilyn surprised her by making a rare, direct request, "Mrs. Murray, would you find me a house? I want to find a Mexican house...as much like Dr. Greenson's as possible. Would you help me?" Mrs.

Murray stated she would be delighted to assist.

Murray described Marilyn's house hunting as a discreet mission to locate an authentic hacienda remindful of the Greenson home. Marilyn initially preferred a property with a view of the Pacific Ocean, but her budget prohibited such extravagance. She was drawn to the view of the water visible from her psychiatrist's home and from the mammoth beachfront home of the Lawfords.

In *Why Norma Jean Murdered Marilyn Monroe*, author Lucy Freeman described Greenson's home as both a design masterpiece and Marilyn's inspiration, based upon interviews with the psychiatrist's widow, Hilde, and their daughter, Joan. The Monterey-style Spanish Colonial home, with a second-story cantilevered balcony, was set high atop a hill on Franklin Street near the Brentwood Country Club and Golf Course. The home had a rear waterfront view of both the Pacific Palisades and the ocean a few miles west. The paneled living room, adorned with a hand-hewn beamed ceiling and lined with bookcases, occupied nearly half the first floor. An antique wooden table was centered in front of the huge fireplace embellished with hand painted tiles imported from Mexico. These colorful tiles, many set by Mrs. Murray, extended low along the living room walls and also enlivened the kitchen.

Murray scheduled clandestine appointments for Marilyn to view prospective properties with borrowed keys from real estate agents. On occasion, Patricia Newcomb would come along to view a home and offer feedback. In her last interview with *Life* magazine, Marilyn recalled the hostility of one owner who demanded that she leave the premises upon learning Marilyn's identity. Murray writes that in late January 1962, a real estate agent suggested a house in Brentwood as he ended his business day. The agent provided directions to a cozy 2,300 square foot home at the end of a cul-de-sac named Fifth Helena Drive near San Vicente Boulevard and Carmelina Drive.

Murray followed the directions and discovered the L-shaped home tucked behind a large gate and whitewashed brick wall covered by blooming bougainvillea vines. The red barrel tiled roof of the garage was visible above the seven-foot wall. Inside the gate, a red brick driveway led to a garage. Attached to the garage, on the right, was a guesthouse. This structure was separated from the kitchen in the main house by a walled garden. The kitchen formed the short leg of the residence's L-shape. The remainder of the main house was perpendicular to the kitchen and set behind a lawn with a flagstone path leading to the front door.

Surrounded by a high wall, the three-bedroom, two-bath home was private and secluded. It featured lush gardens, a swimming pool, a small, detached guesthouse, and a garage. A motion picture studio accountant built the house in 1929 on an acre of rolling lawn with a sloping rear view overlooking the valley below. Its Spanish Colonial architecture boasted cathedral beamed ceilings, arched doorways, textured adobe stucco walls, and deep-sill Spanish windows. The living room windows had their own little roofs and iron gratings. Step-up entrances created levels and interesting architectural detailing.

Murray waited patiently for the current owners to locate their real estate agent so that she might tour the interior. She heard the cries of a baby and sounds of children playing inside. Once inside, Mrs. Murray stepped up from the entryway into a wide living room featuring a fireplace and glass doors opening to the swimming pool. She stepped up again through an arched entrance to a hallway to the right of the living room that led to three bedrooms. The master bedroom faced the home's front, and included a kiva fireplace in the corner and an en suite bath. Behind the master bedroom were two smaller bedrooms adjoined by a bathroom. As many homes built during the Great Depression, closet space was limited. Mrs. Murray noticed the interior's natural lighting provided by many casement windows and exterior glass doors.

Continuing to explore this charming home, Murray grew excited by its potential. To the left of the living room was a small dining room sandwiched between a kitchen in front and a sunroom toward the rear. The glass-enclosed sunroom, marred by an unattractive heating system, led outside to the pool. Outside, eucalyptus trees, hillocks of baby's breath, and German moss grew on the long, narrow lot and a coastal breeze blew from the Pacific Ocean.

Murray quickly arranged to secure the key for Marilyn's private viewing while the family was away. Murray later remembered Marilyn's first reaction to the home. Marilyn studied and memorized the home's every detail, brick by brick. She liked that the home had the feel of being lived in by several generations. Its simplicity, privacy and sturdy construction earned Marilyn's approval. Most of all, Marilyn found comfort in the property's inconspicuousness and the inscription on the front doorstep.

"There's a six- or eight-foot wall for privacy," she told photographer George Barris, "and my mailbox has no name on it, but the mailman knows who lives here. I don't know if you noticed there are fourteen red stone squares leading to my front door, where there is a ceramic tile coat of arms with the motto *Cursum Perficio*, meaning 'end of my journey.' I hope it's true...It's small, but I find it rather cozy that way. It's quiet and peaceful—just what I need right now."

While the Latin inscription foreshadowed events to come, Marilyn continued to live in the moment, inspired to decorate the outdated kitchen and baths with bright, colorful Mexican tiles similar to those in the Greenson home. She planned to reproduce the warm feeling of her psychiatrist's kitchen, where she had enjoyed family gatherings and domestic routine. Marilyn saw beyond the contemporary furnishings, unimaginative decor, and unsightly exposed heating system. She envisioned the thirty-year old home restored to its original, authentic Spanish colonial ambiance. Outside, Marilyn visualized a wooden platform terrace with seats constructed under a shade tree at the end of the sloped backyard. Intrigued, Marilyn sought DiMaggio's advice.

Joe accompanied Marilyn and Mrs. Murray to view the property and to offer his opinion. Mrs. Murray later recalled DiMaggio lowering his head in the car as they drove into the neighborhood to avoid being recognized by residents. He also wished to prevent rumors of house-hunting with his former wife due to the fact that throughout the previous year, the media speculated about a reconciliation and remarriage. After receiving positive feedback from DiMaggio, Marilyn had background checks completed on the neighbors and learned one was a university professor. After her death, neighbor Abe Landau told an interviewer that the community was excited about Marilyn's presence and watched the studio limousine whisk her down the streets in the mornings.

Other neighbors, the John and Joan Maucieri family on Dunoon Drive, would share with Mrs. Murray memories of their famous neighbor's curiosity about them. The back of the Maucieri home buttressed the rear of Marilyn's property. On the morning of Joan's birthday, the family celebrated by having a brunch made by the young daughters on the patio. They noticed Marilyn, in a red kimono, standing on the hill at the edge of her property quietly watching them. The Maucieri family chose not to acknowledge her. Embarrassed, Marilyn slowly walked up the hill toward her home. The family later wished they had asked her to join them.

Another neighbor on Third Helena Drive was Hanna Fenichel, a prominent psychoanalyst and educator known for her work in the field of early child development and association with the School for Nursery Years in Los Angeles. She was also active in the Marxist faction of the Psychoanalytic Institute and a friend of Dr. Greenson's. Marilyn had met her several times at Sunday afternoon chamber music receptions at the Greenson home.

With the neighbors' backgrounds cleared, Marilyn sought spiritual validation. She called psychic Kenny Kingston in San Francisco and requested his blessing. "I felt uncomfortable as we drove to the end of the cul-de-sac," he would recall. "But Marilyn was like an excited child. There were too many trees that cast ominous shadows on the property and I felt it would further her depression." At that point, not even metaphysical persuasion could stop her.

Marilyn purchased the home on lot twenty, tract number 5462 for $75,500 from William and Aileen Doris Pagen who, along with their children, had outgrown it. She made a down payment of $42,500 and qualified for a fifteen-year mortgage in the amount of $37,335.78 at six and one-half percent interest with the City National Bank of Beverly Hills. Marilyn used as collateral her 1963 deferred salary payment of $100,000 from her ten-percent share of *Some Like It Hot*. Monthly payments of $320 would commence on March 1, 1962. If Marilyn remained in the home and continued the payments at the mortgage's rate, the loan would be paid in 1977, when she would be age fifty.

Marilyn's new attorney Milton Rudin, Greenson's brother-in-law, drew up the sales contract. He also transferred Marilyn's professional representation from MCA to his own firm. In her Doheny Drive apartment, Marilyn hesitated before signing the escrow papers and excused herself to the bedroom, where she cried. "I could never imagine buying a home alone," Marilyn told journalist Alan Levy. "But I've always been alone, so why couldn't I imagine it?"

The Los Angeles that greeted Marilyn in 1962 sharply contrasted with the Los Angeles of her youth and with her concurrent metropolitan lifestyle in Manhattan. The population of Los Angeles had soared to about six million. Asphalt bands of seemingly endless freeways carried high-volume traffic through the smog-clouded city spotted by neon-lighted hamburger stands and coffee shops resembling spaceships. In the Hollywood Hills, a futuristic octagon-shaped dwelling was sandwiched between Mediterranean-style estates once built by silent film stars. Through its Case Study House program, *Arts & Architecture* magazine had purchased sites and commissioned architects to demonstrate innovative structural and design concepts. The twenty-eight homes resulting from this competition brought modern motif and relaxed living to this city of sunshine and motion picture stars.

Brentwood is neither a township nor city, but a section of West Los Angeles located in the foothills of the Santa Monica Mountains. It is bordered in the north by Mount St. Mary's College, in the south by the Brentwood Country Club, in the east by the University of California Los Angeles, and in the west by Topanga State Park. The hills and canyons that comprise Brentwood were once part of the land grant made by Juan Alvarado, Governor of the California, to Francisco Sepulveda in 1839. The 48,000 acres, titled Rancho San Vicente y Santa Monica, eventually became the communities of Brentwood and Santa Monica.

Motion picture actors, seeking a relatively anonymous lifestyle, purchased estates in Brentwood and avoided the spotlight of tour buses cruising the streets of Beverly Hills. Actress Joan Crawford resided in a Georgian-style mansion on Bristol Avenue in Brentwood Heights from the 1930s until 1956 and Gary Cooper, Ida Lupino, and their respective spouses had resided there as well. By 1962, Brentwood had evolved into a prominent community. Upscale shops, restaurants, and businesses dominated San Vicente Boulevard, between Barrington Avenue and Bundy Drive, creating a pedestrian-friendly commercial village.

Brentwood Country Mart reigned as the area's commercial anchor. Opened in November 1948 at 26th Street and San Vicente Boulevard, the Mart contained many shops along its winding walkways and brick courtyards. Its rural architecture, reminiscent of a red barn, and green awnings suggested a miniature version of the famous Farmer's Market located on Fairfax Avenue. Marilyn's rented Cadillac limousine and uniformed driver would be seen parked outside the Mart as she shopped inside wearing dark sunglasses and a brunette wig beneath a silk kerchief.

Enveloped in a womb of privacy, minutes away from the doctor who guided her, and in close proximity to her employer, Marilyn became a resident in a community distanced from the nightlife of the Sunset Strip and the pretension of Beverly Hills. She was now a practical, maturing lady seeking quiet and stability. If the formula for success in real estate is adhering to the mantra "location, location, location," Marilyn was poised for a wise investment. On a personal level, this was the first home she owned independent of a husband, and it had no connection to painful memories or past marriages. The house was a clean canvas for the life she wished to create.

CHAPTER TWENTY: ROBERT F. KENNEDY

While Marilyn bravely purchased a modest home as a single woman and planned its restoration, another public figure prepared to reveal the results of an extensive restoration of a grand, historic residence. On Valentine's Day 1962, three out of four television viewers watched First Lady Jacqueline Kennedy give a tour of the newly refurbished interior of the White House. As the first primetime documentary targeted to a female audience and featuring voice-over narration by a woman, the First Lady's tour became the most widely viewed documentary during the early years of television.

Soon after the inauguration in 1961, the First Lady cringed at the White House's lack of authenticity. Gutted and structurally rebuilt within its exterior shell during the Truman administration, the presidential mansion was decorated with reproduction furnishings and contemporary fabrics. Jacqueline Kennedy's education and cultured background inspired her to elevate the residence to a historical showpiece for the nation. Using her power to have the White House declared a national museum, the First Lady successfully raised funds and solicited donations of authentic American furnishings and period pieces.

Author Michael Curtin explored the significance of the First Lady's public unveiling of her project in the changing role of women in the early 1960s. "The final product..." Curtin writes, "effectively represents changing attitudes about the public and private roles of American women." Although Jacqueline Kennedy appeared traditionally domestic in her role as a guide, she actually narrated the tour and educated the public on the historical significance of the furnishings and art. Broadcast correspondent Charles Collingswood's role was secondary as he frequently walked out of frame, permitting the First Lady to speak directly to the viewers. Only at end of the tour when President Kennedy appeared did she regress to a subordinate role as wife and mother.

Little is known of Marilyn's impression of Jacqueline Kennedy, but two weeks before the White House tour, Marilyn had met the First Lady's brother-in-law and would document her positive impression of him in letters to Arthur Miller's family. Despite the many differences in their backgrounds and careers, Marilyn and Robert Kennedy shared similar social and political values and supported liberal causes. They were also only six and one-half months apart in age, and both had enormous charisma and self-deprecating senses of humor that made them disarming to others and to each other.

In 1960, Robert Francis Kennedy (1925-1968) published the book *The Enemy Within*, describing his investigation into corruption within the Teamsters, a trade union for truck drivers and warehouse workers, and its connection to organized crime. Now the Attorney General of the United States under his brother's administration, Kennedy came to Los Angeles to discuss Budd Schulberg's adaptation of his book into a motion picture and planned to visit the Lawfords. Kennedy's wife, Ethel, allegedly wanted to meet Marilyn and believed she should portray her in the film adaptation of *The Enemy Within.* "I think she's underrated," Ethel allegedly said according to the research of J. Randy Taraborrelli. "I think she's done some very good work and I'd be honored to have her play me in the movie."

After graduating from Harvard University, Kennedy earned a law degree from the University of Virginia. He served in the United States Navy at the end of World War II, but was never called into action. In 1950, Kennedy married Ethel Skakel who gave birth to thirteen children, the youngest born six months after Robert's assassination. Senator Joseph McCarthy appointed him as an assistant counsel to the Senate subcommittee on investigations in 1953, but he soon resigned. After McCarthy's fall from power, Kennedy rejoined the Senate's permanent subcommittee on investigations and served as chief counsel and staff director. When his aggressive interrogation of Teamster President James Hoffa was televised in 1957, Kennedy achieved wide public attention.

Nine months into his term as United States Attorney General, Kennedy faced challenges of the civil rights movement. In May, the Congress on Racial Equality (CORE) had begun to organize Freedom Rides in an attempt to end segregation in the transportation system in the South, and to test the president's commitment to civil rights. An interracial group would board a bus destined for a Southern city. White activists would sit in the rear, and African-American activists in the front. At rest stops, the white activists would gather in the areas designated only for blacks, and the African-Americans would do the same in areas clearly marked for "white only." When angry mobs in Alabama and Mississippi targeted the Freedom Riders with assault or threatened them with violence, Robert Kennedy intervened with local officials to provide protection.

On Thursday, February 1, Peter and Patricia Lawford invited Marilyn to meet Robert Kennedy along with Judy Garland, Gene Kelly, Tony Curtis, Janet Leigh, Kim Novak, Dean Martin, and Angie Dickenson. By most accounts, Ethel did not attend this Hollywood reception in her husband's honor. Marilyn turned to Daniel Greenson as she prepared for an introduction to the Attorney General. Together they outlined questions about the increase of troops in Vietnam, the House Un-American Activities Committee, civil rights, and J. Edgar Hoover. Marilyn jotted them down on an index card.

The day before the dinner party, she consulted with Patricia Newcomb—whose passions included civil rights—and confessed a desire to be in touch with current social issues. "[Marilyn] identified with all the people who were denied civil rights," Newcomb told Donald Spoto. The press agent read Marilyn's prepared a list of questions and later contended this was the reason why the press reported the Attorney General spent more time talking with Marilyn than the other guests.

Marilyn wanted Kennedy to appreciate her intellect and social consciousness, but by no means did she want to completely obliterate her beauty, so she commissioned a black lace cocktail dress designed by Norman Norrell. When Mrs. Murray entered the room while Marilyn was being fitted into the skin-tight sheath, the housekeeper's expression indicated apprehension. "Be brave, Mrs. Murray," Marilyn giggled. "Be brave." The housekeeper quietly stepped out of the room.

The Lawfords strategically sat Kennedy between Marilyn and Kim Novak. Marilyn didn't need her cue card as she engaged the Attorney General in conversation about political events. "That evening Marilyn was quite sober—a terrifically nice person—fun to talk with, warm and interested in serious issues," Joan Braden told J. Randy Taraborrelli. "They had an instant rapport, not surprising in that they were both charismatic, smart people…Bobby enjoyed talking to intelligent, beautiful women, and Marilyn certainly fit the bill. She was also inquisitive in a childlike way, which I think he found refreshing. I found her to be delightful, and everyone at the party was completely enthralled by her and rather dazzled by her presence."

After dinner, the Lawfords played contemporary music on the stereo, including Chubby Checker's "Let's Twist Again." The teenage dance craze had raged in adult society during the previous autumn when the black tie and cocktail dress set started swiveling its hips in discothèques and in salons across Manhattan and Beverly Hills. A November 1961 issue of *Life* featured an article about the "older generation's" interest in the Twist with photographs of Jean Smith Kennedy, Tennessee Williams, and Greta Garbo at the Peppermint Lounge in New York. *Billboard* magazine referenced the phenomenon in an October 1961 article citing new dance songs such as "The High Society Twist."

When the record dropped from the Lawfords' phonograph spindle, and the needle made contact with the groove in the 45-rpm disc, Marilyn brought Kennedy into the large family room and taught him how to rotate his hips to Chubby Checker's tune. At ease with her body and known by her friends to move sensually like a trained dancer or a graceful feline, Marilyn was the master at this game without a need for crib notes. The record played over and over on the stereo to the delight of the other guests who stopped dancing, formed a circle around them, and cheered.

According to Gloria Romanoff, a party guest, Kennedy made a telephone call during the party. "Guess who's standing next to me?" Kennedy asked his ailing father. "Marilyn Monroe!" Kennedy handed the receiver to Marilyn, who introduced herself and spoke to the seventy-three-year-old patriarch. Recovering from a serious cerebral hemorrhage sustained in December, Joseph Kennedy was unable to speak or walk.

Marilyn followed up with a note to the elder Kennedy. His daughter, Jean Kennedy Smith, wrote a note of thanks to Marilyn on letterhead bearing the address "North Ocean Boulevard, Palm Beach, Florida," Joseph Kennedy's sixteen-room winter home on Millionaires' Row. Anthony Summers reprinted the note, discovered by Inez Melson in Marilyn's locked filing cabinet, in *Goddess: The Secret Lives of Marilyn Monroe*:

> *Mother asked me to write and thank you for your sweet note to Daddy—He really enjoyed it and you were very cute to send it—Understand that you and Bobby are the new item! We all think you should come with him when he comes back East! Again, thanks for the note—Love, Jean Smith*

Summers cites the note as "evidence" of both an affair between Marilyn and the Attorney General and an implication of the Kennedy family's acceptance of his philandering. However, it seems more realistic that Smith's note graciously acknowledged Marilyn's kindness to the President's infirmed father. The "item" arguably references in jest Monroe and Kennedy's mirthful spectacle on the dance floor at the Lawford home.

Several biographers cite Edwin Guthman, Robert Kennedy's press aide, as a witness to the Attorney General driving Marilyn home the night of the Lawford party because she had become intoxicated. Guthman has been quoted as claiming to have assisted Kennedy by helping to carry Marilyn into her apartment and onto her queen-sized bed. However, this is likely Monroe apocrypha. A receipt from Carey Cadillac Company dated the day of the party refutes Guthman's version. The receipt documents a driver collecting Marilyn at eight o'clock in the evening at her apartment on Doheny Drive, delivering her to the Lawfords' home where she stayed until three o'clock in the morning, and returning her home.

Edward Barnes corroborates the version documented by the yellowing receipt. Hired by the Lawfords as a valet to park cars along Beach Road, Barnes recounted to J. Randy Taraborrelli his observation of another parking attendant violating the rules of the Secret Service by asking to photograph Marilyn as she left the party. An agent confiscated the camera, and a sober Marilyn jumped to the attendant's defense. When press aide Edward Guthman explained to her that agents were present to guard the Attorney General, Marilyn defied the agent who snatched the camera. "It is not okay to steal someone's camera," she snapped. "You give back that camera right now." The agent complied, and Marilyn posed for the valet. This anecdotal recollection of Marilyn standing up against the Secret Service may also be part of the Monroe legend. Marilyn called DiMaggio twice at the Hotel Lexington in New York hours after meeting Bobby Kennedy and left her last message with an operator at 2:45 in the morning.

At noon the next day, there was another Bobby on Marilyn's mind: Bobby Miller, her twelve-year-old former stepson. Before leaving for Los Angeles International Airport to catch a flight to New York, Marilyn sat down and typed him a letter referencing his parents' opposition to her Christmas present to him, the introduction to Kennedy, and the purchase of her new home. The entire four-page letter was published in *MM—Personal from the Private Archive of Marilyn Monroe* and addressed to "*Dear Bobbybones*":

> *The first thing I want to say is that I am very disappointed that you don't get to have your telephone. I don't quite understand why it didn't work out, and I am very sorry, but remember that in a few years you will be able to do more things that you want... I still think, and agree with you, that it would be fun to have a phone and I can't see any harm in it, especially since I want to give it to you as your Christmas present, and you feel you have a need for it...*

Marilyn mentioned having also sent him a sweater for Christmas but returns to the issue of using the cash gift intended for a phone to start a savings account in his name or for another gift of his choice. She acknowledged the boy's desire to send her a gift but assured him that one is unnecessary since his allowance was limited and intended for school supplies. Marilyn turned to the topic of her new home and its high gates that guarded against intruders and extended an invitation with promise to cover the cost of plane fare and meet him at the airport:

> *I would love—for whichever vacation it can be arranged—if you and Janie wanted to—at least for a part of the vacation, even if it is for a few days, or a week—you are welcome to stay as long as you wanted to... You are always welcome... I miss you very much...*

Marilyn detailed her introduction to Robert Kennedy and asserted, "*I think you would like him.*" She described the Attorney General as intelligent, having a "*terrific*" sense of humor, and good dancing skills. She focused mainly on their political conversation:

> *I was mostly impressed with how serious he is about Civil Rights. He answered all of my questions... [and] asked if I had been attending some kind of meetings. (Ha ha!) I laughed and said "no," but these are the kind of questions that the youth of America want answers to and want things done about.*

Marilyn ended with mention of her travel to New York later in the day and invitation to take him to lunch or dinner and a movie. "*I think we all know what we mean to each other,*" she wrote, "*don't we. At least I know I love you kids and I want to be your friend and stay in touch.*" Marilyn concluded with a return to the topic of the telephone:

> *Golly I'm sorry about the phone, but you will grow up before you know it and things like telephones will be possible and not out of reach. I love you and miss you, and, give my love to Janie.*

She also referenced topics likely mentioned in Bobby's letters to her and recalled details of his life: an arm injury, a skiing trip, and mid-term exams. She even followed up on the results of a particular math test. Marilyn delicately forgave his sister's lack of recent communication, redirected him to a time when he would earn more responsibilities, and campaigned for him to be allowed to play billiards. She also responded to his recommendation of William Golding's *Lord of the Flies*. Marilyn's love for the stepchildren and desire to remain active and involved in their lives resonates in this correspondence.

On the same day, Marilyn wrote to her former father-in-law, Isidore Miller, regarding her plans to travel to New York within a few hours, her introduction to Robert Kennedy, and an invitation for the elderly man to be a guest in her new home:

> *Do give my invitation some serious thought, because remember you haven't been west of the Rockies yet...But, most of all, I would love to have you spend the time with me. Last night I attended a dinner in honor of the Attorney General, Robert Kennedy. He seems rather mature and brilliant for his thirty-six years, but what I liked best about him, besides his Civil Rights program, is that he's got such a wonderful sense of humor...I send all my love and I miss you.*

It was important for Marilyn to inform her support system of her interaction with Robert Kennedy, and the attraction between her and the attorney general was simple for all to understand. Kennedy was the physically slim-built seventh child of an affluent family who competed for his father's attention, and according to Peter Edelman, had empathy for the disenfranchised. He was also direct and sincere, and like Marilyn, had an endearing, self-effacing sense of humor.

Chapter Twenty-One: February–March 1962

After a short excursion to New York to attend the Old Vic Theatre's production of *Macbeth*, Marilyn returned to Los Angeles. A few days later, she arrived at the Beverly Hills Hotel in a purple dress with matching scarf, what she called the "purple people-eater wardrobe" (referencing a 1958 novelty song), for a conversation with Alan Levy for *Redbook*. During the marathon six-hour interview in the hotel's dining room, Marilyn picked at pink grapefruit while candidly discussing her three marriages, career, and psychiatric treatment.

When Levy complimented Marilyn's reduction to less than 120 pounds and size 8 slacks, Marilyn quipped, "I'm not only proud of my firm bosom, but I'm proud of my firm character." The interview continued another three hours in her apartment. When Levy referenced Alan Snyder's observation of Marilyn being in her best condition for quite some time and attributing it to her single status, she concurred: "It's better to be unhappy alone than unhappy with someone—so far."

Redbook published the interview, titled "Marilyn Monroe: A Good, Long Look at Myself," in its August issue, released just weeks before Marilyn's death. Levy probed for Marilyn's appraisal of her marriage to Miller. "At the beginning of our marriage, there was a pupil-teacher relationship," she explained. "I learned a great deal from it, but there was more to the marriage than that. A good marriage is a very delicate balance of many forces, I think." She credited Miller for introducing her to the importance of political freedom in society and noted that the emotional background one brings to a relationship is more important than formal education, dismissing the rumors of the disparity in education ending the marriage.

Levy pressed for dirt about Miller, but never vengeful or vindictive, Marilyn stood firm. "Under the present circumstances I feel it would be indelicate to even try to answer publicly," she said, referring to his recent announcement of plans to marry Inge Morath. "To answer publicly I feel it would be trespassing..." Levy told Marilyn that he noted no rancor and bitterness regarding her failed marriages and admired her friendliness after divorce. "It's not like fighting a duel," she explained. "Besides, I have three former stepchildren..." Her face lit up when the conversation turned to Joe DiMaggio, Jr., and Jane and Bobby Miller. "Their lives that are forming are very precious to me," Marilyn said. "And I know that I had a part in forming them."

Marilyn refused to discuss her feelings about her inability to bear a child and returned to the topic of her stepchildren. "I take a lot of pride in them," she said. "Because they're from broken homes...I think I love them more than I love anyone." Of course, the interview turned to the wide public speculation about reconciliation between Marilyn and DiMaggio. "I've always been able to count on Joe as a friend after that first bitterness of our parting faded," she clarified. "I fell in love with two of the nicest men I had met up to that time and was lucky enough to marry them."

Moving on to another important part of Marilyn's past, Levy questioned Marilyn about her psychiatric hospitalization, and she discussed it with courage and honesty. "Payne Whitney gives me a pain," Marilyn joked. "It was obviously an error in judgment to place me in Payne Whitney. The doctor who recommended it realized it and tried to rectify it." She expressed pride in confronting the specialists by advising them to have their own heads examined. Marilyn expressed belief in psychoanalysis "but in a sane way."

"I haven't reached a dramatic crossroads yet," Marilyn said of her career, although she acknowledged having reached the comedy crossroads in *Some Like It Hot*. "I'm looking forward to eventually becoming a marvelous—excuse the word marvelous—character actress," she announced for her future in films, insightfully aware of the need to plan for the day she would no longer fit the bill for a sexy leading lady. "Like Marie Dressler, like Will Rogers. I think they've left this kind of appeal out of the movies today. The emphasis is on spring love. But people like Will Rogers and Marie Dressler were people who, as soon as you looked at them, you paid attention because you knew: They've lived; they've learned."

Posthumously, biographers painted Marilyn's final year as a tumultuous search for a man to rescue her or validate her worth, but Levy learned her priority was her career. "I'm trying to find myself as a person," Marilyn had once disclosed to him. "Sometimes that's not easy to do. Millions of people live their entire lives without finding themselves. But it is something I must do. The best way for me to find myself as a person is to prove to myself that I'm an actress." She also confided to the journalist, "I am trying to prove to myself that I am a person. Then maybe I'll convince myself that I am an actress."

* * *

Marilyn's first step in finding herself was by laying down roots. She approached the restoration and decoration of her new home as passionately as she prepared for a film role. She painstakingly researched authentic Mexican design and landscaping and organized an eleven-day trip to Mexico to purchase native furnishings and decorations for the home. The trip became a personal and creative success marked by Marilyn's ability to sleep without the use of barbiturates. Frank Sinatra arranged her entry into the country along with Miguel Aleman, President of Mexico from 1946 to 1952.

Mrs. Murray arrived at Hotel Montejo in Mexico a week earlier than Marilyn in order to scout for appropriate shops and venders. Her former brother-in-law, Churchill Murray, a producer of an English language radio program, lived in Mexico City and served as a guide. He also assisted in selecting ceramic tiles for Marilyn's consideration.

Marilyn first traveled to Miami Beach to visit her former father-in-law, Isidore Miller, who was spending the winter season at the Sea Isle Hotel, an Art Deco architectural masterpiece on Collins Avenue (now The Palms Hotel & Spa). She remained devoted to the recent widower, whom she routinely telephoned on Sunday evenings. She sent him a telegram dated February 17 reading: "Arriving Eastern Airlines flight 605 at 9:05 tonight. Have reservations at Fountainebleau. Love you."

Miller waited for her at the airport where another man asked who he was expecting. "I could see that the man was aghast that such an old man was waiting for Marilyn Monroe," he told *Good*

Housekeeping in 1963. When Marilyn arrived, the man told her that there was a tall, elderly man looking for her. "That's Mr. Miller," she proudly stated. "I came to Florida to see him."

Marilyn and the elder Miller dined at the Fontainebleau Hotel's Club Gigi and strolled arm in arm on Collins Avenue. When other pedestrians recognized her, Miller expressed sorrow for the public constantly infringing upon her privacy. "When they stop doing that," Marilyn explained, "I'm finished."

The couple attended a cabaret show at the Minaret. The show was a disappointment, but Marilyn chose not to leave early in order to avoid insulting the performers. Later that night, she and the elder Miller visited in her suite at the Fountainebleau, the curvaceous luxurious resort designed by Morris Lapidus [The iconic property appears in Jerry Lewis' *The Bell Hop* (1960) and in the sweeping aerial shot that opens *Goldfinger* (1964)]. She told him of Arthur's marriage earlier that day to Inge Morath, who was pregnant. Isidore fell silent. Arthur hadn't told his father of his wedding plans. Marilyn assured Isidore that a letter was probably on the way.

The next day, Marilyn hosted a dinner for Miller and several of his retired friends. When Isidore returned to the Sea Isle, he found two hundred dollars stuffed in his pocket by his former daughter-in-law. He called her because he wanted to return the money. "I know you spent more than that on me," Marilyn protested. "Do me a favor and take it. I won't feel right if you don't." "Marilyn wanted to make me feel right," he would say. "She wanted me to protect her, but she also protected me."

Isidore followed up with a letter dated February 23, typed on Sea Isle stationary:

> *I can't tell you in words just how much your trip to Florida meant to me. I don't ever remember having such a good time!*
>
> *The guests of the Sea Isle Hotel can't get over how beautiful you looked the night you were there; they were so thrilled to see you in person they are still talking about it. Your visit was the best excitement they have had all season and expect to have. I thought you would be interested in seeing the enclosed picture of us taken in the "Gigi Club" at the Fountainebleau Hotel.*

Please let me hear from you soon.
Again, many, many thanks for a WONDERFUL visit.
With love,
Dad

Marilyn also visited DiMaggio, who was staying at the Yankee Clipper Hotel in Miami for the Yankees spring training. He accompanied her to Miami International Airport, where an entourage of Patricia Newcomb and hairdresser George Masters waited along with Marilyn's baggage.

Marilyn wore a black and white print blouse, white Capri slacks and white pumps. Her five pieces of luggage were packed with silk dresses and silk blouses in bright solid colors and prints by Italian designer Emilio Pucci. Photographers captured Marilyn and DiMaggio kissing at the gate before she climbed the steps to the plane carrying a cosmetics case, with Newcomb and Masters in tow. Marilyn finally arrived in Mexico City on February 20, and registered into a two-bedroom suite at the four-year-old Hilton Continental Hotel (an earthquake would destroy the resort in 1985). At first, Marilyn questioned the need for two guards holding post at her door, but soon swarms of newsmen congregated in the public areas and corridors, convincing her of the necessity for increased security. Outside, Mexican fans chanted their pronunciation of her name, "Maraleen," but respected her privacy without incident.

While in Mexico, Marilyn met Mexican comic actor Cantinflas (1911-1993) and was enthusiastically received by other members of the Mexican film industry. Screenwriter José Bolaños (1935-1994), who wrote *La Cucaracha* (1958), starring Emilio Fernandez, brazenly showered her with attention. Dark and attractive, he was nine years younger than Marilyn. Obviously smitten, Bolaños sent flowers on a silver platter to Patricia Newcomb in an attempt to arrange a private meeting with Marilyn. Mrs. Murray voiced alarm at his ingratiating overtures.

Bolaños boldly followed Marilyn to Taxco and appeared below her hotel window one evening with dueling mariachi bands. Wrapped in a kimono, Marilyn leaned over her balcony with her arms outstretched in welcome. Concerned that the romantic serenade would disturb other guests, she acknowledged the performers but avoided reinforcing the spectacle. So that no one below would hear, Marilyn muttered in earshot of Mrs. Murray, "Go away, you crazy Mexicans." Upon learning of this extravagant display of attraction, Newcomb seized an opportunity to generate publicity for Marilyn and arranged to fly Bolaños to Los Angeles as Marilyn's escort to the Golden Globe Award ceremony scheduled March 5.

Newcomb coordinated one of two press conferences in the hotel's Grand Ballroom attended by a crowd of two hundred. Newsreels of the event showed a svelte and glamorous Marilyn wearing a bouffant hairstyle similar to the one she would don in *Something's Got to Give*. Clutching a flowing chiffon scarf, she swirled around for the photographers, modeling a light green jersey sheath by Pucci. Marilyn's figure filled out the dress's simple straight lines. When reporters complimented the outfit, she quipped, "You should see it on a hanger." It was perhaps her favorite dress, and she would be buried wearing it six months later.

Taking position on a raised platform, Marilyn sipped champagne and graciously charmed the journalists and photographers with her quick wit and charisma. She answered questions about her search for Mexican pieces for her new home and the impending production of a new film at Fox. When asked to comment on a journalist recently referring to her as a female Charlie Chaplin, Marilyn responded, "I consider that a flattering exaggeration."

When Marilyn sat on a sofa to engage in a lengthier interview, the reporters extended microphones into her personal space, but the Mexican press invaded her privacy in worse ways than the American press had in the past. As she demurely crossed her legs, her dress's knee-length hemline rose slightly, and the cameramen disrespectfully focused their lenses on her pelvic region, employing a rude and deplorable intrusion. One photographer seated on the floor tactlessly snapped a shot of Marilyn published long after her death that revealed her lack of undergarments.

Reporters commented on Marilyn's three divorces and asked if she would consider marriage again. "I'm keeping my eyes open," she said. "I haven't given up." When asked to comment on Miller's recent marriage to Inge Morath, Marilyn responded, "I learned a lot from him and I'm glad. I wish him the best." Another reporter pressed her about a possible remarriage to DiMaggio, and she smiled and said, "We tried that once." When a reporter asked Marilyn to comment on Mexico's men, her eyes widened and she replied, "Mexican men are very warm and very intense...and Mexican women are very beautiful." The crowd cheered. The press conference was an enormous success, and Mexican magazines splashed images of Marilyn and printed quotations of her witty comments.

On the day following Marilyn's arrival, Fred Vanderbilt Field (1905-2000) and his wife, with whom Marilyn shared mutual friends in Connecticut, called on her at 5:00 PM for an hour-long visit. Field was a collector of pre-Columbian artifacts and director of the American Russian Institute. Coincidently, he was also a friend of Dr. Greenson's mother. Despite being born into wealth, Field supported Communist causes, earning him the moniker "the Reds' pet blueblood." He was a descendant of Commodore Cornelius Vanderbilt, a shipping and railroad tycoon; Samuel Osgood, the country's first postmaster general; and Cyrus Field, responsible for laying the first trans-Atlantic cable. Field's wife, Nieves Orozco, was a favorite model of artist and muralist Diego Rivera.

Field had worked for the Institute of Pacific Relations; a non-government organization dedicated to resolving the problems of nations in the Pacific Rim and tagged a hotbed for subversives in the 1950s. He had also served as executive director of the American Peace Mobilization, an organization that urged the United States to avoid entering into World War II but was cited as a Communist front group by the Attorney General in 1947. Field moved to Mexico in 1953 and studied archaeology after being convicted of contempt of court by refusing to reveal who had posted bond for four Communists who jumped bail.

Marilyn and the Fields established immediate rapport and extended their time together by planning a three-day shopping excursion to Cuernavaca, Taxco, and Tallares Borda. The Fields stated they would be delighted to serve as her guides and outlined specific shops. Fred Vanderbilt Field said Marilyn's politics were "excellent...She told us of her strong feelings about civil rights, for black equality, as well as her admiration for what was being done in China, her anger at red-baiting and McCarthyism and her hatred of J. Edgar Hoover... She was beautiful beyond measure...warm, attractive, bright and witty; curious about things, people and ideas...also incredibly complicated." Marilyn also confided in the Fields about her miscarriages and her divorce from Miller. She talked of retiring from films to find a man, a combination of DiMaggio and Miller, "who would be decent to her but also her intellectual leader and stimulant." She also spoke of wanting to live in the country and change her life completely.

To determine if Marilyn needed protection for the three-day trip, she and the Fields took a day trip to Toluca, about twenty miles south of Mexico City, to shop in the open market. Mrs. Murray and Churchill Murray joined the expedition, which had expanded to a convoy of two cars and three presidential guards. Like Field, Churchill Murray was a left-wing expatriate living in exile in Mexico for his communist affiliations in the United States. Marilyn's connection to those with socialist beliefs extended to Dr. Greenson, active in the Arts, Sciences and Professions Committee that promoted communist ideology on the West Coast. Her medical doctor, Hyman Engelberg, was also a prominent member of the committee.

Marilyn's association with alleged members of the American Communist Group in Mexico (ACGM) flagged the highest level of US Intelligence. A memorandum to the FBI, dated March 6, 1962, documented her social engagements during her stay. Two FBI informants apparently had undercover contact with Mrs. Murray, incorrectly referred to in the report as Eunice Churchill. She allegedly described Marilyn as "disturbed" by Arthur Miller's recent marriage and having "leftist" political views "rubbed off from Miller." Field's name is repeatedly censored with a black marker in the released copy of the memorandum in all but one paragraph reporting her "considerable curiosity" about him.

Additionally, there is mention of Marilyn's recent contact with Robert Kennedy at the Lawford estate. She was likely viewed as a potential threat to national security based upon her recent political conversation with Kennedy and subsequent conversations with alleged communists or communist sympathizers in Mexico. The documents also advises "extreme care should be used in reporting any of this information to avoid disclosure of sources who were associating closely with subject during her visit to Mexico."

While in Toluca, Marilyn bought colorful handcrafted items, baskets, glassware, and linens including a black and red bordered

Aztec tapestry from the open plazas. Marilyn was especially enthused by a hand-embroidered tablecloth with colorful Mexican figures in the weave and decided it would complement her breakfast nook trestle table. With the success of the day trip, Marilyn, the Fields, and Mrs. Murray ventured off early the next morning in the Fields' European compact car for a three-day excursion to the rugged terrain of Taxco, a silver mining city. The group enjoyed a leisurely lunch on the terrace of Las Mananitas restaurant overlooking a vast lawn where peacocks strutted.

In Talleres Borda, Taxco, Marilyn met local artists in a silver shop closed to the public for her visit. She ordered glass and metal sconce light fixtures, a silver-framed mirror for the dining room, and large mirrors for her bedroom. Marilyn also purchased authentic Mexican living room chairs with hand-carved backs and legs and a chess set of silver and gold.

Later that evening, Marilyn and her companions dined outdoors at a hotel and enjoyed the music of native singers and guitar players. The group retired early only to be awakened at midnight by José Bolaños and his dueling mariachi bands. On the second day, Marilyn and her companions had lunch in Cuernavaca and toured actress Merle Oberone's authentic Mexican home for decorating inspiration. Afterward, the Fields arranged for Marilyn to meet William Spratling at his home fifteen miles from town.

William Spratling (1900-1967), formerly a professor of architecture at Tulane University, entertained Marilyn and her companions at his ranch amid banana trees and sugar cane. Spratling had visited Mexico over thirty years before to research village life and remained to open a silver shop where he earned the title of "Father of Contemporary Mexican Silver." Marilyn admired her host's round mahogany dining table with scalloped octagonal base and learned it was made at one of his shops. Coincidentally, its scalloped design matched the tables Marilyn purchased from a New York antique shop. She asked Spratling to design a copy of the table for her dining room.

Spratling shared with Marilyn his fateful conversation in 1931 with the U. S. Ambassador to Mexico, Dwight Morrow. The ambassador explained that Taxco was the site of silver mines for centuries but never developed into a location where jewelry and silver pieces could be designed and created. Inspired, Spratling opened a shop and hired a goldsmith from Iguala to create silver jewelry from his original designs. Partnering artisans soon joined the shop and eventually opened their own shops, expanding the artistic community. Marilyn, who considered herself an advocate for the working man, was fascinated by her host's system of apprenticeship, which resulted in a boost of the local culture's economy. Later in the day, Spratling opened his workshops for Marilyn's inspection. She delighted in his pack of large dogs, which followed them throughout the tour.

Spratling, a gay man, found a good listener in Marilyn. He entertained her with stories about promoting the work of his friend, Diego Rivera, and assembling the first exhibit of Mexican arts held in the United States, opening at the Metropolitan Museum, one of her favorite haunts in New York. Spratling also discussed his involvement in the New Orleans literary colony along with William Faulkner, with whom he co-authored *Sherwood Anderson and Other Famous Creoles* the year of Marilyn's birth.

At the Byrna Gallery, Marilyn invested in three oil paintings. She was especially challenged in choosing between two paintings of an adobe at twilight. Marilyn selected the one that had a light on in the window. "This one looks lived in," she told Mrs. Murray. "It has so much more warmth."

Marilyn and her traveling companions visited the archaeological site of Teotihuacan, forty-five miles from Mexico City, thought to have been built in 100 BC. The ruin is a labyrinth of ancient palaces, temples, homes, workshops, markets, and avenues surrounding huge pyramids constructed in honor of the sun and moon. Marilyn briefly paused in Chiconcuac de Juárez, a small town dedicated to the production of traditional clothing, and browsed a store owned by the Delgado family, where she purchased a handmade cotton sweater. She was frequently photographed wearing it during the remainder of her life.

Back in Mexico City, Marilyn accepted invitations to events hosted by prominent Mexican citizens who wished to meet her. She was first approached at the Hilton Hotel by Emilio "El Indio" Fernandez (1904-1986), Mexican actor, screenwriter, and director, who had introduced her to tequila at an earlier reception. Fernandez invited Marilyn to his estate in Coyoacán and told her there would be only a few people present along with him and his wife, Mexican actress Columba Dominguez. Marilyn consented based upon those conditions, but when she arrived at Fernandez's palatial stone home with Mrs. Murray, twenty-five guests in formal attire greeted her. After socializing for a respectful length of time, Marilyn leaned toward Mrs. Murray and whispered, "Let's get out of here."

According to a recently released FBI report, the next day Marilyn had a date with a man whose name is censored in the released document, to see the film *Torero* (1956), an Oscar-nominated documentary about an aspiring bullfighter who must overcome his fear of bulls and crowds. According to the report, five minutes before her date was to arrive, Marilyn canceled, and her date was reportedly "furious." Not mentioned in the FBI document, she also joined Jean Pierre Piquet, the attractive manager of the Continental Hilton Hotel, at a reception he hosted in the showroom. The two were photographed toasting with glasses of champagne as they enjoyed the music of a Mariachi band. Afterward, Marilyn greeted the performers.

An FBI informant reported that on February 27, Marilyn attended a reception for Princess Antonia DeBraganza, Infant of Portugal, at the home of Dennis Bourke. The informant must have been incorrect about the honorary guest, as the Princess died in 1913. It is possible that Bourke's reception was for Anita DeBraganza (1885-1977), an American socialite married to Prince Miguel of Braganza. The event was described as nonpolitical in nature and attended by staffs of various embassies. Throughout the evening, Marilyn reportedly expressed curiosity about Fred Vanderbilt Field to those in attendance.

Churchill Murray arranged a reception in Marilyn's honor and gave her the option of meeting artists or diplomats and government officials; Marilyn chose diplomats. The event included live music and dancing, and the men took turns dancing with her. After dancing a fox trot with her host, Marilyn told Eunice, "Your brother-in-law is so nice. He told me all about how he met you in Chicago when you were sixteen. And how you were his best friend until his older brother stole you away." Mrs. Murray noted how her employer took an interest in the lives of those around her. Marilyn's discussion with the government officials primarily focused on social problems, and she related her personal experience in an orphanage. One official invited her to visit an orphanage in Mexico City, citing how inspiring her personal story could be for the children.

Wearing a colorful, clinging geometric-print sheath, which she would model for a photo session with Bert Stern in June, Marilyn visited the National Institute for the Protection of Children, a Catholic orphanage. She spent time with the children and met with the nuns who coordinated adoptions. When told the orphanage also provided breakfasts for needy neighborhood children, Marilyn recalled her own childhood and replied, "I know what it means to go without breakfast." She completed an application to adopt one or more of the orphaned children before writing a check for a one thousand dollar donation. Impulsively, she tore up the check and wrote another for the sum of $10,000. Before leaving the country, Marilyn spoke to the press about adopting a Mexican child. Evelyn Moriarty said, "It was around this time that I first heard talk of Marilyn trying to adopt a child...that her trip to Mexico was for more than buying furniture."

Journalist Glenn Thomas Carter accompanied Marilyn on a night out in Acapulco where she observed an eight-year-old boy entertaining customers. In an article in *Motion Picture* magazine, Carter alleges that Marilyn broke down in tears when the boy disclosed to her that he was an orphan and that his foster parents taught him to dance and pickpocket American tourists. The boy asked to live with her in California, and she promised him she would try to make this happen. The next day, Marilyn recruited José Bolaños as interpreter, and he agreed to accompany her to the foster parents' home to arrange for a possible adoption. Eunice Murray made no mention of this child in her published memoir of the trip.

During her visit to Isidore Miller and throughout her stay in Mexico, behind closed doors, Marilyn was preoccupied with Arthur's marriage to a woman pregnant with his child. Another woman was helping Miller realize the dream he and Marilyn had held during their marriage. Despite years of efforts to bear a child, Marilyn remained childless during an era when motherhood was the paramount goal for a woman. One can surmise she ached for a child of her own, and adoption was now her only recourse. However, Marilyn's feelings about adoption would soon change. "I don't think a single person should adopt children," she would tell George Barris in June.

In the same geometric-patterned sheath, Marilyn next visited an estate home where Spanish director and writer Luis Bunuel (1900-1983) was filming *El Angel Exterminador.* The surrealistic plot involved the hosts of a formal dinner and their guests inexplicably unable to leave the room. Trapped together for several days, chaos ensues. The cast included a baby bear rented from a circus that chases several sheep into the house, thus providing an opportunity for the guests to slaughter, roast, and consume the animals to stay alive. The film's star, Silvia Pinal (born 1931), later said Marilyn arrived "impeccably groomed" and contrasted glaringly with the cast, who were covered in honey and dirt so that they appeared unkempt and grimy. For twenty-three-year-old actress Jacqueline Andere, Marilyn's arrival rivaled the entrance of a live bear on the set. "We saw her come in with a glass of champagne," Andere remembered. "First the bear, and now Marilyn Monroe. It was too much for me, the age I was."

Marilyn stood behind the camera as Bunuel took over from an animal handler and taught the bear to emit a growl while it perched on a swinging chandelier. The director seemed more patient coaching the beast than his human actors. She watched him whisper into the animal's ear and complete the scene in one take. Marilyn told Bunuel the scene was superb and jokingly asked if he had whispered into the bear's ear for motivation for the scene. He found humor in her questions. Then Marilyn asked, "But what does it mean?" Marsha Kinder published their dialogue. "What does it mean to you?" he countered.

"It means that the growls a bear makes while hanging on a chandelier make more sense than all the noise of the tiresome, uncaring people trapped in the room," she replied. "Exactly what I intended," Bunuel replied, applauding her astute interpretation. They embraced; it was a meeting of the minds. "Now tell *me,*" Bunuel said, "how do *you* see life?" "I see life as long, meaningless…" Marilyn began as the sound of a plane roared overhead. "Talking, everybody just talking…obviously." In another version of this conversation, Bunuel quipped, "The bourgeois are always talking." Mishearing him, Marilyn replied, "Yes, the bourgeois are always walking." The interaction inspired Bunuel's 1972 film *The Discreet Charm of the Bourgeoisie* about interruptions that prevent six Parisians from dining.

Bunuel included a recurring, surrealistic sequence of the dinner party guests dressed in formal attire continuously strolling along a barren country road.

As Marilyn's visit to Mexico approached its end, her new friends hosted a farewell celebration. She would return Mr. and Mrs. Field's warm hospitality by having them stay at her apartment in New York in the spring. On June 7, the management company of her apartment wrote Marilyn a letter objecting to this arrangement, citing violation of her lease and threatening a notice for the couple to vacate:

> *It has come to our attention that while you were away, you permitted others to live at your apartment, in violation of the terms of your lease. At this time, we do not wish to cause you any embarrassment by serving these people as well as yourself a notice to vacate, and by not doing so, we do not waive your rights under the lease, but merely wish to save you from an unpleasant situation…We are calling this to your attention so that in the future you will not again permit others to use your apartment, thereby creating a situation which will be embarrassing to you.*

May Reis intervened. "*This is a nasty letter and I think it deserves a nasty reply,*" she angrily wrote in a note to Cherie Redmond. "*Marilyn has had guests in the apt here for the last two weeks, and they will be here for another week…The problem may be that Mrs. Field is Mexican—though I'm only guessing…In view of the tone of the letter perhaps M's lawyer should answer it and I hope tell the management where to get off.*"

On the morning of Friday, March 2, Marilyn began dressing for her departure from Mexico and discovered that Mrs. Murray had packed her shoes the night before in luggage that had been transported to the airport. She borrowed Mrs. Murray's white bedroom slippers to board the plane. In a Pucci blouse, white Capri slacks, and a mink coat draped over her shoulders, Marilyn walked onto the tarmac on the arm of Jean Pierre Piquet, manager of the Hilton Continental. She waved to reporters from the door of the plane. "Adios, muchachos!" she said before taking a seat next between Patricia and Mrs. Murray. Marilyn turned to the housekeeper, remarked that the slippers were comfortable, and offered to purchase them from her. Murray appreciated her employer's good humor about the mishap.

Anticipating Marilyn's arrival in Los Angeles, Mrs. Murray's son-in-law, Norman Jeffries, Jr., and his brother worked diligently to prepare the house by cleaning and waxing the woodwork, washing the walls, and removing the kitchen cabinets. Roy Newell, the plumbing contractor, installed a temporary kitchen in the guest home including a sink, refrigerator, and stove combined in one unit. Sloane's installed untreated white wool wall-to-wall carpeting imported from India. Ray Tolman, the cabinetmaker, created a breakfast table and benches for the kitchen nook from rare black walnut saved for a special job.

* * *

Marilyn arrived in Los Angeles in time to attend the Hollywood Foreign Press Association's 19th annual Golden Globe Award ceremony and formal dinner at the Beverly Hilton Hotel scheduled on March 5. She was voted World Film Favorite Female, compensation for being snubbed for a nomination in the category of best dramatic actress for *The Misfits*. Actresses nominated in that category included Geraldine Page, Leslie Caron, Shirley MacLaine, Claudia McNeil, and Natalie Wood.

Before the visit to Mexico, Marilyn had received news of the award and told Patricia Newcomb, "I guess I can go to dinner with Sydney Skolsky." The two women now arranged for José Bolaños, a thirty-five-year-old handsome, fit Latino with a thick head of jet black hair, to escort Marilyn at her own expense with reservations at the Beverly Hills Hotel rather than a five-foot two-inch, fifty-six year old, bespeckled, married father of two who never learned to drive a car.

Dr. Engelberg allegedly administered a drug injection to Marilyn on Saturday, March 3, the same day as her first session with Dr. Greenson in over a month and the day Bolaños arrived in Los Angeles and checked into the Beverly Hills Hotel. Engelberg allegedly administered injections to Marilyn again on Sunday and Monday, the day of the award ceremony. Donald Spoto noted that Engelberg's wife's 1962 divorce petition alleged that the doctor had administered hypnotic and barbiturate drugs to calm her during the collapse of their thirty-year marriage. After Marilyn's session, she did not join Bolaños. Instead she spent the weekend at the Greenson home and returned there after the award ceremony.

Pleased with his services in Mexico, Marilyn called upon George Masters to prepare her for the event. He teased her hair into a full-volume bouffant style. In a modern take on her trademark look, Marilyn chose a fitted gown of emerald green sequins designed by Norman Norell. Two Fox wardrobe technicians transformed the scooped-neck of the gown into a backless halter. A small strip of matching sequined fabric attached to each armhole created the halter behind Marilyn's neck. She completed the outfit with diamond and emerald earrings, a gift from Frank Sinatra. Marilyn looked beautiful, and for the first time in many years was escorted by a young, attractive male. With his thick black hair, heavily lidded eyes, and full lips, Bolaños was sexy, even if Susan Strasberg thought he looked like a gigolo.

Marilyn and Bolaños arrived early at the Beverly Hilton Hotel, holding hands and attracting intense media attention. Patricia Newcomb predicted this pairing would have the gossip columnists buzzing about "Marilyn's new Latin lover." Susan Strasberg described Marilyn's entrance: "Something happened that knocked me out. There was a room full of the biggest stars in the world, and when Marilyn walked in and made her way slowly to the table, her dress was so tight she could hardly move; some people in the room stood on chairs, just to get a look at her, like kids. I'd never seen stars react to another star like that. Marilyn seemed oblivious of them all; she was in one of her armored vapor clouds."

The maître'd escorted the couple to their assigned seats at a table directly in front of the stage. "[Bolaños'] pants were so tight that he had to ease himself onto his seat at a slant," Strasberg wrote. "Between [Marilyn's] dress and his pants, there wasn't an inch to spare." Photographers clamored to take pictures of them sipping cocktails and chatting during dinner. Matchmaker Patricia Newcomb joined them at table number 9.

As the ceremony began, Bolaños turned his and Marilyn's chairs so that they faced the stage. By snuggling, caressing, and practically cuddling her, Bolaños seemed to be making the most of his opportunity to be perceived as romantically linked with the biggest female star of the American film industry. Throughout the evening, Marilyn whispered into his ear, her arm entwined with his. She received another embrace from Judy Garland as the singer stepped down from the stage near table number 9 after receiving the lifetime achievement award.

As the previous year's recipient of World Film Favorite award, Rock Hudson stood at the podium to present the trophy to the new winner. By the time he announced Marilyn's name, Dr. Engelberg's injections had mixed with the dinner cocktails, inebriating the next World Film Favorite. Hudson reached for Marilyn's hand and assisted her onto the stage. They embraced, and Hudson stepped back beside Master of Ceremonies, Steve Allen, as Marilyn moved to the microphone. Local television coverage deleted her slurred acceptance speech, which remains undocumented to date.

The typed notes for a World Film Favorite Award posthumously discovered in Marilyn's gold compact most likely corresponded to her speech in acceptance. They read in part: "*This is a wonderful surprise for me—being named most popular in the world. Up until last week I never left Redlands [a suburb in San Bernadino County]... [I'm] moved—thrilled.*"

Seated at a distance along with Ann-Margaret, Rita Moreno, and George Chakiris, Susan Strasberg watched her "befogged" friend "weave in front of the microphone life a hypnotized cobra." This was not "the clear-eyed, agile-witted, sensitive person" Strasberg knew. Hudson escorted Marilyn off the stage amid thunderous applause to a makeshift press room in a corner of the hotel.

Flanked by Hudson and Charlton Heston, who received the World Film Favorite Male Award, Marilyn spoke to the reporters and posed for the photographers. As Bolaños remained at the table with Patrician Newcomb, Marilyn and Hudson hugged, snuggled, and admired the award's engraving at the instructions of the Fox publicity department. They were instructed to present themselves to the press as a romantic pairing to promote their reputations as sex symbols and to generate the public's interest in their being cast together in a future film. According to Strasberg, despite being tipsy, Marilyn "exuded innocence and a vibrant life force that surrounded her like an aura."

That evening, a limousine returned Bolaños to the Beverly Hills

Hotel before delivering Marilyn to the Greenson home. Upon her return to the United States, Marilyn discovered that a national magazine had published her Doheny Drive address. Alarmed, she decided to move into her new home before the major renovations began and summoned DiMaggio for assistance. She told friends, "I'll walk on the bare floors. I'll eat out. But I want to sleep in my house. I'll feel so much safer there."

Seemingly, Greenson's disapproval extended to DiMaggio. In an interview with Donald Spoto, a student analyst under Greenson's clinical supervision would later recount an incident on the morning following the Golden Globe Award ceremony in early March 1962. Marilyn, under Greenson's care, was ensconced in the doctor's upstairs guest room. DiMaggio arrived at the residence and requested to see her. Learning her former husband had arrived, Marilyn asked Greenson to send him to her. Greenson forbade the couple to see each other, keeping DiMaggio downstairs. Marilyn grew increasingly agitated. The student compared the situation to a patient confined to a hospital against her will and demanding to see her family or visitors. "Greenson insisted on detaining Joe," the student said, "and Marilyn was eventually close to a tantrum..." Spoto does not reveal the former student's identity.

Greenson's projections on Marilyn and the control he had over her relationship disturbed the young student. She and DiMaggio appeared to be re-enacting her admission to Payne Whitney Hospital the previous year. Again, DiMaggio prevailed without having to threaten to dismantle the Greenson home brick by brick.

Chapter Twenty-Two: March–April 1962

Aficionados would be drawn to Marilyn's last home as a touchstone to her brief and extraordinary life. The home would serve as a shrine, along with her crypt in Westwood Memorial Cemetery, where fans and admirers could pay homage to the goddess' memory. In 1988, Irish New Age recording artist Enya would release a haunting song, "Cursum Perficio", on her *Watermark* album, inspired by the inscription on the home's threshold. The hacienda's address would even be printed on movie star maps sold in Hollywood gift shops and on street corners along Sunset Boulevard.

Marilyn's life in Brentwood began on the weekend of March 8th and 9th, when Joe DiMaggio assisted in moving her possessions and few furnishings from the Doheny Drive apartment to Fifth Helena Drive. He stayed with her for several days in the virtually bare home before turning her over to the handiwork of trusted friend Ralph Roberts. Roberts installed black draperies over the bedroom windows to create the darkness needed to battle Marilyn's chronic insomnia.

During the era before portable cell phones, he also installed long extension cords that allowed Marilyn to chat on the phone while moving freely throughout the house. Roberts had spent many Saturday evenings with Marilyn, grilling steaks on the outdoor barbecue at apartment and dining with her. "I'd cook steaks and baked potatoes on the barbeque in her backyard and make a salad," Roberts recounted in Susan Strasberg's memoir. "She wanted to bottle my salad dressing before Paul Newman did his." Roberts shared a special brotherly relationship with Marilyn and soothed her with therapeutic deep tissue massage when her anxiety and insomnia intensified. He knew her deepest secrets but respected her confidence by never disclosing them and choosing never to publish a book about her. Marilyn had placed her trust in an appropriate friend.

Marilyn took great care to slowly transform the hacienda into her dream home. She asked the contractors to focus on quality and workmanship rather than speed. Without the support of a professional interior decorator, she created a private refuge from her fame. The thick white carpeting and textured alabaster walls provided a stark pallet for the contrasting bright colors of the Mexican tiles and art. Dark, rustic wood furniture complemented the dark beamed ceilings. Marilyn continued the theme by paneling the living room wall adjacent to the sunroom, copying the paneled walls in Dr. Greenson's living room.

Marilyn placed a low wooden coffee table with scalloped design in front of her fireplace, copying the similar antique table that she admired in front of Greenson's fireplace. Its surface was comprised of leather stretched over wood. Four hardwood folding benches with cushions and tassels encircled the table, creating a casual conversation area. She positioned a settee bench against the entry area wall. The scallop pattern was repeated in its carved design. Above the bench, Marilyn displayed the painting of the adobe purchased in Mexico and signed by the artist, Olga. The living room window treatments of padded cornices and formal drapery panels were made of white on white damask fabric.

A red sofa designed by Norman Norell in New York arrived several days before Marilyn's death. It remained in shipping wrap in the guesthouse. The sofa would later be upholstered in gold velour and owned by a collector in Los Angeles. Marilyn had ordered leather and wood armchairs, but until they arrived, she used an Italian settee with matching side chairs from the Doheny Drive apartment. She would accidentally tear the seat cushion of one chair with the heel of her pump when she posed for photographs to accompany the interview with Richard Meryman for *Life*.

Also in the living room, an Aztec calendar tracked the days, and a white knight was missing from the chess set displayed on a rustic table against the paneled wall. Beside the chess set stood an Indian hammered brass vessel mounted as a lamp. A bronze ashtray in the shape of a swan rested on a surface in this room. Its head was turned backward forming a handle, and its tail feathers served as rests for cigars or cigarettes. Marilyn also displayed an oil painting of a male figure playing a guitar and another by the Parisian artist Poucette, titled *La Toureau* and dated 1962, depicted the silhouette of a bull against a dramatic red landscape.

Hoping to recreate the tile pattern framing the psychiatrist's fireplace opening, Marilyn asked the workmen to remove the bricks bordering her own fireplace. They began the process on April 10, the day of costume and makeup tests for *Something's Got to Give.* Marilyn returned home from the studio to find the tiles already framing the fireplace. Fox electrician James A. Gough arrived with his son to find Marilyn and Mrs. Murray happily cleaning the fireplace's newly discovered original Mexican tile previously hidden under a layer of plaster and bricks. Marilyn broke away from the task and led Gough and his son on a tour of the home and garden. The electrician was surprised by the house's modesty.

A Mexican hanging star of frosted glass and leaded copper served as the dining room chandelier. Produced in William Spratling's shop in Taxco, this striking piece was suspended from a chain over the dining table. The table's scallop-designed stretcher treatments between its eight legs created an octagonal base. Accompanying hand-made chairs featured leather seats attached by ornamental rows of brass tacks. Marilyn placed a small china cabinet next to the dining room window facing the front of the house. On the dining room wall, Marilyn displayed a dramatic mirror framed by triangular mirror pieces leaded in copper. An original painting by Nova Taylor titled *Thistles #7*, hung on the opposite wall near the sunroom. It depicted blue flowers in a yellow vase against an orange and red background.

The completed kitchen was a masterpiece by Custom Kitchens by St. Charles on Sunset Boulevard. Copper pots and pans suspended from a long, shiny copper stove hood. The wall behind the stove was tiled in yellow and blue. Tiles also framed the Hotpoint cooking range and continued along the wall to create a splashboard. Marilyn purchased the stainless steel sink, Hotpoint appliances, and Kitchenmaid dishwasher from Kafton Sales Company on North Highland Avenue. The exposed side of the modern rectangular

Hotpoint refrigerator of brushed chrome was painted blue to match the tiles (a collector in Los Angeles would preserve the appliance's customized tint). Typically, the refrigerator contained only smoked sturgeon, rye bread, bagels, cream cheese and lox.

A trestle table was positioned in front of a window, creating a nook. Two matching plank benches were mounted to the nook's walls on either side of the table. One bench sported a red cushion with tassels and the other had a matching cushion in bright yellow. On the opposite side of the nook partition was a tiled service area housing a tall pantry and low cabinet with a countertop. A star light fixture illuminated the service area, and a door led to the patio connecting to the guesthouse.

Marilyn told photographer George Barris that she planned to host dinner parties for her friends. Her culinary talents included stews, homemade pasta, and guacamole. She often served peas and carrots because she liked the color combination on the plate. Marilyn's specialty was Yiddish dishes formerly cooked for Arthur Miller such as borscht, chicken soup and matzo balls. After Marilyn's death, handwritten recipes for rum cake and beef bourguignon were found between the pages of her copy of *The Joy of Cooking*, authored by Irma Rombauer and Marion Rombauer Becker.

The small sunroom was bright and cheerful. Its uncovered windows overlooked the kidney-shaped pool. Marilyn rarely swam in it but encouraged guests to do so. The sunroom was furnished with a low, armless love seat of wicker stretched over a solid wood frame with two matching chairs and foot rests. A three-tier liquor cart with glass shelves displayed spirits. Other furnishings included two walnut five-shelf bookcases and a tea table. An Aztec tapestry covered nearly the entire wall adjacent to the dining room. Four cartoon-like, wirework figures of Mexican musician hung on the opposite wall. They depicted men in wide sombreros playing a trumpet, violin, guitar and clarinet.

The master bedroom was about fifteen feet square and had a kiva fireplace in the corner with a pointed top resembling a witch's hat. A white satin comforter and fitted damask dust ruffle covered the bed. Matching damask fabric was used in the draperies covering the room's three windows. A makeshift nightstand was positioned on the left side of the bed suggesting that Marilyn preferred sleeping on this side. Its small size accommodated a small lamp with shade. In the days before her death, Marilyn purchased a nightstand to replace the one photographed at the death scene. It arrived on the day of her death and remained in the living room. An earthenware jug marked *Un Recuerdo de Toluca* rested beside the bed stand.

A phonograph was typically plugged into the electrical outlet near Marilyn's bed. Her nightly ritual involved stacking Frank Sinatra records on its spindle; her former lover's soothing voice singing her to sleep. A hand-carved eight-drawer dresser from Mexico contained her folded garments. Inside a dresser drawer, she kept an envelope filled with photographs of Bobby and Janie Miller, Joe DiMaggio, Jr., and James Haspiel.

Blue and yellow tiles brightened the master bathroom's walls and sink countertop. They also bordered the tub and shower area alongside stone-color tiles. Some of the tiles were decorated with hand-painted orange flowers with yellow leaves. A complementary blue and yellow embroidered floral design surrounded a monogrammed letter "M" on white terry cloth bath towels.

A Jack and Jill second bath was accessible through the guest bedroom and third bedroom. The guest bedroom contained a twin bed and two walnut cabinets. The third bedroom was converted to a fitting and dressing room. The limited closet space prompted Marilyn to purchase a large wardrobe cabinet. The dressing room contained a custom-made three-piece mirror, moved from the Doheny apartment, and joined by piano hinges. The mirror would reflect Marilyn as she was fitted for designer Jean Louis' sleek costumes for *Something's Got to Give* and the diaphanous gown of silk soufflé gauze and glass beads worn to the President's birthday gala.

The dressing room closet stored Marilyn's West Coast casual garments. She had a fondness for the simple style and bright solid colors of Emilio Pucci. Marilyn owned many of the Italian designer's straight-lined jersey silk dresses, with matching waist ties, in a variety of hues such as mauve, shocking pink, royal blue, turquoise and taupe. Her sportswear wardrobe was comprised of a wide selection of jewel-print blouses, Capri slacks, and stiletto pumps by Ferragamo. These modern fashions contrasted with her East Coast department store and couture dresses of black, white and beige.

In Mexico City, Marilyn had purchased a Mexican colonial

wardrobe at Versalles, S.A., for additional storage. However, the Mexican government had limited exportation to prevent the country's loss of precious antiques. The piece was delivered to Cheli Air Force Base. By 1964, it would remain in the Brentwood garage of William Pagen, the previous owner of Marilyn's home. Somehow, it had been incorrectly shipped to his new home in Los Angeles.

Marilyn shopped with Mrs. Murray at The Mart, owned by Bill Alexander, on Santa Monica Boulevard in West Hollywood. She purchased a wall hanging depicting Adam, Eve, and the Serpent in an apple tree. She displayed it in the hallway near her bedroom. Both its commentary on relationships and placement near the bedroom may have reflected Marilyn's sense of humor.

For the guesthouse, Marilyn ordered red Mexican carpeting hand-woven by natives. Mura Bright, a Los Angeles contact for Mexican arts and decorative pieces, took the guest room's measurements in centimeters to assure the carpet's perfect fit. Maf-Honey slept on an old beaver coat in this space, creating an animal odor for which Marilyn apologized to visitors when she proudly led them through the rooms. Mexican artists painted flowers and vines on the ceiling beams. Similarly, a striking mural was painted on the ceiling of the bath in the guesthouse.

Marilyn envisioned adding an apartment over the garage and hired an architect to prepare a sketch of the design. Repeating the home's Spanish motif, the apartment's design included a balcony, outside stairway, and dark beam ceilings. She planned to relocate her cook, Hattie Stevenson, from New York to the small space. The garage was cluttered with delivery boxes and pieces not yet placed in the house. Marilyn did not own a car, but spoke of someday purchasing a white Jaguar.

Beside the pool, Marilyn placed Eames patio furniture including a chaise lounge, side chair with ottoman, round table, and settee. Wearing a candy-kiss shaped straw hat, she planted an herb garden, a variety of flowering plants, and citrus trees from Frank's Nursery. She researched plants and cacti indigenous to the Mexican climate and received an annual subscription to Horticulture magazine as a Christmas gift from Jane and Bobby Miller. An issue was discovered at her bedside when she died. Marilyn also planted a tree in the walled patio between the kitchen and guesthouse.

She hired Mexican brick masons to build a low wall around the tree, and gardener Mr. Tateishi planted white azaleas beneath the tree. The brick masons also paved paths in the garden courtyard, where herbs grew in clay pots. Marilyn impulsively chiseled out several edge tiles near the kitchen and planted a flower in the middle of each edge tile. She hung antique bronze wind chimes, a gift from Carl Sandburg, in one of the trees surrounding the house.

"I live here all alone with my snowball, my little white poodle..." Marilyn told photographer George Barris. "Oh, sure, I'd rather be married and have children and a man to love—but you can't always have everything in life the way you want it. You have to accept what comes your way."

Chapter Twenty-Three: **President John F. Kennedy**

Norman and Hedda Rosten, visiting Los Angeles on a film assignment, were some of Marilyn's first guests in her new hacienda. On a Sunday afternoon, Marilyn called them at a nearby hotel to be her guests at a reception at the Greenson home. Norman asked if psychiatrists were allowed to entertain their patients at home. "He's a great person and has a wonderful family," Marilyn responded, avoiding the question. "You'll like them all and vice versa."

Upon arrival to the Greenson home, Marilyn formally introduced Norman to the psychoanalyst as her "poet friend" and Hedda as "a dear person." In an obvious attempt at providing evidence of her contact with healthy couples, Marilyn emphasized, "They're happily married." The Rostens soon realized that not only did Marilyn invite them to meet the family; they were also welcomed to stay and listen to chamber music in the living room. She and the Rostens returned several more times as Greenson's guests. Norman would later write about walking into the kitchen to interrupt Marilyn and screenwriter Ira Wallach arguing about politics.

Before returning home to Brooklyn, Hedda joined Norman and Marilyn for dinner with playwright and screenwriter William Inge. Marilyn assured Hedda she would closely monitor Norman in her absence and guard him from predatory females. Hedda raised her eyebrows. "You don't know this town," Marilyn warned. "It's full of husbands on the prowl." DiMaggio joined them at the restaurant, and Marilyn introduced Norman as a writer. "Didn't you just leave a writer?" her former husband jokingly asked.

Norman had given Marilyn a tape recording of his poetry reading for a local radio station. Like the white knight in her chess set, Marilyn carried the tape in a handbag as a transitional object and purchased an audiotape player. One evening after Hedda's departure, Marilyn invited Norman to visit and listen to the tape with her before he went off to a screening in Hollywood and she retired to her bedroom to sleep. Exhausted, she warned him of her likely dozing before the tape ended and instructed him to slip out to his engagement if she fell asleep. Norman recalled Marilyn receiving him in her pajamas, serving him coffee, and, indeed, falling asleep as they listened to his delivery of prose. As the poet left, he found himself feeling protective of his lonely friend and wishing someone else had the charge of looking after her.

* * *

Since her triumphant appearance at the fundraiser at Fifi Fell's apartment in February, Marilyn lingered in President Kennedy's mind. He had experienced her vitality, wit, beauty, and grace. At her best, Marilyn was enormously engaging and possessed a charisma that compared to the gravitational pull of a planet. As an official trip to California approached, Kennedy appointed his contacts to plan a rendezvous with the woman who had both enchanted and upstaged him on Park Avenue.

First as a pampered son of an affluent Eastern family and later as a powerful world leader, Kennedy routinely seduced the women he desired. Posthumously, rumors emerged of Kennedy's dalliances with scores of attractive women during his marriage and subsequent presidency. Desired by millions of males from Topeka to Tibet, the quintessential love goddess of her time may have represented a trophy or conquest for Kennedy's ego.

The president had originally accepted an invitation to be a guest at the home of Frank Sinatra, but the singer's reputation of cavorting with mobsters increased risk for the administration. Instead, the President stayed at the home of Bing Crosby, Sinatra's archrival crooner and a registered Republican.

Before reaching the tranquil desert atmosphere of Palm Springs, Air Force One touched down in California on March 23. President Kennedy met with bio-defense scientists at the Radiation Lab at the University of California at Berkeley. He also visited Vandenberg Air

Force Base, where he personally inspected the launch facilities for retaliatory missiles and watched an Atlas soar over the Pacific and land within one mile of its target.

The following morning, Marilyn arrived at the Greenson home to wash her hair in their guest bath. She explained that plumbers were installing a new water heater in her hacienda, and she needed to be ready for Peter Lawford to take her to Palm Springs to meet the president. Greenson worried about his patient setting herself up for being hurt and exploited by another selfish man. It is also possible that Marilyn's arrival at Greenson's home to wash her hair may have served as an excuse to flaunt her recklessness and solicit his protection.

In Palm Springs, the president spent fifty minutes visiting with former President Dwight D. Eisenhower at the Crosby estate. Since February, Eisenhower and his wife, Mamie, had rented a home located on the eleventh fairway of the Eldorado Country Club's golf course and enjoyed the relaxing desert ambience. According to Eunice Murray, while the current and former presidents discussed world affairs, Peter Lawford arrived at Marilyn's hacienda to escort her to Cosby's estate where, after Eisenhower's departure, she would be sequestered in a secluded detached guest cottage.

Special assistant David Powers accompanied Kennedy on this trip. His alleged role was to greet visitors and escort them to the President, a job he performed, according to the *New York Times*, with "startling unpretentiousness and lack of formality." According to his obituary in the *New York Times*, Powers introduced Prime Minister Harold Macmillan of Britain as "the greatest name in England," and to the Shah of Iran he said, "I want you to know you're my kind of Shah." It is undocumented if or how Powers presented Marilyn to the president or if he deferred that role to Lawford.

In the early evening, the president hosted an exclusive formal dinner in Crosby's sprawling 6,700-square-foot estate in Thunderbird Heights, a private community in Rancho Mirage. Philip Watson, former Los Angeles county assessor, told Anthony Summers the president and Marilyn appeared together in public as a couple during a less formal reception at the cottage and outside on the terrace against the hillside backdrop. He described the president wearing a turtleneck sweater and Marilyn wearing a "kind of a robe thing," likely an evening hostess outfit of the era. "There were a lot of people poolside, and some people were wandering in and out…" Watson recalled. "Marilyn was there and the president was there and they were obviously together. There was no question in my mind that they were having a good time."

According to Watson, it was obvious to him and the other invited guests that the couple were intimate and staying together for the evening. At the time, Jacqueline Kennedy was thousands of miles away on a goodwill tour of India and Pakistan with her sister, Lee Radizwell. As the president indiscreetly courted the world's most desired actress, his dutiful wife rode an elephant and met both Indira Ghandi and Prime Minister Nehru.

"[Marilyn] was delightful, a little bit nervous perhaps," recalled Peter Summers, a Kennedy political strategist who handled relations with the television networks, "but I think her nervousness was because she was in a new territory with people who were political animals. She wasn't totally at ease. I did feel that she was impressed by Kennedy's charm and charisma, that she was almost starry-eyed… But she was totally able to hold her own conversationally; she was very bright."

Later that night, Ralph Roberts received a phone call from Marilyn. He alleged she called directly from the bedroom she shared with the president in Palm Springs. Without disclosing a name, Marilyn told Roberts that a companion in her presence was suffering from back pain and needed advice. "She asked me about the soleus muscle which she knew something about from the Mabel Ellsworth Todd book," Roberts later said, "and she had obviously been talking about this with the president, who was known to have all sorts of ailments, muscle and back trouble." Allegedly, the president took the phone from Marilyn's hand and, in his Bostonian accent, personally thanked Roberts for his time. "Of course, I didn't reveal that I knew who he was," Roberts would say, "and he didn't say."

After returning home on Sunday, Marilyn called Roberts and confirmed that her Bostonian companion was indeed the leader of the free world. "I told him he should get a massage from you, Ralph," she said nefariously, "but he said, 'It wouldn't really be the same.' I think I made his back feel better." Marilyn told Roberts this was the only time she had an affair with the president and gave an impression that it had not been a significant episode for either of them. "Of course she was titillated beyond belief, because for a year he had been trying, through Lawford, to have an evening with her," Roberts would tell Donald Spoto. "A great many people thought, after that weekend, that there was more to it...it happened once, that weekend, and that was it."

In an apparent act of religious hypocrisy, Kennedy and aide David Powers attended a Catholic mass the next morning at the Sacred Heart Church before boarding Air Force One en route to Washington, where General Lauris Norstad and Indira Ghandi were scheduled to meet with the president the following day. Bing Crosby later named his 1400 square foot master bedroom the Kennedy Suite in honor of the president's visit. The estate is now a rental property boasting as the site of likely the only tryst between the president and the actress.

Former Florida Senator George Smathers (1913-2007) told J. Randy Taraborrelli that the president saw Marilyn only once more when he took her sailing on a motorboat down the Potomac River. Kennedy also invited Hubert Humphrey (1911-1978) with whom she shared common political views to stimulate conversation. Humphrey was a liberal leader in the United States Senate from 1949 to 1965, vice president in Lyndon B. Johnson's administration from 1965-1969, and a presidential candidate for the Democratic Party in 1968. "We got back at 11:30 at night," Smathers recalled. "There was no hanky-panky between her and JFK that night, I know because I asked him the next day and he would have happily said so. But, anyway, Jackie knew all about that trip. In fact, we were dancing at the White House hall and she said to me, 'Don't think I'm naïve to what you and Jack are doing with all those pretty girls—like Marilyn—sailing on the Potomac under the moonlight. It's all so sophomoric, George.'"

After her historic rendezvous with the president in Rancho Mirage, Marilyn returned to Los Angeles early on Sunday, March 26. She expected to spend the day with Norman Rosten, scheduled to leave Los Angeles in the late afternoon. Rosten found Marilyn "heavy-lidded" and hung-over when she finally stumbled out of her bedroom in a robe. She remained silent about her weekend exploits as they gallery-hopped in Beverly Hills, but her behavior exposed an underlying anxiety about men or a particular man.

At Edgardo Acosta's gallery on North Bedford Drive, a bronze copy of a Rodin statue caught Marilyn's eye. It depicted male and female figures in a passionate embrace. The man's stance was dominant and brutal, while the woman's posture was passive. Rosten later wrote that the statue's symbolism triggered Marilyn's own issues about relationships, compelling her to impulsively purchase it for seven hundred fifty dollars. With Rosten at her side, she immediately brought the statue to Dr. Greenson's home for his interpretation. Marilyn wanted to know the piece's meaning. "He's hurting her," she said, "but he wants to love her, too." The intensity of her reaction to the piece disturbed her friend. Back at her hacienda, Marilyn positioned the sculpture on her coffee table and stepped back to examine it. She reminded Rosten of his flight, and he left with a promise to come back and swim in her pool. Marilyn would die before Rosten could fulfill the pledge.

After her alleged tryst with the president, Marilyn spoke more directly but discreetly with Sidney Skolsky about "the president," never referring to him by name. "Marilyn was extremely fond of the President," Skolsky wrote. "She always mentioned him with kindness and in the most pleasant terms. Despite her fondness for the president, Marilyn did not regard Jacqueline Kennedy with envy or animosity."

Based upon the president's schedule published by the John Fitzgerald Kennedy Presidential Library, he and Marilyn can be placed together on four occasions: at Fifi Fell's apartment in Manhattan, Bing Crosby's estate in Palm Springs, Madison Square Garden, and the Manhattan home of Arthur Krim. An earlier meeting in late 1961 at Peter Lawford's beach home is more difficult to document. On November 18, 1961, Kennedy delivered a speech at a Democratic Party dinner held in his honor at the Hollywood Palladium in Los Angeles. Afterward, he allegedly visited the Lawfords. However, that same evening, Douglas Kirkland was photographing Marilyn at the Bel-Air Hotel. Donald Spoto places this first meeting in October 1961.

Posthumously, the Kennedy-Monroe affair has been romanticized by tabloid books and articles and generally accepted by popular culture. Nowhere is it officially documented. For Marilyn, formerly a neglected child, the relationship fulfilled a fantasy and offered some validation of her worth. Sidney Skolsky described her as "the little orphan waif indulging in free love with the leader of the free world;" however, she indulged with "great discretion."

"In retrospect, we can argue that good taste, discretion, even national security prohibited the few reporters who knew the facts from reporting them," Skolsky wrote of the Kennedy-Monroe relationship. "The truth, I believe, is that freedom of the press, like other freedoms, is more dangerously fragile than we care to confront. I accept my share of the blame."

Throughout United States history, presidents had extramarital affairs, but if the media gained knowledge of these shenanigans, it was not customary to make the information public. This ended in 1998 with President Bill Clinton's highly publicized affair with Monica Lewinsky, a twenty-one year-old White House intern, which culminated to an impeachment trial on grounds of perjury. As the press published lurid details of Lewinsky performing oral sex on Clinton in the Oval Office, his inserting a cigar tube into her vagina, and her preserving a blue dress containing his semen, the president vehemently denied the accusations on national television. While shaking his fist, Clinton told Americans: "*I* did *not* have sex with *that* woman." Later, Clinton admitted the affair, qualifying that her performing oral sex upon him did not constitute his engaging in "real" sex with her. The public had never before been privy to the particulars of a sitting president's sexual dalliances.

When Kennedy discussed world affairs with Dwight D. Eisenhower (president from 1953-1961), as Marilyn was en route to the Palm Springs rendezvous, it is unlikely the two men digressed to the topic of extramarital affairs. However, in this matter, Eisenhower and Kennedy apparently had much in common. During World War II, General Eisenhower left his wife Mamie in the United States when he was deployed to Europe. There, Kay Summersby, a young woman and former British model, was assigned to him as personal driver. Eisenhower died in 1969, and eight years later, Summersby published *Past Forgetting: My Love Affair with Dwight D. Eisenhower.*

CHAPTER TWENTY-FOUR: APRIL TO MAY 1962

Marilyn's final, uncompleted film would inspire two documentaries, *Marilyn Monroe: The Final Days* (2001) and *Marilyn: Something's Got to Give* (1990), as well as an investigative book, *Marilyn: The Last Take*, by Peter Harry Brown and Patte B. Barham, released to coincide with the thirtieth anniversary of her death.

Only brief dazzling excerpts of *Something's Got to Give* would appear in documentaries on Marilyn's life, most recycled from Fox's retrospective, *Marilyn* (1963) and said to be gleaned from the entirety of only about eight usable minutes of footage. Then in 1990, an investigative Fox News reporter, Henry Schipper, set out on a mission to locate surviving scenes by accessing a newly computerized index of Fox Entertainment's archives. He hit pay dirt upon the discovery of six crates of film reels that vindicated Marilyn's reputation as an actress.

"The studio had said that she drifted through her scenes in a drug-induced haze," Schipper reported. "And it has been accepted ever since that her work on *Something's Got to Give* was a sad finale to an otherwise spectacular career. This film proves the studio wrong. In fact, Monroe never looked better. Her work there is on par with the rest of her career—funny, touching and, at times, superb. She was lighting up the screen as only she could."

"She is mature, serene, fragile—but graceful and resplendent, too," author Donald Spoto concurred upon viewing. "None of the emotions were manufactured: they were, to the contrary, deeply felt, imagined, lived in some way. The laughter with the children moments later is neither cute nor manic, but joyous, wise, confident that somehow all will be well…this [is] the effort of a responsible and sensitive actress evoking recognizable human feeling and continuing to grow as an artist, just as she wished." Editors eventually compiled about thirty-seven minutes of the footage into a reconstructed, coherent short film.

Dialogue between Marilyn and Dean Martin in the final scene filmed eerily encapsulates the impact of the discovered footage. In a different context, the lines appear as if Marilyn is speaking from the grave about the malice that had been spread about her final performance. After presenting the shoe salesman masquerading as the man who spent five years on the island with her, Ellen asks her husband if he is satisfied. Nick responds that he is completely content with her explanation. Ellen asks if he now feels ashamed of his suspicions of her. "Terribly," he replies.

* * *

The 34th Academy Awards were held on April 9, 1962 at Santa Monica Civic Auditorium with Bob Hope as host. Andy Williams sang the winning original song, "Moon River," from *Breakfast at Tiffany's,* by Henry Mancini and Johnny Mercer. Fred Astaire presented the Best Picture Award to producer Robert Wise for *West Side Story*, and Burt Lancaster presented Sophia Loren the Best Actress Oscar for *Two Women*, an Italian foreign language film. Marilyn's dramatic performance in *The Misfits* had failed to earn a nomination. The following morning, April 10, *Something's Got to Give* commenced with Marilyn's hair and costume tests.

Jean-Louis' watercolor renderings of Marilyn's elegant costumes, several made of imported Chinese silk, appear suitable for Audrey Hepburn, Grace Kelly, Doris Day, or Lana Turner. Most recently, he had designed sophisticated wardrobes for Turner, Day, and Susan Hayward in several recent films: *Imitation of Life* (1959), *Pillow Talk* (1959), *Portrait in Black* (1960), and *Back Street* (1961). Discovered by Irene Dunne, French-born Jean-Louis (1907-1997) was plucked from Hattie Carnegie's fashion house in New York and hired by Columbia Studios. His iconic creation, a strapless black silk gown worn by Rita Hayworth in *Gilda* (1946) in the "Put the Blame on Mame" musical number, achieved acclaim. After thirteen years at Columbia, Louis moved to Universal Studios where he designed for a string of films by director Ross Hunter. In 1962, Louis was freelancing in film costume design while focusing on his own ready-to-wear fashion line. Nominated for ten Academy Awards, Louis won for

The Solid Gold Cadillac (1956). Having dressed a fuller Marilyn for *The Misfits*, Louis immediately noticed her drastic reduction to one hundred-fifteen pounds and determined his designs no longer needed to disguise a protruding belly.

"The change in her was breathtaking," Louis later said of Marilyn at this point in her career. "It was made even more startling because [she] had just lost twenty-five pounds. She had never been so slim and glowing. And, because she was to wear a bikini in several scenes, she had been working out—and walking a great deal." Marilyn felt thrilled for an opportunity to wear high-fashion clothes for the first time in her career. Deborah Burke of Stamford, Connecticut, purchased one of the dresses Louis designed for Marilyn from eBay online auction for $57,000, and confirmed its measurements as a svelte 34-24-34.

Marilyn's wardrobe included an ensemble of a sheath with a high neckline and low plunge in back of white silk with a pattern of red roses and green vines with a white spring coat; a lime green bikini, full in the middle and narrow at the sides, accompanied by a short beach wrap with pattern of poppies; and a sheath with spaghetti straps in white silk with pattern of black stylized flowers and vining. Jean-Louis also created a stunning two-piece beige suite trimmed with blonde mink at the hem, sleeves, and collar, with matching mink tam and accessorized with a brooch.

For Ellen's nanny uniform, he designed a white long-sleeve fitted shirtdress with cinch belt. For the rescue scene aboard the submarine, Marilyn's character would wear a denim men's shirt and baggy denim jeans accompanied by a bouffant wig with long ponytail. For Nick's dream sequence when he fantasizes about Ellen on the island with Burkett, Jean-Louis designed a revealing island outfit consisting of a leopard loincloth and vines. Sydney Guilaroff designed seven hairstyles including a teased bouffant with elements of a "flip," a style Marilyn had preferred during the year.

Peter Levathes recognized the risk in casting Marilyn as an upper-middle-class wife and mother because he could not predict the public's reaction to a Monroe who looked and dressed differently than in previous films. However, the new style would persist as Marilyn's iconic representation for the next five decades along with the pleated white halter dress from *The Seven Year Itch* and the strapless pink gown from *Gentlemen Prefer Blondes.*

Marilyn arrived on the Fox lot wearing her favorite Jean-Louis black suit for costume and hairstyle tests on April 10, but her director was absent; Cukor oddly refused to direct the tests. "It was a terrible breach of studio etiquette..." William Travilla said. "If this had happened to Elizabeth Taylor, they would have been looking for another star. Liz would have walked." Allan "Whitey" Snyder, Bunny Gardel, and Marjorie Pletcher attended to Marilyn as she delayed in her dressing room. The studio executives had disliked Marilyn's tests for *Let's Make Love*, and she had much at stake. After pacing the set, Henry Weinstein visited the dressing room to coax his reluctant star onto the soundstage. "Mr. Weinstein, what do you have to do when you get up in the morning?" Marilyn asked. "Do you have to put on makeup? Or eye shadow? And what about hair? Does it take fifty minutes to style your hair?" The producer swiftly retreated.

Barbara Eden, Fox's twenty-seven year-old blonde starlet, was filming *Five Weeks in a Balloon* with Red Buttons in an adjacent sound stage as Marilyn prepared for her tests. Having starred in the television series based upon *How To Marry a Millionaire*, she was three years away from her iconic role in *I Dream of Jeannie* as a genie set free from her bottle by an astronaut. Eden had never met Marilyn, but heard much about her from shared stand-in Evelyn Moriarty.

On this particular morning, Moriarty approached Eden and said in her charming New York accent, "Barbara, my *other* star has asked to meet you." Eden, dressed like a clown in baggy plaid pants and a large white shirt, felt ill prepared for an impromptu introduction. Before she could respond, Moriarty grabbed her hand and brought her to stage fourteen where Marilyn's trailer was illuminated by a circle of white light in the middle of the cavernous space. When Marilyn stepped out of the trailer wearing Jean-Louis' black suit, Evelyn announced, "Marilyn, I want you to meet my *other* star." In her memoir, Eden described Marilyn as a "vision of loveliness" who was warm and gracious to the fledgling actress. "She just glows," Eden wrote. "There is something in the ether swirling around her..."

Finally, after many delays, Marilyn was ready to face the camera and stepped onto the set. Under Franz Planer's flattering lighting, she sat on a swiveling stool and slowly spun around to display her hairstyle from every angle for the silent camera. Smiling and giggling, she radiated with bright eyes and delicate beauty. In silent close-ups, she stood before the cinemascope cameras, endlessly and playfully spinning around, smiling, and talking to the crew. This footage is reproduced in documentary films and on the Internet. Marilyn's look and demeanor is more natural than in previous films. With puckered lips, she blows the teased wave of her hair from her eyes. She sensuously shakes her head to allow the waves of her hair to fall away from her face. Just as Barbara Eden had observed, Marilyn seemed to glow from an internal illumination.

In medium and long shots, Marilyn is stunning. Her feline-like movement, observed by Susan Strasberg and Eunice Murray, is more evident than ever. At one point, she is obviously told to walk away from the camera to show the back of her dress. There was little space on the set to ambulate, so she raises her hands and spins around as she reaches the edge, her head thrown back in laughter. As Marilyn models the bikini, she slips off the wrap, allowing it to fall to her high-heeled mules, and covers the scar from gall-bladder surgery with her hand. (Studio photo refinishers would remove the imperfection in stills taken during the costume tests for mass publication around the world.) "It was the most daring swimsuit yet on-screen," Jean-Louis would assert. "And Monroe, with her new svelte figure, looked sensational in it."

While viewing the tests that evening, Weinstein was delighted and thought Marilyn had bravely departed from her established image in a self-reinvention. Fox Vice President, Phil Feldman, and Director of Operations, Stanley Hough, declared the tests as a radiant triumph and sent them to Spyrous Skouras at the New York office. Studio executives on both coasts unanimously agreed that their star was at her peak and the film could be a success. The tests would be posthumously released to the public in Fox's retrospective documentary, *Marilyn*, released the following year.

The next day, Weinstein had an appointment with Marilyn. She failed to arrive, and the producer nervously pacing the set, which was dressed like George Cukor's mansion. When the studio limousine driver reported that there was no answer to repeated knocks on the door, Weinstein panicked and went to his office to call Marilyn's home. After twenty rings, no one answered. Weinstein immediately called a secondary, emergency number. When Marilyn answered on eleventh ring and spoke in a slurred voice, Weinstein sensed danger and promised to immediately rush over to her home. "There's only one bedroom," Marilyn replied. "Where will you sleep?" Although disoriented, she was aware of it raining outside and cautioned the producer to drive safely to avoid an accident.

Summoned by Weinstein, Greenson examined Marilyn and determined she had over-medicated but did not require emergency medical intervention. Frightened and unfamiliar with drug use common among film actors, Weinstein sent a memorandum to his superiors recommending postponement of the production. Fox rejected this suggestion. The studio retained a $10 million insurance policy on Marilyn with Continental Casualty Company of New York and Lloyd's of London. If she were diagnosed with a medical crisis such as cardiac arrest or cancer, coverage would pay a claim, but mental illness and addiction were ineligible. Marilyn always seemed to have psychological problems, the executives rationalized to Weinstein, and still she always finished a film.

On Friday, April 13, Marilyn flew to New York to consult with Lee and Paula Strasberg before principal photography was scheduled to begin on April 23. Lee suffered from a nasty upper respiratory infection but reviewed each scene of the film with his student. Marilyn placed Paula on salary for three thousand dollars per week for private coaching and emotional hand holding on the set in Los Angeles.

As the plane touched ground on Thursday, April 19, Marilyn was suffering from the infection caught from her acting coach. By Sunday, she had a migraine headache, loss of voice, congestion, and labored respiration. Mrs. Murray called Henry Weinstein to alert him of his star's fever soaring to 101 degrees, making it impossible for her to report to work on Monday morning. Dr. Engelberg reserved a bed at Cedars of Lebanon Hospital where physicians diagnosed a massive sinus infection. When Fox sent the studio physician, Dr. Siegel, to Marilyn's home to confirm the illness, he diagnosed a secondary throat infection.

A black cloud now appeared over the film's production. While Marilyn was in Manhattan, the set's swimming pool's seam sprung a leak and flooded the soundstage. From April 23 to 27, she remained at home in bed at the recommendation of the studio physician. However, each day of the first week, Marilyn called for the studio limousine but could not get herself to work. On one morning, Mrs. Murray found her passed out in the bathroom.

When the chauffeur returned to Fifth Helena Drive on Monday, April 30, he expressed concern to Marilyn about her obvious symptoms, but she insisted upon reporting to the studio and arrived nearly thirty minutes early for her makeup call at 6:30 AM. Due to her sore throat and fever, Cukor filmed seven hours of close shots of Marilyn as her character arrives home after being gone for five years and sees her children at play. The next day, however, Marilyn fainted under a hairdryer in her dressing room and had to go home. Executives had ordered the studio physician to prescribe stimulant drugs to rouse her to work, worsening the illness. By the third week of production, Marilyn completed several crucial scenes with the child actors despite her symptoms.

In the reunification scene, Ellen watches her children playing in the pool. Marilyn conveyed emotion through her tears and facial expression without the assistance of speaking lines. The surviving film allows us to observe the actress who impressed the Actors Studio in scenes from *Anna Christie* and *A Streetcar Named Desire.* Marilyn's work on this film suggested the professional heights she might later achieve. She looked splendid and beautiful in Jean-Louis' elegant and sophisticated costumes. Marilyn's face had matured, become more slender, and she moved gracefully onscreen as she spoke in her natural voice.

Curiously, Cukor spent two weeks on Ellen Arden's entrance, producing one hour of film for only one page of script. His peculiarly slow-paced direction of Marilyn after her tardy appearance on set seems to have sabotaged both his leading lady and the film's progress. He dallied with multiple close shots and minimal dialogue with no visible differences among the many repeated takes. While editing the scene, David Bretherton could not identify a major mistake and believed Marilyn had never looked or acted better.

When Shah Mohammed Reza Pahlavi and Empress Farah of Iran visited Fox Studios during their goodwill tour of the United States, *Something's Got to Give*, the only film in production on the lot, served as a highlight. Fox's Movietone News covered the event, but

Marilyn refused to participate in welcoming the leader of a Muslim country.

"I don't know the status of Iran's relationship with Israel," she explained to Henry Weinstein as justification for her absence. The producer contacted Rabbi Max Nussbaum at Temple Israel, a synagogue in Los Angeles founded by many Jewish men in the film industry, including Fox producer Sol Wurtzel. Nussbaum had wed Elizabeth Taylor to Eddie Fisher and served as spiritual advisor to Sammy Davis, Jr. The rabbi advised that "it would be very good indeed" if Marilyn were to be photographed with the Shah. With the rabbi's blessing, Marilyn arrived, albeit late and unable to film, and the Shah watched a scene wherein Steve Allen and Cyd Charisse indirectly discussed Nick's assumed impotence upon his marriage to Bianca.

* * *

On May 7, in Twentieth Century Fox Studio's soundstage fourteen, director George Cukor shouted, "Action!"

Ellen greets her children who are swimming in the pool and asks if they remember her.

Timmy has no memory of her, but Lita—younger—says she does.

Timmy advises Ellen to ignore his sister because she's "crazy" and asks if she will be staying with them.

Ellen gently asks the children if they would like her to stay, and Timmy wonders where she would sleep.

Ellen presses if they would like her to stay if they could make arrangements. Timmy warmly affirms.

In another sequence, the script calls for Ellen's son, portrayed by child actor Robert Christopher Morely, to dive into the swimming pool and accidently get hurt. Marilyn, under the glare of klieg lights, runs toward him as he climbs up the pool ladder. Morely cried on cue and played the boy concealing his tears, a daunting task for a young actor. When boys in the South Sea Islands get hurt and don't want to show their feelings, Marilyn says, they bravely ask someone to cry for them. She offers to cry for her son as she had done many times during their separation. The child smiles as Marilyn embraces him. Cukor instructed cameraman Franz Planer to cut.

On the set of *Something's Got to Give*, Marilyn delivered a powerful performance. She was constantly aware that the young girl portraying her daughter was the age of her own first child, had it lived.

Marilyn's personal pain motivated her acting to a deeper level and created convincing scenes. The film, had it been completed, may have changed her screen image.

Robert Christopher Morely and Alexandra Heilweil hit their marks beside Marilyn in a set dressed as a garden and swimming pool. The three actors sat on an artificial lawn. Franz Planer moved the large Cinemascope camera closer for a medium shot. Alexandra said she was cold, and Marilyn immediately rubbed the child's arm. Cukor shouted, "Camera…and action!"

Marilyn embraced both children simultaneously, closed her eyes, and expressed her love for them, calling them her "two best sweethearts in the whole world." On the verge of tears, she shifted to pure joy as the three actors rolled on the floor giggling. The delightful shot was completed in one take.

"I'm just sorry in retrospect that I pulled away when she wanted to console me," Robert Christopher Morley would say as an adult decades later, "but, I do remember when she knelt down to help me out of the pool. She was very tender…and in the fantasy world of being on the set and shooting the movie it was very, very nice to have Marilyn be my mother."

"I remember looking up at her, and it was as if she drifted out of a mist," Alexandra Heilweil later recalled, as a woman of Marilyn's age. "To this day, she is the model of femininity to me. I think it was the way she carried herself and the sweetness of her voice—totally feminine and totally elegant."

"Marilyn was magnificent," Alexandra's mother, Eva Wolas Heilweil, would say. "You never really knew how sick she was. And I can tell you, she was sick indeed."

On May 8, Marilyn stood on the set shaking with chills and grew so weak that she needed to rest on the set's patio furniture. Studio maid Hazel Washington observed the oral thermometer registering Marilyn's fever of 101. Dr. Seigel examined Marilyn in the dressing room and ordered her home until the following week, meeting the Screen Actors Guild's requirement for excused absence. Paula Strasberg and her sister, Bea Glass, arrived at Marilyn's hacienda with Jewish penicillin (homemade chicken soup) and nursed the patient back to health.

On Monday, May 14, Marilyn spent nine hours working with

the children. In the afternoon, she shot a scene with a nine-year-old Cocker Spaniel named Jeff, and his handler, Rudd Weatherwax, under 94 degree lighting. In the sequence, Ellen gingerly squats beside the edge of the pool talking to her children for the first time as the family dog—Tippy—greets her, recognizing his long-lost mistress. She notices the family pet has gained weight during her absence. Over twenty of perhaps thirty takes survive of Marilyn repeatedly delivering her lines letter-perfect. She also tells the children that Tippy remembers her because she used to visit a long time ago. Tippy had also been the name of Norma Jeane's childhood pet that had been tragically killed; perhaps Marilyn requested the dog in the film be given the same name in order for her to summon real emotions in the true Method approach to acting.

For once, Marilyn was not responsible for delaying production; Jeff repeatedly missed his trainer's cues to bark and failed to hit his mark beside her. Marilyn remained patient and nurturing, cuddling the dog and laughing when he pawed at her hair and moved out of frame. She even tried coaching the dog herself when he would not respond to Weatherwax. At one point, Jeff knocked her over. "He's getting better," she squealed, laughing wildly and clapping her hands. In unedited close shots of the dog from Marilyn's point of view, one can hear her whispering to Weatherwax that the dog is tired. In all takes of Marilyn's lines with the problematic Cocker Spaniel, she "never looked or acted better," according to film editor David Bretherton.

"Here's a director who finally got his star back!" observed Susan Strasberg. "What kind of man would spend the entire day filming a scene with an uncooperative dog and the whole night rewriting the script?" According to Harry Brown and Patte B. Barham, Cukor's obsessive focus on Marilyn's interaction with the children in the reunion scene monopolized two weeks of production and twenty-seven hours of film to complete nine lines of dialogue. Three-quarters of the one hundred thirty-one takes were identical with the exception of four significant errors. Cukor also shot twenty-six versions of Marilyn's dialogue with Robert Christopher Morley. Not only did Marilyn question Cukor's motives, she also took objection to his rude behavior toward the child actors and believed he was projecting his disdain of her on to them.

Cukor's behavior was only one of Marilyn's many annoyances. She had consented to the film based upon Nunnally Johnson's screenplay. However, once production began, couriers arrived each night at her hacienda to deliver Walter Bernstein's daily rewrites of scenes scheduled for filming the following morning. The studio printed the new pages on blue paper for differentiation from the original script, written on white paper. Marilyn spent evenings in bed memorizing new lines and planning every gesture. The gradual deviation from the original plot and last minute changes angered her. At dawn, studio maid Hazel Washington made black coffee and encouraged an exhausted Marilyn to drink several cups.

Henry Weinstein schemed to have the new revisions transcribed from blue to white paper, but Marilyn noticed his deception. Since the color of the revised pages was the same as the original script, Marilyn did not have the benefit of a clear prompt for modified dialogue, making it difficult to identify and then learn new lines. It is unclear why studio executives would sabotage her preparation and risk the film's financial success.

One morning, Marilyn arrived on set prepared to shoot fifteen pages of script, but the set and crew were not ready for her. Cukor had relocated the production to the Balboa Bay Club in Newport Harbor to film a scene aboard a yacht with Tom Tryon and five young starlets. Given Marilyn's many absences, Cukor seemed to simply abandon hope of her arrival on the set.

The production schedule for Friday, May 18 included a fantasy sequence of Nick Arden's imaging his wife and her male companion stranded on the island paradise as Adam and Eve in the Garden of Eden. To prepare, Tom Tryon rehearsed swinging like Tarzan on the limb of an artificial tree. Marilyn, dressed in a leopard loincloth, would take a bite of an apple. The scene was rescheduled, but Marilyn would never film it.

On the afternoon of Thursday, May 17, Marilyn left the set with written permission from Fox executives after a morning of work to attend a command performance for President Kennedy in New York. As Marilyn flew to New York for the president's birthday gala, she memorized lines for impending scenes; art imitated life.

"Who is the president now?" Ellen Arden asks upon her rescue from the island. "Kennedy," she is told.

"Which one?" she replies.

The early dismissal, combined with Marilyn's confirmed lingering upper respiratory infection and significant absenteeism, would ultimately shut down the production and derail her career, but Fox's poor treatment of Marilyn must be viewed in context of the condition of the motion picture industry in the early 1960s. The studio contract player system was falling apart, costs were skyrocketing and profits were declining.

The studio executives denied Marilyn's illness and ordered their physician to prescribe and administer injections of amphetamines to increase her energy to work. Dr. Engelberg prescribed antibiotic drugs and administered vitamin and liver extract injections to boost her resistance. Despite Marilyn's lingering upper respiratory infection and a multitude of drugs in her system, surviving footage displays no evidence of a temperamental actress. Marilyn apologized when she flubbed a line (which was often the case), but alternative takes reveal that she eventually completed the scenes successfully. She soothed and reassured a child actor when director George Cukor lost his patience. When Marilyn stumbled on words, she cried, "You're going to hate me!" or "Sorry, sorry, sorry." After stumbling on a line in a series of retakes, she resorted to humor: "We're getting there, George."

"She had a sense of humor and she didn't take herself seriously around the crew," recalled art director and assistant producer Gene Allen, "I mean, she wasn't any prima donna, and she was full of fun, but she was also looking for that escape."

"She'd be waiting around while they changed the lighting or whatever because the assistant director, Buck Hall, never told her that she could leave," said stand-in Evelyn Moriarty. "Most other people would have walked away, but not her. You could feel the tension on the set. They treated her like a piece of meat. On the other hand, the crew—the technicians, the electricians, the grips, the extras—all adored her. It was the production office that hated her."

Meanwhile, Christopher Mankiewicz served as second assistant director on the set of Fox's *Cleopatra* in Rome and was assigned the arduous task of micro-managing Elizabeth Taylor and driving the high-maintenance diva to the studio every day. Taylor's contract stipulated her excusal from work during her menstrual cycle, and she took advantage of this clause. Taylor's assistant would call the youthful Mankiewicz with such frequency about his boss' cramps that his father, director Joe Mankiewicz, tracked her periods on chart mounted on a wall in his office. Compared to Taylor, working with Marilyn should have been a cakewalk.

Chapter Twenty-Five: **The JFK Birthday Gala**

Just as Arthur Miller had been welcomed to the White House in May, Marilyn now received her summons from the Kennedy administration. Dated April 11, 1962, a letter on embossed White House stationery arrived at Marilyn's hacienda:

> *Many, many thanks for your acceptance of the invitation to appear at the President's Birthday Party at Madison Square Garden on May 19. Your appearance will guarantee a tremendous success for the affair and a fitting tribute to President Kennedy.*
> *With every good wish,*
> *Sincerely,*
> *Kenneth O'Donnell*
> *Special Assistant to the President*

This pièce de résistance command performance for the leader of the free world provided Marilyn with validation of her value as a human being. "She would have come back from the dead to be there," Mrs. Murray wrote.

On Saturday, May 19, at 8:30 in the evening, the Democratic Party hosted the fundraiser to reimburse the cost of the 1960 presidential election. Taking place ten days before the president's forty-fifth birthday, the event was staged as a birthday salute to the Commander-in-Chief at the cost of one thousand dollars per ticket. A series of performances by famous actors culminated in the birthday celebration, complete with an enormous cake. It was Peter Lawford's idea for Marilyn to sing "Happy Birthday" to the president in her sexy, whispery voice in the event's climax. Broadway producer Richard Adler, who wrote *Damn Yankees* and *The Pajama Game*, was in charge of musical portion of the show.

For seven decades, Madison Square Garden at Fifth Street and Eighth Avenue, an ornate Moorish building designed by Stanford White, served as a venue primarily for boxing matches. Two months before the birthday gala, the Garden was the site of a tragic death during the 1962 welterweight championship bout between Emile Griffith and Benny "Kid" Paret. In the anticipation of the match, Paret insulted Griffith and implied that he was gay. In the twelfth round, Paret became entangled in the ring's ropes, and Griffith delivered a relentless pounding that proved fatal ten days later.

Tragedy at the Garden existed in fiction as well. A few months after the gala, the climactic assassination sequence of the *Manchurian Candidate* (1962) was filmed in the historic venue. The plot involved a Communist conspiracy to brainwash an American war hero to assassinate a presidential candidate on stage during an election convention speech. Director John Frankenheimer filmed the assassination of the candidate, portrayed by actor Robert Riordan, on the Garden's stage by a bullet from the rifle of the sniper, Laurence Harvey, perched high in a lighting booth. The film was released in October 1962 but was removed from distribution and shelved for a generation due to its parallel to President Kennedy's November 1963 assassination by alleged sniper Lee Harvey Oswald, perched high in the Texas School Book Depository.

Marilyn chose Isidore Miller as her escort for the historic evening. "He came here an immigrant and I thought this would be one of the biggest things in his life," she said. "He's about seventy-five or eighty years old and I thought this would be something that he would be telling his grandchildren about." Patricia Newcomb would accompany them.

Although Marilyn promised Richard Adler that she would perform in a sedate, high-neck, silk black Norman Norell dress, she secretly schemed to make a splash with an unforgettable, show-stopping gown. She called upon designer Jean-Louis as co-conspirator. "I want you to design a truly historic dress, a dazzling dress that's one of a kind," Marilyn told him, keeping the event a secret. She described a full-length gown that "only Marilyn Monroe could wear."

"Marilyn had a totally charming way of boldly displaying her body and remaining quite elegant at the same time," Louis said. "So I designed an apparently nude dress—the nudist dress—relieved only by sequins and beading." Louis had designed similar gowns for Marlene Dietrich in the early 1950s when she began performing in concert, dying silk soufflé fabric to match her skin tone to create the illusion, when seen from a distance, that she only wore sequins and beads against her bare skin.

In March, Louis presented Marilyn with sketches of two designs for her gown. One was backless with high, draping neckline and long sleeves. The other was a sheath with a low, scooped décolleté to be worn with long, white gloves. Marilyn chose the latter but deleted the gloves. Louis ordered flesh-colored silk soufflé gauze woven from fine thread on miniature looms in France. Once it arrived in Los Angeles, he noted it feeling like soft skin. Louis and his assistants descended upon Marilyn's home and disappeared with her behind the closed door of her spare bedroom while Mrs. Murray paced in the living room. Marilyn stood naked for days before the mirrors as Louis and his couture cutters designed the pattern against her body. As the dress was unlined and Marilyn would wear no undergarments, twenty individually cut layers of gauze were used to mask her breasts and two hundred tiny panels were stitched into the sheath for modesty.

The dress contained a clear plastic zipper and tiny hooks sewn by hand to ensure that it fit like a second skin. "It was impossible for her to wear undergarments with this kind of dress," said Nancy Valentino, senior vice president of marketing at Christie's Auction House, who examined the size 5 gown when it was sold for $1.26 million in 1999. "She was literally sewn into it, and I think what's interesting is she wanted it to be so close-fitting that it was cut to her body and actually measured to her body."

Once the dress was constructed, a team of seamstresses took over a month to painstakingly hand-sew six thousand rhinestone beads and sequins in a carefully calculated, graduated sequence of rosettes and tiny drops. Between the gauze fabric and rhinestones, Marilyn would appear on stage in the spotlight "as if she was covered in a spiderweb of glittering beads, and nothing else." The beading would reflect the lights, take on their colors, and glow as if illuminated from within. Marilyn spent $12,000 on Louis' creation at a time when the average American annual income was $5,556 and the average new home cost $12,500.

Before leaving for New York, Marilyn practiced her sensual rendition of the song for Joan Greenson and in doing so, shared her growing anxiety. To console her, Joan gave her a copy of the children's book *The Little Engine That Could.* The story about a small train's attempt to carry precious cargo over tall mountains is an allegory meant to build confidence in children and allay self-doubt. Marilyn would leave Joan's childhood book in her apartment, and it would be auctioned as her personal property in 1999.

When Marilyn needed support or reassurance at a time when Dr. Greenson was unavailable, she carried a transitional object representing him and the strength he inspired. For the command performance, Marilyn symbolically chose the white knight piece of her chess set. Without breeching patient-psychotherapist confidentiality, Greenson referenced this in his publication *Explorations in Psychoanalysis*:

> *The young woman had recently been given a gift of a carved ivory chess set...As she looked at the set through the sparkling light of a glass of champagne, it suddenly struck her that I looked like the white knight of her chess set. The realization evoked in her a feeling of comfort...The white knight was a protector, it belonged to her, she could carry it wherever she went, it would look after her, and I could go on my merry way...without having to worry about her.*

At 12:30 in the afternoon, Peter Lawford and Milton Ebbins arrived by helicopter outside soundstage 14 on the Fox lot to whisk Marilyn, Paula Strasberg, and Patricia Newcomb to Los Angeles International Airport for a flight to New York City. With an 8 millimeter movie camera in hand, James Haspiel waited outside Marilyn's apartment and filmed her arrival in a sleek black limousine. The driver opened the door, and Marilyn stepped out in casual attire and embraced May Reis, who caressed her cheek. Marilyn chatted gaily with Reis and the driver before waving to Hapiel's camera and entering the building.

On Friday, the following morning, Marilyn received a breach of contract letter from Fox's legal department for leaving the set and traveling to New York. Richard Adler spent three hours in her apartment rehearsing "Happy Birthday" with Adler playing the white baby grand piano. Concerned about her sounding too sexy, the producer urged Marilyn to keep her promise to wear a high neck gown.

Haspiel haunted the sidewalk outside 444 East Fifty-Seventh Street, trusty camera in hand, and filmed Marilyn as she left for a rehearsal at Madison Square Garden, accompanied by Pat Newcomb. Wearing a lime green Pucci blouse, white capris, white pumps, and a mink coat draped over her shoulder, Marilyn could pass for any attractive, blonde resident of the Upper East Side. She wore cat-eye sunglasses and had another pair perched on her head.

At the Garden, Marilyn worked with Richard Allan, Jack Benny, and jazz pianist Hank Jones, hired to accompany her vocals. In a 2005 interview with New Public Radio, Jones recalled Marilyn fretting through the rehearsal. "She was very nervous and upset..." he said. "But who wouldn't be nervous singing 'Happy Birthday' to the president?" Marilyn diligently rehearsed the song and carefully choreographed gestures, with Newcomb and Reis in the wings for moral support. Photographer Victor R. Helou preserved her efforts on film.

On the next evening, May 18th, hairdresser Kenneth arrived at Marilyn's apartment to groom her for a meeting with Richard Meryman, an associate editor of *Life.* The magazine planned a series of celebrity interviews exploring fame and wished to begin with Marilyn's perspective on its impact on her life. John Springer accompanied her to the meeting at the Savoy-Plaza Hotel where Meryman waited at the bar of the hotel with another staff writer, Barbara Villet.

The quartet sat together, drinking champagne, as they discussed the concept for the interview. In a summer issue, *Life* would publish a verbatim transcript of her responses to their questions. "The legend may become extinct before publication," Marilyn mused. When this caused concerned expressions, Marilyn added, "Not the girl, but the legend." As the discussion concluded, Marilyn told her companions that Peter Lawford was staying upstairs at the hotel in preparation for the birthday salute and suggested they drop in on him. He had encouraged her to contact him when she arrived in town.

The three companions consented and followed Marilyn into the elevator. As the elevator doors opened on the tenth floor, she hesitated in confusion about which direction to turn in the corridor before leading them a door and knocking. When the door opened, Springer remembered seeing an athletic, tanned young man standing in nothing but a hotel towel. Marilyn announced that she was looking for Mr. Lawford and acknowledged he must be staying in another room. The young man stared at her. Dazed with awe, the young man stuttered a reply that Lawford was not present and then slowly closed the door. Marilyn burst into giggles. "He probably thinks he's drunk," she said. "He's seeing pink Marilyns." The group returned to the lobby and learned at the front desk that Lawford was registered but out for the evening. Meryman and Villet departed, and Springer invited Marilyn to join him and his wife for dinner. She declined and returned to her home.

On the morning of the gala, Marilyn called Joan Greenson in Los Angeles, in a time zone three hours earlier, for last minute support. She warbled her brief song birthday song and added verses modified for the occasion. In the late afternoon, a make-up artist and hairdresser arrived at Marilyn's apartment to prepare her.

For many years, hairdresser Mickey Song would claim that Marilyn arrived at Madison Square Garden with hair in curlers for him to perform the comb out and styling. According to Song, who worked for the president and attorney general as a personal barber, Robert Kennedy urged Marilyn to allow Song to style her hair. When interviewed for *Marilyn: The Last Take*, Song claimed Marilyn asked him to create "something historic" and took credit for styling the exaggerated flip on the right side of her head.

As quoted in *Marilyn: The Last Take*, Song recounted overhearing Robert Kennedy arguing with Marilyn behind closed doors in the dressing room at Madison Square Garden. Allegedly, when Kennedy left the dressing room, he called her "a rude bitch." When the author interviewed Song in his Los Angeles apartment in 1998, the hairdresser denied ever telling this version and alleged that the authors of *Marilyn: The Last Take* had fabricated it. For many years, Song spoke at memorial services held annually on the anniversary of Marilyn's death in the chapel where her funeral had been held in

1962. Song's description of his alleged brief encounter with Marilyn varied little year after year and never included mention of Robert Kennedy's presence backstage at the Garden.

Song's claims are another example of Monroe apocrypha often applied to prove a relationship between Monroe and Robert Kennedy. The myth of Song styling her hair for the gala is now debunked, beginning with Jean Louis' sketch of the gown depicting the hairstyle Marilyn would wear. During this period, Marilyn chose George Masters and Kenneth Batelle to style her hair when in residence at her New York apartment. Batelle, known professionally as Kenneth, styled Jacqueline Kennedy's hair when he was employed at Helena Rubinstein's salon in the 1950s. He groomed President Kennedy and the First Lady for the Inauguration and received media publicity as the artist behind Jacqueline's bouffant hairstyles. Additionally, photographs of Marilyn in the elevator of her apartment home on the evening of May 19—fully coiffed and dressed in the gown she would wear only once for this occasion—have appeared on the Internet. Despite Song's claim, she did not leave her apartment wearing curlers.

A faded yellow carbon copy from Lilly Dache Beauty Salon on East Fifty-Sixth Street sold at Bonhams Auctions on June 14, 2009 in Los Angeles; and indisputably solved the mystery of Marilyn's hairdresser for this historic occasion. Handwritten by a sales clerk, it reads, "*Miss Monroe/ 5/18/62 5/19/62 /Kenneth/Services at home/Fri & Saturday $150.*" According to the auction catalogue, a white register slip attached to the receipt documented Marilyn's having paid the bill on June 13 with "check #1689." The name "Kenneth" clearly refers to stylist Kenneth Batelle who was employed by Lilly Dache until he opened his own salon in a Renaissance Revival townhouse on East Fifty-Fourth Street in 1963. He continued to operate a salon in New York until his death, and his website cited credit for Marilyn's asymmetric bouffant flip for her appearance at the birthday gala. Despite this false claim, Mickey Song spoke well of Marilyn and may indeed have met her. He died in 2005.

Other documents uncovered after Marilyn's death detail the steps leading to her grand entrance at the gala. According to another invoice, Marie Irvine of Elmhurst, Long Island, charged Marilyn $125 for applying her make-up for the event. Another receipt shows Marilyn's limousine limousine driver collected Isidore Miller in Brooklyn, drove Marilyn and Miller to dinner at the Four Season restaurant, and then deposited them at Madison Square Garden for the gala.

At 8:30 PM, on Saturday, May 19, seventeen thousand people filled Madison Square Garden for the Democratic Party fundraiser. The arena was decorated in red, white, and blue balloons, and a huge wooden stage was constructed and decorated in a patriotic theme. The president's box at the center of the Garden was draped in bunting and adorned with the Presidential Seal. President Kennedy sat in the center of the front row, and smoked a cigar. Robert Kennedy sat in the third row, with his wife, Ethel, directly in front of him in the second row. The president's sisters, Eunice and Patricia, sat near their mother, Rose. The First Lady was conspicuously absent, having fled to Virginia where she became a last-minute participant in the Loudoun Hunt Horse Show at Glen Ora and earned a third place ribbon.

The call sheet denotes Marilyn's appearance as number 35 of 39, but the plan for the evening was a running joke about her tardiness. Peter Lawford would introduce her again and again, but Marilyn would not appear until the finale to sing "Happy Birthday" as two men in chef hats carried out a six-foot birthday cake.

Opera soprano Maria Callas, then the lover of wealthy Greek shipping magnate Aristotle Onassis, performed early in the show. In a twist of fate, by the end of the decade Onassis would end the relationship with Callas and marry Kennedy's widow, Jacqueline. Robert Champion, a hairdresser from the salon at the Bergdorf-Goodman department store in Manhattan, styled Callas' hair for the performance and remained with her throughout the evening. In his unpublished memoirs, he described bedlam backstage as the celebrities readied for their appearances. Champion waited outside Callas' dressing room, one of many large spaces spread along a long corridor.

Champion, Callas, and Marilyn walked together to the deep pit behind the stage to await the cues. Dressed in white, Peggy Lee joined them. The group stood for a long time feeling the heat of the many lights illuminating from the stage. "I kept checking their make-up, as we all stood there perspiring," Champion wrote in his unpublished memoir *He Made Stars Shine.* Milton Ebbins also stood beside Marilyn for support.

After the orchestra played a birthday overture, opera baritone Robert Merrill sang "The Star Spangled Banner," an anthem he would perform for years at the season opening game of the New York Yankees. Jack Benny, the master of ceremonies, took the stage with a comedic monologue. "The amazing thing to me," he said, poking fun of the president's penchant for rocking chairs to ease back pain from a war injury, "is how a man in a rocking chair can have such a young wife."

The Jerome Robbins Ballet performed excerpts from *New York Export: Opus Jazz*, a 1958 "ballet in sneakers," conveying the story of urban youth through Latin and African American rhythms. Actor-singer-dancer-comedian Danny Kaye (*Hans Christian Anderson* and *White Christmas*) performed with the Johnny Mann Singers. The Presentation of Colors by the United States Armed Forces was followed by appearances by Henry Fonda, Shirley MacLaine, and Peter Lawford.

In a voluminous green silk gown patterned with pink cabbage roses, Maria Callas sang two arias from Bizet's *Carmen.* In appreciation for her participation, the President would send her a silver bowl from Tiffany & Company with a signed photograph. Elliott Reid, Marilyn's co-star in *Gentlemen Prefer Blondes*, performed a JFK impersonation that rivaled that of Vaughn Meader, lampooned the president's thick Bostonian accent on television and later released a satirical comedy album *The First Family.* Songwriter and jazz vocalist Peggy Lee (best known for her 1958 hit "Fever") and crooner Bobby Darin ("Splish Splash," "Mack the Knife," and "Beyond the Sea") each sang in the spotlight. Proboscis-endowed Jimmy Durante, the self-proclaimed "Schnozzola," performed with his partner, Eddie Jackson, recreating their familiar vaudeville act.

The improvisational comedy duo Mike Nichols and Elaine May, whose Broadway standup debut won a Grammy in 1962 for Best Comedy Performance, read a series of fake telegrams addressed to the president from heads of state. The pair would collaborate on the screenplay for *The Birdcage* (1996). Nichols would also direct classic films such as *Who's Afraid of Virginia Woolf?* (1966), *The Graduate* (1967), and *Working Girl* (1988). He is currently married to news anchor Diane Sawyer.

A strong African-American presence among the performers reflected the president's commitment to civil rights: Ella Fitzgerald; Harry Belafonte; South African singer, Marion Makeba; and Diahann Carroll. Since March, Carroll had been appearing in *No Strings* on Broadway as an African-American female in an interracial romance not indicated in the musical's script. She would win a Tony for her performance, and by the end of the decade, star in the television series *Julia* as the first African-American female in a non-stereotyped leading role.

Throughout the evening, Peter Lawford stood at the podium, and introduced Marilyn; his introduction followed by a drum roll and a spotlight. Invariably, there was no Monroe, and the next act performed. The anticipation of the crowd reached frenzy by the end of the evening, when Adler had planned her entrance. Off stage, Marilyn listened to the show as Robert Champion refreshed her lipstick, powdered her nose, and checked her blusher.

An edited, grainy television recording of Marilyn's performance is often included in documentaries and is available on the Internet. "On the occasion of your birthday, this lovely lady is not only punctitudinous but punctual," Lawford says. "Mr. President, Marilyn Monroe..." He gestures toward an area illuminated by a spotlight as a drum rolls. No Marilyn. Lawford laughs and fills the time: "A woman about whom it truly may be said, she needs no introduction," and then imitating the president's Bostonian accent, "*But let me just say*, here she is..." There is another drum roll. No Monroe. "But I'll give her an introduction anyway, because in the history of show business perhaps there has been no one female who's meant so much, who's done more..."

The crowd roars with thunderous applause as Marilyn, with assistance from Robert Champion or with a gentle push from Milton Ebbins—depending upon whose version one believes—ascends the makeshift steps at the rear of the stage and steps into the spotlight. She looks radiant, and the audience goes wild. Coyly clutching her white ermine stole to her neck in an effort to delay the unveiling of Jean-Louis' tightfitting, restrictive creation, Marilyn runs across the stage to the podium in tiny steps befitting a geisha due to the tightness of her gown. Lawford places his left arm around her and delivers the punch line suggested by comedian Bill Dana, "Mr. President, the *late* Marilyn Monroe."

As Lawford removes Marilyn's stole, she thanks him, flicks the microphone with her two fingers—sending a reverberation thorough the cavernous arena—and repositions it. The thousands of rhinestones in her gown reflect the bright lights, and Marilyn is an ethereal vision with platinum hair, white-toned body and face make-up, and a virtual white light of costume. The crowd goes wild.

"I was honored when they asked me to appear at the President's birthday rally," Marilyn told *Life*. "There was like a hush over the whole place when I came on to sing 'Happy Birthday'—like if I had been wearing a slip, I would have thought my slip was showing or something. I thought, 'Oh, my gosh, what if no sound comes out!'"

Marilyn covers her eyes with her hands to shield them from the glaring spotlights and scans the audience. "I remember when I turned to the microphone," she would recall, "I looked all the way up and back and thought, that's where'd I'd ordinarily be...way up there under one of those rafters, close to the ceiling, after I paid my $2." About thirty seconds pass as Marilyn collects herself and allows the audience to settle down. "It's sort of like an embrace," Marilyn said of the reaction. "Then you think, by God, I'll sing this song if it's the last thing I ever do, and for all the people." Marilyn exhales into microphone only to arouse louder roars and stronger applause. She turns her head in the direction of Hank Jones at the piano, straining to hear him repeatedly play the key over the cheers of the crowd. Hesitatingly, Marilyn begins to sing "Happy Birthday" in a slow, whispery voice as her name is shouted by a voluble male voice in the audience. She veers from her sexy manner to sing the line "Mr. President" with reverence and dignity, changing her body language by standing erect.

As Marilyn grips the podium, she segues into "Thanks, Mr. President," written by Richard Adler to the melody of "Thanks for the Memory," a song made famous by Bob Hope:

Thanks, Mr. President,
For all the things you've done,
The battles that you've won,
The way you deal with U.S. Steel,

And our problems by the ton,
We thank you, so much.

Marilyn runs her right hand up her thigh and stomach. She pulls her hand away before reaching her breast, with a cupping gesture in synchronization with the line, "our problems by the ton." The fourth line refers to Kennedy recently having taken on the steel industry (then in the position similar to that of the oil industry today) and forcing it to reduce its inflated prices.

"Everybody, 'Happy Birthday!'" Marilyn shouts as she uses her arms and hands to conduct the audience and orchestra, and the massive crowd sings to the president. With a sweeping motion of her arms, she jumps into the air, seemingly spontaneous in her excitement. Photographs of the rehearsal, though, show that Adler had choreographed this movement. Marilyn retreats off stage as the enormous cake is carried into the arena. Richard Adler described the serenade as "mass seduction." In a photograph of the presidential box, President Kennedy sits at center with his chin resting on his hand, Robert and Ethel Kennedy smile broadly, and Patricia Lawford's expression is stoic.

At the end of the evening, President Kennedy addressed the crowd with a speech that juxtaposed humor with current serious social events, and thanked many of the individual performers. He voiced pride "to be in a political party which can produce this extraordinary talent."

"Miss Monroe left a picture to come all the way East," the president commented, "and I can now retire from politics after having had 'Happy Birthday' sung to me in such a sweet and wholesome way." This punchline received an enthusiastic reaction from the audience. Afterward, Kennedy visited the performers backstage. Marilyn described their interaction to Richard Meryman: "I think I did something wrong when I met the president. Instead of saying, 'How do you do?' I just said, 'This is my former father-in-law, Isidore Miller.' I should have said, "How do you do, Mr. President.' But I had already done the singing, so well, you know. I guess nobody noticed it."

Robert Champion joined Callas in her dressing room, and she presented him with a record album of her singing a collection of

French arias. The stage director knocked on the door and entered, informing Callas that other performers were waiting outside in the hallway and wishing to pay their respects to her. "Show them in," Callas said. Champion interrupted Callas as she received the visitors to report Marilyn had expressed an interest in formally meeting her. Callas consented, and Champion went to Marilyn's dressing room and brought her to meet the diva. He obtained signatures of the celebrities visiting Callas' dressing room on the record album and auctioned it in 2010. Victor R. Helous photographed Marilyn with Callas and her guests, who included Richard Blackwell, the designer and fashion critic who gained notoriety for annually publishing his list of the worst dressed celebrities. Marilyn had the dubious honor of having her name appear on Blackwell's list. Helous currently sells copies of the photographs on his website.

Arthur and Mathilde Krim hosted a private party in honor of the President at their Manhattan home following the salute. In 1987, *Life* magazine published photographs of the reception in an article titled "Cocktails at Camelot." Arthur Krim (1910-1994) was an American entertainment lawyer who later served as finance chairman of United States Democratic Party and advisor to President Lyndon B. Johnson. He and attorney Robert Benjamin purchased United Artists from Charles Chaplin and Mary Pickford in 1951, a motion picture studio corporation without a physical studio.

They distributed and owned movies created by independent filmmakers and ushered in the independent production system that exists today. Krim headed Orion Pictures from 1982-1992. A record fourteen of his films won the Best Picture Oscar, ten with United Artists and four with Orion, including *West Side Story* (1961), *Midnight Cowboy* (1969), *One Flew Over The Cuckoo's Nest* (1975), *Rocky* (1976), *Annie Hall* (1977), and *Silence of the Lambs* (1991).

Coincidently, *The Manchurian Candidate* was released through United Artists, and as the studio's president, Krim cringed at its subject matter, fearful that it might be received as un-American and might also encourage political assassinations. The film's co-star, Frank Sinatra, contacted President Kennedy to persuade Krim to make the film. Allegedly, it was Kennedy's phone call to Krim that started production. Ironically, its director, John Frankenheimer, drove Robert Kennedy to the Ambassador Hotel on the evening he was assassinated by Shiran Shiran in 1968.

Krim's wife, Mathilde (born 1926), was noteworthy in her own right. Holding a doctorate degree from the University of Geneva, Switzerland, she had been part of the research team that developed the method for prenatal determination of gender. In 1962, Mathilde served as a research scientist at Sloan-Kettering Institute for Cancer Research. In the 1980s, she hosted publicized charity events to raise funds for AIDS research.

Marilyn arrived at the Krims' on the arm of Isidore Miller and accompanied by Patricia Newcomb, who wore a gold lamé damask cocktail dress with matching wrap. Secret Service agent Anthony Sherman opened the door of Marilyn's limousine. Noticing he held a guest list, she smiled and said, "Hello, sir. I'm Marilyn Monroe.'" Every moment of Sherman's assignment to the president was historic, but his encounter with Marilyn was the most memorable.

Marilyn hovered over Isidore Miller making sure his plate was full and he had a chair in which to sit. "Sit down, Dad," Marilyn insisted. "I can't sit when everybody else is standing," he replied. She urged, "Sit, I want you to."

Mathilde Krim remembered her guest: "There was a softness to her that was very appealing. She was—well, just extraordinarily beautiful." Other guests included members of Kennedy's family and administration, performers from the gala, and other political personalities. They included New York City's Mayor Robert F. Wagner; Kennedy aides, Kenneth O'Donnell and Larry O'Brien; Robert Sargent Shriver, the first director of the Peace Corps, and Eunice Kennedy Shriver, the president's sister; Steven Edward Smith, political strategist in JFK's 1960 presidential campaign, and Jean Kennedy Smith, the president's sister; and Anna Rosenberg, regional director of the War Manpower Commission, who had been awarded the Medal of Freedom in 1945 and who was the first female recipient of the Medal for Merit.

Historian and aide to President Kennedy, Arthur Schlesigner, Jr. (1917-2007) spent a significant amount of time chatting with Marilyn, with whom he shared mutual friends, Joe and Olie Rauth. "The image of this exquisite, beguiling and desperate girl will always stay with me..." he wrote in his personal journal published in 2007.

"I do not think I have seen anyone so beautiful; I was enchanted by her manner and her wit, at once so masked, so ingenuous and so penetrating. But one felt a terrible unreality about her—as if talking to someone under water. Bobby and I engaged in mock competition for her; she was most agreeable to him and pleasant to me, but one never felt her to be wholly engaged. She receded into her own glittering mist."

Adlai Stevenson (1900-1965), Kennedy's appointed Ambassador to the United Nations and former Democratic Party Presidential Candidate in the 1952 and 1956 elections, wrote that he approached Marilyn "only after breaking through the strong defenses established by Robert Kennedy, who was dodging around her like a moth around a flame." Kennedy's wife, Ethel, must not have been amused. Stevenson described Marilyn as "wearing skin and beads," but added, "I didn't see the beads!"

White House photographer Cecil Stoughton took a photograph of Marilyn sandwiched between RFK and JFK that would be published after the subjects' deaths. The trio stands beside a bookcase and two windows in a corner of the room. In profile, Marilyn is clearly speaking as she holds a champagne glass low against her right side. She is possibly holding the chess piece—a transitional object representing Dr. Greenson's support—in a handkerchief in her left hand. Robert Kennedy stands to her right. The president, turned away from the camera, stands to Marilyn's left and is clearly listening to her.

In the far right of the photo, facing Marilyn, a smiling Arthur Schlesigner, Jr., or possibly, Isadore Miller, stands in profile, holding a drink and a cigar. A female wearing a damask suite, possibly Patricia Newcomb, stands beside him. Behind the president, in the far corner of the room, Harry and Julie Belafonte chat with an unidentified male seen from behind. The photo is often published cropped—depicting only Marilyn, the attorney general, and the president—and often presented as evidence of her affairs with each man. Stoughton also photographed Steven Edward Smith with his arm around Marilyn but no author has alleged a relationship between the two.

Later in the evening, Diahann Carroll performed and Jimmy Durante played piano and sang as the guests stood as audience. Photographs show Marilyn seated beside Miller near a railing. "It's certainly her beauty I remember most," Carroll recalled. "As I sang, I distinctly remember being somewhat distracted by her gaze."

The Monroe apocrypha alleges that she spent the night with the president at the Carlyle Hotel. In reality, she left the Krims' residence in the early morning hours, returned Isidore Miller to Brooklyn, and went home. "Dad, come back to the coast with me tomorrow," she said. "Later, Marilyn," Miller replied, weary from the night. "Maybe in November." She blew him a kiss and walked away. It was the last time he would ever see her.

James Haspiel claims to have seen a barefoot Marilyn arrive home to Fifty-Seventh Street, holding her shoes and with her hair combed out and looking like "white spun gold." This would also be the last time he saw her. "I can tell you with *authority*, that I was with Marilyn at her apartment ten minutes to four in the morning," Haspiel writes in *Marilyn: The Ultimate Look at the Legend*. "Categorically, Marilyn was not asleep at the Carlyle Hotel, and I didn't notice the President anywhere nearby us, either!"

In their final interaction, Haspiel targeted Marilyn with an angry outburst. "Oh, Jimmy…" she said, appearing fatigued and visibly upset. Haspiel refuses to disclose the rest of the encounter but admits to telling her to "go to hell." Perhaps Marilyn was too tired to pose for more home movies or sign autographs but Haspiel wrote with regret, "I was never destined to forget the very last worlds [she] heard come forth from my tongue, in an unfortunate moment…"

Marilyn's appearance at the fundraiser was an enormous success for both the event and her career. The press warmly greeted her with questions about her experience at the gala when she arrived in Los Angeles. "I liked it," Marilyn replied. "I like celebrating birthdays. I enjoy knowing that I'm alive; and you can underline alive." She spoke of losing her good luck charm, likely the white knight, in New York, and of feeling extremely fatigued. Now facing the consequences of taking off a day and a half from production of *Something's Got to Give*, Marilyn would need a bit of luck and stamina to battle with the studio.

Dean Martin's manager Mort Viner slammed Marilyn. "That was poor form on her part," he said. "It showed where her priorities were, anyway, didn't it? But Dean told me, 'Hey you can't blame her, Mort. Look, if Jackie Kennedy has asked me to fly cross country to sing "Happy Birthday" to her, I woulda gone.'"

Fox production records document Marilyn's dismissal with permission from the set on Thursday, May 17 at 12:30 pm, but the studio would use her appearance in New York as evidence of breach of contract. "That was stupid," Henry Weinstein would say thirty decades later in the documentary *Marilyn: Something's Got to Give*, "and had I been more experienced I'd have said, 'Marilyn I'll go with you; we'll get more publicity for the picture,' which would be the natural thing to do. I should walk with a sign saying *Something's Got to Give* instead of worrying about whether she's gone or what the studio thinks." In hindsight, Weinstein regretted having opposed Marilyn's appearance, not sending Fox's newsreel crew and photographers to Madison Square Garden, and failing to publicize the event as advertising for his film.

Chapter Twenty-Six: **May to June 1962**

In May, the cast and crew of *Cleopatra* occupied the island of Ischia in the Gulf of Naples to film the Battle of Actium scenes. Just as a helicopter had whisked Monroe to New York City for a command performance, another transported Taylor and Burton to the Regina Isabella seaside resort. There, paparazzo Marcello Geppetti snapped the infamous photo of a swimsuit-clad Elizabeth Taylor and Richard Burton lying together and passionately kissing on the white deck of a yacht off the Amalfi Coast. A seismic shock reverberated across the globe.

Marilyn returned to Los Angeles on Sunday, May 20, and reported to work on the following morning. Fox executives may have sneered at her absence on Friday, but the week began with the Vatican and U.S. leaders' denouncement of the studio's other leading lady. Geppetti's famous shot hit the media and knocked Marilyn off magazine covers. By mid-week, Georgia Congresswoman Iris F. Blitch addressed the House of Representatives on the topic of the adulterous lovers with hope that Attorney General Robert Kennedy would "take the measures necessary to determine whether or not the two are ineligible for reentry into this country on the grounds of undesirability." At least temporarily, the heat was off Marilyn.

When Dean Martin reported to work with one-hundred-degree fever on May 21, Marilyn consulted with Dr. Siegel who advised against her performing with Martin during his illness. In a bizarre twist that further slowed the production, Cukor filmed twenty-six identical takes of letter-perfect dialogue between Marilyn and Christopher Morley. On Wednesday, May 23, Fox cleared stage fourteen for the nude swimming scene, the film's obvious pull for an audience. In the script, Ellen takes a moonlit skinny dip in the swimming pool while her husband meets with a life insurance agent inside the house. "My, listen to that splashing..." the agent (Phil Silvers) says, "they must be doing the *breast* stroke. I hope the pool is heated." Nick drolly replies, "It's being heated right now."

Sniffing an opportunity for hype, Patricia Newcomb had called photographer Lawrence Schiller of *Paris-Match* and *Life* and advised him to pack plenty of rolls of film and spend the day on the set. The Fox publicity department invited photographer William Woodfield to the closed set to shoot the sequence from another angle.

Marilyn and Cukor conspired to make the nudity appear improvised, but carefully choreographed each step. Jean-Louis had designed a flesh-colored, strapless bikini top and bottom of the silk soufflé used for the birthday gala gown to simulate nudity, even though Marilyn would remove the top for realism. Cukor instructed Marilyn to begin the scene wearing the bikini and coached the cinematographer, Billy Daniels, to announce that the line of the swimsuit was visible through the camera lens. Cukor borrowed his scheme from Elizabeth Taylor, whose similar bathing suit in a nude bathing scene for *Cleopatra* was visible beneath the water.

According to Allan Snyder, Marilyn obsessed about the possibly of indecency and requested he view the scene beside the camera lens to ensure that her breasts and pelvic area remained out of view. Additionally, Cukor intended to film the sequence in long and medium shots to maintain propriety. This historic moment marked the first time a major motion picture actress appeared nude in a mainstream film. Understandably, pandemonium swept the Fox lot as word spread.

In his memoir *Marilyn & Me*, Schiller described his preparatory meeting with Marilyn and Patricia on Fifth Helena Drive. "Nice to see you again," he said, referring to their work together on the set of *Let's Make Love.* "You, too Larry," Marilyn responded, remembering his earlier remark about being the Big Bad Wolf. "You get any badder since I last saw you?" "Quite a bit," he replied. Before getting down to business, Marilyn asked to borrow his "one good eye" to assist her in selecting tiles for the renovation of the kitchen. Patricia seemed confused by their exchange of private jokes. Marilyn offered Schiller an exclusive opportunity to photograph her partially nude for the first time since Tom Kelly's calendar pose thirteen years earlier. He knew the sale of the pictures would afford him a new house for his wife and baby, and she knew the pictures would push Elizabeth Taylor off magazine covers, so it was a win-win for both parties. "You're already famous," Schiller told Marilyn. "Now you're gonna to make *me* famous."

On the day of the shoot, Marilyn jumped into the pool and dog-paddled, kicking her legs in the water and splashing. She remained in the ninety-five-degree water for four hours, swimming a total of ninety minutes. "Come on in," Ellen calls to Nick, who watches above from a second-story bedroom window. "The water's so refreshing, you know…after you've finished with…you-know-what." Although Dean Martin was sick and at home, the script placed his character upstairs in the house with his new wife, scheming to prevent her discovery of his first wife. Nick orders Ellen out of the pool only to discover she is nude. He commands her back into the pool and throws down a robe. Upon a cue from Cukor, Marilyn removed her bikini top and placed it on the edge of the pool. Schiller's and Woodfield's Nikon motorized cameras shot dozens of frames per second.

In the film and in publicity stills, Marilyn swims to the edge of the pool and lifts her right leg over the edge, keeping her body hidden in the water and behind the pool's rim. A female script supervisor reads Dean Martin's line in a static voice, "Get back in there." Marilyn giggled, dropped her leg into the water, and swam backward. Her skin glistened, and her eyes sparkled.

After splashing around, Marilyn emerged from the water and sat on the edge of the pool, facing away from the cameras, and looked back over her shoulder while she dried her hair with a towel. The bottom of her nude-colored bikini was visible, only now it was rolled down like a thong. Allan "Whitey" Snyder and Agnes Flanagan stepped to the edge of the pool to attend to Marilyn's makeup and hair.

In a daring move suggesting Botticelli's painting of Venus rising nude from the sea, Marilyn removed the bikini bottom and emerged completely nude from the pool. In the sequence, her character puts on a blue, terry cloth robe. Marilyn carefully concealed her nipples, but some of the Schiller's shots revealed her breasts and buttocks. While heading back to the dressing room, Marilyn asked Agnes if the stunt was in poor taste, but the elderly hairdresser assured her that indeed, it had not been suggestive.

Journalist Vernon Scott of the *Los Angeles Herald Examiner* covered the stunt and interviewed Marilyn. "The set was closed, all except for members of the crew, who were very sweet," she told him afterward. "I told them to close their eyes or turn their backs, and I think they all did."

"She has a beautiful body," Cukor proudly announced. "Better than ever."

"I was a little embarrassed by the fact I don't swim very well," Marilyn confessed. "I only dog-paddle but I'm buoyant and I can float. I only went under once but I popped right back to the surface." She referenced her approaching birthday and quipped, "I thought I'd celebrate a little early in my birthday suit." Echoing her nude calendar scandal then years before, Marilyn reveled in the display of her fit body. After she viewed the rushes, she told Scott, "There's really nothing terribly immodest about the shots."

"She felt secure that day…" Henry Weinstein recalled. "I really thought the worst was over." Fox's Board of Directors was equally pleased, especially with Marilyn's perfect attendance all week. While Marilyn fell in good graces with the studio, Skouras' correspondence to Zanuck revealed violence in the tumultuous Taylor-Burton relationship and Taylor's two attempts at suicide by overdoses of Nembutal and Seconal.

On May 24, Marilyn filmed a scene with Cyd Charisse. Despite a low-grade fever and earache, Marilyn returned the following day to perform with Charisse and Dean Martin, now recovered from his cold. The sequence entailed Ellen greeting Nick and Bianca upon their return from their honeymoon, as she poses as their household's new Swedish governess, Miss Ingrid Tic. Marilyn carried their luggage through the courtyard and spoke in a superb Greta Garbo accent: "Honeymoon is over, yah?"

Marilyn's fever rose over the weekend, and she received injections of antibiotics. She called in sick on Monday. On Tuesday, May 29, dressed in a blue robe, she shot the scene with Dean Martin that would follow the nude film sequence in the film. Nick confronts Ellen with knowledge of her male companion on the island. She fumbles with an excuse about intending to tell him, but she knew how upset he gets about "*little* things."

Martin stumbled on his lines when Marilyn's character explained that her male companion had broken his leg and was therefore incapacitated during the first six months they lived together on the island: "Six months? That still leaves four and a half years!" When Nick quarrels about her omission, Ellen turns the tables by asking how long it should take for a man to tell a woman that his wife has returned. It takes only two seconds, she insists, and he hasn't said it in two days.

After returning to the set on May 31 following a short respite for Memorial Day, Marilyn appeared elegant in a cashmere suit with blonde mink trim and matching mink hat as she filmed on the set of an exclusive department store. In the sequence, shoe clerk Wally Cox assists Ellen in trying on a pair of shoes in her size, but they are obviously too tight. While trying to squeeze her foot into the shoe, she nearly slides off the chair and realizes her foot has grown from going barefoot on the island for five years. Suddenly, Ellen schemes to solicit the clerk to pose as Steven, her island companion. When she invites him to lunch, the clerk nervously says he brings his lunch to the store. Ellen leans forward and whispers that she would be "ever so grateful" if he would go out to lunch with her. As David Bretherton edited the scene, he noted Marilyn's performance was perfect.

Allan Snyder noticed an extra with platinum hair and a striking resemblance to Marilyn on set during the filming of the scene in the department store. He mentioned it to Marilyn, who consulted with the assistant director. She reminded him of the studio's standing order on all her films prohibiting the use of blonde extras. When the assistant director confronted Cukor, the director shut down production for four hours. Later, the studio's publicity department used this incident to claim Marilyn was paranoid.

* * *

At dusk, Lawrence Schiller arrived at Marilyn's home to review the contact sheets of her nude swim. She answered the door herself and suggested they go for a drive in Patricia Newcomb's Thunderbird to "get Dom." Schiller was perplexed but did not ask questions. Marilyn drove to Schwabb's drugstore on Sunset Boulevard, parked under a streetlight, went inside, and returned with a bottle of Dom Perignon. After they arrived back at her place, Schiller handed Marilyn an envelope containing the filmstrips. Before she took them, she reached into her purse and removed a loupe and pinking shears. He recognized the loupe but asked about the sharps. As Marilyn held the filmstrip up to the illumination of the streetlight and snipped a few frames, she explained pinking shears were used to cut fabric when hemming a dress. As Douglas Kirkland had done five months earlier, Schiller cringed as Marilyn destroyed the images she rejected.

* * *

Marilyn completed the last performance of her illustrious career on sound stage fourteen on her thirty-sixth and final birthday. She filmed a comic scene with Dean Martin and Wally Cox, starting the workday at 9:37am and ending at 6:05 pm. Marilyn's character, fearing her husband's reaction to the attractive playboy with whom she spent five years alone on the island, introduces Cox's character, the shoe salesman, as the man with whom she lived on the island. Martin's character has already discovered the playboy's identity, but humors his wife by quizzing the coached imposter. They lived in huts, Ellen explains. The show salesman clarifies, "*Separate* huts." Nick asks where they lived during the rainy season. Ellen replies that they moved into the trees. The salesman interjects, "*Separate* trees."

Cukor printed fourteen takes of the scene in medium and close shots, and each time Marilyn's delivery was perfect. Marilyn reported on time for nine consecutive workdays and completed ten scenes. Marilyn and Paula retreated to the dressing room behind the studio's commissary during the lunch break. Out of her costume and in a white terrycloth robe, Marilyn lounged on the sofa under a round window as Paula served her a light lunch and angel food cake. Meanwhile, Evelyn Moriarty coordinated a surprise birthday celebration on the set with a sheet cake purchased from Humphrey's Bakery at the Farmer's Market for seven dollars, collected from the cast and crew. The cake was decorated with sparklers and a plastic doll wearing a bikini and swimming in a pool, depicting the infamous nude swimming scene. Evelyn hid the cake in a prop room, and Cukor demanded that she present it only after production wrapped in order to "get a good day's work" from Marilyn.

Studio artist Joseph Krutak designed a greeting card announcing "Happy Birthday (Suit)" with a cartoon likeness of Marilyn wrapped in a short robe with the label "Ladies Wardrobe." Moriarty obtained over eighty signatures from the entire cast and crew. Paula Strasberg drew a heart with an arrow through it, and Cox wrote, "*Wally Cox loves you.*" Martin signed, "*You sure are something, Dino.*" Crewmember Mack Gray wrote, "*To the most beautiful girl...If only I was the marrying type.*"

Bags of telegrams arrived on set including one from DiMaggio: "*Happy Birthday, hope today and future years bring you sunny skies and all your heart desires. As ever, Joe.*" Jack Lemmon, Robert Wagner, and Marlon Brando sent flowers, and Peter and Patricia Lawford sent a case of champagne. Lew Wasserman of MCA and Frank Sinatra sent gift baskets.

Marilyn had received permission from the wardrobe department to wear the fur-trimmed beige suit and matching hat to a charity baseball event that evening. Weinstein gave his blessing to borrow the suit but warned her against going out in the night air. "I don't think I'll stay for the whole game," Marilyn told columnist James Bacon. "Though I would if Joe were playing. He's the only ball player I care about."

At the end of the day, Marilyn changed out of her costume into a print blouse and white Capri slacks but continued wearing the blonde mink beret. It was now her turn to be serenaded with a chorus of "Happy Birthday", and received her card and birthday cake decorated with sparklers. Pat Newcomb, Mrs. Murray, and freelance photographer George Barris attended, crowding around Marilyn as she cut the cake. Barris arrived in Los Angeles specifically to see Marilyn after consulting with Robert Atherton of *Cosmopolitan* for a major eight- to ten-page cover story on her.

Marilyn turned to her body make-up artist Bunny Gardel, assisting her in serving the cake, and asked her how many years they had worked together. "About ten," Gardel replied. Marilyn laughed, "That's a nice round number." Gardel regulary made a point to tell Marilyn that she had a nicely rounded figure.

Lawrence Schiller, photographing the celebration, approached Marilyn regarding the sales of the photographs he had taken of her nude swimming sequence. Schiller asked Marilyn what she would like in exchange for his and Woodfield's photographs. Marilyn smiled and jokingly requested a slide projector to view them. Moved to tears, Schiller acknowledged her generosity and speculated that sale of the images to the media would likely fund a new house for his family. He joked about making a wooden sign with the inscription "The house that Marilyn Monroe bought" and hanging it over the front door. "At least I'll be helping to make your wife happy," Marilyn said, serving Schiller a piece of cake. "I'll be happy, too, to see all those covers with me on them and not Liz." However, before leaving the studio, Marilyn had reconsidered and expressed her reservations about releasing the photographs to the press.

Marilyn warmly embraced George Barris and reminded him of their agreement to work on a book together. While discussing the article for *Cosmopolitan*, they considered concurrently working on a book in which Marilyn would refute all the lies the studio had released about her to the press.

Fox clearly gave Elizabeth Taylor preferential treatment. In February, the studio had spent five thousand dollars on her birthday celebration in Rome but would now charge Marilyn for the coffee served at hers from the studio commissary. (Henry Weinstein agreed to pay for the cake and returned everyone's donation.) Additionally, Taylor had been afforded a Rolls Royce Silver Cloud, a fourteen-room villa, a six-room on-set dressing suite decorated with expensive antiques, meals provided at the cost of \$150 per day, and a \$500 per week liquor allowance. As Marilyn celebrated with Martin, Cox, Weinstein, and Cukor in her crowded dressing room, she must have felt like Fox's stepchild and may have been reminded of the days when she lived in the orphanage, wore an orphan's uniform, and was treated differently than the other children at school.

After the party had ended, Marilyn and Wally Cox were driven to the Montana Drive home in Santa Monica that was likely the residence shared by Cox and Marlon Brando. The two men hosted a brief celebration at their home before Marilyn changed again into the elegant beige suit and rushed off to Dodger Stadium, where she escorted Dean Martin's young son to a benefit for the Muscular Dystrophy Association. There, she threw the first ball, introduced a boys choir, and spoke to the crowd on behalf of the charity. Albert "Albie" Gregory Pearson (born 1934), a twenty-seven-year-old, left-handed center fielder for the Los Angeles Angels, escorted her onto the field. At five-foot five inches in height, Pearson was the shortest man to receive Rookie of the Year (1958).

The last public photographs of Marilyn show her talking to children in wheelchairs and waving to the crowds at Dodger Stadium while holding the fur hat that had blown from her head in the strong night wind. Receipts from the Carey Cadillac Car Renting Service documented Marilyn's travel from the studio to "*601 Montana Dr.-Dodger Stadium-Chasen's-Home-La Scala-Studio-Home-La Scala-Home.*"

Dan and Joan Greenson joined Marilyn at her home before midnight to share a bottle of champagne, and presented her with a crystal champagne glass engraved with her name. "Now, I'll know who I am when I'm drinking," Marilyn squealed with delight. Returned to the siblings after her death, it would be auctioned in June 2010 along with Dr. Greenson's psychoanalysis couch.

Contradicting George Barris' impression that Marilyn was happy and hopeful, Joan Greenson believed it had been a rather melancholy birthday. "I may be smiling," Marilyn told her when sharing photographs of the on-set party, "but my eyes are dead." Within days, Marilyn's mood worsened. "I think she was just depressed," Joan would say. "She was just in a terrible place this time." Marilyn had called upon the Greenson siblings for much-needed support in her psychiatrist's absence. Greenson and his wife had left in May for a five-week tour of Europe and Israel, and a visit with Hilde Greenson's mother, who had recently suffered a cerebral hemorrhage in Switzerland. Joan and Daniel Greenson rushed to Marilyn's side, finding her in bed with a black sleeping mask covering her eyes.

"This woman was desperate," Daniel Greenson told Anthony Summers. "She couldn't sleep—it was the middle of the afternoon—and she said how terrible she felt about herself, how worthless she felt. She talked about being a waif, that she was ugly, that people were only nice to her for what they could get from her. She said she had no one, that nobody loved her. She mentioned not having children. It was a whole litany of depressive thoughts." Panicked, the siblings contacted Milton Wexler and Dr. Milton Uhley, their father's colleagues, to intervene.

As Henry Weinstein feared, the night air at Dodger Stadium exacerbated Marilyn's sinus infection over the weekend. She was treated for sinusitis at Cedars of Lebanon Hospital on Sunday, June 3. On Monday, Marilyn called in sick at 5:55 am with a fever of one hundred degrees. Dr. Lee E. Siegel, Fox's medical director, examined her at home and confirmed an illness to Feldman. The production log contained an entry verifying Marilyn's excused illness.

The men at Fox were unsympathetic to Marilyn's condition. Executives disbelieved Siegel's medical report and accused Marilyn of malingering and manipulating the doctor. In an act of sabotage, Cukor discredited Marilyn by telling the studio brass he had watched Marilyn's completed scenes and determined her work inferior. Then the executioner's axe fell. Milton Gould, financial lawyer and head of the studio's executive committee, ordered Marilyn's termination. Milton Rudin called the studio on Tuesday morning to report Marilyn was able to return to work but was told the crew was not prepared for her. Executives warned him of intent to sue his client for breach of contract. Both Rudin and Weinstein contacted Greenson in Europe to sound the alarm.

Marilyn's increased depressive symptoms arguably intensified due to lack of access to Dr. Greenson while he was in Europe and risk of dismissal by Fox. *The Diagnostic and Statistical Manual IV* identifies "frantic efforts to avoid real or imagined abandonment" as one of the diagnostic features of Borderline Personality Disorder. Those with the disorder tend to experience intense abandonment fears and inappropriate anger even when faced with a separation and may perceive the separation as a rejection that implies they are inherently "bad." This panic is related to an intolerance of being alone and a need to have other people with them. Frantic efforts to avoid abandonment may include impulsive actions such as self-injury or suicidal behaviors. If Marilyn took her own life three months later, the act may have resulted from her fear of abandonment from someone she loved or intensely depended upon, or her perception that she would somehow remain alone and unloved. Without conclusive evidence, a specific trigger for her "probable" or possible" suicidal impulse remains unclear and is subject to conjecture.

Leaving his wife in Switzerland, Greenson cut his vacation short, canceled a meeting in New York with his publisher, and returned to

Los Angeles. He arrived at Marilyn's house on June 6 directly from the airport. In a letter to Marianne Kris dated August 20, Greenson explored his own countertransference and his famous patient's symptoms of Borderline Personality Disorder: "If I behaved in a way which hurt her, she acted as though it was the end of the world and could not rest until peace had been re-established..."

Not only was Marilyn emotionally hurt, she was now physically injured with bruises on both lower eyelids. On June 7, Greenson accompanied his patient to the Beverly Hills office of plastic surgeon Michael Gurdin and reported she had slipped and fell in her shower. Marilyn appeared heavily sedated and expressed fear of a broken nose, but Greenson answered most of Gurdin's questions related to her injury. Marilyn refused an X-ray. The plastic surgeon found no evidence of a fracture and concluded the bruising was consistent with either a fall or having been struck in the face.

Having taken charge of assessing his patience's injuries, Greenson immediately shifted to salvaging her career. He called Rudin and announced Marilyn was capable of returning to the film. Curiously, neither of Marilyn's advocates reported the fall and injury to the studio, which, arguably, could have excused her absence. Greenson also failed to inform Engelberg or to solicit his medical intervention. Given these omissions, Donald Spoto alleged Greenson might have been responsible for Marilyn's injuries.

Biographer Richard Ben Cramer, aware of DiMaggio's past domestic violence against Marilyn, speculated he might have become physically abusive toward her again as he had been intimately involved with her at the time of her injuries. Cramer theorized DiMaggio used Marilyn's termination to urge her to retire and marry him so they could finally be happy together without the burden of her fame, but it escalated into a "terrible fight" during which DiMaggio assaulted Marilyn in an episode of rage.

On Friday, June 8, Greenson attended a meeting at Fox with Milton Rudin; Frank Ferguson, vice-president; and Phil Feldman. "I can persuade Marilyn to go along with any reasonable request," Greenson vouched. Eccentrically, he also professed the ability to participate in the film's editing process. When Rudin returned to his office two hours later, he received a message from Feldman stating Fox was no longer interested in further negotiations and would instead seek legal remedies. As reported by Sheila Graham in *Citizen-News*, attorneys from the firm of Musick, Peeler, and Garrett drafted a lawsuit suing Marilyn Monroe Productions for $500,000.

"Why did they make [my father] come back from Europe when they already intended to fire her anyway?" Joan Greenson wondered. Greenson was unaware of the confrontation that had occurred in Europe on Marilyn's birthday and its relevance to the future of her employment. According to Jack Brodsky and Nathan Weiss (authors of *The Cleopatra Papers: A Correspondence*), Peter Levathes had arrived on the set of *Cleopatra* in Rome with two studio vice presidents and an attorney, with the intent to terminate Elizabeth Taylor. However, both Taylor's and her director's personal production companies were partners with Fox in the production.

In a showdown with the Fox team, attorneys for the independent production companies threatened termination of the studio, a take-over of the film, and litigation that could tie up its release for years. Taylor also wielded the power she had inherited from deceased husband, Michael Todd: rights to the Todd-AO Wide Screen process used by Fox in addition to Cinemascope. Defeated, Levathes agreed to a final fifteen weeks of production. With only $2.1 million invested in the Monroe property, Fox executives agreed to pull the plug on *Something's Got to Give* and continue with its larger investment in *Cleopatra.* When informed of Marilyn's termination, Henry Weinstein swiftly resigned and instantly went to work at MGM Studios. "This was a purely political move, and I wanted no part of it," he said. "They couldn't get rid of Taylor, so they decided to show they were strong men and fire Monroe—in Taylor's place."

Journalist Murray Schumach's series of articles in the *New York Times* lambasting Fox executives as "spineless" also influenced the studio's decision to sacrifice Marilyn. One particular article, titled "Weakness Seen in Film Industry," cited Fox as having no authority over its stars. "It looked as if Skouras and his appointed head Levathes were losing control of their talent," Weinstein recalled. "And so [Marilyn] was a pawn—an interesting pawn, a sad pawn; it's tragic, it's funny—but a pawn. And that's the real Hollywood story."

In Europe, Darryl F. Zanuck was outraged. "He felt the dismissal of Monroe was a startling indication of the rudderless course Fox was taking," wrote his biographer Leonard Mosley. "Zanuck felt Levathes had decided to rid himself of this temperamental star, and this act convinced him of the man's poor judgment. He was the wrong person in control." After Zanuck viewed raw footage of both *Something's Got to Give* and *Cleopatra*, he predicted success for the Monroe film and failure for Taylor's. On June 6, Zanuck fired an angry telegram to the studio's board demanding Marilyn's reinstatement. "It was the only time in my life that I saw my dad frightened," daughter Darrilyn Zanuck would say. "When he talked of the mishandling of the Monroe film and of *Cleopatra*, I could see that he was desperately concerned about the future of the company. Normally, my father was absolutely fearless."

Billy Wilder learned of his former leading lady's professional crisis while filming *Irma La Douce* with Shirley MacLaine in a role he knew was well-suited for Marilyn's talents. He spoke with resolve to a reporter for *Show Business Illustrated*: "I can tell you my mouth is watering to have her in another picture," he said with resolve. "The idea that she may be slipping is like saying a model is out of fashion when a hundred sculptors are just waiting to get their chisels in a choice piece...Marilyn is very talented and a huge box office star. And that's what matters. After all, if her picture is running in Manchester and a man tell his wife, 'There's a Monroe picture showing.' The wife doesn't turn and say, 'We don't want to see her, she's always rowing with directors.' They go and see her, and that's why I want her." Having grown fond of Marilyn since working with her on *River of No Return*, Otto Preminger also came to her defense by informing the media he was ready and willing to direct her in a suitable film.

Fox's poor treatment of Marilyn must be viewed in context of the condition of the motion picture industry in the early 1960s. The studio contract player system was falling apart, costs were skyrocketing and profits were declining. Executives had denied Marilyn's illness from the start and ordered their physician to prescribe and administer injections of amphetamines to increase her energy to work. Dr. Engelberg concurrently prescribed antibiotic drugs and administered vitamin and liver extract injections to boost Marilyn's resistance. When these attempts failed to keep Marilyn working, the executives panicked.

Fox chose to depict Marilyn to the media as in breach of contract, malingering, unprofessional, and even seriously mentally ill in an attempt to recoup a portion or all of the cost of the film. If she indeed, could be proven psychiatrically unstable and unable or unwilling to fulfill her contract, the studio could file a claim with the insurance company and sue her. Conclusive evidence of the quality of Marilyn's performance, ranging from adequate to exceptional, existed on the footage owned and controlled by Fox. Three decades would pass and many executives would die before the truth would emerge.

Marilyn fell into a serious depressive episode and lay sequestered and protected in her bedroom. Patricia Newcomb kept vigil by sleeping on the floor at the foot of the bed. Mrs. Murray brought trays of food to the bedroom door only to find it locked; Newcomb would emerge, take the tray, and close the door. Greenson apparently closely monitored his patient with one-to-one supervision until she could be left alone. He would charge her estate for a session at her home on June 8 and sessions in his office on June 9 and 10. In its August 22, 1962 issue, the *Los Angeles Times* reported Sydney Guilaroff's unsuccessful attempts to visit Marilyn on Fifth Helena Drive during the same weekend.

On Monday, June 11, Fox officially suspended production. Referencing Marilyn's relatively recent psychiatric hospitalization and publicized family history of mental illness, Peter Levathes told the media, "We've let the inmates run the asylum and they've practically destroyed it."

Philip Feldman leveraged Lee Remick's contract and had her photographed in Marilyn's costumes with Cukor. The twenty-seven-year-old star had excelled in *Anatomy of a Murder* (1959) and *Days of Wine and Roses* (1962). Fox's lead publicists, Perry Lieber and John Campbell, issued negative statements about Marilyn in Remick's name. "I never said any those things," Remick later said. "Since it was a publicity stunt, they released all those statements in my name. It was all very degrading."

"I have the greatest respect for Lee Remick," Dean Martin told Vernon Scott, "but I signed to do this film with Marilyn Monroe." Marilyn was both touched and appreciative of her friend's loyalty and proudly showed Joan Greenson the headlines of the *New York Daily News* announcing, "No MM, No Martin."

"She was thrilled by that," Joan Greenson recalled. "She campaigned for him instead of James Garner." In retaliation, Harry Brand mounted a new media attack on Dean Martin as Fox slapped the actor with a $3 million lawsuit citing breach of contract and an "unprofessional attitude." Martin fired back by suing the studio for $6.8 million for damage to his professional reputation. A battle of litigation now raged on the Fox lot.

Feldman approached Kim Novak, Doris Day, and Shirley MacLaine to replace Marilyn, but in support of their colleague, the actresses declined his offer. Earl Wilson called Marilyn for a statement and published it the following day. She said, "I'm ready and eager to get back to the set on Monday."

Instead of reinstating Marilyn, Fox executives initiated a campaign to malign her to the press in justification of their actions. They claimed Marilyn's absence for the president's birthday gala was her final act of defiance. However, surviving documentation reveals she had obtained approval for this leave of absence, as we know that the studio oddly chose not to capitalize on the event for publicity purposes.

Harry Brand, once commissioned by the studio to create Marilyn's stardom, was now ordered to ruin her career. His publicists released statements alleging Marilyn was high while filming the swimming scene and had disrobed in a state of madness. They claimed Marilyn called in sick for several days, yet had been seen at Hollywood nightclubs. In the *New York Times*, Murray Schumach quoted Levathes, saying, "Miss Monroe is not just being temperamental; she is mentally ill, perhaps seriously." Levathes later admitted, "I never said that nor did I feel that way." Sheila Graham also received inaccurate information and falsely quoted Henry Weinstein in accusing Marilyn of malingering. Hedda Hopper published George Cukor's prediction of the end of Marilyn's career. Fox even fabricated a press conference that never took place and released fictitious statements assigned to Weinstein, Levathes, and Cukor.

In an attempt to clear Marilyn's name and repair damage to her reputation, Patricia Newcomb released statements to the Associated Press and United Press International confirming the studio physician's diagnosis of Marilyn's illness. In a *coup de grace*, Fox publicists published an ad in *Variety Weekly* as if it were written by the crew of *Something's Got to Give,* sarcastically thanking Marilyn for putting them out of work. Vernon Scott wrote that Marilyn "has taken the bread out of the mouths of men who depend on this film to feed their families."

Marilyn, always akin to those who worked behind the cameras, felt devastated by this ultimate betrayal. She retreated to her home and Patricia Newcomb transcribed one hundred four telegrams of apology to each member of the crew. "*Please believe me it was not my doing,*" Marilyn dictated. "*I so looked forward to working with you.*" During their research for *Marilyn: The Last Take*, Brown and Barham contacted twenty-three of the thirty surviving crewmembers, and all denied participation in an effor to discredit Marilyn. In fact, most of them sympathized with her. Special effects artist Paul Worzl later said: "There was tremendous support for her from the entire crew—indeed, from all the craftsmen on the lot. We all knew the score."

Marilyn reached Zanuck, her former nemesis and current ally, by telephone in Paris while he was editing *The Longest Day*. Allan Snyder heard the conversation from Marilyn's side. She also called Spyros Skouras for help, but he was recovering from prostate surgery. Judge Samuel Rosenman, formerly a speech writer for President Franklin Delano Roosevelt, New York Superior Court Justice, and Fox's chairman of the board of directors, was also a friend of Joseph P. Kennedy when Kennedy was Ambassador to Great Britain. Brown and Barham referenced a document note in the Skouras collection stating Robert Kennedy contacted Rosenman and convinced him to reconsider Marilyn's termination. This might account for Marilyn's rash of calls to the Justice Department's main switchboard on June 23, July 2, July 16, and July 17.

Marilyn's own longtime affair with the public may have been most influential in Fox's reevaluation. Stunning images of a slim and beautiful Monroe swimming nude appeared on thirty-two magazine covers and produced an excitement similar to the one caused by the discovery of her nude calendar pose a decade earlier. Her loyal audience wanted to know when the film would be released. Bags of telegrams poured onto the Fox lot, and its switchboard received mass calls from fans requesting Marilyn's return.

One man particularly disturbed by the photographs of Marilyn's skinny dip was Arthur Miller. He believed Marilyn was above performing in scenes designed to objectify her body. For years she had struggled to be taken seriously, only to revert to swimming naked in a pool. However, the same could be said of Miller's gratuitous paddleball scene in *The Misfits*. To her former husband, Marilyn's skinny dip signified she had surrendered her fight against being cast as age-worn "prey."

On the contrary, Marilyn had shifted to survivor mode, and her unique brand of exhibitionism guaranteed the resurrection of her career. Within days, Fox called for negotiations but these efforts were not reported to the press. At first, Philip Feldman and Charles Einfeld, Director of Marketing, wished to publicly humiliate Marilyn; they demanded that she participate in a press conference and read an apology scripted by the studio, or that her publicists release it to the press. Levathes vetoed this plan as downright hostile and demeaning.

"As a person, my work is important to me," Marilyn told Alan Levy. "My work is the only ground I've ever had to stand on." However, in mid-1962, she was forced to fight for her career and her professional reputation. Marilyn was a survivor whose resilience overcame the unfortunate circumstances of her childhood, multiple traumas, depressive episodes, and numerous losses. She rose to the top of her profession as a beloved actress whose name was known from Nairobi to Tasmania. She had stood up to Fox's tyranny in 1955 and emerged the victor. Surely, the studio's vengeance could not destroy her.

Chapter Twenty-Seven: **Life on Fifth Helena Drive**

Marilyn's life on Fifth Helena Drive during the spring and summer of 1962 was dramatically happier and more social than it had been in the previous year, despite her ongoing battle with Twentieth Century-Fox Studios. Her weight reduced to 117 pounds, and friends commented on the improvement in both her appearance and mental state. "She never looked better," recalled Marjorie Pletcher, Marilyn's studio wardrobe assistant. "She was in great spirits." Patricia Newcomb corroborated this impression in a 1992 interview with columnist Liz Smith: "Everybody who knew her in that last year knew she was in just about the best physical shape of her life. She was also in a positive mood then, except for small things."

Marilyn's routine in the last six months of her life was simple. When not involved in negotiations to resume the production of *Something's Got to Give*, she attended yoga lessons with Virginia Dennison, frequently watched children play at nearby Barrington Park, and tossed a ball to Maf-Honey in the Fifth Helena Drive cul-de-sac during twilight hours. On pleasant days, Marilyn practiced Tai Chi, an ancient Chinese form of meditation based on channeling energy, tinkered in her garden, and strolled Santa Monica Beach, which she had visited since childhood.

Marilyn was a regular patron of La Scala Italian Restaurant in Beverly Hills. Dining with friends, she preferred secluded booth fifteen at the end of a labyrinth of an aisle and next to the entrance of the wine cellar. Owner and operator Jean Leon immigrated to Los Angeles from Spain, and at the age of seventeen, began his career at Villa Capri in Hollywood. In 1956, he opened La Scala to great critical acclaim and was the first Italian restaurateur in Los Angeles to serve white truffles and make his own pasta. The restaurant was one of Marilyn's favorites and had served six presidents.

At Renna's salon in Beverly Hills, Marilyn underwent Dr. G.W. Campbell's treatments that increased blood flow to facial muscles. French esthetician Madame Renna partnered with her husband, dentist Dr. Campbell, to perfect a formula derived from honey and touted to minimize the effects of aging. Having been a client at the salon since the early 1950s, Marilyn usually scheduled and paid for two consecutive sessions to assure that she received a full hour treatment, as she now often arrived late. She and Campbell discussed religion, philosophy, and alternative spiritualities. The doctor loaned her several self-help books including *Your Key to Happiness* by Harold Sherman.

Wally Cox often visited and made Marilyn laugh. They seemed an unlikely pair. Once after a cocktail party at the Lawford estate, Cox drove Marilyn home so slowly and cautiously, that she joked he might be arrested for impeding traffic. On a typical weekday, Mrs. Murray arrived around eight o'clock in the morning to perform housekeeping duties. She often began the day by preparing Marilyn's breakfast of egg whites poached in safflower oil. Marilyn saved the yolks to make pound cakes for her friends but limited herself to angel food cake.

Mrs. Murray also collected Marilyn's mail from the box mounted on the wall surrounding the hacienda. Sometimes packages arrived from the widow of Marilyn's former acting instructor, Michael Chekhov. Xenia Chekhov sent gifts of warm nightgowns, concerned that Marilyn slept nude. With a differing motive, DiMaggio sent a package containing his pajamas. Joe DiMaggio was Marilyn's constant companion, and rumors of their remarriage had circulated in the media since her divorce from Miller. "Believe me, there is no spark to be kindled," Marilyn told Alan Levy. "I just like being with him and we have a better understanding than we've ever had."

DiMaggio visited Marilyn's hacienda in late June and three times in July, when they rode bicycles rented from Hans Ohrt Bicycle Shop along San Vicente Boulevard. With the kitchen under renovation, they ordered take-out meals and ate on the floor of the living room. Marilyn told Joe about her application to the orphanage in Mexico to adopt one or more children. After dinner, she usually served DiMaggio tea and listened to his troubles.

Marilyn's and DiMaggio's respective biographers, Donald Spoto and Richard Ben Cramer, would offer evidence that the couple discussed a future together and secretly planned to remarry on August 8, ironically, the day of Marilyn's burial. Cramer published a letter to Marilyn from DiMaggio during this period:

> *Had an early dinner at the Colony with George [Solotaire]...It's always nice to hear your voice and I well realize your phone bill runs into astronomical figures. I'd like to be able to tear mine up without opening the envelope this month—as I have talked to Joe [Jr.] quite a bit this month, trying to help resolve some of his present problems. You have been quite a help to me in so much as discussing Joe's affairs...And dear, I want to thank you beyond words for helping relieve mine...I'm always interested in your activities... Now I hope that the happiness we all seek comes to you soon—so that friends who give a damn will relish right along with you. I better wrap this up as I feel mushiness coming on. And so my dearest, good night!*
> *Much love, Joe*

Marilyn's other frequent companion was Rudy Kautzky, the young driver whom she requested from a local limousine service. He chauffeured her to the Brentwood Country Mart, Briggs' Deli, Jorgenson's for grocery shopping, San Vicente Pharmacy, and to Elizabeth Arden's salon for beauty treatments. Whenever he waited for Marilyn to be ready for her day of errands, Kautzky played with Maf-Honey in the yard.

Habitually over-involved in the lives of her clients, Patricia Newcomb spent considerable time at Marilyn's hacienda. Similarly, Marilyn routinely hired associates with poor professional boundaries. Secretary Cherie Redmond worked from Marilyn's home several days each week but maintained a professional distance and denied Mrs. Murray's unreasonable requests for signed blank paychecks from her employer.

"[Marilyn] was really taking control of her life and asserting herself that summer," Ralph Roberts recalled. "And she saw that

Greenson was severing all the close relationships, one by one." Marilyn recognized this controlling pattern and allegedly contemplated discharging Greenson. Mrs. Murray continued to carry out Greenson's orders for Marilyn's life. Ralph Roberts described the housekeeper as intimidating, manipulative, and divisive of Marilyn and her friends. He and Marilyn conspired to maintain their close association by scheduling massage appointments after nine o'clock in the evening, after Murray had gone home. Roberts typically entered the home without ringing the doorbell. On one awkward occasion, Roberts and Mrs. Murray accidently confronted each other, and the housekeeper grimaced with disapproval.

Against doctor's orders, Marilyn detached herself from Mrs. Murray. Former housekeeper Florence Thomas claimed Marilyn contacted her to replace Mrs. Murray. Marilyn's increased need for interpersonal boundaries indicated she was growing healthier. Greenson, however, objected and attempted to exercise increased control over his patient.

Marilyn spent the majority of her time attending psychotherapy sessions with Dr. Greenson at his office, his home, or her own house. According to Greenson's creditor's claim against the Marilyn Monroe Estate, during the last thirty-five days of Marilyn's life, she received treatment from Greenson thirty-two times. His itemized claim would reflect four occasions when he provided both office and home visits on the same day.

Alone at night, Marilyn sometimes lit a fire in her bedroom's kiva fireplace. "Sometimes I wonder what the night time is for," she wrote to Dr. Greenson. "It almost doesn't exist for me—it all seems like one long, long horrible day." Sometimes Marilyn awakened with a scream in a cold sweat, likely a long-term effect of childhood sexual abuse. Both Dr. Greenson and Dr. Engelberg treated these symptoms of past trauma by prescribing massive dosages of barbiturates but they only exacerbated her depression, clouded her consciousness, and impaired her judgment.

"Sleep became the real focus of her life and of my father's treatment," Joan Greenson said. "She would do almost anything to get to sleep. But the more she tried the more she couldn't." Marilyn attributed her night terrors and insomnia to her childhood experiences in the orphanage and foster homes. During the night, children were removed; the next morning, she discovered them gone. Marilyn felt insecure in the dark, fearing she might be spirited away.

Regardless of these dark moments, Marilyn committed random acts of kindness for which she was famous. When Patricia Newcomb's car broke down, Marilyn bought her a new Ford Thunderbird. Hairdresser Agnes Flanagan admired a bench in Marilyn's garden and discovered a similar one delivered to her home within days. Marilyn spontaneously treated stand-in Evelyn Moriarty to a shopping spree in New York, and handed her New York maid an envelope filled with hundred dollar bills. Marilyn's compassion and generosity extended beyond material and monetary gifts; friends were hesitant to inform her of their ills, as she was known to rush over to their homes with cold remedies and other comforts for recovery.

* * *

On Friday, June 13, Attorney General and Mrs. Robert Kennedy received a witty telegram from Marilyn at their estate Hickory Hill, in McLean, Virginia, declining a dinner invitation in honor of Patricia and Peter Lawford. She metaphorically described herself as "*involved in a freedom ride protesting the loss of the minority rights belonging to the few remaining earthbound stars.*" The reference to civil rights cleverly and amusingly illustrated Marilyn's dispute with Fox. "*After all,*" she wrote, "*all we demanded was our right to twinkle.*"

Marilyn missed a wild and wet outdoor dance at the Kennedy estate on Saturday, June 16. Lyndon and Lady Bird Johnson, British Ambassador David Ormsby Gore, Supreme Court Associate Justice Byron "Whizzer" White, and Harry Belafonte were among the three hundred guests who danced to the music of Lester Lanin and his orchestra. *Time* magazine described it as a "Big Splash at Hickory Hill," and *U.S. News and World Report* announced, "Fun in the New Frontier: Who Fell, Who Was Pushed." Ethel, known for staging pranks and games at her soirees, erected a bridge across the width of the sixteen by forty foot swimming pool, where she set a table and two chairs for herself and astronaut John Glenn.

Before the end of the evening, she jumped in the pool fully dressed in a red gown. Arthur Schlesinger and Mrs. Spencer Davis, wife of a Washington broker, plunged along with their hostess. Ethel's vivaciousness balanced her husband's shy and socially uncomfortable demeanor. She regularly mixed celebrities at her dining table, seating an aristocratic diplomat next to a migrant labor organizer. Had Marilyn ventured to Hickory Hill, she might have found herself seated next to John Glenn, dunked in the pool, or dancing the twist with Harry Belafonte.

Ethel Kennedy's invitation disputes the allegations of an affair between her husband and Marilyn. Robert Kennedy's administrative assistant John Seigenthaler attested that Ethel teased her husband incessantly about him having danced with Marilyn; in turn, Robert teased her about having a crush on Byron White (1917-2002). Ethel's taunting did not end with Marilyn; she also ribbed Robert about having kissed Maya Plisetskaya (born 1925), prima ballerina of the Bolshoi Ballet. Kennedy was later targeted by rumors of a dalliance with Patricia Newcomb. After he took her horseback riding at Hickory Hill, he sent her a mock bill for $1.50 signed "Charlie Generous." Newcomb mailed Kennedy a check payable to "Charlie Generous" and signed it as "Bertha Bronco."

FBI director J. Edgar Hoover sent Courtney Evans, Justice Department liaison, to speak to Kennedy about rumors of his alleged affair with a young woman in El Paso, Texas. According to Evan's memo dated August 20 documenting the confrontation, the attorney general voiced awareness of gossip of an affair with Marilyn as well, and denied all allegations.

In the last weeks of her life, Marilyn's career continued to thrive despite Fox's efforts to tarnish her professional reputation. She discussed prospective film projects including a comedy about a train heist co-starring members of the Rat Pack. Telegrams arrived at her hacienda offering work in the United States and Europe. Photographs of the nude swimming scene appeared in magazines throughout the summer. The June 22 cover of *Life* featured Marilyn wrapped in a blue, terry cloth robe with the headline "The Skinny Dip You'll Never See on the Screen." She also graced the covers of seventy magazines in thirty-two countries. There was promise and hope for Marilyn to realize her dreams and emerge as a survivor. "I'm thirty-six years old," she told photographer George Barris. "I'm just getting started."

* * *

Bertram "Bert" Stern (1929-2013), fashion and celebrity portrait photographer, may arguably be best known for *The Complete Last Sitting*, a monumental collection of 2,500 photographs of Marilyn Monroe taken over a three day period, six weeks before her death and commissioned by *Vogue*. Since the last half-century, these fashion, portrait, and nude studies have shaped the iconic image of Marilyn Monroe.

Marilyn initially posed for Stern in a second-floor suite at the Bel-Air Hotel while the photographer played Everly Brothers records on the Hi-fi. She arrived five hours late accompanied by hairdresser George Masters at 7 o'clock in the evening. "She was a total surprise," Stern reminisced in his memoir. "She was no older woman, voluptuous, aging. She had lost a lot of weight, and the loss had transformed her...She had wrapped a scarf around her hair, and she wore no makeup. Nothing. And she was gorgeous...I took a deep breath and said, 'You're beautiful.'" Marilyn responded: "Really? What a nice thing to say."

Stern wished to achieve an iconic portrait of Marilyn much like Edward Steichen's of Greta Garbo. He brought along props to inspire her creativity: sheer scarves, a black knotted veil, beaded necklaces, and champagne glasses filled with Dom Perignon as props. After reassurance that her gallbladder surgery scar would be eliminated from the prints by a few strokes of an airbrush, Marilyn agreed to pose topless under the caveat of not removing her green Jax Carpi slacks. As she held a geometric-pattern diaphanous scarf across her bare breasts, Marilyn asked Stern, "How's this for thirty-six?" The photographer approved. Within time, Marilyn shed her slacks. She even seemed proud of her scar 'like a soldier exhibiting a medal for some war wound," Susan Strasberg noted. Stern snapped the shutter as she accidently dropped a scarf and reached for it in mid-air. In this photo Marilyn looks startled and painfully vulnerable.

While the Everly Brothers crooned "Dream" in the background, Marilyn returned to her roots as a consummate photographer's model. When needing reassurance, she beckoned Masters into the room for feedback: "George, what do you think about these scarves and doing nudes?" Fortunately for Stern, the hairdresser endorsed each pose. Intuitively, Marilyn followed Stern's lead, telepathically communicating with him.

At the headquarters of *Vogue* on Madison Avenue in Manhattan, editors Jessica Daves and Diana Vreeland raved about Stern's developed output and enthusiastically arranged for an additional three sessions on June 23, 24, and 26. They hired Kenneth to style Marilyn's hair and sent him to Los Angeles with Editor Babs Simpson, who furnished her fashion wardrobe.

Like an eager suitor, Stern staged spacious bungalow ninety-six at the Bel-Air Hotel as a portrait studio complete with chilled bottles of Dom Perignon and Chateau Lafite-Rothschild for Marilyn's pleasure. His assistants, Peter Deal and Leif-Erik Nygards, hovered along with Babs Simpson and Patricia Newcomb. During the course of three days, Stern preserved for future generations a plethora of color and monochrome images of an outstandingly beautiful Marilyn reflecting a variety of moods and frozen in time as age thirty-six. "Marilyn had the power," Stern would write. "She was the wind, the comet shape that Blake draws blowing around a sacred figure. She was the light, and the goddess, and the moon. The space and the dream, the mystery and the danger. But everything else altogether too, including Hollywood, and the girl next door that every guy wants to marry, I could have hung up my camera, run off with her, lived happily ever after..."

Marilyn modeled a sleeveless black cocktail dress with bouffant skirt accessorized with strings of pearls; a high neck, backless black gown with a bouffant hairstyle; a snug black gown with sequin opera gloves; a white pillbox hat with lace veil; a white suit with coat; and various furs. In a classic pose, Marilyn's nude knee peeks through a floor-length chinchilla coat. Marilyn wore fashionable coats with wide-brim hats of the era. Eventually, Stern lured her into the bedroom to pose in lingerie and nude under the sheets. Viewed retrospectively, the work seems contemporary, with Marilyn appearing less iconic but less static than she had in studio publicity stills taken a decade earlier.

In the bedroom, Stern claims their bodies met as Marilyn snuggled close to him. He interpreted her body language as receptive to an intimate encounter and leaned in to kiss her. "No," she said. Indeed, their relationship remained chaste. After hours of work, Marilyn was exhausted and muttered, "Where have *you* been so long?" She swiftly fell asleep. In stocking feet, Stern climbed on the bed, stood above her, and captured her asleep in profile against the pillow. Nygards took a now-famous, stunningly composed nude photograph of Marilyn asleep on her stomach in bed, her hand cradling her face, her pelvis turned sideways facing the camera with a hint of pubic hair in shadow, a dreamy smile on her face, and a tuft of blonde hair covering one of her closed eyes.

While Nygards captured a sleeping Marilyn, Stern still lacked the iconic pose he desired. In a last attempt, Stern asked his subject to lay on the floor with her hair cascading and glitter sprinkled on her face and shoulders. He erected scaffolding from a table and chairs and shot from above, looking down at Marilyn, bringing her closer to him with his Nikon lens. With Marilyn in a receptive pose, and the photographer above her in a position of power, the composition suggests the perspective of a partner making love to her. Douglas Kirkland had composed similar nude studies, but Marilyn remained at a less intimate distance.

Marilyn had consumed several glasses of champagne and writhed from side to side, playing with beaded necklaces and giggling. From above in a simulated sexual position, Stern snapped the shutter on his prized portrait: Marilyn lying on the floor, her mouth wide open in genuine, spontaneous laughter. When the final session ended, Babs Simpson asked Stern with sincere apprehension what would happen to that "poor girl."

Stern sent Marilyn a portion of original transparencies and contact sheets, but retained the original negatives. She returned the images to Stern, many defaced with x's made in permanent marker or with a hairpin. Stern was furious at first and later published the ones she rejected. Viewed in the aftermath of her apparent suicide, Marilyn would appear to be rejecting and obliterating herself.

Weeks later, *Vogue* editors discarded Stern's color portraits and selected only twenty moody black and white portraits for publication. "It was true, there was something haunting about the pictures they had chosen," Stern would say. "All those black dresses, dark clothing, dark backgrounds...the layout had an elegiac quality. It was strange and eerie. Because Marilyn was still alive."

* * *

As Marilyn returned home from the long shoot at the Bel-Air Hotel on Stone Canyon Road, Robert Kennedy checked in to the

Beverly Hills Hotel on Sunset Boulevard. Later that evening, he addressed the National Insurance Association at Statler-Hilton Hotel at the intersection of Figueroa and Wilshire. According to documentation, Marilyn and Kennedy spent time together at the Lawfords' home afterward. Creditors' claims submitted to the court by Allan Snyder and Agnes Flanagan following Marilyn's death verify make-up and hairstyling services provided on the same day to prepare Marilyn for her appearance at the Lawford beach home.

Snyder's claim itemizes "personal makeup to attend dinner at Peter Lawfords home honoring Robert Kennedy. Call 7:30 PM." Flanagan's merely cites "Hairstyling for Dinner Party/Peter Lawfords Home." Marilyn arrived at the Lawfords' home two hours late, and according to the *Hollywood Reporter*, where Patricia Lawford served her a "cold chop." According to Mrs. Murray's memoir, Kennedy arrived at Marilyn's home alone in a white convertible Cadillac the next day and stayed for an hour. Murray observed the visit and noted that before getting into his car to leave, the attorney general saluted his hostess.

The salute forecasted the female warrior's defeat of her formidable opponent. On June 27, the Board of Directors of Twentieth Century Fox Studios met in its New York offices on West Fifty-Sixth Street for a corporate showdown. Darryl F. Zanuck arrived prepared to gain back control of the studio by amassing additional stock and overthrowing Milton Gould, John Loeb, and the other members of the board. Spyros Skouras, recovered from surgery, conspired to combine his 100,000 shares of stock with Zanuck's 280,000 shares and resign. Zanuck told Nunnally Johnson that *Something's Got to Give* would be completed to Marilyn's satisfaction under his regime and, combined with her one remaining film, could earn the studio upwards of $20 million in profit. Board members attacked Zanuck's character with accusations about his private life and extramarital affairs, but in the end voted nine to two to elect Zanuck as chairman. Milton Gould, the man who fired Monroe, resigned, and Zanuck's son, Richard, would soon become the corporation's president.

Based upon makeup and hairstyling invoices, Marilyn met with studio officials on June 28 and July 12 to discuss salvaging *Something's Got to Give* and developing her remaining film. Levathes arrived at the hacienda at Marilyn's invitation for a conference with Phil Feldman and marveled at her punctuality. She greeted them wearing a severe hairstyle, horn-rimmed glasses and a conservative beige suit designed by Norman Norell. During the dialogue, Marilyn walked between neat rows of hundreds of photographs on the white-carpeted floor of her living room and closely studied the images. She asked Levathes for assistance in choosing Bert Stern's portraits of her for publication, declaring her reliance on his good judgment, possibly conveyance of a developing trust in him.

While serving Levathes and Feldman chilled caviar and canapés, Marilyn identified further comic potential in the film's storyline and shared ideas for her character's struggle with adjusting to her return to civilization. She insisted that a woman who had been stranded on a desert island would not eat delicately with utensils and suggested that the character use her hands to eat in a restaurant. Marilyn also proposed that the character, unaccustomed to wearing shoes on the island, frequently leave the house barefoot.

Levathes delighted in his leading lady's character development and found her savvy and the antithesis of the image Fox had created. "I found, surprisingly, that she was an astute businesswoman in many ways," he said. "She was very rational. You couldn't have had a better meeting with an actress. She had kind of a renewed interested in the project that was infectious. I was finally confident that the picture would be made. In fact, I even authorized a new rewrite of the script incorporating Marilyn's ideas." Unbeknown to Levathes and Feldman, Patricia Newcomb listened to the conversation from a bedroom with her ear pressed to the door and busily took notes.

Marilyn triumphed. Fox eventually renegotiated her contract into a million dollar deal and planned to resume production in late August. The studio even conceded to replace George Cukor with Jean Negulesco, who directed Marilyn in the successful *How To Marry A Millionaire*, and to revert to the original version of the script preferred by Marilyn. Dean Martin would return in September after completing a nightclub act at the Sands, and the film would wrap in October. Marilyn asked for Levathes' personal involvement in the production and promised the studio would complete the film it desperately needed. She would receive $500,000 for *Something's Got to Give* with a bonus if it were completed on schedule. From the start, the studio had strategically cast her in *Something's Got to Give* fully aware of her tremendous box office draw, and it now depended upon the film's Christmas release to recuperate financial losses from *Cleopatra* by year's end.

The studio also promised Marilyn $500,000 for her third and final commitment—a lavish, stylized production with seventy-two costumes changes and matching hairstyles. Produced by the owner of the corporation providing her public relations, Arthur P. Jacobs, and directed by J. Lee Thompson (1914-2002), *I Love Louisa* would eventually be made with Shirley MacLaine and released in 1964 as *What a Way to Go!* The story follows Louisa May Foster, a romantic young woman, who marries for love rather than money despite the wishes of her mother and finds herself a neglected wife. When all four husbands die after achieving wealth, Louisa becomes a rich but unhappy widow and believes she is the victim of a curse. The film would afford Marilyn opportunities to co-star with a series of leading men including Gene Kelly, Dean Martin, Paul Newman, Dick Van Dyke, and Frank Sinatra and to parody recent films such as *Cleopatra*.

Although *Something's Got to Give* would resume production in the fall, the resilient Marilyn Monroe had no intention of spending the remaining summer weeks idle. As promised during her birthday celebration on Fox's Stage 14, Marilyn participated in interviews with photographer George Barris in preparation for a book about her life. On the heels of working with Stern, Marilyn casually posed for Barris in an equally outstanding shoot for *Cosmopolitan* magazine on June 29, 30, and July 1. Snyder applied her make-up, and Agnes Flanagan styled her hair. Barris started taking pictures as Marilyn's longtime friends prepared her. Marilyn's face showed no traces of the tribulations of the last two months. On the contrary, she looked youthful and natural in silk blouses, Capri slacks, a bikini bathing suit, and bundled in a bulky wool sweater purchased during the trip to Mexico. These photographs would appear timeless when viewed retrospectively.

Marilyn had suggested the sessions take place in her own home, but Barris had thought its barely furnished condition might create a depressing backdrop. Instead, he selected the modern North Hollywood Hills home and patio of Tim Leimert at 1635 Blue Jay

Way. Leimert, a CBS radio correspondent who had been the first to announce the dropping of the atomic bomb on Japan when he was in the armed forces, might have been best known as the stadium announcer for UCLA football games for thirty-eight years. His family invested in California real estate and developed Leimert Park, among others, in Los Angeles. Leimert's cousin, Anabel Shaw, had appeared with Marilyn in *Dangerous Years* (1947).

When Barris brought Marilyn to the house, Leimert's maid, Louise, shook Marilyn's hand and gasped: "Is that really you?"

With a giggle, Marilyn confirmed people had been referring to her as *the* Marilyn Monroe.

At a secluded section of Santa Monica Beach, Barris photographed his subject frolicking in the waves, wrapped in a towel, and resting in the sand. Teenage boys gathered at a respectful distance and mimicked Marilyn's poses to their amusement and to hers. Nearby, a woman, wearing a large straw hat covering her face, silently watched Marilyn. Later, Barris would learn the mysterious woman was retired motion picture actress Mae West, Marilyn's predecessor as an icon of sensuous femininity. West later told Barris of her admiration for Marilyn's beauty and talent.

Cosmopolitan cut the photographic essay when Marilyn died, but Barris would publish the interview along with many of the images in his "Twilight of a Star" series in *New York Daily News* in the weeks following her death.

On Friday, July 1 at 7 o'clock in the evening, Barris took his last photograph of Marilyn as the sun set over the Pacific Ocean. "This is for you, George," Marilyn said, puckering her lips and blowing him a kiss. When a strong wave carried away one of Barris' shoes, Marilyn said, "The ocean apparently needs it more than you do."

* * *

"If Marilyn Monroe was glad to see you," Richard Meryman would write, "her 'hello' will sound in your head all your life—the breathless warmth of the emphasis in the 'lo,' her well-deep eyes turned up toward you and her face radiantly crinkled in a wonderfully girlish smile."

During the weeks following Marilyn's appearance at President Kennedy's birthday gala in New York, Richard Meryman, an associate editor of *Life* magazine, followed-up on Marilyn's interest in an article exploring her perspective on fame. The legendary interview took place over the course of three days in the wake of Marilyn's termination from the production of *Something's Got to Give* and would forever be known as her last words.

Patricia Newcomb arranged for Merryman to conduct the six-hour audiotaped interview in Marilyn's house beginning on July 4. In it Marilyn is presented as a bright, insightful, articulate, and down-to-earth woman. The tapes preserved Marilyn's style of speech, expression, and range of emotions. Marilyn had matured, and gone was the whispery-voiced caricature that she had presented to the press for over a decade. Compared to her 1955 televised interview with Edward R. Murrow on *Person to Person*, Marilyn had transformed into another woman.

Meryman was clearly touched by the charismatic child-woman he discovered living in the house on Fifth Helena Drive, corroborating Susan Strasberg's impression that "she still exuded innocence and a vibrant life force that surrounded her like an aura." He recorded his memories in an article titled "A Last Long Talk with a Lonely Girl" published in *Life* after Marilyn's death and an HBO documentary *Marilyn: The Last Interview*. As Marilyn led Meryman through the rooms of her home, she enthusiastically told him where she would place the furniture she had ordered, and described what was special about each purchase. She explained how the folding stools in the living room were ingeniously carved from single pieces of wood.

Following Marilyn outside, Meryman commented on the abundance of flowers in the garden. As her face brightened, Marilyn said, "I don't know why, but I've always been able to make things grow." Opening the door to the detached guest house, which she was converting to an apartment, Marilyn shared her intention to offer is as a getaway for friends in distress. "Maybe they'll want to live here where they won't be bothered until things improve for them," she said.

Meryman perceived "the house was saturated in paranoia" with an eerie "me-against-the-world" quality. Aside from finding Marilyn to be surprisingly unsexy, he was astounded by her excellent taste in decorating. Meryman especially admired a Chinese horse carved in wood from San Francisco's China Town. When he had difficulty setting up his tape recorder, Marilyn offered help and the use of the recorder given to her by Norman Rosten. At one point in the interview, after midnight, she suggested grilling steaks. They searched the refrigerator for food, finding it nearly empty.

On another day, Mrs. Murray interrupted the second part of the interview to serve hamburgers. At first, Marilyn refused to eat, leading to a negotiation between the two women. Eventually, Marilyn consented to eat only half. The interview paused again for thirty minutes as Marilyn accepted a phone call from co-star Wally Cox. Meryman noticed that she concealed the telephone under cushions in her furniture. As Marilyn spoke to her friend, she lay on the floor, giggling and rolling around, dragging the long extension cord with her. Meryman noted her limitless energy, suggesting that he may have observed her entering a manic episode. At times she punctuated her statements with a laugh that ended with a squeak.

"If I am a star, the people made me a star," Marilyn asserted. "There was no studio and no person. The people did." "Sometimes it's nearly impossible," she said of being a celebrity. "It stirs up envy...When you're famous, every weakness is exaggerated...Fame is like caviar. It's good to have caviar, but if you have caviar every damn day...too much caviar."

Marilyn expressed anger toward those who fired her but never referred directly to the studio or executives by name: "If you have a cold, how dare you have a cold. I mean the executives can get colds and stay home forever and call it in." She also indirectly described the studio executives as angry, rejecting parents, and represented herself as a child in pain. "This industry should behave like a mother whose child has just run out in front of a car," she said. "But instead of clasping the child to them, they start punishing the child."

"A sex symbol becomes a thing, and I just hate to be a thing," Marilyn lamented. She continued after disolving into a girlish giggle, saying, "But then if I'm going to be a symbol of something, I'd rather have it sex than some other things we've got symbols of."

"What the world needs now is a greater feeling of kinship," Marilyn calmly articulated, referring to both the state of the world and the condition of her relationship with Fox. "We are all brothers, after all—and that includes movie stars, laborers, Negroes, Jews, Arabs—everyone."

Marilyn reiterated her desire for acceptance over wealth: "I want to be an artist and an actress with integrity. As I said once before, I don't care about the money. I just want to be wonderful."

Near the end of the interview, Meryman irritated Marilyn when he asked about her method of "cranking" herself as she prepared for a scene. "I don't crank anything—I'm not a Model T," Marilyn pointedly slurred, clearly under the influence of champagne. "I think that's kind of disrespectful to refer to it that way. I'm trying to work at an art form, not in a manufacturing establishment."

According to Meryman, Marilyn initially rejected his suggestion that photographs accompany the article. "I don't want everybody to see exactly where I live, what my sofa or my fireplace looks like," she said. "Do you know the book *Everyman*? Well, I want to stay just in the fantasy of everyman." Marilyn reconsidered and posed for pictures by Allan Grant at her home on July 6, her final professional photo session. Wearing high-heeled pumps and orange blouse with matching slacks, Marilyn sat in a carved Italian chair in her dining room and emoted her reactions to Meryman's question as Patricia Newcomb read them aloud.

Afterward, Marilyn gave Grant a tour of the house. He would recall, "She was very enthusiastic and had great plans for each room. As she talked, she stopped being the provocative, sexy movie star. I suddenly saw a real flesh and blood woman, warm and sweet. At the same time, I felt her reaching out for someone or something. I was quite moved. She told me about the books she read and her interest in designing furniture, and all the things nobody knew or cared about…"

Meryman returned for one last visit on July 9 to deliver a verbatim transcription of the interview. Marilyn carefully reviewed each line, reading it aloud to make certain each phrase sounded exactly like her. She requested the deletion of a remark about secretly giving money to those in need. With the interview approved, Meryman walked down the flagstone path to his car, as she stood alone in the doorway. He turned to say goodbye. "Please don't make me look like a joke," Marilyn pled. Meryman agreed and kept his promise. "Hey, thanks," she said, as the journalist got into his car.

Marilyn's words echoed in Meryman's mind as he drove away: "I now live in my work and in a few relationships with the few people

I can really count on. Fame will go by and, so long, I've had you, fame. If it goes by, I've always known it was fickle. So at least it's something I experienced, but that's not where I live."

Chapter Twenty-Eight: The Last Days/ July–August 3, 1962

It was the summer of 1962; telephones had dials, Cadillacs had tailfins. Race riots divided Selma, Alabama, John Steinbeck won the Nobel Prize in literature, and Seattle hosted the World's Fair. Television audiences watched *Route 66* and *The Dick Van Dyke Show* on their black and white console sets, and according to Joshua Greene in *Milton's Marilyn*, sometime in early July, his mother, Amy, dreamed about Marilyn. "She's alone," Amy told her husband, Milton, the next morning. "She doesn't have anybody she can trust. She was sending me signals to tell you to go to Los Angeles." Milton made excuses about leaving in three days to cover the new French fashion collections. Amy urged him to pass on the assignment and go help Marilyn.

Milton consented to contact Marilyn and agreed to assign a replacement photographer if she seemed in need of his support.

"Amy had this dream..." Milton began when Marilyn answered her telephone.

"It's incredible that Amy felt my needing to talk to you," Marilyn interrupted.

According to Amy, Marilyn and Milton chatted for about three hours, and he offered to immediately travel to Los Angeles. Marilyn insisted she was not in crisis and urged Greene to attend to his professional commitment. She sounded in good spirits, so instead they planned to meet sometime in August. Meanwhile, DiMaggio visited Marilyn on July 8 and two days later, Fred Vanderbilt Fields and his wife left Mexico and arrived as Marilyn's guests at her apartment in New York.

Fox continued negotiations with Marilyn on July 12. After the meeting ended, she told Peter Levathes that she was a "very unfortunate woman" whose nonsensical legendary status always made her a "disappointment" to people. Throughout the ordeal and subsequent arbitration, Levathes had come to respect and admire Marilyn. "She had depth," he told Donald Spoto, "No one compared with Marilyn Monroe." Upon their last meeting, she seemed healed from Fox having terminated her and reminded him of a "young and beautiful starlet" eager to finish the film. In a telephone call shortly before her death, Marilyn told Levathes to imagine an unrecognizable Marilyn Monroe who actually arrives on time to the set.

Sidney Skolsky and Marilyn had been collaborating for years on a film biography in which she would portray her childhood idol, Jean Harlow. In his memoir, Skolsky wrote of having driven with Marilyn on July 15 to Indio, near Palm Springs, to research their subject. He recalled having interviewed Harlow's mother, Jean Bello, who was operating a novelty shop in her daughter's memory. According to Skolsky, the elderly woman agreed to cooperate with the project and bestowed upon Marilyn her blessing to depict the blonde legend. However, Bello died in 1958; Skolsky obviously confused the time frame or, perhaps, the visited Harlow's father, Mont Clair Carpenter, who survived Marilyn by twelve years. Skolsky also claimed to have scheduled an appointment with Marilyn on August 5 to outline the script.

Paula Strasberg and DiMaggio visited Marilyn on the weekend of July 21-22, following another surgical effort to correct chronic endometriosis at Cedars of Lebanon Hospital. Future biographers allude this hospitalization was related to an elective abortion; however, Marilyn's gynecologist, Leon Krohn, asserted she never terminated a pregnancy by her own choice. The documentation of vast amounts of painkilling drugs prescribed by Engelberg in the preceding weeks supports the probability of corrective surgery.

As she recovered, Marilyn told Paula of feeling a strong drive to perform on the stage. Upon returning to New York, Paula and her husband Lee spread the word about Marilyn's interest in the theater as Lee was equally interested in directing her in Shakespeare's *Macbeth.* Immediately, packages began arriving at the hacienda containing scripts for dramas, comedies, and musicals. DiMaggio returned to work but called almost every day inquiring about Marilyn's recuperation.

Peter and Patricia Lawford invited Marilyn to Lake Tahoe for the weekend to see Frank Sinatra perform at the Cal-Neva Lodge. Ralph Roberts and Rupert Allan told Donald Spoto that Marilyn had called DiMaggio and asked him to meet her there. She urged her former husband to register at the nearby Silver Crest Motel in fear of them being seen together, as he and Sinatra were feuding.

After Marilyn's session with Dr. Greenson on Friday, July 25, she and the Lawfords left Los Angeles in Sinatra's twin-engine Martin named *Christina*, after his daughter, and landed first in San Francisco, where Patricia boarded a commercial flight to the East Coast. Peter and Marilyn continued to Reno, but in some accounts of this weekend, Patricia also stayed at the Cal-Neva and departed for Hyannis Port late on Sunday. First Lady Jacqueline Kennedy celebrated her thirty-third birthday on Saturday, July 28, sailing off the coast of Hyannis Port. She and the president also attended mass at St. Xavier's Church the following day before sailing on Lewis Bay with friends, including Charles and Betty Spalding.

Dean Martin was performing in the Cal-Neva's Native American themed showroom on Friday evening. This is documented in the 2005 release of a live recording of his performance titled *Live From Lake Tahoe 1962*, contained in *The Essential Dean Martin.* The performance was recorded on Friday, July 27, 1962. During the weekend, Marilyn and Martin discussed co-starring in *I Love Louisa*, her last obligation under the Fox contract.

Many unsubstantiated and contradictory accounts of Marilyn's short stay at the Cal-Neva blend fact, fiction, and urban legend. The preposterous claims range from Marilyn being drugged sexually abused and photographed; conducting an affair with mobster Samuel Giancana; and being resuscitated from a suicide attempt. These myths fuse with local lore of the Cal-Neva serving as the location of trysts for Marilyn and President Kennedy and resurface each time the owner of the property threatens demolition of its vintage cabins.

"The juiciest piece of the Kennedy rumors," wrote the *Tahoe Daily Tribune/North Lake Tahoe Bonanza* on July 27, 1997, "stems from an alleged secret rendezvous with actress Marilyn Monroe on the North Shore." According to Nevada state archivist Guy Rocha, Kennedy's only documented visit to Lake Tahoe occurred while he sought the Democratic Party's nomination for the presidency. Nevada Governor Grant Sawyer arranged for then-Senator Kennedy to address a joint session of the Legislature in Carson City on February 1, 1960.

Afterward, Kennedy attended a reception at the Governor's Mansion and spoke at a civic auditorium. Kennedy also visited the Cal-Neva Lodge after a stop at Squaw Valley, the site of the 1960 Winter Olympics. At the time, Marilyn was filming *Let's Make Love in* Los Angeles. "The stories, however, about a liaison between Kennedy and Monroe at Lake Tahoe are unsupported," wrote Rocha, "and may well represent a titillating, modern-day presidential version of the 'George Washington slept here' myth."

Unsubstantiated allegations of a link between Marilyn and Chicago mobster Samuel Giancana were made primarily by Jeanne Carmen, an actress and model, and evolved over the decades following Marilyn's death. Carmen's preposterous claims grew into Giancana's having had an affair with Marilyn; and conspiring with other mobsters to destroy either the president or attorney general, or both. An earlier link between the president and Giancana appeared in 1975 when the *Washington Post* reported on Judith Campbell Exner's claim of being a mistress to both Giancana and President Kennedy. Exner's original confession of an affair with the president in a press conference grew into bizarre claims about her role in a conspiracy involving Kennedy and the Mafia in which she may have delivered communications between the two regarding Fidel Castro. White House telephone logs document more than eighty calls from Exner to Kennedy's secretary, Evelyn Lincoln, and evidence of Lincoln's calling Exner.

Giancana's link to Sinatra and the Cal-Neva dates back to the mobster allegedly arranging for the singer to obtain a $1.75 million loan to refurbish the Cal-Neva Lodge. Under surveillance by federal agents, Giancana could not be seen publicly in Nevada casinos. In July 1963 while Giancana was staying at the Cal-Neva, he argued in public with the road manager for the McGuire Sisters, a popular singing trio. Giancana was involved with Phyllis McGuire, introduced to him by Sinatra. During the quarrel, witnesses recognized the

Chicago mobster, and the incident came to the attention of the Nevada Gaming Control Board. The board launched an investigation and charged Sinatra for willingly permitting an outlawed person into his gambling establishment. When Sinatra failed to provide proof to refute the charge, he lost his gambling license and was forced to sell his interests in both the Cal-Neva Lodge and the Sands Hotel.

Alex D'Arcy, a close friend of mobster Johnny Roselli, and Marilyn's co-star in *How To Marry a Millionaire*, told Donald Spoto, "There was absolutely never any affair between Marilyn and any of these [mobsters]. In fact, there was no connection between Marilyn and the mob at all! She was in Lake Tahoe that weekend [July 27-29], and I saw Marilyn eating dinner. Giancana and his crowd weren't there, and I would have known if they were."

While entertainer Buddy Greco sat with his manager, Sinatra, Lawford, and several other men on the deck outside Sinatra's chalet overlooking gigantic boulders and the lake beyond, a limousine pulled up to the driveway. Out of it stepped, in Greco's words, "This gorgeous woman in dark glasses."

"She's dressed all in green," Greco recalled decades later as if he were reliving Marilyn's arrival that weekend, "everything green: coat, skirt and scarf. Before I realized who it was, I thought, 'My God, what a beautiful woman.'"

Marilyn and Greco had met earlier at the Crescendo Club where he played jazz piano, but were never properly introduced. When Sinatra presented her to Greco on the deck, the pianist said, "You won't remember me, but I was the piano player when you auditioned for the Benny Goodman band in 1948." Marilyn became emotional at the recollection and embraced him. "She had such warmth—and I was moved," he remembered.

Of Greco's thirty-six snapshots of Marilyn's visit, only six survive. The rest, secured by Greco in a vault in the World Trade Center, were destroyed in the terrorist attacks on September 11, 2001. The entertainer auctioned the remaining photographs in 2009. In most of them, Marilyn is all smiles. One, taken by Greco's manager, depicts Marilyn embracing him with a bare-chested Sinatra seated in the background with a newspaper on his lap. Contemporary tabloid reporters have made inferences about Sinatra's sidelong expression, but perhaps the sun glared in his eyes. Another photograph depicts Greco and Sinatra seated and Lawford, wearing dark short pants, perched on the railing of the deck. Other photographs depict Marilyn and Lawford standing in the opening of a glass door, Marilyn holding a drinking glass.

Another insight into Marilyn's visit appeared in a letter to the editor of *Life,* published in its August 28, 1962 issue. Mrs. Ed Stocker of North Highlands, California, writes that she and her husband met Marilyn two weeks to the day of her death. The couple sat at an adjoining table at the Cal-Neva and spoke with Marilyn the entire evening. "You could only feel pity for this 'Love Goddess,'" Stocker recounted. Marilyn wore a long black velvet coat in the summer heat, a crumpled green chiffon scarf over long, straight hair, and an enormous pair of sunglasses, which drew attention. According to this dinner companion, Marilyn seemed like a "lost little girl" who made a "sad attempt" to join in the gaiety of her spirited friends throughout the evening.

Fred Lawrence Guiles, however, asserted Marilyn was never in Lake Tahoe that weekend; he theorized the story was a cover for an abortion of a Kennedy baby at Cedars of Lebanon Hospital. This myth is dispelled by her autopsy, performed one week later, indicating recent menstruation.

Donald H. Wolfe alleged the Lawfords brought Marilyn to Lake Tahoe to convince her not to call a press conference to air her grievances about one or both Kennedy brothers. Anthony Summers alleged she was drugged and photographed while being sexually abused in an attempt to extort the Kennedys. Subsequent authors morphed this outrageous claim into tabloid stories of an unconscious Marilyn being gang-raped by mafia bodyguards and sexually assaulted by female prostitutes hired by mobsters to extort either the Kennedys or Marilyn. Summers' report of an anonymous photo laboratory technician advising Sinatra to destroy photographs of Marilyn "in utter disarray" that weekend may have inspired this tale.

According to Lois Banner's research, Betsy Hammes—present at the resort that weekend—believed Sinatra's aides had assisted Marilyn to her cabin when she became nauseated or was possibly induced to vomit a probable overdose of barbiturates. Allegedly, Sinatra's camera was used to photograph the incident. According to photographer

William Woodfield, who claimed to have seen the seven frames of the film, the images were blurry. The people involved were unidentifiable, and the situation was unclear. He recalled the group of males and the one female in the frames were fully clothed and no sex acts were involved. One male seemed to be standing over the female, who appeared to be crawling on the floor on her hands and knees. Woodfield surmised the female was either being helped, or was being degraded and treated like an animal. The photographs have never been produced, so the certainty of their existence is suspect. If indeed they existed, the motivation for having taken them is unclear. Greenson would note no assault in Marilyn's last days.

Some biographers have made less sinister and more romantic claims, asserting that DiMaggio proposed remarriage during this weekend and Marilyn agreed to a wedding in early August. "I heard she and Joe DiMaggio talked about getting married again," Buddy Greco told Britain's *Daily Mail*, "but I don't know." Reports by eyewitnesses allege Marilyn stood by the Cal-Neva Lodge's pool and stared up the hill where DiMaggio stood smiling down at her.

According to the baseball legend's biographer Richard Ben Cramer, during the last week in July, DiMaggio met with his employer Valmore Monette in Smithfield, Virginia to announce his resignation and plan to return to California to marry Marilyn. "He thought things would be different than they had been before and that everything would work out well for them now," Monette told Donald Spoto. "I know that was why he left us and was going back [west] in 1962." Maury Allen (1932-2010) sportswriter and columnist for the *New York Post*, corroborated this information.

Monette's claim of a remarriage between Marilyn and DiMaggio trace back to a notice in the *Los Angeles Herald-Examiner* published on August 14, 1962, six days after Marilyn's funeral. The article cites the former employer, stating that DiMaggio terminated his job to be near his ex-wife, and that he worried about her well-being during her last week. Mention of the remarriage also appeared in Gay Talese's article "The Silent Season of a Hero," in the July 1966 issue of *Esquire*: "He was possessive of her that year, his close friends say, because Marilyn and he had planned to remarry; but before they could she was dead..."

When the weekend visit to Lake Tahoe ended, DiMaggio flew

back to New York to retrieve some possessions from his suite at the Hotel Lexington. He invited George Solotaire to return with him to Los Angeles via San Francisco, where he would deposit his things at the home on Beach Street in the Marina District. DiMaggio would also attend a charity baseball game at Candlestick Park on Saturday, August 4 along with his brothers, Dominic and Vincent. DiMaggio planned to return to Los Angeles late Sunday evening in time for the wedding, scheduled for Wednesday, August 8. He and Marilyn intended to invite about fifteen guests to the ceremony in her garden, given no advance notice in an effort to avoid a media ambush.

* * *

On Monday, July 30, Mrs. Murray arrived early to discover Marilyn strolling along the back wall behind the house and paging through a book on authentic Mexican gardens, a gift from the housekeeper. Marilyn wandered across her property, muttering about her vision of a "garden of color" and indecision about how many bougainvillea vines to plant along the wall. "There was a peaceful expression on her face when she was out there," the housekeeper observed.

According to Inez Melson, Marilyn's last week was spent helping Joe DiMaggio Jr., to the chagrin of his father. The young man had been responsible for an automobile accident—resulting in a four hundred dollar claim for damages to the car of the other driver involved—and went to Marilyn for help. Joe Sr. became angry upon learning Joe Jr. accepted the cash and ordered his son to return to money. "I won't give you a check," he told his son, "because if I give you a check to give to her, she will never cash it. I'll give you the money."

Shortly before Marilyn died, Joe Sr. gave Joe Jr. four hundred dollars to repay Marilyn. Following her death, Melson and DiMaggio Sr. searched Marilyn's home and coat pockets in search of the money and finally gave up. In the next few weeks, Melson inventoried the contents of Marilyn's home for the estate and hired an appraiser, Mr. Gilbert. He scrutinized every object in the home, including a tiny vase with a long neck displayed on the coffee table in the living room. When the appraiser peered into the vase, he discovered four tightly rolled up one hundred dollar bills.

* * *

On July 31, Marilyn made a series of calls to finalize her plans for the next month. First she contacted dress manufacturer Henry Rosenfeld in New York, and asked that he escort her to the premiere of an Irving Berlin musical, *Mr. President*, directed by Joshua Logan, at National Theatre in Washington, D.C. Norman and Hedda Rosten intended to join them in seeing Marilyn's former co-star, Robert Ryan, portray the fictional President Stephen Decatur Henderson, who loses re-election following a calamitous visit to the Soviet Union. The show's opening would be a star-studded event with President Kennedy and his wife also in attendance.

Next, Marilyn telephoned the Strasberg apartment in Central Park West to organize another short trip. She instructed their secretary to arrange for her east coast maid, Lena Pepitone, to obtain a key to the New York apartment. She also alerted her New York cook, Hattie Stevenson, to prepare for her arrival on Monday or Tuesday to join the Strasbergs in attending a Broadway show. Finally, Marilyn spoke with Gene Kelly, who had invited her to co-star with him in another musical with a World War I setting. She agreed to meet with him on Sunday, August 5 to discuss the project.

On August 1, Cherie Redmond typed a memo to Hedda Rosten expressing concern about Marilyn's reaction to Mrs. Murray's intention to travel to Europe. The housekeeper delayed finalizing her reservations to avoid inconveniencing her employer, a trait Redmond perceived as loyalty. The memo debunks future speculation that Mrs. Murray afforded the trip through a payoff for her silence over the circumstances of Marilyn's death. Redmond also requested the transfer of funds to cover checks Marilyn had issued to Paula Strasberg totaling $15,000 and to John Strasberg in the sum of $406.30. The later check likely covered insurance payments for the Ford Thunderbird Marilyn had promised to fund when she originally gave him the automobile.

Later in the day, Marilyn spent four hours with Mrs. Murray at Frank's Nurseries and Flowers on Wilshire Boulevard ordering tuberoses, orange king bougainvillea, hanging begonias, Mexican lime, and Valencia orange trees; totaling $93.08. Included in this purchase were a variety of hummingbird feeders and hummingbird seed. In June 2009, Bonhams Auction house would offer for sale the carbon copy receipt dated August 1. An additional notation on the bottom of the receipt reads, "*ask for Mr. Jeffrey,*" referencing Eunice Murray's son-in-law, Norman Jefferies.

Marilyn and Mrs. Murray also stopped at the boutique of architect, interior designer, and world traveler William Alexander (1909-1997), who jokingly proposed marriage to Marilyn after she made a few purchases. "I'll think about it," Marilyn politely responded with a giggle. She added, "I'm so happy, because I'm going to be married to someone I was married to once before."

On Thursday, August 2, Marilyn went to Dr. Greenson's office for psychotherapy session. He conducted a second session at her home later in the day. Ralph Roberts told Donald Spoto that Marilyn now ruminated about discharging the doctor. "Her resentment of Greenson had reached the breaking point," Roberts recalled. The psychoanalyst had made an effort to isolate Marilyn from many in her life, but when he tried again to eject DiMaggio, Marilyn rebelled. Patricia Newcomb would validate this. "Marilyn was very angry about his not being there for her," Newcomb said. "Several times, she threatened to fire Greenson—to leave him, but I never took her threats seriously."

"These patients are seductive…Rich and famous people need the therapist twenty-four hours a day and they are insatiable," Greenson wrote in an unpublished article, "Special Problems in Psychotherapy with the Rich and Famous," in 1978 (now archived in the Special Collections Section of the UCLA library and unavailable until 2039). "They are also able to give up completely in the sense they are doing to you what was done to them by their parents or their servants. You are their servant and can be dismissed without notice." Greenson seemed to be describing aspects of Borderline Personality Disorder and sidestepped the possibility of his own enabling of this behavior.

Marlon Brando verified these claims of Marilyn setting limits with those around her. He reported that she called him, and they spoke for hours. Marilyn was becoming more emotionally healthy and was starting to believe that Strasberg and others were trying to use her. They spoke for the last time two or three days before she died. Marilyn invited Brando to dinner at her hacienda. "I already made plans for the evening and couldn't, but I promised to call the following week to set a date for dinner," he wrote. "She said, 'Fine,' and that was it...She didn't seem depressed to me, and I don't think that if she had been sleeping with [Kennedy] at the time she would have invited me over for dinner."

At some point in the day, publicist John Springer wrote a short note to Marilyn from his Manhattan office on East Forty-Ninth Street: "*New York misses you. I miss you. Come home.*" She was on the verge of becoming a very fine dramatic actress, he believed, and only recently had begun to feel secure in her own acting ability. "[Marilyn] would have returned to New York," Springer later said. "She was already established as a great comedienne and satirist and she was developing as a dramatic actress." He envisioned her tackling more challenging and serious roles in theater and television, occasionally returning to the screen to play a strong character.

In the twilight hours of Thursday, August 2, 1962, a white Volkswagen Beetle drove slowly through Marilyn's green gates and parked on the brick driveway in front of the guesthouse. Its driver and passenger walked along Marilyn's fieldstone path toward the door. The couple, makeup artist Allan Snyder and wardrobe assistant Marjorie Pletcher, had completed work at Universal Studios and were visiting an ecstatic Marilyn. "We'll have a real celebration," she had said in her invitation.

"It was a pleasant, festive, and quiet evening," Snyder recalled in an interview with Michelle Justice and Roman Hryniszak, editors of *Runnin' Wild*. "Marilyn was very radiant and happy, as we knew it would only be a few weeks before starting her movie again."

Marilyn spoke enthusiastically about returning to the original script by Nunnally Johnson. Aside from celebrating the return to *Something's Got to Give*, the small group conversed happily about Allan and Marjorie's current work. Snyder recalled:

> We sat out by the pool sipping champagne and nibbling on caviar watching Maf play on the grass, trying to be the center of attention, as only puppies can do. It was warm and balmy and the conversation was the usual for us. She wanted to know all about our work. We were both doing pictures at Universal Studios at the time, but not together, I was working with David Niven and Mitzi Gaynor, a dear friend of [Marilyn's and ours], and Marge was working with Doris Day [and Cary

> Grant on *That Touch of Mink*], I think. She had to show us the latest additions on the house and telling us about the furniture that was being made in Mexico and would be finished in the not-so-distant future…you know…the land of mañanas. She was proud to show Margie that she was still thin and wouldn't have to refit any costumes for the picture.

"She was excited and happy that night, which was the last time I ever saw her," Pletcher remembered. "We were going to begin shooting in a matter of weeks." Close-up work would begin September 4, Marilyn explained, and principal shooting would commence September 16 when Dean Martin became available. "Because of our early schedule," Snyder said, "it wasn't a late evening and we were on our way home having set a date for the following week to get together again." He would never again see Marilyn alive.

Marilyn performed her nightly routine of removing the telephone from her bedroom, placing it in the spare bedroom, covering it with pillows, and closing her bedroom door to sleep in total silence. Maf-Honey barked incessantly as the Santa Ana winds blew from the Mojave Desert and rustled through Marilyn's towering eucalyptus trees, keeping his mistress awake during the night. Marilyn's remedy was to restrict the dog to the detached guesthouse after dark. Marilyn retired to her bedroom, lit a fire, and continued reading *Captain Newman, M.D.*, a fictionalized account of Dr. Greenson's experience serving in World War II.

* * *

The Associated Press announced Robert J. Kennedy's arrival with his wife and children in San Francisco on Friday, August 3. He was scheduled to deliver a speech to the American Bar Association on Monday, but the weekend was reserved for pleasure with family friends. The following morning, the Kennedy family traveled sixty miles south to the Bates Ranch in Gilroy, in the Santa Cruz Mountain appellation, near Mount Madonna, to visit John Bates (1918-2004), his wife Nancy, and three children. The Bates raised cattle and grew Cabernet Sauvignon grapes. A graduate of Stanford and Berkley Universities, Bates served as Judicial Board President of the San Francisco Bar. During the Kennedy administration, he turned down an invitation to serve as assistant to the Attorney General in order to fulfill a commitment to his law firm.

The Bates' ranch hand, Roland Snyder, confirmed saddling horses for both families, who rode to Mount Madonna. Bates showed photographs of the Kennedy family's visit to Anthony Summers in the documentary, *Say Goodbye to the President* (1985). The next morning, the Kennedy and Bates families attended Catholic Mass in Gilroy, as documented by *The Gilroy Dispatch*, before the Kennedys drove back to San Francisco to the home of Paul Fay, appointed by President Kennedy as undersecretary of the Navy. Donald Spoto documents two other couples joining them in the city, Edward and Georgina Callan and Joseph Tydings and his wife. Callan was a stockbroker and yachtsman; and President Kennedy had appointed Joseph Tydings (born 1928) as United States Attorney for Maryland.

Across the country in Manhattan, Dorothy Kilgallen's gossip column "The Voice of Broadway" in the *New York Journal-American* led with a veiled reference to Marilyn's love life, "Marilyn Monroe's health must be improving. She's been attending select Hollywood parties and has become the talk of the town again. In California, they're circulating a photograph of her that certainly isn't as bare as the famous calendar, but is very interesting...And she's cooking in the sex-appeal department, too; she's proved vastly alluring to a handsome gentleman who is a bigger name than Joe DiMaggio in his heyday. So don't write off Marilyn as finished." The ambiguous reference to the photograph remains a mystery (and may have been a shot of the nude swimming scene in *Something's Got to Give*); however, many future biographers would speculate the "handsome gentleman" was Robert Kennedy.

An alleged Central Intelligence Agency document dated August 3, 1962, and apparently signed by James Angleton, chief of counterintelligence, appeared on the Internet in the twenty-first century. It referred to wiretaps of conversations between Kilgallen and Howard Rothberg, her friend and interior decorator who owned an antique shop in New York but had no direct link to Marilyn. Erroneously touted by some biographers as fact, the report merely summarizes the content of Rothberg's commentary to the columnist.

According to the report (its authenticity remains undocumented), Rothberg alleged that Marilyn attended parties hosted by the Hollywood "inner circle" and experienced a "break up" with the

Kennedys. He further alluded to Marilyn having "secrets to tell" and claimed the president visited an unidentified air force base to inspect objects from "outer space." Kilgallen responded with knowledge of rumors of a crashed spacecraft and dead bodies, told to her by an unidentified British cabinet official when she served as a London correspondent for the International News Service in the 1950s. The document outlines other allegations, including Marilyn calling the attorney general to complain about he and the president ignoring her; her threatening to hold a press conference to "tell all." Marilyn also purportedly made references to military bases in Cuba, the president's plan to kill Fidel Castro, and her "diary of secrets" being leaked to newspapers.

In her column on July 15, 1959, Kilgallen implied that the CIA was conspiring with organized crime to assassinate Castro; the only substantiated fact in the CIA report. Made public following Kennedy's assassination, Operation Mongoose was a classified program to overthrow the Castro government in Cuba. Initiated in November 1961 and headed by Brigadier General Edward G. Lansdale, Assistant for Special Operations to the Secretary of Defense, the program included General Maxwell D. Taylor and Attorney General Robert Kennedy.

The alleged CIA document plausibly spawned decades of absurd conspiracy theories about Marilyn having affairs with government officials and being murdered to prevent her from disclosing national secrets, such as the persisting unsubstantiated rumors of an Unidentified Flying Object crashing in Roswell, New Mexico in 1947. The source of these claims seems to be telephone conversations between an interior decorator to his gossip columnist friend. The CIA report itself by no means suggests the validity of any of the information; it merely demonstrates identification of a prominent journalist potentially publishing claims that may pose a potential national security risk. We shall see how Kilgallen's colleague Robert Slatzer parlayed these rumors into his own notoriety after Kilgallen's death in 1965 by an overdose of drugs combined with alcohol.

As the seeds of these bizarre rumors first took root, long before their growth into preposterous urban legend in the last half century, Marilyn arose early and refreshed. She had experienced none of her usual sleeping problems and avoided the use of sleeping pills. After preparing her own coffee and grapefruit, Marilyn dressed and went to the guesthouse to let Maf-Honey out. She called Elizabeth Courtney, the fitter for fashion designer Jean-Louis, and requested that she deliver a gown for final alteration the next day, along with a formal suit for a special occasion. Realizing the next day was Saturday, Marilyn called back and rescheduled to Monday, stating she did not wish to interrupt Louis' weekend.

Composer Jule Styne called from New York and offered Marilyn a leading role co-starring Frank Sinatra in Styne's new film, a musical version of *A Tree Grows In Brooklyn*. Investors had committed one million dollars based on Marilyn's casting alone. Over the phone, Marilyn sang a song from the film's score, "Run For Your Life". She and Styne planned to meet in New York on August 9. Based upon a book and a 1945 film adaptation, the musical focuses on a working class family at the turn of the century. Preteen Francie idolizes her optimistic but alcoholic father who works as a singing waiter and spends his meager paycheck in neighborhood saloons. Her hard-working mother is disappointed by years of her husband's broken promises. In a supporting role, exuberant Aunt Cissy lightens the drama with romantic misadventures with a series of men. It is uncertain if Styne envisioned Marilyn in the role of the mother or the aunt, but most early versions of the script proposed the casting of Judy Garland as Aunt Cissy.

Marilyn was in demand in the United States and Europe. Later in the day, a telegram arrived from Italy offering her an eleven million dollar motion picture contract with rights to select scripts, directors, and co-stars. *Esquire* also offered an in-depth interview and accompanying photo essay.

With many offers on the table, Marilyn's mind must have been filled with internal dialogue as she met with Dr. Greenson for a ninety-minute psychotherapy session at his office. After stopping at Briggs Emporium Deli on San Vicente and ordering $49.07 in catered food for an unknown event, Marilyn returned home, where Dr. Engelberg administered an injection of an unknown medication and wrote a prescription for twenty-five tablets of Nembutal. On July 25, Dr. Lee Seigel had issued a prescription for Nembutal and refilled it on August 3. Marilyn filled the original prescription at San Vicente Pharmacy on July 31, and an invoice to her estate showed a charge of $3.75; the refill also appeared on the same invoice for the amount of $6.05.

Engelberg's last prescription reveals his possible lack of communication with Marilyn's other doctors or lack of awareness of Marilyn's efforts to obtain prescriptions from other health care providers. Greenson had advised weaning Marilyn off Nembutal, and Engelberg had limited her intake of the barbiturate to one pill per day. At the time, Engelberg was described as distracted with his acrimonious divorce, and some of Marilyn's friends later perceived his dispensing the prescription had been an oversight.

Next, Marilyn interrupted gynecologist Dr. Leon Krohn's golf game by calling him at the Hillcrest Golf Club. She mysteriously told him she had something very important to discuss and invited him to dinner that evening. Later, depending upon various biographers' versions, either Krohn or Marilyn called back and postponed. According to Donald Spoto, they rescheduled to August fifth, coincidentally the fifth anniversary of her miscarriage. Krohn had given Marilyn both medical and personal advice, having been a supportive friend during her divorce from DiMaggio. Perhaps Marilyn was planning to reveal her remarriage to DiMaggio or to discuss the possibility of eventually having children.

Marilyn then placed another call to handyman Ray Tolman in Fullerton to arrange for the remaining renovation of her house, before Arthur P. Jacobs called to confirm a meeting to discuss *I Love Louisa* with director J. Lee Thompson on Monday evening at 5 o'clock. As the day progressed, Marilyn left a message for her former publicist Rupert Allan, requesting that he represent her again. When he did not return her call, Marilyn contacted Ralph Roberts for assistance in reaching the publicist. In his studio cottage on North Palm Avenue, Roberts called Rupert Allan at Marilyn's request and relayed her message.

Allan had recently returned from Monaco, where he worked for Princess Grace. Roberts urged him to contact Marilyn and congratulate her on the *Life* interview. "Ralph reached me," Allan would later admit, "but I had jet lag after the flight from France and a bad case of bronchitis I had picked up in Monaco. I knew if I spoke one word to Marilyn, she would insist on coming over with chicken soup and aspirin, and I was really too sick for that."

Patricia Newcomb's more mild case of bronchitis did not prevent her from accepting Marilyn's invitation to dine with her and Peter Lawford at La Scala in Beverly Hills. "Why don't you come out here and stay for the night?" Marilyn asked Patricia. "You'll have all the privacy you want, you can sun in the back yard and rest." Marilyn requested her favorite booth, number fifteen, tucked privately in the back at the end of a long, winding aisle and next to the wine cellar. "We'll bake those germs right out of you," she told Patricia over dinner.

If claims of a remarriage to DiMaggio were indeed factual, Marilyn spent her last week preparing a small wedding ceremony and reception in the garden of her home. She granted DiMaggio's wish to invite only a small group of their closest friends, perhaps no more than fifteen, and agreed to dodge publicity by waiting until the last moment to inform them. Marilyn's request to Jean-Louis for a gown and formal suit may have been related to the wedding and honeymoon. Reportedly, the couple planned to travel to Long Island, New York City, or Cape Cod. These plans appeared consistent with Marilyn's disclosure to antique dealer William Alexander.

According to psychic Kenny Kingston, Marilyn called him Friday night and discussed her impending marriage. To celebrate, she planned to wear a disguise and walk along the shore on Santa Monica Beach. Marilyn's last words to him were, "Love is the one immortal thing about us. Without love, what else can life mean?"

Kingston would relate no premonition for tragedy in his friend, but across the Atlantic, an eccentric woman with no personal ties to Marilyn experienced a forewarning. In Paris, Milton and Amy Green were dining in a restaurant with Marlene Dietrich and Alicia Darr Corning Clark, a sometimes artist and actress who claimed to have been engaged to John F. Kennedy before his marriage to Jacqueline Bouvier. A year earlier, Alicia's name appeared in Dorothy Kilgallen's gossip column for her whirlwind courtship to Alfred Corning Clark, the grandson of Edward Clark, co-founder of Singer sewing machines. She was thirty-three, and he was forty-five. In less than three weeks after meeting, Clark gave Alicia a $95,000 diamond engagement ring. The couple married in September 1961, and she became his sixth wife. Thirteen days after the wedding, Clark died of natural causes, leaving Alicia a widow with a lifetime income from two trust funds.

According to Amy, Alicia was intoxicated at dinner. She turned to Amy and Milton and slurred, "Well, how's your friend Marilyn?" Amy explained that Milton had recently spoken to her and sounded fine. Alicia blurted out, "She's going to die soon." Milton's face blanched. Angry at the inappropriate outburst, Marlene Dietrich told her to shut up. Alicia lifted her cocktail to her lips and added, "She's going to commit suicide."

Chapter Twenty-Nine: August 4, 1962

On August 4, 1962, the communities of Brentwood, Palisades, and Beverly Hills awoke to a clear and bright Saturday morning.

At the Ferus Gallery, a contemporary art gallery on La Cienega Boulevard, director Irving Blum featured East Coast artist Andy Warhol's first solo show of Pop Art produced with a semi-mechanized silkscreen process. On display since July 9, the exhibition was closing that evening. Each of Warhol's thirty-two canvases depicted a Campbell's Soup can, one of each of the varieties the company offered. Actor Dennis Hopper had been the first of five attendees to purchase a canvas for one hundred dollars, but Blum bought them all back to keep the set intact. "When people confronted these pictures for the first time, they didn't know how to deal with them," Blum would say. "The paintings were extremely controversial. There was a lot of amusement. People felt that they were somehow slightly ridiculous." A nearby supermarket piled up real Campbell's soup cans in their window and advertised them as "the real thing for only 29 cents a can."

In town for the exhibition, Warhol would hear the news of Marilyn's death the following morning, and she would serve as his muse. The artist would purchase Gene Korman's publicity portrait of her from *Niagara*, crop it, and create his well-known, mass-produced silkscreen series of Marilyn in various colors, presenting her as an infinitely reproducible image and icon.

At 8 o'clock in the morning in nearby Brentwood, Mrs. Murray arrived at Marilyn's hacienda in car driven by Henry D'Antonio, who was servicing her 1957 Dodge Coronet at his garage. He agreed to deliver Mrs. Murray's green Dodge to Marilyn's driveway sometime in the afternoon. Mrs. Murray planned to supervise the planting of shrubs and citrus trees in the rear garden. Both she and Marilyn expected landscapers from Frank's Nursery to deliver the plants before noon. D'Antonio's son, Anthony, then age eight, would later tell Michelle Morgan that while his father performed light handiwork for Marilyn, such as changing exterior light bulbs, Marilyn played catch with Anthony. "She would slip some loose change into my pocket," the younger D'Antonio said, "holding her finger to her lips as this was our secret."

Mrs. Murray had planned a tour of Europe with her sister and brother-in-law later in the month. The Greg Schreiner collection includes a personal check to Mrs. Murray in the amount of two hundred dollars signed by Marilyn and dated August 4, 1962. According to Donald Spoto's theory based upon information from Patricia Newcomb, Marilyn had terminated Mrs. Murray's employment and issued the check for a month's severance wages. Allegedly, Mrs. Murray was completing her last day of work. The sum of two hundred dollars for a month of part-time work seems accurate for the economy of 1962. There is no mention of a dismissal from employment in Mrs. Murray's memoir.

Arthur Miller's father, Isidore, called early and was told Marilyn was dressing and would call him back. She never did. The elder Miller found this out of character as Marilyn usually interrupted important business to return his calls. Norman Jeffries arrived later and began restoring the brick kitchen floor. While kneeling on the floor, he noticed a pair of feet. Marilyn had arisen early and wandered into the kitchen wrapped in a large bath towel. She drank grapefruit juice as her breakfast.

Marilyn casually explained to Mrs. Murray that Patricia Newcomb had spent the night following their dinner together and planned to spend the afternoon lounging poolside. The next morning, neighbors would tell police officers that they heard a woman coughing in Marilyn's back yard. By nine o'clock, as the temperature in Los Angeles rose to eighty degrees, Marilyn called Ralph Roberts and asked him to acquire an unreleased record by a singer she hoped to promote. They discussed dinner plans to grill steaks on the patio, their weekly routine, and agreed to confirm plans later in the afternoon.

Journalist Sidney Skolsky made his routine weekend call to Marilyn. His daughter, Steffi, allegedly told Anthony Summers that she listened to the conversation on an extension and heard Marilyn say she might be going to the beach that evening, possibly referring to the Lawford home, and that Patricia Newcomb was feeling jealous of her for an uncertain reason.

Additional phone calls inundated Marilyn with felicitations on the *Life* magazine interview in the August third edition currently on newsstands. Actor and friend Marlon Brando was one of the first to congratulate her, and they talked for hours.

Marilyn also initiated a thirty-two minute call to Hedda and Norman Rosten in New York. Norman recorded the conversation in his memoir. Cheerfully, Marilyn asked if the couple had read her interview. They had and complimented its spirit. Marilyn lamented about delays in the arrival of her new furniture from Mexico. "We'll go to Washington together," she said, referring to the benefit performance of *Mr. President* in late September. "I have box seats for us," Marilyn said. "We have to start living, right?"

Rosten noticed Marilyn racing from one subject to another. She said she missed them and suggested they visit her in Los Angeles. Marilyn even tempted them by offering to have the pool warmed. If they both couldn't come, she asked if Hedda would come alone. Next, Marilyn inquired about their daughter, Patricia, aged sixteen, and sent her love to the girl. In turn, Norman relayed a message from their mutual friend, poet Ettore Rell, who enjoyed Marilyn's interview and believed she owed him a letter. "Let's all start to live before we get old," Marilyn told Rosten. She ended the conversation to accept another long distance call but promised to call him again on Monday.

Before noon, photographer Lawrence Schiller stepped through the open front gates and found Marilyn kneeling by a flowerbed beside the guesthouse, pulling weeds and pruning flowering shrubs. The Los Angeles County coroner later noted that Marilyn needed a manicure, likely a result of her gardening on her last day alive. Schiller's agenda was to convince her to appear on the front and back cover of *Playboy* magazine's December 1962 tenth anniversary issue. The concept involved an image of a demure Marilyn completely enveloped in a white fur coat on the front cover. The back cover pose would depict an image of her shot from behind and taken simultaneously, revealing bare buttocks. The accompanying article would include Schiller's semi-nude photos of the skinny-dipping scene in *Something's Got to Give.*

On this day, Marilyn seemed doubtful about posing semi-nude on the magazine's back cover, although she welcomed publicity in the wake of her dismissal from Fox. Patricia Newcomb had launched a publicity campaign for Marilyn to replace Elizabeth Taylor on the covers of national magazines. Taylor's love life eclipsed Marilyn in the media for some time. Taylor's affair with Richard Burton, combined with her many life-threatening illness, a suicide attempt, and tantrums on the set of *Cleopatra*, offered far more sensation than Marilyn's current career crisis.

Marilyn gave Schiller a tour of her home before he departed for Palm Springs, then retired to the sunroom to review the photographs in question. Lounging on a wicker settee, she marked each photograph as approved or rejected. She wrote across the back of several prints, granting her permission for publication in *Playboy.* What prompted Marilyn's final decision is unclear. Upon his return from Palm Springs on Monday, Schiller found a plain envelope containing the marked photographs slipped under his studio door, and would wonder who delivered them, and when.

Workmen from The Mart delivered a bedside table selected by Marilyn the previous Wednesday. She wrote them a check and stored the piece in the living room. Marilyn also accepted the delivery of a white Roman chest from Pilgrim's Modern Furniture on Wilshire Boulevard and wrote a check for $228.80, possibly the last check she signed. Many of the furnishings ordered in Mexico had been lost. Shipments had been sent to the wrong address, and incorrect bills arrived at the hacienda. From his home in Mexico, Fred Fields and his wife assisted in correcting the errors with local vendors. He wrote in a letter to Mrs. Murray: "*Nieves [Field's wife] is going to call them up and I have asked her to use her most violent Spanish.*"

Miles north in San Francisco, DiMaggio arrived for a charity baseball game. In the airport gift shops and newsstands, he saw *Life* magazine's advertising campaign featuring large cards of an arrestingly beautiful Marilyn in scenes from *Something's Got to Give*. DiMaggio paged through the current issue of *Paris Match* displaying her on its cover. He was scheduled to arrive in Los Angeles Sunday evening to join Marilyn.

Patricia Newcomb slept until noon. Mrs. Murray prepared her an omelette using the fresh herbs growing in clay pots in the courtyard off the kitchen, and Patricia ate breakfast at the trestle table in the kitchen. Marilyn joined her houseguest at the table, tracing a pattern on its surface with her fingers, but refused to eat. Patricia and Marilyn lounged poolside in the early afternoon. Decades later, some claimed Marilyn seemed angry or resentful at Patricia for flaunting a night of sound sleep when her hostess had experienced a particularly restless night. For a guest to have bragged about sleeping twelve hours in Marilyn's house, said Murray, "was like feasting in front of a starving person."

Either in the late morning or early afternoon, hairdresser Agnes Flanagan arrived for a social call. The brief visit was interrupted when a messenger delivered a package to Marilyn. She opened the package to discover a stuffed toy tiger and carried it out to the pool area, where she sat in silence. Puzzled by this reaction, Flanagan left believing Marilyn suddenly seemed seriously depressed. The following day, two stuffed animal toys would be photographed on the lawn behind the pool. The sender's identity would remain a mystery.

During the mid-afternoon, Marilyn's incessant thoughts of DiMaggio prompted her to take out a sheet of stationery and a ballpoint pen. Somewhere in the house, in her bedroom, in the sunroom, or poolside, she began a letter to her alleged fiancé in her unmistakable slanted, bubble handwriting:

> *Dear Joe,*
> *If I can only succeed in making you happy, I will have succeeded in the biggest and most difficult thing there is—that is, to make one person completely happy. Your happiness means my happiness, and*

The rest of her thoughts would remain a mystery. The unfinished letter would be found folded at its midpoint and inserted between the pages of Marilyn's address book. It is possible Marilyn had been interrupted by a phone call congratulating her on the *Life* article, the delivery of plants or furnishings, or the arrival of her psychiatrist.

The plants ordered three days earlier arrived and were placed in the courtyard between the kitchen and guesthouse, their roots encased in burlap, awaiting installation.

Three hours ahead, in Hyannis Port, President Kennedy posed informally with his wife and children at dusk for White House photographer Cecil Stoughton on the porch of their home with Nantucket Sound in the background. Jacqueline wore a casual summer gingham dress, and the president's sleeves were rolled up.

Sometime between two and four o'clock, Henry D'Antonio and his wife returned Mrs. Murray's car to Marilyn's driveway on their way home to nearby San Vicente Boulevard. Brazenly, the housekeeper invited them inside to see the completed kitchen as Marilyn rested in her bedroom. According to Murray, at some point during the day, Marilyn asked, "Do we have any oxygen?" Murray relayed the odd request to Dr. Greenson, but his reaction remains undocumented.

At two o'clock, twenty-one-year-old Joe DiMaggio Jr. called collect from Camp Pendleton, in nearby Orange County, only to hear the operator talk to Mrs. Murray, who said Marilyn was not at home. During the LAPD's interrogation of Joe DiMaggio, Jr., he indicated having made a total of three phone calls to Marilyn's home that day, only one of which Mrs. Murray mentioned to police. When he placed the second call at 4:30, Mrs. Murray repeated Marilyn's unavailability to the operator.

Dr. Greenson arrived at Marilyn's hacienda between four-thirty and five-fifteen. According to Anthony Summers, Greenson found her somewhat depressed and drugged. Marilyn allegedly felt angry and resentful toward Patricia Newcomb for sleeping soundly for twelve hours as Marilyn had slept poorly. Greenson instructed Patricia to leave. Marilyn looked out from her bedroom hallway as Patricia moved toward the front door carrying her overnight bag.

According to Fred Lawrence Guiles, Patricia thought Marilyn's eyes conveyed a silent apology. Patricia smiled and promised to call in the morning. In Mrs. Murray's version, Patricia sprang up and left without a word. Greenson suggested Mrs. Murray take Marilyn for a restful drive along the Pacific Coast Highway and arranged for the housekeeper to spend the night, which was unusual.

At five o'clock, Peter Lawford called Marilyn and invited her to a small dinner party at his home while his wife, Patricia, remained in Hyannis Port, where she had been since the previous weekend. Marilyn declined. She had never trusted Lawford but considered his wife a good friend.

Ralph Roberts phoned between 5:30 and 6:00 to confirm dinner plans for Sunday before shopping for groceries. A man's voice, undoubtedly Greenson's, answered: "She's not in just now." The male abruptly ended the call. Greenson was waiting for a call back from Engelberg to meet him at Marilyn's house, according to the internist's wife. Allegedly, Engelberg declined Greenson's request.

Donald Spoto's interview with William Asher, television director of *The Donna Reed Show* and *Twilight Zone*, placed Greenson's arrival earlier in the afternoon. Asher remembered Marilyn arriving at the Lawford's home between three and four o'clock, while he was visiting Lawford along with several others, and that she appeared unsteady in the sand.

Greenson left around seven o'clock to prepare for a dinner date with his wife and some friends after spending about two and a half hours with Marilyn. Greenson's lengthy visit may have been monopolized by his disapproval of Marilyn's decision to remarry DiMaggio. This is supported by Donald Spoto's quoting of Greenson's letter to Dr. Marianne Kris dated August 20: "I was aware that she was somewhat annoyed with me. She often became annoyed when I did not absolutely and wholeheartedly agree [with her]...She was angry with me. I told her we would talk more, that she should call me on Sunday morning." Spoto also claimed Greenson and Marilyn discussed her threats of terminating therapy and dismissing Mrs. Murray.

During his third and final call at 7 o'clock, Joe DiMaggio, Jr. successfully reached Marilyn when Mrs. Murray summoned her to the phone. He estimated the time of the call, when later interviewed by police, based upon his having concurrently watched a live broadcast television the sixth or seventh inning of the Angels-Orioles baseball game in Baltimore, a three-hour time difference. Spoto estimated the time as seven o'clock Pacific Time and ten o'clock Eastern Time, taking into account the three hour time difference. Marilyn and her former stepson spoke for about fifteen minutes while the young man followed the game on his television. Joe Jr. announced his broken engagement to Pamela Ries. Marilyn had warned him of a youthful marriage, drawing on her own experience of marriage at age sixteen to James Dougherty. She validated her former stepson's decision and conveyed encouragement.

In the preceding months, Joe Jr. had been struggling with his decision to leave Yale University after his freshman year and join the Marines. Marilyn had intervened several times between the young man and his father. Joe Jr. remained estranged from his own mother, actress Dorothy Arnold, and Marilyn served as a mother figure.

As a child, Joe Jr. seemed ignored by his parents. One would imagine DiMaggio playing catch with his son. Instead, the boy entertained himself by riding up and down the elevator of the Waldorf Astoria Hotel, where the family lived. The time Joe Jr. spent with Marilyn and his father during their nine-month marriage was the most stability the young man had ever recalled.

DiMaggio appreciated Marilyn's love and concern for his son. Biographer Richard Ben Cramer published a letter DiMaggio wrote to her on Hotel Lexington stationery: "*...I have talked to Joe [Jr.] quite a bit this month, trying to help resolve some of his present problems. You have been quite a help to me in so much as discussing Joe's affairs... And dear, I want to thank you beyond words for helping relieve my mind.*"

According to her statement to the police, Mrs. Murray confirmed a call from Joe Jr., estimated at about 7:30 while Marilyn was in her bedroom. Murray could hear Marilyn's voice rising with elation. Immediately afterward, Marilyn called Greenson, who was shaving in preparation for dinner with his wife. She cheerfully reported the good news about Joe Jr.'s broken engagement. "There're not getting married after all," she happily told the doctor. "Isn't that great news?"

Greenson confirmed to police that Marilyn's call occured at about seven-forty, while he was shaving for dinner. In addition to reporting the broken engagement, she allegedly asked if the doctor had taken her vial of Nembutal. He had not. They agreed to talk the following day.

A persistent Lawford called again, pressing Marilyn to join his dinner guests. She declined the invitation a second time.

A neighbor watched Marilyn tossing a ball to Maf-Honey in the back yard as the sun set over Brentwood. The dog retrieved the ball several times, and then she put him to bed in the guesthouse on an old, white beaver coat given to her by Arthur Miller following one of her miscarriages. The next day would be the fifth anniversary of one of Marilyn's failed pregnancies. She must have painfully remembered the date.

"I don't think we'll take that drive after all, Mrs. Murray," Marilyn said once back inside the hacienda. The housekeeper feigned understanding, but would only learn later that Greenson had made the suggestion of a drive along the Pacific Coast Highway.

Marilyn retired to her bedroom at eight o'clock in the evening, softly calling to Mrs. Murray as she closed the door, "Goodnight, Honey." Mrs. Murray heard Frank Sinatra records playing on the Hi-fi in Marilyn's bedroom.

"As far as I am concerned, the happiest time is now," Marilyn told George Barris only a few weeks earlier. "There's a future, and I can't wait to get to it!"

* * *

In San Francisco, Vince was the only one of the three DiMaggio brothers to get a hit in three innings of the Old Timers Day Charity Game played at Candlestick Park where Joe was presented with a silver-plated engraved trinket box. After the game, Joe joined Lefty O'Doul, O'Doul's stepson, and other friends for a multi-course dinner and a show at Bimbo's 365 Club on Columbus Avenue. Featuring jugglers, chorus girls, stand-up comics, and crooners, the famous nightclub may have been hosting DiMaggio's bachelor party.

In his home on Ocean Drive, Peter Lawford continued planning a dinner party. In the August 8, 1962 issue of the *Los Angeles Herald-Examiner*, Harrison Carroll reported that Lawford's guests included Milton Ebbins and his wife, Lynne Sherman; George Durgom; and Joseph and Delores Naar. In the 1980s, Anthony Summers followed this lead and interviewed Lawford's dinner guests. Producer George Durgom, onetime member of the Glenn Miller Band, was known throughout the entertainment industry as "Bullets" for his foot speed. He was also a personal manager for Sammy Davis, Jr. and Frank Sinatra. Durgom told Summers that on the evening of August 4, he had been a guest at Lawford's home, where his host had ordered a Chinese dinner from a local restaurant. Durgom also confirmed that Marilyn turned down Lawford's invitation.

Television producer Joseph Naar and wife Dolores, who lived a few miles away from Lawford, also claimed to have been dinner guests. Naar told Summers that Lawford had asked the couple to drive Marilyn to his home on their way to dinner. Directly following Marilyn's death, Lawford told police he called Marilyn at seven o'clock but she declined his invitation to dinner. The Naars confirmed this to Summers two decades later.

In 1975, Lawford reported having called Marilyn at 5 o'clock on the last evening of her life, and she accepted his invitation but never showed. He claimed to have called her again at 7:30, and she sounded depressed. "Say goodbye to Pat. Say goodbye to Jack and say goodbye to yourself, because you're a nice guy..." were allegedly Marilyn's last words to him. In 1982, Lawford told the District Attorney that Marilyn's phone was busy when he called the second time, and it stayed busy for thirty minutes.

In the 1980s, George Durgom claimed Lawford became panicked during dinner and wanted to check on Marilyn. Durgom persuaded his host to avoid becoming involved in a situation that might leak to the media, since Lawford was related to the President of the United States. Durgom also stated the concern arose later than 7 o'clock. Heeding his friend's warning, Lawford called his manager, Milton Ebbins, to take action. Ebbins, in turn, located Lawford's attorney, Milton Rudin—Dr. Greenson's brother-in-law—at a party at the home of Margaret Allenberg.

According to a Re-Interview Report by the LAPD Lieutenant Grover Armstrong dated August 10, 1962; Milton Rudin received a call at 8:25, relayed to him at 8:30, requesting that he call Milton Ebbins. At 8:45, Rudin called Ebbins, who said he had received a call from Lawford. Ebbins stated Lawford had called Marilyn at home, that her voiced seemed to "fade out," and when Lawford tried to call back, Marilyn's line was busy. Ebbins then instructed Rudin to call Marilyn to determine if she were safe. If she seemed to be in any danger, Ebbin told Rudin to contact her doctor. Rudin told police that he called Marilyn's home at nine o'clock, and Eunice Murray answered. Rudin expressed concern for Marilyn. When Murray confirmed that Marilyn was fine, Rudin dismissed the possibility of her being in any danger or distress. "If only [Rudin] had told [me] that he had received a worried call from someone..." Murray wrote in her memoir, suggesting that the series of calls led to a diluted and nonspecific reason for concern.

The Naars reported to Anthony Summers that they left Lawford's home early, and Lawford called them after they arrived home on Moreno Avenue to request they check on Marilyn at her home. Lawford expressed worry because Marilyn had called him and said she feared she had taken too many sleeping pills. As the Naars dressed in preparation to drive the half-mile to Marilyn's home, Rudin called back to say there was no need for alarm because he learned that Greenson had given her a sedative. Joseph Naar also reported observing no concern about Marilyn during the dinner party, which they attended from 8 to 10 o'clock.

Rupert Allan would never believe Marilyn had called Lawford during an emergency. Marilyn despised Lawford, and her only connection to him was the close relationship she had with Patricia Kennedy Lawford. Allan asserted Marilyn would more likely have turned to Patricia if in crisis. Furthermore, Marilyn wouldn't have tried to reach Patricia at the beach since she was aware her friend was visiting Hyannisport.

An obscure, contradictory version of the evening appeared in Sandra Shevey's *The Marilyn Scandal.* According to the author, actress Jan Sterling claimed Kirk Douglas and his wife, Anne Buydens, had invited Marilyn to a dinner party at their home off Sunset Boulevard. "They were waiting and waiting and were very disappointed when Marilyn didn't show up," Sterling said. Patricia Lawford was out of town, and Marilyn believed Peter was misbehaving in her absence by inviting girls to dinner parties. Allegedly, Marilyn literally or figuratively referred to the girls as "a couple of hookers."

The original LAPD Death Report and Follow-Up Report, written by Sergeant R. E. Byron, summarized the statements made by Eunice Murray, Dr. Greenson, and Dr. Engelberg at the death scene. Byron reiterated their statements: Marilyn retired at eight o'clock. At an unspecified point in the evening, Mrs. Murray noticed the illumination of an electric light in Marilyn's bedroom and knocked on the door, but Marilyn did not respond. At 3:30, when the housekeeper noticed that the light remained illuminated, she knocked again and tried to open the door. Alarmed, she called Greenson, who instructed her to pound on the door. She followed his directions, but there was no response. Greenson then told her go outside and peer through the bedroom window.

Using a fireplace poker to reach through the deep recessed front windowsill and push back the draperies, Murray discovered Marilyn laying on her stomach in bed, nude and uncovered in the chilly air, her hand clutching a telephone receiver. Murray called Greenson back within five minutes and reported that Marilyn looked "strange." Greenson stated he would come to the home immediately and instructed Mrs. Murray to call Dr. Engelberg.

Joan Greenson heard the telephone ring in the house, her parents' muffled voices, and the engine of her father's car starting. She went downstairs to the kitchen and asked her mother if anything was wrong. Hildi Greenson told her daughter there was a problem at Marilyn's house. Dr. Greenson reported leaving his home about a mile away and arriving at 3:30 (according to the original report) and 3:40 (according to the follow-up report). He used the fireplace poker to break one of the unbarred low side bedroom casement windows, reached in to unlatch and open it, and climbed into the bedroom. Greenson removed the telephone from Marilyn's hand and noticed rigor mortis. "We've lost her," he said to Murray. "It was unbelievable," Greenson would write, "so simple and final and over."

Dr. Engelberg, who also lived within a mile, arrived at either 3:35 or 3:50 (depending on differing versions in the two reports), and pronounced Marilyn dead. Neither doctor made an attempt to resuscitate, as the discoloration of the body indicated she had been dead for several hours.

Byron noted that one of the witnesses reported calling the police at four o'clock, and the police complaint log confirmed the call at 4:25. Dr. Engelberg placed the call to the Central Los Angeles Police switchboard, and it was transferred to the West Los Angeles desk. Within minutes, Sergeant Jack Clemmons, who would later become a controversial figure in Marilyn's death, took the call and arrived at the scene with two police radio patrolmen in another vehicle. In a newspaper article, Inspector Edward Walker LAPD judged the delay as unusual but raised no suspicion. "So far as the doctors were concerned," he told the press, "there was no evidence of crime, and the first doctor already knew she was dead. I have no criticism to make of them."

In 1982, Engelberg told the Los Angeles District Attorney that he pronounced Marilyn dead around three o'clock. When asked about allegations of his being called at midnight, he replied, "Absolutely not." When asked about the delay in calling the police, Engelberg responded: "We were stunned. We were talking over what happened, what she had said...Ordinarily, when you pronounce somebody dead, you don't call the police. You call the mortician. I was the one who—I guess—eventually said, 'Gee, I think in this case, we'd better call the police.'"

With assistance from Sergeant Marvin Iannone, Sergeant Byron took over the investigation from Clemmons at five o'clock and noted no calls were made from Marilyn's phone (476-1890) "during the hours of this occurrence," and the police were in the process of checking on calls made from the other phone (472-4830). Greenson told Byron he last saw Marilyn alive at 5:15 p.m., and she had complained of insomnia. Byron noted about fifteen bottles of prescription medication on the bedside table. An empty bottle of Nembutal refilled two days prior should have contained nearly fifty pills.

Arthur P. Jacobs called Patricia Newcomb at four o'clock. "Something's happened to Marilyn," he said and paused. "She's dead." Someone drove Patricia to the hacienda. She arrived in a coat thrown over pajamas and broke down, crying hysterically. Later, Newcomb would clarify she did not see Marilyn's body. Milton Rudin arrived after calling Inez Melson. When Melson arrived, she immediately asked to see the body. In the bedroom, she saw full and empty pill bottles crowded on the nightstand and dresser. Melson walked into the bathroom and saw allergy pills, tranquilizers, and sleeping tablets on the cabinet shelves. "I had an impulse to run though those two rooms, snatching up the bottles and hiding them in my bag," she would say, "but I knew this was impossible."

When Clemmons' shift ended, he called James Dougherty, now a Los Angeles Police Officer to report the news. Dougherty turned to his second wife, Patricia, lying next to him in bed and said, "Say a prayer for Norma Jeane. She's dead." In another Death Report dated August 10, Sergeant Byron summarized Mrs. Murray's admission of only two calls to the house on the evening of Marilyn's death: DiMaggio Jr.'s and Rudin's. Byron noted: "It is this officer's opinion that Mrs. Murray was vague and possibly evasive in answering questions pertaining to the activities of Miss Monroe during this time. It is not known whether this is, or is not intentional."

In Mrs. Murray's memoir, she claimed she was awoken by a "sixth sense" in the cot in the dressing room and walked into the hall, where she immediately saw the telephone cord running from the jack in the third bedroom to under Marilyn's bedroom door. Murray claimed that when Rudin had called earlier, she had walked through the Jack and Jill bath into the third bedroom and not through the hall; and therefore, did not see the cord leading to Marilyn's room.

After originally reporting that she had seen a light under Marilyn's door (as documented by the *New York Times* on August 6, 1962), Murray later clarified that it was actually the cord that alarmed her. Marilyn typically put the phone "to bed" under pillows at night so that a call would not disturb her sleep. Murray stated the thick white wool carpeting under Marilyn's door would not have allowed light to shine through, but that she later observed the light on in Marilyn's bedroom when she peered through the window, and became confused when she spoke to police.

Mrs. Murray called her son-in-law, Norman Jeffries, to repair the broken window. By this time, reporters had arrived and began taking photographs and filming the death scene. In newsreels, Jeffries is visible in the bedroom using a cord from the draperies to secure the handles of a window in preparation for repairs while police walked through the bedroom.

In the succeeding decades, Marilyn's death would be moved to an earlier point in the evening. The advanced state of rigor mortis placed time of death perhaps as much as six to eight hours prior to the discovery of the body.

In interviews conducted by Anthony Summers and in several documentaries produced long after Marilyn's death, actress Natalie Trundy Jacobs claimed she first became aware of trouble on Fifth Helena Drive before midnight. While celebrating her birthday at the Ferrante and Teicher concert at the Hollywood Bowl, a messenger came to the box where she was seated with fiancé, Arthur P. Jacobs, and film director and producer, Mervyn LeRoy, and his wife.

Natalie recounted the messenger summoning Jacobs to the phone because Marilyn was either near death or dead. Jacobs asked the

LeRoys to drive Natalie home to her apartment on Canon Drive a few doors away from Patricia Newcomb's. "I don't know why, but I had the distinct impression it was [Milton] Rudin who called Arthur at the Bowl," Natalie told Donald Spoto, "and that he [Rudin] had been called by Greenson from Marilyn's home." Natalie reported no further knowledge of the events surrounding Marilyn's death. "Arthur said it was horrendous," she would say. "He never gave me any details, and I never asked him. He said only that it was too dreadful to discuss."

In 1985, Walter Schaefer of Schaefer Ambulance Company told Anthony Summers another version of the night and claimed one of his ambulances transported Marilyn in coma to the Santa Monica Hospital, where she expired either en route or upon arrival. Other reports circulated about someone close to Marilyn calling an ambulance and dismissing it on arrival because she had died and law prohibited transportation of a corpse by an ambulance.

* * *

Time and *Life* Editor Richard Stolley was one of the first to receive the flash and dispatched reporter Tommy Thompson and freelance photographer Leigh Wiener to Marilyn's address. Photographer William Woodfield and journalists Joe Hyams and James Bacon soon arrived at Marilyn's home, where neighbors gathered in night robes and slippers in the cul-de-sac of Fifth Helena Drive. Within minutes, a mass of reporters arrived. Cameramen captured Los Angeles Police officers guarding the home as the press swarmed the grounds, documenting every detail for the eagerly awaiting masses.

The Coroner's Office contracted local mortuaries under a rotation system to provide services during the weekend, when less than fifty percent of mortuary employees were scheduled to work. Guy Hockett, one of the owners of Westwood Village Memorial Cemetery's mortuary services, was on-call during the month of August. Coincidently, Marilyn's half-sister and DiMaggio would choose this cemetery for her place of entombment.

Hockett and his son, Don, arrived on the scene in a 1957 white Ford station wagon and were led to the master bedroom. Advanced rigor mortis was evident upon a cursory examination of the body. She was lying in a semi-fetal position, and it took about five minutes for Guy Hockett to straighten the body.

The Hocketts gently lifted Marilyn's body onto the gurney, folded her hands across her abdomen, shrouded her in a baby blue woolen blanket, and secured her with leather straps at the waist and feet. Marilyn's once celebrated body was then wheeled across the front door threshold, over the tiles inscribed "Cursum Perficio," and placed into the station wagon. Police opened Marilyn's scalloped gates, and Don Hockett drove the white Ford to Westwood Village Mortuary, on the grounds of the cemetery where Marilyn's maternal grandmother and guardian were buried. Several reporters followed the van to photograph the body's destination. Guy Hockett stayed behind to distract some of the reporters and solicited a ride back to the mortuary from a police officer.

Don parked the van at the entrance of the mortuary's preparation room and awaited his father's arrival. Within minutes, reporters and photojournalists arrived and gathered outside on the grounds of the adjoining cemetery. Some snapped pictures of Marilyn's covered body in the back of the station wagon.

When Guy Hockett arrived, he and his son wheeled the body inside, and several reporters trespassed into the building. Alan Abbott, mortuary assistant, observed other reporters trying to open doors and windows. Alarmed, he concealed the body in a broom closet until security could be arranged. One reporter offered Abbott ten thousand dollars to photograph the body. After the arrival of twenty Pinkerton guards and eviction of the reporters, the Hocketts placed the body on the embalming table. Shortly after eight o'clock, two deputies from the coroner's office, Charles Pace and Frank Dambacher, arrived to collect the body for transport to the Los Angeles Coroner's Office at the Hall of Justice for autopsy.

Even in death, paparazzi and reporters followed Marilyn. Hers was one of the first celebrity deaths to receive intense coverage in the fairly new television medium. Stamped indelibly in our cultural memory are newsreel images of Marilyn's blanketed body being wheeled on a gurney out of the mortuary's French door by coroner's deputies, through a gauntlet of press photographers, to the coroner's black van. Many have mistakenly assumed that this is footage of Marilyn's body leaving her home, based upon its editing. The van delivered the remains to the first floor of the Hall of Justice where a coroner's aide attached a tag to the left toe indicating case number 81128, and other aides placed the body in stainless steel crypt 33.

Photographer Bud Gray of the *Herald-Examiner* and freelance photographer Leigh Weiner bribed the attendants with bottles of expensive scotch to permit their illicit photographing of the body. One opened the crypt door and pulled out the drawer containing Marilyn's remains. Werner took a disturbing photograph of Marilyn's foot protruding from under a sheet. He also photographed Marilyn's uncovered face, appearing serenely lovely yet somewhat swelled in post mortem. Word spread throughout the Hall of Justice that Marilyn Monroe's corpse rested on the first floor, and coroner's deputies in uniforms flanked the crypt, guarding the corpse as it awaited autopsy.

At the hacienda, Patricia Newcomb sat quietly in the third bedroom where she had spent Friday night as the authorities prepared to seal the house. The police could not coax her to leave, and she practically required eviction. Mrs. Murray offered to drive her to the corner of Carmelina and Sunset, where her psychiatrist had arranged to collect her in his car.

Sergeant Marvin Iannone escorted Murray, Jeffries, and Newcomb from the kitchen's side entrance into the small courtyard and through its gate. Cameras followed Mrs. Murray and Newcomb as they fled to the housekeeper's car parked in the brick driveway. The footage appears in documentaries and on the Internet. Murray wears a Mexican poncho and a white skirt, her hair matted. Her son-in-law accompanies her and opens her door. A distraught Patricia Newcomb, in sunglasses and a polo coat over pajamas, shouts, "You bloodsuckers! You vampires! You can't even let her die in peace, can you?" She gets in the passenger side of the car. Raising her hand to shield her face, Patricia screams to the photographers, "Keep shooting, vultures!" A reporter in a suit perched on the wall surrounding the home snaps her picture.

Mrs. Murray returned to the apartment she shared with her daughter, Jacqueline, who told her that she and her twin sister, Patricia, had been driving along San Vicente Boulevard at 7:30 the previous evening and had considered stopping at Marilyn's home to visit their mother. If they had visited, would the outcome have been different?

Part IV:

Icon

Chapter Thirty: The Death of Marilyn Monroe

Marilyn died between Saturday, August fourth, and Sunday, August fifth, in her bedroom in the hacienda on Fifth Helena Drive. Early on Sunday morning, at neighboring Santa Monica beach—where Marilyn bathed as a child and strolled only weeks before—teen girls and surfer boys blasted their radios as noisy sea gulls flew overhead. The disc jockey interrupted Shelley Fabres' *Johnny Angel* and played *Marilyn*, recorded by Ray Anthony and his orchestra a decade earlier, as a tribute.

"Marilyn Monroe is dead of suicide at age thirty-six," the radio announcer reported. "We grasp at straws as if knowing how she died will bring her back. Not since Jean Harlow have the standards of feminine beauty been so embodied in one woman. Marilyn Monroe; dead at thirty-six." The time of death did not allow a death notice in the morning newspapers, so reports came from television and radio broadcasts.

Patricia Newcomb received over six hundred telephone calls from journalists around the world wanting to know *why* Marilyn was gone. She felt it was her job to do what she could for her client and friend. While the world learned of Marilyn's death from radio broadcasts and news wires, communication of the event spread among her friends and employees.

A flurry of telephone calls notified those within Marilyn's inner circle of her passing. Dr. Hyman Engelberg contacted DiMaggio at eight o'clock in his home on Beach Street in San Francisco, waking him with the dreadful news of a terrible accident. "And the rest Joe heard in fragments, as his world fell apart," wrote Richard Ben Cramer. United Airlines held a nine o'clock plane en route to Los Angeles for Di Maggio. Newspapers documented his arrival at the airport in a condition "stooped by grief," "silent," and "ashen."

Berniece and Paris Miracle returned home to Gainesville, Florida, from a week's vacation to a phone call from Paris' sister about the news. They had been traveling in a car with a broken radio. With the local airport closed due to an Eastern Airlines strike, Berniece traveled farther to Tampa International Airport and secured a flight to Los Angeles.

The Miracles' daughter, Mona Rae, age twenty-two, heard the news and immediately went to a nearby chapel to pray. She had recently received a letter signed, "*Love, Marilyn, your Auntie.*" In the letter, Marilyn expressed pride in her niece attending college, a desire to know her better, and advice about her niece's impending engagement. "*I'm sure [your fiancé] must be wonderful if you love him,*" Marilyn wrote. "*And the whole world must be a beautiful place because he's there—you see, your old Auntie isn't so old—I know how it is.*" Mona Rae reread the letter and its message about avoiding both haste and hesitation in approaching marriage. "*You have time,*" Marilyn wrote, "*time for everything.*"

Mrs. Murray called chauffeur Rudy Kautzky from the Carey Cadillac Company. Paula Strasberg called her daughter in Rome and scolded herself in guiltily: "If only I had stayed in California instead of coming home." Distraught, Lee Strasberg told his wife, "Marilyn promised me that if she ever felt tempted to kill herself, she'd call me first."

In Brooklyn, Isidore Miller shaved in front of his bathroom mirror when Eric, his ten year-old grandson, said, "Gramp, Marilyn is dead." Miller dismissed the news until his daughter, Joan Copeland, confirmed it. "[Marilyn] wanted help and nobody was near her," Miller told Flora Rheta Schreiber of *Good Housekeeping*. "I had spoken to her only ten days before. She sounded happy."

In Paris, Milton Greene turned to his wife, Amy, when they heard the news. "You were right," she said sadly. "I should have gone to her."

When Ralph Roberts contacted his answering service, he learned of a call the previous evening from "a fuzzy-voiced woman" whom he assumed was Marilyn. Had she tried to contact him for help?

Allan Snyder's son called him with the news. In total disbelief,

Snyder drove to Marilyn's house and received confirmation from a police officer guarding the property.

"She seemed normal that last day I saw her," Patricia Newcomb would say. "But of course she was under the care of a psychiatrist... and never should have been given as many Nembutal pills as she was given by Engelberg. Engelberg was supposed to let Greenson know if he gave her such a prescription but that week he was having trouble with his wife and he forgot about it [The doctor had separated from his wife of twenty-nine years, Esther, in early May]. It is hard to understand negligence such as that. If there is any doctor to blame, it's Engelberg."

In a letter to Dr. Marianne Kris, Greenson recounted Engelberg's oversight: "On Friday night she had told the internist that I had said it was all right for her to take some Nembutal, and he had given it to her without checking with me, because he had been upset for his own personal reasons. He had just left his wife."

In an interview with author Sandra Shevey, screenwriter Henry Ephron recalled many in the Hollywood community blaming Greenson and Engelberg for Marilyn's death. When Engelberg arrived at the Beverly Hills Tennis Club on Sunday morning to play a game of tennis, a group of members slammed him against the lockers. "We were so angry," Ephron stated.

A dark cloud fell over the Greenson family home on Franklin Street. "It was just devastating," Joan later said, "I don't think my father ever got over it...He had never had a patient die before that he was taking care of other than from a natural [death]." Daniel Greenson suspected Marilyn took her own life. "My father was hurt by the fact that she killed herself," he would tell Christopher Turner of *The Telegraph* in 2010, "and he would tell himself that it was accidental." Joan added, "[My father] always felt that it was an accident that she killed herself." The psychiatrist believed Marilyn's mental health had improved and that her tolerance for barbiturates and sleeping medication decreased in direct response to his having slowly weaned her off them.

Stanley J. Coen's article, "Narcisstic Temptations to Cross Boundaries and How to Manage Them," published in the *Journal of the American Psychoanalytic Associate*, referenced Greenson's apparent countertransference in the life of his arguably most impressive and tempting patient. Without passing judgment on Greenson, Coen identifies the warning signs of the amount of time the doctor devoted to Marilyn at the expense of other patients and his family, his involvement in her career, and his talking about her with others. "Marilyn Monroe, the cinematic goddess, has entranced generations of movie-goers," Coen wrote in 2007. "Even she herself could become caught up, very ambivalently, in the spell of being Marilyn Monroe. How difficult it would be for an analyst, especially a male analyst, not to become caught up in the exciting drama of being her analyst and become tempted to live this out. What restraint, self-abnegation, and responsible self-awareness it would take for an analyst to be able to contain and manage such temptations for the sake of the patient's analysis."

"I believe she was in a manic phase, and something happened to suddenly depress her and she grabbed pills," Hyman Engelberg speculated in the film documentary *Marilyn: The Final Days*. "She had plenty of pills at bedside. I think she was suddenly depressed and in that sense it was intentional. Then I think she thought better of it when she felt herself going under because she called Peter Lawford. So, while it was intentional at the time, I do believe she changed her mind."

In an interview with Alfred Robbins for the *New York Journal-American*, Patricia Newcomb recounted Marilyn's last days:

> I had arrived at Marilyn's house on Friday. I was fighting a bad case of bronchitis and had decided to enter a hospital for complete rest, but Marilyn called me and said, "Why don't you come out here?"...It was typical of Marilyn, this concern for friends. So I accepted her invitation. I found her in wonderful spirits. Some furnishings had just arrived from Mexico. She was in a very good mood—a very happy mood. Friday night we had dinner at a quiet restaurant near her home. Saturday she was getting things done inside the house. She loved it... When I last saw her, nothing about her mood or manner changed.

Newcomb stated Marilyn waved goodbye to her from the front door and said, "I'll see you tomorrow. Toodle-oo!"

A reporter from *New York Post* called Eunice Murray at home and conducted an interview over the phone. By Monday morning, her address was published, and reporters kept vigil outside the apartment on Ocean Avenue. Murray agreed to a brief interview with three journalists and later claimed they twisted her words and misquoted her in the published description of Marilyn appearing as disturbed or depressed following a final call that came after DiMaggio Jr.'s. This triggered a media buzz about the mysterious final caller who might hold a clue to the fatal overdose. Fingers pointed to José Bolaños.

On August 9, the *New York Daily News* reported that police searched for the Mexican screenwriter to determine if he had been the last caller. Bolaños' friend and attorney, Jorge Barragan, claimed Marilyn had planned to marry the screenwriter in Cuernavaco in September. Barragan stated Bolaños asked him to make plans for the wedding and Marilyn was scheduled to arrive in Mexico on September 15. However, Bolaños' mother told reporters she had no knowledge of these plans.

In the same article, the *Daily News* reported Peter Lawford had called Marilyn at 7 o'clock on Saturday evening to invite her to dinner, and she had called him earlier for his wife's phone number in Hyannisport. Believing Marilyn felt lonely, Lawford called her back to join him and his friends, but she reported feeling tired and planning to retire early. "She did sound sleepy," he told the *Daily News*, "but I've talked to her a hundred times and she sounded no different."

Other friends told a similar story. "I saw no signs of despondency when I talked to her," Carl Sandburg told *Look* magazine. "She gave me the impression of happiness...I didn't rise and escort her to the elevator when it came time for her to leave. I've never been good at manners. But I am eighty-four-years-old. I hope she forgave me...I wish I could have been with her that day...I believe I could have persuaded her not to take her life. She had so much to live for."

By late-morning on Sunday, Maggy Anthony, born in Hollywood, arrived at Marilyn's hacienda with her husband, photojournalist Gene Anthony. The couple had recently returned from an assignment in Germany for an international magazine. They arrived at the moment Mrs. Murray returned to the home with mortician Guy

Hockett and Inez Melson. Gene snapped photographs of Marilyn's white terry cloth robe draped over the Eames patio furniture beside the pool, and the stuffed animal toys scattered on the lawn. Murray guided the Anthonys, Hockett, and Melson around the property. Gene shot a photograph of Murray standing next to a row of unplanted trees delivered the previous day as well as Hockett locking the front door after retrieving Marilyn's Emilio Pucci dress and other personal furnishings for her burial. The photojournalist also took interior shots through the windows.

Peter Evans, a reporter in New York, flew to Los Angeles that morning to cover the story and drove to the house. "I can still recall the haunting sound of the antique wind chimes—a gift to her from the poet Carl Sandburg—that hung beside her pool, on which floated a child's plastic yellow duck. It was a melancholy sight. I had known her a little and it made me sad."

Before noon, maid Hazel Washington and husband Rocky, a Los Angeles police detective, arrived at Fifth Helena Drive to collect a card table loaned to Marilyn when she had moved into her home and awaited the delivery of furnishings. Washington noticed representatives from Twentieth Century Fox Studios searching through Marilyn's files. Frank Neill and three other publicists allegedly purged files of all documents pertaining to the corporation, including verbatim notes taken by Patricia Newcomb during Marilyn's reinstatement meeting with Levathes.

While radio broadcasts and telephone calls notified the world of the devastating news on Sunday morning, Deputy Medical Examiner Dr. Thomas Tsunetomi Noguchi arrived for his weekend shift at the Los Angeles Coroner's Office in the Hall of Justice. A memo from Coroner Theodore Murphey ordered him to perform an autopsy on Marilyn Monroe. At first, Noguchi believed the deceased merely shared the same name as the legendary actress.

Born in Japan in 1927, Noguchi graduated from Tokyo's Nippon Medical School in 1951 and served an internship at the University of Tokyo School of Medicine Hospital. Shortly thereafter, he immigrated to the United States and served a second internship at Orange County General Hospital and residencies at Loma Linda University School of Medicine and Barlow Sanatorium in Los Angeles. He was appointed a deputy coroner for Los Angeles County in 1961.

Deputy District Attorney John Miner (1918-2011) allegedly observed Noguchi's execution of the autopsy. An associate clinical professor at the University of Southern California Medical School and lecturer at the Los Angeles Psychoanalytic Institute, Miner had left his private law practice in 1959 to join the District Attorney's Office.

Eddy Day, an autopsy attendant, prepared the body for Noguchi's examination scheduled at 10:30. "We were both very touched," Miner recalled his first viewing the body with Noguchi. "We had a sense of real sadness, and the feeling that his young woman could stand up and get off the table any minute." When asked by journalist John Preston from *The Telegraph* how Marilyn looked in death, Noguchi quoted the Latin poet, Petrarch: "*It's folly to shrink in fear, if this is dying. For death looked lovely in her lovely face.*"

As a coroner working with the assumption that every corpse may be a potential victim of murder, Noguchi, aided by Miner, checked for hypodermic needle marks and evidence of physical violence. "We both examined the body very carefully with a magnifying glass," Miner later said. "There was no indication that the drugs had been administered by way of a hypodermic needle. If there had been marks, they would have been apparent on such a very careful examination of the body." Noguchi wrote "No needle marks" on the autopsy report's diagram of the body.

Just above Marilyn's left hip, Noguchi discovered a dark reddish-blue bruise. "A slight ecchymotic area is noted in the left hip and left side of the lower back," he wrote in the report. Judging by its color, the bruise appeared fresh. Noguchi observed fixed post-mortem lividity—dark purple discoloration of the skin resulting from the settling of blood—in the face, neck, chest, upper arms and right side of abdomen. This was consistent with Dr. Greenson and Mrs. Murray discovering the body face down in bed. Faint lividity was noted in the back and posterior arms and legs, possibly resulting from the repositioning of the body in the gurney and morgue crypt.

Marilyn's body measured 65.5 inches and weighed 117 pounds. The nearly empty stomach contained about 20 cubic centimeters of a "brownish mucoid fluid." Viewed under a polarized microscope, the contents of both the stomach and duodenum [beginning portion of the small intestine] indicated no refractile crystals [residue of the pills]. The stomach displayed hemorrhage [profuse bleeding], and the colon showed "marked congestion [excessive tissue fluid] and purplish discoloration." Both lungs were "moderately congested with some edema [swelling]," and their rear portion showed "severe congestion."

Following the dissection, Noguchi prepared specimens of the kidneys, stomach, urine, intestines, and blood for toxicological study by Dr. R. J. Abernethy on Monday morning. The entire procedure lasted five hours.

During the medical invasion of his former wife's remains, DiMaggio suffered in the first class cabin of the United Airlines flight. The plane landed at eleven o'clock, and he rushed to the Hall of Justice to claim the body. Attendants slid Marilyn out of the crypt drawer and lifted the sheet from her face. DiMaggio was not prepared for what he saw and "made a noise in the back of his throat and turned away." He signed consent forms to release the body to Westwood Village Memorial Park, and friend Harry Hall drove him to the Miramar Motel. DiMaggio emitted a guttural roar of pain and doubled over in tears. After a few hours, he contacted Marilyn's half-sister, Berniece Miracle, and asked permission to begin the funeral arrangements until she could arrive from Florida.

Harry Hall accompanied DiMaggio to Marilyn's house, where the coroner's seal on the front door announced prosecution to anyone who entered. Police guards allowed DiMaggio entry, and he headed straight to the master bedroom. Police handed DiMaggio the note Marilyn had started writing to him.

At 8 o'clock on Monday morning, Abernethy ordered the testing of specimens for ethanol and barbiturates and documented the seven drugs found at the scene of death:

- 27 capsules of Librium, dated June 7, 1962 for 50 units
- 17 capsules of Librium, dated July 10, 1962 for 100 units
- 26 tablets of Sulfathallidine [sic], prescription dated July 25, 1962 for 36 units
- An empty vial labeled Nembutal, dated August 3, 1962 for 25 units
- 10 capsules of Chloral Hydrate, originally dated July 25, 1962 and refilled July 31 for fifty units

- An empty vial labeled Noludar, dated November 4, 1961 for fifty units
- 32 capsules of Phenergan, prescription number 20857 dated August 3, 1962 for 25 units.

[Abernethy added a correction to the description of Phenergan, indicating the unlabeled vial was marked 'MED' and contained 24 units. The original prescription indicated used for sleep.]

Manufactured by Abbott Laboratories under the brand name Nembutal, pentobarbital is a barbiturate that depresses the central nervous system and produces a continuum of effects from mild sedation to total anesthesia. In the 1950s and 1960s, medical literature documented the risk of barbiturate overdose and the drug's potential for physical and psychological addiction, which eventually led to the scheduling of the drug as controlled substance in 1970. Benzodiazepines have replaced barbiturates in the treatment of anxiety and insomnia, as they are significantly less dangerous in an overdose. Hoffmann-La Roche Laboratories introduced the first benzodiazepine, chlordiazepoxide, under the brand name Librium in 1960.

Chloral hydrate, once prescribed for the treatment of insomnia and as a sedative, was displaced in the mid-20th century by barbiturates and later by benzodiazepines. Today, it is commonly used as an ingredient in the veterinary anesthetic Equithesin.

Noludar, a sedative used for treating insomnia, was withdrawn from the United States market in June 1965 and replaced by newer drugs with fewer side effects such as benzodiazepines.

Phenergan is an antihistamine used to treat allergy symptoms and prevent motion sickness. Due to its sedative side effect, it is also prescribed as a sleep aid.

Sulfathalidine, used in the treatment and management of pain, was prescribed to Marilyn specifically for abdominal cramps, likely resulting from chronic endometriosis.

In recent years, Marilyn's prescriptions have appeared on the Internet and reveal the vast amount of medications she received during her last weeks, which were not recovered from the scene of death. On June 5, while Greenson was in Switzerland, Engelberg issued a prescription for 50 units of Valmid, a short-acting sedative.

Greenson returned to Los Angeles the following day and accompanied Marilyn to plastic surgeon Michael Gurdin. On June 7, Engelberg prescribed chloral hydrate. On June 15, shortly after Fox halted production on *Something's Got to Give*, Engelberg prescribed a month's supply of Paruate, dosed three times daily, typically used to treat depression, anxiety, and migraine headaches. Three days later, he prescribed Perodan, a painkilling combination of the opiate oxycodone and aspirin, for "severe pain or cramps."

On July 1, Engelberg wrote Marilyn a prescription for the stimulant Dexedine. On July 10, he prescribed 50 units Valmid, 25 units of Secondal, and 25 units of Tuinal, with directions to take one unit of each "for sleep." Secondal and Tuinal are barbiturates. On the same day, Engelberg ordered the Librium later recovered by police. On July 17, Engelberg prescribed 24 units of Darvon Compound "for pain." The painkilling drugs were likely the internist's intervention in the days leading to Marilyn's gynecological surgery on the weekend of July 21-22 to correct chronic endometriosis.

"I didn't give her Secondal," Engelberg would insist in the documentary *Marilyn Monroe: The Final Years*. "I never gave her chloral hydrate. She must have bought it in Tijuana." During the 1982 investigation into Marilyn's death, Engelberg told Alan B. Tomich, "I knew nothing about chloral hydrate. I never used choral hydrate." However, the surviving prescriptions suggest otherwise. It was Engelberg's interventions that prompted Patricia Newcomb's finger pointing and caused Henry Ephron and others to slam the internist against lockers at the Beverly Hills Tennis Club.

Chapter Thirty-One: The World Mourns

On Monday morning, August 6th, headlines of Marilyn's death reverberated globally. Marilyn's death from a presumed intentional or accidental overdose of prescribed sedative drugs shocked the world and elicited sympathy from the Vatican and Russian press. Moscow's government newspaper *Izvestia* declared: "Hollywood gave birth to her and killed her." The Vatican's *L'Osservatre Romano* read, "A victim of a mentality and a way of life which she was forced to be the symbol. Her death transcends the limits of personal tragedy and acquires social reverberations." A small Asian village proclaimed a day of mourning. Marilyn's obituary consumed more front-page newspaper space than the Cuban Missile Crisis would in October. Millions across the globe mourned for the former foster child whose Cinderella story had once been inspiring but did not have a happy ending.

According to journalists Peter Brown and Patte B. Barham, for the first time since the Bel Air fire in 1961, the *Los Angeles Herald* and *Los Angeles Times* produced extra editions. In huge black type, the *Times*' headline pronounced, "MARILYN, DEAD."

"Marilyn Monroe Dead—Pills Near," broadcasted the *New York Times*. "Brilliant Stardom and personal tragedy punctuated the life of Marilyn Monroe…Sad child, unhappy star: Help she needed to find self-eluded Marilyn all her life."

"Marilyn Monroe Dead in Probable Suicide," declared the *Baltimore Sun*.

A later edition of the *Los Angeles Times* proclaimed: "Marilyn Monroe Found Dead/Sleeping Pill Overdose Blamed."

The *New York World-Telegram* used only her universally known initials: "MM: Accident or Suicide? Body of Star Lies Unclaimed."

Cartoonist Burris Jenkins Jr. of the *New York Journal-American* depicted Marilyn's death in a rendering of her lifeless arm lying across the bed, her hand clutching the telephone. Through the bedroom window, spotlights illuminate the Hollywood sign towering over the city of Los Angeles. The piece is titled "No Answer."

When Arthur Miller read the headlines, he felt disgust and resentment. The same press that had mocked her—and whose scorn she had taken in earnest—was now mourning her loss. "To have survived, she would have had to be either more cynical or even further from reality than she was," Miller would write. "Instead, she was a poet on a street corner trying to recite to a crowd pulling at her clothes."

Critic Bosley Crowther, frequently disparaging in his reviews of Marilyn's performances, abruptly re-evaluated his opinion of her. "For all her acknowledged ability as a screen comedienne and, indeed, in roles of a particular sort, Marilyn Monroe was not generally regarded as an artist submerged in her art," he wrote. "The irony of this popular image was that it tended to obscure in an excess of sheer sex symbolization the certain skills and competencies of the star." Crowther summarized Marilyn's personality as generous, good-humored, warm, and eager for honest self-improvement, and reflected upon critics having speculated that she would have someday shed her sex symbol image.

Reporters turned to those who knew Marilyn to share their reactions and condensed her life into a sound bite. "She was the child in all of us," Newcomb told *Newsweek*, offering a theory for Marilyn's universal appeal.

"Pat and I loved her dearly," Lawford told reporters. "She was probably one of the most marvelous and warm human beings I have ever met. Anything else I could say would be superfluous." Marilyn had left behind a new pair of sandals at the Lawford home during a visit in July. Peter discovered them after her death and had them bronzed.

"I heard the flash over the air at 7 AM," said Kay Gable. "And I went to mass and prayed for her."

"I'm sure it was an accident," said Dean Martin. "She was at my home a few days ago and she was happy…I just can't believe it. She was a wonderful person and a wonderful talent."

"When your best friend kills herself, how do you feel?" Patricia Newcomb asked reporters rhetorically in response to their questions. "What do you do?"

"She will go on eternally," predicted Jacqueline Kennedy with astute accuracy.

"Impossible...it isn't possible," cried singer Connie Francis. "She was one of my best friends, and though I have been expecting her to do something like this for some time, I still can't believe it. Since Marilyn left Arthur Miller she had never been the same. She became very unhappy."

"Everybody stopped work," Marlon Brando would recall, "and you could see all that day the same expressions on their faces, the same thought: 'How can a girl with success, fame, youth, money, beauty . . . how could she kill herself?' Nobody could understand it because those are the things that everybody wants, and they can't believe that life wasn't important to Marilyn Monroe, or that her life was elsewhere."

Gloria Steinem learned of Marilyn's death during a student meeting in Europe. She would vividly recall the room and people present, a phenomenon usually reserved for the deaths of family members or a president. "She was an actress, a person on whom no one's fate depended," Steinem wrote, "and yet her energy and terrible openness to life had made a connection to strangers."

"If anything was amiss, I wasn't aware of it," Joe DiMaggio, Jr. told the *New York Daily News*.

Lee Strasberg spoke to the *New York Herald-Tribune*: "She did not commit suicide...If it had been suicide, it would have happened in quite a different way. For one thing, she wouldn't have done it without leaving a note. There are other reasons, which cannot be discussed, which makes us certain she did not intend to take her life." Lee continued, "For us Marilyn was a devoted friend, a colleague, a member of our family...it is difficult to accept the fact her zestful life has been ended by this dreadful accident."

"She was an extremely talented woman who was just beginning to do the things she wanted to do," Susan Strasberg said from Rome. "She wanted to work in the theater and..." The actress was unable to contain her grief and could not complete the telephone interview. Later on, she walked twenty-two steep steps to the thirteen-hundred-year-old Church of Santa Maria in Ara Coeli and lit dozens of candles for Marilyn, asking her soul's forgiveness for not always validating her.

Frank Sinatra responded to reporters that he was deeply saddened. "I'll miss her very much," he said simply.

Elizabeth Taylor learned of Marilyn's death in Gastaad, Switzerland, where she had retreated to a chalet in the Swiss ski resort after her affair with Richard Burton went public. She expressed sadness and shock: "I did not know her very well, but what I knew of her I liked enormously."

From his villa in Portofino Italy, British actor Rex Harrison said, "What a terrible tragedy. I always thought she was wonderful, she was one of the most talented comediennes I've ever seen."

In England, Laurence Olivier said, "She was exploited beyond anyone's means."

Stage actor Michael Redgrave (1908-1985), performing in the Chichester Festival Theatre's opening season in the title role in Chekhov's *Uncle Vanya* under the direction of Olivier, praised Marilyn as "a great artist."

"She was a fine actress," said actress Sophia Loren in Tirrenia, Italy. "A beautiful woman and an outstanding person, she was a real star. Now all we can do is pray for her."

Truman Capote was in Spain writing *In Cold Blood.* "I was walking in a little Spanish town. I saw these headlines saying: 'Marilyn Monroe, Morte,'" he remembered. "I was shocked, even though you knew she was the kind of person this might happen to." In a letter to literary critic Newton Arvin, Capote wrote: "*Cannot believe that Marilyn M. is dead. She was such a good-hearted girl, so pure really, so much on the side of the angels. Poor little baby. God Bless her.*"

French filmmaker Jean Cocteau wrote to screenwriter Francoise Sagan: "She was a soul burning bright in the dark of our times...It is the darkness of that time that extinguished her light."

Reporters stopped director Billy Wilder in an airport in Paris. "I said whatever I said, probably not all that kind," he would say. "Then in the cab on the way to the hotel I suddenly saw the placards through the cab window. They never told me, those SOBs..."

"What can one say after such awful news?" Tony Curtis said. "It is simply terrible. She was a nice person and a fabulous actress."

"We lost a unique and, as far as I'm concerned, wonderful person; it's a shame," Jack Lemmon said from New York. "I'm shocked and just totally and completely thrown for a loss."

"I just feel terrible," said actress Edie Adams. "Marilyn and I were good friends. She often called to talk over her problems with Ernie [Kovacs] and me."

"I am deeply shocked," said Gene Kelly. "All show business must mourn. There was no one like her."

"I knew and acted with Marilyn Monroe," *Niagara* co-star Joseph Cotten would write. "I am proud of having had that privilege. May she rest in peace."

"She did an awful lot to boost things up for movies, when everything was at a low state," co-star Betty Grable remarked. "There'll never be anyone like her for looks, for attitude, for all of it."

"Nobody discovered her," Darryl F. Zanuck professed, "she earned her own way to stardom...I disagreed and fought with her on many occasions, but...in spite of her temperament...she never let the public down."

"I join all her friends in Hollywood who had the privilege of knowing her," said producer A. C. Lyles. "We remember her with devotion and love. Each of us felt a personal loss, and the industry was deprived of a great talent at an early age."

Spencer Tracy broke down when heard the sad news on the set of *It's a Mad, Mad, Mad, Mad World* with Edie Adams and Sid Caesar. "You think they would have stopped shooting for a minute out of respect," he remarked to Caesar. "A star dies and the studio doesn't stop for a minute...There was no respect."

"She retained her uniqueness, humanity, and innocence of outlook in a Hollywood that often crushed sensitivity and a sense of fair play," Eunice Murray wrote. "This was the secret of her radiant, magnetic personality, so different from the ordinary. Lesser spirits often survived in Hollywood by cutting themselves off from inner goodness and lost their uniqueness."

Norman Rosten received the call reporting Marilyn's death while seated at his desk, above which he displayed a post card with an image of a jet plane that she had mailed him years earlier. Her message read: "*Guess where I am? Love, Marilyn.*" The inscription seemed poignant now that she was gone. "As I see it, Marilyn took an (accidental?) overdose," he wrote, "it fitted her character, given the forces crowding in upon her. She hungered for death; let us give her that victory." Marilyn's last Christmas gift to Rosten was a tailored brown shirt, which he continued to wear decades after her death. "When it became frayed, I hand-washed it, prolonging its life and wear," he would write, "it's still with me, endlessly repaired. Some call it madness but I call it touch-memory. I still put on that shirt on special occasions."

While on a beach retreat with her girlfriends, sister-in-law, and their children, Jane Russell had found herself preoccupied with Marilyn. "I wished I had her phone number, because I knew she belonged there [with us]," she wrote in her memoir, *My Path & My Detours*, "where we were all laughing about our problems. The next day [my husband] Robert arrived from a hunting trip and said, 'Marilyn Monroe's dead, I heard it on the radio.' We were stunned. If only, if only..."

Upon hearing the news about his former girlfriend, Norma Jeane, Bill Pursel thought, "She didn't find the little cottage and white picket fence; the three children and loving dog she sought."

Shelley Winters was told in upstate New York just before taking a waterskiing lesson and went numb. She experienced a delayed grief reaction later on the skis. Crying hysterically, she deliberately fell off the skis and required rescue from the water. "I wonder if there's a heaven if we'll be together," Winters said of her friend and former roommate. "She had all the beauty that God could bestow but then He took it away. He let us live and He took Marilyn away...I loved Marilyn."

Actress Debbie Reynolds expressed condolences to Marilyn's family: "It's a terrible loss. I join my prayers with theirs that Marilyn now has found the peace that she so desperately looked for but never found." Reverend Billy Graham had told Reynolds of having dreamt that Marilyn would soon die. Recovering from a stillbirth, Reynolds had delegated Sydney Guilaroff to check on Marilyn, but the hairdresser told her of having recently visited Marilyn and noticing no reason for concern. "Sydney, you have to go back," Reynolds implored. "This is very important. This is a possible death."

"I was beside myself with the feeling of guilt that I had failed in my task," Reynolds wrote in *Debbie: My Life*. "We could have done something, anything that might have at least helped her through one more terrible night alone." Two weeks later Graham disclosed to Reynolds of his visions of other Hollywood personalities whose lives were in jeopardy and suggested a meeting at her home with others in the industry to raise the alarm. "Marilyn was still very much on people's minds," Reynolds recalled. "There was a lot of hurt and pain expressed—people trying desperately to find their way in life." The session lasted over three hours, and—according to Reynolds—Graham's motivation for facilitating it stemmed from intense feelings of guilt.

Arthur Miller told the *New York Post* he wouldn't be attending the funeral: "She's not really there anymore." In *Timebends*, Miller described his grieving process in poetic detail. Marilyn was so "vivid" in his mind, ever-present in his life. It took Miller weeks to break out of the denial of her death. He expected to meet with her again, talk "sensibly" about the "foolishness" they had experienced together, and even fall in love with her again. "I could still see her coming across the lawn, or touching something, or laughing," Miller wrote, "at the same time though I confronted the end of her as one might stand watching a sinking sun."

Journalist Neal Pattern interviewed actresses Rosalind Russell, Carroll Baker, and Lisa Kirk as they disembarked the Queen Mary, docked in New York following a transatlantic voyage. "Marilyn Monroe was a perfectionist and a very fine actress," Russell asserted. "She knew she was the sex symbol, but she performed with great wit, never with vulgarity. I understand she had been in poor health. When that happens you need a family and friends—she had too few of both."

"I feel that many factors may have been involved in her death, chief of them loneliness," opined actress and singer Lisa Kirk, best known for her role in the original Broadway production of Cole Porter's long-running musical, *Kiss Me, Kate*. "A suicide? She had so much to live for—yet who can say?"

"Marilyn must have suffered greatly emotionally," said Carroll Baker. "Like all other actresses, she had learned to handle her work and career, but the difficult part of a star's life is often the personal element. She was all alone, with no one to look after her or to care for her—and with no one for her to look after or to care for."

Working on *My Fair Lady* at Warner Brothers Studios, George Cukor realized the depth of Marilyn's emotional pain and regretted having not been more helpful and patient to her. Before his own death in 1983, the director attributed Marilyn's demise to her own innocence in fighting against the power and money of the motion picture industry.

As celebrities philosophized, the management of Grauman's Chinese Theatre displayed a mammoth spray of flowers beside Marilyn's hand and foot prints in the forecourt, where fans gathered at all hours in homage to the fallen star. The impact of Marilyn's death was enormous on the public who attended her films, mailed thousands of fan letters to her each week, and purchased magazines covering her private life.

Across town on North Mission Road, Los Angeles County Coroner Theodore Curphey held a press conference at the Coroner's Office, declaring that Marilyn Monroe had not died from natural causes but may have accidentally self-administered an overdose of sedative drugs. He also announced that his office would be collaborating with the Los Angeles Suicide Prevention Team in developing a "psychological autopsy," incorporating postmortem interviews with survivors to determine whether her death was caused by intentional suicide or accident. The independent investigating team consisted of Dr. Robert Elkon Litman (1921-2010), a psychiatrist and professor at UCLA; Dr. Norman Farberow (born 1918), a psychologist and founding father of modern suicidology educated at UCLA; and Dr. Norman D. Tabachnick (born 1926), professor of clinical psychology at UCLA Medical School.

The Los Angeles Suicide Prevention Team also held a press conference and announced commencement of "exhaustive interviews regarding the probable suicide of Marilyn Monroe." Funded by a grant from the National Institute on Mental Health, the team's Suicide Prevention Center opened in a dilapidated, abandoned tuberculosis ward on the grounds of Los Angeles County Hospital in 1958. The center served as the prototype for such centers across the United States and expanded into the nation's first 24-hour suicide crisis hotline in 1964.

The general public had little understanding of Bipolar Disorder and depression, so fingers pointed to Hollywood as the cause of

Marilyn's death. Few comprehended the complexity of her psyche, but many had opinions about the values of the motion picture industry and the way it treated its arguably principal female star. Studio executives had bullied her, gossip columnists had harassed her, some critics had ridiculed her, and her home studio had fired her. Life in Hollywood and in the media spotlight was known to be detrimental for the individual and her relationships. And where were Marilyn's friends when she needed them the most? Why was she left alone to die? To many, those who represented Hollywood had blood on their hands.

"I suppose all the sob sisters in the world will now start to go to work," Hedda Hopper predicted in her column. "In a way, we're all guilty. We built her up to the skies, we loved her, but we left her lonely and afraid when she needed us the most." A common rescue fantasy emerged in popular culture; sympathetic men imagined that if only they had loved her, they could have saved her; likewise, sympathetic women imagined if only they could have been her friend, they could have saved her.

Like her mother, Susan Strasberg often spoke in analogies and metaphors. "An iron butterfly, some people have called [Marilyn]," she said. "Butterflies are very beautiful, give great pleasure, and have very short life-spans." Strasberg believed the public's love for Marilyn endured because "she showed us her humanity. We don't remember her because she exposed her body. We remember her because she exposed her soul."

"At the core of her, she was really strong," Patricia Newcomb would say many years after Marilyn's death, "and that was something we tended to forget, because she seemed so vulnerable, and one always felt it was necessary to watch out for her."

Photographer Sam Shaw and his family knew more than Marilyn Monroe; they knew Norma Jeane. As one of Marilyn's dearest and closest friends who saw the real woman as she casually played with his children, laughed along with her, and took her phone calls at all hours of the day and night, Shaw spoke from his heart: "Everybody knew about her insecurities, but not everybody knew what fun she was, that she never complained about the ordinary things of life, that she never had a bad word to say about anyone, and that she had a wonderful spontaneous sense of humor."

Chapter Thirty-Two: The Funeral

"This woman had a very good sense of humor," Amy Greene remembered of Marilyn, "and one night we were talking about when we all die, and she said, 'I want Ella Fitzgerald to sing, I want Frank to sing. I want everyone to toast champagne and have a good time. Would you see to that, please?'"

The Greenes and Marilyn's other friends in New York and Connecticut had no role in organizing a memorial service. Half-sister Berniece Miracle, business manager Inez Melson, and Joe DiMaggio coordinated the funeral in Los Angeles. They invited only a select group of Marilyn's closest friends and members of her entourage, and released the following statement to the press:

We sincerely hope that the many friends of Marilyn will understand that we are deeply appreciative of their desire to pay last respects to Marilyn whom we all loved. We hope that each person will understand that last rights must of great necessity be as private as possible so that she can go to her final resting place in the quiet she always sought. We could not in good conscience ask one personality to attend without perhaps affecting many, many others and for this reason alone, we have kept the number of persons to a minimum. Please—all of you—remember the gay, sweet Marilyn and say a prayer of farewell within the confines of your home or your church.
Berniece Miracle
Inez Melson
Joe DiMaggio

Marilyn's funeral was the first service held in the Westwood Village Memorial Park Cemetery's modern and austere A-frame Chapel of Palms on Wednesday, August 8, 1962 at one o'clock in the afternoon. DiMaggio and Miracle chose the location as Marilyn's former guardian, Grace Goddard, and childhood mentor, "Aunt" Ana Lower, were buried there. The cemetery is located on Glendon Avenue, buttressed by a residential neighborhood, near the intersection of Westwood and Wilshire. Today it is completely camouflaged by high-rise office towers in one of the most congested traffic areas of Los Angeles.

"I know exactly what I want on my tombstone!" Marilyn had once told Amy Greene. "Here lies Marilyn Monroe. Thirty-four, twenty-four, thirty-six. Period!" However, there would be no tombstone. Instead, DiMaggio spent eight hundred dollars on crypt number twenty-four in the open-air Mausoleum of Memories. In a bank of forty-eight marble faced crypts, four rows from top to bottom, and twelve crypts across, Marilyn's is located in the second vertical row from the left and second horizontal row from the ground. Its plaque reads simply: "*Marilyn Monroe 1926–1962.*"

During the production of *Gentlemen Prefer Blondes*, Marilyn asked her longtime personal and studio makeup artist, Allan "Whitey" Snyder, to apply her makeup for her funeral. She was only twenty-six, and he was eight years older. Marilyn would certainly outlive him, Snyder thought. He promised to grant her final wish and joked that the body was to be delivered to him warm for preparation. Continuing this private joke, Marilyn presented him with a gold money clip inscribed: "*Whitey Dear, While I'm still warm. Marilyn.*"

With the money clip in his pocket and a bottle of gin concealed in his cosmetics case, Snyder arrived at the mortuary with his future wife, Marjory Pletcher, Marilyn's longtime wardrobe assistant. "There she was on an iron table," Snyder said. "I had to go over and grab her right away, put my hand on her head. I'm a coward and I would've run down the street, but I touched her and it was alright."

Snyder and Pletcher couldn't help but recall the long hours of preparing their friend for her screen performances. To pass the time, Marilyn had engaged in many running jokes, including the ones about her death and funeral. While Whitey had applied her makeup, Marilyn jested about someday being displayed at her wake in a sheer black negligee, and the undertaker custom-making an hourglass-shaped casket to accommodate the curves in her body. They would all break into laughter, Marilyn's rising high above the others.

Now in the mortuary, the mood was melancholy and the only sounds were sobs. Aided by mortician Allan Abbott, Snyder and Pletcher spent three days lovingly preparing Marilyn for her final appearance. Abbott made a promise to his wife to share details of the preparation each evening when he returned home after work.

The embalmer performed a surgical procedure behind Marilyn's neck to reduce postmortem facial and neck swelling. After shaving some hair at the base of her skull, he made a small incision on the back of her neck and sutured the skin tight. The procedure stretched the muscles severed during the autopsy and restored Marilyn's facial and neck contours. Abbott retrieved a lock of Marilyn's shaved blonde hair from the garbage can and preserved it as a personal relic.

As Abbott assisted Pletcher in dressing Marilyn's body in the chartreuse Emilio Pucci dress, Mary Hamrock, a partner of the mortuary, entered the embalming room. "Mrs. Hamrock stated that the body didn't look like Marilyn Monroe because she was too flat-chested," Abbott recalled. "The embalmer explained that the autopsy had rendered her physique in that condition. The family had provided the mortuary with a pair of breast enhancers, but they were too small to compensate for the effects of the postmortem." Mrs. Hamrock removed the falsies from the dress, discarded them and proceeded to restore Marilyn's breasts with cotton batting. After she had finished, she took a few steps back, placed her hands on her hips, and declared, "Now that looks like Marilyn Monroe!"

Sidney Guilaroff entered the preparation room and fainted at the sight of Marilyn in death's repose but soon recovered to fulfill his role as hairdresser. He gently concealed her once lush hair—now damaged by removal of the brain during the autopsy—beneath a blonde wig from Fox studio's wardrobe department styled in the bouffant flip coiffure from *Something's Got to Give*. Abbott was amazed by the collective skills of Snyder, Pletcher, and Guilaroff in transforming Marilyn from unrecognizable to a beautiful china doll.

Manufactured by the famous Belmont Casket Company of Columbus, Ohio, Marilyn's solid bronze casket was known at that time as the "Cadillac of Caskets." The hermetically sealing, antique silver-finished, 48-ounce "Masterpiece" model was lined with champagne-colored satin-silk.

While Marilyn's entourage worked magic within the mortuary, cemetery director Guy Hockett gave press photographers a tour of Marilyn's crypt and the graves of her relatives. He told them of Marilyn having spent many hours over the years seated on a bench near Ana Lower's grave. The din created by workers erecting scaffolding for the newsreel crews and photographers muffled his voice.

On the evening of Tuesday, August 7, a gathering of about fifty stood in front of the gates of the mortuary. Inside the chapel, a grieving DiMaggio spent the night prior to the service before Marilyn's open bronze casket talking to her and praying. When Allan Snyder arrived to touch up the makeup, he found DiMaggio bent over in the pew, silently staring at Marilyn, his hands wrung together in his lap, until he had to return to the motel to dress for the funeral services. Marilyn wore a chartreuse Pucci jersey sheath, unadorned by jewelry, but accessorized by a green scarf. She held a small bouquet of pink teacup roses, a gift from DiMaggio, who also provided a blanket of flowers atop the casket.

On the day of the funeral, guards at the cemetery gates barred Peter and Patricia Lawford, Frank Sinatra, Mitzi Gaynor, Sammy Davis, Jr., Ella Fitzgerald, Bill Alexander (who had jokingly proposed marriage to Marilyn one week before), and others from attending. Twelve year-old Marcia Adlend handed a bouquet of flowers over the fence to a guard who promised to place them at Marilyn's tomb. DiMaggio invited only one journalist into the chapel, Walter Winchell.

Workers in a tall office building across the street from the cemetery gathered on the rooftop for a bird's eye view of the funeral service. A massive, somber crowd of about eight hundred, monitored by law enforcement, lined the streets and peered over the low cemetery walls and through the chain-link fence. The curious would be allowed into the cemetery once the service ended. Caucasians, Latinos, African-Americans, young, old, and middle aged paid their last respects to the fallen star, illustrating her diverse appeal. Some rested on the scaffolding constructed for the media. One young woman was injured when she fell from her perch in a tree branch. An older woman collapsed from the heat, and police officers carried her into the shade.

Florist delivery vans arrived with elaborate sprays sent by President Adolfo Lopez Mateo of Mexico, Frank Sinatra, Jack Benny, Spyros Skouras, and Arthur Miller. Jane and Bobby Miller sent wreaths. A heart-shaped floral arrangement contained dozens of roses. An anonymous wreath bore the full text of Elizabeth Barrett Browning's sonnet, *How Do I Love Thee?* Journalist William Neugenbauer reported that an attractive, thirty-three-year-old man in a Petrocelli suit—who also drove a white Jaguar—visited a floral shop in New Jersey to order the fifty dollar arrangement. In life, Marilyn had requested that her mourners make donations to children's hospitals in lieu of flowers.

Eight guards from Pinkerton, paid one hundred fifty dollars each, protected the casket and maintained order. They wore blue-gray uniforms, white scarves around their necks, black belts across their chests, and pistols in holsters at their waists. The four pallbearers included Allan Snyder, Sidney Guilaroff, and two men who provided hearses and manpower to funeral directors in Los Angeles, Ronald Hast and Allan Abbott.

DiMaggio, tearful and silent, and Joe Jr., on a thirty-six-hour pass and wearing his Marine dress uniform, left the Miramar Hotel and rode in a chauffeured white limousine to the cemetery. Crying, Joe reached across the long back seat and took his son's hand. They held hands until they arrived at the chapel. Joe Jr. would later say that this was the closest he ever felt to his father.

The funeral guest list did not resemble a list of *Who's Who* in Hollywood, but illustrated Marilyn's connection to her former husband, half-sister, long-term friends, and employees. George Solotaire accompanied his friend, Joe DiMaggio, and DiMaggio's son. Reverend Floyd Darling escorted Berniece Miracle. Psychoanalyst Ralph Greenson and his wife, Hilde, attended along with their adult children, Joan and Daniel. Acting coaches Lee and Paula Strasberg accompanied Lotte Gosslar, a mime instructor from whom Marilyn had received coaching in the early 1950s.

DiMaggio invited Anna and Mary Karger, mother and sister of Fred Karger, with whom Marilyn had engaged in a significant relationship early in her career. Although Marilyn had been crushed by Karger's refusal to marry her, she maintained a lasting relationship with his family. Berniece invited Erwin "Doc" Goddard, widower of Marilyn's childhood legal guardian Grace Goddard, and his current wife, Anne, and Grace's sister and brother-in-law, Enid and Sam Knebelcamp, Marilyn's former foster parents.

In addition to housekeeper Eunice Murray and publicist Patricia Newcomb, several other employees were invited to attend Marilyn's private service. They included makeup artist Allan Snyder was joined by his wife, Beverly, and daughter, Sherry. Dresser Marjorie Pletcher was present along with hairdressers Sydney Guilaroff, Agnes Flanagan, and Pearl Porterfield.

Marilyn's friend and masseur Ralph Roberts arrived with May Reis, her secretary and household manager since 1957. Inez Melson, Marilyn's business manager since the early 1950s and guardian to her mother, Gladys, came with her husband, Patrick. Aaron Frosch, Marilyn's attorney in New York and executor of her will, paid his respects, along with her California attorney Milton Rudin, who was also Dr. Greenson's brother-in-law. Rudy Kautzky, a driver for the Carey Limousine Service, and African-American maid, Florence Thomas, were also included. They also had become members of Marilyn's surrogate family.

Arthur Miller was conspicuously absent. "To join in what I knew would be a circus of cameras and shots and luridness was beyond my strength," he wrote. Inez invited Rabbi Goldburg, who had solemnized the Monroe-Miller Jewish wedding ceremony, but he was on vacation in Europe and did not attend.

Thick drapery masked the glass walls of the chapel and concealed the service inside. A blanket of white roses, carnations and orchids with a ribbon inscribed "*With Love*" covered the casket. Before the guests were allowed into the chapel, attendants told them that the family was with the body. Joan Greenson thought if Marilyn had a family, perhaps she would be alive and there would be no need to gather in sadness.

In the chapel, non-denominational minister, Reverend A.J. Sloden, delivered the Twenty-Third Psalm, excerpts from the Fourteenth Chapter of John, Psalm 46 and Psalm 139, and led the mourners in reciting the Lord's Prayer. He based his remarks upon the quotation, "How fearfully and wonderfully she was made by the Creator." Sloden called Marilyn a "grand, great woman" whose death "caused a wave of sorrow to be felt by millions." The organist, Margaret Hockett, played movements from Tchaikovsky's *Sixth Symphony* and Bach and Gounod's "Ave Maria." Judy Garland's recording of "Over the Rainbow" resonated at Marilyn's request. Berniece audiotaped the service, preserving the mourners' sobs, Patricia Newcomb's and Joan Greenson's being the most audible.

DiMaggio had approached Carl Sandburg to speak at the service, but the elderly poet declined due to illness and his belief of having not known Marilyn sufficiently. Instead, a tearful Lee Strasberg stood at the podium and delivered a moving eulogy in a voice trembling and cracking with emotion:

> *I know she would not have wanted us to mourn... but grief is human... and words must be spoken...*
>
> *Marilyn Monroe was a legend.*
>
> *In her lifetime she created a myth of what a poor girl from a deprived background could attain. For the entire world she became a symbol of the eternal feminine. But I have no words to describe the myth and the legend. I did not know this Marilyn Monroe.*
>
> *We, gathered here today, knew only Marilyn... a warm human being, impulsive and shy, sensitive and in fear of rejection, yet ever avid for life and reaching out for fulfillment. I will not insult the privacy of your memory of her... a privacy she sought and treasured... by trying to describe her whom you knew to you who knew her. In our memories of her she remains alive, not only a shadow on a screen or a glamorous personality.*
>
> *For us, Marilyn was a devoted and loyal friend, a colleague constantly reaching for perfection. We shared her pain and difficulties and some of her joys. She was a member of our family. It is difficult to accept the fact that her zest for life has been ended by this dreadful accident.*
> *Despite the heights and brilliance she attained on the screen, she*

was planning for the future; she was looking forward to participating in the many exciting things which she planned. In her eyes and in mine her career was just beginning. The dream of her talent, which she had nurtured as a child, was not a mirage. When she first came to me I was amazed at the startling sensitivity which she possessed and which had remained fresh and undimmed, struggling to express itself despite the life to which she had been subjected.

Others were as physically beautiful as she was, but there was obviously something more in her, something that people saw and recognized in her performances and with which they identified. She had a luminous quality...a combination of wistfulness, radiance, yearning...to set her apart and yet make everyone wish to be a part of it, to share in the childish naiveté which was at once so shy and yet so vibrant.

This quality was even more evident when she was on the stage. I am truly sorry that the public who loved her did not have the opportunity to see her as we did, in many of the roles that foreshadowed what she would have become. Without doubt she would have been one of the really great actresses of the stage.

Now it is all at an end. I hope her death will stir sympathy and understanding for a sensitive artist and woman who brought joy and pleasure to the world.

I cannot say goodbye. Marilyn never liked goodbyes, but in the peculiar way she had of turning things around so that they faced reality...I will say au revoir. For the country to which she has gone, we must all someday visit.

Strasberg choked back sobs as he spoke the final two paragraphs. Having presented a heartfelt and moving tribute to his beloved student and friend, he walked slowly back to his chair beside Paula and wiped his tears.

At the end of the service, mortuary attendants slid back the rose blanket covering the casket and opened is outer lid and the top half of its inner lid. Clanking noises muted sobs, and a shock of Marilyn's blonde hair became visible to Joan Greenson who became horrified, having never seen a corpse. "I have never seen Marilyn look so beautiful," said Fox publicist Don Prince, "like a small child."

After the mourners passed the casket for final respects, DiMaggio approached. He leaned over and kissed Marilyn, and repeated, "I love you" again and again. Attendants sealed and bolted the lids, replaced the blanket of roses, and the pallbearers wheeled the casket down the aisle, toward the chapel doors. The mourners filed behind. When the double doors opened, a thunderous cacophony of camera shutters sliced into the silence as the procession walked into the sunlight outside. The pallbearers slid the casket in to the mortuary's new 1962 Cadillac Eureka funeral coach, flanked by the eight Pinkerton guards.

The procession of mourners slowly walked behind the hearse as the casket was transported from the chapel to the nearby crypt where another brief service was held. Three rows of folding chairs had been set for some of the guests, but many stood. DiMaggio appears grief-stricken in newsreels and photographs as he walked beside his son in the position directly behind the hearse, reserved for the widowed spouse.

As Reverend Sloden administered the final rights, the pallbearers glided the casket into the crypt. Snyder was the last to pat the casket and walk away. "Okay, honey," he whispered, "sleep tight." As the mourners comforted DiMaggio and departed, cemetery workers swiftly sealed the crypt. George Solotaire experienced chest spasms and rested in mortuary office before being helped into a limousine.

As the invited drove away, the guards opened the gates and allowed the uninvited curious to enter the grounds. A wave of fans snatched flowers from the floral tributes as souvenirs, nearly tearing them apart. "Marilyn Monroe meant a lot to me," a short-order cook who had recently immigrated from Italy told columnist James Bacon as he clutched one of DiMaggio's roses. "I'll always keep this flower pressed. It will remind me of a girl who had even a worse start in life than I had—but who became famous all over the world."

As Marilyn was laid to rest, Ida Bolender wrote a letter to Berniece addressed to the hacienda on Fifth Helena Drive—the house number and street name had appeared in the newspaper articles covering the death—inviting her to spend the night before departing from the airport. Ida identified herself as Norma Jeane's caregiver and enclosed a newspaper clipping of a photograph, taken by Berniece's grandmother, of the child at age fourteen months in a polka-dot dress and bonnet. Ida offered to share other photographs of Norma Jeane taken during the time she lived in the Bolender home.

The next day, DiMaggio stopped by the cemetery office before leaving Los Angeles to leaf through hundreds of telegrams offering condolences. He wished to stop by the crypt, but about twenty-five faithful fans crowded around it. Guy Hockett approached the group and explained that DiMaggio wanted a moment of privacy. The group stepped aside. "So, in the end, she was his," wrote Richard Ben Cramer. "Because in death, he did possess her—as he never quite could in life."

Before leaving with mob-connected cronies Harry Hall and Sugar Brown for Mexico, where he would not understand the news reports, DiMaggio headed to the Parisian Florist on Sunset Boulevard and opened an account. He arranged for a bouquet of red roses to be delivered to Marilyn's crypt three times weekly, just as he had promised her while they were married. DiMaggio maintained this agreement for twenty years.

* * *

Marilyn was the first celebrity interred at the small, peaceful cemetery. She would be joined in death with friends Natalie Wood, Peter Lawford, Billy Wilder, Dean Martin, Sammy Cahn, Nunnally Johnson, Gene Kelly, and Truman Capote. Lawford's remains would be relocated due to lack of payment for the crypt. Marilyn would also become neighbors in death to co-workers Eve Arden (*We're Not Married*), Richard Conte (with whom she filmed a powerful 1950 screen test for *Cold Shoulder*), Jim Backus (*Don't Bother to Knock*), Jack Lemmon (*Some Like It Hot*), and her boss, Darryl F. Zanuck.

The body of Terryl Lee Yeigh, known as Darbi Winters, occupies the crypt located next to the one directly above Marilyn's. Winters was a sixteen-year-old California starlet who had just begun her career in modeling and acting when she disappeared on October 18, 1962. Her stepfather told her mother that the young model had gone out on a date. Two days later, Terryl's mother found the body under her bed. Her stepfather, Amos Emery Yeigh, strangled Terryl in a drunken, jealous rage because he thought her acting career was ruining his marriage. Ironically, Terryl had told her mother just weeks before that she wanted to be buried close to Marilyn Monroe one day.

Hugh Hefner, the publisher of *Playboy* magazine, would purchase the vault next to Marilyn's for $75,000 in 1992. In September 1962, he purchased Lawrence Schiller's photographs of Marilyn's nude swim, but waited to publish them in the January 1964 issue to avoid exploitation of her death.

In August 2009, widow Elsie Poncher, whose dead husband was laid to rest in the crypt directly above Marilyn's, relocated his casket to another burial space and offered his valuable vault at auction to help pay off the mortgage on her Beverly Hills home. Bidding started at $500,000 and skyrocketed to $4.6 million in just three days. Richard Poncher allegedly purchased the vault from Joe DiMaggio. As he lay dying, the eight-one-year-old warned his wife, "If you don't put me upside down over Marilyn, I'll haunt you the rest of my life." Poncher was buried in 1986, facing down to prevent turning his back on Marilyn.

Chapter Thirty-Three: The Investigation & Results of the Autopsy

The autopsy report, completed by coroner Thomas Noguchi on August 13, 1962, determined Marilyn died of acute barbiturate poisoning by a massive overdose. No traces of alcohol were found in her system. Reports of Chemical Analysis indicated 4.5 mg per cent of barbiturates in the blood, the absence of phenobarbital (a common barbiturate), and 8 mg per cent of chloral hydrate in the blood specimen. The liver specimen indicated 13 mg per cent of pentobarbital or Nembutal.

The amount of Nembutal found in her body was four times the toxic level and three times the minimum amount for death to occur, the equivalent of between 47 to 60 pills according to varying sources. The amount of chloral hydrate was just under the lethal dose or about 17 pills. Her liver temperature of 89 degrees taken at 10:30 am on August 5 indicated time of death between 10 PM and 2 AM. "An accidental overdose of that magnitude was extremely unlikely," stated Noguchi. "From my forensic experience with suicide victims, I believe that the sheer number of pills Monroe ingested was too many to swallow 'accidentally.'"

The official certificate of death indicated "acute barbiturate poisoning, ingestion of overdose." In the space designated for specification of accident, suicide, or homicide, "Probable Suicide" was typed. Lionel Grandison signed as physician coroner under the stamped name for Coroner Curphey and indicated the date as August 28, 1962. Charles Maxwell signed as embalmer. Time of death was estimated at 3:40 AM on August 5, although the body's advanced rigor mortis and discoloration indicated Marilyn had died several hours before.

On August 17, the world learned the cause of Marilyn's death. In a white lab coat and puffing a cigar, Dr. Theodore Curphey sat at a table flanked by Dr. Litman and Dr. Farberow in a tiny inquest room at Hall of Justice surrounded by seventy-five journalists and television technicians. He read from a prepared statement:

Miss Monroe had suffered from psychiatric disturbances for a long time. She experienced severe fears and frequent depressions. Mood changes were abrupt and unpredictable. Among symptoms of disorganization, sleep disturbances were prominent, for which she had been taking sedative drugs for many years. She was thus familiar with and experienced in the use of sedative drugs and well aware of their dangers.

Recently, one of the objectives of her psychiatric treatments had been reduction of her intake of drugs. This has been partially successful during the last two months. She was reported to be following doctor's orders in her use of the drugs; and the amount of drugs found in her home at the time of her death was not unusual.

In our investigation, we have learned that Miss Monroe had often expressed wishes to give up, to withdraw, and even to die. On more than one occasion in the past, when disappointed and depressed, she had made a suicide attempt using sedative drugs. These occasions, she had called for help and had been rescued. From the information collected about the events of the evening of August 4th, it is our opinion that the same pattern was repeated except for the rescue. It has been our practice with similar information collected in other cases in the past to recommend a certification for such death as probable suicide.

After Curphey read the statement, the press bombarded the forensics team with questions. "Any person who takes any depressing drug, the pattern of death is pretty much the same," Curphey explained, "they lose their ability to judge and to act, they lose muscular power, and they slip into coma." He estimated Marilyn must have quickly gulped about 47 Nembutal and 17 chloral hydrate capsules.

"She was psychiatrically disturbed," affirmed Dr. Litman, "but to say she was mentally unbalanced would improperly state it." Dr. Farberow asserted Marilyn exhibited no physical dependency on drugs. "Marilyn Monroe played the greatest role in her career when she killed herself," Curphey told the media, "because she called the attention of the world to the problem of suicide."

Dr. David Phillips of the University of California began systematic scientific investigations on copycat suicide in the 1970s. The largest possible copycat effect he found was for Marilyn Monroe. During the month of her suicide, there were an additional 303 suicides in the United States alone, an increase of 12 percent. In general, highly publicized stories increase the U.S. national suicide rate by only 2.51 percent during the first month of media coverage.

Within a decade of Marilyn's death, those who believed she did not die from an oral overdose of drugs referenced the autopsy report as "proof" of foul play. If she had orally ingested Nembutal, conspiracy theorists allege, the undigested residue of the drug would have been evident in the stomach, and traces of the drug's "yellow dye" would have been detected in the digestive system. The absence of both, they assert, suggests the drug was administered by either an enema or suppository. However, these allegations are actually invalidated by the autopsy report, as well as by medical facts.

The autopsy findings support the conclusion of an oral ingestion of drugs. The report described "marked congestion" and "hemorrhage" of the stomach lining. This inflammation is consistent with the irritant of an oral overdose. Nembutal, in fact, does not leave the trace of a yellow dye. Unfortunately, the liquid content of the stomach was not tested to determine if it contained residue from the drug's gelatin capsules. Oversight only fueled the fire for conspiracy theories for years to follow.

In an episode of the television series *Unsolved History* (2003), Dr. Nicholas V. Cozzi conducted a scientific experiment in which he simulated Marilyn's overdose to determine whether or not residue of the pills would be detected. He used a beaker to replicate a human stomach, added the drugs, and then took samples of the stomach at ten-minute intervals to illustrate the amount of Nembutal absorbed by her system.

Nembutal would have absorbed quickly and its gelatin capsule dissolved, and the stomach lining would have shown massive irritation, likely caused by the chloral hydrate. Cozzi determined at about an hour, the level of Nembutal in her blood would have caused death by respiratory depression and then cardiac arrest. Other experts believe Marilyn could have lived a long as between one and one-half to two hours after ingestion of the drugs. She likely took a large fatal overdose, rather than having taken smaller dosages of drugs during the course of the day.

The amount of drugs in Marilyn's system was consistent with the medications available to her. The drug levels in the blood and liver were consistent with a gastric ingestion and suggested she probably lived for a period of time after the overdose. Noguchi documented "marked congestion" of the colon and its "purplish discoloration." He described the fecal contents as "light brown and formed" and documented the bladder contents as 150 cubic centimeters of "clear, straw-colored fluid."

Many conspiracy theorists point to the congestion and discoloration of the colon as evidence of a drug-laced enema or suppository. However, if either had been administered, it would have irritated the colon lining, and the bowels and bladder would likely have evacuated stool and urine. According to the autopsy report, the lining of colon was normal, and the stool was fully formed. There is no mention of inflammation of the mucous lining of the colon. The purple discoloration of the outside of colon was likely due to vascular congestion developed after death.

There was also no evidence that Marilyn was a victim of a violent homicide. She was found locked in her bedroom from the inside. The skeletomuscular system showed no evidence of fractures, and the body revealed no signs of trauma. Examination of the chest, sternum, and heart muscle likewiwse showed no signs of trauma, and no blood was found around heart or lungs. These finding contradict later allegations of a physician plunging a hypodermic needle into Marilyn's heart in an attempt either to resuscitate or kill her.

Despite the autopsy's negation of Marilyn both having undergone a tubal ligation to prevent pregnancy and being pregnant at the time of death, both rumors circulated for a half-century. According to the autopsy report, "The tubes are intact. The opening of the fimbria [fringelike opening of the fallopian tubes] are patent.

The right ovary demonstrates recent corpus luteum hemmorrhagieum [menstruation]. The left ovary shows corpora lutea and albicantis." Additionally, postmortem examination contradicted the rumor that Marilyn had recently engaged in sexual activity with a lover. "The examination I made included contents of vaginal passages which were made on a smear and studied under a microscope," Noguchi is quoted in saying in the July 16, 1973 issue of *Time*. "There was no indication of sexual intercourse."

Suicide threats, attempts, and gestures peak in individuals diagnosed with Borderline Personality Disorder in their twenties, but—according to modern studies—the average age of those who completed suicide range from age thirty to thirty-seven. The conclusion of these studies indicates those with the disorder may not kill themselves early in the course of the disorder, when treatment providers and members of their support systems are most alarmed by their impulsivity, but later, when those with the disorder do not recover or treatment has failed. Marilyn's ultimate fate appeared to support this deduction.

A prominent theory from the perspective of mental health professionals is that Marilyn's death resulted from her psychiatric disorders. The fact that Marilyn had been making plans in her final weeks and reportedly left no suicide note leads many to believe she was at low risk for suicide. However, in studies by Richard Hall, Dennis Platt, and Ryan Hall, of patients who have made serious suicide attempts but survived because of medical intervention, only ten percent left a suicide note, and nearly seventy percent had no suicidal thoughts prior to their impulse suicide attempt.

These serious attempts appeared more spontaneous. The patients tended to display depressive symptoms such as feelings of worthlessness, helplessness, hopelessness, insomnia; anxiety and panic episodes; severe lack of energy and severe inability to experience joy. Other predictive indicators included: presence of a mood disorder (such a Bipolar Disorder), recent severe interpersonal conflict, loss of an important relationship, inability to maintain a job, and drug abuse.

If Marilyn had suffered from Borderline Personality Disorder (BPD) alone, or in combination with a depressive or mood disorder, she would have lacked the ability to successfully manage painful emotional challenges in her relationships. According to Marsha

Linehan, a leading specialist in the area, those with BPD may express intense emotional pain by self-harming or suicidal behavior in an attempt to regulate their mood or escape from unbearable life situations. Linehan uses the example that withholding pain medication from a cancer patient could lead those patients unable to regulate their severe physical pain by self-destructive behavior in an attempt to cope.

In recent years, journal articles on endometriosis have suggested the condition contributed to Marilyn's death by necessitating addictive painkilling narcotics and aggravating her psychological problems. Doctors may have been prescribing dangerous drugs of the era to reduce her sometimes unbearable physical pain, and Marilyn may also have been using the drugs to self-medicate the condition's resultant emotional pain, as it left her unable to have the child she so desperately wanted.

Perhaps no conclusion is more poignant than that of the coroner who sifted through the evidence when he performed the autopsy. "No one will ever be able to definitely say what went on that evening," Noguchi would accurately predict, "which…transformed Marilyn Monroe from a beautiful and talented actress…to a dying movie star—and an undying legend."

Chapter Thirty-Four: Studio Without Its Queen

Hollywood compared the near-bankrupt Twentieth Century Fox Studios to the sinking of the *Titanic* a half-century earlier. By August 1962, employees earning more than $20,000 per year received a fifty per cent salary decrease.

The studio outlasted Marilyn by less than two days. Represented by Louis Nizer in a corporate take-over, Darryl Zanuck overthrew the Levathes administration, closed the New York office, temporarily shut down the studio, and suspended all film and television projects. On Monday, August 6, the corporation reorganized and released eight hundred employees, including film Editor David Bretherton, who received his pink slip while editing scenes of *Something's Got to Give.* Eventually, Zanuck and his son, Richard, resuscitated the corporation on a significantly smaller scale.

In addition to salvaging *Cleopatra*, Zanuck had an uncompleted comedy with a deceased leading lady. During production of *Saratoga* in 1937, Jean Harlow died at the age of twenty-six from uremic poisoning, leaving ten percent of her scenes incomplete. Forged with a blonde body-double, MGM Studios staged the remaining scenes with the heroine's face hidden from the viewer by distance shots and heavily veiled hats. Interactions between Harlow's character and co-stars were filmed from an "over the shoulder" vantage point, with the body-double's back to the camera and the lens focused on the co-star. In some scenes, an impersonator's voice dubbed Harlow's lines. In others, lengthy one-sided telephone calls enabled part of the dialogue. Hollywood now buzzed about the release of *Something's Got to Give* with a body-double for Marilyn in the scenes she had not lived to film, but Fox decided to shelve the film, instead.

A week after her death, theater chains across the country launched Marilyn Monroe film festivals, and by late 1963, Fox re-released nearly all her major films. The public and critics alike reevaluated Marilyn's performances and discovered a deeper appreciation for her talents. Journalist Sheila Graham futilely petitioned the American Academy of Motion Picture Arts and Sciences to award a posthumous honorary Oscar to Marilyn.

As fans flocked to theaters and paid to watch Marilyn Monroe films released in the previous decade, Darryl F. Zanuck—motivated by profit—appointed a production team to edit her best scenes from fifteen of her Fox films into a documentary titled simply *Marilyn*. Narrated by Rock Hudson, it became the first documentary listed among the top twenty box office hits. However, her most successful recent films for rival studios were glaringly omitted.

"After Marilyn Monroe's death, it might have been expected that a vast cult would develop," wrote *Time* in its May 31, 1963 review, "necrophilic and worshipful…But the cult of Marilyn has turned out to be more esoteric. Her memory is tended by the somewhat intellectuals. And the theme of their compassions is a touching waif who was destroyed by a cruel world she never made."

A. H. Weiler of the *New York Times* reviewed Fox's "sentimental if not incisive tribute" to its late superstar "who once helped fill the company's coffers", and cited "no effort to delve into the essentials that gave her that rare attribute 'star quality.'" Weiler highlighted Marilyn's projection of "emotion with genuine force and artistry" in *Bus Stop*, fixated on her adroit abilities in comedies, and affirmed that she sang and danced with "decidedly unusual girlish aplomb" in musicals. The compilation demonstrated Marilyn's progress from an emerging star to the culmination of the screen tests for *Something's Got to Give*.

On the year anniversary of Marilyn's death, fans and flowers arrived at her crypt. A heart-shaped floral arrangement from the Netherlands bore a card with the message: "The story's not over; our love protects you."

* * *

Cleopatra filmed for a total of two hundred twenty-five days. The rough cut was eight hours in duration before director Mankiewicz made additional cuts and invited the new studio president for a screening. Zanuck left the screening room in a panic after five hours of "chaos, overwrought dialogue, and semineurotic performances." Released on June 12, 1963, the epic was labeled "a monumental mouse" by the *New York Herald Tribune.*

"Miss Taylor is monotony in a slit skirt," opined the *New Statesman.* Judith Crist of the *New York Herald Tribune* wrote, "There is no depth of emotion in her kohl-laden eyes and no modulation in a voice that too often rises to fishwife levels." Two weeks after her film's release, Zanuck sued Taylor and Burton for $50 million claiming damages from their "deplorable and amoral conduct." The couple divorced respective spouses, married in 1964, and divorced in June 1973. In a bizarre turn of events, they remarried in 1975 and divorced twenty-one months later. Burton died in 1984, Taylor in 2011.

Cleopatra was the highest grossing film of 1963, earning $26 million, yet failed to profit the studio as it cost $44 million; it holds the title of the only film ever to be the highest grossing film of the year only to run at a loss to its creators.

Something's Got to Give did not lay dormant for long. Fox rewrote the script (once again), renamed it *Move Over Darling*, and cast Doris Day, James Garner, and Polly Bergen in the roles intended for Monroe, Martin, and Charisse, under the direction of Michael Gordon. Thelma Ritter portrayed Nick Arden's mother, and Don Knotts depicted the shoe clerk. Chuck Connors co-starred as Steven Burchett. Edgar Buchanan replaced John McGiver as the judge, and John Astin replaced Phil Silvers as the insurance agent. A broad comic scene with Ellen Arden's going through a car wash in a convertible substituted Marilyn's sexy nude swimming scene and better suited Day's screen image.

Doris Day performed the film's title song, "Move Over, Darling," played over the opening credits. Her background chorus featured West Coast session singers Darlene Love and the Blossoms. Released during the Christmas season in 1963, the *New York Times* gave *Move Over Darling* a lukewarm reception, noting "mildly comic" physical humor and declaring the leading stars acted "loquaciously redundant and overly energetic" in situations that call for "defter and lighter touches." Bosley Crowther awarded notice only to Edgar Buchanan as a "bumbling, irascible" judge who got "a laugh" and to

Thelma Ritter as "a properly lovable curmudgeon of a mother-in-law." The critic pounded a final nail in the coffin by saying, "When some of Miss Day's gambits to recapture her spouse have failed, Miss Ritter acidly suggests, 'better think of something else.' That advice could apply to *Move Over, Darling*, too."

Released in 1965, Peter Levathes' project, *Sound of Music*, virtually resuscitated Fox. Costing $8 million, the beloved musical earned $110 million and won the Best Picture Oscar. The Fox Corporation would be sold five times in twenty years and become part of Robert Murdoch's media empire in late 1980s, including *The Wall Street Journal* and HarperCollins Publishers. Even though Fox would continue to thrive and make millions, arguably no other single star will ever come close to equaling the recognition and wealth Marilyn Monroe brought to the studio.

Chapter Thirty-Five: Aftermath

On August 8, 1962, Marilyn Monroe, the woman, was laid to rest; and Marilyn Monroe, the legend and the myth, was born.

The untimely death of a celebrity is generally followed by a communal mourning ritual and subsequent enthrallment facilitated by the global media. We can trace this trend to celebrity deaths of twentieth and twenty-first centuries: Rudolph Valentino (1926), Jean Harlow (1937), James Dean (1955), Marilyn Monroe (1962), Elvis Presley (1977), John Lennon (1980), Princess Diana (1997), Michael Jackson (2009), and Whitney Houston (2012). One expert likens the fascination with deceased celebrities to a modern-day religious movement.

"I would call celebrity worship a new form of religious culture that is very popular in the 20th century," explained Gary Laderman, professor of religion at Emory University and author of *Rest in Peace: A Cultural History of Death and the Funeral Home in 20th Century America*. "We live in a society that venerates a celebrity, and people may have very complicated relationships with them. They may not even know the fallen celebrity, yet they draw quite a bit of meaning from them, which is what religion does. It helps to construct meaning in their lives. Fans are able to draw meaning from this image appearing in the media, and they try to work in some way to maintain those connections."

While DiMaggio planned Marilyn's memorial service, the presses stopped at *Vogue* magazine so that publishers might insert an appropriate solemn commemorative in the Monroe-Stern photo layout planned for the September 1962 issue. The magazine celebrated Marilyn's maturity and instinctive elegance and acknowledged her ability to make millions of people love her and sympathize with her unhappiness. "That she withstood the incredible, unknowable pressures of her public legends as long as she did is evidence of the stamina of the human spirit," the editor wrote. "The waste seems almost unbearable if out of her death comes nothing of insight into her special problems."

On August 10, 1962, two days after Marilyn's funeral and one week before the coroner's finding of probable suicide, the CBS television network's news show, *Eyewitness,* sought to explore the reason why she ended her own life. Hosted by Charles Collingswood, who interviewed Jacqueline Kennedy for the televised White House tour, the program delved into Marilyn's character and final descent.

Director George Cukor spoke of Marilyn as a "poor darling" to CBS and stated: "For all her flash…[she was] a very distinguished creature." When interviewer Robert Shackney asked if she had been temperamental, Cukor protectively replied, "Yes, but so is everybody else…Everyone has doubts, difficulties, and fears." The director also praised Marilyn's mind and unique style. "You had to produce her more than direct her," he said. "If left to her own devices, she could be quite original, quite enchanting."

Also interviewed, fellow blonde actress Kim Novak related to the feeling of being the studio's commodity. "'Never forget you're just a piece of meat,'" Novak quoted the executives at Columbia Studio. She also referred to Marilyn's remarks in *Life* about the industry's mistreatment of its profitable stars: "Marilyn said it so well."

Lee Strasberg, interviewed by Harry Reasoner, associated Marilyn's "tragic" early childhood experiences with her "deep disturbances" and commented on the damage to her psyche caused by "by those who maligned her in life."

Playwright Clifford Odets poetically described Marilyn's burdening "dark companion" of childhood rejections and instability, saying they produced both her "severe" lack of self-esteem and inflexibility. "She has been a legend in her lifetime…she will be an even greater legend," he accurately predicted. "I feel it in the air everywhere I go…The legend is spreading…She will be more vivid, fresher, greener in death than she was in life." But even Odets could not have imagined the extent of Marilyn's posthumous appeal.

The August 17 issue of *Life* featured its eighth cover portrait of Marilyn, photographed by Lawrence Schiller. Marilyn's expression was wistful and she wore a beige mink hat from *Something's Got to Give*. With a somber black background, the cover was titled "Memories of Marilyn." An article, "Remember Marilyn," accompanied an eleven-page pictorial review of her life beginning with Andre deDienes' picture of Norma Jeane at nineteen, sitting on an asphalt highway, on the brink of fame. Reflecting on her fresh face, curly hair in pigtails, simple blouse, and skirt patterned with tiny stars, *Life* supposed she "already had the look of a girl who was made to be remembered." The magazine affectionately celebrated her "air of decency and almost childlike innocence."

Paris Match devoted thirty-six pages to its tribute, one page for each year of Marilyn's life. *Time*, on the other hand, passed on a cover image of her for its August 10 issue and published a cynical article titled, "The Only Blonde in the World." The author eulogized her as "swept by panics, smothered by doubts and fears," and having "conducted a kittenish romance with the intelligentsia." The author further ranted that "everything she said sounded as if she were talking about Zen Buddhism" and her death was inevitable. This cynicism met with harsh criticism by a man of the cloth, whose response was published in the next issue's "Letters to the Editor" section. Reverend Martin L. Deppe of Mandell Methodist Church in Chicago used sexualized imagery in blasting *Time* for playing God and lamented Marilyn facing a "Last Judgement" by the "quick, merciless thrusts" of a male journalist.

Time magazine recognized a growing rescue fantasy among Marilyn's fans and the general public. Her "unique charisma" caused many a male to believe that if only a "well-intentioned, understanding person like me" could have known her, he would have been able to protect her from self-inflicted harm. Similarly, in death, Marilyn inspired the women who once resented her "frolicsome sexuality" to rally behind her "simple noble wish to be taken seriously." The fantasy has grown with each generation that learns of Marilyn through popular culture, the media, and the plethora of biographies published each year.

Unlike previous celebrity deaths, Marilyn's untimely passing by apparent suicide inspired writers, philosophers, activists, and other scholars—such as Claire Booth Luce, Edward Wagenknecht, and later, Norman Mailer and Gloria Steinem—to find meaning in the circumstances of her famous life and struggles and to provide a narrative to make sense of the tragic ending of a modern icon. Marilyn's suicide exposed the secret internal pain and suffering behind the public image of a carefree and glamorous sex symbol who seemed on the surface to have achieved what had been most valued in our culture: beauty, fame, money, success, and love. However, her early death afforded a cautionary tale on failed marriage, childlessness, and the downside of fame.

Controversial novelist and philosopher Ayn Rand (1905-1982) was among the first to explore and even canonize Marilyn in a contemporary essay. Born and educated in Russia, Rand moved to the United States the year of Marilyn's birth and worked as a screenwriter in Hollywood and a playwright on Broadway before she published her two best-selling novels, *The Fountainhead* (1943) and *Atlas Shrugged* (1957). Rand's philosophical paradigm drew harsh literary criticism but a popular following. Her essay, *Through Your Most Grievous Fault*, appeared in the *Los Angeles Times* on August 19, 1962 and examined the culture's reaction to Marilyn's death, as well as its fickle pattern of celebrity idolatry transforming to celebrity vilification. Excerpts of Rand's main points are as follows:

> If there ever was a victim of society, Marilyn Monroe was that victim—of a society that professes dedication to the relief of the suffering, but kills the joyous...To survive it and to preserve the kind of spirit she projected on the screen—the radiantly benevolent sense of life, which cannot be faked—was an almost inconceivable psychological achievement that required a heroism of the highest order...She preserved her vision of life through a nightmare struggle, fighting her way to the top. What broke her was the discovery, at the top, of as sordid an evil as the one she had left behind—worse, perhaps, because it was incomprehensible. She had expected to reach the sunlight; she found, instead, a limitless swamp of malice...An actress, dedicated to her art with passionate earnestness...who went through hell to make her own boundaries, to offer people the sunlit universe of her own vision...but who was ridiculed for her desire to

> play serious parts...Anyone who has ever felt resentment against the good for being the good and has given voice to it is the murderer of Marilyn Monroe.

Diana Trilling (1905-1996), a cultural critic, writer for *The Nation*, and member of a circle of scholars known as the "New York intellectuals" was another of the first females to publish a celebration of Marilyn's remarkable feminine vitality and artistic contribution. Trilling expressed personal surprise at her own reaction to an excerpt of Marilyn's performance in a trailer for *Bus Stop* on television. Marilyn radiated a "glow of something beyond the ordinarily human," Trilling stated, and admitted never before experiencing such a strong emotional reaction to any other actress. Trilling described Marilyn as "alive in a way not granted for the rest of us" and having exhibited "a charge of vitality" which "altered our imagination of life." Trilling concludes that in having accomplished this, Marilyn was the master of a wondrous art form.

Like Rand, Trilling mourned Marilyn as a collective and personal loss and compared her suicide to Ernest Hemingway's:

> Of Ernest Hemingway, for example, I feel much as I do of Marilyn Monroe, that he was unable to marshal any adequate defense against the painful events of his childhood...He was an innocent man, not a naive man, though not always intelligent. Marilyn Monroe offers us a similar paradox. Even when she symbolized an extreme of experience, of sexual knowingness, she took each new circumstance of life, as it came to her or as she sought it, like a newborn babe. And yet this was what made her luminous—her innocence. The glow was not rubbed off her by her experience of the ugliness of life because finally, in some vital depth, she had been untouched by it.

Other contemporary female writers like Claire Booth Luce (1903-1987) saw little beyond Marilyn as a symbol of feminine charm and beauty, or as a victim. Luce's theory about Marilyn's death appeared in the August 7, 1964 issue of *Life,* featuring a rather pensive portrait by Milton Greene and the headline "What Really Killed Marilyn." Inside, Luce's essay "The 'Love Goddess' Who Never Found Any

Love," defended Hollywood against growing accusations of culpability for Marilyn's demise. "Her despair at the end was perhaps akin to that of a painter who discovers he is going blind, or of a pianist whose hands are becoming arthritic," Luce postulated, reducing Marilyn solely to sexual artifice. "Surely she realized that the mob worship of her for her pure sexuality could not last more than a few years longer. Breasts, belly, bottom must one day sag. She was 36, and her mirror had begun to warn her." This flawed hypothesis, minimizing and simplifying Marilyn's final depression into a fear of aging, exemplifies the era in which it was written.

With more accuracy, Luce explored the negative impact of Marilyn's childhood sexual abuse. Norma Jeane's offender instilled a tangled perception of sex, money, and guilt when he gave her a nickel to keep the secret of molestation. Interestingly, Luce, a conservative author and playwright, offered no insight into Marilyn's symptoms of depression as the cause of her suicide. This article, like many written during Marilyn's lifetime, compared her to the fairy tale character of Cinderella, but Luce explains the twist of a doomed—rather than happy—ending: "Cinderella lives happily ever after only in the fairy tale. In real life, no matter how many clothes she puts on—or takes off—her heart remains embittered and her spirit soiled by the ashes she swept in childhood."

Luce, who had served as a U.S. Congresswoman and associated with the conservative wing of the Republican Party, observed a rather shallow irony in her essay: "Marilyn died, really, on a Saturday night. The girl whose translucent beauty had made her the 'love object' of millions of unknown lonely or unsatisfied males had no date that evening."

* * *

In January 1964, Lincoln Center Repertory Theatre announced its inaugural production of an original Arthur Miller play directed by Eli Kazan, their first collaboration in thirteen years. Miller had first met Marilyn through Kazan in 1951, after she had attempted suicide in response to Johnny Hyde's death. The triangle's association now came full circle in 1964, albeit without Marilyn. The play's title, *After the Fall*, was inspired by a novella by Camus about a man struggling with guilt and shame after the suicide of a woman he loved. Miller's work seemed an effort to exorcise Marilyn's ghost and offer a testimonial to the world of his inability to have saved her. "*I loved that girl!*" extolls the protagonist. However, critics such as Graham McCann noted the script's "shocking absence of love."

After the Fall is a memory play about a New York lawyer, Quentin, racked by self-doubt and guilt. The character appears to be an autobiographical exploration of Miller's conscious, delving into his relationships with women, a national communist witch-hunt, and the Holocaust. Like Miller, Quentin was once a communist who had married three times. His first wife accused him of treating her as if she did not exist. His second wife, Maggie, was a switchboard operator who became a sexy jazz vocalist. Miller depicts her as shrewish and self-destructive. Quentin's current wife is an intelligent European. Quentin occasionally speaks directly to the audience, and characters wander in and out of scenes, giving the appearance of flashbacks.

Quentin emerges as a self-absorbed know-it-all incapable of loving or grieving. When a friend kills himself before Quentin can legally defend him against charges of communism, he feels relieved. To Maggie, his second wife, Quentin offered the promise of a savior, but left her feeling as though he had betrayed, and so she perceives him as a traitor. Maggie struggles with painful childhood memories and suicidal impulses, which cause Quentin to tell her, "*You want to die, Maggie, and I really don't know how to prevent it.*" After her suicide by an overdose, he feels grateful for the end of his long anguish.

After the Fall opened on January 23, 1964 with Jason Robards as Quentin and Barbara Loden as Maggie. Tom Prideaux, who reviewed the play for *Life* in its February 7, 1964 issue, noted Miller's "hints of self-infatuation" and satisfaction in being adored by women. Miller's empathic treatment of the suicide of Willy Lowman in *Death of a Salesman* is absent for Maggie in *After the Fall.* He depicts her suicidality as a character flaw rather than a manifestation of depression and mental illness. As Maggie's suicide attempts become more lethal, Quentin leaves her. "*A suicide kills two people*," he tells her, "*that's what it's for! So I am removing myself, and perhaps it will lose its point.*"

Quentin briefly touches on Maggie's victimization by her parents, the culture's puritanical sexual code, and her exploitation as an entertainer. If Maggie indeed channels Marilyn, the play reveals a lack of insight into the source of her despair. Later in life, Miller would identify the serious damage created by Marilyn's early childhood abuse and neglect, but little of this understanding exists in *After the Fall.* Barbara Leaming, a contemporary Monroe biographer, argues Miller exploited her "propensity for self-destruction" to justify his leaving her at the precise time when she was recognizably ill.

Wearing a blonde wig, Loden gave Maggie many of Marilyn's mannerisms, and Miller gave Maggie more biographical elements of his wife than he had given Roslyn in *The Misfits*. In an essay for *Life* arguably abounding with defensiveness and classic denial, Miller insisted Maggie "is not in fact Marilyn Monroe." The character, he explained, represented a human's incapability to "discover in himself the seeds of his own destruction."

Audiences and critics begged to differ. Critic Tom Prideaux argued Miller "not invites, insists on, really" the Marilyn-Miller resemblance. In spite of Miller's vehement repudiation, the play invited numerous comparisons. Maggie's mother attempted to smother her in childhood (a reference to grandmother Della Monroe holding a pillow against Norma Jeane's face); Maggie reveres her vocal coach, Ludwig Reiner (a reference to acting coach Lee Strasberg); she attempts to locate her estranged father in rural California; she dangerously mixes pills and alcohol; and she harbors a strong, fundamental mistrust of others.

Miller also alludes to Maggie's promiscuity early in her career, which was motivated by a need to express gratitude. Maggie's success as a popular singer is based less on her vocal talent than on her strong sexual appeal to men. Quentin speaks of her being "*chewed and spat out by a long line of grinning men!*" Maggie even agonizes about critics not taking her seriously as a performer. "*I'm a joke that brings in money!*" she cries, echoing Marilyn's plea to journalist Richard Meryman to not depict her as a joke.

As Maggie, Marilyn is reduced to a lifeless stereotype—a castrating, shrieking harpy, and Quentin is presented as a long-suffering victim. Fred Lawrence Guiles contended Marilyn would have recognized the fiction in Maggie and applauded the thematic elements of Miller's work. Ironically, the material could have served as a vehicle for Marilyn's stage debut; however, its creation was clearly influenced by her death and may have evolved into a very different work or may never have been finished had she lived.

Disgusting the public as a vulgar attack on a culturally beloved martyr, *After the Fall* was largely despised by critics. "We see little of those flashes of intuitive intelligence that one expects of her," wrote Tom Prideaux of the Monroe-inspired character. Walter Kerr of the *Herald Tribune* noted Quentin/Miller as self-righteous and the play "[resembling] a confessional which Arthur Miller enters as a penitent and from which he emerges a priest." Robert Brustein, writing for the *New Republic*, labeled it "a three and one half hour breach of bad taste." Many people took particular offense at Quentin comparing his pain to the pain of the Jews in the Holocaust, and fellow playwright Noël Coward angrily wrote: "His philosophy is adolescent and sodden with self-pity. His taste is non-existent...Out of all this pretentious, turgid verbosity emerges the character of a silly, dull man with a mediocre mind."

Marilyn, though sometimes controversial, had been generally celebrated and revered by the culture. The romanticized rags-to-riches Cinderella story of an abused waif who searched for love and validation had endeared her to the public, and death by her own hand only deepened public sympathy. Only seven years had passed since Marilyn stood loyally beside her husband during his legal tribulations and in death it seemed he was depicting her as an apathetic tart while her biggest detractors were now canonizing her. "Ironically, in exposing Marilyn as he did," Barbara Leaming observed, "Miller, who had refused to name names, became something of an 'informer' himself."

Miller had failed to include Marilyn's noble qualities and defining characteristics. Even Miller's attorney, Joe Rauh, lambasted the playwright's ingratitude for Marilyn's support during the HUAC trial: "Couldn't he at least give her credit for having been ready to sacrifice everything for him?" Many of Marilyn's friends who shared friendships with Miller during their marriage felt personally betrayed. The Rostens and Strasbergs were aghast. Berniece Miracle felt ill and angry.

Despite the fact that Marilyn hurt her by engaging in an affair with her husband, Simone Signoret came to her defense: "It's sad that a Kazan-Miller reassociation was celebrated across a box called a coffin. A coffin for a blonde. It seems to me that they disfigured her, at least in part; in any case, they betrayed what was best in her." John Springer vowed never to forgive Miller for depicting Marilyn as vicious, drug-addicted, and promiscuous. "None of her sweetness or vulnerability came into that character..." he said. "He piously proclaimed later that he certainly didn't mean Marilyn. That's bullshit!"

Whether or not Maggie truly represented Miller's perception of Marilyn simply did not matter. The play opened seventeen months after Marilyn's death and was written by her third husband, the man who had offered a biographical representation of her in *The Misfits* only three years earlier. Once again, art appeared to be imitating life. Both the public and critics expected either a poignant enlightenment about Marilyn's personal struggle, or a reverent silence like DiMaggio's. Robert Brustein found it "astonishing that a playwright, whose major business is perception, could live with this unfortunate woman for over four years, and yet be capable of no greater insight than those of...a professional theatre columnist." If Marilyn's endorsement of Miller during the Communist witch hunts had, indeed, improved public opinion of him, *After the Fall* degraded him as disloyal and denigrating.

Rather than spin the obvious elements of his real life into inspiration for a dramatic piece, common for playwrights such as Eugene O'Neill and Tennessee Williams, Miller asked for his play to be judged strictly on its own merits. "I feel it is ingenuous for him to hope this..." wrote Tom Prideaux. "It comes with the territory." In return, Miller accused his harshest critics of hypocrisy for having scoffed at Marilyn's ambitions, been "overtly vicious to her both professionally and in print," and now crying "in outrage that Maggie's suffering should be connected with Marilyn's." Undeniably, there was some truth to this charge, but roles had reversed; Miller now appeared to conspire with Marilyn's former detractors, after they evolved to appreciate and glorify her in death.

Joe DiMaggio survived Marilyn by thirty-seven years. Unlike her other two husbands, he remained faithful to Marilyn in death, never remarrying, declining to speak of her in public, and steadfastly refusing to exploit their relationship. The public perceived this as demonstration of his eternal love and devotion. "You know,

Morris," DiMaggio once said to Morris Engelberg, "instead of kissing [Marilyn] on the altar, I kissed her in her casket." Engelberg told author Jay Margolis, "No woman in the world will ever be loved the way he loved her. He loved her in life and in death." Continuing to show his undying love for her, DiMaggio endlessly played a recording of his and Marilyn's song, "Embraceable You," in his car.

* * *

Marilyn Remembered, a Los Angeles fan club organized by Greg Schreiner in 1982, conducted a memorial service each August 5th at the Westwood Memorial Cemetery chapel and at Marilyn's crypt. Memorial services follow the original funeral, and include the playing of an audiotape of the eulogy with the preserved sobs of Marilyn's mourners. Some of Marilyn's surviving friends and co-workers participated as guest speakers at the tributes and other gatherings. The fan club also donated a marbled bench with a bronze plaque inscription to Marilyn, and placed it near her crypt.

Newspapers, magazines and television documentaries marked the tenth, twentieth, thirtieth, fortieth, and fiftieth anniversaries of her death, reviving her each decade and reinterpreting her life based upon contemporary actresses. She has been compared to Farrah Fawcett in the 1970s, Jessica Lange in the 1980s, Madonna in the 1990s, Charlize Theron in the 2000s, and Scarlett Johansson in the 2010s.

As the sexy blonde star of the television series *Charlie's Angels*, Fawcett (1947-2009) posed for a pin-up poster in a red bathing suit that sold 12 million copies and hung on the walls of American teen males' bedrooms, dormatories, and locker rooms across the nation. Like Marilyn's nude calendar, it propelled her into stardom in the mid-1970s. At the age of thirty-seven, Fawcett tackled the dramatic roles of an abused wife in *The Burning Bed* (1984) and the empowered victim of an attempted rape in *Extremities* (1986) before returning to her sexy roots in the 1990s by posing for *Playboy*.

Life compared Jessica Lange (born 1949), also a sexy blonde with enormous acting skill, to Marilyn when she skyrocketed to fame in the early 1980s. Lange began her career as a giant ape's hostage in the remake of *King Kong* (1976). She earned two Oscar nominations in 1982 for her sexy role in *Tootsie* and for her portrayal of actress Frances Farmer—who suffered from mental illness—in *Frances*. In

Tootsie, Lange portrayed a soap opera actress who rejects an actor, but develops a close relationship with him after he disguises himself in drag in order to find work and becomes her co-star. The role is reminiscent of Marilyn's character, Sugar in Some *Like It Hot*, but Lange resented the comparison to a tragic figure who many critics refused to regard as a serious actress. Lange's illustrious career and current relevancy as a leading dramatic actress over the age of sixty suggest the dramatic heights Marilyn would have achieved, had she lived thirty years after her time or past the age of forty.

Blonde (sometimes) singer-songwriter, icon, and "Queen of Pop" Madonna (born 1958) parodied Marilyn's screen image in the 1985 music video *Material Girl*, television comedy sketches in *Saturday Night Live*, public appearances, and a 1991 *Vanity Fair* photo spread. She emerged as a sex symbol of the 1980s and 1990s through provocative lyrics, dance moves, music videos, and her erotic photo book, *Sex* (1992). Unlike Marilyn, Madonna achieved an unprecedented level of power in her industry as an artist and businesswoman. She founded an entertainment company and is recognized as the best-selling female recording artist of all time.

Charlize Theron (born 1975) perhaps shares the most strikingly physical similarity to Marilyn. She rose to fame following a career as a runway and advertising model in a series of films roles during the turn of the century such as a sexy Scandinavian hit woman in *2 Days in the Valley* (1996), an oversexed supermodel in Woody Allen's *Celebrity* (1998), and a female employee who launches a class action sexual harassment suit against a major corporation in *North Country* (2005). Through obliterating her considerable beauty by gaining weight, wearing prosthetic dentures, and thinning her blonde tresses, Theron transformed into serial killer Aileen Wuornos in *Monster* (2003) and delivered a powerhouse performance that earned the Best Actress Oscar. In 2006, the media reported on Theron starring in Tom Hanks' biopic of Marilyn's life, which never came to fruition, but the actress appeared with a computer-generated likeness of Marilyn in a television commercial for a Dior fragrance.

Finally, Scarlett Johansson (born 1984), deemed one of sexiest women in Hollywood by several men's magazines and garnering acclaim as an actress, echoes Marilyn today. Playing smart, sexy blondes in both comedies and dramas—*Lost in Translation* (2003),

Match Point (2005), and *Vicky Cristina Barcelona* (2008)—Johansson's career suggests the roles for which a young Marilyn would have been suited if she had exploded on the scene in the early 2000s rather than the early 1950s. Portraying actress Janet Leigh in *Hitchcock* (2012), about the production of the film *Psycho*, Johansson bore an uncanny resemblance to Marilyn circa 1959-1960.

Marilyn's successors had the advantage of working in the film industry during an era when women yielded more power than in the previous generation. Actresses of today benefit from the culture accepting sensuality, intelligence, and serious drama as consonant rather than mutually exclusive. Unrestricted by the typecasting Hollywood studio system as well as narrow and puritanical societal attitudes toward women and sexuality, these modern actresses exercise freedom in seeking opportunities to broaden their range in roles and to explore facets of their talents for which Marilyn was fighting. Even without today's choices, Marilyn remains relevant, revered, and beloved as a national treasure who evokes deep compassion in millions globally, in a way none of her successors may ever achieve.

Chapter Thirty-Six: The Estate

Marilyn's will established $100,000 in trust to ensure a comfortable retirement for her mentally ill mother, Gladys Baker, dedicated secretary, May Reis, and the elderly widow of her acting coach, Mrs. Michael Chekhov. "She decided to keep me without worries until it die," Chekhov told *Life*. Following their deaths, the trust would transfer to her New York psychiatrist, Dr. Marianne Kris, for the furtherance of a psychiatric institution of her choice. Marilyn also included financial bequests to her half-sister, Berniece Miracle, and to poet Norman Rosten and his wife for the education of their daughter, Patricia.

Attorney Aaron Frosch fulfilled his role as executor by filing the will for probate in New York County Surrogate Court rather than in California, avoiding the reduction of these legacies by a high state inheritance tax. Unencumbered by the debts, tax claims or pending lawsuits, the value of Marilyn's estate was estimated at nearing $1 million. According to an article in *Time*, "for all her troubled personal life, her business affairs seemed in extraordinarily good order." Marilyn and her attorney never anticipated the perpetuated value of her image for licensing, a recent phenomenon specific to legends Elvis Presley, James Dean, and herself—but with no precedence in her lifetime.

Marilyn designated acting coach, Lee Strasberg, as the recipient of her personal effects and clothing with a charge to "distribute these, in his sole discretion, among my friends, colleagues and those to whom I am devoted." Marilyn divided the remainder of her estate among May Reis and Dr. Kris at twenty-five percent each—stipulating Kris donate her share to charity—and the balance to Lee Strasberg. Gloria Lovell, Marilyn's former neighbor on Doheny Drive, adopted Maf-Honey.

Just days before her death, Marilyn allegedly scheduled an appointment with Milton Rudin on Monday, August 6 for the purpose of changing the will. Her specific plans for modification remain unknown.

On September 6, Inez Melson wrote to DiMaggio of her suspicions of Frosch and the Strasbergs colluding to place undue influence on Marilyn, so that they might profit from her death. Coincidentally, a photograph of Frosch and Paula leaving his office shortly after Marilyn's death was published in newspapers. Melson apologized for sounding like an episode of the television courtroom drama *Perry Mason* and requested DiMaggio's assistance in investigating Marilyn's destinations during the seven hours she employed rental car services on the day "our baby executed her will."

Melson also referenced the oddity of Frosch and his secretary, Louise White, having signed the will as witnesses under Marilyn's signature. In fear of Gladys receiving an insufficient annual income from the trust, Melson challenged the will in court. Judge S. Samuel Falco heard the testimony of Frosch and White and dismissed Melson's charges on October 30, based upon inadequate proof.

Marilyn's estate amounted to $930,626 with $183,941 in cash and $830,646 in debt. Assets included ten percent share of royalties from *Some Like It Hot* and *The Misfits*, an RCA record contract, rights to the autobiography, *My Story*, and one hundred one shares of Marilyn Monroe Productions. The estate was rich in assets but low in cash. According to Lois Banner, Marilyn avoided heavy taxes by setting up her salary as deferred income. When she was no longer alive to claim deductions, the $150,000 per year income fell into a high tax bracket.

Frosch neglected to renew Marilyn Monroe Productions' distribution rights to *The Prince and the Showgirl* and lost the potential for revenue needed to fulfill Marilyn's bequests. The estate made its first beneficiary payment in 1971 to May Reis. The Rostens received a payment for their daughter's education in 1975, seven years after she graduated college. Mrs. Michael Chekhov's estate received the first payment in 1976, six years following her death. Frosch failed to pay Rockhaven Sanitarium in entirety for Gladys' care and made numerous management errors in his financial favor. In 1981, Marianne Kris sued Frosch for plundering the estate, validating Cherie Redmond's mistrust in him while Marilyn was alive.

Marilyn entrusted Lee Strasberg with the task of distributing her personal effects and clothing among friends and colleagues, but the bulk of her property from the New York apartment and Brentwood hacienda would be preserved in a vault at J. Santini & Brothers Fireproof Storage in New York for the following thirty-seven years. Like a grieving mother, Paula Strasberg had completely cleaned out Marilyn's residences with the help of a maid, saving nearly everything, even greasy oven mitts. In early 1963, the Strasbergs rejected a proposal of a museum to display Marilyn's wardrobe and possessions, and told *Life* of plans to auction them as a benefit for the Actors Studio.

Paula succumbed to cancer in 1966, and a year later, Anna Mizrahi auditioned for admission to the Actors Studio. The Venezuelan-born actress lost to Jack Nicholson, but her consolation was found in marrying the widowed Strasberg, nearly forty years her senior. When Strasberg died in 1982, ownership of Marilyn's property transferred to his second wife, whom Marilyn never knew. John and Susan Strasberg had close, personal relationships with Marilyn, but their father had disinherited them.

Anna Mizrahi Strasberg received the bulk of Monroe's estate as a result of the residuary clause in her will stipulating "all the rest, residue and remainder of my estate, both real and personal" be bequeathed to May Reis, Dr. Kris, and Lee Strasberg—the latter receiving fifty percent of the estate. When Strasberg died in 1982, his inheritance passed to his wife, Anna.

Strasberg launched Marilyn Monroe LLC, a licensing business in 1982, and hired Los Angeles attorney Roger Richman to control publicity rights over Marilyn Monroe's image. Under Richman's management between 1983 and 1995, Marilyn's estate earned over $7.5 million from many licensing deals, such as a Marilyn Monroe boutique at Bloomingdale's New York department store; print and television advertisements for Absolut vodka; cosmetics manufactured by Revlon Inc.; and an assortment of calendars, coffee mugs, T-shirts, porcelain dolls, collector plates, and Christmas tree ornaments. The proceeds went to Strasberg and the Anna Freud Center, formerly Hampstead Child Therapy Clinic, in London, which inherited Marianne Kris' stake.

After Aaron Frosch's death in 1989, the New York County Surrogate's Court appointed Anna Strasberg as the administrator of the Monroe estate and, in 2001, granted her permission to close the estate and transfer its remaining assets to Marilyn Monroe LLC.

* * *

When Milton Rudin arrived at Marilyn's hacienda on the morning of August 5, 1962, he summoned Inez Melson to unlock Marilyn's filing cabinets, remove her personal diaries and documents, and secure them. As the court-appointed guardian of Gladys Baker, Melson qualified as Marilyn's closest relative. Rudin later petitioned the probate court to designate Melson as administrator of Marilyn's property in Los Angeles in order to liquidate the hacienda and possessions by auction. Melson became the gatekeeper of over ten thousand documents, the contents of two filing cabinets—one tan and one gray—purchased by Marilyn in New York in 1958 and relocated to California in 1962. Marilyn sent the tan cabinet to her dressing room on the Fox lot and the gray one to Norman Jeffries for eventual delivery to her hacienda.

Melson fulfilled her legal obligation by selling the hacienda, auctioning the furnishings, and shipping remaining items to Lee Strasberg as beneficiary of personal effects as stipulated in the will. However, she hoarded a trove of Marilyn's most personal articles. Arguably, her motivation was both protection of Marilyn's privacy and her emotional attachment to Marilyn through some of her most personal articles.

By shipping the tan cabinet to her own home in the Hollywood Hills and purchasing the gray one under an assumed name at the auction she held, Melson guarded what Lois Banner referred to as the "Rosetta Stones of Marilyn Monroe scholarship" until her death in 1986. Melson kept Marilyn's reproduction of a Rodin's sculpture, her emerald green gown by Norman Norell, and the JFK Birthday gala gown by Jean-Louis. Although Melson told the media she intended someday to donate the pieces to a museum dedicated to preserving Marilyn's memory, Anna Strasberg demanded their return. Melson complied.

According to an article in the October 2008 issue of *Vanity Fair*, "The Things She Left Behind," the contents of Marilyn's filing cabinets passed to Ruth Conroy, Melson's sister-in-law, until her death in 2001. Conroy's son, Millington Conroy, inherited the collection and contacted photographer Mark Anderson to document it, and Lois Banner to compose accompanying text for publication. Anna Strasberg sued Conroy in 1995 for false ownership, and a jury acted as King Solomon by delivering a verdict to divide the collection between them. Strasberg appealed the case based upon Melson's acquisition that the contents of the gray cabinet were under an assumed name. The collection was ultimately shared with the public through the publication of *Fragments: Poems, Intimate Notes, Letters by Marilyn Monroe* (2010) edited by Bernard Comment and Stanley Buchthal, and *MM-Personal: From the Private Archive of Marilyn Monroe* (2011) by Lois Banner.

* * *

On the day of Marilyn's death, Dr. Gilbert Nunez and his wife, Betty, placed a sales contract on her home with their realtor. An additional six prospective buyers also signed contracts with their respective realtors on the same day. While the courts reviewed the validity of the will, a bidding war ensued and resulted in legal action. The judge ruled that the property would be sold at a purchase price ten percent over the highest bid. In September 1963, the Nunez family became the new owners at a price five times the market value, and purchased many of the home's contents, including Marilyn's Hoover upright vacuum sweeper. For many years, the home and furnishings would be preserved and the interior would look very much as Marilyn had left it. In May 1997, the Nunez family would offer at auction many of Marilyn's furnishings and possessions including a kitchen chopping block, expected to sell for $800-1,200, dressing mirror ($15,000-20,000), gardening hat ($4,000-6,000), and dining room table ($20,000-25,000).

Following Marilyn's death, the house at 12305 Fifth Helena Drive experienced many incarnations. Subsequent owners made significant structural changes. The space between the guesthouse and main house was converted into interior space. As a result, the shade tree Marilyn planted in the patio next to her kitchen was removed. The guesthouse was converted to a rental property, and the kitchen was enlarged and modernized. A studio was built beside the pool near the rear bedrooms. Eventually, the bright Mexican tiles chosen by Marilyn were removed, and collectors spent in excess of $800 for one piece of them. Terracotta tile floors replaced the white wool carpeting. Finally, the original scalloped wooden fence purchased by Marilyn from Raese Period Furniture was replaced with an electronic steel barrier. During the 1984 Olympics, held in Los Angeles, the owner removed the original gates to make the house less recognizable to the many tourists invading the city that year who might locate the house by this familiar feature.

Film director Michael Ritchie purchased Marilyn's former home in 1994 from Jill Middleman for $995,000. It remained vacant and in a dreadful state of disrepair. Rumors spread in the media that it would be leveled for the construction of a larger home or that it would be relocated to a Hollywood theme park in California or Florida. Public records show Cynthia and Henry Rust subsequently purchased the house for $925,000 in 1996.

Marilyn's hacienda, expanded to four bedrooms, three bathrooms, and 2,624 square feet of living space, listed at $3,595,000 in July 2010 on the website of David Offer's Prudential California Realty. Described as "sprawling and authentic," the listing sparked instant reaction from potential buyers, as some waited outside the gate the next day to tour the home. According to the *Los Angeles Times*, the hacienda was in escrow within two weeks and sold above its asking price for $3.85 million.

* * *

In October 1999, Anna Strasberg offered the personal property of Marilyn Monroe for auction at Christie's in New York. The auction's total sale would exceed $13,000,000 and set a world record for the sale of a woman's costume by the $1,267,000 purchase of the JFK birthday gala gown. Debbie Reynolds' auction of the white dress from *The Seven Year Itch* would ultimately fetch an astronomical $5,600,000 in June 2011.

Many considered the auction a blatant disregard for Marilyn's wishes. This did not prevent thousands of diversified fans from viewing the relics tastefully on display at Christie's New York location at Rockefeller Plaza. Curiosity about Marilyn's belongings rivaled interest in the treasures from the tomb of Egyptian pharaoh Tutankhamun. The exhibition toured Los Angeles, London, Paris, Buenos Aires, and St. Petersburg, Florida before returning to Manhattan for the two-day auction, broadcast on the American

Movie Classics cable television network and the Internet. The hardcover 411-page auction catalogue sold out at $85 per copy.

Examination of the relics Marilyn left in the care of Strasberg would redefine her at the close of the century. She would emerge as an actress and intellectual serious about her craft and ambitious in self-improvement. Marilyn's library revealed her interests in world literature, art, religion, philosophy, and psychology. Many of her books contained handwritten personal references in the margins. "We were also impressed at how hard she worked on each and every line of dialogue she spoke…" wrote Nancy Valentino of Christie's, who perused Marilyn's heavily annotated film scripts and prompt books in preparation for the auction. "What she made look easy and natural was actually the result of endless study, precise concentration, and extreme passion with discipline."

When employees of Christie's unpacked and catalogued the clothing, they noticed a faint scent of Marilyn's favorite perfume, *Chanel No. 5*. Traces of Marilyn lingered through the tiny imprints of her toes in the insoles of her shoes. Her wardrobe was surprisingly unpretentious and conservative. "Marilyn was pretty simple and didn't own many expensive things," observed Greg Schreiner of *Marilyn Remembered* fan club.

Three notes by Marilyn were especially chilling. On a sheet of lined paper, she wrote, "*if I have to kill myself, I must do it.*" Another note on engraved personal stationery reads, "*he does not love me.*" A handwritten poem was discovered folded in a book. Titled "A Sorry Song," it contains the lines: "*They say I'm lucky to be alive/it's hard to figure out/when everything I feel—hurts!*" One doubts Marilyn ever wanted these private laments shared with the world, but Strasberg sold them for nearly fifty thousand dollars rather than donating them to surviving blood relatives or to the Smithsonian Institute.

Over three thousand bidders attended the auction with admission based on a lottery. Christie's Auction House installed one hundred telephone lines, double the normal capacity, to accommodate phone bids from passionate buyers around the globe. Many challenged the successful hammer bidders to create a permanent museum in honor of Marilyn's legacy as a waif who captured the collective heart of America.

Massimo Ferragamo reclaimed a pair of red beaded satin pumps originally created for the actress by his father, Salvatore; where they joined the family's shoe museum in Florence, Italy. Aspiring chef Nicole Martin obtained Marilyn's yellow enamel Le Creuset cookware and well-worn copper pots for $22,000, and planned to use them to host high-profile charity dinner celebrations. Edward Meyer of *Ripley's Believe It Or Not* secured Marilyn's Mexican sweater for $167,500, a makeup box for $266,500 and last driver's license, issued July 11, 1962. Robert Schagrin and Peter Siegel acquired her *Union Prayer Book for Jewish Worship*. DiMaggio's diamond eternity wedding ring, missing one of its thirty-six stones, sold for $772,500. Singer Mariah Carey purchased the baby grand piano for $662,500. Marilyn's 1959 and 1962 Golden Globe Awards fetched $140,000 and $184,000 respectively.

Over $600,000 derived from the sale of Marilyn's massive personal library benefitted the Literacy Foundation, a New York literacy organization. The library included first editions of Kerouac and Hemingway, *Dr. Spock's Baby and Childcare Book*, and the work of Joyce, Camus, and Tolstoy. Over $400,000 derived from the sale of her furs benefitted the World Wildlife Fund.

The painting of an adobe, once displayed above a Mexican bench in the Brentwood hacienda, sold to a collector who had acquired the bench from an earlier auction and reunited the two pieces in his Los Angles home. The vessel inscribed *Un Recuerdo de Toluca*, displayed beside Marilyn's bed, fetched $8,050, in lot 451 along with nine other pieces of Mexican pottery.

Arguably, Marilyn would have been appalled by an auction of her personal possessions as she entrusted them to her mentor for distribution among those she loved. With due respect to Anna Strasberg, Marilyn's specific instructions to Lee Strasberg indicate she had given thought to the manner of dispersing her property with no intention of strangers purchasing them at auction. Mercifully, Strasberg and Christie's exercised taste in archiving and displaying the property like museum curators. The media, however, observed this as an opportunity for everyman to "purchase a piece of Monroe." Marilyn would likely have endorsed the donation of a portion of the proceeds to charities.

Julien's auction house offered a smaller collection of Marilyn's personal property in June 2005, comprising only two hundred eighty-seven lots of mostly clothing, correspondence, and ephemera. Her 1962 personal address and telephone book revealed for once and all those whom she considered friends. Its exclusion of those who claimed to have known her, many the authors of sensational books, gave Marilyn a voice to rebuke their allegations long after death silenced her.

* * *

Just as Marilyn's will was contested and the sale of her hacienda involved litigation by competing buyers, nearly five decades later, she was again the center of a bitter legal dispute over the control of licensing rights to her lucrative image. Elvis Presley reins as the highest-earning deceased celebrity, but Marilyn ranks ninth on the short list—despite her death occurring first—with $27 million in income in 2011. Anna Strasberg and CMG Worldwide, her Indiana-based business partner, sued the families of several deceased photographersfor violation of publicity rights by their exclusion of Marilyn Monroe LLC (MM LLC) from the profits earned from their portraits of Marilyn.

The central issue in four lawsuits in Indiana, New York, and California was Marilyn's residency at the time of death, an issue worth a fortune to the five litigants. Publicity rights fall under the jurisdiction of state laws, unlike copyrights, which are protected by federal law. California grants postmortem publicity rights, permitting heirs to profit, and New York does not acknowledge the publicity rights of dead celebrities or the ability to bequeath them in a will. Marilyn was a resident of New York when she died in her California home.

As the majority owner of rights, Strasberg insisted Marilyn was a resident of California. The families of photographers Tom Kelley, Joshua Greene, and Sam Shaw—who inherited ownership of copyrighted images of Marilyn and licensed the photos to the manufacturers of calendars, drinking mugs, and handbags—declared that she was a resident of New York.

Litigant Joshua Greene, son of Milton Greene, manages his father's prolific archive. He accused MM LLC and CMG of "killing the goose that lays the golden egg," since manufacturers avoided licensing contracts that included payment of fees to more than one holder of rights. Larry Shaw and Tom Kelley Jr. abandoned their own photography businesses to manage their deceased fathers' archives of Marilyn Monroe photographs. Shaw's archive earned more than $100,000 annually in licensing fees, and Kelley's earned about $300,000 from the famous "red velvet" nude portraits.

In 2006, a Target department store in Indiana sold Marilyn t-shirts with the inscription "Shaw Family Archives" (SFA). As holder of Marilyn's postmortem right of publicity, MM LLC sued SFA in both New York and California. Both District Courts held that that at the time of Marilyn's death, no right of publicity existed under California, New York, or Indiana law, and that the estate and MM LLC had no legal right to profit from Marilyn's celebrity.

In 2007, the Shaw Family Archives (SFA) countersued CMG in the Southern District of New York. The legal issue was whether MM LLC held the actress's post-mortem right of publicity. Shaw's children argued that MM LLC and CMG could only declare ownership of property actually owned by Marilyn at the time of her death.

On May 4, 2007, the court found SFA was entitled to a judgment because Marilyn was not a resident of Indiana at the time of her death and, therefore, she could not transfer her right of publicity through her will. Indeed, Marilyn was either a resident of California or New York, and neither state recognized a postmortem right of publicity. Marilyn's will did not mention a right of publicity, and no federal law governs the right of publicity. In New York, the right of publicity does not survive the decedent. Since Marilyn died before California's Celebrity Rights Act was passed in 1985, and the state of New York does not recognize a right of publicity after the celebrity's death, her name and image entered the public domain in those states as well as any other state that does not recognize the postmortem right of publicity.

In October of 2007, California Governor Arnold Schwarzenegger signed Senate Bill 771 into law, creating descendible rights of publicity that last seventy years after death and retroactively applied to any person deceased after January 1, 1938. This allowed post-mortem right of publicity to transfer to non-family members named in the residuary clause in a will, contingent upon the decedent being a resident of California at the time of death. Along with the Screen Actors Guild, Anna Strasberg had lobbied for the passage of the law, which was made retroactive and, thus, applied to Marilyn's estate.

The passage of this progressive and controversial law did not settle the case. In May 2008, the District Court for the Central District of California held that Marilyn was a resident of New York at the time of her death, since the executors of her estate had chosen New York as her place of residence by probating her will there. Since New York does not allow postmortem rights of publicity, Marilyn's estate could not claim those rights under California law. By the selection of New York over California, the executors prevented the residuary beneficiary, MM LLC, from acquiring exclusive control of Marilyn's postmortem right of publicity. Their choice to probate the estate in New York was solely based upon California inheritance taxes being higher than New York's.

The Ninth United States Circuit Court of Appeal in San Francisco ruled in September 2012 that MM LLC had no legal power to prevent The Milton Greene Archives from selling her image without paying for publicity rights. "This is a textbook case for applying judicial estoppel," wrote Judge Kim McLane Wardlaw in her ruling. "Monroe's representatives took one position on Monroe's domicile at death for forty years, and then changed their position when it was to their great financial advantage; an advantage they secured years after Monroe's death by convincing the California legislature to create rights that did not exist when Monroe died. Marilyn Monroe is often quoted as saying, 'If you're going to be two-faced, at least make one of them pretty.' There is nothing pretty in Monroe LLC's about-face on the issue of domicile."

In a footnote to its ruling, Judge Wardlaw astutely pointed to Marilyn having prophesized the clash over rights to her image and its conclusion, saying, "We observe that the lengthy dispute over the exploitation of Marilyn Monroe's persona has ended in exactly the way that Monroe herself predicted more than fifty years ago." [Marilyn said:] 'I knew I belonged to the public and to the world, not because I was talented or even beautiful but because I had never belonged to anything or anyone else.'"

Chapter Thirty-Seven: **The Legend & The Myth**

Part One: **Conspiracy Theories**

Nearly fifty years of conspiracy theories have reduced Marilyn to a one-dimensional victim in an over-simplified 'whodunit' similar to the children's game of *Clue. Colonel Mustard committed the murder in the Library with the candlestick* becomes *Robert Kennedy killed Marilyn in the bedroom with a lethal injection.* Tabloid television of the late twentieth and early twenty-first centuries thrived on the public's hunger for conspiracy theories involving the government and entertainment industry with equal doses of sex and violence thrown in to appeal to our most primal drives.

Year after year, new books, articles, and television "documentaries" sell recycled versions of a Monroe murder plot. The conspiracy theories become circular, newer ones refer to or expand upon previous theories, and in some cases, contradict them. The theories introduced by Frank Capell, Robert Slatzer, Jack Clemmons, Lionel Grandison, and Jeanne Carmen, were later accepted by biographers Anthony Summers and Donald H. Wolfe, and debunked by Donald Spoto. However, the reiteration of these estimations influenced both the media and the general public to accept them as fact.

Why are we so enthralled by conspiracies theories? Scholar Mark Fenster effectively explains conspiracy theories in the post-Watergate and post-9/11 era as our cultural means of interpreting and narrating the abundance of information hurled at us by global mass media. Robert Alan Goldberg argues this is a timeworn practice. Since the colonial period, Americans have entertained notions of vast, subversive plots. In *Enemies Within*, Goldberg says the media's validation and distribution of conspiracy theories, combined with the behavior of elected officials having damaged public faith and confidence, have created fertile ground for disturbed rhetoric and thinking in America.

Why is Marilyn Monroe the focus of so many conspiracy theories? She has been culturally defined as a sexy victim, used by powerful men, and dead before her time. Conspiracy theories have historically followed those who died in youth or mid-life: Princess Diana of Wales (often compared to Marilyn and who also died at age thirty-six), Michael Jackson, Natalie Wood, Elvis Presley, and President John F. Kennedy. Occasionally, new information, such as unpublished images, interviews, personal letters or diaries written by Marilyn herself, humanize her and erase the stream of sleaze journalism. Susan Strasberg accurately described this phenomenon through the metaphor of Marilyn as a lotus rising out of the mud.

Sarah Churchwell was the first to explore five decades of fictionalization of Marilyn's life story and the fabrication of conspiracy theories regarding her demise in the scholastic book, *The Many Lives of Marilyn Monroe*:

> The Kennedys' alleged sexual liaison with Marilyn is thus presented as a political liability, whether because she herself was threatening to blow the whistle, or because someone else was. In these stories she is either assassinated by an enemy of the Kennedys to incriminate them, or she is assassinated by the Kennedys or their associates in order to protect their secrets.

We can trace the theories to several authors with dubious credibility, starting with Frank A. Capell and Robert Slatzer, who painted the villain as Robert Kennedy or a "dissident faction of the CIA." Milo Speriglio pointed the finger at Teamsters Union leader Jimmy Hoffa and organized crime boss Sam Giancana. Later, Speriglio accused Joseph Kennedy of hiring Giancana to kill Marilyn because she was pregnant with a Kennedy child. Speriglio's spurious claim was irrefutably ruled out by the autopsy, but conspiracy theorists invalidate the autopsy report as a part of the massive cover-up. Over time, many others stepped forward with more outrageous allegations. In fact, Sarah Churchwell pinpointed one sweeping Internet theory that attributes Marilyn's death to all of the most popular conspiracies combined, thereby satisfying the public's obsession with them;

allegedly, Marilyn knew too much about the Bay of Pigs, the Cuban Missile Crisis, and the UFO that crashed at Roswell, New Mexico, and was therefore silenced by the United States government.

The method of murder varies among the many theories, but there are three possibilities that consistently remain at the top of the list: lethal injection, enema, or suppository. All three involve sexualized metaphoric penetration of the love goddess, as they negate or manipulate the official finding of the autopsy report. Evidence of the murder is professed to be in the form of telephone records, wiretaps, a personal diary, and even Marilyn's own audiotaped voice. All evidence of the murder is reported to be "confiscated," "destroyed," or "missing" and witnesses verify the alleged existence of the evidence through claims of having seen or heard it; however, no witnesses testified under oath.

This all leads to the big question: How did these fables originate?

The earliest murder theory began with ultra-conservative author Frank A. Capell (1907-1980), who introduced the *The Strange Death of Marilyn Monroe* in his self-published "Herald of Freedom," an "anti-Communist educational bi-weekly" pamphlet in 1964. He was the first to name Robert Kennedy as Marilyn's lover, implicate him in her death, and suggest she was murdered by lethal injection, disguised as a suicide. Capell had served as chief of the Subversive Activities Department for the Sheriff of Westchester Country, New York, and harbored hatred of the Kennedys and liberals in general.

By today's standards, Capell would be the equivalent of a fanatic Tea Party member doubtful of President Obama's citizenship. In 1964, Robert Kennedy emerged as an eventual democratic contender for presidency, and Capell's motivation appeared to have been to destroy this possibility through conjecture. Sarah Churchwell cited Capell having quoted controversial columnist Walter Winchell as his main source in *The Strange Death of Marilyn Monroe*, and Winchell having quoted Capell; so in the end, Capell was "simply quoting himself."

Capell was the first to dispute an oral overdose based upon lack of residue of the drugs in Marilyn's stomach and to question the length of time between discovery of the body and the call to the police. He carefully and indirectly implicated Kennedy in Marilyn's death through a series of rhetorical questions: "Was Marilyn about to do some talking? Did she think her involvement was more serious, expecting perhaps a divorce and marriage to her? Since Marilyn could destroy him either by talking or with written evidence, did he decide to take drastic action?" Capell may have borrowed this technique from Winchell, who perfected the use of slang in reporting stories that, if reported with precise semantics, might have led to legal challenges.

Capell also suggested Engelberg's participation in the plot based upon his pronouncing the time of death as when the body was discovered, rather than taking in to account the advanced state of rigor mortis. Intimating a broad conspiracy, Capell cast suspicion on other members of Marilyn's inner circle as accessories to a crime. He alleged Eunice Murray "came into a bit of money," alluding to a bribe for her silence, and took an extended European vacation. In reality, Murray had planned the trip while Marilyn was alive. In Capell's words, Patricia Newcomb was "whisked to Hyannisport and thence to Europe, also for an extended vacation..." and later "placed on government payroll," implying that she had accepted money in exchange for silence. Capell published Newcomb's application for the position of "Information Specialist (motion pictures)" for the United States Information Agency which she began on May 6, 1963. Newcomb later resigned to work for Pierre Salinger's campaign for United States Senate, only to be rehired as a consultant with the Justice Department.

A photograph of Newcomb with President Kennedy, Jean Kennedy Smith, and Patricia Kennedy Lawford aboard his sailboat, *Manitou*, appears on the Internet and has been used to suggest she served as an accomplice to the Kennedys' alleged cover-up of Marilyn's death. The photograph is dated August 12, 1962, four days after the funeral. It is possible that Newcomb accompanied Patricia Lawford back to Hyannisport after the funeral. However, the photograph proves nothing.

The Strange Death of Marilyn Monroe points to the Kennedys or one of their enemies, such as Jimmy Hoffa, as having ordered the wire-tapping of Marilyn's telephones and the bugging of her house. Capell names Bernard Spindel or Fred Otash as the wire tapper. According to the news articles, police raided Spindel's Manhattan house in 1966 and confiscated his collection of tapes. No recordings of Marilyn and the Kennedys have ever been produced, but subsequent conspiracy theorists rely upon testimonials by sources who claim to have heard them. Had the mafia or J. Edgar Hoover had access to audiotaped evidence of an affair, either or both powers would have used it to destroy Robert Kennedy's presidential campaign in 1968.

Capell's credibility crumbles upon further investigation. He associated with Jack Clemmons, the first police officer to arrive at Marilyn's death scene. Clemmons shared Capell's conservative political view and fraternized with the Police and Fire Rescue Association, a conservative group whose mission was to expose "subversive activities which threaten our American way of life." The most compelling evidence discrediting both men is found in an article in the March 5, 1965 issue of *Time* that reported they were indicted by a Los Angeles grand jury for involvement in circulating a forged affidavit smearing the name of California Senator Thomas Kuchel. Having provoked racist groups by supporting the Civil Rights Act of 1964, Kuchel campaigned against Barry Goldwater, a champion of conservatism and leader of right-wing extremists and racists who supported nuclear war, the elimination of civil rights, and abolishment of social welfare programs.

Capell and Clemmons claimed the affidavit was signed by a police officer who had arrested Kuchel in 1949 for drunkenness and engaging in a homosexual act. When Kuchel learned of the document, he requested an investigation by the Los Angeles Police Department and FBI. Both organizations had no record of any such arrest. Two weeks before the indictment, Clemmons resigned from the LAPD. Ultimately, Capell pled guilty, and charges against Clemmons were dropped. These men are the originators of Marilyn Monroe murder theories pointing the finger at Attorney General Robert F. Kennedy, a liberal politician.

In Capell's addendum to the 1967 edition of *The Strange Death of Marilyn Monroe*, he wrote that unidentified neighbors saw Robert Kennedy enter and leave Marilyn's home. At the time of the publication, Kennedy was campaigning for the 1968 presidential election. In a 1969 addendum, a year after Kennedy's assassination, Capell further claimed that Marilyn was hospitalized shortly before her death after becoming pregnant, alluding to the abortion of a Kennedy fetus when she was supposedly in Lake Tahoe the last weekend of her life. Witnesses and photographs of this trip to Lake Tahoe have surfaced in the media and on the Internet, dispelling Capell's abortion scenario.

In 1973, mainstream author Norman Mailer took Capell's fanatical ranting and introduced murder into the mix in his heavily fictionalized biography, *Marilyn: A Biography.* Mailer questioned the validity of Mrs. Murray's use of the fireplace poker to push aside the draperies in Marilyn's bedroom window on the night of Marilyn's death. Because she was an insomniac, he asserted, Marilyn had stapled her bedroom draperies to the wall to block out any light that might disturb her sleep. However, Mailer was mistaken; Ralph Roberts had stapled closed the bedroom draperies on the floor to ceiling window in the apartment on Doheny Drive but not in the house on Fifth Helena Drive. Evidence of the draperies not being stapled closed is seen in newsreels of Marilyn's window taken on the morning after her death, and in grainy police photographs of Mrs. Murray holding back the draperies inside the room.

Based upon the autopsy report of Marilyn's empty stomach, Mailer alluded to a doctor having used a stomach pump in an attempt to revive her. He even incorrectly asserted the overdose would not have been fatal if she had actually taken it on a full stomach. Mailer also doubted Marilyn's accidently overdosing on her bedtime dosage of barbiturates because she was found completely nude, and her nightly ritual supposedly included sleeping with a bra and eye mask on. Indeed, if she had committed suicide, Mailer never considered the possibility of a depressed woman abandoning her nightly routine on the evening she intentionally ingested an overdose.

In addition, Mailer related an account of FBI agents removing the hardcopy records of Marilyn's final toll calls from the telephone company in Santa Monica on the morning of after her death. It is a story, he writes, "whose author does not choose to give his name."

Mailer's speculation of murder is both suggestive and equivocal. "Why not see her death as the seed of assassinations to follow," he proposes. "For who is the first to be certain it was of no interest to the CIA, or to the FBI, or to the Mafia, and half the secret police of the world, that the brother of the president was reputed to be having an affair with a movie star who had once been married to a playwright denied a passport for 'supporting Communist movement.'"

He continues this dance, suggesting a crime and then citing a lack of evidence to support it:

> Political stakes were riding on her life, and even more on her death.... If she could be murdered in such a way as to appear as a suicide in despair at the turn of her love, what a point of pressure could be maintained afterward against the Kennedys. So one may be entitled to speak of a motive for murder. Of course, it is another matter to find that evidence exists.

Mailer's best-selling work—at the price of $19.95 for a three-pound hardcover edition—both expensive and heavy for its day, made money, but he faced interrogation by this swaggering style of journalism and disregard for facts. In an interview on the CBS news series *60 Minutes* in the summer of 1973, Mike Wallace pressed him to clarify his stand on the possibility of Marilyn's murder. Mailer virtually confessed to having embellished the facts for profit. Wallace published a segment of the confrontation in *Close Encounters: Mike Wallace's Own Story*:

Mailer: I needed the money very badly.

Wallace: You don't believe she was murdered, though, really...

Mailer: If you ask me to give a handicapper's estimate of what it was, I'd say it's ten to one that it was an accidental suicide...

Wallace: And do you believe that Bobby Kennedy was there, had been with her, that night? At her house?

Mailer: Well, no...

Wallace: But facts, Norman!

Mailer: I did not have the time to do both.

Jaded by three significant events occurring in the decade following Marilyn's death, the public was willing to contemplate Mailer's doubt about her suicide. He introduced his theory ten years after President John F. Kennedy's assassination, four years after Senator Edward Kennedy's Chappaquiddick incident, and one year after President Nixon's Watergate scandal. The time was ripe for the public to accept a conspiracy tying a married politician, especially a Kennedy, to the death of a beautiful young woman.

Let us begin with Kennedy's assassination in Dallas on November 22, 1963. While driving alongside his wife in an open convertible Lincoln Continental, he was fatally struck in the head by a bullet and died. Dallas police swiftly arrested his alleged assailant, Lee Harvey Oswald, who was gunned down by Jack Ruby the following day while being transferred from police headquarters to the county jail. The Warren Commission concluded in 1964 that Oswald acted alone, but sixty-six percent of the public polled by Fox News in 2004 believed the assassination was "part of a larger conspiracy" while only twenty-five percent thought it was the "act of one individual."

The poll's results paralleled previous surveys conducted by Louis Harris and Associates in 1967, 1975 and 1981, when about two-thirds also believed the slaying was part of a larger conspiracy. The leading conspiracy theories accuse the CIA, KGB, Mafia, FBI director J. Edgar Hoover, sitting Vice President Lyndon B. Johnson, Cuban president Fidel Castro, anti-Castro Cuban exile groups, and the Federal Reserve, or some combination of them.

Fast-forward six years later to July 19, 1969. The body of Mary Jo Kopechne, age 28, was discovered underwater in a channel on Chappaquiddick Island, Massachusetts, inside a capsized automobile belonging to her driver, Edward "Ted" Kennedy, John and Robert's youngest brother. After the discovery, Kennedy told the police that during the previous night Kopechne was his passenger when he took a wrong turn and accidentally drove his car off a bridge into the water. He admitted to swimming to safety, returning to his hotel, removing his wet clothes, and going to bed.

Although the senator made several telephone calls that night, he never informed authorities of the accident; nor did he summon help to rescue Kopechne, who may have lived for a period of time before drowning. Kennedy pled guilty to a charge of leaving the scene of an accident after causing injury and received a suspended sentence of two months in jail. Initially, the incident was overshadowed in the media by the first moon landing on July 20 but soon became a national scandal and may have influenced Kennedy's decision not to campaign for presidency in the 1972 and 1976 elections.

The Watergate political scandal began with the arrest of five men for breaking and entering into the Democratic National Committee headquarters at the Watergate office complex in Washington, D.C., on June 17, 1972. The ensuing investigation exposed the Nixon administration's efforts to cover up its involvement in the burglary and resulted in the indictment, trial, conviction, and incarceration of several chief Nixon administration officials. The crime eventually led to President Richard Nixon's resignation in 1974, the first and only of a United States President. Vice President Gerald Ford succeeded Nixon and issued a full and unconditional pardon of the former president, immunizing him from prosecution for any crimes he had or may have committed during his term. The incident shook the public's faith in the office of the presidency and in politicians in general like no other in recent times.

In 1974, Robert Slatzer published the fiscally ideal follow-up to Mailer: *The Life and Curious Death of Marilyn Monroe*. Slatzer was the first to introduce Marilyn's "red diary," its alleged "documentation" of her affair with Robert Kennedy, and Kennedy's broken promise to marry her. By this time in history, the Kennedy administration's secrets had been leaked to the media. Slatzer mingled the affair with allegations of the lovers discussing matters of national security, including the Bay of Pigs Invasion, a plot to kill Fidel Castro, the Vietnam War, and the Kennedys' enemies in organized crime. Author Mel Ayton notes all books claiming Marilyn knew about secret murder plots were published after congressional hearings into the CIA's illegal activities.

Slatzer also insists Marilyn did not intentionally or accidently overdose. Collaborating with private detective Milo Speriglio, he alleged Marilyn could not have ingested the pills as no drinking vessel was found at her bedside and the plumbing in her en suite bathroom had been turned off. A researcher with access to Monroe biographies and the Internet easily refutes Slatzer's points. In a police file photograph of a police officer pointing to the medication vials on

Marilyn's bedside table published in many books and on the Internet, a cylindrical drinking vessel is visible on the floor next to the bed; and although the water was turned off during renovations to Marilyn's home in March, when she went to the Greenson home to wash her hair for a weekend trip to Rancho Mirage, it could arguably have been turned back on five months later in August.

Slatzer supported the notion of a fatal injection and cited as evidence the lack of yellow dye, ostensibly left by Nembutal, in Marilyn's digestive tract. Slatzer also alleged the CIA confiscated her telephone records and that her house was bugged to record incriminating evidence against the Kennedys. Slatzer interviewed Jack Clemmons, who publicly alleged that Marilyn's body had been moved and placed in a position on her bed incongruent with the circumstances of her death. In summary, Slatzer detailed a massive government conspiracy and filled all the gaps with information provided by an anonymous informant identifying himself by the pseudonym, Jack Quinn.

Slatzer's most bizarre claim was his undocumented and unproven marriage to Marilyn in Mexico on October 4, 1952. He made this claim long before Marilyn's personal files and documents were released to the media or sold at auctions. However, her careful records included a canceled check written to a store in Los Angeles and signed by Marilyn on the day of the supposed marriage in Mexico, and therefore disproved Slatzer's claim. In his attempt to establish credibility as a heroic and protective former husband, Slatzer only cast further suspicion and doubt upon himself.

The basis of Slatzer's conspiracy theory appears linked to an alleged FBI document dated August 3, 1962. The document reportedly detailed columnist Dorothy Kilgallen's telephone conversation with interior decorator Howard Rothberg about rumors of a Monroe-Kennedy affair and Monroe's knowledge of government secrets. Slatzer had a professional association with Kilgallen, and while she was away on vacation in 1952, he wrote for her column, "The Talk of Broadway." Slatzer's apparent relationship with Kilgallen may have granted him awareness of her conversation with Rothberg and inspired further speculation long after the columnist's death in 1965.

Soon after releasing his book, Slatzer held a press conference and formally requested the District Attorney for Los Angeles County reopen Marilyn's case. The grand jury denied his bid. The foreword of Slatzer's book, written by Marilyn's makeup artist, Allan "Whitey" Snyder, provided Slatzer's most compelling link to her. Even this would be unmasked as apparent fraud by an Italian television producer in a letter to Peggy Wilkins, author of a Monroe website, and quoted by David Marshall in *The DD Group: An Online Investigation into the Death of Marilyn Monroe*:

> I never found him convincing...The only thing that almost convinced me of his friendship with MM was the Snyder introduction to his book...A few days later, I met Allan Snyder and, after the interview, I asked him how well he knew Slatzer when Marilyn was alive. His reply came as a surprise: he didn't know him at all and never even heard of him until the day Slatzer asked him to write the introduction. Then he also said that he always trusts people and Slatzer had told him that he had been close to Marilyn for many years and since he didn't know all of her friends, he had believed it, plus he had been paid for writing that little thing (or maybe just for signing it?).

Lionel Grandison climbed aboard Slatzer's conspiracy bandwagon and made the television circuit with his provocative claim of signing Marilyn's death certificate under duress by Theodore Curphey. The retired coroner vehemently denied the accusation, and the coroner's office quickly clarified Grandison's former role as a clerk and not an investigator. Most disturbingly, Grandison provided lurid descriptions of sexual assaults on Marilyn's body allegedly perpetrated by necrophiliac employees of the coroner's office. Grandison was soon discredited by the disclosure of his leaving the coroner's office in late 1962 following an arrest on forgery charges for using a deceased person's gasoline credit card to make a purchase.

Similarly, Jack Clemmons made the rounds on television with his repeated assertion, "Marilyn Monroe was murdered." In 1981, Grandison, Slatzer, Speriglio, and Clemmons appeared together as a quartet of paranoid obsessives proclaiming the assassination of Marilyn Monroe in an episode of the television series *In Search Of.*

In 1975, Mrs. Murray and a co-author, former sister-in-law Rose

Shade, responded to Slatzer in *Marilyn: The Last Months.* Marilyn referred to Slatzer's "sensational rumors about Bobby Kennedy's arriving at the house that afternoon with a physician, reportedly to sedate a hysterical Marilyn." Murray discounted the neighbor witness hosting a card party and stated Slatzer received this information "from the daughter of a woman, now deceased, who said she attended such a party." Murray cited only three other houses on Marilyn's cul-de-sac still inhabited by the people who had been Marilyn's neighbors. Murray also recalled a very conspicuous visit by Kennedy, sometime in June, in an open convertible without secret service agents. She asserted that the visit "could definitely not have been on Saturday, August 4, because the entire family was out of town on the day of the tragedy."

In the 1975 paperback edition of *Marilyn: A Biography*, Norman Mailer added a chapter titled "The Murder File" and admitted to having told an "unfinished story where fact, supposition, speculation, and inaccuracy were all laid in side by side." Vowing to further investigate the circumstances of Marilyn's death, he summarized the main discrepancies as outlined by Robert Slatzer in a press release. The addenda also synopsized Slatzer's recently published hypothesis and doubted the veracity of Marilyn's blowing the whistle on Kennedy:

> It is a difficult scenario...Nor does it make sense that the Kennedys would commit murder, which is Slatzer's all-but-suggested thesis. In those years, the Presidency was its own natural force for censorship. If Marilyn had threatened to expose the Kennedys to the newspapers, they would have not been exposed so very much. Her version might have been printed, although not necessarily on the front pages, but their rebuttal would have been natural—a grievous and tragic situation, a lovely, talented, and highly disturbed woman with fantasies. It was her career rather than theirs which would have suffered most. The Kennedys were skilled in handling scandal.

Mailer's argument seems plausible given the era in which Marilyn died, before empowered women broke the silence on powerful men in highly publicized scandals: Donna Rice and Gary Hart, Anita

Hill and Justice Clarence Thomas, Monica Lewinsky and Bill Clinton. However, Marilyn was neither vicious nor vindictive; she spoke well of her husbands after divorce and graciously responded to insults by Joan Crawford and Tony Curtis.

Nearly every claim of Marilyn's murder includes assertion of her having called a press conference scheduled August 6, the Monday after her death, to publicly announce an affair with the president or the attorney general or both, which seems ludicrous. At the time, the press protected government officials and would not report on such matters; it would have spelled career suicide for Marilyn, and her publicists would certainly not have allowed it. Additionally, in press coverage of her death, there is no mention that such an event was scheduled. Psychic Kenny Kingston has offered the only plausible reference of a press conference. He claimed that on three days before her death, Marilyn told him, "I want to be refreshed and ready for my press conference." According to Kingston, Marilyn's planned bombshell disclosure had nothing to do with the Kennedys: "Marilyn was going to reveal that she and Joe DiMaggio were going to re-marry on August 8. They'd planned their clothing, ordered the flowers...everything was set."

Private detective Milo Speriglio published *Marilyn Monroe: Murder Cover-Up* in 1982. He repeated Clemmon's claims that the lack of a drinking glass at the death scene excluded the possibility of an oral overdose of drugs and that Marilyn's body was moved after her death. Speriglio also included Grandison's claims of having signed the death certificate under duress after key documents and evidence went missing from the police file. Speriglio added speculation of Marilyn having died elsewhere and her body having been returned to the bed. He also implicated Robert Kennedy in repeating Capell's and Slatzer's allegations of an unidentified neighbor on Fifth Helena Drive hosting a card party and witnessing Robert Kennedy arrive at Marilyn's house the afternoon of her death with a man carrying a doctor's bag.

In Speriglio's book, Clemmons also reported observing Mrs. Murray operate a washer and dryer in the house while police investigated the death, alluding to the destruction of physical evidence of a murder. However, photographs of Marilyn's home and its floor plan reveal no washer or dryer. The architect's blueprint of Marilyn's kitchen, also on the Internet, contains no washer or dryer. Although it is possible both appliances existed in the detached garage or guesthouse, interior photographs of them in the structure have not appeared.

Speriglio accused a "dissident faction of the CIA" of murdering Marilyn, words practically lifted from Slatzer's *The Life and Curious Death of Marilyn Monroe.* The private detective also reported offering a $10,000 reward for recovery of Marilyn's red diary. Ted Jordan, an actor known for a small role on television series *Gunsmoke* and once married to burlesque queen Lily St. Cyr, claimed to have possession of the diary. When interviewed by Speriglio, Jordan stated that the red diary contained only Marilyn's poetry and that he had buried it somewhere in Ohio.

In 1989, Ted Jordan published *Norma Jean: My Secret Life With Marilyn Monroe*, an apparently fictitious account of a long-term relationship with her, similar to Robert Slatzer's claims. Jordan alleged that Marilyn promised to marry him but instead engaged in an affair with his uncle, Big Band leader Ted Lewis, to advance her career. He also alleged that she had a lesbian affair with Lili St. Cyr (1918-1999), a burlesque strip artist. Jordan offered no photographic evidence or documentation of Marilyn's connection to him, his uncle, or St. Cyr, but foolishly published a photograph of Marilyn with her attorney Jerry Giesler in a foreign edition of the book, under which a caption falsely named the elderly attorney as Jordan's Uncle Ted. HBO adapted the book into the forgettable *Marilyn & Norma Jean* (1996), a largely fictionalized biopic starring Ashley Judd and Mira Sorvino.

In August 1982, Los Angeles County District Attorney John Van de Kamp announced that the country Board of Supervisors unanimously passed a motion to request an investigation into Marilyn's death, in response to allegations of improper handling of the case by former coroner's clerk Lionel Grandison, initially and erroneously referenced as a "coroner's aide." In addition to Grandison's allegation that he was coerced into signing the death certificate, he claimed some of the evidence went missing, including Monroe's "red diary" containing "incriminating murder evidence," the "original" autopsy file, and a scribbled note found at the death scene.

Following a three-month investigation, in December 1982, the

Los Angeles County District Attorney's Office discounted and rejected allegations of murder in a 29-page report prepared by Assistant District Attorney Ronald H. Carroll and Investigator Alan Tomich. Many witnesses had testified under oath, and Grandison was simply not credible. "The facts, as we have found them, do not support a finding of foul play," Van de Kamp announced in a press conference. Murder, he avowed, "would have required a massive, in-place conspiracy covering all the principals at the death scene...the actual killer or killers; the chief medical examiner-coroner; the autopsy surgeon to whom the case was fortuitously assigned; and most all of the police officers assigned to the case as well as their supervisors in the LAPD..."

Dr. Thomas Noguchi refuted the rash of conspiracy theories in *Coroner to the Stars*, published in 1983. In the years after Marilyn's death, his duties as Los Angeles County coroner afforded his dissection of other famous corpses such as Robert Kennedy, Janis Joplin, John Belushi, and Natalie Wood. He explained no samples were taken from Marilyn's stomach because it was standard procedure in the early 1960s to rely on blood analysis to determine presence of drugs. Noguchi dispelled the myth that Nembutal leaves a trace of yellow dye and asserted Marilyn's body bore no fresh injection mark. The injections administered by Dr. Engelberg had healed, and any lethal injection would not have had time to heal. Noguchi affirmed his original conclusion of a "*very* probable" suicide.

In the early 1980s, Walter Schaefer, owner of Schaefer Ambulance Company in Los Angeles, stated an ambulance was summoned to Marilyn's home the night of her death. He named former employees Ken Hunter and Murray Leibowitz as the respondents to a call to Marilyn's home while she was still alive but comatose. Hunter told the District Attorney Marilyn was dead when he and his work partner arrived and they left as police arrived. Anthony Summers located Leibowitz, who changed his name to Leib and denied being on duty that night.

James Hall soon surfaced as Schaefer's former employee and asserted he arrived at Marilyn's house after 3 o'clock in the morning and was led to the detached guesthouse. He reported finding Marilyn comatose, Patricia Newcomb distraught and screaming, and Peter Lawford attempting to calm Newcomb. Hall avowed having successfully resuscitated Marilyn with help from his partner, when a doctor interrupted and took command by plunging a hypodermic needle, presumed to contain adrenaline, into her heart. Marilyn's condition worsened and the doctor pronounced her dead. In later versions, Hall stated the doctor inserted the needle at an incorrect angle and hit a rib. When the doctor pushed the needle further inside Marilyn, she expired at that moment. According to Engelberg's testimony to the District Attorney, Greenson called him between 2:30 and 3:00 in the morning, earlier than documented in the original police report, but no ambulance was called.

Anthony Summers expanded an article for *Sunday Express* into *Goddess: The Secret Lives of Marilyn Monroe*. Published in 1985, it boasted six hundred fifty interviews. According to Sarah Churchwell, Summers' sources "related what they believe, not what they demonstrably know." Indeed, the interviews repeat second or third hand accounts of what others allegedly claimed. Perhaps Summers' most provocative allegation is the government covering up Robert Kennedy's secret visit to Los Angeles the day of Marilyn's death when, officially, Kennedy and his family were guests of John Bates in San Francisco.

Concurrent with the book, Summers narrated the BBC documentary, *The Last Days of Marilyn Monroe* (1985)—also released as *Say Goodbye to the President* (1985)—based upon his research. Most dubious among Summers' many sources are Robert Slatzer, Jeanne Carmen, and Deborah Gould. The third wife of Peter Lawford, Gould was age twenty-five when she married him at age fifty-two in 1976. Although the marriage lasted only a few months, Gould purports to know the details of Marilyn's affairs with John and Robert Kennedy and her death. Lawford's last wife, Patricia Seaton, contradicted Gould's claims in statements made to journalist Neal Travis of the *New York Post.* Seaton insisted Gould fabricated the stories.

Jeanne Carmen (1930-2007) emerged as one of Summers' leading sources and later joined with Slatzer in claiming a relationship with Marilyn unknown to her other friends and undocumented by personal phone books or photographs. Formerly a pin-up model, trick-shot golfer, and B movie actress, Carmen often appeared with Slatzer in television shows, but Slatzer failed to mention her in his original book. While Slatzer claimed to have been Marilyn's confidante and to have an insider's knowledge of her relationship with Robert Kennedy, Carmen took it a step further by claiming to be an eyewitness to the affair. After Carmen's death, her son, Brandon James, published *Jeanne Carmen: My Wild, Wild Life*, writing in first person as his mother and disclaiming the book as an "artistic interpretation." In the end, Carmen is reported to have engaged in her own affairs with Robert Kennedy and Frank Sinatra. Carmen's son suggests she held on to the dark secrets despite many interviews throughout the years so that he might publish them in a book.

In Summers' version of events, Robert Kennedy arrived by helicopter to Los Angeles and ended his relationship with Marilyn on the last day of her life. A devastated Marilyn overdosed, called for help, was transported to the hospital where she died, and her body was returned home. Lawford destroyed all evidence of any association with the Kennedys, and J. Edgar Hoover seized her telephone records to eliminate evidence of her communication with them. "The cumulative force of all this detail is overwhelming," wrote Sarah Churchwell, "but none of it actually proves anything."

In a postscript in the 2012 edition of *Goddess: The Secret Lives of Marilyn Monroe*, Summers cited a significant change in Eunice Murray's account. "While being interviewed by me for the BBC, she delivered herself of the version usually offered for public consumption," he wrote. "Then, as the camera crew were starting to clear up, she said suddenly, 'Why, at my age, do I still have to cover this thing?'" However, Murray does not make this statement on film in the documentary. What we see is a frail and feeble Mrs. Murray responding to Summers' questions, her lucidity questionable due to her advanced age. The use of editing appears to connect Mrs. Murray's eyewitness account to Summers' suppositions.

In Summers' voiceover, he reports Marilyn was alive when a doctor and an ambulance arrived at the home. The camera cuts to Murray saying, "When he arrived, she was not dead…because I was there then in the living room." However, the context of the statement is unclear. She could be referring to Greenson's arrival in the afternoon to conduct a therapy session but the implication is that Greenson was called to the home after Marilyn's overdose, and she was still alive but possibly unconscious.

In cutting to a dialogue with Mrs. Murray, Summers alludes to her confirming Kennedy's presence at Marilyn's home on the last day of her life, but the context of this dialogue is also unclear and Summers' questions seem leading:

> "You believe that he was here," Summers says, his intonation sounding as a statement and not a question.
>
> "At Marilyn's house?" Murray asks, her voice rising.
>
> "Yes."
>
> "Oh, sure."
>
> "That afternoon," Summers states.
>
> "Yeah."
>
> "And you think that is the reason that she was so upset," Summers states.

The hair-splitting exploration into the possibility of Kennedy's visit to Marilyn's house on the last day of her life was gratuitous, because in the end, Summers believes she died of an accidental overdose and was not murdered. "All of the long discussion of murder becomes a paralipsis..." Churchwell concluded, "in which the writer indulges in conspiracy theory as long as possible, before concluding (reluctantly?) that Monroe actually died by her own hand. The entire Kennedy narratives turns about to be incidental, as well as speculative."

Borrowing from Summers' exhaustive research and interviews, Milo Speriglio published *The Marilyn Conspiracy* in 1986, followed by an episode of the television series *The Reporters* titled *Marilyn: A Case for Murder* (1988). Slatzer rehashed nearly two decades of conjecture in his book *The Marilyn Files* released in 1992 accompanied by a live television broadcast of the same title, narrated by Bill Bixby.

In 1992, Peter Brown and Patte B. Barham reconstructed a time line of Marilyn's death in *Marilyn: The Last Take*. The author suggested that her death was covered up by Twentieth Century-Fox

Studios, but carefully proposed the idea as hypothetical. In 1998, Donald H. Wolfe presented as fact Marilyn's death as a political assassination. Mrs. Murray's former son-in-law, Norman Jeffries, who for decades remained silent, served as his main source. Destitute and dying, Jeffries claimed that Robert Kennedy and an unidentified doctor arrived at Marilyn's home in response to her mounting rage. They later discovered her comatose in the guest-house and called for help. Borrowing from James Hall and Walter Schaeffer, Dr. Greenson arrived at the same time as an ambulance. Diverging from Hall's original version, Greenson attempted to inject adrenaline into Marilyn's heart but missed the target and hit a rib. Marilyn died, and Greenson and Lawford perpetrated a cover-up to protect Kennedy.

Donald H. Wolfe repeated the story of the now-deceased, bridge-playing neighbor who allegedly saw Kennedy, and a man carrying a doctor's bag, entering Marilyn's house during twilight of her last day alive, and named her as Elizabeth Pollard. Wolfe wrote that Pollard reported her observation to Jack Clemmons shortly after Marilyn's death, but police discredited her, as Kennedy was believed to have been in San Francisco. Wolfe used the second-hand report of Betty Pollard, Elizabeth's daughter, to confirm the allegation.

Donald Spoto's well-documented and definitive *Marilyn Monroe: The Biography* cited one hundred fifty interviews and more than 35,000 pages of previously sealed documents. This best-selling book debunked previous murder theories and exonerated the Kennedys in Marilyn's death, but fumbled in its own speculative version. Spoto hypothesized that Dr. Greenson ordered an enema of chloral hydrate to sedate Marilyn without knowledge of her having ingested Nembutal throughout the course of her last day. Mrs. Murray administered the enema and subsequently contacted Greenson in a panic when she discovered Marilyn comatose. The two attempted to resuscitate Marilyn, but in the end she still died. Together, the psychoanalyst and housekeeper performed a cover-up to erase evidence of their unintended homicide. It is a fantastic ending to an otherwise scholarly biography.

Over the years, John Miner, the man who observed Dr. Noguchi perform Marilyn's autopsy, discussed having interviewed Dr. Greenson in the days following Marilyn's death, and claimed the psychoanalyst played a thirty-minute tape recording she made for him. Repeatedly, Miner publicly opined Marilyn did not end her own life based upon the content of the recording.

"Dr. Greenson very graciously extended me an opportunity for quite a lengthy interview, one in which I heard tapes that were made by Miss Monroe," Miner told Speriglio. "Afterward, I wrote a very short memorandum for Coroner Curphey. It stated that as a result of the interview I had with him, it was my conviction that Miss Monroe did not commit suicide." Miner never specified if the tape convinced him of an accidental overdose, murder, or some other circumstance. A copy of Miner's memorandum has never surfaced, and he refused to disclose the content of the recording. "I gave my word to the man and he's dead," he told Speriglio. "So I don't expect ever to reveal it. It's possible that a judge could order me to reveal it and put me in jail for contempt of court if I refused. I hope I never have to cross that bridge." The Greenson family professed no knowledge of such a recording so it remained elusive along with the mythical "confiscated" wiretaps and the "missing" red diary.

In 2003, Matthew Smith published *Victim: The Secret Tapes of Marilyn Monroe,* based upon "transcripts" of the "missing" audiotape Marilyn allegedly recorded for Dr. Greenson. Smith had never heard the alleged audiotape and could not produce a copy. In these unproven "free associations," Marilyn reportedly summarized her life and background history of each person she mentions as if she structured her soliloquy for a future biographer. This preposterous premise borrows from the claim of John Miner, who for years stated he hoped never to be legally ordered to disclose the contents of the tape. However, on the forty-fifth anniversary of Marilyn's death, Miner released what he called an "extensive" and "nearly verbatim" transcript of the supposed tape to the *Los Angeles Times*.

Why had Miner finally breached his promise to Dr. Greenson? Supposedly because the psychiatrist should be considered a suspect in her death, some biographers suggest. Ronald Carroll, a former Los Angeles County assistant district attorney who conducted the 1982 review of Marilyn's death, which included interviews with Miner, told the *Los Angeles Times* that Miner had disclosed no hint of having possession of a transcript. Miner died at age ninety-two on

February 25, 2010.

According to Sarah Churchwell, Matthew Smith had "gone the furthest toward presenting a tissue of conjecture and unsubstantiated claims as documentary fact" like an "eighth-generation photocopy." She astutely wrote about the alleged existence of the recording "display[ing] remarkable prescience, and helpfulness, on the part of Marilyn. Apparently, in her last days, she decided...to share with Dr. Greenson her thoughts about many of the most controversial aspects of her story...it was so thoughtful of Marilyn to dispose of so many of our questions about her life just before she died, and to offer summary versions of *all* her most famous relationships to the psychiatrist she'd been seeing daily for two years..."

In *Marilyn: The Passion and The Paradox*, Lois Banner published new insights into John Miner with whom she claims to have worked at UCLA. Despite his previous allegations, Miner told her he had never interviewed Greenson, but had heard Marilyn's tapes and learned about her fixation on enemas. Miner also claimed to have interviewed actresses in Hollywood about their sexual practices for Alfred Kinsey; however, the Kinsey Institute had no record of this. Banner became even more suspicious when Miner lectured her on his own extensive knowledge of enemas as a sexual practice and suggested they collaborate on a biography on the Marquis de Sade, a Seventeenth Century French masochist.

According to Banner, after Miner filed for bankruptcy, he approached *Vanity Fair* about selling his story about the alleged transcript but could only produce a few vague notes on a legal notepad. For that reason and possibly others, *Vanity Fair* refused to buy the story. Miner instead sold his story to Matthew Smith in 2003 and to *Playboy* in 2005. Most damning, Banner wrote that Miner had been convicted for offering to perform enemas on several women at the District Attorney's office, resulting in the revocation of his license to practice law. Published in 2012, Banner's revelations suggest Miner fabricated the claim based upon his own sexual interests, not Marilyn's, and used his former position to appear credible.

Dennis Hopper biographer Peter L. Winkler branded Miner's claim of the transcripts as a hoax in a compelling letter to *Playboy* magazine, in response to its coverage of the bombshell. If Miner's motivation for finally revealing the information was truly based upon his desire for a new investigation into her death, Winkler asserted, it was incumbent to have told the authorities when Marilyn died or during the previous re-examination of the case in 1982. During that investigation, Miner had mentioned the tapes but not their content. Furthermore, Winkler reported, Greenson's widow, Hildegard, had recently told the *Los Angeles Times* that her husband never discussed the tapes.

"Anyone with a little bit of imagination could wade through some of the books, articles and documentaries on Monroe and cobble together Miner's transcripts," Winkler wrote in his letter to *Playboy*. "Over the years, numerous people have come forward claiming they have fantastic new revelations about Marilyn Monroe. They invariably turn out to be people with a tenuous or nonexistent connection to Monroe who want to become at least a footnote to her legend or are trying to cash in on her late in their lives. Miner is no exception."

In a similar exposé, *Marilyn: Intimate Exposures* (2011) Susan Bernard published testimonies of the children of John Bates, Robert Kennedy's host at the Bates Ranch in Gilroy, California, on Saturday, August 4, debunking the allegation that he was with Marilyn in Los Angeles. Bernard also printed the family's snapshots of their visit to the ranch given to her father, photographer Bruno Bernard. This disproved the possibility of Kennedy being present at Marilyn's home that evening due to the geographical distance between the two, with Los Angeles being about five hours away by car from Gilroy. As noted by Mel Ayton, the area's deep canyons in the Santa Cruz Mountains made the ranch inaccessible by helicopter, and the nearest airstrip was in San Jose, about an hour away by car.

A more recent conspiracy theory circulating in the media involves Australian film director Philippe Mora who, in 2010, discovered an FBI file dated October 19, 1964. Available on the Internet, the file contains a report by a "former Special Agent" detailing a claim about Marilyn as the murder victim of a scheme in which she was provided a means to fake a suicide attempt. Lawford, Greenson, Newcomb, and Murray are named as co-conspirators. The FBI cover page states the agent "does not know the source and cannot evaluate the authenticity of the information." However, this disclaimer does not stop conspiracy mongers/enthusiasts from accepting yet another theory.

In this version, Marilyn's friends and employees somehow tricked her into killing herself, with the full knowledge of Robert Kennedy, her alleged lover. She was induced to take an overdose of the drug Seconal with the understanding that she would be saved. In reality, Marilyn was left to die in her bed. According to the report, on the night of her death, Robert Kennedy called Lawford from San Francisco and asked if she was dead yet. However, Marilyn died from an overdose of Nembutal and chloral hydrate, not Seconal.

The motive seems to have been to prevent Marilyn from publicly disclosing her affair with Robert Kennedy after she realized he would never divorce his wife, Ethel, and marry her. Additionally, Kennedy had defaulted on his promise to use his influence to get her reinstated by Twentieth Century Fox. However, evidence surfaced in the early 1990s showing Fox had rehired Marilyn.

For every charge of Robert Kennedy's affair with Marilyn, there exists a counter charge. Denial of the Monroe-Kennedy affair by both Marilyn's friends and Kennedy's associates appear in many scholarly biographies; even Marilyn denied it to one of her closest confidantes.

"Have you heard any stories about me and Bobby?" Marilyn asked Ralph Roberts. "They aren't true. He's not my type." According to Sidney Skolsky, she only mentioned Robert Kennedy in connection to the president. Those closely associated with the Kennedys concurred with Marilyn's confidantes. "I know there was no affair," asserted JFK's aide, Edwin Guthman (1919-2008). "I was there. I saw what was going on."

"I was intimately associated with him for years and know everything he ever did," said JFK's aide Kenneth O'Donnell (1924-1977). "And I know for a fact that this Marilyn Monroe story is absolute bullshit." To add to the conclusion that nothing happened between the two, Florida Senator George Smathers (1913-2007) told J. Randy Taraborrelli, "She was sad and lonely and she would call, [and] he would talk to her and calm her down. There was no affair with Bobby, though."

"He was such a sympathetic kind of person," said Robert Kennedy's former personal secretary, Angela Novello. "He never turned away from anyone who needed help, and I'm sure he was well aware of her problems. He was a good listener, and I think that is what she needed more than anything." Novello, who died in 2011 at age ninety-three, cited RFK's frequent practice of accepting calls from Judy Garland although the two were never linked romantically.

In Laurence Leaming's interview with Joseph and Delores Naar for *The Kennedy Men* (2001), the couple described RJK hovering over Monroe at a Lawford event. When the attorney general attempted to cut in while Marilyn danced with Naar, she discreetly made a gesture simulating vomiting. However, President Kennedy's special assistant, Arthur Schlesinger, Jr., had a different impression of the couple's connection. "There was at once something magical and desperate about her," he wrote of Marilyn's allure. "Bobby, with his curiosity, his sympathy and absolute directness of response to distress, in some way got through the glittering mist surrounding Marilyn as few did."

* * *

Part Two: **Debunked Myths**

Marilyn's image has been maligned by other sordid and debunked claims over the years, including allegations of her appearance in a pornographic film early in her career. The release of amateur "sex tapes" depicting modern-day celebrities in sex acts are now commonplace in America. Paris Hilton, Pamela Anderson, Rob Lowe, and Vice Presidential candidate John Edwards have been the subject of such recent scandals; however, gossip of "blue movies" depicting nude motion picture actresses, filmed before they achieved fame, date back to the days of Joan Crawford.

In April 2007, the media reported the $1.5 million purchase of a fifteen-minute film allegedly depicting Marilyn Monroe engaged in a sex act with an unidentified male. Keya Morgan surfaced as the broker of the sale for the anonymous purchaser and informed the media that he personally verified Marilyn's identity based upon her cosmetically enhanced facial mole. Morgan further stated that the pornographic film's anonymous owner had secured it in an effort to protect Marilyn's legacy and vowed never to release it.

Conveniently, Morgan also announced that he was in the process of filming a documentary about Marilyn's life and death, casting suspicion on the entire bombshell as a publicity stunt. Even without evidence of the film—not even a blurred or censored frame was made public—the story received national attention. This apparent hoax was arguably based upon a 1965 FBI file that pertained to the rumor of a "French-style movie which depicted Marilyn Monroe, deceased actress, in unnatural acts with an unknown male." The rumor stated the film was "obtained prior to the time Monroe achieved stardom and that subsequently Joe DiMaggio attempted to purchase this film for $25,000."

In 2009, Morgan released a silent home movie he had purchased of Marilyn, circa 1955, smoking an obviously commercially manufactured cigarette with unidentified females, and claimed it was photographic evidence of her smoking marijuana. Morgan quoted the anonymous photographer of the film as having verifed the cigarette's content. This apparent hoax seemed connected to publicity of the documentary, which incidentally, was never released. With this second bombshell, Morgan displayed a pattern for speaking to the media on behalf of "anonymous" owners of unseen and undocumented films that allegedly depicted Marilyn in compromising situations. What Morgan didn't realize was that one of the women in the home movie was Mary Karger, Anne Karger's daughter; and it was likely filmed at the elder's apartment during Marilyn's separation from DiMaggio in late 1954 or during reshooting of scenes for *The Seven Year Itch* in early 1955.

In July 2011, Argentinian collector Mikel Barsa announced his intention to auction an original 16-mm pornographic film depicting a heterosexual couple engaged in sexual acts; the footage had been circulating on the Internet. It was likely the film described by Keya Morgan four years earlier. Barsa claimed the female in the film was a teenaged, overweight Marilyn Monroe, circa 1947, before cosmetic surgery. The auction was scheduled on August 7, two days after the anniversary of Marilyn's death.

Although the female in the film bore a slight resemblance to Marilyn in her youth, she possessed a squared, masculine jawline, wide gaps between her teeth, and a straight hairline. Compared to the many photographs of Norma Jeane during the same period—when she was modeling for various photographers including Tom Kelley—the woman in the film appears older, heavier, less feminine, and her facial and body contours are unlike Norma Jeane's. The most convincing evidence that she is someone other than Norma Jeane is the absence of the distinct widow's peak hairline that appeared in every photograph of Norma Jeane from her youth until her death.

The 1965 FBI file likely referred to this film as the one sought by DiMaggio and wrongly linked to Marilyn. According to NBC

News senior investigative producer Jim Popkin, FBI officials told NBC that a manual search of records found no evidence of the bureau ever having in its possession a pornographic home movie of Marilyn Monroe. David Hardy, chief of the FBI Record/Information Dissemination Section, conducted a search by a team of seven analysts who spent over thirty hours combing files at a record center in Virgina, and found no evidence of the existence of such a film.

In the 1970s, Marilyn was erroneously credited for another graphic film, albeit less pornographic, whose star bore a vague resemblance to her. This star was Arline Hunter (born 1931), a pin-up model and B-movie actress is best known as *Playboy* magazine's Playmate of the Month in August 1954, her magazine pose inspired by Marilyn's red velvet sitting with Tom Kelley. Early in her career, Hunter appeared in the notorious 1940s soft-core film *The Apple Knockers and the Coke*, also titled *The Girl, the Coke, and the Apple*.

For many years, the girl in the film was believed to be Marilyn, and the brief movie sold commercially as her secret "stag film." In the black-and-white film, Hunter is on a picnic. She sits on a blanket and removes her blouse and bra. Reclining, Hunter lifts her skirt to expose her legs. She stands, removes her skirt, and poses in panties. Reclining again, Hunter removes an apple from her picnic basket and rolls it over her breasts and nipples. She sips Coca Cola from a phallic bottle, spilling some of it on her breasts, in an apparent simulation of oral sex.

In the 1950s, Hunter recreated many of Marilyn's pin-up poses while donning copies of Marilyn's costumes from Fox films. Hunter appeared in low-budget movies such as *White Lightnin' Road* (1967) and *The Art of Burlesque* (1968). She also costarred with the Three Stooges in *Outer Space Jitters* (1959) and with Mamie Van Doren in *Sex Kittens Go to College* (1960).

Efforts to defame Marilyn by linking her to a sex tape seem inspired by a tendency to liken her to contemporary public figures and depict her as having engaged in behaviors common to some contemporary celebrities. Although Marilyn is deceased, she remains "alive" in the media as a historical figure by appearing on magazine covers and being the subject of articles, books, and television shows. The media repeats speculative stories about Marilyn having threatened to blow the whistle on an affair with a Kennedy, her possible bisexuality, and possible use of illicit drugs. This trend may also stem from the same perception of her as contemporary.

Those making these apparently erroneous claims overlook Marilyn as the product of a bygone era, and instead depict her as "ahead of her time." Exploitation is another and most probable motivation to link her to sex tapes, affairs with politicians, bisexuality, and drug use. In death, she is unprotected and unable to defend herself, remaining vulnerable to those seeking financial gain, notoriety, and publicity through her defamation. Another example of this abuse occured when Anthony Summers stirred controversy when he reproduced a horrific image of Marilyn's post-autopsy face in *Goddess: The Secret Lives of Marilyn Monroe.* "Certainly to publish death in quite this way, and to profit from its shock value, seems transgressive," declared Sarah Churchwell.

Many of Marilyn biographers and those who personally knew her criticized Summers' lack of propriety. "It is a particularly great misfortune that Summers should find it necessary for his narrative to include a photograph of Monroe's corpse," Graham McCann wrote. "It is not so much what she looks like that appalls, but rather the feeling that this is the ultimate intrusion, on our part as well as on the author's. It is a needless gesture from the author, a cynical sign, one which reflects very badly on his profession."

Photographer Eve Arnold was equally revolted and lashed out in her 1987 memoir:

> To see this abomination is an affront to those of us who knew her and respected her as a woman and a talent, who photographed her with affection and concern, who tried to show her with her foibles and her problems but also with her humor and her warmth and her humanness.

The disturbing image now circulates on the Internet along with obviously digitally manufactured images depicting Marilyn in her deathbed. As Susan Strasberg observed, Marilyn's good spirit rises like a lotus growing from the mud of atrocities written about her. "They are writing fiction and saying it is true," Evelyn Moriarty said. "It's mind boggling."

"The myth of Marilyn Monroe derived from the peculiarities of these accounts," Sarah Churchill asserted, "Their dubious authenticity, their attempts to establish the truth about a mythical figure, their propensity for espousing cultural dogma (and for being sanctimonious while they're at it), their tendency toward the collective and the aggregate: all of these make the writing about Marilyn Monroe an apocrypha..."

The plethora of published fabrications about Marilyn inspired Ralph Roberts to write a memoir so the truth about a woman he had grown to love and respect during the three years of their friendship could finally be told. The heart breaking part is that he could not interest a publisher in a manuscript containing no sex scandals, even though the one person in the world in whom Marilyn felt safe confiding had written it.

* * *

Marilyn Monroe has become an icon whose myth grows stronger with each passing year, as the real Marilyn Monroe fades and distorts with each attempt at biography and with the deaths of those who actually knew her.

The iconic Marilyn is globally recognized in the portrait wearing in the gold lamé dress with plunging neckline, the pose in the white billowing dress from *The Seven Year Itch*, and Fox's publicity portraits with heavily-lidded eyes, painted mole, red lips, and open, smiling mouth. The United States postal stamp released in 1996 depicts her in a more subdued but iconic pose. Those born decades after her death recognize her as a symbol of feminine sexuality and beauty; a cautionary tale about the dangers of drugs, spinsterhood, and even childhood sexual abuse; and a reminder of mid-century filmmaking.

Indeed, Marilyn's screen image did not reflect the woman behind the facade. She created this public characterization as a means of achieving fame only, to fight against it until her death. When Marilyn looked upon the giant cutout of her skirt-blowing scene in *The Seven Year Itch*, she found the image incongruent with her self-perception and believed it was an inaccurate representation of her true identity. Would she wish to be remembered this way? Would she rather have been forgotten? Or would she rather be remembered through a distorted cultural memory?

In death, as when she was living, Marilyn inspires us to project our own subjective interpretations and fantasies onto her extraordinary life. Fred Lawrence Guiles wrote she "was kind of a living abstraction. She was what you believed her to be." Joel Oppenheimer explored this in his series of interviews in *Marilyn Lives!* (1980). Marilyn insightfully recognized the consequence of this projection. "People had a habit of looking at me as if I were some kind of mirror instead of a person," she said.

Perhaps Gloria Steinem most accurately identified our cultural obsession with Marilyn when she eloquently wrote of Marilyn's youthful death inspiring the posthumous fascination that has endured for half a century: "It is the lost possibilities of Marilyn Monroe that capture our imaginations. It is the lost Norma Jeane, looking out of Marilyn's eyes, who captures our hearts." Today, she remains a motherless and fatherless child whose ambition and vulnerability touched millions of people across the globe beginning over sixty years ago and likely continuing into the future. "Could we have helped Marilyn survive?" Gloria Steinem asks. "There can be no answer…If we learn from [her life], she will live on in us."

Marilyn Monroe will endure along with Cleopatra, Pocahontas, Anne Frank, Eva Peron, and Helen Keller. She wanted to leave behind the legacy of being a good mother and a good actress and arguably died believing she had accomplished neither. Marilyn never set out to leave the legacy we acknowledge today. The way she lived her life fascinates many born after her death and establishes her as both transcendental and unforgettable.

A decade before he received the Best Director Oscar for *The Last Picture Show* (1971), director and film historian Peter Bogdanovich worked as a film programmer at the Museum of Modern Art in New York and was touched by Marilyn at her peak. He captured the essence of Marilyn's lasting appeal in his book *Who the Hell's In It: Conversations with Hollywood's Legendary Actors*:

> She is the most touching, strangely innocent—despite all the emphasis on sex—sacrifice to the twentieth-century art of cinematic mythology, with real people as gods and goddesses. While Lillian Gish had been film's first hearth goddess, Marilyn was the last love goddess of the screen, the final Venus or Aphrodite. The minute she was gone, we started to miss her and that sense of loss has grown, never to be replaced. In death, of

course, she triumphed at last, her spirit being imperishable, and keenly to be felt in the images she left behind to mark her brief visit among us.

On the fiftieth anniversary of her death, a large group of people born during Marilyn's career and long after her death gathered in the same chapel where her funeral service took place to honor the woman behind the myth and the legend. "Please hold a good thought for me," she had asked her closest friends. Generations continue to discover her finer qualities and hold good thoughts for her.

"Does she have the last laugh now!" said Gail Levin, the Emmy Award-winning producer/director of PBS' *American Masters* episode *Marilyn Monroe: Still Life* (2006). "Actually, better than the last laugh—the last word. She kept it light, she had a soft touch, and I don't think there's a woman today who's got that. She was a very rare creature, very delicate, very brilliant. She had this meteoric rise and then poof. And that was exactly what she was meant to do and be."

Shortly before the eleventh anniversary of Marilyn's death, Sir Elton John recorded his composition of "Candle in the Wind" with lyrics by Bernie Taupin for the album *Goodbye Yellow Brick Road*. The song celebrates her from the perspective of gay man who honors the spirit of a tortured woman who was brutalized by straight male lust, but is somewhat inaccurate in that no one set her on a treadmill or created the superstar that she became. A live version of the song was released in 1987 and immortalized Marilyn for future generations.

Imagining Marilyn had lived to age eighty-six in 2012, film critic Roger Ebert hoped she would have quietly disappeared like Doris Day. "Her legacy would never die," Ebert wrote in *Playboy*. "I believe she would have become a sweet little old lady, and a good friend."

CHAPTER THIRTY-EIGHT: THOSE SHE LEFT BEHIND

The telling of Marilyn Monroe's life would be incomplete without inclusion of the paths taken after her death by those significant to her. As Marilyn would have been age eighty-eight in 2014, most members of her support system are deceased. Here is what happened to those she left behind:

GLADYS BAKER & BERNIECE MIRACLE

Directly following Marilyn's funeral, Berniece visited Gladys at Rockhaven and found her bizarrely wearing nurse's garb. The woman displayed no reaction to her daughter's death. Attorney Chester Howell, who hosted Norma Jeane's wedding at his home, guided Berniece in transferring Gladys' guardianship from Inez Melson to her.

In 1963, Gladys escaped from Rockhaven by sliding down a rope of knotted uniforms nailed to a third-floor windowsill and scaling a high fence. Police found her twelve miles away in a church in the San Fernando Valley. The terms of Marilyn's will to provide for Gladys' care had not been fulfilled, so Berniece supplemented her meager Social Security check. After transfer to Camarillo State Hospital, Gladys attempted suicide. She was released in 1967 to Berniece in Gainesville and settled in a retirement home, Collino Court, in 1970. In 1977, the court released Marilyn's will from probate, making available $100,000 in trust for Gladys' care. On occasion, she was photographed by the tabloids and seen riding through town on an adult tricycle. Gladys died of heart failure on March 11, 1984, surviving her daughter for over two decades.

Berniece retired from her career as a bookkeeper at the University of Florida and continued to avoid the media. Paris dodged reporters by pretending to be divorced, a widower, or the gardener, and by inciting rumors of Berniece's death. Mona Rae, their daughter, graduated from the University of Florida in 1962 and accepted a job in another city, where her relationship to Marilyn remained a secret. She studied acting with Lee Strasberg and worked as a teacher, media specialist, and an author. Berniece and Mona Rae collaborated on *My Sister Marilyn: A Memoir of Marilyn Monroe* in 1994. "Some things that have been published about Marilyn's life are such fabrications that further comment would be less than worthy," Berniece wrote. "But of all the distortions that have circulated since her death, I have always wanted most keenly to erase the myth that Marilyn had no family to love her."

James Dougherty

After his divorce from Norma Jeane Baker, James Dougherty wed Patricia Scoman in 1947. The couple had three daughters and divorced in 1972. In the mid-1960s, Dougherty appeared on CBS' *To Tell the Truth* as "Marilyn Monroe's real first husband." He worked for the Los Angeles Police Department for twenty-five years, serving as a detective and training the first special weapons and tactics group (SWAT).

After Dougherty retired in 1974, he married a third time to Rita Lambert and relocated to Arizona, and later to his wife's native state of Maine, settling in Sabattus. Dougherty published *The Secret Happiness of Marilyn Monroe* in 1976 and *To Norma Jeane with Love, Jimmie* in 2001. His marriage to Norma Jeane was featured in the 2004 documentary, *Marilyn's Man*. "I'm still haunted," Dougherty said in the film, tears filling his eyes. "I wish I can ask her some questions. Talk some things over with her. I believe in an afterlife. I believe someday, after I've died—God willing—I'll see her in heaven." In 2005, Dougherty died from complications of leukemia at age eighty-four, in San Rafael, California, where he had settled after his wife's death two years earlier.

Joseph DiMaggio

A lyric in Simon and Garfunkel's song "Mrs. Robinson" for the film *The Graduate* (1967) referenced DiMaggio as an icon of a bygone era: "Where have you gone, Joe DiMaggio?" Initially, the retired baseball legend was offended by the reference but soon came to appreciate the emerging Baby Boomer generation's nostalgia for his role as a cultural hero. Retired young, DiMaggio matured into a distinguished, white-haired gentleman who survived Marilyn by thirty-seven years.

A heavy smoker for much of his adult life, DiMaggio was admitted to Memorial Regional Hospital in Hollywood, Florida, on October 12, 1998, for lung cancer surgery. He remained there for ninety-nine days. DiMaggio returned to his Florida home on January 19, 1999, where he died on March 8 at age eighty-four.

JOSEPH DIMAGGIO, JR.

After military service, Joe DiMaggio, Jr. held decent jobs but never kept them for long. He married Sue Adams, who had two daughters from a previous marriage, and the couple relocated to Martinez, California. Joe Jr. managed a polyurethane foam business for his father, but this position was also short lasting.

The younger DiMaggio felt that no matter how hard he worked he could not please his father. Young Joe drank heavily and targeted his wife with domestic violence. His drinking escalated to amphetamine abuse, and the business was lost. Joe Junior and his wife divorced in 1974, and two years later, he was seriously injured in an automobile accident. A portion of Joe Junior's brain was surgically removed, which resulted in drastic mood changes, outbursts of anger, and poor impulse control.

As time passed, Joe Junior lived a marginal life drifting from job to job and from address to address, while Joe Senior developed a close relationship with his estranged son's ex-wife and stepdaughters. Sadly, Joe Sr. cruised the streets searching for his troubled son.

When his father died, Joe Junior was living in a trailer and working in a junkyard. The two had not seen each other in three years. Joe Senior left his son a trust fund of $20,000 annually and forty-five percent from the sale of his firm, Yankee Clipper Enterprises. Joe Junior barely benefited from the inheritance as he died at age fifty-seven, six months after his father's death on August 7, 1999.

THE SHAW FAMILY

Sam Shaw's daughters, Meta Stevens Shaw and Edith Marcus Shaw, operate their father's archives in New York. His son, Larry Shaw, died in 2008. All three siblings participated in an episode of the Public Broadcasting System's series, *American Masters,* titled *Marilyn Monroe: Still Life.*

THE GREENE FAMILY

Milton Greene continued his prolific career as a fashion and celebrity photographer, his work exhibited at the International Center of Photography in New York, the Art Institute of Chicago, and the Smithsonian Institute in Washington, D.C. He collaborated with Norman Mailer on *Of Women and Their Elegance* before his death on August 8, 1985.

After Milton's death, Amy married Charles Andrews (1916-2004) who produced the popular television series *The Arthur Godfrey Show, Today,* and *Candid Camera.* Amy served as a beauty editor at *Glamour* for ten years, developed the Beauty Checkers line with Henri Blendel, and collaborated with Molly Pomerance on the makeup guide, *The Successful Face*, in 1989.

Milton and Amy's sons, Joshua and Anthony, published the heavily illustrated *Milton's Marilyn* and participated in the 1994 documentary film *Marilyn Monroe: Life After Death.* Joshua, whom Marilyn babysat, authored books on food, gardening, and home furnishings. He has been president of his father's archives since 1993, after his own photographic work was published in *Vogue, House & Garden,* and *House Beautiful.* Anthony died in 2012.

NORMAN ROSTEN

"My wife believed I loved Marilyn," Norman Rosten wrote, "but so did she...Possibly it was the love of a parent for a child, an older daughter, a family member."

Rosten's writing continued to reflect his life as a resident of Brooklyn. He wrote the screenplay for Sidney Lumet's 1962 film of Arthur Miller's play, *A View from the Bridge.* Rosten's other plays included *Mardi Gras, The Golden Door* and *Come Slowly, Eden!*, a portrait of Emily Dickinson. Beginning with his novel *Under the Boardwalk*, about a boy from Coney Island approaching adolescence,

Rosten focused on writing fiction. In the 1970s, he published *Over and Out, Love in All Its Disguises,* and *Neighborhood Tales.* In 1979, Borough President Howard Golden named Mr. Rosten poet laureate of Brooklyn, a title retained until his death. In 1973, Rosten published intimate memories in *Marilyn: An Untold Story,* a rebuttal to Norman Mailer's more sensational book. He and Sam Shaw also collaborated on *Marilyn Among Friends.* Later, Rosten wrote the libretto for *Marilyn,* Ezra Laderman's opera, performed in 1993.

Rosten presented artist Melanie Hope Greenberg with his unpublished collection of children's poems about Brooklyn. Upon his death in 1995, Greenberg returned them to his daughter and heir, Patricia Rosten Filan, a librarian in the history department of Brooklyn Public Library's Central Branch. Filan and Greenberg collaborated in publishing them under the title *A City Is* with illustrations by Greenberg. Hedda Rosten died in January 1984 at age sixty-eight.

THE STRASBERG FAMILY

Lee Strasberg went on to groom more recent actors such as Ellen Burstyn, Harvey Keitel, Al Pacino, Robert DeNiro, Dustin Hoffman, Jack Nicholson, and Julia Roberts. Paula Strasberg, described by her daughter as a "combination delicatessen, pharmacist, Jewish mother," died in 1966 at age fifty-six. Lee married Anna Mizrahi who in 1969 purchased property located at 7936 Santa Monica Boulevard in West Hollywood as a gift to her husband and developed the Marilyn Monroe Theatre, a Los Angeles branch of the Actors Studio, where Lee held classes.

Since his death in 1982 at age eighty, the theater serves as a prestigious stage venue for the premiere of plays and film screenings. Lee appeared in *The Godfather Part II* (1974) and earned an Academy Award nomination for Best Actor in a Supporting Role. The day before his death, Strasberg had been elected to the American Theatre Hall of Fame.

Susan Strasberg lost the role of *Anne Frank* in director George Stevens' film adaptation of the play, believing Stevens feared the interference of her mother, who had become a pariah in Hollywood because of the trouble she instigated by advocating for Marilyn's interests. After failed relationships and a slump in her career, Strasberg began using drugs in 1965. Even though there wasn't room in her house for two egos, she married actor Christopher Jones, with whom she used LSD. Their daughter, Jennifer, was born with a congenital birth defect caused by the drugs. Strasberg and Jones were divorced after one year of marriage.

Strasberg worked in television and wrote her autobiography, *Bitter Sweet*, in 1980, followed up with *Marilyn and Me: Sister, Rivals, Friends*. Financially strapped and with no health insurance, Strasberg sold a cherished string of pearls that Marilyn had given to Paula for $100,000. "I wear these pearls whenever I need confidence or strength," she told *The Toronto Star* in 1992. "I can feel Marilyn's and Mother's energy, and I can know they are with me." After selling one of her most prized possessions, she died alone of breast cancer at age sixty in 1999 in a friend's Manhattan apartment.

John Strasberg worked at the National Film Board of Canada and was executive director of the Lee Strasberg Theater Institute. In the 1980s, he co-founded The Mirror Repertory Company in New York. His former acting school, The Real Stage, had branches in New York, Paris, and Montreal. In 1996, he opened John Strasberg Studios and in 2005 founded the Accidental Repertory Theater in New York City. "She really looked at me as if she saw me," Strasberg said of Marilyn. "It wasn't that I wanted people to look at me, but I knew the difference when she did."

ARTHUR MILLER

Marilyn remained Arthur Miller's muse even in death, inspiring the plots of two plays and several characters in others. Miller produced *After the Fall* in 1964, his first work since *The Misfits*. His final play, *Finishing the Picture*, opened in Chicago in the fall of 2004, and was based on the experience of filming *The Misfits*. Facets of Marilyn's personality crept into the characters of Cathy May in *Mr. Peters' Connections* and Florence in *Fame*. The family drama, *The Price*, produced in 1968, became his most successful play since *Death of a Salesman*.

Miller's third wife, Inge, gave birth to their first child, Rebecca, in September 1962. Miller loved his older children, but his sister, Joan Copeland, told journalized Suzanna Andrews that Rebecca held a special place in his heart.

Many of Miller's plays throughout the 1970s were critical and commercial failures, and during the early 1990s he wrote three plays: *The Ride Down Mt. Morgan* (1991), *The Last Yankee* (1992), and *Broken Glass* (1994). A film adaptation of *The Crucible* starring Daniel Day-Lewis and Winona Ryder opened in 1996. In celebration of its fiftieth anniversary, *Death of a Salesman* was revived on Broadway in 1999 and received a Tony Award for best revival.

Miller, who produced his greatest work before his marriage to Marilyn, received laurels in later years. He was awarded the National Medal of Arts, the Dorothy and Lillian Gish Prize, and Spain's Principe de Asturias Prize for Literature, the latter in honor of being "the undisputed master of modern drama." In 2001, the National Endowment for the Humanities selected Miller for the Jefferson Lecture, the American government's highest honor for achievement in the humanities.

Miller's third wife, Inge Morath, died of lymphatic cancer in 2002. Two years later, the eighty-nine-year-old Miller announced that he had been living with a thirty-four-year-old minimalist painter, Agnes Barley, at his Connecticut farm since 2002 and intended to marry her.

Family surrounded Miller when he died of heart failure after a battle against cancer, pneumonia, and congestive heart failure at his home in Roxbury, Connecticut. He took his last breath on February 10, 2005, coincidently the 56th anniversary of the Broadway debut of *Death of a Salesman.*

Miller was survived by his children by his first wife, producer Robert Miller and Jane Miller Doyle; and two children by Morath, writer and film director Rebecca Miller Day-Lewis, married to the actor Daniel Day-Lewis, and Daniel Miller, a son with Down Syndrome secretly and virtually obliterated from Miller's public and personal life.

Jane Miller married Tom Doyle in 1963, the sculptor who had been married to the artist Eva Hesse. Since the 1960s, Doyle has been creating dynamic sculptures carved from beams of cherry, oak, butternut and sassafras woods. Jane is a self-taught weaver who began making rag rugs more than twenty-seven years ago using a technique called Taquete. Her rugs are often used as hanging art, due to their distinctive design. The couple lives in Western Connecticut.

Miller's obituary in *The Denver Post* called him "the moralist of the past American century," and *The New York Times* eulogized his "fierce belief in man's responsibility to his fellow man—and [in] the self-destruction that followed on his betrayal of that responsibility." These accolades conflicted with Suzanna Andrews' shocking expose titled "Arthur Miller's Missing Act" in the September 2007 issue of *Vanity Fair*. Andrews brought to light the truth about the deceased playwright's abandoned child.

According to the article, Miller had never publicly acknowledged the existence of Daniel. Miller omitted the child in his 1987 memoir, *Timebends*. Daniel's name did not appear in his mother's obituary in the *New York Times* and was only mentioned in the *Los Angeles Times* obituary of his father.

Daniel is believed to have been born in November 1966. Broadway producer Robert Whitehead told biographer Martin Gottfried that Miller seemed "overjoyed" by the birth of a son and considered naming the boy Eugene after playwright Eugene O'Neill, whose work had impressed him. The next day, however, Miller called Whitehead to report the doctors had diagnosed the infant with Down Syndrome, a genetic anomaly marked by an extra twenty-first chromosome. According to Whitehead, Arthur used the word "mongoloid" to describe the child and institutionalized him at a home for infants in Manhattan. At age four, Daniel transferred to the Southbury Training School in Connecticut, located only miles from Miller's farm in Roxbury. Writer Francine du Plessix Gray told Andrews that Morath visited Daniel every Sunday, but that Miller never made an effort to see him until father and son met through Daniel's involvement in an advocacy rights conference in the mid-1990s.

Suzanna Andrews ended the expose by quoting Miller's poignant line from *Timebends*: "A character is defined by the kinds of challenges he cannot walk away from. And by those he has walked away from that cause him remorse."

RALPH ROBERTS

In 1980, Ralph Roberts broke his silence by writing a memoir about Marilyn to counter the lies and distortions published by those who barely or never knew her. May Reis and Lee Strasberg supported this endeavor. Before his death in 1999, Roberts cooperated with biographer Donald Spoto. Excerpts from Roberts' unpublished manuscript, *Mimosa*, currently appear on a website created by Steve Jacobs.

The Greenson Family

Romeo "Ralph" Greenson died of congestive heart failure on November 24, 1979. The documents in his archive relating to Marilyn Monroe are sealed until January 1, 2039.

Joan Greenson Aebi graduated with a Master's Degree in Fine Arts from Otis Art Institute and was the owner and curator of the Greenson Gallery Workshop, committed to the exhibition of emerging artists in Southern California. It hosted the first photography-as-fine art exhibition in Southern California and first Neon Sculpture exhibition. Joan continues to create ceramic sculptures in Pasadena and maintains a website that displays them.

Daniel P. Greenson graduated from the University of Southern California Keck School of Medicine in 1964 before receiving a medical license in 1965. He served as chairperson of the San Francisco Psychoanalytic Institute's Education Committee. After practicing psychiatry in Berkley for nearly forty years, Daniel surrendered the license in 2003.

Hyman Engelberg

In the Fox documentary *Marilyn: The Final Days* (2001), Hyman Engelberg says: "I believe she was in a manic phase, and something happened to suddenly depress her, and she grabbed pills there. She had plenty at the bedside. I think she was suddenly depressed, and in that sense, it was intentional. Then, I think she thought better of it, when she felt herself going under, because she called Peter Lawford. So, while it was intentional at the time, I do believe she changed her mind…" Engelberg died in a nursing home of natural causes at age ninety-two in 2005.

Patricia Newcomb Wigan

Patricia Newcomb left the Arthur P. Jacobs Company soon after Marilyn's death and continued her career in public relations working with Barbra Streisand, among other celebrities. She later worked as an information specialist for the United States Information Agency under the direction of George Stevens, Jr., son of the film director George Stevens. Newcomb resigned to work for Pierre Salinger's campaign for United States Senate in 1964 and subsequently served as a consultant to the Justice Department. In 1969, Newcomb formed Pickwick Public Relations with partners Lois Weber Smith, who was Marilyn's former publicist, Gerry Johnson, and Pat Kingsley.

Columnist Dorothy Manners reported that Newcomb refused a sizeable sum to sell her memories of Marilyn to the press. "As well as being Marilyn's friend, I was her press agent," Newcomb was quoted by Manners. "A reputable press agent doesn't sell information about a client—even when the association is ended by death." Manners also reported Newcomb's termination by Jacobs due to her acceptance of an invitation to join Peter and Patricia Lawford in Hyannis Port as she recovered from Marilyn's death.

According to the *Los Angeles Times*, Newcomb served as vice president of production at MGM Studios. She eventually married Gareth Wigan (1931-2010), an Oxford graduate who began his career as a talent agent in the London office of MCA and later founded his own agency. After selling his agency to EMI in 1970, Wigan relocated to Los Angeles and forged Hollywood's global strategies. He was a production executive at 20th Century Fox, co-vice chairman at Columbia TriStar Motion Picture Group, co-founder of The Ladd Company, and production consultant at Columbia Studios. Wigan's legacy included partial responsibility for memorable blockbusters such as *Star Wars* (1977), *Alien* (1979), and the Oscar-winning *Chariots of Fire* (1981). In 2008, Newcomb was last publicly photographed with Wigan at an opening of the Los Angeles Opera.

PATRICIA AND PETER LAWFORD

Shortly after President Kennedy's assassination in 1963, Patricia Lawford could no longer tolerate Peter's heavy drinking, extramarital affairs, and gradual addiction to drugs. She filed for a legal separation, and the couple officially divorced in 1966. In accordance with her religious beliefs, she never remarried.

Peter Lawford married Mary Rowan, the daughter of comedian Dan Rowan, in 1971. Lawford was forty-eight, and his bride was only twenty-one. The couple divorced in January 1975. In June 1976, Lawford married aspiring actress Deborah Gould, age twenty-five, whom he had known for only three weeks. Lawford and Gould separated two months later and divorced in 1977. While separated from Gould, Lawford wasted no time in partnering with another young woman. He met seventeen-year-old Patricia Seaton, who later became his fourth and final wife in July 1984, six months before his death.

On Christmas Eve 1984, Lawford died at Cedars-Sinai Medical Center in Los Angeles from cardiac arrest, complicated by kidney and liver failure after years of drug and alcohol addiction. His body was cremated, and his ashes were interred in a crypt at Westwood Village Memorial Park Cemetery near Marilyn's. Owing to a dispute between Patricia Seaton Lawford and the cemetery, Lawford's ashes were removed and scattered by his widow in the Pacific Ocean off the coast of California.

After her divorce, Patricia Kennedy Lawford battled alcohol addiction and suffered a bout with cancer. She worked with the John F. Kennedy Library and Museum, as well as with the National Center on Addiction, and was a founder of the National Committee for the Literary Arts. Patricia died in 2006 at age eighty-two from tongue cancer in her Manhattan home, survived by four children and ten grandchildren.

Eunice Murray

Housekeeper Eunice Murray lived quietly in various locations in West Los Angeles. After the death of her sister, Carolyn, in 1972, Murray married her widowed brother-in-law, Franklin Blackmer, a Swedenborgian minister. She relocated to Bath, Maine, until his death shortly thereafter. Returning to Santa Monica, Murray rented a guest cottage from the relatives of the actor, Richard Cromwell, where she wrote a memoir, *Marilyn: The Last Months* (co-authored by sister-in-law Rose Shade), in 1975. In 1985, Murray appeared in the BBC documentary, *The Last Days of Marilyn Monroe* (later released as *Say Goodbye to the President*), interviewed by Anthony Summers inside her apartment. Later, Murray lived with her daughter in Tucson, Arizona, until her death in July 1994.

Donald H. Wolfe published theories about Marilyn's murder based largely on an interview he conducted with Norman Jeffries who had been Murray's son-in-law and Marilyn's handyman. In 1992, while bound to a wheelchair in his Arkansas home, an infirmed Jeffries revealed to Wolfe alleged secrets about the events surrounding Marilyn's death. Jeffries claimed Murray was innocent of murder but participated in the cover-up by talking openly to police officials, newspaper reporters, and authors. He died shortly thereafter in 1993.

* * *

In 2005, Julien's auctioned Marilyn's tan personal telephone and address book from 1962 containing the names of those significant in her final months. Notable names included: Joe DiMaggio, Joe DiMaggio Junior, Marie DiMaggio, Dr. Hyman Engelberg, Dr. Ralph Greenson, Milton Rudin, Henry Weinstein, Lee and Paula Strasberg, Jean Kennedy Smith (JFK's sister), Peter and Patricia Lawford, Arthur Miller, Joan Copeland (Arthur Miller's sister), Bernice Miracle, May Reis, Dr. Marianne Kris, Montgomery Clift, Jack Benny, Frank Sinatra, Henry Fonda, Jane Russell, Eli Wallach, Shelley Winters, Jack Lemmon, Yves Montand, Ben Gazzara, Rex Harrison, Thelma Ritter, Dinah Shore Montgomery (singer), Gene Kelly, Ernie Kovacs (comedian), George Cukor, David & Jennifer Selznick, Sidney Skolsky, Spyros Skouras, Carl Sandburg, Saul Bellow, Sean O'Casey (Irish playwright), Clifford Odets, Louis Untermeyer (poet), Earl Wilson, Ann Landers (advice columnist), Richard Avedon, John Huston, Oscar Levant (composer and talk show host), Arthur P. Jacobs, Inez Melson, Joe Wolhandler and John Springer (her New York press agents), Jay Kanter and Mort Viner (her agents at MCA), James R. Kinney (Maf-Honey's veterinarian in New York), Dr. Erno Laszlo (dermatologist), aesthetician Madame Renna, Charles Lang Jr. (cinematographer for *Some Like It Hot*), Evelyn Moriarty, Jean Negelesco, Ettore Rella (playwright). It is significant that the names of Robert Slatzer and Jeanne Carmen did not appear in the book.

Most people who have a phone book of this size could not say with confidence that they keep in touch with every person who has an entry, but not Marilyn. If your name appeared in her book, you would likely receive a call late at night, after you fell asleep, when you would immediately recognize the whispery voice. Most of all, even though her phone book was ever expanding, when Marilyn called, she made you feel special.

Part V:

Legacy

Chapter Thirty-Nine: The Marilyn Monroe Half-Centennial Memorial

Several hundreds of Marilyn Monroe's fans gathered in Los Angeles for the half-centennial anniversary of her death on Sunday, August 5, 2012 to celebrate the icon's life and offer testimony to the enduring power of her memory. They traveled from as far as Germany, France, Italy, Spain, Belgium, New Zealand, and Venezuela to honor a woman who passed long before most of them were born. Reporters and news crews attempted to pinpoint the basis of her posthumous mass adulation. Hanna Nixon made a four thousand mile pilgrimage from Scotland. When Kate Parkinson-Morgan of the *Brentwood Patch* asked the secret of Marilyn's international appeal, she replied, "She wasn't afraid to show her fragility."

"Marilyn's fans see some part of themselves in her," said Leslie Kasperowicz, a freelance writer from Oregon, of the empathy elicited by Marilyn's remarkable life. "They identify with her in many ways. The struggle Marilyn faced to find herself in spite of the heavy pressure of fame, and the way she never lost her humanity—these things mean a lot to her fans." Marilyn identified her own capacity for empathy as having originated from a lack of consistent love and care in childhood, and as having caused her mistrust and fear of the world. "There were no benefits, except what it could teach me about the basic needs of the young, the sick and the weak," Marilyn wrote in preparation for an interview in 1962. "I have great feeling for all the persecuted ones in the world."

"We've been planning this event for more than a year—organizing speakers and everything," explained Scott Fortner, representing Marilyn Remembered Fan Club, a Los Angeles organization founded by Greg Schreiner. "But we didn't expect so many people to attend...

there are hundreds." Schreiner, a music instructor at UCLA and collector of classic film memorabilia and costumes, has organized a memorial service every year since 1982. "Interest in Marilyn is greater than ever," he said.

"This milestone service was the biggest public memorial event in the park's history," said Jessica Dunn, Westwood Village Memorial Park spokeswoman. Although numerous other motion picture legends are buried at the site, none has a dedicated fan base like Marilyn's.

"Just like the fans who came in August of '62 and waited outside in the hot sun," said David Marshall, "the 2012 Marilyn fans are an incredibly diverse group, old and young, any race and creed you can think of, gay and straight, male and female, some with walkers, some in wheelchairs, and all of them with the smarts to recognize Marilyn Monroe was an exceptional human being and worthy of our appreciation fifty years later."

A group of twenty-something and thirty-something young women with bleached blonde hair and wearing moles painted on their cheeks and reproductions of Marilyn's most recognizable dresses stood where Joe DiMaggio wept long ago on Wednesday afternoon, August 8, 1962. A line formed where Marilyn's original mourners sat in folding chairs on the grass in front of the wall of crypts. Fans waited patiently as each handed a companion a camera and posed for photographs standing at Marilyn's crypt. One man apologized for his smile by explaining he had waited many years to visit Marilyn's final resting place. A woman reassured him that his idol would approve of his joy.

At the cemetery's gate on the fiftieth anniversary, a 1950s Buick Roadmaster was parked where Pinkerton guards had turned away Ella Fitzgerald and Sammy Davis Jr. A large painting of Marilyn was displayed where pallbearers rolled her casket out of the chapel and into the black hearse. A welcome table stood where Ralph Greenson, his wife, their son and daughter had waited to enter the chapel. The fans know by heart the frequently published photograph of the family in mourning attire and the tormented look in the psychiatrist's eyes. Looking at the solemn faces of those gathered outside the chapel and tent, some recalled the black and white news coverage available on YouTube and in many documentaries—all those sad faces of fans lining the cemetery fence that sunny afternoon when John F. Kennedy was president and man had not yet landed on the moon.

"So here we are fifty years later," said David Marshall, author of two books about Marilyn, "maybe not the same hundreds of fans who had dressed up in their summer finest to say good-bye to their favorite movie star but the next generation that now forms the Marilyn Community. From the look on the faces of the people slowly moving along that short distance to the crypt, I can see that fifty years later the shock of Marilyn Monroe's death may not be as intense but the loss is still as strongly felt."

Marilyn seems to reach all ages in the new millennium. A six-year-old girl arrived holding her grandmother's hand. In the girl's other hand, she held a Barbie doll dressed in a costume from one of Marilyn's films. When asked about her interest in the long-departed icon, the child says, "Grandma and I watch Marilyn movies on DVD."

The delivery of a dozen roses three times each week to Marilyn's final resting place from DiMaggio ended on the twentieth anniversary of her death. However, the crypt is never unadorned by floral displays. It is one the most visited burial sites in Los Angeles and is noted in most tour books. Only Elvis Presley's grave at Graceland receives more visitors. The marble wall of Marilyn's crypt has been replaced multiple times because of a steady stream of fans caressing, embracing and kissing it. Today the marble is stained by lipstick marks from kisses left behind by recent female visitors.

Nearby, a gray marble bench bears the inscription "In Remembrance of Marilyn Monroe from Her Many Fans." Many fans, indeed, have come for the first time. Joel Morgan, 16, traveled from South Wales in a wheelchair. Deborah Bakker, 21, from Zaandam, Holland, came with her brother and uncle. The list goes on: Marco van der Munnik, 46, from Amsterdam; Ramon Bertolini, 31, from Paris; Manel Torquet Oliva, 55, from Spain; Shaney Evans, 42, and her daughter, Aimee, 24, from the United Kingdom; Ernest Galindo, 38, from Venezuela; Gianandrea Colombo, 30, from Italy; and Janet Wheeler, 46, who traveled the farthest from Australia.

"Since I was twelve, my dream was to place red roses at Marilyn's crypt," said Paul Maggs, 38, from Kent, England. "This year my dream came true, and to meet all these other fans from around the world is just incredible. I also plan to get her signature tattooed on my arm while in Los Angeles; a constant reminder of my amazing visit."

Roy Harvey, 74, told reporters he spent every August 5 at Marilyn's crypt for the past twenty-five years. He faithfully travels by plane from his home in Manhattan to Westwood every year. Niva Pemberton stepped in front of him to lay a bouquet of flowers on the ground. A resident of San Diego, she decorates the tomb with red roses every time she visits Los Angeles. "Marilyn Monroe is someone who will never stop being loved," Pemberton said.

Heaps of floral bouquets, pictures, drawings, notes, letters, and collages accumulate five feet from the wall of marble crypts, covering the walkway. One is immediately reminded of the makeshift altar of tributes in front of Buckingham Palace when Princess Diana died in 1997 and at Ground Zero after the 9/11 attacks.

A green florist's card bears an anonymous printed message: "*Thank you for teaching me I am a survivor. With love.*" On a black-and-white glossy portrait of Marilyn, several people signed their name in black marker beside the printed messages: "We love you so much! Your beauty never fades! We were blessed to have you." On parchment with pink and green silk butterflies attached, a young fan wrote with spiritual adoration:

> *It's been fifty years. It's almost impossible to believe. Dear Marilyn, how sweet you are. People have come from different parts of the world to be with you this week and this day. You are loved, Marilyn. This night will be hard to sleep but that is only because I will be thinking of you. We have been gathering all together these past few days, celebrating your life and your legacy. It's brought so many people together. Oh, Marilyn, I know you are here with us today... You have touched my life in every single way. There is not a moment I can go without having your picture with me. You are so wonderful and I would love to tell you 'thank you' for everything you have done, because you have helped me through all my struggles and have always been there for me, even when no one was. I love you always, Marilyn.*
> *Love, Monica*

The modernistic chapel where Marilyn's funeral took place was reserved for two hundred sponsors of the event. Unlike the day of the original service, the white draperies are pulled back, exposing the interior through glass walls. Outside, a tent is erected over five rows of folding chairs for more fans watching and listening to a live stream of the service. Others are scattered or gathered in clusters across the lawn, standing on graves.

Inside the A-frame structure, crystal chandeliers hung from the ceiling. Flat-screen televisions mounted on the walls displayed recognizable and rare images of Marilyn. In the spot where Marilyn's open casket once stood, a large painted portrait in close-up of her profile is displayed. She is laughing with her head thrown back. Its inspiration is a photograph taken on the set of *Something's Got to Give* of George Cukor embracing her. Flanking the artwork are about a dozen large floral sprays, some with ribbons reading, "*Holding a good thought—Scott,*" "*Immortal Marilyn Fan Club,*" "*Some Like It Hot Fan Club,*" and "*French Fan Club.*"

Host Greg Schreiner introduced the guest speakers, some of them being the few surviving people in Hollywood who actually knew or worked with Marilyn. Stanley Rubin, producer of the film *River of No Return*, recalled Marilyn fighting the studio powers for serious roles. Academy Award winner George Chakiris, who danced alongside Marilyn in musical production numbers in *Gentlemen Prefer Blondes* and *There's No Business Like Show Business*, remembered Marilyn's professionalism and hard work. Nancy Jeffries, another foster child placed with Norma Jeane Baker in the Bolender home, shared her childhood memories.

Author James Spada likened Marilyn to an ambassador, bringing people together from across the globe to share in their collective adoration of her. As a teen in Staten Island, New York, he founded the first Marilyn Monroe Fan Club during her lifetime. Spada reflected upon having believed interest in his idol peaked when he published *Monroe: Her Life in Pictures* on the twentieth anniversary of her death and marveled that interest in her continues with NBC's television series *Smash* and the recent film *My Week with Marilyn.*

Lois Banner, a professor of history and gender studies at the University of Southern California and author of the recently released *Marilyn: The Passion and the Paradox* said, "I look at her as an extraordinary expression of what it means to be an American and what it is to achieve the American dream."

George Barris remembered warm and intimate conversations with Marilyn while they collaborated on a photo spread for *Cosmopolitan* and discussed producing a memoir. The eighty-seven year old photographer also recounted in detail her final thirty-sixth birthday celebration on the set of her unfinished film *Something's Got to Give* as if it occurred yesterday.

Celebrating his fiftieth wedding anniversary in Santa Barbara with his family, Don Murray sent a tribute that was read to the assembly. "Movie lovers all over the world have given her a greater honor," he wrote, "as the most incandescently unforgettable star in the history of movies. And if you see her in *Bus Stop*, you'll see that, while movie lovers like you have made her famous, she has achieved her greatest ambition and made herself wonderful." Speakers also read tribute letters from photographer Lawrence Schiller and photographer Sam Shaw's surviving children.

Joshua Greene updated the assemblage on the legal status of licensing by Marilyn's estate. Joshua was age eight in 1962 and at her fiftieth memorial, was older than his father had been when Marilyn died. His mother, Amy Greene, widow of Milton, spoke last, displaying her sharp wit. At age eighty-three, Amy's face still held the beauty from her appearance with Marilyn and Milton on *Person To Person*. Her jet black hair faded to white, Amy suggested that Marilyn would also have retained her beauty at eighty-six. Amy and retired agent Jay Kanter, twenty-five-years-old at the time of the formation of Marilyn Monroe Productions, invited questions from those gathered. Amy recalled Marilyn sending her and Milton two dozen roses for their wedding. "Marilyn was a class act," she said with conviction. Amy revealed that only one of her husband's thousands of photographs of Marilyn is displayed in her home in New York—the "graduation portrait" taken during hairdressing tests for *The Prince and the Showgirl*.

A young blonde woman wearing red lipstick evocative of Marilyn stood outside the glass wall, her hands clutched together under her chin, as she listened to the service piped outside by speakers. Singer Sue Ann Pinner performed "Do Not Stand at My Grave and Weep."

As the service neared its end, the recorded voice of Lee Strasberg delivered Marilyn's eulogy once again and validated the overpowering truth that she was a loved, human woman and working actress long before she was an icon and source material for future generations. Hearing Strasberg's voice, still in shock and choking up, brought many members of the assembly to tears.

Following the service, fans gathered for a luncheon in the fellowship hall of the Westwood Presbyterian Church, which stands within walking distance of the cemetery. A Marilyn-inspired piece by artist Victoria Fuller was also auctioned to raise funds for Hollygrove Children and Family Services, the former orphanage where Norma Jeane Baker lived long before she became a legend. As fans recognized each other from online chat and introduced themselves to one another, Marilyn's recorded voice enveloped them, singing "Bye Bye Baby" and "I'm Through With Love."

The Internet keeps Marilyn's memory alive and her fans connected. YouTube has thousands of excerpts from her films, newsreels, and interviews. An online community of Marilyn Monroe fans on Facebook engages in ongoing discussions about her personal and professional life, and theories about her death, and post never-ending news articles and newly discovered photographs of her. "It feels kind of like a cross between a high school reunion and a college mixer" remarked David Marshall.

An evening screening of Marilyn's least-favorite film, *River of No Return*, at the Egyptian Theatre followed the fiftieth memorial service and ended a weeklong schedule of events. The week's organizer was Mary Sims, the owner of "Immortal Marilyn," the largest online fan club dedicated—according to its website—to "a strong, determined woman with a soft heart and fragile soul." As a full-time caregiver to her exceptional-needs son, Gary, Sims spends her days at his side. Her self-proclaimed obsession with Marilyn provides a diversion during brief respite breaks. Projecting loving maternal energy, it's easy to understand Sims' empathy and compassion for the waif from Hawthorn who became the world's biggest star.

The week of events dedicated to Marilyn's memory began with a tour of the Hotel del Coronado Resort in San Diego, where a pregnant Marilyn filmed her greatest commercial film, *Some Like It Hot*, during the autumn of 1958. Marilyn's fans know that her Golden

Globe Award-winning performance came at the price of her tragic miscarriage. The historic hotel's gift shop plays the film on loop and sells high-end merchandize with her image, and its beachside restaurant, Shearwater, serves a "Some Like It Hot" dessert.

While many collectors of Marilyn Monroe memorabilia hide them away out of public sight, Scott Fortner and Greg Schreiner displayed their combined collection of personal property of Marilyn Monroe—the largest in the world—in *Marilyn: The Exhibit, An Intimate Look at the Legend* at the Hollywood Museum. On Thursday, August 2, these two leading authorities on all things Monroe invited the media on a personal tour of the collection and the stories behind remarkable pieces.

Opened on June 1—Marilyn's birthday—the exhibit's one thousand items, previously owned by Marilyn, filled the three thousand square foot third floor of the former Max Factor building on the corner of North Highland and Hollywood Boulevards. There were annotated motion picture scripts, personal letters, professional contracts, personal wardrobe items, furniture and artwork from her Brentwood home, and a University High School *Chieftain* 1942 Yearbook filled with messages from her classmates. Even the driving cap once belonging to Marilyn's preferred chauffer, Rudy Kautzsky, was displayed alongside detailed driver logs of her transportation schedules.

Fortner owns the green Pucci blouse Marilyn wore during rehearsals for President Kennedy's birthday gala at Madison Square Garden and a prescription bottle for Hydrodiuril found next to her bed at the time of her death. By admission, he is most fascinated by a Kodak Brownie camera given to her by "Aunt" Ana Lower. "For me, it's amazing to think I possess the first camera ever owned by the most photographed woman in the world," Scott Fortner said.

"Marilyn was actually a very charitable person," Fortner said in an interview with Marijane Gray, "so I find that being able to share my collection in a way that raises money for people in need is very rewarding for me. In a way, it's almost like carrying on Marilyn's legacy. The charity exhibit I sponsored in March of this year raised tens of thousands of dollars for local children in need of health care, food, and housing."

Fortner's popular blog, themarilynmonroecollection.com, updates fans on the surprisingly steady flow of information published by the media. He is frequently interviewed by Reuters and the Associated Press, and has appeared on television in *Mysteries at The Museum* and *Inside Edition*.

Greg Schreiner guided reporters, news cameras, and patrons of the museum toward a once-white silk charmeuse gown delicately draped on a Victorian fainting couch and worn by Marilyn wore in nearly every scene in *The Prince and the Showgirl*. Yellowed with age, the garment rested beside a flat-screen monitor running a loop of the film. He pointed to furnishings behind glass in a climate-controlled environment such as a Hotpoint refrigerator, snug love seat, and bedroom dresser from Marilyn's Spanish Colonial hacienda on Fifth Helena Drive in Brentwood.

"I fell in love with Marilyn when my parents took me to see *Some Like It Hot*," Schreiner told the media. "I looked up at the screen and saw this incredible creature and I said I've got to start collecting this lady." Decades ago, he spent a mere one hundred dollars on a check Marilyn had written to housekeeper Eunice Murray on the last day of her life, which is now valued upwards of $10,000. Most of the exquisite dresses and shoes in Schreiner's collection were concurrently staged at Museo Salvatore Ferragamo in Florence, Italy.

Across the street from the Hollywood Museum, three attendants wheeled a wax figure of Marilyn outside on the sidewalk in front of Madame Tussaud's Wax museum on Hollywood Boulevard. She is modeled signing her name in the cement in the forecourt of Grauman's Chinese Theatre—next door—in June 1953. The figure immediately attracted a crowd of tourists. A Japanese family on vacation in the United States lurched forward to take photos with the likeness. Young women put their arms around Marilyn's shoulder and kissed her on the cheek while companions took pictures with cell phones. The crowd's passion resembled the affection afforded to icons of saints on religious feast days in Europe.

That evening, Scott Fortner hosted a 1950s-themed pool party at the Orchid Suites in Hollywood and brought several authors of Monroe biographies for a book signing. Morgan Blackbyrne, from Ontario, dressed like Hugh Hefner in a red velvet smoking robe, waited until his girlfriend, Monroe lookalike Nadine Banville, had finished singing "I'm Going to File My Claim" in a reproduction of the saloon girl costume from *River of No Return* before he proposed marriage to her in front of the crowd. Morgan also provided the first public screening of his grandfather's 8-millimeter color home movies of Marilyn and Joe DiMaggio on North Redington Beach, Florida in 1961.

International Marilyn Monroe tribute artist Suzie Kennedy made a planned late entrance, depicting her role model in true form. The previous day, she appeared in Palm Springs under a twenty-five foot sculpture depicting the iconic subway skirt-blowing scene from *The Seven Year Itch.* For the pool party, Monroe's doppelganger wore an exact copy of the white and blue polka-dot sheath cocktail dress from the same film and filled the air with the scent of *Chanel of No. 5.* Kennedy now has a busy schedule traveling the world for photo shoots, print and television advertising campaigns, corporate events, and live ensemble celebrity tribute performances.

On Friday of the fiftieth anniversary week, a "Homes and Haunts Tour" of various Los Angeles addresses related to Marilyn's life ended with a champagne toast at Santa Monica Beach at sunset. Marilyn posed there for her final photo shoot with George Barris just weeks before her death. As the sun dipped under the Pacific, Marilyn sat in the sand bundled in her wool sweater from Mexico with a blanket over her legs. "This is for you, George," she said, puckering her lips and blowing a kiss. He snapped the shutter of his camera. That picture would become more poignant for being the last color photograph taken of her.

People from all over the world exited three charter buses and gathered virtually in the same spot to toast the life of a woman they had never met, but meant so much to them. In the distance, Elton John's recorded voice sang "Candle in the Wind," a moving tribute from the *Goodbye Yellow Brick Road* album released in 1973. Everyone raised their glasses and in unison and saluted, "To Marilyn! This is for you!"

On Saturday, August 4, in an unprecedented move Twentieth Century-Fox Studios opened its historic Café de Paris commissary to fans for a luncheon in celebration of Marilyn's illustrious career. Unlike Universal and Warner Brothers Studios, her home studio remains closed to the public, and had never hosted an event in honor of a deceased contract performer. On this fiftieth anniversary, the studio opened its doors for members of *Marilyn Remembered* and

Immortal Marilyn and hosted a VIP tour of the lot where—before she was a legend—Marilyn was employed as a working actress over a span of sixteen years and made the majority of her films.

Fox served the guests a buffet lunch in the elegant dining hall where Marilyn ate meals with favorite costume designer, William Travilla, and makeup artist, Allan "Whitey" Snyder, and where she personally hosted a production party for her fellow cast of *Let's Make Love*. The Best Picture Academy Award presented to Darryl Zanuck for *All About Eve*—the first Fox film in which Marilyn gained notice—attracted attention from behind glass in a display cabinet at the hall's entrance.

Like an apparition of residual spiritual energy, professional Monroe tribute artist Memory Monroe sauntered across the gleaming parquet floor in an exact reproduction of the red velvet gown designed by Oleg Cassini. Only these diehard fans recognized the reference. Memory's performance art echoed Marilyn's dramatic staged entrance at the studio's formal dinner for visiting film exhibitors in the spring of 1951. In a brilliant example of effective self-promotion, Monroe attracted powerful attention and persuaded Darryl Zanuck and Spyros Skouras to leverage her casting in substantial film roles.

Guides escorted the guests to the exterior of the two-story Spanish building that once housed Marilyn's dressing room and the Elizabethan bungalow that sometimes served as her headquarters. They passed the enormous sound stages where Marilyn worked ten-hour days sometimes six days per week to produce the on-screen magic revealed in Fox's release of seven restored films for the half-centennial, in the box set titled *Forever Marilyn Blu-Ray Collection.* Priced for retail at one hundred dollars, the collection also included re-mastered editions of two films that Marilyn made for rival studios. Fox also re-released a treasure trove three-volume box set of seventeen films on DVD under the title *Marilyn: The Premiere Collection.*

Fox's motivation to open its doors to the fans of its arguably high-earning, deceased star also served as an effective marketing strategy. Fifty years since the studio's payroll department discontinued her paycheck, Marilyn continues to earn her studios a sizeable profit. Fox has released a Marilyn Monroe film collection for each generation since the advent of home video entertainment, re-releasing the body of her work with each technological advance. The studio released collections in VHS format in 1982, 1987, and 1992. Marilyn's image on the covers of more obscure early films in which she played a walk-on or minor role with only a few minutes of screen time sell the films that might otherwise be overlooked by consumers.

On Saturday, August 4, the fiftieth anniversary of the last day of Marilyn's life, Sunny Thompson performed an astounding one-woman show in *Marilyn: Forever Blonde* at the El Portal Theatre in North Hollywood. "It is truly one of the greatest performances of the stage," hailed the *San Francisco Chronicle.* Written by Sunny's husband, Greg Thompson, the play is based upon sources of Marilyn's actual words from actual interviews published during her lifetime and alleged quotes from reputedly scurrilous biographies. Regardless of the mixed accuracy of the material, the play humanizes Marilyn like no other attempt at a theatrical biography.

Sunny Thompson was an uncanny Monroe with astonishing gestural and vocal authenticity. She rivaled every previous stage and screen impersonation of the legend and emerged as the Meryl Streep of Monroe characterization. Her voice sometimes mirrored Marilyn's breathless whisper from the movies, when the character was self-parodying, but leveled into a more natural tone when speaking conversationally to the audience. The performance ascertained that Thompson studied recordings of Marilyn's interviews for Richard Meryman and Georges Belmont.

Visually, Thompson evoked the legend, even to an audience of predominantly diehard fans. Having perfected makeup skills throughout the 1980s and '90s when performing a visual and vocal impersonation of Marilyn in cabaret acts and on television, make-up artist Jimmy James was responsible for accurately recreating her face upon Sunny's. Audience members in the first few row only had to squint their eyes ever so slightly to suspend reality and imagine the real Monroe ten feet before them. In the tenth row, squinting was unnecessary.

In one humorous scene, a bare-shouldered Thompson lounges in a bathtub filled with realistic-looking bubbles as she chats to the audience. When she suddenly stands up, fully clothed—the audience erupts into laughter. "It's all just make believe," she says innocently.

In the final scene, Sunny, as Marilyn, looks up with tears in her eyes and says, "All I ever wanted was to be loved." A moment later she dies in bed, and the stage fades to black. The scene played at half-past ten, the presumed time of Marilyn's death exactly fifty years earlier. "Sunny gives us a glimpse of Marilyn's effervescent spirit," remarked Shar Daws, who attended the performance. "She wasn't downtrodden; she had strength, wit and intelligence, she knew what she wanted and nothing was going to stop her achieving her goals and realizing her dreams."

Afterward, Sunny and Greg Thompson participated in a question-and-answer session with the audience. As herself, Sunny displays softness and gentleness of spirit that channels Marilyn without any pretentiousness. "I have a deep admiration and respect for Marilyn's talent, her warm charm, and empathize with her insecurities and need for reassurance," she declares on the play's website. "I love her style, her shrewd marketing sense and her compassion for humanity. Perhaps it is the kindness and compassion behind her eyes that make her so unforgettably beautiful. She was a powerful and thoughtful person, far ahead of her time." The actress' authentic impersonation is clearly the result of painstaking research, experimentation, rehearsal and a personal identification with Monroe.

Greg Thompson's script was also a labor of love. He confessed to having fallen in love with Marilyn at age eleven in 1953. "She asked for nothing more from a man than his attention," he says on the play's website. "Marilyn Monroe was a vulnerable, insecure child-woman searching desperately for someone to love and respect her for who she really was. I couldn't do it then, perhaps I can do it now."

Before the performance, the owners of El Portal Theatre dedicated its new entertainment space as The Monroe Forum, with a ribbon-cutting ceremony attended by several celebrities and a few former colleagues of Marilyn. Former co-star in *Bus Stop*, Don Murray, delivered a touching tribute to Marilyn's talent and enduring appeal. He was accompanied by his son, Christopher Murray, whose mother, Hope Lang, also appeared in the film.

Also in attendance was actress Renee Taylor, who took classes with Marilyn at the Actors Studio in New York, stage and screen actor Theodore Bikel, Councilman Tom La Bonge, and Joe Razo, the Principal of Lankershim Elementary School located behind the theater. The dedication was partly inspired by the fact that Norma Jeane watched films at the theater in the 1930s, when she lived in a nearby foster home and attended the school.

If the spirit of young Norma Jeane Baker lurked in the El Portal Theatre where she once watched her idols—Jean Harlow and Clark Gable—on the silver screen, she would have been moved by the affection apparent in the words of Marilyn's former leading man. "The woman who wanted most of all to be loved and considered 'wonderful' ultimately achieved her goal," Don Murray told those gathered to celebrate her thirty-six years of life and fifty years of legendary status.

* * *

Marilyn Monroe has become an icon for the motion picture industry, representing its heights and depths, and may be the most beloved actress in its history. She possessed abundant charisma, incredible screen presence, and perfect comic timing. No other American public figure is as loved, with the exception of Elvis Presley and Oprah Winfrey. Marilyn also remains an iconic representation of a love goddess, an idealized female, and an actress of the Golden Age of Hollywood. She left behind more than the legacy of a brilliant film career by increasing our awareness of mental illness and the impact of childhood trauma and abuse.

Mary Sims, who reserved a block of seats in the theater for members of her fan club, watched the faces of those congregated and softly quoted an anonymous source: "'Immortality lies not in the things you leave behind, but in the people your life has touched.'"

Little Norma Jeane Baker grew up wanting nothing more than to be loved; and as Marilyn Monroe, she achieved this goal, becoming one of the most charismatic and beloved women on the planet. Once you discover Marilyn, she will forever remain in your heart.

Appendix: Selected Marilyn Monroe Film Synopses

The Prince and the Showgirl (1957)

In 1911, the Grand Duke Charles, Regent of the Balkan State of Carpathia (Laurence Olivier)—formerly the Prince of Hungary before marriage—arrives in London to attend George V's coronation. His companions include his mother-in-law, the Queen Dowager (Sybil Thorndike), and his sixteen-year-old son, King Nicolas VIII (Jeremy Spenser), who will succeed him in eighteen months. The Grand Duke is both a widower and womanizer.

The British Foreign Office assigns Deputy Head of the Far Eastern Division Peter Northbrook (Richard Wattis) to attend to the Grand Duke's needs at the Carpathian Embassy. Northbrook takes the Duke to see a musical, *The Coconut Girl*, at the Avenue Theatre, starring Maisy Springfield (Jean Kent). Backstage, he greets the cast in a receiving line and becomes infatuated with an American chorus girl, Elsie Marina (Monroe)—formerly Elsie Stolzenburg—whose shoulder strap breaks during their memorable introduction.

Later that evening, Elsie receives an invitation to a midnight supper at the Carpathian embassy. After changing into a carefully selected white evening gown, she is escorted by Northbrook to the Embassy. He coaches her on the correct form of address for royal and imperial leaders, "Your Grand Ducal Highness" or "Serene Highness," and on members of the royal family. Elsie is overwhelmed and remarks that the pressure of protocol reminds her of that of an opening night. Northbrook advises her to speak only when directly addressed.

Elsie is impressed with the elaborate décor of the Embassy, which Northbrook denounces as vulgar. "Well, give me vulgarity!" Elsie responds. When he leads her to an upstairs private drawing room, Elsie is surprised to find no other guests. The footmen deliver a table set for only two, and Elsie is offended when she discovers she has been invited for a tryst in the Duke's private quarters. She tries to flee, informing Northbrook, "There's a *word* for what you are, and it's not Deputy Head of the Far Eastern Department!"

As Northbrook chases Elsie down the stairs and tries to convince her to stay, she indicates that she has fought her way out of many tête-à-têtes and is familiar with the moves of seduction. "'*It-will-be-more-fun-serving-ourselves-don't-you-think?*'" she recites, predicting the words of the Regent. "And then after supper, '*Miss-Marina-you-must-be-very-tired-why-don't-you-put-your-feet-up-on-this-nice-sofa?*'" Northbrook begs Elsie to stay, and offers to assist in her departure after dinner by pretending her elderly aunt has been hospitalized for injuries sustained in an auto accident. As Elsie rushes out the door, the Duke greets her but pays no attention to her use of a string of incorrect titles. Finally, Elsie mutters under her breath, "The hell with it!"

While the Duke escorts Elsie to the second floor drawing room, he attempts to charm her with clichéd expressions, which she recognizes as obvious seductive overtures. The footmen signal Elsie when she should remain standing in the presence of royalty, and she looks to them for an indication of the appropriate time to sit. Elsie also studies their practice of never turning their backs toward the Duke when exiting the room.

The evening quickly proceeds with Duke reciting the twaddle Elsie had predicted. He serves her champagne and shots of vodka, something she has never consumed, before he telephones the Carpathian ambassador. Feeling ignored, Elsie pours herself champagne and feasts alone on the buffet. She bristles upon overhearing the Duke discuss the arrest of a political dissenter and recoils at his pejorative remarks about "stupid" Americans who protested the arrest on the principle of democratic rights.

The telephone conversation also reveals the Duke's suspicion that Germany is working against him by building an alliance with his misguided son. Elsie reminds the Duke of her American citizenship and pointedly makes a toast to President Taft. Nicholas abruptly enters and protests the arrest, and Elsie jumps to her feet upon hearing he is a king. The Duke asserts himself as current ruler of Carpathia even though Nicholas will soon ascend the throne. He banishes the boy to his room and rescinds his telephone privileges.

The hearing-impaired Queen Dowager and her lady-in-waiting return to the Embassy after an evening out. The Dowager is enchanted by Elsie and speaks to her in French, but Elsie knows only one response, "*oui*". The ineffectual but charming conversation convinces the Dowager that Elise is a friend of the great actress Sarah Bernhardt.

Elsie questions the Duke about his deceased wife, and he describes a politically motivated marriage arranged by officials of their respective governments. Elsie finds his life shocking because "there's no love in it." To avoid sharing the sofa with her host, she moves to a chair; the Duke resumes efforts to seduce her by kicking an ottoman at her feet, taking a seat on it, and complimenting her appearance. When he attempts to take Elsie into his arms with a corny line, she bursts into laughter and pushes him across the room. "That's just terrible!" she cries. "Don't pull the 'Grand Duke' with me." He is humiliated, and they mitigate the tension by consuming another shot each of vodka.

Now intoxicated, Elsie brazenly expresses disappointment in the Duke's lack of romantic prowess. She discloses having expected passionate music, dim lights, and erotic perfumes, as well as her inability to resist them. "Better luck next time," Elsie says, "but not with me." Offended by her direct manner, the Duke summons a driver to take Elsie home. She exits the drawing room in search of her wrap and remembering protocol, catches herself and backs out of the door. Stinging from Elsie's criticism, the Duke scolds his footmen for their failure to provide music, dim the lights, and perfume the room. In a last attempt at seduction, he instructs the men to create a romantic ambience before Elsie's return.

When Elsie returns with her wrap, the Duke manipulates her by apologizing and acknowledging the lack of love in his life. Taking advantage of her tipsy state, he describes himself as a sleeping prince waiting to be awakened to life by the kiss of a beautiful woman. The Duke serves Elsie another drink and invites her to recline on the sofa girl as a valet begins playing the violin in the corridor. The Duke compliments Elsie's beauty and attempts to kiss her. Enjoying the amorous attention, Elsie reciprocates with compliments but becomes preoccupied with the Duke's hair gel. Finally, she kisses him. Northbrook interrupts the Duke's victory by barging into the room with news of the hospitalization of Elsie's fictitious aunt. Inebriated, Elsie dismisses him before passing out on the floor, and the footmen carry her to a guestroom.

The next morning, the Duke prepares for the coronation as he and Nicholas discuss the riots and arrests in Carpathia. A hung-over Elsie emerges from the guestroom wrapped in sheets, sashays into the Duke's quarters, collects the vodka bottle, and exits. Appalled, the Duke describes her to Northbrook as having "the mind of backward child, the muscles of a boxer, and an approach to life of stomach-turning sentimentality." He also admits that Elsie elicited uncharacteristically schmaltzy remarks that, if overheard, would make him a laughing stock. Most maddening to the Duke, she was "rendered insensible by an amount of vodka" which in Carpathia would be served to a four-year-old child as a "mild tonic." He asks Northbrook to invite Lady Sunningdale to dinner that evening after the coronation.

Now dressed and refreshed, Elsie greets the Duke with a declaration of having fallen madly in love with him. "You do need more love in your life, so now you've got it," she says adoringly. The Duke responds with indifference, but Elsie realizes he must assume his royal demeanor and quotes his amorous remarks from the previous evening.

After the Duke leaves the drawing room, Elsie hears an organ grinder's tune on the street outside and practices a dance from her show. Nicholas silently watches and asks her to place a telephone call for him to the German ambassador. She happily agrees and hands the phone to him as she gazes out the window as the King speaks in German. She spots her friends in a theatrical troupe standing on the sidewalk across to watch the coronation parade; they see her in the window and call out to her.

Elsie gestures for them to be quiet, having overheard Nicholas' plan to conspire with the Bulgarian Army to overthrow his father and ascend the throne. She also reveals having been born in Milwaukee and understanding German. When Nicholas warns her of the danger of her knowledge of his plan, Elsie confidently replies, "I'm an *American citizen*—nobody can do anything to me!" Nicholas asks if she will tell his father, but Elsie dashes off to the balcony to tell her friends that she is in love and plans to join them later to watch the parade. The Duke, she says, has no sense of humor and "not a bit of charm."

The Duke returns in his formal royal tunic adorned with epaulettes and decoration and formally presents Elsie with a parting gift, a medal with his crest. She surmises that "there are quite a few of these things being worn around Europe" and requests that he pin it on the low décolletage of her gown. As the Duke bids Elsie farewell, she realizes the fairytale may be ending and asks if this is when she must awaken from her dream. When the Duke kisses Elsie, she giggles as his epaulettes tickle her. Infuriated with her childlike and spontaneous joy, he leaves. "Life is rather sad sometimes," Elsie laments to Northbrook as he escorts her into the hall and downstairs.

The Dowager summons Elsie and appoints her as lady-in-waiting for the coronation, decorating her with jewels and a formal veil. When the Dowager instructs the Duke to endow Elsie with a Carpathian order, he protests that it is an order reserved only for a "very personal service" to the head of the state. "No doubt she will do you one someday," the Dowager retorts. The Duke relents, and formally invests Elsie with the Order of Perseverance, Second Class. However, she relinquishes the medal when their parting is delayed.

The open horse-drawn carriage transports Elsie and the royal family to the cononation at Westminster Abbey. Elsie waves excitedly to her theater friends when they pass them on the street, and her spontaneous joy charms the dour Duke. During the lengthy coronation, Elsie is moved to tears.

Upon returning to the embassy after the ceremony, Elsie and Nicholas discuss his political plans. The Duke confronts them about the telephone call and demands that his son divulge the disloyal message he delivered. When Nicholas refuses, the Duke banishes him to his room under the supervision of a colonel and prohibits him from attending the coronation ball. The Duke rhetorically asks Elsie what he should do with such a son. If he were seriously seeking her guidance, Elsie replies, she would offer a heartfelt recommendation.

The Duke presumes it would involve a criticism about the lack of love in his life.

This is exactly Elsie's sentiment. The Duke swears in German, and Elsie nonchalantly translates. He realizes she understands German and asks her to reveal the message she overheard in Nicholas' telephone call. Elsie refuses, and like a sage, calls the treatment of his son "just plain bad policy." To whom is he likely to disclose his plot, she argues, the jailor colonel or his "dream prince of a beautiful father" who has rescinded his invitation to the ball? Realizing her time with the Duke must come to an end, Elsie requests a farewell kiss and the parting present.

Having contemplated Elsie's advice to be less strict and more loving, the Duke summons Nicholas and permits him to attend the ball. Elsie eavesdrops from behind a lute. When the Duke's tone becomes too harsh, Elsie plucks the string of the instrument as a cryptic signal to soften his approach. The Duke permits Nicholas to attend the ball, but the young king agrees only if Elsie accompanies him. She consents, and Nicholas promotes her to a first-class order. Once again, Elsie returns the Duke's parting medal, curtsies properly and backs out of the room.

At the coronation ball, the Duke invites Lady Lucy Sunningdale (Maxine Audley) to a midnight supper at the embassy and finds Elsie and Nicolas sitting on the grand staircase where they are composing a manifesto to present to his father. The Duke invites Elsie to dance, and as they waltz, she negotiates reconciliation by relaying Nicholas' conditions, including a general election. When the Duke balks, Elsie promotes the advantages of a democracy. Worried that he is falling in love with Elsie, the Duke abruptly ends the evening and sends her and his son home.

Back in the embassy drawing room, Northbrook reports to the Duke that Elsie and Nicholas went for a ride on a public bus, walked to the embassy, and were dancing the Fox Trot in the steward's room to the ragtime accompaniment of the valet's violin. Elsie enters and assumes the table set for Lucy Sunningdale is intended for her. Secretly, Northbrook promises the Duke that he will escort Lucy to a different room and call upon him on the pretense that the ambassador has summoned him.

Elsie presents Nicholas' manifesto to the Duke. It proclaims support of his father contingent upon several conditions. While the Duke considers a response, Elsie turns the tables and trumps him with a beautifully staged seduction scene; employing the same manipulation he used the previous evening. She pours him vodka and asks if he would be more comfortable reclined on the sofa. Elsie has also arranged for the valet to be accompanied by an orchestra of servants playing romantic music out in the hall.

After Elsie snuggles with the Duke on the sofa and serenades him, he professes his deep love for her. She reciprocates, and they embrace. When Northbrook interrupts on cue with a fictitious message from the ambassador, the Duke angrily sends him away. Alone with Elsie, the Duke arrives at a solution to the conflict with his son. He will release the jailed dissenter, gain public favor, and win the general election. Serving as a diplomat, Elsie successfully averted war.

The next morning, a dismayed Nicolas tells Northbrook that his father uncharacteristically embraced him, called him a "darling boy," and asked if he felt the lack of love in his life. Northbrook also finds the Grand Duke transformed with joy and emotion. The Duke compliments Northbrook, acts kindly to the servants, and kisses the young king. He also instucts Northbrook to obtain a passport for Elsie to travel Carpathia in preparation for their marriage, and to provide flowers, furs, jewelry, and dresses. Most uncharacteristically, he orders that Elsie has *carte blanche*. Northbrook's eyebrows rise by such generosity. "As *blanche* as she cares," the Duke insists.

Elsie, the Duke, and Nicholas gather in the conservatory as the royal family prepares to return to their return to their home. Before leaving for the train station, the young king tells her the previous evening was the most pleasant he ever spent in his life and presents her with a brooch of the Royal Carpathian Arms.

Alone with the Duke, Elsie announces the time has come for her to be the voice of reason. She acknowledges the importance of his role as leader and honors his reputation as "the best political brain in Europe." The Duke outlines his plan to abdicate his throne to Nicholas in eighteen months, and she replies that her contract with the theatrical troupe will also end in eighteen months. Alas, only the ending of their respective responsibilities will allow them to finally be together.

In a sad realization, Elsie reckons, "So there we are." The Duke alludes to the potential for unexpected events to keep them apart. "This is goodbye," he sadly concludes. "*Au revoir*," Elsie whispers, tears filling her eyes.

As the Duke presents Elsie with the parting gift, she bites on the medal with her teeth to distinguish it from the others presented to her. The Dowager bids a final farewell to Elsie, giving her a medallion, an autographed photograph, and a suggestion of "an occasional change of dress."

Elsie and the Duke exchange a final farewell from a distance. She extends the farewell by requesting that he mail an autographed photograph to the theater; forlorn, she leans against the doorframe and watches the royal family's departure. She collects her parting gifts and takes a final look at the embassy, her mind filled with memories of the past two days. With a borrowed raincoat over her gown, Elsie retreats through the long reception hall and exits the front doors. Jack Cardiff's camera focuses on the rear of her body walking away; however, unlike in *Niagara*, the camera's focus in not on sexualizing the character, but instead on her sadness.

* * *

SOME LIKE IT HOT (1959)

Some Like It Hot opens in Chicago, 1929. A hearse delivers a casket filled with bootlegged whiskey to the Mozzarella Funeral Parlor, a front for a speakeasy owned by Spats Colombo (George Raft). Outside, mobster Toothpick Charlie (George E. Stone) double-crosses his rival kingping by disclosing the establishment's password to Police Sergeant Mulligan (Pat O'Brien). By saying he has arrived for "Grandma's funeral," the sergeant is ushered to a secret room where festivities and illegal alcohol consumption are taking place. He is led to a ringside table to enjoy the wild floorshow and is served coffee spiked with a variety of liquors. Onstage, two jazz musicians, bass fiddle player Jerry (Jack Lemmon) and saxophonist Joe (Tony Curtis), bicker about how to spend their first week's as they perform. Joe convinces Jerry to bet their wages on a dog races. When the police raid the speakeasy, the musicians flee with their instruments.

Joe and Jerry pawn their overcoats to bet on the dog races and find themselves underdressed for a blizzard. They consult with manager Sig Poliakoff (Billy Gray), begging for the three-week gig in Florida, not realizing the positions are for an all-female band, Sweet Sue (Joan Shawlee) and Her Society Syncopaters, managed by Mr. Beinstock (Dave Barry). The band is headed to the Seminole Ritz in Miami, but the saxophone player eloped with a Bible salesman and the bass fiddle player got pregnant. Two musicians are needed by the time the band's train leaves the station that evening, but Joe and Jerry are "not the right shape" to be hired. The snappy dialogue is priceless. Poliakoff tells them they must be younger than twenty-five. Jerry insists they can pass for younger. Poliakoff says they must be blonde. Jerry suggests they dye their hair. Poliakoff concludes with their needing to be girls. Jerry blurts, "We could…" until Joe cuts him off with an emphatic, "No, we couldn't."

Hungry and cold, Jerry suggests they borrow clothes from the girls in the chorus and call themselves Josephine and Geraldine. While putting gas in a borrowed car in a parking garage, the men witness the St. Valentine's Day Massacre when Spats Colombo and his henchmen seek revenge on Toothpick Charlie and his gang. The musicians watch as rapid-fire machine guns blast the lineup of men. When the gas tank overflows, the gangsters see Joe and Jerry. The sound of police sirens distracts the mobsters, and the two musicians escape to safety.

Joe calls Poliakoff, and in a feminine voice, accepts the gig. In the next scene, the men wobble in high heels in full drag down a train platform. Sugar Kane (Monroe), formerly Sugar Kowalczyk, breezes past them and serves as an authentic female role model. Joe introduces himself as "Josephine" to Beinstock and Sweet Sue and announces he and "Geraldine" are the "new girls." "Brand new," adds Jerry, who impulsively changes his name from Geraldine to Daphne.

Josephine and Daphne meet the other band members and retreat to the ladies lounge to adjust their false breasts. They stumble upon Sugar swigging down bourbon from a flask hidden in her garter belt. "I can stop any time I want to," she says of her drinking against the band's policy, only she doesn't want to stop, especially when she's blue. Sugar recounts the sad story of her life, metaphorically explaining that she always gets the "fuzzy end of the lollipop."

On the moving train, the band rehearses *Runnin' Wild*. At the end of the number, Sugar's flask falls to floor before Beinstock and Sweet Sue. To rescue Sugar from immediate termination, Daphne claims the flask is hers and receives a lecture about the band's prohibition against liquor and men. They wouldn't be "caught dead with men," Daphne insists, calling them "hairy beasts with eight hands." Daphne and Sugar have now bonded. "Good-night, Honey!" Sugar later whispers from her berth while taking off her dress.

During the night, Sugar, wearing a negligee, climbs up to Daphne's upper berth to thank her for taking the blame for her flask. She offers to return the favor in any way. Seeing Sweet Sue approaching, Sugar quickly climbs into the berth. "That's one of 'em," Daphne says. In this hilarious scene, Sugar snuggles up next to Daphne, recalling times she cuddled up with her sister and pretended they were lost in a dark cave. Jerry fights off his increasing arousal, reminding himself aloud that, "I'm a girl."

Unaware that Daphne's twitching is due to masculine arousal, Sugar grows alarmed by her new friend's tremors. She discovers Daphne's cold feet under the covers and offers to warm them by rubbing them with her own feet, exacerbating Jerry's arousal.

Daphne feigns illness, and Sugar tries to leave due to her low resistance. To prevent Sugar from leaving, Daphne recommends a shot of whiskey and suggests a secret party, coyly saying it may turn into a surprise party. "This will put hair on your chest," Sugar announces while handing her a drink in a paper cup.

Sugar informs the other girls of the party, and they cram into the upper birth with bottles of vermouth, a cocktail shaker, a corkscrew, cheese, and crackers. Girls wearing skimpy nightclothes surround Daphne and begin drinking and snacking. One girl waves a sausage in Daphne's face and asks if anyone would like salami. The phallic reference is blatant.

Joe/Josephine is awakened by the party in the berth above and is exasperated by the site of his buddy's shenanigans. Sugar leaves to break a chunk of ice into cubes for the cocktails and Josephine follows her into the ladies lounge. Sugar discloses her negative experiences with all-male bands and her pattern of falling in love with saxophone players who use and abuse her (the role Joe has played in relation to women). Sugar elaborates on her attraction to saxophone players, emphasizing her preference for men who play tenor sax. "All they have to do is play eight bars of *Come to Me, My Melancholy Baby*," she says. "And my spine turns to custard, and I get goose-pimply all over—and I come to them."

Sugar announces that she will be twenty-five in June, and she wants to settle down with a millionaire who is sweet and gentle. Back in the berth, the party grows out of control when the girls tickle Daphne and drop ice cubes down her nightgown. Fearful of being unmasked as a man, Jerry pulls the cord above his pillow activating the emergency brake, sending the girls out of his berth and onto the floor as the train screeches to a halt.

The band soon arrives at the Seminole Ritz Hotel on Miami Beach. Sugar and Josephine commiserate about the advanced age of the row of millionaires reading the *Wall Street Journal* in rocking chairs on the resort's verandah. One predatory millionaire, Osgood Fielding III (Joe E. Brown), is instantly attracted to Daphne. He tells her that he admires a girl with a shapely ankle, and Daphne quips, "Me, too."

Osgood makes a pass at Daphne in the elevator, and she slaps him furiously. Meanwhile, a fresh bellhop is harassing Josephine in the hotel room. Behind a closed door, Joe and Jerry exchange experiences of negative treatment by obnoxious, predatory males and begin empathizing with women. Joe expresses interest in remaining with the female band in order to court Sugar, while Jerry wants to end the masquerade and join a male band. Joe convinces Jerry that if they shed the disguises, Spats Colombo will likely locate and kill them.

When Sugar invites the "girls" to rent bathing suits and frolic on the beach, Joe begs off to take a bath, and Jerry agrees to join her, anticipating delight at applying sun-tanning lotion on each other. Once they leave for the beach, Joe pulls Beinstock's stolen suitcase from under his bed. Inside, he discovers a naval hat, sportswear and a pair of glasses. With the information Sugar has shared with him, he schemes to impersonate a wealthy millionaire with the qualities she desires.

On the beach, Sugar and Daphne play ball in the surf. Sugar admires Daphne's flat-chested figure because clothes hang better on her new friend than they do on her. Disguised in Beinstock's yachting jacket, captain's hat and glasses, Joe appears on the sand carrying the *Wall Street Journal*. When Sugar runs past him to catch a stray beach ball, Joe trips her. Sugar is smitten. Imitating Cary Grant's voice, Joe introduces himself as Junior, an oil magnate. He discusses his wealth and the size of his yacht—with phallic allusions—moored in the gulf. The conversation turns to rises in the stock market and Sugar fibs about being a society debutant who, as a lark, has joined a band with sorority sisters. She asks if he collects shells. Junior says he inherited his passion for shells from his father and grandfather. In fact, they named their oil company after it. "Shell Oil?" Sugar gasps.

When Daphne discovers the couple chatting, Sugar introduces her as another collegiate and invites Junior to their performance that evening. Daphne realizes that Junior is Joe, and drags Sugar back to the hotel. Later, Osgood invites Daphne aboard his yacht with plans to entertain her following the show. Joe, accepting the invitation on behalf of Daphne, pressures Jerry to instead go dancing with Osgood and plans to sneak aboard the yacht with Sugar with hopes to seduce her.

In the Seminole Ritz's ballroom, Sugar sings *I Wanna Be Loved By You* while wearing a diaphanous gown. Wilder tantalizes the audience through placement of the spotlight upon her. The bottom curve of the light acts as a neckline over the bodice of the dress that appears sheer, like bare skin. The spotlight dips, "exposing" Marilyn's breasts.

"Monroe and Wilder turn it into one of the most mesmerizing and blatantly sexual scenes in the movies," wrote film critic Roger Ebert many years later. "Wilder places her in the center of a round spotlight that does not simply illuminate her from the waist up, as an ordinary spotlight would, but toys with her like a surrogate neckline, dipping and clinging as Monroe moves her body higher and lower in the light with teasing precision." It is a striptease—without the actual removal of clothing—accompanied by Marilyn innocently singing. "To experience that scene is to understand why no other actor, male or female, has more sexual chemistry with the camera than Monroe," Ebert concluded.

A bouquet of flowers from Osgood arrives on the bandstand for Daphne, and Joe inserts a card from Junior to Sugar. After reading the message inviting her to Junior's yacht after the show, Sugar rushes off to meet him. Joe changes into the Junior disguise and races off to the pier to meet Sugar in a motorboat; he pulls off his dangling earrings just as she arrives. Unable to control the direction of Osgood's motorboat, Joe drives it backward with Sugar reclining beside him.

Aboard the yacht, Joe has difficulty locating where Osgood intended to entertain Daphne. They enter a drawing room with champagne and an evening meal. Sugar notices a swordfish mounted on the wall. Joe says it's a herring. She is amazed at how the big fish are stuffed into little glass jars. Joe suggests they shrink when marinated.

When Sugar expresses discomfort at being completely alone with a man in the middle of the ocean, Junior confesses that she is perfectly safe, as he is unable to reach arousal with women after the tragic loss of his fiancée at the Grand Canyon. Both he and the fiancée, he explains, unable to see without their glasses, took them off to kiss, and the fiancée accidentally fell into the abyss.

Junior feigns impotence in order to motivate Sugar into seducing him—a reversal of the stereotypical aggressive male and passive female roles. He recounts a history of unsuccessful treatments by Sigmund Freud, the Mayo brothers, and French upstairs maids. Eager to help, Sugar administers passionate kisses to him, as he lies prone on the sofa like a psychoanalysis patient. In her copy of the script, Marilyn wrote, "*Trust it, enjoy it, be brave*" and "*Getting drunk on kisses*" to inspire her performance.

After pretending not to feel aroused during the long period of necking, Junior finally announces that Sugar's treatment is effective. She agrees, noting that the lenses of his eyeglasses are steaming up. Junior's foot rises, symbolic of penile erection. She kisses him more sweetly than erotically, and is simultaneously seducing and being seduced.

The scene is inter-spliced with Daphne and Osgood competing to lead one another in a tango to the Latin music of a Cuban band on the dance floor of a roadhouse. They transfer a single red rose from each other's teeth as they change positions in the dance.

As the sun rises, Junior escorts Sugar back to the hotel as Osgood drunkenly returns to his yacht. Back in their room, Jerry/Daphne, now totally immersed in his feminine alter ego, joyfully tells Joe about his/her engagement to Osgood after an evening of romantic tango dancing. At the direction of Wilder, Lemmon punctuated each line of the riotous dialogue with a shake of the maracas so that the audience had time to laugh, and thus, ensured none of the witty lines were lost.

Jerry returns to his masculine senses and shows Joe his diamond bracelet and box of white orchids, engagement presents from Osgood. The men quickly don their feminine disguises when Sugar joins them to share her love for Junior and to describe their glorious evening together as "suicidally beautiful." Enraptured, she swears off liquor.

When Spats Colombo and his henchmen arrive at the hotel as "delegates for the Friends of Italian Opera convention" followed by Sergeant Mulligan, Joe and Jerry uncomfortably share the elevator with the mobsters. One gangster says the "women" look familiar. Back in their room, the musicians decide to flee. Joe, a changed man, does not want to abandon Sugar like the previous saxophone players in her life. He plans a farewell that includes giving her the diamond bracelet. In a Cary Grant accent, Joe calls Sugar to regretfully report that he is marrying the daughter of a Venezuelan oil magnet to merge their two companies.

Initially shocked, Sugar accepts the news graciously and thanks him for the inside information on the stock market value of Venezuelan oil. During the conversation, Joe kicks the box of orchids with the diamond bracelet inside, across the hall toward Sugar's hotel door. She is surprised by his parting gift of diamond and surmises they "must be worth their weight in gold." Tears stream down Sugar's face as she tries to maintain composure during the painful end of their relationship.

Within moments, a devastated Sugar enters Josephine and Daphne's hotel room, searching for liquor. Joe sees Sugar's pain from his feminine perspective. Josephine tries to convince Sugar that she will soon forget him. No matter where she may travel, Sugar laments; she will always see a Shell gas station on the corner.

Joe and Jerry escape from the window of their hotel room and are spotted by Colombo and his men. They change into costumes as a bellboy and an elderly millionaire in a wheelchair and hide under the banquet table where the "Friends of Italian Opera" have assembled from the various regions of Chicago. In the presence of other organized crime groups, the syndicate boss, Little Bonaparte (Nehemiah

Persoff), chastises Colombo for gaining the attention of law enforcement by killing Toothpick Charlie and his men. Bonaparte surprises Spats with a huge birthday cake in commemoration of his birthday. As the group sings, "For He's a Jolly Good Fellow", Spats grows suspicious since his birthday is a few months away. Therefore, it is not a surprise when, instead of a beautiful girl, hit man Johnny Paradise (Edward G. Robinson Jr.) emerges from the cake with a machine gun and executes Colombo and his men. The musicians have now witnessed another mob hit. They escape with a few gangsters tailing them as Police Sergeant Mulligan arrests the bad guys.

Joe and Jerry return to their protective feminine garb. Outside the hotel ballroom, Jerry arranges the pair's escape by telephoning Osgood and agreeing to elope aboard his yacht. Hearing Sugar on the bandstand, Joe approaches her. "The song is a poignant testament to her personality both on and off the screen," wrote Graham McCann and "is one of the most audacious and yet touching moments in American screen comedy." Tears steam down Sugar's face. Marilyn's voice is controlled, and she sings with Method acting behind each phrase. "She puts heartbreak in the lyrics and sings on the verge of emotional collapse," wrote Carl Rollyson, "a collapse that the actress—in weak physical and emotional health throughout the shooting of the film—undoubtedly felt for both herself and Sugar…"

Joe, dressed as Josephine, approaches a tearful Sugar on the bandstand to kiss her goodbye and reveal his true identity. With feminine understanding and masculine desire, he tells her that no guy is worth such pain, and tenderly kisses her on the lips. Sugar opens her eyes and screams, "Josephine!" Sweet Sue is horrified. In an instant, Sugar realizes Josephine and Junior are one—Joe—and her love for both his masculine and feminine personalities. The gangsters pursue Joe and Jerry who flee to the pier; where Osgood awaits to take them aboard his yacht to marry Daphne. Sugar follows on a bicycle and is introduced to Osgood as a flower girl. Joe removes his wig and admits his dishonestly. Sugar forgives him, and the couple passionately embraces.

The closing scene is one of the most memorable finales in motion picture history. Daphne/Jerry attempts to convince Osgood that she is an unsuitable spouse, but Osgood is undaunted. Daphne confesses that she smokes; Osgood doesn't care. Daphne admits that she has lived with a saxophone player; Osgood forgives her. Daphne announces she can never have children; Osgood offers to adopt. Finally, Jerry rips off his wig, and in his male voice, reveals that he is a man. Oblivious, Osgood replies, "Well—nobody's perfect."

* * *

LET'S MAKE LOVE (1960)

During the main titles of *Let's Make Love*, male vocalists sing the title song as Marilyn breathlessly warbles only the chorus. "Don't just lay there," Marilyn says in a voiceover. "Honey, do something!" She punctuates with a naughty giggle as the screen fades to black. The film opens in documentary style, recounting the family history of French billionaire Jean-Marc Clement (Yves Montand). The first Clement struck it rich in France by discovering gold in a potato crop and subsequent generations of Clements amassed a huge fortune in real estate, oil, and railroads while they seduced curvaceous females; the latter metaphorically referred to as an "interest in balloons." The audience learns that the contemporary Clement is ensconced at his company's headquarters in New York.

As Clement examines the classic French impressionistic art he has obtained at auction, he meets with his attorney Mr. Whales (Wilfrid Hyde-White) and public relations agent, Howard Coffman (Tony Randall). Coffman expresses apprehension about an article in *Variety* reporting an off-Broadway musical satirizing Clement's reputation as a pompous, rich playboy. With experience in the entertainment industry, Coffman advises Clement against litigating to shut down the production and incurring bad publicity. Instead, Coffman strategizes for the billionaire to attend a rehearsal at The Circle in the Round Theatre and minimize damage to his image by demonstrating a sense of humor.

At the theater in Greenwich Village, Clement is immediately attracted to Amanda Dell (Monroe), the musical's leading female singer and dancer rehearsing a number with a chorus of male dancers. She pulls off the sweater covering her dance leotard and throws it into the dark audience, where it lands on Clement's face. The musical's director mistakes Clement as an actor auditioning for the role of the billionaire. Interested in courting Amanda, Clement plays along by posing as an amateur actor. He assumes the name Alexander Dumas when Amanda tells him about studying the famous French author in night school, where she is earning a high school diploma. "I got tired of being ignorant," she explains. "I never knew what people were referring to." Clement notices Amanda knitting between scenes and asks what she is creating. "I haven't decided yet," she says, displaying an unidentifiable mass. "It keeps my hands busy."

Amanda coaches Clement, posing as Dumas, on how to impersonate the playboy billionaire in Method acting style. She scorns the billionaire as a "crude" and "rich louse." Amanda also tells him of her disapproval of Clement expecting women "to drop dead with the honor" of his interest, and his preference to juggle several women at once. She prefers sincere—even nervous—men. Intrigued, Clement asks Amanda on a date, but she declines in order to study for a geography exam. The musical's male lead, Tony Danton (Frankie Vaughan)—a recovering alcoholic who appears to be Amanda's potential love interest—performs a humorous song and amuses her, irritating Clement.

When the producer, Oliver Burton (David Burns), requests a fresh joke to fill a gap between acts, Clement is eager to impress Amanda and confidently begins to tell a corny joke garnered laughs from members of his company's board, but the members of the acting troupe deliver the punch line before he gets to the end. Amanda gently advises him not to be discouraged and explains that the troupe does it to everyone when they know the joke.

Clement pursues Amanda by joining the acting troupe and purchasing second-hand clothing to play the part of a struggling actor. He also tries to impress her by the presentation of a diamond bracelet and by demanding that Coffman commission a comedy writer (Joe Besser) to ghostwrite a joke for him to perform. Meanwhile, Clement's private detectives trail Amanda and report that she secretly meets a reputedly married man in a church, but this news does not sway his attraction.

Clement's plan backfires when Burton coincidentally invites the comedy writer to watch a rehearsal, and the writer accuses Clement of stealing his material. When Clement claims to have purchased the joke from a stranger, Amanda comes to his defense by attesting she overheard the transaction. Clement is used to women who are interested in him for his money and is moved by Amanda's noble intention. He claims to sell costume jewelry between acting jobs and offers to sell her the diamond bracelet for five dollars. "The box looks like it's worth more than that!" she says, agreeing to buy it. Another dancer (Mara Lynn) admires the bracelet as a gift for her sick mother, and Amanda graciously offers it to her. Later, the dancer tells Clement her mother is long deceased. To retrieve the bracelet, he explains that its gems were exposed to radioactive atomic rays to produce their sparkle and will make the skin on her wrist peel. Horrified, the dancer removes the bracelet from her wrist, throws it at Clement, and takes back her money.

Leaving the theater together, Amanda and Clement walk down the street as his limousine follows them. Marilyn's heavily annotated script includes mention of her costume, movements, and motivation: "low heels, beret and raincoat…she moves differently—feels the whole thing (pure Method acting)." They get into a taxicab, and Amanda pays the fare. She gets out in front of a church, and Clement urges her to coach him in acting. Like Paula Strasberg, she assists him in finding motivation for his role as the playboy billionaire, but ends the evening and enters the church. Clement spies through an open window and watches Amanda embrace an older man in clergy attire who is revealed to be her father. When Clement falls into the bushes, they rush outside suspecting a young hoodlum, and watch a dark figure escape into the back seat of a limousine. "They even have chauffeurs now!" exclaims Amanda's father.

An edited pivotal scene outside the church—obviously scripted by Miller—established the emotional connection between Amanda and Clement. The deleted dialogue could likely have been a conversation in the Miller living room on East Fifty-Seventh Street. When Amanda explains that she'd like to be "wonderful" and entertain people, Clement cynically suggests only one in a hundred audience members really cares about her acting—the rest are "foolish, perspiring strangers" for whom she is working "like a slave." Amanda describes the exhilaration she feels during a good performance and her connection to the audience: "You're home. Like in a family."

"*How well I know*," Marilyn printed next to this last line on her working copy of the script, which describes how an audience's feedback makes her feel lifted off the ground and in a home. She changed the words "ground" to "*earth*" and "home" to "*sheltered*." In the margin, she scribbled, "*how true*."

Abe Miller (Dennis King Jr.), the manager of the theater, receives a notice from its owner demanding that the troupe pay a year's rent in advance. Coffman traces the ownership to Clement Enterprises and angrily accuses Clement of betraying the troupe and putting them out of work. Clement gathers Whales is behind the demand, acting to preserve his reputation. He confides in Coffman that he knows men respect him only for his wealth and women love his money and not his mind. Only Amanda speaks to him directly, and not to his money and name, Clement says. He wants her.

Clement instructs Whales to pose as a retired merchant interested in financing the musical for a fifty-one percent control, and Burton agrees to the partnership. When Whales see Amanda, he predicts, "There'll be children!" He grows concerned when he notices her affection toward Tony, and encourages Clement to reveal his true identity to her to ensure their marriage. Clement refuses, in hope Amanda will fall in love with him and not his money and power.

To develop his comedic skills, Clement hires Milton Berle (playing himself) to coach him in a pantomime of a man riding a crowded subway. Clement also arranges for the famous comedian to visit the theater and request a demonstration of his skit. Impressed with Clement's ability to amuse Berle, Burton offers him an extended contract. When Clement demands a pay raise for both himself and for Amanda, Burton terminates him, but Whales wields his fifty-one percent control and vetoes the termination. Amanda is awestruck by Clement's expertise in negotiation.

As Amanda and Tony rehearse a romantic musical number, titled "Let's Make Love," Clement fantasizes about taking Tony's place. He hires Bing Crosby and Gene Kelly (playing themselves) to coach him in singing and dancing. Later at a rehearsal of another song, "Incurably Romantic," Whales replaces Tony with Clement. At the end, Amanda and Clement embrace and kiss passionately. "We're getting somewhere!" Whales exclaims.

Amanda walks in on Burton confronting Tony, who has relapsed with alcohol in fear of losing his role to Clement. Tony threatens to leave show business after a series of performances in unsuccessful shows by announcing he wants to leave the show. Amanda reminds Tony that he is an actor first and cannot run away from his true calling. She offers to go to dinner with Clement so that Tony will have an opportunity for perform the song for Whales.

During dinner in a Chinese restaurant, Clement impresses Amanda with his fluency in Chinese and five other languages. He's in the wrong profession, she tells him. Amanda compliments Clement's dignity and suggests he apply for a job with the United Nations or with an international company. When she asks him to be completely honest and to trust her, he confesses his love for her. Amanda feels ashamed of her own dishonesty and confesses having gone with him to dinner as a scheme to give Tony the chance at the number. She explains that she was only trying to help Tony because acting is his genuine passion, and for Clement, it is only a temporary job. Furthermore, she expresses her attraction to him. He proposes marriage and reveals his true identity as Jean-Marc Clement. Convinced he has over-identified with his role and has become delusional, Amanda becomes frightened and flees.

Back at the theater, Clement confesses to Amanda that he hired Milton Berle, Bing Crosby, and Gene Kelly to coach him. She feels responsible for instructing him to "get into character" and encourages him to be himself. Money is unimportant to her, Amanda explains, so she is willing to get a job and work.

These are the exact words Clement has longed to hear a woman utter. They kiss, and Amanda asks, "Who are you?" When Clement insists that he is, indeed, the billionaire, she perceives his response as ridicule and bursts into tears. As Clement and Whales watch Amanda perform with Tony, Clement orders Wales to file an injunction to close the show for an invasion of privacy. This move, Clement believes, will ultimately convince her of his true identity. During the number, Amanda wears a white halter dress with full chiffon skirts in shades of pink and magenta.

The musical's company gathers upon receiving notice of the injunction. Clement suggests that the producer send Amanda directly to the billionaire to charm him into dropping the injunction. "I can murder him!" she hisses. Whales suggests Clement accompany her since he, like the billionaire, is French.

Amanda, Clement, Coffman, Burton, and Whales march into Clement's headquarters. She asks the billionaire's receptionist (Madge Kennedy) for an audience with him. The receptionist stares curiously at Clement and escorts Amanda and her employer into a conference room, where they are met by his private secretary who greets them. Amanda asks to see Mr. Clement, and the secretary looks directly at her employer and affirms his availability. Amanda is suspicious of the strange reactions of the receptionist and secretary.

The secretary escorts them to a private office, where Amanda starts pacing and Clement sits behind the desk. Amanda becomes alarmed when Clement goes through his mail and uses his intercom to summon the staff to take dictation. Pulling Clement from the desk chair, Amanda pleads with him to see a psychiatrist.

Astonished, Amanda watches Clement dictate in Italian. He pauses and advises her to have a seat. Realizing his true identity, Amanda faints in a chair. Regaining consciousness, she admonishes him for maintaining the charade after she had revealed her love for him. Humiliated and angry, she flees; sliding in her high-heels across the polished marble floors, and enters a private elevator. As the doors close, Clement speaks through the intercom, begging her to return. When Amanda refuses, he uses a control button to return the elevator car to the top floor.

When the elevator door opens, Clement gets inside as Amanda protests. Coffman turns to Whales and says, "What a life!" Inside the elevator, Amanda asks Clement how he could bear watching her be made a fool. He serenades her with a reprise of "Let's Make Love," and she turns her back to him. Clement embraces Amanda from behind as she realizes his alias was based upon the author of the book she had been reading. She begins to soften and rests her head against his chest.

As Clements sings in a sexy voice, he kisses Amanda's neck, and she turns to face him. They kiss, and she speaks the lyrics, "It's warm here." She removes the bolero jacket of her suit as Clement continues kissing her neck and repeats the chorus, "Let's make love." Amanda giggles about the surprised reaction she expects from the other students in night school. They passionately kiss to a fade-out.

* * *

THE MISFITS (1961)

Guido (Eli Wallach), a mechanic, drives a tow-truck into the driveway of Isabelle Steers' boarding home in Reno. He gets out and appraises the damage to a Cadillac parked in the driveway. With her arm in a sling, Isabelle (Thelma Ritter) greets him and explains the car is new, despite its damage. Her boarder, Mrs. Roslyn Taber (Monroe), received the car from Mr. Taber on the occation of their divorce, Isabelle explains. The men in town keep crashing into it just to start a conversation with its beautiful driver. She also reports having broken her arm during the celebration of her former boarder's divorce. "I misbehaved," Isabelle shamefully admits. From a second-story window, Roslyn calls for the landlady's assistance.

Upstairs, Roslyn sits before the mirror of a vanity applying makeup and memorizing her divorce testimony. Isabelle enters and coaches her in learning responses to the attorney's questions. Rather than recite the inaccurate reason for divorce, Roslyn asks why she can't be truthful and say, "you could touch him, but he wasn't there."

If that was a legitimate justification for divorce, Isabelle argues, there would be less than a dozen remaining married couples in the entire country. She predicts that Roslyn's divorce will go smoothly, as her serving as a witness in Roslyn's case will be her seventy-seventh time as a witness in a divorce, which must be a good omen.

Guido honks the horn, and Roslyn goes to the window. He tells her that his employer will call with an estimate of the cost for repair. Noticing Roslyn's beauty, Guido offers to drive her and Isabelle to the courthouse.

As Guido assists the women out of his truck in front of the courthouse, he offers to take Roslyn around the country until she returns home to Chicago. She is ambivalent, and thanks him for his kindness. As the women approach the courthouse, Roslyn sees her husband, Raymond (Kevin McCarthy). He tries to coax her out of the divorce. "You can't have me now that you want me," she asserts.

Guido meets his friend Gay (Clark Gable), a cowboy in his fifties, at the train station, where he is seeing off a recent divorcée (Marietta Tree) as she returns home. Gay and the woman had a brief affair, and he seems happy to be rid of her. The two men discuss leaving town for the mountains to capture Mustangs. Gay advises Guido to quit his job at the garage, as he might make a habit of trading his independence as a fellow cowboy for wages.

After the divorce hearing, Roselyn and Isabelle go to Harrah's casino for a cocktail. Roslyn discretely removes the wedding band from her finger and places it in her purse. Melancholy and lonely, she expresses longing for her mother, who disappeared with a patient for long stretches of time when Roslyn was a child. Isabelle suggests Roslyn settle in Reno, where she could teach dancing. Bursting into tears, Roslyn misses her mother, but recovers and thanks Isabelle for her friendship. An obedient dog sitting near the bar beside its owner catches Roslyn's attention, and she calls to him and feeds him peanuts. The owner, Gay, turns from his seat at the bar, and admires Roselyn. Guido, seated beside him, provides an introduction to the two women.

Gay identifies himself as a cowboy. Familiar with cowboys, Isabelle labels them as "good for nothing." Being a cowboy is "better than wages," Gay insists. He is happy to learn that Roslyn isn't educated. "They always want to know what a man thinks," he says. Roslyn supposes they might be trying to get to know the men better. Gay remarks there are others ways to get to know a man, and Roslyn reacts with discomfort to his sexual implication.

Guido encourages Roslyn to explore the country, and Gay promotes it as a place where she can "just live." The sound of a simple, unencumbered existence intrigues her. When Guido offers to loan her his house, Roslyn impulsively decides to rent a car and go there with Isabelle. As the group rises to exit, Guido announces he is quitting his job and joining them.

Following the men's truck, Roslyn drives a rented station wagon as Isabelle educates her on "unreliable" cowboys as the "last real men." Disillusioned by her divorce, Roslyn argues that no one else is any different. Meanwhile in the truck, Guido describes Roslyn's naiveté and sexual allure. "She's real prime," Gay replies with lust in his voice.

The group arrives at the isolated, partially finished cabin, and Guido gives Roslyn a tour. In the bedroom, she notices his wedding picture. Guido explains that his wife died in the bed. She had become ill during pregnancy, and he could not transport her to a hospital. Roslyn learns that Guido's wife died senselessly because his car had a flat tire and he did not have a spare. He and his wife were childhood sweethearts, Guido explains with deep emotion, and Roslyn realizes he could no longer live in the house after her death. Overwhelmed by the intensity of the conversation, Roslyn changes the subject and returns to the living room, where Isabelle prepares sandwiches. When Guido returns to the truck for groceries, Gay describes his friend's deceased wife as an uncomplaining good sport. "She's dead because he didn't have a spare tire," Roslyn remarks, shaken by the irony.

Guido returns with liquor, and Gay serves cocktails. Isabelle recounts the reasons she remained in Reno after traveling from Virginia nineteen years earlier for her divorce. She and the men discover that they have a friend in common—a man with one arm named Andy—and Roslyn suggests they try to find him. Isabelle advises her to stop believing in the ability to change fate. Abruptly, Roslyn suggests turning on the car radio for music, and Guido jumps up to do so.

Gay urges Roslyn to consider staying at the house. They dance to the music, and Guido enters, surprised. Isabelle tells him Roslyn used to teach dancing before she was married. Guido breaks in and tells Roslyn she dances more gracefully than his wife. She tells Guido that since he loved his wife, he could have taught her anything, even to be graceful. "We're all dying, aren't we?" Roslyn asks with desperation. "All the husbands and all the wives...And we're not teaching each other what we really know."

Having drunk into the night, the group is intoxicated when they leave the house, and Roslyn runs barefoot on the lawn. Guido attempts to kiss her, but she pulls away and dances in the moonlight, eventually resting against a tree and hugging its trunk. As Gay gently leads her to car, Roslyn is moved by his worry about her. "Will you have a spare tire?" she pleads.

Gay drives Roslyn home in her rented station wagon as she sleeps. Gay stops the car, and Roslyn awakens to find him admiring her. He asks her what makes her so sad and reaches forward to embrace her. Roslyn withdraws, stating she doesn't feel the same way toward him. Gay resumes driving and offers support to Roslyn is she decides to stay at Guido's house and start a new life. When she asks Gay if he has a home, he looks out at the vast desert and says,

"Right here."

Time passes. Roslyn sleeps in the bed in Guido's house as Gay stands over her, gazing lovingly. Gay kisses her, and she awakens. Gay returns to the kitchen to prepare breakfast, and Roslyn enters in a robe and offers to take over the cooking. He serves her and delights in her hearty appetite. "You like me, huh?" Roslyn asks.

Gay inquires if Roslyn has borne children, and she discloses having not wanted children with her former husband. She believes children shouldn't be brought into an unhappy marriage and recounts her experience with a "so-called happily married couple." The wife was in the hospital delivering a child, Roslyn tells Gay, while the husband was calling her behind his wife's back.

Gay remarks about nothing lasting forever and confides that his wife had an affair with his cousin. He also discusses his adult son and daughter. Roslyn and Gay commiserate about the rapidly changing world.

Gay professes his attachment to Roslyn and suggests fixing up the house and living there together. "Let's just live," she says remembering their conversation in the bar the day they met. Outside, Roslyn discovers a cement block to use as a step for the front door and playfully walks in and out the door like a gleeful child.

In a montage, Gay watches Roslyn's buttocks bounce as she rides a horse, she splashes in Pyramid Lake with his dog, and embraces Gay on a blanket on the beach. As more time passes, Gay and Roslyn tend to the garden as Guido flies overhead in a single engine propeller plane. She marvels at watching lettuce grow from seeds, but Gay becomes irritated by a rabbit eating the lettuce and vows to shoot it. Roslyn says she can't stand to see anything killed and begs him to spare the wild animal. Gay disregards Roslyn's reverence for all living things, and her tone changes. "You don't respect what I feel," she snaps. "*And I don't care about the lettuce!*"

Guido pays a surprise visit with Isabelle, and they are amazed by all the changes Roslyn has made to make the home comfortable. Guido is especially shocked by Gay's sudden domestication. Isabelle wraps her arm around Roslyn's waist and acknowledges her finding herself. Isabelle turns to Gay and says he finally "made contact with a real woman." Touched by Roslyn's display of his wedding picture in the living room, Guido confesses his inability to finish the house.

Roslyn has swept into his life and has transformed it into his ideal.

Guido invites Gay to join him in capturing wild Mustang horses and reports spotting about fifteen from his plane. Gay recalls when hundreds of horses roamed the desert. Isabelle chastises the men for pestering wild animals. The group decides to go to the rodeo in Dayton to find another cowboy to enlist in the hunt.

The four misfits drive toward Dayton and stop at a gas station, where they happen upon cowboy Perce Howland (Montgomery Clift) sitting beside a phone booth. The men greet Perce, who is in town for the rodeo and awaiting a call from his mother. Gay and Guido invite him along in the capture of Mustangs, but the plans are interrupted when the telephone rings. Perce's conversation with his mother reveals tension in their relationship, conflict with his stepfather, and the fact that his face had finally healed from previous rodeos. After hanging up the receiver, Perce gets into the car.

Arriving in Dayton, the group heads straight to a bar, where Roslyn plays with a young boy's paddleball as the patrons gamble on her ability to repeatedly hit the ball. Guido takes cash bets as Roslyn surprises them all by her skill at paddleball. When a patron slaps her buttocks, Guido challenges him to a fight, and the man apologizes.

Roslyn gives some of the cash from Guido's gambling win to an elderly woman (Estelle Winwood) soliciting donations to build a fence around a cemetery to prevent cowboys from pasturing their horses on the graves. Meanwhile, Isabelle runs into her former husband and his new wife—her former best friend—and leaves the band of misfits in order to entertain the couple at her home.

At the rodeo, Perce expresses his interest in Roslyn to Gay and asks permission to pursue her; Gay affirms that she belongs to him. Later, when Perce gets thrown from a bucking horse, Roslyn is horrified and begs him to withdraw from the contest and go to the hospital. He refuses, and Gay sternly scolds her to stop taking charge of the situation. Roslyn cannot understand his insensitivity. Perce returns into the ring to ride a bull, and she offers him the winnings from the bar in compensation for the cash prize. "They don't mind getting busted up," Guido tells Roslyn. When Perce falls off a bull and is rendered unconscious, the bull charges him, and Gay jumps into the ring to save him.

Roslyn weeps alone in the station wagon, and Gay gets in the car to deliver the news about Perce's recovery. "People are dying and people are just standing around," Roslyn cries. He tells her about having risked his own life by dragging Perce out of ring and to safety. In gratitude, Roslyn kisses Gay's hand and sobs about Perce's accident. Gay reasons that everyone must die someday.

Gay and Roslyn reunite with Guido, Perce, and an ambulance attendant (Ralph Roberts), who bandages Perce's head and injects him with a pain-killing drug. Guido resentfully tells Roslyn to direct her sympathy to someone who will appreciate it. Roslyn and the men have cocktails at a dance hall in Dayton. The men become intoxicated as she maternally looks after them. Perce thanks Roslyn for caring about his welfare, and Gay slurs a request for her to dance with his injured friend.

As Perce and Roslyn dance a western two-step, he becomes dizzy and disoriented so they exit the dance hall. Roslyn sits on an abandoned car seat surrounded by discarded beer cans and bottles, and Perce rests his head on her lap. Dressed in a silk cocktail dress and heels, Roslyn is misplaced among the debris, just as she is an urban alien in a country town.

Perce asks Roslyn if she belongs to Gay. She sadly responds that she doesn't know where she belongs. He compliments the trust in Roslyn's eyes and advises her not to allow the men in her life to "grind" her up. Perce recounts being abandoned by a girlfriend and some friends the last time he was injured in a rodeo, and Roslyn is appalled by the desertion. Unlike Gay and Guido, he is new to drifting. After the death of his father on the family ranch, his mother quickly remarried and gave the ranch to her new husband. Perce's stepfather offered him a job on the ranch he expected to inherit, and his mother concurred. Perce asks Roslyn on whom he can depend.

"Maybe we're not supposed to remember anyone's promises," Roslyn speculates.

A drunken Gay finds them and leads them back into the bar to meet his children, coincidently in town for the rodeo. When Gay cannot locate them, he stumbles outside and stands on the roof of a parked car. He shouts out to his children to come to him. Roslyn is horrified by another example of abandonment and its resulting pain in the man she loves. Gay falls off the car onto the dirt road, and she cradles his head and weeps.

Guido speeds home under the influence of alcohol as Gay and Perce are passed out in the back seat of the car. Roslyn begs him to slow down to avoid killing them all, referencing a female friend who sustained disfiguring injuries at the hands of a reckless male behind the wheel. "We're all blind bombardiers," Guido slurs, recalling his service in the war when he bombed nine cities. He compares dropping a bomb to telling a lie. As Guido professes his attraction to Roslyn, his driving becomes more erratic. She soothes him and pleads with him to drive at a safer speed.

Back at the house, Guido drunkenly tries to finish the building by hammering a piece of lumber in the moonlight. Intoxicated and annoyed, Gay yells at him for stepping on the flowers he planted for Roslyn. Awakening, Perce becomes tangled in his bandages and falls backward into a pile of lumber. Overwhelmed by their rowdy drunkenness, Roslyn manages to get Guido and Perce into the living room, where they pass out on the sofas. Maternally, she covers them with blankets.

Gay irritably tells Roslyn he has done more for her than he had done for his former wife. She fearfully wonders aloud if some day Gay will no longer love her and recalls his anger over her reaction to Perce's injury. Gay asks if Roslyn's father ever spanked her and kissed her afterwards. Only strangers spanked her, she tells him, because her father was never around long enough. Roslyn embraces Gay and begs him to love her. They reconcile, and Gay goes into the house. Collapsing against the house and staring up at the moon, Roslyn desperately whispers, "*Help.*"

Gay, Roslyn, Guido, and Perce camp in the desert the night before the Mustang hunt. For the first time, Roslyn learns the horses will be sold to dealers and killed for use as dog food. Revolted, she stomps off to the flatbed of the truck to sleep. Gay appeals to her, justifying that he is doing what he has always done, capturing horses and selling them to dealers. During the settlement of the west, he explains, the horses were used for pulling plows and as children's riding horses. Now the world has changed; the west is industrialized, and children ride scooters. Gay hunts horses to be free and avoid a structured job in the urban age.

Roslyn is unwavering. A kind man can't kill, she argues. Gay is like everyone else. Maybe she is, too, he gently debates. People do what they enjoy and what feels comfortable, but eventually external forces turn what they do into something bad. Gay compares his capture of horses to her having danced in nightclubs. She danced for artistic expression, but the audience gawked at her body and turned her art into something pornographic. He could judge her for dancing and showing off her body, but instead, he respects her. "This is how I dance," Gay explains. Roslyn is honored by his reverence toward her, and they kiss.

The next day, while flying his plane low to the ground, Guido herds the Mustangs into the desert salt flats. Six horses charge into the open area where Gay, Roslyn, and Perce stand waiting on the truck's flatbed. Perce recalls when the desert was populated by hundreds of horses and says it seems senseless to hunt only six. The lesser number makes the act more despicable. Looking through binoculars, Roslyn sees what appears to be a family of Mustangs: a stallion, his four mares, and a spring colt.

Guido drives the truck with Roslyn as his passenger alongside the charging horses. Gay and Perce stand on the flat bed of truck and throw lassoes around the horses' necks. Heavy truck tires are attached to the end of the ropes for weight to slow down the horses. Through the truck window, Roslyn watches a trapped equine with pain in her eyes. The colt runs beside its mother.

They men park use lassoes to rope the horse to the ground. Roslyn runs out of the truck and pulls at Gay's rope. He pushes her away, and she falls to the ground. "We're through!" he shouts. Defeated, she walks back to the truck and buries her face in her hands.

With the horse brought to the ground, Gay binds its legs together with rope. He tells the others it must seem senseless from Roslyn's perspective. The fewer killed, he reckons, the worse it looks. He considers giving her the horses. Overhearing the conversation, Roslyn offers to pay him $200. Emasculated and offended, Gay walks away. "I sell to dealers only," he barks. They are interested only in purchasing a horse, not his manhood and freedom.

Guido offers to stop the capture and pleads with Roslyn to give him a chance. He professes to know what she is about and wants to prove himself to her. Guido tells her to give him a reason, and he'll stop the trapping of the horses. Roslyn is offended by his demand for a reason and chastises him for self-pity.

After the capture of another mare, Gay tallies the dollar amount for the total of all horses. Enraged, Roslyn runs into the desert and screams at them, calling them liars and murderers for exploiting the animals for money and their independent lifestyle.

"Aided by her training in the Stanislavsky method, Marilyn makes the moment direct, real, deeply felt and potent," writes Carl Rollyson. "It is the dramatic climax of a film with a very thin narrative line, and it permits the final resolution in which the horses are freed and Roslyn consequently reconciled with Gay."

Guido contemptuously rants about women never being satisfied with a hardworking man, but Gay listens to Roslyn's tirade and tells him to shut up. The colt touches its hoof on its mother, lying bound and prostrate. Roslyn returns to the cab of the truck, exhausted, and Perce offers to free the horses. She warns that it will only lead to a fight. Impulsively, Perce gets behind the wheel of the truck—Roslyn beside him—and drives to each bound horse and cuts the ropes. "Go home!" Roslyn whispers.

Proving his virility and independence, Gay ropes the stallion, and it takes off running, dragging him on the desert floor. He wrestles it to the ground and collapses over its body. "We don't need anyone," Guido tells Gay with excitement. Gay pushes him aside and resolutely cuts the rope tethering the stallion to the tire. The horse disappears into the darkness of the desert.

Spent, Gay sits against the side of the truck and unleashes: "They changed it…smeared it all over with blood. It's like roping a dream. I've got to find another way to be alive." As Gay instructs Perce to free the last mare. Roslyn approaches Gay, and he offers to drive her back in his truck. Perce bids farewell to Roslyn, and she tells him to stop getting hurt. Guido hollers at Gay for submitting to Roslyn's values and mocks him for surrendering his freedom and independence for a job with wages.

Gay drives back to the other truck, where Roslyn retrieves his dog and brings it into the cab. When she embraces the pet, the couple's eyes lock for the first time since Gay's transformation. "I bless you," he says lovingly. Roselyn moves against him, resting her head on his shoulder. He puts his arm around her. Roslyn speaks of Gay's earlier proposal of their bringing a brave child into the world. She is no longer afraid of this possibility. Roslyn asks how he finds his way home in the darkness, and Gay explains that the star will lead them there.

NOTES

PART I: MRS. ARTHUR MILLER
CHAPTER ONE: *THE PRINCE AND THE SHOWGIRL*

"the best combination since black and white": Quoted in Summers, *The Many Lives of Marilyn Monroe*, 1985, p. 162.

"[Olivier's] position at one time in England": Quoted in Shevey, *The Marilyn Scandal*, 1987, p. 262.

"She idealized Olivier...": Miller, *Timebends: A Life*, 1987, p. 418.

"[Marilyn] was prepared to write...": Darlow, *Terrance Rattigan: The Man and His Work*, 2000.

"Some people have been unkind...": Quoted in Manning, "The Woman and the Legend," *Photoplay*, October 1956, p. 98.

"Marilyn's Elsie is from the first frame...": Spoto, *Marilyn Monroe: The Biography*, 1993, p. 378-379.

"The play is about a man...": Quoted in Shevey, p. 260.

"Where I had feared that my...": Quoted in Shevey, p. 261.

"low forms of sex relationship...": Quoted in Buskin, *Blonde Heat: The Sizzling Film Career of Marilyn Monroe*, 2002, p. 209.

"awakening of a sleeping prince...": Quoted in Buskin, p. 209.

"[Marilyn] was practically perfect...": Quoted in Buskin, p. 210.

"[Marilyn] has an innocence...": Quoted in Zolotow, *Marilyn Monroe*, 1960, p. 299.

"She was withdrawn...": Quoted in Buskin, p. 209.

"jolly, ginny neurotic old bird, " "smokes continuously...": Quoted in Clark, *The Prince, The Showgirl, and Me*, 1996, p. 49.

"I have two ulcers from this film...": Quoted in Greene & Kotsilias-Davies, *Milton's Marilyn*, 1995, p. 77.

"MGM agreed to loan me out…": Guilaroff, *Crowning Glory: Reflections of Hollywood's Favorite Confidante*, 1996, p. 152.
"Just watch me": Quoted in Arnold, *Marilyn Monroe*, 2005, p. 66.
"It has long been my hope…": Quoted in Zolotow, 1960, p. 268.
"He has always been my idol": Quoted in Spoto, 1993, p. 342.
"She is a brilliant comedienne…": Quoted in ibid, p. 342.
"I don't want to play the brothers…": Quoted in ibid.
"I think it begins with a G…": Quoted in Zolotow, 1960, p. 269.
"the simple dignity of a performer announcing a new project": Miller, *Timebends: A Life*, 1987, p. 387.
"*My* corporation owns…": Quoted in Zolotow, 1960, p. 269.
"Shall I take my coat off, boys?": Quoted in DiLorenzo & Wilson, "Marilyn Can Act Too, Sez Olivier," *The New York Daily News*, February 10, 1956.
"How would you feel…": Quoted in Zolotow, 1960, p. 270.
"By the end of the day…": Olivier, *Confessions of an Actor*, 1982, p. 206.
"Please, don't tell her what to do": Quoted in Summers, p. 162.
"Please do not expect her…": Logan, *Movie Stars, Real People, and Me*, 1978, p. 85-86.
"I will not get upset…": Quoted in ibid, p. 86.
"Moore fancies himself as God's gift to women…": Clark, 1996, p. 34.
"secretly thinks that he will get to meet…": Clark, 1996, p. 34.
"They all want to be the one…": Clark, 1996, p. 48.
"solid wall…": Miller, 1987, p. 413.
"She walks…": Quoted in Kidder, 2003, p. 148
"cold as a refrigerated fish…": Quoted in Meyers, *The Genius and the Goddess: Arthur Miller and Marilyn Monroe*, 2010, p. 160.
"The Customs officers…": Clark, 1996, p. 64.
"Are all your conferences…": Quoted in Zolotow, 1960, p. 295.
"Well, this is a little quieter …": Quoted in Zolotow, 1960, p. 295.
"Marilyn *will not* be staying with us…": Quoted in Shevey, p. 256.
"That's an interesting idea": Quoted in Walker, *Vivien: The Life of Viven Leigh*, 1987, p. 225.
"MM is carrying quite…": Clark, p. 135.
"Well, we are going to bed": Quoted in Clark, p. 66.
"unable to take his eyes…": Miller, 1987, p. 413.

"a pair of bewildered pigeons": Miller, 1987, p. 414.
"I hope she's jealous": Quoted in Clark, p. 53.
"Considering I'm in England...": Quoted in Zolotow, 1960, p. 297.
"Lady Macbeth...": Quoted in Zolotow, 1960, p. 297.
"at present that is just a dream...": Quoted in Spoto, 1993, p. 369.
"Seeing my own pictures": Quoted in Zolotow, 1960, p. 297.
"I like, well, jazz...": Quoted in Zolotow, 1960, p. 297.
"I have a terrible time...": Quoted in Zolotow, 1960, p. 297.
"Compared to California...": Quoted in Meyers, 2010, p. 160.
Conversation between Marilyn and Miller at window recreated, based upon quotation in Miller, 1987, p. 414.
"After that we changed...": Quoted in Buskin, p. 210.
"as formal and artificial as his plays": Clark, p. 116.
"[Marilyn] held court in a tent...": Quoted in Morgan, *Marilyn Monroe: Private and Undisclosed*, 2007, p. 96.
"And what about the poor little animals...": Quoted in Shevey, 1987, p. 257.
"We all love Marilyn...": Quoted in Miller, 1987, p. 441.
"I regard her as an actress...": Quoted in "Cinema: Who Could Resist?" *Time*, January 30, 1956.
"a thoroughly ill-mannered and rude girl...": Quoted in Spoto, 1993, p. 376.
"enchantingly unspoilt": Clark, 1996, p. 86.
"clubby professionalism," "almost elementary explanation": Rosten, *Marilyn: An Untold Story*, 1973, p. 43.
"None of his demeaning subtleties...": Clark, p. 87.
"Her manner to me got steadily...": Olivier, 1982, p. 209.
"He talks to me as if he's slumming": Quoted in Strasberg, *Marilyn and Me: Sisters, Rivals, Friends*, 1992, p. 116.
"What am I doing here...": Quoted in Julien, *Property from the Estate of Marilyn Monroe*, 2005, p. 72.
"All you have to do is be sexy...": Quoted in Churchwell, *The Many Lives of Marilyn Monroe*, 2004, p. 247.
"Larry, I don't have to act sexy...": Quoted in Shevey, p. 264.
"half-digested, spit-balled imagery...": Miller, 1987, p. 420.
"terribly," "intimate," " brilliant instincts," "a frightened unicorn": Logan, p. 114.

"For God's sake…": Quoted in Shevey, p. 264.
"Can't you count either?": Quoted in Mills, *Marilyn: On Location*, 1990, p. 107.
"[Marilyn's] system was spontaneity": Quoted in Shevey, p. 265.
"[Vivien Leigh] was a wonderful actress…": Quoted in Shevey, p. 264.
"I sensed Sir Laurence…": Guilaroff p. 152-153.
"Don't you realize…": Quoted in Clark, p. 110.
"My dear, you mustn't concern…": Quoted in Clark, p. 105.
"[Dame Sybil] has become MM's dear old granny…": Clark, p. 108.
"Come on, John darling…": Quoted in Morley, *John Gielgud: The Authorized Biography*, 2002, p. 272.
"No, not at all…": Interview with Dame Sybil Thorndike in "Dame Sybil Thorndike Defending Marilyn Monroe." YouTube.com. n.d. http://www.youtube.com/watch?v=dVX3PLBfAM4.
"You did well in that scene…": Quoted in Guiles, *Norma Jean: The Life of Marilyn Monroe*, 1969, p. 235.
"But then when I saw the film…": Quoted in Buskin, p. 210-211.
"When working, on the set…": Quoted in Zolotow, 1960, p. 299.
"I didn't think…": Quoted in Greene & Kotsilias-Davies, p. 82.
"She was no actress…": Quoted in Mills, p. 107.
"All my life, Marilyn…": Quoted in Clark, p. 103.
"My dear, you really must recognize…": Quoted in Guiles, *Legend: The Life and Death of Marilyn Monroe*, 1984, p. 311.
"a masterpiece of improvisation": Spoto, 1993, p. 379.
"The more they cursed…": Clark, p. 121.
"She quite unintentionally ruined…": Quoted in Morgan, p. 203.
"All I could see…": Clark, p. 111.
"Oh Colin…": Quoted in ibid.
"It was something about how disappointed…": Quoted in Mills, p. 108.
"It's so terrible…": Quoted in Strasberg, 1992, p. 122.
"Marilyn, don't you sometimes…": Recreated, based on Strasberg, 1992, p. 122.
"Of course…": Recreated, based on ibid.
"You must admit…": Recreated, based on ibid.

"Maybe that's true..." Recreated, based on ibid.
"letter from hell": Miller, *After the Fall*, 1964, p. 76.
London doctors confirming pregnancy in August: research of Spoto, 1993, p. 375.
pregnancy documented in September: Clark, p. 142.
"Miss Monroe is a talented comedienne...": *London Times*, quoted in Spoto, 1993, p. 377.
"Adult patient...": Quoted in Schneider, *Marilyn's Last Sessions*, 2011, n. p.
"ever, really": Monroe, *Fragments*, 2010, p. 115.
"merciless pain": Ibid, p. 109.
"shapes of monsters": Ibid, p. 111.
"She had dropped the experience...": Strasberg, 1992, p. 123.
"Olivier talked at us..." & "He was charming...": Strasberg, 1992, p. 121.
"Larry has no right...": Quoted in Zolotow, 1960, p. 300.
"Marilyn Monroe's close-fitting dress...": Quoted in Nickens & Zeno, *Marilyn in Fashion: The Enduring Influence of Marilyn Monroe*, 2012, p. 235.
"Why should someone like Marilyn...": Quoted in ibid.
"[Sitwell] clearly regarded Marilyn Monroe...": Spender, "Lady Natasha Spender Remembers Edith Sitwell," Telegraph.co.uk, June 8, 2008. http://www.telegraph.co.uk/culture/donomigrate/3553964/Lady-Natasha-Spender-remembers-Edith-Sitwell.html
"She was very quiet and had great...": Quoted in Glendinning, *Edith Sitwell: A Unicorn Among Lions*, 1981, p. 305.
"She was what my mother...": Quoted in Meyers, 2010, p. 111.
"It's like we all feel...": Quoted in Rollyson, *Marilyn Monroe: A Life of the Actress*,1993, p. 124.
"a shy exhibitionist, a Garbo...": Quoted in Young, *The Rattigan Version: Sir Terrance Rattigan and the Theatre of Character*, 1998, p. 119.
"I am just a pretty as you are!": Quoted in Guiles, 1969, p. 239.
"That's a very proper curtsy": Quoted in Zolotow, 1960, p. 306.
"Curtsying isn't difficult...:" Quoted in Zolotow, 1960, p. 306.
"You see, we often live at Windsor Castle": Quoted in Zolotow, 1960, p. 306.

"Do you really bicycle": Quoted in ibid, p. 306.
"I love riding...": Recreated & based upon quote in ibid.
"How long will you be vising our country...": Recreated & based upon quote in ibid.
"Only two weeks more...": Recreated & based upon quote in ibid.
"She radiates a wonderful...": "A Nervous Marilyn Meet Neighbor, Queen Elizabeth," *The Milwaukee Journal*, October 30, 1956, n.p.
"Marilyn Monroe, the sleek...": Photograph caption in *The Daily Mirror.*
"as intelligent as she was pleasant...": Photograph caption in *The Spectator.*
"The Queen is a lady...": Quoted in Bret, *Clark Gable: Tormented Star*, 2008, p. 220.
"That evening was one of the most important...": Quoted in Brambilla, *Marilyn Monroe: The Life, The Myth*, 1996, p. 180-181.
"God...": Quoted in Guiles, 1984, p. 324.
"I hope you will all forgive me...": Quoted in Buskin, p. 210.
"[Marilyn] was impeccable...": Quoted in Shevey, p. 261-262.
"triumphal visit to Britain...": Quoted in Zolotow, 1960, p. 307.
"It's the British who are supposed...": Quoted in Zolotow, 1960, p. 307.
"It seemed to be raining ...": Quoted in Morgan, p. 207.
"I want to thank everyone...": Quoted in Shevey, p. 259.
"Miss Monroe's a wonderful person...": Quoted in Shevey, p. 259.
"I wished I had got better stuff...": Quoted in McDonough, *All the Available Light*, 2002, p. 160.
"flattened out," "inferior," "flatter performances...": Quoted in Spoto, 1993, p. 388.
"Jump cutting kills the points..." "The story gets lost..." "American audiences are not as moved..." "make every effort to save our picture": Quoted in Spoto, 1993, p. 388.
"That crowd nearly...": Quoted in Battelle, "Star Calls It 'Wonderful,' Fans Mob, Muss Marilyn in N.Y. Movie Premiere," *The Miami News*, June 14, 1957, n.p.
"Marilyn can always...": Quoted in ibid, n.p.

"Only she has more…": Quoted in ibid, n.p.
"When you look at the film…": Quoted in Shevey, p. 264.
"Marilyn Monroe…has never seemed…": Archer Winsten, *New York Post*, quoted in Ricci & Conway, *The Complete Films of Marilyn Monroe*, 1990, p. 138.
"This, I am sure, is Miss Monroe's best…": *Los Angeles Times*, quoted in Adam Victor, *The Marilyn Encyclopedia*, 1999, p. 240.
"The unpredictable waverings…": Alton Cook, *New York World-Telegram and Sun*, quoted in Ricci & Conway, p. 138.
"The film emerges as the season's sparkling…": Gilbert, *New York Mirror.*
"*The Prince and the Showgirl* lifts…": *Time* review quoted in Buskin, p. 211.
"We are bound to tell you Miss Monroe…": Crowther, "Screen: Prince and Girl," *The New York Times*, June 14, 1957.
"*The Prince and the Showgirl* is great fun…": *New York Herald Tribune*
"play beautifully together…": Quoted in Rollyson, p. 134.
"Apart from the whimsicality of teaming…": *The New Yorker* review quoted in Victor, *The Marilyn Encyclopedia*, 1999, p. 240.
"I just don't think I tried…": Quoted in Rollyson, *Marilyn Monroe, A Life of the Actress*, 1993, p. 125.
"No one had such a look…": Olivier, *On Acting*, 1987, p. 316.
"I was fifty…": Olivier, 1982, p. 213.
"I was good as could be…": Ibid, p. 213.
"It's making money…": Quoted in Barris, "Twilight of a Star," *New York Daily News*, August, 14, 1962.
"were glued together…": Quoted in Kaufman, "Mystery Surrounds 'My Week With Marilyn'." *LaTimes.com.* December 11, 2011.
"NO!": Interview with Amy Greene, August 5, 2012.
"The Marilyn legend…": Quoted in Kaufamn, ibid.

Chapter Two: Manhattan, Autumn 1956/ Winter & Spring 1957

"Just be her husband!": recreated based on quote in Guiles, 1969, p. 222.

"She was ultrasensitive…": Quoted in Wolfe, *The Last Days of Marilyn Monroe*, 1998, p. 306.

"Marriage makes me feel more womanly…": Quoted in David, "Which Was the True Marilyn?" *The Milwaukee Journal*, April 12, 1964, p. 5.

"Marilyn is a perfectionist…": Quoted in Levin, "Marilyn Monroe: I'm Learning About Marriage," *Redbook*, Feburary 1957.

"Movies are my business…": Quoted in Summers, p. 168.

"Women in the home…": Quoted in Cott, *No Small Courage: A History of Women in the United States*, 2000, p. 497.

"Of all the accomplishments…": "The First Baby: Photographed by Suzanne Szasz," *Life*, December 24, 1956.

"had mothers that were fatherly…": Quoted in Coughlan, "Changing Roles in Modern Life," *Life*, December 24, 1956, p. 115.

"all mature childless women…": Quoted in Douglas & Nowak, *The Fifties: The Way We Really Were*, 1977, p. 155.

"A great many children…": Quoted in ibid., p. 154.

"that increasing and strident…": Quoted in ibid, p. 164.

"disease of working women," "out-distanced by his wife": Coughlan (1956).

"surprisingly inexpensive…": Miller, 1987, p. 445.

"One day they may be worth…": Quoted in "Gorgeous Cheesecake Photo Presented by Marilyn as a Tip to Her Carpet Installer." RRAuctions.com., n.d., http://www.rrauction.com/gorgeous_marilyn_monroe_cheesecake_signed_photo.cfm (accessed December 15, 2012).

"I never intrude except…": Quoted in Shevey, p. 268.

"I need to be here to get my husband's…": Quoted in Wolfe, p. 310.

"That's Marilyn…": Quoted in Summers, p. 169.

"I know it's considered chic…": Quoted in Shevey, p. 268.

"charming and hospitable hostess": Zolotow, 1960, p. 314.

"deliriously happy in her new role as housewife": Quoted in Shevey, p. 268.

"I take a lot of pride in them...": Quoted in Levy, "Marilyn Monroe: A Good Long Look at Myself," *Redbook*, August 1962, p. 74.

"May was alone...": Quoted in Spoto, 1992, p. 397-398.

"May is steadfastly loyal to Marilyn...": Miracle, *My Sister Marilyn: A Memoir*, 1994., p. 132.

"He had the vulnerability of age...": Miller, 1987, p. 446.

"Mother, your sauce is delicious": recreated, based on Strasberg, 1992, p. 130.

"People have always...": recreated, based on ibid, p. 130.

"Witch kind?": Quoted in ibid, p. 130.

"The two things she most wanted...": Quoted in Holden, *Behind the Oscar: The Secret History of the Academy Awards*, 1993, p. 218.

"It seems Marilyn doesn't...": Quoted in Leaming, 1998, *Marilyn Monroe*, p. 282.

"Take more": Quoted in Greene & Kotsilias-Davies, p. 86.

"Arthur took away...": recreated based on quotation from Amy Greene in Spoto,1992, p. 390.

"highly ambitious person," "feel anything profound": Quote in Guiles, 1984, p. 261.

"Mrs. [Millicent] Hearst...": *The Mike Wallace Interviews*, "Elsa Maxwell", directed by Bob Eisenhardt, 2001.

"Marilyn Monroe was an invention...": quoted in Hambourg & Mia Fineman, *Avedon's Endgame*, 2002, n.p.

"The famous portrait...": Hambourg & Fineman, ibid.

"The Israelis were asked...": Quoted in Kaplan, "Dodger Photographer Highlighted Game Off Field." New Jersey Jewish Online/Sports, Njjewishnews.com. June 21, 2007. http://njjewishnews.com/njjn.com/062107/sptsDodgerPhotographer.html

"We'd hear no more of falling...": Quoted in "Sign Her Up!" *Soccer Star*, Volume 5, June 15, 1957.

"I could not use the name...": Quoted in Murphey, *Congressional Theatre: Dramatizing McCarthyism on Stage, Film, and Television*, 1999, p. 68.

"A wife's place…": Quoted in Leaming, p. 284.
"I would like to say…": Interview with Marilyn Monroe in various newsreels & documentaries
"By sprinkling…": Luce, "Success in the Sewer," *Time*, August 29, 1955.
"She talked mostly about children…": Quoted in Steinem, *Marilyn: Norma Jean*, 1986, p. 85-87.
"a child of her own…": Miller, 1987, p. 457.
"deaf to his cautionary tone": Ibid., p. 457.
"a new kind of confidence…": Ibid., p. 457.
"thrilled, euphoric": Strasberg, 1992, p. 163.
"I really hope my baby…": recreated based on Strasberg, 1992, p. 163.
"oblivious": Shaw & Rosten, *Marilyn Among Friends*, 1987, p. 98.

CHAPTER THREE: AMAGANSETT, SUMMER 1957

"I was gaga": quoted in Ketchum, "Long Island Journal," *Nytimes.com*, July 14, 1996. http://www.nytimes.com/1996/07/14/nyregion/long-island-journal-428370.html?src=pm (accessed June 8, 2012).
"I can arrange for Chris…": Quoted in Gottried, *Arthur Miller: His Life and Work*, 2004, p. 312.
"I don't think I ever saw…": Quoted in Zolotow, 1960, p. 315.
"She made all the meals…": Quoted in ibid., p. 315.
"perilously off-balance": Rosten, *Marilyn: An Untold Story*, 1973, p. 52.
"confidently and with flair": Lee & Lee, "Marilyn Monroe's Stuffing Recipe Stars in a Remake," *Nytimes.com*, November 9, 2010.
"We were amazed…": Quoted in ibid.
"Marilyn had enough of the child…": Rosten, p. 47.
"Okay, Papa": Quoted in Nasser, "Marilyn's Amagansett." *Hampton Style*, August 1, 2008. http://danshamptons.com/content/hamptonstyle/2008/aug_1/03.html (accessed June 10, 2010).
"Come on…": Rosten, p. 51.

"knew those types," "civilians," "obsessed," "grinning vengefulness…" "confront her humanity…": Miller, 1987, p. 532-533.

2009 study tracking bipolar disorder and schizophrenia within families: Potash & Bienvenu, "Neuropsychiatric Disorders: Shared Genetics of Bipolar Disorder and Schizophrenia," Nature Reviews Neurology, 5, June 2009: 299-300.

"I can't tell you…": Quoted in Rosten, p. 46.

"Make believe…": Quoted in ibid, p. 46.

"*I'm either in the heights…*": Quoted in Strasberg, 1992, p. 132.

"We celebrated…": Quoted in Morgan, p. 212.

"Marilyn seemed interested…": Quoted in ibid, p. 212.

"What a frightening power she had…": Miller, 1987, p. 459

"Marilyn wants as many [children]…": Quoted in Morgan, p. 213.

"*Thank you for the lovely card…*": Quoted in Haspiel, *Marilyn: The Ultimate Look at the Legend*, 1991, p. 152-154.

"*I am glad you are enjoying camp so much…*": Image of letter in Banner, *MM—Personal from the Private Archive of Marilyn Monroe*, 2011, p. 222.

"I'm feeling wonderful…": Quoted in Morgan, p. 213.

"A baby makes a marriage…": Quoted in Strasberg, 1992, p. 270.

"There were no words anymore…": Miller, 1987, p. 458.

"There was a great sadness….": Quoted in Gottried, p. 312.

"Whatever the reasons…": Rosten, p. 47.

"her fierce tenderness": Miller, "Please Don't Kill Anything," *Redbook*, October 1961.

"Alive…": Quoted in Rosten, p. 75.

"delightedly": Miller, 1987, p. 459.

"*Bob, I was wondering…*": Image of letter in Banner, 2011, p. 223.

"*Janie, I really am trying to be a good dog…*": Image of letter in ibid, p. 224.

"Outshone even by her stepmother's absence," "I had never seen anyone…": Kaye, "Remembering Marilyn Monroe," *Premiere*, August 1998: 93.

"Magic is best served by ignorance…": Ibid, p. 63.

"Marilyn possessed a revolutionary idealism…": Miller, 1987, p. 467.

"I'm a new man": Quoted in Gottried, p. 316.

"[she] still she hangs like a bat…": Quoted in Clayton, *Marilyn Monroe: Unseen Archives*, 2004, p. 360.

CHAPTER FOUR: CONNECTICUT & MANHATTAN, AUTUMN & WINTER 1957

"What do you think of Miss Monroe…": *The Mike Wallace Interviews,* "Frank Lloyd Wright", directed by Bob Eisenhardt, 2001.
"I think Miss Monroe's architecture…": Ibid.
"For Mrs. Miller and Mr. Miller…": ibid.
"Whether people are fully conscious of this or not…": Quoted in *franklloydwright.org*, n.d. http://www.franklloydwright.org/about/licensing.html (retrieved January 1, 2012).
"Since I lost my baby…": Quoted in Strasberg, 1992, p. 271.
"a kind of old saltbox…": Quoted in Summers, 1985, p. 173.
"We do long so much for a child…": Quoted in Morgan, p. 214.
"Her impulse was royal…": Miller, 1987, p. 467.
"like a reigning queen of a small country": Ibid., p. 468.
"All our friends agreed …": Quoted in Shevey, p. 271.
"It was my fault…": recreated based on quote in Rosten, p. 68.
"All the time I was married to Arthur Miller…": Quoted in Levy, p. 74.
"She eventually came down and she was very sweet…": Quoted in Morgan, p. 219.
"Where are you taking…" recreated based on Guiles, 1969, p. 244.
"He may return…": recreated and based on quote in ibid, p. 244.
"The calf lives here!": recreated and based on quote in ibid, p. 244.
"You can't do that…": quoted in Morgan, p. 220.
"Marilyn decided she had to go out…": Quoted in ibid, p. 219.
"Mr. Polar Bear," "Mr. Bird," "*For Paris, Love & Kisses…*": Quoted in Miracle, p. 136.
"*we are in the middle of knocking down walls,*" "*Everyone thinks I am a marvelous cook, thanks to you,*" "*so wonderful*": Image of letter in Banner, 2011, p. 221.
"There were so few…": Quoted in Strasberg, 1992, p. 199.

Chapter Five: January to July 1958

"feels that you people would really make…": Image of letter in Banner, 2011, p. 116.

"I can't image that Marilyn Monroe…": Quoted in Thomas, "Maria Schell is a Marilyn Monroe Fan," *Lowell Sun*, June 17, 1957, p. 16.

"She is an honest actress…": Quoted in Mosby, "Part in 'Karamasov' Marilyn Pined For," *Del Rio News Herald*, August 6, 1957, p. 3.

"fascinating," & "very deep and very lovely…": Quoted in Kobal, *People Will Talk*, 1985, p. 140.

"Contrary to…": Buys, "Was Marilyn Monroe Really a Size 16?" *thesundaytimes.co.uk*, n.d. website no longer available (accessed January 2, 2011).

"[Marilyn] didn't have a long body…": Ibid.

The waist size of surviving belts and clothing from early in Marilyn's career ranged from 22 to 26 inches: Scott Fortner Collection.

"One of the smallest mannequins…": Quoted in "Golden Girl: An Auction of Marilyn Monroe's Possessions Reveals an Achingly Human Story Behind Glamorous Façade," *People*, August 16, 1999, p. 56.

twenty-two inch waist and bust measurement averaging thirty-four inches: Postrel, "Plump? No, Teeny," *The St. Petersburg Times*, June 27, 2011.

"A sack allows you to move…": Quoted in Spada & Zeno, *Monroe: Her Life in Pictures*, 1982, p. 138.

"She shouldn't wear it…": Quoted in Spoto, 1993, p. 396.

"But I've never even been to West Berlin!": quoted in Spoto, 1993, p. 396.

"reassured himself, and the audience, of his own goodness": Leaming, p. 301.

"It might vaguely appear…": Crowther, "Get Ready for Heartbreak..." *The New York Times*, June 25, 1958.

"I think I've been pregnant…": Quoted in Rosten, p. 72.

"May I see the baby?" "You don't know how lucky…" "Take good care of her": Quoted in "Star Crossing."

"I want this speech rewritten...": Quoted in Rosten, p. 84.
"an honor which the artist perhaps...": Quoted in Meyers, p. 177.
"magnificent": Quoted in Leaming, p. 331.

Part II: Living Legend
Chapter Six: *Some Like It Hot* Part I

"We had to find the hammerlock...": Quoted in Shevey, p. 274.
"Sometimes I would run into [Marilyn] ...": Diamond, "Marilyn Monroe and the 30-Proof Coffee Break: The Making of an American Classic," *The Chicago Tribune*, January 12, 1986.
"the dream girl of every red-blooded...": Quoted in Wilder & Diamond. *Some Like It Hot*, 1959, p. 37.
"wonderful": Quoted in Rollyson, 1993, p. 148.
"She gets the point...": Quoted in Shevey, p. 275.
"flashily-dressed broad...": Quoted in Wilder & Diamond, *Some Like It Hot*, 1959, p. 23.
"a tasteless and characterless ingénue," "worthless," "affront": Quoted in Guiles, 1984, p. 355.
"something out of nothing": Ibid, p. 355.
"I've got a real problem, Lee": Quoted in Guiles, 1984, p. 339.
"You've never really had a girlfriend...": Quoted in Maslon, *Some Like It Hot: The Official 50th Anniversary Companion*, 2009, p. 68.
"Should I do my next picture...": Quoted in Rosten, p. 71.
"We watched and bought...": Ibid, p. 71-72.
"An apparition in white materialized in the doorway...": Quoted in Summers, 1985, p. 176.
"It's still in the right places...": Quoted in Leaming, p. 310.
"Why do reporters ask if I'm happy or unhappy...": Quoted in *Photoplay*, "Behind the Scenes with 'Some Like It Hot,'" n.d.
"You see, I'm not a quick study...": Quoted in Wolfe, p. 318.
"She is more touching than ever...": Quoted in Ventura, p. 99.
"How was that for you...": Quoted in Leaming, p. 314.
"She had a tremendous sense of a joke...": Quoted in Guiles, 1984, p. 342.
"Neither I nor my husband...": Quoted in Leaming, p. 312.

"twenty cent tart": Quoted in Phillips, *Some Like It Wilder: The Life and Controversial Films of Billy Wilder*, 2010, p. 217.

"Into the darkness stepped Marilyn Monroe...": Fonda, *My Life So Far*, 2005, p. 115-116.

"You still haven't got it, dear...": Quoted in Guiles, 1984, p. 343.

"great humiliation": Quoted in ibid.

"The constant flubbing...": Wolfe, p. 319.

"relaxing a little more..." "go a bit further on the next try": Quoted in Spoto, 1993, p. 401.

"I have to make contact...": Quoted in Mills, p. 116.

"Go ahead and make contact...": Quoted in ibid, p. 116.

"She was a sweet lady...": Quoted in McCann, p. 105.

"It used to be you'd call her at 9:00...": Quoted in Johnson, "Here's A Realistic Look at Moviemaking Business," *Ocala Star-Banner*, August 3, 1962.

"I vowed then that if I did another...": Quoted in Victor, p. 324.

"Don't talk to me now....": Quoted in Shevey, p. 278.

"Arthur, you get her here at nine...": Quoted in Shevey, p. 281.

"I have an aunt in Vienna...": Quoted in Shearer, "How Much Time and Trouble Is Marilyn Monroe Worth?" *Oakland Tribune*, December 7, 1958, p. 31.

"Maybe it's a psychological hurdle...": Quoted in Wood, *The Bright Side of Billy Wilder*, 1970, p. 155.

"Diamond...was a fastidious screenwriter...": Quoted in Shevey, p. 277.

"I have never watched a film...": Whitcomb, "The New Marilyn," *Cosmopolitan*, March 1959, p. 68-71.

"prompt...": Quoted in ibid, p. 68.

"fragile...": Quoted in ibid, p. 70.

"MM is really all woman...": Quoted in ibid, p. 71.

"Marilyn, contrary...": Quoted in ibid, p 68.

"This situation...": Quoted in Maslon, p. 105.

"Marilyn Monroe was dynamite!": Quoted in Butterfield, "Memories of Marilyn," *Sandiego-online.com*, June 21, 1998. http://Sandiego-online.com/retro/marretr4.stm (accessed June 8, 2012).

"She had a childlike naiveté...": Quoted in ibid, n.p.

"She was beautiful and an inspiration...": Quoted in ibid, n.p.

"Marilyn Monroe was magic…": Interview with Sandra Warner in *Memories from the Sweet Sues: The All-Girl Band Featurette in Some Like It Hot/Collector's Edition DVD*, MGM, 2001.
"This will be great for the baby!": Quoted in Guiles, 1969, p. 260.
"It was the ultimate stage fright…": Quoted in Summers, 1985, p. 81.
"I thought it would take…": Quoted in Buskin, p. 220.
"She has become a better actress…": Quoted in Zolotow, 1960, p. 321-322.
"Marilyn was tortured by insecurity…": Leigh, *There Really Was a Hollywood*, 1984, p. 251.
"The greatest thing about Monroe…": Quoted in Victor, p. 323.
"She knew what she was right…": Wolfe, p. 320.
"I knew we were in mid-flight…": Quoted in Buskin, p. 220.
"There was a method to her madness": Wolfe, p. 320.
"Anyone can remember lines…": Quoted in Mills, p. 122.
"Don't give up the ship…": Quoted in Rosten, p. 76-77.
"I would have written this…": Image of letter published in Rosten, n. p.
"Darling Girl": Quoted in Spoto, 1993, p. 403.
"Thank you for your Halloween…": Quoted in Rosten, p. 77-78.
"Kissing Marilyn is like…": recreated based on Zolotow, 1960, p. 323 & many other sources
"Why would you say…": recreated and based on quote in ibid, p. 323.
"Paula, you act…": recreated and based on quote in ibid, p. 323.
"He only said that because I wore…": Quoted in Malone, *The Defiant One: A Biography of Tony Curtis*, 2013, p. 86.
"I'd really like to do a picture with Marilyn…": Quoted in "Charlton Heston Would Trade Biblical Roles for Comedy," *Desert Times*, June 3, 1960, n.p.
"When you watch that scene…:" Ebert, "Some Like It Hot (Chicago Sun Times)," rogerebert.com. January 9, 2000. http:"rogerebert.suntimes.com/apps/pbcs.dll/article?AID+/20000109/REVIEWS08/1090301/1023 (accessed June 8, 2012).
"She would come…": Quoted in quoted in Shevey, p. 279.

"fabulous...wonderful...": Interview with Tony Curtis in *Nostalgic Look Back in Some Like It Hot/Collector's Edition DVD*, MGM, 2001.
"underscore[ing] one of the unsung...": LaSalle, "Some Like It True: Curtis' Monroe Tale Unlikely," *Sfgate.com*, November 6, 2009. http://www.sfgate.com/cgi-bin/article.cgi?f=/c/a/2009/11/05/MVPF1LN.DTL (accessed June 8, 2012).
"There is only way he could comment...": Image of document in Banner, 2011, p. 82.
"You've read there was some actor...": Quoted in Meryman, "Marilyn Monroe Lets Her Hair Down About Being Famous: 'Fame My Go By and So Long, I've Had You'...An Interview," *Life*, August 3, 1962, p. 32.
"Drop dead": Quoted in Hoyt, *Marilyn: The Tragic Venus*, 1973, p. 202.
"Go screw!": Quoted in Guiles, 1969, p. 260.
"Fuck you!": Quoted in Rollyson, 1993, p. 159.
"Go fuck yourself!": Quoted in Mailer, *Marilyn: A Biography*, 1975, p. 17.
"Maybe she doesn't consider...": Quoted in Rollyson, 1993, p. 159.
"how a future generation of women...": Mailer, 1975, p. 17.
"adamant refusal...": Quoted in Guiles, 1969, p. 260.
"The effect of this is to deny...": Churchwell, p. 251.
"It *was* moving...": Quoted in quoted in McCann, p. 108-109.
"It makes one think of the last paintings...": Quoted in Ventura, p. 100.
"It's the least I can do...": Quoted in Guiles, 1969, p. 264.
"Trust it, enjoy it, be brave," "Getting drunk on kisses": Christie's, *The Personal Property of Marilyn Monroe*, 1999, p. 333.
"You remember what Curtis said...": Ebert, 2000.
"The song is a poignant testament...": McCann, p. 107.
"She puts heartbreak...": Rollyson, 1993, p. 156.
"But that's another story...": Wilder & Diamond, *Some Like It Hot*, 1959.
"He was lying naked on the broken stone...": *Suddenly Last Summer*, directed by Joseph L. Mankiewicz, Columbia Pictures, 1959.

"You could not hear anything going…": Quoted in Buskin, p. 221.
"She insisted on going on…": Quoted in Shevey, p. 281.
"I am eating better…": Quoted in Victor, p. 324.
"Well, I have discussed this project…": Quoted in Victor, p. 324.
"attack" "contemptible" "unjust" "cruel" "despite you…": Quoted in Zolotow, *Billy Wilder in Hollywood*, 1996, p. 265.
"overwork or inconsiderate treatment" "coddled" "overwhelming lack of popularity" quoted in ibid, p. 266.
"thrown her out…": Quoted in ibid, p. 266.
"she did her job…" "while your published remarks…": Quoted in Shevey, p. 282.
"the salt of the earth": quoted in Riese & Hitchens, *The Unabridged Marilyn: Her Life from A to Z*, 1987, p. 552.
"The salt of the earth told…": Quoted in ibid, p. 552.
"I hereby acknowledge that good wife Marilyn…": Quoted in Shevey, p. 282.
"under duress" "influence of barbiturates" "suffering from high blood pressure" "brainwashed": Quoted in Victor, p. 324.
"that shit they put in the papers" "love": Quoted in Shevey, p. 280.
"roared": Quoted in ibid, p. 280.
"She is a very great actress…": Quoted in Gehman, "Charming Billy," *Playboy*, December 1960, p. 70.
"You're always running into people's…": Quoted in Meryman, August 3, 1962, p. 32.
"I don't understand why people…": Quoted in ibid.
"beat her into submission" & "made her a monster": Churchwell, p. 251.
"I miss her…": Quoted in Victor, p. 324.
"We just happen to miss her like hell…": Quoted in Guiles, 1969, p. 261.
"Never a week passes …": Quoted in Ventura, p. 106.
"She was an absolute genius as a comic actress…": Quoted in Summers, 1985, p. 178.
"the funniest man in the world": Interview with Marilyn Monroe newsreels of the premiere of *Some Like It Hot.*
"To get down to cases…": Archer Winsten, *New York Post*, quoted in Ricci & Conway, 1990, p. 145.

"Mr. Wilder, abetted by such…": A. H. Weiler, *The New York Times*, quoted in ibid, p. 145.

"*Some Like It Hot*, directed…": Hift, *Variety*, quoted in ibid, p. 145.

"superb": Quoted in "The Essentials: Critics' Corner: *Some Like It Hot*," *TCM.com*, n. d. http://www.tcm.com/essentials/article.html?cid=71637&mainArticleId=463894 (accessed June 1, 2013).

"Directing Marilyn Monroe in a movie…": Quoted in "Walk Like This, Marilyn," *Life*, April 20, 1959, p. 101.

"Monroe steals [the film]…": Ebert, 2000, n.p.

"Some Like It Hot was like the perfect…": Interview with Sandra Warner in *Memories from the Sweet Sues: The All-Girl Band Featurette*, 2001.

Chapter Eight: November–December 1958

"Because of some recent complications…": Image of telegram in Julien, *Property From the Estate of Marilyn Monroe*, 2005, p. 68.

"Between exposures…": Quoted in "Fabled Enchantresses: Marilyn Monroe in a Remarkable Recreation of her Predecessors, *Life*, December 22, 1958, p. 137.

"enchantress" "embodies the fancies" "In our time…": Miller, "My Wife, Marilyn: Playwright Pays Affectionate Tribute to Her Feat, *Life*, December 22, 1958, p.146.

"beauty" "spontaneous joy": Miller, 1958, p. 146.

"Her miraculous sense of sheer play had been unloosed": Ibid, p. 145.

"It's grimly ironic…": Image of letter in Banner, 2011, p. 181.

"You pat right here…": Quoted in Taraborrelli, *The Secret Life of Marilyn Monroe*, 2009, p. 313.

"Get me my mink!": Quoted in Meyers, p. 184.

"Then why didn't he slap me…": ibid, p, 184.

"preprogrammed": Quoted in Strasberg, 1992, p. 170-171.

"If I expressed everything…": Quoted in ibid, p. 138.

"Help help…": Quoted in Rosten, 1973, n.p.

Chapter Nine: 1959

"Who'd know the difference…": Quoted Rosten, p. 55.
"I would and all the people…": Quoted in ibid, p. 55.
"Marilyn dear—About the movie…": Quoted in Banner, 2011, p. 236.
"I'm very old-fashioned…": Quoted in Belmont, p. 20.
"I like to cook…": Quoted in ibid, p. 20.
"I like people…": Quoted in ibid, p. 20.
"a fragile thing…": Huston, p. 130.
"I think Marilyn is bound to make an almost overwhelming…": Quoted in Thurman, *Isak Dineson: The Life of a Storyteller*, 1995, p. 425.
"Well, you can take the week off…": Quoted in Massee, p. 221.
"She was most charming…": Ibid, p. 221.
"We agreed on a number of things…": Quoted in Victor, p. 260.
"Carl Sandburg, who's in his eighties…": Quoted in Meyers, p. 176.
"The first time…": Quoted in Michaels, p. 88.
"She's the most sociable…": Quoted in ibid, p. 88.
"She doesn't come in here…": Quoted in ibid, p 88.
"Hey, mister…": Quoted in ibid, p. 88.
"But somebody said…": Quoted in ibid, p. 89.
"Oh they're tearing down…": Quoted in ibid, p. 89.
"Proud to be the guest…": Quoted in Meyers, p. 175.
"I have yet to see anything…": Quoted in ibid, p. 175.
"I always felt she had picked…": Quoted in ibid, p. 176.
"*I have no prejudice…*" "*I don't consider myself…*" "*How do I know…*": Quoted in "Walk Like This, Marilyn," Life, p. 104.
"Even when a nervous photographer…": Quoted in Spoto, 1992, p. 408.
"successfully managed the difficult transition…": *Current Biography 1959*, 1959.
"Do you have a couple of words…": Interview with Marilyn Monroe in "Marilyn Monroe Given Italian Award for Best Foreign Actress 14-5-1959," *YouTube.com*. n.d. http://www.youtube.com/watch?v=T8_XRx1YXvE (accessed March 8, 2012).

"Marilyn was always my first choice…": Quoted in Paris, *Audrey Hepburn*, 2002, p. 170.
"terrifically good": Quoted in Clarke, p. 269.
"Paramount double-crossed me…": Quoted in ibid, p. 269.
"I can buy flowers…": Quoted in Morgan, p. 218.
"I'm sorry to report…": Quoted in ibid, p. 218.
"the pain is increasing by the minute": Quoted in Rosten, p. 72.
"dead" "There is no love…": Monroe, *Fragments*, p. 127.
"I've been scared…": Quoted in Lewin, "Marilyn Monroe," *London Daily Express*, May 6, 1959, n.p.
"They seemed to be dancing…": Bosworth, "The Newman Chronicles, *Vanityfiar.com*, September 2008. http://www.vanityfair.com/culture/features, 2008/09/newman200809 (accessed December 14, 2012).
"Young man! Has anyone…": Williams, *A Streetcar Named Desire*, 1995, p. 65.
"I gave him a close-up of Monroe…": Quoted in Guiles, 1984, p. 361.
"She *has* to be there!": Quoted in ibid, p. 360.
"I think it's a very wonderful thing…": Quoted in Guiles, 1969, p. 266.
"Do you think…": Quoted in ibid, p. 266.
"I hope he does:" Quoted in ibid, p. 266.
"We must be late!": Quoted in Guiles, 1984, p. 361.
"I think we'll all get blind…": Quoted in Miles, "Stars Turn Out for Hollywood's Welcome to Russian Chieftan," *The Los Angeles Times*, September 20, 1959, n.p.
"You are a very lovely…": Quoted in Wolfe, p. 327.
"There should be more…": Quoted in Guiles, 1984, p. 361.
"My husband…": Quoted in Wolfe, p. 327.
"Ah, yes…": Quoted in Zolotow, 1960, p. 339.
"I very much like to go to Disneyland…": Quoted in Gabler, *Walt Disney: The Triumph of the American Imagination*, 2006, p. 566.
"It was the worst choice…": Quoted in Carlson, "Nikita Khrushchev Goes to Hollywood," *Smithsonian*, July 2009.
"I feel this is a historic…": Quoted in Miles, 1959.
"Marilyn was always my first…": Quoted in Inge, *Truman Capote: Conversations*, 1987, p. 317.

"terrifically good": Quoted in Eisenhower, *After Romanticism*, 2008, p. 51.
"Paramount double-crossed…": Quoted in Voss, *Truman Capote and the Legacy of In Cold Blood*, p. 152-153.
"Earthquakes, storms, wars…": *Times Talk*, "Babe in Boyland," 1959, p. 3.
"With my high heels?": Quoted in Digh, *Creative Is a Verb: If You're Alive, You're Creative*, 2011, p. 147
"In a burst of energy…": Quoted in "Why In the World Are the Windsors Jumping? Photographed by Philippe Halsman," *Life*, November 9, 1959, p. 102.
"When an adult woman jumps…": Quoted in ibid, p. 107.
"radiantly beautiful…": Roberts, "Ralph Roberts Manuscript," *RalphRoberts.com*, n. d., p. 2. http://www.ralphroberts.com/mauscriptpage1.htm (accessed June 8, 2012).
"Miss Holliday, you're wonderful…": Quoted in ibid, p. 2.
"Do you know…": Quoted in ibid, p. 3.
"She's one of my closest…": Quoted in ibid, p. 3.
"I have always felt…": Image of letter in Zanuck in "Letter from Richard D. Zanuck to Marilyn Monroe Dated December 4, 1959," *Bonhams.com*, June 13, 2010.
http://www.bonhams.com/auctions/18245/lot/1009/ (accessed February 9. 2013).
"fairy godmother," and "a new flowering life": Plath, p. 732.

CHAPTER TEN: *LET'S MAKE LOVE*

"Marilyn Monroe is the greatest farceuse…": Quoted in Haspiel, *The Unpublished Marilyn*, 2000, p. 179.
"[Marilyn] had this absolutely…": Quoted in Mills, p. 131.
"not worth the paper…": Miller, *Timebends: A Life*, 1987, p. 466.
"blocks of time," "to try to save her…": Ibid, p. 466.
"It was a bad miscalculation…": Ibid, p. 466.
"He comes from good Italian…": Quoted in Gordon, "Marilyn Meets Montand, *Look*, July 5, 1960.

"[Marilyn] was always on time...": Quoted in Hutchinson, *Marilyn Monroe*, 1982, p. 74.
"America—Marilyn Monroe": Quoted in Hoyt, p. 217.
"The wide-eyed naïve...": Quoted in Haspiel, 2000, p. 177.
"She was nothing but a pro...": Quoted in Crown, *Marilyn at Twentieth Century Fox*, 1987, p. 182.
"Marilyn was a smiling...": Quoted in Spoto, 1992, p. 413.
"Next to my husband...": Quoted in Gordon, p. 96.
"There is nobody like her...": Quoted in ibid, 93.
"They possess internal engines...": Quoted in ibid, p. 96.
"in bed with an adhesion": Image of telegram dated January 15, 1960 in Julienslive.com. http://www.julienslive.com/view-auctions/catalog/id/55/lot/18187/ (accessed February 21, 2013).
"What you paid...": Quoted in Shevey, p. 292-293.
"She was very nice...": Quoted in Morgan, p. 221.
"I don't want to say...": Quoted in Morgan, p. 221.
"She's one of the few stars...": Quoted in Zolotow, p. 335.
"*What am I afraid of?...*": Quoted in Rollyson, 1993, p. 147.
"Marilyn is not a great dancer...": Quoted in "Yves Montand Uses His Gallic Charm as Marilyn's Movie Lover. Marilyn's Own Earnest Eccentricities Offer a Compelling Human Study in Filming *Let's Make Love*. Photographed by John Bryson," Life, August 15, 1960, p. 68.
"I really was awful...": Quoted in Spoto, p. 421.
"The universe sparkles...": Image of telegram in Banner, 2011, p 94.
"with the worst actress...": Quoted in Leaming, p. 344.
"You are just scared...": Recreated and based on quote in ibid, p. 344.
"Everything she do is original...": Quoted in Gordon, p. 93.
"In a whole picture...": Quoted in Ricci & Conway, 1990, p. 14.
"She was a wonderful person...": Interview with Evelyn Moriarty, 1999.
"She treated me more like a friend...": Quoted in Haspiel, 2000, p. 170.
"If she walked...": Interview with Evelyn Moriarty, 1999.
"My next weekend off ..." Image of telegram in Banner, 2011, p. 110.

"When Arthur was in town…": Skolsky, *Don't Get Me Wrong—I Love Hollywood*, 1975, p. 227.
"I am always drawn…": Quoted in Pettus, "Starry, Starry Night," *Gourmet Magazine*, February 2001, p. 123.
"Marilyn had an openness…": Quoted in ibid, p. 123
"who lived together as neighbors…": Signoret, *Nostalgia Isn't What It Used to Be*, 1979, p. 330.
"the most beautiful peasant …": Ibid, p. 330.
"Meet me in the kitchen…": recreated and based on a quote in ibid, p. 331.
"a kid who's delaying the moment for lights out": Ibid, p. 337.
"You can do whatever…": Quoted in ibid, p. 338.
"Please forgive…": Quoted in ibid., p. 339.
"had started to be angry…": Ibid, p. 340.
"Hi, Larry from *Look*…" Quoted in Schiller, p. 4.
"the Big Bad Wolf": Quoted in ibid., p. 4.
"For him to snub…": Quoted in Taraborrelli, p. 318.
"The H-bomb…": Quoted in Levy, p. 77.
"more liberal than many of the Democrats": Image in Banner, 2011, p. 182.
"she sits at the foot of your table": Ibid, p. 183.
"it's a little…": Ibid, p. 183.
"I didn't want…": Ibid, p 183.
"Nix on Nixon": Ibid, 183.
"Over the hump…": Ibid, p. 183.
"Stymied with Symington": Ibid, p. 183.
"Back to Boston…": Ibid, p. 183.
"The next Oscar…": quoted in Wolfe, p. 338.
"desperate depression." Quoted in Leaming, p. 353.
"I just let her go ahead…": Belmont, p. 13.
"Shh, excuse us—it's being taped:" Interview with Marilyn Monroe in *Marilyn on Marilyn*, BBC, 2001.
"My one desire…": Quoted in Belmont, p. 19.
"When I dreamed of love…": Quoted in ibid, p. 19.
"If I'm generally anything…": Interview with Marilyn Monroe in *Marilyn on Marilyn*.
"I'm only thirty-four…": Quoted in Belmont, p. 21.
"I like people…": Quoted in ibid, p. 21.

"I'm so impetuous…": Quoted in ibid, p. 20.
"Above all…": Quoted in ibid, p. 20.
"Love and work…": Quoted in ibid, p. 19.
"I have never known her so happy…": Image of letter dated April 30, 1960 in *Bonhams.com*, April 20, 2011. http://www.bonhams.com/auctions/19377/lot/92/s (accessed February 21, 2013).
"Go say good-night…": Quoted in Wolfe, p. 339.
"It was the dullest…": Quoted in ibid, p. 339.
"An actress whose name…": Quoted in ibid, p. 339.
"Locations in those days…": MacLaine, *My Lucky Stars*, 1995, p. 318.
"*When he sees me on the screen…*": Note on display at Christie's Auction House, New York, *The Personal Property of Marilyn Monroe*, October 1999.
"what may have happened…": Signoret, p. 342-343.
"you're too damned…" Recreated and based upon quote in Guiles, 1969, p. 278.
"I have been to see…": Quoted in Shevey, p. 83.
"I don't understand…": Quoted in ibid, p. 83.
"a real southern girl" Quoted in Guiles, 1984, p. 367.
"They all know you…": Quoted in Shevey, p. 293.
"marvelous time": Image of letter in Julien, 2005, p. 50.
"*It was your good thoughts…*": Image of letter dated June 22, 1960 in Bonhams.com, June 16, 2008. bonhams.com/auctions/16091/lot/3017/ (accessed February 9, 2013.
"How are you, Miss Monroe?": Quoted in Nash, *Baby, Let's Play House: Elvis Presley and the Women Who Love Him*, 2010, p. 327-328.
"offensive sex suggestiveness": Quoted in Buskin, p. 229.
"for the longest and most remunerative": Quoted in ibid, p. 229.
"I'm possibly mad…": Quoted in Sikov, p. 446.
"She is a simple…": Quoted in Spoto, 1993, p. 442 & quoted in Wagenknecht, *Marilyn Monroe: A Composite View*, 1969, p. 24.
"her revenge": Signore, p. 348.
"The real problem…": Quoted in Wagenknecht, p. 24
"Marilyn was wracked …": Quoted in Taraborrelli, p. 321.

"Not for a moment…": Quoted in Wolfe, p. 340.
"The old Monroe…": Crowther, "The Screen: Milton Berle Steals Show in 'Let's Make Love,'" *New York Times*, September 9, 1960, p. 36.
"poor excuse" "ambling…" "who…": Ibid, p. 36.
"She never knew…" and "She's gone…": Signoret, p. 349.
"I think [Marilyn and Montand] both felt attraction…": MacLaine, p. 325.
"It was a sweet adventure…": Ibid, p. 312.
"intrusive and insensitive." Ibid, p. 313.
"He knew he had been insensitive…": MacLaine, p. 326-327.
"For me she was somebody…": Interview with Montand, *Good Morning America*, August 5, 1982.
"One of two things…": Signoret, p. 335.
"well worth an act…":. Ibid, p. 336.

Chapter Eleven: Spring & Summer 1960

"cold and unresponsive": Quoted in Summers, 1985, p. 189.
"rapidly coming to the end of his rope": Quoted in ibid, p. 189.
"I promised she would sleep with less medication…": Quoted in ibid, p 189.
"Let us be modest about…": Quoted in Freeman, *Why Norma Jean Killed Marilyn Monroe*, 1992, p. 2.
"Can't I lie on the couch…": Quoted in ibid, p. 2.
"I'm hurt because you didn't think…": Quoted in ibid, p. 2.
"taking a beating, like a soldier in a war": Quoted in ibid, p. 9.
"I remember things from my childhood…": Quoted in ibid, p. 10.
"As she becomes more anxious…": Quoted in Summers, 1985, p. 189.
"You're both narcissists…": Quoted in Spoto, 1993, p. 429.
"I told you to wait in the car": Quoted in Shevey, p. 296.
"You don't have that kind of equipment": Quoted in Badman, *Marilyn Monroe: The Final Years*, 2010, p. 23.
"I have to get out of the car…": Quoted in Haspiel, 1991, p. 174.
"Would it be all right to have it on…": Quoted in Roberts, p. 5.

"The night of the most important…": Quoted in ibid, p. 5.
"It is time, in short, for a new generation…": Quoted in Podell, *Speeches of the American Presidents*, 1988, p. 602.

Chapter Twelve: *The Misfits* Part I

"ultimate motion picture": Quoted in Leaming, p. 363.
"The movie is about a world of change…": Quoted in Brater, *Arthur Miller: A Playwright's Life and Works*, 2005, p. 114.
"It's supposed to be a Western…": Quoted in Miller, 1987, p. 462.
"It's sort of an Eastern Western…": Quoted in ibid, p. 462.
"I've always felt a misfit": Quoted in Brater, p. 124.
"He's the same man…": Quoted in ibid, p. 114.
"mumble arid aphorisms": Spoto, 1993, p. 431.
"I want you to do it": Quoted in Guiles, 1984, p. 354.
"There was a depth in her…": Quoted in ibid, p. 379.
"Working with John ten years later…": Quoted in Goode, *The Making of The Misfits*, 1986, p. 202.
"Each of them…": Quoted in ibid, p. 17.
"If anyone were average…": Quoted in Guiles, 1969, p. 292.
"He's the only person I know…": Quoted in Bosworth, *Montgomery Clift: A Biography*, 2007, p. 330.
"I look at him and see the brother…": Quoted in Mills, p. 140.
"I have the same problem as Marilyn…": Quoted in Weatherby, *Conversations with Marilyn*, 1992, p. 75.
"They're not going to pay…": Quoted in Miller, 1987, p. 469.
"Instead of having to stop…": Quoted in Buskin, p. 234.
"standing in a minefield..": Quoted in Summers, 1985, p. 195
"There's something extremely alert…": Quoted in Arnold, *Marilyn Monroe*, 2005, p. 72-73.
"a photographic phenomenon": Ibid, p. 72.
"Once she was ready…": Ibid, p. 72.
"I'm thirty-four years old…": Quoted in ibid, p. 91.
"fierce in their dedication to her": Ibid, p. 97.
"They're around her…": Quoted in Guiles, 1969, p. 289-290.
"What was so amazing…": Quoted in Guiles, 1984, p. 385.

"The legend, which I thought a kind of joke…": Quoted in Guiles, 1969, p. 290.
"Trouble has already…": Recreated and based upon quote in Roberts, p. 6.
"What I do for Marilyn…": Quoted in Guiles, 1969, p. 291.
"Rhett Butler…": Quoted in Hoyt, p. 220.
"astonishingly beautiful…": Quoted in Wolfe, p. 352.
"If she couldn't sleep…": Quoted in Buskin, p. 234.
"with screaming headaches…": Quoted in Wolfe, p. 353.
"Chaos was on us all": Miller, 1987, p. 474.
"Marilyn had the difficult scene…": Quoted in Goode, p. 43.
"It was far…": Miller, 1987, p. 464.
"I'm so lonely…": Quoted in Guilaroff, p. 158.
"You know, Sydney…": Quoted in ibid, p. 159.
"Marilyn, I could be your father": Quoted in ibid, p. 159.
"The next morning…": Quoted in Goode, p. 38.
"[Paula] kept saying that she wanted…": Arnold, p. 96.
"seriousness so profound…": Miller, 1987, p. 465.
"You're a branch on a tree...": Quoted in Meyers, p. 220.
"Think garlic; he's eaten garlic": Quoted in Strasberg, 1992, p. 216.
"When she was herself, show could be marvelously…": Quoted in Mills, p. 142.
"If you were pro-Marilyn…": Weatherby, p. 31.
"She felt lonely, isolated…": Quoted in Spoto, 1993, p. 434.
"sulking around…": Quoted in Wolfe, p. 353.
"Hey, King…": *TV Guide, TV Guide Film & Video Companion*, 2004, p. 646.
"What is Eli…": Recreated and based upon quote in Roberts, p. 9.
"He's leading me…": Recreated and based on quoted in ibid, p. 9.
"She was the master…": Arnold, p. 72.
"Let's get the people away…": Quoted in ibid, p. 93.
"Marilyn and Monty were intrigued…": Quoted in ibid, p. 74.
"audition in front of the gods…": Miller 1987, p. 140.
"I look at him and see the brother…": Quoted in ibid, p. 140.
"psychic twins" & "recognized disaster…": Guiles, 1984, p. 382.
"If you do that again…": Capua, *Montgomery Clift: A Biography*, 2002, p. 128.

"We're only going for a walk..." Quoted in Guiles, 1969, p. 299.
"He had a wild look...": Quoted in ibid, p 299.
"We hear you're Arthur's girlfriend...": Recreated and based on quote in ibid, p. 301.
"If she knows that much...": Ibid, p. 301.
"behaved as though Marilyn was a woman...": Miller, 1987, p. 471.
"The place was full of so-called men...": Quoted in McCann, p. 159.
"With Gable [Marilyn] was at her best...": Arnold, p. 92.
"We were rehearsing...": Quoted in Summers, 1985, p. 192.
"I had reservations...": Recreated and based on quotations in Roberts, p. 7.
"Thank you..." Recreated and based on quote in ibid, p 7.
"May I come in...": Recreated and based on quote in Guiles, 1984, p. 384.
"Marilyn loved...": Quoted in Guiles, 1984, p. 384.
"I want to get away from...": Quoted in Roberts, p. 14.
"happy people": Quoted in Guiles, 1969, p. 294.
"He's such a sweet man...": Quoted in ibid, p. 295.
"Grouchy Grumps": Quoted in ibid, p. 295.
"No!...": Quoted in Roberts, p. 10.
"The big Reno blackout...": Quoted in Guiles, 1969, p. 294.
"You can afford to be late...": Quoted in Arnold, p. 96.
"I can't tolerate this behavior...": Quoted in Strasberg, 1992, p. 218-219.
"She was a flower of iron...": Miller, 1987, p. 481.
"agonizing pain" & "Rafe...": Roberts, p. 16.
"I was not an observer...": Quoted in Arnold, p. 97.
"We had the Errol Flynn of directors...": Quoted in Buskin, p. 236.
"She was a ghost of herself," "helpless" "overgrown child," & "vampire...": Strasberg, 1992, p. 220.
"Had Marilyn been more sophisticated...": Quoted in Leaming, p. 372.
"I'm looking forward to getting back to work...": Quoted in Morgan, p. 227.
"looking wonderfully self-possessed..." Miller, 1987, p. 485.

"Her incredible resilience…": Ibid, p. 485.
"That's terrible…": Quoted in Summers, 1985, p. 193.
"When the 10,000…": Arnold, p. 92.
"Working with her was fantastic…": Quoted in LaGuardia, *Monty: A Biography of Montgomery Clift*, 1977, p. 215.
"Compared to the multiple takes…": Rollyson, 1993, p. 179.
"You can all go to hell": Quoted in Goode, p. 209.
"They don't care…": Quoted in Grobel, *The Hustons*, 2000, p. 494.
"People like to manufacture…": Quoted in Buskin, p. 238.
"Wonderful" & "concerned…": Weatherby, p. 43.
"Butchers! Killers!...": Miller, *The Misfits* (1961).
"These words come up…": Rollyson, 1993, p. 181.
"jumping in and out…" "wear and tear" & "must have…: Weatherby, p. 54.
"The public in America…": Quoted in ibid.
"And if you're…": Recreated and based on quotation in Weatherby, p. 59.

CHAPTER THIRTEEN: *THE MISFITS* PART II

"Marilyn, here is the gentleman…": Recreated and based on quotation in Guiles, 1984, p. 386.
"I am so happy…": Recreated and based on quotation in Hoyt, p 221.
"Look at those legs…": Quoted in Arnold, p. 97.
"Yes, but she's no Janice Mars…": Recreated and based on quotation in Roberts, p. 22.
"I'm sorry…": Quoted in ibid, p. 22.
"Mrs. Florence Edwards…": Guiles, 1969, p. x.
"Arthur writes scripts…": Quoted in Guiles, 1984, p. 391.
"What should I ask…": Quoted in Goode, p. 246.
"Don't think, honey…": Quoted in ibid, p.246.
"You, a sensitive fellow…": Miller, *The Misfits* (1961).
"I've loved him like a brother…": Quoted in Roberts, p. 9.
"Whitey, remember…": Quoted in Arnold, p. 136.
"All my life I've played…": Quoted in Kobal, *Marilyn Monroe: A Life on Film*, 1974, p. 613.

"I have no protection...": Quoted in Roberts, p. 24.
"You can't overdo...": Quoted in Miller, 1987, p. 485.
"It's a spiritual autobiography...": Quoted in Goode, p. 257.
"I now have two things...": Quoted in Bret, *Clark Gable: Tormented Star*, 2008, p. 252.
"I do believe it was essential...": Quoted in Goode, p. 259.
"The real trouble with Monroe...": Quoted in Buskin, p. 234.
"Eli you're going to be working...": Quoted in Guiles, 1969, p. 306.
"illicit relationship" & "an over-emphasis of nudity...": Quoted in Buskin, p. 239.
"The low moral tone...": Quoted in Buskin, p. 238
"Seemingly misunderstood...": Cannon, "The Misfits: A Review by Damien Cannon," *Film.u-net.com*, 1998. http://www.film.u-net.com/Movies/Reviews/Misfits.html (accessed February 15, 2013).
"Gable has never done anything better...": Kate Cameron in *New York Daily News* quoted in Buskin, p. 239.
"powerful experience..." "characters at once more lifelike...": Alpert, "S. R. Goes to the Movies: Arthur Miller, Screenwriter," *Saturday Review*, February 4, 1961, p. 27 & 47.
"A picture that I can only call superb..." Beckley, "The Misfits," *New York Herald Tribune*, February 2, 1961, n.p.
"In this era when sex and violence...": Ibid, n.p.
"vivid" "thrilling," "completely blank," and "unfathomable," "kicks up such a ruckus," "breathless horror," "everything turn[ing] upon her," "just doesn't come off": Crowther, "John Huston's 'The Misfits'; Gable and Monroe Star in Script by Miller," *The New York Times*, February 2, 1961, n.p.
"At face value...": Tube, "The Misfits," *Daily Variety*, February 1, 1961, n.p.
"Nuances of which may seriously...": Ibid, n.p.
"Terrible...": Quoted in *FilmFacts*, February 17, 1961, p. 12.
"Miss Monroe has seldom looked worse...": *Hollywood Reporter*, quoted in Victor, p. 200.
"Marilyn Monroe (in a bikini yet) looks like an aunt...": *Limelight* quoted in Buskin, p. 239.
"Monroe and Gable make a congenial pair...": *Los Angeles Mirror* quoted in ibid, p. 239.

"Her familiar breathless, childlike…": "The Misfits," *Variety*, February 1, 1961, n.p..

"Miss Monroe plays the stripper…": Hart, "The Misfits," *Films in Review*, February 1961, n.p.

"Marilyn Monroe, the Saint of Nevada Desert...": Mekas, "Movie Journal," *Village Voice*, February 9, 1961, n.p.

"As Roslyn, Marilyn carries the film…": Mellen, *Marilyn Monroe*, 1973, p. 133.

"The more tormented Monroe's private…": Rollyson, 1993, p. 154.

"The film seemed purely a torture for her….": Quoted in Victor, p. 199.

"I had to use my wits…": Quoted in Taraborrelli, p. 337.

"Absolutely NOT!": Quoted in Capua, *Montgomery Clift: A Biography*, 2002, p. 148.

"Clark was one of the kindness…": Quoted in Parsons, "Marilyn Monroe's Life As a Divorcee," *Modern Screen*, October, 1961, n.p.

CHAPTER FOURTEEN: OCTOBER–DECEMBER 1960

"Proof of her eminence …": Zinsser, "How Cinderella Became a National Institution," *The New York Times*, October 30, 1960, p. 30.

"To Jim Hapsiel…": Haspiel, 1991, p. 184

"I don't care how long…": Quoted in McLellan, "John Springer, 85; Press Agent to Illustrious Array of Entertainers, *The Los Angeles Times*, November 1, 2001, n.p.

"Who's Morris Greene…": Miller, 1987, p. 490.

"Who's Morris Green!...": Quoted in ibid, p. 490.

"Are you coming home?": Recreated and based on quote in Miller, 1987, p. 521.

"Only to collect my things": Quoted in Leaming, p. 376.

"I will not discuss my personal life": Marilyn Monroe speaking in various newsreels & documentaries.

"The most unlikely marriage…": Quoted in Gottfried, *Arthur Miller: His Life and Work*, 2004, p. 337.

"The breakup of her marriage…": Quoted in Guiles, 1984, p. 396.

"To the other Venus": Arnold, p. 154.

"I hear from a couple…": image of letter in Julien, p. 51.
"Clark Gable was one…": Quoted in Victor, p. 115.
"You have recently submitted…": Image of letter in "Letter Regarding Clark Gable's Insurance Policy Dated February 25, 1960," *Bonhams.com*, December 9, 2007. http://bonhams.com/auctions/15427/lot/2017/ (accessed February 8, 2013).
"I kept him waiting…": Quoted in Skolsky, 1975, p. 230.
"How does it feel…": Quoted in Miracle, p. 165.
"I'm not doing well…": Quoted in Taraborrelli, p. 339.
"I don't see how things…": Quoted in ibid, p. 339.
"Who will be the next ambassador …": Buchwald, "Let's be Firm on Monroe Doctrine." *Washington Post*, November 19, 1960, n.p.
"*Loving good wishes…*": *Gladys Pearl Eley.*" Julien, p. 54.
"forest full": Monroe, Letter to Dr. Greenson, in Shaun Usher, "Men Are Climbing to the Moon But They Don't Seem Interested in the Beating Human Heart," Lettersofnote.com, January 28, 2011. http://www.lettersofnote.com/2011/01/men-are-climbing-to-moon-but-they-dont.html (accessed June 1, 2012).
"Who sent them?": Recreated and based on quote in ibid.
"The card just…": Recreated and based on ibid.
"Pat, there is…": Recreated and based on ibid.
"First of all…": Quoted in ibid.
"What are you doing Christmas?": Ibid.
"Nothing, I'm just visiting…": Recreated and based on ibid.
"I must say I was bleary…": Ibid.
"Marilyn knew where…": Quoted in *Allen, Where Have You Gone,* Joe DiMaggio?, 1975, p. 189.

CHAPTER FIFTEEN: JANUARY–JUNE 1961

"My dear…": Quoted in Summers, 1985, p. 202.
"The fewer people who know …": Image of note in Banner, 2011, p. 306.
"in his sole discretion…" & "to be used…": Image of the Last Will and Testament of Marilyn Monroe appearing on the Internet & various sources.

"*I don't think those squares…*" & "*you can call…*": Image of letter in Banner, 2011, p. 239.
"I felt Marilyn could do…": Quoted in Guiles, 1984, p. 400-401.
"I went back to the Maugham…": Quoted in Woodard, "Marilyn Monroe and 'Rain,' the Project That Never Came to Be, Part 2," in Elisa Jordan's *Examiner.com*, January, 7, 2013. http://www.examiner.com/article/marilyn-monroe-and-rain-the-project-that-never-came-to-be-part-2 (accessed January 13, 2013).
"My hope is Marilyn Monroe…": Quoted in ibid.
"Let the word go forth …": Quoted in Clarke, *Ask Not: The Inauguration of John F. Kennedy and the Speech that Changed the World*, 2010 (ebook).
"I've been expecting…": Recreated and based upon Roberts.
"So the one time she was late…": Recreated and based upon ibid.
"I am too, and I know Marilyn is…": Quoted in Leaming, p. 380.
"I am upset and I don't feel…": Quoted in Spoto, p. 455.
"every kind of celebrity, non-celebrity, would-be celebrity": Roberts, p. 25.
"everything" & "intrigued": Quoted in Roberts, p. 25.
"charming telegram of good wishes…" & "I am sure…": Image of telegram in Banner, 2011, p. 186.
"It was sad…": Quoted in Rosten, p. 91.
"I opened the living room window…": Quoted in Guiles, 1984, p. 401.
"for the study and treatment…": Quoted in ibid, p 401.
"Marilyn was admitted…": Quoted in Guiles, 1969, p. 318.
"What are you doing…": Quoted in ibid, p. 317.
"screamed out…": Monroe, Letter to Dr. Greenson, in Shaun Usher, "Men Are Climbing to the Moon But They Don't Seem Interested in the Beating Human Heart," *Lettersofnote.com.*
"very disturbed depressed patients" & "Open that door…": Quoted in Meryman, "TV Film Uncovers Rare Photos of Marilyn Monroe: Behind the Myth the Face of Norma Jean," *Life*, November 4, 1966.
"I'd have to be nuts if I like it here": Monroe, Letter to Dr. Greenson, in Shaun Usher, "Men Are Climbing to the Moon But They Don't Seem Interested in the Beating Human Heart," *Lettersofnote.com.*

"There was no empathy…": Ibid.
"Well,that any good interior…": Ibid.
"Well, Miss Monroe…": Recreated based on upon ibid.
"I tried to explain…": Ibid.
"a pathetic and vague creature" & "strong armed": Ibid.
"I figured, it's a squeaky wheel…" & "If you are going…": Ibid.
"corny" & "the furthest thing…": Ibid.
"ox of a woman," "high-school …" "a very, very sick girl," "for many years," & "Don't you think that …": Ibid.
"We felt so protective toward her…": Quoted in Meryman, "TV Film Uncovers Rare Photos of Marilyn Monroe: Behind the Myth the Face of Norma Jean," *Life*, November 4, 1966, n.p.
"It was like a nightmare…." & "I was a curiosity…": Quoted in Summers, 1985, p. 228.
"extremely disturbed" and "potentially self-destructive." Quoted in Spoto, 1993, p. 456.
"Dr. Kris as put me…": Letter published in Spoto, 1993, p. 457& Summers, 1985, p. 200.
"brick by brick": Quoted in Badman, p. 47.
"Dearest Marilyn, It seems to me…": Image of Nan Taylor's letter in Banner, 2011, p. 188.
"Turkey foot…": Image of Walter Winchell's telegram in Banner, 2011, p. 187.
"She was like a hurricane unleashed…": Quoted in Strasberg, 1992, p. 228.
"The only thing that saved…": Quoted in ibid, p. 228.
"The best reappraisals…": Image of letter "Letter from Marlon Brando to Marilyn Monroe dated February 27, 1961," Christies.com, June 30, 2005. http://www.christies.com/lotfinder/LotDetailsPrintable.aspx?intObjectID=4537758 (accessed February 12, 2013).
"She had a hell of a year…": Quoted in Morgan, p. 258.
"Just now when I looked…" "I see a sad," "secretly," "tender" & "It was sort of a fling…": Monroe, Letter to Dr. Greenson, in Shaun Usher, "Men Are Climbing to the Moon But They Don't Seem Interested in the Beating Human Heart," *Lettersofnote.com.*
"from her body…": Rosten, p. 93.
"Why are you so unhappy?": Quoted in ibid, p. 92.

"I've been paying the best doctors…": Quoted in ibid, p. 92.
"I feel wonderful…": Interview with Marilyn Monroe in various newsreels & documentaries. "Well I put [him] in the hospital today…": Quoted in Gottfried, p.342.
"Marilyn must have found…": Freeman, 1992, p. 34.
"for the furtherance…": Image of *The Last Will and Testament of Marilyn Monroe* appearing on the Internet and in various sources
"I'm beginning to look at things…": Quoted in Parton, "A Revealing Last Interview with Marilyn Monroe," *Look*, February 19, 1979, p. 24.
"for a man…" "support…" "just can't…" "*she's there*…" Quoted in ibid, p. 25
"She was a girl…": Quoted in ibid, p. 24.
"with a sense of having met…": Quoted in Guiles, 1969, p. 320.
"If you were a man..": Quoted in ibid, p. 320.
"care package" & I know that station wagon…": Quoted in Roberts, p. 26.
"MM—pale of figure…": Sider, "Marilyn, Mmmmmm, Visits Us," *St Petersburg Times*, March 23, 1961.
"The only time I remember…": Quoted in "Suncoast: A Sun Gilds a Lily." *St. Petersburg Times*, March 31, 1961.
"Do let me know…": Julien, 2005, p. 51.
"It would be so pleasant…": ibid.
"I lost to a tracheotomy": Quoted in Bret, *Elizabeth Taylor: The Lady, The Lover, The Legend 1932-2011*, 2011, p. 141.
"All I could see ahead…": Quoted in Hyams, "Crack-Up," *Photoplay*, January 1957.
"The studio people want me…": Quoted in Steinem, "Marilyn Monroe: The Woman Who Died Too Soon," *Ms*, August 1972, p. 41.
"Above all, I try to help her…": Quoted in Summers, 1985, p. 231.
"It must be terrible to be orphaned at 71": Quoted in Conner, *Hollywood's Most Wanted: The Top 10 Book of Lucky Breaks, Prima Donnas, Box Office Bombs, and Other Oddities*, 2002, p. 107.

"We hear Marilyn Monroe's version…": Quoted in Woodard, "Marilyn Monroe and 'Rain,' the Project That Never Came to Be, Part 3," in Elisa Jordan's *Examiner.com*, January 12, 2013. http://www.examiner.com/article/marilyn-monroe-and-rain-the-project-that-never-came-to-be-part-3 (accessed January 13, 2013).
"We blondes seem…": Quoted in Guiles, 1969, p. 429-430.
"Dear Dr. Greenson: In this world…": Image of telegram published in Summers, 1985, p. 207.
"I'm very happy…": Quoted in Rudd, "Now That I am 35," *The London Daily Mail*, June 5, 1961.
"When I just can't take it…": Quoted in deDienes, *Marilyn Mon Amour*, 1985.p. 154.
"nothing…": Quoted in ibid, p. 154.
"Oh, please, don't!...": Quoted in ibid, p. 155.
"I was ashamed…": Ibid, p. 155.
"You look like a goddamned…": Zehme, *The Way You Wear Your Hat: Frank Sinatra and the Lost Art of Livin'*, 2009, p. 69.
"I've never had such a good…": Quoted in Parsons, "Marilyn Monroe's Life As a Divorcee," *Modern Screen*, October, 1961, n.p.
"All eyes were on Marilyn…": Quoted in Taraborrelli, p. 365.
"off the record": Quoted in ibid, p. 365.
"Even Marilyn Monroe was there…" Parsons, 1961, n.p.
"Oh, we're just old friends…": Quoted in ibid, n.p.
"I've always been able to count…": Quoted in ibid, n.p.
"Arthur is a brilliant man…": Quoted in ibid, n.p.
"For the first time in many years…": Quoted in ibid n.p,.
"It's always seemed strange…": Quoted in ibid, n.p.
"That's my real love…": Quoted in ibid, n.p.
"Oh, not that again": Quoted in Meyers, p. 250.
"Shut up, Norma Jeane…": Quoted in ibid, p. 250.
"Believe me, I would have loved…": Quoted in Thomas, "Singer Pat Boone Tells All; Well, Almost All," Ocala Banner, June 10, 2007, n.p.
"I've always wanted to play Sadie…": Quoted in Woodard, "Marilyn Monroe and 'Rain,' the Project That Never Came to Be, Part 3," in Elisa Jordan's *Examiner.com*, January 12, 2013. http://www.examiner.com/article/marilyn-monroe-and-rain-the-project-that-never-came-to-be-part-3 (accessed January 13, 2013).

"I've seen so much of the old…": Quoted in Torre, "Television and Radio News and Views," *Steubenville Herald Star*, June 9, 1961, p. 34.

"That is a coup if I ever heard one": Ibid.

"It's not that I have any concern…": Quoted in Guiles, 1969, p. 322.

CHAPTER SIXTEEN: JUNE–DECEMBER 1961

"highly nervous, frightened, and confused." Cottrell as told to Hayden in "I Was Marilyn Monroe's Doctor," *Ladies' Home Companion*, January 1965, n.p.

"During the days…": Quoted in ibid, n.p.

"Look at the stars…": Quoted in ibid, n.p.

"It was scary…": Quoted in Spoto, 1993, p. 467-468.

"She looked fresh and rested…": Arnold, p. 155.

"That was the last time I saw her…": Ibid, p. 155.

"It was like watching a print come up in the developer…": Ibid, p. 155.

"Dear fellas, I know it's been a long, hot vigil…": Image of letter appearing in press coverage.

"I hope all your roses…": Telegram in the Scott Fortner Collection.

"I need you to be with me…": Quoted in Miracle, p. 149.

"Thank goodness he's not too heavy…": Quoted in ibid, p. 151.

"Marilyn told me she never talked…": Quoted in ibid, p. 181.

"Whatever anybody did for her…": Quoted in ibid, p. 162.

"If she didn't give, she'd get bad publicity…: Quoted in ibid, p. 162.

"I need those pills!..": Quoted in ibid, p. 153.

"I have so many problems…": Quoted in Miracle, p. 158.

"I've known her a lot longer…": Quoted in Taraborrelli, p. 366.

"I faced Marilyn, and we grinned…": Miller, 1987, p. 506.

"That's why I was in pain…": Quoted in ibid, p. 506.

"I made the decorator stop…": Quoted in Murray, p. 16.

"From the man you tried to see…": Quoted in Guiles, 1969, p. 325.

"It was such a sad sight…": Quoted in Taraborrelli, p. 379.

"[She] thought the waiter...": Quoted in ibid, p. 374.

"I felt it would alleviate...": Quoted in C. Turner, "Marilyn Monroe on the Couch," Telegraph.co.uk, June 23, 2010. http://www.telegraph.co.uk/culture/film/7843140/Marilyn-Monroe-on-the-couch.html (accessed June 8, 2012).

"impressed": S. Coen, "Narcissistic Temptations to Cross Boundaries and How to Manage Them," Journal of the American Psychoanalytical Association, December 2007.

"She treated me as a younger sister..": Interview with Joan Greenson in *The Last Days of Marilyn Monroe*, 1985.

"She would give me older sisterly advice...": Quoted in C. Turner, 2010.

"Good Lord...": Quoted in Freeman, Freeman, p. 15.

"Until she came along...": Quoted in C. Turner, 2010.

"Who the hell do you think you are...": Quoted in Meryman, August 3, 1962, p. 32.

"She gave me self-confidence...": Quoted in C. Turner, 2010.

"It may have been foolhardy...": Quoted in ibid.

"My father's heart...": Quoted in ibid.

"She never saw things...": Quoted in Freeman, p. 18.

"I was her therapist...": Quoted in Spoto, 1993, p. 449.

"I firmly believe she'd be alive...": Quoted in Woodard, "Marilyn Monroe and 'Rain,' the Project That Never Came to Be, Part 3," in Elisa Jordan's *Examiner.com*, January 12, 2013. http://www.examiner.com/article/marilyn-monroe-and-rain-the-project-that-never-came-to-be-part-3 (accessed January 13, 2013).

"The things she was most interested...": Quoted in Summers, 1985, p. 241.

"Have you ever been in a house...": Quoted in ibid, p. 241.

"appalled at the emptiness...": Quoted in ibid, p. 205-206.

"terrible loneliness": Quoted in ibid, p. 204.

"She went through a severe depressive...": Quoted in Summers, 1985, p. 243.

"Dear Dad Darling...": Image of telegram in "September 22, 1961 Telegram from Marilyn Monroe to Joe DiMaggio," Huntuactions.com, n. d., http//:www.huntauctions.com/online/imageviewer.cfm?auction_num=27&lot_qual= (accessed June 12, 2012).

"a person's privilege…" "I don't believe it's a since or a crime…" & "although it doesn't get…": Quoted in Rollyson, 1993, p. 186.
"Pat is the one with head…": Lawford, *Symptoms of Withdrawal: A Memoir of Snapshots and Redemptions*, 2005, p. 6.
"She reminds me of my Aunt Grace…": Quoted in Taraborrelli, p. 324.
"[Marilyn] had a quiet voice…": Quoted in Lawford, p. 327.
"Come on in…": Quoted in Murray, p. 13.
"sensuous catlike grace of motion": Quoted in ibid, p. 32.
"Marilyn, despite her lack of education…": Quoted in ibid, p. 29.
"already given him enough…": Quoted in ibid, p. 25.
"fawning or flattery": Quoted in ibid, p. 65.
"Dr. Greenson thinks…": Quoted in Spoto, 1993, p. 471.
"an artistic interpretation…": Quoted in James, *Jeanne Carmen: My Wild, Wild Life as a New York Pin Up Queen Trick Shot Golfer & Hollywood Actress*, 2007, p. vii.
"amazingly pleasant and playful…": Quoted in Taraborrelli, p. 380.
"Sit here…" "girl next door," & "[Marilyn's] smile…": Kirkland, p. 11.
"I was young…": Quoted in Taraborrelli, p. 380.
"She's sometimes…" Quoted in Kirkland, p. 6.
"more spiritual…" & "flowing slow motion: Ibid, p. 13.
"I think…": Ibid, p. 27-28.
"Why don't you…": Quoted in ibid, p. 41-42.
"We talked about simple things…": Ibid, p. 58.
"When I worked in a factory…": Quoted in ibid, p. 106-107.
"I like this girl because…": Quoted in ibid, p. 81-82.
"You have ten minutes": Quoted in Morgan, p. 265.
"From Marilyn Monroe to Barbara Heinz…": Quoted in Badman, p. 29.
"I know that writing on the little napkin…": Letter in the Scott Fortner Collection.
"Marilyn is no more like she is on screen…": Ibid.
"I'm sorry I'm late…": Quoted in "'Marilyn Monroe: The Visit' Photographs with Carl Sandburg Taken by Len Steckler in 1961 For Sale," NYDailyNews.com, February 7, 2010. http://www.nydailynews.com/entertainment/gossip/marilyn-monroe-visit-photographs-carl-sandburg-len-steckler-1961-sale-

article-1.198507#ixzz2LB4Qmf1C (accessed February 17, 2013).

"*For years I have been struggling...*": Image of letter in Monroe, *Fragments*, 2010, p. 196.

"presumptuous": Ibid, p. 196.

"*Dear Marlon, I need your opinion...*": Image of note in "A Marilyn Monroe Handwritten Note to Marlon Brando and His Return Telegram to Her," Bonhams.com, December 17, 2006. http://www.Bonhams.com/auctions/14034/lot/1000/ (accessed February 17, 2013).

"Tried to reach you...": Image of note in ibid.

"Who would believe that there were...": Quoted in Guiles, 1984, p. 414.

"All the kids in the house...": Quoted in Murray, p. 28.

"an old married couple": Quoted in Summers, 1985, p. 243.

"I can't give it to her..." & "It's not fatal...": Quoted in Strasberg, 1992, p. 234.

PART III: THE LAST MONTHS
CHAPTER SEVENTEEN: *SOMETHING'S GOT TO GIVE*

"If I could, I would launch a torpedo...": Quoted in Brown & Barnham, *Marilyn: The Last Take*, 1992, p. 52.

"I want to grow old without face-lifts...": Quoted in Rollyson, 1993, p. 185.

"being on hand for the fall..." & "a small tropical town...": Quoted in Brown & Barnham, p. 15.

"This is just a reminder that we miss...": Image of letter in Halperin, *Heritage Music & Entertainment Memorabilia Auction Catalogue*, Ivy Press, 2007, p. 138.

"He was a great writer...": Interview with David Brown in *Marilyn Monroe: The Final Days*, 2001.

"Not a story for MM," "It's for a man and just any two girls," "Not funny," "At one point in the story..." & "all the fags...": Image of script notations in Christie's, 1999, p. 48.

"We've got a dog here...": Image of script notation in ibid, p. 78.

"I can do without you...": Image of script notation in ibid, p. 76.

"She plays a record player…" "You know the old saying—cast your broad upon the waters," & "Not funny": Image of script and notations in ibid, p. 76.

"Too flat…": Image of script notation in ibid, p. 342.

"sentimental schmaltz": Image of script and notation in ibid, p. 341.

"New producer…How come?": Image of script and notation in ibid, p. 48.

"You know, Henry…": Quoted in Brown & Barnham, p. 18.

"Before you, Henry…": Quoted in ibid, p. 38.

"Have you been trapped…": Quoted in Hoyt, p. 237.

"Tell them you're a call girl…": Quoted in ibid, p. 239.

"She was quick…": Quoted in Brown & Barnham, p. 58.

"She was perfectly pleasant…": Quoted in ibid, p. 62.

"Let's face it": Quoted in Spoto, 1993, p. 504.

"Remember, you've got Marilyn Monroe": Quoted in ibid, p. 503.

CHAPTER EIGHTEEN: JANUARY 1962

"There is something naïve and lovely about her…": Quoted in Levy, p. 76.

"Marilyn was a good talker…": Quoted in "Tribute to Marilyn from a friend…Carl Sandburg," *Look*, September 11, 1962, p. 92.

"The bigger the people are…": Quoted in Meryman, August 3, 1962, p. 33.

"There were no pretenses about Marilyn Monroe….": Quoted in "Tribute to Marilyn from a friend…Carl Sandburg," *Look*, September 11, 1962.

"*A beautiful Saturday morning…*": Image of letter in "Letter from Joe DiMaggio Dated January 27, 1962," *Christies.com*, June 19, 2007. http://www.christies.com/lotfinder/LotDetailsPrintable.aspx?intObjectID=4927037 (February 9, 2013).

"*Just read where you are back…*": Image of letter in "Letter from Ann Landers to Marilyn Monroe Dated January 24, 1962," *Bonhams.com*, December 20, 2009. http://auctions/17544/lot/2005/ (accessed January 5, 2013).

"Marilyn was immensely sad...": Quoted in Badman, p. 65.
"I'm really sorry...": Quoted in Barrell, "Fly Me to the Stars," *The Sunday Times*, February 1, 2004.
"For you, I would wait a week": Quoted in ibid.
"When she walked in, Christ Almighty...": Quoted in Taraborrelli, p. 406.
"Finally! You're here...": Quoted in ibid, p. 406.
"Then she was descended upon...": Quoted in ibid, 406.
"She was overjoyed with this bit of news...": Skolsky, 1975, p. 234.
"Sex to Jack Kennedy...": Dickerson, *On Her Trail: My Mother, Nancy Dickerson, TV News' First Woman Star*, 2006, p. 26.

CHAPTER NINETEEN: *CURSUM PERFICIO*: FEBRUARY 1962

"Nowhere": Quoted in Badman, p. 244.
"To put it bluntly..." Quoted in Levy, p. 77.
"She was not the usual movie idol...": Quoted in "Tribute to Marilyn from a friend...Carl Sandburg," *Look*, September 11, 1962, p. 91.
"In no way was she put on or artificial...": Quoted in Summers, 1985, p. 205.
"fortress where I can feel safe...": Quoted in Guiles, 1984, p. 417.
"There's a six- or eight-foot wall for privacy": Quoted in Barris, p. 143.
"The doctor thought the house...": Interview with Eunice Murray in *The Legend of Marilyn Monroe*, 1966.
"I encouraged her to buy the house...": Quoted in Spoto, 1993, p. 478.
"Mrs. Murray, would you find me a house...": Quoted in Murray, p. 33.
"I felt uncomfortable as we drove...": Quoted in Porter, "Psychic Medium Kenny Kingston Reveals 'The Marilyn Monroe I Knew,'" *Voices.yahoo.com*, November 28, 2011, http://voices.yahoo.com/psychic-medium-kenny-kingston-reveals-marilyn-10490545.html (accessed December 20, 2012).
"I felt badly because I was buying...": Quoted in Murray, p. 49.

"I could never imagine buying a home alone..." Quoted in Levy, p. 40.

Chapter Twenty: Robert F. Kennedy

"The final product..." Curtin, "A Tour of the White House with Mrs. John F. Kennedy," *Museum.tv.* http://www.museum.tv/eotvsection.php?entrycode=tourofthew (accessed January 11, 2013).
"I think she's underrated...": Quoted in Taraborrelli, p. 400.
"The day before [the dinner party]...": Quoted in Spoto, 1993, p. 490.
"Be brave, Mrs. Murray...": Quoted in Murray, p. 101.
"That evening Marilyn was quite sober...": Quoted in Taraborrelli, p. 400-401.
"Mother asked me to write...": Image of letter in Summers, 1985, p. 245.
"It is not okay to steal someone's...": Quoted in Taborelli, p. 403.
"The first thing...": Banner, 2011, p. 238.
"I would love...": Ibid, p. 239.
"I think you would like him" & "terrific": Ibid, p. 230.
"I was mostly impressed ...": Ibid, p. 230.
"I think we all know...": Ibid, p. 231.
"Golly I'm sorry about the phone...": Ibid, p. 231.
"Do give my invitation...": Image of letter in Banner, 2011, p. 232-233.

Chapter Twenty-One: February–March 1962

"I'm not only proud...": Quoted in Levy, p. 40.
"At the beginning of our marriage...": Quoted in ibid, p. 74.
"Under the present circumstances...": Quoted in ibid, p. 74.
"To answer publicly..." Quoted in ibid, p 74.
"It's not like fighting a duel..." Quoted in ibid, p. 76.
"Their lives that are forming... ": Quoted in ibid, p. 74.
"I take a lot of pride in them...": Quoted in Levy, p. 74.

"Payne Whitney gives me a pain…": Quoted in ibid, p. 76.
"But in a sane way": Quoted in ibid, p. 76.
"I've always been able to count…": Quoted in ibid, p. 76.
"I haven't reached a dramatic cross-roads…": Quoted in ibid, p. 77.
"I'm looking forward to eventually…": Quoted in ibid. p. 77.
"I'm trying to find myself as a person…": Quoted in ibid, p. 77.
"There has been a slight alteration…": Quoted in ibid, p. 77.
"Arriving Eastern…": Quoted in Schreiber, "Remembrance of Marilyn," *Good Housekeeping*, January 1963, p. 135.
"I could see that the man…": Quoted in ibid, p. 135.
"That's Mr. Miller…": Quoted in ibid, p. 135.
"When they stop…": Quoted in ibid, p. 135.
"I know you spent…": Quoted in ibid, p. 135.
"Marilyn wanted to make me feel…": Quoted in ibid, p. 135.
"I can't tell you in words…": Letter in the Scott Fortner Collection.
"Go away, you crazy…": Quoted in Murray, p. 62.
"You should see it on a hanger": Quoted in ibid, p. 56.
"I consider that…": Quoted in Badman, p. 105.
"I'm keeping my eyes…": Quoted in ibid, p. 105.
"I learned a lot from him…": Ibid, p. 105.
"We tried that once": Ibid, p.105.
"Mexican men…": Ibid, p. 105.
"excellent...She told us of her strong…" & "who would be decent…": Quoted in Summers, 1985, p. 254.
"This one looks lived in…": Quoted in Murray, p. 82.
"Let's get out of here": Quoted in ibid, p. 64.
"Your brother-in-law is so nice…": Quoted in ibid, p. 65.
"It was around this time…": Quoted in Morgan, p. 270.
"I used to feel [that] for every child…": Quoted in Barris, p. 131.
"We saw her come in with a glass…": Quoted in "A Proposito de Bunuel (Regarding Luis Bunuel)—Screenplay," *AmericanBuddha.com*, n. d. http://www.american-buddha.com/bunuel.screenplay5.htm (accessed June 3, 2012).
"But what does it mean?": Quoted in Kinder, *Luis Bunuel's The Discreet Charm of the Bourgeoisie*, 1999, p. 36.
"What does it mean to you?": Quoted in ibid, p. 36.
"It means that the growls…": Quoted in ibid, p. 36.
"Exactly what I intended": Quoted in ibid, p. 36.

"Now tell *me*…": Quoted in ibid, p. 36.
"I see life a long, meaningless…": Quoted in ibid, p. 36-37.
"The bourgeois are always talking...": Quoted in "Life in Film: Runa Islam," Frieze.com, March 2007. http://www.frieze.com/issue/article/life_in_film_runa_islam/ (accessed December 22, 2012).
"It has come to our attention…": Image of letter in Julien, 2005, p. 52.
"This is a nasty letter…": Image of note in ibid, p. 52.
"I guess I can go to dinner…": Quoted in Spoto, 1993, p. 496.
"Marilyn's new Latin lover" & "Something happened…": Strasberg, 1992, p. 238-239.
"[Bolanos's] pants were so tight…": Ibid, p. 239.
"This is a wonderful surprise…": Image of note in Christie's, p. 214.
"befogged," "weave in front…" & "the clear-eyed…": Strasberg, 1992, p. 239.
"exuded innocence…": Ibid, p. 239.
"I'll walk on the bare floors…": Quoted in Murray, p. 68.
"Greenson insisted on detaining…": Quoted in Spoto, 1993, p. 500-501.

Chapter Twenty-Two: March–April 1962

"I'd cook steaks…": Quoted in Strasberg, 1993, p. 251.
"I'll think about it": Quoted in Murray, p. 121.
"I live here all alone…": Quoted in Barris, p. 143.

Chapter Twenty-Three: President John F. Kennedy

"He's a great person…": Quoted in Rosten, p. 98.
"poet friend," "a dear person," & "They're happily married": Quoted in ibid., p. 99.
"You don't know this town…": Quoted in ibid, p. 102.
"Didn't you just leave a writer?": Rosten, p. 103.
"kind of a robe thing": Quoted in Summers, 1985, p. 259.

"There were a lot of people...": Quoted in Taraborrelli, p. 410.
"[Marilyn] was delightful...": Quoted in Steinem, *Marilyn: Norma Jeane*, 1986, p. 120.
"She asked me about...": Quoted in Spoto, 1993, p. 487.
"Of course, I didn't reveal...": Quoted in Summers, 1985, p. 260.
"I told him he should get a massage...": Quoted in ibid, p. 260.
"Of course she was titillated...": Quoted in Spoto, 1993, p. 487.
"We got back at 11:30 at night...": Quoted in Taraborrelli, p. 417.
"heavy-lidded": Rosten, p. 112.
"He's hurting her...": Quoted in ibid, p. 115.
"Marilyn was extremely fond...": Skolsky, 1975, p. 234.
"the little orphan waif..." & "great discretion": Ibid, p. 233.
"In retrospect, we can argue...": ibid, p. 233.
"had the instincts of a Turkish sultan in Istanbul": Sullivan, Michael John, *Presidential Passions: The Love Affairs of America's Presidents*, 1992, p. 92.

CHAPTER TWENTY-FOUR: APRIL TO MAY 1962

"The studio had said...": Quoted in Brown & Barnham, p. 5.
"She is mature, serene, fragile...": Spoto, 1993, p. 510-511.
"The change in her was breathtaking...": Quoted in Brown & Barnham, p. 30.
"It was a terrible breach...": Quoted in ibid, p. 30.
"Mr. Weinstein, what do you...": Quoted in Brown & Barnham, p. 35.
"Barbara, my *other* star...": Quoted in Eden with Leigh, *Jeannie Out of the Bottle*, 2011, p. 3.
"Marilyn, I want you to meet...": Quoted in ibid, p. 3.
"She just glows...": Ibid, p. 3.
"It was the most daring swimsuit...": Quoted in Brown & Barnham, p. 36.
"There's only one bedroom...": Quoted in ibid, p. 39.
"I don't know what Iran's relationship...": Interview with Henry Weinstein in *Marilyn: Something's Got To Give*, 1990.
"I'm just sorry in retrospect...": Interview with Robert Christopher Morley in ibid.

"I remember looking up at her…": Interview with Alexandra Heilweil in ibid.
"Marilyn was magnificent…": Quoted in Brown & Barnham, p. 107.
"never looked or acted better," & "Of course, I had…": Quoted in ibid, p. 115.
"Here's a director…": Quoted in ibid, p. 111-112.
"She had a sense of humor…": Quoted in Buskin, p. 251.
"She'd be waiting around…": Quoted in ibid, p 251.

CHAPTER TWENTY-FIVE: THE JFK BIRTHDAY GALA

"*Many, many thanks for your acceptance…*": Image of letter in Taraborrelli, n. p.
"She would have come back…": Murray, p. 100.
"He came here an immigrant…": Meryman, August 3, 1962, p. 36.
"I want you to design…": Christies, 1999, p. 92.
"Marilyn had a totally charming…": Ibid, p. 92.
"It was impossible for her…": Quoted in LoBianco, "Jeane Louis Profile—Films in Bold Air on TCM," TCM.com. http://www.tcm.com/this-month/article/133187%7C0/Jean-Louis-Profile.html (accessed February 24, 2013).
"as if she was covered…": Quoted in Christie's, 1999, p. 92.
"The young woman had recently been given…": Quoted in Wolfe, p. 407.
"She was very nervous…": "Remembering Hank Jones, 'The Dean Of Jazz Pianists,'" NPR.org, May 17, 2010. http://www.npr.org/templates/story/story.php?storyId=126884916 (accessed February 24, 2013).
"The legend may become extinct…": Quoted in Guiles, 1969, p. 331.
"He probably thinks he's drunk…Quoted in ibid, p. 332.
"something historic": Quoted in Brown & Barnham, p. 147.
"a rude bitch": Quoted in ibid, p. 147.
"Miss Monroe/ 5/18/62…": Image of receipt in "Marilyn Monroe Madison Square Garden Make-up Receipt," Julienslive.com, n.

d. http://www.julienslive.com/view-auctions/catalog/id/66/lot/24814/ (accessed February, 17. 2013).

"I kept checking their make-up…": Champion, *He Made Stars Shine*, p. 132 and quoted in "Robert Champion Auction," Willishenry.com, October 29, 2005. http://www.willishenry.com/auctions/05/autograph%20session%20two%2005/autographs__documents_auction.htm (accessed June 3, 2012).

"The amazing thing…" Quoted in Badman, p. 150.

"On the occasion…" "Mr. President, Marilyn Monroe…" "A woman about whom…" "*But let me just say…*" "But I'll give her an introduction…" "Mr. President, the *late* Marilyn Monroe": Peter Lawford in newsreels of the event in various documentaries.

"I was honored when they asked me…": Quoted in Meryman, August 3, 1962, p. 36.

"I remember when I turned to the microphone…": Quoted in ibid, p. 36.

"It's sort of like an embrace…": Quoted in ibid, p. 36.

"Thanks, Mr. President/For all the things…": Marilyn Monroe in newsreels of the event in various documentaries.

"mass seduction": Quoted in Mahoney, *Sons and Brothers: The Days of Jack and Bobby Kennedy*, 1999, p. 161.

"to be in a political party…": Kennedy, "Remarks in Response to New York's Birthday Salute to the President. May 19, 1962," www.jfklink.com. http://www.jfklink.com/speeches/jfk/publicpapers/1962/jfk201_62.html.

"Miss Monroe left a picture…": Ibid.

"I think I did something wrong…": Quoted in Meryman, August 3, 1962, p. 36.

"Hello, sir. I'm Marilyn Monroe": Quoted in Taraborrelli, p. 437.

"Sit down, Dad": Quoted in Schreiber, p. 135.

"I can't sit when everybody…": Quoted in ibid, p. 135.

"Sit, I want you to": Quoted in ibid, p. 135.

"There was a softness…": Quoted in Spoto, 1993, p. 521.

"The image of this exquisite, beguiling…": Schlesinger, p. 590.

"only after breaking through the strong defenses…": Ibid, p. 590.

"wearing skin and beads" & "I didn't see the beads!": Ibid, p. 590.
"It's certainly her beauty I remember...": Quoted in Taraborrelli, p. 437.
"Dad, come back to the coast...": Quoted in Schreiber, p. 135.
"Later, Marilyn...": Quoted in ibid, p; 135.
"white spun gold": Haspiel, 1991, p. 196.
"I can tell you with *authority*...": Ibid, p. 194-196.
"go to hell": Ibid, p. 196.
"I was never destined to forget...": Ibid, p. 196.
"I liked it...": Quoted in Morgan, p. 275.
"That was poor form on her part...": Quoted in Taraborrelli, p. 431-432.
"That was stupid": Interview with Henry Weinstein in *Marilyn: Something's Got To Give*, 1990.

CHAPTER TWENTY-SIX: MAY TO JUNE 1962

"take the measures necessary...": Quoted in "'Ostracize Them:' Lawmaker Denounces Liz, Burton," *Reno Gazette*, May 23, 1962.
"Nice to see you again": Quoted in Schiller, p. 34.
"You, too Larry": Quoted in ibid, p. 34.
"You get any badder...": Quoted in ibid, p. 34.
"Quite a bit": Quoted in ibid, p. 34.
"one good eye": Quoted in ibid, p. 34.
"You're already famous...": Quoted in Guiles, 1969, p. 336.
"The set was closed...": Quoted in Scott, "Marilyn Celebrates Her Natal Day By Cavorting in Her Birthday Suit," *Los Angeles Herald-Examiner*, date unknown, n.p.
"She has a beautiful body...": Quoted in ibid, n.p.
"I was a little embarrassed...": Quoted in ibid, n.p.
"I thought I'd celebrate...": Quoted in ibid, n.p.
"There's really nothing terrible...": Quoted in ibid, n.p.
"She felt secure that day...": Interview with Henry Weinstein in *Marilyn: Something's Got To Give*, 1990.
"get Dom": Quoted in Schiller, p. 64.
"get a good day's work": Interview with Evelyn Moriarty in *Marilyn: Something's Got To Give*, 1990.

"I don't think I'll stay for the whole game...": Quoted in "Personal Portrait: The Saga of Marilyn Monroe," *The Washington Observer*, August 9, 1962.
"About ten": Quoted in Hoyt, p. 245.
"That's a nice round number." Ibid, p. 245.
"I'm going to have a little wooden...": Quoted in Schiller, p. 82.
"At least I'll be helping...": Quoted in Guiles, 1969, p. 336.
"...601 Montana Dr.-Dodger Stadium-Chasen's-Home-La Scala-Studio-Home-La Scala-Home": Image of receipt in "Receipts from Carey Cadillac Company of California," bonhams.com, June 16, 2008.
http://www.bonhams.com/auctions/16091/lot/3015/ (accessed February 24, 2013).
"Now, I'll know...": Quoted in Summers, 1985, p. 273.
"I may be smiling...": Interview with Joan Greenson in *Marilyn: Say Goodbye to the President*, 1985.
"I think she was just depressed...": Ibid.
"This woman was desperate...": Quoted in Summers, 1985, p. 273-274.
"frantic efforts to avoid...": American Psychiatric Association, *Diagnostic and Statistical Manual of Mental Disorders Fourth Edition Text Revision*, 2000, p. 654.
"If I behaved in a way which hurt her...": Quoted in Spoto, 1993, p. 529.
"terrible fight": Cramer, *Joe DiMaggio: The Hero's Life*, 2000, p. 410.
"I can persuade Marilyn...": Quoted in Wolfe, p. 422.
"Why did they make [my father] come back...": Quoted in Brown & Barnham, p. 206-207.
"This was a purely political move...": Quoted in ibid, p. 205.
"spineless:" Schumach, "Weakness Seen in Film Industry," *New York Times*, June 8, 1962, p. 38.
"It looked as if Skouras...": Quoted in Spoto, 1993, p. 535.
"He felt the dismissal of Monroe...": Mosley, *Zanuck: The Rise and Fall of Hollywood's Last Tycoon*, 1984, p. 270.
"It was the only time in my life...": Quoted in Brown & Barnham, p. 269.
"I can tell you my mouth is watering...": Quoted in Victor, p. 324.

"She had a sense of humor...": Quoted in Buskin, p. 251.
"She'd be waiting around...": Quoted in ibid, p. 251.
"We've let the inmates...": Quoted in "MM, Dean Out, Studio Decides to Cancel Film, *Tuscaloosa News*, June 12, 1962.
"I never said any those things": Quoted in Brown & Barnham, p. 227.
"I have the greatest respect...": Quoted in "No Marilyn, No Dean; Martin Stands on That," *Desert News Salt Lake Telegram*, June 11, 1962.
"She was thrilled by that": Quoted in Brown & Barnham, p. 228.
"I'm ready and eager...": Quoted in Guiles, 1969, p. 338.
"Miss Monroe is not just being temperamental": Quoted in Schumach, "Hollywood Loss," *New York Times*, August 12, 1962, p. X7.
"has taken the bread out of the mouths...": Quoted in Wolfe, p. 423.
"Please believe me...": Quoted in Summers, 1985, p. 274.
"There was tremendous support...": Quoted in Brown & Barnham, p. 179.
"prey": Miller, p. 528.
"As a person, my work...": Quoted in Levy, p. 77.

Twenty-Seven: Life on Fifth Helena Drive

"She never looked better": Quoted in Summers, 1985, p. 301.
"Everybody who knew her...": Quoted in Cunningham, *The Ultimate Marilyn*, 1998, p. 176.
"Believe me, there is no spark...": Quoted in Levy, p. 76.
"Had an early dinner at the Colony...": Quoted in Cramer, 2000, p. 398-399.
"She was really taking control...": Quoted in Spoto, 1993, p. 546.
"Sometimes I wonder what the night...": Quoted in Monroe, *Fragments*, p. 208.
"Sleep became the real focus...": Quoted in Brown & Barnham, p. 275.

"involved in a freedom ride..." &"After all...": Image of telegram published in Summers, 1985, p. 282.
"Charlie Generous" & "Bertha Bronco": Hilty, Robert Kennedy: Brother Protector, 1997, p. 248.
"I'm thirty-six years old...": Quoted in Barris, 1995, p. 126.
"She was a total surprise...": Stern, *The Last Sitting*, 1982, p. 39.
"Really?": Ibid, p. 39.
"How's this for thirty-six?": Quoted in Spoto, 1993, p. 538.
"like a soldier exhibiting a medal...": Strasberg, 1992, p. 236.
"George, what do you think...": Quoted in Stern, p. 42.
"Marilyn had the power...": Quoted in Schneider, *Marilyn's Last Sessions*, 2011.
"Where have *you* been so long?" Quoted in Stern, p. 144.
"What's going to happen to that poor girl?" Quoted in ibid, p. 162.
"It was true...": Quoted in ibid, p. 184.
"I found, surprisingly...": Quoted in Brown & Barnham, p. 247.
"Is that really you?" Quoted in Barris, 1995, p. xv.
"Sometimes I can hardly...": Quoted in ibid, p. xv.
"This is for you, George": Quoted in Barris, 1995, p. 151.
"The ocean apparently needs...": Quoted in ibid, p. 151.
"If Marilyn Monroe was glad...": Meryman, "A Last Long Talk With A Lonely Girl," *Life*, August 17, 1962, p. 32.
"she still exuded innocence...": Strasberg, 1992, p. 239.
"A place for friends...": Quoted in Meryman, August 17, 1962, p. 32.
"I don't know why...": Quoted in ibid, p. 32.
"the house was saturated in paranoia" & "me-against-the-world": Quoted in Hoyt, p. 249-250.
"If I am a star...": Quoted in Meryman, August 3, 1962, p. 34.
"Sometimes it's nearly impossible..." Interview with Marilyn Monroe in *Marilyn: The Last Interview*, 1992.
"It stirs up envy....When you're famous...": Ibid
"If you have a cold...": Quoted in Meryman, August 3, 1962, p. 34.
"An industry, I don't think...": Quoted in ibid, p. 34.
"A sex symbol becomes a thing...": Quoted in ibid, p. 36.
"What the world needs now...": Quoted in Dinkin & Dinkin, *Infertility and the Creative Spirit*, 2010, p. 295-296.

"I want to be an artist..." Quoted in Spoto, 1993, p. 544.
"I don't crank anything...": Interview with Marilyn Monroe in *Marilyn: The Last Interview*, 1992.
"I don't want everybody to see...": Quoted in Meryman, August 17, 1962, p. 32.
"She was very enthusiastic...": Quoted in Murray, p. 116.
"Please don't make...": Quoted in Spoto, p. 545.
"I now live in my work...": Quoted in Meryman, August 3, 1962, p. 38.

Chapter Twenty-Eight: The Last Days: July–August 3 1962

"She's alone...": Recreated, based upon quotation in Greene & Kotsilias-Davies, p. 91.
"Amy had this dream...": Quoted in ibid, p. 91.
"It's incredible that Amy...": recreated, based upon quotation in ibid, p. 91.
"very unfortunate woman," "disappointment": Quoted in Spoto, 1993, p. 547.
"She had depth," "enormously complex," "underlying suffering," & "young and beautiful starlet": Quoted in ibid, p. 548.
"The juiciest piece...": Rocha, "Myth #21 - Marilyn Monroe: Mystery and Myth," Nevada State Library and Archives. http://nsla.nevadaculture.org/index.php?option=com_content&task=view&id=693&Itemid=418
"The stories, however...": Ibid.
"There was absolutely...": Quoted in Spoto, p. 549.
"This gorgeous woman...": Quoted in Peter Evans, "Marilyn Monroe's Last Weekend," MailOnline.com, August 2, 2010. http://www.dailymail.co.uk/femail/article-1299496/Marilyn-Monroes-weekend-told-time-eyewitnesss-account-row-Frank-Sinatra-friends-fear-signed-death-warrant.html (accessed December 13, 2012).
"She's dressed all in green": Quoted in ibid.
"You won't remember me...": Quoted in ibid.
"She had such warmth...": Quoted in ibid.

"You could only feel pity..." "lost little girl," & "sad attempt": Quoted in "Letters to the Editor," *Life*, August 28, 1962.
"in utter disarray": Quoted in Summers, 1993, p. 294.
"I heard she...": Quoted in "The Last Ever Pictures of Marilyn Monroe, Taken the Weekend Before She Died," *Dailymail.co.uk*, May 11, 2009. http://dailyhmail.co.uk/tvshowbiz.article-1180108/The-pictures-Marilyn-Monroe-taken-weekend-died.html (accessed June 8, 2012)
"He thought things...": Quoted in Spoto, p. 549.
"He was possessive...": Quoted in *The Gay Talese Reader: Portraits and Encounters*, 2003, p. 91.
"garden of color": Quoted in Brown & Barnham, p. 290.
"There was a peaceful...": Quoted in ibid, p. 290
"I won't give you a check...": Quoted in Melson, *Marilyn Monroe: Confidential*, unpublished, in the Christelle Montagner Collection, n.p.
"ask for Mr. Jeffrey": Image of receipt in "Receipt from Frank's Nursery dated August 1, 1962," Bonhams.com, June 14, 2009. http://bonhams.com/auctions/17108/lot/6009/ (accessed February 17, 2013)
"I'll think about it": Quoted in Spoto, p. 560.
"Her resentment of Greenson...": Quoted in Spoto, 1993, p. 558.
"Marilyn was very angry...": Quoted in ibid, p. 558.
"These patients are seductive...": Greenson, *Special Problems in Psychotherapy with the Rich and Famous*, (August 18, 1978) in The Ralph R. Greenson Papers Special Collection at the University of Southern California at Los Angeles.
"I already made plans...": Brando, *Songs My Mother Taught Me*, 1994, p.154-155.
"New York misses...": Quoted in Gibson, "Marilyn Monroe May Have Made It As Actress, Says Publicist," *Ocala Star-Banner*, May 12, 1988, n.p.
"[Marilyn] would have returned...": Quoted in ibid, n.p.
"We'll have a real celebration": Quoted in Justice & Hryniszak, "Interview with Allan Snyder," *Runnin' Wild, All About Marilyn* quarterly newsletter, issue no.13, January 1994.
"It was a pleasant...": Quoted in ibid

"We sat out by the pool sipping…": Quoted in ibid.
"She was excited…": Quoted in Brown & Barham, p. 296.
"Because of our early…": Quoted in Justice & Hrynisak.
"Marilyn Monroe's health…": Quoted in Kilgallen, "Voice of Broadway," *New York Journal American*, August 3, 1962.
"inner circle," "break up," "secrets to tell," "outer space," & "diary of secrets": Image of alleged CIA report dated August 3, 1962 in Abovetopsecret.com, n.d. http://www.abovetopsecret.com/forum/thread513308/pg4 (accessed February 24, 2013).
"Ralph reached me": quoted in Wolfe, p. 450.
"Why don't you come…": Quoted in Spoto, 1993, p. 565.
"We'll bake those germs…": Quoted in Guiles, 1969, p. 348.
"Love is the one immortal…": Quoted in Porter, 2011.
"Well, how's your friend Marilyn?": Based on interview with Amy Greene in Feinberg, "Amy Greene, Scene-Stealer of 'Love, Marilyn,' on Her House Guest Marilyn Monroe," *The Hollywood Reporter*, November 9, 2012. http://www.hollywoodreporter.com/race/amy-greene-love-marilyn-385836 (accessed November 12, 2012).

Chapter Twenty-Nine: August 4, 1962

"When people confronted these pictures…": Quoted in Comenas, "Andy Warhol Pre-Pop." Warholstars.com, p. 11. http://www.warholstars.org/warhol1/11roylichtenstein.html (accessed December 18, 2012).
"She would slip some…": Quoted in Morgan, p. 282.
"[Marilyn] was becoming a much healthier…": Brando, 2000, p. 155.
"She didn't seem depressed…": Ibid, p. 155.
"We'll go to Washington…": Quoted in Rosten, p. 120-121.
"Let's all start to live…": Quoted in ibid, p. 121.
"Nieves is going to call…": Quoted in Murray, p. 119.
"was like feasting…": ibid, p. 124.
"Dear Joe, If I can only…": image of note in "A Marilyn Monroe Letter Handwritten to Joe DiMaggio, probably 1962,"

bonhams.com, December 21, 2008. http://www.bonhams.com/auctions,16151/lot/1009 (accessed February 24, 2013).

"Do we have any oxygen?": Quoted in Murray, p. 127.

"She's not in just now": Quoted in Guiles, 1969, p. 350.

"I was aware that she was somewhat...": Quoted in Spoto, p. 568.

"...I have talked to Joe [Jr.]...": Quoted in Cramer, p. 398.

"There're not going to be married...": Quoted in Murray, p. 130.

"I don't think we'll take...": Quoted in ibid, p. 130.

"Goodnight, Honey": Quoted in Guiles, 1969, p. 351.

"As far as I am concerned...": Quoted in Barris, 1995, p. 138.

"Say goodbye to Pat...": Quoted in "Marilyn Monroe Death Files Released," *Spartanburg Herald-Journal*, September 24, 1985.

"If only [Rudin] had told [me]...": Murray, p. 132.

"They were waiting and waiting...": Quoted in Shevey, p. 28.

"We've lost her": Quoted in Murray, p. 137.

"It was unbelievable...": Quoted in Summers, 1985, p. 312.

"So as far...": Quoted in "Marilyn Monroe Dead, Pills Near," *New York Times*, August 6, 1962."

"Absolutely not": Quoted in Margolis, *Marilyn Monroe: A Case for Murder*, 2011, p. 287.

"We were stunned...": Quoted in ibid, p. 287.

"Something's happened to Marilyn...": Quoted in Guiles, 1969, p. 353.

"There were pill bottles...":Quoted in Guiles, 1984, p. 442.

"Say a prayer for Norma Jeane...": Quoted in ibid, p. 443.

"It is this officer's opinion that Mrs. Murray...": *Marilyn Monroe Death Report*, Los Angeles Police Department, dated August 10, 1962.

"sixth sense": Murray, p. 134.

"I don't know why...": Quoted in Spoto, 1993, p. 574.

"Arthur said it was horrendous...": Quoted in ibid, p. 588.

"It took about five minutes...": Quoted in Summers, p. 313.

"You bloodsuckers! ...": Quoted in Brown & Barnham, p. 319.

PART IV: ICON
CHAPTER THIRTY: THE DEATH OF MARILYN MONROE

"Marilyn Monroe is dead of suicide at age 36…": Audio of radio broadcast in *The Last Days of Marilyn Monroe*, 1985.

"And the rest Joe heard in fragments…": Cramer, p.414.

"stooped by grief," "silent," & "ashen": Quoted in ibid, p. 415.

"*Love, Marilyn…*" "*I'm sure [your fiancé]…*" "*You have time…*": Image of letter in http://www.invaluable.com/auction-lot/marilyn-monroe-handwritten-signed-note-to-her nie-68-c-f27b813bbf.

"If I had been understanding…": Quoted in Strasberg, 1992, p. 256.

"She promised me…": Quoted in ibid, p. 257.

"Gramp, Marilyn is dead": Quoted in Schreiber, p. 30.

"[Marilyn] wanted help…": Quoted in ibid, p. 30.

"You were right…": Quoted in Greene & Kotsilias-Davies, p. 92.

"a fuzzy-voiced woman": Quoted in Guiles, 1984, p. 438.

"She seemed normal that last day…": Quoted in Guiles, 1984, p. 441.

"On Friday night…": Quoted in Spoto, p. 586.

"We were so angry": Quoted in Shevey, p.30.

"It was just devastating": Interview with Joan Greenson in taking care of other than from a natural [death]." *Marilyn Monroe: Life After Death*, 1994.

"My father was hurt…": Quoted in Christopher Turner.

"[My father] always felt that it was an accident…": Quoted in ibid.

"Marilyn Monroe, the cinematic goddess…": Coen, "Narcissistic Temptations to Cross Boundaries and How to Manage Them," *Journal of the American Psychoanalytical Association*, December 2007, 55, p. 1176.

"I believe she was in a manic phase…": Interview with Hyman Engelberg in *Marilyn Monroe: The Final Days*.

"I had arrived at Marilyn's house…": Quoted in Badman, p. 246.

"I'll see you tomorrow…": Quoted in ibid, p. 258.

"She did sound sleepy…": Quoted in "MM on Death Night," *New York Daily News*, August 9, 1962.

"I saw no signs of despondency...": Quoted in "Tribute to Marilyn from a friend...Carl Sandburg," *Look*, September 11, 1962.

"I can still recall the haunting sound...": Quoted in Evans, "Marilyn Monroe's Last Weekend," MailOnline.com, August 2, 2010. http://www.dailymail.co.uk/femail/article-1299496/Marilyn-monroe-weekend-told-eyewitness-account-row-Frank-Sinatra-friends-fear-signed-death-warrant.html (accessed December 13, 2012).

"We were both very touched...": Quoted in Summers, 1985, p. 318.

"We both examined the body...": Quoted in Wolfe, p. 28.

"made a noise in the back...": Cramer, p. 415.

"Then the noise came out of Joe...": Cramer, p. 415.

"I didn't give her Secondal...": Interview with Hyman Engelberg in *Marilyn Monroe: The Final Years.*

"I knew nothing about chloral hydrate...": Quoted in Margolis, p. 287.

CHAPTER THIRTY-ONE: THE WORLD MOURNS

"Hollywood gave birth to her and killed her": Luce, "The 'Love Goddess' Who Never Found Any Love," *Life*, August 7, 1964.

"A victim of a mentality...": Quoted in Brown & Barnham, p. 324.

"She gave Hollywood color...": Thomas, "Pieces All Cling Together In Unhappy Actress' Death," *Spokane Daily Chronicle*, August 6, 1962.

"To have survived...": Miller, 1987, p. 532.

"For all her acknowledged ability...": Crowther, "Actress as a Symbol," *The New York Times*, August 6, 1962.

"She was the child...": Quoted in Waters, "Taking a New Look at MM," *Newsweek*, October 16, 1972.

"Pat and I loved her...": Quoted in Summers, 1985, p. 316.

"I heard the flash...": Quoted in "Stars Mourn the Loss of a Friend and a Great Talent," *New York World-Telegram*, August 6, 1962.

"I'm sure it was an accident…": Quoted in Gardella, "Hollywood Mourns for 'A Warm Human Being,'" *New York Daily News*, August 6, 1962.

"When your best friend kills herself…": Quoted in "Marilyn Found Dead; Pill Bottle Near Bed," *New York Daily News*, August 6, 1962.

"She will go on eternally": Quoted in Madison, "From Book-Reading to Norma Jeane to Hollywood's Blonde Bombshell: The Metamorphosis of Marilyn Monroe...As You've Never Seen Her Before," *Dailymail.com*, November 10, 2011. http://www.dailymail.co.uk/femail/article-2059643/Marilyn-Monroe-pictures-Norma-Jeane-Hollywoods-blonde-bombshell.html#ixzz2MJcEuBlW (accessed March 1, 2013).

"Impossible...it isn't possible…": Quoted in "MM: Accident or Suicide? Body of Star Lies Unclaimed," *New York World-Telegram*, August 6, 1962.

"Everybody stopped work…": Quoted in Victor, p. 41-42.

"She was an actress…": Steinem, *Outrageous Acts and Everyday Rebellions*, 2012, p. 259.

"If anything was amiss…": Quoted in "Seek Mexican in MM Mystery Call," *New York Daily News*, August 8, 1962.

"She did not commit suicide…": Quoted in "Stars Mourn the Loss of a Friend and a Great Talent," *New York World-Telegram*, August 6, 1962.

"a quality second to no actress…": Quoted in Summers, 1985, p. 315.

"For us Marilyn was a devoted friend...": Quoted in "Stars Mourn the Loss of a Friend and a Great Talent," *New York World-Telegram*, August 6, 1962.

"She was an extremely talented…": Quoted in ibid.

"I'll miss her very much": Quoted in Summers, 1985, p. 31.

"I did not know her very well…": "Stars Mourn the Loss of a Friend and a Great Talent," *New York World-Telegram*, August 6, 1962.

"What a terrible tragedy…:" Quoted in ibid.

"she was exploited…": Quoted in Free Press Wire Service, "Monroe Death Said 'Terrible Lesson' for Star-Exploiters: Olivier Blames Ballyhoo," *Immortal.marilyn.com*, n.d.

http://immortalmarilyn.com/TwilightArticles.html (accessed March 1, 2013).

"a great artist": Quoted in ibid.

"She was a fine actress...:" Quoted in "Stars Mourn the Loss of a Friend and a Great Talent," *New York World-Telegram*, August 6, 1962.

"She gave so much...": Quoted in Morgan, p. 298.

"I was walking in a little Spanish...": Capote, "An Abbess in High-Heeled Shoes," *People.com*, October 1980. http://www.people.com/people/archive/article/0,,20077726,00.html (accessed March 1, 2013).

"Cannot believe that Marilyn M. is dead...:" Quoted in Clark, *Too Brief a Treat: The Letters of Truman Capote*, 2004, p. 359.

"She was a soul burning bright...": Gilmore, *Inside Marilyn Monroe*, 2007, p. 15.

"I said whatever I said...": Quoted in Summers, 1985, p. 315.

"What can one say after such awful...": Quoted in Free Press Wire Service, "Monroe Death Said 'Terrible Lesson' for Star-Exploiters: Olivier Blames Ballyhoo."

"We lost a unique...": Quoted in "Stars Mourn the Loss of a Friend and a Great Talent," *New York World-Telegram*, August 6, 1962.

"I just feel terrible...": Quoted in Quoted in Free Press Wire Service, "Monroe Death Said 'Terrible Lesson' for Star-Exploiters: Olivier Blames Ballyhoo."

"I am deeply shocked...": Quoted in Gardella.

"I knew and acted with Marilyn Monroe...": Cotten, *Vanity Will Get You Somewhere*, 1987, p. 112.

"She did an awful lot to boost...": Quoted in Reise & Hitchens, *The Unabridged Marilyn: Her Life from A to Z*, 1987, p. 343.

"I know she would become a great actress...": Quoted in Free Press Wire Service, "Monroe Death Said 'Terrible Lesson' for Star-Exploiters: Olivier Blames Ballyhoo."

"Nobody discovered her...": Quoted in Summers, 1985, p. 315.

"I disagreed and fought with her...": Quoted in "Zanuck Hails a True Star," periodical untitled, date unknown.

"I join all her friends in Hollywood...": Quoted in Morgan, p. 299.

"You think they would have stopped...": Quoted in Curtis, *Spencer Tracy: A Biography*, 2011, p. 808-809.
"She retained her uniqueness...": Quoted in Murray, p. 150-151.
"Nieves and I are alone..": Quoted in ibid, p. 55.
"Guess where I am?...": Quoted in Rosten, p. 124.
"As I see it, Marilyn took...": Shaw & Rosten, p. 188.
"When it became frayed...": Ibid, p. 140.
"I wished I had her phone number...": Russell, *Jane Russell: My Path & My Detours*, 1985, p. 163.
"She didn't find the little cottage...": Quoted in Morgan, p. 298.
"I wonder if there's a heaven...": Quoted in Gilmore, p. 163.
"It's a terrible loss...": Quoted in Free Press Wire Service, "Monroe Death Said 'Terrible Lesson' for Star-Exploiters: Olivier Blames Ballyhoo," *Immortal.marilyn.com*, n.d. http://immortalmarilyn.com/TwilightArticles.html (accessed March 1, 2013).
"Sydney, you have to go back...": Reynolds, *Debbie: My Life*, 1988, p. 255.
"I was beside myself...": Ibid., p. 256.
"Marilyn was still very much...": Ibid, p. 256.
"She's not really there anymore": Quoted in Summers, 1985, p. 314.
"vivid," "sensibly," "foolishness," & "I could still see her coming...": Miller, 1987, p. 531.
"Marilyn Monroe was a perfectionist...": Quoted in Patterson, "3 Stars Pity Lonely Marilyn," *New York Daily News*, date unknown.
"I feel that many factors...": Quoted in ibid.
"Marilyn must have suffered...": Quoted in ibid.
"I suppose all the sob sisters...": Quoted in Rollyson, 1993, p. 177.
"There was something exceptional...": Capote, "An Abbess in High-Heeled Shoes," *People.com*, October 1980. http://www.people.com/people/archive/article/0,,20077726,00.html (accessed March 1, 2013).
"An iron butterfly, some people...": Strasberg, *Bittersweet*, 1981, p. 157.
"she showed us her humanity...": Interview with Susan Strasberg in *Marilyn Monroe: Life After Death*, 1994.

"At the core of her…": Quoted in Victor, p. 52.
"Everybody knows…": Quoted in ibid, p. 52.

CHAPTER THIRTY-TWO: THE FUNERAL

"This woman had a very good…": Interview with Amy Greene in *Marilyn Monroe: Life After Death.*
"We sincerely hope…": Press release in national newspapers
"I know exactly what I want…": Interview with Amy Greene in *Marilyn Monroe: Life After Death.*
"Whitey Dear…": Image of engraving in Crown, p. 210.
"Whitey, you promised…": Quoted in Cramer, p. 417.
"I'll be there…": ibid, p. 417.
"There she was on an iron table…": Quoted in Crown, p. 210.
"Mrs. Hamrock stated that the body…": Interview with Allan Abbott in *Marilyn Monroe: Life After Death.*
"Now that looks like Marilyn Monroe!": Interview with Allan Abbott in ibid.
"Cadillac of Caskets": "Marilyn Monroe's Funeral," Abbottandhast.com, n. d. http://www.abbottandhast.com/mmfuneral.html (accessed March 17, 2013).
"To join in what I knew would be a circus…": Miller, 1987, p. 531.
"grand, great woman" & "caused a wave of sorrow…": "Marilyn Monroe Funeral Is Held in Hollywood," *The New York Times,* August 9, 1962, p. 22.
"I know she would not have wanted us to mourn…": Lee Strasberg's eulogy from an audiotape provided by Greg Schreiner in 1998.
"I have never seen Marilyn…": Quoted in "Weeping DiMaggio Kisses Marilyn in Final Farewell," *The Springfield Union*, August 9, 1962.
"Okay, Honey" & "sleep tight." Interview with Allan Snyder in *Marilyn Monroe: Life After Death.*
"Marilyn Monroe meant a lot to me…": Quoted in Bacon, "Fans Are Orderly During Marilyn Monroe Services," *Los Angeles Herald-Examiner*, August 9, 1962.

"So, in the end, she was his....": Cramer, p. 420.
"If you don't put me upside down over Marilyn...": Quoted in Gottlieb, "For Sale: Eternity with Marilyn Monroe," *LaTimes.com*, August 14, 2009. http://articles.latimes.com/2009/aug/14/local/me-marilyn14 (accessed March 1, 2013).

Chapter Thirty-Three: The Investigation & Results of the Autopsy

"An accidental overdose of that magnitude ...": Quoted in Wolfe, p. 40.
"Miss Monroe had suffered from psychiatric disturbances...": Press release published in national newspapers and read by Theodore Curphey in a press conference in newsreels and various documentaries.
"Any person who takes any depressing drug...": Press conference by Theodore Curphey in newsreels and various documentaries.
"She was psychiatrically disturbed...": Quoted in "Her Greatest Role," periodical unknown, August 18, 1962.
"Marilyn Monroe played the greatest role...": Quoted in ibid.
Suicide rates increasing directly following Marilyn's death: Phillips, Lundie, & Paight, "Effects of Mass Media News Stories on Suicide with New Evidence on Story Content," in *Suicide Among Youth: Perspectives on Risk and Prevention*, by Cynthia Pfeiffer (editor), 1989.
"The examination I made included...": Quoted in Margolis, p. 59.
Studies about impulsive suicide attempts: Hall, Platt, & Hall, "Suicide Risk Assessment: A Review of Risk Factors for Suicide in 100 Patients Who Made Severe Suicide Attempts: Evaluation of Suicide Risk in a Time of Managed Care," *Psychosomatics*, Volume 40 (January-February 1999), pp. 18-27.
Studies about Borderline Personality Disorder: Linehan, *Cognitive-behavioral Treatment of Borderline Personality Disorder*, 1993, p. 15 & 18.
"No one will ever be able...": Quoted in Margolis, p. 26.

CHAPTER THIRTY-FOUR: STUDIO WITHOUT ITS QUEEN

"After Marilyn Monroe's death…": "Hollywood: Marilyn, My Marilyn," *Time*, May 31, 1963.
"sentimental if not incisive tribute": Weiler, "Screen: Marilyn Monroe Compilation," *The New York Times*, July 18, 1963, p. 15.
"who once helped fill the company's coffers": Ibid, p. 15.
"no effort to delve into the essentials…": Ibid, p. 15.
"emotion with genuine force and artistry": Ibid, p. 15.
"decidedly unusual girlish aplomb": Ibid, p. 15.
"Fans will be poignantly reminded…": Ibid, p. 15.
"chaos, overwrought dialogue…": Quoted in Brown & Barham, p. 365.
"a monumental mouse": Quoted in ibid, p. 366.
"Miss Taylor is overweight..": Quoted in Kelly, *Elizabeth Taylor: The Last Star*, 1981, p. 191.
"When she portrays…": Quoted in ibid, p. 191.
"Miss Taylor is monotony in a slit skirt": Quoted in ibid, p. 191.
"There is no depth of emotion…": Quoted in ibid, p. 191.
"deplorable and amoral conduct": Quoted in Brown & Barham, p. 367.
"mildly comic": Crowther, "Screen: Eight New Movies Arrive for the Holidays," *The New York Times*, December 26, 1963.
"loquaciously redundant…": Ibid.
"defter and lighter touches": Ibid.
"bumbling, irascible judge": Ibid.
"laugh": Ibid.
"a properly lovable curmudgeon…": Ibid.
"When some of Miss Day's gambits…": Ibid.

CHAPTER THIRTY-FIVE: AFTERMATH

"I would call celebrity worship…": Quoted in Hughes, "Tupac Lives! Why Fans Are Fascinated By Stars Who Die Tragically," *Ebony*, August, 2003, p. 114.
"That she withstood the incredible, unknowable…": "Marilyn Monroe," *Vogue*, September 1, 1962, p. 190.

"poor darling," Interview with George Cukor, *Eyewitness* (CBS), "Who Killed Marilyn Monroe?," August 10, 1962.
"for all her flash…": Ibid.
"Yes, but so is everybody else…": Ibid.
"distinguished mind": Ibid.
"You had to produce…": Ibid.
"If left to her own…": Ibid.
"'Never forget you're just a piece of meat'…": Interview with Kim Novak in ibid.
"tragic," "deep disturbances," & "pressure created…": Interview with Lee Strasberg in ibid.
"dark companion": Interview with Clifford Odets in ibid.
"severe": Ibid.
"If she had been more cynical…": Ibid.
"She has been a legend in her lifetime…": Ibid.
"She already had the look of a girl...": "Remember Marilyn," *Life*, August 17, 1962, p. 63.
"air of decency and almost childlike innocence": Ibid.
"swept by panics…": "The Only Blonde in the World," *Time*, August 10, 1962.
"Within hours after her death…": Quoted in Letters to the Editor, *Time*, August 17,1962, p. 3.
"Marilyn Monroe's unique charisma…": Quoted in Dolleris, Hello, Norma Jean, 2010, p. 153.
"If there ever was a victim…": Rand, "Through Your Most Grievous Fault," in *The Voice of Reason: Essays in Objectivist Thought* by Ayn Rand, ed., Leonard Peikoff and Peter Schwartz, 1989.
"glow of something…" "alive in a way…" "a charge of vitality…": Trilling, "The Death of Marilyn Monroe," *Poemhunter. com.* http://www.poemhunter.com/quotations/hunting/page-5/ (accessed June 8, 2012).
"Of Ernest Hemingway…": Ibid.
"Her despair at the end…:" Luce, Clare Boothe, "The 'Love Goddess' Who Never Found Any Love," *Life*, August 7, 1964, p. 70.
"Cinderella lives only happily ever …": Ibid, p. 78.
"Marilyn died…": Ibid, p. 78.

"I loved that girl!": Miller, *After the Fall*, 1964.
"shocking absence of love": McCann, *Marilyn Monroe*, 1988, p. 161.
"You want to die…": Miller, *After the Fall*, 1964.
"hints of self-infatuation" Prideaux, "Marilyn's Ghost Takes the Stage: A Desperate Search by a Troubled Hero," *Life*, February 7, 1964, p. 64.
"A suicide kills…": Miller, *After the Fall*, 1964.
"used her propensity…": Leaming, p. 430.
"is not in fact Marilyn Monroe" & "the human animal's…": Miller, "With Respect For Her Agony—But With Love," *Life*, February 7, 1964, p. 66.
"not invites, insists on, really": Prideaux, p. 64.
"chewed and spat…": Miller, *After the Fall*, 1964.
"I'm a joke that brings in money!": Ibid.
"We see little of those flashes…": Pridaeux, p. 64.
"[resembling] a confessional…": "How N.Y. Critics Rate Miller's 'After the Fall,'" *The Capital Times*, January 27, 1964.
"a three and one half hour breach…": Quoted in Churchwell, p. 80.
"His philosophy is adolescent…": Quoted in Payn, *The Noel Coward Diaries*, 1982, p. 558.
"Ironically, in exposing Marilyn…": Leaming, p. 430.
"Couldn't he at least give her credit…": Ibid, p. 431.
"It's sad that a Kazan-Miller…": Quoted in McCann, p. 160.
"None of her sweetness or vulnerability …": Quoted in Greene & Kotsilias-Davies , p. 91.
"astonishing that a playwright…": Quoted in Churchwell, p. 80.
"I feel it is ingenuous…": Prideaux, p. 64.
"overtly vicious…": Miller, "With Respect For Her Agony—But With Love," Life, February 7, 1964, p. 66.

Chapter Thirty-Six: The Estate

"for all her troubled personal life…": *Time*, August 24, 1962, p. 30.
"She decided to keep me…": Quoted in "The Growing Cult of Marilyn," *Life*, January 25, 1963, p. 94.

"distribute these, in his sole discretion…": Images of *The Last Will & Testament of Marilyn Monroe*, published on the Internet & in various sources

"our baby executed her will": Image of letter in Banner, 2011, p. 324.

"We were also impressed at how hard she worked…": Quoted in Christie's, 1999, p. 9.

"Marilyn was pretty simple…": Interview with Greg Schreiner, August 2, 2012.

"killing the goose that lays the golden egg": Koppel, "Blonde Ambition: A Battle Erupts Over the Right to Market Marilyn," *Online.wsj.com.* http://online.wsj.com/article/SB114463306707721479.html (accessed March 17, 2013).

"This is a textbook case for applying judicial estoppel…": Judge Wardlaw quoted in *Milton H. Greene Archives, Inc., v. Marilyn Monroe LLC & Anna Strasberg*, United States Court of Appeals for the Ninth Circuit, August 30, 2012, p. 29.

"We observe that the lengthy dispute…": Ibid, p. 29.

Chapter Thirty-Seven: The Legend & The Myth

"The Kennedys' alleged sexual liaison…": Churchwell, p. 313.

"simply quoting himself": Ibid., p. 299.

"Was Marilyn about to do some talking?...": Capell, p. 57 & 69.

"came into a bit of money": Ibid, p. 63.

"whisked to Hyannisport…" & "placed on government payroll": Ibid, p. 63.

"Had he [known more], Hoover…": Gentry, *J. Edgar Hoover: The Man and the Secrets*, 1991, p. 494.

"subversive activities…": Turner, *Power and the Right*, 1971, p. 224.

Capell & Clemons' legal issues: "California: The Smear," *Time*, March 5, 1965.

"whose author does not choose…": Mailer, p. 242.

"Why not see her death…": Ibid.

"Political stakes were riding on her life…": Ibid., p. 242 & 244.

"Mailer: I needed the money...": Quoted in Wallace & Gates, *Close Encounters: Mike Wallace's Own Story*, 1984, p. 336.
"part of a larger conspiracy" & "act of one individual": "Poll: Most Believe 'Cover-Up' of JFK Assassination Facts," FoxNews.com, June 18, 2004. http://wwfoxnews.com/story/0,2933,102511,00.html (accessed February 25, 2013).
"I never found him convincing...": Quoted in Marshall, *The DD Group: An Online Investigation Into the Death of Marilyn Monroe*, 2005, p. 235-236.
"sensational rumors about Bobby Kennedy's arriving...": Murray, p. 128.
"from the daughter...": Ibid, p 128.
"could definitely not have been on Saturday...": Ibid., p. 129.
"unfinished story...": Mailer, p. 340.
"It is a difficult scenario...": Mailer, 1975, p. 350.
"I want to be refreshed...": Quoted in Porter, "Psychic Medium Kenny Kingston Reveals 'The Marilyn Monroe I Knew,'" Voices.yahoo.com, November 28, 2011. http://voices.yahoo.com/psychic-medium-kenny-kingston-reveals-marilyn-10490545.html (accessed December 20, 2012).
"Marilyn was going to reveal...": Quoted in ibid.
"The facts...": Quoted in Hyman, "Authorities Reject Claim Marilyn Monroe Was Murdered," *The St. Petersburg Times*, December 29, 1982.
"would have required a massive...": Quoted in ibid.
"*very* probable": Noguchi & DiMona, *Coroner to the Stars*, 1983, p. 81.
"sheer wealth of anecdotal...": "related what they believe..." Churchwell, p. 88.
"The cumulative force...": Ibid, p. 300.
"While being interviewed...": Summers, *The Secret Lives of Marilyn Monroe*, 2012, n.p.
"When he arrived, she was not dead...": Interview with Eunice Murray in *The Last Days of Marilyn Monroe*, 1985.
"You believe...": Ibid.
"At Marilyn's house?": Ibid.
"Yes": Ibid.

"Oh, sure": Ibid.
"That afternoon": Ibid.
"Yeah": Ibid.
"And you think…": Ibid.
"All of the long discussion of murder…": Churchwell, p. 301.
"Dr. Greenson very graciously…": Quoted in Slatzer, *The Marilyn Files*, 1992, p. 149.
"I gave my word…": Quoted in ibid, p. 150.
"gone the furthest…": Churchwell, p. 323.
"eighth-generation photocopy": Ibid, p. 323.
"display[ing] remarkable…": Ibid, p. 323.
"Anyone with a little bit of imagination…": Winkler, "Precious Cargo: Refreshingly Bitter and Twisted Observations of Life's Passing Parade: The Death of Marilyn Monroe & My Letter to Playboy," *Preciouscargoblogspot.com*, February 16, 2006. http://preciouscargo.blogspot.com/2006/12/death-of-marilyn-monroe-my-letter-to/html (accessed July 15, 2012).
"Have you heard any stories…": Quoted in Summers, 1985, p. 296.
"I know there was no affair…": Quoted in Taraborrelli, p. 426.
"I was intimately…": Quoted in ibid, p. 426.
"She was sad and lonely…": Quoted in ibid, p. 426.
"He was such a sympathetic…": Quoted in Summers, 1985, p. 248.
"There was at once something…": Schlesinger, *Robert Kennedy and His Times*, 2002, p. 591.
"Certainly to *publish* death…": Churchwell, p. 308.
"It is a particularly great…": McCann, *Marilyn Monroe*, 1988, p. 188.
"To see this abomination…": Arnold, 2005, p. 141.
"They are writing fiction…": Quoted in Victor, p. 206.
"The myth of Marilyn Monroe…": Churchwell, p. 8.
"was kind of a living abstraction…": Quoted in Churchwell, p. 187.
"People had a habit…": Monroe, *My Story*, p. 183.
"It is the lost possibilities…": Steinem, 1986, p. 180.
"Could we have helped Marilyn…": Ibid, p. 180.
"She is still…": Bogdanovich, *Who the Hell's in It: Conversations with Hollywood's Legendary Actors*, 2005, p. 491-492.

"Does she have the last…": Quoted in "Marilyn Monroe: Filmmaker Interview—Gail Levin," *Pbs.org*, July 19, 2006. http://www.pbs.org/wnet/americanmasters/episodes/marilyn-monroe/filmmaker-interview-gail-levin/63/ (accessed December 30, 2012).

"Her legacy would never die…": Ebert, "A Sense of Control," *Playboy*, December 2012, p. 173.

Chapter Thirty-Eight: Those She Left Behind

"Some things that have…": Miracle, p. iv.

"I'm still haunted…": Interview with James Dougherty in *Marilyn's Man*, 2004.

"You, know, Morris…": Quoted in Margolis, *Marilyn Monroe: A Case for Murder*, 2011, p. 15.

"He'd play it over and over again…": Quoted in ibid, p. 16.

"My wife believed I loved Marilyn…": Shaw & Rosten, p. 192.

"combination delicatessen…": Strasberg, *Bittersweet*, 1981, p. 60.

"I wear these pearls whenever…": Quoted in Smith, "Frank Actress," *People*, February 8, 1999.

"When I looked into her eyes…": Quoted in Strasberg, 1992, p. 30

"were almost never in the picture": Quoted in Andrews, "Arthur Miller's Forgotten Son," *Vanity Fair*, September 2007.

"the moralist of the past…": Moore, "Arthur Miller: 1915-2005: He'll Be Remembered as America's Great Moralist," *DenverPost.com*. February 21, 2005. http://www.denverpost.com/nacchio/ci_14998567 (accessed March 1, 2013).

"fierce belief in man's…": Isherwood, "An appreciation: A Morality That Stared Down Sanctimony." *NYTimes.com*. February 12, 2005. http://theater.nytimes.com/2005/02/12/theater/newsandfeatures/12appr.html (accessed March 1, 2013).

"It would be easy to judge…": Andrews, 2007.

"I believe she was in a manic phase…": Interview with Hyman Engelberg in *Marilyn: The Final Days*.

PART V: LEGACY
CHAPTER THIRTY-NINE: THE MARILYN MONROE HALF-CENTENNIAL MEMORIAL

"She wasn't afraid...": Quoted in Parkinson-Morgan," Fans Honor Marilyn Monroe at Westwood Village Memorial Park: Hundreds Turn Out to Celebrate the Life of the Late Hollywood Starlet at Her Fiftieth Anniversary Memorial Service," *Brentwood Patch*, August 6, 2012. http://brentwoodpatch.com/articles/marilyn-remembered-at-westwood-memorial#photo-10957324 (accessed November 18, 2012).

"Marilyn's fans see...: Interview with Leslie Kasperowicz, August 5, 2012.

"There were no benefits...": Monroe, *Fragments*, 2010, p. 223.

"We've been planning this event...": Quoted in Parkinson-Morgan.

"Just like the fans...": Interview with David Marshall, August 5, 2012.

"So here we are fifty years...": Interview with David Marshall, August 5, 2012.

"Grandma...": Interview with Scott Fortner, August 5, 2012.

"Since I was twelve...": Interview with Paul Maggs, August 5, 2012.

"Marilyn Monroe is someone...": Quoted in Parkinson-Morgan.

"Dear Marilyn...": Quoted from actual letter left at Marilyn Monroe's crypt on August 5, 2012 and photographed by author.

"I look at her as an extraordinary expression...": Lois Banner's remarks at the *Marilyn Remembered* Memorial Service on August 5, 2012 in Los Angeles.

"Movie lovers all over the world...": Don Murray's remarks at the *Marilyn Remembered* Memorial Service on August 5, 2012 in Los Angeles.

"Marilyn was a class act": Amy Greene's remarks at the *Marilyn Remembered* Memorial Service on August 5, 2012 in Los Angeles.

"It feels kind of like...": Interview with David Marshall, August 5, 2012.

"For me, it's amazing…": interview with Scott Fortner, August 5, 2012.
"Marilyn was actually a very charitable…": Quoted in Immortal Marilyn website, *ImmortalMarilyn.com*. http://.immortalmarilyn.com/index.html (accessed January 1, 2013).
"I fell in love with Marilyn…": Schreiner's remarks at the media opening of the Marilyn Monroe Collection at the Max Factor Museum on August 2, 2012.
"It is truly one of the greatest performances…": Quote from *San Francisco Chronicle* in *Gregthompsonproductions.com* (accessed January 1, 2013).
"Sunny gives us a glimpse…": Quoted in ImmortalMarilyn.com.
"I have a deep admiration and respect…": Greg Thompson from http://www.gregthompsonproductions.com/mfb.php.
"She asked for nothing…": Ibid.
"The woman who wanted…": Don Murray's remarks at the ribbon-cutting ceremony at the Monroe Forum/El Portel Theatre on August 5, 2012.

APPENDIX: SELECTED MARILYN MONROE FILM SYNOPSES

"Monroe and Wilder turn it…": Ebert, "Some Like It Hot (*Chicago Sun Times*)," *rogerebert.com*. January 9, 2000. http:"rogerebert.suntimes.com/apps/pbcs.dll/article?AID+/20000109/REVIEWS08/1090301/1023 (accessed June 8, 2012).
"Trust it, enjoy it, be brave," "Getting drunk on kisses": *Christie's, The Personal Property of Marilyn Monroe*, 1999, p. 333.
"The song is a poignant testament…": McCann, p. 107.
"She puts heartbreak…": Rollyson, 1993, p. 156.
"low heels, beret…": Image of script in Christie's, 1999, p. 336.
"foolish…" & "like a slave": Ibid, p. 336.
"you're home…" "How well I know," "earth," "sheltered," & "how true": Ibid, p. 336.
"Aided by her training…": Rollyson, 1993, p. 138-139.

Bibliography

"120 Years of Popular Culture at Christis's South Kensington in June." *Christies.com*, June 2013. http://www.christies.com/about/press-center/releases/pressrelease.aspx?pressreleaseid=6468 (accessed June 28, 2013).

"A Proposito de Bunuel (Regarding Luis Bunuel)—Screenplay." *American Buddha*, n.d. http://www.american-buddha.com/bunuel.screenplay5.htm (accessed June 3, 2012).

"A Short Interview with Marilyn." *YouTube.com*. n.d. http://youtube.com/watch?v=uDHY2rhaYWQ (accessed January 21, 2013).

ABC Stage 67, "*The Legend of Marilyn Monroe*". Directed by Dan Eriksen. November 30, 1966.

"Academy Awards 1954 Complete Part 2," *YouTube.com*. www.youtube.com/watch?v=Fl0E7cpvE8.

Adams, Bruce. "Joe DiMaggio's San Francisco." *sfgate.com*. May 27, 2009. http://www.sfgate.com/cgi-bin/article.cgi?f=/c/a/2009/05/17/SPIT17KU1Q.DTL (accessed March 17, 2013).

Adams, Cindy. *Lee Strasberg: The Imperfect Genius of the Actors Studio.* Garden City: Doubleday, 1980. Adams, Val. "Marilyn Monroe May Star on TV." The New York Times, January 6, 1961: 53.

—. "N.A.B. Convention Opens in Capital." *The New York Times*, May 8, 1961.

—. "TV 'Play of the Week' Considers Presenting First Original Work." *The New York Times*, November 25, 1960.

A & E, "Marilyn Monroe: The Child Goddess." Directed by Donatella Baglivo. 1994.

A & E Biography, "Marilyn Monroe: The Mortal Goddess." Directed by Kevin Burns and Jeff Scheftel and Andrew Thomas. 2001.

Albelli, Alfred. "MM Left the Million $ She Look Like." *The New York Daily News*, n.d.

Allan, Rupert. "Marilyn Monroe...A Serious Blonde Who Can Act." *Look*, October 23, 1951: 40-44, 46.

"Alleged CIA Report Dated August 3, 1962." *Abovetopsecret.com*. n.d. http://www.abovetopsecret.com/forum/thread513308/pg4 (accessed February 24, 2013).

Allen, Maury. "Rare Photo Book Captures Brooklyn Team's Magic." *Thecolumnists.com*. n.d. http://www.thecolumnists.com/allen/allen117.html (accessed December 13, 2012).

American Masters, "Marilyn Monroe: Still Life". Directed by Gail Levin. 2006.

American Movie Classics Backstory: "Bus Stop". Directed by Michele Farinola. 2001.

American Movie Classics Backstory, "The Seven Year Itch". Directed by Michele Farinola and Mimi Freedman. 2000.

American Psychiatric Association. *Diagnostic and Statistical Manual of Mental Disorders Fourth Editon Text Revision*. Washington, DC: American Psychiatric Association, 2000.

Anderson, Janice. *Marilyn Monroe*. London: Hamlyn, 1983.

Andrews, Suzanna. "Author Miller's Forgotten Son." *Vanity Fair*, September 2007.

"Andy Warhol Pre-Pop." *Warholstars.com*. n.d. http://www.warholstars.org/warhol1/11roylichtenstein.html (accessed June 8, 2012).

Archer, Eugene. "Movie to Be Made by Publicity Firm." *The New York Times*, September 4, 1962.

Arnold, Eve. *Marilyn Monroe*. New York: Harry N. Abrams, 2005.

—. *Marilyn Monroe: An Appreciation*. New York: Alfred A. Knopf, 1987.

Attanasio, Ed. "He Played with the Yankee Clipper." *Broowaha.com.* January 14, 2008. broowaha.com/articles/2912/he-played-with-the-yankee-clipper-dariolodigiani#Fcf7b9qBuuw71Uwl. 9 Sports Corner (accessed September 16, 2012).

—. "Opening Day Brings Out the Predictions." *Marinatime.com.* April 2010. http://www.marinatimes.com/apr10/sports-sports-corner.html (accessed September 16, 2012).

Ayton, Mel. "The 'Assassination' of Marilyn Monroe." *Crimemagazine.com.* July 24, 2005. http://www.crimemagazine.com/assassination-marilyn-monroe (accessed June 8, 2012).

Bacall, Lauren. *By Myself.* New York: Alfred A. Knopf, 1979.

—. *By Myself and Then Some.* New York: HarperCollins, 2006.

Bacon, James. "Marilyn Monroe Has Faults, But Not in Box Office Appeal." *Idahoe State Journal,* July 15, 1960.

—. "Fans Are Orderly During Marilyn Monroe Services." *Los Angeles Herlad-Examiner,* August 9, 1962.

—. "Personal Portrait: The Saga of Marilyn Monroe." *The Washington Observer,* August 9, 1962.

Badman, Keith. Marilyn Monroe: The Final Years. New York: St. Martin's Press, 2010.

Bailey, George. *Marilyn Monroe and the Making of "Niagara".* Canada: Premier Impressions, 1998.

Baker, Norma Jeane. "What Is Your Favorite Type of Girl." *The Emersonian,* June 29, 1941.

Baker, Steven. "Actor Corey Feldman Says Pedophilia No. 1 Problem for Child Stars, Contributed to Demise of Corey Haim." *Abcnews.com.* August 10, 2011. http://abcnews.go.com/Entertainment/corey-feldman-pedophilia-problem-child-actors-contributed-demise/story?id=14256781 (accessed January 1, 2013).

Banner, Lois. *Marilyn: The Passion and Paradox.* New York: Bloomsbury USA, 2012.

—. *MM-Personal: From the Private Archive of Marilyn Monroe.* New York: Abrams, 2011.

Barbas, Samantha. *The First Lady of Hollywood: A Biography of Louella Parsons.* Berkley, CA: University of California Press, 2006.

Barham, Peter Brown and Patte B. *Marilyn: The Last Take.* New York: Signet, 1993.

—. *Marilyn: The Last Take.* New York: Dutton/Penguin Group, 1992.

Barrell, Tony. "Fly Me to the Stars." *The Sunday Times*, February 1, 2004.

Barris, George. *Marilyn: Her Life in Her Own Words: Marilyn Monroe's Revealing Last Words and Photographs.* New York: Citadel Press, 1995.

—. "Twilight of a Star." *New York Daily News*, August 14, 1962.

Battelle, Phyllis. "Star Calls It 'Wonderful,' Fans Mob, Muss Marilyn at N.Y. Movie Premiere." *The Miami News*, June 14, 1957.

Beckley, Paul V. "The Misfits," *New York Herald Tribune*, February 2, 1961.

Belmont, Georges. *Marilyn Monroe and the Camera.* Munich: Schirmer/Mosel, 1989.

Benny, Jack Benny and Joan. *Saturday Nights at Seven: The Jack Benny Story.* New York: Warner Books, 1990.

Bernard, Susan. *Bernard of Hollywood's Marilyn: Images by Hollywood's Great Glamour Photographer.* New York: St. Martin's Press, 1993.

—. *Marilyn: Intimate Exposures.* New York: Sterling, 2011.

Bernstein, Walter. "Monroe's Last Picture Show." *Esquire*, July 1973.

Bloom, Ken. *Broadway: Its History, People, and Places.* New York: Routledge, 2004.

Bogdanovich, Peter. *Who the Hell's in It: Conversations with Hollywood's Legendary Actors.* New York: Random House, 2005.

Bosworth, Patricia. *Montgomery Clift: A Biography.* New York: Proscenium, 2007.

—. "The Mentor and the Movie Star." *Vanityfair.com.* June 2003. http://www.vanityfair.com/hollywood/features/2003/06/marilyn-monroe-and-lee-strasberg-200306 (accessed December 14, 2012).

—. "The Newman Chronicles." *Vanityfair.com.* September 2008. http://www.vanityfair.com/culture/features/2008/09/newman200809 (accessed December 14, 2012).

Brambilla, Giovanbattista. *Marilyn Monroe: The Life, The Myth.* New York: Rizzoli, 1996.

Brando, Marlon. "Letter from Marlon Brando to Marilyn Monroe dated February 27, 1961." *Christies.com*, June 30, 2005. http://www.christies.com/lotfinder/LotDetailsPrintable.aspx?intObjectID=4537758 (accessed February 12, 2013).

Brando, Marlon with Robert Lindsey. *Songs My Mother Taught Me.* New York: Random House, 1994.

Brater, Enoch. *Arthur Miller: A Playwright's Life and Works.* New York: Thames & Hudson, 2005.

Brenneman, Richard E. *Americanancestors.org, "Notable Kin—New England in Hollywood, Part Three: The Possible Rhode Island Ancestry of Marilyn Monroe".* n.d. http://www.americanancestors.ord/notable-kin-the-possible-rhode-island-ancestry-of-marilyn-monroe/ (accessed January 29, 2013).

Bret, David. *Clark Gable: Tormented Star.* Philadelphia, PA: Da Capo Press, 2008.

—. *Elizabeth Taylor: The Lady, The Lover, The Legend 1932-2011.* Vancouver: Greystone Books, 2011.

—. *Joan Crawford: Hollywood Martyr.* Philadelphia, PA: Da Capo Press, 2008.

Brierly, Dean. "Photographing Marilyn Monroe in 'The Seven Year Itch'." *Black and White*, September 2008.

—. *Photographyinterviews.blogspot.com, "George Zimbel: Framing Perfection".* August 3, 2009. http://photographyinterviews.blogspot.com/2009/08/george-zimbel-framing-perfection-year.html (accessed January 21, 2013).

Brustein, Robert. "Arthur Miller: Mea Culpa." *New Republic*, February 8, 1964.

Bryan, CDB. "Say Goodbye to Camelot." *Rolling Stone*, December 5, 1985.

Buchwald, Art. "Let's Be Firm on the Monroe Doctrine." *The Washington Post*, November 19, 1960.

Buckley, Michael. *theatermania.com, "Darlin' Eileen".* n.d. http://www.theatermania.com/new-york-city-theater/news/01-2002/darlin-eileen_1871.html (accessed February 3, 2013).

"Bush's Famous Family Tree." *CBSnews.com*. February 11, 2009. http://www.cbsnews.com/2100-500202_162-3424359.html (accessed January 29, 2013).

Buskin, Richard. *Blonde Heat: The Sizzling Screen Career of Marilyn Monroe*. New York: Billboard Books, 2001.

Buys, *Sara. thesundaytimes.co.uk, "Was Marilyn Monroe Really a Size 16?"*. n.d. (accessed January 2, 2011).

Byronic.tumblr.com. April 11, 2010. http://byronic.tumblr.com/post/512837760/guys-in-ties-88-robert-mitchum-photographed-at (accessed January 18, 2013).

Cahn, Robert. "Marilyn Monroe Hits a New High." *Collier's*, July 9, 1954.

—. "The 1951 Model Blonde." *Collier's*, September 8, 1951.

Cahn, Sammy. "Marilyn Monroe Letter from Sammy Cahn (dated June 14, 1960)." *Juliensauctions.com*. 2005. http://www.juliensuauctions.com/auctions/2005/Marilyn-Monroe/results.html (accessed January 20, 2013).

Calin-Russell, Kathleen. "What's In A Name? The Selling of Marilyn Monroe's Beverly Hills and Manhattan Homes." *Unique Homes*, August-September 1996.

Calta, Louis. "Marilyn Monroe to Divorce Miller." *The New York Times*, November 12, 1960: 1.

—. "Taxes Draining Marilyn Monore Estate." *The New York Times*, June 26, 1965: 21.

Cannon, Damien. *Film.u-net. com, "The Misfits: A Review"*. 1998. http://www.film.u-net.com/Movies/Reviews/Misfits.html (accessed February 15, 2013).

Capell, Frank A. *The Strange Death of Marilyn Monroe*. New Jersey: Herald of Freedom, 1969.

The Capital Times. "How N. Y. Critics Rate Miller's 'After the Fall'." January 27, 1964.

Capote, Truman. *Marilyn Monroe: Photographs 1945-1962*. New York: W. W. Norton, 1994.

—. *Music for Cameleons*. New York: Random House/Vintage, 1994.

—. *People.com, "An Abbess in High-Heeled Shoes"*. October 1980. http://www.people.com/people/archive/article/0,,20077726,00.html (accessed March 1, 2013).

—. *Portraits and Observations: The Essays of Truman Capote.* New York: Modern Library Paperbacks, 2008.

Capua, Michelangelo. *Montgomery Clift: A Biography.* Jefferson: MacFarland & Company, 2002.

Carlson, Peter. "Nikita Khrushchev Goes to Hollywood." *Smithsonian*, July 2009.

—. *Smithsonianmag.com, "Nikita Khrushchev Goes to Hollywood.* July 2009. http://www.smithsonianmag.com/history-archaeology/Nikita-in-Hollywood.html (accessed June 8, 2012).

Carroll, Jock. *Falling For Marilyn: The Lost Niagara Collection.* New York: Freidman/Fairfax Books, 1996.

Champion, Robert Freeman. *He Made Stars Shine.* Unpublished manuscript, n.d.

Chapman, Don. *Hotspotshawaii.com, "Clubhouses: The Next Generation".* n.d. http://hotspotshawaii.com/Chapman9.html (accessed March 1, 2013).

The Chicago Sun-Times. "News From the Casting Couch." June 10, 2005: 52.

Christie's. *Entertainment Memorabilia: Monday 19 November 2001.* New York: Christie's East, 2001.

Christie's New York. *The Personal Property of Marilyn Monroe.* New York: Christie's, 1999.

Churchwell, Sarah. *The Many Lives of Marilyn Monroe.* New York: Henry Holt and Company, 2004.

City Herald. "Marilyn Monroe Hit with Penalty." March 1, 1956.

Clark, Colin. *The Prince, the Showgirl, and Me.* New York: St. Martin's Press, 1996.

Clark, Gerald. *Too Brief a Treat: The Letters of Truman Capote.* New York: Random House, 2004.

Clarke, Thurston. *Ask Not: The Inauguration of John F. Kennedy and the Speech that Changed the World.* New York: Penguin Books, 2010.

Clayton, Marie. *Marilyn Monroe: Unseen Archvies.* New York: Barnes & Noble Books, 2004.

Clemente, T. J. *Easthamptonpatch.com, "Reflections on Marilyn Monroe's Time in the Hamptons".* July 7, 2012.

http://easthampton.patch.com/blog_posts/reflection-on-marilyn-monroes-time-in-the-hamptons (accessed January 1, 2013).
—. *EastHamptonPatch.com, Issue #02, "Marilyn Monroe and Arthur Miller's Two Summers in the Hamptons"*. April 6, 2007, (accessed May 3, 2010).
Clinton, Paul. *Edition.cnn.com, "Controversy Over Oscars Heats Up"*. March 16, 1999. http://edition.cnn.com/SHOWBIZ/Movies/9903/16/kazan.oscar/index.html (accessed January 25, 2013).
Cogerson. *Cogerson.HubPages.com, "Marilyn Monroe: Box Office Results with Inflation for her Best and Worst Movies"*. n.d. http://cogerson.hubpages.com/hub/Marilyn-Monroe-Box-Office-Results (accessed June 3, 2012).
Coen, MD, Stanley J. "Narcissistic Temptations to Cross Boundaries and How to Manage Them." *Journal of the American Psychoanalytical Association*, December 2007: 1169-1190.
Coen, Richard. "The Paper Chase." *Talk*, September 2001.
CBS Eyewitness, "Who Killed Marilyn Monroe?". Directed by Charles Collingwood. August 10, 1962.
Collins, Joan. *Second Act*. New York : Doubleday, 1996.
Comenas, Gary. *Warholstars.com, "Andy Warhol Pre-Pop"*. n.d. http://www.warholstars.org/warhol1/11roylichtenstein.html (accessed December 8, 2012).
Condon, Bill and Linda Wolfe. *Kinsey: Public and Private*. New York: NewmarketPress, 2004.
Conner, Floyd. *Hollywood's Most Wanted: The Top 10 Book of Lucky Breaks, Prima Donnas, Box Office Bombs, and Other Oddities*. Dulles: Potomac Books, 2002.
Conover, David. *Finding Marilyn*. New York: Grosset & Dunlap, 1981.
Cook, A., J. Spinazzola, J. Ford, C. Lanktree, et al. "Complex Trauma in Children and Adolescents." *Psychiatric Annals*, May 2005: 390-398.
Cook, Jim. "The Miller-Monroe Romance: Marilyn in Love with Author for 5 Years." *The Toledo Blade*, July 12, 1956.
Cooper, Gary. "Letter from Gary Cooper to Marilyn Monroe dated June 22, 1960." *Bonhams.com*. June 16, 2008.

bonhams.com/auctions/16091/lot/3017/ (accessed February 9, 2013).

Cordon, Ingrid M., Margaret-Ellen Pipe, Liat Sayfan, Annika Melinder, and Gail S. Goodman. "Memory for Traumatic Experiences in Early Childhood." *Developmental Review, 24*, 2004.

Corliss, Richard. *Time.com, "Marilyn Monroe 50 Years Later: in Time and Out of Time"*. August 3, 2012. entertainment.time.com/2012/08/03/marilyn-monroe-50-years-later-in-time-and-out-of-time/ (accessed December 16, 2012).

Cott, Nancy F. *No Small Courage: A History of Women in the United States*. New York: Oxford Press, 2000.

Cotten, Joseph. *Vanity Will Get You Somewhere*. New York: Avon Books, 1987.

Cottrell, Dr. Richard as told to C. Gervin Hayden. "I Was Marilyn Monroe's Doctor." *Ladies' Home Companion*, January 1965.

Coughlan, Robert. "Changing Roles in Modern Life." *Life*, December 24, 1956: 109-111.

Coughlan, Sean. *news.bbc.co.uk, "What Was Bobby Kennedy?"*. January 30, 2007. http://news.bbc.co.uk/2/hi/uk_news/magazine/6309127.stm (accessed August 8, 2011).

Cowles, Fleur. *Friends & Memories*. London: J, Cape, 1975.

—. *She Made Friends and Kept Them: An Anecdotal Memoir.* New York: HarperCollins, 1996.

Cramer, Richard Ben. *Joe DiMaggio: The Hero's Life.* New York: Simon & Schuster, 2000.

Cravens, Hamilton (editor). *Great Depression: People and Perspectives.* Santa Barbara, CA: ABC-CLIO, LCC, 2009.

Crown, Lawrence. *Marilyn at Twentieth Century Fox*. London: Comet/Planet, 1987.

Crowther, Bosely. "Screen: Prince and Girl." *The New York Times*, June 14, 1957: 22.

Crowther, Bosley. "Actress as a Symbol." *The New York Times*, August 6, 1962.

—. "'Don't Bother to Knock,' Starring Marilyn Monroe and Richard Widmark, Opens at Globe." *The New York Times*, July 19, 1952: 8.

—. "Get Ready for Heartbreak..." *The New York Times*, June 25, 195

—. "John Huston's 'The Misfits'; Gable and Monroe Star in Script by Miller," *The New York Times*, February 2, 1961.

—. "Look at Marilyn!" *The New York Times*, June 12, 1955.

—. "Screen: Eight New Movies Arrive for the Holidays." *The New York Times*, December 26, 1963.

—. "The Proof of Marilyn." *The New York Times*, September 9, 1956: X1.

—. "The Screen: Marilyn Monroe Arrives." *The New York Times*, September 1, 1956: F19.

—. "The Screen: Milton Berle Steals Show in 'Let's Make Love'." *The New York Times*, September 9, 1960: 36.

Cunningham, Ernest W. *The Ultimate Marilyn*. Los Angeles: Renaissance Books, 1998.

Current Biography 1959. New York: H. W. Wilson Company, 1959.

Curtin, Michael. *museum.tv, "A Tour of the White House with Mrs. John F. Kennedy"*. n.d. http://www.museum.tv/eotvsection.php?entrycode=tourofthew (accessed January 11, 2013).

—. *Redeeming the Wasteland: Television Documentary and Car War Politics*. New Brunswick: Rutgers University Press, 1995.

Curtis, James. *Spencer Tracy: A Biography*. New York: Alfred A. Knopf, 2011.

Cypert, Rick. *The Virtue of Suspense: The Life and Works of Charlotte Armstrong*. Selinsgrove: Susquehanna University Press, 2008.

Dalton, David. *James Dean: Mutant King: A Biography*. New York: St. Martin's Press, 1983.

"Dame Sybil Thorndike Defending Marilyn Monroe." *YouTube.com*. n.d. http://www.youtube.com/watch?v=dVX3PLBfAM4 (accessed December 27, 2012).

Darlow, Michael. *Terrance Rattigan: The Man and His Work*. London: Quartet Books, 2000.

Davis, Charles. "Sad Child, Unhappy Star." *The Los Angeles Times*, August 6, 1962.

David, Lester. "Which Was the True Marilyn?" *The Milwaukee Journal*, April 12, 1964: 5.

Davis, Ronald L. *Just Making Movies: Company Directors on the Studio System*. Jackson: University Press of Mississippi, 2005.

de Dienes, Andre. *Marilyn Mon Amour*. New York: St. Martin's Press, 1985.

De La Hoz, Cindy. *Marilyn Monroe: Platinum Fox*. Philadelphia: Running Press, 2007.

Dean, Bob. "Marilyn to Wed Again?" *Photoplay*, May 1961.

Desert News. "Charlton Heston Would Trade Biblical Roles for Comedy." June 3, 1960.

Desert News Salt Lake Telegram. "No Marilyn, No Dean; Martin Stands on That." June 11, 1962.

Diamond, I. A. L. "Marilyn Monroe and the 30-Proof Coffee Break: The Making of an American Classic." *The Chicago Tribune*, January 12, 1986.

Dickerson, John. *On Her Trail: My Mother, Nancy Dickerson, TV News' First Woman Star*. New York: Simon & Schuster, 2006.

Digh, Patti. *Creative Is a Verb: If You're Alive, You're Creative*. Guilford : Globe Pequot Press, 2011.

Dillon, Nancy. "Winning Bidder in eBay Auction for Spot Above Marilyn Monroe's Crypt Can't Afford $4.6M Price Tag." *Nydailynews.com*. August 25, 2009. http://articles.nydailynews.com/2009-08-25/news/17932890_1_bidder-crypt marilyn-monroe (accessed June 15, 2013).

DiLorenzo, Josephine and Theo Wilson. "Marilyn Can Act Too, Sez Olivier." *The New York Daily News*, February 10, 1956.

DiMaggio, Joe. "Letter from Joe DiMaggio to Marilyn Monroe dated January 27, 1962." *Christies.com*. June 19, 2007 http://www.christies.com/lotfinder/LotDetailsPrintable.aspx?intObjectID=4927037 (accessed February 9, 2013).

—. "Letter to Joe DiMaggio to Marilyn Monroe dated January 27, 1962." *Christies.com*. June 19, 2007. http://www.christies.com/lotfinder/lot/dimaggio-joseph-4927037details.aspx?pos=8&intObjectID=4927037&sid=&page=3?intObjectID=4927037. (accessed June 10, 2010).

"DiMaggio's and Monroe's Keepsakes Auctioned." *abcnews.go.com.* March 31, 2006. http://abcnews.go.com/GMA/story?id=1781543&page=1 (accessed August 20, 2012).

Dinkin, Roxane and Robert J. Dinkin. *Infertility and the Creative Spirit.* Burlington, IL: iUniverse, 2010.

Dirk, Tim. "Niagara." *Filmsite.org.* n.d. http://www.filmsite.org/some.html (accessed March 27, 2008).

—. "Some Like It Hot." *Filmsite.org.* n.d. http://www.filmsite.org/misf.html (accessed March 27, 2008).

Doll, Susan. *Marilyn: Her Life & Legend.* Lincolnwood: Publications International, LTD, 1990.

Dolleris, Sue. *Hello, Norma Jean.* Honolulu, HI: Savant Books and Publications, 2010.

Doty, Alexander. *Making Things Perfectly Queer: Interpreting Mass Culture.* Minneapolis: University of Minnesota Press, 1993.

Dow, Jason. "My Encounter with Mariln Monroe." *We Prefer Marilyn,* July/August 1989.

Drury, Allen. "Arthur Miller Admits Helping Communist-Front Groups in '40s; But Playwright Denies Being Under 'Discipline'." *The New York Times,* June 22, 1956: 1.

Dunne, Dominick. *The Way We Lived Then: Recollections of a Well-Known Name Dropper.* New York: Corwn Publishers, 1999.

"Early Recording By Marilyn Monroe." *The New York Times.com.* August 16, 1995. http://www.nytimes.com/1995/08/16/arts/early-recording-by-monroe.html (accessed January 19, 2013).

"East of Eden Film Premiere (1955) – Feat. Marilyn Monroe, Jack Warner, John Steinbeck." YouTube.com., n. d. http://www.youtube.com/watch?v=JEP5CSXV4xA (accessed January 1, 2012).

Ebert, Roger. "A Sense of Control." *Playboy,* December 2012.

—. "Some Like It Hot (Chicago Sun Times)." *rogerebert.com.* January 9, 2000. http://rogerebert.suntimes.com/apps/pbcs.dll/article?AID+/20000109/REVIEWS08/1090301/1023 (accessed June 8, 2012).

Eden, Barbara and Wendy Leigh. *Jeannie Out of the Bottle*. New York: Crown Archetype, 2011. *Edmonton Journal*. "Marilyn Monroe Still Hunting for a Husband." February 23, 1961.

Edwards, Owen. "The Persistence of Marilyn." *American Photographer*, July 1984.

Eisenhauer, Robert G. *After Romanticism*. New York: Peter Lang Publishing, 2008.

Eisenhower, Mamie. "If I Were A Bride Today." *Today's Woman*, 1953.

Elise, Pettus. "Starry, Starry Night." *Gourmet Magazine*, February 2001.

Elizabeth. "Quigley's Annual List of Box-Office Champions, 1932-1970." *ReelClassics.com*. October 23, 2003. http://www.reelclassics.com/Articles/General/quigleytop10-article.htm (accessed June 8, 2012).

The Emersonian. "A Peek into the Future." June 20, 1941.

Engelberg, Morris and Marv Schneider. *DiMaggio: Setting the Record Straight*. Minnesota: MVP Books, 2004.

"The Essentials: Critics' Corner: *Some Like It Hot*." *TCM.com*, n.d. http://www.tcm.com/essentials/article.html?cid=71637&mainArticleId=463894 (accessed June 1, 2013).

Evans, Mike. *Marilyn Handbook*. Portland, OR: Octopus Books, 2004.

Evans, Peter. "Marilyn Monroe's Last Weekend." *MailOnline.com*. August 2, 2010. http://www.dailymail.co.uk/femail/article-1299496/Marilyn-Monroes-weekend-told-time-eyewitness-account-row-Frank-Sinatra-friends-fear-signed-death-warrant.html (accessed December 13, 2012).

Exner, Judith and Ovid Demaris. *My Story*. New York: Grove Press, 1978.

Farber, Manny. "Blame the Audience." *The Nation*, December 19, 1952.

"FBI Records: The Vault: Freedom of Information and Privacy Acts, Subject: Marilyn Monroe." *FBI.gov*. n.d. http://vault.fbi.gov/Marilyn%20Monroe (accessed February 13, 2013).

Federal Bureau of Investigation. *Marilyn Monroe: The FBI Files*. Minneapolis: Filiquarian Publishing, LLC, 2007.

Feinberg, Scott. "Amy Greene, Scene-Stealer of 'Love, Marilyn,' on Her House Guest Marilyn Monroe." *HollywoodReporter.Com.* November 9, 2012. http://www.hollywoodreporter.com/race/amy-greene-love-marilyn-385836. (accessed November 12, 2012).

Feingersh, Ed and Bob LaBrasca. *Marilyn: March 1955: Photographs From the Michael Ochs Archives.* New York: Delta, 1990.

Feldman, Charles K. "Inter-office Memo to Darryl Zanuck, dated October 22, 1954." iCollector.com. December 16, 2011. http://www.icollector.com/Marilyn-Monroe-extensive-archive-of-production-and-publicity-material-from-The-Seven-Year-Itch_i11537134 (accessed June 28, 2013).

Fenster, Mark. *Conspiracy Theories: Secrecy and Power in American Culture.* Minneapolis: University of Minnesota Press, 2008.

Ferris, Paul. *Dylan Thomas: The Biography.* Washington, DC: Counterpoint, 2000.

Fichtl, Paula. *Day to Day Life with the Freud Family.* Hamburg: Hoffman & Campe, 1987.

Finkelhor, David et al. "Sexual Abuse in a National Survey of Adult Men and Women: Prevalence, Characteristics and Risk Factors." *Child Abuse and Neglect,* 1990: 19-28.

Finn, Michelle. *Marilyn's Addresses.* London: Smith Gryphon Publishers, 1995.

Flinn, Caryl. *Brass Diva: The Life and Legend of Ethel Merman.* Los Angeles: University of California Press, 2007.

Flint, Peter B. "Joan Crawford Dies at Home." *The New York Times,* May 11, 1977.

Flynn, Chris. *Faces of Fukuoka.* Fukuoka, Japan: The Nishinippon Newspaper Company, 1999.

Fonda, Jane. *My Life So Far.* New York: Random House, 2005.

Fowler, Will. *Reporters: Memoirs of a Young Newspaperman.* Santa Monica, CA: Roundtable Publications, 1991.

Fox News. "Poll: Most Believe 'Cover-Up' of JFK Assassination Facts." *FoxNews.com.* June 18, 2004. http://www.foxnews.com/story/0,2933,102511,00.html (accessed February 25, 2013).

Franklin, Joe and Laurie Palmer. *The Marilyn Monroe Story*. New York: Rudolph Field, 1954.

Free Press Wire Service. "Monroe Death Said 'Terrible Lesson' for Star-Expoiters: Olivier Blames Ballyhoo." *Immortal.marilyn.com*. n.d. http://immortalmarilyn.com/TwilightArticles.html (accessed March 1, 2013).

Freedman, Jonathan. *Klezmer America: Jewishness, Ethnicity, Modernity.* New York: Columbia University Press, 2008.

Freeman, Lucy. *Why Norma Jean Killed Marilyn Monroe*. Chicago: Global Rights, 1992.

—. *Why Norma Jean Killed Marilyn Monroe: A Psychological Portrait*. Mamaroneck, NY: Hastings House, 1992.

Gable, Kay. "Marilyn Monroe Letter from Kay Gable (dated April 11, 1961)." *Juliensauctions.com*. 2005. http://www.juliensuactions.com/auctions/2005/Marilyn-Monroe/results.html (accessed January 20, 2013).

Gabor, Zsa Zsa. *My Story*. New York: Crest, 1961.

—. *One Lifetime is Enough*. New York: Delacorte, 1991.

Gaffney, Dennis. "Joe DiMaggio Jr." *pbs.org*. n.d. http://www.pbs.org/wgbh/amex/dimaggio/peopleevents/pande03.htm (accessed January 1, 2012).

Gardella, Kay. "Hollywood Mourns for 'A Warm Human Being'." *New York Daily News*, August 6,1962.

Gehman, Richard. "Charming Billy." *Playboy*, December 1960.

Geist, Kenneth L. *Pictures Will Talk: The Life and Films of Joseph L. Mankiewicz*. New York: Scribner's, 1978.

Gelb, Arthur. "Producers Vying on 'Golden Kazoo'." *The New York Times*, February 20 1956.

Gentry, Curt. *J. Edgar Hoover: The Man and the Secrets*. London: W. W. Norton & Company, 1991.

Gertz, Stephen J. "Heartbreaking Marilyn Monroe Letter Estimated at $30,000-$50,000." *Booktryst.com*. n.d. http://www.booktryst.com/2012/11/heartbreaking-marilyn-monroe-letter.html (accessed December 16, 2012).

Gibson, Gwen. "Marilyn Monroe May Have Made It As Actress, Says Publicist." *Ocala Star-Banner*, May 12, 1988.

Gilmore, John. *Inside Marilyn Monroe*. Los Angeles: Amok Books, 2007.

Gingsberg, Allen. "The Howl." *Wussu.com*. n.d. http://www.wussu.com/poems/agh.htm (accessed June 8, 2012).

Ginsberg, Allen. *Howl and Other Poems.* San Fransciso, CA: The City Lights Pocket Bookshop, 1956.

Glatzer, Jenna. *The Marilyn Monroe Treasures.* London: Metro Books, 2008.

Glendinning, Victoria. *Edith Sitwell: A Unicorn Among Lions.* London: Weidenfeld & Nicolson, 1981.

Goldberg, Robert Alan. *Enemies Within: The Culture of Conspiracy in Modern America.* New Haven, CT: Yale University Press, 2001.

Goldburg, Robert. "Letter from Rabbi Robert Goldburg dated September 29, 1961." *Bonhams.com*. n.d. bonhams.com/auctions/17544/lot/2006/ (accessed January 5, 2013).

Good Morning America (ABC). August 5, 1982.

Goode, James. *The Making of the Misfits.* New York: Limelight, 1986.

Goodman, Ezra. "To Aristophanes & Back." *Time*, May 14, 1956.

Gordon, Stanley. "Marilyn Meet Montand." *Look*, July 5, 1960: 91-96.

"Gorgeous Cheesecake Photo Presented by Marilyn as a Tip to Her Carpet Installer." *RRAuctions.com*. n.d. http://www.rrauction.com/gorgeous_marilyn_monroe_cheesecake_signed_photo.cfm (accessed December 15, 2012).

Gottlieb, Jeff. "For Sale: Eternity with Marilyn Monroe." *LaTimes.com.* August 14, 2009. http://articles.latimes.com/2009/aug/14/local/me-marilyn14 (accessed March 1, 2013).

Gottman, John. *Why Marriages Succeed or Fail: And How You Can Make Yours Last.* New York: Simon & Schuster, 1994.

Gottried, Martin. *Arthur Miller: His Life and Work.* Cambridge: Da Capo Press, 2004.

Graham, Sheila. "Marilyn Talks About Joe and Babies." *Modern Screen*, September 1954.

Granger, Farley with Robert Calhoun. *Include Me Out: My Life From Goldwyn to Broadway.* New York: St. Martin's Press, 2008.

Green, Timothy. "I Am an Electic Eel in a Pool of Catfish." *Life*, January 4, 1963.

Greene, Joshua and James Kotsilias-Davies. *Milton's Marilyn.* New York: Schirmer/Mosel, 1995.

Greenson, Ralph. "Special Problems in Psychotherapy with the Rich and Famous." University of Southern California Press. The Ralph R. Greenson Papers Special Collection, August 19, 1978.

Gregory, R. "Clinical Challenges in Co-occurring Borderline Personality and Substance Abuse Disorders." *Psychiatric Times, XXIII*, November 1, 2006: 650.

Grenier, Cynthia. "Motion Picture Activities Along the Seine." *The New York Times*, September 25, 1960.

Grobel, Lawrence. *The Hustons.* Lantham: Cooper Square Books, 2000.

—. *The Hustons.* New York: Avon, 1989.

Grohol, John H. "Characteristics of Borderline Personality Disorder." *Psychcentral.com.* 2007. http://psychcentral.com/lib/2007/characteristics-of-borderline-personality-disorder/ (accessed June 17, 2012).

Guilaroff, Sydney and Cathy Griffin. *Crowning Glory: Reflections of Hollywood's Favorite Confidante.* Santa Monica, CA: General Publishing Group, 1996.

Guiles, Fred Lawrence. *Legend: The Life and Death of Marilyn Monroe.* New York: Stein and Day, 1984.

—. *Norma Jean: The Life of Marilyn Monroe.* New York: McGraw-Hill, 1969.

Gussow, Mel. "The Last Movie Tycoon." *New York Magazine*, February 1, 1971: 27-41.

—. "John Springer, 85, Hollywood Publicist, Dies." *The New York Times*, November 1, 2001.

Haedrich, Marcel. *Coco Chanel: Her Life, Her Secrets.* New York: Little, Brown and Company, 1972.

Hall, Richard C., Platt, Dennis E., & Hall, Ryan C. W. "Suicide Risk Assessment: A Review of Risk Factors for Suicide in 100 Patients Who Made Severe Suicide Attempts: Evaluation Of Suicide Risk in a Time of Managed Care." *Psychosomatics, Volume 40* (January-February 1999), pp. 18-27.

Halperin, James L. (editor). *Heritage Music & Entertainment Memorabilia Auction Catalogue*, Dallas, TX: Ivy Press, 2007.

Halsman, Philippe. *Halsman Sight and Insight.* New York: Doubleday, 1972.

—. "Shooting Marilyn." *Popular Photography*, June 1953.

Hambourg, Maria Morris and Mia Fineman. *Avedon's Endgame.* New York City: Abrams and the Metropolitan Museum of Art, 2002.

Hamilton Cravens, editor. *Great Depression: People and Perspectives.* Santa Barbara, CA: ABC-CLIO, LLC, 2009.

Harnish, Larry. "Chasing Marilyn Monroe." *Latimes.com.* June 2, 2007. http://latimesblogs.latimes.com/thedailymirror/2007/06/marilyn_monroe.html (accessed January 21, 2013).

Harris, Radie. *Radie's World.* New York: Putnam, 1975.

Hart, Henry. "The Misfits," *Films in Review*, February 1961.

Harvey, John H., T. L. Orbuch, and A. L. Webber. "A Social Psychology Model of Account-Making in Response to Severe Stress." *Journal of Language and Social Psychology, 9*, 1990: 191-207.

Harvey, Steve. "Marilyn Monroe Secrets Were Safe—at Least for a While." *Latimes.com.* June 5, 2011. http://articles.latimes.com/2011/jun/05/local/la-me-0605-then-20110605 (accessed January 21, 2013).

Hasley, Kevin J. *Hollywood 3: A Collector's Ransom Catalogue.* Beverly Hills, CA: Self-published, May 18, 1997.

—. "Profiles in History: Hollywood Memorabilia Auction 13: Auction Catalogue." Beverly Hills, CA: self-published, December 17, 2002.

Haspiel, James. *Marilyn: Becoming the Legend.* New York: Hyperion, 1994.

—. *Marilyn: The Ultimate Look at the Legend.* New York: Henry Holt, 1991.

Haspiel, James Robert. "How A Cinema Legend Was Born: The Screen Testing of Marilyn Monroe." In *American Classic Film Features*, by John C. Tibbetts and James M. Welsh. Lanham, Maryland: Scarecrow Press, 2010.

Haspiel, James. *The Unpublished Marilyn.* Edinburgh: Mainstream Publishing, 2000.

What's My Line? Directed by Franklin Heller. September 12, 1954.
Henaghan, Jim. "So Far to Go Alone!" *Redbook*, June 1952.
"Her Greatest Role," periodical unknown, August 18, 1962.
Herman, Gary. *The Book of Hollywood Quotes*. London: Omnibus Press, 1979.
Hertel, Howard and Don Neff. "Unclad Body of Star Discovered on Bed; Empty Bottle Near." *The Los Angeles Times*, August 6, 1962.
Heston, Charlton. *In the Arena: An Autobiography*. New York: Simon & Schuster, 1995.
Heymann, C. David. Liz: *An Intimate Biography of Elizabeth Taylor.* New York: Atria Books, 2011.
Hilty, James W. *Robert Kennedy: Brother Protector.* Philadelphia: Temple University Press, 1997.
Hine, Thomas. *Populuxe*. New York: Knopf, 1986.
Holden, Anthony. *Behind the Oscar: The Secret History of the Academy Awards*. New York: Simon and Schuster, 1993.
Hollis, Alpert, "S. R. Goes to the Movies: Arthur Miller, Screenwriter," *Saturday Review*, February 4, 1961, p. 27 & 47.
Hollywood Greats: Marilyn Monroe (BBC). Directed by Sue Mallinson. Performed by Barry Norman. 1979.
Hoppe, Art. "Joe DiMaggio Weds Marilyn Monroe at City Hall." *The San Francisco Chronicle*, January 15, 1954.
Hopper, Hedda. "Howard Hughes is on the Mend." *The Los Angeles Times*, July 29, 1946.
"How Bobby Betrayed Marilyn." *Smh.com*. March 17, 2007.
http://www.smh.com.au/news/world/how-bobby-betrayed-marilyn/2007/03/16/1173722744316.html
(accessed March 17, 2013).
Hoyt, Edwin P. *Marilyn: The Tragic Venus*. New York: Chilton, 1965.
Hughes, Zondra. "Tupac Lives! Why Fans Are Fascinated by Celebrities Who Die Tragically." *Ebony*, August 2003.
Huston, John. *An Open Book*. New York: Da Capo Press, 1994.
Huston, Nanci G. "Roxbury A Quiet Place for Famous Authors to Savor Life Out of the Spotlight." *Newstimes.com*. March 22, 2010. http://www,newstimes.com/news/article/Roxbury-a-quiet-place-for-famous-authors-to-savor-417465.php (accessed June 8, 2012).

Hutchinson, Tom. *Marilyn Monroe.* New York: Exeter Books, 1982.

Hyams, Joe. "Crack-Up." *Photoplay,* January 1957.

Hyman, Jackie. "Authorities Reject Claim Marilyn Monroe Was Murdered." *The St. Petersburg Times,* December 29, 1982.

Inge, M. Thomas. *Truman Capote: Conversations.* Jackson: University Press of Mississippi, 1987.

Intimate Portrait: Marilyn Monroe. Directed by Tom Yaroschuk. 1996.

"Investigation of the Unauthorized Use of United States Passports—Part 3. Hearings Before the Committee on Un-American Activities House of Representatives Eighty-fourth Congress Session." *Archive.org.* June 12 and 13, 1956. http://archive.org/stream/investigationofu0304unit/investigationofu0304unit_djvu.txt (accessed March 17, 2013).

Isherwood, Charles. "An Appreciation: A Morality That Stared Down Sanctimony." *Nytimes.com.* February 12, 2005 http://theater.nytimes.com/2005/02/12/theater/newsandfeatures/12appr.html (accessed March 1, 2013).

The Jack Benny Show "Honolulu Trip" (CBS). Directed by Ralph Levy and Hilliard Marks. September 13, 1953.

James, Brandon. *Jeanne Carmen: My Wild, Wild Life as a New York Pin Up Queen, Shot Golfer & Hollywood Actress.* Lincoln: iUniverse, 2007.

Jamison, Barbara Berch. "If At First You Do Succeed." *The New York Times,* June 20, 1954.

Jennings, Bob. "Six Thousand Thunderbird Stampede, Mob Stage to See Marilyn." *StarsandStripes.com.* February 23, 1954. http://www.stripes.com/news/6-000-thunderbirds-stampede-mob-stage-to-see-marilyn-1.6395 (accessed August 31, 2012).

—. "Twenty-fifth's Roaring Thousands Greet Singing, Slinking Blonde Bomber." *StarsandStripes.com.* February 19, 1954. http://www.stripes.com/news/from-the-s-s-archives-25th-s-roaring-thousands-greet-singing-slinking-blonde-bomber-1.101081 (accessed August 31, 2012)

Johnson, Dean. "Unforgettable Marilyn." *The Orlando Sentinel,* August 5, 1982.

Johnson, Erskine. "Here's A Realistic Look at Moviemaking Business." *Ocala Star-Banner*, August 3, 1962.

—. "Marilyn Monroe Confesses Mother Alive, Living Here." *Los Angeles Daily News*, May 3, 1952.

Johnston, Laurie. "If You're Thinking of Living in Sutton Place." *Nytimes.com*. May 27, 1984. http://www.nytimes.com/1984/05/27/realestate/if-you-re-thinking-of-living-in-sutton-place.html (accessed June 8, 2012).

Jordan, Ted. *Norma Jean: My Secret Life with Marilyn Monroe*. New York: William Morrow, 1989.

Joyce, James. *Ulysses: A Reproduction of the 1922 First Edition*. Mineola, NY: Dover, 2002.

Julien, Darren. *Property From the Estate of Marilyn Monroe*. West Hollywood, CA: Julien's Auctions, 2005.

Justice, Michelle and Roman Hryniszak. "Interview with Allan Snyder." *Runnin' Wild (All About Marilyn quarterly newsletter)*, January 1994.

Justice, Michelle. "Marilyn Doesn't Live Here Anymore." *Runnin' Wild (All About Marilyn newsletter)*, 1988.

Kacich, Tom. *Hot Type: 150 Years of the Best Local Stories From the News-Gazette*. Champaign: Sports Publishing, 2002.

Kaplan, Fred. *1959: The Year Everything Changed*. Hoboken, NJ: John Wiley & Sons, 2009.

Kaplan, Ron. "Dodger Photographer Highlighted Game Off the Field." *New Jersey Jewish Online/Sports, Njjewishnews.com*. June 21, 2007. http://njjewish-news.com/njjn.com/062107/sptsDodgerPhotographer.html (accessed June 8, 2012).

Kaplan, Sam Hall. *LA Lost & Found: An Architectural History of Los Angeles*. New York: Crown Trade Paperbacks, 1987.

Kasher, Sam. "Marilyn and Her Monsters." *Vanityfair.com*. November 2010. http://www.vanityfair.com/hollywood/features/2010/11/marilyn-monroe-201011 (accessed June 8, 2012).

Kashner, Sam and Nancy Schoenberger. *A Talent for Genius: The Life and Times of Oscar Levant*. Los Angeles: Silman-James Press, 1994.

Kashner, Sam. "Discovery of Marilyn's Secret Papers." *Vanity Fair*, October 2008.

—. "Marilyn and Her Monsters." *Vanity Fair*, November 2010.

—. "The Things She Left Behind." *Vanity Fair*, October 2008.

Kaufman, Amy. "Mystery Surrounds 'My Week With Marilyn'." *LaTimes.com*. December 11, 2011. http://articles.latimes.com/2011/dec/10/entertainment/la-et-marilyn-accuracy-20111210 (accessed September 27, 2012).

Kaye, Elizabeth. "Remembering Marilyn Monroe." *Premiere*, August 1998: 93.

Kazan, Elia. *A Life*. New York: Alfred A. Knopf, 1988.

—. "Elia Kazan Love Letter to Marilyn Monroe." *Ephemera.com*. n.d. http://ephemera.typepad.com/ephemera/2009/08/elia-kazan-love-letter-to-marilyn-monroe.html (accessed February 12, 2013).

Kearney, Christine. "New Photos of Marilyn Monroe Up For Sale." *Reuters.com*. 2010. http://www.reuters.com/article/2010/02/05/us-finearts-marilyn-idUSTRE6141S220100205 (accessed December 17, 2012).

Kelly, Kitty. *Elizabeth Taylor: The Last Star*. New York: Simon & Schuster, 1981.

Kendler, Kenneth S., C. Bulik, J. Silberg, J. Hettema, J. Myers, C. Prescott. "Childhood Sexual Abuse and Adult Psychiatric and Substance Use Disorders in Women: An Epidemiological and Cotwin Control Analysis." *Archives of General Psychiatry*, 2000: 953-959.

Kennedy, John F. *Remarks in Response to New York's Birthday Salute to the President*. May 19, 1962. Jfklink.com.http://www.jfklink.com/speeches/jfk/publicpapers/1962/jfk201_62.html. (accessed October 19, 2013).

Ketcham, Diane. "Long Island Journal." *Nytimes.com*. July 14, 1996. http://www.nytimes.com/1996/07/14/nyregion/long-island-journal-428370.html?src=pm (accessed June 8, 2012).

Key, Ovor. "Marilyn Monroe: The Legend Becomes a Cult." *The Rocky Mountain News*, December 2, 1973.

Kidder, Clark. *Marilyn Monroe: Cover to Cover.* Iola, WI: Krause Publications, 2003.

Kilgallen, Dorothy. "Voice of Broadway." *New York Journal American*, August 3, 1962.

—. "Voice of Broadway." *New York Journal American*, September 18, 1952.

—. "Voice of Broadway." *New York Journal American*, August 28, 1952.

Kinder, Marsha. *Luis Brunel's The Discreet Charm of the Bourgeoisie.* New York: Cambridge University Press, 1999.

King, Susan. "Marilyn Monroe: People Who Knew Her Recall the Real Person." *The Los Angeles Times*, August 4, 2012.

Kirkland, Douglas. *An Evening wih Marilyn.* New York: Welcome Books, 2005.

Kobal, John. *Marilyn Monroe: A Life on Films.* New York: Hamlyn, 1974.

—. *People Will Talk.* New York: Knopf, 1985.

Koegler, Horst. "Lotte Goslar: 1907-97." *Dance Magazine*, January 1998.

Koppel, Nathan. "A Battle Erupts Over the Right to Market Marilyn (*The Wall Street Journal*)." *Post-gazette.com.* March 17, 2012. http://www.post-gazette.com/stories/business/news/a-battle-erupts-over-the-right-to-market-marilyn-429397/ (accessed June 8, 2012).

—. "Blonde Ambition: A Battle Erupts Over the Right to Market Marilyn." *Online.wsj.com.* n.d. http://online.wsj.com/article/SB114463306707721479.html (accessed March 17, 2013).

Kovan, Florice Whyte. "Ben Hecht & Marilyn Monroe: Hecht Wrote Marilyn Monroe's Memoir 'My Story'." *BenHechtBooks.net.* 2001. http://benhechtbooks.net/ben_hecht__marilyn_ monroe (accessed July 13, 2012).

Laderman, Gary. *Rest in Peace: A Cultural History of Death and the Funeral Home in 20th Century America.* New York: Oxford University Press, 2003.

LaGuardia, Robert. *Monty: A Biography of Montgomery Clift.* Westminster, MD: Arbor House, 1977.

Lambert, Gavin. *On Cukor.* New York: Putnam's, 1972.

Landers, Ann. "Letter from Ann Landers to Marilyn Monroe dated January 24, 1962." *Bonhams.com.* December 20, 2009. bonhams.com/auctions/17544/lot/2005/ (accessed January 5, 2013).

Largo, Michael. *Genius and Heroin: The Illustrated Catalogue: Creativity, Obsession, and Reckless Abandon Through the Ages.* New York: HarperCollins, 2008.

Larry King Live "June Allison Discusses Her Career (CNN). July 4, 2001.

Larry King Live "Marilyn Monroe" (CNN). August 5, 1997.

LaSalle, Mick. "A Marilyn Monroe Story." *Sfgate.com.* August 13, 2012. http://blog.sfgate.com/mlasalle/2012/08/13/a-marilyn-monroe-story/ (accessed November 5, 2012).

—. "Some Like It True: Curtis' Monroe Tale Unlikely." *Sfgate.com.* November 6, 2009. http://www.sfgate.com/cgi-bin/article.cgi?f=/c/a/2009/11/05/MVPF1AE1LN.DTL. (accessed June 8, 2012).

The Last Days of Marilyn Monroe (BBC). Directed by Christopher Ogliati. 1985.

"The Last Ever Pictures of Marilyn Monroe, Taken the Weekend Before She Died." *Dailymail.com.* May 11, 2009. http://dailymail.co.uk/tvshowbiz.article-1180108/The-pictures-Marilyn-Monroe-taken-weekend-died.html (accessed June 8, 2012).

Lawford, Christopher. *Symptoms of Withdrawal: A Memoir of Snapshots and Redemptions.* New York: William Morrow, 2005.

Leaf, Earl. "A New Marilyn Comes Back." *Movie Spotlight*, April 1954.

Leaf, MD, Norman. *Are Those Real? True Talkes of Plastic Surgery from Beverly Hills.* Bloomington, IN: iUniverse, 2010.

Leaming, Barbara. *Marilyn Monroe.* New York: Crown, 1998.

Lear, Martha Weinman. "Blonde on Blonde: Marilyn and Judy Holliday." *Fame*, November 1988.

Leclair, J. E. "From a Private Eye's Confidential Report: The Real Reason for Marilyn Monroe's Divorce!" *Confidential*, September 1957.

Lee, Henry. "An Ex-husband Can Be a Girl's Best Friend." *New York Daily News*, January 22, 1961.

Lee, Matt and Ted Lee. "Marilyn Monroe's Stuffing Recipe Stars in a Remake." *Nytimes.com*. November 9, 2010. http://www.nytimes.com/2012/11/10/dining/10marilyn.html?_r=0 (accessed June 8, 2012).

Leigh, Janet. *There Really Was a Hollywood.* Garden City: Doubleday & Company, 1984.

Leigh, Wendy. *True Grace: The Life and Times of An American Princess.* New York: St. Martin's Press, 2008.

The Legend of Marilyn Monroe. Directed by Terry Sanders. 1966

"Letter Regarding Clark Gable's insurance policy dated February 25, 1960." *Bonhams.com.* December 9, 2007. bonhams.com/auctions/15427/lot/2017/ (accessed February 8, 2013).

"Letters to the Editor," *Life*, August 28, 1962.

Levin, Robert J. "Marilyn Monroe: I'm Learning About Marriage." *Redbook*, Feburary 1957.

Levine, Debra. "Hollywood's Dance History: Jack Cole Made Marilyn Monroe Move." *Latimes.com.* August 9, 2009. http://www.latimes.com/entertainment/news/arts/la-ca-marilyn-monroe9-2009aug09,0,5569636.story (accessed December 17, 2012).

Levy, Alan. "Marilyn Monroe: A Good Long Look at Myself." *Redbook*, August 1962.

Lewin, David. "Marilyn Monroe." *London Daily Express*, May 6, 1959.

Lewis, Jerry and James Kaplan. *Dean and Me: A Love Story.* New York: Doubleday, 2005.

Lewis, Robert. *Slings and Arrows: Theatre in My Life.* New York: Applause Books, 1996.

Life. "Apprentice Goddesses." January 1, 1951: 36-41.

Life. "Cocktails at Camelot." June 1987.

Life. "Fabled Enchantresses: Marilyn Monroe in a Remarkable Recreation of Her Predecessors: Lillian Russell, Theda Bara, Clara Bow, Marlene Dietrich, Jean Harlow: Photographed by Richard Avedon." December 22, 1958: 137.

Life. "Hollywood Topic A-Plus." April 7, 1952.

Life. "Marilyn Monroe: A Skinny Dip You'll Never See." June 22, 1962: 90-92.

Life. "Marilyn, Part of a Jumping Gallery." November 9, 1959.

Life. "Memories of Marilyn." August 17, 1962: 63-70.

Life. "Parting Shots: For Marilyn, A Look Back in Adoration." September 8, 1972.

Life. "Powerful Stars Meet to Play-act Romance." August 15, 1960: 64-67.

Life. "Remember Marilyn." September 8, 1972: 63-71.

Life. "She Wears a Borrowed Dress to Her Party." November 29, 1954.

Life. "The First Baby: Photographed by Suzanne Szasz." December 24, 1956.

Life. "The Growing Cult of Marilyn." January 25, 1963.

Life. "They Fired Marilyn: Her Dip Lives On." June 22, 1962.

Life. "Walk Like This, Marilyn." April 20, 1959.

Life. "Why in the World Are the Windsors Jumping? Photographed by Philippe Halsman." November 9, 1959.

Life. "Yves Montand Uses His Gallic Charms as Marilyn's Movie Lover. Marilyn's Own Earnest Eccentricities Offer a Compelling Human Study in Filming Let's Make Love. Photographed by John Bryson." August 15, 1960.

"Life in Film: Runa Islam." *Frieze.com*. March 2007. http://www.frieze.com/issue/article/life_in_film_runa_islam/ (accessed December 22, 2012).

Linehad, Marsha. *Cognitive-behavioral Treatment of Borderline Personality Disorder*. New York: Guilford Press, 1993.

Lippe, Richard. "The Misfits." *FilmReference.com*. n.d. http://www.filmreference.com/Films-Mi-My/The-Misfits.html (accessed June 8, 2012).

Lipton, Harry. "Marilyn's the Most!" *Motion Picture*, May 28, 1956.

Lipton, James. *Inside "Inside"*. New York: Dutton/Penguin Group, 2007.

LoBianco, Lorraine. "Jean Louis Profile—Films in Bold Air on TCM." *TCM.com*. n.d. http://www.tcm.com/this-month/article/133187%7C0/Jean-Louis-Profile.html (accessed February 24, 2013).

Logan, Joshua. *Movie Stars, Real People, and Me*. New York: Dell Publishing Company, 1978.

Look. "Tribute to Marilyn from a Friend...Carl Sandburg." September 11, 1962.
"Lot of Original Telephone Messages Received by Joe DiMaggio from Marilyn Monroe, c. 1960-62." *HuntAuctions.com*. n.d. http://www.huntauctions.com/online/imageviewer.cfm?auction_num=27&lot_num=874&lot_qual= (accessed December 18, 2012).
The Los Angeles Times. "Housekeeper Discloses: Mystery Phone Call Received by Marilyn." August 7, 1962.
The Los Angeles Times. "Marilyn and DiMaggio on Their Way to Japan." January 30, 1954.
Luce, Clare Boothe. "The 'Love Goddess' Who Never Found Any Love." *Life*, August 7, 1964: 68-78.
Luce, Henry Robinson. "Success in the Sewer." *Time*, August 29, 1955.
Lundberg, Ferdin and Marynia L. Foot Farnham. *Modern Woman: The Lost Sex*. New York: Harper & Brothers, 1947.
Lyle, Jae. "Does This Picture Tell More Than It Should?" *Photoplay*, October 1960.
MacLaine, Shirley. *My Lucky Stars*. New York: Bantam Books, 1995.
Madison, Jennifer. "From Book-Reading to Norma Jeane to Hollywood's Blonde Bombshell: The Metamorphosis of Marilyn Monroe...As You've Never Seen Her Before." *Dailymail.com*. November 10, 2011. http://www.dailymail.co.uk/femail/article-2059643/Marilyn-Monroe-pictures-Norma-Jeane-Hollywoods-blonde-bombshell.html#ixzz2MJcEuBlW (accessed March 1, 2013).
Mahoney, Richard D. *Sons and Brothers: The Days of Jack and Bobby Kennedy*. New York: Arcade Publishing, 1999.
Mailer, Norman. "A Biography of Tom Kelley." *Durangodowntown.com*. n.d. http://www.durangodowntown.com/kelleystudio/tksr.htm (accessed January 6, 2013).
—. *Marilyn: A Biography*. New York: Warner Books, 1975.
—. *Marilyn: A Biography*. New York: Grosset & Dunlap, 1973.
Maker, Elizabeth and Bruce Weber. "Arthur Miller's Refuge Amid the Pines." *Nytimes.com*. February 20, 2005.

http://www.nytimes.com/2005/02/20/nyregion/thecity/20CONN.html?pagewanted=print&_r (accessed December 17, 2012).

Mallon, Gerald P. and Peg McCartt Hess. *Child Welfare for the Twenty-first Century: A Handbook of Practices, Policies, and Programs.* New York: Columbia University Press, 2005.

Malson, Laurence. *Some Like It Hot: The Official 50th Anniversary Companion.* New York: Collins Design, 2009.

Mankiewicz, Joseph L. *All About Eve.* New York: Random House, 1951.

—. "All About the Women in 'All About Eve'." *New York Magazine*, October 16, 1972.

Mann, William J. *Behind the Screen: How Gays and Lesbians Shaped Hollywood.* New York: Viking Press, 2001.

Manning, Dorothy. "The Woman and the Legend." *Photoplay*, October, 1956.

Mansfield, Stephanie. "Wild and Woody." *The Chicago Sun-Times*, July 5, 1996.

Marchese, John. "Channeling a Bombshell, One Jazzy Note at a Time." *The New York Times*, August 5, 2011.

Margolis, Jay. *Marilyn Monroe: A Case for Murder.* Bloomington: iUniverse, 2011.

Marilyn in Manhattan. Directed by John Parsons Peditto. 1998.

Marilyn Monroe. Directed by Art Lieberman. Performed by Mike Wallace. 1963.

"Marilyn Monroe and Arthur Miller at a Press Conference." *YouTube.com.* n.d. http://youtube.com/watch?v=b_P2FFIVV8A (accessed March 8, 2012).

"Marilyn Monroe—Announcing Separation from Joe DiMaggio." *YouTube.com*, n.d., http://www.youtube.com/watch?v=5_CdnJxqskQ (accessed June 1, 2012).

"Marilyn Monroe—Attorney Jerry Giesler Press Conference." *YouTube.com*, 1954. http://www.youtube.com/watch?v=rrjft31ogOw (accessed June 1, 2012).

Marilyn Monroe: Beyond the Legend. Directed by Gene Feldman. 1987.

"Marilyn Monroe—Cross-Examination By The Press June 21st 1956," *YouTube.com*, n.d., http://www.youtube.com/watch?v=YZMrcfHamVE (accessed June 23, 2013).

"Marilyn Monroe Died Here." *RealEstateStalker.blogspot.com.* July 14, 2010. http://realestalker.blogspot.com/2010/07/marilyn-monroe-died-here.html (accessed June 8, 2012).

"Marilyn Monroe—Filmmaker Interview: Gail Levin." Pbs.org. July 19, 2006. http://www.pbs.org/wnet/americanmasters/episodes/marilyn-monroe/filmmaker-interview-gail-levin/63/ (accessed December 30, 2012).

"Marilyn Monroe Given Italian Award for Best Foreign Actress 14-5-1959." *YouTube.com*. n.d. http://www.youtube.com/watch?v=T8_XRx1YXvE (accessed March 8, 2012).

"Marilyn Monroe—Hal Schaefer Interviewed [*E! Entertainment News*]", *YouTube.com*, n. d., http://www.youtube.com/watch?v=rzGJc3UOmaY (accessed June 1, 2012).

"Marilyn Monroe—Interviewed At Call Me Madam Premiere 1953 FOOTAGE," *YouTube.com*, n. d., http://www.youtube.com/watch?v=uPAd59uBETk (accessed June 1, 2012).

"Marilyn Monroe Interviewed at Idlewild Airport Circa 1954." *YouTube.com*, Accessed January 21, 2013.

"Marilyn Monroe Letter from Apartment Management Company." *Julienslive.com*. 2005. http://www.juliensauctions.com/auctions/2005/Marilyn-Monroe/results.html (accessed February 17, 2013).

Marilyn Monroe: Life After Death. Directed by Gordon Freedman. 1994.

"Marilyn Monroe Madison Square Garden Make-up Receipt." *Julienslive.com*. n.d. http://www.julienslive.com/view-auctions/catalog/id/66/lot/24814/ (accessed February 17, 2013).

"Marilyn Monroe Pays a Traffic Fine," *Youtube.com*, n.d., http://www.youtube.com/watch?v=II7eYqnvJmQ (accessed June 1, 2012).

"Marilyn Monroe Phone Book 1962." *LiveAuctionWorld.com.* May 20, 2010. http://www.liveauctionworld.com/Marilyn-Monroe-Phone-Book-1962_i9479626 (accessed February 10, 2013).

"Marilyn Monroe Rare Footage—Arriving In Hollywood To Film *Bus Stop* Feb 26, 1956," *Youtube.com*, n.d., http://www.youtube.com/watch?v=gk4HdrS8xOs (accessed June 22, 2013).

"Marilyn Monroe—Rare Radio Interview 1955 ½ [NBC, *Monitor*]," *Youtube.com*, n.d., http://www.youtube.com/watch?v=Ab0PvSbocs8&list=PL214A0C965504B52&index=1(accessed June 23, 2013).

"Marilyn Monroe Returns to Hollywood, Talks to Press. Speaks to the Press (Bus Stop)." *YouTube.com*, (accessed March 8, 2012).

"Marilyn Monroe—The Complete Rare Screen Test 1950." *YouTube.com.* http://www.youtube.com/watch?v=_FH2dzjH5Ek (accessed January 6, 2013).

Marilyn Monroe: The Final Days. Directed by Patty Ivins. 2001.

"Marilyn Monroe's Former Maid Who Wrote Tell All Book Dies of a Heart Attack at 86." *Dailymail.co.uk.* June 9, 2011. http://www.dailymail.co.uk/news/article-2001363/Marilyn-Monroes-maid-biographer-dies-heart-attack-aged-86.html (accessed June 8, 2012).

"Marilyn Monroe's Funeral." *Abbottandhast.com.* n.d. http://www.abbottandhast.com/mmfuneral.html (accessed March 17, 2013).

"Marilyn Monroe's Last Weekend Alive: New Details." *Gossipcenter.com.* August 2, 2010. http://gossipcenter.com/marilyn-monroe/marilyn%E2%80%99s-last-weekend-alive-new-details-395818 (accessed June 8, 2012).

Marilyn on Marilyn (BBC). Directed by Paul Kerr. 2001.

Marilyn's Man. Directed by Schani Krug. 2004.

Marilyn: Something's Got To Give. Directed by William Knoedelseder and Henry Schipper and Ken Turner. 1990.

Marilyn: The Last Interview (HBO). Directed by James A. Edgar. 1992.

Markel, Lester. "Marilyn Monroe Letter to Journalist (dated May 23, 1960)." *Juliensauctions.com*. 2005. http://www.juliensuactions.com/auctions/2005/Marilyn-Monroe/results.html (accessed January 20, 2013).

Marshall, David. *The DD Group: An Online Investigation into the Death of Marilyn Monroe*. Bloomington: iUniverse, 2005.

Martin, Pete. *Pete Martin Call On*. New York: Simon and Schuster, 1962.

—. "The New Marilyn Monroe." *Saturday Evening Post*, May 19, 1956.

—. "The New Marilyn Monroe." *Saturday Evening Post*, May 12, 1956.

—. "The New Marilyn Monroe." *Saturday Evening Post*, May 5, 1956.

—. *Will Acting Spoil Marilyn Monroe?* New York: Doubleday, 1956.

Mason, Jeffrey Daniel. *Stone Tower: The Political Theatre of Arthur Miller*. Ann Arbor, MI: University of Michigan Press, 2011.

Massee, Jordan. *Accepted Fables: An Autobiography*. Macon, GA: Henchard Press, LTD, 2005.

Mast, Gerald. *Howard Hawks, Storyteller*. New York: Oxford University Press, 1982.

McCann, Graham. *Marilyn Monroe*. New Brunswick: Rutgers University Press, 1988.

McCarthy, Todd. *Howard Hawks: The Grey Fox of Hollywood*. New York: Grove Press, 1997.

McDonald, Thomas. "Production Unit Treks to 'Biggest Little City' for Colorful Canvas." *The New York Times*, August 21, 1960: X7.

McDonough, Yona Zeldis. *All the Available Light: A Marilyn Monroe Reader*. New York: Touchstone, 2002.

McDougal, Dennis. *The Last Mogul: Lew Wasserman, MCA, and the Hidden History of Hollywood*. New York: Da Capo Press, 2001.

McGilligan, Patrick. *Backstory 3: Interviews with Screenwriters of the 60s*. Berkley, CA: University of California Press, 1997.

McKinley, Jesse. "A Boy's Film of a Day With Marilyn Monroe". *NyTimes.com.* February 18, 2003. http://www.nytimes.com/2003/02/18/arts/a-boy-s-film-of-a-day-with-marilyn-monroe.html (accessed June 8, 2012).

McKinney, Susan M. *An American Legend.* New York: New York Daily News Books, 1999.

McLellan, Dennis. "John Springer, 85; Press Agent to Illustrious Array of Entertainers." *The Los Angeles Times*, November 1, 2001.

Meadows, Audrey and Joseph A. Daley. *Love, Alice: My Life as a Honeymooner.* New York: Crown, 1994.

"Meeting Marilyn Monroe." *Connectionnewspapers.com.* August 16-20, 2012. http://connectionarchives.com/PDF/2012/081512/Springfield.pdf (accessed January 20, 2013).

Mekas, Jonas. "Movie Journal." *Village Voice*, February 9, 1961.

Mellen, Joan. *Marilyn Monroe.* New York: Pyramid, 1973.

Melson, Inez. "Letter to E. S. Goddard, dated November 23, 1953." *Cursumperficio.net*, n.d. http://www.cursumperficio.net/CD/Peop/Ent/Mels/Letter/Mels7.jpg.

—. "Marilyn Monroe Confidential." Unpublished manuscript. Christelle Montagner Collection, n.d.

Memories from the Sweet Sues: The All-Girl Band Featurette in Some Like It Hot/Collector's Edition DVD, MGM, 2001.

Mendini, Doublas A. "Goodbye, Norma Jean." *Entertainment*, July 31, 1998.

Merrill, Gary. *Bette, Rita, and the Rest of My Life.* Augusta, ME: Lance Tapley, 1988.

Meryman, Richard. "A Last Long Talk with a Lonely Girl." *Life*, August 17, 1962.

— "Marilyn Monroe Lets Her Hair Down About Being Famous: 'Fame My Go By and So Long, I've Had You'...An Interview." *Life*, August 3, 1962.

— "TV Film Uncovers Rare Photos of Marilyn Monroe: Behind the Myth the Face of Norma Jean." *Life*, November 4, 1966.

Meyers, Jeffrey. "Marilyn and the Literati." *Michigan Quarterly Review.* n.d. http://quod.lib.umich.edu/cgi/t/text/text-idx?cc=mqr;c=mqr;c=mqrarchive;idno=act2080.0047.102;rgn=main;view=text;xc=1;g=mqrg (accessed June 3, 2012).

Meyes, Jeffrey. *The Genius and the Goddess: Arthur Miller and Marilyn Monroe.* Champaign: University of Illinois Press, 2010.

The Miami News, "Landlady's Error Put Marilyn in A Bed in Physician's Apartment." October 17, 1954.

Michaels, Evan. "What Was Marilyn Monroe Doing at 685 Third Avenue?" *Photoplay*, August 1959.

The Mike Wallace Interview, "Elsa Maxwell." Directed by Bob Eisenhardt. 2001.

The Mike Wallace Interview, "Frank Lloyd Wright". Directed by Bob Eisenhardt. 2001

Miles, Marvin. "Stars Turn Out for Hollywood's Welcome to Russian Chieftan." *The Los Angeles Times*, September 20, 1959.

Miller, Arthur. *After the Fall.* New York: Viking, 1964.

—. *The Crucible*. New York: Viking, 1953.

—. "Letter from Arthur Miller to George Cukor dated April 30, 1960." *Bonhams.com*. April 20, 2011. http://www.bonhams.com/auctions/19377/lot/92/ (accessed February 21, 2013).

—. "My Wife Marilyn: Playwright Pays Affectionate Tribute to Her Feat." *Life*, December 22, 1958: 137.

—. "With Respect For Her Agony—But With Love." *Life*, February 7, 1964.

—. "Please Don't Kill Anything." *Redbook*, October 1961.

—. Miller, Arthur. *Timebends: A Life.* New York: Grove Press, 1987.

Miller, Douglas T. and Maria Nowak. *The Fifties: The Way We Really Were.* Garden City: Doubleday & Company, 1977.

Miller, Isidore. "Marilyn Monroe Letters from Isidor Miller (February 8, 1962)." *Julientsauctions.com*. 2005. http://juliensliveauctions.com/auctions/2005/Marilyn-Monroe/results.html (accessed January 20, 2013).

Miller, Merle. "The Wife Who Works." *Esquire*, April 1954.

Mills, Bart. *Marilyn: On Location.* London: Pan Books, LTD, 1990.

Milton H. Greene Archives, Inc., Plaintiff-Appellee v. Marilyn Monroe LLC, A Delaware Limited Liability Company; Anna Strasberg, an individual, Defendants-Appellants, and CMG Worldwide Inc., an Indiana Corporation, United States Court of Appeals for the Ninth Circuit, opinion by Circuit Judge Wardlaw, August 30, 2012.

The Milwaukee Journal. "A Nervous Marilyn Meet Neighbor, Queen Elizabeth." October 30, 1956.

Miracle, Berniece and Mona Rae Miracle. *My Sister Marilyn: A Memoir.* Chapel Hill: Algonquin Books, 1994. www.MonaRaeMiracle.com

—. *My Sister Marilyn: A Memoir.* Bloomington, IN: iUniverse, 2013. www.MonaRaeMiracle.com

"The Misfits," *FilmFacts*, February 17, 1961.

"The Misfits," *Variety*, February 1, 1961.

Monroe, Marilyn. "18-Year-Old Marilyn Monroe Amazing Autograph Letter Signed." *Profilesinhistory.com.* December 16, 2011. http://bid.profilesinhistory.com/18-year-old-Marilyn-Monroe-amazing-autograph-letter-signed_i11537108 (accessed February 13, 2013).

—. "1960 Marilyn Monroe Signed Letter." *Robert Edwards Auctions.* 2004. http://www.robertedwardauctions.com/auction/2004/785.html (accessed February 13, 2013).

—. "Failure Was My Spur." *Filmland*, January 1953.

—. "How I Stay in Shape." *Pageant*, September 1952.

—. "I Want Women To Like Me." *Photoplay*, November, 1952.

—. "Important March 1, 1954 Marilyn Monroe Autographed Handwritten Letter As Sent to Joe DiMaggio." *HuntAuctions.com*, n.d., http://www.huntauctions.com/online/imageviewer.cfm?auction_num=27&lot_num=866&lot_qual= (accessed January 1, 2012).

—. "Letter from Marilyn Monroe to Marlon Brando undated." *Bonhams.com.* December 17, 2006. http://www.bonhams.com/auctions/14034/lot/1000/ (accessed February 17, 2013).

—. "Letter from Norma Jeane Dougherty to Berniece Miracle dated June 4, 1945." *Everlasting-Star.net.* Apri 17, 2011. http://blog.everlasting-star.net/2011/04/ (accessed February 13, 2013).

—. "Letter from Norma Jeane Dougherty to Grace Goddard dated September 14, 1942." *Bonhams.com.* April 20, 2011. bonhams.com/auctions/19377/lot/521/

(accessed February 13, 2013).
—. Letter to Dr. Greenson, in Shaun Usher, "Men Are Climbing to the Moon But They Don't Seem Interested in the Beating Human Heart," *Lettersofnote.com*, January 28, 2011. http://www.lettersofnote.com/2011/01/men-are-climbing-to-moon-but-they-dont.html (accessed June 1, 2012).
—. "Letter Written by Marilyn Monroe." *Divine Marilyn Blog.* n.d. http://divinemarilyn.canalblog.com/archives/2011/11/20/22741 275.html (accessed February 12, 2013).
—. "Letters to the Editor Column." *Redbook*, July 1952.
—. "Marilyn Monroe Letter to Edwin Goddard." *Julienslive.com.* n.d. http://www.julienslive.com/view-auctions/catalog/id/55/lot/18223/ (accessed January 20, 2013).
—. "Marilyn Monroe Letter to Her Half Sister." *Juliensauctions.com.* 2005. http://www.juliensauctions.com/auctions/2005/Marilyn-Monroe/results.html (accessed January 20, 2013).
—. "Marilyn Monroe Western Union Telegram (November 26, 1958)." *Juliensauctions.com.* 2005. http://www.juliensauctions.com/auctions/2005/Marilyn-Monroe/results.html (accessed January 20, 2013).
—. "Marilyn Monroe/Norma Jeane Handwritten Letter (dated June 4, 1945)." *Julienslive.com.* n.d. http://www.julienslive.com/view-auctions/catalog/id/36/lot/11599/ (accessed February 13, 2013).
—. "Note from Marilyn Monroe to Joe DiMaggio undated." *Bonhams.com.* December 21, 2008. http://www.bonhams.com/auctions/16151/lot/1009/ (accessed February 24, 2013).
—. "How I Stay in Shape." *Pageant*, September 1952.
—. "Restore Paper, Conservation by J. Franklin Mowery." *Restorepaper.com.* n.d. http://www.restorepaper.com/services.stain-reduction/ (accessed June 12, 2012).
—. "World's Premiere Auctions, Lot 68: Marilyn Monroe Handwritten Signed Note to Her Niece on 'Mrs. Arthur Miller' Stationery." Invaluable.com, July 28, 2013. http//www.invaluable.com/auction-lot/Marilyn-monroe-hand-

written-signed-note-to-her-nie-68-c-f27b813bbf (accessed August 30, 2013)

Monroe, Marilyn and Bernard Comment (editor) and Stanley Buchthal (narrator). *Fragments, Poems, Intimate Notes, Letters.* New York: Farrar, Straus & Giroux, 2010.

Monroe, Marilyn with Ben Hecht and foreward by Joshua Greene. *My Story: Illustrated Edition.* New York: Taylor Trade, 2006.

Montagner, Christelle. *Cursum Perficio...My Journey Ends Here.* n.d. http://www.cursum.perficio.net/IndexA.html (accessed June 3, 2013).

Moore, John. "Arthur Miller: 1915-2005: He'll Be Remembered as America's Great Moralist." *DenverPost.com.* February 21, 2005. http://www.denverpost.com/naccio/ci_14998567 (accessed March 1, 2013).

Morgan, Michelle. *Marilyn Monroe: Private and Undisclosed.* New York: Carroll & Graf, 2007.

Morley, Sheridan. *John Gielgud: The Authorized Biography.* New York: Simon & Schuster, 2002.

Mosby, Aline. "Part in 'Karamasov' Marilyn Pined For." *Del Rio News Herald,* August 6, 1957: 3.

—. "'They're Just Jealous of Miss Monroe' Says Betty Grable." *Los Angeles Daily News,* March 16, 1953.

—. "Marilyn Monroe Admits She's Nude Blonde of Calendar." *Los Angeles Express,* March 13, 1952.

Mosley, Leonard. *Zanuck: The Rise and Fall of Hollywood's Last Tycoon.* New York: McGraw-Hill, 1984.

Muir, Dorothy. "The Real Marilyn Monroe at 13..." *The National Tattler,* October 7, 1973.

Muir, Florabel. "Eight to Share in MM's Estate." *New York Daily News,* August 11, 1962.

—. "Expect an Uninvited Mob at Funeral Today." *The New York Times,* August 8, 1962.

—. "Final Verdict on Finale: Probable Suicide." *New York Daily News,* August 18, 1962.

—. "Florabel Muir Reporting ." *Los Angeles Mirror,* February 10, 1953.

—. "Expect an Uninvited Mob at Funeral Today." *The New York* Times, August 8, 1962.

—. "Marilyn is Free; Love Caught Cold from Joe." *The New York Daily News*, October 28, 1954.

Murphey, Brenda. *Congressional Theatre: Dramatizing McCarthyism on Stage, Film, and Televisioin.* Cambridge: Cambridge Univeristy Press, 1999.

Murray, Eunice. *Marilyn: The Last Months.* New York: Pyramid, 1975.

Nash, Alanna. *Baby, Let's Play House: Elvis Presley and the Women Who Loved Him.* New York: It Books/Harpercollins, 2010.

Nasser, Julie. "Marilyn's Amagansett." *Hampton Style.* August 1, 2008. http://danshamptons.com/content/hamptonstyle/2008/aug_1/03.html (accessed June 10, 2010).

Nelson, Hal. "Looking It Over with Hal Nelson—Before a Star Was Born." *Rockford Morning Star*, n.d.

Neugebauer, William. "From Me to Marilyn/$50 Roses Are Anonymous." *New York Daily News*, August 8, 1962.

The New York Daily News. "Joe and Marilyn Spend First Night in $4 Motel." January 16, 1954.

The New York Daily News. "Joe to Marilyn at Rites: 'I Love You'." August 9, 1962.

The New York Daily News. "Marilyn Found Dead; Pill Bottle Near Bed." August 6, 1962.

The New York Daily News. "MM on Death Night." August 9, 1962.

The New York Daily News. "Seek Mexican in MM Mystery Call." August 8, 1962.

The New York Daily News. "Was It Romance, or Just Business?" August 8, 1962.

The New York Daily News. "Lawford: I Phoned MM on Death Nite." August 8, 1962.

The New York Daily News. "A Shaken DiMaggio Flies to Hollywood." August 6, 1962.

The New York Daily News. "Bolanos Says Last Good-Bye with Flowers." August 18, 1962.

The New York Times. "Actress Loses Baby." August 3, 1957: 9.

The New York Times. "Brilliant Stardom and Personal Tragedy Punctuated the Life of Marilyn Monroe." August 6, 1962.

The New York Times. "Dean Martin Quits Movie Over Monroe Dismissal." June 10, 1962: 56.

The New York Times. "DiMaggio is Divorced." October 28, 1954: 46.

The New York Times. "Fans Cite Film Stars." March 7, 1962: 28.

The New York Times. "First Scene Put Her in Limelight." August 6, 1962.

The New York Times. "Fox, Irked Over Film Delays, May Sue Marilyn Monroe." June 7, 1962: 30.

The New York Times. "Marilyn Monroe Cited." June 28, 1958: 14.

The New York Times. "Marilyn Monroe Dead, Pills Near." August 6, 1962.

The New York Times. "Marilyn Monroe Faces Surgery." November 6, 1954.

The New York Times. "Marilyn Monroe Fund Starts." June 1, 1963.

The New York Times. "Marilyn Monroe Has Operation." November 9, 1954: 30.

The New York Times. "Marilyn Monroe Here." November 22, 1956.

The New York Times. "Marilyn Monroe in Hospital." May 25, 1961.

The New York Times. "Marilyn Monroe in Hospital." August 2, 1957: 11.

The New York Times. "Marilyn Monroe in Hospital." April 13, 1956.

The New York Times. "Marilyn Monroe in Hospital." February 9, 1961: 25.

The New York Times. "Marilyn Monroe Meets a Neighbor—the Queen." October 30, 1956: 43.

The New York Times. "Marilyn Monroe Resting Well." July 1, 1961: 8.

The New York Times. "Marilyn Monroe Sued." July 12, 1957: 17.

The New York Times. "Marilyn Monroe Sues." January 22, 1961: 86.

The New York Times. "Marilyn Monroe to Divorce DiMaggio." October 5, 1954: 23.

The New York Times. "Marilyn Monroe Undergoes Surgery." June 30, 1961: 33.

The New York Times. "Marilyn Monroe, Arthur Miller Married in White Plains." June 30, 1956: 19.

The New York Times. "Marilyn Monroe's Hearing Set." October 21, 1954: 30.

The New York Times. "Marilyn Monroe's Million: Nothing After Taxes." June 22, 1965: 24.

The New York Times. "Marilyn Monroe's Mother and Halfsister Get Bequest." August 10, 1962: 9.

The New York Times. "Miller Files Appeal." February 22, 1958: 6.

The New York Times. "Millers Remarried." July 3, 1956: 16.

The New York Times. "Movie Premiere to Aid Milk Fund." May 26, 1957.

The New York Times. "New Role for Marilyn." January 8, 1955: 10.

The New York Times. "Niagara Falls Vies with Marilyn Monroe." January 22 1953.

The New York Times. "Olivier and Monroe to Co-star in Film." February 10, 1956: 16.

The New York Times. "Paula Strasberg, Drama Coach, Dies." May 1, 1966: 87.

The New York Times. "Simple Rite Set for Miss Monroe." August 8, 1962.

The New York Times."Star Scores Associate." April 12, 1957: 22.

The New York Times. "Tragic Beauty: Marilyn Monroe." November 12, 1960: 14.

The New York Times. "Tribute Amazes Unknown Singer." August 6, 1963.

New York World-Telegram. "MM: Accident of Suicide? Body of Star Lies Unclaimed." August 6, 1962.

New York World-Telegram. "Stars Mourn the Loss of a Friend and a Great Talent." August 6, 1962.

Newcastle, Jack. "George Axelrod and the Great American Sex Farce." *The cad.net.* n.d. http://the cad.net/Theatre/george-axelrod.html (accessed January 21, 2013).

Newman, Robert P. *The Cold War Romance of Lillian Hellman and Joe Melby.* Chapel Hill, NC: University of North Caroline Press, 1989.

Newsweek. "I Love You...I Love You..." August 20, 1962.

Nicholson, Stuart. *Ella Fitzgerald: A Biography of the First Lady of Jazz.* New York: Macmillian Publishing Company, 1993.

Nickens, Christopher and George Zeno. *Marilyn in Fashion: The Enduring Influence of Marilyn Monroe.* Philadelphia: Running Press, 2012.

Nixon, Marnie with Stephen Cole. *I Could Have Sung All Night.* New York: Billboard Books, 2006.

Noguchi, Thomas T. with Joseph DiMona. *Coroner to the Stars.* New York: Simon & Schuster, 1983.

Nostalgic Look Back in Some Like It Hot/Collector's Edition DVD, MGM, 2001.

O'Brien, Michael. "The Exner File—Judith Campbell Exner, John F. Kennedy's Mistress WashingtonMonthly)." *Findarticles.com.* December 1999 http://findarticles.com/p/articles/mi_m1316/is_12_31/ai_58170292/ (accessed August 5, 2012).

Odets, Clifford. *Golden Boy.* New York: Dramatists Play Services, Inc., 1964.

O'Hagan, Andrew. *The Life and Opinions of Maf the Dog, and of His Friend Marilyn Monroe.* Boston: Houghton Mifflin Harcourt, 2010.

O'Hara, Maureen with John Nicoletti. *'Tis Herself a Memoir.* New York: Simon & Schuster, 2004.

"Old Friend Releases Marilyn Monroe Keepsakes." *ABC Good Morning America.* July 17, 2006. http://abcnews.com/GMA/Entertainment/story?id=220193&page=1 (accessed November 25, 2012).

Oliver, Amy. "Why Wallis Hated Marilyn and How the Duke of Windsor Was a 'Sad, Small, Pathetic Figure'." *MailOnline.com.* March 12, 2012. http://www.dailymail.co.uk/femailarticle2113756/Why-Wallis-Simpson-hated-Marilyn-Monroe-revealed-Charles-Picks-memoirs.html (accessed March 17, 2013).

Olivier, Laurence. *Confessions of an Actor.* New York: Simon & Schuster, 1982.

—. *On Acting.* New York: Simon & Schuster, 1987.

O'Malley, Sheila. "Don't Bother to Knock." *The Sheila Variations.* June 2, 2010. http://www.sheilaomalley.com/?p=10125 (accessed July 4, 2012).

O'Neill, Eugene. *Anna Christie.* Stilwell, KS: Digireads.com Publishing, 2005.

Oppenheimer, John. *Marilyn Lives!* New York: Delilah Books, 1981.

Ortega, Tony. "Jonas Mekas Loves Marilyn Monroe." *Village Voice Blogs.* November 14, 2008.

http://blogs.villagevoice.com/runninscared/2008/11/clip_job_mekas.ph (accessed August 5, 2011).

Ortiz, Johnny. *My Life Among the Icons: A Fascinating Memoir of a Raconteur Whose Life Intersected with the Giants of Sports and the Glamour of Hollywood*. Bloomington, IN: AuthorHouse, 2001.

Oser, Alan S. "Spotlight on Walter Bernstein." *Eldercountry.com.* April 2010. http://www.eldercountry.com/spotlight/apr_010.shtml (accessed June 8, 2012).

Ottawa Citizen. "Marilyn Monroe Loses Baby After 106-Mile Trip to Hospital." August 2, 1957.

Packard, Eleanor. "Vatican Voices Pity for Marilyn." *Periodical untitled*, August 6, 1962.

Paris, Barry. *Audrey Hepburn*. New York: Berkley Publishing, 2002.

Parker, Ray and Roby Heard. "What Made Marilyn and Joe Bust Up?" *Los Angeles Mirror*, October 5, 1954.

Parkinson-Morgan, Kate. "Fans Honor Marilyn Monroe at Westwood Village Memorial Park: Hundreds Turn Out to Celebrate the Life of the Late Hollywood Starlet at Her Fiftieth Anniversary Memorial Service." *Brentwood Patch*. August 6, 2012. http://brentwoodpatch.com/articles/marilyn-remembered-at-westwood-memorial#photo-10957324 (accessed November 18, 2012).

Parsons, Louella. "In Hollywood with Louella Parsons: Marilyn Monroe Gets First Starring Role in Cold Shoulder." *Desert News*, July 19, 1950.

—. "Marilyn Monroe's Life As a Divorcee." *Modern Screen*, October 1961.

Parton, Margaret. "A Revealing Last Interview with Marilyn Monroe." *Look*, February 19, 1979.

Patterson, Neal. "3 Stars Pity Lonely Marilyn." *New York Daily News*, date unknown.

Payn, Graham (editor). *The Noel Coward Diaries*. New York: Little, Brown & Company, 1982.

Pearson, Drew. "Merman, Monroe Mull Over Male/Female Fashions." *The Tuscaloosa News*, August 30, 1954.

People. "Do A Dead Man's Files Finally End Marilyn Monroe's Search for Her Dad?" *People*, March 9, 1981.

People. "Golden Girl: An Auction of Marilyn Monroe's Possessions Reveals an Achingly Human Story Behind a Glamorous Facade." *People*, August 16, 1999.

Pepitone, Lena with William Stadiem. *Marilyn Monroe Confidential.* New York: Simon & Schuster, 1979.

Person To Person (CBS). Directed by Don Hewitt. Performed by Edward R. Murrow. April 8, 1955.

Phillips, David P. and Lundie L. Carstensen and Daniel Paight. "Effects of Mass Media News Stories on Suicide with New Evidence on Story Content." In *Suicide Among Youth: Perspectives on Risk and Prevention*, by Cynthia Pfeiffer (editor). Washington, DC: American Psychiatric Press, 1989.

Phillips, Gene D. *Some Like It Wilder: The Life and Controversial Films of Billy Wilder.* Lexington: The University Press of Kentucky, 2010.

Photoplay. "Behind the Scenes with 'Some Like It Hot'." n.d.

Plant, Tony. "How Did Marilyn Monroe Die?" *Southern Wings Aircraft.* n.d. http://Southernwingsaircraft.com/howmarilyndied.htm; (accessed November 12, 2012).

—. *SouthernWingAircraft*.com. n.d. http://southernwingsaircraft.com/howmarilyndied.html (accessed June 8, 2012).

Plath, Sylvia and Karen V. Kukil (editor). *The Unabridged Journals of Sylvia Plath.* New York: Anchor Books, 2000.

Player, Ernie. "You Don't Really Know Monroe, Says Clifton Webb." *Picturegoer*, June 11, 1955.

Podell, Janet. *Speeches of the American Presidents.* New York: H. W. Wilson, Company, 1988.

Ponder, Jon. "Wrong Door Raid: The Celebrity Scandal That Irked Sinatra, Made a Fool of

DiMaggio—All at Marilyn Monroe's Expense." *Sunsetstrip.com.* December 7, 2010. http://www.sunsetstrip.com-2010/12/07/wrong-door-raid/ (accessed January 20, 2013).

Porter, Valerie. "Psychic Medium Kenny Kingston Reveals 'The Marilyn Monroe I Knew'." *Voices.yahoo.com*. November 28, 2011. http://voices.yahoo.com/psychic-medium-kennykingston-reveals-marilyn-10490545.html (accessed December 20, 2012).

Postrel, Virginia. "Plump? No, Teeny." *The St. Petersburg Times*, June 27, 2011.

Potash, James B. and O. Joseph Bienvenu. "Neuropsychiatric Disorders: Shared Genetics of Bipolar Disorder and Schizophrenia." *Nature Reviews Neurology*, 5, June 2009: 299-300.

Preston, John. "Dr. Thomas Noguchi: LA Coroner Confidential." *Telegraph.co.uk*. September 10, 2009. http://www.telegraph.co.uk/culture/film/612682/Dr-Thomas- Noguchi-LA-coroner-confidential.html (accessed June 8, 2012).

Prideaux, Tom. "Marilyn's Ghost Takes the Stage: A Desperate Search by a Troubled Hero." *Life*, February 7, 1964.

Pryor, Thomas M. "Fox to Film Life of Jean Harlow." *The New York Times*, June 4 , 1956: 25.

—. "Marilyn Monroe Cast in 'Can-Can'." *The New York Times*, April 22, 1958.

—. "Marilyn Monroe Gets Comedy Role." *The New York Times*, April 25, 1958: 30.

—. "Marilyn Monroe Gets Film Offer." *The New York Times*, May 5, 1956: 13.

—. "Marilyn Monroe Wins Pact Fight." *The New York Times*, January 5, 1956: 27.

—. "Rita Hayworth Signs Film Pact." *The New York Times*, February 20, 1956.

—. "Warners to Back Movie By Monroe." *The New York Times*, March 2, 1956: 17.

Quirk, Lawrence J. and William Schoell. *Joan Crawford: The Essential Biography.* Lexington: University of Kentucky Press, 2002.

Quirk, Lawrence J. *Fasten Your Seat Belts: The Passionate Life of Bette Davis.* New York: William Morrow, 1987.

QuoteInvestigator.com. October 4, 2010. http://quoteinvestigator.com/2010/10/04/kissing-marilyn/ (accessed June 8, 2012).

Rand, Ayn. "Through Your Most Grievous Fault." In *The Voice of Reason: Essays in Objectivist Thought*, by Ayn Rand (editor) and Leonard Peikoff and Peter Schwartz. New York: New America Library, 1989.

Randall, Tony. "Marilyn Monroe Telegram from Tony Randall." *Julienslive.com.* n.d. http://www.julienslive.com/view-auctions/catalog/id/55/lot/18187/ (accessed February 21, 2013).

"Receipt from Frank's Nursery dated August 1, 1962." *Bonhams.com.* June 14, 2009. http://www.bonhams.com/auctions/17108/lot/6009/ (accessed February 17, 2013).

"Receipt from Lilly Dache Beauty Salon dated May 25, 1962." *Bonhams.com.* n.d. http://m.bonhams.com/auctions/17108/lot/6002/ (accessed February 17, 2013).

"Receipts from Carey Cadillac Renting Company of Californnia." *Bonhams.com.* June 16, 2008. http://www.bonhams.com/auctions/16091/lot/3015/ (accessed February 24, 2013).

Red Bank Register. "Had Everything—But Happiness." August 6, 1962.

Red Bank Register. "Suicide or Accident? Marilyn Monroe's Death Probed." August 6, 1962.

Reilly, Maureen E. Lynn. *Hollywood Costume Design by Travilla.* Atglen, PA: Schiffer Publishing, 2003.

Reise, Randall and Neal Hitchens. *The Unabriged Marilyn: Her Life from A to Z.* New York: Congdon & Weed, 1987.

"Remember Marilyn." *Life*, August 17, 1962, p. 63-71.

"Remember Marilyn." *Life*, September 8, 1972.

"Remembering Hank Jones, 'The Dean of Jazz Pianists'." *NPR.org.* May 17, 2010. http://www.npr.org/templates/story/story.php?storyId=126884916 (accessed February 24, 2013).

Remembering Marilyn. Directed by Andrew Solt. Performed by Lee Remick. 1988.

Reno Gazette. "'Ostracize Them': Lawmaker Denounces Liz, Burton." May 23, 1962.

Reuters. "'Marilyn Monroe: The Visit' Photographs with Carl Sandburg Taken by Len Steckler in 1961 for Sale." *NyDailyNews.com.* February 7, 2010. http://www.nydailynews.com/entertainment/gossip/marilyn-monroe-visit-photographs-carl-sandburg-len-steckler-1961-sale-article-1.198507#ixzz2LB4Qmf1C (accessed February 17, 2013).

Reuters.com. "Marilyn Monroe Crypt Auction Fails Again." November 2, 2009. http://www.reuters.com/article/2009/11/02/us-monroe-idUSTRE5A10PP20091102 (accessed June 15, 2012).

Reynolds, Debbie and David Patrick Columbia. *Debbie: My Life.* New York: William Morrow and Company, 1988.

Ricci, Michael Conway and Mark. *The Films of Marilyn Monroe.* New York: The Citadel Press, 1990.

—. *The Films of Marilyn Monroe.* Secaucus: Citadel, 1964.

Richards, Sylvie F. F. "Marilyn Monroe's Will and the Right of Publicity: Residency Matters Sunday." *Richardsesq.wordpress.com.* June 27, 2010. http://richardseq.wordpress.com/2010/06/27/marilyn-monroes-will-of-publicity-residency-matters/ (accessed March 17, 2013).

"Robert Chamption Auction." *Willishenry.com.* October 29, 2005. http://www.willishenry.com/auctions/05/autograth%20session %20two%2005.autographs documents_auction.htm (accessed June 3, 2012).

Roberts, Ralph. *Mimosa.* Unpublished manuscript. Ralph Roberts Collection, n.d.

—. "Ralph Roberts Manuscript." *RalphRoberts.com.* n.d. http://www.ralphroberts.com/manuscriptpage1.htm (accessed June 8, 2012).

Rocha, Guy. "Myth #21—Marilyn Monroe: Mystery and Myth." *Nevada State Library and Archives.* September 1997. http://snla.nevadaculture.org/index.php?option=com-content task=view&id=693&Itemid=418 (accessed June 8, 2012).

Rollyson, Carl. *Marilyn Monroe: A Life of the Actress.* Cambridge, MA: DaCapo Press, 1993.

Rollyson, Carl. "More Than a Popcorn Venus: Contemporary Women Reshape the Myth of Marilyn Monroe (Journal of American Culture, Fall 1987)." *Onilnelibrary.wiley.com.* June 7, 2004. http://onlinelibrary.wiley.com/doi/10.1111.j.1542-734X.1987_19.x/abstract (accessed December 3, 2011).

Rose, Frank. *The Agency: William Morris and the Hidden History of Show Business.* New York: HarperCollins, 1996.

Ross, Sid. "How Marilyn Monroe Sees Herself." *Parade Magazine*, October 12, 1952.

Rosten, Marjorie. *Popcorn Venus: Women, Movies and the American Dream.* New York: Avon Books, 1974.

Rosten, Norman. *Marilyn: An Untold Story.* New York: New American Library/Signet, 1973.

Rudd, Jonah. "Now That I Am 35." *The London Daily Mail*, June 5, 1961.

Rudnick, Paul. "The Blonde Marilyn Monroe." *Time.com.* June 14, 1999.
http://www.time.com/time/magazine/article/0,9171,991257,00.html#ixzzib0gBjHjc (accessed February 2, 2013).

Russell, Diana E. H. *The Secret Trauma: Incest in the Lives of Girls and Women.* New York: Basic Books, 1986.

Russell, Jane. *Jane Russell: My Path & My Detours.* New York: Franklin Watts, 1985.

Rutledge, Leigh W. *The Gay Fireside Companion.* New York: Alyson Publications, 1989.

Ryan, Pat. "Marilyn's Manhattan, Both Public and Private." *NyTimes.com.* January 7, 2011.
http://query.nytimes.com/gst/fullpage.html?res9E03E5D6133AF934A35752C0A9679D8D63&&scpmarilyn%20monroe%20prodctions&st=cse (accessed March 17, 2013).

Sanders, George. *Memories of a Professional Cad: The Autobiography of George Sanders.* London: G. P. Putnam's Sons, 1960.

Sandiego-online.com, "Memories of Marilyn". June 21, 1998. Sandiego-online.com/retro/marretr4.stm (accessed June 8, 2012).

Sarasota-Herald Tribune. "Marilyn Monroe Will Seek Divorce from Joe DiMaggio." October 5, 1954.

Schiller, Lawrence. *Marilyn & Me: A Photographer's Memories.* New York: Nan A. Talese/Doubleday, 2012.

—. "A Splash of Marilyn." *Vanity Fair*, June 2012.

Schlesinger, Arthur M., Jr. *Robert Kennedy and His Times.* New York: First Mariner Books/Houghton Mifflin Company, 2002.

—. *Robert Kennedy and His Times.* Boston: Houghton Mifflin, 1978.

Schneider, Michel. *Marilyn's Last Sessions.* Edinburg: Canongate Books, LTD, 2011.

Schreiber, Flora Rheta. "Rememberance of Marilyn." *Good Housekeeping*, January 1963: 30-32, 135.
Schulman, Irving. *Harlow: An Intimate Biography.* Lincoln, NE: iUniverse, 2000.
Schumach, Murray. "Fox Dimisses Marilyn Monroe and Files a Suit for $500,000." *The New York Times,* June 9, 1962: 19.
—. "Hollywood Amour." *The New York Times,* February 14, 1960: X7.
—. "Hollywood 'Darling'." *The New York Times,* June 9, 1962: 121.
—. "Hollywood Encore." *The New York Times,* June 3, 1962: 125.
—. "Hollywood Loss." *The New York Times,* August 12, 1962: X7.
—. "Illness of Star Disrupts Filming." *The New York Times,* August 30, 1960: 24.
—. "Marilyn Monroe Funeral Is Held in Hollywood." *The New York Times,* August 9, 1962: 22.
—. "Marilyn Monroe's Death Is Called Suicide." *The New York Times,* August 18, 1962: 10.
—. "Simone Signoret Discusses Film." *The New York Times,* March 25, 1960.
Schwartz, Benjamin. "Becoming Cary Grant." *Theatlantic.com.* January-February 2007. http://www.theatlantic.com/magazine/archive/2007/01/becoming-cary-grant/305548/ (accessed January 8, 2013).
Scott, Marion. "Secret Marilyn; Celebrity Snapper's Unseen Photos of the World's Most Famous Movie Star. (Scottish Daily Record & Sunday Mail)." *Thefreelibrary.com.* 2009. http://www.thefreelibrarycom/Secret+Marilyn%3B+CELEBRITY+SNAPPER'S++UNSEEN+PHOTOS+OF+THE+WORLD'S+MOST...-a0197614763 (accessed January 24, 2013).
Scott, Vernon. "Marilyn Celebrates Her Natal Day By Cavorting in Her Birthday Suit." *Los Angeles Herald-Examiner,* 1962.
—. "Marilyn Monroe: Memory Still Cherished By Millions of Fans." *Los Angeles Herald-Examiner,* July 16, 1972.
—. "Marilyn Monroe: A Quiet Legend." *Rocky Mountain News,* July 16, 1972.
"Screenlegends.com Presents: Photos of Marilyn Monroe by Victor Helou." *Screenlegends.com.* n.d. http://screenlegends.com/History.htm (accessed June 8, 2012).

Schumach, Murray. "Weakness Seen in Film Industry." *The New York Times*, June 8, 1962: 38.

Seaman, Barbara. *Lovely Me: The Life of Jacqueline Susann.* New York: Seven Stories Press, 1996.

Server, Lee. *Ava Gardner: Love Is Nothing*. New York: St. Martin's Press, 2007.

Shalit, Gene. *Great Hollywood Wit: A Glorious Cavalcade of Hollywood Wisecracks, Zingers, Japes, Quips, Slings, Jests, & Sass from the Stars.* New York: St. Martin's Press, 2002.

Sharbutt, Jay. "'20/20' Probe: ABC Reviews Kennedy-Monroe Story." *Articles.latimes.com.* October 7, 1985. http://articles.latimes.com/1985-10-17/entertainment/ca-16725_1_ abc_news (accessed June 8, 2012).

Shaw, Sam and Norman Rosten. *Marilyn Among Friends.* New York: Henry Holt and Company, 1987.

Shaw, Sam. *The Joy of Marilyn in the Camera Eye.* New York: St. Martin's Press, 1979.

Shaw, Stewart, with files from Bill Fortier. "Jasper Remembers Marilyn Monroe." *Edmonton.ctvnews.ca.* June 21, 2013. http://edmonton.ctvnews.ca/jasperremembers-marilyn-monroe1.1336637#xzz2XXczBc00 (accessed June 27, 2013)

Shearer, Lloyd. "How Much Time and Trouble is Marilyn Monroe Worth?" *Oakland Tribune*, December 7, 1958.

—. "Marilyn Monroe—Why Won't They Let Her Rest in Peace?" *Parade*, August 5, 1973.

Shevey, Sandra. *The Marilyn Scandal.* New York: William Morrow & Company, 1987.

Sider, Don. "Marilyn Mmmmmm Visits Us." *The St. Petersburg Times*, March 23, 1961.

Sigel, Robert. "Forever Marilyn Part 2: There's No Business Liek Show Business in Cinemascope!" *Blu-ray.com.* August 16, 2012. http:www.blu-ray.com/new/?id=9279 (accessed August 24, 2012).

"Significant Joe DiMaggio Journal with Handwritten Notes Regarding Marilyn Monroe, c. 1955." *HuntAuctions.com.* n.d. http://www.huntauctions.com/online/imageviewer.cfm?auction_num=27&lot_num=880&lot_qual= (accessed June 3, 2012).

Signoret, Simone. *Nostalgia Isn't What It Used to Be.* New York: Penguin, 1979.

Sikov, Ed. *On Sunset Boulevard: The Life and Times of Billy Wilder.* New York: Hyperion, 1998.

Silbert, M. D. and A. M. Pines. "Sexual Child Abuse as an Antecedent to Prostitution." *Child Abuse and Neglect, 5,* 1981: 407-411.

Silverman, Stephen M. *The Fox That Got Away: The Last Days of the Zanuck Dynasty at Twentieth Century-Fox.* Secaucus: Lyle Stuart, 1988.

Sitell, William. "Between the Lines (Telegraph Magazine, March 2011)." *Sitwellsociety.com.* March 2011. http://sitwellsociety.com/documents/WilliamSitwellBETWEEN THELINES.pdf (accessed June 8, 2012).

Sitwell, Edith. *Taken Care Of: An Autobiography.* London: Bloomsbury Reader, 2011.

Skolsky, Sidney. *Don't Get Me Wrong—I Love Hollywood.* New York: Putnam's, 1975.

Slatzer, Robert F. *The Life and Curious Death of Marilyn Monroe.* Los Angeles: Pinnacle Books, 1977.

—. *The Marilyn Files.* New York: SPI Books/Shapolsky Press, 1992.

Slatzer, Robert. "Voice of Broadway." *New York Journal American,* September 12, 1952.

Smith, David L. *Sitting Pretty: The Life and Times of Clifton Webb.* Jackson: University Press of Mississippi, 2011.

Smith, Kyle. "Frank Actress." *People.com.* February 8, 1999. http://www.people.com/people/archive/article/0,,20127526,00.html (accessed March 17, 2013).

—. "Frank Actress." *People*, February 8, 1999.

Smith, Liz. "The Exner Files." *Vanity Fair*, January 1997: 30, 32, 34, 37-40, 42-43.

Smith, Matthew. *Marilyn's Last Words: Her Secret Tapes and Mysterious Death.* New York: Carroll & Graf Publishers, 2003.

Soccer Star, Volume 5. "Sign Her Up!" June 15, 1957.

Soloff, P. H., K. G. Lynch, T. M. Kelly, K. M Malone, and J. J. Mann. "Characteristics of Suicide Attempts of Patients with Major Depressive Episode and Borderline Personality Disorder." *American Journal of Psychiatry*, 157, 2000: 601-608.

Spada, James and George Zeno. *Monroe: Her Life in Pictures.* New York: Doubleday, 1982.

Spartanburg Herald-Journal. "Marilyn Monroe Death Files Released." September 24, 1985.

Spender, Lady Natasha. "Lady Natasha Spender Remembers Edith Sitwell." *Telegraph.co.uk.* June 8, 2008. http://www.telegraph.co.uk/culture/donomigrate/3553964/Lady-Natasha-Spender-remembers-Edith-Sitwell.html (accessed December 16, 2012).

Speriglio, Milo. *Marilyn Monroe: Murder Cover-Up.* Van Nuys, CA: Seville, 1982.

—. *The Marilyn Conspiracy.* New York: Pocket Books, 1986.

Spoto, Donald. "Marilyn Monroe: The Nomadic Life of a Screen Legend." *Architectural Digest*, April 1994.

—. *Marilyn Monroe: The Biography.* New York: HarperPaperbacks, 1994.

—. *Marilyn Monroe: The Biography.* New York: HarperCollins, 1993.

St. Joseph Gazette. "Marilyn Gives $1000 to Help Needy Children." March 2, 1962.

Stagg, Sam. *Close Up on Sunset Boulevard: Billy Wilder, Norma Desmond, and the Dark Hollywood Dream.* New York: St. Martin's Press, 2002.

Staggs, Sam. *All About "All About Eve".* New York: St. Martin's Press, 2000.

Stapleton, Maureen and Jane Scovell. *One Hell of a Life: An Autobiography.* New York: Simon & Schuster, 1995.

Stebner, Beth. "My Day with Marilyn." *Dailymail.co.uk.* February 7, 2012. http://www.dailymail.co.uk/news/article-2097537/Marilyn-Monroe-pictures-effortless-glamour-hidden-drawer-50-YEARS.html (accessed January 6, 2013).

Steen, David. "Marilyn Inc." *Film Comment*, September/October 1982.

Stein, Sadie. "Some Like It Hot: For the Last Time: What Size Was Marilyn Monroe?" *Jezebel.com.* June 22, 2009. http:jezebel.com/5299793/for-the-last-time-what-was-marilyn-monroe (accessed June 8, 2012).

Steinam, Gloria. *Outrageous Acts and Everyday Rebellions.* New York: Open Road Publishing, 2012.

Steinam, Gloria with photographs by George Barris. *Marilyn: Norma Jeane.* New York: Henry Hold, 1986.

Stern, Bert. *The Last Sitting.* New York: William Morrow & Company, 1982.

Stillman, Deanne. "California Girl." *Buzz*, August 1997.

—. "'The Mistfits' at 50: Honoring the Horse and an Iconic Western." *Truthdig.com.* February 13, 2011 http://truthdig.com/report/item/the_misfits_at_50_honoring_the_horse_and_an_iconic_western_20110213/ (accessed June 8, 2012).

Strasberg, Susan. *Bittersweet.* New York: Signet/New American Library, 1981.

—. *Marilyn and Me: Sisters, Rivals, Friends.* New York: Warner books, 1992.

Stump, Al. "The Beautiful and the Dead...Hollywood's Unsolved Mysteries." *Los Angeles Herald-Examiner*, January 6, 1980.

Suddenly Last Summer. Directed by Joseph L. Mankiewicz. Columbia Pictures, 1959.

Sullivan, Michael John. *Presidential Passions: The Love Affairs of America's Presidents.* New York: SPI Books/Shapolsky Publishers, 1992.

Summer, Anthony. *Goddess: The Secret Lives of Marilyn Monroe.* New York: Macmillian, 1985.

Summers, Anthony. *Goddess: The Secret Lives of Marilyn Monroe.* New York: Open Road Media, 2012.

Tackery, Ted. "Emmedline Snively." *Los Angeles Herlald Examiner*, August 7, 1961.

Talese, Gay. "The Silent Season of a Hero." *Esquire*, July 1966.

—. *The Gay Talese Reader: Portraits and Encounters.* New York: Walker Publishing Company, 2003.

—. "12 Suicides Here Set a Day's Mark." *The New York Times*, August 14, 1962: 33.

Taraborrelli, J. Randy. *The Secret Life of Marilyn Monroe.* New York: Grand Central Publishing, 2009.

Taubman, Howard. "A Cheer for Controversy; While Discussion Rages, Miller's 'After the Fall' Remains Visible at the New Repertory Theater." *The New York Times*, February 2, 1964: X1.

Taylor, Rumsey. "The Seven Year Itch: The Title Credits." *Notcoming.com.* August 8, 2005. http://www.notcoming.com/saulbass/caps_7yearitch.php (accessed January 31, 2013).

Telegraph Sunday Magazine. "The Marilyn Industry." March 1, 1981.

"The Seven Year Itch." *Moviediva.com.* n.d. http://www.moviediva.com/MD_root/reviewpages/MDSevenYearItch.htm (accessed January 21, 2013).

The Springfield Union. "Weeping DiMaggio Kisses Marilyn in Final Farewell." August 9, 1962.

The St. Petersburg Times. "Suncoast: A Sun Gilds a Lily." March 31, 1961.

Thomas, Bob. "Bob Thomas Column." *Hollywood Citizen-News,* March 2, 1953.

—. "Maria Schell is a Marilyn Monroe Fan." *Lowell Sun*, June 17, 1957: 16.

—. "Marilyn Monroe Too Sexy—Joan Crawford Decalres." *Mansfield News Journal*, March 8, 1953.

—. "Singer Pat Boone Tells All: Well, Almost All." *Ocala Banner*, June 10, 2007.

—. "Pieces All Cling Together in Unhappy Actress' Death." *Spokane Daily Chronicle,* August 6, 1962.

—. "20 Years After Her Death, Marilyn's Magic Lives On." *The Chicago Times,* August 1, 1982.

—. "Maria Schell in Role Eyed By Marilyn." *The San Mateo Times,* June 17, 1957.

Thomas, Evan. *Robert Kennedy: His Life.* New York: Simon & Schuster, 2002.

Thomas, James. "Wilder's Winning Ways." *London Daily Express,* April 19, 1961.

Thompson, Greg. Gregthompson.com/mfb.php (accessed January 1, 2013).

Thompson, Howard. "Gable's Last Film Slated Here Feb. 1." *The New York Times,* December 31, 1960.

Thomson, David. "Baby Go Boom!" *Film Comment*, September/October 1982.

Thurman, Judith. *Isak Dineson: The Life of a Storyteller.* New York: St. Martin's Press, 1995.

Time. "California: The Smear." March 5, 1965.
Time. "Cinema: The Co-Stars." February 20, 1956.
Time. "Cinema: The New Pictures, Sep. 19, 1960." September 19, 1960.
Time. "Cinema: The Winner." January 16 1956.
Time. "Cinema: Who Could Resist?" January 30, 1956.
Time. "Fleur's Flair." September 12, 1949.
Time. "Hollywood: Marilyn, My Marilyn." May 31, 1963.
Time. "Hollywood: Monroe Doctrine." June 22, 1962.
Time. "Hollywood: Popsie & Poopsie." November 21, 1960.
Time. "Hollywood: Thrilled with Guilt." August 17, 1962.
Time. "Letters to the Editor." August 17, 1962.
Time. "The Administration: Big Splash at Hickory Hill." June 29, 1961.
Time. "The Only Blonde in the World." August 10 1962.
Time. "The Presidency: Happy Birthday." June 1, 1962.
Time. "The Press: Conquest." July 30, 1956 .
Times Talk (newsletter of The New York Times). "Babe in Boyland." 1959: 3.
Today Show (NBC). October 21, 1963.
Torre, Marie. "Marilyn Monroe." *New York Herald-Tribune TV and Radio Magazine,* week of August 14-20, 1955.
—. "Television and Radio News and Views." *Steubenville Herald Star,* June 9, 1961: 34.
—. "TV Production of 'Rain' Seems More Like a Drought." *The St. Petersburg Times,* June 7, 1961.
Towles, Dan. "Chilling Wind, Cheering Mob Greet Marilyn, Joe in Tokyo." *Stars and Stripes.* February 2, 1954. http://wwwstripes.com/news/chilling-wind-cheering-mob-greet-marilyn--joe-in-tokyo-1.174209 (accessed August 21, 2012).
Towles, Don. "Monroe Sidesteps Queries on Tour, Family, Lingerie." *Stars and Stripes.* February 3, 1954. http://www.stripes.com/news/monroe-sidesteps-queries-on-tour-family-lingerie-1.85777(accessed August 31, 2012).
Tozian, Greg. "20 years After Her Death, Mystique Lives On." *The Tampa Tribune,* August 5, 1982.
Tresniowski, Alex. "Golden Girl." *People.com.* August 16, 1999.

http://www.people.com/people/archive/article/0,,20128959,,00 html (accessed June 8, 2012).

Trilling, Diana. "The Death of Marilyn Monroe." In *Claremont Essays.* New York: Harcourt Brace, 1964.

—. "The Death of Marilyn Monroe." *Poemhunter.com.* n.d. http://www.poemhunter.com/quotations/hunting/page-5/ (accessed June 8, 2012).

Turner, Christopher. "Marilyn Monroe on the Couch." *Telegraph.co.uk.* June 23, 2010. http://www.telegraph.co.uk/culture/film/7843140/Marilyn-Monroe-on-the-couch.html (accessed June 8, 2012).

Turner, Roy. "Saturday's Child." *Members.tripod.com.* n.d. http://members.tripod.com/~trevor_ford/Roy_Turner (accessed June 8, 2012).

Turner, Roy. *Saturday's Child.* Unpublished manuscript, n.d.

Turner, William W. *Power and the Right.* Berkley, CA: Pamparts Press, 1971.

Tuscaloosa News. "MM, Dean Out, Studio Decides to Cancel Film." June 12, 1962.

Tuz, Susan. "Paparazzi Have Feeding Frenzy with Miller and Monroe in the 1950s." *Newstimes.com.* March 22, 2010. http://www.newstimes.com/new/article/Paparazzi-have-feeding-frenzy--with-Miller-and-417464.php (accessed March 17, 2013).

Unsolved History "The Death of Marilyn Monroe". Directed by James Younger. 2003.

Usher, Sam. "Who Do You Think You Are—Marilyn Monroe?" *Lettersofnote.com.* October 27, 2011. http://www.lettersofnote.com/2011/10/who-do-you-think-you-are-marilyn-mornoe.html (accessed February 13, 2013).

Valentine, Maggie. *The Show Starts on the Sidewalk: An Architectural History of the Movie Theatre, Starring S. Charles Lee.* New Haven, CT: Yale University Press, 1994.

Ventura, Michael. *Marilyn Monroe: From Beginning to End: Newly Discovered Photographs by Earl Leaf from the Michael Ochs Archives.* London: Blandford Press, 1997.

Victor, Adam. *The Marilyn Encyclopedia.* New York: The Overlook Press, 1999.

"Vintage 1950s Commercial with Marilyn Monroe for Royal Triton." *YouTube.com.* n.d. http://www.youtube.com/watch?v=JXH2UGP4H1Q (accessed January 6, 2013).

Vogue. "Marilyn Monroe." September 1, 1962.

Voss, Ralph F. *Truman Capote and Legacy of In Cold Blood.* Tuscaloosa: The University of Alabama Press, 2001.

Wagenknecht, Edward (editor). *Marilyn Monroe: A Composite View.* Philadelphia: Chilton Book Company, 1969.

Walker, Alexander. *Vivien: The Life of Viven Leigh.* New York: Grove Press, 1987.

Walker, Michael. "The Photography of Sam Shaw." *HollywoodReporter.com.* January 25, 2011. http://www.hollywoodreporter.com/news/photography-sam-shaw-75208 (accessed June 8, 2012).

Wallace, Mike and Gary Paul Gates. *Close Encounters: Mike Wallace's Own Story.* New York : William Morrow and Company, 1984.

Wallace, Tom. "He Sure Made Time on the Couch with Marilyn Monroe!" *Confidential,* May 1957: 20-23.

Wallach, Eli. *The Good, the Bad, and Me: In My Anecdotage.* New York: Mariner Books, 2006.

Warren, Doug. *Betty Grable: The Reluctant Movie Queen.* New York: St. Martin's Press, 1981.

Waters, Harry. "Taking a New Look at MM." *Newsweek,* October 16, 1972.

Waxman, Leanne. "Baseball Legend Stems 20-Year Flow of Roses to Dead Actress." *The Tampa Tribune,* October 1, 1982.

Weatherby, W. J. *Conversations with Marilyn.* New York: Paragon House, 1992.

—. "The Naked Wonder in Her Face." *Guardian.co.uk.* November 2, 1960. http://guardian.co.uk/news/1960/nov/03/mainsection.fromthearchive (accessed June 8, 2012).

Webb, Clifton with David Lee Smith. *Sitting Pretty: The Life and Times of Clifton Webb.* Jackson: University Press of Mississippi, 2011.

Weiler, A. H. "'River Kwai' Wins 3 Critic Awards." *The New York Times,* December 31, 1957.

—. "Screen: Marilyn Monroe Compilation." *The New York Times,* July 18, 1963: 15.

Weiner, Lee. *Marilyn: A Hollywood Farewell.* Los Angeles: Self-published, 1990.

Weiner, Tim. "J. F. K Turns to the CIA to Plug a Leak." *Nytimes.com.* July 1, 2007. http://nytimes.com/2007/07/01/weekinreview/01word.htm (accessed June 17, 2012).

Weiss, Jack Brodsky and Nathan. *The Cleopatra Papers: A Correspondence.* New York: Simon & Schuster, 1963.

Welkos, Robert W. "Death of a Star Still an Enigma." *Chicagotribune.com.* August 8, 2005. http://articles.chicagotribune.com/2005-08-08/news/050808134_1_probable-suicide-lee-strasberg-dr-ralph-greenson/2 (accessed January 3, 2013).

—. "Death of a Star Still an Enigma, 43 Years After Marilyn Monroe Was Found Dead in Her Bed..." *The Los Angeles Times,* August 8, 2005.

Weston, Robert. "Niagara." *Filmmonthly.com.* n.d. http://www.filmmonthly.com/film_noir/niagara.html (accessed March 27, 2008).

What's My Line? Directed by Franklin Heller. September 12, 1954.

Where Have You Gone, Joe DiMaggio? New York: Dutton, 1975.

Whitcomb, Jon. "Marilyn Monroe—The Sex Symbol Versus the Good Wife." *Cosmopolitan*, December 1960.

—. "The New Marilyn." *Cosmopolitan*, March 1959: 68-70.

Wilder, Billy and I. A. L Diamond. *Some Like It Hot: The Screenplay.* Monterey Park: OSP Publishing, 1994.

Wilder, Billy and I. A. L. Diamond. *Some Like It Hot.* New York: New American Library, 1959.

Williams, Dick. "Marilyn Wants to Turn It Off." *The Mirror*, March 10, 1953.

—. "Should Marilyn Turn It Down?" *The Mirror*, February 13, 1953.

Wilson, Earl. "David Wayne Discovers Who Marilyn Monroe Is." *Sarasota Herald-Tribune*, June 24, 1956.

—. "Marilyn Monroe Will Divorce Arthur Miller." *Los Angeles Mirror,* November 11, 1960.—. "Marilyn Monroe Letter from Reporter." Juliensuauctions.com. 2005. http://www.julienslive.com/auctions/2005/Marilyn-Monroe/results.html (accessed January 20, 2013).

—. "In Defense of Marilyn." *Modern Screen*, June 1955.

—. "Six Red Roses, Thrice Weekly." *Press-Telegram*, August 8, 1968.

Winkler, Peter L. "Precious Cargo: Refreshingly Bitter and Twisted Observations of Life's Passing Parade: The Death of Marilyn Monroe & My Letter to Playboy." *Preciouscargoblogspot.com* February 16, 2006. http://preciouscargo.blogspot.com/2006/12/death-of-marilyn-monroe-my-letter-to/html (accessed July 15, 2012).

Winter, Joysa. "Marilyn Monroe Was a Sincere Convert to Judaism, Rabbi's Letters Reveal." *Examiner.com.* March 6, 2010. http://www.examiner.com/article/marilyn-monroe-was-a-sin-cere-convert-to-judaism-rabbi-s-letters-reveal (accessed July 5, 2012).

Winters, Shelley. *Shelley II: The Middle of My Life.* New York: Simon & Schuster, 1989.

—. *Shelley: Also Known As Shirley.* New York: Ballantine Books, 1981.

Wit, Carter. "Marilyn and Joe in Japan (Japan-zine.com)." *OnMarilynmonroe.ca.* October 2000. http://www.marilynmonroe.ca/camera/tickets/index.html (accessed January 20, 2013).

Wolfe, Donald H. *The Last Days of Marilyn Monroe.* New York: William Morrow, 1998.

Wood, Tom. *The Bright Side of Billy Wilder.* New York: Doubleday, 1970.

Woodard, Eric Monroe. "Marilyn Monroe and 'Rain,' the Project That Never Came to Be, Part 1." *Examiner.com.* January 6, 2013. http://www.examiner.com/article/marilyn-monroe-and--rain-the-project-that-never-came-to-be-part-1 (accessed January 13, 2013).

—. "Marilyn Monroe and 'Rain,' the Project That Never Came to Be, Part 2." *Examiner.* com. January 7, 2013. http://www.examiner. com.article/marilyn-monroe-and-rain-the-project-that-never-came-to-be-part-2 (accessed January 13, 2013).

—. "Marilyn Monroe and 'Rain,' The Project That Never Came to Be, Part 3." *Examiner.com.* January 12, 2013. http://www.examiner.com/article/marilyn-monroe-and-rain-the-project-that -never-came-to-be-part-3 (accessed January 13, 2013).

Woodard, Eric Monroe with David Marshall. *Hometown Girl.* United States: HG Press, 2004.

Yankee, Luke. *Just Outside the Spotlight: Growing Up with Eileen Heckart.* New York: Back Stage Books, 2006.

Yates, Ronald. "Marilyn Monroe Mystery Lives On." *Periodical untitled,* date unknown.

Young, Bertram A. *The Rattigan Version: Sir Terrance Rattigan and the Theatre of Character.* New York: Atheneum, 1998.

Zanuck, Darryl F. "Interoffce Correspondence to Billy Wilder, dated September 20, 1954." *Icollector.com* December 16, 2011. http://www.icollector.com/Marilyn-%20Monroe-extensive-archive-of-production-and-publicity-material-from-The-Seven-%20Year-Itch_i11537134 (accessed June 28, 2013).

"Zanuck Hails a True Star." *Periodical untitled.* Date unknown.

Zanuck, Richard D. "Letter from Richard D. Zanuck to Marilyn Monroe dated December 4, 1959." *Bonhams.com.* June 13, 2010. http://www.bonhams.com/auctions/18245/lot/1008/ (accessed February 9, 2013).

Zec, Donald. "Marilyn and Me: Mirror Showbiz Legend on His Amazing Friendship with the Sex Goddess Movie Icon Who Died 50 ears Ago." *Mirror.co.uk.* August 3, 2012. http://www.mirror.co.uk/3am/celebrity-news/marilyn-monroe-and-me-mirror-showbiz-1207829 (accessed December 8, 2012).

Zehme, Bill. *The Way You Wear Your Hat: Frank Sinatra and the Lost Art of Livin'.* New York: HarperCollins, 2009.

Zenter, Joe. "The Filming of an Unsettling Desert Classic." *Desertusa.com.* n.d. http://www.desertusa.com/mag05.nov/misfits.html (accessed November 30, 2012).

Zinsser, William K. "How Cinderella Became a National Institution." *The New York Times,* October 30, 1960: 30.

Zolotow, Maurice. *Billy Wilder in Hollywood.* New York: Proscenium Publisher, 1996.
—. *Marilyn Monroe.* New York: Harcourt Brace, 1960.

INDEX

Abbott, Allan 548, 575, 577
ABC Television Network 51
Abernethy, R. J. 560, 561
Academy of Motion Picture Arts & Sciences (Oscar Awards) 11, 17, 21, 22, 35, 75, 76, 94, 123, 131, 136, 137, 138, 141, 165, 174, 180, 190, 199, 201, 202, 203, 215, 216, 218, 227, 230, 247, 248, 250, 251, 281, 292, 293, 314, 332, 333, 364, 374, 380, 391, 423, 448, 473, 592, 594, 605, 606, 649, 655, 660, 669, 675
Acosta, Edgardo 444
Actors Studio 11, 61, 65, 75, 104, 119, 122, 173, 184, 185, 192, 193, 249, 284, 307, 314, 330, 453, 611, 655, 677
Adams, Edie 285, 567
Adams, Sue 653
Addinsell, Richard 25
Adlend, Marcia 576
Adler, Buddy 198, 203, 204, 207, 333, 341
Adler, Richard 462, 465, 470, 471, 472
Adler, Stella 386
African Queen, The 22, 247, 255,
After the Fall 46, 122, 125, 135, 230, 600, 601, 602, 604, 656
Aguilar, Arturo Soa 307
"Ain't That a Kick in the Head?" 381
Albee, Edward 172
Aldrich, (United States Ambassador) Winthrop 34, 77
Aldrich, Mrs. Winthrop 34
Aleman, Miguel 415
Alexander, William "Bill" 436, 524, 531, 576
Alien 660
All About Eve 250, 675
Allan, Richard 465
Allan, Rupert 32, 73, 134, 153, 160, 206-7, 215, 216, 219, 223, 224, 225, 228, 254, 260, 261, 276, 277, 278, 288, 301, 306, 517, 530, 543
Allen, Angela 255, 256, 261, 267
Allen, Gene 382, 458
Allen, Maury 521
Allen, Steve 386, 387, 429, 454
Allyson, June 187

Alport, Hollis 293
Alvarado, Juan 403
American Film Institute 11, 129, 131, 161, 218
American in Paris, An 203
American Masters 650, 654
American National Exhibition 186
American Prince: A Memoir 154
Among Those Present 396
Anatasia 75
Anatomy of a Murder 199, 492
Anchors Away 203
And God Created Woman 55
Andere, Jacqueline 425
Anderson, Daphne 23, 41
Anderson, Mark 7, 613
Anderson, Pamela 644
Andrews, Charles 654
Andrews, Julie 33, 342
Andy Griffith Show, The 386
Angleton, James 527
Anna Christie 5, 136, 453
Annie Hall 473
Ann-Margret 241, 259
Anthony, Gene 557
Anthony, Maggy 557
Anthony, Ray 553
Apartment, The 131, 133, 197, 226, 227, 332
Apple Knockers and the Coke, The 646
Arden, Elizabeth 118, 499
Arden, Eve 582
Arena, Sal 2, 121
Aristophane 51
Arlen, Harold 286, 335
Armstrong, Grover 542
Arnold, Alan 53
Arnold, Dorothy 540
Arnold, Eve 3, 25, 27, 253, 255, 260, 267, 274, 278, 283, 287, 288, 305, 345, 647
Arnoul, Françoise 77
Around the World in 80 Days 198
Art of Burlesque 646
Arthur 35
Arthur Godfrey Show, The 654
Arthur, Jean 376
Arvin, Newton 566
As You Like It 22
Asher, William 539
Ask Any Girl 212
Astaire, Fred 339, 385, 387, 448
Astin, John 593
Atherton, Robert 485
Atlas Shrugged 593
Audley, Maxine 24, 684
Auntie Mame 163
Auric, Georges 176
Avanti 131
"Ave Maria" 579
Avedon, Richard 78, 79, 152, 164, 168, 211, 375, 662
Avedon's Endgame 79
Axelrod, George 189, 239
Ayton, Mel 629, 642
Babette's Feast 174
Baby Doll 57, 65, 75, 78, 179, 250
Backus, Jim 582
Bacon, James 332, 485, 547, 581
Bad Seed, The 75
Baker. Bud 254
Baker, Carroll, 57, 65. 75, 569
Baker, Gladys Pearl Baker 123, 250, 307, 308, 312, 314, 360, 578, 609, 610, 612

Bakker, Deborah 2, 667
Baldwin, Alec 85
Ball, Lucille 76
Banas, Bob 207
Bancroft, Anne 391
Band Wagon, The 385
Bankhead, Tallulah 250
Banner, Lois 93, 216, 469, 520, 610, 612, 613, 649, 669
Banville, Nadine 673
Bara, Theda 152, 167, 375
Bardot, Brigitte 54, 55, 206
Barefoot Contessa, The 22
Barham, Patte B. 494, 563, 638
Barley, Agnes 657
Barragan, Jorge 557
Barris, George 7, 62, 401, 424, 434, 437, 485, 486, 487, 502, 508, 509, 541, 670, 674
Barry, Dave 687
Barsa, Mikel 645
Basinger, Kim 85
Bass, Mary 86, 87, 115
Bass, Richardson 115
Batelle, Kenneth 318, 344, 345, 467
Bates, John 526, 527, 636, 642
Battista, Fulgencio 217
Battle of the River Plate, The 53
Bautzer, Gregson 223
Beardsley, Percy 184
Beaton, Cecil 71
Bacall, Lauren 239, 337
Beckett 35
Beckley, Paul V. 294
Beggar's Opera, The 23
Behan, Brendan 315
Belafonte, Harry 470, 475, 501, 502
Belafonte, Julie 475
Bell, Book and Candle 199
Bell Hop, The 416
Bell Jar, The 194
Bell, Rex 251
Bell, Vanessa 348
Bello, Jean 516
Bellow, Saul 73, 178, 662
Bells Are Ringing 192, 194, 205, 283, 381
Bells of St. Mary's, The 202
Belmont, Georges 7, 13, 173, 219, 220, 676
Ben-Hur 199, 218
Benny, Jack 339, 465
Bergen, Polly 593
Berglass, Dr. Bernard 93
Bergman, Ingrid 12, 75, 197, 322
Berle, Milton 697, 698
Berlin, Irving 335, 523
Berliner Ensemble 50
Bernard, Bruno 642
Bernard, Susan 642
Bernhardt, Sarah 19, 20, 24, 681
Bernstein, Leonard 114
Bernstein, Walter 384, 385, 457
Bertolini, Ramon 2, 667
Besser, Joe 203, 695
Beymer, Richard 341
"Beyond the Sea" 469
Bicycle Thief, The 380
Bikel, Theodore 677
Billionaire, The 190, 194, 197
Billy May Orchestra 72
Billy Wilder in Hollywood 159
Bird, Lady Pamela 66
Birdcage, The 469
Bishop, Joey 337, 339

Bixby, Bill 638
Black Narcissus 22
Blackbyrne, Morgan 3, 673
Blackmer, Carolyn Joerndt
Blackmer, Franklin 361, 661
Blackwell, Richard 473
Blass, Bill 70
Blendel, Henri 654
Blitch, Iris F. 479
Blixen, Baroness Karen (see Isak Dineson)
Block, Mervin 179
Bloomgarden, Kermit 66, 86, 93, 98, 124, 125
Bloomgarden, Virginia 98
Blossoms, The 593
Blue Angel 112, 113, 117, 135, 180, 373
Blue Book Modeling Agency 215
Blum, Irving 533
Bobo 109
Bogart, Humphrey 247, 337
Bogdanovich, Peter 649
Bolaños, José 417, 418, 421, 424, 427, 428, 429, 557
Bolender, Ida 581
Bolshoi Theatre Ballet 52, 502
Bond, Gordon 54
Bonhams Auction 467, 523
Boone, Pat 241, 341
Born Yesterday 197
Bosworth, Patricia 116, 185
Bourke, Dennis 423
Bow, Clara 138, 152, 167, 168, 251
Boys' Night Out 380
Braden, Joan 408
Brains Trust, The 51
Branagh, Kenneth 63
Brand, Harry 223, 493
Brando, Marlon 118, 190, 193, 205, 216, 276, 312, 324, 354, 356, 368, 380, 386, 485, 486, 524, 535, 565
Brant, Henry 251
Braziller, George 115
Braziller, Marsha 115
Breakfast at Tiffany's 189, 190, 270, 286, 314, 380, 387, 448
Breathless 171, 297
Brecht, Bertolt 50
Breen Office 22
Bretherton, David 453, 456, 483, 591
Brevard, Aleshia 285, 286
Bridge Over the River Kwai 111
Brigadoon 385
Bright, Mura 436
British Academy Awards 60
British Broadcasting Channel (BBC) 36, 41, 51, 636, 637, 661
Broadway Melody of 1938 247, 268
Brodsky, Jack 490
Broken Glass 657
Brothers Karamazov, The 26, 51, 118, 119, 188, 193
Brown, Andreas 111
Brown, David 187, 194, 380, 382
Brown, Helen Gurley 380
Brown, Joe E. 132, 152, 160, 227, 382, 689
Brown, Peter Harry 447, 456, 494, 563, 638
Brown, Sugar 582
Browning, Elizabeth Barrett 577

Browning Version, The 18, 24
Bruce, Lenny 171, 286
Brustein, Robert 603, 604
Brynner, Yul 118, 123, 199
Buchanan, Edgar 593
Buchanan, Wiley T. 188
Buchthal, Stanley 613
Buchwald, Art 160, 307
Bundle of Joy 76
Bunuel, Luis 425, 426
Burke, Billie 43
Burke, Deborah 449
Burns, David 695
Burton, Richard 342, 374, 479, 482, 536, 566, 593
Burroughs, William 171
Burstyn, Ellen 655
Bus Stop 11, 28, 33, 34, 47, 60, 66, 67, 75, 76, 239, 240, 301, 592, 599, 670, 677
Bushell, Tony 22
Buskin, Richard 7, 279
But Not For Me 212
Butch 109
Butch Cassidy and the Sundance Kid 342
Butterfield, Virginia 148
Butterfield 8 332
Buttons, Red 59, 450
Buydens, Anne 543
Buys, Sara 120
"Bye Bye Baby" 671
Bye Bye Birdie (film) 259
Byron, R. E. 543, 544, 545
Caesar, Sid 567
Cagney, James 133
Cahn, Sammy 203, 225, 339, 582
Calder, Alexander 104
Call of the Wild 248
Callan, Edward and Georgina 527
Callas, Maria 224, 468, 469, 472, 473
Campbell, John 492
Camelot 342, 473
Campbell, G. W. 335, 498
Camus, Albert 72, 600, 616
Can Can 123, 188, 203, 392
Candid Camera 654
Candida 23
"Candle in the Wind" 650, 674
Cannon, Damian 293
Cantinflas 417
Capell, Frank 621-626, 633
Capote, Truman 189, 190, 192, 286, 566. 582
Captain Newman, MD 526
Cardiff, Jack 17, 22, 34, 39, 41, 56, 72, 304, 686
Carey, Jim 132
Carey, Mariah 616
Carmen 469
Carmen, Jeanne 363, 518, 621, 636, 637, 662
Carnegie, Hattie 448
Caron, Leslie 203, 383, 427
Carpenter, Mont Clair 516
Carpozi, George 306
Carr, Joan 29
Carr, Joseph 76
Carr, Virginia 175
Carroll, Diahann 169, 470, 475
Carroll, Ronald H. 635, 640
Carter, Glenn Thomas 424
Cartier-Bresson, Henri 253
Caspary, Vera 240
Cassini, Oleg 390, 675

Casson, Lewis 23, 34
Castro, Fidel 217, 518, 528, 623, 629, 675
Cat on a Hot Tin Roof 124
Cather, Willa 193
Caucasian Chalk Circle 50
CBS Television Network 313, 314, 359, 386, 509, 596, 627, 652
Celebration 240, 241, 341, 379
Chagall 115
Chakiris, George 429, 669
Champion, Robert 468, 470, 472, 473
Chanel No. 5 32, 615, 674
Chappell, Billy 25
Chaplin, Charles 42, 133, 197, 212, 322, 418, 473
Chariots of Fire 660
Charisse, Cyd 385, 454, 482, 593
Charles, Ray 335
Chayefsky, Paddy 122, 123
Checker, Chubby 237, 408
Chekhov, Michael 136, 224, 281, 312, 498, 566, 609, 610
Chekhov, Xenia 224, 281, 312, 498, 609, 610
Chevalier, Maurice 123, 141
"Chicken Feed: The Last Frontier of the Quixotic Cowboy" (See "The Misfits, or Chicken Feed: The Last Frontier of the Quixotic Cowboy")
Child Study Center at Yale University 75
Chorus Line, A 386
Christie's Auction House 393, 463, 614, 615, 616
Children's Hour, The 353, 380
Churchwell, Sarah 4, 6, 12, 150, 155, 161, 622, 623, 636, 637, 638, 641, 647
Cindy 109
City Is, A 655
Clark, Alfred Corning 531
Clark, Alicia Darr Corning 531, 532
Clark, B. C. 331
Clark, Colin 22, 24, 25, 28, 30, 31, 34, 36, 38, 40, 43, 44, 47, 62, 63
Clark, Edward 531
Clark, Lord Kenneth 28
Clash By Night 181, 207
Clay, Tom 356
Clement, Rene 125
Clemente, T. J. 100
Clemmons, Jack 544, 545, 621, 625, 630, 631, 633, 639
Cleopatra (film) 327, 374, 375, 376, 458, 479, 480, 490, 491, 508, 536, 591, 592, 593, 649
Cleopatra 375
Cleopatra Papers: A Correspondence, The 490
Clerk, Clive 386
Cliburn, Van 191, 224
Clift, Montgomery 123, 157, 200, 248, 249, 251, 256, 257, 261, 264, 265, 266, 270, 271, 278, 279, 280, 283, 284, 285, 287, 291, 292, 293, 298, 311, 318, 662, 704
Clinton, President Bill 455, 633
Close Encounters: Mike Wallace's Own Story 622
Coco, Imogene 277

Cocoon 194, 383
Cocteau, Jean 566
Coen, Stanley J. 351, 352, 555, 556
Cold Shoulder 582
Cole, Jack 199, 206, 208, 210, 224
Collected Plays of Arthur Miller, The 177
Collier, Marion 148
Collingswood, Charles 406, 596
Colombo, Gianandrea 3, 667
Colton, John 313, 341
Colum, Padraic 125
Columbia Studios 203, 248, 391, 448, 596, 660
Come Fly with Me 72
Come Slowly, Eden! 654
"Come to Me, My Melancholy Baby" 689
Comment, Bernard 7
Como, Perry 192, 202
Complete Last Sitting, The 503
Complete Poems of Carl Sandburg, The 175
Connolly, Mike 313
Connors, Chuck 593
Conroy, Millington 613
Conroy, Ruth 612, 613
Conte, Richard 582
Conversation Piece 114
Conversations with Marilyn 281
Cooper, Gary 224, 225, 340, 403
Cooper, Lady Diana 34
Copeland, Joan 60, 114, 123, 554, 656, 662
Coroner to the Stars 635
Cotes-Preedy, Admiral 28
Cotten, Joseph 567
Cottrell, Dr. Richard 343, 344
Council for the Encouragement of the Arts 23
Country Girl, The 202
Courtney, Elizabeth 502, 529
Covici, Pascal 178
Coward, Noël 114, 334, 603
Cowles, Fleur (see Fleur Cowles Meyer)
Cox, Wally 386, 483, 484-486, 498, 511
Cramer, Richard Ben 489, 499, 521, 540, 553, 582
Crawford, Cheryl 185, 222, 223
Crawford, Joan 5, 54, 55, 197, 314, 330, 374, 403, 633, 644
Crist, Judith 27
Cromwell, Richard 661
Crosby, Bing 202, 440, 443, 444, 697, 698
Crown, Lawrence 204
Crowther, Bosley 61, 123, 163, 179, 229, 230, 294, 564, 593
Crucible, The 122, 200, 657
Crystal Star Award 11, 60, 187, 176
Cukor, George 117, 187, 188, 197, 198, 203, 206-208, 210, 218, 220, 224, 225, 229, 239, 240, 333, 373, 380, 382, 384, 385, 450, 451, 453-458, 479-484, 486, 488, 492, 493, 507, 570, 596, 662, 669
Culver, Calvin 386
Curphey, Theodore 570, 585, 586, 587, 631, 640
"Cursum Perficio" (song) 431
Curtin, Michael 405

Curtis, Jamie Lee 149
Curtis Management Group Worldwide (CMG) 617, 618
Curtis, Tony 131, 132, 137, 140, 141, 143-145, 149, 150-155, 157, 158, 160, 161, 187, 235, 335, 407, 566, 633, 686
Dache, Lilly 467
Daddy Long Legs 387
D'Agostino, Dennis 79
Dahl, Arlene 395
Daly, John 217
Dambacher, Frank 548
Damn Yankees 462
Dana, Bill 471
Dandridge, Dorothy 215
Dangerous Years 509
Daniels, Billy 480
D'Antonio, Anthony 534
D'Antonio, Henry 533, 534, 538
Darby O'Gill and the Little People 250
D'Arcy, Alex 519
Darin, Bobby 469
Dark Secret of Harvest Home, The 386
Darling, (Rev.) Floyd 577
Darlow, Michael 18
Darvi, Bella 379
Daves, Jessica 504
David di Donatello Prize 11, 60, 180, 187, 338
Davidson, Bruce 211
Davies, Marion 335
Davis, Bette 5, 12, 259, 356, 374, 386
Davis, Miles 171
Davis, Jr., Sammy 101, 141, 255, 337, 338, 340, 454, 541, 576, 666
Davis, Mrs. Spencer 501
Daws, Shar 3, 4, 677
Dawson, Beatrice "Bumble" 24, 34
Day, Doris 198, 212, 215, 374, 391, 448, 493, 525, 593, 650
Day, Eddy 559
Day-Lewis, Daniel 657
Day to Day Life with the Freud Family: The Reminiscences of Paula Fichtl 48
Days of Wine and Roses 492
DD Group: An Online Investigation Into the Death of Marilyn Monroe, The 631
Dead, The 252
Deal, Borden 179
Deal, Peter 504
Dean, James 595, 609
Death of a Salesman 111, 250, 251, 314, 601, 656, 657
Debbie: My Life 568
DeBraganza, Anita 423
DeBraganza, Princess Antonia 423
Debuskey, Christine 86, 87
Debuskey, Merle 86, 87
de Dienes, Andre 324, 336, 597
Dee, Sandra 272
Deep Blue Sea, The 18
Defiant Ones, The 131, 141
de Kooning, Willem 86
DeNiro, Robert 655
Dennison, Virginia 497
Deppe, (Rev.) Martin L. 597
De Rachelle 51
Derby, Jane 118
De Sica, Vittorio 380

Desk Set 112
Deskey, Donald 58
Deutsch, Adolph 139
Diagnostic and Statistical Manual IV 488
Diamond, I. A. L. 129-131, 140, 145, 152, 157, 165, 226
"Diamonds Are a Girl's Best Friend" 206
Diana, Princess 595, 622, 668
Diary of Anne Frank, The 91, 215
Dick Van Dyke Show, The 515
Dickenson, Angie 337, 407
Dickerson, Nancy 396
Diebold Family 104
Dietrich, Marlene 112, 113, 152, 167, 283, 463, 531, 532
Dillon, Carmen 25
DiMaggio, Dominic 522
DiMaggio, Joseph "Joe" 2, 81, 88, 89, 113, 123, 156, 169, 200, 205, 222, 229, 276, 283, 285, 301, 306, 308, 309, 315, 317, 322, 323, 325, 326, 329, 330-332, 336, 339, 341, 343, 346-348, 357, 362, 369, 383, 392, 401, 410, 414, 417, 418, 420, 430, 431, 435, 439. 485, 489, 498, 499, 515-517, 521, 522, 524, 527, 530, 531, 536-541, 545, 547, 553, 557, 560, 565, 573, 574, 576, 577, 579, 581-583, 595, 604, 605, 610, 616, 633, 645, 646, 652, 653, 662, 666, 667, 674
DiMaggio, Jr., Joseph "Butch" 73, 522, 539,540, 577, 653, 662
DiMaggio, Marie 662
DiMaggio, Vincent 522
Dinah Shore Show 201
Dineson, Isak 174, 175
Dinner at Eight 43, 136
Dirk, Tim 129
Discreet Charm of the Bourgeoisie, The 425
Dominuez, Columba 423
Donero, Don 270
Donfeld 188, 239
Donini, Filipo 180
Donna Reed Show, The 68, 539
Donovan, Casey (see Calvin Culver)
Don't Bother to Knock 322, 582
Dors, Diana 111
Dostoyevsky, Fyodor 118, 119
Dougherty, James "Jim" 3, 123, 540, 545, 652
Douglas, Kirk 543
Douglas, Melvyn 376
Douglas, William O. 217
Doyle, Tom 657
Dr. Jekyll and Mr. Hyde 314
Dr. Spock's Baby and Childcare Book 616
"Dream" 503
Dressler, Marie 136, 414
Driving Miss Daisy 194, 383
Dubrow, Dr. Hilliard 93
Duke and Duchess of Baccleuch 34
Duke and Duchess of Windsor 77, 78, 191
Duke, Doris 81
Dumas, Alexander 224, 695
Dunbar's Cove 179
Dunn, Jessica 3, 666
Dunne, Irene 376, 448
Durante, Jimmy 469, 475

Durgom, George 541, 542
Duse, Eleanora 20, 175
Eady Plan 50
Eagels, Jeanne 313, 314
Eames, Charles 186, 436, 558
East of Eden 179
Easter Parade 358
Ebbins, Milton 395, 464, 469, 470, 541, 542
Ebert, Roger 154, 165, 650, 690
Ebony 109
Ed Sullivan Show, The 68
Eden, (British Prime Minister) Anthony 30
Eden, Barbara 450, 451
Edith Sitwell: A Unicorn Among Lions 53
Edward VIII 147
Edwards, Blake 286
Edwards, Florence 286
Edwards, John 644
Einstein, Albert 71, 288
Eisenhower, President Dwight D. 55, 92, 99, 390, 441, 445
Eisenhower, Mamie 441, 445
Ekberg, Anita 54
El Angel Exterminador 425
Eldridge, Florence 314, 341
Elephant Walk 21
Ella in Hollywood 335
Ellington, Duke 335
Ellison, Ralph 99
"Embraceable You" 605
Enemies Within 621
Enemy Within, The 406
Engelberg, Hyman 2, 91, 234, 237, 255, 275, 420, 427, 429, 452, 458, 489, 491, 500, 516, 529, 530, 539, 543, 544, 545, 553, 555, 556, 561, 562, 624, 635, 636, 659, 662
Engelberg, Morris 605
Entratter, Jack 338
Enya 431
Ephron, Henry 555, 562
Ericson, June 286
Ernie Kovacs Show 285
Erwitt, Elliott 264, 265, 270
Esque, Harold 331
Essential Dean Martin, The 517
Evans, Aimee 3
Evans, Courtney 502
Evans, Peter 558
Evans, Shaney 3, 667
Evening with Marilyn, An 634
Evening with Yves Montand, An 200
Everly Brothers 503
"Everybody's Somebody's Fool" 334
Exner, Judith Campbell 518
Explorations in Psychoanalysis 464
Eyewitness 596
Fabres, Shelley 553
Fairbanks, Douglas 34
Fairbanks, Jr., Douglas 133
Falco, S. Samuel 610
"Falling in Love Again" 112
Fame 656
Fanfare d'Amour 129
Fanfaren der Liebe (*Fanfares of Love*) 129
Farah of Iran, Empress 453
Farberow, Norman 570, 586, 587
Farewell to Arms, A 111
Father Knows Best 68
Faubus, Orval 99
Faulkner, William 123, 422

Fay, Paul 527
Faye, Alice 198
Feld, Donald Lee (see Donfeld)
Feldman, Charles 18, 376
Feldman, Phil 451, 488
Felini, Federico 297
Fell, Fifi 394, 395, 440, 444
Fell, John Randolph 394
Feminine Mystique, The 390
Fenichel, Hanna 353, 402
Fenichel, Otto 234
Ferguson, Frank 489
Fernandez, Emilio 417
Ferragamo, Massimo 615
Ferragamo, Salvatore 67, 435, 615, 673
Ferrante and Teisher 546
Ferrer, José 314-316, 341, 356
"Fever" 469
Fichtl, Paula 48
Field, Cyrus 419
Field, Frederick Vanderbilt 419-421, 423, 426, 515, 536
Finch, Peter 21
Fineman, Mia 79
Finishing the Picture 656
Finkbine, Sherri 391
Fire Over England 21
First Family, The 469
Fisher, Eddie 187, 220, 338, 340, 374, 454
Fitzgerald, Ella 72, 284, 335, 470, 573, 576, 666
Fitzgerald, F. Scott 253
Five Marvelous Astons 132
Five Weeks in a Balloon 450
Flaming Star 225
Flanagan, Agnes 187, 224, 255, 261, 264, 265, 271, 272, 283, 285, 357, 481, 501, 506, 508, 537, 578
Fletcher, Lucy 139
Flower Drum Song 251
Flynn, Errol 274
Focus 108
Fonda, Henry 141, 142, 187, 469, 662
Fonda, Jane 141, 212
Fonteyn, Dame Margot 34
Ford, Gerald 629
Ford, Mrs. Edsel 191
Ford II, Mrs. Henry 191
Forever Marilyn Blu-Ray Collection 675
Fortner, Scott 2, 665, 672, 673
Fortune Cookie, The 131
Fountainhead, The 598
Fox Studios 68, 69, 111, 113, 114, 117, 123, 125, 134, 135, 144, 179, 180, 181, 184, 186-190, 195, 197-200, 204-207, 210, 211, 213, 214, 218, 225, 228-230, 238-41, 243, 259, 285, 302, 313, 319, 333-335, 341, 355, 356, 367, 373-376, 379, 380, 385, 387, 391, 418, 423, 428, 429, 433, 447, 450-454, 457, 458, 464, 465, 477, 479, 480, 482, 486, 488-495, 497, 501, 502, 506-508, 511, 516, 517, 536, 558, 562, 575, 581, 591-594, 612, 628, 638, 643, 646, 648, 659, 660, 674, 675
Fragments: Poems, Intimate Notes, Letters by Marilyn Monroe 7, 325, 368, 613

Franchetti, Baronessa Afdera 142
Francis, Connie 334, 565
Frank, Anne 649, 655
Frankenheimer, John 189, 462, 473
Franklin, Rebecca 315
Freeman, Lucy 328, 353, 399
Frees, Paul 143
Freidan, Betty 390
Freud 200, 274, 358
Freud, Anna 47, 48, 74, 235, 611
Freud, Martha 47
Freud, Sigmund 45, 48, 74, 183, 234, 291, 292, 326, 358, 691
From Here to Eternity 248, 250
Fromm, Eric 92
Frontiere, Dominic 204
Frosch, Aaron 305, 311, 312, 316, 317, 578, 609, 610, 612
Fuller, Victoria 671
"Fur Elise" 71
Furse, Roger 25
Gable, Clark 157, 182, 240, 244, 246-248, 256, 257, 259-262, 264-268, 270, 274-277, 279, 286, 290-294, 296-298, 302-307, 319, 331, 339, 340, 678, 700
Gable, John Clark 339, 340,
Gable, Kay 257, 276, 303, 305, 319, 331, 339, 564
Galindo, Ernesto 3, 667
Garbo, Greta 12, 54, 136, 322, 374, 408, 482, 503
Gardel, Bunny 224, 255, 268, 450, 485
Gardener, Ava 32
Garland, Judy 135, 139, 187, 188, 197, 200, 247, 268, 302, 332, 333, 358, 364, 407, 429, 529, 579, 644
Garner, James 239, 380, 493, 593
Gates, Phyllis 249
Gatto, John 224
Gavin, John 385
Gaynor, Mitzi 131, 132, 272, 525
Gazzara, Ben 662
Gehman, Richard 207
Gentlemen Prefer Blondes 450, 469, 574, 669
Geppetti, Marcello 479
Gershwin, George 233
Gershwin, Ira 335
Ghandi, Indira 442
Ghost Writer, The 292
Giancana, Samuel 270, 517-519, 622
Gibbs, A. H. 138
Gideon 341
Gielgud, Sir John 34, 35, 40
Giesler, Jerry 634
Gigi 25, 137, 141, 218
Gilda 448
Gillon, Margaret 44, 57
Ginsberg, Allen 171
Girl Can't Help It, The 68
Girl, the Coke, and the Apple, The 646
Gish, Lillian 649, 657
Givenchy, Hubert 190, 286
Glass, Bea 455
Glass Menagerie, The 224
Glendinning, Victoria 53
Glenn, John H. 391, 393, 501, 502
Glenn Miller Band 541

Gober, Bert 270
Godard, Jean-Luc 297
Goddard, Anne 578
Goddard, Erwin "Doc" 578
Goddard, Grace 359, 574, 578
Goddess, The 122, 123
Goddess: The Secret Lives of Marilyn Monroe 7, 409, 636, 637, 647
Godfather Part II, The 655
Goethe 91
Going My Way 202
Goldberg, Robert Alan 621
Goldburg, Rabbi Robert 190, 358, 578
Golden Door, The 654
Golden Globe Award 11, 76, 165, 214, 215, 219, 230, 250, 293, 297, 418, 427, 430, 616
Golden, Howard 655
Goldfinger 416
Golding, William 411
Goldman, Milton 193
Goldstein, Robert 379
Goldwater, Barry 625
Goldwyn, Samuel 133
Gomez, Judge Miguel 317
Gone With the Wind 21, 157, 222, 248, 291, 297
Good Boy 138
Good Morning America 231
Goodbye, Charlie 239-241, 333, 335, 373
Goodbye Yellow Brick Road 650
Goode, John 253
Gordon, Stanley 208, 364, 365
Gore, David Ormsby 501
Goslar, Lotte 224, 334
Gottfried, Martin 658
Gough, James A. 433
Gould, Beatrice & Bruce 329
Gould, Deborah 636, 661
Gould, Milton 488, 506
Gounod, Charles-François 579
Grable, Betty 281, 567
Graduate, The 469, 652
Graham, (Rev.) Billy 568, 569
Graham, Martha 252
Graham, Sheilah 75, 76, 240, 490, 493, 592
Grammy Award 165, 332
Grandison, Lionel 621, 631, 633-635, 585
Grant, Allan 512,
Grant, Cary 130, 197, 199, 391, 690, 692
Grant, Duncan 348
Granz, Norman 335
Gray, Billy 687
Gray, Bud 549
Gray, Francine du Plessix 658
Gray, Marijane 3, 4, 672
Great St. Trinian's Train Robbery, The 23
Greatest Story Ever Told, The 334
Greco, Buddy 519-521
Greenberg, Melanie Hope 655
Greene, Amy Franco 2, 24, 27, 29-31, 42, 52, 59, 63, 74, 77, 554, 573, 574, 654, 670
Greene, Anthony 59, 654
Greene, Joshua 2, 4, 31, 515, 617, 654, 670
Greene, Milton 2, 4, 5, 11, 18, 19, 22, 24, 25, 28, 29, 31, 34, 42, 47, 49, 50, 52, 55, 57-60, 66, 67, 74, 76, 77, 114, 515, 554, 573, 599, 617, 619, 654, 670

Greenschpoon, Joel and Katharine 233, 234, 353
Greenson, Daniel P. 234, 352-355, 369, 397, 407, 487, 555, 577, 659
Greenson, Dr. Romeo "Ralph" 69, 222, 233-237, 275, 276, 291, 308, 322, 325, 326, 334-336, 345, 349, 351-358, 360-362, 368, 369, 373, 382, 398, 399, 401, 402, 419, 420, 427, 428, 430, 432, 439, 441, 444, 452, 464, 475, 487-490, 492, 500, 517, 521, 524, 526, 529, 530, 538-545, 547, 555, 556, 559, 561, 562, 577, 578, 579, 581, 630, 636, 637, 639-642, 659, 662, 666
Greenson Rudin, Elizabeth 234, 353
Greenson, Hildegard "Hilde/Hildi" Troesch 234, 235, 353, 544, 355, 361, 399, 487, 577, 642
Greenson (Aebi), Joan 234, 352-355, 369, 394, 399, 464, 466, 487, 490, 492, 493, 500, 544, 555, 577, 578, 579, 581, 659
Greenson, Juliet 233, 353
Greenwald, Michael 3
Grey, Joe 138
Griffith, D. W. 133
Griffith, Emile 462
Grimes, Steven 218
Grober, Bert "Wingy" 270
Group Theatre 330
Gruner, George and family 70
Guilaroff, Sydney 24, 25, 35, 40, 187, 204, 252, 254, 259, 315, 449, 492, 568, 575, 577, 578
Guiles, Fred Lawrence 5, 6, 43, 66, 77, 155, 186, 223, 247, 255, 256, 266, 269, 286, 319, 369, 398, 520, 538, 602, 649
Gunsmoke 634
Gurdin, Maria 348
Guthman, Edwin 409, 410, 643
Haas, Ernst 264
Haines, William "Billy" 382
Hall, Arsenio 213
Hall, Buck 458
Hall, Harry 560, 582
Hall, James 635, 639
Halsman, Philippe 191, 192
Hambourg, Maria Morris 79
Hamilton, Jack 364-365
Hamlet 17, 22
Hammes, Betsy 520
Hamrock, Mary 575
Hand, Judge Learned 191
Hans Christian Anderson 469
Happiest Days of Your Life, The 23
"Happy Days are Here Again" 141
Hardwick, Paul 23
Harlow, Jean 136, 152, 167, 211, 212, 248, 516, 553, 591, 595, 678
Harris, Radie 72, 104, 107,
Harrison, Rex 33, 566, 662
Hart, Gary 632
Harvey 132
Harvey, Laurence 201, 462
Harvey, Roy 3, 668
Haspiel, James 2, 93, 110, 162, 176, 181, 241, 301, 435, 464, 465, 476
Hast, Ronald 577

Hathaway, Henry 289, 356
Haworth, Ted 165
Hayton, Lennie 330
Hayward, Susan 448
Hayworth, Rita 181, 314, 358, 448
He Made Stars Shine 469
Hearst, Millicent 78, 84
Hearst, William Randolph 78
Heart Is A Lonely Hunter, The 174
"Heat Wave" 206
Heaven Knows, Mr. Allison 247
Hefner, Hugh 583, 673
Heilweil, Alexandra 455
Heilweil, Eva Wolas 455
Heinz, Barbara 366-367
Hellman, Lillian 353, 380
Helous, Victor R. 473
Hemingway, Ernest 113, 357, 599, 616
Henry V 17
Hepburn, Audrey 12, 190, 215, 270, 286, 380, 387, 448
Hepburn, Katharine 5, 12, 75, 112, 157, 197, 215, 247
Hermann, Bernard 238
Hesse. Eva 657
Heston, Charlton 154, 200, 429
"Hey You with the Crazy Eyes" 203
Hickey, William 29
High Time 332
Hill, Anita 632-633
Hill, George Roy 342
Hilton, Paris 644
Hiroshima, Mon Amour 297
Hirsch, Foster 62
Hitchcock, Alfred 164, 199, 238, 281, 385, 607
Hitler, Adolph 153-155, 160
Hobson's Choice 23
Hockett, Don 547, 548
Hockett, Guy 547, 548, 558, 576, 582
Hockett, Margaret 579
Hoffa, James 406, 622, 624
Hoffman, Dustin 165, 655
Hollaender, Friedrich 112
Holliday, Judy 76, 131, 140, 192, 193, 197, 205, 277, 283
Hohenberg, Dr. Margaret 47, 74, 237
Hollywood Chamber of Commerce 212
Hollywood Foreign Press 165, 212, 214, 293, 427
Hollywood Walk of Fame 212, 213
Holm, Celeste 353
Home and Beauty 376
Hometown Story 358
Hoover, (President) Hubert 191
Hoover, J. Edgar 407, 419, 502, 625, 628, 637
Hope, Bob 448, 471, 202, 313, 332
Hopkins, Gerard Manley 52
Hopkins, Miriam 43
Hopper, Dennis 533, 641
Hopper, Hedda 227, 276, 335, 339, 356, 493, 571
Horn, Lena 330
Horns for the Devil 69
Hostage, The 315
Hough, Stanley 451
Houston, Walter 314
How Do I Love Thee? 577
How to Be Very, Very Popular 383
How to Marry a Millionaire 450, 507, 519

Howard, Shemp 203
Howell, Chester 651
Hoyt, Edwin P. 155, 357
Hryniszak, Roman 4, 525
HUAC (House Un-American Activities Committee) 87, 603
Hudson, Rock 198, 200, 218, 249, 429, 592
Hughes, Howard 205
Hugo 2, 85, 87, 90, 93, 97, 98, 100, 121, 173, 184, 305, 349
Huie, William Bradford 179
Humphrey, Hubert 217, 443
Hunt Auctions 309,
Hunter, Ross 448
Huston, Anjelica 251
Huston, John 39, 174, 182, 183, 213, 241, 245, 247, 249, 251, 252, 254-258, 260-268, 274, 275, 277-281, 284, 287, 289-292, 295-297, 662
Huston, Walter Antony 251
Hutchinson, Dora 394
Hutchinson, Tom 53, 202
Hunt, Roger 31
Hunter, Arline 646
Hunter, Ken 635
Huston, Jack 251
Hyams, Joe 158, 159, 547
Hyde, Johnny 123, 272, 350, 600
Hyde-White, Wilfrid 202, 225, 694
Hyman, Elliott 183
I Could Go On Singing 333
I Dream of Jeannie 450
"I Found A Dream" 25
I Love Louisa 508, 517, 530
"I Wanna Be Loved By You" 138, 690
Iannone, Sgt. Marvin 545, 549
"I'm Going to File My Claim" 673
"I'm Through With Love" 138, 671
Imitation of Life 215, 251, 272, 448
Immortal Marilyn 3, 669, 671, 675
Importance of Being Ernest, The 24
Importance of Living, The 136
In Cold Blood 566
"Incurably Romantic" 203, 697
Indiscreet 197
Inside Edition 673
Invasion of the Body Snatchers 250
Irma la Douce 131, 133, 226, 491
Irvine, Marie 467
Island of Pachyderms, The 231
It Happened in Brooklyn 358
It Happened One Night 248, 297
It Should Happen to You 131
Italian Cultural Institute 180
It's a Mad, Mad, Mad, Mad World 567
"Itsy Bitsy Teeney Weeney Yellow Polka Dot Bikini" 265
I've Got a Secret 387
Jackson, Anne 104
Jackson, Donald 113
Jackson, Eddie 469
Jackson, Janet 26, 385
Jackson, Michael 595, 622
Jackson, Shirley 136
Jacobs, Arthur P. 18, 31, 301, 302, 307, 508, 530, 545, 546, 659, 660, 662
Jacobs, Steve 659
Jailhouse Rock 111
James, Brandon 363, 637
James, Lorenzo 298

Jaws 194, 383
Jeakins, Dorothy 204, 205, 252
Jeanne Carmen: My Wild, Wild Life 637
Jeff 456
Jeffries, Nancy 669
Jeffries, Jr., Norman 427, 534, 546, 612, 639, 661
Jenkins, Jr., Burris 564
Jerome Robbins Ballet 469
Joerndt, Wilhelm and Mary 360
Johansson, Scarlett 605-607
John, (Sir) Elton 650, 674
"Johnny Angel" 553
Johnny Mann Singers 469
Johnson, Dorris 383
Johnson, Gerry 660
Johnson, Lady Bird 501
Johnson, Lyndon B. 302, 443, 473, 501, 628
Johnson, Nunnally 381, 383, 457, 506, 525, 582
Jones, Christopher 656
Jones, Hank 465
Jones, Jennifer 222, 341
Jordan, Louis 123
Jordan, Ted 634
Josephy, Robert 46
Journey, The 199
Joy of Cooking, The 87, 434
Joyce, James 5, 616
Judd, Ashley 634
Judgment at Nuremberg 333
Judy at Carnegie Hall 332
Julia 470
Julien's Auction House 37, 269, 616, 662
Jump Book 191
Jurgens, Curt 112
Justice, Michelle 4, 525
Invisible Man 99
Kafka, Franz 53
Kahn, Gus 138
Kalmar, Bert 138
Kane, Helen 138
Kanter, Jay 18, 662, 670
Kaplan, Fred 171
Karger, Anne 54, 156, 250, 577, 645
Karger, Fred 269, 341, 577, 578
Karger, Mary 645
Karolinska Institute 90
Kasperowicz, Leslie 3, 4, 665
Kaufman, Amy 63
Kautzky, Rudy 224, 255, 260, 261, 264, 274, 289, 499, 554, 578, 672
Kaye, Danny 131, 469
Kaye, Elizabeth 98-99
Kaye, Virginia 93
Kazan, Elia 57, 65, 73, 179, 222, 244, 251, 600, 603
Kazickas, Joe 100
Kazickas, Lucy 100
Keaton, Diane 387
Keitel, Harvey 655
Kelley, Tom 617, 618, 645, 646
Keller, Helen 391
Kelly, Gene 202, 203, 210, 216, 385, 407, 408, 523, 567, 582, 697, 698, 662
Kelly, (Princess) Grace 141, 301, 448, 530
Kelly, Nancy 75
Kennedy, Caroline 389, 396
Kennedy, Edward 628-629

Kennedy, Ethel Skakel 301, 406, 407, 468, 472, 475, 501, 502, 643
Kennedy, (President) John Fitzgerald 2, 77, 121, 217, 241, 259, 302, 307, 316, 317, 319, 337, 338, 359, 360, 363, 389, 390, 394, 395, 396, 406, 440, 441, 442, 443, 444, 445, 457, 461, 462, 466, 467, 468, 472, 473, 474, 475, 509, 517, 518, 520, 523, 525, 526, 527, 528, 531, 538, 622, 623, 624, 625, 627, 628, 629, 630, 632, 633, 637, 639, 643, 644, 647, 660, 661, 667, 672
Kennedy, Jr., John Fitzgerald 389
Kennedy, Jacqueline Bouvier 77, 319, 389, 390, 396, 405, 406, 442-444, 467, 468, 476, 517, 531, 538, 549, 565, 596
Kennedy, Joseph P. 74, 359, 409, 494, 622
Kennedy, Madge 203, 699
Kennedy Men, The 644
Kennedy, (Attorney General) Robert Francis 301, 302, 406, 407, 408, 409, 410, 411, 412, 420, 466, 467, 468, 472, 474, 475, 479, 494, 501, 502, 505, 506, 520, 525, 526, 527, 528, 621, 622, 623, 624, 625, 627, 628, 629, 630, 632, 633, 635, 636, 637, 638, 639, 642, 643, 644, 647
Kennedy, Rose 358
Kennedy, Suzie 3, 674
Kent, Jean 24, 62, 679
Kerouac, Jack 99, 171, 616
Kerr, Deborah 75, 76
Khrushchev, (Soviet Premier) Nikita 144, 186-189, 198, 204, 337
Kid for Two Farthings, A 23
Kilgallen, Dorothy 527, 528, 531, 630
Kilarr, Stanley 268-269
Kind of Blue 171
King, Dr. Martin Luther 92
King George V 18, 19, 23, 679
King George VI 17
King and I, The 75, 76
King, Coretta Scott 92
Kingsley, Pat 660
Kingston, Kenny 402, 531, 633
Kinney, James R. 662
Kirk, Lisa 569
Kirkland, Douglas 360, 363-366, 444, 484, 505
Kirkland, Sally 167
Kitt, Eartha 60
Knebelcamp, Enid 578
Knebelcamp, Sam 578
Knotts, Don 386, 593
Kohner, Susan 215
Konzal, Joseph 178
Kopechne, Mary Jo 628
Korman, Gene 533
Kovacs, Ernie 285, 567, 662
Krasner, Lee 86
Krasna, Norman 197, 198, 230
Krim, Arthur 444, 473, 474, 476
Krim, Mathilde 473, 474, 476
Kris, Dr. Marianne 74, 75, 233, 237, 307, 308, 312, 319, 320, 323-325, 328, 334, 349, 355, 489, 539, 555, 609-611, 662

Kris, Ernst 74
Krohn, Leon 148, 335, 516, 530
Krutak, Joseph 224, 485
Kubrick, Stanley 251
Kuchel, Thomas 625
Kupchik, George 76
Kyo, Machiko 76
La Bonge, Tom 677
L'Academie du Cinema 167
La Cucaracha 417
Ladd Company, The 660
Laderman, Ezra 655
Laderman, Gary 595
La Dolce Vita 297
Lady Chatterley's Lover 171
Lancaster, Burt 131, 448
Landers, Ann (columnist) 393, 662
Landers, Ann 147
Lanin, Lester 501
Lang Jr., Charles 137, 165, 380, 662
Lange, Jessica 605-606
Lansdale, Edward G. 528
Lapidus, Morris 416
Lark, The 192
LaRue, Frank 256, 261, 283, 285, 286
LaSalle, Mick 154
Last Days of Marilyn Monroe, The (book) 6
Last Days of Marilyn Monroe, The (film) 352, 636, 661
Last Picture Show, The 649
Last Yankee, The 657
Laszlo, Erno 662
Laughter is a Wonderful Thing 132
Laughton, Charles 23, 226
Laura 319
Lawford, Christopher 359
Lawford, Patricia Kennedy 338-360, 394, 399, 406-409, 420, 444, 472, 485, 498, 501, 506, 517, 520, 535, 543, 564, 576, 624, 644, 660-662
Lawford, Peter 337-339, 358-360, 394, 399, 406-409, 420, 441, 443, 444, 461, 464-466, 468-471, 485, 498, 501, 506, 517, 519, 520, 531, 535, 538-543, 556, 557, 564, 576, 582, 624, 635-637, 639, 642, 643, 644, 659-662
Lawrence of Arabia 391
Lawrence, T. E. 391
Leaf, Earl 137, 156
Leaming, Barbara 6, 122, 208, 218, 276, 602, 603
Leaming, Laurence 644
Leatherbee, Mary 167
Leave It to Beaver 68
Leave it to Me 206
Lederer, Pauline Friedman (see Ann Landers)
Lee, Harper 238
Lee, Lillian 301
Lee, Peggy 468, 469
Lee, Matt 88
Lee, Ted 88
Leeds, Dalia 82
Leibowitz, Murray 635
Leigh, Janet 149, 187, 238, 385, 407, 607
Leigh, Vivien 18, 21, 27, 29, 30, 33, 34, 37, 39, 49, 157, 185, 235
Leimert, Tim 508-509

Lemmon, Jack 131, 132, 140, 141, 143, 145, 152, 153, 156-158, 165, 224, 226, 485, 567, 582, 662, 686, 691
Lennon, John 595
LeRoy, Mervyn 391, 546-547
Les Diaboliques 201
Let's Make It Legal 131
Let's Make Love (film) 2, 13, 168, 187, 194, 197-232, 233, 235, 238, 243, 252, 256, 270, 272, 285, 287, 338, 375, 450, 480, 518, 675, 694-699
"Let's Make Love" (song) 225, 694, 697, 699
"Let's Twist Again" 408
Levant, Oscar 662
Levathes, Peter 379, 449, 490-493, 495, 506, 507, 516, 558, 591, 594
Levin, Gail 650
Levin, George 76
Levy, Alan 7, 216, 397, 402, 413-415, 495, 498
Lewinsky, Monica 445, 633
Lewis, Jerry 233, 380, 381, 416
Lewis, Ted 634
Liberace 81, 255
Lieber, Perry 492
Life Among the Savages 136
Life and Curious Death of Marilyn Monroe, The 629, 634
Life and Opinions of Maf the Dog, and of His Friend Marilyn Monroe, The 348
Life Story of an Ugly Duckling 136
Lincoln, Abraham 396
Lincoln, Evelyn 518
Lindberg Story, The 18
Lipkin, Dr. 320
Liszt, Franz 230
Litman, Robert Elkon 570, 586, 587
Little Caesar 133
Little Engine That Could, The 464
Little Foxes, The 353
Little Rock Nine 99
Little Women 358
Live From Lake Tahoe 1962 517
Livingston, Fud 138
Loden, Barbara 601-602
Loeb, John 506
Loewenstein, Rudolph 152,
Logan, Joshua 17, 28, 38, 185, 187, 330, 341, 523
Loggia, Robert 314
Longest Day, The 494
Lopez, Jennifer 120
Lord of the Flies 411
Lord of the Rings: Return of the King 218
Loren, Sophia 448, 566
Lorre, Peter 235
Loss for Roses, A 240
Lost Lady 193
Louis, Jean 252, 265, 270, 288, 338, 435, 448-451, 453, 462, 467, 470, 480, 529, 531, 612
Love, Darlene 593
Love in All Its Disguises 655
Love in the Afternoon 131
Lovell, Gloria 349, 362, 367, 609
Lover Come Back 198
Lowe, Rob 644
Lower, Ana 47, 574, 576, 672
Luce, Claire Booth 598-600

Lumet, Sidney 654
Lupino, Ida 403
Lyles, A. C. 567
Lynn, Mara 696
Lysistrata 51
Lytess, Natasha 39, 123, 250
Maas, Willard 172
Macbeth 413, 516
"Mack the Knife" 469
Mackintosh, Robert 168
MacLaine, Shirley 123, 188, 189, 209, 212, 215, 216, 221, 226, 227, 230, 231, 332, 337, 364, 380, 427, 469, 508
Macmillan, (Prime Minister) Harold 441
MacMurray, Fred 226, 376
Madden, Owney 133
Madonna 79, 605, 606
Maf-Honey 348, 349, 366, 436, 497, 499, 525, 526, 529, 540, 609, 662
Maggs, Paul 3, 667
Magnani, Anna 180
Magnum 25, 253, 264, 268, 270, 292
Maiden Voyage 66
Mailer, Norman 598, 626-629, 632, 654-655
Makeba, Marion 470
Making of Some Like It Hot, The 154
Malneck, Matty 138, 139
Maltin, Leonard 141, 154
"Mambo Italiano" 381
Mamoulian, Rouben 375
Manchurian Candidate, The 387, 462, 473
Mancini, Henry 448
Mankiewicz, Christopher 458-459
Mankiewicz, Joseph L. 375, 459, 592
Mann, Roderick 226
Manners, Dorothy 660
Manning, Dorothy 20
Mansfield, Jayne 68, 111, 192
Many Lives of Marilyn Monroe, The 4, 6, 622
Marais, Jean 77
March, Fredric 112, 123, 314, 341
Mardi Gras 654
Margolis, Jay 605
Marilyn (film) 592
"Marilyn" (song) 553
Marilyn (opera) 655
Marilyn: A Biography 5, 626, 632
Marilyn: A Case for Murder 638
Marilyn Among Friends 5, 655
Marilyn: An Untold Story 5, 655
Marilyn and Eve 345
Marilyn & Me 480
Marilyn and Me: Sisters, Rivals, Friends 6, 45, 75, 656
Marilyn & Norma Jean 634
Marilyn Conspiracy, The 638
Marilyn Files, The 638
Marilyn: Forever Blonde 676-677
Marilyn: Intimate Exposures 642
Marilyn Lives! 649
Marilyn Monroe: Life After Death 654
Marilyn Monroe LLC 611-612, 617-619
Marilyn Monroe: Murder Cover-Up 633

Marilyn Monroe Productions 25, 28, 58, 76, 107, 179, 182, 246, 335, 376, 490, 610, 670
Marilyn Monroe: Still Life 650, 654
Marilyn Monroe: The Biography 6, 639
Marilyn Monroe: The Final Days 380, 447, 556, 659
Marilyn on Location 45
Marilyn Remembered 1, 3, 605, 615, 665, 674
Marilyn's Man 652
Marilyn Scandal, The 7, 159, 543
Marilyn: Something's Got to Give 447, 477
Marilyn: The Exhibit, An Intimate Look at the Legend
Marilyn: The Last Interview 672
Marilyn: The Last Months 6, 362, 398, 632, 661
Marilyn: The Last Take 447, 466, 494, 638
Marilyn: The Passion and the Paradox 641, 669
Marilyn: The Premiere Collection 675
Marilyn: The Tragic Venus 155
Marilyn: The Ultimate Look at the Legend 476
Marilyn: The Untold Story 5, 95, 655
Markel, Lester 190-191, 216-217
Marlowe, Anne 313
Marquis de Sade 641
Marquis of Lafayette 78
Mars, Janice 193, 284
Marshall, David 3, 4, 631, 666, 667, 671
Martin, Dean 123, 202, 334, 337-340, 350, 380-381, 385, 387, 391, 407, 448, 476-477, 479, 481, 482, 484-486, 492, 493, 507, 508, 517, 526, 564, 582, 593
Martin, Jeanne 338, 350
Martin, Mary 114, 206, 229
Martin, Nicole 616
Marx, Barbara 340
Marx Brothers 130
Massee, Jordan 175-175
Masters, George 318-319, 417, 428, 467, 503
Mastroianni, Marcello 390
Mateo, Adolfo Lopez 577
Mating Game, The 202
Maucieri, Joan and John 401-402
Maugham, Somerset 313, 315, 318, 356, 376
Maverick 380
Maxwell, Charles 585
Maxwell, Elsa 77-78
May, Elaine 469
Mayer, Louis B. 248, 359
MCA (Music Corporation of America) 117, 134, 182, 246, 402, 485, 660, 662
McCann, Graham 143, 601, 647, 693,
McCarthy, (Senator) Joseph 251, 406, 419
McCarthy, Kevin 249, 250, 258, 700
McCoy, Clyde 139
McCullers, Carson 174-175
McCullers, Reeves 174
McGiver, John Irwin 387, 593

McGuire, Phyllis 518
McGuire Sisters 518
McHugh, Jimmy 137
McIntyre, Alice 256
McLaughlin, Judge Charles F. 76, 80
McNeil, Claudia 427
McQuade, Jimmy 176-177
Meader, Vaughn 469
Mekas, Jonas 4, 296
Mellen, Joan 298
Melson, Inez 6, 367, 409, 522, 545, 558, 573, 578, 610, 612, 613, 651, 662
"Memories Are Made of This" 381
Mendelson, Anne 88
Menken, Marie 172
Mercer, Johnny 335, 387, 448
Merrill, Robert 469
Meryman, Richard 4, 7, 13, 161, 322, 432, 465, 466, 472, 509-512, 602, 676
Metty, Russell 251, 258, 275, 280, 287, 295, 297
Metro Goldwyn Mayer Studios (MGM) 25, 36, 109, 118, 148, 194, 203, 205, 211, 240, 248, 330, 333, 358, 359, 385, 490, 591, 660
Meyer, Edward 616
Meyer, Fleur Cowles 174
Michaels, Evan 176-178
Middle of the Night 122-123
Middleman, Jill 614
Midnight Cowboy 473
Midnight Lace 198
Milk Fund for Babies 59, 83
Miller, Arthur 3, 17, 18, 25-35, 38, 42, 44-54, 56, 57, 59, 60, 62, 63, 65-67, 69-74, 76-78, 80-83, 85-101, 103-111, 113-115, 117-119, 122-125, 133-135, 138-139, 141-142, 144, 147-148, 152, 155-157, 159-160, 162-163, 168-169, 173-177, 180-184, 187-190, 193-194, 199-201, 203, 205-206, 208-209, 211, 213-216, 218, 220, 222, 228, 230, 235-236, 239, 241, 243-251, 253-262, 264-268, 270-273, 275-277, 280, 284, 286-291, 293-295, 297-298, 303-309, 314, 316-318, 339, 347-349, 352, 369, 398, 406, 413-414, 418, 420, 424, 434, 461, 495, 498, 534, 541, 564, 565, 569, 577, 578, 600-604, 654, 656-658, 662, 696
Miller, Augusta 73, 87, 327-328
Miller, Daniel 657-658
Miller, Frank 262, 266
Miller, Isidore 73, 327-328, 411-412, 415-417, 424, 462, 468, 472, 474-476, 534, 554
Miller (Doyle), Jane 71, 73, 89, 98, 99, 142, 152, 177, 181, 182, 205, 308, 346, 414, 436, 577, 657
Miller, Mary (See Mary Grace Slattery)
Miller, Rebecca 656, 657
Miller, Robert "Bobby" 71, 73, 89, 90, 93, 94, 97, 98, 99, 139, 152, 181, 182, 203, 205, 308, 346, 369, 410, 411, 414, 435, 436, 577

Million Dollar Request Radio 356
Mills, Bart 45
Mills, John 34
Mills, Mary 34
Milton Greene Archives 619
Min and Bill 136
Miner, John 559, 639-642
Mines, Harry 256, 264
Minnelli, Vincente 123, 194, 235, 335
Miracle, Berniece 6, 73, 135, 312, 554, 560, 573, 574, 577, 603, 609, 651-652, 662
Miracle, Mona Rae 4, 6, 135, 554, 651-652
Miracle, Paris 115, 554, 652
Miracle on 34th Street 250
Miracle Worker, The 391
Mirisch Brothers 134
Mirisch Company 131, 135
Mirisch, Harold 137
Mirisch, Walter 135
Misfits, The 2, 4, 11, 110, 113, 117, 125, 135, 182-183, 199-200, 211, 213, 218, 220, 228-229, 238-242, 243-281, 283-299, 302, 305-307, 311, 315, 318, 333, 343, 348, 353, 357, 427, 448, 449, 495, 602, 604, 610, 656, 700-709
"Misfits or Chicken Feed: The Last Frontier of the Quixotic Cowboy, The" 93, 96
Miss Sadie Thompson 314
Mister Roberts 131
Mitchell, Laurie 148
Mitchell, Margaret 248
Mitchell, Philip 251
Mitchum, Robert 247, 297
Mizrahi (Strasberg), Anna 611-618, 655
MM—Personal from the Private Archive of Marilyn Monroe 7, 93, 97, 139, 216, 410, 613
Monette, Valmore H. 308, 383, 521
Monkey Business 131
Monroe, Della 602
Monroe: Her Life in Pictures 669
Monroe, Memory 675
Monroe Six 176, 241
Montand, Yves 194, 200, 201, 205, 206, 208-211, 213-215, 218, 220-224, 226-231, 233, 238-241, 267, 271, 276, 287, 662, 694
Montgomery, Robert H. 76
Moon and Sixpence, The 313
"Moon River" 190, 448
Moore, Dudley 35
Moore, John 26, 70, 118, 121, 122, 135
Moore, Lord Garrett 29, 31
Mora, Philippe 642
Morality of Sigmund Freud, The 358
Morath (Miller), Inge 111, 253, 254, 267, 272, 281, 304-305, 414, 416, 418, 657
Morehouse, Ward 315
Morely, Robert Christopher 454-455
Moreno, Rita 429
Morgan, Joel 3, 667
Morgan, Keya 644-645
Morgan, Michelle 1, 7, 35, 44, 109, 534

Moriarty, Evelyn 2, 209, 210, 255, 261, 267, 274, 275 280, 315, 398, 424, 350, 358, 384, 385, 501, 647, 662
Morrissey, Jimmy 367
Morrow, Dwight 421
Mosby, Aline 118
Moskowitz, Joseph 117, 356
Motion Picture Code 22
Moulin Rouge 247
Move Over Darling (film) 198, 593-594
"Move Over Darling" (song) 593
Mr. President 523, 535
Mr. Hobbs Takes a Vacation 387
Mr. Peters' Connections 656
Mrs. Doubtfire 165
Mud on the Stars 179
Murder on the Orient Express 35
Murdoch, Robert 594
Murphey, Theodore 558
Murray, Christopher 677
Murray, Churchill 361, 415, 420, 423
Murray, Eunice Joerndt 234, 235, 335, 359, 360-362, 369, 398-401, 407, 415, 417-418, 424, 426-427, 433, 436, 441, 451-453, 463, 485, 492, 498-500, 506, 511, 522-524, 533-534, 536-546, 549, 554, 557-559, 567, 578, 624, 626, 631-633, 635, 637-639, 642, 661-662, 673
Murray, Don 670, 677-678
Murray, Jacqueline 361
Murray, John 234, 235, 361
Murray, (Colonel) John M. 234
Murray, Marilyn 361, 549
Murray, Patricia 361, 549
Murrow, Edward R. 13, 510
Music Man, The 114
"My Blue Heaven" 72
My Fair Lady 33, 202, 381, 570
My Favorite Martian 226
My Favorite Wife 376
My Geisha 230
"My Heart Belongs to Daddy" 206, 229, 285
My Life So Far 141
My Lucky Stars 221
My Path & My Detours 568
My Sister Marilyn 4, 6, 346, 652
My Story 4, 6, 13, 610
My Week with Marilyn 36, 62, 669
"Myself Exercising" 53
Mysteries at The Museum 673
Naar, Delores 541-543, 644
Naar, Joseph 541-543, 644
Nabokov, Vera 224
Nabokov, Vladimir 206, 224
Naked Lunch 171
Nash, Alanna 225
Nasser, Julia 89
National Institute of Arts and Letters 125
Negulesco, Jean 507
Nehru, (Prime Minister) Jawaharlal 442
Neighborhood Tales 655
Neill, Frank 558
Neugenbauer, William 577
New Fannie Farmer Boston Cooking-School Cook Book, The 87
New Steve Allen Show, The 387
New York Export: Opus Jazz 469

New York Psychoanalytic Institute 74, 559, 659
New Watergate Theatre Club 51
Newcomb, Carmen Adams 301
Newcomb, (Margot) Patricia 2, 18, 123, 288-289, 301-305, 308-309, 315-316, 326-327, 329, 348, 350, 361, 366, 394, 399, 407, 417-418, 427-429, 462, 464-465, 474-475, 480, 483, 485, 492-494, 497, 499, 501-502, 504, 507, 510, 512, 524, 531, 534-538, 545, 547, 549, 553, 555-556, 558, 562, 564-565, 571, 578-579, 624, 635, 642, 659-660
Newell, Roy 427
Newman, Eve 139, 144
Newman, Jack 177
Newman, Lionel 203-204
Newman, Paul 124, 185, 312, 431, 508
Niagara 3, 112, 205, 252, 289, 533, 567, 685
Nicholas, Joan 148
Nichols, Mike 469
Nicholson, Jack 387, 611, 655
Niesen, Gertrude 284
Niven, David 525
Nivola, Constantino 86
Nixon, Hanna 3, 4, 665
Nixon, Richard M. 191, 217, 349, 628-629
Nizer, Louis 591
No Strings 470
Noguchi, Thomas Tsunetomi 558-560, 585, 588-590, 635, 639
Norell, Norman 118, 428, 432, 462, 507, 612
Norma Jean: My Secret Life With Marilyn Monroe 634
Norma Jean: The Life and Death of Marilyn Monroe 5, 286
Norstad, (General) Lauris 443
North, Alex 251-252, 292
North By Northwest 199, 203
North, Sheree 111,
Norton, Mildred 335
Nostalgia Isn't What It Used to Be 230
Not Tonight, Josephine! 124, 129
Novak, Kim 111, 123, 199, 239, 341, 356, 380, 407, 408, 493, 596
Novello, Angela 643
Nugent, Sir Terence and Lady Nugent 34
Nunez, Betty 613
Nunez, Gilbert 613
Nun's Story, The 215, 380
Nussbaum, (Rabbi) Max 454
Nygards, Leif-Erik 504-505
Obama, Barack 623
O'Brien, Larry 474
O'Brien, Pat 133, 686
O'Casey, Sean 216, 662
Ocean's 11 203, 337, 381
Odets, Clifford 181, 224-225, 596, 662
O'Donnell, Kenneth 461, 474, 643
O'Doul, "Lefty" Francis Joseph 285, 541
Of Human Bondage 112, 313, 355-356
Of Mice and Men 284
Of Women and Their Elegance 654

Offer, David 614
O'Hagan, Andrew 348-349
O'Hara, Maureen 81
Ohrt, Hans 498
Old Man and The Sea, The 113
Olivier, Sir, Laurence 18, 17, 20-45, 47, 49, 50, 52, 53, 56-63, 313, 566, 679
On the Avenue 198
On the Road 99
On the Town 203
Onassis, Aristotle 468
One Flew Over The Cuckoo's Nest 473
One Two Three 131
O'Neill, Eugene 5, 315, 604, 658
Oppenheimer, Joel 649
Oppenheimer, Robert 191
Orozco, Nieves 419, 536
Orry-Kelly, Jack 137-138, 165, 182
Osborn, Paul 66, 179
Oscar Awards (see Academy of Motion Picture Arts & Sciences)
Osgood, Samuel 419
Ostrow, Jack 311
Oswald, Lee Harvey 462, 628
Otash, Fred 624
Other, The 386
O'Toole, Peter 391
Out of Africa 174
Outer Space Jitters 646
Over and Out 655
"Over the Rainbow" 286, 332, 579
Owens, Clyde 114
Owens, Kitty 114
Pace, Charles 548
Pacino, Al 655
"Paddleball" 252
Pagen, Aileen Doris and William 402, 436
Pahlavi, (Shah) Mohammed Reza Pahlavi 453-454
Paine, Thomas 155
Pajama Game, The 462
Palmer, Edith 269, 286
Palmer, Lilli 212, 215
Paramount Studios 137, 189, 190, 197, 287, 288, 289, 290, 291, 380
Paret, Benny "Kid" 462
Paris, Barry 189
Paris Blues 93, 99, 190, 312
Parkinson-Morgan, Kate 665
Parone, Edward 261, 281
Parsons, Louella 34, 35, 137, 298, 339,
Parton, Margaret 328-329
Past Forgetting: My Love Affair with Dwight D. Eisenhower 445
Patrick, Gail 376
Patricola, Miss 138
Pattern, Neal 569
Peacock, Robert 115
Pearson, Albert "Albie" Gregory 486-487
Peck, Gregory 199, 238, 391
Pepitone, Lena 113, 156, 159, 162, 180, 346, 523
Period of Adjustment 387
Perkins, Anthony 238
Peron, Eva 649
Perry Como Show, The 192
Perry Mason 133, 610
Person to Person 13, 510, 670
Perultz, Carl 117
Peters, Jean 205

Petrarch, Francesco 559
Peyton Place 111
Phil Silvers Show, The 386
Philadelphia Story, The 197
Philco Television Playhouse 386
Philippe, Claude 77
Philippe, Gerard 77
Photoplay 20, 176
Piaf, Edith 200
Pickford-Fairbanks Studios 133
Pickford, Mary 133, 473
Picnic 185
Pillow Talk 198, 200, 212, 215, 448
Piquet, Jean Pierre 423, 426
Pinal, Silvia 425
Pinewood Studios 28, 32, 35, 38, 44, 49, 50, 51, 52, 57, 209
Pinner, Sue Ann 670
Place in the Sun, A 248, 249
Planer, Franz 380, 450, 454, 455
Plath, Sylvia 194
Playhouse 90 314
"Please Don't Kill Anything" 95
Pletcher, Marjorie 148, 224, 450, 497, 525-526, 574, 575, 578
Plisetskaya, Maya 502
Plod, Inspector 31
Plummer Jr., Bob 277
Pocahontas 649
Pocketful of Miracles 259
Poitier, Sidney 131, 141, 31
Polaire, Hal 155
Polar, Dan 115
Pollard, Betty 639
Pollard, Elizabeth 639
Pollard, Michael 189
Pollock, Jackson 86
Pomerance, Molly 654
Poncher, Elsie 583
Poncher, Richard 583
Porgy and Bess 140, 141, 212
Porter, Cole 123, 206, 335, 569
Porterfield, Pearl 211-212, 270, 578
Portrait in Black 448
Portrait of Clare 23
Potter, Jeffrey 85, 94
Potter, Job 86
Potter, Penny 85
Poucette 433
Powell, Bud 156
Powell, Dick 187, 198
Powers, David 395, 441, 443
Preminger, Otto 141, 491
Presley, Elvis 111, 200, 224, 225, 259, 595, 609, 617, 622, 667, 678
Preston, John 559
Preston, Robert 114
Price, The 656
Prideaux, Tom 601-604
Prince and the Showgirl, The 17-63, 66, 67, 69, 78, 111, 119, 134, 156, 168, 176, 180, 182, 610, 670, 673, 679-686
Prince Miguel of Braganza 423
Prince, the Showgirl, and Me, The 36
Princess Margaret 54-55
Private Life of Sherlock Holmes, The 131
Prizzi's Honor 252
Proctor, Jim 87, 88
Professor's House, The 193
Profiles in Courage 395

Profiles in History Auction House 121
Project XX 313
Prowse, Juliette 188, 337, 392
Psycho 164, 238, 385, 607
Psychoanalytic Study of the Child, The 75
Public Enemy, The 133
Pucci, Emilio 344, 351, 392, 394, 417, 418, 426, 435, 465, 558, 575, 576, 672
Pulitzer Prize 73, 83, 160, 175, 178, 238, 289, 395
Pursel, Bill 568
"Put the Blame on Mame" 448
Qualye, Anthony 35, 54
Queen Elizabeth II 21, 52, 53-55
Radizwell, Lee 442
Raft, George 133, 686
Rain 3, 313-315, 318, 333, 335, 341-342
Rainmaker, The 75
Raintree County 111, 248
Rand, Ayn 598-599
Randall, Tony 198, 202, 215, 218, 694
Rattigan, Terence 18-22, 24, 25, 27, 34, 35, 53, 54, 61
Rauh, Joe 80, 317, 603
Rauh, Olie 80, 317
Rat Pack 203, 336, 337, 340, 358, 381, 385, 390, 502
Ray, Johnny 29
Razo, Joe 677
Reasoner, Harry 596
Rebecca 17
Red Shoes, The 22
Redford, Robert 342
Redgrave, Michael 566
Redmond, Cherie 311-312, 426, 499, 523, 610
Reed, Donna 76
Reed, Rex 332
Reflections in a Golden Eye 174
Reid, Elliott 469
Reis, May 73, 78, 114, 136, 233, 238, 250, 255, 256, 261, 264, 269, 270, 274, 276, 283, 287, 288, 303, 307, 311, 312, 316, 323, 326, 328, 332, 343, 346, 347, 426, 464, 465, 578, 609, 610, 611, 658, 662
Reis, Virginia 73
Reiss, Marilyn 238-239
Rella, Ettore 115, 662
Rella, Jesse 115
Remick, Lee 179, 194, 199, 492
"Rendezvous" 252
Renna, Madame 498, 662
Renner, Elmer "Bones" 270
Reporters, The 638
"Requiem for a Heavyweight" 314
Requiem for a Nun 194
Resnais, Alain 297
Rest in Peace: A Cultural History of Death and the Funeral Home in 20th Century America 595
"Return to Me" 381
Reynolds, Debbie 76, 121, 187, 220, 335, 374, 568-569, 614
Rice, Donna 632
Richman, Roger 611
Ride Down Mt. Morgan, The 657
Rie, Dr. Oskar 74
Rief, Phillip 358
Ries, Pamela 539

Rights of Man 155
Riordan, Robert 462
Ripley's Believe It Or Not 616
Ritchie, Michael 614
Ritter, Thelma 247, 250, 258, 267, 282, 593-594, 662, 700
River of No Return 491, 669, 671, 673
Rivera, Diego 419, 422
Rizzo, Willy 393-394
Robards, Jr., Jason 125, 601
Robbins, Alfred 556
Robbins, Dr. Bernard 358
Robbins, Jerome 469
Roberts, Gainsborough David 120
Roberts, Julia 655
Roberts, Ralph 6, 45, 46, 134, 187, 192-193, 194, 205, 241, 251, 255, 256, 257, 261, 262-263, 264, 265, 268, 269, 270-273, 275, 276, 277, 283-284, 285-286, 287-288, 289, 290, 303, 316, 317-318, 319, 324, 329, 330, 347-348, 349, 362-363, 431, 442-443, 499-500, 517, 524, 530, 534, 539, 554, 578, 626, 643, 648, 658-659, 705
Robinson, Jr., Edward G. 133, 693
Rockefeller Center Sidewalk Superintendents Club 91
Rockefeller, Jr., John D. 58
Rockefeller, Laurence S. 91
Rockefeller, Nelson 216
Rockettes 59
Rockford Files, The 380
Rocky and Bullwinkle 143
Rocha, Guy 518
Roche, Serge 71
Rocky 473
Rodgers and Hammerstein 114
Rodgers and Hart 335
Rodgers, (Dr.) Mortimer 185
Rodgers, Richard 114, 335
Rogers, Will 414
Rollyson, Carl 4, 6, 132, 278, 280, 298, 693, 708
Roman Catholic Legion of Decency 164, 292-293
Roman Holiday 380
Romanoff, Gloria 323, 350, 362, 408
Romanoff, Mike 350, 362
Romeo and Juliet 114
Romero, Cesar 339
Romper Room 391
Room at the Top 201, 215
Roosevelt, (President) Franklin Delano 494
Roosevelt, Theodore 395
Roots of Heaven, The 183
Roselli, Johnny 519
Rose Tattoo, The (play) 250
Rose Tattoo, The (film) 180
Rosenberg, Anna 474
Rosenfeld, Henry 523
Rosenman, Samuel 494
"Roslyn" 252
Rosten, Hedda 31, 36, 50, 89, 159, 173, 201, 311, 312, 317, 326, 439, 523, 655
Rosten, Norman 5, 88, 89, 90, 91, 95, 108, 121, 124, 125, 135, 151, 170, 172, 278, 318, 318, 355, 443, 511, 535, 567, 609, 654-655

Rosten (Filan), Patricia 99, 109, 347, 655
Roth, Janet 367
Rothberg, Howard 527, 630
"Round-Up Suite" 252
Route 66 515
Rowan, Dan 660
Rowan, Mary 660
Rubinstein, Helena 467
Ruby, Harry 138
Ruby, Jack 628
Rudd, Jonah 336
Rudin, Elizabeth (see Elizabeth Greenson Rudin) 234, 353
Rudin, Mickey 270
Rudin, Milton 240, 311, 312, 353, 376, 402, 488, 489, 542, 543, 545, 546, 547, 578, 610, 612, 662
"Run For Your Life" 529
"Runnin' Wild" 138, 139, 687
Russell, Jane 568, 662
Russell, Lillian 152, 167
Russell, Rosalind 163, 391, 569
Rust, Cynthia and Henry 614
Ryan, Robert 523
Ryder, Winona 657
Sadie Thompson 313-315, 318, 329, 341-342
Sagan, Francoise 566
Saint Joan 23
Salinger, Pierre 302, 624, 660
Samuel Goldwyn Studios 133
Sanctuary, The 194, 240, 241
Sandburg, Carl 175, 178, 334-335, 346, 367, 391-392, 394, 397, 437, 557, 558, 579, 662
SANE (National Committee for a Sane Nuclear Policy) 92, 216
Sane Society, The 92
Sawyer, Diane 470
Scarface 133
Saratoga 248, 591
Sartre, Jean-Paul 183, 291,
Save the Tiger 131
Sawyer, Gail 254
Sawyer, Grant 254, 518
Say Goodbye to the President 527, 636, 661
Schaefer, Walter 547, 635
Schagrin, Robert 616
Schary, Dore 109
Schell, Maria 118-119,
Schenck, Joseph 184, 223, 275
Schiller, Lawrence 5, 214, 480-481, 483-486, 535-536, 583, 597, 670
Schipper, Henry 447
Schlesinger, Jr., Arthur 474, 475, 501, 644
Schlesinger, Carl 92
Schneider, Helene 114
Schneider, Isidore 114
Schofield, Paul 356
Schreiner, Greg 1, 2, 3, 534, 605, 615, 665-666, 669, 672-673
Schreyeck, Elaine 43
Schreiber, Flora Rheta 554
Schreiber, Lew 111-112
Schulberg, Budd 406
Schulman, Arnold 261, 376, 380, 381, 383
Schumach, Murray 490, 493
Schwartz, Emanuel 141
Schwartz, Helen 141
Schwarzenegger, Arnold 213, 618

Schweitzer, Dr. Albert 92
Scoman, Patricia 652
Scott, Randolph 376
Scott, Vernon 341, 482, 492, 494
Screen Actor's Guild 159, 214, 250, 455, 618
Seaton, Patricia 636, 661
"Second Time Around, The" 332
Secret Happiness of Marilyn Monroe, The 652
Selznick, David O. 21, 222, 223, 662
Sennett, Matt 130
Separate Tables 18
Serafina 209
Sergeants 3 337
Serling, Rod 313, 314, 341,
Sesame, Imperial, and Pioneer Club 52
Seven Arts Productions 183, 246
Sex Kittens Go to College 646
Shackney, Robert 596
Shade, Rose 661
Shaggy Dog, The 163
Shakespeare, William 114, 516
Shaw, Anabel 509
Shaw, Anne 89, 173
Shaw, Artie 72
Shaw, Edie 89, 618, 654
Shaw Family Archives 618
Shaw, George Bernard 23
Shaw, Larry 89, 617, 618, 654
Shaw, Lee (see Aleshia Brevard)
Shaw, Meta 89, 618, 654
Shaw, Sam 5, 83, 87, 89, 93, 100, 173, 175, 214, 312, 571, 617, 654, 655, 670
Shawlee, Joan 133, 687
Shearer, Norma 197
Shepard, Alan 318
Sherman, Harold 498
Sherman, Lynne 541
Sherwood Anderson and Other Famous Creoles 422
Shevey, Sandra 223, 238, 543, 555
Shinbone Alley 60
Shiran, Shiran 474
Shore (Montgomery), Dinah 662
Short, Bobby 70
Show Boat 132
Shriver, Eunice Kennedy 474
Shriver, Robert Sargent 474
Shurlock, Geoffrey 22
Sick Humor of Lenny Bruce, The 171
Siegel, Lee 455, 529
Signoret, Simone 168, 200, 201-202, 205, 210-213, 215, 216, 218, 222, 227, 228, 230, 231, 267, 305, 603
Silence of the Lambs 473
Silk Stockings 385
Silvers, Phil 233, 386, 480, 593
Simmel, Ernst 234
Simon and Garfunkle 652
Simpson, Babs 504, 505
Simpson, Wallace 147
Sims, Gary 671
Sims, Mary 3, 671, 678
Sinatra, Frank 38, 56, 72, 123, 131, 155, 188, 201, 202, 203, 233, 235, 250, 270, 276, 317, 326, 334, 336, 339, 340, 348, 362, 364, 376, 385, 390, 392, 393, 415, 428, 435, 440, 473, 485, 508, 517, 529, 541, 566, 576, 577, 637, 662

Singin' in the Rain 203, 385
Sitwell, Dame Edith 52-53
Sixth Symphony 579
60 Minutes 627
Skakel, Jr., George 301
Skipsey, Eric 366
Skolsky, Sidney 205, 210, 306, 395, 427, 444, 445, 516, 535, 643, 662
Skouras, Spyros 113, 133, 135, 187, 188, 213, 230, 333, 373, 379, 451, 482, 490, 494, 506, 577, 662, 675
Slattery (Miller), Mary Grace 122
Slatzer, Robert 81, 528, 621, 622, 629-634, 636, 638, 662
Sleeping Beauty 20
Sleeping Car to Trieste 24
Sleeping Prince, The 27, 49, 53, 55
Sleeping Tiger, The 24
Sloden, (Rev.) A. J. 578-579, 581
Smash 669
Smathers, (Senator) George 443, 643
Smith, Jean Kennedy 338, 409, 474, 624, 662
Smith, Liz 497
Smith, Lois Weber 309, 660
Smith, Matthew 640-641
Smith, Percy 238
Smith, Steven Edward 474-475
"Smoke Gets in Your Eyes" 72
Snow White 20
Snyder, Allan "Whitey" 24, 31, 187, 214, 255, 257, 264, 279, 283, 284, 285, 315, 360, 413, 450, 480, 481, 483, 494, 506, 508, 525, 526, 554-555, 574, 575, 576, 577, 578, 581, 631, 675
Snyder, Beverly 578
Snyder, Roland 527
Snyder, Sherry 578
Solid Gold Cadillac, The 76, 449
Solomon, Lindy 118
Solomon, Sandy Sue 118
Solomon and Sheba 199
Solotaire, George 315, 346, 499, 522, 577
Soma, Enrica 251
Some Came Running 123, 337, 381
Some Like It Hot (film) 11, 129-145, 147-165, 167, 175, 178, 179, 186, 191, 197, 198, 200, 212, 215, 218, 226, 227, 257, 307, 383, 402, 414, 582, 606, 610, 662, 671, 672, 673, 686-694
"Some Like It Hot" (song) 138
"Someone to Watch Over Me" 338
Somerset Maugham TV Theatre 313
Something's Got to Give 2, 187, 198, 367, 373-387, 418, 433, 435, 447, 448, 453, 454, 476, 477, 490, 491, 494, 497, 506-508, 510, 525, 527, 536, 562, 575, 591-593, 597, 669, 670
Sondheim, Stephen 114
Song, Mickey 2, 466-467
Song without End 230
"Sorry Song, A" 615
Sorvino, Mira 634
Sotheby's 121, 135
Soule, Henri 315
Sound and the Fury, The 123, 199
Sound of Music, The 114, 594

South Pacific 132, 272
South Sea Bubble 33
Spada, James 3, 669
Spartacus 251
"Special Problems in Psychotherapy with the Rich and Famous" 235, 524
"Specialization" 203, 224
Spellbound 281
Spender, Lady Natasha 52
Spenser, Jeremy 19, 23, 679
Speriglio, Milo 622, 629, 631, 633, 634, 638, 640
Spewack, Bella and Sam 380
Spindel, Bernard 624
"Spinning Wheel" 71
Splendor in the Grass 222
"Splish Splash" 469
Spock, Dr. Benjamin 92, 616
Spoto, Donald 6, 20, 32, 43, 58, 73, 145, 152, 179, 246, 275, 325, 360, 363, 380, 398, 407, 427, 430, 443, 444, 447, 489, 499, 516, 517, 519, 521, 524, 527, 530, 534, 539, 547, 621, 639, 659
Spratling, William 3, 421-422, 433,
Springer, John 134, 160, 302, 307, 315, 320, 325, 326, 327, 330, 344, 351, 365, 465-466, 525, 604, 662
St. Cyr, Lily 339, 634
Stack, Robert 339
Stadiem, William 113, 162
Stanley, Kim 122
Stapleton, Maureen 193, 241, 277, 350, 351
Star is Born, A 197, 314, 333
"Star Spangled Banner, The" 469
Star Wars 660
Star Without Light 200
State Fair 241, 259
Steckler, Len 367-368
Steichen, Edward 503
Stein, Irving 18, 47, 76, 77
Steinbeck, John 329, 515
Steinberg, Dr. Oscar 183
Steinem, Gloria 4, 6, 12, 82, 565, 598, 649
Stekel, Wilhelm 234
Sten, Anna 119
Stengel, Marjorie 311, 349, 392
Sterling, Jan 543
Stern, Bertram "Bert" 5, 424, 502-505, 507, 508, 595
Stern, Phil 158
Steve Allen Show, The 387
Stevens, Diane 307-308, 351
Stevens, George 655, 660
Stevens, Jr., George 660
Stevenson, Adlai 55, 217, 241, 475
Stevenson, Hattie 73, 114, 311, 436, 523
Stewart, James 18, 199, 224, 328
Stewart, Robert 328
Sting, The 342, 383
Stocker, Mrs. Ed 320
Stolley, Richard 547
Stone, George E. 133, 686
Story of The Misfits, The 253
Story on Page One, The 181
Stothart, Herbert 138
Stoughton, Cecil 475, 538
Stradling, Harry 199
Strahm, Shirlee 255, 267, 268

Strange Death of Marilyn Monroe, The 623, 624, 625
Strasberg, Anna (See Anna Mizrahi)
Strasberg, John 115, 116, 142, 170, 186, 368, 523, 611, 655-656
Strasberg, Lee 11, 28, 31, 37, 39, 45, 49, 50, 66, 74, 75, 90, 115, 134, 142, 149, 162, 170, 173, 184, 186, 189, 192, 233, 239, 240, 273, 276, 308, 311, 312, 313, 314, 317, 323, 324, 332, 333, 341, 342, 347, 368, 379, 452, 523, 524, 554, 565, 577, 579-580, 596, 602, 603, 609, 610, 611, 612, 615, 616, 652, 655-656, 658, 662, 671
Strasberg, Paula 25, 28, 31, 37, 38, 39, 42, 43, 45, 49, 50, 56, 61, 75, 90, 115, 136-137, 140, 141, 142, 152, 153, 158, 162, 170, 173, 184, 189, 192, 208, 209, 220, 222, 235, 250, 255, 256, 257, 260, 261, 262-264, 267, 268, 272, 273, 275, 276, 284, 285, 289, 291, 292, 308, 311, 313, 314, 323, 324, 332, 334, 347, 369, 379, 452, 455, 464, 484, 485, 516, 523, 554, 577, 580, 603, 610, 611, 655-656, 662, 696
Strasberg, Susan 6, 38, 39, 45, 48, 49, 75, 82, 85, 91, 95, 104, 115, 141, 142, 169, 170, 183, 184, 276, 311, 315, 327, 368, 428, 429, 431, 451, 456, 503, 510, 565, 571, 611, 622, 647, 655-656
Streetcar Named Desire, A 21, 49, 185, 199, 251, 453
Streisand, Barbra 659
Stripper, The 341
Styne, Jule 192, 529
Styx, Mrs. 262, 263
Suddenly, Last Summer 157, 215, 248
"Sugar Blues" 138, 139
Sugar Finney 109
Sullivan, Ed 59, 68,
"Summer Place, A" (song) 238
Summer Place, A (film) 272
Summers, Anthony 7, 149, 235, 277, 339, 356, 409, 441, 487, 520, 527, 535, 538, 541-542, 543, 546, 547, 621, 635, 636, 637-638, 647, 661
Summers, Peter 442
Summersby, Kay 445
"Summit Ridge Drive" 72
Svendsen, Clara 174
Swanson, Gloria 314, 359, 396
Swanson on Swanson 396
"Sway" 381
Sweet Bird of Youth 179
Sweet Smell of Success 131
Swiss Family Robinson 375
Symington, Stuart 217
Tabachnick, (Dr.) Norman D. 570
Talese, Gay 521
Talmack, Mattie 118, 135
Talmadge, Norma 184
Tandy, Jessica 185, 313
Tanner Family 104
Taper Collection 178
Taraborrelli, J. Randy 169, 183, 338, 351, 359, 395, 406, 408, 409, 443, 643

Tashlin, Frank 68, 376, 380
Tateishi, Sam 437
Taupin, Bernie 650
Taylor, Curtice "Tucky" 109, 110
Taylor, Elizabeth 21, 124, 157, 187, 188, 215, 220, 249, 327, 332, 338, 340, 358, 364, 374, 375, 389, 450, 454, 458, 479, 480, 481, 486, 490, 536, 566
Taylor, Frank 108, 109, 182, 187, 218, 243, 247, 251, 253, 254, 275, 287, 290, 291, 292, 297, 306, 324
Taylor, Mark 109
Taylor, Maxwell D. 528
Taylor, Mike 109
Taylor, Nan 108, 251, 324
Taylor, Nova 433
Taylor, Renee 677
Tchaikovsky, Pyotr Ilyich 579
Teahouse of the August Moon 76
Tender is the Night 253, 383
Tennant, Cecil 27, 32, 42
Terms of Endearment 364
Texaco Star Theatre 202
Texas John Slaughter 385
"Thanks for the Memory" 471
"Thanks, Mr. President" 471
That Touch of Mink 198, 391, 526
"That's Amore" 381
There's No Business Like Show Business 139, 669
Theron, Charlize 605, 606
They Shoot Horses, Don't They? 212
Thomas, Bob 118
Thomas, Clarence 633
Thomas, Danny 367
Thomas, Dylan 52
Thomas, Florence 500, 578
Thompson, Greg 3, 676-677
Thompson, J. Lee 508, 530
Thompson, Tommy 547
Thompson, Sunny 3, 676
Thorndike, (Dame) Sybil 19, 23, 24, 34, 40, 61, 209, 679
Three Faces of Eve, The 111, 383
Three Stooges 203, 646
Thrill of It All, The 198
Tierney, Gene 319
Time and Tide 179, 199, 200
Timebends 92, 95, 199, 258, 273, 348, 569, 658
Titanic 218, 591
"To a Wild Rose" 71
To Kill A Mockingbird 238, 391
To Norma Jeane with Love, Jimmie 652
To Tell the Truth 652
To the Actor 136
Today 654
Todd, Mabel Ellsworth 442
Todd, Michael 490
Tolman, Ray 427, 530
Tolstoy, Leo 72, 616
Tomich, Alan B. 562, 635
Tone, Franchot 330
Tonight Show, The 386
Too Many Husbands 376
Tootsie 165, 605, 606
Topping, Dan 331
Torero 423
Torquet, Manel 3, 667
Torre, Marie 342
Touch of Evil 251
Towers, George 382
Toys in the Attic 314, 353

Tracy, Spencer 112, 113, 117, 567
Travilla, William 204, 450, 675
Travis, Neal 636
Tree, Marietta Peabody 251, 259
Tree Grows In Brooklyn, A 529
Trial, The 53
Trilling, Diana 599
TriStar Motion Picture Group 660
Trouble in Paradise 43
Truman, (President) Harry S. 32, 405
Trundy (Jacobs), Natalie 546-547
Tryon, Tom 385-386, 457
Tugboat Annie 136
Turner, Christopher 353, 555
Turner, Lana 111, 358, 374, 448
Turner, Roy 4
Twentieth Century-Fox Studios (see Fox)
Twilight 251
Twilight Zone, The 539
"Twist, The" 237, 355, 408, 502
Two Women 448
Tydings, Joseph 527
Uhley, (Dr.) Milton 486
Uncle Vanya 566
Under the Boardwalk 654
Union Prayer Book for Jewish Worship 616
United Artists 22, 133, 134, 183, 226, 246, 263, 274, 275, 391, 473
Universal Studios 111, 200, 274, 391, 448, 525
Untermeyer, Louis 168, 662
Valentino, Nancy 12, 120, 463, 615
Valentino, Rudolph 595
Van Buren, Abigail 393
Van de Kamp, John 634, 635
van der Munnik, Marco 3, 4, 667
Van Doren, Mamie 111, 646
Van Dyke, Dick 508, 515
Vanderbilt, (Commodore) Cornelius 419
Van Gogh, Vincent 156
Van Heusen, Jimmy 203
Vaughn, Frankie 202, 225
Vertigo 199
Victim: The Secret Tapes of Marilyn Monroe 640
Victor/Victoria 380
Vidor, Charles 112
Vidor, Doris 220, 223, 230, 275
View from the Bridge, A 51, 654
Villet, Barbara 465-466
Viner, Mort 476, 662
Viva Las Vegas 259
"Volare" 381
von Sternberg, Josef 112
von Trapp Family Singers 114
Vreeland, Diana 504
Wagenknecht, Edward 598
Wagner, Robert 485
Wagner, Robert F. 60, 474
Wald, Jerry 181, 197, 198, 201, 207, 240, 241, 341
Walker, Edward 544
Wall Street: Money Never Sleeps 292
Wallace, Mike 627
Wallach, Eli 71, 104, 249, 261, 262, 268, 272, 279, 292, 662, 700
Walmsley, Gene 277
Walston, Ray 226
Walter 139

Walters, Barbara 36
Wardlaw, (Judge) Kim McLane 619
Warhol, Andy 79, 533
Warner, Jack 18, 22, 57, 58, 60,
Warner Brothers Studios 18, 21, 57, 58, 59, 132, 357, 391, 570, 674,
Warner-Hollywood Studios 133
Warner, Sandra 148, 157, 165
Warren, Chief Justice Earl 81
Warren Commission 628
Watermark 431
Watson, Philip 441-442
Washington, Hazel 224, 255, 455, 457, 558
Washington, Rocky 558
Wasserman, Lew 485
Wattis, Richard 23, 679
Wauters, Eddie 79
Wayne, John 214, 244, 390
Weatherby, W. J. 253, 261, 264, 267, 279, 280, 281, 357, 374,
Weatherwax, Rudd 456
Webb, Alan 34
Webb, Clifton 334
Weiler, A. H. 163, 592
Weinstein, Henry 353, 382, 383, 384, 391, 392, 450, 451, 452, 454, 457, 477, 482, 485, 486, 488, 490, 493, 662
Weiss, Nathan 490
Weissberger, Arnold 193
We're Not Married 383, 582
West, Mae 295, 364, 509
West Side Story 114, 448, 473
Westbrook-Van Cleave, Toni 277
Wexler, (Dr.) Milton 235, 351, 487
What a Way to Go! 508
What's My Line? 387
Wheeler, Janet 3, 667
"Where the Boys Are" 334
Whitcomb, Jon 117, 147, 164, 307
White, Byron "Whizzer" 501, 502
White Christmas (film) 469
"White Christmas" (song) 202
White Lightnin' Road 646
White, Louise H. 610
White, Stanford 462
Whitehead, Robert 658
Whitney, Grace Lee 148
Who's Afraid of Virginia Woolf? 172, 469
Who's Got the Action? 387
Who's Who Current Biography 1959 179
Who the Hell's In It 649
Widmark, Richard 104
Wiener, Leigh 547
Wigan, Gareth 660
Wild River 200, 248
Wilder, Billy 18, 39, 124, 129-135, 137, 139, 140, 142-145, 147, 149-152, 155-161, 163-165, 179, 186, 187, 197, 208, 226, 291, 297, 491, 566, 582, 690, 691
Wilding, Michael 249
Wilkins, Peggy 4, 631
Will Success Spoil Rock Hunter? 192, 202, 380
Williams, Andy 448
Williams, Clarence 139
Williams, Edwina 224
Williams, Leona 139
Williams, Robin 165

Williams, Tennessee 157, 179, 185, 224, 225, 240, 250, 379, 408, 604
Wilson, Earl 78, 304, 305, 493, 662
Winchell, Walter 244, 324, 335, 576, 623, 624
Windfohr, Robert 105, 107
Winfrey, Oprah 678
Winkler, Peter L. 641-642
Winokur, Julius 311
Winslow Boy, The 18
Winters, Darbi 582
Winters, Shelley 215, 233, 568, 662
Winwood, Estelle 250, 272, 704
Wisdom, Norman 44
Wise, Robert 448
Wolhandler, Joe 662
Wolfe, Donald H. 6, 142, 143, 145, 150, 151, 234, 237, 520, 621, 639, 661-662
"Woman" 86
Women, The 197
Woman in Question, The 24
Wood, Leo 138
Wood, Natalie 188, 222, 348, 391, 427, 582, 622, 635
Woodfield, William 480-481, 486, 521, 547
Woodward, Joanne 111, 123, 185, 199, 312, 341
Working Girl 469
World of Bob Hope, The 313
World Upside Down 231
Wright, Frank Lloyd 3, 103, 105, 107, 171
Writers Guild 214, 230
Wurtzel, Sol 454
Wuthering Heights 17
Wyler, Augusta "Gussie" 255
Wyler, William 187
Yeigh, Amos Emery 583
Yeigh, Terryl Lee (see Darbi Winters)
"You Made Me Love You" 247, 268
Young Lions, The 381
Young, Loretta 76, 248
Youngstein, Max 263, 274, 290
Your Key to Happiness 498
Yulstra, Joe 176
Yuska, Stella 118
Yutand, Lin 136
Zanders, Ida Mae 148
Zanuck, Darrilyn 491
Zanuck, Darryl F. 373, 379, 482, 490, 491, 494, 506, 567, 582, 591-593, 675
Zanuck, Richard D. 194, 382
Zec, Donald 31
Zeigler, Jane 349
Zinsser, William K. 301
Zolotow, Maurice 6, 32, 54, 72, 87, 88, 149, 159, 301, 305

About the Author

Gary Vitacco-Robles is a Licensed Mental Health Counselor and National Certified Counselor in practice in the Tampa Bay Area. He holds a master's degree in Counselor Education from the University of South Florida, and for twenty years has worked with children and families who have survived sexual/physical abuse or neglect.

Seeing the resilient survivor underneath Marilyn Monroe's famous persona, Gary felt a deep admiration and connection toward her; thus beginning Gary's dream to honor both Marilyn's strength and the inspiration she became for future generations.

Gary is happily married and lives on Florida's Gulf Coast.

CPSIA information can be obtained
at www.ICGtesting.com
Printed in the USA
BVOW06*2034160217
475782BV00022B/80/P

9 781593 937782